Eighth Edition

Bond Markets, Analysis, and Strategies

FRANK J. FABOZZI, CFA
Professor of Finance
EDHEC Business School

Boston   Columbus   Indianapolis   New York   San Francisco   Upper Saddle River
Amsterdam   Cape Town   Dubai   London   Madrid   Milan   Munich   Paris   Montreal   Toronto
Delhi   Mexico City   São Paulo   Sydney   Hong Kong   Seoul   Singapore   Taipei   Tokyo

Editor in Chief: Donna Battista
Acquisitions Editor: Tessa O'Brien
Editorial Project Manager: Amy Foley
Editorial Assistant: Elissa Senra-Sargent
Director of Marketing: Patrice Jones
Senior Marketing Assistant: Ian Gold
Senior Managing Editor: Nancy Fenton
Senior Production Project Manager:
Nancy Freihofer
Senior Manufacturing Buyer: Carol Melville

Text Designer: S4Carlisle Publishing Services
Cover Designer: Jane Conte
Manager, Rights and Permissions: Hessa Albader
Cover Photo: Zoe/Fotolia
Full-Service Project Management: S4Carlisle
Publishing Services
Composition: S4Carlisle Publishing Services
Printer/Binder: Edwards Brothers Malloy
Cover Printer: Lehigh-Phoenix Color
Text Font: Minion Pro

Credits and acknowledgments borrowed from other sources and reproduced, with permission, in this textbook appear on the appropriate page within text or on pages 732–733.

Microsoft® and Windows® are registered trademarks of the Microsoft Corporation in the U.S.A. and other countries. Screen shots and icons reprinted with permission from the Microsoft Corporation. This book is not sponsored or endorsed by or affiliated with the Microsoft Corporation.

Many of the designations by manufacturers and sellers to distinguish their products are claimed as trademarks. Where those designations appear in this book, and the publisher was aware of a trademark claim, the designations have been printed in initial caps or all caps.

Library of Congress Cataloging-in-Publication Data
Fabozzi, Frank J.
  Bond markets, analysis, and strategies/Frank J. Fabozzi. — 8th ed.
    p. cm.
  Includes index.
  ISBN-13: 978-0-13-274354-9
  ISBN-10: 0-13-274354-X
  1. Bonds.   2. Investment analysis.   3. Portfolio management.   4. Bond market.   I. Title.
  HG4651.F28 2013
  332.63'23—dc23

                       2011031156

10 9 8 7 6 5 4

ISBN-10:   0-13-274354-X
ISBN-13: 978-0-13-274354-9

To the memory of my parents, Josephine and Alfonso Fabozzi.

Contents

Preface

The first edition of *Bond Markets, Analysis, and Strategies* was published in 1989. The objective was to provide coverage of the products, analytical techniques for valuing bonds and quantifying their exposure to changes in interest rates, and portfolio strategies for achieving a client's objectives. In the six editions subsequently published and in the current edition, the coverage of each of these areas has been updated. In the product area, the updating has been primarily for the latest developments in nonagency residential mortgage–backed securities, asset-backed securities, bank loans, and credit derivatives (more specifically credit default swaps). The updating of the coverage on bond portfolio management has been for factor models for constructing bond portfolios and controlling a portfolio's interest rate risk.

Each edition has benefited from the feedback of readers and instructors using the book at universities and training programs. Many discussions with portfolio managers and analysts, as well as my experiences serving on the board of directors of several funds and consulting assignments, have been invaluable in improving the content of the book.

I am confident that the eighth edition continues the tradition of providing up-to-date information about the bond market and the tools for managing bond portfolios.

NEW TO THIS EDITION

With the exception of Chapter 1, all chapters now end with key points rather than a summary. The key points are in the form of bullet points, which should make it is easier for students to review the major points made in the chapter.

The chapter "Collateralized Debt Obligations (CDOs)" was deleted in this edition. Given that there has not been any issuance of this product with the exception of collateralized loan obligations, and highly unlikely there will be future issuance, coverage was deleted. Collateralized loan obligations are covered in Chapter 7.

New Chapters

Chapter 23 Bond Portfolio Construction   This chapter is dedicated to the different approaches used by portfolio managers to construct bond portfolios. It begins with describing what the Markowitz mean-variance framework for constructing portfolios is, and the limitations of applying it to bond portfolio construction. The two common approaches for portfolio construction—the cell-based approach and the multi-factor approach—are explained. The primary focus is on how a multi-factor model can be used to identify the sources of risk of a portfolio. An extensive illustration is provided.

Chapter 29 Credit Default Swaps   In the seventh edition, Chapter 30 ("Credit Derivatives") provided a general description of the different types of credit derivatives. Since by far the major credit derivative used for trading credit risk and controlling portfolio credit risk is the credit default swap, this new chapter describing this product and its applications has been included in the current edition.

Significantly Revised Chapters

Chapter 6 Treasury and Agency Securities   Thoroughly revised to expand the discussion on agency securities.

Chapter 7 Corporate Debt Instruments   Completely revised to cover bank loans (particularly leveraged loans) and collateralized loan obligations.

Chapter 8 Municipal Securities   Revised to eliminate the details of the different types of municipal revenue bonds and to include Build America Bonds.

Chapter 9 International Bonds   Significantly changed to describe products and to describe sector performance.

Chapter 12 Agency Collateralized Mortgage Obligations and Stripped Mortgage–Backed Securities   Revised to update its coverage on stripped mortgage–backed securities.

Chapter 13 Nonagency Residential Mortgage–Backed Securities   Extensively revised to describe the market following the subprime mortgage meltdown that can be traced back to the summer of 2007.

Chapter 22 Bond Portfolio Management Strategies   Now includes topics that had previously been in Chapter 23 ("Active Bond Portfolio Management Strategies") and Chapter 24 ("Indexing"). The revised chapter provides a more structured discussion of bond portfolio management strategies that describes active and passive strategies, as well as a description of the bond portfolio management team.

Chapter 25 Bond Performance Measurement and Evaluation   This chapter, which was Chapter 26 in the seventh edition, provides a more in-depth coverage showing how bond attribution models can be used to identify the active management decisions that contribute to the portfolio's performance and give a quantitative assessment of the contribution of these decisions. This chapter includes an extensive illustration that builds on the illustration in Chapter 23.

Chapter 26 Interest-Rate Futures Contracts   Previously Chapter 27, it includes two major changes: an update to the types of interest-rate futures contracts currently traded and an extensive illustration to demonstrate how interest-rate futures can be used to control portfolio risk.

Chapter 28 Interest-Rate Swaps, Caps, and Floors   Previously Chapter 29, now includes an extensive illustration to explain how interest-rate swaps and swaptions can be used to control portfolio risk.

Online Appendix

Additional content is available on the companion website at www.pearsonhighered.com/fabozzi/.

Chapter 20 Appendix   Wachovia's credit report of the Lear Corporation

INSTRUCTOR SUPPLEMENTS

The following supplements are available to adopting instructors:

Instructor's Resource Center Register.Redeem.Login

www.pearsonhighered.com/irc is where instructors can access a variety of print, media, and presentation resources that are available with this text in downloadable, digital format.

It gets better. Once you register, you will not have additional forms to fill out or multiple usernames and passwords to remember to access new titles and/or editions. As a registered faculty member, you can log in directly to download resource files, and receive immediate access and instructions for installing Course Management content to your campus server.

Need help? Our dedicated Technical Support team is ready to assist instructors with questions about the media supplements that accompany this text. Visit http://247pearsoned .custhelp.com/ for answers to frequently asked questions and toll-free user support phone numbers. The following supplements are available to adopting instructors. Detailed descriptions of the following supplements are provided on the Instructor's Resource Center:

Electronic Instructor's Manual with Solutions

Prepared by Dr. Rob Hull of Washburn University School of Business. The Instructor's Manual contains chapter summaries and suggested answers to all end-of-chapter questions.

PowerPoint Presentation

Prepared by Dr. Rob Hull of Washburn University School of Business. The PowerPoint slides provide the instructor with individual lecture outlines to accompany the text. The slides include all of the figures and tables from the text. These lecture notes can be used as is or professors can easily modify them to reflect specific presentation needs.

ACKNOWLEDGMENTS

I am grateful to the following individuals who assisted in different ways as identified below:

- Cenk Ural (Barclays Capital) for the extensive illustrations used in Chapters 4, 23, and 25.
- Karthik Ramanathan (Fidelity Management and Research Company/Pyramis Global Advisors) for the data used in Chapter 9.
- Anand Bhattacharya (Arizona State University) and William Berliner (Berliner Consulting & Research) for their feedback on Chapter 10.
- Oren Cheyette (Barclays) and Alex Levin (Andrew Davidson & Co.) for reviewing and commenting on Chapter 21.
- Jane Howe for allowing me to use some of our joint work in Chapter 20.
- Tim Backshall for reviewing and commenting on Chapter 21.
- Peter Ru for preparing the hedging illustrations in Chapters 26 and 27.
- Donald Smith (Boston University) for providing the correct methodology for valuing interest rate caps and floors in Chapter 28.
- Mark Paltrowitz (BlackRock Financial Management) for the illustrations in Chapters 26 and 28.

I thank Wachovia Securities for allowing me to include the Chapter 20 Appendix, the research report coauthored by Eric Sell and Stephanie Renegar.

I am indebted to the following individuals who shared with me their views on various topics covered in this book: Moorad Choudry (Royal Bank of Scotland), Sylvan Feldstein (Guardian Life), Michael Ferri (George Mason University), Sergio Focardi (EDHEC Business School), Laurie Goodman (Amherst Securities), Frank Jones (San Jose State University), Andrew Kalotay (Andrew Kalotay Associates), Martin Leibowitz (Morgan Stanley), Jack Malvey (BNY Mellon), Steven Mann (University of South Carolina), Lionel Martellini (EDHEC Business School), Wesley Phoa (The Capital Group Companies), Philippe Priaulet (Natexis Banques Populaires and University of Evry Val d'Essonne), Scott Richard (Wharton), Ron Ryan (Ryan ALM), Richard Wilson, David Yuen (Franklin Advisors), and Yu Zhu (China Europe International Business School).

Thanks also go to the following reviewers of this eighth edition: Ying Wang, University at Albany; Berry K. Wilson, Pace University; Jeffrey A. Schultz, Christian Brothers University; Ghassem Homaifar, Middle Tennessee State University; Michael Stutzer, University of Colorado at Boulder; Tao-Hsien Dolly King, University of North Carolina at Charlotte; David Brown, University of Florida; Peter Ritchken, Case Western Reserve University.

I also received extremely helpful comments from a number of colleagues using the text in an academic setting. These individuals helped me refine previous editions, and I am sincerely appreciative of their suggestions. They are:

Şxenay Ağca, George Washington University
Michael J. Alderson, St. Louis University
John Edmunds, Babson College
R. Philip Giles, Columbia University
Martin Haugh, Columbia University
Deborah Lucas, Northwestern University
Davinder K. Malhotra, Philadelphia University
John H. Spitzer, University of Iowa
Joel M. Vanden, Dartmouth College
Russell R. Wermers, University of Colorado at Boulder
Xiaoqing Eleanor Xu, Seton Hall University

Introduction

1

A bond is a debt instrument requiring the **issuer** (also called the **debtor** or **borrower**) to repay to the lender/investor the amount borrowed plus interest over a specified period of time. A typical ("plain vanilla") bond issued in the United States specifies (1) a fixed date when the amount borrowed (the principal) is due, and (2) the contractual amount of interest, which typically is paid every six months. The date on which the principal is required to be repaid is called the **maturity date**. Assuming that the issuer does not default or redeem the issue prior to the maturity date, an investor holding a bond until the maturity date is assured of a known cash flow pattern.

For a variety of reasons to be discussed later in this chapter, since the early 1980s a wide range of bond structures has been introduced into the bond market. In the residential mortgage market particularly, new types of mortgage designs were introduced. The practice of pooling individual mortgages to form mortgage pass-through securities grew dramatically. Using the basic instruments in the mortgage market (mortgages and mortgage pass-through securities), issuers created derivative mortgage instruments such as collateralized mortgage obligations and stripped mortgage-backed securities that met the specific investment needs of a broadening range of institutional investors.

SECTORS OF THE U.S. BOND MARKET

The U.S. bond market is the largest bond market in the world. The market is divided into six sectors: U.S. Treasury sector, agency sector,[1] municipal sector, corporate sector, asset-backed securities sector, and mortgage sector. The **Treasury sector** includes securities issued by the U.S. government. These securities include Treasury bills, notes, and bonds. This sector plays a key role in the valuation of securities and the determination of interest rates throughout the world.

The **agency sector** includes securities issued by federally related institutions and government-sponsored enterprises. The distinction between these issuers is described in Chapter 6. The securities issued are not backed by any collateral and are referred to as **agency debenture securities**. This sector is the smallest sector of the bond market.

The **municipal sector** is where state and local governments and their authorities raise funds. This sector is divided into two subsectors based on how the interest received by investors is taxed at the federal income tax level. The tax-exempt market is the largest sector where interest received by investors is exempt from federal income taxes. Historically, the taxable sector was a small sector of the municipal bond market. However, in 2009 the U.S. federal government introduced a new type of taxable bond, Build America Bonds, that significantly increased the size of the taxable sector of the municipal bond market. The municipal bond market includes two types of structures: (1) tax-backed bonds and (2) revenue bonds.

The **corporate sector** includes securities issued by U.S. corporations and securities issued in the United States by non–U.S. corporations. Issuers in the corporate sector issue bonds, medium-term notes, structured notes, and commercial paper. In addition to their issuance of these securities, corporations borrow funds from banks. At one time commercial banks that made these loans held them in their loan portfolio. Today, certain commercial loans are traded in the market. The corporate sector is divided into the investment-grade and noninvestment-grade sectors. The classification is based on the assignment of a credit rating determined by a third-party commercial entity. We will discuss credit ratings in Chapter 7.

An alternative to the corporate sector where a corporation can raise funds is the **asset-backed securities sector**. In this sector, a corporation pools loans or receivables and uses the pool of assets as collateral for the issuance of a security. Captive finance companies, that is, subsidiaries of operating companies that provide funding for loans to customers of the parent company to buy the product manufactured, are typically issuers of asset-backed securities. Harley-Davidson Financial Services, Ford Motor Credit Company, and Caterpillar Financial Services Corporation are just a few examples. Probably the most well-known asset-backed securities (although a very tiny part of the market) are those issued by performing

---

[1] In later chapters, we will see how organizations that create bond market indexes provide a more detailed breakdown of the sectors.

artists such as David Bowie, Ashford & Simpson, and James Brown, backed by music royalty future receivables.[2] The various types of asset-backed securities are described in Chapter 15.

The mortgage sector is the sector where the securities issued are backed by mortgage loans. These are loans obtained by borrowers in order to purchase residential property or to purchase commercial property (i.e., income-producing property). The mortgage sector is thus divided into the **residential mortgage sector** and the **commercial mortgage sector**. The residential mortgage sector, which includes loans for one- to four-family homes, is covered in Chapters 10 through 13. The commercial mortgage sector, backed by commercial loans for income-producing property such as apartment buildings, office buildings, industrial properties, shopping centers, hotels, and health care facilities, is the subject of Chapter 14.

Chapter 10 discusses the different types of residential mortgage loans and the classification of mortgage loans in terms of the credit quality of the borrower: prime loans and subprime loans. The latter loans are loans to borrowers with impaired credit ratings. Also, loans are classified as to whether or not they conform to the underwriting standards of a federal agency or government-sponsored enterprise that packages residential loans to create residential mortgage-backed securities. Residential mortgage-backed securities issued by a federal agency (the Government National Mortgage Association or Ginnie Mae) or Fannie Mae or Freddie Mac (two government-sponsored enterprises) are referred to as **agency mortgage-backed securities**. Chapter 11 is devoted to the basic type of such security, an **agency mortgage pass-through security**, while Chapter 12 covers securities created from agency mortgage pass-through securities: **collateralized mortgage obligations** and **stripped mortgage-backed securities.**

Residential mortgage-backed securities not issued by Ginnie Mae, Fannie Mae, or Freddie Mac are called **nonagency mortgage-backed securities** and are the subject of Chapter 13. This sector is divided into securities backed by prime loans and those backed by subprime loans. The securities in the latter sector, referred to as **subprime mortgage-backed securities,** have had major difficulties due to defaults. The turmoil in the financial marked caused by the defaults in this sector is referred to as "the subprime mortgage crisis."

Non-U.S. bond markets include the Eurobond market and other national bond markets. We discuss these markets in Chapter 9.

OVERVIEW OF BOND FEATURES

In this section, we provide an overview of some important features of bonds. A more detailed treatment of these features is presented in later chapters.

Type of Issuer

A key feature of a bond is the nature of the issuer. There are three issuers of bonds: the federal government and its agencies, municipal governments, and corporations (domestic and foreign). Within the municipal and corporate bond markets, there is a wide range of issuers, each with different abilities to satisfy their contractual obligation to lenders.

---

[2] David Bowie was the first recording artist to issue these bonds, in 1997, and hence these bonds are popularly referred to as "Bowie bonds." The bond issue, a $55 million, 10-year issue, was purchased by Prudential and was backed by future royalties from a substantial portion of Bowie's music catalogue.

Term to Maturity

The term to maturity of a bond is the number of years over which the issuer has promised to meet the conditions of the obligation. The maturity of a bond refers to the date that the debt will cease to exist, at which time the issuer will redeem the bond by paying the outstanding principal. The practice in the bond market, however, is to refer to the **term to maturity** of a bond as simply its **maturity** or **term**. As we explain subsequently, there may be provisions in the indenture that allow either the issuer or bondholder to alter a bond's term to maturity.

Generally, bonds with a maturity of between one and five years are considered **short-term**. Bonds with a maturity between five and 12 years are viewed as **intermediate-term**, and **long-term** bonds are those with a maturity of more than 12 years.

There are three reasons why the term to maturity of a bond is important. The most obvious is that it indicates the time period over which the holder of the bond can expect to receive the coupon payments and the number of years before the principal will be paid in full. The second reason that term to maturity is important is that the yield on a bond depends on it. As explained in Chapter 5, the shape of the yield curve determines how term to maturity affects the yield. Finally, the price of a bond will fluctuate over its life as yields in the market change. As demonstrated in Chapter 4, the volatility of a bond's price is dependent on its maturity. More specifically, with all other factors constant, the longer the maturity of a bond, the greater the price volatility resulting from a change in market yields.

Principal and Coupon Rate

The **principal value** (or simply **principal**) of a bond is the amount that the issuer agrees to repay the bondholder at the maturity date. This amount is also referred to as the **redemption value**, **maturity value**, **par value**, or **face value**.

The **coupon rate,** also called the **nominal rate**, is the interest rate that the issuer agrees to pay each year. The annual amount of the interest payment made to owners during the term of the bond is called the **coupon**.[3] The coupon rate multiplied by the principal of the bond provides the dollar amount of the coupon. For example, a bond with an 8% coupon rate and a principal of $1,000 will pay annual interest of $80. In the United States and Japan, the usual practice is for the issuer to pay the coupon in two semiannual installments. For bonds issued in certain European bond markets, coupon payments are made only once per year.

Note that all bonds make periodic coupon payments, except for one type that makes none. The holder of a **zero-coupon bond** realizes interest by buying the bond substantially below its principal value. Interest is then paid at the maturity date, with the exact amount being the difference between the principal value and the price paid for the bond.

Floating-rate bonds are issues where the coupon rate resets periodically (the coupon reset date) based on a formula. The formula, referred to as the **coupon reset formula,** has the following general form:

$$\text{reference rate} + \text{quoted margin}$$

---

[3] Here is the reason why the interest paid on a bond is called its "coupon." At one time, the bondholder received a physical bond, and the bond had coupons attached to it that represented the interest amount owed and when it was due. The coupons would then be deposited by the bondholder to obtain the interest payment. Although in the United States most bonds are registered bonds and, therefore, there are no physical "coupons," the term coupon interest or coupon rate is still used.

The quoted margin is the additional amount that the issuer agrees to pay above the reference rate. For example, suppose that the reference rate is the 1-month London interbank offered rate (LIBOR), an interest rate that we discuss in later chapters. Suppose that the quoted margin is 150 basis points. Then the coupon reset formula is

1-month LIBOR + 150 basis points

So, if 1-month LIBOR on the coupon reset date is 3.5%, the coupon rate is reset for that period at 5.0% (3.5% plus 150 basis points).

The reference rate for most floating-rate securities is an interest rate or an interest rate index. The mostly widely used reference rate throughout the world is the **London Interbank Offered Rate** and referred to as LIBOR. This interest rate is the rate at which the highest credit quality banks borrow from each other in the London interbank market. LIBOR is calculated by the British Bankers Association (BBA) in conjunction with Reuters based on interest rates it receives from at least eight banks with the information released every day around 11 a.m. Hence, often in debt agreements LIBOR is referred to as BBA LIBOR. The rate is reported for 10 currencies:[4] U.S. dollar (USD), UK pound sterling (GBP), Japanese yen (JPY), Swiss franc (CHF), Canadian dollar (CAD), Australian dollar (AUD), euro (EUR), New Zealand dollar (NZD), Swedish krona (SEK), and Danish krona (DKK). So, for example, the AUD BBA LIBOR is the rate for a LIBOR loan denominated in Australian dollars as computed by the British Bankers Association.

There are floating-rating securities where the reference rate is some financial index such as the return on the Standard & Poor's 500 or a nonfinancial index such as the price of a commodity. An important non-interest rate index that has been used with increasing frequency is the rate of inflation. Bonds whose interest rate is tied to the rate of inflation are referred to generically as **linkers**. As we will see in Chapter 6, the U.S. Treasury issues linkers, and they are referred to as Treasury Inflation Protection Securities (TIPS).

While the coupon on floating-rate bonds benchmarked off an interest rate benchmark typically rises as the benchmark rises and falls as the benchmark falls, there are issues whose coupon interest rate moves in the opposite direction from the change in interest rates. Such issues are called **inverse-floating-rate bonds** (or simply, **inverse floaters**) or **reverse floaters**.

In the 1980s, new structures in the high-yield (junk bond) sector of the corporate bond market provided variations in the way in which coupon payments are made. One reason is that a leveraged buyout (LBO) or a recapitalization financed with high-yield bonds, with consequent heavy interest payment burdens, placed severe cash flow constraints on the corporation. To reduce this burden, firms involved in LBOs and recapitalizations issued **deferred-coupon bonds** that let the issuer avoid using cash to make interest payments for a specified number of years. There are three types of deferred-coupon structures: (1) deferred-interest bonds, (2) step-up bonds, and (3) payment-in-kind bonds. Another high-yield bond structure requires that the issuer reset the coupon rate so that the bond will trade at a predetermined price. High-yield bond structures are discussed in Chapter 7.

In addition to indicating the coupon payments that the investor should expect to receive over the term of the bond, the coupon rate also indicates the degree to which the

---

[4] The symbol in parentheses following each currency is the International Organization for Standardization three-letter code used to define a currency.

bond's price will be affected by changes in interest rates. As illustrated in Chapter 4, all other factors constant, the higher the coupon rate, the less the price will change in response to a change in market yields.

Amortization Feature

The principal repayment of a bond issue can call for either (1) the total principal to be repaid at maturity, or (2) the principal repaid over the life of the bond. In the latter case, there is a schedule of principal repayments. This schedule is called an **amortization schedule**. Loans that have this feature are automobile loans and home mortgage loans.

As we will see in later chapters, there are securities that are created from loans that have an amortization schedule. These securities will then have a schedule of periodic principal repayments. Such securities are referred to as **amortizing securities**. Securities that do not have a schedule of periodic principal repayment are called **nonamortizing securities**.

For amortizing securities, investors do not talk in terms of a bond's maturity. This is because the stated maturity of such securities only identifies when the final principal payment will be made. The repayment of the principal is being made over time. For amortizing securities, a measure called the **weighted average life** or simply **average life** of a security is computed. This calculation will be explained later when we cover the two major types of amortizing securities—mortgage-backed securities and asset-backed securities.

Embedded Options

It is common for a bond issue to include a provision in the indenture that gives either the bondholder and/or the issuer an option to take some action against the other party. The most common type of option embedded in a bond is a **call provision**. This provision grants the issuer the right to retire the debt, fully or partially, before the scheduled maturity date. Inclusion of a call feature benefits bond issuers by allowing them to replace an outstanding bond issue with a new bond issue that has a lower coupon rate than the outstanding bond issue because market interest rates have declined. A call provision effectively allows the issuer to alter the maturity of a bond. For reasons explained in the next section, a call provision is detrimental to the bondholder's interests.

The right to call an obligation is also included in most loans and therefore in all securities created from such loans. This is because the borrower typically has the right to pay off a loan at any time, in whole or in part, prior to the stated maturity date of the loan. That is, the borrower has the right to alter the amortization schedule for amortizing securities.

An issue may also include a provision that allows the bondholder to change the maturity of a bond. An issue with a **put provision** included in the indenture grants the bondholder the right to sell the issue back to the issuer at par value on designated dates. Here the advantage to the investor is that if market interest rates rise after the issuance date, thereby reducing the bond's price, the investor can force the issuer to redeem the bond at the principal value.

A **convertible bond** is an issue giving the bondholder the right to exchange the bond for a specified number of shares of common stock. Such a feature allows the bondholder to take advantage of favorable movements in the price of the issuer's common stock. An **exchangeable bond** allows the bondholder to exchange the issue for a specified number of common stock shares of a corporation different from the issuer of the bond. These bonds are discussed and analyzed in Chapter 19.

Some issues allow either the issuer or the bondholder the right to select the currency in which a cash flow will be paid. This option effectively gives the party with the right to choose the currency the opportunity to benefit from a favorable exchange rate movement. Such issues are described in Chapter 9.

The presence of embedded options makes the valuation of bonds complex. It requires investors to have an understanding of the basic principles of options, a topic covered in Chapter 17 for callable and putable bonds and Chapter 18 for mortgage-backed securities and asset-backed securities. The valuation of bonds with embedded options frequently is complicated further by the presence of several options within a given issue. For example, an issue may include a call provision, a put provision, and a conversion provision, all of which have varying significance in different situations.

Describing a Bond Issue

There are hundreds of thousands of bond issues. Most securities are identified by a nine-character (letters and numbers) CUSIP number. CUSIP stands for Committee on Uniform Security Identification Procedures. The CUSIP International Numbering System (CINS) is used to identify foreign securities and includes 12 characters. The CUSIP numbering system is owned by the American Bankers Association and operated by Standard & Poor's. CUSIP numbers are important for a well-functioning securities market because they aid market participants in properly identifying securities that are the subject of a trade and in the clearing/settlement process.

The CUSIP number is not determined randomly but is assigned in such a way so as to identify an issue's key differentiating characteristics within a common structure. Specifically, the first six characters identify the issuer: the corporation, government agency, or municipality. The next two characters identify whether the issue is debt or equity and the issuer of the issue. The last character is simply a check character that allows for accuracy checking and is sometimes truncated or ignored; that is, only the first characters are listed.

The debt instruments covered are

- asset-backed securities
- banker acceptances
- certificates of deposits
- collateralized debt obligations
- commercial paper
- corporate bonds
- medium-term notes
- mortgage-backed securities
- municipal bonds
- structured products
- U.S. federal government agencies
- U.S. Treasury securities: bonds, bills, and notes

There are also derivatives and credit derivatives covered.

In general when bonds are cited in a trade or listed as holdings in a portfolio, the particular issue is cited by issuer, coupon rate, and maturity date. For example, three bonds issued by Alcoa Inc. and how they would be referred to are shown in the following table.

Coupon	Maturity	
5.95%	Feb. 1, 2037	Alcoa, 5.95%, due 2/1/2037 or Alcoa, 5.95s 2/1/2037
6.15%	Aug. 15, 2020	Alcoa, 6.15%, due 8/15/2020 or Alcoa, 6.15s 8/15/2020
6.75%	July 15, 2018	Alcoa, 6.75%, due 7/15/2018 or Alcoa, 6.75s 7/15/2018

RISKS ASSOCIATED WITH INVESTING IN BONDS

Bonds may expose an investor to one or more of the following risks: (1) interest-rate risk, (2) reinvestment risk, (3) call risk, (4) credit risk, (5) inflation risk, (6) exchange-rate risk, (7) liquidity risk, (8) volatility risk, and (9) risk risk. While each of these risks is discussed further in later chapters, we describe them briefly in the following sections. In later chapters, other risks, such as yield curve risk, event risk, and tax risk, are also introduced. What is critical in constructing and controlling the risk of a portfolio is the ability to quantify as many of these risks as possible. We will see this in later chapters, particularly in our coverage of factor models in Chapter 23.

Interest-Rate Risk

The price of a typical bond will change in the opposite direction from a change in interest rates: As interest rates rise, the price of a bond will fall; as interest rates fall, the price of a bond will rise. This property is illustrated in Chapter 2. If an investor has to sell a bond prior to the maturity date, an increase in interest rates will mean the realization of a capital loss (i.e., selling the bond below the purchase price). This risk is referred to as **interest-rate risk** or **market risk**.

As noted earlier, the actual degree of sensitivity of a bond's price to changes in market interest rates depends on various characteristics of the issue, such as coupon and maturity. It will also depend on any options embedded in the issue (e.g., call and put provisions), because, as we explain in later chapters, the value of these options is also affected by interest-rate movements.

Reinvestment Income or Reinvestment Risk

As explained in Chapter 3, calculation of the yield of a bond assumes that the cash flows received are reinvested. The additional income from such reinvestment, sometimes called **interest-on-interest**, depends on the prevailing interest-rate levels at the time of reinvestment, as well as on the reinvestment strategy. Variability in the reinvestment rate of a given strategy because of changes in market interest rates is called **reinvestment risk**. This risk is that the prevailing market interest rate at which interim cash flows can be reinvested will fall. Reinvestment risk is greater for longer holding periods, as well as for bonds with large, early cash flows, such as high-coupon bonds. This risk is analyzed in more detail in Chapter 3.

It should be noted that interest-rate risk and reinvestment risk have offsetting effects. That is, interest-rate risk is the risk that interest rates will rise, thereby reducing a bond's price. In contrast, reinvestment risk is the risk that interest rates will fall. A strategy based on these offsetting effects is called immunization, a topic covered in Chapter 24.

Call Risk

As explained earlier, bonds may include a provision that allows the issuer to retire or "call" all or part of the issue before the maturity date. The issuer usually retains this right in order to have flexibility to refinance the bond in the future if the market interest rate drops below the coupon rate.

From the investor's perspective, there are three disadvantages to call provisions. First, the cash flow pattern of a callable bond is not known with certainty. Second, because the issuer will call the bonds when interest rates have dropped, the investor is exposed to reinvestment risk (i.e., the investor will have to reinvest the proceeds when the bond is called at relatively lower interest rates). Finally, the capital appreciation potential of a bond will be reduced because the price of a callable bond may not rise much above the price at which the issuer will call the bond.[5]

Even though the investor is usually compensated for taking call risk by means of a lower price or a higher yield, it is not easy to determine if this compensation is sufficient. In any case the return or price performance of a bond with call risk can be dramatically different from those obtainable from an otherwise comparable noncallable bond. The magnitude of this risk depends on various parameters of the call provision, as well as on market conditions. Techniques for analyzing callable bonds are explained in Chapter 17.

Credit Risk

It is common to define **credit risk** as the risk that the issuer of a bond will fail to satisfy the terms of the obligation with respect to the timely payment of interest and repayment of the amount borrowed. This form of credit risk is called **default risk**. Market participants gauge the default risk of an issue by looking at the **credit rating** assigned to a bond issue by one of the three rating companies—Standard & Poor's, Moody's, and Fitch. We will discuss the rating systems used by these rating companies (also referred to as rating agencies) in Chapter 7 and the factors that they consider in assigning ratings in Chapter 20.

There are risks associated with investing in bonds other than default that are also components of credit risk. Even in the absence of default, an investor is concerned that the market value of a bond issue will decline in value and/or that the relative price performance of a bond issue will be worse than that of other bond issues, which the investor is compared against. The yield on a bond issue is made up of two components: (1) the yield on a similar maturity Treasury issue, and (2) a premium to compensate for the risks associated with the bond issue that do not exist in a Treasury issue—referred to as a spread. The part of the risk premium or spread attributable to default risk is called the **credit spread**.

The price performance of a non-Treasury debt obligation and its return over some investment horizon will depend on how the credit spread of a bond issue changes. If the credit spread increases—investors say that the spread has "widened"—the market price of the bond issue will decline. The risk that a bond issue will decline due to an increase in the credit spread is called **credit spread risk**. This risk exists for an individual bond issue, bond issues in a particular industry or economic sector, and for all bond issues in the economy not issued by the U.S. Treasury.

Once a credit rating is assigned to a bond issue, a rating agency monitors the credit quality of the issuer and can change a credit rating. An improvement in the credit quality

---

[5] The reason for this is explained in Chapter 17.

of an issue or issuer is rewarded with a better credit rating, referred to as an **upgrade**; a deterioration in the credit quality of an issue or issuer is penalized by the assignment of an inferior credit rating, referred to as a **downgrade**. An unanticipated downgrading of an issue or issuer increases the credit spread sought by the market, resulting in a decline in the price of the issue or the issuer's debt obligation. This risk is referred to as **downgrade risk**.

Consequently, credit risk consists of three types of risk: default risk, credit spread risk, and downgrade risk. Furthermore, these risks do not disappear if there is a financial guaranty by a nongovernment third-party entity such as a private insurance company. This point was made clear to market participants at the end of 2007 when specialized insurance companies that provide financial guarantees faced financial difficulties and the downgrading of their own credit rating.

Finally, there is a form of credit risk that involves transactions between two parties in a trade. This risk is called **counterparty risk**. Here are two examples. There are strategies that involve borrowing funds to purchase a bond. The use of borrowed funds to purchase a bond is referred to as leveraging and is explained in Chapter 22. In this transaction, the lender of funds is exposed to counterparty risk because there is the risk that the borrower will fail to repay the loan. A second example of where counterparty risk is faced is when there is a trade in a derivative instrument. In later chapters, we will describe derivative instruments. Some of these instruments are traded on an exchange, and in such trades, the exchange, as will be explained, becomes the ultimate counterparty to the trade. In such cases, the market views counterparty risk as minimal. In stark contrast, for derivative instruments that are over-the-counter instruments, the counterparty is an entity other than an exchange. In such trades, there is considerable concern with counterparty risk; fortunately there are risk management mechanisms that counterparties to such trades can employ to minimize counterparty risk.

Inflation Risk

Inflation risk or **purchasing-power risk** arises because of the variation in the value of cash flows from a security due to inflation, as measured in terms of purchasing power. For example, if investors purchase a bond on which they can realize a coupon rate of 7% but the rate of inflation is 8%, the purchasing power of the cash flow actually has declined. For all but floating-rate bonds, an investor is exposed to inflation risk because the interest rate the issuer promises to make is fixed for the life of the issue. To the extent that interest rates reflect the expected inflation rate, floating-rate bonds have a lower level of inflation risk.

Exchange-Rate Risk

From the perspective of a U.S. investor, a non–dollar-denominated bond (i.e., a bond whose payments occur in a foreign currency) has unknown U.S. dollar cash flows. The dollar cash flows are dependent on the exchange rate at the time the payments are received. For example, suppose that an investor purchases a bond whose payments are in Japanese yen. If the yen depreciates relative to the U.S. dollar, fewer dollars will be received. The risk of this occurring is referred to as **exchange-rate** or **currency risk**. Of course, should the yen appreciate relative to the U.S. dollar, the investor will benefit by receiving more dollars.

Liquidity Risk

Liquidity or **marketability risk** depends on the ease with which an issue can be sold at or near its value. The primary measure of liquidity is the size of the spread between the bid price and the ask price quoted by a dealer. The wider the dealer spread, the more the liquidity risk. For individual investors who plan to hold a bond until it matures and have the ability to do so, liquidity risk is unimportant. In contrast, institutional investors must mark to market their positions to market periodically. **Marking a position to market**, or simply **marking to market**, means that the portfolio manager must periodically determine the market value of each bond in the portfolio. To get prices that reflect market value, the bonds must trade with enough frequency.

Volatility Risk

As explained in Chapter 17, the price of a bond with certain types of embedded options depends on the level of interest rates and factors that influence the value of the embedded option. One of these factors is the expected volatility of interest rates. Specifically, the value of an option rises when expected interest-rate volatility increases. In the case of a bond that is callable, or a mortgage-backed security, in which the investor has granted the borrower an option, the price of the security falls, because the investor has given away a more valuable option. The risk that a change in volatility will affect the price of a bond adversely is called **volatility risk**. In our coverage of factor models in Chapter 23, we will see that the measure used to quantify volatility is referred to as *vega* and that this measure draws from option theory, which we discuss in Chapter 27.

Risk Risk

There have been new and innovative structures introduced into the bond market. Unfortunately, the risk/return characteristics of these securities are not always understood by money managers. **Risk risk** is defined as not knowing what the risk of a security is. When financial calamities are reported in the press, it is not uncommon to hear a money manager or a board member of the affected organization say "we didn't know this could happen." Although a money manager or a board member may not be able to predict the future, there is no reason why the potential outcome of an investment or investment strategy is not known in advance.

There are two ways to mitigate or eliminate risk risk. The first approach is to keep up with the literature on the state-of-the-art methodologies for analyzing securities. Your reading of this book is a step in that direction. The second approach is to avoid securities that are not clearly understood. Unfortunately, it is investments in more complex securities that offer opportunities for return enhancement. This brings us back to the first approach.

OVERVIEW OF THE BOOK

The next four chapters set forth the basic analytical framework necessary to understand the pricing of bonds and their investment characteristics. How the price of a bond is determined is explained in Chapter 2. The various measures of a bond's potential return are illustrated and evaluated critically in Chapter 3, which is followed by an explanation of the price-volatility characteristics of bonds in Chapter 4. The factors that affect the yield of a bond are explained in Chapter 5, and the important role of the term structure of interest rates (i.e., the relationship between maturity and yield) is introduced.

In Chapters 6 through 15 the various sectors of the debt market are described. As Treasury securities provide the benchmark against which all bonds are valued, it is imperative to have a thorough understanding of the Treasury market. Treasury securities, Treasury derivative securities (zero-coupon Treasury securities or "stripped" Treasury securities), and federal agency securities are introduced in Chapter 6. In Chapters 7 through 9 the investment characteristics and special features of U.S. corporate debt, municipal securities, and non-U.S. bonds, respectively, are explained.

Chapters 10 through 13 focus on residential mortgage-backed securities. The various types of residential mortgage instruments are described in Chapter 10. Residential mortgage pass-through securities issued by Ginnie Mae, Freddie Mac, and Fannie Mae are discussed in Chapter 11, and derivative mortgage-backed securities (collateralized mortgage obligations and stripped mortgage-backed securities) issued by these three entities are described in Chapter 12. While Chapters 11 and 12 cover what is referred to as agency mortgage-backed securities, Chapter 13 covers nonagency mortgage-backed securities, which include subprime mortgage-backed securities. Chapter 14 explains commercial mortgage loans and commercial mortgage-backed securities. Asset-backed securities are covered in Chapter 15.

In the next four chapters, methodologies for valuing bonds are explained. Chapter 16 provides the basics of interest rate modeling. The lattice method for valuing bonds with embedded options is explained in Chapter 17, and the Monte Carlo simulation model for mortgage-backed securities and asset-backed securities backed by residential loans is explained in Chapter 18. A byproduct of these valuation models is the option-adjusted spread. The analysis of convertible bonds is covered in Chapter 19.

Chapters 20 and 21 deal with corporate bond credit risk. Chapter 20 describes traditional credit analysis. Chapter 21 provides the basics of credit risk modeling, describing the two major models: structural models and reduced-form models.

Portfolio management is discussed in Chapters 22 through 25. Chapter 22 explains the objectives of bond portfolio management and the various types of portfolio strategies. Chapter 23 demonstrates how to construct portfolios using a factor model and to control portfolio risk. Liability-driven strategies (immunization and cash flow matching strategies and strategies for managing defined pension plans) are covered in Chapter 24. Measuring and evaluating the investment performance of a bond portfolio manager are explained in Chapter 25.

In the last four chapters, the various instruments that can be used to control portfolio risk are explained. Chapter 26 covers interest-rate futures contracts; Chapter 27 covers interest-rate options; Chapter 28 covers interest-rate swaps, caps, and floors. Coverage includes the pricing of these contracts and their role in bond portfolio management. Credit derivatives, more specifically credit default swaps (one type of credit derivative), are the subject of Chapter 29.

QUESTIONS

1. What is the cash flow of a 10-year bond that pays coupon interest semiannually, has a coupon rate of 7%, and has a par value of $100,000?

2. What is the cash flow of a seven-year bond that pays no coupon interest and has a par value of $10,000?

3. Give three reasons why the maturity of a bond is important.

4. Explain whether or not an investor can determine today what the cash flow of a floating-rate bond will be.

5. Suppose that the coupon reset formula for a floating-rate bond is

   1-month LIBOR + 220 basis points

   a. What is the reference rate?
   b. What is the quoted margin?
   c. Suppose on a coupon reset date that 1-month LIBOR is 2.8%. What will the coupon rate be for the period?

6. What is a deferred coupon bond?

7. What is meant by a linker?

8. **a.** What is meant by an amortizing security?
   b. Why is the maturity of an amortizing security not a useful measure?

9. What is a bond with an embedded option?

10. What does the call provision for a bond entitle the issuer to do?

11. **a.** What is the advantage of a call provision for an issuer?
    b. What are the disadvantages of a call provision for the bondholder?

12. What does the put provision for a bond entitle the bondholder to do?

13. Export Development Canada issued a bond on March 17, 2009. The terms were as follows:

    Currency of denomination: Japanese yen (JPY)
    Denomination: JPY100,000,000
    Maturity date: March 18, 2019, or an optional redemption date
    Redemption/payment basis: Redemption at par value
    Interest payment dates: March 18 and September 18 in each year
    Optional redemption dates: The issuer has the right to call the instruments in whole (but not in part) at par starting on March 18, 2012.
    Interest rate:
        Fixed rate for the first three years up to but excluding March 18, 2012: 1.5%
        March 18, 2012 – September 18, 2012 1.75% – 6 month JPY LIBORBBA
        September 18, 2012 – March 18, 2013 1.75% – 6 month JPY LIBORBBA

March 18, 2013 – September 18, 2013 2.00% – 6 month JPY LIBORBBA
September 18, 2013 – March 18, 2014 2.00% – 6 month JPY LIBORBBA
March 18, 2014 – September 18, 2014 2.25% – 6 month JPY LIBORBBA
September 18, 2014 – March 18, 2015 2.25% – 6 month JPY LIBORBBA
March 18, 2015 – September 18, 2015 2.50% – 6 month JPY LIBORBBA
September 18, 2015 – March 18, 2016 2.50% – 6 month JPY LIBORBBA
March 18, 2016 – September 18, 2016 2.75% – 6 month JPY LIBORBBA
September 18, 2016 – March 18, 2017 2.75% – 6 month JPY LIBORBBA
March 18, 2017 – September 18, 2017 3.00% – 6 month JPY LIBORBBA
September 18, 2017 – March 18, 2018 3.00% – 6 month JPY LIBORBBA
March 18, 2018 – September 18, 2018 3.25% – 6 month JPY LIBORBBA
September 18, 2018 – March 18, 2019 3.25% – 6 month JPY LIBORBBA

a. What is meant by JPY LIBORBBA?
b. Describe the coupon interest characteristics of this bond.
c. What are the risks associated with investing in this bond if the investor's home currency is not in Japanese yen.

14. What are a convertible bond and an exchangeable bond?

15. How do market participants gauge the default risk of a bond issue?

16. Comment on the following statement: "Credit risk is more than the risk that an issuer will default."

17. Explain whether you agree or disagree with the following statement: "Because my bond is guaranteed by an insurance company, I have eliminated credit risk."

18. **a.** What is counterparty risk?
    b. Give two examples of transactions where one faces counterparty risk.

19. Does an investor who purchases a zero-coupon bond face reinvestment risk?

20. What is meant by marking a position to market?

21. What is meant by a CUSIP number, and why is it important?

Pricing of Bonds

LEARNING OBJECTIVES

After reading this chapter, you will understand

- the time value of money
- how to calculate the price of a bond
- that to price a bond it is necessary to estimate the expected cash flows and determine the appropriate yield at which to discount the expected cash flows
- why the price of a bond changes in the direction opposite to the change in required yield
- that the relationship between price and yield of an option-free bond is convex
- the relationship between coupon rate, required yield, and price
- how the price of a bond changes as it approaches maturity
- the reasons why the price of a bond changes
- the complications of pricing bonds
- the pricing of floating-rate and inverse-floating-rate securities
- what accrued interest is and how bond prices are quoted

In this chapter, we explain how the price of a bond is determined, and in the next we discuss how the yield on a bond is measured. Basic to understanding pricing models and yield measures is an understanding of the time value of money. Therefore, we begin this chapter with a review of this concept.

REVIEW OF TIME VALUE OF MONEY

The notion that money has a time value is one of the basic concepts in the analysis of any financial instrument. Money has time value because of the opportunity to invest it at some interest rate.

Future Value

To determine the future value of any sum of money invested today, equation (2.1) can be used:

$$P_n = P_0 (1 + r)^n \qquad (2.1)$$

where

n = number of periods
P_n = future value n periods from now (in dollars)
P_0 = original principal (in dollars)
r = interest rate per period (in decimal form)

The expression $(1 + r)^n$ represents the future value of $1 invested today for n periods at a compounding rate of r.

For example, suppose that a pension fund manager invests $10 million in a financial instrument that promises to pay 9.2% per year for six years. The future value of the $10 million investment is $16,956,500; that is,

$$P_6 = \$10,000,000(1.092)^6$$
$$= \$10,000,000(1.69565)$$
$$= \$16,956,500$$

This example demonstrates how to compute the future value when interest is paid once per year (i.e., the period is equal to the number of years). When interest is paid more than one time per year, both the interest rate and the number of periods used to compute the future value must be adjusted as follows:

$$r = \frac{\text{annual interest rate}}{\text{number of times interest is paid per year}}$$

$$n = \text{number of times interest is paid per year} \times \text{number of years}$$

For example, suppose that the portfolio manager in the first example invests $10 million in a financial instrument that promises to pay an annual interest rate of 9.2% for six years, but the interest is paid semiannually (i.e., twice per year). Then

$$r = \frac{0.092}{2} = 0.046$$
$$n = 2 \times 6 = 12$$

and

$$P_{12} = \$10,000,000(1.046)^{12}$$
$$= \$10,000,000(1.71546)$$
$$= \$17,154,600$$

Notice that the future value of $10 million when interest is paid semiannually ($17,154,600) is greater than when interest is paid annually ($16,956,500), even though the same annual rate is applied to both investments. The higher future value when interest is paid semiannually reflects the greater opportunity for reinvesting the interest paid.

Future Value of an Ordinary Annuity

When the same amount of money is invested periodically, it is referred to as an **annuity**. When the first investment occurs one period from now, it is referred to as an **ordinary**

annuity. The future value of an ordinary annuity can be found by finding the future value of each investment at the end of the investment horizon and then adding these future values. However, it is easier to compute the future value of an ordinary annuity using the equation

$$P_n = A\left[\frac{(1 + r)^n - 1}{r}\right] \tag{2.2}$$

where A is the amount of the annuity (in dollars). The term in brackets is the **future value of an ordinary annuity of \$1** at the end of n periods.

To see how this formula can be applied, suppose that a portfolio manager purchases \$20 million par value of a 15-year bond that promises to pay 10% interest per year. The issuer makes a payment once a year, with the first annual interest payment occurring one year from now. How much will the portfolio manager have if (1) the bond is held until it matures 15 years from now, and (2) annual payments are invested at an annual interest rate of 8%?

The amount that the portfolio manager will have at the end of 15 years will be equal to

1. the \$20 million when the bond matures
2. 15 annual interest payments of \$2,000,000 (0.10 × \$20 million)
3. the interest earned by investing the annual interest payments at 8% per year

We can determine the sum of the second and third items by applying equation (2.2). In this illustration, the annuity is \$2,000,000 per year. Therefore,

$$A = \$2,000,000$$
$$r = 0.08$$
$$n = 15$$

and

$$P_{15} = \$2,000,000\left[\frac{(1.08)^{15} - 1}{0.08}\right]$$
$$= \$2,000,000\left[\frac{3.17217 - 1}{0.08}\right]$$
$$= \$2,000,000[27.152125]$$
$$= \$54,304,250$$

The future value of the ordinary annuity of \$2,000,000 per year for 15 years invested at 8% is \$54,304,250. Because \$30,000,000 (15 × \$2,000,000) of this future value represents the total dollar amount of annual interest payments made by the issuer and invested by the portfolio manager, the balance of \$24,304,250 (\$54,304,250 − 30,000,000) is the interest earned by reinvesting these annual interest payments. Thus, the total dollars that the portfolio manager will have at the end of 15 years by making the investment will be

Par (maturity) value	\$20,000,000
Interest payments	30,000,000
Interest on reinvestment of interest payments	24,304,250
Total future dollars	\$74,304,250

As you shall see in Chapter 3, it is necessary to calculate these total future dollars at the end of a portfolio manager's investment horizon in order to assess the relative value of a bond.

Let's rework the analysis for this bond assuming that the interest is paid every six months (based on an annual rate), with the first six-month payment to be received and immediately invested six months from now. We shall assume that the semiannual interest payments can be reinvested at an annual interest rate of 8%.

Interest payments received every six months are $1,000,000. The future value of the 30 semiannual interest payments of $1,000,000 to be received plus the interest earned by investing the interest payments is found as follows:

$$A = \$1,000,000$$

$$r = \frac{0.08}{2} = 0.04$$

$$n = 15 \times 2 = 30$$

$$P_{30} = \$1,000,000 \left[\frac{(1.04)^{30} - 1}{0.04} \right]$$

$$= \$1,000,000 \left[\frac{3.2434 - 1}{0.04} \right]$$

$$= \$1,000,000 \left[56.085 \right]$$

$$= \$56,085,000$$

Because the interest payments are equal to $30,000,000, the interest earned on the interest payments reinvested is $26,085,000. The opportunity for more frequent reinvestment of interest payments received makes the interest earned of $26,085,000 from reinvesting the interest payments greater than the $24,304,250 interest earned when interest is paid only one time per year.

The total future dollars that the portfolio manager will have at the end of 15 years by making the investment are as follows:

Par (maturity) value	$20,000,000
Interest payments	30,000,000
Interest on reinvestment of interest payments	26,085,000
Total future dollars	$76,085,000

Present Value

We have explained how to compute the future value of an investment. Now we illustrate how to work the process in reverse; that is, we show how to determine the amount of money that must be invested today in order to realize a specific future value. This amount is called the **present value**. Because, as we explain later in this chapter, the price of any financial instrument is the present value of its expected cash flows, it is necessary to understand present value to be able to price fixed-income instruments.

What we are interested in is how to determine the amount of money that must be invested today at an interest rate of r per period for n periods to produce a specific future value. This can be done by solving the formula for the future value given by equation (2.1) for the original principal (P_0):

$$P_0 = P_n\left[\frac{1}{(1 + r)^n}\right]$$

Instead of using P_0, however, we denote the present value by PV. Therefore, the present value formula can be rewritten as

$$PV = P_n\left[\frac{1}{(1 + r)^n}\right] \tag{2.3}$$

The term in brackets is the present value of \$1; that is, it indicates how much must be set aside today, earning an interest rate of r per period, in order to have \$1 n periods from now.

The process of computing the present value is also referred to as **discounting**. Therefore, the present value is sometimes referred to as the **discounted value**, and the interest rate is referred to as the **discount rate**.

To illustrate how to apply equation (2.3), suppose that a portfolio manager has the opportunity to purchase a financial instrument that promises to pay \$5 million seven years from now with no interim cash flows. Assuming that the portfolio manager wants to earn an annual interest rate of 10% on this investment, the present value of this investment is computed as follows:

$$r = 0.10$$
$$n = 7$$
$$P_7 = \$5,000,000$$
$$PV = \$5,000,000\left[\frac{1}{(1.10)^7}\right]$$
$$= \$5,000,000\left[\frac{1}{1.948717}\right]$$
$$= \$5,000,000[0.513158]$$
$$= \$2,565,791$$

The equation shows that if \$2,565,791 is invested today at 10% annual interest, the investment will grow to \$5 million at the end of seven years. Suppose that this financial instrument is actually selling for more than \$2,565,791. Then the portfolio manager would be earning less than 10% by investing in this financial instrument at a purchase price greater than \$2,565,791. The reverse is true if the financial instrument is selling for less than \$2,565,791. Then the portfolio manager would be earning more than 10%.

There are two properties of present value that you should recognize. First, for a given future value at a specified time in the future, the higher the interest rate (or discount rate), the lower the present value. The reason the present value decreases as the interest rate increases should be easy to understand: The higher the interest rate that can be earned on any sum invested today, the less has to be invested today to realize a specified future value.

The second property of present value is that for a given interest rate (discount rate), the further into the future the future value will be received, the lower its present value. The reason is that the further into the future a given future value is to be received, the more opportunity there is for interest to accumulate. Thus, fewer dollars have to be invested.

Present Value of a Series of Future Values

In most applications in portfolio management, a financial instrument will offer a series of future values. To determine the present value of a series of future values, the present value of each future value must first be computed. Then these present values are added together to obtain the present value of the entire series of future values.

Mathematically, this can be expressed as follows:

$$PV = \sum_{t=1}^{n} \frac{P_t}{(1 + r)^t} \qquad (2.4)$$

For example, suppose that a portfolio manager is considering the purchase of a financial instrument that promises to make these payments:

Years from Now	Promised Payment by Issuer
1	$ 100
2	100
3	100
4	100
5	1,100

Assume that the portfolio manager wants a 6.25% annual interest rate on this investment. The present value of such an investment can be computed as follows:

Years from Now	Future Value of Payment	Present Value of $1 at 6.25%	Present Value of Payment
1	$ 100	0.9412	$ 94.12
2	100	0.8858	88.58
3	100	0.8337	83.37
4	100	0.7847	78.47
5	1,100	0.7385	812.35
		Present value =	$1,156.89

Present Value of an Ordinary Annuity

When the same dollar amount of money is received each period or paid each year, the series is referred to as an **annuity**. When the first payment is received one period from now, the annuity is called an **ordinary annuity**. When the first payment is immediate, the annuity is called an **annuity due**. In all the applications discussed in this book, we shall deal with ordinary annuities. To compute the present value of an ordinary annuity, the present value of each future value can be computed and then summed. Alternatively, a formula for the present value of an ordinary annuity can be used:

$$PV = A \left[\frac{1 - \dfrac{1}{(1 + r)^n}}{r} \right] \qquad (2.5)$$

where A is the amount of the annuity (in dollars). The term in brackets is the **present value of an ordinary annuity of $1 for _n_ periods**.

Suppose that an investor expects to receive $100 at the end of each year for the next eight years from an investment and that the appropriate discount rate to be used for discounting is 9%. The present value of this ordinary annuity is

$$A = \$100$$
$$r = 0.09$$
$$n = 8$$

$$PV = \$100\left[\frac{1 - \dfrac{1}{(1.09)^8}}{0.09}\right]$$

$$= \$100\left[\frac{1 - \dfrac{1}{1.99256}}{0.09}\right]$$

$$= \$100\left[\frac{1 - 0.501867}{0.09}\right]$$

$$= \$100[5.534811]$$

$$= \$553.48$$

Present Value When Payments Occur More Than Once per Year

In our computations of the present value, we have assumed that the future value to be received or paid occurs each year. In practice, the future value to be received may occur more than once per year. When that is the case, the formulas we have developed for determining the present value must be modified in two ways. First, the annual interest rate is divided by the frequency per year.[1] For example, if the future values are received semiannually, the annual interest rate is divided by 2; if they are paid or received quarterly, the annual interest rate is divided by 4. Second, the number of periods when the future value will be received must be adjusted by multiplying the number of years by the frequency per year.

PRICING A BOND

The price of any financial instrument is equal to the present value of the expected cash flows from the financial instrument. Therefore, determining the price requires

1. an estimate of the expected cash flows
2. an estimate of the appropriate required yield

The expected cash flows for some financial instruments are simple to compute; for others, the task is more difficult. The required yield reflects the yield for financial instruments with **comparable risk**, or **alternative (or substitute) investments**.

The first step in determining the price of a bond is to determine its cash flows. The cash flows for a bond that the issuer cannot retire prior to its stated maturity date (i.e., an option-free bond[2]) consist of

1. periodic coupon interest payments to the maturity date
2. the par (or maturity) value at maturity

---

[1] Technically, this is not the proper way for adjusting the annual interest rate. The technically proper method of adjustment is discussed in Chapter 3.

[2] In Chapter 17, we discuss the pricing of bonds (i.e., callable, putable, and convertible bonds).

Our illustrations of bond pricing use three assumptions to simplify the analysis:

1. The coupon payments are made every six months. (For most domestic bond issues, coupon interest is, in fact, paid semiannually.)
2. The next coupon payment for the bond is received exactly six months from now.
3. The coupon interest is fixed for the term of the bond.

Consequently, the cash flow for an option-free bond consists of an annuity of a fixed coupon interest payment paid semiannually and the par or maturity value. For example, a 20-year bond with a 10% coupon rate and a par or maturity value of $1,000 has the following cash flows from coupon interest:

$$\text{annual coupon interest} = \$1,000 \times 0.10$$
$$= \$100$$
$$\text{semiannual coupon interest} = \$100/2$$
$$= \$50$$

Therefore, there are 40 semiannual cash flows of $50, and a $1,000 cash flow 40 six-month periods from now. Notice the treatment of the par value. It is *not* treated as if it is received 20 years from now. Instead, it is treated on a basis consistent with the coupon payments, which are semiannual.

The required yield is determined by investigating the yields offered on comparable bonds in the market. By comparable, we mean option-free bonds of the same credit quality and the same maturity.[3] The required yield typically is expressed as an annual interest rate. When the cash flows occur semiannually, the market convention is to use one-half the annual interest rate as the periodic interest rate with which to discount the cash flows.

Given the cash flows of a bond and the required yield, we have all the analytical tools to price a bond. As the price of a bond is the present value of the cash flows, it is determined by adding these two present values:

1. the present value of the semiannual coupon payments
2. the present value of the par or maturity value at the maturity date

In general, the price of a bond can be computed using the following formula:

$$P = \frac{C}{1 + r} + \frac{C}{(1 + r)^2} + \frac{C}{(1 + r)^3} + \cdots + \frac{C}{(1 + r)^n} + \frac{M}{(1 + r)^n}$$

or

$$P = \sum_{t=1}^{n} \frac{C}{(1 + r)^t} + \frac{M}{(1 + r)^n} \qquad (2.6)$$

where

P = price (in dollars)
n = number of periods (number of years times 2)
C = semiannual coupon payment (in dollars)
r = periodic interest rate (required annual yield divided by 2)
M = maturity value
t = time period when the payment is to be received

---

[3] In Chapter 4, we introduce a measure of interest-rate risk known as duration. There, instead of talking in terms of bonds with the same maturity as being comparable, we recast the analysis in terms of duration.

Because the semiannual coupon payments are equivalent to an ordinary annuity, applying equation (2.5) for the present value of an ordinary annuity gives the present value of the coupon payments:

$$C\left[\frac{1 - \dfrac{1}{(1 + r)^n}}{r}\right] \qquad (2.7)$$

To illustrate how to compute the price of a bond, consider a 20-year 10% coupon bond with a par value of $1,000. Let's suppose that the required yield on this bond is 11%. The cash flows for this bond are as follows:

1. 40 semiannual coupon payments of $50
2. $1,000 to be received 40 six-month periods from now

The semiannual or periodic interest rate (or periodic required yield) is 5.5% (11% divided by 2).

The present value of the 40 semiannual coupon payments of $50 discounted at 5.5% is $802.31, calculated as

$$C = \$50$$
$$n = 40$$
$$r = 0.055$$

$$= \$50\left[\frac{1 - \dfrac{1}{(1.055)^{40}}}{0.055}\right]$$

$$= \$50\left[\frac{1 - \dfrac{1}{8.51332}}{0.055}\right]$$

$$= \$50\left[\frac{1 - 0.117463}{0.055}\right]$$

$$= \$50[16.04613]$$

$$= \$802.31$$

The present value of the par or maturity value of $1,000 received 40 six-month periods from now, discounted at 5.5%, is $117.46, as follows:

$$\frac{\$1,000}{(1.055)^{40}} = \frac{\$1,000}{8.51332} = \$117.46$$

The price of the bond is then equal to the sum of the two present values:

Present value of coupon payments	$802.31
+ Present value of par (maturity value)	117.46
Price	$919.77

Suppose that, instead of an 11% required yield, the required yield is 6.8%. The price of the bond would then be $1,347.04, demonstrated as follows.

The present value of the coupon payments using a periodic interest rate of 3.4% (6.8%/2) is

$$\$50\left[\frac{1 - \dfrac{1}{(1.034)^{40}}}{0.034}\right] = \$50[21.69029]$$

$$= \$1,084.51$$

The present value of the par or maturity value of $1,000 received *40 six-month periods from now* discounted at 3.4% is

$$\frac{\$1,000}{(1.034)^{40}} = \$262.53$$

The price of the bond is then as follows:

Present value of coupon payments	$1,084.51
+ Present value of par (maturity value)	262.53
Price	$1,347.04

If the required yield is equal to the coupon rate of 10%, the price of the bond would be its par value, $1,000, as the following calculations demonstrate.

Using a periodic interest rate of 5.0% (10%/2), the present value of the coupon payments is

$$\$50\left[\frac{1 - \dfrac{1}{(1.050)^{40}}}{0.050}\right] = \$50[17.15909]$$

$$= \$857.97$$

The present value of the par or maturity value of $1,000 received *40 six-month periods from now* discounted at 5% is

$$\frac{\$1,000}{(1.050)^{40}} = \$142.05$$

The price of the bond is then as follows:

Present value of coupon payments	$ 857.95
+ Present value of par (maturity value)	142.05
Price	$1,000.00

Pricing Zero-Coupon Bonds

Some bonds do not make any periodic coupon payments. Instead, the investor realizes interest as the difference between the maturity value and the purchase price. These bonds are called **zero-coupon bonds**. The price of a zero-coupon bond is calculated by substituting zero for C in equation (2.6):

$$P = \frac{M}{(1 + r)^n} \tag{2.8}$$

Equation (2.8) states that the price of a zero-coupon bond is simply the present value of the maturity value. In the present value computation, however, the number of periods used for discounting is not the number of years to maturity of the bond, but rather double the number of years. The discount rate is one-half the required annual yield. For example, the price of a zero-coupon bond that matures 15 years from now, if the maturity value is $1,000 and the required yield is 9.4%, is $252.12, as shown:

$$M = \$1,000$$
$$r = 0.047 \left[= \frac{0.094}{2} \right]$$
$$n = 30 (= 2 \times 15)$$
$$P = \frac{\$1,000}{(1.047)^{30}}$$
$$= \frac{\$1,000}{3.96644}$$
$$= \$252.12$$

Price–Yield Relationship

A fundamental property of a bond is that its price changes in the opposite direction from the change in the required yield. The reason is that the price of the bond is the present value of the cash flows. As the required yield increases, the present value of the cash flow decreases; hence the price decreases. The opposite is true when the required yield decreases: The present value of the cash flows increases, and therefore the price of the bond increases. This can be seen by examining the price for the 20-year 10% bond when the required yield is 11%, 10%, and 6.8%. Exhibit 2-1 shows the price of the 20-year 10% coupon bond for various required yields.

Exhibit 2-1   Price–Yield Relationship for a 20-Year 10% Coupon Bond

Yield	Price	Yield	Price
0.045	$1,720.32	0.110	$919.77
0.050	1,627.57	0.115	883.50
0.055	1,541.76	0.120	849.54
0.060	1,462.30	0.125	817.70
0.065	1,388.65	0.130	787.82
0.070	1,320.33	0.135	759.75
0.075	1,256.89	0.140	733.37
0.080	1,197.93	0.145	708.53
0.085	1,143.08	0.150	685.14
0.090	1,092.01	0.155	663.08
0.095	1,044.41	0.160	642.26
0.100	1,000.00	0.165	622.59
0.105	958.53		

If we graph the price–yield relationship for any option-free bond, we will find that it has the "bowed" shape shown in Exhibit 2-2. This shape is referred to as convex. The convexity of the price–yield relationship has important implications for the investment properties of a bond, as we explain in Chapter 4. Also note the price in Exhibit 2-2 where the graph of the price–yield relationship intersects the price axis (i.e., the vertical axis). That price is the maximum price for the bond and corresponds to the value of the undiscounted cash flows of the bond; that is, it is the sum of all the coupon payments and the par value.

Relationship Between Coupon Rate, Required Yield, and Price

As yields in the marketplace change, the only variable that can change to compensate an investor for the new required yield in the market is the price of the bond. When the coupon rate is equal to the required yield, the price of the bond will be equal to its par value, as we demonstrated for the 20-year 10% coupon bond.

When yields in the marketplace rise above the coupon rate at *a given point in time*, the price of the bond adjusts so that an investor contemplating the purchase of the bond can realize some additional interest. If it did not, investors would not buy the issue because it offers a below-market yield; the resulting lack of demand would cause the price to fall and thus the yield on the bond to increase. This is how a bond's price falls below its par value.

The capital appreciation realized by holding the bond to maturity represents a form of interest to a new investor to compensate for a coupon rate that is lower than the required yield. When a bond sells below its par value, it is said to be selling at a **discount**. In our earlier calculation of bond price, we saw that when the required yield is greater than the coupon rate, the price of the bond is always lower than the par value ($1,000).

When the required yield in the market is below the coupon rate, the bond must sell above its par value. This is because investors who have the opportunity to purchase the

Exhibit 2-2   Shape of Price–Yield Relationship for an Option-Free Bond

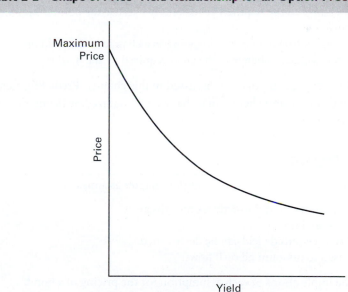

bond at par would be getting a coupon rate in excess of what the market requires. As a result, investors would bid up the price of the bond because its yield is so attractive. The price would eventually be bid up to a level where the bond offers the required yield in the market. A bond whose price is above its par value is said to be selling at a **premium**. The relationship between coupon rate, required yield, and price can be summarized as follows:

$$\text{coupon rate} < \text{required yield} \leftrightarrow \text{price} < \text{par (discount bond)}$$
$$\text{coupon rate} = \text{required yield} \leftrightarrow \text{price} = \text{par}$$
$$\text{coupon rate} > \text{required yield} \leftrightarrow \text{price} > \text{par (premium bond)}$$

Relationship Between Bond Price and Time If Interest Rates Are Unchanged

If the required yield does not change between the time the bond is purchased and the maturity date, what will happen to the price of the bond? For a bond selling at par value, the coupon rate is equal to the required yield. As the bond moves closer to maturity, the bond will continue to sell at par value. Its price will remain constant as the bond moves toward the maturity date.

The price of a bond will *not* remain constant for a bond selling at a premium or a discount. Exhibit 2-3 shows the time path of a 20-year 10% coupon bond selling at a discount and the same bond selling at a premium as it approaches maturity. Notice that the discount bond increases in price as it approaches maturity, assuming that the required yield does not change. For a premium bond, the opposite occurs. For both bonds, the price will equal par value at the maturity date.

Reasons for the Change in the Price of a Bond

The price of a bond will change for one or more of the following three reasons:

1. There is a change in the required yield owing to changes in the credit quality of the issuer.
2. There is a change in the price of the bond selling at a premium or a discount, without any change in the required yield, simply because the bond is moving toward maturity.
3. There is a change in the required yield owing to a change in the yield on comparable bonds (i.e., a change in the yield required by the market).

Reasons 2 and 3 for a change in price are discussed in this chapter. Predicting a change in an issue's credit quality (reason 1) before that change is recognized by the market is one of the challenges of investment management.

COMPLICATIONS

The framework for pricing a bond discussed in this chapter assumes that:

1. The next coupon payment is exactly six months away.
2. The cash flows are known.
3. The appropriate required yield can be determined.
4. One rate is used to discount all cash flows.

Let's look at the implications of each assumption for the pricing of a bond.

Exhibit 2-3 Time Path for the Price of a 20-Year 10% Bond Selling at a Discount and Premium as It Approaches Maturity

Year	Price of Discount Bond Selling to Yield 12%	Price of Premium Bond Selling to Yield 7.8%
20.0	$ 849.54	$1,221.00
19.5	850.51	1,218.62
19.0	851.54	1,216.14
18.5	852.63	1,213.57
18.0	853.79	1,210.90
17.5	855.02	1,208.13
17.0	856.32	1,205.24
16.5	857.70	1,202.25
16.0	859.16	1,199.14
15.5	860.71	1,195.90
15.0	862.35	1,192.54
14.5	864.09	1,189.05
14.0	865.94	1,185.43
13.5	867.89	1,181.66
13.0	869.97	1,177.74
12.5	872.17	1,173.67
12.0	874.50	1,169.45
11.5	876.97	1,165.06
11.0	879.58	1,160.49
10.5	882.36	1,155.75
10.0	885.30	1,150.83
9.5	888.42	1,145.71
9.0	891.72	1,140.39
8.5	895.23	1,134.87
8.0	898.94	1,129.13
7.5	902.88	1,123.16
7.0	907.05	1,116.97
6.5	911.47	1,110.53
6.0	916.16	1,103.84
5.5	921.13	1,096.89
5.0	926.40	1,089.67
4.5	931.98	1,082.16
4.0	937.90	1,074.37
3.5	944.18	1,066.27
3.0	950.83	1,057.85
2.5	957.88	1,049.11
2.0	965.35	1,040.02
1.5	973.27	1,030.58
1.0	981.67	1,020.78
0.5	990.57	1,010.59
0.0	1,000.00	1,000.00

Next Coupon Payment Due in Less Than Six Months

When an investor purchases a bond whose next coupon payment is due in less than six months, the accepted method for computing the price of the bond is as follows:

$$P = \sum_{t=1}^{n} \frac{C}{(1 + r)^v (1 + r)^{t-1}} + \frac{M}{(1 + r)^v (1 + r)^{n-1}} \tag{2.9}$$

where

$$v = \frac{\text{days between settlement and next coupon}}{\text{days in six-month period}}$$

Note that when v is 1 (i.e., when the next coupon payment is six months away) equation (2.9) reduces to equation (2.6).

Cash Flows May Not Be Known

For option-free bonds, assuming that the issuer does not default, the cash flows are known. For most bonds, however, the cash flows are not known with certainty. This is because an issuer may call a bond before the stated maturity date. With callable bonds, the cash flow will, in fact, depend on the level of current interest rates relative to the coupon rate. For example, the issuer will typically call a bond when interest rates drop far enough below the coupon rate so that it is economical to retire the bond issue prior to maturity and issue new bonds at a lower coupon rate.[4] Consequently, the cash flows of bonds that may be called prior to maturity are dependent on current interest rates in the marketplace.

Determining the Appropriate Required Yield

All required yields are benchmarked off yields offered by Treasury securities, the subject of Chapter 5. The analytical framework that we develop in this book is one of decomposing the required yield for a bond into its component parts, as we discuss in later chapters.

One Discount Rate Applicable to All Cash Flows

Our pricing analysis has assumed that it is appropriate to discount each cash flow using the same discount rate. As explained in Chapter 5, a bond can be viewed as a package of zero-coupon bonds, in which case a unique discount rate should be used to determine the present value of each cash flow.

PRICING FLOATING-RATE AND INVERSE-FLOATING-RATE SECURITIES

The cash flow is not known for either a floating-rate or an inverse-floating-rate security; it will depend on the reference rate in the future.

Price of a Floater

The coupon rate of a floating-rate security (or **floater**) is equal to a reference rate plus some spread or margin. For example, the coupon rate of a floater can reset at the rate on a

---

[4] Residential mortgage-backed securities, discussed in Chapters 11 through 13, are another example; the individual borrowers have the right to prepay all or part of the mortgage obligation prior to the scheduled due date.

three-month Treasury bill (the reference rate) plus 50 basis points (the spread). The price of a floater depends on two factors: (1) the spread over the reference rate, and (2) any restrictions that may be imposed on the resetting of the coupon rate. For example, a floater may have a maximum coupon rate called a **cap** or a minimum coupon rate called a **floor**. The price of a floater will trade close to its par value as long as (1) the spread above the reference rate that the market requires is unchanged, and (2) neither the cap nor the floor is reached.[5]

If the market requires a larger (smaller) spread, the price of a floater will trade below (above) par. If the coupon rate is restricted from changing to the reference rate plus the spread because of the cap, then the price of a floater will trade below par.

Price of an Inverse Floater

In general, an inverse floater is created from a fixed-rate security.[6] The security from which the inverse floater is created is called the **collateral**. From the collateral, two bonds are created: a floater and an inverse floater. This is depicted in Exhibit 2-4.

The two bonds are created such that (1) the total coupon interest paid to the two bonds in each period is less than or equal to the collateral's coupon interest in each period, and (2) the total par value of the two bonds is less than or equal to the collateral's total par value. Equivalently, the floater and inverse floater are structured so that the cash flow from the collateral will be sufficient to satisfy the obligation of the two bonds.

For example, consider a 10-year 7.5% coupon semiannual-pay bond. Suppose that $100 million of the bond is used as collateral to create a floater with a par value of $50 million and an inverse floater with a par value of $50 million. Suppose that the coupon rate is reset every six months based on the following formula:

$$\text{Floater coupon: reference rate} + 1\%$$
$$\text{Inverse floater coupon: } 14\% - \text{reference rate}$$

Notice that the total par value of the floater and inverse floater equals the par value of the collateral, $100 million. The weighted average of the coupon rate of the combination of the two bonds is

$$0.5(\text{reference rate} + 1\%) + 0.5(14\% - \text{reference rate}) = 7.5\%$$

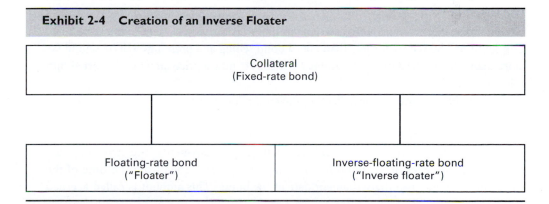

Exhibit 2-4   Creation of an Inverse Floater

Collateral
(Fixed-rate bond)

Floating-rate bond
("Floater")

Inverse-floating-rate bond
("Inverse floater")

---

[5] In between coupon reset dates, the floater can trade above or below par.
[6] Inverse floaters are also created using interest-rate swaps without the need to create a floater.

Thus, regardless of the level of the reference rate, the combined coupon rate for the two bonds is equal to the coupon rate of the collateral, 7.5%.

There is one problem with the coupon formulas given here. Suppose that the reference rate exceeds 14%. Then the formula for the coupon rate for the inverse floater will be negative. To prevent this from happening, a floor is placed on the coupon rate for the inverse floater. Typically, the floor is set at zero. Because of the floor, the coupon rate on the floater must be restricted so that the coupon interest paid to the two bonds does not exceed the collateral's coupon interest. In our hypothetical structure, the maximum coupon rate that must be imposed on the floater is 15%. Thus, when a floater and an inverse floater are created from the collateral, a floor is imposed on the inverse and a cap is imposed on the floater.

The valuation of the cap and the floor is beyond our discussion at this point. Here, it is sufficient to point out that the price of an inverse floater is found by determining the price of the collateral and the price of the floater. This can be seen as follows:

$$\text{collateral's price} = \text{floater's price} + \text{inverse's price}$$

Therefore,

$$\text{inverse's price} = \text{collateral's price} - \text{floater's price}$$

Notice that the factors that affect the price of an inverse floater are affected by the reference rate only to the extent that it affects the restrictions on the floater's rate. This is quite an important result. Some investors mistakenly believe that because the coupon rate rises, the price of an inverse floater should increase if the reference rate decreases. This is not true. The key in pricing an inverse floater is how changes in interest rates affect the price of the collateral. The reference rate is important only to the extent that it restricts the coupon rate of the floater.

PRICE QUOTES AND ACCRUED INTEREST

Price Quotes

Throughout this chapter, we have assumed that the maturity or par value of a bond is $1,000. A bond may have a maturity or par value greater or less than $1,000. Consequently, when quoting bond prices, traders quote the price as a percentage of par value.

A bond selling at par is quoted as 100, meaning 100% of its par value. A bond selling at a discount will be selling for less than 100; a bond selling at a premium will be selling for more than 100. The examples in Exhibit 2-5 illustrate how a price quote is converted into a dollar price.

In later chapters, we will describe the convention for quoting specific security types.

Accrued Interest

When an investor purchases a bond between coupon payments, the investor must compensate the seller of the bond for the coupon interest earned from the time of the last coupon payment to the settlement date of the bond.[7] This amount is called **accrued**

---

[7] The exceptions are bonds that are in default. Such bonds are said to be quoted **flat**; that is, without accrued interest.

Exhibit 2-5	Price Quotes Converted into a Dollar Price		
(1) **Price Quote**	**(2)** **Converted to a Decimal [= (1)/100]**	**(3)** **Par Value**	**(4)** **Dollar Price [= (2) × (3)]**
97	0.9700000	$ 10,000	$ 9,700.00
85½	0.8550000	100,000	85,500.00
90¼	0.9025000	5,000	4,512.50
80⅛	0.8012500	10,000	8,012.50
76⁵⁄₃₂	0.7615625	1,000,000	761,562.50
86¹¹⁄₆₄	0.8617188	100,000	86,171.88
100	1.0000000	50,000	50,000.00
109	1.0900000	1,000	1,090.00
103¾	1.0375000	100,000	103,750.00
105⅜	1.0537500	25,000	26,343.75
103¹⁹⁄₃₂	1.0359375	1,000,000	1,035,937.50

interest. The computation of accrued interest depends on the type of bond. For a Treasury coupon security (discussed in Chapter 6), accrued interest is based on the actual number of days the bond is held by the seller. For corporate and municipal bonds, accrued interest is based on a 360-day year, with each month having 30 days.

The amount that the buyer pays the seller is the agreed-upon price plus accrued interest. This is often referred to as the **full price** or **dirty price**. The price of a bond without accrued interest is called the **clean price**.

KEY POINTS

- The price of a bond is the present value of the bond's expected cash flows, the discount rate being equal to the yield offered on comparable bonds. For an option-free bond, the cash flows are the coupon payments and the par value or maturity value. The higher (lower) the required yield, the lower (higher) the price of a bond.
- For a zero-coupon bond, there are no coupon payments. The price of a zero-coupon bond is equal to the present value of the maturity value, where the number of periods used to compute the present value is double the number of years and the discount rate is a semiannual yield.
- A bond's price changes in the opposite direction from the change in the required yield. The reason is that as the required yield increases (decreases), the present value of the cash flow decreases (increases).
- A bond will be priced below par, at par, or above par depending the bond's coupon rate and the yield required by investors. When the coupon rate is equal to the required yield, the bond will sell at its par value. When the coupon rate is less (greater) than the required yield, the bond will sell for less (more) than its par value.
- Over time, the price of a premium or discount bond will change even if the required yield does not change. Assuming that the credit quality of the issuer is unchanged, the

price change on any bond can be decomposed into a portion attributable to a change in the required yield and a portion attributable to the time path of the bond.

- The price of a floating-rate bond will trade close to par value if the spread required by the market does not change and there are no restrictions on the coupon rate.
- The price of an inverse floater depends on the price of the collateral from which it is created and the price of the floater.
- Accrued interest is the amount that a bond buyer who purchases a bond between coupon payments must pay the bond seller. The amount represents the coupon interest earned from the time of the last coupon payment to the settlement date of the bond.

QUESTIONS

1. A pension fund manager invests $10 million in a debt obligation that promises to pay 7.3% per year for four years. What is the future value of the $10 million?

2. Suppose that a life insurance company has guaranteed a payment of $14 million to a pension fund 4.5 years from now. If the life insurance company receives a premium of $10.4 million from the pension fund and can invest the entire premium for 4.5 years at an annual interest rate of 6.25%, will it have sufficient funds from this investment to meet the $14 million obligation?

3. a. The portfolio manager of a tax-exempt fund is considering investing $500,000 in a debt instrument that pays an annual interest rate of 5.7% for four years. At the end of four years, the portfolio manager plans to reinvest the proceeds for three more years and expects that for the three-year period, an annual interest rate of 7.2% can be earned. What is the future value of this investment?

   b. Suppose that the portfolio manager in Question 3, part a, has the opportunity to invest the $500,000 for seven years in a debt obligation that promises to pay an annual interest rate of 6.1% compounded semiannually. Is this investment alternative more attractive than the one in Question 3, part a?

4. Suppose that a portfolio manager purchases $10 million of par value of an eight-year bond that has a coupon rate of 7% and pays interest once per year. The first annual coupon payment will be made one year from now. How much will

the portfolio manager have if she (1) holds the bond until it matures eight years from now, and (2) can reinvest all the annual interest payments at an annual interest rate of 6.2%?

5. a. If the discount rate that is used to calculate the present value of a debt obligation's cash flow is increased, what happens to the price of that debt obligation?

   b. Suppose that the discount rate used to calculate the present value of a debt obligation's cash flow is x%. Suppose also that the only cash flow for this debt obligation is $200,000 four years from now and $200,000 five years from now. For which of these cash flows will the present value be greater?

6. The pension fund obligation of a corporation is calculated as the present value of the actuarially projected benefits that will have to be paid to beneficiaries. Why is the interest rate used to discount the projected benefits important?

7. A pension fund manager knows that the following liabilities must be satisfied:

Years from Now	Liability (in millions)
1	$2.0
2	3.0
3	5.4
4	5.8

Suppose that the pension fund manager wants to invest a sum of money that will satisfy this liability stream. Assuming that any amount that can be invested today can earn an annual interest rate of 7.6%, how much must be invested today to satisfy this liability stream?

8. Calculate for each of the following bonds the price per $1,000 of par value assuming semiannual coupon payments.

Bond	Coupon Rate (%)	Years to Maturity	Required Yield (%)
A	8	9	7
B	9	20	9
C	6	15	10
D	0	14	8

9. Consider a bond selling at par ($100) with a coupon rate of 6% and 10 years to maturity.

   a. What is the price of this bond if the required yield is 15%?

   b. What is the price of this bond if the required yield increases from 15% to 16%, and by what percentage did the price of this bond change?

   c. What is the price of this bond if the required yield is 5%?

   d. What is the price of this bond if the required yield increases from 5% to 6%, and by what percentage did the price of this bond change?

   e. From your answers to Question 9, parts b and d, what can you say about the relative price volatility of a bond in high- compared with low-interest-rate environments?

10. Suppose that you purchased a debt obligation three years ago at its par value of $100,000 and nine years remaining to maturity. The market price of this debt obligation today is $90,000. What are some reasons why the price of this debt obligation could have declined since you purchased it three years ago?

11. Suppose that you are reviewing a price sheet for bonds and see the following prices (per $100 par value) reported. You observe what seem to be several errors. Without calculating the price of each bond, indicate which bonds seem to be reported incorrectly and explain why.

Bond	Price	Coupon Rate (%)	Required Yield (%)
U	90	6	9
V	96	9	8
W	110	8	6
X	105	0	5
Y	107	7	9
Z	100	6	6

12. What is the maximum price of a bond?

13. What is the "dirty" price of a bond?

14. Explain why you agree or disagree with the following statement: "The price of a floater will always trade at its par value."

15. Explain why you agree or disagree with the following statement: "The price of an inverse floater will increase when the reference rate decreases."

3

Measuring Yield

LEARNING OBJECTIVES

After reading this chapter, you will understand

- how to calculate the yield on any investment
- how to calculate the current yield, yield to maturity, yield to call, yield to put, and cash flow yield
- how to calculate the yield for a portfolio
- how to calculate the discount margin for a floating-rate security
- the three potential sources of a bond's return
- what reinvestment risk is
- the limitations of conventional yield measures
- how to calculate the total return for a bond
- why the total return is superior to conventional yield measures
- how to use horizon analysis to assess the potential return performance of a bond
- the ways that a change in yield can be measured

In Chapter 2, we showed how to determine the price of a bond, and we described the relationship between price and yield. In this chapter, we discuss various yield measures and their meaning for evaluating the relative attractiveness of a bond. We will also explain the ways in which a change in yield is calculated. We begin with an explanation of how to compute the yield on any investment.

COMPUTING THE YIELD OR INTERNAL RATE OF RETURN ON ANY INVESTMENT

The yield on any investment is the interest rate that will make the present value of the cash flows from the investment equal to the price (or cost) of the investment. Mathematically, the yield on any investment, y, is the interest rate that satisfies the equation

$$P = \frac{CF_1}{1 + y} + \frac{CF_2}{(1 + y)^2} + \frac{CF_3}{(1 + y)^3} + \cdots + \frac{CF_N}{(1 + y)^N}$$

This expression can be rewritten in shorthand notation as

$$P = \sum_{t=1}^{N} \frac{CF_t}{(1 + y)^t} \tag{3.1}$$

where

CF_t = cash flow in year t
P = price of the investment
N = number of years

The yield calculated from this relationship is also called the **internal rate of return**.

Solving for the yield (y) requires a trial-and-error (iterative) procedure. The objective is to find the interest rate that will make the present value of the cash flows equal to the price. An example demonstrates how this is done.

Suppose that a financial instrument selling for $903.10 promises to make the following annual payments:

Years from Now	Promised Annual Payments (Cash Flow to Investor)
1	$ 100
2	100
3	100
4	1,000

To compute yield, different interest rates must be tried until the present value of the cash flows is equal to $903.10 (the price of the financial instrument). Trying an annual interest rate of 10% gives the following present value:

Years from Now	Promised Annual Payments (Cash Flow to Investor)	Present Value of Cash Flow at 10%
1	$ 100	$ 90.91
2	100	82.64
3	100	75.13
4	1,000	683.01
	Present value =	$931.69

Because the present value computed using a 10% interest rate exceeds the price of $903.10, a higher interest rate must be used, to reduce the present value. If a 12% interest rate is used, the present value is $875.71, computed as follows:

Years from Now	Promised Annual Payments (Cash Flow to Investor)	Present Value of Cash Flow at 12%
1	$ 100	$ 89.29
2	100	79.72
3	100	71.18
4	1,000	635.52
		Present value = $875.71

Using 12%, the present value of the cash flow is less than the price of the financial instrument. Therefore, a lower interest rate must be tried, to increase the present value. Using an 11% interest rate:

Years from Now	Promised Annual Payments (Cash Flow to Investor)	Present Value of Cash Flow at 11%
1	$ 100	$ 90.09
2	100	81.16
3	100	73.12
4	1,000	658.73
		Present value = $903.10

Using 11%, the present value of the cash flow is equal to the price of the financial instrument. Therefore, the yield is 11%.

Although the formula for the yield is based on annual cash flows, it can be generalized to any number of periodic payments in a year. The generalized formula for determining the yield is

$$P = \sum_{t=1}^{n} \frac{CF_t}{(1 + y)^t} \tag{3.2}$$

where

CF_t = cash flow in period t
n = number of periods

Keep in mind that the yield computed is now the yield for the period. That is, if the cash flows are semiannual, the yield is a semiannual yield. If the cash flows are monthly, the yield is a monthly yield. To compute the *simple* annual interest rate, the yield for the period is multiplied by the number of periods in the year.

Special Case: Investment with Only One Future Cash Flow

In one special case, it is not necessary to go through the time-consuming trial-and-error procedure to determine the yield. This is where there is only one future cash flow from the investment. When an investment has only one future cash flow at period $n(CF_n)$, equation (3.2) reduces to

$$P = \frac{CF_n}{(1 + y)^n}$$

Solving for yield, y, we obtain

$$y = \left[\frac{CF_n}{P}\right]^{1/n} - 1 \qquad (3.3)$$

To illustrate how to use equation (3.3), suppose that a financial instrument currently selling for $62,321.30 promises to pay $100,000 six years from now. The yield for this investment is 8.20%, as follows:

$$y = \left[\frac{\$100,000.00}{\$62,321.30}\right]^{1/6} - 1$$
$$= (1.60459)^{1/6} - 1$$
$$= 1.082 - 1$$
$$= 0.082 \text{ or } 8.2\%$$

Note in equation (3.3) that the ratio of the future cash flow in period n to the price of the financial instrument (i.e., CF_n/P) is equal to the future value per $1 invested.

Annualizing Yields

In Chapter 2, we annualized interest rates by multiplying by the number of periods in a year, and we called the resulting value the **simple annual interest rate**. For example, a semiannual yield is annualized by multiplying by 2. Alternatively, an annual interest rate is converted to a semiannual interest rate by dividing by 2.

This simplified procedure for computing the annual interest rate given a periodic (weekly, monthly, quarterly, semiannually, and so on) interest rate is not accurate. To obtain an effective annual yield associated with a periodic interest rate, the following formula is used:

$$\text{effective annual yield} = (1 + \text{periodic interest rate})^m - 1$$

where m is the frequency of payments per year. For example, suppose that the periodic interest rate is 4% and the frequency of payments is twice per year. Then

$$\text{effective annual yield} = (1.04)^2 - 1 = 1.0816 - 1$$
$$= 0.0816 \text{ or } 8.16\%$$

If interest is paid quarterly, the periodic interest rate is 2% (8%/4), and the effective annual yield is 8.24%, as follows:

$$\text{effective annual yield} = (1.02)^4 - 1 = 1.0824 - 1$$
$$= 0.0824 \text{ or } 8.24\%$$

We can also determine the periodic interest rate that will produce a given annual interest rate by solving the effective annual yield equation for the periodic interest rate. Solving, we find that

$$\text{periodic interest rate} = (1 + \text{effective annual yield})^{1/m} - 1$$

For example, the periodic quarterly interest rate that would produce an effective annual yield of 12% is

$$\text{periodic interest rate} = (1.12)^{1/4} - 1 = 1.0287 - 1$$
$$= 0.0287 \text{ or } 2.87\%$$

CONVENTIONAL YIELD MEASURES

There are several bond yield measures commonly quoted by dealers and used by portfolio managers. In this section, we discuss each yield measure and show how it is computed. In the next section, we critically evaluate yield measures in terms of their usefulness in identifying the relative value of a bond.

In our illustration of each measure, we will first use a hypothetical bond so that we do not have to worry about dealing with a bond that is traded between coupon dates. We will then provide the yield measure for an actual bond. The specific bond that we will use is an Iowa State Hospital Revenue Bond issued by the University of Iowa Hospitals and Clinics. The bond is a municipal revenue bond, a bond structure that we will describe in Chapter 8. Information for this bond issue follows:

CUSIP: 46256QDN3
Price on November 5, 2010: 99.531
Coupon rate: 4.5%
Maturity date: 09/01/2036
Bond Rating: Aa2 (Moody's); S&P (AA)
Call schedule: First callable on 9/1/2020 at par value (100) and continuously
    callable on 30 days notice
Sinking fund schedule:
9/1/2033 $1,675,000 at par
9/1/2034 $1,750,000 at par
9/1/2035 $1,850,000 at par

Current Yield

Current yield relates the annual coupon interest to the market price. The formula for the current yield is

$$\text{current yield} = \frac{\text{annual dollar coupon interest}}{\text{price}}$$

For example, the current yield for a 15-year 7% coupon bond with a par value of $1,000 selling for $769.42 is 9.10%:

$$\text{current yield} = \frac{\$70}{\$769.42} = 0.0910 \text{ or } 9.10\%$$

For the Iowa State Hospitals Revenue issue, the current yield using a par value of $100 is

$$\text{current yield} = \frac{\$4.50}{\$99.531} = 4.52\%$$

The current yield calculation takes into account only the coupon interest and no other source of return that will affect an investor's yield. No consideration is given to the capital gain that the investor will realize when a bond is purchased at a discount and held to maturity; nor is there any recognition of the capital loss that the investor will realize if a bond purchased at a premium is held to maturity. The time value of money is also ignored.

Yield to Maturity

In the first section of this chapter, we explained how to compute the yield or internal rate of return on any investment. The yield is the interest rate that will make the present value of the cash flows equal to the price (or initial investment). The **yield to maturity** is computed in the same way as the yield (internal rate of return); the cash flows are those that the investor would realize by holding the bond to maturity. For a semiannual pay bond, the yield to maturity is found by first computing the periodic interest rate, y, that satisfies the relationship

$$P = \frac{C}{1 + y} + \frac{C}{(1 + y)^2} + \frac{C}{(1 + y)^3} + \cdots + \frac{C}{(1 + y)^n} + \frac{M}{(1 + y)^n}$$

$$P = \sum_{t=1}^{n} \frac{C}{(1 + y)^t} + \frac{M}{(1 + y)^n} \tag{3.4}$$

where

P = price of the bond
C = *semiannual* coupon interest (in dollars)
M = maturity value (in dollars)
n = number of periods (number of years $\times$ 2)

For a semiannual pay bond, doubling the periodic interest rate or discount rate (y) gives the yield to maturity. However, recall from our discussion of annualizing yields that doubling the periodic interest rate understates the effective annual yield. Despite this, the market convention is to compute the yield to maturity by doubling the periodic interest rate, y, that satisfies equation (3.4). The yield to maturity computed on the basis of this market convention is called the **bond-equivalent yield**.

The computation of the yield to maturity requires an iterative procedure. To illustrate the computation, consider the bond that we used to compute the current yield. The cash flow for this bond is (1) 30 coupon payments of $35 every six months, and (2) $1,000 to be paid 30 six-month periods from now.

To get y in equation (3.4), different interest rates must be tried until the present value of the cash flows is equal to the price of $769.42. The present value of the cash flows of the bond for several periodic interest rates is as follows:

Annual Interest Rate (%)	Semiannual Rate y (%)	Present Value of 30 Payments of $35[a]	Present Value of $1,000 30 Periods from Now[b]	Present Value of Cash Flows
9.00	4.50	$570.11	$267.00	$837.11
9.50	4.75	553.71	248.53	802.24
10.00	5.00	538.04	231.38	769.42
10.50	5.25	532.04	215.45	738.49
11.00	5.50	508.68	200.64	709.32

[a]The present value of the coupon payments is found using the formula

$$\$35 \left[\frac{1 - \dfrac{1}{(1 + y)^{30}}}{y} \right]$$

[b]The present value of the maturity value is found using the formula

$$\$1,000 \left[\frac{1}{(1 + y)^{30}} \right]$$

When a 5% semiannual interest rate is used, the present value of the cash flows is $769.42. Therefore, y is 5%, and the yield to maturity on a bond-equivalent basis is 10%. It is much easier to compute the yield to maturity for a zero-coupon bond because equation (3.3) can be used. As the cash flow in period n is the maturity value M, equation (3.3) can be rewritten as[1]

$$y = \left[\frac{M}{P}\right]^{1/n} - 1 \tag{3.5}$$

For example, for a 10-year zero-coupon bond with a maturity value of $1,000, selling for $439.18, y is 4.2%:

$$
\begin{aligned}
y = \left[\frac{\$1,000}{\$439.18}\right]^{1/20} - 1 &= (2.27697)^{0.05} - 1 \\
&= 1.042 - 1 \\
&= 0.042
\end{aligned}
$$

Note that the number of periods is equal to 20 semiannual periods, which is double the number of years. The number of years is not used because we want a yield value that may be compared with alternative coupon bonds. To get the bond-equivalent annual yield, we must double y, which gives us 8.4%.

The yield-to-maturity measure takes into account not only the current coupon income but also any capital gain or loss that the investor will realize by *holding the bond to maturity*. In addition, the yield to maturity considers the timing of the cash flows. The relationship among the coupon rate, current yield, and yield to maturity looks like this:

Bond Selling at:	Relationship
Par	Coupon rate = current yield = yield to maturity
Discount	Coupon rate < current yield < yield to maturity
Premium	Coupon rate > current yield > yield to maturity

Bond Calculators

Although we have walked through the steps to calculate the yield to maturity, as well as the bond's price in the previous chapter, in practice software is available to calculate this measure. Moreover, in most instances when a bond is offered to an investor by a broker, the yield-to-maturity measure or one of the other measures discussed below is reported.

For example, on Yahoo! Finance information on bond prices is provided at http://finance.yahoo.com/bonds/market_summary/article/200001/bond_ticker.

On that website, one can find most publicly traded bond issues. In the box "Find Bonds by Name" suppose that we entered the name "Alcoa". A screen listing the bonds by Alcoa

---

[1] That is, M is substituted for CF_n.

would appear. When this was done on November 5, 2010, the following information was obtained for the first five bond issues by Alcoa on the list:[2]

Price	Coupon (%)	Maturity	YTM (%)
103.79	5.900	02/01/2027	5.542
108.59	5.870	02/23/2022	4.870
110.92	6.150	08/15/2020	4.739
107.70	5.720	02/23/2019	4.591
114.41	6.750	07/15/2018	4.507

The last column shows the yield to maturity. All five bonds are not callable.

When one wants the yield only knowing the bond price (or price knowing the bond yield), handheld calculators, add-in functions to spreadsheets, and, most conveniently, bond calculators are available online that provide the computation. This overcomes the difficulty of dealing with the issue of bonds traded between coupon periods. For example, SmartMoney has an online bond calculator available at http://www.smartmoney.com/investing/bonds/bond-calculator-7917/.

For example, let's take the first bond issue for Alcoa listed in the table above and use the SmartMoney bond calculator by entering the coupon, maturity date (the calculator only uses the month, not the date), and the price. The calculator produces a value of 5.54%, which agrees with the yield to maturity in the table above.

For the Iowa State Hospitals Revenue Bond the SmartMoney bond calculator would produce a value of 4.53%.

Yield to Call

As explained in Chapter 1, the issuer may be entitled to call a bond prior to the stated maturity date. When the bond may be called and at what price are specified at the time the bond is issued. The price at which the bond may be called is referred to as the **call price**. For some issues, the call price is the same regardless of when the issue is called. For other callable issues, the call price depends on when the issue is called. That is, there is a **call schedule** that specifies a call price for each call date.

For callable issues, the practice has been to calculate a **yield to call** as well as a yield to maturity. The yield to call assumes that the issuer will call the bond at some assumed call date and the call price is then the call price specified in the call schedule. Typically, investors calculate a **yield to first call** or **yield to next call**, a **yield to first par call**, and **yield to refunding**. The yield to first call is computed for an issue that is not currently callable, while the yield to next call is computed for an issue that is currently callable. The yield to refunding is computed assuming the issue will be called on the first date the issue is refundable. (In Chapter 7, we see that an issue may be callable but there may be a period when the issue may not be called using a lower cost of funds than the issue itself; that is, the issue is nonrefundable.)

The procedure for calculating the yield to any assumed call date is the same as for any yield calculation: Determine the interest rate that will make the present value of the expected cash flows equal to the bond's price. In the case of yield to first call, the expected cash flows are the coupon payments to the first call date and the call price as specified in the call schedule.

---

[2] The data are provided to Yahoo! Finance by ValuBond, Inc.

For the yield to first par call, the expected cash flows are the coupon payments to the first date at which the issuer may call the bond at par value plus the last cash flow of par value.

Mathematically, the yield to call can be expressed as follows:

$$P = \frac{C}{1+y} + \frac{C}{(1+y)^2} + \frac{C}{(1+y)^3} + \cdots + \frac{C}{(1+y)^{n^*}} + \frac{M^*}{(1+y)^n}$$

$$P = \sum_{t=1}^{n^*} \frac{C}{(1+y)^t} + \frac{M}{(1+y)^{n^*}} \tag{3.6}$$

where

M^* = call price (in dollars)
n^* = number of periods until the assumed call date (number of years $\times$ 2)

For a semiannual pay bond, doubling the periodic interest rate (y) gives the yield to call on a bond-equivalent basis.

To illustrate the computation, consider an 18-year 11% coupon bond with a maturity value of $1,000 selling for $1,169. Suppose that the first call date is 8 years from now and that the call price is $1,055. The cash flows for this bond if it is called in 13 years are (1) 26 coupon payments of $55 every six months, and (2) $1,055 due in 16 six-month periods from now.

The value for y in equation (3.6) is the one that will make the present value of the cash flows to the first call date equal to the bond's price of $1,169. The process of finding the yield to first call is the same as that for finding the yield to maturity. The present value at several periodic interest rates is as follows:

Annual Interest Rate (%)	Semiannual Rate y (%)	Present Value of 16 Payments of $55[a]	Present Value of $1,055 16 Periods from Now[b]	Present Value of Cash Flows
8.000	4.0000	$640.88	$563.27	$1,204.15
8.250	4.1250	635.01	552.55	1,187.56
8.500	4.2500	629.22	542.05	1,171.26
8.535	4.2675	628.41	540.59	1,169.00
8.600	4.3000	626.92	537.90	1,164.83

[a]The present value of the coupon payments is found using the formula

$$\$55\left[\frac{1 - \frac{1}{(1+y)^{16}}}{y}\right]$$

[b]The present value of the call price is found using the formula

$$\$1,055\left[\frac{1}{(1+y)^{16}}\right]$$

Because a periodic interest rate of 4.2675% makes the present value of the cash flows equal to the price, 4.2675% is y, the yield to first call. Therefore, the yield to first call on a bond-equivalent basis is 8.535%.

Suppose that the first par call date for this bond is 13 years from now. Then the yield to first par call is the interest rate that will make the present value of $55 every six months for the next 26 six-month periods plus the par value of $1,000 26 six-month periods from now equal to the price of $1,169. It is left as an exercise for the reader to show that the semiannual interest rate that equates the present value of the cash flows to the price is 4.3965%. Therefore, 8.793% is the yield to first par call.

A bond calculator can also be used to compute the yield to call for any call date. When using the calculator, the call date of interest is used in lieu of the maturity date and the call price is used instead of the maturity price. For the Iowa State Hospitals Revenue Bond, two call dates were used for purposes of this illustration. The first call date for this issue is September 1, 2020, and the bond is callable at par. The yield to call assuming a call date of September 1, 2020, using the SmartMoney bond calculator is 4.56%. Assuming, instead, a call date of September 1, 2028, the yield to call is 4.54%.

Yield to Sinker

As explained in Chapter 1, some bond issues have a sinking fund provision. This requires that the issuer retire a specified amount at the scheduled dates. The yield calculated assuming the bond will be retired at a specific sinking fund payment date is called the **yield to sinker**. The calculation is the same as the yield to maturity and the yield to call: use the sinking fund date of interest and the sinking fund price.

For the Iowa State Hospitals Revenue Bond, there are three sinking fund dates. The first is September 1, 2033. Using the SmartMoney bond calculator, the yield to sinker is 4.53%.

Yield to Put

As explained in Chapter 1, an issue can be putable. This means that the bondholder can force the issuer to buy the issue at a specified price. As with a callable issue, a putable issue can have a put schedule. The schedule specifies when the issue can be put and the price, called the put price.

When an issue is putable, a **yield to put** is calculated. The yield to put is the interest rate that makes the present value of the cash flows to the assumed put date plus the put price on that date as set forth in the put schedule equal to the bond's price. The formula is the same as equation (3.6), but M is now defined as the put price and n^* as the number of periods until the assumed put date. The procedure is the same as calculating yield to maturity and yield to call.

For example, consider again the 11% coupon 18-year issue selling for $1,169. Assume that the issue is putable at par ($1,000) in five years. The yield to put is the interest rate that makes the present value of $55 per period for 10 six-month periods plus the put price of $1,000 equal to the $1,169. It is left to the reader to demonstrate that a discount rate of 3.471% will result in this equality. Doubling this rate gives 6.942% and is the yield to put.

Yield to Worst

A practice in the industry is for an investor to calculate the yield to maturity, the yield to every possible call date, and the yield to every possible put date. The minimum of all of these yields is called the **yield to worst**.

For the Iowa State Hospitals Revenue Bond, the yield to maturity, the yield to call for all call dates, and the yield to sinker for all sinking fund dates were computed. The lowest was 4.53%.

Cash Flow Yield

In later chapters, we will cover fixed income securities whose cash flows include scheduled principal repayments prior to maturity. That is, the cash flow in each period includes interest plus principal repayment. Such securities are called **amortizing securities**. Mortgage-backed securities and asset-backed securities are examples. In addition, the amount that the borrower can repay in principal may exceed the scheduled amount. This excess amount of principal repayment over the amount scheduled is called a **prepayment**. Thus, for amortizing securities, the cash flow each period consists of three components: (1) coupon interest, (2) scheduled principal repayment, and (3) prepayments.

For amortizing securities, market participants calculate a **cash flow yield**. It is the interest rate that will make the present value of the projected cash flows equal to the market price. The difficulty is projecting what the prepayment will be in each period. We will illustrate this calculation in Chapter 11.

Yield (Internal Rate of Return) for a Portfolio

The yield for a portfolio of bonds is not simply the average or weighted average of the yield to maturity of the individual bond issues in the portfolio. It is computed by determining the cash flows for the portfolio and determining the interest rate that will make the present value of the cash flows equal to the market value of the portfolio.[3]

Consider a three-bond portfolio as follows:

Bond	Coupon Rate (%)	Maturity (years)	Par Value	Price	Yield to Maturity (%)
A	7.0	5	$10,000,000	$ 9,209,000	9.0
B	10.5	7	20,000,000	20,000,000	10.5
C	6.0	3	30,000,000	28,050,000	8.5

To simplify the illustration, it is assumed that the coupon payment date is the same for each bond. The portfolio's total market value is $57,259,000. The cash flow for each bond in the portfolio and for the entire portfolio follows:

Period Cash Flow Received	Bond A	Bond B	Bond C	Portfolio
1	$ 350,000	$ 1,050,000	$ 900,000	$ 2,300,000
2	350,000	1,050,000	900,000	2,300,000
3	350,000	1,050,000	900,000	2,300,000
4	350,000	1,050,000	900,000	2,300,000
5	350,000	1,050,000	900,000	2,300,000
6	350,000	1,050,000	30,900,000	32,300,000
7	350,000	1,050,000	—	1,400,000
8	350,000	1,050,000	—	1,400,000
9	350,000	1,050,000	—	1,400,000
10	10,350,000	1,050,000	—	11,400,000
11	—	1,050,000	—	1,050,000
12	—	1,050,000	—	1,050,000
13	—	1,050,000	—	1,050,000
14	—	21,050,000	—	21,050,000

---

[3] In Chapter 4, we discuss the concept of duration. A good approximation to the yield for a portfolio can be obtained by using duration to weight the yield to maturity of the individual bonds in the portfolio.

To determine the yield (internal rate of return) for this three-bond portfolio, the interest rate must be found that makes the present value of the cash flows shown in the last column of the preceding table equal to $57,259,000 (the total market value of the portfolio). If an interest rate of 4.77% is used, the present value of the cash flows will equal $57,259,000. Doubling 4.77% gives 9.54%, which is the yield on the portfolio on a bond-equivalent basis.

Yield Spread Measures for Floating-Rate Securities

The coupon rate for a floating-rate security changes periodically based on the coupon reset formula which has as its components the reference rate and the quoted margin. Since the future value for the reference rate is unknown, it is not possible to determine the cash flows. This means that a yield to maturity cannot be calculated. Instead, there are several conventional measures used as margin or spread measures cited by market participants for floaters. These include spread for life (or simple margin), adjusted simple margin, adjusted total margin, and discount margin.[4]

The most popular of these measures is discount margin, so we will discuss this measure and its limitations below. This measure estimates the average margin over the reference rate that the investor can expect to earn over the life of the security. The procedure for calculating the discount margin is as follows:

Step 1: Determine the cash flows assuming that the reference rate does not change over the life of the security.

Step 2: Select a margin (spread).

Step 3: Discount the cash flows found in step 1 by the current value of the reference rate plus the margin selected in step 2.

Step 4: Compare the present value of the cash flows as calculated in step 3 with the price. If the present value is equal to the security's price, the discount margin is the margin assumed in step 2. If the present value is not equal to the security's price, go back to step 2 and try a different margin.

For a security selling at par, the discount margin is simply the spread over the reference rate.

To illustrate the calculation, suppose that a six-year floating-rate security selling for 99.3098 pays a rate based on some reference rate plus 80 basis points. The coupon rate is reset every six months. Assume that the current value of the reference rate is 10%. Exhibit 3-1 shows the calculation of the discount margin for this security. The second column shows the current value of the reference rate. The third column sets forth the cash flows for the security. The cash flow for the first 11 periods is equal to one-half the current value of the reference rate (5%) plus the semiannual spread of 40 basis points multiplied by 100. In the twelfth six-month period, the cash flow is 5.4 plus the maturity value of 100. The top row of the last five columns shows the assumed margin. The rows below the assumed margin show the present value of each cash flow. The last row gives the total present value of the cash flows.

For the five assumed yield spreads, the present value is equal to the price of the floating-rate security (99.3098) when the assumed margin is 96 basis points. Therefore, the discount margin on a semiannual basis is 48 basis points and 96 basis points on an annual

---

[4] For a discussion of these alternative measures, see Chapter 3 in Frank J. Fabozzi and Steven V. Mann, *Floating Rate Securities* (New York: John Wiley & Sons, 2000).

Exhibit 3-1 Calculation of the Discount Margin for a Floating-Rate Security

Maturity: six years
Coupon rate: reference rate + 80 basis points
Reset every six months

Period	Reference Rate	Cash Flow[a]	Present Value of Cash Flow at Assumed Annual Margin (basis points)				
			80	84	88	96	100
1	10%	5.4	5.1233	5.1224	5.1214	5.1195	5.1185
2	10	5.4	4.8609	4.8590	4.8572	4.8535	4.8516
3	10	5.4	4.6118	4.6092	4.6066	4.6013	4.5987
4	10	5.4	4.3755	4.3722	4.3689	4.3623	4.3590
5	10	5.4	4.1514	4.1474	4.1435	4.1356	4.1317
6	10	5.4	3.9387	3.9342	3.9297	3.9208	3.9163
7	10	5.4	3.7369	3.7319	3.7270	3.7171	3.7122
8	10	5.4	3.5454	3.5401	3.5347	3.5240	3.5186
9	10	5.4	3.3638	3.3580	3.3523	3.3409	3.3352
10	10	5.4	3.1914	3.1854	3.1794	3.1673	3.1613
11	10	5.4	3.0279	3.0216	3.0153	3.0028	2.9965
12	10	105.4	56.0729	55.9454	55.8182	55.5647	55.4385
		Present value =	100.0000	99.8269	99.6541	99.3098	99.1381

[a] For periods 1–11: cash flow = 100 (reference rate + assumed margin)(0.5); for period 12: cash flow = 100 (reference rate + assumed margin)(0.5) + 100.

basis. (Notice that the discount margin is 80 basis points, the same as the spread over the reference rate when the security is selling at par.)

A drawback of the discount margin as a measure of the potential return from investing in a floating-rate security is that the discount margin approach assumes that the reference rate will not change over the life of the security. Second, if the floating-rate security has a cap or floor, this is not taken into consideration.

POTENTIAL SOURCES OF A BOND'S DOLLAR RETURN

An investor who purchases a bond can expect to receive a dollar return from one or more of these sources:

1. the periodic coupon interest payments made by the issuer
2. any capital gain (or capital loss—negative dollar return) when the bond matures, is called, or is sold
3. interest income generated from reinvestment of the periodic cash flows

The last component of the potential dollar return is referred to as **reinvestment income**. For a standard bond that makes only coupon payments and no periodic principal payments prior to the maturity date, the interim cash flows are simply the coupon payments. Consequently, for such bonds the reinvestment income is simply interest earned from reinvesting the coupon interest payments. For these bonds, the third component of the potential source of dollar return is referred to as the **interest-on-interest component**. For amortizing securities, the reinvestment income is the interest income from reinvesting both the coupon interest payments and periodic principal repayments prior to the maturity date. In our subsequent discussion, we will look at the sources of return for non-amortizing securities (that is, bonds in which no periodic principal is repaid prior to the maturity date).

Any measure of a bond's potential yield should take into consideration each of these three potential sources of return. The current yield considers only the coupon interest payments. No consideration is given to any capital gain (or loss) or interest on interest. The yield to maturity takes into account coupon interest and any capital gain (or loss). It also considers the interest-on-interest component. However, as will be demonstrated later, implicit in the yield-to-maturity computation is the assumption that the coupon payments can be reinvested at the computed yield to maturity. The yield to maturity, therefore, is a *promised* yield—that is, it will be realized only if (1) the bond is held to maturity, and (2) the coupon interest payments are reinvested at the yield to maturity. If neither (1) nor (2) occurs, the actual yield realized by an investor can be greater than or less than the yield to maturity.

The yield to call also takes into account all three potential sources of return. In this case, the assumption is that the coupon payments can be reinvested at the yield to call. Therefore, the yield-to-call measure suffers from the same drawback as the yield to maturity in that it assumes coupon interest payments are reinvested at the computed yield to call. Also, it assumes that the bond will be called by the issuer on the assumed call date.

The cash flow yield, which will be more fully discussed in Chapter 11, also takes into consideration all three sources as is the case with yield to maturity, but it makes two additional assumptions. First, it assumes that the periodic principal repayments are reinvested at the computed cash flow yield. Second, it assumes that the prepayments projected to obtain the cash flows are actually realized.

Determining the Interest-on-Interest Dollar Return

Let's focus on nonamortizing securities. The interest-on-interest component can represent a substantial portion of a bond's potential return. The potential total dollar return from coupon interest and interest on interest can be computed by applying the future value of an annuity formula given in Chapter 2. Letting r denote the semiannual reinvestment rate, the interest on interest plus the total coupon payments can be found from the equation

$$\begin{matrix} \text{coupon interest} \\ + \\ \text{interest on interest} \end{matrix} = C\left[\frac{(1 + r)^n - 1}{r}\right] \tag{3.7}$$

The total dollar amount of coupon interest is found by multiplying the semiannual coupon interest by the number of periods:

$$\text{total coupon interest} = nC$$

The interest-on-interest component is then the difference between the coupon interest plus interest on interest and the total dollar coupon interest, as expressed by the formula

$$\text{interest on interest} = C\left[\frac{(1 + r)^n - 2}{r}\right] - nC \tag{3.8}$$

The yield-to-maturity measure assumes that the reinvestment rate is the yield to maturity.

For example, let's consider the 15-year 7% bond that we have used to illustrate how to compute current yield and yield to maturity. If the price of this bond per $1,000 of par value is $769.40, the yield to maturity for this bond is 10%. Assuming an annual reinvestment rate of 10% or a semiannual reinvestment rate of 5%, the interest on interest plus total coupon payments using equation (3.7) is

$$\begin{array}{c}\text{coupon interest} \\ + \\ \text{interest on interest}\end{array} = \$35\left[\frac{(1.05)^{30} - 1}{0.05}\right]$$

Using equation (3.8), the interest-on-interest component is

$$\begin{aligned}\text{interest on interest} &= \$2,325.36 - 30(\$35) \\ &= \$1,275.36\end{aligned}$$

Yield to Maturity and Reinvestment Risk

Let's look at the potential total dollar return from holding this bond to maturity. As mentioned earlier, the total dollar return comes from three sources:

1. total coupon interest of $1,050 (coupon interest of $35 every six months for 15 years)
2. interest on interest of $1,275.36 earned from reinvesting the semiannual coupon interest payments at 5% every six months
3. a capital gain of $230.60 ($1,000 minus $769.40)

The potential total dollar return if the coupons can be reinvested at the yield to maturity of 10% is then $2,555.96.

Notice that if an investor places the money that would have been used to purchase this bond, $769.40, in a savings account earning 5% semiannually for 15 years, the future value of the savings account would be

$$\$769.40(1.05)^{30} = \$3,325.30$$

For the initial investment of $769.40, the total dollar return is $2,555.90.

So, an investor who invests $769.40 for 15 years at 10% per year (5% semiannually) expects to receive at the end of 15 years the initial investment of $769.40 plus $2,555.90. Ignoring rounding errors, this is what we found by breaking down the dollar return on the bond assuming a reinvestment rate equal to the yield to maturity of 10%. Thus, it can be seen that for the bond to yield 10%, the investor must generate $1,275.36 by reinvesting the coupon payments. This means that to generate a yield to maturity of 10%, approximately half ($1,275.36/$2,555.96) of this bond's total dollar return must come from the reinvestment of the coupon payments.

The investor will realize the yield to maturity at the time of purchase only if the bond is held to maturity and the coupon payments can be reinvested at the computed yield to maturity. The risk that the investor faces is that future reinvestment rates will be less than the yield to maturity at the time the bond is purchased. This risk is referred to as **reinvestment risk**.

There are two characteristics of a bond that determine the importance of the interest-on-interest component and therefore the degree of reinvestment risk: maturity and coupon. For a given yield to maturity and a given coupon rate, the longer the maturity, the more dependent the bond's total dollar return is on the interest-on-interest component in order to realize the yield to maturity at the time of purchase. In other words, the longer the maturity, the greater the reinvestment risk. The implication is that the yield-to-maturity measure for long-term coupon bonds tells little about the potential yield that an investor may realize if the bond is held to maturity. For long-term bonds, the interest-on-interest component may be as high as 80% of the bond's potential total dollar return.

Turning to the coupon rate, for a given maturity and a given yield to maturity, the higher the coupon rate, the more dependent the bond's total dollar return will be on the reinvestment of the coupon payments in order to produce the yield to maturity anticipated at the time of purchase. This means that when maturity and yield to maturity are held constant, premium bonds are more dependent on the interest-on-interest component than are bonds selling at par. Discount bonds are less dependent on the interest-on-interest component than are bonds selling at par. For zero-coupon bonds, none of the bond's total dollar return is dependent on the interest-on-interest component, so a zero-coupon bond has zero reinvestment risk if held to maturity. Thus, the yield earned on a zero-coupon bond held to maturity is equal to the promised yield to maturity.

Cash Flow Yield and Reinvestment Risk

For amortizing securities, reinvestment risk is even greater than for nonamortizing securities. The reason is that the investor must now reinvest the periodic principal repayments in addition to the periodic coupon interest payments. Moreover, as explained later in this book when we cover the two major types of amortizing securities—mortgage–backed securities and asset-backed securities—the cash flows are monthly, not semiannually as with nonamortizing securities. Consequently, the investor must not only reinvest periodic coupon interest payments and principal, but must do it more often. This increases reinvestment risk.

There is one more aspect of nonamortizing securities that adds to their reinvestment risk. Typically, for nonamortizing securities the borrower can accelerate the periodic principal repayment. That is, the borrower can prepay. But a borrower will typically prepay when interest rates decline. Consequently, if a borrower prepays when interest rates decline, the investor faces greater reinvestment risk because he or she must reinvest the prepaid principal at a lower interest rate.

TOTAL RETURN

In the preceding section, we explained that the yield to maturity is a **promised** yield. At the time of purchase, an investor is promised a yield, as measured by the yield to maturity, if both of the following conditions are satisfied:

1. The bond is held to maturity.
2. All coupon interest payments are reinvested at the yield to maturity.

We focused on the second assumption, and we showed that the interest-on-interest component for a bond may constitute a substantial portion of the bond's total dollar return. Therefore, reinvesting the coupon interest payments at a rate of interest less than the yield to maturity will produce a lower yield than the yield to maturity.

Rather than assuming that the coupon interest payments are reinvested at the yield to maturity, an investor can make an explicit assumption about the reinvestment rate based on personal expectations. The **total return** is a measure of yield that incorporates an explicit assumption about the reinvestment rate.

Let's take a careful look at the first assumption—that a bond will be held to maturity. Suppose, for example, that an investor who has a five-year investment horizon is considering the following four bonds:

Bond	Coupon (%)	Maturity (years)	Yield to Maturity (%)
A	5	3	9.0
B	6	20	8.6
C	11	15	9.2
D	8	5	8.0

Assuming that all four bonds are of the same credit quality, which is most attractive to this investor? An investor who selects bond C because it offers the highest yield to maturity is failing to recognize that the investment horizon calls for selling the bond after five years, at a price that depends on the yield required in the market for 10-year 11% coupon bonds at the time. Hence, there could be a capital gain or capital loss that will make the return higher or lower than the yield to maturity promised now. Moreover, the higher coupon on bond C relative to the other three bonds means that more of this bond's return will be dependent on the reinvestment of coupon interest payments.

Bond A offers the second highest yield to maturity. On the surface, it seems to be particularly attractive because it eliminates the problem of realizing a possible capital loss when the bond must be sold prior to the maturity date. Moreover, the reinvestment risk seems to be less than for the other three bonds because the coupon rate is the lowest. However, the investor would not be eliminating the reinvestment risk because after three years the proceeds received at maturity must be reinvested for two more years. The yield that the investor will realize depends on interest rates three years from now on two-year bonds when the proceeds must be rolled over.

The yield to maturity does not seem to be helping us to identify the best bond. How, then, do we find out which is the best bond? The answer depends on the investor's expectations. Specifically, it depends on the investor's planned investment horizon. Also, for bonds with a maturity longer than the investment horizon, it depends on the investor's expectations about required yields in the market at the end of the planned investment horizon. Consequently, any of these bonds can be the best alternative, depending on some reinvestment rate and some future required yield at the end of the planned investment horizon. The total return measure takes these expectations into account and will determine the best investment for the investor, depending on personal expectations.

The yield-to-call measure is subject to the same problems as the yield to maturity. First, it assumes that the bond will be held until the first call date. Second, it assumes that the coupon interest payments will be reinvested at the yield to call. If an investor's planned investment horizon is shorter than the time to the first call date, the bond may have to be sold for less than its acquisition cost. If, on the other hand, the investment horizon is longer than the time to the first call date, there is the problem of reinvesting the proceeds from the time the bond is called until the end of the planned investment horizon. Consequently, the yield to call does not tell us very much. The total return, however, can accommodate the analysis of callable bonds.

Computing the Total Return for a Bond

The idea underlying total return is simple. The objective is first to compute the total future dollars that will result from investing in a bond assuming a particular reinvestment rate. The total return is then computed as the interest rate that will make the initial investment in the bond grow to the computed total future dollars.

The procedure for computing the total return for a bond held over some investment horizon can be summarized as follows. For an assumed reinvestment rate, the dollar return that will be available at the end of the investment horizon can be computed for both the coupon interest payments and the interest-on-interest component. In addition, at the end of the planned investment horizon the investor will receive either the par value or some other value (based on the market yield on the bond when it is sold). The total return is then the interest rate that will make the amount invested in the bond (i.e., the current market price plus accrued interest) grow to the future dollars available at the end of the planned investment horizon.

More formally, the steps for computing the total return for a bond held over some investment horizon are as follows:

Step 1: Compute the total coupon payments plus the interest on interest based on the assumed reinvestment rate. The coupon payments plus the interest on interest can be computed using equation (3.7). The reinvestment rate in this case is one-half the annual interest rate that the investor assumes can be earned on the reinvestment of coupon interest payments.

Step 2: Determine the projected sale price at the end of the planned investment horizon. The projected sale price will depend on the projected required yield at the end of the planned investment horizon. The projected sale price will be equal to the present value of the remaining cash flows of the bond discounted at the projected required yield.

Step 3: Sum the values computed in steps 1 and 2. The sum is the total future dollars that will be received from the investment, given the assumed reinvestment rate and the projected required yield at the end of the investment horizon.[5]

Step 4: To obtain the semiannual total return, use the formula

$$\left[\frac{\text{total future dollars}}{\text{purchase price of bond}} \right]^{1/h} - 1$$

where h is the number of six-month periods in the investment horizon. Notice that this formula is simply an application of equation (3.3), the yield for an investment with just one future cash flow.

Step 5: As interest is assumed to be paid semiannually, double the interest rate found in step 4. The resulting interest rate is the total return.

---

[5] The total future dollars computed here differ from the total dollar return that we used in showing the importance of the interest-on-interest component in the preceding section. The total dollar return there includes only the capital gain (or capital loss if there was one), not the purchase price, which is included in calculating the total future dollars; that is,

total dollar return = total future dollars − purchase price of bond

To illustrate computation of the total return, suppose that an investor with a three-year investment horizon is considering purchasing a 20-year 8% coupon bond for $828.40. The yield to maturity for this bond is 10%. The investor expects to be able to reinvest the coupon interest payments at an annual interest rate of 6% and that at the end of the planned investment horizon the then-17-year bond will be selling to offer a yield to maturity of 7%. The total return for this bond is found as follows:

Step 1: Compute the total coupon payments plus the interest on interest, assuming an annual reinvestment rate of 6%, or 3% every six months. The coupon payments are $40 every six months for three years or six periods (the planned investment horizon). Applying equation (3.7), the total coupon interest plus interest on interest is

$$\begin{array}{c}\text{coupon interest} \\ + \\ \text{interest on interest}\end{array} = \$40\left[\frac{(1.03)^6 - 1}{0.03}\right] = \$40\left[\frac{1.194052 - 1}{0.03}\right]$$

$$= \$40[6.4684]$$
$$= \$258.74$$

Step 2: Determining the projected sale price at the end of three years, assuming that the required yield to maturity for 17-year bonds is 7%, is accomplished by calculating the present value of 34 coupon payments of $40 plus the present value of the maturity value of $1,000, discounted at 3.5%. The projected sale price is $1,098.51.[6]

Step 3: Adding the amounts in steps 1 and 2 gives total future dollars of $1,357.25.

Step 4: To obtain the semiannual total return, compute the following:

$$\left[\frac{\$1,375.25}{\$828.40}\right]^{1/6} - 1 = (1.63840)^{0.16667} - 1 = 1.0858 - 1$$
$$= 0.0858 \text{ or } 8.58\%$$

Step 5: Double 8.58%, for a total return of 17.16%.

There is no need in this case to assume that the reinvestment rate will be constant for the entire investment horizon. An example will show how the total return measure can accommodate multiple reinvestment rates.

Suppose that an investor has a six-year investment horizon. The investor is considering a 13-year 9% coupon bond selling at par. The investor's expectations are as follows:

1. The first four semiannual coupon payments can be reinvested from the time of receipt to the end of the investment horizon at a simple annual interest rate of 8%.

---

[6] The present value of the 34 coupon payments discounted at 3.5% is

$$\$40\left[\frac{1 - \frac{1}{(1.035)^{34}}}{0.035}\right] = \$788.03$$

The present value of the maturity value discounted at 3.5% is

$$\frac{\$1,000}{(1.035)^{34}} = \$310.48$$

The projected sale price is $788.03 plus $310.48, or $1,098.51.

2. The last eight semiannual coupon payments can be reinvested from the time of receipt to the end of the investment horizon at a 10% simple annual interest rate.
3. The required yield to maturity on seven-year bonds at the end of the investment horizon will be 10.6%.

Using these three assumptions, the total return is computed as follows:

Step 1: Coupon payments of $45 every six months for six years (the investment horizon) will be received. The coupon interest plus interest on interest for the first four coupon payments, assuming a semiannual reinvestment rate of 4%, is

$$\text{coupon interest} + \text{interest on interest} = \$45\left[\frac{(1.04)^4 - 1}{0.04}\right]$$

$$= \$191.09$$

This gives the coupon plus interest on interest as of the end of the second year (four periods). Reinvested at 4% until the end of the planned investment horizon, four years or eight periods later, $191.09 will grow to

$$\$191.09(1.04)^8 = \$261.52$$

The coupon interest plus interest on interest for the last eight coupon payments, assuming a semiannual reinvestment rate of 5%, is

$$\text{coupon interest} + \text{interest on interest} = \$45\left[\frac{(1.05)^8 - 1}{0.05}\right]$$

$$= \$429.71$$

The coupon interest plus interest on interest from all 12 coupon interest payments is $691.23 ($261.52 + $429.71).

Step 2: The projected sale price of the bond, assuming that the required yield is 10.6%, is $922.31.[7]

Step 3: The total future dollars are $1,613.54 ($691.23 + $922.31).

Step 4: Compute the following:

$$\left[\frac{\$1,613.54}{\$1,000.00}\right]^{1/12} - 1 = (1.61354)^{0.08333} - 1$$

$$= 1.0407 - 1$$

$$= 0.0407 \text{ or } 4.07\%$$

Step 5: Doubling 4.07% gives a total return of 8.14%.

---

[7] The present value of the coupon payments discounted at 5.3% is

$$\$45\left[\frac{1 - \dfrac{1}{(1.053)^{14}}}{0.053}\right] = \$437.02$$

The present value of the maturity value discounted at 5.3% is

$$\frac{\$1,000}{(1.053)^{14}} = \$485.29$$

The projected sale price is $437.02 plus $485.29, or $922.31.

APPLICATIONS OF THE TOTAL RETURN (HORIZON ANALYSIS)

The total return measure allows a portfolio manager to project the performance of a bond on the basis of the planned investment horizon and expectations concerning reinvestment rates and future market yields. This permits the portfolio manager to evaluate which of several potential bonds considered for acquisition will perform best over the planned investment horizon. As we have emphasized, this cannot be done using the yield to maturity as a measure of relative value.

Using total return to assess performance over some investment horizon is called **horizon analysis**. When a total return is calculated over an investment horizon, it is referred to as a **horizon return**. In this book, we use the terms *horizon return* and *total return* interchangeably.

Horizon analysis is also used to evaluate bond swaps. In a bond swap, the portfolio manager considers exchanging a bond held in the portfolio for another bond. When the objective of the bond swap is to enhance the return of the portfolio over the planned investment horizon, the total return for the bond being considered for purchase can be computed and compared with the total return for the bond held in the portfolio to determine if the bond being held should be replaced. We discuss several bond swap strategies in Chapter 22.

An often-cited objection to the total return measure is that it requires the portfolio manager to formulate assumptions about reinvestment rates and future yields as well as to think in terms of an investment horizon. Unfortunately, some portfolio managers find comfort in measures such as the yield to maturity and yield to call simply because they do not require incorporating any particular expectations. The horizon analysis framework, however, enables the portfolio manager to analyze the performance of a bond under different interest-rate scenarios for reinvestment rates and future market yields. Only by investigating multiple scenarios can the portfolio manager see how sensitive the bond's performance will be to each scenario. Chapter 22 explains a framework for incorporating the market's expectation of future interest rates.

CALCULATING YIELD CHANGES

When interest rates or yields change between two time periods, there are two ways that in practice the change is calculated: the absolute yield change and the percentage yield change.

The **absolute yield change** (also called the **absolute rate change**) is measured in basis points and is simply the absolute value of the difference between the two yields. That is,

$$\text{absolute yield change (in basis points)} = |\text{initial yield} - \text{new yield}| \times 100$$

For example, consider the following three yields over three months:

Month 1: 4.45%
Month 2: 5.11%
Month 3: 4.82%

Then the absolute yield changes are computed as shown below:

$$\text{absolute yield change from month 1 to month 2}$$
$$= |4.45\% - 5.11\%| \times 100 = 66 \text{ basis points}$$
$$\text{absolute yield change from month 2 to month 3}$$
$$= |5.11\% - 4.82\%| \times 100 = 29 \text{ basis points}$$

The **percentage yield change** is computed as the natural logarithm of the ratio of the change in yield as shown below:

$$\text{percentage yield change} = 100 \times \ln(\text{new yield/initial yield})$$

where ln is the natural logarithm.

Using the three monthly yields earlier, the percentage yield changes are

absolute yield change from month 1 to month 2 $= \ln(5.11\%/4.45\%) = 13.83\%$
absolute yield change from month 2 to month 3 $= \ln(4.82\%/5.11\%) = -5.84\%$

KEY POINTS

- For any investment, the yield or internal rate of return is the interest rate that will make the present value of the cash flows equal to the investment's price (or cost). The same procedure is used to calculate the yield on any bond.
- The conventional yield measures commonly used by bond market participants are the current yield, yield to maturity, yield to call, yield to sinker, yield to put, yield to worst, and cash flow yield.
- The three potential sources of dollar return from investing in a bond are coupon interest, reinvestment income, and capital gain (or loss).
- Conventional yield measures do not deal satisfactorily with all of these sources. The current yield measure fails to consider both reinvestment income and capital gain (or loss). The yield to maturity considers all three sources but is deficient in assuming that all coupon interest can be reinvested at the yield to maturity. The risk that the coupon payments will be reinvested at a rate less than the yield to maturity is called reinvestment risk.
- The yield to call has the same shortcoming; it assumes that the coupon interest can be reinvested at the yield to call. The cash flow yield makes the same assumptions as the yield to maturity, plus it assumes that periodic principal payments can be reinvested at the computed cash flow yield and that the prepayments are actually realized.
- Total return is a more meaningful measure for assessing the relative attractiveness of a bond given the investor's or the portfolio manager's expectations and planned investment horizon.
- The change in yield between two periods can be calculated in terms of the absolute yield change or the percentage yield change.

QUESTIONS

1. A debt obligation offers the following payments:

Years from Now	Cash Flow to Investor
1	$2,000
2	2,000
3	2,500
4	4,000

Suppose that the price of this debt obligation is $7,704. What is the yield or internal rate of return offered by this debt obligation?

2. What is the effective annual yield if the semiannual periodic interest rate is 4.3%?

3. What is the yield to maturity of a bond?

4. What is the yield to maturity calculated on a bond-equivalent basis?

5. **a.** Show the cash flows for the following four bonds, each of which has a par value of $1,000 and pays interest semiannually:

Bond	Coupon Rate (%)	Number of Years to Maturity	Price
W	7	5	$884.20
X	8	7	948.90
Y	9	4	967.70
Z	0	10	456.39

   b. Calculate the yield to maturity for the four bonds.

6. A portfolio manager is considering buying two bonds. Bond A matures in three years and has a coupon rate of 10% payable semiannually. Bond B, of the same credit quality, matures in 10 years and has a coupon rate of 12% payable semiannually. Both bonds are priced at par.

   a. Suppose that the portfolio manager plans to hold the bond that is purchased for three years. Which would be the best bond for the portfolio manager to purchase?

   b. Suppose that the portfolio manager plans to hold the bond that is purchased for six years instead of three years. In this case, which would be the best bond for the portfolio manager to purchase?

   c. Suppose that the portfolio manager is managing the assets of a life insurance company that has issued a five-year guaranteed investment contract (GIC). The interest rate that the life insurance company has agreed to pay is 9% on a semiannual basis. Which of the two bonds should the portfolio manager purchase to ensure that the GIC payments will be satisfied and that a profit will be generated by the life insurance company?

7. Consider the following bond:

   Coupon rate = 11%
   Maturity = 18 years
   Par value = $1,000
   First par call in 13 years
   Only put date in five years and putable at par value
   Suppose that the market price for this bond is $1,169.

   a. Show that the yield to maturity for this bond is 9.077%.
   b. Show that the yield to first par call is 8.793%.
   c. Show that the yield to put is 6.942%.
   d. Suppose that the call schedule for this bond is as follows:
   Can be called in eight years at $1,055
   Can be called in 13 years at $1,000
   And suppose this bond can only be put in five years and assume that the yield to first par call is 8.535%. What is the yield to worst for this bond?

8. **a.** What is meant by an amortizing security?
   b. What are the three components of the cash flow for an amortizing security?
   c. What is meant by a cash flow yield?

9. How is the internal rate of return of a portfolio calculated?

10. What is the limitation of using the internal rate of return of a portfolio as a measure of the portfolio's yield?

11. Suppose that the coupon rate of a floating-rate security resets every six months at a spread of 70 basis points over the reference rate. If the bond is trading at below par value, explain whether the discount margin is greater than or less than 70 basis points.

12. An investor is considering the purchase of a 20-year 7% coupon bond selling for $816 and a par value of $1,000. The yield to maturity for this bond is 9%.

   a. What would be the total future dollars if this investor invested $816 for 20 years earning 9% compounded semiannually?
   b. What are the total coupon payments over the life of this bond?
   c. What would be the total future dollars from the coupon payments and the repayment of principal at the end of 20 years?
   d. For the bond to produce the same total future dollars as in part a, how much must the interest on interest be?
   e. Calculate the interest on interest from the bond assuming that the semiannual coupon payments can be reinvested at 4.5% every six months and demonstrate that the resulting amount is the same as in part d.

13. What is the total return for a 20-year zero-coupon bond that is offering a yield to maturity of 8% if the bond is held to maturity?

14. Explain why the total return from holding a bond to maturity will be between the yield to maturity and the reinvestment rate.

15. For a long-term high-yield coupon bond, do you think that the total return from holding a bond to maturity will be closer to the yield to maturity or the reinvestment rate?

16. Suppose that an investor with a five-year investment horizon is considering purchasing a seven-year 9% coupon bond selling at par. The investor expects that he can reinvest the coupon payments at an annual interest rate of 9.4% and that at the end of the investment horizon two-year bonds will be selling to offer a yield to maturity of 11.2%. What is the total return for this bond?

17. Two portfolio managers are discussing the investment characteristics of amortizing securities. Manager A believes that the advantage of these securities relative to nonamortizing securities is that because the periodic cash flows include principal repayments as well as coupon payments, the manager can generate greater reinvestment income. In addition, the payments are typically monthly so even greater reinvestment income can be generated. Manager B believes that the need to reinvest monthly and the need to invest larger amounts than just coupon interest payments make amortizing securities less attractive. Whom do you agree with and why?

18. Assuming the following yields:

    Week 1: 3.84%
    Week 2: 3.51%
    Week 3: 3.95%

    a. Compute the absolute yield change and percentage yield change from week 1 to week 2.
    b. Compute the absolute yield change and percentage yield change from week 2 to week 3.

4

Bond Price Volatility

LEARNING OBJECTIVES

After reading this chapter, you will understand

- the price–yield relationship of an option-free bond

- the factors that affect the price volatility of a bond when yields change

- the price-volatility properties of an option-free bond

- how to calculate the price value of a basis point

- how to calculate and interpret the Macaulay duration, modified duration, and dollar duration of a bond

- why duration is a measure of a bond's price sensitivity to yield changes

- the spread duration measure for fixed-rate and floating-rate bonds

- how to compute the duration of a portfolio and contribution to portfolio duration

- limitations of using duration as a measure of price volatility

- how price change estimated by duration can be adjusted for a bond's convexity

- how to approximate the duration and convexity of a bond

- the duration of an inverse floater

- how to measure a portfolio's sensitivity to a nonparallel shift in interest rates (key rate duration and yield curve reshaping duration)

As explained in Chapter 2, a major risk associated with investing in bonds is interest rate risk. Therefore, in implementing bond trading strategies and portfolio strategies it is imperative to be able to quantify an exposure of a position or a portfolio to interest rate risk. Accordingly, the purpose of this chapter is twofold. First, an explanation of the price volatility characteristics of a bond are explained. Second, several measures for quantifying the exposure of a position or a portfolio to interest rate risk are presented and illustrated.

REVIEW OF THE PRICE–YIELD RELATIONSHIP FOR OPTION-FREE BONDS

As we explain in Chapter 2, a fundamental principle of an option-free bond (i.e., a bond that does not have an embedded option) is that the price of the bond changes in the direction opposite to that of a change in the required yield for the bond. This principle follows from the fact that the price of a bond is equal to the present value of its expected cash flows. An increase (decrease) in the required yield decreases (increases) the present value of its expected cash flows and therefore decreases (increases) the bond's price. Exhibit 4-1 illustrates this property for the following six hypothetical bonds, where the bond prices are shown assuming a par value of $100 and interest paid semiannually:

1. a 9% coupon bond with 5 years to maturity
2. a 9% coupon bond with 25 years to maturity
3. a 6% coupon bond with 5 years to maturity
4. a 6% coupon bond with 25 years to maturity
5. a zero-coupon bond with 5 years to maturity
6. a zero-coupon bond with 25 years to maturity

When the price–yield relationship for any option-free bond is graphed, it exhibits the shape shown in Exhibit 4-2. Notice that as the required yield rises, the price of the option-free bond declines. This relationship is not linear, however (i.e., it is not a straight line). The shape of the price–yield relationship for any option-free bond is referred to as **convex**.

The price–yield relationship that we have discussed refers to an instantaneous change in the required yield. As we explain in Chapter 2, the price of a bond will change over time as a result of (1) a change in the perceived credit risk of the issuer, (2) a discount or premium bond approaching the maturity date, and (3) a change in market interest rates.

Exhibit 4-1   Price–Yield Relationship for Six Hypothetical Bonds

Required Yield (%)	Price at Required Yield (coupon/maturity in years)					
	9%/5	9%/25	6%/5	6%/25	0%/5	0%/25
6.00	112.7953	138.5946	100.0000	100.0000	74.4094	22.8107
7.00	108.3166	123.4556	95.8417	88.2722	70.8919	17.9053
8.00	104.0554	110.7410	91.8891	78.5178	67.5564	14.0713
8.50	102.0027	105.1482	89.9864	74.2587	65.9537	12.4795
8.90	100.3966	100.9961	88.4983	71.1105	64.7017	11.3391
8.99	100.0395	100.0988	88.1676	70.4318	64.4236	11.0975
9.00	100.0000	100.0000	88.1309	70.3570	64.3928	11.0710
9.01	99.9604	99.9013	88.0943	70.2824	64.3620	11.0445
9.10	99.6053	99.0199	87.7654	69.6164	64.0855	10.8093
9.50	98.0459	95.2539	86.3214	66.7773	62.8723	9.8242
10.00	96.1391	90.8720	84.5565	63.4881	61.3913	8.7204
11.00	92.4624	83.0685	81.1559	57.6712	58.5431	6.8767
12.00	88.9599	76.3572	77.9197	52.7144	55.8395	5.4288

Exhibit 4-2 Shape of Price–Yield Relationship for an Option-Free Bond

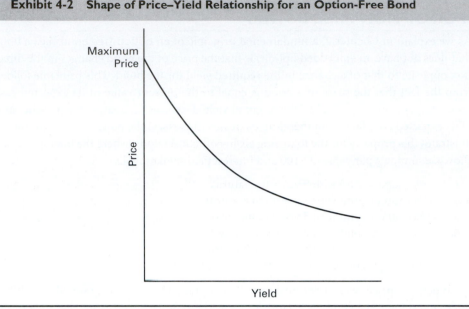

PRICE VOLATILITY CHARACTERISTICS OF OPTION-FREE BONDS

Exhibit 4-3 shows, for the six hypothetical bonds in Exhibit 4-1, the percentage change in the bond's price for various changes in the required yield, assuming that the initial yield for all six bonds is 9%. An examination of Exhibit 4-3 reveals several properties concerning the price volatility of an option-free bond:

Property 1: Although the prices of all option-free bonds move in the opposite direction from the change in yield required, the percentage price change is not the same for all bonds.

Property 2: For very small changes in the yield required, the percentage price change for a given bond is roughly the same, whether the yield required increases or decreases.

Property 3: For large changes in the required yield, the percentage price change is not the same for an increase in the required yield as it is for a decrease in the required yield.

Property 4: For a given large change in basis points, the percentage price increase is greater than the percentage price decrease.

The implication of property 4 is that if an investor owns a bond (i.e., is "long" a bond), the price appreciation that will be realized if the required yield decreases is greater than the capital loss that will be realized if the required yield rises by the same number of basis points. For an investor who is "short" a bond, the reverse is true: The potential capital loss is greater than the potential capital gain if the required yield changes by a given number of basis points.

An explanation for these four properties of bond price volatility lies in the convex shape of the price–yield relationship. We will investigate this in more detail later in the chapter.

Characteristics of a Bond That Affect Its Price Volatility

There are two characteristics of an option-free bond that determine its price volatility: coupon and term to maturity.

Characteristic 1: For a given term to maturity and initial yield, the lower the coupon rate, the greater the price volatility. This characteristic can be seen by comparing the 9%, 6%, and zero-coupon bonds with the same maturity.

Characteristic 2: For a given coupon rate and initial yield, the longer the term to maturity, the greater the price volatility. This can be seen in Exhibit 4-3 by comparing the five-year bonds with the 25-year bonds with the same coupon.

An implication of the second characteristic is that investors who want to increase a portfolio's price volatility because they expect interest rates to fall, all other factors being constant, should hold bonds with long maturities in the portfolio. To reduce a portfolio's price volatility in anticipation of a rise in interest rates, bonds with shorter-term maturities should be held in the portfolio.

Exhibit 4-3　Instantaneous Percentage Price Change for Six Hypothetical Bonds

Six hypothetical bonds, priced initially to yield 9%:
9% coupon, 5 years to maturity, price = $100.0000
9% coupon, 25 years to maturity, price = 100.0000
6% coupon, 5 years to maturity, price = 88.1309
6% coupon, 25 years to maturity, price = 70.3570
0% coupon, 5 years to maturity, price = 64.3928
0% coupon, 25 years to maturity, price = 11.0710

Yield (%) Changes to:	Change in Basis Points	Percentage Price Change (coupon/maturity in years)					
		9%/5	9%/25	6%/5	6%/25	0%/5	0%/25
6.00	−300	12.80	38.59	13.47	42.13	15.56	106.04
7.00	−200	8.32	23.46	8.75	25.46	10.09	61.73
8.00	−100	4.06	10.74	4.26	11.60	4.91	27.10
8.50	−50	2.00	5.15	2.11	5.55	2.42	12.72
8.90	−10	0.40	1.00	0.42	1.07	0.48	2.42
8.99	−1	0.04	0.10	0.04	0.11	0.05	0.24
9.01	1	−0.04	−0.10	−0.04	−0.11	−0.05	−0.24
9.10	10	−0.39	−0.98	−0.41	−1.05	−0.48	−2.36
9.50	50	−1.95	−4.75	−2.05	−5.09	−2.36	−11.26
10.00	100	−3.86	−9.13	−4.06	−9.76	−4.66	−21.23
11.00	200	−7.54	−16.93	−7.91	−18.03	−9.08	−37.89
12.00	300	−11.04	−23.64	−11.59	−25.08	−13.28	−50.96

Exhibit 4-4 Price Change for a 100-Basis-Point Change in Yield for a 9% 25-Year Bond Trading at Different Yield Levels

Yield Level (%)	Initial Price	New Price[a]	Price Decline	Percent Decline
7	$123.46	$110.74	$12.72	10.30
8	110.74	100.00	10.74	9.70
9	100.00	90.87	9.13	9.13
10	90.87	83.07	7.80	8.58
11	83.07	76.36	6.71	8.08
12	76.36	70.55	5.81	7.61
13	70.55	65.50	5.05	7.16
14	65.50	61.08	4.42	6.75

[a]As a result of a 100-basis-point increase in yield.

Effects of Yield to Maturity

We cannot ignore the fact that credit considerations cause different bonds to trade at different yields, even if they have the same coupon and maturity. How, then, holding other factors constant, does the yield to maturity affect a bond's price volatility? As it turns out, the higher the yield to maturity at which a bond trades, the lower the price volatility.

To see this, compare the 9% 25-year bond trading at various yield levels in Exhibit 4-4. The first column shows the yield level the bond is trading at, and the second column gives the initial price. The third column indicates the bond's price if yields change by 100 basis points. The fourth and fifth columns show the dollar price change and the percentage price change. Note in these last two columns that the higher the initial yield, the lower the price volatility. An implication of this is that for a given change in yields, price volatility is greater when yield levels in the market are low, and price volatility is lower when yield levels are high.

MEASURES OF BOND PRICE VOLATILITY

Money managers, arbitrageurs, and traders need to have a way to measure a bond's price volatility to implement hedging and trading strategies. Three measures that are commonly employed are (1) price value of a basis point, (2) yield value of a price change, and (3) duration.

Price Value of a Basis Point

The **price value of a basis point** (PVBP), also referred to as the **dollar value of an 01** (DV01), is the change in the price of the bond if the required yield changes by 1 basis point. Note that this measure of price volatility indicates **dollar price volatility** as opposed to percentage price volatility (price change as a percent of the initial price). Typically, the price value of a basis point is expressed as the absolute value of the change in price. Owing to property 2 of the price–yield relationship, price volatility is the same for an increase or a decrease of 1 basis point in required yield.

We can illustrate how to calculate the price value of a basis point by using the six bonds in Exhibit 4-1. For each bond, the initial price, the price after increasing the required yield by 1 basis point (from 9% to 9.01%), and the price value of a basis point (the difference between the two prices) are as follows:

Bond	Initial Price (9% yield)	Price at 9.01%	Price Value of a Basis Point[a]
5-year 9% coupon	100.0000	99.9604	0.0396
25-year 9% coupon	100.0000	99.9013	0.0987
5-year 6% coupon	88.1309	88.0945	0.0364
25-year 6% coupon	70.3570	70.2824	0.0746
5-year zero-coupon	64.3928	64.3620	0.0308
25-year zero-coupon	11.0710	11.0445	0.0265

[a]Absolute value per $100 of par value.

Because this measure of price volatility is in terms of dollar price change, dividing the price value of a basis point by the initial price gives the percentage price change for a 1-basis-point change in yield.

Yield Value of a Price Change

Another measure of the price volatility of a bond used by investors is the change in the yield for a specified price change. This is estimated by first calculating the bond's yield to maturity if the bond's price is decreased by, say, X dollars. Then the difference between the initial yield and the new yield is the yield value of an X dollar price change. The smaller this value, the greater the dollar price volatility, because it would take a smaller change in yield to produce a price change of X dollars.

Duration

In Chapter 2, we explained that the price of an option-free bond can be expressed mathematically as follows:[1]

$$P = \frac{C}{1 + y} + \frac{C}{(1 + y)^2} + \cdots + \frac{C}{(1 + y)^n} + \frac{M}{(1 + y)^n} \tag{4.1}$$

where

P = price of the bond
C = semiannual coupon interest (in dollars)
y = one-half the yield to maturity or required yield
n = number of semiannual periods (number of years $\times$ 2)
M = maturity value (in dollars)

---

[1] Equation (4.1) assumes that the next coupon payment is exactly six months from now and that there is no accrued interest. As we explain at the end of Chapter 2, it is not difficult to extend the model to account for the first coupon payment occurring less than six months from the valuation date and to adjust the price to include accrued interest.

To determine the approximate change in price for a small change in yield, the first derivative of equation (4.1) with respect to the required yield can be computed as

$$\frac{dP}{dy} = \frac{(-1)C}{(1+y)^2} + \frac{(-2)C}{(1+y)^3} + \cdots + \frac{(-n)C}{(1+y)^{n+1}} + \frac{(-n)M}{(1+y)^{n+1}} \tag{4.2}$$

Rearranging equation (4.2), we obtain

$$\frac{dP}{dy} = -\frac{1}{1+y}\left[\frac{1C}{1+y} + \frac{2C}{(1+y)^2} + \cdots + \frac{nC}{(1+y)^n} + \frac{nM}{(1+y)^n}\right] \tag{4.3}$$

The term in brackets is the weighted average term to maturity of the cash flows from the bond, where the weights are the present value of the cash flow.

Equation (4.3) indicates the approximate dollar price change for a small change in the required yield. Dividing both sides of equation (4.3) by P gives the approximate percentage price change:

$$\frac{dP}{dy}\frac{1}{P} = -\frac{1}{1+y}\left[\frac{1C}{1+y} + \frac{2C}{(1+y)^2} + \cdots + \frac{nC}{(1+y)^n} + \frac{nM}{(1+y)^n}\right]\frac{1}{P} \tag{4.4}$$

The expression in brackets divided by the price (or here multiplied by the reciprocal of the price) is commonly referred to as **Macaulay duration**;[2] that is,

$$\text{Macaulay duration} = \frac{\dfrac{1C}{1+y} + \dfrac{2C}{(1+y)^2} + \cdots + \dfrac{nC}{(1+y)^n} + \dfrac{nM}{(1+y)^n}}{P}$$

which can be rewritten as

$$\text{Macaulay duration} = \frac{\displaystyle\sum_{t=1}^{n}\frac{tC}{(1+y)^t} + \frac{nM}{(1+y)^n}}{P} \tag{4.5}$$

Substituting Macaulay duration into equation (4.4) for the approximate percentage price change gives

$$\frac{dP}{dy}\frac{1}{P} = -\frac{1}{1+y} \times \text{Macaulay duration} \tag{4.6}$$

Investors commonly refer to the ratio of Macaulay duration to $1 + y$ as **modified duration**; that is,

$$\text{modified duration} = \frac{\text{Macaulay duration}}{1+y} \tag{4.7}$$

Substituting equation (4.7) into equation (4.6) gives

$$\frac{dP}{dy}\frac{1}{P} = -\text{modified duration} \tag{4.8}$$

---

[2] In a 1938 National Bureau of Economic Research study on bond yields, Frederick Macaulay coined this term and used this measure rather than maturity as a proxy for the average length of time that a bond investment is outstanding. [See Frederick Macaulay, *Some Theoretical Problems Suggested by the Movement of Interest Rates, Bond Yields, and Stock Prices in the U.S. Since 1856* (New York: National Bureau of Economic Research, 1938).] In examining the interest rate sensitivity of financial institutions, Redington and Samuelson independently developed the duration concept. (See F. M. Redington, "Review of the Principle of Life Office Valuation," *Journal of the Institute of Actuaries*, 1952, pp. 286–340; and Paul A. Samuelson, "The Effect of Interest Rate Increases on the Banking System," *American Economic Review*, March 1945, pp. 16–27.)

Equation (4.8) states that modified duration is related to the approximate percentage change in price for a given change in yield. Because for all option-free bonds modified duration is positive, equation (4.8) states that there is an inverse relationship between modified duration and the approximate percentage change in price for a given yield change. This is to be expected from the fundamental principle that bond prices move in the opposite direction of the change in interest rates.

Exhibits 4-5 and 4-6 show the computation of the Macaulay duration and modified duration of two five-year coupon bonds. The durations computed in these exhibits are in terms of duration per period. Consequently, the durations are in half-years because the cash flows of the bonds occur every six months. To adjust the durations to an annual figure, the durations must be divided by 2, as shown at the bottom of Exhibits 4-5 and 4-6. In general, if the cash flows occur m times per year, the durations are adjusted by dividing by m; that is,

$$\text{duration in years} = \frac{\text{duration in } m \text{ periods per year}}{m}$$

Exhibit 4-5   Calculation of Macaulay Duration and Modified Duration for Five-Year 9% Bond Selling to Yield 9%

Coupon rate: 9.00%
Term (years): 5
Initial yield: 9.00%

Period, t	Cash Flow[a]	PV of $1 at 4.5%	PV of CF	$t \times$ PVCF[b]
1	$ 4.50	0.956937	4.306220	4.30622
2	4.50	0.915729	4.120785	8.24156
3	4.50	0.876296	3.943335	11.83000
4	4.50	0.838561	3.773526	15.09410
5	4.50	0.802451	3.611030	18.05514
6	4.50	0.767895	3.455531	20.73318
7	4.50	0.734828	3.306728	23.14709
8	4.50	0.703185	3.164333	25.31466
9	4.50	0.672904	3.028070	27.25262
10	104.50	0.643927	67.290443	672.90442
			100.000000	826.87899

[a]Cash flow per $100 of par value.

$$\text{Macaulay duration (in half years)} = \frac{826.87899}{100.000000} = 8.27$$

$$\text{Macaulay duration (in years)} = \frac{8.27}{2} = 4.13$$

$$\text{Modified duration} = \frac{4.13}{1.0450} = 3.96$$

[b]Values are rounded.

Exhibit 4-6   **Calculation of Macaulay Duration and Modified Duration for Five-Year 6% Bond Selling to Yield 9%**

Coupon rate: 6.00%
Term (years): 5
Initial yield: 9.00%

Period, t	Cash Flow[a]	PV of $1 at 4.5%	PV of CF	$t \times$ PVCF[b]
1	$ 3.00	0.956937	2.870813	2.87081
2	3.00	0.915729	2.747190	5.49437
3	3.00	0.876296	2.628890	7.88666
4	3.00	0.838561	2.515684	10.06273
5	3.00	0.802451	2.407353	12.03676
6	3.00	0.767895	2.303687	13.82212
7	3.00	0.734828	2.204485	15.43139
8	3.00	0.703185	2.109555	16.87644
9	3.00	0.672904	2.018713	18.16841
10	103.00	0.643927	66.324551	663.24551
Total			88.130923	765.89520

[a]Cash flow per $100 of par value.

$$\text{Macaulay duration (in half years)} = \frac{765.89520}{88.130923} = 8.69$$

$$\text{Macaulay duration (in years)} = \frac{8.69}{2} = 4.35$$

$$\text{Modified duration} = \frac{4.35}{1.0450} = 4.16$$

[b]Values are rounded.

Macaulay duration in years and modified duration for the six hypothetical bonds are as follows:

Bond	Macaulay Duration (years)	Modified Duration
9%/5-year	4.13	3.96
9%/25-year	10.33	9.88
6%/5-year	4.35	4.16
6%/25-year	11.10	10.62
0%/5-year	5.00	4.78
0%/25-year	25.00	23.92

Rather than use equation (4.5) to calculate Macaulay duration and then equation (4.7) to obtain modified duration, we can derive an alternative formula that does not require the extensive calculations required by equation (4.5). This is done by rewriting the price of a bond in terms of its two components: (1) the present value of an annuity, where the annuity is the sum of the coupon payments, and (2) the present value of the par value. That is, the price of a bond per $100 of par value can be written as follows:[3]

$$P = C\left[\frac{1 - \dfrac{1}{(1 + y)^n}}{y}\right] + \frac{100}{(1 + y)^n} \tag{4.9}$$

By taking the first derivative of equation (4.9) and dividing by P, we obtain another formula for modified duration:

$$\text{modified duration} = \frac{\dfrac{C}{y^2}\left[1 - \dfrac{1}{(1 + y)^n}\right] + \dfrac{n(100 - C/y)}{(1 + y)^{n+1}}}{P} \tag{4.10}$$

where the price is expressed as a percentage of par value. Macaulay duration can be expressed by multiplying equation (4.10) by $(1 + y)$. To illustrate how to apply equation (4.10), consider the 25-year 6% bond selling at 70.357 to yield 9%. Then

$C = 3(0.06 \times 100 \times 1/2)$
$y = 0.045\,(0.09 \times 1/2)$
$n = 50$
$p = 70.357$

Substituting into equation (4.10) yields

$$\text{modified duration} = \frac{\dfrac{3}{(0.045)^2}\left[1 - \dfrac{1}{(1.045)^{50}}\right] + \dfrac{50(100 - 3/0.045)}{(1.045)^{51}}}{70.357}$$

$$= \frac{1{,}481.481(0.88929) + 176.5704}{70.357}$$

$$= 21.23508$$

Converting to an annual number by dividing by 2 gives a modified duration of 10.62. Multiplying by 1.045 gives 11.10, which is Macaulay duration.

Properties of Duration

As can be seen from the various durations computed for the six hypothetical bonds, the modified duration and Macaulay duration of a coupon bond are less than the maturity. It should be obvious from the formula that the Macaulay duration of a zero-coupon bond is equal to its maturity; a zero-coupon bond's modified duration, however, is less than its maturity. Also, the lower the coupon, generally the greater the modified and Macaulay duration of the bond.[4]

There is a consistency between the properties of bond price volatility we discussed earlier and the properties of modified duration. We showed earlier that when all other factors are constant, the longer the maturity, the greater the price volatility. A property of modified duration is that when all other factors are constant, the longer the maturity, the greater

---

[3] The first term in equation (4.9) is the present value of the coupon payments from equation (2.7) discounting at y.
[4] This property does not hold for long-maturity deep-discount bonds.

the modified duration. We also showed that the lower the coupon rate, all other factors being constant, the greater the bond price volatility. As we have just seen, generally the lower the coupon rate, the greater the modified duration. Thus, the greater the modified duration, the greater the price volatility.

Finally, as we noted earlier, another factor that will influence the price volatility is the yield to maturity. All other factors constant, the higher the yield level, the lower the price volatility. The same property holds for modified duration, as can be seen in the following table, which shows the modified duration of a 25-year 9% coupon bond at various yield levels:

Yield (%)	Modified Duration
7	11.21
8	10.53
9	9.88
10	9.27
11	8.70
12	8.16
13	7.66
14	7.21

Approximating the Percentage Price Change

If we multiply both sides of equation (4.8) by the change in the required yield (dy), we have the following relationship:

$$\frac{dP}{P} = -\text{modified duration} \times dy \tag{4.11}$$

Equation (4.11) can be used to approximate the percentage price change for a given change in required yield.

To illustrate the relationship, consider the 25-year 6% bond selling at 70.3570 to yield 9%. The modified duration for this bond is 10.62. If yields increase instantaneously from 9% to 9.10%, a yield change of +0.0010 (10 basis points), the *approximate* percentage change in price using equation (4.11) is

$$-10.62(+0.0010) = -0.0106 \text{ or } -1.06\%$$

Notice from Exhibit 4-3 that the actual percentage change in price is −1.05%. Similarly, if yields decrease instantaneously from 9% to 8.90% (a 10-basis-point decrease), the approximate percentage change in price using equation (4.11) would be +1.06%. According to Exhibit 4-3, the actual percentage price change would be +1.07%. This example illustrates that for small changes in the required yield, modified duration gives a good approximation of the percentage change in price.

Instead of a small change in required yield, let's assume that yields increase by 200 basis points, from 9% to 11% (a yield change of +0.02). The approximate percentage change in price using equation (4.11) is

$$+10.62(+0.02) = -0.2124 = -21.24\%$$

How good is this approximation? As can be seen from Exhibit 4-3, the actual percentage change in price is only −18.03%. Moreover, if the required yield decreased by 200 basis points, from 9% to 7%, the approximate percentage change in price based on duration would be +21.24%, compared with an actual percentage change in price of +25.46%. Modified duration provides not only a flawed approximation but also a symmetric percentage price change, which, as we point out earlier in this chapter, is not a property of the price–yield relationship for bonds when there are large changes in yield.

We can use equation (4.11) to provide an interpretation of modified duration. Suppose that the yield on any bond changes by 100 basis points. Then, substituting 100 basis points (0.01) into equation (4.11), the following is obtained:

$$\frac{dP}{P} = -\text{modified duration}\,(0.01) = -\text{modified duration}\,(\%)$$

Thus, *modified duration can be interpreted as the approximate percentage change in price for a 100-basis-point change in yield.*

Approximating the Dollar Price Change

Modified duration is a proxy for the percentage change in price. Investors also like to know the dollar price volatility of a bond. Of course, equation (4.2) can be used to compute the dollar price volatility. Alternatively, multiplying both sides of equation (4.8) by P gives

$$\frac{dP}{dy} = (-\text{modified duration})P \qquad \qquad \textbf{(4.12)}$$

The expression on the right-hand side is called **dollar duration**:

$$\text{dollar duration} = -(\text{modified duration})P \qquad \qquad \textbf{(4.13)}$$

When we know the percentage price change and the initial price, the estimated dollar price change using modified duration can be determined. Alternatively, the estimated dollar price change can be obtained by multiplying both sides of equation (4.11) by P, giving

$$dP = -(\text{modified duration})P(dy)$$

From equation (4.13) we can substitute dollar duration for the product of modified duration and P. Thus,

$$dP = -(\text{dollar duration})(dy) \qquad \qquad \textbf{(4.14)}$$

For small changes in the required yield, equation (4.14) does a good job in estimating the change in price. For example, consider the 6% 25-year bond selling at 70.3570 to yield 9%. The dollar duration is 747.2009. For a 1-basis-point (0.0001) increase in the required yield, the estimated price change per $100 of face value is

$$dP = -(\$747.2009)(0.0001)$$
$$= -\$0.0747$$

From Exhibit 4-1, we see that the actual price is 70.2824. The actual price change would therefore be 0.0746 (70.2824 − 70.3570). Notice that the dollar duration for a 1-basis-point change is the same as the price value of a basis point.

Now, let's see what happens when there is a large change in the required yield for the same bond. If the required yield increases from 9% to 11% (or 200 basis points), the approximate dollar price change per $100 par value is

$$dP = -(\$747.2009)(0.02)$$
$$= -\$14.94$$

From Exhibit 4-1, we see that the actual price for this bond if the required yield is 11% is 57.6712. Thus, the actual price decline is 12.6858 (57.6712 − 70.3570). The estimated dollar price change is more than the actual price change. The reverse is true for a decrease in the required yield. This result is consistent with what we illustrated earlier. When there are large movements in the required yield, dollar duration or modified duration is not adequate to approximate the price reaction. Duration will overestimate the price change when the required yield rises, thereby underestimating the new price. When the required yield falls, duration will underestimate the price change and thereby underestimate the new price.

Spread Duration

Market participants compute a measure called *spread duration*. However, this measure is used in two ways. One use is for fixed-rate bonds and the other for floating-rate bonds.

Consider first fixed-rate bonds. As we have explained, duration is a measure of the change in the value of a bond when rates change. The interest rate that is assumed to shift is the Treasury rate. However, as explained in the next chapter, for non-Treasury bonds the yield for such securities is equal to the Treasury yield plus a spread to the Treasury yield curve. The spread represents compensation for credit risk. The price of a non-Treasury bond is exposed to a change in the spread, and we referred to this in Chapter 1 as credit spread risk. The credit spread can change even though Treasury yields are unchanged because the spread required by the market changes. A measure of how a non-Treasury bond's price will change if the spread sought by the market changes is referred to as **spread duration**. For a Treasury security, the spread duration is zero.

Spread duration is used in different ways even when dealing with fixed-rate bonds. As we will see in future chapters, there are different spread measures.[5] Consequently, in using this measure it is important to know what spread measure is being used. A spread duration for a fixed-rate security is interpreted as follows: It is the approximate change in the price of a fixed-rate bond for a 100-basis-point change in the spread.

As explained in Chapter 2, a floating-rate security's price sensitivity will depend on whether the spread that the market wants changes. Recall that the spread is reflected in the quoted margin in the coupon reset formula. The quoted margin is fixed over the life of a typical floater. Spread duration is a measure used to estimate the sensitivity of a floater's price sensitivity to a change in the spread. A spread duration of 1.4 for a floater would mean that if the spread the market requires changes by 100 basis points, the floater's price will change by about 1.4%.

Portfolio Duration

Thus far, we have looked at the duration of an individual bond. The duration of a portfolio is simply the weighted average duration of the bonds in the portfolios. That is, the duration

---

[5] Specifically, for fixed-rate bonds there is the nominal spread, zero-volatility spread, and option-adjusted spread.

Exhibit 4-7   Four-Bond Portfolio

Bond	Market Value	Portfolio Weight	Duration
A	$10 million	0.10	4
B	$40 million	0.40	7
C	$30 million	0.30	6
D	$20 million	0.20	2

of each bond in the portfolio is weighted by its percentage within the portfolio. For example, consider a four-bond portfolio with a total market value of $100 million shown in Exhibit 4-7. The portfolio weight for a bond is simply the market value of the bond divided by the total market value of $100 million. The portfolio duration is then

$$0.1 \times 4 + 0.4 \times 7 + 0.3 \times 6 + 0.2 \times 2 = 5.4$$

The portfolio's duration is 5.4 and it is interpreted as follows: If *all* the yields affecting the four bonds in the portfolio change by 100 basis points, the portfolio's value will change by approximately 5.4%.

Portfolio managers look at their interest rate exposure to a particular issue in terms of its **contribution to portfolio duration**. This measure is found by multiplying the weight of the issue in the portfolio by the duration of the individual issue. That is,

contribution to portfolio duration = weight of issue in portfolio × duration of issue

For example, for the four-bond portfolio in Exhibit 4-7 (whose portfolio duration was computed previously), the contribution to portfolio duration for each issue is shown in the last column of Exhibit 4-8.

Moreover, portfolio managers look at portfolio duration for sectors of the bond market. The procedure is the same for computing the contribution to portfolio duration of a sector as it is for computing the contribution to portfolio duration of an individual issue. A spread duration for a portfolio of fixed-rate bonds can also be computed. In this case, the portfolio duration is divided into two durations. The first is the duration of the portfolio with respect to changes in the level of Treasury rates. The second is the spread duration.

Exhibit 4-8   Calculation of Contribution to Portfolio Duration for Four-Bond Portfolio

Bond	Market Value	Weight in Portfolio	Duration	Contribution to Portfolio Duration
A	$ 10,000,000	0.10	4	0.40
B	40,000,000	0.40	7	2.80
C	30,000,000	0.30	6	1.80
D	20,000,000	0.20	2	0.40
Total	$100,000,000	1.00		5.40

Exhibit 4-9 Sector Distribution and Contribution to Duration for a Portfolio

Sector	Portfolio Weight	Sector Duration	Contribution to Portfolio Duration
Treasury	0.295	7.25	2.14
Government Related	0.036	1.94	0.07
Corporates	0.379	4.85	1.84
Agency MBS	0.290	5.17	1.50
Total	1.000	–	5.55

To illustrate the above, let's use a portfolio that will be used in Chapter 23 where we explain how to construct a bond portfolio. For that portfolio, Exhibit 4-9[6] shows the four sectors in which the portfolio manager has invested. We will explain each sector in the chapters to follow. For now, "Agency MBS" refers to agency residential mortgage-backed securities that will be discussed in Chapter 11; "Corporates" refers to corporate bonds and other forms of corporate credit. Shown in the second column of the exhibit is the allocation to each sector in the portfolio. The duration of each sector is shown in the third column. Actually, the duration for each sector except for the Treasury sector is calculated using a more complex model than presented in this chapter to obtain the prices to substitute into the duration formula. This will be discussed in later chapters. The last row in the contribution to portfolio duration column shows the duration of the portfolio: 5.55.

As will be explained in Chapter 22, performance of a typical manager is measured relative to a benchmark, typically a bond index. Suppose that the portfolio manager who has constructed the portfolio shown in Exhibit 4-9 has a benchmark that is the Barclays Capital U.S. Aggregate Index. Exhibit 4-10 shows the index weight for that benchmark and the contribution to index duration by sector (the second and third columns respectively). The benchmark for the portfolio is shown in the last row of the third column: 5.41.

Notice that the duration for both the portfolio and the index is approximately the same. Such a portfolio is said to be **duration neutral**. This would suggest that both would change by roughly 5.5% for a 100-basis-point change in interest rates. But as can be seen,

Exhibit 4-10 Sector Distribution and Contribution to Duration for the Barclays Capital U.S. Aggregate Index

Sector	Index Weight	Sector Duration	Contribution to Index Duration
Treasury	0.333	5.32	1.77
Government Related	0.068	5.88	0.40
Corporates	0.266	6.50	1.73
Agency MBS	0.333	4.53	1.51
Total	1.000	–	5.41

---

[6]The portfolio was constructed by Cenk Ural of Barclays Capital.

there are different exposures to the different sectors. As mentioned earlier, spread duration can be used to estimate the exposure to the different sectors; and, in the same way that contribution to duration for the portfolio and the index can be calculated, so can a contribution to spread duration.

CONVEXITY

The three measures for price volatility that we described in the preceding section are good measures for small changes in yield or price. We have explained how these measures are related. Exhibit 4-11 does this more formally.

Because all the duration measures are only approximations for small changes in yield, they do not capture the effect of the convexity of a bond on its price performance when yields change by more than a small amount. The duration measure can be supplemented with an additional measure to capture the curvature or convexity of a bond. In this section, we tie together the convex price–yield relationship for a bond and several of the properties of bond price volatility discussed earlier.

In Exhibit 4-12, a tangent line is drawn to the price–yield relationship at yield y^*. The tangent shows the rate of change of price with respect to a change in interest rates at that point (yield level). The slope of the tangent line is closely related to the price value of a basis point. Consequently, for a given starting price, the tangent (which tells the rate of absolute price changes) is closely related to the duration of the bond (which tells about the

---

Exhibit 4-11   Measures of Bond Price Volatility and Their Relationships to One Another

Notation:

D = Macaulay duration
D^* = modified duration
PVBP = price value of a basis point
y = yield to maturity in decimal form
Y = yield to maturity in percentage terms ($Y = 100 \times y$)
P = price of bond
m = number of coupons per year

Relationships:

$$D^* = \frac{D}{1 + y/m}$$ by definition

$$\frac{\Delta P/P}{\Delta y} \approx D^*$$ to a close approximation for a small Δy

$\Delta P/\Delta Y \approx$ slope of price–yield curve   to a close approximation for a small ΔY

$$\text{PVBP} \approx \frac{D^* \times P}{10,000}$$ to a close approximation

For bonds at or near par:
PVBP = $D^*/100$ to a close approximation
$D^* \approx \Delta P/\Delta Y$ to a close approximation for a small ΔY

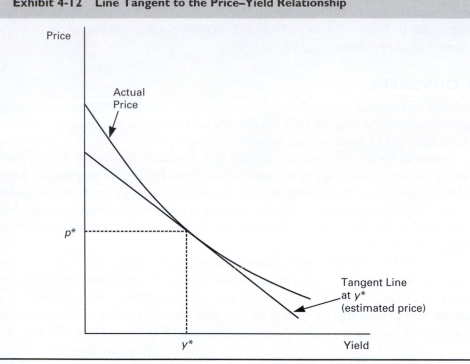

Exhibit 4-12   Line Tangent to the Price–Yield Relationship

rate of percentage of price changes). The steeper the tangent line, the greater the duration; the flatter the tangent line, the lower the duration. Thus, for a given starting price, the tangent line and the duration can be used interchangeably and can be thought of as one and the same method of estimating the rate of price changes.

Notice what happens to duration (steepness of the tangent line) as yield changes: As yield increases (decreases), duration decreases (increases). This property holds for all option-free bonds, as we noted earlier.

If we draw a vertical line from any yield (on the horizontal axis), as in Exhibit 4-13, the distance between the horizontal axis and the tangent line represents the price approximated by using duration starting with the initial yield y^*. The approximation will always understate the actual price. This agrees with what we demonstrated earlier about the relationship between duration (and the tangent line) and the approximate price change. When yields decrease, the estimated price change will be less than the actual price change, thereby underestimating the actual price. On the other hand, when yields increase, the estimated price change will be greater than the actual price change, resulting in an underestimate of the actual price.

For small changes in yield, the tangent line and duration do a good job in estimating the actual price. However, the farther away from the initial yield y^*, the worse the approximation. It should be apparent that the accuracy of the approximation depends on the convexity of the price–yield relationship for the bond.

Exhibit 4-13   Price Approximation Using Duration

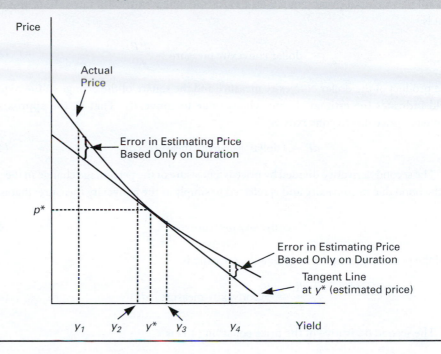

Measuring Convexity

Duration (modified or dollar) attempts to estimate a convex relationship with a straight line (the tangent line). Is it possible to specify a mathematical relationship that provides a better approximation to the price change of the bond if the required yield changes?

We can use the first two terms of a Taylor series to approximate the price change as follows:[7]

$$dP = \frac{dP}{dy}dy + \frac{1}{2}\frac{d^2P}{dy^2}(dy)^2 + \text{error} \tag{4.15}$$

Dividing both sides of equation (4.15) by P to get the percentage price change gives us

$$\frac{dP}{P} = \frac{dP}{dy}\frac{1}{P}dy + \frac{1}{2}\frac{d^2P}{dy^2}\frac{1}{P}(dy)^2 + \frac{\text{error}}{P} \tag{4.16}$$

The first term on the right-hand side of equation (4.15) is equation (4.14); that is, it is the dollar price change based on dollar duration. Thus, the first term in equation (4.15) is our approximation of the price change based on duration. In equation (4.16), the first term on the right-hand side is the approximate percentage change in price based on modified duration.

The second term in equations (4.15) and (4.16) includes the second derivative of the price function [equation (4.1)]. It is the second derivative that is used as a proxy measure

---

[7] A Taylor series, discussed in calculus textbooks, can be used to approximate a mathematical function. Here, the mathematical function to be approximated is the price function.

to correct for the convexity of the price–yield relationship. Market participants refer to the second derivative of price [equation (4.1)] as the **dollar convexity measure** of the bond; that is,

$$\text{dollar convexity measure} = \frac{d^2P}{dy^2} \tag{4.17}$$

The product of the dollar convexity measure and the square of the change in the required yield indicates the estimated price change due to convexity. That is, the approximate change in price due to convexity is

$$dP = (\text{dollar convexity measure})(dy)^2 \tag{4.18}$$

The second derivative divided by price is a measure of the percentage change in the price of the bond due to convexity and is referred to simply as the **convexity measure**; that is,

$$\text{convexity measure} = \frac{d^2P}{dy^2}\frac{1}{P} \tag{4.19}$$

and the percentage price change due to convexity is

$$\frac{dP}{P} = \frac{1}{2}(\text{convexity measure})(dy)^2 \tag{4.20}$$

The second derivative of the price equation (4.1) is

$$\frac{d^2P}{dy^2} = \sum_{t=1}^{n} \frac{t(t+1)C}{(1+y)^{t+2}} + \frac{n(n+1)M}{(1+y)^{n+2}} \tag{4.21}$$

Exhibits 4-14 and 4-15 demonstrate how to calculate the second derivative [equation (4.21)], the annualized dollar convexity measure, and the annualized convexity measure for the two five-year coupon bonds. The convexity measure is in terms of periods squared. To convert the convexity measures to an annual figure, equations (4.17) and (4.19) must be divided by 4 (which is 2 squared). In general, if the cash flows occur m times per year, convexity is adjusted to an annual figure as follows:

$$\text{convexity measure in years} = \frac{\text{convexity measure in } m \text{ periods per year}}{m^2}$$

Annualized convexity measure and annualized dollar convexity measure for our six hypothetical bonds can be summarized as follows:

Bond (per $100 par)	Second Derivative	Annualized Convexity Measure (per $100 par)	Annualized Dollar Convexity Measure
9%/5-year	7,781.02	19.45	$ 1,945.26
9%/25-year	64,288.42	160.72	16,072.00
6%/5-year	7,349.45	20.85	1,837.36
6%/25-year	51,476.26	182.92	12,869.70
0%/5-year	6,486.30	25.18	1,621.42
0%/25-year	25,851.93	583.78	6,463.02

Exhibit 4-14   Calculation of Convexity Measure and Dollar Convexity Measure for Five-Year 9% Bond Selling to Yield 9%

Coupon rate: 9.00%
Term (years): 5
Initial yield: 9.00%
Price: 100

Period, t	Cash Flow[a]	$\dfrac{1}{(1.045)^{t+2}}$	$t(t+1)CF$	$\dfrac{t(t+1)CF}{(1.045)^{t+2}}$
1	$4.50	0.876296	9	7.886
2	$4.50	0.838561	27	22.641
3	$4.50	0.802451	54	43.332
4	$4.50	0.767895	90	69.110
5	$4.50	0.734828	135	99.201
6	$4.50	0.703185	189	132.901
7	$4.50	0.672904	252	169.571
8	$4.50	0.643927	324	208.632
9	$4.50	0.616198	405	249.560
10	$104.50	0.589663	11,495	6,778.186
			12,980	7,781.020

[a]Cash flow per $100 of par value.

$$\text{Second derivative} = 7,781.02$$

$$\text{Convexity measure (half years)} = \frac{7,781.020}{100.0000} = 77.8102$$

$$\text{Convexity measure (years)} = \frac{77.8102}{4} = 19.4526$$

$$\text{Dollar convexity measure} = 100 \times 19.4526 = 1,945.26$$

Alternatively, the second derivative can be determined by taking the second derivative of equation (4.9). By doing so, we can simplify equation (4.21) as follows:

$$\frac{d^2P}{dy^2} = \frac{2C}{y^3}\left[1 - \frac{1}{(1+y)^n}\right] - \frac{2Cn}{y^2(1+y)^{n+1}} + \frac{n(n+1)(100 - C/y)}{(1+y)^{n+2}} \qquad (4.22)$$

To illustrate how to use equation (4.22), consider the 25-year 6% bond selling at 70.357 to yield 9%. The second derivative is

$$\frac{2(3)}{(0.045)^3}\left[1 - \frac{1}{(1.045)^{50}}\right] - \frac{2(3)(50)}{(0.045)^2(1.045)^{51}} + \frac{50(51)(100 - 3/0.045)}{(1.045)^{52}}$$

$$= 65,843.62(0.88929) - 15,695.14 + 8,617.31$$

$$= 51,476.26$$

This agrees with the value reported earlier.

Exhibit 4-15 **Calculation of Convexity Measure and Dollar Convexity Measure for Five-Year 6% Bond Selling to Yield 9%**

Coupon rate: 6.00%
Term (years): 5
Initial yield: 9.00%
Price: 88.1309

Period, t	Cash Flow[a]	$\dfrac{1}{(1.045)^{t+2}}$	$t(t+1)CF$	$\dfrac{t(t+1)CF}{(1.045)^{t+2}}$
1	$3.00	0.876296	6	5.257
2	$3.00	0.838561	18	15.094
3	$3.00	0.802451	36	28.888
4	$3.00	0.767895	60	46.073
5	$3.00	0.734828	90	66.134
6	$3.00	0.703185	126	88.601
7	$3.00	0.672904	168	113.047
8	$3.00	0.643927	216	139.088
9	$3.00	0.616198	270	166.373
10	$103.00	0.589663	11,330	6,680.891
			12,320	7,349.446

[a]Cash flow per $100 of par value.

$$\text{Second derivative} = 7,349.45$$

$$\text{Convexity measure (half years)} = \frac{7,349.45}{88.1309} = 83.3924$$

$$\text{Convexity measure (years)} = \frac{83.3924}{4} = 20.8481$$

$$\text{Dollar convexity measure} = 88.1309 \times 20.8481 = 1,837.36$$

Approximating Percentage Price Change Using Duration and Convexity Measures

Equation (4.16) tells us that the percentage price change of a bond can be estimated using both duration and convexity measure. To illustrate how this is done, consider the 25-year 6% bond selling to yield 9%. The modified duration for this bond is 10.62, and the convexity measure is 182.92. If the required yield increases by 200 basis points, from 9% to 11%, the approximate percentage change in the price of the bond is

percentage change in price due to duration from equation (4.11)
$$= -(\text{modified duration})(dy)$$
$$= -(10.62)(0.02) = -0.2124 = -21.24\%$$

percentage change in price due to duration from equation (4.20)
$$= \frac{1}{2}(\text{convexity measure})(dy)^2$$
$$= \frac{1}{2}(182.92)(0.02)^2 = 0.0366 = 3.66\%$$

The estimated percentage price change due to duration and convexity is

$$-21.24\% + 3.66\% = -17.58\%$$

From Exhibit 4-3, we see that the actual change is -18.03%. Using duration and convexity measures together gives a better approximation of the actual price change for a large movement in the required yield. Suppose, instead, that the required yield decreases by 200 basis points. Then the approximate percentage change in the price of the bond using modified duration and convexity is

percentage change in price due to duration from equation (4.11)
$$= -(\text{modified duration})(dy)$$
$$= -(10.62)(0.02) = +0.2124 = +21.24\%$$

percentage change in price due to convexity from equation (4.20)

$$= \frac{1}{2}(\text{convexity measure})(dy)^2$$

$$= \frac{1}{2}(182.92)(-0.02)^2 = 0.0366 = 3.66\%$$

The estimated percentage price change due to duration and convexity is

$$+21.24\% + 3.66\% = 24.90\%$$

From Exhibit 4-3, we see that the actual change is $+25.46\%$. Once again, using both duration and convexity measure provides a good approximation of the actual price change for a large movement in the required yield.

Some Notes on Convexity

There are three points that should be kept in mind regarding a bond's convexity and convexity measure. First, it is important to understand the distinction between the use of the term *convexity*, which refers to the general shape of the price–yield relationship, and the term *convexity measure*, which is related to the quantification of how the price of the bond will change when interest rates change.

The second point has to do with how to interpret the convexity measure. Recall that for duration, the interpretation of this measure is straightforward. A duration of 4, for example, is interpreted as the approximate percentage change in the price of the bond for a 100-basis-point change in interest rates. How do we interpret a convexity measure? It's not that simple because the approximate percentage change in price due to convexity is affected by the square of the change in rates, as shown in equation (4.20). In that equation, the approximate percentage change in price due to convexity is the product of three numbers: (1) 1/2, (2) convexity measure, and (3) the square of the change in yield.

The final point is that in practice different vendors of analytical systems and different writers compute the convexity measure in different ways. To see why, look back at equation (4.16) and focus on the second term on the right-hand side of the equation. In equation (4.19), we used part of that equation to define the convexity measure. Specifically, the convexity measure is the product of the second derivative and the reciprocal of the price. Suppose instead that we defined the convexity measure from the second term of equation (4.16) to be

$$\text{convexity measure} = \frac{1}{2}\frac{d^2P}{dy^2}\frac{1}{P}$$

That is, the convexity measure shown is just one-half the convexity measure given by equation (4.19). Does it make a difference? Not at all. We must just make sure that we make the adjustment to the relationship between the approximate percentage price change due to convexity and the convexity measure accordingly. Specifically, in equation (4.20), the relationship would be changed as follows:

$$\frac{dP}{P} = (\text{convexity measure}) \times (dy)^2$$

The bottom line is that the approximate percentage price change due to convexity is the same regardless of whether the preceding equation or equation (4.20) is used. This relates to our second point. The interpretation of the convexity measure on a stand-alone basis is not meaningful because different vendors and writers may scale the measure in different ways. What is important is relating the convexity measure and the change in yield (squared).

Value of Convexity

Up to this point, we have focused on how taking convexity into account can improve the approximation of a bond's price change for a given yield change. The convexity of a bond, however, has another important investment implication, which is illustrated in Exhibit 4-16. The exhibit shows two bonds, A and B. The two bonds have the same duration and are offering the same yield; they have different convexities, however. Bond B is more convex (bowed) than bond A.

What is the implication of the greater convexity for B? Whether the market yield rises or falls, B will have a higher price. That is, if the required yield rises, the capital loss on bond B will be less than it will be on bond A. A fall in the required yield will generate greater price appreciation for B than for A.

Generally, the market will take the greater convexity of B compared with A into account in pricing the two bonds. That is, the market will price convexity. Consequently,

Exhibit 4-16   Comparison of Convexity of Two Bonds

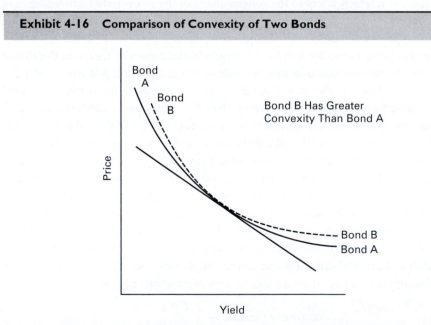

although there may be times when a situation such as that depicted in Exhibit 4-16 will exist, generally the market will require investors to "pay up" (accept a lower yield) for the greater convexity offered by bond B.

The question is: How much should the market want investors to pay up for convexity? Look again at Exhibit 4-16. Notice that if investors expect that market yields will change by very little—that is, they expect low interest rate volatility—the advantage of owning bond B over bond A is insignificant because both bonds will offer approximately the same price for small changes in yield. In this case, investors should not be willing to pay much for convexity. In fact, if the market is pricing convexity high, which means that A will be offering a higher yield than B, investors with expectations of low interest rate volatility would probably be willing to "sell convexity"—that is, to sell B if they own it and buy A. In contrast, if investors expect substantial interest rate volatility, bond B would probably sell at a much lower yield than A.

Properties of Convexity

All option-free bonds have the following convexity properties.

Property 1: As the required yield increases (decreases), the convexity of a bond decreases (increases). This property is referred to as **positive convexity**.

An implication of positive convexity is that the duration of an option-free bond moves in the right direction as market yields change. That is, if market yields rise, the price of a bond will fall. The price decline is slowed down by a decline in the duration of the bond as market yields rise. In contrast, should market yields fall, duration increases so that percentage price change accelerates. With an option-free bond, both these changes in duration occur.

This is portrayed graphically in Exhibit 4-17. The slope of the tangent line in the exhibit gets flatter as the required yield increases. A flatter tangent line means a smaller duration

---

Exhibit 4-17   Change in Duration as the Required Yield Changes

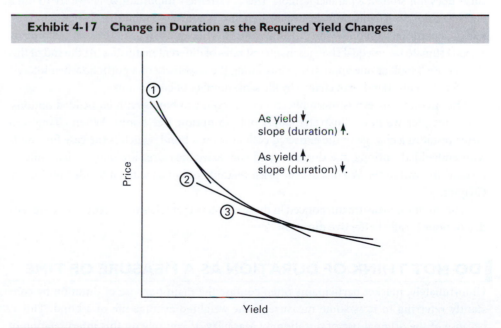

as the required yield rises. In contrast, the tangent line gets steeper as the required yield decreases, implying that the duration gets larger. This property will hold for all option-free bonds. Also, from this graphical presentation we can see that the convexity is actually measuring the rate of change of the dollar duration as market yields change.

Property 2: For a given yield and maturity, the lower the coupon, the greater the convexity of a bond.

This can be seen from the computed convexity of our hypothetical bonds. Of the three five-year bonds, the zero-coupon bond has the highest convexity, and the 9% coupon bond has the lowest convexity. The same is true of the 25-year bonds.

Property 3: For a given yield and modified duration, the lower the coupon, the smaller the convexity.

The investment implication of property 3 is that zero-coupon bonds have the lowest convexity for a given modified duration.

ADDITIONAL CONCERNS WHEN USING DURATION

Our illustrations have demonstrated that relying on duration as the sole measure of the price volatility of a bond may mislead investors. There are two other concerns about using duration that we should point out.

First, in the derivation of the relationship between modified duration and bond price volatility, we started with the price equation (4.1). This price equation assumes that all cash flows for the bond are discounted at the same discount rate. The appropriateness of this assumption is examined in Chapter 5 where we analyze the yield curve. Essentially, the derivation of equation (4.3) assumes that the yield curve is flat and all shifts are parallel. In Chapter 22, we show the limitations of applying duration when this assumption does not hold, and the yield curve does not shift in a parallel fashion. This is extremely important when we try to use a portfolio's duration to quantify the responsiveness of a portfolio's value to a change in interest rates. If a portfolio has bonds with different maturities, the duration measure may not provide a good estimate for unequal changes in interest rates of different maturities. At the end of this chapter, we'll look at one approach to measuring the sensitivity of a portfolio when interest rates for all maturities do not change by the same number of basis points.

Our second concern is misapplication of duration to bonds with embedded options. The principles we have illustrated apply only to option-free bonds. When changes in yields result in a change in the expected cash flow for a bond, which is the case for bonds with embedded options, the duration and convexity measures are appropriate only in certain circumstances. We discuss the price volatility of bonds with embedded options in Chapters 17 and 18.

The duration measure introduced in those chapters that takes into account any embedded options is called **effective duration.**

DO NOT THINK OF DURATION AS A MEASURE OF TIME

Unfortunately, market participants often confuse the main purpose of duration by constantly referring to it as some measure of the weighted average life of a bond. This is because of the original use of duration by Macaulay. If you rely on this interpretation of duration, it will be difficult for you to understand why a bond with a maturity of 20 years can have a duration greater than 20 years. For example, in Chapter 12, we discuss collateralized mortgage obligation (CMO) bond classes. Certain CMO bond classes have a greater duration than the underlying mortgage loans. That is, a CMO bond class can have a duration of 40 although the underlying mortgage loans from which the CMO is created can have a maturity of 30 years. Also, some CMO bond classes have a negative duration. How can this happen?

The answer to this puzzle is that duration is the approximate percentage change in price for a small change in interest rates. In fact, as explained earlier, a good way to remember duration is that it is the approximate percentage change in price for a 100-basis-point change in interest rates.

Certain CMO bond classes are leveraged instruments whose price sensitivity or duration, as a result, are a multiple of the underlying mortgage loans from which they were created. Thus, a CMO bond class with a duration of 40 does not mean that it has some type of weighted average life of 40 years. Instead, it means that for a 100-basis-point change in yield, that bond's price will change by roughly 40%.

Similarly, we interpret the duration of an option in the same way. A call option can have a duration of 20 when the time to expiration of the option is one year.[8] This is confusing to someone who interprets duration as some measure of the life of an option. What it means is that if yields change by 100 basis points for the bond underlying the option, the value of the option will change by approximately 20%.

APPROXIMATING A BOND'S DURATION AND CONVEXITY MEASURE

In our explanation of duration, we started with the price of an option-free bond and then calculated the sensitivity of the bond to a change in interest rates by computing the first and second derivatives. The first derivative is related to duration. A limitation of calculating duration using equation (4.4) or equation (4.5) is that it assumes that the cash flows are known. However, ignoring defaults, it is only in the case of option-free bonds that the cash flows are known. For bonds with embedded options, the cash flows are unknown even in the absence of defaults. For a callable bond, for example, when the issuer might call the bond is unknown. For a putable bond, when the bondholder might put the bond is unknown. For residential mortgage-backed securities, when the borrowers in the pool of mortgage loans will prepay is unknown.

This does not present a problem since we understand that duration is related to percentage price change. Hence, a simple formula can be used to calculate the approximate duration of a bond or any other more complex derivative securities or options described throughout this book. All we are interested in is the percentage price change of a bond when interest rates change by a small amount. This can be found by the following procedure:[9]

Step 1: Increase the yield on the bond by a small number of basis points and determine the new price at this higher yield level. We denote this new price by P_+.

---

[8] We see how to measure the duration of an option in Chapter 27.
[9] Recall that in calculus, the first derivative of the tangent to a curve is the limit. Equation (4.23) is nothing more than approximating the tangency to the curve.

Step 2: Decrease the yield on the bond by the same number of basis points and calculate the new price. We will denote this new price by P_-.

Step 3: Letting P_0 be the initial price, duration can be approximated using the following formula:

$$\text{approximate duration} = \frac{P_- - P_+}{2(P_0)(\Delta y)} \qquad (4.23)$$

where Δy is the change in yield used to calculate the new prices (in decimal form). What the formula is measuring is the average percentage price change (relative to the initial price) per 1-basis-point change in yield.

To see how good this approximation is, let's apply it to the 25-year 6% coupon bond trading at 9%. All the necessary information is provided in Exhibit 4-2. The initial price (P_0) is 70.3570. The steps are as follows:

Step 1: Increase the yield on the bond by 10 basis points from 9% to 9.1%. Thus, Δy is 0.001. The new price (P_+) is 69.6164.

Step 2: Decrease the yield on the bond by 10 basis points from 9% to 8.9%. The new price (P_-) is 71.1105.

Step 3: Because the initial price, P_0, is 70.3570, the duration can be approximated as follows:

$$\text{approximate duration} = \frac{71.1105 - 69.6164}{2(70.3570)(0.001)} = 10.62$$

How good is the approximation? The modified duration as calculated by using equations (4.5) and (4.7) is 10.62.

If an investor is interested in the duration of any financial instrument, equation (4.23) can be used. However, to use the equation, it is necessary to have a good pricing model to get the new prices in steps 1 and 2. These models are discussed in later chapters. *It is important to emphasize here that duration is a by-product of a pricing model. If the pricing model is poor, the resulting duration estimate is poor.*

In practice, no commercial software uses equations (4.4) or (4.5). Rather, it uses equation (4.23). Different vendors have their own rules for determining how much to change interest rates to compute the prices in equation (4.23). For option-free bonds, any small change in interest rates will provide about the same value. For bonds with embedded options, the change in interest rates used must be reasonable enough to pick up how the value of the option will change.

Similarly, the convexity measure of any bond can be approximated using the following formula:

$$\text{approximate convexity measure} = \frac{P_+ + P_- - 2P_0}{P_0(\Delta y)^2} \qquad (4.24)$$

Using our previous illustration, the approximate convexity measure is

$$\text{approximate convexity measure} = \frac{71.1105 + 69.6164 - 2(70.3570)}{70.3570(0.001)^2} = 183.3$$

As reported previously, the convexity measure calculated by formula is 182.92. Thus, equation (4.24) does a fine job.

As we noted earlier, the convexity measure can be measured in a different way. Equation (4.24) can be rewritten to include 2 in the denominator. All this means is that when the percentage change in price due to convexity is computed using equation (4.20), the 1/2 should be eliminated.

Duration of an Inverse Floater

In Chapter 2, we discussed how an inverse floater is created and how it is priced. Here we will look at the duration of an inverse floater. The duration of the inverse floater is related to the duration of the collateral and the duration of the floater. Assuming that the duration of the floater is close to zero, it can be shown that the duration of an inverse floater is as follows:[10]

$$\text{duration of inverse floater} = (1 + L)(\text{duration of collateral}) \times \frac{\text{collateral price}}{\text{inverse price}}$$

where L is the ratio of the par value of the floater to the par value of the inverse floater. For example, if collateral with a par value of $100 million is used to create a floater with a par value of $80 million and an inverse floater with a par value of $20 million, L is 4 ($80 million/ $20 million).

It is easy to see why an inverse's duration is a multiple of the collateral. Suppose that the par value of the collateral of $100 million is split as follows: $80 million for the floater and $20 million for the inverse floater. Suppose also that the collateral and inverse are trading at par so that the ratio of the prices is 1 and that the duration for the collateral is 8. For a 100-basis-point change in interest rates, the collateral's price will decline by 8% or $8 million (8% times $100 million). Assuming that the floater's price does not change when interest rates increase, the $8 million decline must come from the inverse floater. For the inverse floater to realize a decline in value of $8 million when its value is $20 million, the duration must be 40. That is, a duration of 40 will produce a 40% change in value or $8 million (40% times $20 million). Thus, the duration is five times the collateral's duration of 8. Or equivalently, because L is 4, it is (1 + 4) times the collateral's duration.

Notice that even if the maturity of the collateral is 30 years, the duration of the inverse is greater than the maturity of the collateral. Investors who interpret duration as some time of weighted life of a security would be surprised by this result.

MEASURING A BOND PORTFOLIO'S RESPONSIVENESS TO NONPARALLEL CHANGES IN INTEREST RATES

We noted earlier in this chapter when we identified the shortcoming of duration that this measure may be inadequate in measuring how a security's price or a portfolio's value will change when interest rates do not change in a parallel manner. (We will discuss how yield curve shifts in Chapter 5.) This is particularly the case for a bond portfolio. As a result, it is necessary to be able to measure the exposure of a bond or bond portfolio to shifts in the yield curve. There have been several approaches that have been suggested for measuring this

---

[10] William R. Leach, "A Portfolio Manager's Perspective of Inverses and Inverse IOs," Chapter 9 in Frank J. Fabozzi (ed.), *Advances in the Valuation and Management of Mortgage-Backed Securities* (New Hope, PA: Frank J. Fabozzi Associates, 1998).

exposure. There have been several approaches to measuring yield curve risk. The two major ones are yield curve reshaping duration and key rate duration. We describe each below.[11]

Yield Curve Reshaping Duration

The first approach concentrates on the sensitivity of a portfolio to a change in the slope of the yield curve. The initial step in this approach is to define what is meant by the slope of the yield curve. Market participants have used different definitions. Some define yield curve slope as the difference in the Treasury yield curve at two maturity levels. For instance, the yield curve slope can be defined as the difference between the yield on a proxy for the long-term Treasury bond (30-year Treasury) and the two-year on-the-run Treasury. Some have defined the short maturity point as the six-month rate.

One of the first measures of this approach was introduced by three researchers at Salomon Brothers (now Salomon Smith Barney), Klaffky, Ma, and Nozari.[12] They called the measure that they suggest **yield curve reshaping duration**. They focus on three maturity points on the yield curve: two-year, 10-year, and 30-year. Using these three points they then calculate the spread between the 10-year and two-year yield and refer to this as the spread for the short end of the yield curve; the spread between the 30-year and the 10-year is computed and referred to as the spread for the long end of the yield curve. Klaffky, Ma, and Nozari refer to the sensitivity of a portfolio to changes in the short end of the yield curve as **short-end duration** (SEDUR) and to changes in the long-end of the yield curve as **long-end duration** (LEDUR). These concepts, however, are applicable to other points on the yield curve.

To calculate the SEDUR of the portfolio, first the change in each security's price is calculated for

1. a steepening of the yield curve at the short end by x basis points
2. a flattening of the yield curve at the short end by x basis points

The portfolio value for a steepening of the yield curve is then computed by adding up the value of every security in the portfolio after the steepening. We will denote this value as $V_{SE,S}$ where V stands for portfolio value, SE for short end of the yield curve, and S for steepening. Similarly, the portfolio value after the flattening is obtained by summing up the value of each security in the portfolio and the resulting value will be denoted by $V_{SE,F}$ where F denotes flattening. The SEDUR is then computed as follows:

$$\text{SEDUR} = \frac{V_{SE,S} - V_{SE,F}}{2(V_0)(\Delta y)}$$

where V_0 is the initial value of the portfolio (the value before any steepening or flattening) and Δy is the number of basis points used to compute the steepening and flattening of the yield curve (x).

Compare the above equation to equation (4.23) for approximating duration. Notice that it is the same formula where V is used instead of P and P_- and P_+ are replaced by $V_{SE,S}$ and $V_{SE,F}$, respectively.

---

[11] The other measures are yield curve reshaping duration and yield curve specific duration. These measures are discussed in Chapter 7 of Frank J. Fabozzi, *Duration, Convexity, and Other Bond Risk Measures* (New Hope, PA: Frank J. Fabozzi Associates, 1999). The discussion in this section on key rate duration is adapted from that chapter.

[12] Thomas E. Klaffky, Y. Y. Ma, and Ardavan Nozari, "Managing Yield Curve Exposure: Introducing Reshaping Durations," *Journal of Fixed Income* (December 1992), pp. 5–15.

To compute the LEDUR of the portfolio, the change in each security's price is first calculated for

1. a flattening of the yield curve at the long end by x basis points
2. a steepening of the yield curve at the long end by x basis points

The value for the portfolio after each shift is computed and denoted by $V_{LE,F}$ and $V_{LE,S}$ where LE denotes the long-end of the yield curve. Then LEDUR is calculated from the following formula:

$$\text{LEDUR} = \frac{V_{LE,F} - V_{LE,S}}{2(V_0)(\Delta y)}$$

SEDUR and LEDUR are interpreted as follows. SEDUR is the approximate percentage change in the value of a portfolio for a 100-basis-point change in the slope of the short-end of the yield curve. LEDUR is the approximate percentage change in the value of a portfolio for a 100-basis-point change in the slope of the long-end of the yield curve.

Key Rate Duration

The most popular measure for estimating the sensitivity of a security or a portfolio to changes in the yield curve is key rate duration. The basic principle of key rate duration is to change the yield for a particular maturity of the yield curve and determine the sensitivity of a security or portfolio to that change holding all other yields constant. The sensitivity of the change in value to a particular change in yield is called **rate duration**. There is a rate duration for every point on the yield curve. Consequently, there is not one rate duration, but a vector of durations representing each maturity on the yield curve. The total change in value of a bond or a portfolio if all rates change by the same number of basis points is simply the duration of a security or portfolio we discussed earlier in this chapter.

The notion of using multiple durations was first suggested in 1988 by Donald Chambers and Willard Carleton; they called it **duration vectors**.[13] Robert Reitano suggested a similar approach in a series of papers and called the durations partial durations.[14] The most popular version of this approach is that developed by Thomas Ho in 1992, who called it rate duration.[15]

Ho's approach focuses on 11 key maturities of a Treasury curve, which we will describe in Chapter 5. The specific curve used in the analysis is called the Treasury spot rate curve; this important curve shows the relationship between maturity and yields on Treasury zero-coupon securities (see Chapter 5 for a detailed discussion). The rate durations are called **key rate durations.** The specific maturities on the spot rate curve for which a key rate duration is measured are three months, one year, two years, three years, five years, seven years, 10 years, 15 years, 20 years, 25 years, and 30 years. Changes in rates between any two key rates are calculated using a linear approximation.

A key rate duration for a particular portfolio maturity should be interpreted as follows: Holding the yield for all other maturities constant, the key rate duration is the approximate

---

[13] Donald Chambers and Willard Carleton, "A Generalized Approach to Duration," *Research in Finance* 7 (1988).
[14] See, for example, Robert R. Reitano, "Non-Parallel Yield Curve Shifts and Durational Leverage," *Journal of Portfolio Management*, Summer 1990, pp. 62–67, and "A Multivariate Approach to Duration Analysis," *ARCH* 2 (1989).
[15] Thomas S. Y. Ho, "Key Rate Durations: Measure of Interest Rate Risk," *Journal of Fixed Income*, September 1992, pp. 29–44.

percentage change in the value of a portfolio (or bond) for a 100-basis-point change in the yield for the maturity whose rate has been changed. Thus, a key rate duration is quantified by changing the yield of the maturity of interest and determining how the value or price changes. In fact, equation (4.23) is used. The prices denoted by P_- and P_+ in the equation are the prices in the case of a bond and the portfolio values in the case of a bond portfolio found by holding all other interest rates constant and changing the yield for the maturity whose key rate duration is sought.

Let's look at three actual portfolios to make the concept of key rate duration more concrete. Exhibit 4-18 shows three portfolios consisting of different maturity Treasury

Exhibit 4-18 Key Rate Durations for Three Treasury Portfolios (March 22, 2006)

Barbell Portfolio		Bullet Portfolio		Ladder Portfolio	
Treasury Issue	Weight (%)	Treasury Issue	Weight (%)	Treasury Issue	Weight (%)
2.625% 05/15/2008	3.71	3.875% 02/15/2013	0.50	14.000% 11/15/2011	36.47
4.000% 02/15/2015	14.95	3.875% 09/15/2010	69.73	10.375% 11/15/2012	13.92
4.250% 08/15/2015	9.12	4.250% 01/15/2011	29.41	12.000% 08/15/2013	7.81
4.500% 02/15/2036	6.90	4.500% 02/15/2036	0.35	12.500% 08/15/2014	8.57
4.625% 02/29/2036	65.31			6.000% 02/15/2026	6.06
				6.750% 08/15/2026	2.58
				5.375% 02/15/2031	2.89
				5.000% 08/15/2011	4.55
				4.000% 02/15/2015	7.74
				4.500% 02/15/2036	4.57
				4.500% 02/15/2016	4.85

	Key Rate Durations		
Vertices	Barbell	Bullet	Ladder
0.0833	0.0000	0.0000	0.0015
0.25	0.0017	0.0014	0.0045
0.50	0.0092	0.0087	0.1273
1	0.0662	0.0290	0.1768
2	1.2480	0.0744	0.2880
3	0.0513	0.1071	0.2430
4	0.0448	1.5132	0.1520
5	0.0790	2.4525	0.2280
7	0.5131	0.0287	0.3626
10	1.3210	0.0060	0.9770
20	0.2520	0.0120	1.1040
30	0.6750	0.0330	0.5940
Duration	4.2613	4.2660	4.2586

Note: *This exhibit was prepared for the author by Dan Sinnreich and Oren Cheyette.*

securities as of March 22, 2006. The duration for each portfolio is the same, 4.26.[16] The key rate durations differ for each portfolio. Look at the 30-year key rate duration for each portfolio. For the first portfolio in the exhibit, the 30-year duration is 0.675. This means that if the 30-year Treasury spot rate changes by 100 basis points and the spot rate for all other maturities does not change, the portfolio's value will change by approximately 0.675%. For the second portfolio, the 30-year key rate duration is close to zero; thus, for a 100-basis-point change in the 30-year Treasury spot rate and holding the spot rate for all other maturities the same, the second portfolio's value will not change. The third portfolio's 30-year key rate duration is 0.594, so its value will change by 0.594% for a 100-basis-point change assuming no change in the spot rate for other maturities.

From this illustration it can be seen that despite the same portfolio duration for all three portfolios (4.26), they will each be expected to react in a different way if the 30-year spot rate changes. Exhibit 4-18 indicates that each portfolio will have quite different reactions to changes in the interest rate for different maturities.

KEY POINTS

- The price–yield relationship for all option-free bonds is convex.
- There are three properties of the price volatility of an option-free bond: (1) for small changes in yield, the percentage price change is symmetric; (2) for large changes in yield, the percentage price change is asymmetric; and (3) for large changes in yield the price appreciation is greater than the price depreciation for a given change in yield.
- The price volatility of an option-free bond is affected by two characteristics of a bond (maturity and coupon) and the yield level at which a bond trades. For a given maturity and yield, the lower the coupon rate the greater the price volatility. For a given coupon rate and yield, the longer the maturity the greater the price volatility.
- For a given coupon rate and maturity, the price volatility is greater the lower the yield.
- There are two measures of bond price volatility: price value of a basis point and duration.
- Modified duration is the approximate percentage change in price for a 100-basis-point change in yield. The dollar duration is the approximate dollar price change.
- Duration does a good job of estimating a bond's percentage price change for a small change in yield. However, it does not do as good a job for a large change in yield. The percentage price change due to convexity can be used to supplement the approximate price change using duration. Together, the duration and convexity measures provide an excellent approximation of the price change when yields change.
- Duration is an approximation of price change assuming a parallel shift in the yield curve.
- Duration should not be interpreted as a measure of the weighted life of a bond. For certain bonds, the modified duration can be greater than the maturity of a bond.
- For a fixed-rate bond, spread duration is a measure of how a non-Treasury bond's price will change if the spread sought by the market changes.
- Duration and convexity can be approximated by looking at how the price of a bond changes when the yield is changed up and down by a small number of basis points.
- For a floating-rate bond a spread duration can be calculated.
- The duration of an inverse floater is a multiple of the duration of the collateral from which it is created.
- The duration of a portfolio is the weighted average duration of the bonds in the portfolio. When a manager attempts to gauge the sensitivity of a bond portfolio to

---

[16] Note that the three portfolios are labeled "Ladder Portfolio," "Barbell Portfolio," and "Bullet Portfolio." We'll see why in Chapter 22.

changes in interest rates by computing a portfolio's duration, it is assumed that the interest rate for all maturities changes by the same number of basis points.

- Contribution to portfolio duration measures how much a holding or a sector contributes to the duration of a portfolio and is found by multiplying the weight of the issue (or sector) in the portfolio by the duration of the individual issue (sector).
- To estimate the sensitivity of a bond portfolio to unequal changes in interest rates, two approaches have been used. The first is yield curve reshaping duration. Here two measures are computed: short-end duration and long-end duration. The former measures the exposure of a portfolio to changes in the short-end of the yield curve and the latter exposure to the long-end of the yield curve. The more popular approach is key rate duration.
- A rate duration is the approximate change in the value of a portfolio (or bond) to a change in the interest rate of a particular maturity assuming that the interest rate for all other maturities is held constant. Practitioners compute a key rate duration, which is simply the rate duration for key maturities.

QUESTIONS

1. The price value of a basis point will be the same regardless if the yield is increased or decreased by 1 basis point. However, the price value of 100 basis points (i.e., the change in price for a 100-basis-point change in interest rates) will not be the same if the yield is increased or decreased by 100 basis points. Why?

2. Calculate the requested measures for bonds A and B (assume that each bond pays interest semiannually):

	A	B
Coupon	8%	9%
Yield to maturity	8%	8%
Maturity (years)	2	5
Par	$100.00	$100.00
Price	$100.00	$104.055

   a. Price value of a basis point
   b. Macaulay duration
   c. Modified duration
   d. The approximate duration using the shortcut formula by changing yields by 20 basis points and compare your answer with the convexity measure calculated in part c.
   e. Convexity measure
   f. The approximate convexity measure using the shortcut formula by changing yields by 20 basis points and compare your answer to the convexity measure calculated in part e.

3. Can you tell from the following information which of the following three bonds will have the

greatest price volatility, assuming that each is trading to offer the same yield to maturity?

Bond	Coupon Rate (%)	Maturity (years)
X	8	9
Y	10	11
Z	11	12

4. For bonds A and B in Question 2:
   a. Calculate the actual price of the bonds for a 100-basis-point increase in interest rates.
   b. Using duration, estimate the price of the bonds for a 100-basis-point increase in interest rates.
   c. Using both duration and convexity measure, estimate the price of the bonds for a 100-basis-point increase in interest rates.
   d. Comment on the accuracy of your results in parts b and c, and state why one approximation is closer to the actual price than the other.
   e. Without working through calculations, indicate whether the duration of the two bonds would be higher or lower if the yield to maturity is 10% rather than 8%.

5. State why you would agree or disagree with the following statement: As the duration of a zero-coupon bond is equal to its maturity, the price responsiveness of a zero-coupon bond to yield changes is the same regardless of the level of interest rates.

6. State why you would agree or disagree with the following statement: When interest rates are low, there will be little difference between the Macaulay duration and modified duration measures.

7. State why you would agree or disagree with the following statement: If two bonds have the same dollar duration, yield, and price, their dollar price sensitivity will be the same for a given change in interest rates.

8. State why you would agree or disagree with the following statement: For a 1-basis-point change in yield, the price value of a basis point is equal to the dollar duration.

9. The November 26, 1990, issue of *BondWeek* includes an article, "Van Kampen Merritt Shortens." The article begins as follows: "Peter Hegel, first v.p. at Van Kampen Merritt Investment Advisory, is shortening his $3 billion portfolio from 110% of his normal duration of six years to 103–105% because he thinks that in the short run the bond rally is near an end." Explain Hegel's strategy and the use of the duration measure in this context.

10. Consider the following two Treasury securities:

Bond	Price	Modified Duration
A	$100	6
B	80	7

Which bond will have the greater dollar price volatility for a 25-basis-point change in interest rates?

11. What are the limitations of using duration as a measure of a bond's price sensitivity to interest-rate changes?

12. The following excerpt is taken from an article titled "Denver Investment to Make $800 Million Treasury Move," which appeared in the December 9, 1991, issue of *BondWeek*, p. 1: "Denver Investment Advisors will swap $800 million of long zero-coupon Treasuries for intermediate Treasuries. . . . The move would shorten the duration of its $2.5 billion fixed-income portfolio. . . ." Why would the swap described here shorten the duration of the portfolio?

13. You are a portfolio manager who has presented a report to a client. The report indicates the duration of each security in the portfolio. One of the securities has a maturity of 15 years but a duration of 25. The client believes that there is an error in the report because he believes that the duration cannot be greater than the security's maturity. What would be your response to this client?

14. **a.** Suppose that the spread duration for a fixed-rate bond is 2.5. What is the approximate change in the bond's price if the spread changes by 50 basis points?
   b. What is the spread duration of a Treasury security?

15. What is meant by the spread duration for a floating-rate bond?

16. Explain why the duration of an inverse floater is a multiple of the duration of the collateral from which the inverse floater is created.

17. Consider the following portfolio:

Bond	Market Value	Duration
W	$13 million	2
X	$27 million	7
Y	$60 million	8
Z	$40 million	14

   a. What is the portfolio's duration?
   b. If interest rates for all maturities change by 50 basis points, what is the approximate percentage change in the value of the portfolio?
   c. What is the contribution to portfolio duration for each bond?

18. "If two portfolios have the same duration, the change in their value when interest rates change will be the same." Explain why you agree or disagree with this statement.

19. Some authors give the following formula for the approximate convexity measure:

$$\frac{P_+ + P_- - 2(P_0)}{2(P_0)(\Delta y)^2}$$

   where the variables are defined as in equation (4.24) of this chapter. Compare this formula with the approximate convexity measure given by equation (4.24). Which formula is correct?

20. **a.** How is the short-end duration of a portfolio computed?
   b. How is the long-end duration of a portfolio computed?
   c. How is the short-end and long-end of a portfolio defined?
   d. Suppose that the SEDUR of a portfolio is 3. What is the approximate change in the portfolio's value if the slope of the short end of the yield curve changed by 25 basis points?

21. **a.** Explain what a 10-year key rate duration of 0.35 means.
   b. How is a key rate duration computed?

5

Factors Affecting Bond Yields and the Term Structure of Interest Rates

LEARNING OBJECTIVES

After reading this chapter, you will understand

- why the yield on a Treasury security is the base interest rate
- the factors that affect the yield spread between two bonds
- what a yield curve is
- a spot rate and a spot rate curve
- how theoretical spot rates are derived using arbitrage arguments from the Treasury yield curve
- what the term structure of interest rates is
- why the price of a Treasury bond should be based on theoretical spot rates
- a forward rate and how a forward rate is derived
- how long-term rates are related to the current short-term rate and short-term forward rates
- why forward rates should be viewed as hedgeable rates
- the various theories about the determinants of the shape of the term structure: pure expectations theory, the liquidity theory, the preferred habitat theory, and the market segmentation theory
- the main economic influences on the shape of the Treasury yield curve
- what the swap curve/LIBOR curve is and why it is used as an interest rate benchmark

In all financial markets throughout the world, there is not one yield offered on all bonds. The yield offered on a particular bond depends on a myriad of factors having to do with the type of issuer, the characteristics of the bond issue, and the state of the economy. In this chapter, we look at the factors that affect the yield offered in the bond market. We begin with the minimum interest rate that an investor wants from investing in a bond, the yield on U.S. Treasury securities. Then we describe why the yield on a non-U.S. Treasury security will differ from that of a U.S. Treasury security. Finally, we focus on one particular factor that affects the yield offered on a security: maturity. The pattern of interest rates on securities of the same issuer but with different maturities is called the term structure of interest rates. The importance of analyzing the term structure of interest rates for U.S. Treasury securities is explained. In the last section of this chapter, we describe another important interest rate benchmark, the swap curve (LIBOR curve).

BASE INTEREST RATE

The securities issued by the U.S. Department of the Treasury are backed by the full faith and credit of the U.S. government. Consequently, historically market participants throughout the world view them as having no credit risk, a view that has recently been challenged. As such, interest rates on Treasury securities are the key interest rates in the U.S. economy as well as in international capital markets. Another important benchmark is the interest rate swap market, and we discuss it later in this chapter.

The minimum interest rate that investors want is referred to as the **base interest rate** or **benchmark interest rate** that investors will demand for investing in a non-Treasury security. This rate is the yield to maturity (hereafter referred to as simply **yield**) offered on a comparable maturity Treasury security that was most recently issued ("on the run"). When we refer to the interest rate offered on a bond, we refer to that interest rate as the yield on the bond. In Chapter 3, we explained how to compute a bond's yield. Exhibit 5-1 shows the yield for U.S. Treasury securities on February 26, 2011. These yields represent the benchmark interest rate. So if an investor wanted to purchase a five-year bond on February 26, 2011, the minimum yield the investor would seek was 3.49%, which is the five-year yield shown in Exhibit 5-1.

BENCHMARK SPREAD

The difference between the yields of any two bonds is called a **yield spread**. For example, consider two bonds, bond A and bond B. The yield spread is then

$$\text{yield spread} = \text{yield on bond A} - \text{yield on bond B}$$

Exhibit 5-1	U.S. Treasury Security Yields on February 26, 2011
Maturity	**Yield**
3-month	0.11
6-month	0.14
2-year	0.72
3-year	1.20
5-year	2.16
10-year	3.41
30-year	4.50

Note: *Yields were reported on finance.yahoo.com. The original source is ValuBond.*

The normal way that yield spreads are quoted is in terms of basis points.

The yield spread reflects the difference in the risks associated with the two bonds. While we have formulated the yield spread in terms of individual bonds, we can also think of the yield spread for sectors of the bond market.

When bond B is a benchmark bond and bond A is a non-benchmark bond, the yield spread is referred to as a **benchmark spread**; that is,

benchmark spread = yield on non-benchmark bond − yield on benchmark bond

The benchmark spread reflects the compensation that the market is offering for bearing the risks associated with the non-benchmark bond that do not exist for the benchmark bond. Thus, the benchmark spread can be thought of as a risk premium.

Some market participants measure the risk premium on a relative basis by taking the ratio of the yield spread to the yield level. This measure, called a **relative yield spread**, is computed as follows:

$$\text{relative yield spread} = \frac{\text{yield on bond A} - \text{yield on bond B}}{\text{yield on bond B}}$$

For example, on February 24, 2011, the Goldman Sachs GP 3.65% coupon maturing in February 2016 traded to yield 3.723%. Since this bond issue had five years to maturity, the appropriate Treasury benchmark would be the five-year Treasury yield of 2.16% reported in Exhibit 5-1. Therefore, the relative yield spread is

$$\text{relative yield spread} = \frac{3.723\% - 2.16\%}{2.16\%} = 0.72 = 72\%$$

The **yield ratio** is the quotient of two bond yields:

$$\text{yield ratio} = \frac{\text{yield on bond A}}{\text{yield on bond B}}$$

For the Goldman Sachs issue, the yield ratio is

$$\text{yield ratio} = \frac{3.723\%}{2.16\%} = 1.72$$

Below, we discuss the following factors that affect the benchmark spread for an issue:

1. the type of issuer
2. the perceived creditworthiness of the issue
3. the term or maturity of the issue
4. the provisions that grant either the issuer or the investor the option to do something
5. the taxability of the interest received
6. the expected liquidity of the issue

Types of Issuers

The bond market is classified by the type of issuer, including the U.S. government, U.S. government agencies, municipal governments, credit (domestic and foreign corporations), and foreign governments. These classifications are referred to as **market sectors**. Different sectors are generally perceived to represent different risks and rewards. Some market sectors are further subdivided into categories intended to reflect common economic characteristics. For example, within the credit market sector, issuers are classified as follows: (1) industrial, (2) utility, (3) finance, and (4) noncorporate. Excluding the Treasury market sector, the other market sectors have a wide range of issuers, each with different abilities to satisfy their contractual obligations. Therefore, a key feature of a debt obligation is the nature of the issuer.

The spread between the interest rate offered in two sectors of the bond market with the same maturity is referred to as an **intermarket sector spread**. The most common intermarket sector spread calculated is the spread between Treasury securities and some sector of the non-Treasury market with the same maturity. The spread between two issues within a market sector is called an **intramarket sector spread**.

Perceived Creditworthiness of Issuer

Default risk refers to the risk that the issuer of a bond may be unable to make timely principal and/or interest payments. Most market participants rely primarily on commercial rating companies to assess the default risk of an issuer. We discuss these rating companies in Chapter 7.

The spread between Treasury securities and non-Treasury securities that are identical in all respects except for quality is referred to as a **credit spread**. It is important to keep in mind what is meant by "identical in all respects except for quality." As explained in Chapters 4 and 7 and discussed further subsequently, issues may have provisions that can be beneficial or detrimental to a bondholder. These provisions are absent in a Treasury issue but may be present in a non-Treasury under examination. For this reason, the credit spread would be distorted because it reflects the value of these other provisions.

Examples of credit spreads on February 26, 2011 are provided in Exhibit 5-2. The Treasury yields for computing the credit spreads are those shown in Exhibit 5-1. As can be seen, for a given maturity, the higher the credit rating, the smaller the credit spread.

Inclusion of Options

It is not uncommon for a bond issue to include a provision that gives either the bondholder or the issuer an option to take some action against the other party. Such embedded options are discussed throughout this book. The most common type of option in a bond issue is the call provision that grants the issuer the right to retire the debt, fully or partially,

Exhibit 5-2	Corporate Bond Yields and Risk Premium Measures Relative to Treasury Yields on February 26, 2011			
Maturity	Rating	Corporate Yield (%)	Treasury Yield (%)	Yield Spread (bps)
5-year	AAA	2.43	2.16	26
5-year	AA	2.79	2.16	63
10-year	AAA	3.88	3.41	47
10-year	AA	4.39	3.41	98

Note: *Yields were reported on finance.yahoo.com. The original source is ValuBond.*

before the scheduled maturity date. The inclusion of a call feature benefits issuers by allowing them to replace an old bond issue with a lower-interest-cost issue should interest rates in the market decline. Effectively, a call provision allows the issuer to alter the maturity of a bond. A call provision is detrimental to the bondholder because the bondholder must reinvest the proceeds received at a lower interest rate.

The presence of an embedded option has an effect on the benchmark spread. In general, market participants will require a larger benchmark spread with an embedded option that is favorable to the issuer (e.g., a call option) than for an issue without such an option. In contrast, market participants will require a smaller benchmark spread for an issue with an embedded option that is favorable to the investor (e.g., a put option or conversion option). In fact, for a bond with an option that is favorable to an investor, the interest rate on an issue may be less than that on a comparable benchmark issue!

Since part of the yield spread is for the value of any embedded options, is there a way to adjust the yield spread to remove that portion that is attributable to them? That is, if a bond is callable, the benchmark spread is greater compared to a noncallable bond due to the risk the investor must accept that the bond may be called when interest rates decline below the issue's coupon rate. Can we remove the portion of the compensation in the benchmark spread that is attributable to the value of the call option given to the issuer? The answer is yes. In Chapter 17, we will discuss an analytical measure called the **option-adjusted spread** (OAS). As the name suggests, the OAS is the spread (i.e., yield spread) after adjusting for the value of the embedded options. In Chapter 18, we will see how the OAS is calculated for corporate bonds, and in Chapter 19, we will see how it is calculated for mortgage-backed securities. As will be seen, it is not a simple calculation but relies on a model for valuing bonds with embedded options.

For now, all that is important for us to understand is that the benchmark spread incorporates the value of any embedded options and the OAS removes that value. That is why if we observe two benchmark spreads in the market at a given point in time, the benchmark spread might at first seem confusing. For example, consider two corporate bonds, one rated double A and one rated triple A. One would expect that absent any embedded options, the lower-rated bond would have a higher benchmark spread. Suppose the opposite is observed in the market (i.e., the lower-rated bond has a lower benchmark spread). The reason could be one or both of the following reasons. First, the higher-rated bond is callable. Hence, the benchmark spread reflects compensation for the call risk. Second, the lower-rated corporate bond may be putable or may be convertible. Either of these features (i.e., embedded options) could result in a lower benchmark spread relative to the higher-rated bond.

Taxability of Interest

Unless exempted under the federal income tax code, interest income is taxable at the federal level. In addition to federal income taxes, there may be state and local taxes on interest income.

The federal tax code specifically exempts the interest income from qualified municipal bond issues from taxation at the federal level. For municipal bonds that qualify for tax exemption, the yield is less than that on Treasuries with the same maturity. This can be seen in Exhibit 5-3, which shows the municipal yield and corporate yield for A-rated issues for three maturities (five, 10, and 20 years as of February 26, 2011). Rather than using yield

Exhibit 5-3	A Rated Municipal Yields versus A Rated Corporate Yields as of February 26, 2011		
Maturity	Municipal Yield (%)	Corporate Yield (%)	Yield Ratio
5-year	2.88	2.99	0.96
10-year	3.82	4.45	0.86
20-year	5.58	5.62	0.99

Note: *Yields were reported on finance.yahoo.com. The original source is ValuBond.*

spreads to show the difference between a municipal bond and a corporate bond with the same maturity and same credit rating, the yield ratio described earlier in this chapter is commonly used. The last column of the exhibit shows the yield ratio.

The yield on a taxable bond issue after federal income taxes are paid is called the **after-tax yield**:

$$\text{after-tax yield} = \text{pretax yield} \times (1 - \text{marginal tax rate})$$

Of course, the marginal tax rate varies among investors. For example, suppose that a taxable bond issue offers a yield of 5% and is acquired by an investor facing a marginal tax rate of 35%. The after-tax yield would then be

$$\text{after-tax yield} = 0.05 \times (1 - 0.35) = 3.25\%$$

Alternatively, we can determine the yield that must be offered on a taxable bond issue to give the same after-tax yield as a tax-exempt issue. This yield, called the **equivalent taxable yield**, is determined as follows:

$$\text{equivalent taxable yield} = \frac{\text{tax-exempt yield}}{1 - \text{marginal tax rate}}$$

For example, consider an investor facing a 35% marginal tax rate who purchases a tax-exempt issue with a yield of 3.4%. The equivalent taxable yield is then

$$\text{equivalent taxable yield} = \frac{0.034}{1 - 0.35} = 0.0523 = 5.23\%$$

Notice that the higher the marginal tax rate, the higher the equivalent taxable yield. For example, in our previous example, if the marginal tax rate is 45% rather than 35%, the equivalent taxable yield would be 6.18% rather than 5.23%:

$$\text{equivalent taxable yield} = \frac{0.034}{1 - 0.45} = 0.0618 = 6.18\%$$

The municipal bond market is divided into two major sectors: tax-backed bonds (the most popular being general obligations bonds) and revenue bonds. The revenue bond sector is further decomposed into various sectors that we discuss in Chapter 8. For the tax-exempt bond market, the benchmark for calculating spreads is not Treasuries. Rather, it is a generic AAA general obligation bond with a specified maturity.

State and local governments may tax interest income on bond issues that are exempt from federal income taxes. Some municipalities exempt interest income from all municipal issues from taxation; others do not. Some states exempt interest income from bonds issued by municipalities within the state but tax the interest income from bonds issued by municipalities outside the state. The implication is that two municipal securities of the same quality rating and the same maturity may trade at some spread because of the relative demand for bonds of municipalities in different states. For example, in a high-income-tax state such as New York, the demand for bonds of municipalities will drive down their yield relative to municipalities in a low-income-tax state such as Florida. Municipalities are not permitted to tax the interest income from securities issued by the U.S. Treasury. Thus, part of the spread between Treasury securities and taxable non-Treasury securities of the same maturity reflects the value of the exemption from state and local taxes.

Expected Liquidity of an Issue

Bonds trade with different degrees of liquidity. The greater the expected liquidity, the lower the yield that investors would require. As noted earlier, Treasury securities are the most liquid securities in the world. The lower yield offered on Treasury securities relative to non-Treasury securities reflects the difference in liquidity. Even within the Treasury market, on-the-run issues have greater liquidity than off-the-run issues. One study finds that while default risk explains the majority of the risk premium between corporate bonds and Treasury securities, a significant factor that affects the risk premium is corporate bond illiquidity.[1]

Financeability of an Issue

A portfolio manager can use an issue as collateral for borrowing funds. By borrowing funds, a portfolio manager can create leverage. We will discuss this strategy in Chapter 22. The typical market used by portfolio managers to borrow funds using a security as collateral for a loan is the repurchase agreement market or "repo" market. We will discuss this market and the repo agreement in Chapter 22.

Basically, when a portfolio manager wants to borrow funds via a repo agreement, a dealer provides the funds. The interest rate the dealer charges is called the repo rate. There is not one repo rate but a structure of rates depending on the maturity of the loan and the specific issue being financed. With respect to the latter, there are times when dealers are in need of particular issues to cover a short position. When a dealer needs a particular issue, that dealer will be willing to offer to lend funds at a lower repo rate than the general repo rate in the market. The dealer is willing to offer attractive financing because it can use the collateral (i.e., the particular issue it needs) to cover a short position for the life of the repo agreement. Because such issues offer below-market financing opportunities, the price of such issues will be bid up, and therefore their yield is less than otherwise comparable issues. The spread between the yield on such issues and issues that do not offer a below-market repo rate reflects the financing advantage. This spread is commonly observed in the Treasury market between on-the-run and off-the-run issues. Consequently, the spread between on-the-run and off-the-run issues of approximately the same maturity reflects not

---

[1] Francis A. Longstaff, Sanjay Mithal, and Eric Neis, "Corporate Yield Spreads: Default Risk or Liquidity? New Evidence from the Credit Default Swap Market," *Journal of Finance* (October 2005), pp. 2213–2253.

only differences in liquidity but any financing advantage. This spread does not only occur between on-the-run and off-the-run issues. There are times in the market when particular off-the-run issues are needed by dealers for various activities that they perform.

Term to Maturity

As we explained in Chapter 2, the price of a bond will fluctuate over its life as yields in the market change. The time remaining on a bond's life is referred to as its **term to maturity** or simply **maturity**. As demonstrated in Chapter 4, the volatility of a bond's price is dependent on its term to maturity. More specifically, with all other factors constant, the longer the term to maturity of a bond, the greater the price volatility resulting from a change in market yields. Generally, bonds are classified into three **maturity sectors**: Bonds with a term to maturity of between one to five years are considered **short term**; bonds with a term to maturity between five and 12 years are viewed as **intermediate term**; and **long-term** bonds are those with a term to maturity greater than 12 years. The spread between any two maturity sectors of the market is called a **maturity spread**. The relationship between the yields on otherwise comparable securities with different maturities is called the **term structure of interest rates**.

TERM STRUCTURE OF INTEREST RATES

The term structure of interest rates plays a key role in the valuation of bonds. For this reason, we devote a good deal of space to this important topic.

Yield Curve

The graphical depiction of the relationship between the yield on bonds of the same credit quality but different maturities is known as the **yield curve**. In the past, most investors have constructed yield curves from observations of prices and yields in the Treasury market. Two factors account for this tendency. First, Treasury securities are free of default risk, and differences in creditworthiness do not affect yields. Therefore, these instruments are directly comparable. Second, as the largest and most active bond market, the Treasury market offers the fewest problems of illiquidity or infrequent trading. The disadvantage, as noted previously, is that the yields may be biased downward because they reflect favorable financing opportunities.

Exhibit 5-4 shows three typical shapes that have been observed for the yield curve. Daily yield curve information is available from a variety of sources on a real-time basis. Historical information about daily yield curves is obtained from 1990 onward from the U.S. Department of the Treasury's website.[2]

From a practical viewpoint, as we explained earlier in this chapter, a key function of the Treasury yield curve is to serve as a benchmark for pricing bonds and to set yields in all other sectors of the debt market: bank loans, mortgages, corporate debt, and international bonds. However, market participants are coming to realize that the traditionally constructed Treasury yield curve is an unsatisfactory measure of the relation between required yield and maturity. The key reason is that securities with the same maturity may actually

---

[2] Website available at: http://www.ustreas.gov/offices/domestic-finance/debt-management/interest-rate/yield_historical_main.shtml.

Exhibit 5-4 Three Shapes That Have Been Observed for the Yield Curve

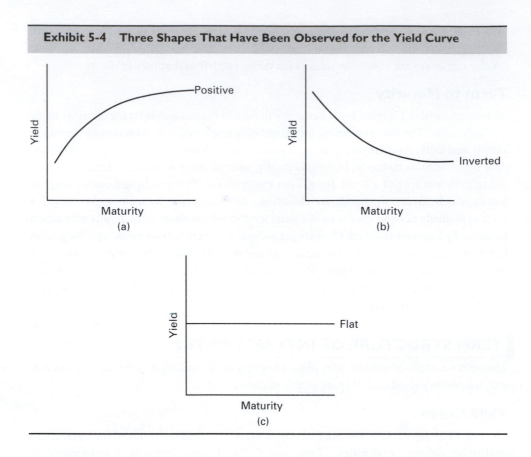

carry different yields. As we explain in the next section, this phenomenon reflects the role and impact of differences in the bonds' coupon rates. Hence, it is necessary to develop more accurate and reliable estimates of the Treasury yield curve. In what follows, we show the problems posed by traditional approaches to the Treasury yield curve and offer the correct approach to building a yield curve. This approach consists of identifying yields that apply to zero-coupon bonds and therefore eliminates the problem of coupon rate differences in the yield-maturity relationship.

Why the Yield Curve Should Not Be Used to Price a Bond

The price of a bond is the present value of its cash flow. However, in our illustrations and our discussion of the pricing of a bond in Chapter 2, we assume that one interest rate should be used to discount all the bond's cash flows. The appropriate interest rate is the yield on a Treasury security, with the same maturity as the bond, plus an appropriate risk premium.

As noted previously, however, there is a problem with using the Treasury yield curve to determine the appropriate yield at which to discount the cash flow of a bond. To illustrate this problem, consider the following two hypothetical five-year Treasury bonds, A and B. The difference between these two Treasury bonds is the coupon rate, which is 12% for A and 3% for B. The cash flow for these two bonds per $100 of par value for the 10 six-month periods (five years) to maturity would be

Period	Cash Flow for A	Cash Flow for B
1–9	$ 6.00	$ 1.50
10	106.00	101.50

Because of the different cash flow patterns, it is not appropriate to use the same interest rate to discount all cash flows. Instead, each cash flow should be discounted at a unique interest rate that is appropriate for the time period in which the cash flow will be received. But what should be the interest rate for each period?

The correct way to think about bonds A and B is not as bonds but as packages of cash flows. More specifically, they are packages of zero-coupon instruments. Thus, the interest earned is the difference between the maturity value and the price paid. For example, bond A can be viewed as 10 zero-coupon instruments: one with a maturity value of $6 maturing six months from now, a second with a maturity value of $6 maturing one year from now, a third with a maturity value of $6 maturing 1.5 years from now, and so on. The final zero-coupon instrument matures 10 six-month periods from now and has a maturity value of $106. Similarly, bond B can be viewed as 10 zero-coupon instruments with maturity values of $1.50 for the first nine six-month periods and $101.50 for the last six-month period. Obviously, in the case of each coupon bond (A or B), the value or price of the bond is equal to the total value of its component zero-coupon instruments.

In general, any bond can be viewed as a package of zero-coupon instruments. That is, each zero-coupon instrument in the package has a maturity equal to its coupon payment date or, in the case of the principal, the maturity date. The value of the bond should equal the value of all the component zero-coupon instruments. If this did not hold, it would be possible for a market participant to generate riskless profits by stripping off the coupon payments and creating stripped securities (see Chapter 6).

To determine the value of each zero-coupon instrument, it is necessary to know the yield on a zero-coupon Treasury with that same maturity. This yield is called the **spot rate**, and the graphical depiction of the relationship between the spot rate and maturity is called the **spot rate curve**. Because there are no zero-coupon Treasury debt issues with a maturity greater than one year, it is not possible to construct such a curve solely from observations of market activity on Treasury securities. Rather, it is necessary to derive this curve from theoretical considerations as applied to the yields of the actually traded Treasury debt securities. Such a curve is called a **theoretical spot rate curve** and is the graphical depiction of the **term structure of interest rate**.

Constructing the Theoretical Spot Rate Curve for Treasuries

A default-free theoretical spot rate curve can be constructed from the yield on Treasury securities.[3] The Treasury issues that are candidates for inclusion are

1. on-the-run Treasury issues
2. on-the-run Treasury issues and selected off-the-run Treasury issues
3. all Treasury coupon securities and bills
4. Treasury coupon strips

[3] This discussion draws from Chapter 5 in Frank J. Fabozzi, *Fixed Income Analysis for the Chartered Financial Analyst* (New Hope, PA: Frank J. Fabozzi Associates, 2000).

Each type of Treasury is explained in the next chapter. After the securities that are to be included in the construction of the theoretical spot rate curve are selected, the methodology for constructing the curve must be determined. The methodology depends on the securities included. If Treasury coupon strips are used, the procedure is simple, because the observed yields are the spot rates. If the on-the-run Treasury issues with or without selected off-the-run Treasury issues are used, a methodology called **bootstrapping** is used. When all Treasury coupon securities and bills are used, then elaborate statistical techniques are used.

On-the-Run Treasury Issues

The **on-the-run Treasury issues** are the most recently auctioned issue of a given maturity. These issues include the three-month, six-month, and one-year Treasury bills; the two-year, three-year, five-year, seven-year, and 10-year Treasury notes; and the 30-year Treasury bond. Treasury bills are zero-coupon instruments; the notes and the bond are coupon securities.

There is an observed yield for each of the on-the-run issues. For the coupon issues, these yields are not the yields used in the analysis when the issue is not trading at par. Instead, for each on-the-run coupon issue, the estimated yield necessary to make the issue trade at par is used. The resulting on-the-run yield curve is called the **par coupon curve**.

The goal is to construct a theoretical spot rate curve with 60 semiannual spot rates, ranging from the: six-month rate to 30-year rate. Excluding the three-month bill, there are only eight maturity points available when only on-the-run issues are used. The 52 missing maturity points are interpolated from the surrounding maturity points on the par yield curve. The simplest interpolation method, and the one most commonly used, is linear extrapolation. Specifically, given the yield on the par coupon curve at two maturity points, the following is calculated:

$$\frac{\text{yield at higher maturity} - \text{yield at lower maturity}}{\text{number of semiannual periods between the two maturity points} + 1}$$

Then, the yield for all intermediate semiannual maturity points is found by adding to the yield at the lower maturity the amount computed here.

For example, suppose that the yield from the par yield curve for the two-year and five-year on-the-run issues is 6% and 6.6%, respectively. There are five semiannual periods between these two maturity points. The extrapolated yield for the 2, 2.5, 3.0, 3.5, 4.0, and 4.5 maturity points is found as follows. Calculate

$$\frac{6.6\% - 6\%}{6} = 0.10\%$$

Then

$$2.5\text{-year yield} = 6.00\% + 0.10\% = 6.10\%$$
$$3.0\text{-year yield} = 6.10\% + 0.10\% = 6.20\%$$
$$3.5\text{-year yield} = 6.20\% + 0.10\% = 6.30\%$$
$$4.0\text{-year yield} = 6.30\% + 0.10\% = 6.40\%$$
$$4.5\text{-year yield} = 6.40\% + 0.10\% = 6.50\%$$

There are two problems with using just the on-the-run issues. First, there is a large gap between some of the maturities points, which may result in misleading yields for those maturity points when estimated using the linear interpolation method. Specifically, the

Exhibit 5-5	Maturity and Yield to Maturity for 20 Hypothetical Treasury Securities[a]		

Period	Years	Yield to Maturity/ Coupon Rate (%)
1	0.5	5.25
2	1.0	5.50
3	1.5	5.75
4	2.0	6.00
5	2.5	6.25
6	3.0	6.50
7	3.5	6.75
8	4.0	6.80
9	4.5	7.00
10	5.0	7.10
11	5.5	7.15
12	6.0	7.20
13	6.5	7.30
14	7.0	7.35
15	7.5	7.40
16	8.0	7.50
17	8.5	7.60
18	9.0	7.60
19	9.5	7.70
20	10.0	7.80

[a]*All bonds with the exception of the six-month and one-year issues are at par (100). For these issues the coupon rate is equal to the yield to maturity. The six-month and one-year issues are zero-coupon instruments that have a price less than par value.*

concern is with the large gap between the five-year and 10-year maturity points and the 10-year and 30-year maturity points. The second problem is that the yields for the on-the-run issues themselves may be misleading because most offer the favorable financing opportunity in the repo market mentioned earlier. This means that the true yield is greater than the quoted (observed) yield.

Now let's look at how the par yield curve is converted into the theoretical spot rate curve using bootstrapping. For simplicity, we will illustrate this methodology to calculate the theoretical spot rate curve for only 10 years. That is, 20 semiannual spot rates will be computed. Suppose that the par yield curve is the one shown in Exhibit 5-5.[4]

To explain the process of estimating the theoretical spot rate curve from observed yields on Treasury securities, we use the data for the price, annualized yield (yield to maturity),

---

[4] Note that the intermediate maturity points in Exhibit 5-5 were not calculated using the linear interpolation procedure.

and maturity of the 20 hypothetical Treasury securities shown in Exhibit 5-5. Each security is assumed to have a market price equal to its par value, so that the yield to maturity and the coupon rate are equal.

Throughout the analysis and illustrations to come, it is important to remember that the basic principle is that the value of the Treasury coupon security should be equal to the value of the package of zero-coupon Treasury securities that duplicates the coupon bond's cash flow.

Consider the six-month Treasury bill in Exhibit 5-5. As explained in Chapter 6, a Treasury bill is a zero-coupon instrument; hence, its annualized yield of 5.25% is equal to the spot rate. Similarly, for the one-year Treasury, the cited yield of 5.5% is the one-year spot rate. Given these two spot rates, we can compute the spot rate for a theoretical 1.5-year zero-coupon Treasury. The price of a theoretical 1.5-year zero-coupon Treasury should equal the present value of three cash flows from an actual 1.5-year coupon Treasury, where the yield used for discounting is the spot rate corresponding to the cash flow. Exhibit 5-5 shows the coupon rate for a 1.5-year Treasury as 5.75%. Using $100 as par, the cash flow for this Treasury security is

$$
\begin{array}{lll}
\text{0.5 year:} & 0.0575 \times \$100 \times 0.5 = & \$\ \ 2.875 \\
\text{1.0 year:} & 0.0575 \times \$100 \times 0.5 = & 2.875 \\
\text{1.5 years:} & 0.0575 \times \$100 \times 0.5 + \$100 = & 102.875
\end{array}
$$

The present value of the cash flow is then

$$
\frac{2.875}{1 + z_1} + \frac{2.875}{(1 + z_2)^2} + \frac{102.875}{(1 + z_3)^3}
$$

where

z_1 = one-half the annualized six-month theoretical spot rate
z_2 = one-half the one-year theoretical spot rate
z_3 = one-half the annual value of the 1.5-year theoretical spot rate

Because the six-month spot rate and one-year spot rate are 5.25% and 5.50%, respectively, we know these facts:

$$
z_1 = 0.02625 \text{ and } z_2 = 0.0275
$$

We can compute the present value of the 1.5-year coupon Treasury security as

$$
\frac{2.875}{1.02625} + \frac{2.875}{(1.0275)^2} + \frac{102.875}{(1 + z_3)^3}
$$

Because the price of the 1.5-year coupon Treasury security is $100, the following relationship must hold:

$$
100 = \frac{2.875}{1.02625} + \frac{2.875}{(1.0275)^2} + \frac{102.875}{(1 + z_3)^3}
$$

We can solve for the theoretical 1.5-year spot rate as follows:

$$
100 = 2.801461 + 2.723166 + \frac{102.875}{(1 + z_3)^3}
$$

$$
94.47537 = \frac{102.875}{(1 + z_3)^3}
$$

$$
(1 + z_3)^3 = 1.028798
$$

$$
z_3 = 0.028798
$$

Doubling this yield, we obtain the bond-equivalent yield of 0.0576 or 5.76%, which is the theoretical 1.5-year spot rate. That rate is the rate that the market would apply to a 1.5-year zero-coupon Treasury security if, in fact, such a security existed.

Given the theoretical 1.5-year spot rate, we can obtain the theoretical two-year spot rate. The cash flow for the two-year coupon Treasury in Exhibit 5-5 is

$$
\begin{array}{lll}
\text{0.5 year:} & 0.060 \times \$100 \times 0.5 = \$ & 3.00 \\
\text{1.0 year:} & 0.060 \times \$100 \times 0.5 = & 3.00 \\
\text{1.5 years:} & 0.060 \times \$100 \times 0.5 = & 3.00 \\
\text{2.0 years:} & 0.060 \times \$100 \times 0.5 + \$100 = & 103.00
\end{array}
$$

The present value of the cash flow is then

$$
\frac{3.00}{1 + z_1} + \frac{3.00}{(1 + z_2)^2} + \frac{3.00}{(1 + z_3)^3} + \frac{103.00}{(1 + z_4)^4}
$$

where z_4 is one-half the two-year theoretical spot rate. Because the six-month spot rate, one-year spot rate, and 1.5-year spot rate are 5.25%, 5.50%, and 5.76%, respectively, then

$$
z_1 = 0.02625 \quad z_2 = 0.0275 \quad z_3 = 0.028798
$$

Therefore, the present value of the two-year coupon Treasury security is

$$
\frac{3.00}{1.002625} + \frac{3.00}{(1.0275)^2} + \frac{3.00}{(1.028798)^3} + \frac{103.00}{(1 + z_4)^4}
$$

Because the price of the two-year coupon Treasury security is $100, the following relationship must hold:

$$
100 = \frac{3.00}{1.002625} + \frac{3.00}{(1.0275)^2} + \frac{3.00}{(1.028798)^3} + \frac{103.00}{(1 + z_4)^4}
$$

We can solve for the theoretical two-year spot rate as follows:

$$
100 = 2.92326 + 2.84156 + 2.75506 + \frac{103.00}{(1 + z_4)^4}
$$

$$
91.48011 = \frac{103.00}{(1 + z_4)^4}
$$

$$
(1 + z_4)^4 = 1.125927
$$

$$
z_4 = 0.030095
$$

Doubling this yield, we obtain the theoretical two-year spot rate bond-equivalent yield of 6.02%.

One can follow this approach sequentially to derive the theoretical 2.5-year spot rate from the calculated values of z_1, z_2, z_3, z_4 (the six-month, one-year, 1.5-year, and two-year rates), and the price and coupon of the bond with a maturity of 2.5 years. Further, one could derive theoretical spot rates for the remaining 15 half-yearly rates.

The spot rates using this process are shown in Exhibit 5-6. They represent the term structure of interest rates for maturities up to 10 years at the particular time to which the bond price quotations refer.

On-the-Run Treasury Issues and Selected Off-the-Run Treasury Issues

As noted previously, one of the problems with using just the on-the-run issues is the large gaps between maturities, particularly after five years. To mitigate this problem, some dealers and vendors use selected off-the-run Treasury issues. Typically, the issues used

Exhibit 5-6	Theoretical Spot Rates	
Period	**Years**	**Spot Rate (%)**
1	0.5	5.25
2	1.0	5.50
3	1.5	5.76
4	2.0	6.02
5	2.5	6.28
6	3.0	6.55
7	3.5	6.82
8	4.0	6.87
9	4.5	7.09
10	5.0	7.20
11	5.5	7.26
12	6.0	7.31
13	6.5	7.43
14	7.0	7.48
15	7.5	7.54
16	8.0	7.67
17	8.5	7.80
18	9.0	7.79
19	9.5	7.93
20	10.0	8.07

are the 20-year issue and 25-year issue. Given the par coupon curve including any off-the-run selected issues, the linear extrapolation method is used to fill in the gaps for the other maturities. The bootstrapping method is then used to construct the theoretical spot rate curve.

All Treasury Coupon Securities and Bills

Using only on-the-run issues, even when extended to include a few off-the-run issues, fails to recognize the information embodied in Treasury prices that are not included in the analysis. Thus, it is argued that it is more appropriate to use all Treasury coupon securities and bills to construct the theoretical spot rate curve. Some practitioners do not use callable Treasury bonds.[5]

When all coupon securities and bills are used, statistical methodologies must be employed to construct the theoretical spot rate curve rather than bootstrapping because there may be more than one yield for each maturity. Several statistical methodologies have

---

[5] A common practice is to filter the Treasury securities universe to eliminate securities that offer advantageous financing in the repo market.

been proposed to estimate the spot rate curve. The most common methodology used is "exponential spline fitting."[6] An adjustment for the effect of taxes and for call features on U.S. Treasury bonds can be incorporated into the statistical model. A discussion of this statistical methodology is beyond the scope of this book.[7]

Treasury Coupon Strips

As explained in the next chapter, Treasury coupon strips are zero-coupon Treasury securities. It would seem logical that the observed yield on strips could be used to construct an actual spot rate curve rather than go through the procedure we describe here. There are three problems with using the observed rates on strips. First, the liquidity of the strips market is not as great as that of the Treasury coupon market. Thus, the observed rates on strips reflect a premium for liquidity.

Second, the tax treatment of strips is different from that of Treasury coupon securities. Specifically, the accrued interest on strips is taxed even though no cash is received by the investor. Thus, they are negative cash flow securities to taxable entities; as a result, their yield reflects this tax disadvantage.

Finally, there are maturity sectors in which non–U.S. investors find it advantageous to trade off yield for tax advantages associated with a strip. Specifically, certain foreign tax authorities allow their citizens to treat the difference between the maturity value and the purchase price as a capital gain and tax this gain at a favorable tax rate. Some will grant this favorable treatment only when the strip is created from the principal rather than the coupon. For this reason, those who use Treasury strips to represent theoretical spot rates restrict the issues included to coupon strips.

Using the Theoretical Spot Rate Curve

We can now apply the spot rates to price a bond. In Chapter 2, we showed how to price a bond assuming that each cash flow is discounted at one discount rate. Exhibit 5-7 shows how to value a Treasury bond properly using the theoretical spot rates. The bond in the illustration is a hypothetical 10-year Treasury security with a coupon rate of 10%.

The third column of the exhibit shows the cash flow per $100 of par value for each of the 20 six-month periods. The fourth column shows the theoretical spot rate for each maturity given in Exhibit 5-6. The fifth column gives the present value of $1 when discounted at the theoretical spot rate shown in the fourth column. The last column gives the present value of the cash flow, found by multiplying the third column by the fifth column. The theoretical price of this bond is the sum of the present values in the last column, $115.4206.

Although we have stated that the price of a Treasury security should be equal to the present value of its cash flow where each cash flow is discounted at the theoretical spot rates, the question is: What forces a Treasury to be priced based on the spot rates? The answer is that arbitrage forces this. For example, the theoretical price of $115.4206 can be

---

[6] Willard R. Carleton and Ian Cooper, "Estimation and Uses of the Term Structure of Interest Rates," *Journal of Finance*, September 1976, pp. 1067–1083; J. Huston McCulloch, "Measuring the Term Structure of Interest Rates," *Journal of Business*, January 1971, pp. 19–31; and McCulloch, "The Tax Adjusted Yield Curve," *Journal of Finance*, June 1975, pp. 811–830.

[7] See Oldrich A. Vasicek and H. Gifford Fong, "Term Structure Modeling Using Exponential Splines," *Journal of Finance*, May 1982, pp. 339–358. For an example of a dealer model, see Arnold Shapiro et al., *Merrill Lynch Exponential Spline Model*, Merrill Lynch & Co., Global Securities Research & Economics Group, Fixed Income Analytics, August 8, 1994.

Exhibit 5-7   Determining the Theoretical Value of a 10% 10-Year Treasury Security Using the Theoretical Spot Rates

Period	Year	Cash Flow	Spot Rate (%)	PV of $1 at Spot Rate	PV of Cash Flow
1	0.5	5	5.25	0.974421	4.872107
2	1.0	5	5.50	0.947188	4.735942
3	1.5	5	5.76	0.918351	4.591756
4	2.0	5	6.02	0.888156	4.440782
5	2.5	5	6.28	0.856724	4.283619
6	3.0	5	6.55	0.824206	4.12103
7	3.5	5	6.82	0.790757	3.953783
8	4.0	5	6.87	0.763256	3.81628
9	4.5	5	7.09	0.730718	3.653589
10	5.0	5	7.20	0.701952	3.509758
11	5.5	5	7.26	0.675697	3.378483
12	6.0	5	7.31	0.650028	3.250138
13	6.5	5	7.43	0.622448	3.112238
14	7.0	5	7.48	0.597889	2.989446
15	7.5	5	7.54	0.573919	2.869594
16	8.0	5	7.67	0.547625	2.738125
17	8.5	5	7.80	0.521766	2.608831
18	9.0	5	7.79	0.502665	2.513325
19	9.5	5	7.93	0.477729	2.388643
20	10.0	105	8.07	0.453268	47.593170
					Theoretical value = 115.4206

viewed as the value of a package of zero-coupon instruments. That is, if this 10% 10-year Treasury security is purchased and then stripped, it will generate proceeds of $115.4206. The stripped Treasury securities created are the securities we describe in Chapter 6.

Now suppose, instead, that the market priced the 10% 10-year Treasury security based on the yield to maturity of 10-year Treasury securities as indicated by the yield curve. As can be seen in Exhibit 5-5, the yield to maturity for 10-year Treasury securities is 7.8%. If the 10% 10-year Treasury security is priced using a discount rate of 7.8%, its price would be $115.0826, a price that is less than its theoretical value. A government securities dealer who had the opportunity to buy this Treasury security for $115.0826 would buy it, then strip it and sell the zero-coupon securities created. As we just noted, the total proceeds from this process would be $115.4206. Thus, the dealer would realize an arbitrage profit of $0.338 per $100 of par value purchased. The actions of dealers to capture this arbitrage profit would drive up the price of this Treasury security. Only when the price reaches $115.4206—the theoretical value when the cash flows are discounted at the theoretical spot rates—will the arbitrage disappear. It is this action that forces Treasury securities to be priced based on the theoretical spot rates.

Spot Rates and the Base Interest Rate

We can now modify our earlier statement about the base interest rate for a given maturity. It is not simply the yield on the on-the-run Treasury security for that maturity, but the theoretical Treasury spot rate for that maturity. It is to the theoretical Treasury spot rates that a risk premium must be added in order to value a non-Treasury security.

Forward Rates

Thus, we have seen that from the yield curve we can extrapolate the theoretical spot rates. In addition, we can extrapolate what some market participants refer to as the market's consensus of future interest rates. To see the importance of knowing the market's consensus for future interest rates, consider the following two investment alternatives for an investor who has a one-year investment horizon.

Alternative 1: Buy a one-year instrument.
Alternative 2: Buy a six-month instrument and when it matures in six months, buy another six-month instrument.

With alternative 1, the investor will realize the one-year spot rate and that rate is known with certainty. In contrast, with alternative 2, the investor will realize the six-month spot rate, but the six-month rate six months from now is unknown. Therefore, for alternative 2, the rate that will be earned over one year is not known with certainty. This is illustrated in Exhibit 5-8.

Suppose that this investor expected that six months from now the six-month rate will be higher than it is today. The investor might then feel that alternative 2 would be the better investment. However, this is not necessarily true. To understand why and to appreciate the need to understand why it is necessary to know what the market's consensus of future interest rates is, let's continue with our illustration.

The investor will be indifferent to the two alternatives if they produce the same total dollars over the one-year investment horizon. Given the one-year spot rate, there is some rate on a six-month instrument six months from now that will make the investor indifferent between the two alternatives. We denote that rate by f.

Exhibit 5-8   Two Alternative One-Year Investments

Total Dollars at End
of One Year per $100
Investment

$$(1 + z_2)^2 \qquad \$100(1 + z_2)^2$$

$$1 + z_1 \qquad 1 + f \qquad \$100(1 + z_1)(1 + f)$$

Today   6 Months   1 Year

The value of *f* can be readily determined given the theoretical one-year spot rate and the six-month spot rate. If an investor placed $100 in a one-year instrument (alternative 1), the total dollars that will be generated at the end of one year is

$$\text{total dollars at end of year for alternative 1} = \$100(1 + z_2)^2 \tag{5.1}$$

where z_2 is the one-year spot rate. (Remember that we are working in six-month periods, so the subscript 2 represents two six-month periods, or one year.)

The proceeds from investing at the six-month spot rate will generate the following total dollars at the end of six months:

$$\text{total dollars at end of six months for alternative 2} = \$100(1 + z_1) \tag{5.2}$$

where z_1 is the six-month spot rate. If the amount in equation (5.2) is reinvested at the six-month rate six months from now, which we denoted *f*, the total dollars at the end of one year would be

$$\text{total dollars at end of year for alternative 2} = \$100(1 + z_1)(1 + f) \tag{5.3}$$

The investor will be indifferent between the two alternatives if the total dollars are the same. This will occur if equation (5.1) is equal to equation (5.3). Setting these two equations equal we get the following:

$$\$100(1 + z_2)^2 = \$100(1 + z_1)(1 + f) \tag{5.4}$$

Solving equation (5.4) for *f*, we get

$$f = \frac{(1 + z_2)^2}{1 + z_1} - 1 \tag{5.5}$$

Doubling *f* gives the bond-equivalent yield for the six-month rate in which we are interested six months from now.

We can illustrate the use of equation (5.5) with the theoretical spot rates shown in Exhibit 5-6. From that exhibit we know that

six-month spot rate = 0.0525; therefore, z_1 = 0.02625
one-year spot rate = 0.0550; therefore, z_2 = 0.02750

Substituting into equation (5.5), we have

$$f = \frac{(1.02750)^2}{1.02625} - 1$$
$$= 0.028752$$

Therefore, the annual rate for *f* on a bond-equivalent basis is 5.75% (2.8752% × 2).

Here is how we use this rate of 5.75%. If the six-month rate six months from now is less than 5.75%, the total dollars at the end of one year would be higher by investing in the one-year instrument (alternative 1). If the six-month rate six months from now is greater than 5.75%, the total dollars at the end of one year would be higher by investing in the six-month instrument and reinvesting the proceeds six months from now at the six-month rate at the time (alternative 2). Of course, if the six-month rate six months from now is 5.75%, the two alternatives give the same total number of dollars at the end of one year.

Now that we have the rate for *f* that we are interested in and we know how that rate can be used, let's return to the question we posed at the outset. From Exhibit 5-7 the six-month spot rate is 5.25%. Suppose that the investor expects that six months from now the six-month rate will be 5.60%. That is, the investor expects that the six-month rate will be higher than its current level. Should the investor select alternative 2 because the six-month rate six months from now is expected to be higher? The answer is no. As we explained earlier, if the rate is less than 5.75%, alternative 1 is the better alternative. Because this investor expects a rate of 5.60%, he should select alternative 1 despite the fact that he expects the six-month rate to be higher than it is today.

This is a somewhat surprising result for some investors, but the reason for this is that the market prices its expectations of future interest rates into the rates offered on investments with different maturities. This is why knowing the market's consensus of future interest rates is critical. The rate that we determined for f is the market's consensus for the six-month rate six months from now. A future interest rate calculated from either the spot rates or the yield curve is called a **forward rate**.

Relationship Between Six-Month Forward Rates and Spot Rates

In general, the relationship between a t-period spot rate, the current six-month spot rate, and the six-month forward rates is as follows:

$$z_t = [(1 + z_1)(1 + f_1)(1 + f_2)(1 + f_3) \ldots (1 + f_{t-1})]^{1/t} - 1 \qquad (5.6)$$

where f_t is the six-month forward rate beginning t six-month periods from now.

To illustrate how to use equation (5.6), let's look at how the five-year (10-period) spot rate is related to the six-month forward rates. Six-month forward rates were calculated for the spot rate given in Exhibit 5-6. The values for f_1 through f_9 are as follows:

$$\begin{aligned} f_1 &= 0.02875 & f_2 &= 0.03140 & f_3 &= 0.03670 & f_4 &= 0.03945 \\ f_5 &= 0.04320 & f_6 &= 0.03605 & f_7 &= 0.04455 & f_8 &= 0.04100 \\ f_9 &= 0.03885 \end{aligned}$$

The six-month spot rate is 2.625% (5.25% on a bond-equivalent basis). Substituting these values into equation (5.6) we have

$$\begin{aligned} z_{10} = &[(1.02875)(1.02625)(1.03140)(1.03670)(1.03945)(1.04320)(1.03605) \\ &(1.04455) \cdot (1.04100)(1.03855)]^{1/10} - 1 = 0.036 = 3.6\% \end{aligned}$$

Note that when doubled this value agrees with the five-year (10-period) spot rate shown in Exhibit 5-6.

Other Forward Rates

We can take this sort of analysis much further. It is not necessary to limit ourselves to six-month forward rates. The spot rates can be used to calculate the forward rate for any time in the future for any investment horizon. As examples, the following can be calculated:

- the two-year forward rate five years from now
- the six-year forward rate 10 years from now
- the seven-year forward rate three years from now

Forward Rate as a Hedgeable Rate

A natural question about forward rates is how well they do at predicting future interest rates. Studies have demonstrated that forward rates do not do a good job in predicting future interest rates.[8] Then why the big deal about understanding forward rates? As we demonstrated in our illustration of how to select between two alternative investments, the reason is that the forward rates indicate how an investor's expectations must differ from the market's consensus in order to make the correct decision.

In our illustration, the six-month forward rate may not be realized. That is irrelevant. The fact is that the six-month forward rate indicated to the investor that if his expectation about the six-month rate six months from now is less than 5.75%, he would be better off with alternative 1.

For this reason, as well as others explained later, some market participants prefer not to talk about forward rates as being market consensus rates. Instead, they refer to forward rates as being **hedgeable rates**. For example, by buying the one-year security, the investor was able to hedge the six-month rate six months from now.

Determinants of the Shape of the Term Structure

If we plot the term structure—the yield to maturity, or the spot rate, at successive maturities— against maturity, what is it likely to look like? Exhibit 5-4 shows three generic shapes that have appeared for the U.S. Treasury yield curve with some frequency over time. Exhibit 5-9 shows five selective daily Treasury yield curves in tabular form.

Panel (a) of Exhibit 5-4 shows an upward-sloping yield curve; that is, yield rises steadily as maturity increases. This shape is commonly referred to as a **positively sloped yield curve**. Market participants differentiate positively sloped yield curves based on the steepness or slope of the curve. The slope is commonly measured in terms of the maturity spread, where the maturity spread is the difference between long-term and short-term yields. While there are many maturity candidates to proxy for long-term and short-term yields, we'll just use the maturity spread between the six-month and 30-year yield in our example.

The first two daily yield curves shown in Exhibit 5-9 are positively sloped yield curves. Notice that the three-month and six-month yields are roughly the same for both dates. However, the steepness of the slope is different. The maturity spread between the 30-year and six-month yield (i.e., the 30-year/six-month spread) was 195 basis points

Exhibit 5-9	U.S. Treasury Yield Curve for Five Selective Dates									
Day	3 mos	6 mos	1 yr	2 yrs	3 yrs	5 yrs	7 yrs	10 yrs	20 yrs	30 yrs	Shape
4/23/2001	3.75	3.78	3.75	3.77	4.15	4.38	4.78	5.06	5.84	5.73	Normal
4/10/1992	3.74	3.88	4.12	5.16	5.72	6.62	7.03	7.37	N/A	7.89	Steep
8/14/1981	N/A	N/A	16.71	16.91	15.88	15.34	15.04	N/A	14.74	13.95	Inverted
1/3/1990	7.89	7.94	7.85	7.94	7.96	7.92	8.04	7.99	N/A	8.04	Flat
1/4/2001	5.37	5.20	4.82	4.77	4.78	4.82	5.07	5.03	5.56	5.44	Humped

Note: *The data for the 4/23/2001, 4/10/1992, 1/3/1990, and 1/4/2001 dates were obtained from the daily yield curves provided by the U.S. Treasury. The data for 8/14/1981 were obtained from various Treasury yield tables published by the U.S. Treasury.*

---

[8] Eugene F. Fama, "Forward Rates as Predictors of Future Spot Rates," *Journal of Financial Economics*, Vol. 3, No. 4, 1976, pp. 361–377.

(5.73% − 3.78%) on 4/23/2001 and 401 basis points (7.89% − 3.88%) on 4/10/1992. The convention in the marketplace is to refer to a Treasury positively sloped yield curve whose maturity spread between the six-month and 30-year yields is 300 basis points or less as a **normal yield curve**; when the maturity spread is more than 300 basis points, the yield curve is said to be a **steep yield curve**.

When a yield curve's maturity spread increases (or in the parlance of the market, "widens"), the yield curve is said to *steepen*; when the maturity spread decreases (i.e., "narrows"), the yield curve is said to *flatten*.

Panel (b) of Exhibit 5-4 shows a downward-sloping or **inverted yield curve**, where yields, in general, decline as maturity increases. There have not been many instances in the recent history of the U.S. Treasury market where the yield curve exhibited this characteristic. The most notable example occurred in August 1981. Exhibit 5-9 shows the daily yield curve for one day in that month, August 14th. Treasury yields at the time were at an historic high. The yield on the two-year maturity was 16.91% and declined for each subsequent maturity until it reached 13.95% for the 30-year maturity.

Finally, panel (c) of Exhibit 5-4 shows a **flat yield curve**. While the exhibit suggests that for a flat yield curve, the yields are identical for each maturity, that is not what is observed in real-world markets. Rather, the yields for all maturities are similar. The yield curve on 1/3/1990 is a flat yield curve. Notice the very small six-month/30-year maturity spread: 10 basis points. A variant of the flat yield is one in which the yield on short-term and long-term Treasuries are similar but the yield on intermediate-term Treasuries are lower.

Two major theories have evolved to account for these observed shapes of the yield curve: **expectations theories** and **market segmentation theory**.

There are several forms of the expectations theory: **pure expectations theory**, **liquidity theory**, and **preferred habitat theory**. Expectations theories share a hypothesis about the behavior of short-term forward rates and also assume that the forward rates in current long-term bonds are closely related to the market's expectations about future short-term rates. These three theories differ, however, as to whether other factors also affect forward rates, and how. The pure expectations theory postulates that no systematic factors other than expected future short-term rates affect forward rates; the liquidity theory and the preferred habitat theory assert that there are other factors. Accordingly, the last two forms of the expectations theory are sometimes referred to as **biased expectations theories**. Exhibit 5-10 depicts the relationships among these three theories.

Pure Expectations Theory

According to the pure expectations theory, the forward rates exclusively represent the expected future rates. Thus, the entire term structure at a given time reflects the market's current expectations of the family of future short-term rates. Under this view, a rising term structure, as in panel (a) of Exhibit 5-4, must indicate that the market expects short-term rates to rise throughout the relevant future. Similarly, a flat term structure reflects an expectation that future short-term rates will be mostly constant, and a falling term structure must reflect an expectation that future short rates will decline steadily.

We can illustrate this theory by considering how the expectation of a rising short-term future rate would affect the behavior of various market participants so as to result in a

---

Exhibit 5-10   Theories about the Term Structure of Interest Rates

Expectations Theory
Asserts the behavior of short-term forward rates and the forward rates in current long-term bonds are closely related to the market's expectations about future short-term rates.

Pure Expectations Theory: Forward rates exclusively represent the expected future rates. Three Interpretations

- Broadest interpretation
- Local expectations interpretation (narrowest interpretation)
- Return-to-maturity expectations interpretation

Biased Expectations Theory: Two theories

- **Liquidity Theory:** Implied forward rates will not be an unbiased estimate of the market's expectations of future interest rates because they embody a liquidity premium.
- **Preferred Habitat Theory:** Term structure reflects the expectation of future interest rates plus a risk premium reflecting the imbalance of demand and supply of funds in a given maturity range.

Market Segmentation Theory
Asserts neither investors nor borrowers are willing to shift from one maturity sector to another to take advantage of opportunities arising from differences between expectations and forward rates.

---

rising yield curve. Assume an initially flat term structure, and suppose that subsequent economic news leads market participants to expect interest rates to rise.

1. Those market participants interested in a long-term investment would not want to buy long-term bonds because they would expect the yield structure to rise sooner or later, resulting in a price decline for the bonds and a capital loss on the long-term bonds purchased. Instead, they would want to invest in short-term debt obligations until the rise in yield had occurred, permitting them to reinvest their funds at the higher yield.
2. Speculators expecting rising rates would anticipate a decline in the price of long-term bonds and therefore would want to sell any long-term bonds they own and possibly to "sell-short" some they do not now own. (Should interest rates rise as expected, the price of longer-term bonds will fall. Because the speculator sold these bonds short and can then purchase them at a lower price to cover the short sale, a profit will be earned.) Speculators will reinvest in short-term debt obligations.
3. Borrowers wishing to acquire long-term funds would be pulled toward borrowing now in the long end of the market by the expectation that borrowing at a later time would be more expensive.

All these responses would tend either to lower the net demand for, or to increase the supply of, long-maturity bonds, and all three responses would increase demand for short-term debt obligations. This would require a rise in long-term yields in relation to short-term yields; that is, these actions by investors, speculators, and borrowers would tilt the term structure upward until it is consistent with expectations of higher future interest rates. By analogous reasoning, an unexpected event leading to the expectation of lower future rates will result in the yield curve sloping down.

Unfortunately, the pure expectations theory suffers from one shortcoming, which, qualitatively, is quite serious. It neglects the risks inherent in investing in bonds and similar instruments. If forward rates were perfect predictors of future interest rates, the future prices of bonds would be known with certainty. The return over any investment period would be certain and independent of the maturity of the instrument initially acquired and of the time at which the investor needed to liquidate the instrument. However, with uncertainty about future interest rates and hence about future prices of bonds, these instruments become risky investments in the sense that the return over some investment horizon is unknown.

There are two risks that cause uncertainty about the return over some investment horizon: price risk and reinvestment risk. The first is the uncertainty about the price of the bond at the end of the investment horizon. For example, an investor who plans to invest for five years might consider the following three investment alternatives: (1) invest in a five-year bond and hold it for five years, (2) invest in a 12-year bond and sell it at the end of five years, and (3) invest in a 30-year bond and sell it at the end of five years. The return that will be realized for the second and third alternatives is not known because the price of each long-term bond at the end of five years is not known. In the case of the 12-year bond, the price will depend on the yield on seven-year debt securities five years from now; and the price of the 30-year bond will depend on the yield on 25-year bonds five years from now. Because forward rates implied in the current term structure for a future 12-year bond and a future 25-year bond are not perfect predictors of the actual future rates, there is uncertainty about the price for both bonds five years from now. Thus, there is price risk; that is, the risk that the price of the bond will be lower than currently expected at the end of the investment horizon. As explained in Chapter 4, an important feature of price risk is that it is greater the longer the maturity of the bond.

The second risk has to do with the uncertainty about the rate at which the proceeds from a bond can be reinvested until the expected maturity date; that is, reinvestment risk. For example, an investor who plans to invest for five years might consider the following three alternative investments: (1) invest in a five-year bond and hold it for five years; (2) invest in a six-month instrument and when it matures, reinvest the proceeds in six-month instruments over the entire five-year investment horizon; and (3) invest in a two-year bond and when it matures, reinvest the proceeds in a three-year bond. The risk in the second and third alternatives is that the return over the five-year investment horizon is unknown because rates at which the proceeds can be reinvested until maturity are unknown.

There are several interpretations of the pure expectations theory that have been put forth by economists. These interpretations are not exact equivalents nor are they consistent with each other, in large part because they offer different treatments of the two risks associated with realizing a return that we have just explained.[9]

The broadest interpretation of the pure expectations theory suggests that investors expect the return for any investment horizon to be the same, regardless of the maturity strategy selected.[10] For example, consider an investor who has a five-year investment horizon. According to this theory, it makes no difference if a five-year, 12-year, or 30-year bond is purchased and held for five years because the investor expects the return from all three

---

[9] These formulations are summarized by John Cox, Jonathan Ingersoll, Jr., and Stephen Ross, "A Reexamination of Traditional Hypotheses about the Term Structure of Interest Rates," *Journal of Finance*, September 1981, pp. 769–799.
[10] Frederich A. Lutz, "The Structure of Interest Rates," *Quarterly Journal of Economics*, 1940–41, pp. 36–63.

bonds to be the same over five years. A major criticism of this very broad interpretation of the theory is that, because of price risk associated with investing in bonds with a maturity greater than the investment horizon, the expected returns from these three very different bond investments should differ in significant ways.[11]

A second interpretation, referred to as the **local expectations theory**, a form of pure expectations theory, suggests that the returns on bonds of different maturities will be the same over a short-term investment horizon. For example, if an investor has a six-month investment horizon, buying a five-year, 10-year, or 20-year bond will produce the same six-month return. It has been demonstrated that the local expectations formulation, which is narrow in scope, is the only one of the interpretations of the pure expectations theory that can be sustained in equilibrium.[12]

The third and final interpretation of the pure expectations theory suggests that the return that an investor will realize by rolling over short-term bonds to some investment horizon will be the same as holding a zero-coupon bond with a maturity that is the same as that investment horizon. (Because a zero-coupon bond has no reinvestment risk, future interest rates over the investment horizon do not affect the return.) This variant is called the **return-to-maturity expectations interpretation**. For example, let's assume that an investor has a five-year investment horizon. By buying a five-year zero-coupon bond and holding it to maturity, the investor's return is the difference between the maturity value and the price of the bond, all divided by the price of the bond. According to return-to-maturity expectations, the same return will be realized by buying a six-month instrument and rolling it over for five years. The validity of this interpretation is currently subject to considerable doubt.

Liquidity Theory

We have explained that the drawback of the pure expectations theory is that it does not consider the risks associated with investing in bonds. There is the risk in holding a long-term bond for one period, and that risk increases with the bond's maturity because maturity and price volatility are directly related.

Given this uncertainty and the reasonable consideration that investors typically do not like uncertainty, some economists and financial analysts have suggested a different theory. This theory states that investors will hold longer-term maturities if they are offered a long-term rate higher than the average of expected future rates by a risk premium that is positively related to the term to maturity.[13] Put differently, the forward rates should reflect both interest-rate expectations and a "liquidity" premium (really a risk premium), and the premium should be higher for longer maturities.

According to this theory, which is called the **liquidity theory of the term structure**, the implied forward rates will not be an unbiased estimate of the market's expectations of future interest rates because they embody a liquidity premium. Thus, an upward-sloping yield curve may reflect expectations that future interest rates either (1) will rise, or (2) will be flat or even fall, but with a liquidity premium increasing fast enough with maturity so as to produce an upward-sloping yield curve.

---

[11] Cox, Ingersoll, and Ross, "A Reexamination of Traditional Hypotheses about the Term Structure of Interest Rates," pp. 774–775.

[12] Cox, Ingersoll, and Ross, "A Reexamination of Traditional Hypotheses about the Term Structure of Interest Rates," pp. 774–775.

[13] John R. Hicks, *Value and Capital*, 2nd ed. (London: Oxford University Press, 1946), pp. 141–145.

Preferred Habitat Theory

Another theory, the preferred habitat theory, also adopts the view that the term structure reflects the expectation of the future path of interest rates as well as a risk premium. However, the preferred habitat theory rejects the assertion that the risk premium must rise uniformly with maturity.[14] Proponents of the preferred habitat theory say that the risk premium would rise uniformly with maturity only if all investors intend to liquidate their investment at the shortest possible date while all borrowers are anxious to borrow long. This assumption can be rejected since institutions have holding periods dictated by the nature of their liabilities.

The preferred habitat theory asserts that to the extent that the demand and supply of funds in a given maturity range do not match, some lenders and borrowers will be induced to shift to maturities showing the opposite imbalances. However, they will need to be compensated by an appropriate risk premium whose magnitude will reflect the extent of aversion to either price or reinvestment risk.

Thus, this theory proposes that the shape of the yield curve is determined by both expectations of future interest rates and a risk premium, positive or negative, to induce market participants to shift out of their preferred habitat. Clearly, according to this theory, yield curves sloping up, down, flat, or humped are all possible.

Market Segmentation Theory

The market segmentation theory also recognizes that investors have preferred habitats dictated by the nature of their liabilities. This theory also proposes that the major reason for the shape of the yield curve lies in asset–liability management constraints (either regulatory or self-imposed) and/or creditors (borrowers) restricting their lending (financing) to specific maturity sectors.[15] However, the market segmentation theory differs from the preferred habitat theory in that it assumes that neither investors nor borrowers are willing to shift from one maturity sector to another to take advantage of opportunities arising from differences between expectations and forward rates. Thus, for the segmentation theory, the shape of the yield curve is determined by the supply of and demand for securities within each maturity sector.

The Main Influences on the Shape of the Yield Curve

A body of work by Antti Ilmanen provides the most comprehensive research on the main influences of the shape of the Treasury yield curve.[16] He finds that the three main influences are

1. the market's expectations of future rate changes
2. bond risk premiums
3. convexity bias

---

[14] Franco Modigliani and Richard Sutch, "Innovations in Interest Rate Policy," *American Economic Review*, May 1966, pp. 178–197.

[15] This theory was suggested in J. M. Culbertson, "The Term Structure of Interest Rates," *Quarterly Journal of Economics*, November 1957, pp. 489–504.

[16] The research first appeared as a report published by Salomon Brothers. Different parts of the research report were then published. See Antti Ilmanen, "Market's Rate Expectations and Forward Rates," *Journal of Fixed Income*, September 1996, pp. 8–22; Antti Ilmanen, "Does Duration Extension Enhance Long-Term Expected Returns?" *Journal of Fixed Income*, September 1996, pp. 23–36; Antti Ilmanen, "Convexity Bias in the Yield Curve," Chapter 3 in Narasimgan Jegadeesh and Bruce Tuckman (eds.), *Advanced Fixed-Income Valuation Tools* (New York: Wiley, 2000); and Antti Ilmanen, "Overview of Forward Rate Analysis," Chapter 8 in Frank J. Fabozzi (ed.), *The Handbook of Fixed Income Securities* (New York, NY: McGraw-Hill, 2005).

In our discussion of the pure expectations theory of the term structure, we explained how market expectations of future rate changes influence the shape of the yield curve. Let's look at the last two influences.

Bond risk premiums are the expected return differentials across Treasury securities of different maturities. As explained in the previous section, there are theories of the term structure of interest rates that hypothesize why expected returns will vary by maturity. However, the theories disagree with respect to whether the risk premium is positive or negative. For example, the liquidity theory of the term structure would argue that the risk premium should increase with maturity; the market segmentation theory says that the bond risk premium can be positive or negative.

Ilmanen investigated the effect of the behavior of the bond risk premium using historical average *returns* on U.S. Treasury securities. Exhibit 5-11 shows the empirical average return curve as a function of average duration (not maturity) for the period 1972 to 2001. (Recall from Chapter 4 that duration is a measure of the price sensitivity of a bond to changes in interest rates.) Also shown in Exhibit 5-11 is the theoretical expected return curve shown by the straight line, which is based on expectations only (the first influence listed previously). Notice that this curve is linear (i.e., it increases linearly with duration). In contrast, notice that the empirical evidence suggests that the bond risk premiums are not linear in duration. Instead, the empirical evidence suggests that at the front-end of the yield curve (i.e., up to a duration of 3), bond risk premiums increase steeply with duration. However, after a duration of 3 the bond risk premiums increase slowly. Ilmanen suggests that the shape shown in Exhibit 5-11 "may reflect the demand for long-term bonds from pension funds and other long-duration liability holders."[17]

Exhibit 5-11   Theoretical and Empirical Bond Risk Premiums

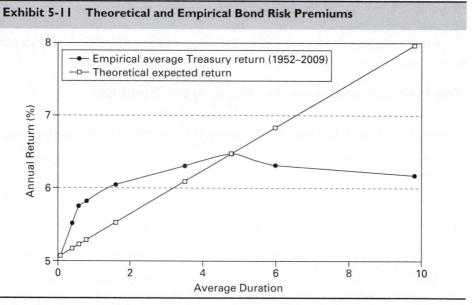

Source: *Provided by Antti Ilmanen.*

---

[17] Ilmanen, "Overview of Forward Rate Analysis," p. 167.

Now let's look to the convexity bias influence, an influence that Ilmanen argues is the least well known of the three influences. Let's recall the concept of convexity described in Chapter 4. When interest rates change by a large number of basis points, a Treasury security's price change will not be the same for an increase and decrease in interest rates. More specifically, the price appreciation when interest rates fall will be greater than the price decline when interest rates rise by the same number of basis points. For example, if interest rates decline by 100 basis points, the price of a Treasury security might appreciate by 20%, but if interest rates increase by 100 basis points, the price of the same Treasury security might decline by only 15%. This attractive property of a bond is due to the shape of the relationship between price and yield described in Chapter 4 and is referred to as the bond's convexity. The longer the maturity, the more convexity the security has. That is, longer-term Treasury securities have a more attractive feature due to convexity than shorter-term Treasury securities. As a result, investors are willing to pay more for longer-term Treasury securities and therefore accept lower returns. This influence on the shape of the Treasury yield curve is what is referred to as the **convexity bias**.

SWAP RATE YIELD CURVE

It is not until Chapter 28 that we discuss an interest rate swap. However, the basic elements of an interest rate swap are important for us to understand here because it is a commonly used interest rate benchmark. In fact, while our focus in this chapter has been on using the Treasury market as an interest rate benchmark, for reasons described briefly in this section, the interest rate swap market in most countries is increasingly used as an interest rate benchmark despite the existence of a liquid government bond market. We will briefly explain how and why here.

In a generic interest rate swap, the parties exchange interest payments on specified dates: one party pays a fixed rate and the other party pays a floating rate over the life of the swap. In a typical swap, the floating rate is based on a reference rate, and the reference rate is typically the London Interbank Offered Rate (LIBOR). LIBOR is the interest rate at which prime banks in London pay other prime banks on U.S. dollars certificates of deposits.

The fixed interest rate that is paid by the fixed rate counterparty is called the **swap rate**. Dealers in the swap market quote swap rates for different maturities. The relationship between the swap rate and maturity of a swap is called the **swap rate yield curve** or, more commonly, the **swap curve**. Because the reference rate is typically LIBOR, the swap curve is also called the **LIBOR curve**.

There is a swap curve for most countries. Exhibit 5-12 shows the U.S. swap curve, Euro swap curve, and U.K. swap curve on February 24, 2011. For Euro interest rate swaps, the reference rate is the Euro Interbank Offered Rate (Euribor), which is the rate at which bank deposits in countries that have adopted the euro currency and are member states of the European Union[18] are offered by one prime bank to another prime bank.

The swap curve is used as a benchmark in many countries outside the United States. Unlike a country's government bond yield curve, however, the swap curve is not a

---

[18] The euro is the official currency of the European Union Member States. The member states include Austria, Belgium, Finland, France, Germany, Ireland, Italy, Luxembourg, the Netherlands, Portugal, Spain, and Slovenia. Countries where the euro is adopted as the official currency are commonly referred to as the Eurozone, Euroland, or Euro area.

Exhibit 5-12 U.S., Euro, and U.K. Swap Rate Curve on February 24, 2011

Years to Maturity	Swap Rate (%) for:		
	U.S.	Euro	U.K.
1	0.46	1.71	1.27
2	0.93	2.14	2.01
3	1.46	2.42	2.47
5	2.37	2.85	3.11
7	3.00	3.15	3.51
10	3.56	3.44	3.87
12	3.80	3.59	4.02
15	4.03	3.75	4.16
20	4.21	3.81	4.22
25	4.29	3.76	4.20
30	4.34	3.66	4.16

Note: *The rates in this table were obtained from CLP Structured Finance's website, www.swap-rates.com.*

default-free yield curve. Instead, it reflects the credit risk of the counterparty to an interest rate swap. Since the counterparty to an interest rate swap is typically a bank-related entity, the swap curve reflects the average credit risk of representative banks that provide interest rate swaps. More specifically, a swap curve is viewed as the *interbank yield curve*. It is also referred to as the *double A rated yield curve* because the banks that borrow money from each other have credit ratings of double A or above. In addition, the swap curve reflects liquidity risk. However, in recent years the liquidity of the interest rate swap has increased to the point where it is now a more liquid market than the market for some government bonds.

One would expect that if a country has a government bond market, the yields in that market would be the best benchmark. That is not necessarily the case. There are several advantages of using a swap curve over a country's government securities yield curve.[19]

First, there may be technical reasons why within a government bond market some of the interest rates may not be representative of the true interest rate but instead be biased by some technical or regulatory factor unique to that market. For example, market participants may need to cover a short position in a particular government bond, and the actions to cover a short position would push up the demand for that particular government bond and would drive down its yield. In the swap market, there is nothing that has to be delivered, so technical market factors have less of an impact. Also, there may be government bonds selling above or below their par value. Moreover, as explained earlier, government tax authorities might tax such bonds differently if they are purchased and held to maturity. As a result, the yields at which these bonds trade in the marketplace will reflect any

---

[19] For a further discussion, see Uri Ron, "A Practical Guide to Swap Curve Construction," Chapter 6 in Frank J. Fabozzi (ed.), *Interest Rate, Term Structure, and Valuation Modeling* (New York: John Wiley & Sons, 2002).

tax advantage or disadvantage. While it may be difficult to appreciate these factors at this point, the key is that the observed interest rate on government securities may not reflect the true interest rate due to these factors. This is not the case for swap rates. There is no regulation of this market, and hence, swap rates represent true interest rates. However, remember that swap rates do reflect credit risk and liquidity risk.

Second, to create a representative government bond yield curve, a large number of maturities must be available. However, in most government bond markets, securities with only a few maturities are issued. For example, as will be seen when we discuss U.S. Treasury securities in the next chapter, the U.S. government issues only four securities with a maturity of two years or more (two, five, 10, and 30 years). While there are a good number of off-the-run issues available from which to construct a government bond yield curve, the yields on such issues may not be true interest rates for the reasons noted previously. In contrast, in the swap market, a wide range of maturities is quoted, as can be seen in Exhibit 5-12. In fact, in the United States, there was a suspension in the issuance of 30-year bonds, and as a result, 30-year Treasury rates were unavailable. Yet, swap dealers quoted 30-year swap rates.

Finally, the ability to compare government yields across countries is difficult because there are differences in the credit risk for every country. In contrast, as explained earlier, the swap curve is an inter-bank yield curve and thereby makes cross-country comparisons of benchmark interest rates easier.

KEY POINTS

- In all economies, there is not just one interest rate but a structure of interest rates.
- The difference between the yield on any two bonds is called the yield spread. When one of the two bonds is a benchmark bond, the yield spread is called a benchmark spread and reflects a risk premium.
- The most commonly used benchmark in the United States is U.S. Treasury securities.
- The factors that affect the spread include (1) the type of issuer (e.g., agency, corporate, municipality), (2) the issuer's perceived creditworthiness as measured by the rating system of commercial rating companies, (3) the term or maturity of the instrument, (4) the embedded options in a bond issue (e.g., call, put, or conversion provisions), (5) the taxability of interest income at the federal and municipal levels, (6) the expected liquidity of the issue, and (7) the financeability of an issue.
- The credit spread is the yield spread or benchmark spread attributable to credit risk. The option-adjusted spread is the measure that is used to adjust for any options embedded in a bond issue.
- The relationship between yield and maturity is referred to as the term structure of interest rates. The graphical depiction of the relationship between the yield on bonds of the same credit quality but different maturities is known as the yield curve.
- There is a problem with using the Treasury yield curve to determine the one yield at which to discount all the cash payments of any bond. Each cash flow should be discounted at a unique interest rate that is applicable to the time period when the cash flow is to be received. Because any bond can be viewed as a package of zero-coupon instruments, its value should equal the value of all the component zero-coupon instruments. The rate on a zero-coupon bond is called the spot rate.

The relationship between the spot rate and maturity is called the term structure of interest rates.

- A default-free theoretical spot rate curve can be constructed from the yield on Treasury securities using either (1) only on-the-run Treasury issues, (2) on-the-run Treasury issues and selected off-the-run Treasury issues, (3) all Treasury coupon securities and bills, and (4) Treasury coupon strips. When the securities used are either (1) or (2), a method known as bootstrapping is used. More complex statistical techniques are used when all Treasury coupon securities and bills are used.

- Under certain assumptions, the market's expectation of future interest rates can be extrapolated from the theoretical Treasury spot rate curve. The resulting forward rate is called the implied forward rate. The spot rate is related to the current six-month spot rate and the implied six-month forward rates.

- Several theories have been proposed about the determination of the term structure: pure expectations theory, the biased expectations theory (the liquidity theory and preferred habitat theory), and the market segmentation theory. All the expectation theories hypothesize that the one-period forward rates represent the market's expectations of future actual rates. The pure expectations theory asserts that it is the only factor. The biased expectations theories assert that there are other factors.

- Empirical evidence suggests that the three main influences on the shape of the Treasury yield curve are (1) the market's expectations of future rate changes, (2) bond risk premiums, and (3) convexity bias.

- The swap rate yield curve also provides information about interest rates in a country and is used as an interest rate benchmark. The swap rate yield curve, or simply swap curve or LIBOR curve, is not a default-free yield curve but rather reflects inter-bank credit risk. In many countries, market participants use the country's swap curve as the benchmark interest rates rather than the country's government bond yield curve.

QUESTIONS

1. Following are U.S. Treasury benchmarks available on December 31, 2007:

Issue	Yield (%)
US/T 3.125 11/30/2009	3.133
US/T 3.375 11/30/2012	3.507
US/T 4.25 11/15/2017	4.096
US/T 4.75 02/15/2037	4.518

On the same day, the following trades were executed:

Issuer	Issue	Yield (%)
Time Warner Cable Inc.	TWC 6.55 05/01/2037	6.373
McCormick & Co. Inc.	MKC 5.75 12/15/2017	5.685
Goldman Sachs Group Inc.	GS 5.45 11/01/2012	4.773

Based on the above, complete the following table:

Issue	Yield (%)	Treasury Benchmark	Benchmark Spread (bps)	Relative Yield Spread	Yield Ratio
TWC 6.55 05/01/2037	6.373				
MKC 5.75 12/15/2017	5.685				
GS 5.45 11/01/2012	4.773				

2. The yield spread between two corporate bond issues reflects more than just differences in their credit risk. What other factors would the yield spread reflect?

3. Why is an option-adjusted spread measure more suitable for a bond with an embedded option than a yield spread?

4. Suppose a client observes the following two benchmark spreads for two bonds:

    Bond issue U rated A: 150 basis points
    Bond issue V rated BBB: 135 basis points

    Your client is confused because he thought the lower-rated bond (bond V) should offer a higher benchmark spread than the higher-rated bond (bond U). Explain why the benchmark spread may be lower for bond U.

5. In the May 29, 1992, *Weekly Market Update* published by Goldman, Sachs & Co., the following information was reported in an exhibit for high-grade, tax-exempt securities as of the close of business Thursday, May 28, 1992:

Maturity (years)	Yield (%)	Yield (%) as a Percentage of Treasury Yield
1	3.20	76.5
3	4.65	80.4
5	5.10	76.4
10	5.80	78.7
30	6.50	82.5

    a. What is meant by a tax-exempt security?
    b. What is meant by high-grade issue?
    c. Why is the yield on a tax-exempt security less than the yield on a Treasury security of the same maturity?
    d. What is the equivalent taxable yield?
    e. Also reported in the same issue of the Goldman, Sachs report is information on intramarket yield spreads. What are these?

6. a. What is an embedded option in a bond?
    b. Give three examples of an embedded option that might be included in a bond issue.

    c. Does an embedded option increase or decrease the risk premium relative to the base interest rate?

7. a. What is a yield curve?
    b. Why is the Treasury yield curve the one that is most closely watched by market participants?

8. What is a spot rate?

9. Explain why it is inappropriate to use one yield to discount all the cash flows of a financial asset.

10. Explain why a financial asset can be viewed as a package of zero-coupon instruments.

11. How are spot rates related to forward rates?

12. You are a financial consultant. At various times you have heard comments on interest rates from one of your clients. How would you respond to each of the following comments?
    a. "The yield curve is upward-sloping today. This suggests that the market consensus is that interest rates are expected to increase in the future."
    b. "I can't make any sense out of today's term structure. For short-term yields (up to three years) the spot rates increase with maturity; for maturities greater than three years but less than eight years, the spot rates decline with maturity; and for maturities greater than eight years the spot rates are virtually the same for each maturity. There is simply no theory that explains a term structure with this shape."
    c. "When I want to determine the market's consensus of future interest rates, I calculate the forward rates."

13. You observe the yields of the Treasury securities at the top of the following page (all yields are shown on a bond-equivalent basis). All the securities maturing from 1.5 years on are selling at par. The 0.5- and 1.0-year securities are zero-coupon instruments.
    a. Calculate the missing spot rates.
    b. What should the price of a 6% six-year Treasury security be?

c. What is the six-month forward rate starting in the sixth year?

Year	Yield to Maturity (%)	Spot Rate (%)
0.5	5.25	5.25
1.0	5.50	5.50
1.5	5.75	5.76
2.0	6.00	?
2.5	6.25	?
3.0	6.50	?
3.5	6.75	?
4.0	7.00	?
4.5	7.25	?
5.0	7.50	?
5.5	7.75	7.97
6.0	8.00	8.27
6.5	8.25	8.59
7.0	8.50	8.92
7.5	8.75	9.25
8.0	9.00	9.61
8.5	9.25	9.97
9.0	9.50	10.36
9.5	9.75	10.77
10.0	10.00	11.20

14. You observe the following Treasury yields (all yields are shown on a bond-equivalent basis):

Year	Yield to Maturity (%)	Spot Rate (%)
0.5	10.00	10.00
1.0	9.75	9.75
1.5	9.50	9.48
2.0	9.25	9.22
2.5	9.00	8.95
3.0	8.75	8.68
3.5	8.50	8.41
4.0	8.25	8.14
4.5	8.00	7.86
5.0	7.75	7.58
5.5	7.50	7.30
6.0	7.25	7.02
6.5	7.00	6.74
7.0	6.75	6.46
7.5	6.50	6.18
8.0	6.25	5.90
8.5	6.00	5.62
9.0	5.75	5.35
9.5	5.50	?
10.0	5.25	?

All the securities maturing from 1.5 years on are selling at par. The 0.5- and 1.0-year securities are zero-coupon instruments.

a. Calculate the missing spot rates.

b. What should the price of a 5% four-year Treasury security be?

15. What Treasury issues can be used to construct the theoretical spot rate curve?

16. What are the problems with using only on-the-run Treasury issues to construct the theoretical spot rate curve?

17. When all Treasury issues are used to construct the theoretical spot rate curve, what methodology is used to construct the curve?

a. What are the limitations of using Treasury strips to construct the theoretical spot rate curve?

b. When Treasury strips are used to construct the curve, why are only coupon strips used?

18. What actions force a Treasury's bond price to be valued in the market at the present value of the cash flows discounted at the Treasury spot rates?

19. Explain the role that forward rates play in making investment decisions.

20. "Forward rates are poor predictors of the actual future rates that are realized. Consequently, they are of little value to an investor." Explain why you agree or disagree with this statement.

21. Bart Simpson is considering two alternative investments. The first alternative is to invest in an instrument that matures in two years. The second alternative is to invest in an instrument that matures in one year and at the end of one year, reinvest the proceeds in a one-year instrument. He believes that one-year interest rates one year from now will be higher than they are today and therefore is leaning in favor of the second alternative. What would you recommend to Bart Simpson?

22. a. What is the common hypothesis about the behavior of short-term forward rates shared by the various forms of the expectations theory?

b. What is price risk and reinvestment risk and how do these two risks affect the pure expectations theory?

c. Give three interpretations of the pure expectations theory.

23. **a.** What are the two biased expectations theories about the term structure of interest rates?
    b. What are the underlying hypotheses of these two theories?
24. **a.** "Empirical evidence suggests that with respect to bond risk premiums that influence the shape of the Treasury yield curve, there is a linear relationship between Treasury average returns and duration." Explain whether you agree or disagree with this statement. If you disagree, explain the type of relationship that has been observed.
    b. What is meant by the "convexity bias" influence on the shape of the Treasury yield curve?

25. **a.** What is meant by the swap rate?
    b. What is meant by the swap curve?
    c. Explain whether you agree or disagree with the following statement: "A country's swap curve is a default-free yield curve."
26. Why do market participants in some countries prefer to use the swap curve rather than the government bond yield curve?
27. A client observes that a corporate bond that he is interested in purchasing with a triple A rating has a benchmark spread that is positive when the benchmark is U.S. Treasuries but negative when the benchmark is the LIBOR curve. The client asks you why. Provide an explanation.

6

Treasury and Federal Agency Securities

LEARNING OBJECTIVES

After reading this chapter, you will understand

- the different types of securities issued by the U.S. Department of the Treasury

- the difference between fixed principal and inflation-protected Treasury securities

- the Treasury auction process

- the secondary market for Treasury securities

- how Treasury securities are quoted in the secondary market

- the zero-coupon Treasury securities market

- the difference between federally related institutions and government-sponsored enterprises that issue debt in the federal agency securities market

- issuers in the federal agency securities market and the types of securities that they issue

The second largest sector of the bond market (after the mortgage market) is the market for U.S. Treasury securities; one of the smallest sectors is the U.S. government agency securities market. We discuss them together in this chapter. As we'll explain in more detail in Chapter 11, a majority of the securities backed by a pool of mortgages are guaranteed by a federally sponsored agency of the U.S. government. These securities are classified as part of the mortgage-backed securities market rather than as U.S. government agency securities.

TREASURY SECURITIES

Treasury securities are issued by the U.S. Department of the Treasury and are backed by the full faith and credit of the U.S. government. Consequently, market participants view them as having minimal credit risk, although in recent years there have been increased concerns due to the growth of the U.S. federal deficit. Interest rates on Treasury securities are the benchmark interest rates throughout the U.S. economy as well as in international capital markets. In Chapter 5, we described this important role played by Treasury securities.

Two factors account for the prominent role of U.S. Treasury securities: volume (in terms of dollars outstanding) and liquidity. The Department of the Treasury is the largest single issuer of debt in the world. The large volume of total debt and the large size of any single issue have contributed to making the Treasury market the most active and hence the most liquid market in the world. The dealer spread between bid and ask price is considerably narrower than in other sectors of the bond market.[1]

All Treasury securities are noncallable. Therefore, investors in Treasury securities are not subject to call risk.

Treasury securities are available in book-entry form at the Federal Reserve Bank. This means that the investor receives only a receipt as evidence of ownership instead of an engraved certificate. An advantage of book entry is ease in transferring ownership of the security. Interest income from Treasury securities is subject to federal income taxes but is exempt from state and local income taxes.

Types of Treasury Securities

The Treasury issues marketable and nonmarketable securities. Our focus here is on marketable securities.[2] Marketable Treasury securities are categorized as **fixed-principal securities** or **inflation-indexed securities**. We describe each type below.

Fixed-Principal Treasury Securities

Fixed-income principal securities include Treasury bills, Treasury notes, and Treasury bonds.

Treasury bills are issued at a discount to par value, have no coupon rate, and mature at par value. The current practice of the Treasury is to issue all securities with a maturity of one year or less as discount securities. As discount securities, Treasury bills do not pay coupon interest. Instead, Treasury bills are issued at a discount from their maturity value; the return to the investor is the difference between the maturity value and the purchase price.

All securities with initial maturities of two years or more are issued as coupon securities. Coupon securities are issued at approximately par and, in the case of fixed-principal securities, mature at par value. Treasury coupon securities issued with original maturities of more than one year and no more than 10 years are called **Treasury notes**. Treasury coupon securities with original maturities greater than 10 years are called **Treasury bonds**.[3]

---

[1] For a further discussion of the Treasury secondary market, see Frank J. Fabozzi and Michael J. Fleming, "U.S. Treasury Securities," Chapter 7 in Frank J. Fabozzi (ed.), *The Handbook of Financial Instruments* (Hoboken, NJ: John Wiley & Sons, 2002). Parts of this chapter draw from that work.

[2] Nonmarketable securities issued by the Treasury include savings bonds that are sold to individuals, and state and local government series (SLGS) securities that are sold to state and local government issuers of tax-exempt securities.

[3] On quote sheets, an "n" is used to denote a Treasury note. No notation typically follows an issue to identify it as a bond.

Treasury Inflation Protection Securities

The U.S. Department of the Treasury issues securities that adjust for inflation. These securities are popularly referred to as **Treasury inflation protection securities**, or TIPS.

TIPS work as follows. The coupon rate on an issue is set at a fixed rate. That rate is determined via the auction process described later in this section. The coupon rate is called the "real rate" since it is the rate that the investor ultimately earns above the inflation rate. The inflation index that the government has decided to use for the inflation adjustment is the non-seasonally adjusted U.S. City Average All Items Consumer Price Index for All Urban Consumers (CPI-U).

The adjustment for inflation is as follows. The principal that the Treasury Department will base both the dollar amount of the coupon payment and the maturity value on is adjusted semiannually. This is called the **inflation-adjusted principal**. For example, suppose that the coupon rate for a TIPS is 3.5% and the annual inflation rate is 3%. Suppose further that an investor purchases on January 1 $100,000 par value (principal) of this issue. The semiannual inflation rate is 1.5% (3% divided by 2). The inflation-adjusted principal at the end of the first six-month period is found by multiplying the original par value by one plus the semiannual inflation rate. In our example, the inflation-adjusted principal at the end of the first six-month period is $101,500. It is this inflation-adjusted principal that is the basis for computing the coupon interest for the first six-month period. The coupon payment is then 1.75% (one-half the real rate of 3.5%) multiplied by the inflation-adjusted principal at the coupon payment date ($101,500). The coupon payment is therefore $1,776.25.

Let's look at the next six months. The inflation-adjusted principal at the beginning of the period is $101,500. Suppose that the semiannual inflation rate for the second six-month period is 1%. Then the inflation-adjusted principal at the end of the second six-month period is the inflation-adjusted principal at the beginning of the six-month period ($101,500) increased by the semiannual inflation rate (1%). The adjustment to the principal is $1,015 (1% times $101,500). So, the inflation-adjusted principal at the end of the second six-month period (December 31 in our example) is $102,515 ($101,500 + $1,015). The coupon interest that will be paid to the investor at the second coupon payment date is found by multiplying the inflation-adjusted principal on the coupon payment date ($102,515) by one-half the real rate (i.e., one-half of 3.5%). That is, the coupon payment will be $1,794.01.

As can be seen, part of the adjustment for inflation comes in the coupon payment since it is based on the inflation-adjusted principal. However, the U.S. government has decided to tax the adjustment each year. This feature reduces the attractiveness of TIPS as investments in accounts of tax-paying entities.

Because of the possibility of disinflation (i.e., price declines), the inflation-adjusted principal at maturity may turn out to be less than the initial par value. However, the Treasury has structured TIPS so that they are redeemed at the greater of the inflation-adjusted principal and the initial par value.

An inflation-adjusted principal must be calculated for a settlement date. The inflation-adjusted principal is defined in terms of an index ratio, which is the ratio of the reference CPI for the settlement date to the reference CPI for the issue date. The reference CPI is calculated with a three-month lag. For example, the reference CPI for May 1 is the CPI-U reported in February. The U.S. Department of the Treasury publishes and makes available on its Web site (www.publicdebt.treas.gov) a daily index ratio for an issue.

The Treasury Auction Process

Treasury securities are sold in the primary market through sealed-bid auctions. Each auction is announced several days in advance by means of a Treasury Department press release or press conference. The announcement provides details of the offering, including the offering amount and the term and type of security being offered, and describes some of the auction rules and procedures. Treasury auctions are open to all entities. The U.S. Treasury securities issued by the U.S. Department of the Treasury on a regular cycle as of February 2011 are listed in Exhibit 6-1.

While the Treasury regularly offers new securities at auction, it often offers additional amounts of outstanding securities. This is referred to as a "reopening" of an issue. The Treasury has established a regular schedule of reopenings for the five- and 10-year issues.

The auction for Treasury securities is conducted on a competitive bid basis. There are actually two types of bids that may be submitted by a bidder: noncompetitive bids and competitive bids. A **noncompetitive bid** is submitted by an entity that is willing to purchase the auctioned security at the yield that is determined by the auction process.

When a noncompetitive bid is submitted, the bidder only specifies the quantity sought. The quantity in a noncompetitive bid may not exceed $5 million. A **competitive bid** specifies both the quantity sought and the yield at which the bidder is willing to purchase the auctioned security.

The auction results are determined by first deducting the total noncompetitive tenders and nonpublic purchases (such as purchases by the Federal Reserve) from the total securities being auctioned. The remainder is the amount to be awarded to the competitive bidders. The competitive bids are then arranged from the lowest yield bid to the highest yield bid submitted. (This is equivalent to arranging the bids from the highest price to the lowest price that bidders are willing to pay.) Starting from the lowest yield bid, all competitive bids are accepted until the amount to be distributed to the competitive bidders is completely allocated. The highest yield accepted by the Treasury is referred to as the **stop-out yield** (or **high yield**). Bidders whose bid is higher than the stop-out yield are not distributed any of the new issue (i.e., they are unsuccessful bidders). Bidders whose bid was the stop-out yield (i.e., the highest yield accepted by the Treasury) are awarded a proportionate amount for which they bid. For example, suppose that $2 billion was tendered for at the stop-out yield but only $1 billion remains to be allocated after allocating to all bidders who bid lower than the stop-out yield. Then each bidder who bid the stop-out yield will receive 50% of the

Exhibit 6-1	**Treasury Securities Issued on a Regular Auction Cycle as of February 2011**		
Bills	**Fixed Principal Notes**	**Fixed Principal Bonds**	**TIPS**
4-week bills	2-year notes	30-year bonds	10-year TIPS
13-week bills	3-year notes		30-year TIPS
26-week bills	5-year notes		
52-week bills	7-year notes		
	10-year notes		

amount for which they tendered. So, if an entity tendered for $5 million, then that entity would be awarded only $2.5 million.

Within an hour following the 1:00 P.M. auction deadline, the Treasury announces the auction results. Announced results include the stop-out yield, the associated price, and the proportion of securities awarded to those investors who bid exactly the stop-out yield. Also announced is the quantity of noncompetitive tenders, the median-yield bid, and the ratio of the total amount bid for by the public to the amount awarded to the public (called the **bid-to-cover ratio**). For notes and bonds, the announcement includes the coupon rate of the new security. The coupon rate is set to be that rate (in increments of 1/8 of 1%) that produces the price closest to, but not above, par when evaluated at the yield awarded to successful bidders.

The detailed results of the auction for the 10-year Treasury note auctioned on February 9, 2011 are shown in Exhibit 6-2. To determine the winning bidders, the bids are arranged from the lowest bid yield to the highest bid yield. The Treasury reported that the lowest bid yield was 3.510%. The high bid yield accepted for the 10-year Treasury note was 3.655%. All bidders that bid less than 3.655% were awarded the amount that they bid.

Now that we know how the winning bidders are determined and the amount that successful bidders will be allotted, the next question is the yield at which they are awarded the auctioned security. All U.S. Treasury auctions are **single-price auctions**. In a single-price auction, all bidders are awarded securities at the highest yield of accepted competitive tenders (i.e., the high yield).

Secondary Market

The secondary market for Treasury securities is an over-the-counter market where a group of U.S. government securities dealers offers continuous bid and ask prices on outstanding Treasuries. There is virtual 24-hour trading of Treasury securities. The three primary trading locations are New York, London, and Tokyo. The normal settlement period for Treasury securities is the business day after the transaction day ("next day" settlement).

The most recently auctioned issue is referred to as the **on-the-run issue** or the **current issue**. Securities that are replaced by the on-the-run issue are called **off-the-run issues**. At a given point in time, there may be more than one off-the-run issue with approximately the same remaining maturity as the on-the-run issue. Treasury securities are traded prior to the time they are issued by the Treasury. This component of the Treasury secondary market is called the **when-issued market**, or **wi market**. When-issued trading for both bills and coupon securities extends from the day the auction is announced until the issue day.

Government dealers trade with the investing public and with other dealer firms. When they trade with each other, it is through intermediaries known as **interdealer brokers**. Dealers leave firm bids and offers with interdealer brokers who display the highest bid and lowest offer in a computer network tied to each trading desk and displayed on a monitor. Dealers use interdealer brokers because of the speed and efficiency with which trades can be accomplished. Interdealer brokers keep the names of the dealers involved in trades confidential. The quotes provided on the government dealer screens represent prices in the "inside" or "interdealer" market.

> **Exhibit 6-2   Example of the Results of a Treasury Auction**

PUBLIC DEBT NEWS

Department of the Treasury • Bureau of the Public Debt • Washington, DC 20239

For Immediate Release
February 09, 2011

CONTACT: Office of Financing
202-504-3550

TREASURY AUCTION RESULTS

Term and Type of Security	10-Year Note
CUSIP Number	912828PX2
Series	B-2021
Interest Rate	3-5/8%
High Yield[1]	3.665%
Allotted at High	58.81%
Price	99.667623
Accrued Interest per $1,000	None
Median Yield[2]	3.620%
Low Yield[3]	3.510%
Issue Date	February 15, 2011
Maturity Date	February 15, 2021
Original Issue Date	February 15, 2011
Dated Date	February 15, 2011

	Tendered	Accepted
Competitive	$77,481,570,000	$23,856,010,600
Noncompetitive	$143,999,500	$143,999,500
FIMA (Noncompetitive)	$0	$0
Subtotal[4]	**$77,625,569,500**	**$24,000,010,100[5]**
SOMA	$550,670,000	$550,670,000
Total	**$78,176,239,500**	**$24,550,680,100**

	Tendered	Accepted
Primary Dealer[6]	$47,803,000,000	$6,731,960,600
Direct Bidder[7]	$5,264,020,000	$118,000,000
Indirect Bidder[8]	$24,414,550,000	$17,006,050,000
Total Competitive	**$77,481,570,000**	**$23,856,010,600**

[1] All tenders at lower yields were accepted in full.
[2] 50% of the amount of accepted competitive tenders was tendered at or below that yield.
[3] 5% of the amount of accepted competitive tenders was tendered at or below that yield.
[4] Bid-to-Cover Ratio: $77,625,569,500/$24,000,010,100 = 3.23

[5] Awards to combined Treasury Direct systems = $79,377,500.
[6] Primary dealers as submitters bidding for their own house accounts.
[7] Non-Primary dealer submitters bidding for their own house accounts.
[8] Customers placing competitive bids through a direct submitter, including Foreign and International Monetary Authorities placing bids through the Federal Reserve Bank of New York.

Source: *U.S. Department of the Treasury*

Price Quotes for Treasury Bills

The convention for quoting bids and offers is different for Treasury bills and Treasury coupon securities. Bids and offers on Treasury bills are quoted in a special way. Unlike bonds that pay coupon interest, Treasury bill values are quoted on a **bank discount basis**, not on a price basis. The yield on a bank discount basis is computed as follows:

$$Y_d = \frac{D}{F} \times \frac{360}{t}$$

where

Y_d = annualized yield on a bank discount basis (expressed as a decimal)
D = dollar discount, which is equal to the difference between the face value and the price
F = face value
t = number of days remaining to maturity

As an example, a Treasury bill with 100 days to maturity, a face value of $100,000, and selling for $99,100 would be quoted at 3.24% on a bank discount basis:

$$D = \$100,000 - \$99,100$$
$$= \$900$$

Therefore,

$$Y_d = \frac{\$900}{\$100,000} \times \frac{360}{100} = 3.24\%$$

Given the yield on a bank discount basis, the price of a Treasury bill is found by first solving the formula for Y_d for the dollar discount (D), as follows:

$$D = Y_d \times F \times t/360$$

The price is then

$$\text{price} = F - D$$

For the 100-day Treasury bill with a face value of $100,000, if the yield on a bank discount basis is quoted as 3.24%, D is equal to

$$D = 0.0324 \times \$100,000 \times 100/360$$
$$= \$900$$

Therefore,

$$\text{price} = \$100,000 - \$900 = \$99,100$$

The quoted yield on a bank discount basis is not a meaningful measure of the return from holding a Treasury bill for two reasons. First, the measure is based on a face-value investment rather than on the actual dollar amount invested. Second, the yield is annualized according to a 360-day rather than a 365-day year, making it difficult to compare Treasury bill yields with Treasury notes and bonds, which pay interest on a 365-day basis. The use of 360 days for a year is a money market convention for some money market instruments, however. Despite its shortcomings as a measure of return, this is the method that dealers have adopted to quote Treasury bills. Many dealer quote sheets, and some reporting services, provide two other yield measures that attempt to make the quoted yield comparable to that for a coupon bond and other money market instruments.

The measure that seeks to make the Treasury bill quote comparable to Treasury notes and bonds is called the **bond equivalent yield**, which we explained in Chapter 3. The **CD equivalent yield** (also called the **money market equivalent yield**) makes the quoted yield on a Treasury bill more comparable to yield quotations on other money market instruments that pay interest on a 360-day basis. It does this by taking into consideration the price of the Treasury bill rather than its face value. The formula for the CD equivalent yield is

$$\text{CD equivalent yield} = \frac{360 Y_d}{360 - t(Y_d)}$$

As an illustration, consider once again the hypothetical 100-day Treasury bill with a face value of $100,000, selling for $99,100, and offering a yield on a bank discount basis of 3.24%.

$$\text{CD equivalent yield} = \frac{360(0.0324)}{360 - 100(0.0324)} = 0.327 = 3.27\%$$

Quotes on Treasury Coupon Securities

Treasury coupon securities are quoted in a different manner than Treasury bills—on a price basis in points where one point equals 1% of par.[4] The points are split into units of *32nds*, so that a price of 96-14, for example, refers to a price of 96 and 14 *32nds*, or 96.4375 per 100 of par value. The following are other examples of converting a quote to a price per $100 of par value:

Quote	No. of *32nds*	Price per $100 par
91-19	19	91.59375
107-22	22	107.6875
109-06	6	109.1875

The 32nds are themselves often split by the addition of a plus sign or a number. A plus sign indicates that half a *32nd* (or a *64th*) is added to the price, and a number indicates how many eighths of *32nds* (or *256ths*) are added to the price. A price of 96-14+, therefore, refers to a price of 96 plus 14 *32nds* plus 1 *64th*, or 96.453125, and a price of 96-142 refers to a price of 96 plus 14 *32nds* plus 2 *256ths*, or 96.4453125. The following are other examples of converting a quote to a price per $100 of par value:

Quote	No. of *32nds*	No. of *64ths*	No. of *256ths*	Price per $100 par
91-19+	19	1		91.609375
107-222	22		2	107.6953125
109-066	6		6	109.2109375

In addition to price, the yield to maturity is typically reported alongside the price.

When an investor purchases a bond between coupon payments, if the issuer is not in default, the buyer must compensate the seller of the bond for the coupon interest earned

---

[4] Notes and bonds are quoted in yield terms in when-issued trading because coupon rates for new notes and bonds are not set until after these securities are auctioned.

from the time of the last coupon payment to the settlement date of the bond. This amount is called **accrued interest**.

When calculating accrued interest, three pieces of information are needed: (1) the number of days in the accrued interest period, (2) the number of days in the coupon period, and (3) the dollar amount of the coupon payment. The number of days in the accrued interest period represents the number of days over which the investor has earned interest. Given these values, the accrued interest (AI) assuming semiannual payments is calculated as follows:

$$\text{AI} = \frac{\text{annual dollar coupon}}{2} \times \frac{\text{days in AI period}}{\text{days in coupon period}}$$

For example, suppose that (1) there are 50 days in the accrued interest period, (2) there are 183 days in a coupon period, and (3) the annual dollar coupon per $100 of par value is $8. Then the accrued interest is

$$\text{AI} = \frac{\$8}{2} \times \frac{50}{183} = \$1.0929$$

The calculation of the number of days in the accrued interest period and the number of days in the coupon period begins with the determination of three key dates: the trade date, settlement date, and date of previous coupon payment. The **trade date** is the date on which the transaction is executed. The **settlement date** is the date a transaction is completed. For Treasury securities, settlement is the next business day after the trade date. Interest accrues on a Treasury coupon security from and including the date of the previous coupon payment up to but excluding the settlement date.

The number of days in the accrued interest period and the number of days in the coupon period may not be simply the actual number of calendar days between two dates. The reason is that there is a market convention for each type of security that specifies how to determine the number of days between two dates. These conventions are called day count conventions. There are different day count conventions for Treasury securities than for government agency securities, municipal bonds, and corporate bonds.

For Treasury coupon securities, the day count convention used is to determine the actual number of days between two dates. This is referred to as the **actual/actual day count convention**. For example, consider a Treasury coupon security whose previous coupon payment was May 15. The next coupon payment would be on November 15. Suppose this Treasury security is purchased with a settlement date of September 10. First, the number of days of accrued interest is calculated. The actual number of days between May 15 (the previous coupon date) and September 10 (the settlement date) is 118 days, as follows:

May 15 to May 31	17 days
June	30 days
July	31 days
August	31 days
September 1 to September 10	9 days
Actual number of days	118 days

The number of days in the coupon period is the actual number of days between May 15 and November 15, which is 184 days. The number of days between the settlement date

(September 10) and the next coupon date (November 15) is therefore 66 days (184 days − 118 days). Notice that in computing the number of days from May 15 to May 31, May 15 is counted in determining the number of days in the accrued interest period; however, the settlement date (September 10) is not included.

STRIPPED TREASURY SECURITIES

The Treasury does not issue zero-coupon notes or bonds. However, because of the demand for zero-coupon instruments with no credit risk, the private sector has created such securities. The profit potential for a government dealer who strips a Treasury security lies in arbitrage resulting from the mispricing of the security. We explained the reason for this in Chapter 5.

To illustrate the process, a process referred to as **coupon stripping**, suppose that $500 million of a 10-year fixed-principal Treasury note with a coupon rate of 5% is purchased by a dealer firm to create zero-coupon Treasury securities. The cash flow from this Treasury note is 20 semiannual payments of $12.5 million each ($500 million times 0.05 divided by 2) and the repayment of principal (also called the **corpus**) of $500 million 10 years from now. As there are 11 different payments to be made by the Treasury, a security representing a single payment claim on each payment is issued, which is effectively a zero-coupon Treasury security. The amount of the maturity value for a security backed by a particular payment, whether coupon or corpus, depends on the amount of the payment to be made by the Treasury on the underlying Treasury note. In our example, 20 zero-coupon Treasury securities each have a maturity value of $12.5 million, and one zero-coupon Treasury security, backed by the corpus, has a maturity value of $500 million. The maturity dates for the zero-coupon Treasury securities coincide with the corresponding payment dates by the Treasury.

Zero-coupon Treasury securities were first created in August 1982 by dealer firms. The problem with these securities were that they were identified with particular dealers and therefore reduced liquidity. Moreover, the process involved legal and insurance costs. In February 1985, the Treasury announced its **Separate Trading of Registered Interest and Principal of Securities** (STRIPS) program to facilitate the stripping of designated Treasury securities. Today, all Treasury notes and bonds (fixed-principal and inflation-indexed) are eligible for stripping. The zero-coupon Treasury securities created under the STRIPS program are direct obligations of the U.S. government. Moreover, the securities clear through the Federal Reserve's book-entry system.

There may be confusion when a market participant refers to a "stripped Treasury." Today, a stripped Treasury typically means a STRIPS product. However, because there are trademark products and other types of pre-STRIPS zero-coupon products still outstanding, an investor should clarify what product is the subject of the discussion. In the chapters that follow, we will refer to stripped Treasury securities as simply "strips."

On dealer quote sheets and vendor screens, STRIPS are identified by whether the cash flow is created from the coupon (denoted ci), principal from a Treasury bond (denoted bp), or principal from a Treasury note (denoted np). Strips created from the coupon are called **coupon strips** and strips created from the principal are called **principal strips**. The reason why a distinction is made between coupon strips and principal strips has to do with the tax treatment by non–U.S. entities, as discussed in the next section.

All fixed-principal notes and bonds that pay interest on the same dates are assigned the same CUSIP number. For example, fixed-principal notes and bonds that pay interest on April 15 and October 15 are stripped. The coupon strips that are payable on the same day have the same CUSIP number. The principal strips of each fixed-principal note and bond, in contrast, are assigned a unique CUSIP number, and principal strips with different CUSIP numbers that pay on the same day are not interchangeable.

Tax Treatment

A disadvantage of a taxable entity investing in stripped Treasury securities is that accrued interest is taxed each year even though interest is not paid. Thus, these instruments are negative cash flow instruments until the maturity date. They have negative cash flow because tax payments on interest earned but not received in cash must be made. One reason for distinguishing between coupon strips and principal strips is that some foreign buyers have a preference for principal strips. This preference is due to the tax treatment of the interest in their home country. The tax laws of some countries treat the interest from a principal strip as a capital gain, which receives a preferential tax treatment (i.e., lower tax rate) compared with ordinary interest income if the stripped security was created from a coupon strip.

Reconstituting a Bond

In our illustration of coupon stripping in Chapter 5, the price of the Treasury security is less than its theoretical price. Suppose, instead, that the Treasury security is greater than its theoretical price. In such cases, investors can purchase in the market a package of zero-coupon Treasury securities such that the cash flow of the package of securities replicates the cash flow of the mispriced coupon Treasury security. By doing so, the investor will realize a yield higher than the yield on the coupon Treasury security. This process is called **reconstitution**.

It is the process of coupon stripping and reconstituting that will prevent the actual spot rate curve observed on zero-coupon Treasuries from departing significantly from the theoretical spot rate curve. As more stripping and reconstituting occurs, forces of demand and supply will cause rates to return to their theoretical spot rate levels. This is, in fact, what has happened in the Treasury market and in other government bond markets throughout the world.

FEDERAL AGENCY SECURITIES

Federal agency securities are securities issued by government-chartered entities. These entities are either federally related institutions or government-sponsored enterprises. *Federally related institutions* are agencies of the federal government. *Government-sponsored enterprises* (GSEs) are privately owned, publicly chartered entities. They are instrumentalities (not agencies) of the U.S. government that like federally related institutions provide them privileges that are not granted to private sector corporations. Despite this difference, we refer to GSEs in this chapter as agencies.

As of February 2011, Freddie Mac, Fannie Mae, Federal Home Loan Bank System, Federal Farm Credit System, and the Federal Agricultural Mortgage Corporation are classified as GSEs. Fannie Mae, Freddie Mac, and Federal Home Loan Bank are responsible for providing credit to the housing sectors. The Federal Agricultural Mortgage Corporation provides the same function for agricultural mortgage loans. The Federal Farm Credit Bank System is responsible for the credit market in the agricultural sector of the economy. In addition to the debt obligations issued by these five GSEs, there are issues outstanding by one-time GSE issuers that have been dismantled. These GSEs include the Financing Corporation, Resolution Trust Corporation, and the Farm Credit Assistance Corporation. One former GSE, Student Loan Marketing Association (Sallie Mae), elected to alter its status.

An important issue associated with federal agency securities is their credit quality. A commonly shared view is that although any agency issue may not carry the explicit guarantee of the U.S. government, there is an implicit guarantee due to their ability to borrow from the U.S. Treasury. However, despite this right to borrow from the Treasury and other privileges that they receive relative to private sector firms, there is no explicit or implicit guarantee. There are, however, issues that have occurred during crisis times where the U.S. government has provided an explicit government guarantee.

Because of the credit risk, federal agency securities trade at a higher yield in the market than U.S. Treasury securities. As with Treasury securities, these securities trade in a multiple-dealer, over-the-counter secondary market but with trading volume significantly less than that in the Treasury market. Primary dealer trading volumes in agency debt securities averaged 11% of U.S. bond daily trading volumes from 2000 to 2010.

There are two types of securities that can be issued. The first are the typical bond used by other issuers in the bond market. This type of debt obligation is referred to as a *debenture*. The other type, and the one that is probably the best known by bond market participants, is a security backed by a pool of residential mortgage loans. This type of debt obligation is called a *mortgage-backed security* and is the subject of several chapters later in this book. Our focus in the remainder of this chapter is on federal agency debentures. The major concern of investors when considering investing in federal agency securities is the credit risk associated with the security.

Below we review the securities issued by the three large active issuers (Fannie Mae, Freddie Mac, and the Federal Home Loan Bank System) and the three smaller active issuers (Farm Credit System, the Federal Agricultural Mortgage Corporation, and a major federally related institution, the Tennessee Valley Authority). It should be noted that as of this writing, Congress has proposed new rules regarding GSEs.

Fannie Mae and Freddie Mac

We'll discuss Fannie Mae and Freddie Mac, the two major suppliers of funds to the residential mortgage market, together because they issue similar debt instruments, as well as currently facing the same legal constraint.

Fannie Mae has issued Benchmark Bills, Benchmark Notes and Benchmark Bonds, Callable Benchmark Notes, Subordinated Benchmark Notes, Investment Notes, callable securities, and structured notes. Benchmark Notes and Benchmark Bonds are noncallable instruments. Fannie Mae issues securities with maturities of 2, 3, 5, 10, and 30 years. Freddie Mac has issued Reference Bills, discount notes, medium-term notes, Reference Notes and Bonds, Callable Reference Notes, Euro Reference Notes (debt denominated in euros) and global bonds. Reference Bills and discount notes are issued with maturities of one year or less. Reference Notes and Bonds have maturities of 2 to 30 years, and Callable Reference Notes have maturities of 2 to 10 years.

There are outstanding issues of both GSEs that are structured notes. As explained in Chapter 7, these debt obligations are customized based on demand from institutional investors. The structured notes issued have been various floating rate, zero-coupon, and step-up securities. There are securities denominated in U.S. dollars as well as issues denominated in a wide range of foreign currencies.

Due to the major downturn in the housing and credit markets beginning in 2007, in September 2008 the entity that regulates Fannie Mae and Freddie Mac, the Federal Housing Finance Agency (FHFA), placed these two GSEs in conservatorship. This meant that the FHFA had complete control over the operations and assets of these two GSEs. The federal government was concerned that the failure of these two GSEs would cause the housing finance market to dry up and cause severe disruptions in the global financial market due to the wide holding of the securities of these two GSEs. Therefore, the U.S. Department of the Treasury put in place financing agreements to ensure that these two entities could continue to satisfy the debt obligations that they issued as well as those that guaranteed securities that we will discuss in Chapters 11 and 12.

Federal Farm Credit Bank System

The *Federal Farm Credit Bank System* (FFCBS) was established by Congress to facilitate the supply of credit to the agricultural sector of the economy. The Farm Credit System consists of three entities: the Federal Land Banks, Federal Intermediate Credit Banks, and Banks for Cooperatives. All financing for the FFCBS is arranged through the Federal Farm Credit Banks Funding Corporation (FFCBFC), which issues consolidated obligations. Interest income is *generally* exempt from state and local income taxes.

The FFCBFC, or simply Farm Credit, issues debt with a broad range of structures and maturities. Farm Credit Discount Notes are similar to U.S. Treasury bills with maturities from one day to 365 days. Farm Credit Designated Bonds can have a noncallable or callable structure that generally has 2- to 10-year maturities at issuance. The callable Designated Bonds have a one-time only redemption feature. Farm Credit Bonds can be customized for institutional investors as structured notes. Farm Credit Master Notes are debt obligations whose coupon rate is indexed to some reference rate. As of February 2011, the debt obligations issued by the FFCBFC are rated triple A.

Federal Agricultural Mortgage Corporation

The purpose of the *Federal Agricultural Mortgage Corporation* (Farmer Mac) is to provide a secondary market for first mortgage agricultural real estate loans. Farmer Mac raises funds by selling debentures and mortgage-backed securities backed by the loans purchased. The latter securities are called *agricultural mortgage-backed securities* (AMBSs). The debentures that are issued include discount notes and medium-term notes.

Federal Home Loan Bank System

The *Federal Home Loan Bank System* (FHL Banks) consists of the 12 district Federal Home Loan Banks and their member banks. Each member bank issues consolidated debt obligations, which are joint and several obligations of the 12 member banks. The debt obligations issues are discount notes with maturities from one to 360 days and longer-term debt that include issues with a bullet maturity, callable, and floating interest rate.

Tennessee Valley Authority

The *Tennessee Valley Authority* (TVA) was established by Congress in 1933 primarily to provide flood control, navigation, and agricultural and industrial development. Created to promote the use of electric power in the Tennessee Valley region, the TVA is the largest public power system in the United States. Because it is a self-funded agency of the U.S. government, the TVA obtains funds from its operating revenues and the capital markets by issuing debt obligations, the TVA's power program financing. This program involves the issuance of debt only for power program purposes, which includes refinancing of existing debt. Although TVA debt obligations are not guaranteed by the U.S. government, the debt obligations issued are triple A rated based on the TVA's status as a wholly owned corporate agency of the U.S. government and its financial strengths.

The TVA issues bonds with a wide range of maturities and targeting individual (retail) and institutional investors. The *TVA Discount Notes* have a maturity of one year or less. They are offered on a continuous basis to investors via investment dealers and dealer banks. The bonds issued, referred to as *TVA Power Bonds*, can have a final maturity of up to 50 years and have a variety of bond structures issued in two programs. One program, the TVA Electronotes^{R} program, targets individual investors. The bonds issued in this program, which are issued monthly and can have maturities up to 30 years, have been standard callable bonds with an interesting put option referred to as an "estate feature." This put option allows the bonds to be redeemed at par value plus accrued interest upon the death of the bondholder. Another part of the TVA Power Bond program targeted to individual investors is the Putable Automatic Rate Reset Securities (PARRS) program. In this program noncallable bonds are issued that have two interesting features. First, they have a fixed coupon rate for the first five years, and then there is an annual reset provision that provides for a reduction in the issue's coupon rate under certain conditions. Second, the bondholder has the right to put the bond at par value plus accrued interest if and when the coupon rate is reduced. The bonds issued in this program trade on the New York Stock Exchange.

For institutional investors, the TVA has global bonds outstanding that are noncallable and are issued in U.S. dollars and in other major currencies. There are also putable issues that may not be called and inflation-indexed bonds.

KEY POINTS

- The U.S. Treasury market is closely watched by all participants in the financial markets because interest rates on Treasury securities are the benchmark interest rates throughout the world.
- The Treasury issues three types of securities: bills, notes, and bonds. Treasury bills have a maturity of one year or less, are sold at a discount from par, and do not make periodic interest payments. Treasury notes and bonds are coupon securities.
- The Treasury issues coupon securities with a fixed principal and an inflation-protected principal. The coupon payment for the latter is tied to the Consumer Price Index and the securities are popularly referred to as Treasury Inflation Protection Securities (TIPS).
- Treasury securities are issued on a competitive bid auction basis, according to a regular auction cycle. The secondary market for Treasury securities is an over-the-counter market, where dealers trade with the general investing public and with other dealers.

- In the secondary market, Treasury bills are quoted on a bank discount basis; Treasury coupon securities are quoted on a price basis.
- Although the Treasury does not issue zero-coupon Treasury securities, government dealers have created these instruments synthetically by a process called coupon stripping. Zero-coupon Treasury securities are created via the U.S. Treasury's STRIPS program.
- The federal agency securities market is the market for the debt instruments issued by federally related institutions and government-sponsored enterprises. Unless otherwise specified, the securities issued by these entities are not explicitly or implicitly guaranteed by the full faith and credit of the U.S. government.

QUESTIONS

1. What are the differences between a Treasury bill, a Treasury note, and a Treasury bond?

2. The following questions are about TIPS.

   a. What is meant by the "real rate"?

   b. What is meant by the "inflation-adjusted principal"?

   c. Suppose that the coupon rate for a TIPS is 3%. Suppose further that an investor purchases $10,000 of par value (initial principal) of this issue today and that the semiannual inflation rate is 1%.

   1. What is the dollar coupon interest that will be paid in cash at the end of the first six months?

   2. What is the inflation-adjusted principal at the end of six months?

   d. Suppose that an investor buys a five-year TIPS and there is deflation for the entire period. What is the principal that will be paid by the Department of the Treasury at the maturity date?

   e. What is the purpose of the daily index ratio?

   f. How is interest income on TIPS treated at the federal income tax level?

3. What is the when-issued market?

4. Why do government dealers use government brokers?

5. Suppose that the price of a Treasury bill with 90 days to maturity and a $1 million face value is $980,000. What is the yield on a bank discount basis?

6. The bid and ask yields for a Treasury bill were quoted by a dealer as 5.91% and 5.89%, respectively. Shouldn't the bid yield be less than the ask yield, because the bid yield indicates how much the dealer is willing to pay and the ask yield is what the dealer is willing to sell the Treasury bill for?

7. Assuming a $100,000 par value, calculate the dollar price for the following Treasury coupon securities given the quoted price:

   a. 84.14

   b. 84.14+

   c. 103.284

   d. 105.059

8. In a Treasury auction what is meant by

   a. a noncompetitive bidder?

   b. the high yield?

9. In a Treasury auction, how is the price that a competitive bidder must pay determined in a single-price auction format?

10. In a Treasury auction, how is the price that a noncompetitive bidder must pay determined in a single-price auction format?

11. Suppose that a Treasury coupon security is purchased on April 8 and that the last coupon payment was on February 15. Assume that the year in which this security is purchased is not a leap year.

    a. How many days are in the accrued interest period?

    b. If the coupon rate for this Treasury security is 7% and the par value of the issue purchased is $1 million, what is the accrued interest?

12. **a.** What is meant by coupon stripping in the Treasury market?

    b. What is created as a result of coupon stripping in the Treasury market?

13. Why is a stripped Treasury security identified by whether it is created from the coupon or the principal?

14. What is the federal income tax treatment of accrued interest income on stripped Treasury securities?

15. What is a government-sponsored enterprise?

16. Explain why you agree or disagree with the following statement: "The debt of government-owned corporations is guaranteed by the full faith and credit of the U.S. government, but that is not the case for the debt of government-sponsored enterprises."

17. In the fall of 2010, the author of this book received an offering sheet for very short-term Treasury bills from a broker. The offering price for a few of the issues exceeded the maturity value of the Treasury bill. When the author inquired if this was an error, the broker stated that it was not and that there were institutional investors who were buying very short-term Treasury bills above their maturity value. What does that mean in terms of the yield such investors were willing to receive at that time?

7

Corporate Debt Instruments

LEARNING OBJECTIVES

After reading this chapter, you will understand

- the different types of corporate debt obligations: corporate bonds, medium-term notes, commercial paper, bank loans, convertible corporate bonds, and asset-backed securities

- the different credit classes in a corporation's capital structure and the seniority of each in the case of bankruptcy

- major provisions of the U.S. bankruptcy law and the principle of absolute priority

- corporate bond ratings and what investment-grade bonds and noninvestment-grade (or high-yield) bonds are

- provisions for paying off a bond issue prior to the stated maturity date

- bond structures that have been used in the high-yield bond market

- the secondary market for corporate bonds

- the private-placement market for corporate bonds

- medium-term notes and their features

- structured medium-term notes and various types of structured notes

- what commercial paper is and the difference between directly placed and dealer-placed commercial paper

- what a bank loan is and the difference between an investment-grade bank loan and a leveraged bank loan

- what a collateralized loan obligation is

- corporate bond default risk, default rates, and recovery rates

- corporate bond downgrade risk and rating transition matrices

- corporate bond spread risk, event risk, and headline risk

Corporate debt instruments are financial obligations of a corporation that have priority over its common stock and preferred stock in the case of bankruptcy. Corporate debt instruments can be classified as follows: (1) corporate bonds, (2) medium-term notes, (3) commercial paper, (4) bank loans, (5) convertible corporate bonds, and (6) asset-backed securities. In this chapter we discuss the first four instruments. We postpone a discussion of convertible corporate bonds until Chapter 19 and asset-backed securities until Chapter 15.

Issuers of corporate debt obligations are categorized into the following five sectors:

- *Public utilities:* Includes electric utilities, communication companies, gas pipeline and transmission companies, and water companies
- *Transportation:* Includes airlines, railroads, and trucking companies
- *Banks/finance:* Includes banks, savings and loan associations, brokerage firms, finance companies, and insurance companies
- *Industrials:* Includes manufacturers, retailers, energy companies, service-related industries, and mining companies
- *Yankee and Canadian:* Includes dollar-denominated bonds issued in the United States by sovereign governments, non-U.S. local governments, non-U.S. corporations, and foreign branches of U.S. corporations

Beyond the type of debt obligation and the corporate debt sectors, corporate instruments are classified based on their credit risk as gauged by the credit rating assigned by the major credit rating companies. We briefly discussed credit risk and credit ratings in Chapter 1 and will expand on the discussion in this chapter. In our discussion, we will see that the two major categories are investment grade and non–investment grade debt instruments. Corporate debt obligations that fall into the non–investment grade category are more popularly referred to as "high-yield debt obligations."

SENIORITY OF DEBT IN A CORPORATION'S CAPITAL STRUCTURE

The capital structure of the firm is the way in which the firm's management has elected to finance itself. In broad terms, the capital structure of a firm consists of common stock, preferred stock, and debt. In corporate finance, the capital structure decision is one of the principal decisions made by a firm's management. The issue—which we do not review in this chapter—is whether there is an optimal capital structure, where optimal means a capital structure that will maximize the market value of equity. Another question in designing a firm's capital structure is how to construct an optimal debt structure. This issue deals with the seniority in the case of bankruptcy of one creditor class relative to other creditor classes. Although optimal capital structure and the optimal debt structure are important topics in corporate finance and in credit risk modeling, our focus here is merely to describe the seniority structure.

The priority of creditors is as follows:

- Senior secured debt
- Senior unsecured debt
- Senior subordinated debt
- Subordinated debt

Senior secured debt is backed by or secured by some form of collateral beyond the issuer's general credit standing. Either real property (using a mortgage) or personal property may be pledged to offer security. A **mortgage bond** grants the creditor a lien against the pledged assets; that is, the creditor has a legal right to sell the mortgaged property to satisfy unpaid obligations that are owed. In practice, foreclosure and sale of mortgaged property is unusual. As explained in the next section, usually in the case of bankruptcy, a reorganization of the issuer provides for settlement of the debt to bondholders for less than the amount of the principal owed. The mortgage lien is important, though, because it gives the mortgage bondholders a strong bargaining position relative to other creditors in determining the terms of any reorganization.

Some companies do not own fixed assets or other real property and so have nothing on which they can give a mortgage lien to secure bondholders. Instead, they own securities of other companies; they are holding companies, and the other companies are subsidiaries. To satisfy the desire of bondholders for security, they will pledge stocks, notes, bonds or whatever other kind of obligations they own. Bonds secured by such assets are called **collateral trust bonds**.

Debt that is not secured is obviously referred to as unsecured. Unsecured bonds are called **debenture bonds**.

Senior unsecured debt is debt that is not secured by a specific pledge of property, but that does not mean that the creditors holding this type of debt have no claim on property of issuers or on their earnings. This creditor class has a claim of general creditors on all assets of the issuer not pledged specifically to secure other debt. In addition, they have a claim on pledged assets to the extent that these assets have more value than necessary to satisfy senior secured creditors.

Creditors holding **subordinated debt** rank after senior secured creditors, after senior unsecured creditors, and often after some general creditors in their claim on assets and earnings. In turn, subordinated debt falls into two categories. Within this class of debt, there are some creditors who have priority in their claims relative to other subordinated debt holders. This class of debt that has seniority within the ranks of subordinated debt is referred to as **senior subordinated debt**.

It is important to recognize that the superior legal status of any debt obligation will not prevent creditors from suffering financial loss when the issuer's ability to generate cash flow adequate to pay its obligations is seriously eroded.

BANKRUPTCY AND CREDITOR RIGHTS

As we have noted earlier, the holder of a corporate debt instrument has priority over the equity owners in the case of bankruptcy of a corporation, and there are creditors who have seniority over other creditors. The U.S. bankruptcy law gives debtors who are unable to meet their debt obligations a mechanism for formulating a plan to resolve their debts through an allocation of their assets among their creditors.[1] One purpose of the bankruptcy law is to set forth the rules for a corporation to be either liquidated or reorganized.

The **liquidation** of a corporation means that all the assets will be distributed to the holders of claims of the corporation and no corporate entity will survive. In a **reorganization**, a new corporate entity will result. Some holders of the claims of the bankrupt corporation will receive cash in exchange for their claims; others may receive new securities in the

---

[1] Congress passed the Bankruptcy Code under its Constitutional grant of authority to "establish . . . uniform laws on the subject of Bankruptcy throughout the United States." The U.S. Bankruptcy Courts are responsible for the supervising and litigating of bankruptcy proceedings.

corporation that results from the reorganization; and still others may receive a combination of both cash and new securities in the resulting corporation.

Another purpose of the bankruptcy act is to give a corporation time to decide whether to reorganize or liquidate and then have the necessary time to formulate a plan to accomplish either a reorganization or liquidation. This is achieved because when a corporation files for bankruptcy, the act grants the corporation protection from creditors who seek to collect their claims.[2] A company that files for protection under the bankruptcy act generally becomes a **debtor in possession** (DIP), and continues to operate its business under the supervision of the court.

The bankruptcy act is composed of 15 chapters, each chapter covering a particular type of bankruptcy. Of particular interest to us are two of the chapters, Chapter 7 and Chapter 11. Chapter 7 deals with the liquidation of a company. Historically, liquidations have been less common than Chapter 11 filings. Chapter 11 deals with the reorganization of a company. In this case, the corporation that declares bankruptcy seeks to emerge from the bankruptcy proceedings as a going concern. The process involved in a traditional Chapter 11 filing is costly (both explicit legal expenses and the potential adverse impact on operating revenues as well as reputation) and takes from a year to 18 months to be resolved.[3]

When a company is liquidated, creditors receive distributions based on the **absolute priority rule** to the extent that assets are available. The absolute priority rule is the principle that senior creditors are paid in full before junior creditors are paid anything. For secured creditors and unsecured creditors, the absolute priority rule guarantees their seniority to equity holders. In liquidations, the absolute priority rule generally holds. In contrast, there is a good body of literature that argues that strict absolute priority has not been upheld by the courts or the Securities and Exchange Commission (SEC).[4] Studies of actual reorganizations under Chapter 11 have found that the violation of absolute priority is the rule rather the exception.[5] Consequently, although investors in the debt of a corporation may feel that they have priority over the equity owners and priority over other classes of debtors, the actual outcome of a bankruptcy may be far different from what the terms of the debt agreement state.

Corporate Debt Ratings

Professional money managers use various techniques to analyze information on companies and bond issues in order to estimate the ability of the issuer to live up to its future contractual obligations. This activity is known as **credit analysis** and is the subject of Chapter 20.

---

[2] The petition for bankruptcy can be filed either by the company itself, in which case it is called a **voluntary bankruptcy**, or by its creditors, in which case it is called an **involuntary bankruptcy**.

[3] A prepackaged bankruptcy and a prenegotiated plan are court restructuring alternatives to a traditional Chapter 11 filing that are less costly and can be confirmed by the court faster.

[4] See, for example, William H. Meckling, "Financial Markets, Default, and Bankruptcy," *Law and Contemporary Problems*, Vol. 41, 1977, pp. 124–177; Merton H. Miller, "The Wealth Transfers of Bankruptcy: Some Illustrative Examples," *Law and Contemporary Problems*, Vol. 41, 1977, pp. 39–46; Jerome B. Warner, "Bankruptcy, Absolute Priority, and the Pricing of Risky Debt Claims," *Journal of Financial Economics*, Vol. 4, 1977, pp. 239–276; and Thomas H. Jackson, "Of Liquidation, Continuation, and Delay: An Analysis of Bankruptcy Policy and Nonbankruptcy Rules," *American Bankruptcy Law Journal*, Vol. 60, 1986, pp. 399–428.

[5] See Julian R. Franks and Walter N. Torous, "An Empirical Investigation of U.S. Firms in Reorganization," *Journal of Finance*, July 1989, pp. 747–769; Lawrence A. Weiss, "Bankruptcy Resolution: Direct Costs and Violation of Priority of Claims," *Journal of Financial Economics*, 1990, pp. 285–314; and Frank J. Fabozzi, Jane Tripp Howe, Takashi Makabe, and Toshihide Sudo, "Recent Evidence on the Distribution Patterns in Chapter 11 Reorganizations," *Journal of Fixed Income*, Spring 1993, pp. 6–23.

Some large institutional investors and many banks have their own credit analysis departments. Other institutional investors do not do their own analysis but instead rely primarily on nationally recognized rating companies that perform credit analysis and issue their conclusions in the form of ratings. The three major rating companies are (1) Moody's Investors Service, (2) Standard & Poor's Corporation, and (3) Fitch Ratings. The rating systems used by these three rating companies are shown in Exhibit 7-1. The factors considered by rating agencies in assigning a credit rating are discussed in Chapter 20.

In all three systems, the term **high grade** means low credit risk, or conversely, high probability of future payments. The highest-grade debt obligations are designated by Moody's by the letters Aaa, and by the other two agencies by AAA. The next highest grade is Aa or AA; for the third grade all rating agencies use A. The next three grades are Baa or BBB, Ba or BB, and B, respectively. There are also C grades. Standard & Poor's and Fitch use plus or minus signs to provide a narrower credit quality breakdown within each class, and Moody's uses 1, 2, or 3 for the same purpose. These refinements in the ratings are referred to as rating "notches."

Debt obligations rated triple A (AAA or Aaa) are said to be **prime**; double A (AA or Aa) are of **high quality**; single A issues are called **upper medium grade**, and triple B are **medium grade**. Lower-rated debt issues are said to have speculative elements or to be distinctly speculative.

Debt obligations that are assigned a rating in the top four categories are said to be **investment-grade**. Issues that carry a rating below the top four categories are said to be **noninvestment-grade**, or more popularly referred to as **high-yield debt** or **junk debt**. Thus, the corporate debt market can be divided into two sectors based on credit ratings: the investment-grade and noninvestment-grade markets. This distinction is important since investment guidelines of institutional investors may prohibit the investment in noninvestment-grade debt obligations.

Rating agencies monitor the bonds and issuers that they have rated. A rating agency may announce that it is reviewing a particular credit rating, and may go further and state that the outcome of the review may result in a downgrade (i.e., a lower credit rating being assigned) or upgrade (i.e., a higher credit rating being assigned). When this announcement is made by a rating agency, the issue or issuer is said to be under credit watch.

CORPORATE BONDS

Corporate bonds are debt obligations issued by corporations. Most corporate bonds are **term bonds**; that is, they run for a term of years, and then become due and payable. Any amount of the liability that has not been paid off prior to maturity must be paid off at that time. The term may be long or short. Generally, obligations due in under 10 years from the date of issue are called **notes**. (However, the term *notes* has been used to describe particular types of securities that can have maturities considerably longer than 10 years.) Corporate borrowings due in 20 to 30 years tend to be referred to as **bonds**. As a practical matter, the distinction between a note and a bond is not important. Term bonds may be retired by payment at final maturity or retired prior to maturity if provided for in the terms of the agreement. Some corporate bond issues are arranged so that specified principal amounts become due on specified dates. Such issues are called **serial bonds**.

Exhibit 7-1	**Summary of Corporate Bond Ratings Systems and Symbols**		
Moody's	S&P	Fitch	Brief Definition
Investment Grade: High Credit Worthiness			
Aaa	AAA	AAA	Gilt edge, prime, maximum safety
Aa1	AA+	AA+	
Aa2	AA	AA	Very high grade, high quality
Aa3	AA−	AA−	
A1	A+	A+	
A2	A	A	Upper medium grade
A3	A−	A−	
Baa1	BBB+	BBB+	
Baa2	BBB	BBB	Lower medium grade
Baa3	BBB−	BBB−	
Distinctly Speculative: Low Credit Worthiness			
Ba1	BB+	BB+	
Ba2	BB	BB	Low grade, speculative
Ba3	BB−	BB−	
B1	B+	B+	
B2	B	B	Highly speculative
B3	B−	B−	
Predominantly Speculative: Substantial Risk or in Default			
	CCC+		
Caa	CCC	CCC	Substantial risk, in poor standing
	CCC−		
Ca	CC	CC	May be in default, extremely speculative
C	C	C	Even more speculative than those above
	CI		CI = Income bonds; no interest is being paid
		DDD	Default
		DD	
	D	D	

Provisions for Paying Off Bonds Prior to Maturity

Some corporate bond issues have call provision granting the issuer an option to buy back all or part of the issue prior to the stated maturity date. Some issues specify that the issuer must retire a predetermined amount of the issue periodically. Various types of corporate call provisions are discussed below.

(1) Traditional call and refunding provisions. An important provision in a bond issue is whether the issuer shall have the right to redeem the entire amount of bonds outstanding on a date before maturity. Issuers generally want this right because they recognize that at some time in the future the general level of interest rates may fall sufficiently below the issue's coupon rate that redeeming the issue and replacing it with another issue with a lower coupon rate would be attractive. This right is a disadvantage to the bondholder.

The **call price** is the price that the issuer must pay to retire the issue and may be a single call price or a **call schedule** that sets forth a call price based on when the issuer exercises the option to call the bond. The call price is referred to as the **regular price** or **general redemption price** because there may also be a **special redemption price** for debt redeemed through the sinking fund (discussed next) and through other provisions such as with the proceeds from the confiscation of property through the right of eminent domain.

Some bonds that are callable require that the issuer pay a premium over the par value when exercising this option. The initial call premium on some outstanding bond issues has been the interest coupon plus par or the initial reoffering price (in some cases it is the higher of the two) scaled down as the issue approaches its maturity date.

At the time of issuance, a callable bond issue may contain a restriction that prevents the issuer from exercising the call option for a specified number of years. Callable bonds with this feature are said to have a **deferred call** and the date at which the issue may first be called is said to be the **first call date**. If, instead, a callable bond does not have any protection against early call, then it is said to be a **currently callable issue**.

Even if a new bond issue is currently callable, there may be restrictions imposed on the issuer from redeeming the bond early. The most common restriction is that prohibiting the refunding of the bonds for a certain number of years. **Refunding** a bond issue means redeeming bonds with funds obtained through the sale of a new bond issue. Bonds that are noncallable for the issue's life are more common than bonds that are nonrefundable for life but otherwise callable.

Sometimes investors are confused by the terms **noncallable** and **nonrefundable**. Call protection is much more absolute than refunding protection. The term **refunding** means to replace an old bond issue with a new one, often at a lower interest cost. In the *Florida Power & Light* case, the judge said:

> The terms *redemption* and *refunding* are not synonymous. A *redemption* is simply a call of bonds. A *refunding* occurs when the issuer sells bonds in order to use the proceeds to redeem an earlier series of bonds. The refunding bond issue being sold is closely linked to the one being redeemed by contractual language and proximity in time so that the proceeds will be available to pay for the redemption. Otherwise, the issuer would be taking an inordinate risk that market conditions would change between the redemption of the earlier issue and the sale of the later issue.[6]

---

[6] *Lucas et al. v. Florida Power & Light Company*, Final Judgment, paragraph 77.

Although there may be certain exceptions to absolute or complete call protection in some cases (such as sinking funds and the redemption of debt under certain mandatory provisions), a noncallable bond still provides greater assurance against premature and unwanted redemption than does refunding protection. Refunding prohibition merely prevents redemption only from certain sources, namely the proceeds of other debt issues sold at a lower cost of money. The holder is protected only if interest rates decline and the borrower can obtain lower-cost money to pay off the debt. There is nothing to prevent the company from calling the bonds within the refunding protected period from debt sold at a higher rate (although the issuer normally would not do so) or from funds obtained through other means. There have been legal actions taken by bondholders against corporations that have redeemed nonrefundable bonds based on the argument that the funds used to redeem an issue were in fact from cheaper sources of financing.

Beginning in early 1986, a number of industrial companies issued long-term debt with extended call protection, not refunding protection. A number are noncallable for the issue's life. For such issues the prospectus expressly prohibits redemption prior to maturity. These noncallable-for-life issues are referred to as **bullet bonds**. Other issues carry 15 years of call protection. However, this does not prevent the issuer from offering to repurchase the issue via a tender offer.

Bonds can be called in whole (the entire issue) or in part (only a portion).When less than the entire issue is called, the specific bonds to be called are selected randomly or on a pro rata basis.

(2) Make whole call provisions. With a traditional call provision, the call price is fixed and is either par or a premium over par based on the call date. With a **make-whole call provision**, the payment when the issuer calls a bond is determined by the present value of the remaining payments discounted at a small spread over a maturity-matched Treasury yield. The specified spread that is fixed over the bond's life is called the **make-whole premium**. Because the spread is small relative to the market spread at issuance, the bondholder is highly likely to benefit when the issuer invokes this option. Thus, the term "make-whole" misrepresents this provision. It is highly likely that when the issuer invokes the option, the bondholder will be made more than whole to compensate for the issuer's action. As of mid 2010, about 7% of the 50,000 corporate bonds had a make-whole call provision.[7]

As an example,[8] consider the Southern California Edison 5½s of 2040. The make-whole call price for this bond will be calculated at the time the call is invoked based on the Treasury yield for a maturity-matched Treasury plus a make-whole premium of 15 basis points. At issuance in 2010, this bond had a maturity of 30 years and was sold at a 90 basis point spread over the then 30-year Treasury yield. What this means is that as long as the spread for this issue exceeds 15 basis points at the time the make-whole call provision is invoked, the bondholder will receive more than the bond's fair market value. The likelihood that the bondholder will be harmed if the option is exercised is minimal because it would typically require a substantial decline in the market spread—in our example a decline from 90 basis points to 15 basis points.

---

[7] Andrew Kalotay, "Making Sense of the Make-whole Call, From Its Origins to BABs," *The Bond Buyer* (July 26, 2010).
[8] This example is taken from Kalotay, "Making Sense of the Make-whole Call, From Its Origins to BABs."

Notice that unlike a traditional call option, there is no reinvestment risk. Also, instead of having to compensate investors for accepting call risk, the make-whole call provision is attractive to an investor. Because of the attractiveness of the make-whole call provision, its exercise by the issuer is less likely to occur than a traditional call.

(3) Sinking fund provision. A corporate bond issue may require the issuer to retire a specified portion of an issue each year. This is referred to as a **sinking fund requirement**. This kind of provision for repayment of corporate debt may be designed to liquidate all of a bond issue by the maturity date, or it may be arranged to pay only a part of the total by the end of the term. If only a part is paid, the remainder is called a **balloon maturity**. The purpose of the sinking fund provision is to reduce credit risk.

Generally, the issuer may satisfy the sinking fund requirement by either (1) making a cash payment of the face amount of the bonds to be retired to the corporate trustee, who then calls the bonds for redemption using a lottery, or (2) delivering to the trustee bonds purchased in the open market that have a total face value equal to the amount that must be retired. If the bonds are retired using the first method, interest payments stop at the redemption date. Usually, the periodic payments required for sinking fund purposes will be the same for each period. A few bond issues might permit variable periodic payments, where payments change according to certain prescribed conditions. Some bond issues include a provision that grants the issuer the option to retire more than the amount stipulated for sinking fund retirement. This is referred to as an **accelerated sinking fund provision**.

Usually, the sinking fund call price is the par value if the bonds were originally sold at par. When issued at a price in excess of par, the call price generally starts at the issuance price and scales down to par as the issue approaches maturity.

Covenants

The promises of corporate bond issuers and the rights of investors who buy them are set forth in great detail in contracts called **bond indentures**. The covenants or restrictions on management are important in the analysis of the credit risk of a corporate bond issue as well as for bank loans. Covenants are described in Chapter 20.

Special Structures for High-Yield Corporate Bonds

As we have noted earlier, noninvestment-grade bonds are issues assigned a credit rating below triple B and are popularly referred to as high-yield corporate bonds and junk bonds. Bond issues in this sector of the bond market may have been either (1) rated noninvestment grade at the time of issuance or (2) rated investment grade at the time of issuance and downgraded subsequently to noninvestment grade. Bond issues in the first category are referred to as **original-issue high-yield bonds**. Bond issues in the second category are either issues that have been downgraded because the issuer voluntarily significantly altered its capital structure so as to increase its debt relative to equity (i.e., significantly increased its financial leverage) as a result of a leveraged buyout or a recapitalization, or issues that have been downgraded for other reasons. The latter issues are commonly referred to as **fallen angels**.

In the early years of the high-yield bond market, all the issues had a conventional structure; that is, the issues paid a fixed coupon rate and were term bonds. Today, however, there are more complex bond structures in the high-yield corporate bond sector, particularly for bonds issued for leveraged buyout (LBO) financing and recapitalizations producing higher debt. The structures we describe next have features that are more attractive to issuers. In an LBO or a recapitalization, the heavy interest payment burden that the corporation assumes places severe cash flow constraints on the firm. To reduce this burden, firms involved in LBOs and recapitalizations have issued bonds with **deferred coupon structures** that permit the issuer to avoid using cash to make interest payments for a period of three to seven years. There are three types of deferred coupon structures: (1) deferred-interest bonds, (2) step-up bonds, and (3) payment-in-kind bonds.

Deferred-interest bonds are the most common type of deferred coupon structure. These bonds sell at a deep discount and do not pay interest for an initial period, typically from three to seven years. (Because no interest is paid for the initial period, these bonds are sometimes referred to as zero-coupon bonds.) **Step-up bonds** do pay coupon interest, but the coupon rate is low for an initial period and then increases ("steps up") to a higher coupon rate. Finally, **payment-in-kind** (PIK) **bonds** give the issuer an option to pay cash at a coupon payment date or give the bondholder a similar bond (i.e., a bond with the same coupon rate and a par value equal to the amount of the coupon payment that would have been paid). The period during which the issuer can make this choice varies from five to 10 years.

Another structure found in the high-yield bond market is one that requires the issuer to reset the coupon rate so that the bond will trade at a predetermined price.[9] The coupon rate may reset annually or even more frequently, or reset only one time over the life of the bond. Generally, the coupon rate at the reset date will be the average of rates suggested by a third part, usually two banks. The new rate will then reflect (1) the level of interest rates at the reset date, and (2) the credit spread the market wants on the issue at the reset date. This structure is called an **extendable reset**.

Notice the difference between an extendable reset bond and a floating-rate issue. In the latter structure, the coupon rate resets according to a fixed spread over some benchmark (i.e., the quoted margin). The amount of the quoted margin or spread reflects market conditions at the time the issue is offered. In contrast, the coupon rate on an extendable reset bond is reset based on market conditions at the time of the reset date. Moreover, the new coupon rate reflects the new level of interest rates and the new spread that investors seek.

The advantage to issuers of extendable reset bonds is that they can be assured of a long-term source of funds based on short-term rates. For investors, the advantage of these bonds is that the coupon rate will reset to the market rate—both the level of interest rates and the credit spread, in principle keeping the issue at par. In fact, experience with reset bonds has not been favorable during the recent period of difficulties in the high-yield bond market. The sudden substantial increase in default risk has meant that the rise in the rate needed to keep the issue at par was so large that it would have insured the bankruptcy of the firm. As a result, the rise in the coupon rate has been insufficient to keep the issue at the stipulated price.

Accrued Interest

As explained in Chapter 2, in addition to the agreed-upon price, the buyer must pay the seller accrued interest. The market convention for determining the number of days in a corporate bond coupon period and the number of days from the last coupon payment to the settlement

---

[9] Most of the bonds have a coupon reset formula that requires the issuer to reset the coupon so that the bond will trade at a price of $101.

date differs from that for a Treasury coupon security. Whereas a calendar year has 365 days (366 days in the case of a leap year), corporate bond interest is computed as if the year were 360 days. Each month in a corporate bond year is 30 days, whether it is February, April, or August. A 12% coupon corporate bond pays $120 per year per $1,000 par value, accruing interest at $10 per month or $0.33333 per day. The accrued interest on a 12% corporate bond for three months is $30; for three months and 25 days, $38.33, and so on. The corporate calendar is referred to as "30/360."

Secondary Market for Corporate Bonds

As with all bonds, the principal secondary market for corporate bonds is the over-the-counter market. The major concern is market transparency. Efforts to increase price transparency in the U.S. corporate debt market resulted in the introduction of a mandatory reporting of over-the-counter secondary market transactions for corporate bonds that met specific criteria. The reporting system, the Trade Reporting and Compliance Engine (also known as "TRACE"), requires that all broker/dealers who are member firms of the Financial Integrity Regulatory Authority (FINRA) report transactions in corporate bonds to TRACE. At the end of each trading day, market aggregate statistics are published on corporate bond market activity. End of day recap information provided includes (1) the number of securities and total par amount traded; (2) advances, declines, and 52-week highs and lows; and (3) the 10 most active investment-grade, high-yield, and convertible bonds for the day.

Electronic Bond Trading: Historically, corporate bond trading has been an OTC market conducted via telephone and based on broker-dealer trading desks, which take principal positions in corporate bonds in order to fulfill buy and sell orders of their customers. There has been a transition away from this traditional form of bond trading and toward electronic trading. The major advantages of electronic trading over traditional corporate bond trading are (1) providing liquidity to the markets, (2) price discovery (particularly for less liquid markets), (3) use of new technologies, and (4) trading and portfolio management efficiencies. As an example of the last advantage, a portfolio manager can load buy/sell orders in a website, trade from these orders, and then clear these orders.

There are the following five types of electronic corporate bond trading systems:

- auction systems
- cross-matching systems
- interdealer systems
- multidealer systems
- single-dealer systems

Auction systems allow market participants to conduct electronic auctions of securities offerings for both new issues in the primary markets and secondary market offerings. Auction systems are not typically used. **Cross-matching systems** bring dealers and institutional investors together in electronic trading networks that provide real-time or periodic cross-matching sessions. Buy and sell orders are executed automatically when matched. **Interdealer systems** allow dealers to execute transactions electronically with other dealers via the anonymous services of "brokers' brokers." The clients of dealers are not involved in interdealer systems. **Multidealer systems** allow customers to execute from among multiple quotes. Multidealer systems, also called **client-to-dealer systems**, typically display to customers the best bid or offer price of those posted by all dealers. The participating dealer usually acts as the principal in the transaction. **Single-dealer systems** permit investors to execute transactions directly with the specific dealer desired; this dealer acts as a principal in the transaction with access to the dealer by the investor, which increasingly has been through the Internet. Single-dealer systems therefore simply replace telephone contact between a single dealer and a customer with Internet contact.

Private-Placement Market for Corporate Bonds

Securities privately placed are exempt from registration with the SEC because they are issued in transactions that do not involve a public offering. SEC Rule 144A allows the trading of privately placed securities among qualified institutional buyers. Not all private placements are Rule 144A private placements. Consequently, the private-placement market can be divided into two sectors. First is the traditional private-placement market, which includes non-144A securities. Second is the market for 144A securities.

Rule 144A private placements are now underwritten by investment bankers on a firm commitment basis, just as with publicly issued bonds. The features in these issues are similar to those of publicly issued bonds. For example, the restrictions imposed on the borrower are less onerous than for traditional private-placement issues. For underwritten issues, the size of the offering is comparable to that of publicly offered bonds.

Unlike publicly issued bonds, the issuers of privately placed issues tend to be less well known. In this way, the private-placement market shares a common characteristic with the bank loan market that we will discuss later in this chapter. Borrowers in the publicly issued bond market are typically large corporations. Issuers of privately placed bonds tend to be medium-sized corporations. Those corporations that borrow from banks tend to be small corporations. Although the liquidity of issues has increased since Rule 144A became effective, it is still not comparable to that of publicly offered issues. Yields on privately placed debt issues are still higher than those on publicly offered bonds. However, one market observer reports that the premium that must be paid by borrowers in the private placement market has decreased as investment banking firms have committed capital and trading personnel to making markets for securities issued under Rule 144A.

MEDIUM-TERM NOTES

A **medium-term note** (MTN) is a corporate debt instrument, with the unique characteristic that notes are offered continuously to investors by an agent of the issuer. Investors can select from several maturity ranges: nine months to one year, more than one year to 18 months, more than 18 months to two years, and so on up to 30 years. Medium-term notes are registered with the SEC under Rule 415 (the shelf registration rule), which gives a corporation the maximum flexibility for issuing securities on a continuous basis. Although we elected to discuss MTNs in our coverage of corporate debt, they are also issued by federal agencies (as we mentioned in the previous chapter), supranational institutions, and sovereign governments.

Using the term *medium-term note* to describe this corporate debt instrument is misleading. Traditionally, the term *note* or *medium-term note* was used to refer to debt issues with a maturity greater than one year but less than 15 years. Certainly, this is not a characteristic of MTNs because they have been sold with maturities from nine months to 30 years and even longer.[10] For example, in July 1993, Walt Disney Corporation issued a security with a 100-year maturity off its MTN shelf registration.

Borrowers have flexibility in designing MTNs to satisfy their own needs. They can issue fixed- or floating-rate debt. The coupon payments can be denominated in U.S. dollars or in a foreign currency. Earlier in this chapter we described the various security structures; MTNs have been designed with the same features.

When the treasurer of a corporation is contemplating an offering of either an MTN or corporate bonds, there are two factors that affect the decision. The most obvious is the cost of the funds raised after consideration of registration and distribution costs. This cost is referred to as the **all-in cost of funds**. The second is the flexibility afforded to the issuer in structuring the offering. The tremendous growth in the MTN market is evidence of the relative advantage of MTNs with respect to cost and flexibility for some offerings. However, the fact that there are corporations that raise funds by issuing both bonds and MTNs is evidence that there is no absolute advantage in all instances and market environments.

Medium-term notes differ from corporate bonds in the manner in which they are distributed to investors when they are initially sold. When they are offered, MTNs are usually sold in relatively small amounts on a continuous or an intermittent basis, whereas corporate bonds are sold in large, discrete offerings. A corporation that wants an MTN program will file a shelf registration with the SEC for the offering of securities. Although the SEC registration for MTN offerings is between $100 million and $1 billion, after the total is sold, the issuer can file another shelf registration.

The issuer then posts rates over a range of maturities: for example, nine months to one year, one year to 18 months, 18 months to two years, and annually thereafter. Usually, an issuer will post rates as a spread over a Treasury security of comparable maturity. For example, in the two- to three-year maturity range, the offering rate might be 120 basis points over the two-year Treasury. Rates will not be posted for maturity ranges that the issuer does not desire to sell. The agents will then make the offering rate schedule available to their investor base interested in MTNs. An investor who is interested in the offering will contact the agent. In turn, the agent contacts the issuer to confirm the terms of the transaction. Because the maturity range in the offering rate schedule does not specify a specific maturity date, the investor can choose the final maturity subject to approval by the issuer. The minimum size that an investor can purchase of an MTN offering typically ranges from $1 million to $25 million. The rate offering schedule can be changed at any time by the issuer either in response to changing market conditions or because the issuer has raised the desired amount of funds at a given maturity. In the latter case, the issuer can either not post a rate for that maturity range or a low rate.

Structured Notes

MTNs created when the issuer simultaneously transacts in the derivative markets (such as a swap or an option) in order to create the security are called **structured notes**. By using the derivative markets in combination with an offering, borrowers are able to create

---

[10] General Motors Acceptance Corporation first used MTNs in 1972 to fund automobile loans with maturities of five years and less. The purpose of the MTN was to fill the funding gap between commercial paper and long-term bonds. It is for this reason that they are referred to as "medium term."

investment vehicles that are more customized for institutional investors to satisfy their investment objectives, even though they are forbidden from using swaps for hedging. Moreover, it allows institutional investors who are restricted to investing in investment-grade debt issues the opportunity to participate in other asset classes to make a market play. For example, an investor who buys an MTN whose coupon rate is tied to the performance of the S&P 500 is participating in the equity market without owning common stock. If the coupon rate is tied to a foreign stock index, the investor is participating in the equity market of a foreign country without owning foreign common stock. In exchange for creating a structured note product, borrowers can reduce their funding costs.

In addition to credit risk and the risk associated with the play that the investor is seeking to make, structured notes expose investors to liquidity risk because structured notes rarely trade in the secondary market.

How do borrowers or their agents find investors who are willing to buy structured notes? In a typical offering of a corporate bond, the sales force of the underwriting firm will solicit interest in the offering from its customer base. That is, the sales force will make an inquiry. In the structured note market, the process is often quite different. Because of the small size of an offering and the flexibility to customize the offering in the swap market, investors can approach an issuer through its agent about designing a security for their needs. This process of customers inquiring of issuers or their agents to design a security is called a **reverse inquiry**.

Structured notes include[11]

- Inverse floating-rate notes
- Equity-linked notes
- Commodity-linked notes
- Currency-linked notes
- Credit-linked notes

We discussed the first type of structured note in Chapter 1 when we covered the different types of coupon payments. Below we briefly describe the others.

Equity-linked notes: An **equity-linked note** (ELN) differs from a conventional bond because the principal, coupon payment, or both are linked to the performance of an established equity index, a portfolio of stocks, or an individual stock. Maturities have ranged from one year to 10 years. Large brokerage firms have their own version of the ELN product. In addition, there are listed equity-linked notes that are designed primarily for retail investors. Examples of these are Equity Participation Notes (EPNs), Stock Upside Notes (SUNs), Structured Upside Participating Equity Receipts (SUPERs), and Synthetic High Income Equity Linked Securities (SHIELDS). The coupon can be fixed or floating and denominated in any currency. The equity-linked payment is typically equal to 100% of the equity appreciation, and redemption at maturity is the par value of the bond plus the equity appreciation.[12]

---

[11] For a more detailed discussion of the different types of structured notes, see John D. Finnerty and Rachael Park, "Structured Notes and Credit-Linked Notes," in Frank J. Fabozzi (ed.), *The Handbook of Fixed Income Securities: 8th Edition* (New York: McGraw-Hill, 2012).

[12] Equity participation is actually flexible and changes depending on whether the ELN includes a coupon payment.

The typical ELN is economically equivalent to a portfolio consisting of a zero-coupon bond and a call option on the equity index that is the ELN's reference asset. The cash flows associated with this type of structured note are as follows. At issuance, the investor purchases the ELN, which represents the initial cash flow. Periodic cash flows are derived exclusively from the performance of the linked equity index. For example, if the index appreciated 8% for the year and equity participation is 100%, then assuming that the notional amount is $1 million, the investor would receive $80,000 as a periodic cash flow. At the maturity date, the terminal cash flow includes the return of principal and the final equity payment. Often, however, cash flows are subject to a cap, which limits the upside participation.

Commodity-linked notes: The payments of a commodity-linked note are tied to the price performance of a designated commodity (such as crude oil, heating oil, natural gas, or a precious metal) or a basket of commodities. At the maturity date, the investor receives the initial principal amount plus a return based on the percentage change in the price of the designated commodity or basket of commodities.

Here is an example of a commodity-linked note issued in April 2010 by Danske Bank and denominated in Danish kroner. The notes do not pay any coupon interest and mature on May 10, 2013. They are priced at 105 at issuance and will be redeemed at a price reflecting the performance of the Dow Jones-UBS Commodity Index. The notes will not be redeemed at a price below 80 or a price higher than indicatively 170 at a cap of 70% of the initial level of the index. The indicative cap is 70% but can be higher depending on the market conditions. The offer specified that the final cap will be fixed on May 6, 2010, at the latest, on the basis of market conditions.

Credit-linked notes: A **credit-linked note** (CLN)[13] is a security whose credit risk is linked to a second issuer (called the reference issuer), and the return is linked to the credit performance of the reference issuer. A CLN can be quite complicated, so we will focus on the basic structure only. The basic CLN is just like a standard bond: It has a coupon rate (fixed or floating), maturity date, and a maturity value. However, in contrast to a standard bond, the maturity value depends on the performance of the reference issuer. Specifically, if a credit event occurs with respect to the reference issuer then (1) the bond is paid off, and (2) the maturity value is adjusted down. How the adjustment is made is described in the prospectus. The compensation for the investor accepting the credit risk of the reference issuer is an enhanced coupon payment.

Typically, CLNs have a maturity of anywhere from three months to several years, with one to three years being the most likely term of credit exposure. The short maturity of CLNs reflects the desire of investors to take a credit view for such a time period.[14]

Currency-linked notes: A **currency-linked note** pays a return linked to a global foreign-exchange index. Typically, this structured note is short-term, paying out a fixed minimum rate of interest determined by the movement in foreign exchange rates over the life of the note. On the maturity date, the note pays the initial principal amount plus return, if any.

For the above structured notes, if there is a negative return for the underlying reference asset or index, the investor might receive less than the initial investment. Structured notes

---

[13] While several structured notes are preceded with the letters "CLN," in the marketplace, the abbreviation CLN is usually reserved for a credit-linked note.

[14] For a further discussion of CLNs, see Mark J. P. Anson, Frank J. Fabozzi, Moorad Choudhry, and Ren-Raw Chen, *Credit Derivatives: Instruments, Applications, and Pricing* (Hoboken, NJ: John Wiley & Sons, 2004).

that guarantee the return of principal (i.e., guarantees a minimum return on the reference asset or index of zero) are called **principal-protected notes**. The issuer of this type of structured note is typically a bank. Consequently, the investor is exposed to the credit risk of the issuing bank.

COMMERCIAL PAPER

Commercial paper is a short-term unsecured promissory note that is issued in the open market and that represents the obligation of the issuing corporation. The minimum round-lot transaction is $100,000, although some issuers will sell commercial paper in denominations of $25,000. There is very little secondary trading of commercial paper. Typically, an investor in commercial paper is an entity that plans to hold it until maturity. This is understandable because an investor can purchase commercial paper in a direct transaction with the issuer that will issue paper with the specific maturity the investor desires.

In the United States, commercial paper ranges in maturity from one day to 270 days. The reason that the maturity of commercial paper does not exceed 270 days is as follows. The Securities Act of 1933 requires that securities be registered with the SEC. Special provisions in the 1933 act exempt commercial paper from registration as long as the maturity does not exceed 270 days. Hence, to avoid the costs associated with registering issues with the SEC, firms rarely issue commercial paper with maturities exceeding 270 days. Another consideration in determining the maturity is whether the commercial paper would be eligible collateral for a bank that wanted to borrow from the Federal Reserve Bank's discount window. To be eligible, the maturity of the paper may not exceed 90 days. Because eligible paper trades at lower cost than paper that is not eligible, issuers prefer to issue paper whose maturity does not exceed 90 days. According to the Federal Reserve Bank of New York, commercial paper usually does not exceed 30 days. To pay off holders of maturing paper, issuers generally use the proceeds obtained by selling new commercial paper. This process is often described as "rolling over" short-term paper. The risk that the investor in commercial paper faces is that the issuer will be unable to issue new paper at maturity. As a safeguard against this **rollover risk**, commercial paper is typically backed by unused bank credit lines. Because there is a commitment fee charged by a bank for providing a credit line, this safeguard increases the effective cost of issuing commercial paper.

There are three types of financial companies: captive finance companies, bank-related finance companies, and independent finance companies. Captive finance companies are subsidiaries of equipment manufacturing companies. Their primary purpose is to secure financing for the customers of the parent company. For example, the three major U.S. automobile manufacturers have captive finance companies: General Motors Acceptance Corporation (GMAC), Ford Credit, and Chrysler Financial. Furthermore, a bank holding company may have a subsidiary that is a finance company, which provides loans to enable individuals and businesses to acquire a wide range of products. Independent finance companies are those that are not subsidiaries of equipment manufacturing firms or bank holding companies.

The three rating agencies have a special rating system for commercial paper as shown in Exhibit 7-2. As with the ratings on other long-term debt obligations, commercial paper ratings are categorized as either **investment grade** or **noninvestment grade**.

Exhibit 7-2   Commercial Paper Ratings[a]

Category	Commercial Rating Company		
	Fitch	Moody's	S&P
Investment grade	F-1+		A-1+
	F-1	P-1	A-1
	F-2	P-2	A-2
	F-3	P-3	A-3
Noninvestment grade	F-S	NP (not prime)	B
			C
In default	D		D

[a] The definition of ratings varies by rating agency.
Source: *Mitchell A. Post, "The Evolution of the U.S. Commercial Paper Market Since 1980," Federal Reserve Bulletin, December 1992, p. 882.*

Directly Placed versus Dealer-Placed Paper

Commercial paper is classified as either direct paper or dealer-placed paper. **Directly placed paper** is sold by the issuing firm directly to investors without the help of an agent or an intermediary. (An issuer may set up its own dealer firm to handle sales.) A large majority of the issuers of direct paper are financial companies. These entities require continuous funds in order to provide loans to customers. As a result, they find it cost-effective to establish a sales force to sell their commercial paper directly to investors. An institutional investor can find information about the rates posted by issuers on Bloomberg Financial Markets, Telerate/Bridge, Reuters, and the Internet (at cpmarket.com).

General Electric Capital Corporation (GE Capital) is an example of a direct issuer, having issued commercial paper for more than 50 years. GE Capital is the principal financial services arm of General Electric Company and is now the largest and most active direct issuer in the United States. The Corporate Treasury unit of GE Capital manages the commercial paper programs of General Electric Company, GE Capital Services, GE Capital, and other GE-related programs. The paper is marketed directly to institutional investors on a continuous basis by Corporate Treasury or through GECC Capital Markets Group, Inc. (an NASD-registered broker-dealer).

Dealer-placed commercial paper requires the services of an agent to sell an issuer's paper. The agent distributes the paper on a best efforts underwriting basis by commercial banks and securities houses.

Tier-1 and Tier-2 Paper

A major investor group in commercial paper is money market mutual funds. There are restrictions imposed on money market mutual funds by the SEC. Specifically, Rule 2a-7 of the Investment Company Act of 1940 limits the credit risk exposure of money market mutual funds by restricting their investments to "eligible" paper. Eligibility is defined in terms of the credit ratings shown in Exhibit 7-2. To be eligible paper, the issue must carry one of the two highest ratings ("1" or "2") from at least two of the nationally recognized statistical ratings agencies. **Tier-1 paper** is defined as eligible paper that is rated "1" by at least two of the rating agencies; **tier-2 paper** is defined as eligible paper that is not a tier-1 security.

BANK LOANS

Bank loans to corporate borrowers are divided into two categories: investment-grade loans and leveraged loans. An **investment-grade loan** is a bank loan made to corporate borrowers that have an investment-grade rating. These loans are typically originated by and retained in the originating bank's portfolio. The reason is that the loans are revolving lines of credit. In such a loan arrangement, a bank sets a maximum amount that can be borrowed by a corporation, and the corporation can take down any part of that amount and repay it at any time. Because of the ability of the corporate borrower to repay at any time and the absence of a maturity date for the loan, an investment-grade bank loan is not sold by the originating bank to institutional investors.

In contrast, a **leveraged loan** is a bank loan to a corporation that has a below-investment-grade rating. A leveraged loan has a maturity, and the interest rate is a floating rate with the reference rate being LIBOR. In fact, when market participants refer to corporate bank loans, they typically mean a leveraged loan. These loans can be sold to institutional investors. A corporation may have as its debt obligations both leveraged loans and high-yield bonds.

Syndicated Bank Loans

A **syndicated bank loan** is one in which a group (or syndicate) of banks provides funds to the borrower. The need for a group of banks arises because the amount sought by a borrower may be too large for any one bank to be exposed to the credit risk of that borrower. Therefore, the syndicated bank loan is used by borrowers who seek to raise a large amount of funds in the loan market rather than through the issuance of securities.

These bank loans are called **senior bank loans** because of their priority position over subordinated lenders (bondholders) with respect to repayment of interest and principal. The interest rate on a syndicated bank loan is a rate that periodically resets at the reference rate plus a spread. The reference rate is typically LIBOR, although it could be the prime rate (that is, the rate that a bank charges its most creditworthy customers) or the rate on certificates of deposits. The term of the loan is fixed. A syndicated loan is typically structured so that it is amortized according to a predetermined schedule, and repayment of principal begins after a specified number of years (typically not longer than five or six years). Structures in which no repayment of the principal is made until the maturity date can be arranged and are referred to as **bullet loans**.

A syndicated loan is arranged by either a bank or a securities house. The arranger then lines up the syndicate. Each bank in the syndicate provides the funds for which it has committed. The banks in the syndicate have the right to sell their parts of the loan subsequently to other banks.

Syndicated loans are distributed by two methods: assignment or participation. Each method has its relative advantages and disadvantages, with the method of assignment being the more desirable of the two.

The holder of a loan who is interested in selling a portion can do so by passing the interest in the loan by the **method of assignment**. In this procedure, the seller transfers all rights completely to the holder of the assignment, now called the **assignee**. The assignee is said to have **privity of contract** with the borrower. Because of the clear path between the borrower and assignee, assignment is the more desirable choice of transfer of ownership.

A **participation** involves a holder of a loan "participating out" a portion of the holding in that particular loan. The holder of the participation does not become a party to the loan agreement and has a relationship not with the borrower but with the seller of the participation. Unlike an assignment, a participation does not confer privity of contract on the holder of the participation, although the holder of the participation has the right to vote on certain legal matters concerning amendments to the loan agreement. These matters include changes regarding maturity, interest rate, and issues concerning the loan collateral. Because syndicated loans can be sold in this manner, they are marketable.

The trading of bank loans is not limited to *performing loans*, which are loans whose borrowers are fulfilling contractual commitments. A market also exists for the trading of nonperforming loans—loans on which the borrowers have defaulted.

Secondary Market for Syndicated Bank Loans

While at one time, a bank or banks who originated loans retained them in their loan portfolio, today those loans can be traded in the secondary market or securitized to create collateralized loan obligations (discussed below) and therefore require periodic marking to market.

The Loan Syndications and Trading Association (LSTA) has helped foster the development of a liquid and transparent secondary market for bank loans by establishing market practices and settlement and operational procedures. This association provides dealer-quotes based on mark-to-market prices. Information provided by the LSTA includes:

- A list of the most volatile loans priced by the LSTA/Thompson Reuters Market-to-Market Pricing at the end of each trading day
- A list of the biggest winners, biggest losers, most volatile, and newest deals in terms of weekly price volatility published each week based on quotes from three or more individual broker/dealers
- At the end of each month a file of all mark-to-market loan prices based on quotes from three or more individual broker/dealers
- At the end of each quarter a file of all mark-to-market loan prices based on quotes from five or more individual broker/dealers

The LSTA in conjunction with Standard & Poor's Leveraged Commentary & Data (LCD) has developed a leveraged loan index (the S&P/LSTA Leveraged Loan 100 Index) to gauge the performance of the different sectors of the syndicated loan market. This index, a market-weighted index of the 100 largest loan facilities[15] in the leveraged loan market, is a total return index.

High-Yield Bond versus Leveraged Loans

Leveraged loans are bank loans in which the borrower is a noninvestment-grade borrower. Hence, leveraged loans and high-yield bonds are alternative sources of debt by noninvestment-grade borrowers. Here, we will summarize the distinguishing characteristics of these sources of debt funding.

The coupon rate on high-yield bonds is typically a fixed interest rate. For leveraged loans, it is a floating rate, with the most common reference rate being three-month LIBOR.

---

[15] A loan facility provided by a bank can be a short-term loan or a line of credit (also called a revolver or revolving credit agreement). A line of credit is a loan that the borrower can take down up to a maximum amount.

With respect to maturity, high-yield bonds usually have a maturity of 10 years and are noncallable until three or five years after issuance. Leveraged loans are shorter term, usually five to eight years, and offer no call protection since they are callable at any time.

Within the capital structure, leveraged loans are the most senior, while high-yield bonds are subordinated to bank loans. With respect to covenants, they are stronger for leveraged loans than high-yield bonds, which is one of the reasons corporate borrowers prefer to issue bonds. Finally, investors are concerned with the amount that can be recovered in the case of a default. Historically, on average, the recovery rate for defaulted leveraged loans is much higher than for defaulted high-yield bonds as will be shown later in this chapter.

Collateralized Loan Obligations

Leveraged loans have been pooled and used as collateral for the issuance of a **collateralized loan obligation** (CLO). A CLO is created using the securitization technology described in later chapters. Here we provide a basic explanation of a CLO.[16]

A CLO is a special purpose vehicle (SPV) that issues debt and equity and from the funds raised invests in a portfolio of leveraged loans. The entity responsible for managing the portfolio of leveraged loans (i.e., the collateral) is the **collateral manager**. Investors in the debt securities that the SPV issues—referred to as bond classes or tranches—are entitled to the cash flows from the portfolio of loans. The cash flow is distributed to the bond classes in prescribed ways that take into account the seniority of those liabilities. The rules described for the distribution of the cash flow are set forth in the CLO's indenture. In addition to the bond classes, there is a security called the **equity tranche** that is entitled to receive the residual cash flows as explained later.

The liability structure of a CLO is referred to as its capital structure. These bond classes are commonly labeled Class A, Class B, Class C, and so forth going from top to bottom of the capital structure in terms of their priority and their credit rating. They run the gamut from the most secured AAA-rated bond class to the lowest-rated bond class in the capital structure. Exhibit 7-3 shows a simplified capital structure for a CLO. Class A in the capital

Exhibit 7-3 Simple, Typical CLO Capital Structure

Bond Class	Percent of Capital Structure	Rating	Coupon
Class A	80	AAA	LIBOR + 26
Class B	8	A	LIBOR + 75
Class C	3	BBB	LIBOR + 180
Class D	2	BB	LIBOR + 475
Equity tranche	7	Not rated	Residual Cash Flow

---

[16] For a more detailed explanation, see Chapter 4 in Stephen Antczak, Douglas J. Lucas, and Frank J. Fabozzi, *Leveraged Finance: Concepts, Methods, and Trading of High-Yield Bonds, Loans, and Derivatives* (John Wiley & Sons, 2009).

structure, the one with the AAA rating, is referred to as the **senior bond class**. The other three bond classes are referred to as **subordinate bond classes**. Notice that in a typical CLO, the coupon rate floats with a reference rate (most commonly LIBOR).

The cash flow credit structure is the dominant credit enhancement mechanism in most CLOs[17] because the specifics of a CLO's cash flow structure determine the credit risk taken on by the bond classes. To understand the cash flow credit structure, the rules for the distribution of collateral interest and collateral principal must be understood. These rules for the distribution of collateral interest and collateral principal, referred to as the **cash flow waterfalls**, specify the order in which bond classes get paid and by doing so enforce the seniority of one CLO creditor over another.

Another key feature of a CLO is the **coverage tests** set forth in the indenture. They are important because the outcomes of these tests can result in a diversion of cash that would have gone to the subordinated bond classes and redirect it to senior bond classes. Although there are several coverage tests, we will describe only one such test here: **par coverage tests**.[18] For each bond class there is the following par coverage test:

$$\text{Class A par coverage test} = \frac{\text{Par value of assets}}{\text{Par value of Class A}}$$

$$\text{Class B par coverage test} = \frac{\text{Par value of assets}}{\text{Par value of Class A} + \text{Par value of Class B}}$$

and so on for the rest of the bond classes in the CLO capital structure.

In addition, it is important to understand that there is a period of time in which collateral principal is not distributed to the bond classes or the equity tranche but is instead reinvested by the collateral manager by purchasing additional loans. This time period is referred to as the **reinvestment period**.

Now let's see how the cash flow waterfalls work in conjunction with the coverage tests and reinvestment period. Here is a typical basic *interest* waterfall in which collateral interest payments are applied to the bond classes in the following order:

1. Pay the trustee for base administrative fees and expenses.
2. Pay the collateral manager for base management fees.
3. Pay Class A its interest expense.
4. If Class A coverage tests are failed, collateral interest is diverted to Class A for principal repayment until Class A coverage tests are met. This results in a reduction in the amount of the liabilities outstanding for Class A.
5. Pay Class B its interest expense.
6. If Class B coverage tests are failed, collateral interest is diverted to the senior-most outstanding bond class (which could be Class A or, if Class A has been paid in full, Class B) for principal repayment until Class B coverage tests are met.
7. Pay Class C its interest expense.
8. If Class C coverage tests are failed, collateral interest is diverted to the senior-most outstanding bond classes for principal repayment until Class C coverage tests are met.

Steps 7 and 8 are repeated for all the remaining bond classes.

---

[17] Some outstanding CLOs carry monoline insurance, which is a form of credit enhancement.
[18] For a discussion of other coverage tests, see Antczak, Lucas, and Fabozzi, *Leveraged Finance: Concepts, Methods, and Trading of High-Yield Bonds, Loans and Derivatives.*

9. An additional coverage test that determines whether an amount of collateral interest must be reinvested in additional collateral during the reinvestment period.
10. Pay additional fees to the trustee.
11. Pay additional fees to the collateral manager.

At this point, if there is any collateral interest remaining it is distributed to the equity tranche in accordance with any profit sharing agreement with the collateral manager.

It should be clear from the above interest waterfall how the coverage tests force a decision to be made about whether to pay collateral interest to a bond class or pay down principal on the senior-most outstanding bond class and how this diversion of collateral interest can potentially greatly increase protection for the senior bond class.

Here is a typical basic *principal* waterfall for the distribution of collateral principal to the bond classes:

1. Collateral principal is diverted to the extent that there were any shortfalls in the amounts due in 1 through 8 of the interest waterfall.
2. During the reinvestment period, collateral principal is used by the collateral manager to purchase new loans.
3. After the reinvestment period, use collateral principal to repay principal of bond classes in order of their priority.
4. Pay amounts due in 9 through 11 of the interest waterfall.
5. With any remaining principal, pay the equity tranche.

CORPORATE DEFAULT RISK

As explained in Chapter 1, credit risk has three dimensions: default risk, credit spread risk, and downgrade risk. With our further understanding of bonds, we'll look at these risks more closely. In this section we focus on corporate default risk. Then the remaining two sections of this chapter describe the two other forms of corporate credit risk.

For a corporate debt obligation, default risk is the risk that the corporation issuing the debt instrument will fail to satisfy the terms of the obligation with respect to the timely payment of interest and repayment of the amount borrowed. In Chapter 20, we'll take a close look at the factors that go into the analysis of the creditworthiness of a corporate debt instrument. The gauge individual investors use is the credit ratings of the three major commercial rating companies: Moody's, Standard & Poor's, and Fitch. Although many institutional investors employ their own credit analysis using the framework described in Chapter 20, their benchmark or starting point is the credit rating assigned by one or more of the rating agencies.

There are different methods for computing historical default rates for corporate debt obligations. Here we report default rates as computed by Professor Edward Altman, the leading researcher in this area. Exhibit 7-4 provides summary information about average default rates for the years 1971 through 2009 for high-yield corporate bonds.

To assess the potential return from investing in corporate debt obligations, more than just default rates are needed. The reason is that default rates by themselves are not of paramount significance. It is perfectly possible for a portfolio of corporate debt obligations to suffer defaults and to outperform a portfolio of U.S. Treasuries at the same time, provided the yield spread of the portfolio is sufficiently high to offset the losses from default. Furthermore, holders of defaulted bonds typically recover a percentage of the face

---

Exhibit 7-4 Default Rates for High-Yield and Distressed Debt (Speculative Grade) Corporate Bonds: 1971–2009[a]

Arithmetic Average Weighted Average

Period	Default Rate (%)	Default Rate (%)[b]
1971–2009	3.33	4.55
1978–2009	3.64	4.56
1985–2009	4.32	4.60
1985–2009		
Fallen Angels	3.88	
Original-Issue Speculative Grade	4.90	

---

[a]Includes straight bonds only
[b]Weighted by par value of amount outstanding for each year
Source: *Statistics obtained from Figures 1 and 11 in Edward I. Altman and Brenda J. Karlin, "Defaults and Returns in the High-Yield and Distressed Debt Market: The Year 2009 in Review and Outlook," Special Report, New York University Salomon Center, Leonard N. Stern School of Business, April 8, 2010.*

amount of their investment: this is called the **recovery rate**. Therefore, an important measure in evaluating investments in corporate debt is the **default loss rate**, which is defined as follows:

$$\text{Default loss rate} = \text{Default rate} \times (100\% - \text{Recovery rate})$$

For instance, a default rate of 5% and a recovery rate of 30% produce a default loss rate of only 3.5% (5% × 70%). Therefore, focusing exclusively on default rates merely highlights the worst possible outcome that a diversified portfolio of corporate bonds would suffer, assuming all defaulted bonds would be totally worthless.

As with default rates, there are different methodologies that can be employed for computing recovery rates. Exhibit 7-5 shows the average dollar recovery per $100 of par value defaulted bonds from 1971 to 2009 by seniority (lien position) as reported by Professor

---

Exhibit 7-5 Average Dollar Recovery per $100 Par Value by Seniority and Original Rating, Corporate Bond Defaults: 1971–2009[*]

Seniority	Investment Grade ($)	Noninvestment Grade ($)	All ($)
Senior Secured	53.21	43.83	46.64
Senior Unsecured	43.69	36.18	39.95
Senior Subordinated	37.10	32.74	32.14
Subordinated	22.52	32.54	31.45

---

[*]Recovery based on mean price.
Source: *Data obtained from Figure 15 in Edward I. Altman and Brenda J. Karlin, "Defaults and Returns in the High-Yield and Distressed Debt Market: The Year 2009 in Review and Outlook," Special Report, New York University Salomon Center, Leonard N. Stern School of Business, April 8, 2010.*

Exhibit 7-6   Discounted Ultimate Recovery Rates by Debt Type

Type of Debt/Seniority	Average Recovery Rate (%)
Bank Loan	82
Senior Secured Debt	65
Senior Unsecured Debt	38
Senior Subordinated Debt	29
Subordinated Bond	27
Junior Subordinated Bond	15
All Bonds	37

Source: *Data obtained from Exhibit 4 in Kenneth Emery, Richard Cantor, David Keisman, and Sharon Ou, "Moody's Ultimate Recovery Database," Special Comment, Moody's Investors Service, April 2007.*

Altman. The recoveries are reported by original rating: investment grade and noninvestment grade (i.e., high yield). The recovery amount is measured in terms of post-default prices. As can be seen, for both credit rating categories, the better the seniority, the higher the recovery. For a given seniority, the recovery rate is greater for original-issue investment grade bonds than for noninvestment grade bonds with the exception of the subordinated bondholders.

Other information on historical recovery rates is provided by Moody's. Instead of using post-default prices, Moody's uses a metric it refers to as ultimate recoveries which is defined as the recovery values that creditors actually receive at the resolution to default, usually at the time of emergence from Chapter 11 bankruptcy proceedings.[19] Exhibit 7-6 reports the discounted ultimate recovery rates by debt type and seniority. As can be seen, the ultimate recovery rate for bank loans is the highest. In fact, the median recovery rate reported by Moody's was 100%.

In addition to the information in Exhibit 7-6, Moody's has determined discounted ultimate recovery rates by security class. Moody's defines three security classes based on the position of creditor in the issuer's capital structure: junior, mezzanine, and senior classes. The recovery rates for those security classes are 21% for junior classes, 58% for mezzanine classes, and 93% for senior classes.[20]

The rating agencies have services that provide other information related to defaults and recoveries that are useful to investors. For example, Moody's publishes for speculative grade bonds and loans an expected loss rating, loss-given-default assessments (LGDA), and, for corporate family ratings, probability-of-default ratings (PDRs).

Fitch and Standard & Poor's developed **recovery rating systems** for corporate bonds. The recovery ratings were introduced by Standard & Poor's in December 2003. The recovery ratings were for secured debt. The S&P recovery ratings use an ordinal scale of 1+ through 5. Each recovery rating category, shown in Exhibit 7-7, corresponds to a specific range of recovery values.

[19] Kenneth Emery, Richard Cantor, David Keisman, and Sharon Ou, "Moody's Ultimate Recovery Database," Special Comment, Moody's Investors Service, April 2007.
[20] As reported in Emery, Cantor, Keisman, and Ou, "Moody's Ultimate Recovery Database."

Exhibit 7-7   S&P Recovery Ratings for Secured Debt

Recovery Rate	Ultimate Recovery of Principal	Indicative Recovery Expectation
1+	Highest expectation of full recovery of principal	100% of principal
1	High expectation of full recovery of principal	100% of principal
2	Substantial recovery of principal	80%–100% of principal
3	Meaningful recovery of principal	50%–80% of principal
4	Marginal recovery of principal	25%–50% of principal
5	Negligible recovery of principal	0%–25% of principal

Exhibit 7-8   Fitch Rating Recovery Rating System

Recovery Rating	Recovery Prospect[a]	Recovery Band[b]
R1	Outstanding	91%–100%
R2	Superior	71%–90%
R3	Good	51%–70%
R4	Average	31%–50%
R5	Below average	11%–30%
R6	Poor recovery	0%–10%

[a] Recovery prospect given default.
[b] Recovery bands in terms of securities that have characteristics in line with securities historically recovering current principal and related interest.
Note: *This exhibit was prepared by the author based on the recovery rating system described in publications by Fitch Ratings.*

In July 2005, Fitch introduced a recovery rating system for corporate bonds rated single B and below. The factors considered in assigning a recovery rating to an issue by Fitch are (1) the collateral, (2) the seniority relative to other obligations in the capital structure, and (3) the expected value of the issuer in distress. The recovery rating system does not attempt to precisely predict a given level of recovery. Rather, the ratings are in the form of an ordinal scale and are referred to accordingly as a *Recovery Ratings Scale*. The Recovery Ratings Scale is given in Exhibit 7-8. Despite the recovery ratings being in relative terms, Fitch also provides recovery bands in terms of securities that have characteristics in line with securities historically recovering current principal and related interest. The recovery bands for each recovery rating are shown in the last column of Exhibit 7-8.

CORPORATE DOWNGRADE RISK

Rating agencies monitor the debt obligations and issuers that they have rated. Corporate downgrade risk is the risk that one or more of an issuer's debt obligations will be downgraded.

The rating agencies accumulate statistics on how ratings change over various periods of time. A table that specifies this information is called a **rating transition matrix** or **rating transition table**. Exhibit 7-9 shows a hypothetical one-year rating transition matrix. Here is how to interpret the table: The rows indicate the rating at the beginning of a year. The columns show the rating at the end of the year. For example, look at the second row. This row shows the transition for a rated bond at the beginning of a year. The number 91.40 in the second row means that on average 91.40% of Aa rated bonds at the beginning of the year remained Aa rated at year end. The value 1.50 means that on average 1.50% of Aa rated bonds at the beginning of the year were upgraded to Aaa. The value 0.50 means that on average 0.50% of Aa rated bonds at the beginning of the year were downgraded to a Baa rating. From Exhibit 7-9, it can be seen that the probability of a downgrade is much higher than an upgrade for investment-grade bonds. That attribute is actually observed in rating transition matrices reported by rating agencies.

CORPORATE CREDIT SPREAD RISK

Corporate credit spread risk is the risk that a debt obligation's price will decline due to an increase in the credit spread sought by the market either for the individual issue, the industry, or the sector. That is, it is the risk of credit spread widening.

There are two unique risks that can change corporate credit spreads: event risk and headline risk. The difference between these two risks is as follows. In the case of **event risk**, upon the announcement of some event there is an almost immediate credit rating downgrade for the adversely impacted corporation, sector, or industry. Hence, event risk is tied to downgrade risk. With **headline risk**, on the other hand, the announcement results in an adverse impact on the credit spread, as with event risk, but does not result in an immediate downgrade of debt.

An example of event risk is a corporate takeover or corporate restructuring. A specific example of event risk is the 1988 takeover of RJR Nabisco for $25 billion through a financing technique known as a **leveraged buyout** (LBO). The new company took on a substantial amount of debt incurred to finance the acquisition of the firm. In the case of

Exhibit 7-9	**Hypothetical One-Year Rating Transition Matrix**						
Rating at Start of Year	Rating at End of Year						
	Aaa	Aa	A	Baa	Ba	B	C or D	Total
Aaa	91.00	8.30	0.70	0.00	0.00	0.00	0.00	100.00
Aa	1.50	91.40	6.60	0.50	0.20	0.00	0.00	100.00
A	0.10	3.00	91.20	5.10	0.40	0.20	0.00	100.00
Baa	0.00	0.20	5.80	88.00	5.00	0.90	0.10	100.00

RJR Nabisco, the debt and equity after the leveraged buyout were $29.9 and $1.2 billion, respectively. Because the corporation must service a larger amount of debt, its bond quality rating was reduced; RJR Nabisco's quality rating as assigned by Moody's dropped from A1 to B3. The impact of the initial LBO bid announcement on the credit spreads for RJR Nabisco's debt was an increase from 100 basis points to 350 basis points.

Event risk can have spillover effects on other firms. Consider once again the RJR Nabisco LBO. An LBO of $25 billion was considered impractical prior to the RJR Nabisco LBO, but the RJR transaction showed that size was not an obstacle, and other large firms previously thought to be unlikely candidates for an LBO became fair game resulting in an increase in their credit spread.

An example of headline risk is a natural or industrial accident that would be expected to have an adverse economic impact on a corporation. For example, an accident at a nuclear power plant is likely to have an adverse impact on the credit spread of the debt of the corporation that owns the plant. Just as with event risk, there may be spillover effects.

KEY POINTS

- Corporate debt obligations require a corporation to pay periodic interest with full repayment of principal at maturity and include corporate bonds, medium-term notes, commercial paper, bank loans, convertible corporate bonds, and asset-backed securities.

- The sectors of the corporate debt market are public utilities, transportation, banks/finance, industrials, and Yankee and Canadian.

- The different creditor classes in a corporation's capital structure include senior secured creditors, senior unsecured creditors, senior subordinated creditors, and subordinated creditors.

- The bankruptcy law governs the bankruptcy process in the United States. Chapter 7 of the bankruptcy act deals with the liquidation of a company. Chapter 11 deals with the reorganization of a company. Creditors receive distributions based on the absolute priority rule to the extent assets are available. This means that senior creditors are paid in full before junior creditors are paid anything. Generally, this rule holds in the case of liquidations. In contrast, the absolute priority rule is typically violated in a reorganization.

- The credit risk of a corporate borrower can be gauged by the credit rating assigned by one or more of the three nationally recognized rating companies. Issues rated in the top four ratings of all raters are referred to as investment-grade bonds; those below the top four ratings are called noninvestment-grade bonds, high-yield bonds, or junk bonds.

- Provisions for paying off a bond issue prior to maturity include traditional call and refunding provisions, make-whole call provisions, and sinking fund provisions.

- The high-yield sector of the corporate bond market is the market for noninvestment-grade corporate bonds. Several complex bond structures are issued in the high-yield sector of the corporate bond market. These include deferred-coupon bonds (deferred-interest bonds, step-up bonds, and payment-in-kind bonds) and extendable reset bonds.

- There are five types of electronic corporate bond trading systems: auction systems, cross-matching systems, interdealer systems, multidealer systems, and single-dealer systems.

- Medium-term notes are corporate debt obligations offered on a continuous basis. They are registered with the SEC under the shelf registration rule and are offered through agents. The rates posted are for various maturity ranges, with maturities as short as nine months to as long as 30 years.

- Medium-term notes have been issued simultaneously with transactions in the derivatives market, particularly the swap market, to create structured MTNs. These products allow issuers greater flexibility in creating MTNs that are attractive to investors who seek to hedge or undertake a market play that they might otherwise be prohibited from doing. Structured notes include inverse floating-rate notes, equity-linked notes, commodity-linked notes, currency-linked notes, and credit-linked notes.

- Commercial paper is a short-term unsecured promissory note issued in the open market that represents the obligation of the issuing entity. It is sold on a discount basis. Generally, commercial paper maturity is less than 30 days. Financial and nonfinancial corporations issue commercial paper, with the majority issued by the former. Direct paper is sold by the issuing firm directly to investors without using a securities dealer as an intermediary; with dealer-placed commercial paper, the issuer uses the services of a securities firm to sell its paper. There is little liquidity in the commercial paper market.

- Bank loans represent an alternative to the issuance of bonds. Bank loans to corporations are classified as investment-grade loans and leveraged bank loans. It is the latter that are sold to institutional investors and traded in a secondary market.

- A collateralized loan obligation is created when leveraged bank loans are pooled and used as collateral for the issuance of debt claims with different seniority. The creation of this product uses securitization technology.

- The potential return from investing in a corporate debt is impacted by both the default rate and the recovery rate or default loss rate.

- In addition to providing credit ratings, the rating agencies have services that provide information related to defaults and recoveries that are useful to investors.

- To help gauge downgrade risk, investors can use the rating transition matrix reported by each rating agency.

- Corporate credit spread risk can be gauged by the historical volatility of spread changes. There are two unique risks that can change corporate credit spreads: event risk and headline risk.

QUESTIONS

1. What is the significance of a secured position if the absolute priority rule is typically not followed in a reorganization?

2. **a.** What is the difference between a liquidation and a reorganization?
   b. What is the difference between a Chapter 7 and a Chapter 11 bankruptcy filing?

3. What is a debtor in possession?

4. What is the principle of absolute priority?

5. Comment on the following statement: "A senior secured creditor has little risk of realizing a loss if the issuer goes into bankruptcy."

6. What is meant by an issue or issuer being placed on a credit watch?

7. Comment on the following statement: "An investor who purchases the mortgage bonds of a corporation knows that should the corporation become bankrupt, mortgage bondholders will be paid in full before the common stockholders receive any proceeds."

8. **a.** What is the difference between refunding protection and call protection?
   b. Which protection provides the investor with greater protection that the bonds will be acquired by the issuer prior to the stated maturity date?

9. **a.** What is a bullet bond?
   b. Can a bullet bond be redeemed prior to the stated maturity date?

10. **a.** What is meant by a make-whole call provision?
    b. What is the make-whole premium?
    c. How does a make-whole call provision differ from a traditional call provision?
    d. Why is a make-whole call provision probably a misnomer?

11. **a.** What is a sinking fund requirement in a bond issue?
    b. Comment on the following statement: "A sinking fund provision in a bond issue benefits the investor."

12. What is the difference between a fallen angel and an original-issue high-yield bond?

13. "A floating-rate note and an extendable reset bond both have coupon rates readjusted periodically. Therefore, they are basically the same instrument." Do you agree with this statement?

14. What is a payment-in-kind bond?

15. **a.** In what ways does an MTN differ from a corporate bond?
    b. What derivative instrument is commonly used in creating a structured MTN?

16. Indicate why you agree or disagree with the following statements:
    a. "Most MTN issues are rated noninvestment grade at the time of offering."
    b. "Typically, a corporate issuer with an MTN program will post rates for every maturity range."

17. What is meant by reverse inquiry?

18. Indicate why you agree or disagree with the following statements pertaining to the private-placement corporate debt market:
    a. "Since Rule 144A became effective, all privately placed issues can be bought and sold in the market."
    b. "Traditionally privately placed issues are now similar to publicly offered securities."

19. The supplemental prospectus of an actual offering by Royal Bank of Canada states the following:

Reference Asset:	SGI Smart Market Neutral Commodity Index (USD – Excess Return) (Bloomberg Ticker: SGICVMX). For a description of the Reference Asset, please see the section below, "The Reference Asset."
Specified Currency:	U.S. Dollars
Minimum Investment:	$1,000
Denomination:	$1,000
Pricing Date:	January 26, 2010
Issue Date:	January 29, 2010
CUSIP:	78008HTY6
Interest Payable:	None
Payment at Maturity (if held to maturity):	The Payment at Maturity will be calculated as follows:

1. If the Reference Asset Performance is **greater than** 0%, then you will receive an amount equal to:

    Principal Amount + [(Principal Amount × Reference Asset Performance)] × Participation Rate

2. If the Reference Asset Performance is **less than or equal to** 0%, then you will receive an amount equal the principal amount of your notes.

Reference Asset Performance:	The Reference Asset Performance, expressed as a percentage and rounded to four decimal places, will be calculated using the following formula:

$$\frac{\text{Final Level} - \text{Initial Level}}{\text{Initial Level}}$$

Participation Rate: 100%

Initial Level:　　109.0694

Term:　　　　　Approximately five (5) years

    a. What type of structured note is this?

    b. What are the risks associated with investing in this structured note?

20. **a.** Why is commercial paper an alternative to short-term bank borrowing for a corporation?

    b. What is the difference between directly placed paper and dealer-placed paper?

    c. What does the yield spread between commercial paper and Treasury bills of the same maturity reflect?

    d. Why does commercial paper have a maturity of less than 270 days?

    e. What is meant by tier-1 and tier-2 commercial paper?

21. **a.** Bank loans are classified as investment-grade and leveraged bank loans. Explain the difference between these two types of loans.

    b. Which of the two types of bank loans is typically sold and traded in the secondary market?

22. **a.** What is a syndicated bank loan?

    b. What is the reference rate typically used for a syndicated bank loan?

    c. What is the difference between an amortized bank loan and a bullet bank loan?

23. Explain the two ways in which a bank can sell its position in a syndicated loan.

24. In a collateralized loan obligation, how is protection afforded to the most senior bond class?

25. Why is a default rate not a good sole indicator of the potential performance of a portfolio of high-yield corporate bonds?

26. What is the difference between a credit rating and recovery rating?

27. What is a rating transition matrix?

28. What is the difference between event risk and headline risk?

8

Municipal Securities

LEARNING OBJECTIVES

After reading this chapter, you will understand

- the two basic security municipal structures: tax-backed debt and revenue bonds

- the flow of funds structure for revenue bonds

- municipal bonds with hybrid structures and special bond security structures such as refunded bonds and insured municipal bonds

- the different types of tax-exempt short-term municipal securities

- what a tender option bond is

- the tax risk that investors face when investing in municipal securities

- yield spreads within the municipal market

- the shape of the municipal yield curve

- the primary and secondary markets for municipal securities

- the taxable municipal bond market

Municipal securities are issued by state and local governments and by entities that they establish. All states issue municipal securities. Local governments include cities and counties. Political subdivisions of municipalities that issue securities include school districts and special districts for fire prevention, water, sewer, and other purposes. Public agencies or instrumentalities include authorities and commissions. The number of municipal bond issuers is remarkable. Bloomberg Financial Markets' database contains more than 50,000 active issuers. Even more noteworthy is the number of different issues. Bloomberg's database contains more than 1.5 million issues with complete description pages. In comparison, there are fewer than 1,000 Treasury issues and around 5,000 corporate bond issues.

Municipal securities are issued for various purposes. Short-term notes typically are sold in anticipation of the receipt of funds from taxes or proceeds from the sale of a bond issue, for example. The proceeds from the sale of short-term notes permit the issuing municipality to cover seasonal and temporary imbalances between outlays for expenditures and tax inflows. Municipalities issue long-term bonds as the principal means for financing both (1) long-term capital projects such as the construction of schools, bridges, roads, and airports; and (2) long-term budget deficits that arise from current operations.

The attractiveness of municipal securities is due to their tax treatment at the federal income tax level. While most municipal bonds outstanding are tax exempt, some issues are taxable at the federal level. The tax treatment of interest at the state and local level varies. The taxation of interest on municipal bonds by each state can be one of the following: (1) all interest is tax exempt regardless of whether the issuer is in-state or out-of-state, (2) all interest is taxable regardless of whether the issuer is in-state or out-of-state, or (3) interest is tax exempt if the issuer is in-state but taxable if the issuer is out-of-state.

Historically, the investors in municipal bonds have included mutual funds, bank trust departments, property and casualty insurance companies, and high net worth individuals. These investors are interested in the tax-exempt feature of municipal bonds. More recently, hedge funds, arbitrageurs, life insurance companies, and foreign banks have become important participants. These investors are not interested in the tax-exempt feature. Instead, their primary interest is in opportunities to benefit from leveraged strategies that seek to generate capital gains.

In this chapter, we discuss municipal securities.

TYPES AND FEATURES OF MUNICIPAL SECURITIES

There are basically two different types of municipal bond security structures: tax-backed bonds and revenue bonds. There are also securities that share characteristics of both tax-backed and revenue bonds.

Tax-Backed Debt

Tax-backed debt obligations are instruments issued by states, counties, special districts, cities, towns, and school districts that are secured by some form of tax revenue. Tax-backed debt includes general obligation debt, appropriation-backed obligations, and debt obligations supported by public credit enhancement programs. We discuss each here.

General Obligation Debt

The broadest type of tax-backed debt is **general obligation debt**. There are two types of general obligation pledges: unlimited and limited. An **unlimited tax general obligation debt** is the stronger form of general obligation pledge because it is secured by the issuer's unlimited taxing power. The tax revenue sources include corporate and individual income taxes, sales taxes, and property taxes. Unlimited tax general obligation debt is said to be secured by the full faith and credit of the issuer. A **limited tax general obligation debt** is a limited tax pledge because for such debt there is a statutory limit on tax rates that the issuer may levy to service the debt.

Certain general obligation bonds are secured not only by the issuer's general taxing powers to create revenues accumulated in a general fund, but also by certain identified fees, grants, and special charges, which provide additional revenues from outside the general fund. Such bonds are known as **double-barreled** in security because of the dual nature of the revenue sources. For example, the debt obligations issued by special-purpose service systems may be secured by a pledge of property taxes, a pledge of special fees/operating revenue from the service provided, or a pledge of both property taxes and special fees/operating revenues. In the last case, they are double-barreled.

Appropriation-Backed Obligations

Agencies or authorities of several states have issued bonds that carry a potential state liability for making up shortfalls in the issuing entity's obligation. The appropriation of funds from the state's general tax revenue must be approved by the state legislature. However, the state's pledge is not binding. Debt obligations with this nonbinding pledge of tax revenue are called **moral obligation bonds**. Because a moral obligation bond requires legislative approval to appropriate the funds, it is classified as an appropriation-backed obligation. The purpose of the moral obligation pledge is to enhance the creditworthiness of the issuing entity. However, the investor must rely on the best efforts of the state to approve the appropriation. Another type of appropriation-backed obligation is lease-backed debt.

Debt Obligations Supported by Public Credit Enhancement Programs

While a moral obligation is a form of credit enhancement provided by a state, it is not a legally enforceable or legally binding obligation of the state. There are entities that have issued debt that carries some form of public credit enhancement that is legally enforceable. This occurs when there is a guarantee by the state or a federal agency or when there is an obligation to automatically withhold and deploy state aid to pay any defaulted debt service by the issuing entity. Typically, the latter form of public credit enhancement is used for debt obligations of a state's school systems.

Some examples of state credit enhancement programs include Virginia's bond guarantee program that authorizes the governor to withhold state aid payments to a municipality and divert those funds to pay principal and interest to a municipality's general obligation holders in the event of a default. South Carolina's constitution requires mandatory withholding of state aid by the state treasurer if a school district is not capable of meeting its general obligation debt. Texas created the Permanent School Fund to guarantee the timely payment of principal and interest of the debt obligations of qualified school districts. The fund's income is obtained from land and mineral rights owned by the state of Texas.

Revenue Bonds

The second basic type of security structure is found in a revenue bond. Such bonds are issued for either project or enterprise financings in which the bond issuers pledge to the bondholders the revenues generated by the operating projects financed. A feasibility study is performed before the endeavor is undertaken to determine whether it can be self-supporting.

For a revenue bond, the revenue of the enterprise is pledged to service the debt of the issue. The details of how revenue received by the enterprise will be disbursed are set forth in the trust indenture. Typically, the flow of funds for a revenue bond is as follows. First, all revenues from the enterprise are put into a revenue fund. It is from the revenue fund that disbursements for expenses are made to the following funds: **operation and maintenance fund**, **sinking fund**, **debt service reserve fund**, **renewal and replacement fund**, **reserve maintenance fund**, and **surplus fund**.[1]

Operations of the enterprise have priority over the servicing of the issue's debt, and cash needed to operate the enterprise is deposited from the revenue fund into the operation and maintenance fund. The pledge of revenue to the bondholders is a net revenue pledge, net meaning after operation expenses, so cash required to service the debt is deposited next in the sinking fund. Disbursements are then made to bondholders as specified in the trust indenture. Any remaining cash is then distributed to the reserve funds. The purpose of the debt service reserve fund is to accumulate cash to cover any shortfall of future revenue to service the issue's debt. The specific amount that must be deposited is stated in the trust indenture. The function of the renewal and replacement fund is to accumulate cash for regularly scheduled major repairs and equipment replacement. The function of the reserve maintenance fund is to accumulate cash for extraordinary maintenance or replacement costs that might arise. Finally, if any cash remains after disbursement for operations, debt servicing, and reserves, it is deposited in the surplus fund. The issuer can use the cash in this fund in any way it deems appropriate.

There are various restrictive covenants included in the trust indenture for a revenue bond to protect the bondholders. A rate, or user charge, covenant dictates how charges will be set on the product or service sold by the enterprise. The covenant could specify that the minimum charges be set so as to satisfy both expenses and debt servicing, or to yield a higher rate to provide for a certain amount of reserves. An additional bond covenant indicates whether additional bonds with the same lien may be issued. If additional bonds with the same lien may be issued, conditions that must first be satisfied are specified. Other covenants specify that the facility may not be sold, the amount of insurance to be maintained, requirements for recordkeeping and for the auditing of the enterprise's financial statements by an independent accounting firm, and requirements for maintaining the facilities in good order.

Revenue bonds include

- airport revenue bonds
- higher education bonds
- hospital revenue bonds
- single-family mortgage revenue bonds
- multifamily revenue bonds
- public power bonds
- resource recovery bonds
- student loan revenue bonds
- toll road and gas tax revenue bonds
- water revenue bonds
- pollution control revenue bonds
- industrial development revenue bonds

---

[1] There are structures in which it is legally permissible for others to tap the revenues of the enterprise prior to the disbursement set forth in the flow of funds structure described next. For example, it is possible that the revenue bond could be structured such that the revenue is first applied to the general obligation of the municipality that has issued the bond.

Hybrid and Special Bond Securities

Some municipal bonds that have the basic characteristics of general obligation bonds and revenue bonds have more issue-specific structures as well. Some examples are insured bonds, bank-backed municipal bonds, refunded bonds, and asset-backed securities.

Insured Bonds

Insured bonds, in addition to being secured by the issuer's revenue, are also backed by insurance policies written by commercial insurance companies. Insurance on a municipal bond is an agreement by an insurance company to pay the bondholder any bond principal and/or coupon interest that is due on a stated maturity date but that has not been paid by the bond issuer. When issued, this municipal bond insurance usually extends for the term of the bond issue, and it cannot be canceled by the insurance company.

At one time, almost half of the newly issued municipal bonds were insured by a monoline insurer. Investors were comfortable with the insurance provided because prior to November 2007, no monoline insurer had defaulted or had its credit rating lowered (i.e., downgraded). That changed in late 2007 due to the participation of monoline insurers in the sub-prime mortgage business. Insuring these bonds, called sub-prime mortgage-backed securities, results in substantial losses for monoline insurers and resulted in a lowering of their credit rating. As a result, the municipal bonds that they insured were downgraded. Consequently, the role played by monoline insurers in the municipal bond market will not be the same in the future.

Letter-of-Credit–Backed Municipal Bonds

Municipal obligations have been increasingly supported by various types of credit facilities provided by commercial banks. The support is in addition to the issuer's cash flow revenues. There are three basic types of bank support: irrevocable line of credit, revolving line of credit, and letter of credit. An **irrevocable line of credit** is not a guarantee of the bond issue, although it does provide a level of security. A **revolving line of credit** is a liquidity-type credit facility that provides a source of liquidity for payment of maturing debt in the event that no other funds of the issuer are currently available. Because a bank can cancel a revolving line of credit without notice if the issuer fails to meet certain covenants, bond security depends entirely on the credit worthiness of the municipal issuer. A **letter-of-credit** (LOC) **agreement** is the strongest type of support available from a commercial bank, and we will discuss it in more detail here.

There are three parties to an LOC: (1) LOC provider, (2) municipal issuer, and (3) bond trustee. The LOC provider is the bank that issues the LOC and is required to advance funds to the trustee if one of any specified events occurs. The municipal issuer is the municipality that is requesting the LOC in connection with the offering of the bond. The municipal issuer agrees to two things: (1) to reimburse the LOC provider for any payments that the LOC provider had to make under the agreement, and (2) to make an LOC fee payment periodically to the LOC provider. The LOC is for a specified length of time and a specified amount such as the principal outstanding of the bond issue plus a certain number of days of accrued interest. The LOC fee is typically from 50 basis points to 200 basis points of the outstanding principal amount of the bond issue.

There are three types of LOC arrangements: (1) direct-pay LOC, (2) standby LOC, and (3) confirming LOC. A **direct-pay LOC** grants the trustee the right to request that the LOC provider provide principal and/or interest for the LOC-backed municipal bond if there is a specified event or default or an inability of the municipal issuer to meet a contractual interest payment or principal at the maturity date. The trustee can make this demand for funds on the LOC provider without requesting that the municipal issuer make the payment first. From a credit perspective, the direct-pay LOC provides the trustee and therefore the bondholders with the most comfort. This is because in contrast to a direct-pay LOC, the other two types of LOC arrangements (standby LOC and confirming LOC) require that the trustee must first request any contractual payment from the municipal issuer before drawing down on the LOC.

The distinction between a **standby LOC** and a **confirming LOC** (also called a **LOC wrap**) is that there are small community banks that are unrated by any of the rating agencies but nevertheless can issue an LOC. As a result, these small banks look to a correspondent bank that is a larger rated bank to confirm their LOC. If the correspondent bank fails to honor its LOC, the smaller bank must do so. That is, the LOC provider is the small bank but the underlying credit is the larger bank. In fact, a confirming LOC can also be provided so that an entity other than a bank can be an LOC provider.

Refunded Bonds

Although originally issued as either revenue or general obligation bonds, municipals are sometimes refunded. A refunding usually occurs when the original bonds are escrowed or collateralized by direct obligations guaranteed by the U.S. government. By this, it is meant that a portfolio of securities guaranteed by the U.S. government is placed in trust. The portfolio of securities is assembled such that the cash flow from all the securities matches the obligations that the issuer must pay. For example, suppose that a municipality has a 7% $100 million issue with 12 years remaining to maturity. The municipality's obligation is to make payments of $3.5 million every 6 months for the next 12 years and $100 million 12 years from now. If the issuer wants to refund this issue, a portfolio of U.S. government obligations can be purchased that has a cash flow of $3.5 million every 6 months for the next 12 years and $100 million 12 years from now.

When this portfolio of securities whose cash flow matches that of the municipality's obligation is in place, the refunded bonds are no longer secured as either general obligation or revenue bonds. The bonds are now supported by the portfolio of securities held in an escrow fund. Such bonds, if escrowed with securities guaranteed by the U.S. government, have little if any credit risk. They are the safest municipal bond investments available.

The escrow fund for a refunded municipal bond can be structured so that the refunded bonds are to be called at the first possible call date or a subsequent call date established in the original bond indenture. Such bonds are known as **prefunded municipal bonds**. Although refunded bonds are usually retired at their first or subsequent call date, some are structured to match the debt obligation to the retirement date. Such bonds are known as **escrowed-to-maturity** bonds.

There are three reasons why a municipal issuer may refund an issue by creating an escrow fund. First, many refunded issues were originally issued as revenue bonds. Included in revenue issues are restrictive-bond covenants. The municipality may wish to eliminate these restrictions. The creation of an escrow fund to pay the bondholders legally eliminates any restrictive-bond covenants. This is the motivation for the escrowed-to-maturity bonds. Second, some issues are refunded in order to alter the maturity schedule of the obligation.

Finally, when interest rates have declined after a municipal security has been issued, there is a tax arbitrage opportunity available to the issuer by paying existing bondholders a lower interest rate and using the proceeds to create a portfolio of U.S. government securities paying a higher interest rate.[2] This is the motivation for the prerefunded bonds.

Asset-Backed Bonds

In recent years, state and local governments began issuing bonds where the debt service is to be paid from so-called dedicated revenues such as sales taxes, tobacco settlement payments, fees, and penalty payments. These structures mimic the asset-backed bonds that are discussed in Chapter 15. Asset-backed bonds are also referred to as **dedication revenue bonds** and **structured bonds**.

These bonds have unique risks compared to other types of revenue bonds. One example is the bonds backed by tobacco settlement payments. In 1998, the four largest tobacco companies (Philip Morris, R. J. Reynolds, Brown & Williamson, and Lorillard) reached a settlement with 46 state attorneys general to pay over the following 25 years a total of $206 billion. States and municipalities began to issue bonds backed by the future payments of the tobacco companies, commonly referred to as **tobacco settlement bonds**. New York City was the first to do so in November 1999 with a bond offering of $709 million. The credit risk associated with these bonds is that they depend on the ability of the tobacco companies to make the payments.

The second example is the New Jersey Economic Development Authority series of cigarette tax revenue bonds issued in 2004. A concern that arose here after the bonds were issued was that the New Jersey 2007 state budget increased the cigarette tax but, at the same time, increased the amount of the cigarette tax revenue that had to be distributed into the State's health care subsidy fund. Hence, there was concern that there would not be a sufficient amount after the allocation to that fund to pay the bondholders.[3]

MUNICIPAL MONEY MARKET PRODUCTS

Tax-exempt money market products include notes and variable-rate demand obligations.

Municipal notes include tax anticipation notes (TANs), revenue anticipation notes (RANs), grant anticipation notes (GANs), and bond anticipation notes (BANs). These are temporary borrowings by states, local governments, and special jurisdictions. Usually, notes are issued for a period of 12 months, although it is not uncommon for notes to be issued for periods as short as three months and for as long as three years. TANs and RANs (also known as TRANs) are issued in anticipation of the collection of taxes or other expected revenues. These are borrowings to even out irregular flows into the treasuries of the issuing entity. BANs are issued in anticipation of the sale of long-term bonds.

---

[2] Because the interest rate that a municipality must pay on borrowed funds is less than the interest rate paid by the U.S. government, in the absence of any restrictions in the tax code, a municipal issuer can realize a tax arbitrage. This can be done by issuing a bond and immediately investing the proceeds in a U.S. government security. There are tax rules that prevent such arbitrage. Should a municipal issuer violate the tax-arbitrage rules, the Internal Revenue Service will rule the issue to be taxable. However, if subsequent to the issuance of a bond interest rates decline so that the issuer will find it advantageous to call the bond, the establishment of the escrow fund will not violate the tax-arbitrage rules.

[3] "New Jersey Economic Development Authority's Cigarette Tax Revenue Bonds Rating Placed On Negative CreditWatch," *BondsOnLine*, September 12, 2006.

Variable-rate demand obligations (VRDOs) are floating-rate obligations that have a nominal long-term maturity but have a coupon rate that is reset either daily or every seven days. The investor has an option to put the issue back to the trustee at any time with seven days' notice. The put price is par plus accrued interest.

FLOATERS/INVERSE FLOATERS

A common type of derivative security in the municipal bond market is one in which two classes of securities, a **floating-rate security** and an **inverse-floating-rate bond**, are created from a fixed-rate bond. The coupon rate on the floating-rate security is reset based on the results of a Dutch auction. The auction can take place anywhere between 7 and 35 days. The coupon rate on the floating-rate security changes in the same direction as market rates. The inverse-floating-rate bond receives the residual interest; that is, the coupon interest paid on this bond is the difference between the fixed rate on the underlying bond and the rate on the floating-rate security. Thus, the coupon rate on the inverse-floating-rate bond changes in the opposite direction of interest rates.

The sum of the interest paid on the floater and inverse floater (plus fees associated with the auction) must always equal the sum of the fixed-rate bond from which they were created. A floor (a minimum interest rate) is established on the inverse floater. Typically, the floor is zero. As a result, a cap (maximum interest rate) will be imposed on the floater such that the combined floor of zero on the inverse floater and the cap on the floater is equal to the total interest rate on the fixed-rate bond from which they were created.

Inverse floaters can be created in one of three ways. First, a municipal dealer can buy in the secondary market a fixed-rate municipal bond and place it in a trust. The trust then issues a floater and an inverse floater. The second method is similar to the first except that the municipal dealer uses a newly issued municipal bond to create a floater and an inverse floater as illustrated in Exhibit 8-1. The third method is to create an inverse floater without the need to create a floater. This is done using the municipal swaps market and is discussed in Chapter 29. The structure used to create the inverse floater is called a **tender option bond** structure.

The dealer determines the ratio of floaters to inverse floaters. For example, an investment banking firm may purchase $100 million of the underlying bond in the secondary market and issue $50 million of floaters and $50 million of inverse floaters. The dealer may opt for a 60/40 or any other split. The split of floaters/inverse floaters determines the leverage of the inverse floaters and thus affects its price volatility when interest rates change. In Chapter 4, we explained that the duration of an inverse floater is a multiple of

Exhibit 8-1   Creation of a Municipal Inverse Floater

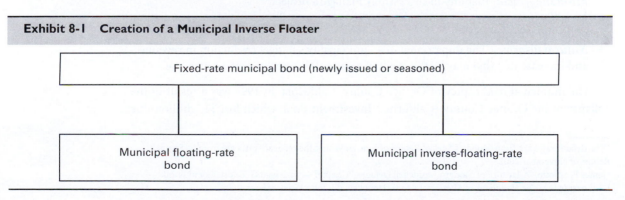

the underlying fixed-rate issue from which it was created. The multiple is determined by the leverage. To date, the most popular split of floaters and inverse floaters has been 50/50. In such instances, the inverse floater will have double the duration of the fixed-rate bond from which it is created. Determination of the leverage will be set based on the desires of investors at the time of the transaction.

The investor in the inverse floater can purchase the corresponding floater at auction and combine her two positions to effectively own the underlying fixed-rate bond. This can be done if interest rates are rising and the investor wishes to close out her inverse floater position. Because the market for inverse floaters is not highly liquid at this time, this represents an easy way to convert her position into a synthetic fixed-rate bond. In the future, the investor may opt to split the issue again, retaining the inverse floater. This is a valuable option for investors. As a result, the yield on this bond will generally be less than the yield on a comparable fixed-rate bond that does not have this option.

CREDIT RISK

Municipal bonds are viewed as having little default risk. The default record as reported by Moody's indicates that for the issues it rated between 1970 and 2006, there were only 41 defaults. This was not always the case. Between 1939 and 1969, 6,195 municipal defaults were recorded. Moreover, cumulative default rates and recovery rates for investment-grade municipal bonds are better than for comparably rated corporate bonds. For example, according to Moody's, over the period of 1970 to 2005, the 10-year cumulative default rate was 2.23% for corporate bonds compared to 0.06% for comparably rated municipal bonds. Moody's also reports that the average recovery rate was only 42% of par for corporate bonds that defaulted compared to 66% for defaulted municipal bonds.[4]

Spiotto provides a history of municipal bond defaults as well as the causes and nature of defaults.[5] These include:

- *Economic conditions:* Defaults caused by downturns in the economy and high interest rates.
- *Nonessential services:* Revenue bonds issued for services that were no longer needed.
- *Feasibility of projects and industries:* Revenue bonds are issued after a feasibility study for a project is completed. The feasibility study may have been too optimistic with respect to the demand for the project or the cost of completing the project.
- *Fraud:* Municipal officials fail to comply with the terms of the relevant documents.
- *Mismanagement:* Inability to successfully manage a project.
- *Unwillingness to pay:* A municipality may simply be unwilling to pay (i.e., repudiation of the debt obligation).
- *Natural disasters:* The impairment of a municipality's budget (reduction in revenue and increase in costs) may be the result of a natural disaster such as a hurricane.

The municipal bankruptcy of Orange County, California, in 1994 was a result of the collapse of the Orange County (California) Investment Pool, which lost $1.7 billion due

---

[4] The default rates are from Moody's Special Report of June 2006, and the recovery rates are from its Special Report of November 2002.
[5] James E. Spiotto, "A History of Modern Municipal Defaults," Chapter 44 in Sylvan G. Feldstein and Frank J. Fabozzi (eds.), *The Handbook of Municipal Bonds* (Hoboken, NJ: John Wiley & Sons, 2008).

to a poorly conceived investment strategy in mortgage-backed securities by the county treasurer. In terms of the list of causes for bankruptcy above, this was the result of both fraud and unwillingness to pay rather than raise county taxes. Another major default was the default of the Washington Public Power System (WPPS) bonds in the early 1980s. The problem with this bond, nicknamed "Whoops," was that the feasibility study severely over-estimated the demand for power. In addition, it involved a legally untested bond structure that did not firmly establish the rights of the bondholders and the obligations of the issuers. In fact, the rights of the bondholders were not upheld by the Washington Supreme Court.

As with corporate bonds, some institutional investors in the municipal bond market rely on their own in-house municipal credit analysts for determining the creditworthiness of a municipal issue; other investors rely on the nationally recognized rating companies. The two leading rating companies are Moody's and Standard & Poor's, and the assigned rating system is essentially the same as that used for corporate bonds.

In evaluating general obligation bonds, the commercial rating companies assess information in four basic categories. The first category includes information on the issuer's debt structure to determine the overall debt burden. The second category relates to the issuer's ability and political discipline to maintain sound budgetary policy. The focus of attention here usually is on the issuer's general operating funds and whether it has maintained at least balanced budgets over the prior three to five years. The third category involves determining the specific local taxes and intergovernmental revenues available to the issuer as well as ob-taining historical information both on tax collection rates, which are important when looking at property tax levies, and on the dependence of local budgets on specific revenue sources. The fourth and last category of information necessary to the credit analysis is an assessment of the issuer's overall socioeconomic environment. The determinations that have to be made here include trends of local employment distribution and composition, population growth, real estate property valuation, and personal income, among other economic factors.[6]

RISKS ASSOCIATED WITH INVESTING IN MUNICIPAL SECURITIES

The investor in municipal securities is exposed to the same risks affecting corporate bonds plus an additional one that may be labeled **tax risk**. There are two types of tax risk to which tax-exempt municipal securities buyers are exposed. The first is the risk that the federal income tax rate will be reduced. The higher the marginal tax rate, the greater the value of the tax exemption feature. As the marginal tax rate declines, the price of a tax-exempt municipal security will decline. When in 1995 there were Congressional proposals regard-ing the introduction of a flat tax with a low tax rate, tax-exempt municipal bonds began trading at lower prices.

The second type of tax risk is that a municipal bond issued as a tax-exempt issue may eventually be declared to be taxable by the Internal Revenue Service. This may occur because many municipal revenue bonds have elaborate security structures that could be subject to future adverse congressional action and IRS interpretation. A loss of the tax exemption feature will cause the municipal bond to decline in value in order to provide a yield comparable to similar taxable bonds. As an example, in June 1980, the Battery Park

---

[6] A comprehensive discussion of the analysis of various revenue bond structures is found in Feldstein and Fabozzi (eds.), *The Handbook of Municipal Bonds*.

City Authority sold $97.315 million in notes, which at the time of issuance legal counsel advised were exempt from federal income taxation. In November 1980, however, the IRS held that interest on these notes was not exempt. The issue was not settled until September 1981, when the Authority and the IRS signed a formal agreement resolving the matter so as to make the interest on the notes tax exempt.

YIELDS ON MUNICIPAL BONDS

As explained in Chapter 5, a common yield measure used to compare the yield on a tax-exempt municipal bond with a comparable taxable bond is the equivalent taxable yield. The equivalent taxable yield is computed as follows:

$$\text{equivalent taxable yield} = \frac{\text{tax-exempt yield}}{1 - \text{marginal tax rate}}$$

For example, suppose that an investor in the 40% marginal tax bracket is considering the acquisition of a tax-exempt municipal bond that offers a yield of 6.5%. The equivalent taxable yield is 10.83%, as follows:

$$\text{equivalent taxable yield} = \frac{0.065}{1 - 0.40} = 0.1083$$

When computing the equivalent taxable yield, the traditionally computed yield to maturity is not the tax-exempt yield if the issue is selling at a discount because only the coupon interest is exempt from federal income taxes. Instead, the yield to maturity after an assumed tax rate on the capital gain is computed and used in the numerator of the formula shown here. The yield to maturity after an assumed tax on the capital gain is calculated in the same manner as the traditional yield to maturity as explained in Chapter 3.

Yield Spreads

Because of the tax-exempt feature of municipal bonds, the yield on municipal bonds is less than that on Treasuries with the same maturity. The yield on municipal bonds is compared to the yield on Treasury bonds with the same maturity by computing the following ratio:

$$\text{yield ratio} = \frac{\text{yield on municipal bond}}{\text{yield on same maturity Treasury bond}}$$

The yield ratio varies over time. For example, according to Bloomberg, from April 28, 2001, to August 31, 2006, the yield ratio for AAA 20-year general obligation bonds ranged from 82.5% on May 31, 2005, to a high of 101% on June 30, 2003, with an average yield ratio of 90.6%. As can be seen, the yield ratio can sometimes exceed 1.

Yield spreads within the municipal bond market are attributable to differences between credit ratings (i.e., credit spreads), sectors within markets (intramarket spreads), and differences between maturities (maturity spreads).

Our statement in Chapter 5 about credit spreads between credit ratings for corporate bonds over the interest-rate cycle is true for municipal bonds: Credit spreads widen during recessionary periods but narrow during periods of economic prosperity. Another factor that can cause changes in the credit spread is a temporary oversupply of issues within a market sector. For example, a substantial new-issue volume of high-grade state general obligation bonds may tend to decrease the spread between high-grade and lower-grade revenue bonds. In a weak market environment, it is easier for high-grade municipal bonds to come to market than weaker ones. Therefore, it is not uncommon for high grades to flood weak markets at the same time there is a relative scarcity of medium- and lower-grade municipal bond issues.

In the municipal bond market, several benchmark curves exist. There are two services that, in the afternoon of each trading day, make available generic "scales" for different maturities and different credit ratings. A scale is simply a yield curve. One is provided by Thomson Municipal Market Data and is known in the industry as the **MMD scale**. The other is provided by Municipal Market Advisors (MMA). In the Treasury and corporate bond markets, it is not unusual to find at different times all three shapes for the yield curve described in Chapter 5. In general, the municipal yield curve is positively sloped.

Bonds of municipal issuers located in certain states yield considerably less than issues of identical credit quality that come from other states that trade in the general market. One reason for this is that states often exempt interest from in-state issues from state and local personal income taxes, whereas interest from out-of-state issues is generally not exempt. Consequently, in states with high income taxes, such as New York and California, strong investor demand for in-state issues will reduce their yields relative to bonds of issuers located in states where state and local income taxes are not important considerations (e.g., Florida).

MUNICIPAL BOND MARKET

Primary Market

A substantial number of municipal obligations are brought to market each week. A state or local government can market its new issue by offering bonds publicly to the investing community or by placing them privately with a small group of investors. When a public offering is selected, the issue usually is underwritten by investment bankers and/or municipal bond departments of commercial banks. Public offerings may be marketed by either competitive bidding or direct negotiations with underwriters. When an issue is marketed via competitive bidding, the issue is awarded to the bidder submitting the best bid.

Usually, state and local governments require a competitive sale to be announced in a recognized financial publication, such as the *Bond Buyer,* which is a trade publication for the municipal bond industry. The *Bond Buyer* also provides information on upcoming competitive sales and most negotiated sales, as well as the results of previous weeks.

The sale of bonds by issuers, both competitively and through negotiation, has also become more efficient and software based. Two companies that offer this service for competitive bond sales are I-Deal/Ipreo, which also provides a software platform for negotiated bond sales, and MuniAuction, which focuses on competitive sales.

An **official statement** describing the issue and the issuer is prepared for new offerings. Municipal bonds have legal opinions that are summarized in the official statement. The relationship of the legal opinion to the safety of the bond is twofold. First, bond counsel determines if the issuer is indeed legally able to issue the bonds. Second, bond counsel verifies that the issuer has prepared for the bond sale properly by having enacted various required ordinances, resolutions, and trust indentures and without violating any other laws and regulations.

Disclosure has become more immediate and accessible. The Securities and Exchange Commission as of mid-2007 has designated four information firms as Nationally Recognized Municipal Securities Information Repositories (NRMSIRs). Official statements from issuers and "material event notices" are available at the NRMSIRs. Although this is not the final solution to ongoing disclosure because the definition of what is "material" is still open to disagreement between bondholders and underwriters, it is a step in the right direction.

Secondary Market

Municipal bonds are traded in the over-the-counter market supported by municipal bond dealers across the country. Markets are maintained on smaller issuers (referred to as **local general credits**) by regional brokerage firms, local banks, and by some of the larger Wall Street firms. Larger issuers (referred to as **general names**) are supported by the larger brokerage firms and banks, many of whom have investment banking relationships with these issuers. There are brokers who serve as intermediaries in the sale of large blocks of municipal bonds among dealers and large institutional investors. Since 2000, bonds in the secondary market as well as some new competitive and negotiated issues began to be auctioned and sold over the Internet by large and small broker-dealers to institutional and individual investors.

In the municipal bond markets, an odd lot of bonds is $25,000 or less in par value for retail investors. For institutions, anything below $100,000 in par value is considered an odd lot. Dealer spreads depend on several factors: For the retail investor, the spread can range from as low as one-fourth of one point ($12.50 per $5,000 par value) on large blocks of actively traded bonds to four points ($200 per $5,000 of par value) for odd-lot sales of an inactive issue. For institutional investors, the dealer spread rarely exceeds one-half of one point ($25 per $5,000 of par value).

The convention for both corporate and Treasury bonds is to quote prices as a percentage of par value with 100 equal to par. Municipal bonds, however, generally are traded and quoted in terms of yield (yield to maturity or yield to call). The price of the bond in this case is called a **basis price**. The exception is certain long-maturity revenue bonds. A bond traded and quoted in dollar prices (actually, as a percentage of par value) is called a **dollar bond**.

A major concern in the secondary market was limited price transparency. In recent years the trading and pricing of municipal bonds have become much more transparent. Actual price and trade information for specific municipal bonds is available on a daily basis at no charge via the Internet at www.investinginbonds.com. It is the home page of the Securities Industry and Financial Markets Association (SIFMA). The trade information provided is from the Municipal Securities Rulemaking Board and Standard & Poor's J.J. Kenny. The original source of the trades reported are transactions between two dealers and a dealer with an institutional or retail customer (individual investor).

The pricing of municipals, marked to market at the end of the trading day, is now done daily. The two most widely used services are FT Interactive Data and J.J. Kenny (Standard & Poor's Securities Evaluations).[7]

There are municipal bond indexes for gauging portfolio performance and the market's performance. These indexes are primarily used by portfolio managers of regulated investment companies (mutual funds and closed-end funds) for performance evaluation purposes as well as the benchmark for exchange-traded funds.

The municipal bond indexes most commonly used by institutional investors are those produced by Barclays Capital (which it inherited from its acquisition of Lehman Brothers).

---

[7] For a description of the methodology and process used by FT Interactive Data, see Gerard Brennan, "Evaluation of Municipal Bonds," Chapter 27 in *The Handbook of Municipal Bonds*.

The broad-based index is the Barclays Capital National Municipal Bond Index. This index covers long-term tax-exempt bonds that are investment grade. Barclays also publishes a High-Yield Municipal Index and enhanced state-specific indexes.

Since 2005, an index has been published that identifies managed money tax-exempt bonds to serve the benchmark needs for investor groups whose permissible investments in the tax-exempt municipal bond market are not likely to be met by the Barclays Capital Municipal Bond Index. That is, while the Barclays Capital Municipal Bond Index provides a description of the market, it is not necessarily a good index for certain institutional investors. The purpose of the Barclays Capital Managed Money Municipal Index is to provide high net worth investors and small institutional investors with a more meaningful benchmark so that management performance can be assessed. There are subindexes of this index for individual states and maturity.

THE TAXABLE MUNICIPAL BOND MARKET

Taxable municipal bonds are bonds whose interest is taxed at the federal income tax level. Because there is no tax advantage, an issuer must offer a higher yield than for another tax-exempt municipal bond. The yield must be higher than the yield on U.S. government bonds because an investor faces credit risk by investing in a taxable municipal bond. The investors in taxable municipal bonds are investors who view them as alternatives to corporate bonds.

Despite the excellent performance of the municipal bond sector in terms of credit risk, in 2008 state and local governments and their agencies faced financial difficulties. To provide assistance to these municipal entities, the American Recovery and Investment Act of 2009 authorized the issuance of a new type of taxable municipal bond, *Build America Bonds* (dubbed BABs). A BAB is a taxable municipal bond wherein the issuer is subsidized for the higher cost of issuing a taxable bond rather than a tax-exempt bond in the form of a payment from the U.S. Department of the Treasury. Under this program, the payment made by the federal government to the issuer is equal to 35% of the interest payments. Issuance of BABs significantly increased the size of the taxable sector of the municipal bond market during its operations in 2009 and 2010. Although the program has been terminated, there is a considerable supply of BABs outstanding. There have been various proposals in Congress to reinstitute this program.

KEY POINTS

- Municipal securities are issued by state and local governments and their authorities. Tax-exempt and taxable municipal securities are available. "Tax exempt" means that interest on a municipal security is exempt from federal income taxation.
- The two basic types of municipal security structures are tax-backed debt and revenue bonds.
- Tax-backed debt obligations are instruments issued by states, counties, special districts, cities, towns, and school districts that are secured by some form of tax revenue. Tax-backed debt includes general obligation debt (the broadest type of tax-backed debt), appropriation-backed obligations, and debt obligations supported by public credit enhancement programs.
- A general obligation bond is said to be double-barreled when it is secured not only by the issuer's general taxing powers to create revenues accumulated in a general

fund but also by certain identified fees, grants, and special charges, which provide additional revenues from outside the general fund.

- Revenue bonds are issued for enterprise financings secured by the revenues generated by the completed projects themselves or for general public-purpose financings in which the issuers pledge to the bondholders the tax and revenue resources that were previously part of the general fund.

- Credit-enhanced municipal bonds include insured bonds and letter-of-credit–backed municipal bonds. Insured bonds, in addition to being secured by the issuer's revenue, are backed by an insurance policy written by commercial insurance companies; letter-of-credit–backed municipal bonds are supported by various types of credit facilities provided by commercial banks. Because of the difficulties faced by monoline insurers, the number of such insured municipal bonds issued today is minimal.

- Prerefunded bonds are no longer secured as either general obligation or revenue bonds when originally issued but are supported by a portfolio of securities held in an escrow fund. If escrowed with securities guaranteed by the U.S. government, refunded bonds are the safest municipal bonds available. A prerefunded municipal bond is one in which the escrow fund is structured so that the bonds are to be called at the first possible call date or a subsequent call date established in the original bond indenture.

- Municipal securities structured as asset-backed securities are backed by "dedicated" revenues such as sales taxes and tobacco settlement payments.

- Municipal notes and variable-rate demand obligations are tax-exempt money market products issued by municipalities.

- Investing in municipal securities exposes investors to credit risk and tax risk. Because of the low historical default rates for municipal bonds, until recently credit risk has been viewed as small. Rating agencies evaluate the credit risk associated with municipal securities just as they do for corporate bonds.

- A tax risk associated with investing in municipal bonds is that the highest marginal tax rate will be reduced, resulting in a decline in the value of municipal bonds. Another tax risk associated with investing in municipal bonds is that a tax-exempt issue may be eventually declared by the Internal Revenue Service to be taxable.

- Because of the tax-exempt feature, yields on municipal securities are lower than those on comparably rated taxable securities. Within the municipal bond market, there are credit spreads and maturity spreads. Typically, the municipal yield curve is upward sloping. Moreover, there are yield spreads related to differences between in-state issues and general market issues.

- While the municipal bond market is dominated by tax-exempt municipal bonds, there are taxable municipal bonds. Most recently, the issuance of Build America Bonds has dramatically increased the municipal taxable bond market. Bonds issued under this federal subsidized program have ceased because the program was terminated at the end of 2010.

QUESTIONS

1. Explain why you agree or disagree with the following statements:
   a. "All municipal bonds are exempt from federal income taxes."
   b. "All municipal bonds are exempt from state and local taxes."

2. If Congress changes the tax law so as to increase marginal tax rates, what will happen to the price of municipal bonds?

3. What is the difference between a tax-backed bond and a revenue bond?

4. Which type of municipal bond would an investor analyze using an approach similar to that for analyzing a corporate bond?

5. In a revenue bond, which fund has priority on funds disbursed from the reserve fund, the operation and maintenance fund, or the debt service reserve fund?

6. "An insured municipal bond is safer than an uninsured municipal bond." Indicate whether you agree or disagree with this statement.

7. Who are the parties to a letter-of-credit–backed municipal bond, and what are their responsibilities?

8. **a.** What are the three different types of letters of credit in a municipal bond, and how do they differ?
   b. Which type of letter-of-credit–backed bond provides the greatest protection for investors?

9. **a.** What is a prerefunded bond?
   b. Why does a properly structured prerefunded municipal bond have no credit risk?

10. Give two reasons why an issuing municipality would want to refund an outstanding bond issue.

11. The following statement appeared in a publication by the Idaho State Treasurer's Office:

   Each year since 1982 the Idaho State Treasurer has issued a State of Idaho Tax Anticipation Note 'TAN'. These notes are municipal securities that are one-year, interest-bearing debt obligations of the State of Idaho. The distinguishing characteristic of a municipal security is that the interest earned on them is exempt from federal income tax. Idaho municipal securities are further exempt from state income taxes. Idaho's TANs are issued in multiples of $5,000 which is the amount paid when the bond matures. Idaho TANs are issued with a fixed interest rate.

   Why is a TAN issued by a municipality?

12. What are the revenues supporting an asset-backed security issued by a municipality?

13. The four largest tobacco companies in the United States reached a settlement with 46 state attorneys general to pay a total of $206 billion over the following 25 years.
   a. States and municipalities, New York City being the first, sold bonds backed by the future

payments of the tobacco companies. What are these bonds called?
   b. What is the credit risk associated with these bonds?

14. **a.** Explain how an inverse-floating-rate municipal bond can be created.
   b. Who determines the leverage of an inverse floater?
   c. What is the duration of an inverse floater?

15. Historically, what have been the causes of municipal bankruptcies?

16. Credit default swaps, a derivative instrument described in Chapter 29, allow investors to buy and sell protection against the default of a municipal issuer. Why do you think it is difficult to find investors who are willing to buy protection against default of a municipal issuer but a large number of investors who are willing to sell such protection?

17. In a revenue bond, what is a catastrophe call provision?

18. What is the tax risk associated with investing in a municipal bond?

19. **a.** What is the equivalent taxable yield for an investor facing a 40% marginal tax rate, and who can purchase a tax-exempt municipal bond with a yield of 7.2?
   b. What are the limitations of using the equivalent taxable yield as a measure of relative value of a tax-exempt bond versus a taxable bond?

20. What can you say about the typical relationship between the yield on short- and long-term municipal bonds?

21. How does the steepness of the Treasury yield curve compare with that of the municipal yield curve?

22. Explain why the market for taxable municipal bonds competes for investors with the corporate bond market.

23. What is the yield ratio, and why is it typically less than 1?

24. **a.** What is a Build America Bond?
   b. What is the current status of the federal government program authorizing the issuance of such bonds?

9

International Bonds

LEARNING OBJECTIVES

After reading this chapter, you will understand

- the classification of global financial markets

- motivation for investing in nondollar-denominated bonds

- non-U.S. issuers of international bonds: sovereign governments, subsovereign governments, supranational agencies, financial institutions, and corporations

- the foreign exchange risk exposure of an investor who invests in nondollar-denominated bonds

- characteristics of bonds issued by non-U.S. entities: Yankee bonds, Regulation 144a private placements, Eurobonds, Euro medium-term notes, global bonds, non-U.S. domestic bonds, and emerging market bonds

- SEC Regulation S and its implications for investing in non-U.S. bonds

- the different types of Eurobond structures

- how to compare yields on U.S. bonds and Eurobonds

- non-U.S. government bond markets

- European covered bonds

- factors considered in the analysis of emerging market sovereign bonds

U.S. investors have become increasingly aware of non-U.S. interest-rate movements and their relationship to U.S. interest rates. In addition, foreign countries have liberalized their bond markets, making them more liquid and more accessible to international investors. In many cases, withholding taxes have been eliminated or reduced. Futures and options markets have been developed on government bonds in several major countries, permitting more effective implementation of hedging and arbitrage strategies. And in general, there is an increased awareness of international bond markets as potential sources of return enhancement and/or risk reduction. As a result, U.S. bond managers have increasingly adopted a global approach and invested in bonds from several countries.

Several reasons have been offered for why U.S. investors should allocate a portion of their fixed income portfolio to nondollar-denominated (i.e., nondollar) bonds. The party line is that diversifying bond investments across countries—particularly with the currency hedged—may provide diversification resulting in a reduction in risk. This is generally demonstrated using modern portfolio theory by showing that investors can realize a higher expected return for a given level of risk (as measured by the standard deviation of return) by adding nondollar bonds in a portfolio containing U.S. bonds. Although there was ample evidence in the 1980s and early 1990s that this might have been true, recent evidence suggests that the reduction in risk may not be that great.[1]

One study suggests that although the diversification benefits may not be that great, a powerful reason for a U.S. investor to invest in nondollar bonds is "the increased opportunities to find value that multiple markets provide," but it is hard to quantify such a benefit because it depends on the investor's talents.[2] That is, nondollar bonds—with the currency hedged—permit investment strategies based on interest rate changes in various countries, thereby providing additional dimensions to the actual investment decision or a broader range of investment choices. Another reason given for nondollar bond investing is that the decision not to hedge the currency component can then be regarded as an active currency play.

In this chapter, we limit our coverage to international bond markets from the perspective of U.S. investors.

CLASSIFICATION OF GLOBAL BOND MARKETS

There is no uniform system for classifying the sectors of the global bond market, although one possible classification is as follows. From the perspective of a given country, the global bond market can be classified into two markets: an internal bond market and an external bond market. The **internal bond market** is also called the **national bond market**. It can be decomposed into two parts: the domestic bond market and the foreign bond market. The **domestic bond market** is where issuers domiciled in the country issue bonds and where those bonds are subsequently traded.

The **foreign bond market** of a country is where bonds of issuers not domiciled in the country are issued and traded. For example, in the United States the foreign bond market is the market where bonds are issued by non-U.S. entities and then subsequently traded. Bonds traded in the U.S. foreign bond market are nicknamed **Yankee bonds**. In Japan, a yen-denominated bond issued by a British corporation and subsequently traded in Japan's bond market is part of the Japanese foreign bond market. Yen-denominated bonds issued by non-Japanese entities are nicknamed **Samurai bonds**. Foreign bonds in the United

[1] See Robert Litterman, "Nondollar Bond Markets: Opportunities for U.S. Portfolio Managers," *Fixed Income Research* (New York: Goldman, Sachs & Co., April 1992); and Michael R. Rosenberg, "International Fixed Income Investing: Theory and Practice," Chapter 49 in Frank J. Fabozzi (ed.), *The Handbook of Fixed Income Securities* (New York: McGraw-Hill, 2001).
[2] Litterman, "Nondollar Bond Markets," pp. 2–3.

Kingdom are referred to as **bulldog bonds**, in the Netherlands as **Rembrandt bonds**, and in Spain as **matador bonds**.

The **external bond market**, also called the **international bond market**, includes bonds with the following distinguishing features:

- They are underwritten by an international syndicate.
- At issuance they are offered simultaneously to investors in a number of countries.
- They are issued outside the jurisdiction of any single country.
- They are in unregistered form.

The external bond market is commonly referred to as the **offshore bond market**, or, more popularly, the **Eurobond market**. The classification used here is by no means universally accepted. Some market observers refer to the external bond market as consisting of the foreign bond market and the Eurobond market.

Another way to classify the world's bond market is in terms of trading blocs. The trading blocs used by practitioners for this classification are the dollar bloc, European bloc, Japan, and emerging markets.[3] The **dollar bloc** includes the United States, Canada, Australia, and New Zealand. The **European bloc** is subdivided into two groups: (1) the **euro zone market bloc** (Germany, France, Holland, Belgium, Luxembourg, Austria, Italy, Spain, Finland, Portugal, and Greece), which has a common currency, the euro; and (2) the **non–euro zone market bloc** (Norway, Denmark, and Sweden). The United Kingdom often trades more on its own, influenced by both the euro zone and the United States, as well as its own economic fundamentals.

The trading bloc construct is useful because each bloc has a benchmark market that greatly influences price movements in the other markets. Investors are often focused more on the spread level of, say, Denmark to Germany, than the absolute level of yields in Denmark.

NON-U.S. BOND ISSUERS AND BOND STRUCTURES

In this section, we describe the various non-U.S. issuers of international bonds, the type of bond structures, and the currencies in which international bonds are issued.

Non-U.S. Bond Issuers

Non-U.S. issuers of international bonds include

- Sovereign governments
- Subsovereign governments
- Supranational agencies
- Financial institutions
- Corporations

Sovereign bonds are issued by central governments. Bonds issued by government entities that are below that of central government are referred to as **subsovereign government bonds**. Such issuers include regions, provinces, states, and municipalities.

---

[3] See Christopher B. Steward, J. Hank Lynch, and Frank J. Fabozzi, "International Bond Portfolio Management," in Frank J. Fabozzi (ed.), *Fixed Income Readings for the Chartered Financial Analyst Program* (New Hope, PA: Frank J. Fabozzi Associates, 2004).

A **supranational agency** is an entity that is formed by two or more central governments through international treaties. The purpose for creating a supranational agency, also referred to as an **international organization**, is to promote economic development for the member countries. Two examples of supranational institutions are the International Bank for Reconstruction and Development, popularly referred to as the World Bank, and the InterAmerican Development Bank. The general objective of the former is to improve the efficiency of the international financial and trading markets. The objective of the latter supranational is to promote economic growth in the developing countries of the Americas. **Financial institutions** are primarily banks, and **corporations** are nonfinancial corporate entities.

Exhibit 9-1 provides information about the amount of outstanding international debt by the nationality of the issuer as of June 2010 as reported by the Bank for International Settlement (BIS). A breakdown is provided for developed countries, developing countries, and offshore centers. For comparison purposes the United States is also shown. (The information is also shown by the type of issuer: governments, financial institutions, and corporate issuers. Information about domestic bond markets is provided later in this chapter.)

Some definitions are in order. Organizations that collect data on international debt issuance use different definitions for categorizing the nationality of issuers. For example, the Organisation of Economic Co-operation and Development (OECD) defines developed and developing countries as follows in its glossary of statistical terms:

> There is no established convention for the designation of "developed" and "developing" countries or areas in the United Nations system. In common practice, Japan in Asia, Canada and the United States in northern America, Australia and New Zealand in Oceania and Europe are considered "developed" regions or areas. In international trade statistics, the Southern African Customs Union is also treated as a developed region and Israel as a developed country; countries emerging from the former Yugoslavia are treated as developing countries; and countries of Eastern Europe and the former USSR countries in Europe are not included under either developed or developing regions.

Exhibit 9-1	International Debt Securities Outstanding by Nationality of Issuer as of June 2010 (in billions of U.S. dollars)			
	All Issuers	**Governments**	**Financial Institutions**	**Corporate Issuers**
All countries	25,574.30	2,196.30	19,435.50	3,119.70
Developed countries	23,130.80	1,634.70	18,692.30	2,803.80
Developing countries	1,367.30	523.70	569.2	274.4
Offshore centers	253.40	37.90	174.00	41.5
United States	6,760.10	10.70	5,390.40	1,359.00

Source: *The data for this exhibit were obtained from Tables 12A, 12B, 12C, and 12D in BIS Quarterly Review, December 2010.*

For the data in Exhibit 9-1 as reported by the BIS, developed countries include Austria, Belgium, Canada, Cyprus, Denmark, Finland, France, Germany, Greece, Iceland, Ireland, Italy, Japan, Luxembourg, Netherlands, New Zealand, Norway, Portugal, Slovakia, Spain, Sweden, Switzerland, the United Kingdom, and the United States.

An **offshore financial center** or **offshore center** is defined by the OECD as

> Countries or jurisdictions with financial centres that contain financial institutions that deal primarily with nonresidents and/or in foreign currency on a scale out of proportion to the size of the host economy. Nonresident-owned or -controlled institutions play a significant role within the centre. The institutions in the centre may well gain from tax benefits not available to those outside the centre.

For the data in Exhibit 9-1 as reported by the BIS, offshore centers include Aruba, Bahamas, Bermuda, Cayman Islands, Hong Kong SAR, Lebanon, Netherlands Antilles, Panama, Singapore, and West Indies UK.

Bond Structures

In previous chapters, we described the various types of bond structures. We find all of these structures in international bonds. Exhibit 9-2 identifies the amount outstanding as of June 2010 of the different types of bond structures (floating rate, straight fixed rate, and equity related), as well as the currencies of the outstanding issues of international bonds and notes. Also shown is the issuance by type of issuer (financial institutions, governments, corporations, and international organizations).

As can be seen from the exhibit, the vast majority of international bonds are straight fixed-rate bonds. The floating-rate bond security is roughly 30% of total issuance, most of which issued by financial institutions. The largest currency denomination is in euros, followed closely by U.S. dollars. The U.K. pound sterling is a distant third.

▌FOREIGN EXCHANGE RISK AND BOND RETURNS

The key factor that impacts the price and the yield of a bond is the currency denomination. From the perspective of a U.S. investor, this means that the price and yield of a U.S. dollar–denominated bond issued by a non-U.S. entity will be principally affected by U.S. interest rates. Consequently, managing a portfolio that contains bonds issued by U.S. entities and dollar-denominated bonds issued by non-U.S. entities requires no special treatment. The addition of non-U.S. issuing entities merely requires credit analysis of the foreign issuer.

In contrast, when a portfolio includes nondollar-denominated issues by non-U.S. entities, there are two additional factors to consider beyond the analysis of the issuer's credit. The first is the movement of interest rates of all the countries where there is currency exposure. The second is the foreign exchange rate movement of all the currencies to which the portfolio has exposure. A **foreign exchange rate** is the amount of one currency that can be exchanged for another currency or the price of one currency in terms of another currency. Thus, each day a currency's value may stay the same, increase, or decrease relative to that of another currency. When a currency declines in value relative to another currency, it is said to have **depreciated** relative to the other currency. Alternatively, this is the same as saying that the other currency has **appreciated**.

Exhibit 9-2 International Bonds and Notes Outstanding by Type, Sector, and Currency as of June 2010 (in billions of U.S. dollars)

Total Issues	24,697.10
Floating Rate	7,482.50
US dollar	2,231.00
Euro	3,936.70
Yen	176.20
Pound sterling	896.50
Swiss franc	18.80
Canadian dollar	29.70
Other currencies	193.60
Financial institutions	7,148.40
Governments	116.00
International organizations	55.80
Corporate issuers	162.2
Straight Fixed Rate	16,772.30
US dollar	7,422.90
Euro	6,690.80
Yen	466.70
Pound sterling	1,097.40
Swiss franc	321.70
Canadian dollar	279.10
Other currencies	493.50
Financial institutions	11,279.40
Governments	2,048.00
International organizations	757.20
Corporate issuers	2,687.70
Equity-Related	442.40
US dollar	221.10
Euro	100.20
Yen	48.20

(*Continued*)

Exhibit 9-2 **International Bonds and Notes Outstanding by Type, Sector, and Currency as of June 2010 (in billions of U.S. dollars) (Continued)**

Pound sterling	8.80
Swiss franc	7.20
Canadian dollar	9.20
Other currencies	47.80
Financial institutions	205.10
Governments	1.00
International organizations	-----
Corporate issuers	236.30
Convertibles	439.30
Warrants	3.10

Currency of Issue

Argentine peso	0.60
Australian dollar	266.30
Baht	3.80
Canadian dollar	318.00
Czech koruna	14.30
Danish krone	4.00
Euro	10,727.70
Hong Kong dollar	60.20
New Taiwan dollar	1.50
New Zealand dollar	36.20
Norwegian krone	55.00
Pound sterling	2,002.70
Rand	34.70
Russian rouble	12.40
Singapore dollar	29.10
Swedish krona	66.80
Swiss franc	347.70
US dollar	9,875.00
Yen	691.10
Zloty	10.20

Source: *The data for this exhibit were obtained from Table 13B in* BIS Quarterly Review, *December 2010.*

From the perspective of a U.S. investor, the cash flows of nondenominated bonds expose the investor to uncertainty as to the cash flow in U.S. dollars. The actual U.S. dollars that the investor receives depend on the foreign exchange rate between the U.S. dollar and the foreign currency at the time the nondollar cash flow is received and exchanged for U.S. dollars. If the foreign currency depreciates (i.e., declines in value) relative to the U.S. dollar, the dollar value of the cash flows will be proportionately less. This risk is referred to as **foreign exchange risk** or **currency risk**. This risk can be hedged with foreign exchange spot, forwards, futures, swaps or options instruments (although there is a cost of hedging).

The return on a portfolio that includes nondollar-denominated bonds consists of three components: (1) income, (2) capital gain/loss in the local currency, and (3) foreign currency gain/loss. To see the importance of the three components, Exhibit 9-3 shows the annual return for each of the three return components for Citigroup World Government Bond Indices for the years 2000 to 2010.[4] Notice the significant contribution of the foreign currency capital gain/loss to the average annual return for the entire 11-year period: 2.8% of the 6.8% total return. Also notice the considerable volatility in the annual return caused by the foreign exchange capital gain/loss component.

Exhibit 9-3	**Annual Returns for the Three Components of the Citigroup World Government Bond Indices: 2000 to 2010**			
Year	Income (%)	Capital Gain/Loss in Local Currency (%)	Foreign Currency Gain/Loss (%)	Annual Return (%)
2000	4.7	0.9	−7.8	−2.2
2001	4.4	0.4	−8.0	−3.2
2002	4.1	2.8	14.0	20.9
2003	3.7	−1.5	16.0	18.2
2004	3.6	1.6	6.6	11.8
2005	3.3	0.6	−12.6	−8.7
2006	3.3	−3.1	6.8	7.0
2007	3.4	−1.0	8.8	11.2
2008	3.4	4.1	2.3	9.8
2009	3.1	−0.7	2.0	4.4
2010	2.9	−0.4	2.7	5.2
2000–2010	3.6	0.3	2.8	6.8

---

[4] The data were provided by Karthik Ramanathan of Fidelity Management and Research Company/Pyramis Global Advisors.

BONDS ISSUED BY NON-U.S. ENTITIES

Bonds issued by non-U.S. entities include

- Yankee bonds
- Regulation 144a private placements
- Eurobonds
- Euro medium-term notes
- Global bonds
- Non-U.S. domestic bonds
- Emerging market bonds

Below we describe each.

Yankee Bonds

Yankee bonds are bonds issued by non-U.S. entities that are registered with the U.S. Securities and Exchange Commission (SEC) and traded in the United States. Issuers in the Yankee bond market are sovereign governments, subsovereign entities, supranational agencies, financial institutions, and corporations.

Historically, more than half of the issuance in the Yankee bond market has been by supranational agencies, Canadian provinces (including provincial utilities), and financial institutions. In the first month of 2011, both the European Investment Bank (a supranational agency) and Germany's KIW issued $5 billion of Yankee bonds. In just the first two weeks of 2011, there were 54 Yankee bonds issued by European banks totaling $36 billion, an amount that exceeded the entire 2010 issuance by European banks.[5] European corporations in recent years have been major issuers of Yankee bonds. For example, in the first eight months of 2010, about 20% of bond issuance by European corporations was in the form of Yankee bonds.[6] Yankee bonds issued by European corporations accounted for about 43% of corporate bonds issued in the United States in 2010 and 37% in 2009.[7]

Regulation 144a Private Placements

As explained in Chapter 7, because they are issued in transactions that do not involve a public offering, the private placement of a bond is exempt from SEC registration. SEC Rule 144A allows the trading of privately placed securities among qualified institutional buyers. Because of the reduced reporting requirements, 144a bond issuance has become an important market for non-U.S. borrowers to raise funds. Although U.S. corporations are the major issuers, European and Australian companies have increasingly raised funds by the sale of 144a bonds. There are no restrictions on the currency denomination; however, the bulk of the outstanding 144a bonds are dollar denominated.

---

[5] Helen Avery, "Yankee Bonds: European Banks Turn to Eager US Investors," *Euromoney*, February 2011, http://www.euromoney.com/Article/2759845/ChannelPage/8959/AssetCategory/14/Yankee-bonds-European-banks-turn-to-eager-US-investors.html.

[6] Richard Milne and Anousha Sakoui, "Europe Leads Way for Yankee Bond Sales," FT.com Financial Times, August 10, 2010, http://www.ft.com/cms/s/0/f781862a-ae0f-11df-bb55-00144feabdc0.html#axzz1FmsYjc4T.

[7] Sapna Maheshwari, "Yankees Scoop Biggest Market Share in 10 Years: Credit Markets," Bloomberg, October 4, 2010, http://www.bloomberg.com/news/2010-10-03/yankees-scoop-biggest-market-share-in-10-years-credit-markets.html.

Eurobonds

The Eurobond market is divided into sectors depending on the currency in which the issue is denominated. For example, when Eurobonds are denominated in U.S. dollars, they are referred to as **Eurodollar bonds**. The Eurodollar bond market is the largest sector within the Eurobond market.

It has become increasingly difficult to classify a bond issue as a foreign bond or a Eurobond based on the distinguishing characteristics that we cited earlier. We noted that the most important characteristic of a Eurobond offering is the composition of the underwriting syndicate. Yet "bought deals"—when there is only one underwriter—are becoming increasingly common. A bond offering in which there is only one underwriter and in which the issue is placed primarily outside the national market of both the issuer and underwriter would not traditionally be classified as a Eurobond offering. Another characteristic of a Eurobond is that it is not regulated by the single country whose currency is used to pay bondholders. In practice, however, only the United States and Canada do not place restrictions on U.S. dollar—or Canadian dollar—denominated issues sold outside their two countries. Regulators of other countries whose currencies are used in Eurobond issues have closely supervised such offerings. Their power to regulate Eurobond offerings comes, from their ability to impose foreign exchange and/or capital restrictions.

Although Eurobonds are typically registered on a national stock exchange (the most common being the Luxembourg, London, or Zurich exchanges), the bulk of all trading is in the over-the-counter market. Listing is purely to circumvent restrictions imposed on some institutional investors who are prohibited from purchasing securities that are not listed on an exchange. Some of the stronger issuers privately place issues with international institutional investors.

With respect to the purchase of Eurodollar bonds by U.S. investors, there are selling restrictions under U.S. securities law for offerings outside of the United States. SEC Regulation S issued in April 1990 sets forth guidelines under which offerings of securities can be made outside the United States without registration under the Securities Act of 1933. There are two fundamental requirements. First, the transaction must be an offshore transaction. Second, there can be no directed selling efforts associated with the offering made in the United States. The requirements beyond these two depend on the status of the issuer under Regulation S. There are three categories of issuers. A Category 1 issuer is a non-U.S., nongovernmental issuer in respect to their debt for purposes of Regulation S if the issuer reasonably believes that there is no substantial U.S. market interest for its debt securities or it has otherwise registered securities with the SEC. For Category 1 issuers, there are no restrictions other than the two mentioned above. Issuers classified as Category 2 have offering restrictions. More specifically, Regulation S requires a restricted period of 40 days (a "seasoning period") before the securities can be sold in the United States. Debt securities of a nonreporting U.S. issuer fall into Category 3 and there are further restrictions beyond those imposed on issuers that fall into Category 2. As a consequence of Regulation S, the new issue market is dominated by European investors since U.S. investors typically do not participate in the new issue market. Instead, U.S. investors can participate in the secondary market only after the seasoning period expires.

The major buyers of Eurodollar bonds are investors who plan to hold the issue in their portfolio. As a result, although the issue size of Eurodollar bond offerings is large, they tend to have less liquidity than Yankee bonds.

Corporate Bonds and Covenants

In Chapter 20, covenants for U.S. corporate bonds will be discussed. In the Eurobond market, there is a debate regarding the relatively weak protection afforded by covenants. The chief reason for this is that investors in corporate Eurobonds are geographically diverse. As a result, it is difficult for potential bond investors to agree on what form of covenants offer true protection.

For investment-grade corporate issues in the Eurobond market, documentation is somewhat standardized. According to David Munves, the key terms and conditions in Eurobond documentation are

- *Governing law:* Most transactions are governed by U.K. law, although New York state law is an occasional alternative.
- *Security:* As a rule, issues are not secured by the company's assets.
- *Negative pledges:* Negative pledges are common. They prohibit an issuer from creating security interests on its assets unless all bondholders receive the same level of security.
- *Subordination:* Except for bank or insurance capital issues, most bonds are sold on a senior basis.
- *Cross-default clauses:* Cross-default clauses state that if an issuer defaults on other borrowings, then the bonds will become due and payable. The definition of which borrowings are covered can vary. The cross-default clause usually carves out defaults in borrowings up to a certain threshold (e.g., $10,000) to prevent a minor trade dispute or overlooked invoice from allowing the bondholders to put the bonds back to the issuer.
- *Prohibition on the sale of material assets:* In order to protect bondholders, most documentation prohibits the sale or transfer of material assets or subsidiaries. As with cross-default clauses, the definition of material can vary considerably.[8]

Securities Issued in the Eurobond Market

The Eurobond market has been characterized by new and innovative bond structures to accommodate particular needs of issuers and investors. There are, of course, the "plain vanilla," fixed-rate coupon bonds, referred to as **Euro straights**. Because these are issued on an unsecured basis, they are usually issued by high-quality entities.

Coupon payments are made annually, rather than semiannually, because of the higher cost of distributing interest to geographically dispersed bondholders. There are also zero-coupon bond issues and deferred-coupon issues, both of which were described in earlier chapters.

Floating-rate notes. There are a wide variety of floating-rate Eurobond notes. The coupon rate on a floating-rate note is some stated margin over the London interbank offered rate (LIBOR), the bid on LIBOR (referred to as LIBID), or the arithmetic average of LIBOR and LIBID (referred to as LIMEAN). The size of the spread reflects the perceived credit risk of the issuer, margins available in the syndicated loan market, and the liquidity of the issue. Typical reset periods for the coupon rate are either every six months or every quarter, with the rate tied to six-month or three-month LIBOR, respectively; that is, the

---

[8] David Munves, "The Eurobond Market," Chapter 6, in Frank J. Fabozzi and Moorad Choudhry (eds.), *The Handbook of European Fixed Income Securities* (Hoboken, NJ: John Wiley & Sons, 2003).

length of the reset period and the maturity of the index used to establish the rate for the period are matched.

Many issues have either a minimum coupon rate (or floor) that the coupon rate cannot fall below and a maximum coupon rate (or cap) that the coupon rate cannot rise above. An issue that has both a floor and a cap is said to be **collared**. There are some issues that grant the borrower the right to convert the floating coupon rate into a fixed coupon rate at some time. There are some issues referred to as **drop-lock bonds**, which automatically change the floating coupon rate into a fixed coupon rate under certain circumstances.

A floating-rate note issue will either have a stated maturity date or it may be a **perpetual** (also called **undated**) **issue** (i.e., with no stated maturity date). For floating-rate notes that do mature, the term is usually greater than five years, with the typical maturity being between seven and 12 years. There are callable and putable floating-rate notes; some issues are both callable and putable.

Dual-currency bonds. There are issues that pay coupon interest in one currency but pay the principal in a different currency. Such issues are called **dual-currency issues**. For the first type of dual-currency bond, the exchange rate that is used to convert the principal and coupon payments into a specific currency is specified at the time the bond is issued. The second type differs from the first in that the applicable exchange rate is the rate that prevails at the time a cash flow is made (i.e., at the spot exchange rate at the time a payment is made). The third type is one that offers to either the investor or the issuer the choice of currency. These bonds are commonly referred to as **option currency bonds**.

Convertible Bonds and Bonds with Warrants

A convertible Eurobond is one that can be converted into another asset. Bonds with attached warrants represent a large part of the Eurobond market. A warrant grants the owner of the warrant the right to enter into another financial transaction with the issuer if the owner will benefit as a result of exercising. Most warrants are detachable from the host bond; that is, the bondholder may detach the warrant from the bond and sell it.

There is a wide array of bonds with warrants: equity warrants, debt warrants, and currency warrants. An **equity warrant** permits the warrant owner to buy the common stock of the issuer at a specified price. A **debt warrant** entitles the warrant owner to buy additional bonds from the issuer at the same price and yield as the host bond. The debt warrant owner will benefit if interest rates decline because a bond with a higher coupon can be purchased from the same issuer. A **currency warrant** permits the warrant owner to exchange one currency for another at a set price (i.e., a fixed exchange rate). This feature protects the bondholder against a depreciation of the foreign currency in which the bond's cash flows are denominated.

Coupon step-up and step-down bonds. In Chapter 1, we described how the coupon rate can step up over time due to either the passage of time or a change in the reference interest rate. A unique structure in the Eurobond market, particularly for large issues of telecom bonds, has been coupon step-up and step-down provisions where the change in the coupon is triggered by a change in the issuer's credit rating. A rating upgrade would result in a lower coupon rate while a rating downgrade would result in a higher coupon rate.

Comparing Yields on U.S. Bonds and Eurodollar Bonds

Because Eurodollar bonds pay annually rather than semiannually, an adjustment is required to make a direct comparison between the yield to maturity on a U.S. fixed-rate bond and that on a Eurodollar fixed-rate bond. Given the yield to maturity on a Eurodollar fixed-rate bond, its bond-equivalent yield is computed as follows:

$$\text{bond-equivalent yield of Eurodollar bond}$$
$$= 2[(1 + \text{yield to maturity on Eurodollar bond})^{1/2} - 1]$$

For example, suppose that the yield to maturity on a Eurodollar bond is 6%. Then the bond-equivalent yield is

$$2[(1.06)^{1/2} - 1] = 0.0591 = 5.91\%$$

Notice that the bond-equivalent yield will always be less than the Eurodollar bond's yield to maturity.

To convert the bond-equivalent yield of a U.S. bond issue to an annual-pay basis so that it can be compared to the yield to maturity of a Eurodollar bond, the following formula can be used:

$$\text{yield to maturity on annual-pay basis}$$
$$= (1 + \text{yield to maturity on bond-equivalent basis}/2)^2 - 1$$

For example, suppose that the yield to maturity of a U.S. bond issue quoted on a bond-equivalent yield basis is 5.5%. The yield to maturity on an annual-pay basis would be

$$[(1.0275)^2 - 1] = 0.0558 = 5.58\%$$

The yield to maturity on an annual basis is always greater than the yield to maturity on a bond-equivalent basis.

Euro Medium-Term Notes

In Chapter 8, we discussed a medium-term note (MTN). In the United States, SEC Rule 415 allows entities to develop a MTN program. **Euro medium-term notes** (EMTN) are debt obligations that are intended primarily for offerings outside of the United States. Typically, EMTNs are intended for European investors. Their denomination can be any currency.

The principal European legislation dealing with EMTN programs is the Prospectus Directive 2003/71/EC (or simply PD) and amendments set forth by the European Union Parliament in mid-2010. For U.S. investors seeking to invest in EMTNs, the sale of these debt obligations must comply with the exemption from registration provided by Regulation S under the U.S. Securities Act of 1933. In addition, some EMTN programs qualify for Rule 144A treatment so that the securities can be sold to qualified institutional investors. As with U.S. MTNs, EMTNs can be coupled with derivatives in order to create the various types of structured products described in Chapter 7.

Global Bonds

A **global bond** is one that is issued simultaneously in several bond markets throughout the world and can be issued in any currency. The three characteristics of a global bond are as follows

1. At issuance, they are sold simultaneously in multiple bond markets throughout the world at the same offering price.
2. They are traded in multiple bond markets throughout the world without restrictions with settlement that is similar to a trade of domestic bonds.
3. The issuance size is large, allowing for multiple tranches by maturity.

A **tranche** means one of several related securities issued simultaneously. Many of the recent issues of global bonds have two tranches that differ by maturity date and coupon rate.

Here are three examples of global bonds, the first two being dollar denominated and the second nondollar denominated.

In 2009, the Republic of Indonesia issued its largest-ever bond offering of US$3 billion in two tranches: a 5-year (US$1 billion) tranche and a 10-year (US$2 billion) tranche. According to the press release, 55% of the 5-year tranche was placed with investors in Asia, 18% in Europe, and 27% in the United States. Half of the 10-year tranche was placed with investors in the United States, 30% in Asia, and 20% in Europe.

In January 2010, the Republic of the Philippines issued a US$1.5 billion dual-tranche offering. The first tranche was a US$650 million due January 2020 (10-year tranche); the second a US$850 million tranche due October 2034 (about a 24.5-year tranche). The geographical allocation for the 10-year tranche was as follows: 23% from the Philippines, 25% from the rest of Asia, 35% from the United States, and 17% from Europe. For the second tranche, the geographical allocation was: 19% came from the Philippines, 21% from the rest of Asia, 40% from the United States, and 20% from Europe.

An example of a nondollar-denominated global bond is the World Bank offering in October 2009 in two tranches: a 5-year tranche (due October 2014) and 10-year tranche (due October 2019). Both tranches are denominated in Australian dollars. The A$800 million 5-year tranche was placed with institutional investors in Australia (67%), Asia (20%), North America (6%), and Europe (7%); the A$600 million 10-year tranche was placed with institutional investors in Australia (37%), Asia (32%), North America (20%), and Europe (11%). According to the World Bank press release on October 7, 2009, "Investors were attracted by the rarity of the issuer in this market, the global recognition of the name, the strength of the credit, the choice of tenors and the liquidity and benchmark size of the transaction."

Non-U.S. Domestic Markets

Domestic bond markets throughout the world offer U.S. investors the opportunity to buy bonds of non-U.S. entities. Exhibit 9-4 shows as of June 2010 the outstanding debt securities for the domestic market for all countries broken down by type of issuer. Also shown in the exhibit is the same information for the U.S. domestic debt securities market. As can be seen, the U.S. domestic debt securities market is roughly 39% of the world's domestic market. The difference between the outstanding domestic debt securities issued by all countries and

Exhibit 9-4	**Outstanding Amount of Domestic Debt Securities as of June 2010 (in billions of U.S. dollars)**			
	All Issuers	Governments	Financial Institutions	Corporate Issuers
All countries	63,708.70	35,387.40	21,470.90	6,850.30
United States	25,081.50	10,326.90	11,909.10	2,845.50
Non-U.S.	38,627.20	25,060.50	9,561.80	4,004.80

Source: *The data for this exhibit were obtained from Table 16B in* BIS Quarterly Review, *December 2010.*

the U.S. domestic debt securities is that of the non-U.S. domestic market. Issuance in the non-U.S. domestic market by type of issuer is as follows: governments, 65%; financial institutions, 25%; and corporations, 10%.

The non-U.S. countries with the five largest domestic debt markets and the amount outstanding as of June 2010 were, according to the BIS (in billions of U.S. dollars)

Japan	$12,456.9
Italy	$3,191.6
China	$2,843.0
France	$2,850.1
Germany	$2,411.3

Below we focus on non-U.S. government bonds, the largest sector of the non-U.S. domestic bond market as well as the European covered bond market.

Non-U.S. Government Bond Markets

Exhibit 9-5 shows government debt securities outstanding in the domestic market by country as of mid 2010.

The institutional settings for government bond markets throughout the world vary considerably, and these variations may affect liquidity and the ways in which strategies are implemented, or, more precisely, affect the tactics of investment strategies. For example,

Exhibit 9-5 Government Debt Securities Outstanding in the Domestic Market by Country as of June 2010 (in billions of U.S. dollars)

All countries	$35,387.4
Argentina	48.1
Australia	253.7
Austria	115.5
Belgium	255.1
Brazil	750.6
Canada	931.4
China	1,591.1
Czech Republic	47.6
Denmark	94.1
Egypt	76.5
Finland	24.8
France	526.8
Germany	1,387.2
Greece	141.4
Hong Kong SAR	85.9

(Continued)

Exhibit 9-5	Government Debt Securities Outstanding in the Domestic Market by Country as of June 2010 (in billions of U.S. dollars) (Continued)
India	564.1
Indonesia	95.4
Ireland	111.6
Italy	1,752.1
Japan	10,536.0
Malaysia	105.0
Mexico	237.7
Netherlands	342.8
Norway	87.8
Poland	167.8
Portugal	90.6
Singapore	91.4
South Africa	97.5
South Korea	444.8
Spain	535.0
Sweden	113.0
Switzerland	115.1
Thailand	144.0
Turkey	215.9
United Kingdom	1,223.2
United States	10,326.9

Source: *The data for this exhibit were obtained from Table 16A in* BIS Quarterly Review, *December 2010.*

in the government bond market different primary market issuance practices may affect the liquidity and the price behavior of specific government bonds in a country. The nature of the secondary market affects the ease and cost of trading. The importance of the benchmark effect in various countries may influence which bonds to trade and hold. In addition, yields are calculated according to different methods in various countries, and these differences will affect the interpretation of yield spreads. Withholding and transfer tax practices also affect global investment strategies.

As explained in Chapter 6, a security can be stripped—that is, each interest payment and the one principal payment can be separated and sold as a separate security. While many Euro government bonds can be stripped, the stripped securities are not as liquid as U.S. Treasury strips. Sovereign governments also issue inflation-linked bonds. As explained in Chapter 6, the U.S. Department of the Treasury issues Treasury notes and bonds indexed to the consumer price index. These securities are referred to as Treasury Inflation Protection Securities (TIPS). Despite not issuing inflation-linked debt obligations until 1997, the United States is by far the largest issuer of inflation-indexed securities. Outside of the United States, the largest government issuer of inflation-linked bonds is the United Kingdom, followed by France. These bonds, popularly referred to as **linkers** in Europe, are typically linked to a consumer price index.

Methods of distribution of new government securities. There are four methods that have been used in distributing new securities of central governments:

- the regular calendar auction/Dutch style system
- the regular calendar auction/minimum-price offering
- the ad hoc auction system
- the tap system

In the **regular calendar auction/Dutch style auction system**, there is a regular calendar auction and winning bidders are allocated securities at the yield (price) they bid.

In the **regular calendar auction/minimum-price offering system**, there is a regular calendar of offerings. The price (yield) at which winning bidders are awarded the securities is different from the Dutch style auction. Rather than awarding a winning bidder at the yield (price) they bid, all winning bidders are awarded securities at the highest yield accepted by the government (i.e., the stop-out yield). For example, if the highest yield or stop-out yield for a government issue at auction is 5.14% and someone bids 5.12%, that bidder would be awarded the securities at 5.12%. In contrast, with the minimum-price offering method, that bidder would be awarded securities at 5.14%, which means a lower price than at the bid price of 5.12%. In Chapter 6, we referred to this auction method as a single-price auction; it is the auction method used in the U.S. government market. The regular calendar auction/minimum-price offering method is used in Germany and France.

In the **ad hoc auction system**, governments announce auctions when prevailing market conditions appear favorable. It is only at the time of the auction that the amount to be auctioned and the maturity of the security to be offered are announced. This is one of the methods used by the Bank of England in distributing British government bonds. From the issuing government's perspective, there are two advantages of an ad hoc auction system over a regular calendar auction. First, a regular calendar auction introduces greater market volatility than an ad hoc auction does because yields tend to rise as the announced auction date approaches and then fall afterward. Second, there is reduced flexibility in raising funds with a regular calendar auction.

In a **tap system**, additional bonds of a previously outstanding bond issue are auctioned. The government announces periodically that it is adding this new supply.

Sovereign bond ratings. Sovereign debt is the obligation of a country's central government. The debt of national governments is rated by the rating agencies. For the reasons discussed subsequently, there are two sovereign debt ratings assigned by rating agencies: a local currency debt rating and a foreign currency debt rating.

Standard & Poor's, Moody's, and Fitch all assign ratings to sovereign bonds. In assigning ratings, there are two general categories of risk that are assessed: economic risk and political risk. The former category is an assessment of the ability of a government to satisfy its obligations. Both quantitative and qualitative analyses are used in assessing economic risk. Political risk is an assessment of the willingness of a government to satisfy its obligations. A government may have the ability to pay but may be unwilling to pay. Political risk is assessed based on qualitative analysis of the economic and political factors that influence a government's economic policies. In our discussion of emerging market sovereign debt later in this chapter, we will discuss these factors further.

The reason for distinguishing between local currency debt ratings and foreign currency debt ratings is that historically, the default frequency differs by the currency denomination of the debt. Specifically, defaults have been greater on foreign currency–denominated debt. The reason for the difference in default rates for local currency debt and foreign currency debt is that if a government is willing to raise taxes and control its domestic financial system, it can generate sufficient local currency to meet its local currency debt obligation. This is not the case with foreign currency–denominated debt. A national government must purchase foreign currency to meet a debt obligation in that foreign currency and therefore has less control with respect to its exchange rate. Thus, a significant depreciation of the local currency relative to a foreign currency in which a debt obligation is denominated will impair a national government's ability to satisfy such obligation.

The implication of this is that the factors S&P analyzes in assessing the credit worthiness of a national government's local currency debt and foreign currency debt will differ to some extent. In assessing the credit quality of local currency debt, for example, S&P emphasizes domestic government policies that foster or impede timely debt service. For foreign currency debt, credit analysis by S&P focuses on the interaction of domestic and foreign government policies. S&P analyzes a country's balance of payments and the structure of its external balance sheet. The areas of analysis with respect to its external balance sheet are the net public debt, total net external debt, and net external liabilities.

The European Covered Bond Market

One of the largest sectors of the European market is the covered bond market. **Covered bonds** are issued by banks. The collateral for covered bonds can be either (1) residential mortgage loans, (2) commercial mortgage loans, or (3) public sector loans. (The use of public sector loans as collateral has been in decline.) They are referred to as "covered bonds" because the pool of loans that is the collateral is referred to as the "cover pool." The cover pool is not static over the life of a covered bond. That is, the composition of the cover pool changes over time.

Covered bonds work as follows. Investors in covered bonds have two claims. The first is a claim on the cover pool. At issuance, there is no legal separation of the cover pool from the assets of the issuing bank. However, if subsequently the issuing bank becomes insolvent, then at that time the assets included in the cover pool are separated from the issuing bank's other assets for the benefit of the investors in the covered bonds. The second claim is against the issuing bank. Because they are issued by strong banks and because the covered pool includes high-quality mortgage loans, covered bonds are viewed as highly secure bonds, typically receiving a triple A or double A credit rating. Covered bonds can be issued in any currency.

Covered bonds in many countries are created using the securitization process that will be described in later chapters. For that reason, covered bonds are often compared to residential mortgage-backed securities (RMBS), commercial mortgage-backed securities (CMBS), and other asset-backed securities (ABS). However, the difference between these securities created from a securitization and covered bonds is fourfold. First, at issuance, the bank that originated the loans will sell a pool of loans to a special purpose vehicle (SPV). By doing so, the bank has removed the pool of loans from its balance sheet. The SPV is the issuer of the securities. In contrast, with covered bonds, the issuing bank holds the pool of loans on its balance sheet. It is only if the issuing bank becomes insolvent that the assets are segregated for the benefit of the investors in the covered bonds. The second difference is that investors in RMBS/CMBS/ABS do not have recourse to the bank that sold the pool of loans to the SPV. In contrast, covered bond investors have recourse to the issuing bank. The third difference is that for RMBS/CMBS/ABS backed by residential and commercial mortgage loans, the group of loans, once assembled, does not change, whereas covered bonds are not static. Finally, covered bonds typically have a single maturity date (i.e., they are bullet bonds), whereas RMBS/CMBS/ABS typically have time-tranched bond classes.

Special legislation is required in a country in order for covered bonds to be issued. The two major issues that laws resulting from the legislation must address are (1) the eligibility of assets that may be included in the cover pool, and (2) the treatment in bankruptcy of the holders of covered bonds. According to a report by the European Central Bank in April 2010,[9] there are 24 countries in Europe that permit financial institutions to issue covered bonds.[10] In the euro zone, the largest issuers of covered bonds are Germany, France, and Spain.

The German mortgage-bond market, called the **Pfandbriefe market**, is the largest covered bond market. In fact, it is about one-third of the German bond market and the largest asset type in the European bond market.[11] The bonds in this market, Pfandbriefe, are issued by German mortgage banks. There are two types of Pfandbriefe that differ based on the borrowing entity for the loan. *Ofentliche Pfandbriefe* are bonds fully collateralized by loans to public-sector entities. These bonds are called Public Pfandbriefe. When the bonds are fully collateralized by residential and commercial mortgages, they are called *Hypotheken Pfandbriefe* or Mortgage Pfandbriefe.

The Pfandbriefe market is further divided into Traditional Pfandbriefe and Jumbo Pfandbriefe. The former represents the market for issues of smaller size. Historically, it has been an illiquid and fragmented market and, as a result, has not attracted much interest from non-German investors. The tap method was used for issuing Traditional Pfandbriefe. The sector of the Pfandbriefe market that has received the greatest interest from global institutional bond investors is the **Jumbo Pfandbriefe** sector. This sector, started in 1995, is referred to as *Jumbo* because the minimum size of an issue is €500 million. Because of its size, it attracted non-German institutional money managers. The liquidity of the Jumbo Pfandbriefe market is further enhanced by the obligations of the dealers participating in an issuance.

Emerging Market Bonds

The financial markets of Latin America, Asia (with the exception of Japan), and Eastern Europe are viewed as emerging markets. There is no formal consensus on the definition of a country that should be classified as an emerging country. One definition is that a

---

[9] *Financial Integration in Europe.*
[10] These are Austria, Bulgaria, Belgium, the Czech Republic, Denmark, Finland, France, Germany, Greece, Hungary, Ireland, Italy, Latvia, Luxembourg, the Netherlands, Poland, Portugal, Romania, Slovakia, Slovenia, Spain, Sweden, Switzerland, and the United Kingdom.
[11] Data from the website of the Association of German Pfandbrief Banks, available at http://www.pfandbrief.org/d/internet.nsf/tindex/en_pfandbrief.htm.

country is classified in the category of emerging markets if it has defaulted at least once on its international debt obligations. A second definition is based on certain macroeconomic criteria of the country. And a rather loose emerging market universe is one that includes all countries that are not considered industrialized or already "developed" and are thus named "lesser developed countries" (LDC) or developing countries. However, even in the absence of a formal definition, there is an understanding amongst institutional and retail investors as to what is meant by an emerging market.

Governments of emerging market countries have issued Brady bonds, Eurobonds, global bonds, and domestic bonds. We have discussed Eurobonds and global bonds earlier in this chapter. **Brady bonds** are basically bonds that represent a restructuring of nonperforming bank loans of governments into marketable securities.[12] Today, however, most countries have retired their outstanding Brady bonds and issue the other three types of bonds. It was the introduction of Brady bonds that resulted in emerging market bonds being treated as a separate asset class. These bonds were purchased by institutions of emerging countries and dedicated international emerging market funds. As these markets developed, there was also interest in these securities from high-yield international funds and institutions. Moreover, the development of credit default swaps (the subject of Chapter 29) on emerging market government debt has facilitated the trading of credit risk.

At one time, the securities issued by governments of emerging market countries were exclusively denominated in U.S. dollars or other major currencies. Today, emerging market local debt issues are denominated in local currency as well as in major currencies. The development of the local market has been fostered by both the growth of local pension funds and foreign investor interest.

Credit Risk

Investing in the government bonds of emerging market countries entails considerably more credit risk than investing in the government bonds of major industrialized countries. Standard & Poor's and Moody's rate emerging market sovereign debt. In the evaluation of the sovereign debt of emerging market countries, both economic and political factors must be considered. Economic analysis involves the analysis of a country's macroeconomic fundamentals. Political factors involve the political analysis of a country. Loucks, Penicook, and Schillhorn discuss macroeconomic fundamentals and political analysis along a timeline: factors that have an immediate, intermediate, and long-term impact on credit quality.[13]

Macroeconomic fundamentals. These factors fall into three general categories:[14]

- Serviceability: immediate impact
- Solvency: intermediate impact
- Structural: long-term impact

---

[12] An agreement for the restructuring of nonperforming bank loans was first worked out between Mexico and the United States by the then-Secretary of the Treasury Nicholas Brady—hence, nicknamed "Brady bonds." The agreement called for U.S. government and multilateral support to provide relief for principal and interest payments owed to banks outside Mexico, if Mexico successfully implemented certain structural reforms. This U.S. government program was then extended to the government debt of other emerging markets.

[13] Maria Mednikov Loucks, John A. Penicook, Jr., and Uwe Schillhorn, "A Disciplined Approach to Emerging Markets Debt Investing," Chapter 4 in Frank J. Fabozzi and Efstathia Pilarinu (eds.), *Investing in Emerging Market Fixed Income Markets* (Hoboken, NJ: John Wiley & Sons, 2002).

[14] Ibid.

Serviceability involves factors that reflect the country's foreign exchange reserve position relative to its debt obligations and liquidity. Two indicators suggested for gauging serviceability, **refinancing risk** and **basic balance**, are defined below:

$$\text{Refinancing Risk} = \frac{\text{Short-term debt stock} + \text{Interest payments} + \text{Amortization on medium and long-term debt}}{\text{Reserves}}$$

$$\text{Basic balance} = \frac{\text{Current account balance} + \text{Foreign direct investment}}{\text{GDP}}$$

Refinancing risk measures the size of the country's debt that has to be refinanced by borrowing from external sources. The lower the value, the less is a country's refinancing risk. The basic balance measures a country's inflow of foreign currency relative to its GDP. The numerator of the ratio is the two sources of a country's inflow of foreign currency: inflows from trade as measured by a country's trade balance and foreign direct investments. The higher the ratio, the less is the serviceability risk.

Solvency involves the ability of a government to service its local and external debt. Ratios that can be used to gauge whether a country can access external financial markets so as to be able to refinance its immediate debt obligations are the **domestic credit ratio**, **external debt ratio**, external service ratio, and **public sector borrowing requirement**. These four solvency measures are given below:

$$\text{Domestic credit ratio} = \frac{(1 + \text{Expected 3-year domestic credit growth}) \times \text{Domestic credit}}{(1 + \text{Expected 3-year GDP growth}) \times \text{GDP}}$$

$$\text{External debt ratio} = \frac{\text{External debt}}{\text{GDP}}$$

$$\text{External service ratio} = \frac{\text{Interest payments} + \text{Amortization on medium- and long-term debt}}{\text{Exports of goods and services} + \text{Income receipts}}$$

$$\text{Public sector borrowing requirement} = \frac{\text{Primary fiscal balance} + \text{Interest payments}}{\text{GDP}}$$

The rationale for the domestic credit ratio is as follows. If a government is efficiently allocating the country's credit to productive investment ventures, over time its GDP growth should exceed its credit growth. Failure to allocate the country's credit to productive investment ventures will result in a lower-than-desired GDP growth. Hence, the lower the domestic credit ratio, the lower the solvency risk is Loucks, Penicook, and Schillhorn argue that one of the reasons for the Asian crisis of 1997 and 1978 was the inefficient allocation of domestic credit. In those years, Thailand's domestic credit ratio exceeded 130% and Malaysia and South Korean's ratios exceeded 150%. These ratios were lowered to near 100% as a result of policies directed at correcting the banking system.

Indicators of the size of a country's debt and debt burden are captured by the external service ratio and external debt ratio. The lower the value of these two ratios, the lower the serviceability risk is.

In the public sector borrowing requirement indicator, the first component of the numerator (primary fiscal balance) indicates a country's current fiscal problems. A continuation of such problems will increase a country's future interest payments. The second component of the numerator is interest payments that reflect prior fiscal problems. A country could have, for example, a primary fiscal surplus but yet have high interest payments due to high interest costs associated with financing prior fiscal deficits. This is, in fact, what occurred in Brazil in 2000. The lower the public sector borrowing requirement, the lower the solvency risk is.

Factors that fall into the structural category involve an assessment of the country's long-term health and, although not directly associated with the default of the sovereign entity, do provide guidance as to the likely development of economic problems when there are poor structural fundamentals. These factors include dependence on specific commodities to generate earnings from exports, indicators of economic well being such as per capita income, and income distribution measures. Two macroeconomic measures used for gauging structural risks are five-year average GDP per capita growth and inflation as measured by the average change year-over-year. The key in the analysis of structural factors is forecasting when the market will focus on them and, as a result, increase service-ability and solvency risks.

Political analysis. Unlike economic factors, political factors are difficult to quantify. These factors include

- Elections: immediate impact
- Systems/institutions: intermediate impact
- Geopolitical significance: long-term impact

With respect to elections, the factors considered are the fairness of elections and the political opposition programs. An example of the immediate impact of these factors is provided by Loucks, Penicook, and Schillhorn. In the May 2000 presidential election in Peru, the incumbent, Alberto Fujimori, won the election. However, there were allegations of fraud. During the election period, the spread on Peruvian bonds increased by 200 basis points compared to the spread on a popular emerging bond market index. In early September 2000, it was found that Fujimori's top security advisor had paid opposition members in congress to switch sides. Shortly thereafter, Fujimori called for new presidential and parliamentary elections and renounced his power. After a series of other scandals associated with the top security advisory, in June 2001 presidential runoffs were held, with one of the candidates being Alan Garcia, former president of Peru. During his administration, he had pushed Peru into a debt crisis in 1987. Because of the uncertainty associated with his possible election to president, the spread on Peruvian bonds once again increased by 200 basis points relative to the same emerging bond market index.

Systems/institutions involve political leadership, regional integration, and social composition stability. Strong leadership both in dealing with challenging economic issues facing a country and dealing with the international financial community is important. Santiso argues that finance or economics ministers play a critical role for emerging market governments by communicating with international financial markets and ensuring market confidence.[15] Moser finds support for this view based on a study of cabinet reshuffles affecting the ministry of finance or economics in 12 Latin American countries from 1992 to 2007.[16] His empirical

---

[15] Javieer Santiso, *The Political Economy of Emerging Markets: Actors, Institutions and Crisis in Latin America* (New York: Palgrave, 2003).
[16] Christoph Moser, "The Impact of Political Risk on Sovereign Bond Spreads – Evidence from Latin America," Department of Economics, University of Mainz, Germany, November 2007.

analysis suggests that such political news (1) instantaneously increases bond spreads and (2) spreads significantly increase in the 40 days leading up to the minister change and then flatten out at a higher level in the subsequent 40 days.

The Free Dictionary defines geopolitics as "The study of the relationship among politics and geography, demography, and economics, especially with respect to the foreign policy of a nation." When an emerging market country faces a major credit crisis, geopolitical significance becomes important. When a credit crisis occurs in an emerging market country that is perceived to have major global repercussions, industrialized countries and supranational agencies have stepped in to commit significant resources to prevent an economic collapse and political instability for that country. Therefore, geopolitical significance is an important political factor to consider.

KEY POINTS

- The global bond market can be classified into two markets: the internal or national bond market, which consists of a domestic bond market and a foreign bond market, and the external or international bond market (or Eurobond market).
- Although it is often stated that the primary motivation for investing in non-U.S. bonds is that it provides diversification benefits, such benefits may not be significant. Rather, investing in non-U.S. bonds gives a money manager the opportunity to capitalize on factors that affect bond prices in non-U.S. markets and permits a currency play.
- Non-U.S. issuers of international bonds include sovereign governments, subsovereign governments, supranational agencies, financial institutions, and corporations.
- Currency denomination is the key factor that impacts the price and the yield of a bond. When a portfolio includes nondollar-denominated issues by non-U.S. entities, bond returns are impacted by the movement of interest rates of all the countries where there is currency exposure and the foreign exchange movement of all the currencies to which the portfolio has exposure.
- The return on a portfolio that includes nondollar-denominated bonds consists of three components: (1) income, (2) capital gain/loss in the local currency, and (3) foreign currency gain/loss.
- Bonds issued by non-U.S. entities include Yankee bonds, Regulation 144a private placements, Eurobonds, Euro medium-term notes, global bonds, non-U.S. domestic bonds, and emerging market bonds.
- Yankee bonds are bonds issued by non-U.S. entities that are registered with the SEC and traded in the United States.
- Because of the reduced reporting requirements, 144a bond issuance has become an important market for non-U.S. borrowers to raise funds.
- The Eurobond market is divided into sectors based on the currency in which the issue is denominated. Many innovative bond structures have been introduced in the Eurobond market.
- Euro medium-term notes are debt obligations that are intended primarily for offerings outside of the United States.
- A global bond is one that is issued simultaneously in several bond markets throughout the world and can be issued in any currency.
- Domestic bond markets throughout the world offer U.S. investors the opportunity to buy bonds of non-U.S. entities. The largest sector of domestic bond markets throughout the world is the government sector.

- Sovereign debt is the obligation of a country's central government. Ratings are assigned separately for local currency–denominated debt and foreign currency–denominated debt. The two general categories analyzed by rating companies in assigning ratings are economic risk and political risk.
- Covered bonds are issued primarily in Europe by banks using predominately residential and mortgage loans as collateral. While covered bonds are often compared to mortgage and asset-backed securities, there are differences in their credit protection and structure.
- Governments of emerging market countries have issued Brady bonds, Eurobonds, global bonds, and domestic bonds. The outstanding amount of Brady bonds is small. Instead, emerging market countries issue the other types of bonds.
- Macroeconomic factors considered in the analysis of emerging market government bonds include serviceability, solvency, and structural factors. Unlike economic factors, political factors are difficult to quantify. These factors include elections, systems/institutions, and geopolitical significance.

QUESTIONS

1. Describe the trading blocs that are used in classifying the world's bond markets.
2. What risk is faced by a U.S. life insurance company that buys British government bonds?
3. "The strongest argument for investing in nondollar bonds is that there are diversification benefits." Explain why you agree or disagree with this statement.
4. What arguments are offered for investing in nondollar bonds?
5. What is the difference between LIBID and LIMEAN?
6. What is the foreign bond market of a country?
7. What is the debate regarding covenants in corporate bonds in the Eurobond market?
8. Explain the step-up and step-down structure used in the Eurobond market.
9. Suppose that the yield to maturity on a Eurodollar bond is 7.8%. What is the bond-equivalent yield?
10. This excerpt, which discusses dual currency bonds, is taken from the *International Capital Market*, published in 1989 by the European Investment Bank:

    The generic name of dual-currency bonds hides many different variations which are difficult to characterize in detail. These variations on the same basic concept have given birth to specific names like Index Currency Option Notes (ICON), foreign interest payment bonds (FIPS), forex-linked bonds, heaven and hell bonds, to name but a few. Despite this diversity it is, however, possible to attempt a broad-brush classification of the various types of dual-currency bonds.

    The first category covers bond issues denominated in one currency but for which coupon and repayment of the principal are made in another designated currency at an exchange rate fixed at the time of issue. A second category comprises dual-currency bonds in which coupon payments and redemption proceeds are made in a currency different from the currency of denomination at the spot exchange rate that will prevail at the time of payment.

    Within this category, one finds the forex-linked bonds, foreign currency bonds and heaven and hell bonds. A final category includes bonds which offer to issuers or the holder the choice of the currency in which payments and/or redemptions are to be made at the future spot exchange rate. ICONs fall into this latter category because there is an implicit option due to the exchange rate revision formula. Usually, these bonds are referred to as option currency bonds.

Irrespective of the above-mentioned categories, all dual-currency bonds expose the issuers and the holders to some form of foreign exchange risk. . . . Pricing dual-currency bonds is therefore an application of option pricing, as the bonds can be looked at as a combination of a straight bond and a currency option. The value of the straight bond component is obtained according to traditional fixed-rate bond valuation models. The pricing of the option component is, ex post, equal to the difference between the dual currency bond price and its straight bond component. . . .

a. Why do all currency bonds "expose the issuers and the holders to some form of foreign exchange risk" regardless of the category of bond?

b. Do you agree that the pricing of all dual-currency bonds is an application of option pricing?

c. Why should the price of the option component be "equal to the difference between the dual currency bond price and its straight bond component"?

11. **a.** Why do rating agencies assign a different rating to the debt of a sovereign entity based on whether the debt is denominated in a local currency or a foreign currency?

b. What are the two general categories of risk analyzed by rating agencies in assigning a sovereign rating?

12. What are the different methods for the issuance of government securities?

13. **a.** What are covered bonds?

b. How do covered bonds differ from residential mortgage-backed securities, commercial mortgage-backed securities, and asset-backed securities?

c. What is the Pfandbriefe market?

14. In the analysis of emerging market sovereign bonds, what is meant by structural factors?

15. In the analysis of emerging market sovereign bonds, why is geopolitical significance important?

16. Why can one consider alleged corruption in a presidential election in an emerging market country or the change in finance minister in an emerging market country headline risk? (Headline risk was described in a prior chapter.)

17. On January 9, Reuters announced a US$2.6 billion bond offering by the Australia and New Zealand Banking Group. The following is reproduced from the announcement:

Issue: US$2.6 bln 144a reg S 2, 3-year
The offer comprised US$1.9 bln 3-year at 100bp/swap and US$700 mln 2-yr at 70bp/Libor.

Participants: (Before the offer was increased) 45 investors.
For the 3-year tranche, 65% from North America, 10% from Europe, 20% Asia, 10% others. For the 2-year tranche: 40% from North America, 20% from Europe, 40% from Asia

Describe this bond offering.

18. On January 9, Reuters announced a US$3.075 billion bond offering by the Commonwealth Bank of Australia. The following is reproduced from the announcement:

Issue: US$3.075 billion of 144a reg S bonds priced on Jan. 9. Offer included US$2.5 bln 3-year bonds at 78bp/swap and US$575 mln 5-year bonds at 85bp/swap.

Participants: Nearly 100 investors in Asia, the U.S. and Europe.
Buyers mostly included asset managers and banks.

Describe this bond offering.

10

Residential Mortgage Loans

LEARNING OBJECTIVES

After reading this chapter, you will understand

- what a mortgage is
- who the major originators of residential mortgages are
- the borrower and property characteristics considered by a lender in evaluating the credit risk of an applicant for a mortgage loan
- what the servicing of a residential mortgage loan involves
- the types of residential mortgage loans based on lien status, credit classification, interest-rate type, amortization type, credit guarantees, loan balances, and prepayments and prepayment penalties
- what a prepayment is
- the cash flow of a mortgage loan
- what a prepayment penalty mortgage is
- the risks associated with investing in mortgages
- the significance of prepayment risk

Although the American dream may be to own a home, the major portion of the funds to purchase one must be borrowed. The market where these funds are borrowed is called the mortgage market. A **mortgage** is a pledge of property to secure payment of a debt. Typically, property refers to real estate. If the property owner (the mortgagor) fails to pay the lender (the mortgagee), the lender has the right to foreclose the loan and seize the property in order to ensure that it is repaid. The types of real estate properties that can be mortgaged are divided into two broad categories: single-family (one- to four-family) residential and commercial properties. The former category includes houses, condominiums, cooperatives, and apartments. Commercial properties are income-producing properties: multifamily properties (i.e., apartment buildings), office buildings, industrial properties (including warehouses), shopping centers, hotels, and health care facilities (e.g., senior housing care facilities).

This chapter describes residential mortgage loans, and the three chapters to follow describe securities created by using residential mortgage loans as collateral. In Chapter 14, we cover commercial mortgage loans and securities backed by commercial mortgage loans.

ORIGINATION OF RESIDENTIAL MORTGAGE LOANS

The original lender is called the **mortgage originator**. The principal originators of residential mortgage loans are thrifts, commercial banks, and mortgage bankers. Mortgage originators may service the mortgages they originate, for which they obtain a **servicing fee**. Servicing of the mortgage involves collecting monthly payments from mortgagors and forwarding proceeds to owners of the loan, sending payment notices to mortgagors, reminding mortgagors when payments are overdue, maintaining records of mortgage balances, furnishing tax information to mortgagors, administering an escrow account for real estate taxes and insurance purposes, and, if necessary, initiating foreclosure proceedings. The servicing fee is a fixed percentage of the outstanding mortgage balance, typically 25 basis points to 100 basis points per year. The mortgage originator may sell the servicing of the mortgage to another party who would then receive the servicing fee.

Here are the choices available to mortgage originators once the loans are made:

- Hold the mortgage in their portfolio.
- Sell the mortgage to an investor that wishes to hold the mortgage in its portfolio or that will place the mortgage in a pool of mortgages to be used as collateral for the issuance of a security.
- Use the mortgage themselves as collateral for the issuance of a security.

When a mortgage originator intends to sell the mortgage, it will obtain a commitment from the potential investor (buyer). Two government-sponsored enterprises (GSEs) and several private companies buy mortgages. Because these entities pool these mortgages and sell them to investors, they are called **conduits**.

When a mortgage is used as collateral for the issuance of a security, the mortgage is said to be **securitized**. In the next three chapters, we will discuss the securitization of residential mortgage loans.

Underwriting Standards

Someone who wants to borrow funds to purchase a home will apply for a loan from a mortgage originator. Most mortgage loans are originated with a 30-year original term, although some borrowers prefer shorter maturities such 20, 15, or 10 years. The potential homeowner completes an application form, which provides financial information about the applicant, and pays an application fee; then the mortgage originator performs a credit evaluation of the applicant. The requirements specified by the originator in order to grant the loan are referred to as **underwriting standards**.

The two primary quantitative underwriting standards are the

- payment-to-income ratio
- loan-to-value ratio

Payment-to-Income Ratio

The **payment-to-income ratio** (PTI) is the ratio of monthly payments to monthly income, which measures the ability of the applicant to make monthly payments (both mortgage and real estate tax payments). The lower the PTI, the greater the likelihood that the applicant will be able to meet the required monthly mortgage payments.

Loan-to-Value Ratio

The difference between the purchase price of the property and the amount borrowed is the borrower's down payment. The **loan-to-value ratio** (LTV) is the ratio of the amount of the loan to the market (or appraised) value of the property. The lower this ratio is, the greater the protection for the lender if the applicant defaults on the payments and the lender must repossess and sell the property. For example, if an applicant wants to borrow $225,000 on property with an appraised value of $300,000, the LTV is 75%. Suppose the applicant subsequently defaults on the mortgage. The lender can then repossess the property and sell it to recover the amount owed. But the amount that will be received by the lender depends on the market value of the property. In our example, even if conditions in the housing market are weak, the lender may still be able to recover the proceeds lent if the value of the property declines by $75,000. Suppose, instead, that the applicant wanted to borrow $270,000 for the same property. The LTV would then be 90%. If the lender had to foreclose on the property and then sell it because the applicant defaults, there is less protection for the lender.

The LTV has been found in numerous studies to be the single most important determinant of the likelihood of default. The rationale is straightforward: Homeowners with large amounts of equity in their properties are unlikely to default. They will either try to protect this equity by remaining current or, if they fail, sell the house or refinance it to unlock the equity. In any case, the lender is protected by the buyer's self-interest. On the other hand, if the borrower has little or no equity in the property, the value of the default option is much greater. In fact, data on the behavior of borrowers after 2006 indicate that they have an increased propensity to voluntarily stop making their mortgage payments once the current LTV (which is defined as the ratio of the current loan balance divided by the estimated market value) exceeds 125%, even if they can afford making monthly payments. This behavior is referred to as a "strategic default."

TYPES OF RESIDENTIAL MORTGAGE LOANS

There are different types of residential mortgage loans. They can be classified according to the following attributes:

- lien status
- credit classification
- interest rate type
- amortization type
- credit guarantees
- loan balances
- prepayments and prepayment penalties[1]

---

[1] See Frank J. Fabozzi, Anand K. Bhattacharya, and William S. Berliner, *Mortgage-Backed Securities: Products, Structuring, and Analytical Techniques* (Hoboken, NJ: John Wiley & Sons, 2007).

Lien Status

The **lien status** of a mortgage loan indicates the loan's seniority in the event of the forced liquidation of the property due to default by the obligor. For a mortgage loan that is a **first lien**, the lender would have first call on the proceeds of the liquidation of the property if it were to be repossessed. A mortgage loan could also be a **second lien** or **junior lien**, and the claims of the lender on the proceeds in the case of liquidation come after the holders of the first lien are paid in full.

Credit Classification

A loan that is originated where the borrower is viewed to have a high credit quality (i.e., where the borrower has strong employment and credit histories, income sufficient to pay the loan obligation without compromising the borrower's creditworthiness, and substantial equity in the underlying property) is classified as a **prime loan**. A loan that is originated where the borrow is of lower credit quality or where the loan is not a first lien on the property is classified as a **subprime loan**. The origination of subprime loans declined dramatically after 2006, when it became evident that loans to subprime borrowers were plagued by poor underwriting, fraud, and an excessive reliance on rising home prices. Between the prime and subprime sector is a somewhat nebulous category referred to as an **alternative-A loan** or, more commonly, an **alt-A-loan**. These loans had been considered to be prime loans (the "A" refers to the A grade assigned by underwriting systems), but they have some attributes that either increase their perceived credit riskiness or cause them to be difficult to categorize and evaluate due to limited income or asset documentation. The origination of alt-A loans declined sharply after 2006 due to the decline in home prices and mortgage credit performance.

In assessing the credit quality of a mortgage applicant, lenders look at various measures. The starting point is the applicant's credit score. There are several firms that collect data on the payment histories of individuals from lending institutions and, using statistical models, evaluate and quantify individual creditworthiness in terms of a credit score. Basically, a credit score is a numerical grade of the credit history of the borrower. The three most popular credit reporting companies that compute credit scores are Experian, Transunion, and Equifax. While the credit scores have different underlying methodologies, the scores generically are referred to as "FICO scores."[2] Typically, a lender will obtain more than one score in order to minimize the impact of variations in credit scores across providers. FICO scores range from 350 to 850. The higher the FICO score is, the lower the credit risk.

The LTV has proven to be a good predictor of default: The higher the LTV is, the greater the likelihood of default. By definition, the LTV of the loan in a purchase transaction is a function of both the down payment and the purchase price of the property. However, borrowers refinance their loans when rates decline. When a lender is evaluating an application from a borrower who is refinancing, the LTV is dependent upon the requested amount of the new loan and the market value of the property as determined by an appraisal. When the loan amount requested exceeds the original loan amount, the transaction is referred to as a **cash-out refinancing**. If instead, there is a refinancing where the loan balance remains unchanged, the transaction is said to be a **rate-and-term refinancing** or

---

[2] This is because credit scoring companies generally use a model developed by Fair, Isaac & Company. The model uses 45 criteria to rank the creditworthiness of an individual.

no-cash refinancing. That is, the purpose of refinancing the loan is to either obtain a better note rate or change the term of the loan.

Lenders calculate income ratios such as the PTI to assess the applicant's ability to pay. These ratios compare the monthly payment that the applicant would have to pay if the loan is granted to the applicant's monthly income. The most common measures are the front ratio and the back ratio. The **front ratio** is computed by dividing the total monthly payments (which include interest and principal on the loan plus property taxes and homeowner insurance) by the applicant's pre-tax monthly income. The **back ratio** is computed in a similar manner. The modification is that it adds other debt payments such as auto loan and credit card payments to the total payments. In order for a loan to be classified as "prime," the front and back ratios should be no more than 28% and 36%, respectively.

The credit score is the primary attribute used to characterize loans as either prime or subprime. Prime (or A-grade) loans generally have FICO scores of 660 or higher, front and back ratios with the above-noted maximum of 28% and 36%, and LTVs less than 90%. For Alt-A loans, there is a wide range in the credit spectrum, from loans that are close to prime in quality to products that are virtually subprime loans in character. While subprime loans typically have FICO scores below 660, the loan programs and grades are highly lender specific. One lender might consider a loan with a 620 FICO score to be a "B rated loan," while another lender would grade the same loan higher or lower, especially if the other attributes of the loan (such as the LTV) are higher or lower than average levels.

Interest Rate Type

The interest rate that the borrower agrees to pay, referred to as the **note rate**, can be fixed or change over the life of the loan. For a **fixed-rate mortgage** (FRM), the interest rate is set at the closing of the loan and remains unchanged over the life of the loan.

For an **adjustable-rate mortgage** (ARM), as the name implies, the note rate changes over the life of the loan. The note rate is based on both the movement of an underlying rate, called the **index** or **reference rate**, and a spread over the index called the **margin**. Two categories of reference rates have been used in ARMs: (1) market-determined rates, and (2) calculated rates based on the cost of funds for thrifts. Market-determined rates include the London Interbank Offered Rate (LIBOR), the one-year Constant Maturity Treasury (CMT), and the 12-month Moving Treasury Average (MTA), a rate calculated from monthly averages of the one-year CMT. The two most popular calculated rates are the Eleventh Federal Home Loan Bank Board District Cost of Funds Index (COFI) and the National Cost of Funds Index. Depository institutions prefer to hold ARMs in their portfolios rather than FRMs because ARMs provide a better matching with their liabilities.

The basic ARM is one that resets periodically and has no other terms that affect the monthly mortgage payment. Typically, the mortgage rate is affected by other terms. These include (1) periodic rate caps, and (2) lifetime rate cap and floor. A **periodic rate cap** limits the amount that the interest rate may increase or decrease at the reset date. The periodic rate cap is expressed in percentage points. Most ARMs have an upper limit on the mortgage rate that can be charged over the life of the loan. This **lifetime rate cap** is expressed in terms of the initial rate. ARMs may also have a lower limit (floor) on the interest rate that can be charged over the life of the loan.

During the period between 2001 and 2007 when ARM issuance was at its height, the most popular form of an ARM was the **hybrid ARM**. For this loan type, for a specified number of years (three, five to seven, and 10 years), the note rate was fixed. At the end of the initial fixed-rate period, the loan resets in a fashion very similar to that of more traditional ARM loans.

Amortization Type

The amount of the monthly loan payment that represents the repayment of the principal borrowed is called the **amortization**. Traditionally, both FRMs and ARMs are **fully amortizing loans**. What this means is that the monthly mortgage payments made by the borrower are such that they not only provide the lender with the contractual interest but also are sufficient to completely repay the amount borrowed when the last monthly mortgage payment is made. Thus, for example, for a fully amortizing 30-year loan, at the end of the 360th month, the last mortgage payment is sufficient to pay off any loan balance so that after that last payment, the amount owed is zero.

Fully amortizing fixed-rate loans have a payment that is constant over the life of the loan. For example, suppose a loan has an original balance of $200,000, a note rate of 7.5%, and a term of 30 years. Then the monthly mortgage payment would be $1,398.43. The formula for calculating the monthly mortgage payment is

$$MP = MB_0 \left[\frac{i(1 + i)^n}{(1 + i)^n - 1} \right]$$

where

MP = monthly mortgage payment ($)
MB_0 = original mortgage balance ($)
i = note rate divided by 12 (in decimal)
n = number of months of the mortgage loan

For example, suppose that

$$MB_0 = \$200,000; i = 0.075/12 = 0.00625; n = 360$$

Then the monthly payment is

$$MP = \$200,000 \left[\frac{0.00625(1.00625)^{360}}{(1.00625)^{360} - 1} \right] = \$1,398.43$$

To calculate the remaining mortgage balance at the end of any month, the following formula is used:

$$MB_t = MB_0 \left[\frac{(1 + i)^n - (1 + i)^t}{(1 + i)^n - 1} \right]$$

where

$$MB_t = \text{mortgage balance after } t \text{ months.}$$

For example, suppose that for month 12 ($t = 12$), we have

$$MB_0 = \$200,000; i = 0.00625; n = 360$$

The mortgage balance at the end of month 12 is

$$MB_t = \$200,000 \left[\frac{(1.00625)^{360} - (1.00625)^{12}}{(1.00625)^{360} - 1} \right] = \$198,156.33$$

To calculate the portion of the monthly mortgage payment that is the scheduled principal payment for a month, the following formula is used:

$$SP_t = MB_0 \left[\frac{i(1 + i)^{t-1}}{(1 + i)^n - 1} \right]$$

where

SP_t = scheduled principal repayment for month t.

For example, suppose that for month 12 ($t = 12$), we have

$$MB_0 = \$200,000; \; i = 0.00625; \; n = 360$$

Then the scheduled principal repayment for month 12 is

$$SP_{12} = \$200,000 \left[\frac{0.00625(1.00625)^{12-1}}{(1.00625)^{360} - 1} \right] = \$158.95$$

Assuming that the borrower has made all monthly payments on a timely basis, then after the last monthly mortgage payment is made, the outstanding balance is zero (i.e., the loan is paid off). This can be seen in the schedule shown in Exhibit 10-1, which is

Exhibit 10-1 Amortization Schedule

Original balance	$200,000.00
Note rate	7.50%
Term	30 years
Monthly payment	$1,398.43

Month	Beginning Balance	Interest	Principal Repayment	Ending Balance
1	$200,000.00	$1,250.00	$148.43	$199,851.57
2	199,851.57	1,249.07	149.36	199,702.21
3	199,702.21	1,248.14	150.29	199,551.92
4	199,551.92	1,247.20	151.23	199,400.69
5	199,400.69	1,246.25	152.17	199,248.52
6	199,248.52	1,245.30	153.13	199,095.39
7	199,095.39	1,244.35	154.08	198,941.31
8	198,941.31	1,243.38	155.05	198,786.27
9	198,786.27	1,242.41	156.01	198,630.25
10	198,630.25	1,241.44	156.99	198,473.26
11	198,473.26	1,240.46	157.97	198,315.29
12	198,315.29	1,239.47	158.96	198,156.33
13	198,156.33	1,238.48	159.95	197,996.38
14	197,996.38	1,237.48	160.95	197,835.43

(Continued)

Exhibit 10-1	Amortization Schedule (Continued)			
Month	Beginning Balance	Interest	Principal Repayment	Ending Balance
...	...	...	...	...
89	$182,656.63	$1,141.60	$ 256.83	$182,399.81
90	182,399.81	1,140.00	258.43	182,141.37
91	182,141.37	1,138.38	260.05	181,881.33
...	...	...	...	...
145	165,499.78	1,034.37	364.06	165,135.73
146	165,135.73	1,032.10	366.33	164,769.40
147	164,769.40	1,029.81	368.62	164,400.77
...	...	...	...	...
173	154,397.69	964.99	433.44	153,964.24
174	153,964.24	962.28	436.15	153,528.09
175	153,528.09	959.55	438.88	153,089.21
...	...	...	...	...
210	136,417.23	852.61	545.82	135,871.40
211	135,871.40	849.20	549.23	135,322.17
212	135,322.17	845.76	552.67	134,769.51
...	...	...	...	...
290	79,987.35	499.92	898.51	79,088.84
291	79,088.84	494.31	904.12	78,184.71
292	78,184.71	488.65	909.77	77,274.94
...	...	...	...	...
358	4,143.39	25.90	1,372.53	2,770.85
359	2,770.85	17.32	1,381.11	1,389.74
360	1,389.74	8.69	1,389.74	0.00

referred to as an **amortization schedule**. (Not all 360 months are shown to conserve space.) The column labeled "Principal Repayment" is the monthly amortization of the loan. Notice that in the 360th month, the ending balance is zero. Also note that in each month, the amount of the monthly mortgage payment applied to interest declines. This is because the amount of the outstanding balance declines each month.

In the case of an ARM, the monthly mortgage payment adjusts periodically. Thus, the monthly mortgage payments must be recalculated at each reset date. This process of resetting the mortgage loan payment is referred to as **recasting the loan**. For example, consider once again a $200,000 30-year loan. Assume that the loan adjusts annually and that the initial note rate (i.e., the note rate for the first 12 months) is 7.5%. How much of the loan will be outstanding at the end of one year? We can determine this from Exhibit 10-1 by looking at the last column ("Ending Balance") for month 12. That amount is $198,156.33. (Alternatively, the formula given earlier can be used.) Now recasting the loan involves computing the monthly mortgage payment that will fully amortize a loan of $198,156.33 for 29 years (348 months) because after one year, there are 29 years remaining on the loan. The note rate used is the reset rate. Suppose that the reset rate is 8.5%. Then the monthly mortgage payment to fully amortize the loan is $1,535.26, and that is the monthly mortgage payment for the next 12 months.

During the years 2001–2007, several types of nontraditional amortization schemes have become popular in the mortgage market. The most popular was the **interest-only product** (or IO product). With this type of loan, only interest was paid for a predetermined period of time called the **lockout period**. Following the lockout period, the loan was recast such that the monthly mortgage payments will be sufficient to fully amortize the original amount of the loan over the remaining term of the loan. The interest-only product could have been an FRM, ARM, or hybrid ARM.

Credit Guarantees

Mortgage loans can be classified based on whether a credit guarantee associated with the loan is provided by the federal government, a government-sponsored enterprise, or a private entity. Loans that are backed by agencies of the federal government are referred to under the generic term of **government loans** and are guaranteed by the full faith and credit of the U.S. government. The Department of Housing and Urban Development (HUD) oversees two agencies that guarantee government loans. The first is the Federal Housing Administration (FHA), a governmental entity created by Congress in 1934 that became part of HUD in 1965. FHA provides loan guarantees for those borrowers who can afford only a low down payment and generally also have relatively low levels of income. The second is the Veterans Administration (VA), which is part of the U.S. Department of Veterans Affairs. The VA guaranteed loans are made to eligible veterans and reservists, allowing them to receive favorable loan terms.

In contrast to government loans, there are loans that have no *explicit* guarantee from the federal government. Such loans are said to obtained from "conventional financing" and therefore are referred to in the market as **conventional loans**. Although a conventional loan might not be insured when it is originated, a loan may qualify to be insured when it is included in a pool of mortgage loans that backs a mortgage-backed security (MBS). More specifically, MBSs are those issued by two government-sponsored enterprises, Freddie Mac and Fannie Mae. Because the guarantees of Freddie Mac and Fannie Mae do not carry the full faith and credit of the U.S. government, they are not classified as government loans. We will discuss this further in the next chapter.

A conventional loan can be insured by a **private mortgage insurer**. From an investor's perspective, the guarantee is only as good as the credit rating of the insurer.

Loan Balances

As explained in the next section, for government loans and the loans guaranteed by Freddie Mac and Fannie Mae, there are limits on the loan balance. The maximum loan size for one- to four-family homes changes every year. The loan limits, referred to as **conforming limits**, for Freddie Mac and Fannie Mae are identical because they are specified by the same statute. Loans larger than the conforming limit for a given property type are referred to as **jumbo loans**. The Economic Stimulus Act of 2008 grants Fannie Mae and Freddie Mac temporary authority to purchase loans beyond the above loan limits in designated high-cost areas.

Prepayments and Prepayment Penalties

Homeowners often repay all or part of their mortgage balance prior to the scheduled maturity date. The amount of the payment made in excess of the monthly mortgage payment is called a **prepayment**. For example, consider the 30-year $200,000 mortgage with a 7.5% note rate. The monthly mortgage payment is $1,398.43. Suppose the homeowner makes a payment of $5,398.43. This payment exceeds the monthly mortgage payment by $4,000. This amount represents a prepayment and reduces the outstanding mortgage balance by $4,000. For example, look at Exhibit 10-1. Suppose that the prepayment is made in month 90. In the absence of the prepayment, the mortgage balance at the end of month 90 is $182,141.37. Because of the prepayment of $4,000, the mortgage balance at the end of month 90 is $178,141.37.

This type of prepayment in which the entire mortgage balance is not paid off is called a **partial payment** or **curtailment**. When a curtailment is made, the loan is not recast. Instead, the borrower continues to make the same monthly mortgage payment. The effect of the prepayment is that more of the subsequent monthly mortgage payment is applied to the principal. For example, once again assume that the prepayment of $4,000 is made in month 90. In the next month, month 91, the amount of interest to be paid is based on $178,141.37. The interest is $1,113.38 (7.5% divided by 12 times $178,141.37), which is less than the amount shown in Exhibit 10-1. Therefore, for month 91, the principal repayment is $1,398.43 minus the interest of $1,113.38, or $285.05, compared to the amount shown in Exhibit 10-1 of $260.05. The net effect of the prepayment is that the loan is paid off faster than the scheduled maturity date. That is, the maturity of the loan is "curtailed."

The more common type of prepayment is one where the entire mortgage balance is paid off. All mortgage loans have a "due on sale" clause, which means that the remaining balance of the loan must be paid when the house is sold. Existing mortgages can also be refinanced by the obligor if the prevailing level of mortgage rates declines or if a more attractive financing vehicle is proposed to them.

Effectively, the borrow's right to prepay a loan in whole or in part without a penalty is a called an option. A mortgage design that mitigates the borrower's right to prepay is the **prepayment penalty mortgage**. This mortgage design imposes penalties if borrowers prepay. The penalties are designed to discourage refinancing activity and require a fee to be paid if the loan is prepaid within a certain amount of time after funding. Penalties are typically structured to allow borrowers to partially prepay up to 20% of their loan each year the penalty is in effect and charge the borrower six months of interest for prepayments on the remaining 80% of their balance. Some penalties are waived if the home is sold and are described as "soft" penalties; hard penalties require the penalty to be paid even if the prepayment occurs due to the sale of the underlying property.[3]

CONFORMING LOANS

As explained in Chapter 6, Freddie Mac and Fannie Mae are government-sponsored enterprises (GSEs) whose mission is to provide liquidity and support to the mortgage market. While Fannie Mae and Freddie Mac are private corporations, they did receive a charter from the federal government. This federal charter allows these GSEs to operate with certain benefits that are not available to other corporations. However, the federal charter imposes limits on their business activities. In September 2008, they were placed under the conservatorship of the U.S. government.

One of the ways that GSEs fulfill their mission is by buying and selling mortgages.[4] The loans they purchase can be held in their portfolios or packaged to create an MBS. The securities they create are the subject of the next chapter. While Fannie Mae and Freddie Mac can buy or sell any type of residential mortgage, the mortgages that are packaged into securities are restricted to government loans and those that satisfy their underwriting guidelines. The conventional loans that qualify are referred to as **conforming loans**. A conforming loan is simply a conventional loan that meets the underwriting standard of Fannie Mae and Freddie Mac. Thus, conventional loans in the market are referred to as **conforming conventional loans** and **nonconforming conventional loans**.

One of the underwriting standards is the loan balance at the time of origination. As noted in the previous section, conventional loans that meet the underwriting standards of the two GSEs are called conforming limits. But there are other important underwriting standards that must be satisfied. These include the following:[5]

- type of property (primary residence, vacation/second home, investment property)
- loan type (e.g., fixed rate, ARM)
- transaction type (rate and term refinances, equity buyouts, cash-out refinances)
- loan-to-value ratio by loan type
- loan-to-value ratio by loan type and transaction type
- borrower credit history
- documentation

Qualifying for a conforming loan is important for both the borrower and the mortgage originator. This is because the two GSEs are the largest buyers of mortgages in the United States. Hence, loans that qualify as conforming loans have a greater probability of being purchased by Fannie Mae and Freddie Mac to be packaged into an MBS. As a result, they have lower interest rates than nonconforming conventional loans.

---

[3] The laws and regulations governing the imposition of prepayment penalties are established at the federal and state levels. Usually, the applicable laws for fixed-rate mortgages are specified at the state level. There are states that do not permit prepayment penalties on fixed-rate mortgages with a first lien. There are states that do permit prepayment penalties but restrict the type of penalty. For some mortgage designs, such as adjustable-rate and balloon mortgages, there are federal laws that override state laws.

[4] The two GSEs must allocate a specific percentage of the loans made for low- and moderate-income households or properties located in targeted geographic areas as designed by the Department of Housing and Urban Development. Such loans are classified as "affordable housing loans."

[5] See, for example, Fannie Mae's publication of January 2007, *Guide to Underwriting with DU*, which covers underwriting conventional loans. "DU" is Fannie Mae's automated underwriting system whose purpose is to assist mortgage lenders in making credit lending decisions.

RISKS ASSOCIATED WITH INVESTING IN MORTGAGE LOANS

The principal investors in mortgage loans include thrifts and commercial banks. Pension funds and life insurance companies also invest in these loans, but their ownership is small compared to that of the banks and thrifts. Investors face four main risks by investing in residential mortgage loans: (1) credit risk, (2) liquidity risk, (3) price risk, and (4) prepayment risk.

Credit Risk

Credit risk is the risk that the homeowner/borrower will default. For FHA- and VA-insured mortgages, this risk is minimal. For privately insured mortgages, the risk can be gauged by the credit rating of the private insurance company that has insured the mortgage. For conventional mortgages that are uninsured, the credit risk depends on the credit quality of the borrower. The LTV ratio provides a useful measure of the risk of loss of principal in case of default. When the LTV ratio is high, default is more likely because the borrower has little equity in the property.

At one time, investors considered the LTV only at the time of origination (called the **original LTV**) in their analysis of credit risk. Because of periods in which there has been a decline in housing prices, the **current LTV** has become the focus of attention. The current LTV is the LTV based on the current unpaid mortgage balance and the estimated current market value of the property. Specifically, the concern is that a decline in housing prices can result in a current LTV that is considerably greater than the original LTV. This would result in greater credit risk for such mortgage loans than at the time of origination.

Liquidity Risk

Although there is a secondary market for mortgage loans, which we discuss in the next chapter, the fact is that bid-ask spreads are large compared to other debt instruments. That is, mortgage loans tend to be rather illiquid because they are large and indivisible.

Price Risk

As explained in Chapter 2, the price of a fixed-income instrument will move in an opposite direction from market interest rates. Thus, a rise in interest rates will decrease the price of a mortgage loan.

Prepayments and Cash Flow Uncertainty

The three components of the cash flow for a mortgage loan are

- interest
- principal repayment (scheduled principal repayment or amortization)
- prepayment

Prepayment risk is the risk associated with a mortgage's cash flow due to prepayments. More specifically, investors are concerned that borrowers will pay off a mortgage when prevailing mortgage rates fall below the loan's note rate. For example, if the note rate on a mortgage originated five years ago is 8% and the prevailing mortgage rate (i.e., rate at which a new loan can be obtained) is 5.5%, then there is an incentive for the borrower to refinance the loan. The decision to refinance will depend on several factors, but the single most important one is the prevailing mortgage rate compared to the note rate. The disadvantage to the investor is that the proceeds received from the repayment of the loan must be reinvested at a lower interest rate than the note rate.

This risk is the same as that faced by an investor in a callable corporate or municipal bond. However, unlike a callable bond, there is no premium that must be paid by the borrower in the case of a residential mortgage loan. Any principal repaid in advance of the scheduled due date is paid at par value. The exception, of course, is if the loan is a prepayment penalty mortgage loan.

KEY POINTS

- A mortgage is a pledge of property to secure payment of a debt with the property typically being a form of real estate.
- The two general types of real estate properties that can be mortgaged are single-family (one- to four-family) residential and commercial properties.
- Residential mortgage loans can be classified according to lien status (first and second liens), credit classification (prime and subprime), interest rate type (fixed-rate and adjustable-rate), amortization type (fully amortizing and interest-only), credit guarantees (government loans and conventional loans), loan balances, and prepayments and prepayment penalties.
- The two GSEs, Fannie Mae and Freddie Mac, can purchase any type of loan; however, the only conventional loans that they can securitize to create a mortgage-backed security are conforming loans, that is, conventional loans that satisfy their underwriting standards.
- The cash flow of a mortgage loan consists of interest, scheduled principal repayment, and prepayments.
- The lender faces four main risks by investing in residential mortgage loans: (1) credit risk, (2) liquidity risk, (3) price risk, and (4) prepayment risk.
- Prepayment risk is the risk associated with a mortgage's cash flow due to prepayments.

QUESTIONS

1. What type of property is security for a residential mortgage loan?
2. What are the two primary factors in determining whether or not funds will be lent to an applicant for a residential mortgage loan?
3. Explain why the higher the loan-to-value ratio is, the greater the credit risk is to which the lender is exposed.
4. What is the difference between a cash-out refinancing and a rate-and-term refinancing?
5. What are the front ratio and back ratio, and how do they differ?
6. What is the difference between a prime loan and a subprime loan?
7. How are FICO scores used in classifying loans?
8. What is an alternative-A loan?
9. What is an FHA-insured loan?
10. What is a conventional loan?
11. **a.** What is meant by conforming limits?
    b. What is a jumbo loan?
12. **a.** When a prepayment is made that is less than the full amount to completely pay off the loan, what happens to future monthly mortgage payments for a fixed-rate mortgage loan?
    b. What is the impact of a prepayment that is less than the amount required to completely pay off a loan?
13. Consider the following fixed-rate, level-payment mortgage:

    maturity = 360 months
    amount borrowed = $100,000
    annual mortgage rate = 10%

a. Construct an amortization schedule for the first 10 months.

b. What will the mortgage balance be at the end of the 360th month assuming no prepayments?

c. Without constructing an amortization schedule, what is the mortgage balance at the end of month 270 assuming no prepayments?

d. Without constructing an amortization schedule, what is the scheduled principal payment at the end of month 270 assuming no prepayments?

14. Explain why in a fixed-rate mortgage the amount of the mortgage payment applied to interest declines over time, while the amount applied to the repayment of principal increases.

15. Why is the cash flow of a residential mortgage loan unknown?

16. In what sense has the investor in a residential mortgage loan granted the borrower (homeowner) a loan similar to a callable bond?

17. What is meant by strategic default behavior?

18. What is the advantage of a prepayment penalty mortgage from the perspective of the lender?

19. Explain whether you agree or disagree with the following statements:

a. "Freddie Mac and Fannie Mae are only allowed to purchase conforming conventional loans."

b. "In packaging loans to create a mortgage-backed security, Freddie Mac and Fannie Mae can only use government loans."

20. **a.** What features of an adjustable-rate mortgage will affect its cash flow?

b. What are the two categories of benchmark indexes used in adjustable-rate mortgages?

21. **a.** What is the original LTV of a mortgage loan?

b. What is the current LTV of a mortgage loan?

c. What is the problem with using the original LTV to assess the likelihood that a seasoned mortgage will default?

22. For mortgage loans, what is prepayment risk?

11

Agency Mortgage Pass-Through Securities

LEARNING OBJECTIVES

After reading this chapter, you will understand

- what a mortgage-backed security is
- the different sectors of the residential mortgage-backed securities market
- what a mortgage pass-through security is
- the cash flow characteristics of mortgage pass-through securities
- the importance of prepayment projections in estimating the cash flow of a mortgage pass-through security
- the weighted average contract rate and weighted average maturity of a pass-through security
- the different types of agency pass-through securities
- what the Public Securities Association prepayment benchmark is and how it is used for determining the cash flow of a pass-through security
- the factors that affect prepayments for agency mortgage-backed securities
- what the cash flow yield is and its limitations
- how the average life of a mortgage pass-through security is calculated
- why prepayment risk can be divided into contraction risk and extension risk
- the market trading conventions of mortgage pass-through securities

A residential mortgage–backed security (RMBS) is created when residential mortgages are packaged together to form a pool of mortgage loans and then one or more debt obligations are issued backed by the cash flow generated from the pool of mortgage loans. "Backed" means that the principal and interest due to the investors in an RMBS come from the principal and interest payments made by the borrowers whose loans are part of the pool of mortgages. A mortgage loan that is included in an RMBS is said to be **securitized**, and the process of creating an RMBS is referred to as **securitization**.

In this chapter and the two that follow, we discuss the different sectors in the RMBS market. In the current chapter, we will focus on what agency mortgage pass-through securities are and general information about RMBS. We begin this chapter with a discussion of the different sectors of the RMBS market. That discussion will provide us with a roadmap for this and the next two chapters.

SECTORS OF THE RESIDENTIAL MORTGAGE–BACKED SECURITY MARKET

Our discussion in the previous chapter on the residential mortgage market will help us understand the different sectors in the RMBS market. As explained in the previous chapter and shown in panel a of Exhibit 11-1, the residential mortgage market can be divided into two subsectors based on the credit quality of the borrower:

- prime mortgage market
- subprime mortgage market

Exhibit 11-1   Breakdown of Residential Mortgage Loan Market and the Sectors of the RMBS Market

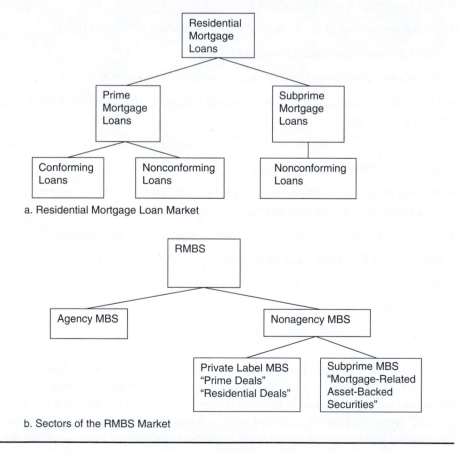

a. Residential Mortgage Loan Market

b. Sectors of the RMBS Market

The prime sector includes (1) loans that satisfy the underwriting standards of Ginnie Mae, Fannie Mae, and Freddie Mac (i.e., conforming loans); and (2) loans that fail to conform for a reason other than credit quality or because the loan is not a first lien on the property (i.e., nonconforming loans). The subprime mortgage sector is the market for loans provided to borrowers with an impaired credit rating or where the loan is a second lien; these loans are nonconforming loans.

All of these loans can be securitized in different sectors of the RMBS market. Loans that satisfy the underwriting standard of the agencies are typically used to create RMBS that are referred to as **agency mortgage-backed securities** (MBS). All other loans are included in what is referred to generically as **nonagency MBS**. In turn, this subsector is classified into **private label MBS**, where prime loans are the collateral, and **subprime MBS**, where subprime loans are the collateral. The names given to the nonagency MBS are arbitrarily assigned. Some market participants refer to private label MBS as "residential deals" or "prime deals." Subprime MBS are also referred to as "mortgage-related asset-backed securities."[1] In fact, market participants often classify agency MBS and private label MBS as part of the RMBS market and subprime MBS as part of the market for asset-backed securities, a sector that we will describe in Chapter 15. This classification is somewhat arbitrary.

In terms of market size, the agency MBS market is the largest sector of the U.S. investment-grade bond market. That is, of all securities that have an investment-grade rating (which includes U.S. Treasury securities), the agency MBS sector is the largest sector. In fact, as of 2010, it was roughly 45% of the investment-grade bond market.

The agency MBS market includes three types of securities:

- agency mortgage pass-through securities
- agency collateralized mortgage obligations (CMOs)
- agency stripped MBS

Agency CMOs and stripped CMOs are created from mortgage pass-through securities. Hence, agency CMOs and agency stripped MBS are routinely referred to as **derivative MBS products**. While Exhibit 11-1 provides a summary of the RMBS market, in recent years, there have been issuances of agency MBS where the loan pool consists of subprime loans. We will mention these in Chapter 12.

Our focus in this chapter is on agency mortgage pass-through securities. In the next chapter, we will describe agency CMOs and agency stripped MBS. In Chapter 13, we look at nonagency MBS.

GENERAL DESCRIPTION OF AN AGENCY MORTGAGE PASS-THROUGH SECURITY

A **mortgage pass-through security**, or simply a pass-through security, is a type of MBS created by pooling mortgage loans and issuing certificates entitling the investor to receive a pro rata share in the cash flows of the specific pool of mortgage loans that serves as the collateral for the security. Because there is only one class of bondholders, these securities are sometimes referred to as **single-class MBS**. As will be explained in the next chapter, what distinguishes pass-through securities from the other two types of agency MBS—agency

---

[1] See Frank J. Fabozzi, Anand K. Bhattacharya, and William S. Berliner, *Mortgage-backed Securities: Products, Structuring, and Analytical Techniques*, 2nd ed. (Hoboken, NJ: John Wiley & Sons, 2010).

CMOs and agency stripped CMOs—is that there are multiple classes of bonds that are backed by the collateral pool.

To illustrate a pass-through security, let's look at an agency pass-through security issued by Fannie Mae on May 1, 2007: *FNMS 05.5000 CL-918462*. The "FNMS" means that it is a security issued by Fannie Mae. The "05.5000" means that the coupon rate for the security is 5.5%. The loan pool that is the collateral for this security is Fannie Mae pool number CL-918462, which turns out to have at issuance 1,103 loans. The "CL" appearing before the pool number is called the **pool prefix**. All agency issuers have their own pool prefix, and it indicates the type of collateral. In the case of Fannie Mae, there is a two-character prefix indicating (1) whether the loans are conventional, government insured, or guaranteed by some entity; (2) whether the note rates for the loans are fixed or adjustable and features about adjustment in the latter case; and (3) the general term to maturity of the loans at issuance. In our Fannie Mae example, "CL" means "Conventional Long-Term, Level-Payment Mortgages; Single-Family; maturing or due in 30 years or less." Other examples of pool prefixes used by Fannie Mae are "CI," which means that the collateral is "Conventional Intermediate-Term, Level-Payment Mortgages; Single-Family; maturing or due in 15 years or less," and "A1," which means that the collateral is "Adjustable-Rate Mortgages; Single-Family; indexed to the one-year Treasury Constant Maturity; 1 percent per interest rate adjustment; lifetime caps are pool-specific."

The total principal of the loan pool for FNMS 05.5000 CL-918462 at the issuance date was $285,296,859 (so the average loan balance at the issuance date was roughly $259,000). If an investor in this security purchased, say, $5,920,000 in principal at issuance, then the investor purchased 2.075% of the issue and is entitled to 2.075% of the cash flow available to investors.

When a pass-through security is first issued, the principal is known. Over time, because of regularly scheduled principal payments and prepayments, the amount of the pool's outstanding loan balance declines. The **pool factor** is the percentage of the original principal that is still outstanding. At issuance, the pool factor is 1 and declines over time. Pool factor information is published monthly.

The cash flow of a pass-through security depends on the cash flow of the underlying loans. As we explained in Chapter 10, the cash flow consists of monthly mortgage payments representing interest, the scheduled repayment of principal, and any prepayments.

Payments are made to the security holders each month. However, neither the amount nor the timing of the cash flow from the loan pool is identical to that of the cash flow passed through to investors. The monthly cash flow for a pass-through security is less than the monthly cash flow of the loan pool by an amount equal to servicing and other fees. The other fees are those charged by the issuer or guarantor of the pass-through for guaranteeing the issue. Therefore, the coupon rate on a pass-through security, called the **pass-through coupon rate**, is less than the mortgage rate on the loan pool by an amount equal to the servicing and guaranteeing fees. For FNMS 05.5000 CL-918462, the pass-through coupon rate is 5.5%.

The timing of the cash flow is also different. The monthly mortgage payment is due from each mortgagor on the first day of each month, but there is a delay in passing through the corresponding monthly cash flow to the security holders. The length of the delay varies by the type of pass-through security.

Because of prepayments, the cash flow of a pass-through is also not known with certainty. The various conventions for estimating the cash flow are discussed later in the chapter.

Not all of the mortgages that are included in the loan pool that are securitized need to have the same note rate and the same maturity. Consequently, when describing a pass-through security, the weighted-average coupon rate and a weighted-average maturity are determined.

A **weighted-average coupon rate** (WAC) is found by weighting the note rate of each mortgage loan in the pool by the amount of the mortgage outstanding at issuance. A **weighted-average maturity** (WAM) is found by weighting the remaining number of months to maturity for each mortgage loan in the pool by the amount of the mortgage outstanding at issuance. This measure is also referred to as the **weighted average loan term** (WALT). For the FNMS 05.5000 CL-918462 security, the WAC at issuance was 6.2%, and the WAM was 360 months. A WAM of 360 months means that the mortgages were newly originated.

After origination of the MBS, the WAM of a pool changes. Fannie Mae and Freddie Mac report the remaining number of months to maturity for a loan pool, which they refer to as the **weighted average remaining maturity** (WARM). Both Fannie Mae and Freddie Mac also report the weighted average of the number of months since the origination of the security for the loans in the pool. This measure is called the **weighted average loan age** (WALA).

Other information about the loan pool is also provided. Exhibit 11-2 shows the pool statistics for FNMS 05.5000 CL-918462 taken from the prospectus supplement. This information is provided to assist the investor in assessing the value of the security or, more specifically, assessing the prepayments that might be expected from the loan pool.

ISSUERS OF AGENCY PASS-THROUGH SECURITIES

Agency pass-through securities are issued by the Governmental National Mortgage Association (Ginnie Mae), the Federal National Mortgage Association (Fannie Mae), and the Federal Home Loan Mortgage Corporation (Freddie Mac). The pass-through securities that they issue are referred to as follows:

Ginnie Mae	Mortgage-Backed Securities (abbreviated MBS)
Fannie Mae	Guaranteed Mortgage Pass-Through Certificates or MBS Certificates (abbreviated MBS)
Freddie Mac	Mortgage Participation Certificates (abbreviated PC)

Do not be confused by the generic term "MBS" and the pass-through certificates that Ginnie Mae and Fannie Mae have elected to refer to as MBS.

Ginnie Mae

As explained in Chapter 6, Ginnie Mae is a federally related institution because it is part of the Department of Housing and Urban Development. As a result, the pass-through securities that it guarantees carry the full faith and credit of the U.S. government with respect to timely payment of both interest and principal. That is, the interest and principal are paid when due even if mortgagors fail to make their monthly mortgage payment.

Exhibit 11-2 Pool Statistics for FNMS 05.5000 CL-918462

FANNIE MAE
MORTGAGE-BACKED SECURITIES PROGRAM
SUPPLEMENT TO PROSPECTUS DATED JANUARY 01, 2006
FANNIE MAE POOL NUMBER CL-918462
CUSIP 31411YMK6
POOL STATISTICS PAGE 2 OF 3

QUARTILE DISTRIBUTION

Loan Size	
MAX	$625,500.00
75%	344,472.00
MED	272,500.00
25%	212,300.00
MIN	148,500.00

Coupon Rate	
MAX	6.7500
75%	6.2500
MED	6.2500
25%	6.1250
MIN	5.9900

LTV	
MAX	100
75%	80
MED	79
25%	68
MIN	19

Credit Score	
MAX	818
75%	770
MED	733
25%	694
MIN	558

Loan Term (# Of Months)	
MAX	360
75%	360
MED	360
25%	360
MIN	300

Loan Age (# Of Months)	
MAX	3
75%	1
MED	0
25%	0
MIN	0

Remaining Maturity (# Of Months)	
MAX	360
75%	360
MED	360
25%	359
MIN	300

LOAN PURPOSE

Type	# Of Loans	% Of UPB	Aggregate UPB
PURCHASE	522	45.71	$130,397,871.91
REFINANCE	581	54.29	154,898,987.31

PROPERTY TYPE

# Of Units	# Of Loans	% Of UPB	Aggregate UPB
1	1095	99.11	$282,751,681.12
2 - 4	8	0.89	2,545,178.10

OCCUPANCY TYPE

Type	# Of Loans	% Of UPB	Aggregate UPB
PRINCIPAL RESIDENCE	1024	93.02	$265,384,181.51
SECOND HOME	52	4.71	13,429,545.31
INVESTOR	27	2.27	6,483,132.40

(Continued)

Exhibit 11-2   Pool Statistics for FNMS 05.5000 CL-918462 (Continued)

FANNIE MAE
MORTGAGE-BACKED SECURITIES PROGRAM
SUPPLEMENT TO PROSPECTUS DATED JANUARY 01, 2006
FANNIE MAE POOL NUMBER CL-918462
CUSIP 31411YMK6
POOL STATISTICS PAGE 3 OF 3

ORIGINATION YEAR

Year	# Of Loans	% Of UPB	Aggregate UPB	Year	# Of Loans	% Of UPB	Aggregate UPB
2007	1103	100.00	$285,296,859.22				

GEOGRAPHIC DISTRIBUTION

State	# Of Loans	% Of UPB	Aggregate UPB	State	# Of Loans	% Of UPB	Aggregate UPB
ALABAMA	15	1.23	$3,518,795.79	MINNESOTA	17	1.41	$4,015,247.95
ALASKA	1	0.08	224,000.00	MISSISSIPPI	4	0.25	723,610.69
ARIZONA	65	5.64	16,100,382.48	MISSOURI	19	1.38	3,930,370.14
ARKANSAS	6	0.48	1,358,461.55	MONTANA	4	0.35	994,471.94
CALIFORNIA	176	18.50	52,773,431.63	NEVADA	29	2.34	6,688,290.67
COLORADO	45	3.83	10,930,647.76	NEW HAMPSHIRE	8	0.67	1,903,164.06
CONNECTICUT	14	1.27	3,624,851.58	NEW JERSEY	49	4.60	13,118,410.38
DELAWARE	3	0.30	865,701.35	NEW MEXICO	8	0.73	2,073,968.30
DISTRICT OF COLUMBIA	1	0.07	209,795.90	NEW YORK	27	2.50	7,132,127.89
FLORIDA	72	6.07	17,306,894.80	NORTH CAROLINA	19	1.60	4,555,181.93
GEORGIA	9	0.64	1,816,368.30	OHIO	21	1.61	4,601,088.09
HAWAII	12	1.71	4,864,341.16	OKLAHOMA	4	0.25	712,778.28
IDAHO	15	1.25	3,552,727.42	OREGON	31	2.45	7,000,479.38
ILLINOIS	67	5.88	16,779,455.25	PENNSYLVANIA	32	2.76	7,876,505.67
INDIANA	11	0.74	2,104,278.78	RHODE ISLAND	3	0.25	722,498.53
IOWA	2	0.16	454,640.32	SOUTH CAROLINA	9	0.82	2,335,065.10
KANSAS	4	0.28	788,720.00	SOUTH DAKOTA	1	0.09	265,635.30
KENTUCKY	10	0.77	2,190,070.01	TENNESSEE	12	0.96	2,751,705.80
LOUISIANA	7	0.63	1,808,778.14	UTAH	40	3.35	9,560,604.89
MAINE	8	0.74	2,118,712.94	VERMONT	3	0.22	641,881.77
MARYLAND	44	4.41	12,595,145.56	VIRGINIA	35	3.50	9,976,537.22
MASSACHUSETTS	42	4.36	12,446,537.19	WASHINGTON	56	5.46	15,584,350.72
MICHIGAN	24	1.90	5,413,948.58	WISCONSIN	19	1.50	4,286,198.03

SERVICER

Servicer Name	# Of Loans	% Of UPB	Aggregate UPB
COUNTRYWIDE HOME LOANS SERVICING, LP	1103	100.00	$285,296,859.22

Source: *Fannie Mae, Mortgage-Backed Securities Program, January 1, 2006, Prospectus Supplement*

We stated at the outset of this section that Ginnie Mae is an issuer of pass-through securities. Technically, that is not correct. Ginnie Mae provides the guarantee, but it is not the issuer. Pass-through securities that carry its guarantee and bear its name are issued by lenders it approves, such as thrifts, commercial banks, and mortgage bankers. Thus, these approved entities are referred to as the "issuers." These lenders receive approval only if the underlying loans satisfy the underwriting standards established by Ginnie Mae. When it guarantees securities issued by approved lenders, Ginnie Mae permits these lenders to convert illiquid individual loans into liquid securities backed by the U.S. government. In the process, Ginnie Mae accomplishes its goal to supply funds to the residential mortgage market and provide an active secondary market. For the guarantee, Ginnie Mae receives a fee, called the **guaranty fee**.

There are two MBS programs through which securities are issued: the Ginnie Mae I program and the Ginnie Mae II program. In the Ginnie Mae I program, pass-through securities are issued that are backed by single-family or multifamily loans; in the Ginnie Mae II program, only single-family loans are included in the loan pool. While the programs are similar, there are differences in addition to the obvious one that the Ginnie Mae I program may include loans for multifamily houses, whereas the Ginnie Mae II program only has single-family housing loans. The most important differences are summarized below:

Ginnie Mae I Program	Ginnie Mae II Program
All mortgages in the pool must have the same note rate.[2]	The note rates for the mortgages in the pool may vary.
The securities issued must have a fixed interest rate.	Some of the securities issued may have an adjustable interest rate.
There is a single issuer who forms the pool.	There may be a single issuer or multiple issuers.

Fannie Mae and Freddie Mac

Although the MBS issued by Fannie Mae and Freddie Mac are commonly referred to as "agency MBS," both are in fact shareholder-owned corporations chartered by Congress to fulfill a public mission.[3] Their stocks trade on the New York Stock Exchange. They do not receive a government subsidy or appropriation and are taxed like any other corporation. As explained in Chapter 6, Fannie Mae and Freddie Mac are government-sponsored enterprises (GSEs). In 1992, Congress established the Office of Federal Housing Enterprise Oversight (OFHEO) to regulate Fannie Mae and Freddie Mac. OFHEO is responsible for overseeing their safety and soundness. In September 2008, both GSEs were placed in conservatorship.

The mission of these two GSEs is to support the liquidity and stability of the mortgage market. They accomplish this by (1) buying and selling mortgages, (2) creating pass-through securities and guaranteeing them, and (3) buying MBS. The mortgages

---

[2] There are exceptions regarding manufactured housing loans.
[3] The securities issued by Fannie Mae and Freddie Mac are sometimes referred to as "conventional pass-through securities." This is because the collateral is typically conventional loans that conform to the underwriting standards of these two GSEs as explained in the previous chapter.

purchased and held as investments by Fannie Mae and Freddie Mac are held in a portfolio referred to as the *retained portfolio*. However, the MBS that they issue are not guaranteed by the full faith and credit of the U.S. government. Rather, the payments to investors in MBS are secured first by the cash flow from the underlying pool of loans and then by a corporate guarantee. Historically however, that corporate guarantee, is the same as the corporate guarantee to the other creditors of the two GSEs. Further government backing was provided in 2008 as part of a bailout of the two GSEs. As with Ginnie Mae, the two GSEs receive a guaranty fee for taking on the credit risk associated with borrowers failing to satisfy their loan obligations.

When issuing MBS, the GSEs provide a prospectus for the offering. What is issued first is what is termed a "prospectus." However, the prospectus contains general information about the securities issued by each GSE and the risks associated with investing in MBS securities in general. The prospectus is amended periodically. It does not provide specific information about the loan pool for a security. That information is provided in a supplement to the prospectus, called the **prospectus supplement** by Fannie Mae and the **pool supplement** by Freddie Mac.

Exhibit 11-3 shows the first two pages of the 72-page Fannie Mae single-family MBS prospectus of June 1, 2007, while Exhibit 11-4 shows the first two pages of the 73-page Freddie Mac Mortgage Participation Certificates prospectus of March 19, 2007. The table of contents of each prospectus is shown in the two exhibits. On page 3 of the Fannie Mae prospectus (not reproduced), it states that, "Each prospectus supplement will include information about the pooled mortgage loans backing that particular issue of certificates and about the certificates themselves." Exhibit 11-2 is an example of pages from a prospectus supplement.

The rules for the formation of pools (i.e., pooling requirements) vary by GSE. For example, in the case of Fannie Mae, when fixed-rate mortgages are used to create a pool, the note rates for the loans in the pool can vary. However, Fannie Mae limits the range of the note rates to 200 basis points.

PREPAYMENT CONVENTIONS AND CASH FLOW[4]

To value a pass-through security, it is necessary to project its cash flow. The difficulty is that the cash flow is unknown because of prepayments. The only way to project a cash flow is to make some assumption about the prepayment rate over the life of the underlying mortgage pool. The prepayment rate assumed is called the **prepayment speed** or, simply, **speed**. The yield calculated based on the projected cash flow is called a **cash flow yield**.

Estimating the cash flow from a pass-through requires making an assumption about future prepayments. Several conventions have been used as a benchmark for prepayment rates: (1) Federal Housing Administration (FHA) experience, (2) the conditional prepayment rate, and (3) the Public Securities Association (PSA) prepayment benchmark. Although the first convention is no longer used, we discuss it because of its historical significance.

In the early stages of the development of the pass-through market, cash flows were calculated assuming no prepayments for the first 12 years, at which time all the mortgages

---

[4] This section and the one to follow are adapted from Chapter 3 of Frank J. Fabozzi and Chuck Ramsey, *Collateralized Mortgage Obligations: Structures and Analysis* (New Hope, PA: Frank J. Fabozzi Associates, 1999).

in the pool were assumed to prepay. This naive approach was replaced by the **FHA prepayment experience** approach. This prepayment assumption, based on the prepayment experience for 30-year mortgages derived from an FHA table on mortgage survival factors, was once the most commonly used benchmark for prepayment rates. It calls for the

---

Exhibit 11-3   First Two Pages of Fannie Mae Single-Family MBS Prospectus (June 1, 2007)

Single-Family MBS Prospectus

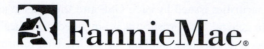

Guaranteed Mortgage Pass-Through Certificates
(Single-Family Residential Mortgage Loans)

The Certificates

We, the Federal National Mortgage Association or Fannie Mae, will issue the guaranteed mortgage pass-through certificates or MBS certificates. Each issue of certificates will have its own identification number and will represent the beneficial ownership in a distinct pool of residential mortgage loans secured by single-family (one-to four-unit) dwellings, or in a pool of participation interests in loans of that type.

Fannie Mae Guaranty

We guarantee to the MBS trust that we will supplement amounts received by the MBS trust as required to permit timely payments of interest and principal on the certificates. We alone are responsible for making payments under our guaranty. **The certificates and payments of principal and interest on the certificates are not guaranteed by the United States, and do not constitute a debt or obligation of the United States or any of its agencies or instrumentalities other than Fannie Mae.**

Consider carefully the risk factors section beginning on page 10. Unless you understand and are able to tolerate these risks, you should not invest in the certificates.

The certificates are exempt from registration under the Securities Act of 1933, as amended, and are "exempted securities" under the Securities Exchange Act of 1934, as amended. Neither the Securities and Exchange Commission nor any state securities commission has approved or disapproved these certificates or determined if this prospectus is truthful or complete. Any representation to the contrary is a criminal offense.

(Continued)

Exhibit 11-3   First Two Pages of Fannie Mae Single-Family MBS Prospectus (June 1, 2007) (Continued)

TABLE OF CONTENTS

Source: *Fannie Mae, June 1, 2007, Prospectus.*

projection of the cash flow for a mortgage pool on the assumption that the prepayment rate will be the same as the FHA experience with 30-year mortgage loans.

Despite the method's past popularity, prepayments based on FHA experience are not necessarily indicative of the prepayment rate for a particular pool, mainly because FHA prepayments are for mortgages originated over all sorts of interest-rate periods. Prepayment rates are tied to interest-rate cycles, however, so an average prepayment rate over various cycles is not very useful in estimating prepayments. Moreover, new

---

Exhibit 11-4 **First Two Pages of Freddie Mac Mortgage Participation Certificates Prospectus (March 19, 2007)**

Freddie Mac

Mortgage Participation Certificates

Mortgage Participation Certificates

Freddie Mac issues and guarantees Mortgage Participation Certificates, or **"PCs."** PCs are securities that represent undivided beneficial ownership interests in, and receive payments from, pools of one- to four-family residential mortgages.

Freddie Mac's Guarantee

We guarantee the payment of interest and principal on the PCs as described in this Offering Circular. **Principal and interest payments on the PCs are not guaranteed by and are not debts or obligations of the United States or any federal agency or instrumentality other than Freddie Mac.** We alone are responsible for making payments on our guarantee.

Tax Status and Securities Law Exemptions

The PCs are not tax-exempt. Because of applicable securities law exemptions, we have not registered the PCs with any federal or state securities commission. No securities commission has reviewed this Offering Circular.

The PCs may not be suitable investments for you. You should not purchase PCs unless you have carefully considered and are able to bear the associated prepayment, interest rate, yield and market risks of investing in them. The *Risk Factors* section beginning on page 8 highlights some of these risks.

(Continued)

Exhibit 11-4   First Two Pages of Freddie Mac Mortgage Participation Certificates Prospectus (March 19, 2007) (Continued)

If you intend to purchase PCs, you should rely only on the information in this Offering Circular, in the disclosure documents that we incorporate by reference in this Offering Circular as stated under *Additional Information* and in the related pool supplement (each, a **"Pool Supplement"**) that we will make available on our internet website as to each PC Pool upon its formation.

We also make available on our internet website certain loan-level information regarding each of the Mortgages backing our PCs based on information furnished to us by the sellers of the Mortgages. We may not have independently verified information furnished to us by sellers regarding the Mortgages backing our PCs and make no representations or warranties concerning the accuracy or completeness of that information. In addition, sellers sometimes provide information about certain mortgages that they sell to us in separate additional supplements (**"Additional Supplements"**).

Each Pool Supplement and Additional Supplement contains information on a pool-level basis as of the date of the issuance of the related PCs. For the convenience of investors, we may post Additional Supplements on our website and furnish them upon request. We have not verified the information in Additional Supplements and make no representations or warranties concerning the accuracy or completeness of that information.

You can find additional and updated information about our PCs on our internet website at www.freddiemac.com/mbs/. We have not authorized anyone to provide you with different information. Any information that may be furnished to you by a third party may not be reliable.

This Offering Circular, any related Pool Supplement, any loan-level information and any incorporated documents may not be correct after their dates.

We are not offering the PCs in any jurisdiction that prohibits their offer.

TABLE OF CONTENTS

Source: *Freddie Mac*

FHA tables are published periodically, causing confusion about the FHA table on which prepayments should be based. Finally, because FHA mortgages are assumable (unlike Fannie Mae, Freddie Mac, and most nonconforming mortgages that have due-on-sale provisions), FHA statistics underestimate prepayments for non-FHA mortgages. Because estimated prepayments using the FHA experience may be misleading, the resulting cash flow is not meaningful for valuing pass-throughs.

Conditional Prepayment Rate

Another benchmark for projecting prepayments and the cash flow of a pass-through requires assuming that some fraction of the remaining principal in the pool is prepaid each month for the remaining term of the mortgage. The prepayment rate assumed for a pool, called the **conditional prepayment rate** (CPR), is based on the characteristics of the pool (including its historical prepayment experience) and the current and expected future economic environment. It is referred to as a conditional rate because it is conditional on the remaining mortgage balance at the beginning of the month.

Single-Monthly Mortality Rate

The CPR is an annual prepayment rate. To estimate monthly prepayments, the CPR must be converted into a monthly prepayment rate, commonly referred to as the **single-monthly mortality rate** (SMM). A formula can be used to determine the SMM for a given CPR:

$$SMM = 1 - (1 - CPR)^{1/12} \tag{11.1}$$

Suppose that the CPR used to estimate prepayments is 6%. The corresponding SMM is

$$\begin{aligned} SMM &= 1 - (1 - 0.06)^{1/12} \\ &= 1 - (0.94)^{0.08333} = 0.005143 \end{aligned}$$

Single-Monthly Mortality Rate and Monthly Prepayment

An SMM of $w\%$ means that approximately $w\%$ of the remaining mortgage balance at the beginning of the month, less the scheduled principal payment, will prepay that month. That is, prepayment for month t is

$$\begin{aligned} = SMM \times (&\text{beginning mortgage balance for month } t \\ &- \text{scheduled principal payment for month } t) \end{aligned} \tag{11.2}$$

For example, suppose that an investor owns a pass-through in which the remaining mortgage balance at the beginning of some month is $290 million. Assuming that the SMM is 0.5143% and the scheduled principal payment is $3 million, the estimated prepayment for the month is

$$0.005143(\$290,000,000 - \$3,000,000) = \$1,476,041$$

Public Securities Association Prepayment Benchmark

The Public Securities Association (PSA)[5] prepayment benchmark is expressed as a monthly series of annual prepayment rates.[6] The PSA benchmark assumes that prepayment rates are low for newly originated mortgages and then will speed up as the mortgages become seasoned.

---

[5] The PSA changed its name to the Bond Market Association (BMA) and then to the Securities Industry and Financial Markets Association (SIFMA). Despite the name changes, the term PSA prepayment benchmark is still used.

[6] This benchmark is commonly referred to as a *prepayment model*, suggesting that it can be used to estimate prepayments. Characterization of this benchmark as a prepayment model is inappropriate. It is simply a market convention of prepayment behavior.

The PSA benchmark assumes the following CPRs for 30-year mortgages: (1) a CPR of 0.2% for the first month, increased by 0.2% per year per month for the next 30 months when it reaches 6% per year, and (2) a 6% CPR for the remaining years. This benchmark, referred to as "100% PSA" or simply "100 PSA," is depicted graphically in Exhibit 11-5. Mathematically, 100 PSA can be expressed as follows:

$$\text{If } t \le 30: \text{CPR} = 6\%(t/30)$$
$$\text{If } t > 30: \text{CPR} = 6\%$$

where t is the number of months since the mortgage originated.

Slower or faster speeds are then referred to as some percentage of PSA. For example, 50 PSA means one-half the CPR of the PSA benchmark prepayment rate; 150 PSA means 1.5 times the CPR of the PSA benchmark prepayment rate; 300 PSA means three times the CPR of the benchmark prepayment rate. A prepayment rate of 0 PSA means that no prepayments are assumed.

The CPR is converted to an SMM using equation (11.1). For example, the SMMs for month 5, month 20, and months 31 through 360 assuming 100 PSA are calculated as follows:

For month 5:

$$\text{CPR} = 6\%(5/30) = 1\% = 0.01$$
$$\text{SMM} = 1 - (1 - 0.01)^{1/12}$$
$$= 1 - (0.99)^{0.83333} = 0.000837$$

For month 20:

$$\text{CPR} = 6\%(20/30) = 4\% = 0.04$$
$$\text{SMM} = 1 - (1 - 0.04)^{1/12}$$
$$= 1 - (0.96)^{0.083333} = 0.0003396$$

For months 31–360:

$$\text{CPR} = 6\%$$
$$\text{SMM} = 1 - (1 - 0.06)^{1/12}$$
$$= 1 - (0.94)^{0.083333} = 0.005143$$

Exhibit 11-5   Graphic Depiction of 100 PSA

The SMMs for month 5, month 20, and months 31 through 360 assuming 165 PSA are computed as follows:

For month 5:

$$CPR = 6\%(5/30) = 1\% = 0.01$$
$$165\ PSA = 1.65(0.01) = 0.0165$$
$$SMM = 1 - (1 - 0.0165)^{1/12}$$
$$= 1 - (0.9835)^{0.083333} = 0.001386$$

For month 20:

$$CPR = 6\%(20/30) = 4\% = 0.04$$
$$165\ PSA = 1.65(0.04) = 0.066$$
$$SMM = 1 - (1 - 0.066)^{1/12}$$
$$= 1 - (0.934)^{0.083333} = 0.005674$$

For months 31 through 360:

$$CPR = 6\%$$
$$165\ PSA = 1.65(0.06) = 0.099$$
$$SMM = 1 - (1 - 0.099)^{1/12}$$
$$= 1 - (0.901)^{0.083333} = 0.007828$$

Notice that the SMM assuming 165 PSA is not just 1.65 times the SMM assuming 100 PSA. It is the CPR that is a multiple of the CPR assuming 100 PSA.

Monthly Cash Flow Construction

We now show how to construct a monthly cash flow for a hypothetical pass-through given a PSA assumption. For the purpose of this illustration, the underlying mortgages for this hypothetical pass-through are assumed to be fixed-rate level-payment mortgages with a WAC of 8.125%. It will be assumed that the pass-through rate is 7.5%, with a WAM of 357 months.

Exhibit 11-6 shows the cash flow for selected months assuming 100 PSA. The cash flow is broken down into three components: (1) interest (based on the pass-through rate), (2) the regularly scheduled principal repayment, and (3) prepayments based on 100 PSA.

Let's walk through Exhibit 11-6 column by column.

Column 1 This is the month.

Column 2 This column gives the outstanding mortgage balance at the beginning of the month. It is equal to the outstanding balance at the beginning of the preceding month reduced by the total principal payment in the preceding month.

Column 3 This column shows the SMM for 100 PSA. Two things should be noted in this column. First, for month 1, the SMM is for a pass-through that has been seasoned three months. That is, the CPR is 0.8%. This is because the WAM is 357. Second, from month 27 on, the SMM is 0.00514, which corresponds to a CPR of 6%.

Column 4 The total monthly mortgage payment is shown in this column. Notice that the total monthly mortgage payment declines over time as prepayments reduce the mortgage balance outstanding. There is a formula to determine what the monthly mortgage balance will be for each month given prepayments.[7]

---

[7] The formula is presented in Chapter 22 of Frank J. Fabozzi, *Fixed Income Mathematics: Analytical and Statistical Techniques,* 4th ed. (New York: McGraw-Hill, 2006).

Exhibit 11-6 Monthly Cash Flow for a $400 Million 7.5% Pass-Through Rate with a WAC of 8.125% and a WAM of 357 Months Assuming 100 PSA

(1) Month	(2) Outstanding Balance	(3) SMM	(4) Mortgage Payment	(5) Interest	(6) Scheduled Principal	(7) Prepayment	(8) Total Principal	(9) Total Cash Flow
1	400,000,000	0.00067	2,975,868	2,500,000	267,535	267,470	535,005	3,035,005
2	399,464,995	0.00084	2,973,877	2,496,656	269,166	334,198	603,364	3,100,020
3	398,861,631	0.00101	2,971,387	2,492,885	270,762	400,800	671,562	3,164,447
4	398,190,069	0.00117	2,968,399	2,488,688	272,321	467,243	739,564	3,228,252
5	397,450,505	0.00134	2,964,914	2,484,066	273,843	533,493	807,335	3,291,401
6	396,643,170	0.00151	2,960,931	2,479,020	275,327	599,514	874,841	3,353,860
7	395,768,329	0.00168	2,956,453	2,473,552	276,772	665,273	942,045	3,415,597
8	394,826,284	0.00185	2,951,480	2,467,664	278,177	730,736	1,008,913	3,476,577
9	393,817,371	0.00202	2,946,013	2,461,359	279,542	795,869	1,075,410	3,536,769
10	392,741,961	0.00219	2,940,056	2,454,637	280,865	860,637	1,141,502	3,596,140
11	391,600,459	0.00236	2,933,608	2,447,503	282,147	925,008	1,207,155	3,654,658
12	390,393,304	0.00254	2,926,674	2,439,958	283,386	988,948	1,272,333	3,712,291
13	389,120,971	0.00271	2,919,254	2,432,006	284,581	1,052,423	1,337,004	3,769,010
14	387,783,966	0.00288	2,911,353	2,423,650	285,733	1,115,402	1,401,134	3,824,784
15	386,382,832	0.00305	2,902,973	2,414,893	286,839	1,177,851	1,464,690	3,879,583
16	384,918,142	0.00322	2,894,117	2,405,738	287,900	1,239,739	1,527,639	3,933,378
17	383,390,502	0.00340	2,884,789	2,396,191	288,915	1,301,033	1,589,949	3,986,139
18	381,800,553	0.00357	2,874,992	2,386,253	289,884	1,361,703	1,651,587	4,037,840
19	380,148,966	0.00374	2,864,730	2,375,931	290,805	1,421,717	1,712,522	4,088,453
20	378,436,444	0.00392	2,854,008	2,365,228	291,678	1,481,046	1,772,724	4,137,952
21	376,663,720	0.00409	2,842,830	2,354,148	292,503	1,539,658	1,832,161	4,186,309
22	374,831,559	0.00427	2,831,201	2,342,697	293,279	1,597,525	1,890,804	4,233,501
23	372,940,755	0.00444	2,819,125	2,330,880	294,005	1,654,618	1,948,623	4,279,503
24	370,992,132	0.00462	2,806,607	2,318,701	294,681	1,710,908	2,005,589	4,324,290
25	368,986,543	0.00479	2,793,654	2,306,166	295,307	1,766,368	2,061,675	4,367,841
26	366,924,868	0.00497	2,780,270	2,293,280	295,883	1,820,970	2,116,852	4,410,133
27	364,808,016	0.00514	2,766,461	2,280,050	296,406	1,874,688	2,171,092	4,451,144
28	362,636,921	0.00514	2,752,233	2,266,481	296,879	1,863,519	2,160,398	4,426,879
29	360,476,523	0.00514	2,738,078	2,252,978	297,351	1,852,406	2,149,758	4,402,736

(Continued)

Exhibit 11-6 Monthly Cash Flow for a $400 Million 7.5% Pass-Through Rate with a WAC of 8.125% and a WAM of 357 Months Assuming 100 PSA (Continued)

(1)	(2)	(3)	(4)	(5)	(6)	(7)	(8)	(9)
Month	Outstanding Balance	SMM	Mortgage Payment	Interest	Scheduled Principal	Prepayment	Total Principal	Total Cash Flow
30	358,326,766	0.00514	2,723,996	2,239,542	297,825	1,841,347	2,139,173	4,378,715
...								
100	231,249,776	0.00514	1,898,682	1,445,311	332,928	1,187,608	1,520,537	2,965,848
101	229,729,239	0.00514	1,888,917	1,435,808	333,459	1,179,785	1,513,244	2,949,052
102	228,215,995	0.00514	1,879,202	1,426,350	333,990	1,172,000	1,505,990	2,932,340
103	226,710,004	0.00514	1,869,538	1,416,938	334,522	1,164,252	1,498,774	2,915,712
104	225,211,230	0.00514	1,859,923	1,407,570	335,055	1,156,541	1,491,596	2,899,166
105	223,719,634	0.00514	1,850,357	1,398,248	335,589	1,148,867	1,484,456	2,882,703
...								
200	109,791,339	0.00514	1,133,751	686,196	390,372	562,651	953,023	1,639,219
201	108,838,316	0.00514	1,127,920	680,239	390,994	557,746	948,740	1,628,980
202	107,889,576	0.00514	1,122,119	674,310	391,617	552,863	944,480	1,618,790
203	106,945,096	0.00514	1,116,348	668,407	392,241	548,003	940,243	1,608,650
204	106,004,852	0.00514	1,110,607	662,530	392,866	543,164	936,029	1,598,560
205	105,068,823	0.00514	1,104,895	656,680	393,491	538,347	931,838	1,588,518
...								
300	32,383,611	0.00514	676,991	202,398	457,727	164,195	621,923	824,320
301	31,761,689	0.00514	673,510	198,511	458,457	160,993	619,449	817,960
302	31,142,239	0.00514	670,046	194,639	459,187	157,803	616,990	811,629
303	30,525,249	0.00514	666,600	190,783	459,918	154,626	614,545	805,328
304	29,910,704	0.00514	663,171	186,942	460,651	151,462	612,113	799,055
305	29,298,591	0.00514	659,761	183,116	461,385	148,310	609,695	792,811
...								
350	4,060,411	0.00514	523,138	25,378	495,645	18,334	513,979	539,356
351	3,546,432	0.00514	520,447	22,165	496,435	15,686	512,121	534,286
352	3,034,311	0.00514	517,770	18,964	497,226	13,048	510,274	529,238
353	2,524,037	0.00514	515,107	15,775	498,018	10,420	508,437	524,213
354	2,015,600	0.00514	512,458	12,597	498,811	7,801	506,612	519,209
355	1,508,988	0.00514	509,823	9,431	499,606	5,191	504,797	514,228
356	1,004,191	0.00514	507,201	6,276	500,401	2,591	502,992	509,269

Column 5 The monthly interest paid to the pass-through investor is found in this column. This value is determined by multiplying the outstanding mortgage balance at the beginning of the month by the pass-through rate of 7.5% and dividing by 12.

Column 6 This column gives the regularly scheduled principal repayment. This is the difference between the total monthly mortgage payment (the amount shown in column 4) and the gross coupon interest for the month. The gross coupon interest is 8.125% multiplied by the outstanding mortgage balance at the beginning of the month, then divided by 12.

Column 7 The prepayment for the month is reported in this column. The prepayment is found by using equation (11.2). So, for example, in month 100, the beginning mortgage balance is $231,249,776, the scheduled principal payment is $332,928, and the SMM at 100 PSA is 0.00514301 (only 0.00514 is shown in the table to save space), so the prepayment is

$$0.00514301(\$231,249,776 - \$332,928) = \$1,187,608$$

Column 8 The total principal payment, which is the sum of columns 6 and 7, is shown in this column.

Column 9 The projected monthly cash flow for this pass-through is shown in the last column. The monthly cash flow is the sum of the interest paid to the pass-through investor (column 5) and the total principal payments for the month (column 8).

Exhibit 11-7 shows selected monthly cash flows for the same pass-through assuming 165 PSA.

Beware of Conventions

The PSA prepayment benchmark is simply a market convention. It is the product of a study by the PSA based on FHA prepayment experience. Data that the PSA committee examined seemed to suggest that mortgages became seasoned (i.e., prepayment rates tended to level off) after 30 months and the CPR tended to be 6%. How, though, did the PSA come up with the CPRs used for months 1 through 29? In fact, these numbers are not based on empirical evidence but on a linear increase from month 1 to month 30 so that at month 30 the CPR is 6%. Moreover, the same benchmark or seasoning process is used in quoting pass-throughs regardless of the collateral: 30- or 15-year loans, fixed- or adjustable-rate loans, and conventional or VA/FHA-insured loans.

Astute money managers recognize that the CPR is a convenient shorthand enabling market participants to quote yield and/or price but that, as a convention in determining value, it has many limitations.

FACTORS AFFECTING PREPAYMENTS AND PREPAYMENT MODELING

A prepayment model is a statistical model that is used to forecast prepayments. It begins by modeling the statistical relationships among the factors that are expected to affect prepayments. Wall Street firms that sell MBS and independent research firms have developed prepayment models.

Exhibit 11-7 Monthly Cash Flow for a $400 Million 7.5% Pass-Through Rate with a WAC of 8.125% and a WAM of 357 Months Assuming 165 PSA

(1)	(2)	(3)	(4)	(5)	(6)	(7)	(8)	(9)
Month	Outstanding Balance	SMM	Mortgage Payment	Interest	Scheduled Principal	Prepayment	Total Principal	Total Cash Flow
1	400,000,000	0.00111	2,975,868	2,500,000	267,535	442,389	709,923	3,209,923
2	399,290,077	0.00139	2,972,575	2,495,563	269,048	552,847	821,896	3,317,459
3	398,468,181	0.00167	2,968,456	2,490,426	270,495	663,065	933,560	3,423,986
4	397,534,621	0.00195	2,963,513	2,484,591	271,873	772,949	1,044,822	3,529,413
5	396,489,799	0.00223	2,957,747	2,478,061	273,181	882,405	1,155,586	3,633,647
6	395,334,213	0.00251	2,951,160	2,470,839	274,418	991,341	1,265,759	3,736,598
7	394,068,454	0.00279	2,943,755	2,462,928	275,583	1,099,664	1,375,246	3,838,174
8	392,693,208	0.00308	2,935,534	2,454,333	276,574	1,207,280	1,483,954	3,938,287
9	391,209,254	0.00336	2,926,503	2,445,058	277,690	1,314,099	1,591,789	4,036,847
10	389,617,464	0.00365	2,916,666	2,435,109	278,631	1,420,029	1,698,659	4,133,769
11	387,918,805	0.00393	2,906,028	2,424,493	279,494	1,524,979	1,804,473	4,228,965
12	386,114,332	0.00422	2,894,595	2,413,215	280,280	1,628,859	1,909,139	4,322,353
13	384,205,194	0.00451	2,882,375	2,401,282	280,586	1,731,581	2,012,567	4,413,850
14	382,192,626	0.00480	2,869,375	2,388,704	281,613	1,833,058	2,114,670	4,503,374
15	380,077,956	0.00509	2,855,603	2,375,487	282,159	1,933,203	2,215,361	4,590,848
16	377,862,595	0.00538	2,841,068	2,361,641	282,623	2,031,931	2,314,554	4,676,195
17	375,548,041	0.00567	2,825,779	2,347,175	283,006	2,129,159	2,412,164	4,759,339
18	373,135,877	0.00597	2,809,746	2,332,099	283,305	2,224,805	2,508,110	4,840,210
19	370,627,766	0.00626	2,792,980	2,316,424	283,521	2,318,790	2,602,312	4,918,735
20	368,025,455	0.00656	2,775,493	2,300,159	283,654	2,411,036	2,694,690	4,994,849
21	365,330,765	0.00685	2,757,296	2,283,317	283,702	2,501,466	2,785,169	5,068,486
22	362,545,596	0.00715	2,738,402	2,265,910	283,666	2,590,008	2,873,674	5,139,584
23	359,671,922	0.00745	2,718,823	2,247,950	283,545	2,676,588	2,960,133	5,208,083
24	356,711,789	0.00775	2,698,575	2,229,449	283,338	2,761,139	3,044,477	5,273,926
25	353,667,312	0.00805	2,677,670	2,210,421	283,047	2,843,593	3,126,640	5,337,061
26	350,540,672	0.00835	2,656,123	2,190,879	282,671	2,923,885	3,206,556	5,397,435
27	347,334,116	0.00865	2,633,950	2,170,838	282,209	3,001,955	3,284,164	5,455,002
28	344,049,952	0.00865	2,611,167	2,150,312	281,662	2,973,553	3,255,215	5,405,527
29	340,794,737	0.00865	2,588,581	2,129,967	281,116	2,945,400	3,226,516	5,356,483

(Continued)

Exhibit 11-7 Monthly Cash Flow for a $400 Million 7.5% Pass-Through Rate with a WAC of 8.125% and a WAM of 357 Months Assuming 165 PSA (Continued)

Month	Outstanding Balance	SMM	Mortgage Payment	Net Interest	Scheduled Principal	Prepayment	Total Principal	Cash Flow
30	337,568,221	0.00865	2,566,190	2,109,801	280,572	2,917,496	3,198,067	5,307,869
⋮								
100	170,142,350	0.00865	1,396,958	1,063,390	244,953	1,469,591	1,714,544	2,777,933
101	168,427,806	0.00865	1,384,875	1,052,674	244,478	1,454,765	1,699,243	2,751,916
102	166,728,563	0.00865	1,372,896	1,042,054	244,004	1,440,071	1,684,075	2,726,128
103	165,044,489	0.00865	1,361,020	1,031,528	243,531	1,425,508	1,669,039	2,700,567
104	163,375,450	0.00865	1,349,248	1,021,097	243,060	1,411,075	1,654,134	2,675,231
105	161,721,315	0.00865	1,337,577	1,010,758	242,589	1,396,771	1,639,359	2,650,118
⋮								
200	56,746,664	0.00865	585,990	354,667	201,767	489,106	690,874	1,045,540
201	56,055,790	0.00865	580,921	350,349	201,377	483,134	684,510	1,034,859
202	55,371,280	0.00865	575,896	346,070	200,986	477,216	678,202	1,024,273
203	54,693,077	0.00865	570,915	341,832	200,597	471,353	671,950	1,013,782
204	54,021,127	0.00865	565,976	337,632	200,208	465,544	665,752	1,003,384
205	53,355,375	0.00865	561,081	333,471	199,820	459,789	659,609	993,080
⋮								
300	11,758,141	0.00865	245,808	73,488	166,196	100,269	266,465	339,953
301	11,491,677	0.00865	243,682	71,823	165,874	97,967	263,841	335,664
302	11,227,836	0.00865	241,574	70,174	165,552	95,687	261,240	331,414
303	10,966,596	0.00865	239,485	68,541	165,232	93,430	258,662	327,203
304	10,707,934	0.00865	237,413	66,925	164,912	91,196	256,107	323,032
305	10,451,827	0.00865	235,360	65,324	164,592	88,983	253,575	318,899
⋮								
350	1,235,674	0.00865	159,202	7,723	150,836	9,384	160,220	167,943
351	1,075,454	0.00865	157,825	6,722	150,544	8,000	158,544	165,266
352	916,910	0.00865	156,460	5,731	150,252	6,631	156,883	162,614
353	760,027	0.00865	155,107	4,750	149,961	5,277	155,238	159,988
354	604,789	0.00865	153,765	3,780	149,670	3,937	153,607	157,387
355	451,182	0.00865	152,435	2,820	149,380	2,611	151,991	154,811
356	299,191	0.00865	151,117	1,870	149,091	1,298	150,389	152,259
357	148,802	0.00865	149,809	930	148,802	0	148,802	149,732

At one time, because of the data limitations on the individual loans in the pool backing a mortgage-backed security, prepayment models viewed borrowers as generic, with the only significant difference in borrowers being due to

1. how borrowers respond, on average, to refinancing opportunities based on their mortgage rate relative to the market rate, and the loan age (i.e., the length of time their mortgage has been outstanding)
2. the type of loan (i.e., fixed rate vs. adjustable rate)

Today, more data are available, particularly for nonagency MBS, regarding borrower and loan attributes. The attributes that modelers have found to be important in the nonagency MBS market have been applied to the agency MBS market using proxy measures where data for individual loans are not available. As a result, more variables are now used to compute prepayments that are attributable to refinancing and housing turnover.

Modelers have developed different prepayment models for agency and nonagency mortgage-backed securities. However, much less borrower and loan data are provided for agency MBS than for nonagency MBS. As a result, prepayment modeling has been done at the pool level rather than the loan level.

An agency prepayment model typically consists of three components:

*   housing turnover
*   cash-out refinancing
*   rate/term refinancing

Here we discuss these factors for agency MBS. Although the factors driving prepayments in a prepayment model typically do not change over time (except when more detailed data become available), the relative importance of the values of the factors does change.

Housing Turnover Component

Housing turnover means existing home sales. The two factors that impact existing home sales include:

*   family relocation due to changes in employment and family status (e.g., change in family size, divorce)
*   trade-up and trade-down activity attributable to changes in interest rates, income, and home prices

In general, housing turnover is insensitive to the level of mortgage rates.

The factors typically used to forecast prepayments due to housing turnover are (1) seasoning effect, (2) housing price appreciation effect, and (3) seasonality effect.

Because of transaction costs and moving costs, one might not expect that a newly acquired home would be sold shortly after it is purchased. The 30-month ramp in the baseline PSA model is a reflection of this view. However, due to periods of substantial refinancing (i.e., refinancing waves), there is evidence that a 30-month aging period is no longer an appropriate description of the seasoning process because the homeowner's tenure in the home (which does not necessarily correspond to the age of the loan due to refinancing) must be recognized. For example, a homeowner who resided in a home for 10 years but refinanced six months ago would view the decision to sell his home differently than someone who just moved into a home six months ago. Consequently, this must be accounted for.

With respect to housing appreciation, over time the LTV of a loan changes. This is due to both the amortization of the loan and the change in the value of the home. There is an incentive for cash-out refinancing (discussed next) if the value of a home appreciates. Thus, in prepayment modeling, to estimate prepayments attributable to housing appreciation, a proxy is needed to capture the change in the value of the LTV for a pool. Modelers do so in building agency prepayment models by constructing a composite *home appreciation index* (HPI).

Finally, there is a well-documented seasonal pattern in prepayments. This pattern, referred to as the **seasonality effect**,[8] is related to activity in the primary housing market, with home buying increasing in the spring and gradually reaching a peak in late summer. Home buying declines in the fall and winter. Mirroring this activity are the prepayments that result from the turnover of housing as home buyers sell their existing homes and purchase new ones. Prepayments are low in the winter months and begin to rise in the spring, reaching a peak in the summer months. However, probably because of delays in passing through prepayments, the peak may not be observed until early fall.

Cash-Out Refinancing Component

Cash-out refinancing means refinancing by a borrower in order to monetize the price appreciation of the property. Obviously, prepayments due to cash-out refinancing will depend on the increase in housing prices in the economy or region where the property is located. Adding to the incentive for borrowers to monetize price appreciation is the favorable tax law regarding the taxation of capital gains. Thus, cash-out refinancing may be economic despite a rising mortgage rate and considering transaction costs. Basically, cash-out refinancing is more like housing turnover refinancing because of its tie to housing prices and its insensitivity to mortgage rates. The proxy measure used for price appreciation in prepayment models is the HPI.

Rate/Term Refinancing Component

Rate/term refinancing means that the borrower has obtained a new mortgage on the existing property to save either on interest cost or by shortening the life of the mortgage with no increase in the monthly payment. The homeowner's incentive to refinance is based on the projected present value of the dollar interest savings from the lower mortgage rate after deducting the estimated transaction costs to refinance.

In prepayment modeling, what measure is used to proxy for the savings incentive for a rate/term refinancing? One simple proxy would be to use the difference between the prevailing mortgage rate and the note rate on the homeowner's loan. However, this is not a good proxy. The reason is that a difference of 100 basis points between the homeowner's note rate and the prevailing mortgage rate has a greater impact on the borrower's savings if the borrower's note rate is 11% rather than 6%. Prepayment modelers have found that a better, although not perfect, proxy for capturing the incentive to refinance is the ratio of the borrower's note rate to the current mortgage rate. This ratio is called the **refinancing ratio**. For agency data, the WAC is the numerator. A refinancing ratio less than 1 means that the borrower's mortgage rate is less than the prevailing mortgage rate, and therefore, there is no incentive for rate/term refinancing; a refinancing ratio of 1 means

---

[8] Do not get seasonality and seasoning confused. Seasonality is the time of the year; seasoning is the aging of a loan.

Exhibit 11-8 Example of an S-Curve for Prepayments

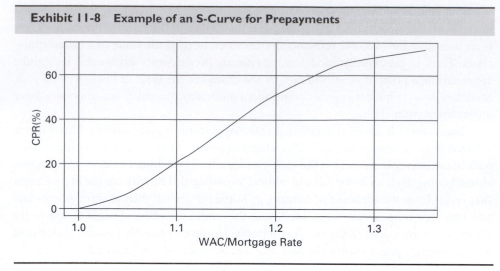

that the borrower has no incentive to refinance because his rate is the same as the market rate. When the refinancing ratio exceeds unity, there is an incentive to refinance.

The refinancing decision is not based solely on the mortgage rate relative to the prevailing market rate but also on a host of other borrower circumstances. This is reflected in the **S-curve for prepayments**, which is graphically illustrated in Exhibit 11-8. The reason for the observed S-curve for prepayments is that as the rate ratio increases, the CPR (i.e., prepayment rate) increases. There is some level of the rate ratio, however, at which the prepayment rate tends to level off. The reason for this leveling off of the prepayment rate is because the only borrowers remaining in the pool are those who cannot obtain refinancing or those who have other reasons why refinancing does not make sense.

The S-curve is not sufficient for modeling the rate/term refinancing. This is because the S-curve fails to adequately account for a borrower attribute that impacts refinancing decisions: the burnout effect. The **burnout effect** occurs because the composition of borrowers in a mortgage pool changes over time due to seasoning and refinancing patterns. More specifically, as mortgage rates decline, those borrowers in the pool who are the most interest-rate sensitive prepay. The balance of the borrowers in the pool are less rate sensitive but, as mortgage rates continue to decline, these borrowers prepay. As mortgage rates continue down, there is less additional prepayment activity, and at some point, the incentive to refinance is "burned out."

CASH FLOW YIELD

Given the projected cash flow and the price of a pass-through, its yield can be calculated. The yield is the interest rate that will make the present value of the expected cash flow equal to the price. A yield computed in this manner is known as a **cash flow yield**.

Bond-Equivalent Yield

For a pass-through, the yield that makes the present value of the cash flow equal to the price is a monthly interest rate. The next step is to annualize the monthly yield. According to market convention, to compare the yield for a pass-through to that of a Treasury or corporate bond, the monthly yield should not be annualized just by multiplying the monthly yield by 12. The reason is that a Treasury bond and a corporate bond pay interest semiannually, whereas a pass-through has a monthly cash flow. By reinvesting monthly cash flows, the pass-through holder has the opportunity to generate greater interest than can be earned by a bondholder who has only semiannual coupon payments to reinvest. Therefore, the yield on a pass-through must be calculated so as to make it comparable to the yield to maturity for a bond.

This is accomplished by computing the **bond-equivalent yield.** As explained in Chapter 3, this is simply a market convention for annualizing any fixed-income instrument that pays interest more than once a year. The bond-equivalent yield is found by doubling a semiannual yield. For a pass-through security, the semiannual yield is

$$\text{semiannual cash flow yield} = (1 + y_M)^6 - 1$$

where y_M is the monthly interest rate that will equate the present value of the projected monthly cash flow to the price of the pass-through. The bond-equivalent yield is found by doubling the semiannual cash flow yield; that is

$$\text{bond-equivalent yield} = 2\left[(1 + y_M)^6 - 1\right]$$

Limitations of Cash Flow Yield Measure

The yield corresponding to a price must be qualified by an assumption concerning prepayments. Although yields are frequently quoted, remember that the yield is based on some underlying prepayment assumption. Consequently, a yield of 9% based on 150% PSA means that it is assumed that the underlying mortgages will prepay at a rate equal to 150% PSA. A yield number without qualification as to the prepayment assumption is meaningless.

In fact, even with specification of the prepayment assumption, the yield number is meaningless in terms of the relative value of a pass-through. For an investor to realize the yield based on some PSA assumption, a number of conditions must be met: (1) the investor must reinvest all the cash flows at the calculated yield, (2) the investor must hold the pass-through security until all the mortgages have been paid off, and (3) the assumed prepayment rate must actually occur over the life of the pass-through. Now, if all this is likely, we can trust the yield numbers. Otherwise, investors must be cautious in using yield numbers to evaluate pass-through securities.

Yield Spread to Treasuries

Although we have explained that it is not possible to calculate a yield with certainty, it has been stated that pass-through securities offer a higher yield than Treasury securities. Typically, the comparison is between Ginnie Mae pass-through securities and Treasuries because both are free of default risk. Presumably, the difference between the two yields primarily represents prepayment risk. The question should be whether the premium the investor receives in terms of higher potential yield for bearing prepayment risk is adequate. This is where option theory applied to pass-through securities has been used. Option theory lets us determine if the pass-through security is offering the proper compensation for accepting prepayment risk.

When we speak of comparing the yield of a mortgage pass-through security to a comparable Treasury, what does "comparable" mean? The stated maturity of a mortgage pass-through security is an inappropriate measure because of prepayments. Instead, market participants have used two measures: Macaulay duration and average life. As we explained in Chapter 4, Macaulay duration is a weighted-average term to maturity where the weights are the present values of the cash flows. The more commonly used measure is the average life.

Average Life

The **average life** of a mortgage-backed security is the average time to receipt of principal payments (scheduled principal payments and projected prepayments), weighted by the amount of principal expected. Mathematically, the average life is expressed as follows:

$$\text{average life} = \sum_{t=1}^{T} \frac{t \times \text{principal received at month } t}{12(\text{total principal})}$$

where T is the number of months. The average life of a pass-through depends on the PSA prepayment assumption. To see this, the average life is shown in Exhibit 11-9 for different prepayment speeds for the pass-through we used to illustrate the cash flow for 100 PSA and 165 PSA in Exhibits 11-6 and 11-7.

PREPAYMENT RISK AND ASSET/LIABILITY MANAGEMENT

An investor who owns pass-through securities does not know what the cash flow will be because that depends on prepayments. The risk associated with prepayments is called **prepayment risk**. To understand prepayment risk, suppose that an investor buys a 10% coupon Ginnie Mae at a time when mortgage rates are 10%. Let's consider what will happen to prepayments if mortgage rates decline to, say, 6%. There will be two adverse consequences. First, we know from the basic property of fixed-income securities that the price of an option-free bond will rise. But in the case of a pass-through security, the rise in price will not be as large as that of an option-free bond because a fall in interest rates increases the borrower's incentive to prepay the loan and refinance the debt at a lower rate. This results in the same adverse consequence faced by holders of callable corporate and municipal bonds. As in the case of those instruments, the upside price potential of a pass-through security is truncated because of prepayments. This characteristic, as we explain in Chapter 17, is referred to as **negative convexity**. This should not be surprising, because a mortgage loan effectively grants the borrower the right to call the loan at par value. The second adverse consequence is that the cash flow must be reinvested at a lower rate. These two adverse consequences when mortgage rates decline are referred to as **contraction risk**.

Exhibit 11-9	Average Life of a Pass-Through Based on Different PSA Prepayment Assumptions								
PSA speed	50	100	165	200	300	400	500	600	700
Average life	15.11	11.66	8.76	7.68	5.63	4.44	3.68	3.16	2.78

Now, let's look at what happens if mortgage rates rise to 15%. The price of the pass-through, like the price of any bond, will decline. But again, it will decline more because the higher rates will tend to slow down the rate of prepayment, in effect increasing the amount invested at the coupon rate, which is lower than the market rate. Prepayments will slow down because home owners will not refinance or partially prepay their mortgages when mortgage rates are higher than the contract rate of 10%. Of course, this is just the time when investors want prepayments to speed up so that they can reinvest the prepayments at the higher market interest rate. This adverse consequence of rising mortgage rates is called **extension risk**.

Therefore, prepayment risk encompasses contraction risk and extension risk. Prepayment risk makes pass-through securities unattractive for certain financial institutions to hold from an asset–liability perspective. Let's look at why particular institutional investors may find pass-throughs unattractive:

1. Thrifts and commercial banks want to lock in a spread over their cost of funds. Their funds are raised on a short-term basis. If they invest in fixed-rate pass-through securities, they will be mismatched because a pass-through is a longer-term security. In particular, depository institutions are exposed to extension risk when they invest in pass-through securities.

2. To satisfy certain obligations of insurance companies, pass-through securities may be unattractive. More specifically, consider a life insurance company that has issued a four-year guaranteed investment contract (GIC). The uncertainty about the cash flow from a pass-through security and the likelihood that slow prepayments will result in the instrument being long term make it an unappealing investment vehicle for such accounts. In such instances, a pass-through security exposes the insurance company to extension risk.

3. Consider a pension fund that wants to satisfy long-term liabilities by locking in prevailing interest rates. Buying a pass-through security exposes the pension fund to the risk that prepayments will speed up and the maturity of the investment will shorten considerably. Prepayments will speed up when interest rates decline, thereby forcing reinvestment of prepayments at a lower interest rate. In this case, the pension fund is exposed to contraction risk.

We can see that some institutional investors are concerned with extension risk and others with contraction risk when they purchase a pass-through security. Is it possible to alter the cash flow of a pass-through so as to reduce the contraction risk and extension risk for institutional investors? This can be done, as we shall see in the next chapter.

It should be understood that prepayments are not necessarily an adverse event for an investor. The effect on investment performance will depend on whether the pass-through is purchased at a discount or at a premium. Prepayments enhance the return from holding a pass-through if it is purchased at a discount for two reasons. First, the investor realizes a capital gain equal to the difference between the par value and the price paid. Second, a pass-through will trade at a discount because the pass-through's coupon rate is lower than the current coupon rate for newly issued pass-throughs. Consequently, prepayments allow the investor to reinvest the proceeds at a higher coupon rate. For a pass-through purchased at a premium to par, prepayments reduce investment returns for two reasons: (1) the investor realizes a capital loss equal to the difference between the price paid and par, and (2) the proceeds must be reinvested at a lower coupon rate.

SECONDARY MARKET TRADING

Pass-throughs are quoted in the same manner as U.S. Treasury coupon securities. A quote of 94-05 means 94 and 5/32nds of par value, or 94.15625% of par value. As explained in our discussion of prepayments, the yield corresponding to a price must be qualified by an assumption concerning prepayments.

As explained earlier, pass-through securities are identified by a pool prefix and pool number provided by the agency. The prefix indicates the type of collateral. The pool number indicates the specific mortgages underlying the pass-through and the issuer of the pass-through.

Many trades occur while a pool is still unspecified, and therefore, no pool information is known at the time of the trade. This kind of trade is known as a "TBA" (to be announced) trade. When an investor purchases, for example, $1 million GNMA 8s on a TBA basis, the investor can receive up to three pools, with pool numbers being announced shortly before the settlement date. Three pools can be delivered because the PSA has established guidelines for standards of delivery and settlement of mortgage-backed securities,[9] under which our hypothetical TBA trade permits three possible pools to be delivered. The option of what pools to deliver is left to the seller, as long as selection and delivery satisfy the PSA guidelines. In contrast to TBA trades, a pool number may be specified. In this case, the transaction will involve delivery of the pool specifically designated.

There are many seasoned issues of the same agency with the same coupon rate outstanding at a given point in time. For example, there are more than 30,000 pools of 30-year Ginnie Mae MBS outstanding with a coupon rate of 9%. One pass-through may be backed by a pool of mortgage loans in which all the properties are located in California, whereas another may be backed by a pool of mortgage loans in which all the properties are in Minnesota. Yet another may be backed by a pool of mortgage loans in which the properties are from several regions in the country. So which pool are dealers referring to when they talk about Ginnie Mae 8s? They do not refer to any specific pool but instead to a generic security, although the prepayment characteristics of pass-throughs with underlying pools from different parts of the country are different. Thus, the projected prepayment rates for pass-throughs reported by dealer firms are for generic pass-throughs. A particular pool purchased may exhibit a materially different prepayment speed from the generic. Moreover, when an investor purchases a pass-through without specifying a pool number, the seller can deliver the worst-paying pools as long as the pools delivered satisfy good delivery requirements.

Prior to March 1999, the PSA delivery standards allowed the seller in a TBA trade to under- or over-deliver by 1% per $1 million traded. So, if $1 million of par value is sold at par, the seller could deliver as little as $990,000 or as much as $1,010,000. The seller would select the amount to deliver based on prevailing prices. This was a valuable option to sellers in a TBA trade and a disadvantage to buyers. In March 1999, the PSA changed its delivery standards so that the seller in a TBA trade may only under- or over-deliver by 0.1%. Consequently, the value of this delivery option to the seller is now minimal.

---

[9] Public Securities Association, *Uniform Practices for the Clearance and Settlement of Mortgage-Backed Securities* (New York: SIFMA, 2008). More specifically, the requirement for good delivery permits a maximum of three pools per $1 million traded, or a maximum of four pools per $1 million for coupons of 12% or more.

KEY POINTS

- The residential mortgage–backed securities market is divided into two sectors: agency MBS and nonagency MBS.

- A residential mortgage–backed security is created when residential loans are pooled and one or more securities are issued whose obligations are to be repaid from the cash flow from the loan pool.

- A mortgage pass-through security is one type of RMBS created when one or more mortgage holders of loans pool them and sell a single debt obligation that is to be repaid from the cash flow of the specific loan pool with each investor entitled to a pro rata share of the cash flow.

- Agency MBS include agency mortgage pass-through securities, agency collateralized mortgage obligations, and agency stripped mortgage-backed securities. The cash flow of the latter two types of MBS is derived from the first type, and hence, they are referred to as derivative MBS.

- The monthly cash flow of a mortgage pass-through security depends on the cash flow of the underlying mortgages and therefore consists of monthly mortgage payments representing interest, the scheduled repayment of principal, and any prepayments. The cash flow is less than that of the underlying mortgages by an amount equal to servicing and any guarantor fees.

- As with individual mortgage loans, because of prepayments, the cash flow of a pass-through is not known with certainty. Agency MBS are issued by Ginnie Mae, Fannie Mae, and Freddie Mac. Ginnie Mae pass-through securities are guaranteed by the full faith and credit of the U.S. government and consequently are viewed as risk-free in terms of default risk. Freddie Mac and Fannie Mae are government-sponsored enterprises, and therefore, their guarantee does not carry the full faith and credit of the U.S. government.

- Estimating the cash flow from a mortgage pass-through security requires forecasting prepayments. The current convention is to use the PSA prepayment benchmark, which is a series of conditional prepayment rates, to obtain the cash flow.

- A prepayment model begins by modeling the statistical relationships among the factors that are expected to affect prepayments. The key components of an agency's prepayment model are housing turnover, cash-out refinancing, and rate/term refinancing.

- Given the projected cash flow and the market price of a pass-through, a cash flow yield can be calculated. Because the PSA prepayment benchmark is only a convention enabling market participants to quote yield and/or price, it has many limitations for determining the value of a pass-through. The yield spread is quoted as the difference between the cash flow yield and the yield to maturity of a comparable Treasury.

- A measure commonly used to estimate the life of a pass-through is its average life.

- The prepayment risk associated with investing in mortgage pass-through securities can be decomposed into contraction risk and extension risk. Prepayment risk makes mortgage pass-through securities unattractive for certain financial institutions to hold from an asset-liability perspective.

- Mortgage pass-through securities are quoted in the same manner as U.S. Treasury coupon securities.

- Mortgage pass-through securities are identified by a pool prefix and pool number. A TBA trade occurs while a pool is still unspecified, and therefore, no pool information is known at the time of the trade. The seller has the right in this case to deliver mortgage pass-through securities backed by pools that satisfy the PSA requirements for good delivery.

QUESTIONS

1. **a.** Explain what is meant by a residential mortgage–backed security.

   b. Describe the sectors of the residential mortgage–backed securities market.

2. What is a mortgage pass-through security?

3. What are the two types of private–label MBS?

4. What are subprime mortgage–backed securities?

5. What is meant by a derivative mortgage-backed security?

6. Describe the cash flow of a mortgage pass-through security.

7. **a.** What are the WAC and WAM of a pass-through security?

   b. After origination of a mortgage-backed security, the WAM changes. What measures are used by Fannie Mae and Freddie Mac to describe the term to maturity of the loans remaining in the loan pool?

8. While it is often stated that Ginnie Mae issues mortgage-backed securities, why is that technically incorrect?

9. What are the different types of agency pass-through securities?

10. How does the guarantee for a Ginnie Mae mortgage-backed security differ from that of a mortgage-backed security issued by Fannie Mae and Freddie Mac?

11. On October 1, 2005, Fannie Mae issued a mortgage pass-through security and the prospectus supplement stated the following:

FANNIE MAE

MORTGAGE-BACKED SECURITIES PROGRAM

SUPPLEMENT TO PROSPECTUS DATED JULY 01, 2004

$464,927,576.00

ISSUE DATE OCTOBER 01, 2005

SECURITY DESCRIPTION FNMS 05.0000 CL-844801

5.0000 PERCENT PASS-THROUGH RATE

FANNIE MAE POOL NUMBER CL-844801

CUSIP 31407YRW1

PRINCIPAL AND INTEREST PAYABLE ON THE 25TH OF EACH MONTH

BEGINNING NOVEMBER 25, 2005

POOL STATISTICS

SELLER	WELLS FARGO BANK, N.A.
SERVICER	WELLS FARGO BANK, N.A.
NUMBER OF MORTGAGE LOANS	1,986
AVERAGE LOAN SIZE	$234,312.06
MATURITY DATE	10/01/2035
WEIGHTED AVERAGE COUPON RATE	5.7500%
WEIGHTED AVERAGE LOAN AGE	1 mo
WEIGHTED AVERAGE LOAN TERM	360 mo
WEIGHTED AVERAGE REMAINING MATURITY	359 mo
WEIGHTED AVERAGE LTV	73%
WEIGHTED AVERAGE CREDIT SCORE	729

a. What does the "pass-through rate" of 5% for this security mean?

b. What is the average note rate being paid by the borrowers in the loan pool for this security?

c. Why does the pass-through rate differ from the average note rate paid by the borrowers in the loan pool for this security?

d. What is the pool number for this security, and why is the pool number important?

e. What is the prefix for this security, and what does a prefix indicate?

f. The "maturity date" for this security is shown as "10/01/2035." An investor in this security might be concerned about its very long maturity (30 years). Why is the maturity date a misleading measure of the security's maturity?

g. If an investor purchased $15 million principal of this security and, in some month, the cash flow available to be paid to the security holders (after all fees are paid) is $12 million, how much is the investor entitled to receive?

h. Every month a pool factor would be reported for this security. If the pool factor for some month is 0.92, what is the outstanding mortgage balance for the loan pool for that month?

i. Why does the weighted average loan term differ from the weighted average remaining maturity?

j. Wells Fargo Bank, N.A. is identified as the seller and the servicer. What does that mean?

k. What does the following mean: "MORTGAGE-BACKED SECURITIES PROGRAM SUPPLEMENT TO PROSPECTUS DATED JULY 01, 2004"?

12. Why is an assumed prepayment speed necessary to project the cash flow of a pass-through?

13. What does a conditional prepayment rate of 8% mean?

14. Indicate whether you agree or disagree with the following statement: "The PSA prepayment benchmark is a model for forecasting prepayments for a pass-through security."

15. a. Complete the following table:

CPR Assuming:

Month	100% PSA	70% PSA	320% PSA
1			
4			
9			
27			
40			
120			
340			

b. Complete the following table:

SMM Assuming:

Month	100% PSA	70% PSA	320% PSA
1			
4			
9			
27			
40			
120			
340			

16. Complete the following table (in thousands of dollars) assuming a prepayment rate of 165 PSA:

Original balance: $100,000,000
Pass-through rate: 9.0%
WAM: 360 months

Month	Outstanding Balance	SMM	Mortage Payment	Interest	Scheduled Principal	Prepayment	Total Principal	Cash Flow
1	100,000	841						
2	99,934	841						

17. What is meant by prepayments due to:

a. housing turnover?

b. cash-out refinancing?

c. rate/term refinancing?

18. a. What factor can be used as a proxy for cash-out refinancing incentives?

b. Why are prepayments attributable to cash-out refinancing likely to be insensitive to changes in mortgage rates?

19. What is the S-curve for prepayments? Explain the reason for the shape.

20. What is the burnout effect?

21. **a.** What is the cash flow yield of a mortgage pass-through security?

    b. What are the limitations of cash flow yield measures for a mortgage pass-through security?

22. What is the bond-equivalent yield if the monthly cash flow yield is 0.7%?

23. What is the average life of a pass-through, and what does it depend on?

a. What are contraction risk and extension risk?

b. Why would a pass-through with a WAM of 350 months be an unattractive investment for a savings and loan association?

24. **a.** What is a TBA trade?

    b. What delivery options are granted to the seller in a TBA trade?

12

Agency Collateralized Mortgage Obligations and Stripped Mortgage-Backed Securities

LEARNING OBJECTIVES

After reading this chapter, you will understand

- why and how an agency collateralized mortgage obligation is created

- what is meant by a REMIC and why are CMOs referred to as REMICs or REMIC structures

- what a sequential-pay CMO is

- how the average life of a sequential-pay CMO compares to that of the collateral from which it is created

- what an accrual tranche is and its effect on the average life of sequential-pay tranches in the CMO structure

- how a floater and an inverse floater are created from a CMO tranche

- what a planned amortization class tranche is and how it is created

- how the prepayment protection for a planned amortization class changes over time

- what a support tranche is and the substantial prepayment risk to which it exposes investors

- what a support bond with a schedule is

- what a notional IO is and how it is created

- how agency stripped mortgage-backed securities are created

- the various types of agency stripped mortgage-backed securities

- the investment characteristics of agency stripped mortgage-backed securities

In this chapter, we discuss two agency mortgage-backed securities that are created from agency mortgage pass-through securities: agency collateralized mortgage obligations and stripped mortgage-backed securities. In the agency mortgage-backed securities markets, these securities are referred to as **derivative mortgage products** since they derive their cash flow from the underlying collateral—a pass-through security or a pool of pass-through securities. Unlike pass-through securities, which have only one bond class, derivative mortgage products have multiple bond classes that are supported by the collateral.

These mortgage products are issued by the same entities that issue agency pass-through securities: Ginnie Mae, Fannie Mae, and Freddie Mac. The credit risk associated with these mortgage products is the same as with agency pass-through securities. The structure in which there are multiple bond classes supported by the loan pool in collateralized mortgage obligations (CMOs) for agency deals that we describe in this chapter is similar to that of nonagency deals discussed in the next chapter. The important difference, and the reason why we discuss them in separate chapters, is that nonagency deals require more complicated structuring because of their greater credit risk. Mechanisms have to be employed in creating multiple class nonagency deals to supplement the support of the bond classes beyond that offered by the loan pool.

AGENCY COLLATERALIZED MORTGAGE OBLIGATIONS[1]

At the close of Chapter 11, we discussed the prepayment risks associated with investing in agency pass-through securities: contraction risk and extension risk. We noted there that some institutional investors are concerned with extension risk when they invest in a pass-through, whereas others are more concerned with contraction risk. Fortunately, redirecting cash flows from a pass-through security to various bond classes makes it possible to redistribute prepayment risk for investors who want to reduce their exposure to prepayment risk. Because the total prepayment risk of a pass-through security will not be changed by altering the cash flows, other investors must be found who are willing to accept the unwanted prepayment risk.

Collateralized mortgage obligations (CMOs) are bond classes created by redirecting the cash flows of mortgage-related products so as to mitigate prepayment risk. The mere creation of a CMO cannot eliminate prepayment risk; it can only transfer the various forms of this risk among different classes of bondholders. The technique of redistributing the coupon interest and principal from the underlying mortgage-related products to different classes, so that a CMO class has a different coupon rate from that for the underlying collateral, results in instruments that have varying risk-return characteristics that may be more suitable to the needs and expectations of investors, thereby broadening the appeal of mortgage-backed products to various traditional fixed-income investors.

The bond classes created are commonly referred to as **tranches**. The principal payments from the underlying collateral are used to retire the tranches on a priority basis according to terms specified in the prospectus.

All three entities that issue agency pass-through securities also issue CMOs, with Ginnie Mae being a late entry into the market, issuing its first CMO in 1994. The CMOs are not referred to as CMOs by these issuers. They are referred to as **REMICs** or **REMIC structures**. REMIC means **Real Estate Mortgage Investment Conduit** and is a provision

---

[1] This section is adapted from Chapters 1 through Chapter 7 of Frank J. Fabozzi and Charles Ramsey, *Collateralized Mortgage Obligations: Structures and Analysis*, 3rd ed. (New Hope, PA: Frank J. Fabozzi Associates, 1999).

in the Tax Reform Act of 1986. This provision in the tax law allows the efficient creation of a CMO structure. Consequently, issuers, both agency and nonagency issuers, structure their CMO deals so as to qualify for REMIC tax treatment. Rather than referring to this multiclass mortgage structure as a CMO, the preference is to refer to it as a REMIC.

Sequential-Pay Tranches

The first CMO was created in 1983 and was structured so that each class of bonds would be retired sequentially. Such structures are referred to as **sequential-pay CMOs**. To illustrate a sequential-pay CMO, we discuss FJF-01,[2] a hypothetical deal made up to illustrate the basic features of the structure. The collateral for this hypothetical CMO is a hypothetical pass-through with a total par value of $400 million and the following characteristics: (1) the pass-through coupon rate is 7.5%, (2) the weighted-average coupon (WAC) is 8.125%, and (3) the weighted-average maturity (WAM) is 357 months. This is the same pass-through that we used in Chapter 11 to describe the cash flow of a pass-through based on some PSA assumption.

From this $400 million of collateral, four bond classes or tranches are created. Their characteristics are summarized in Exhibit 12-1. The total par value of the four tranches is equal to the par value of the collateral (i.e., the pass-through security). In this simple structure, the coupon rate is the same for each tranche and also the same as the coupon rate on the collateral. There is no reason why this must be so, and in fact, typically the coupon rate varies by tranche.

Now remember that a CMO is created by redistributing the cash flow—interest and principal—to the different tranches based on a set of payment rules. The payment rules at the bottom of Exhibit 12-1 describe how the cash flow from the pass-through (i.e., collateral) is to be distributed to the four tranches. There are separate rules for the payment of the coupon interest and the payment of principal, the principal being the total of the regularly scheduled principal payment and any prepayments.

Exhibit 12-1   FJF-01: Hypothetical Four-Tranche Sequential-Pay Structure[a]

Tranche	Par Amount	Coupon Rate (%)
A	$194,500,000	7.5
B	36,000,000	7.5
C	96,500,000	7.5
D	73,000,000	7.5
	$400,000,000	

[a]*Payment rules:*

1. *For payment of periodic coupon interest: Disburse periodic coupon interest to each tranche on the basis of the amount of principal outstanding at the beginning of the period.*
2. *For disbursement of principal payments: Disburse principal payments to tranche A until it is paid off completely. After tranche A is paid off completely, disburse principal payments to tranche B until it is paid off completely. After tranche B is paid off completely, disburse principal payments to tranche C until it is paid off completely. After tranche C is paid off completely, disburse principal payments to tranche D until it is paid off completely.*

---

[2] All CMO structures are given a name. In our illustration, we use FJF, the initials of the author of this book.

In FJF-01, each tranche receives periodic coupon interest payments based on the amount of the outstanding balance at the beginning of the month. The disbursement of the principal, however, is made in a special way. A tranche is not entitled to receive principal until the entire principal of the preceding tranche has been paid off. More specifically, tranche A receives all the principal payments until the entire principal amount owed to that bond class, $194,500,000, is paid off; then tranche B begins to receive principal and continues to do so until it is paid the entire $36,000,000. Tranche C then receives principal, and when it is paid off, tranche D starts receiving principal payments.

Although the priority rules for the disbursement of the principal payments are known, the precise amount of the principal in each period is not. This will depend on the cash flow, and therefore, principal payments, of the collateral, which depends on the actual prepayment rate of the collateral. An assumed PSA speed allows the cash flow to be projected. Exhibit 12-2 shows the cash flow (interest, regularly scheduled principal repayment, and prepayments) assuming 165 PSA. Assuming that the collateral does prepay at 165 PSA, the cash flow available to all four tranches of FJF-01 will be precisely the cash flow shown in Exhibit 12-2.

To demonstrate how the priority rules for FJF-01 work, Exhibit 12-2 shows the cash flow for selected months assuming that the collateral prepays at 165 PSA. For each tranche, the exhibit shows (1) the balance at the end of the month, (2) the principal paid down (regularly scheduled principal repayment plus prepayments), and (3) interest. In month 1, the cash flow for the collateral consists of a principal payment of $709,923 and interest of $2.5 million (0.075 times $400 million divided by 12). The interest payment is distributed to the four tranches based on the amount of the par value outstanding. So, for example, tranche A receives $1,215,625 (0.075 times $194,500,000 divided by 12) of the 2.5 million. The principal, however, is all distributed to tranche A. Therefore, the cash flow for tranche A in month 1 is $1,925,548. The principal balance at the end of month 1 for tranche A is $193,790,076 (the original principal balance of $194,500,000 less the principal payment of $709,923). No principal payment is distributed to the three other tranches because there is still a principal balance outstanding for tranche A. This will be true for months 2 through 80.

After month 81, the principal balance will be zero for tranche A. For the collateral, the cash flow in month 81 is $3,318,521, consisting of a principal payment of $2,032,196 and interest of $1,286,325. At the beginning of month 81 (end of month 80), the principal balance for tranche A is $311,926. Therefore, $311,926 of the $2,032,196 of the principal payment from the collateral will be disbursed to tranche A. After this payment is made, no additional principal payments are made to this tranche as the principal balance is zero. The remaining principal payment from the collateral, $1,720,271, is disbursed to tranche B. According to the assumed prepayment speed of 165 PSA, tranche B then begins receiving principal payments in month 81.

Exhibit 12-2 shows that tranche B is fully paid off by month 100, when tranche C now begins to receive principal payments. Tranche C is not fully paid off until month 178, at which time tranche D begins receiving the remaining principal payments. The maturity (i.e., the time until the principal is fully paid off) for these four tranches assuming 165 PSA

Exhibit 12-2 Monthly Cash Flow for Selected Months for FJF-01 Assuming 165 PSA

	Tranche A			Tranche B		
Month	Balance	Principal	Interest	Balance	Principal	Interest
1	194,500,000	709,923	1,215,625	36,000,000	0	225,000
2	193,790,077	821,896	1,211,188	36,000,000	0	225,000
3	192,968,181	933,560	1,206,051	36,000,000	0	225,000
4	192,034,621	1,044,822	1,200,216	36,000,000	0	225,000
5	190,989,799	1,155,586	1,193,686	36,000,000	0	225,000
6	189,834,213	1,265,759	1,186,464	36,000,000	0	225,000
7	188,568,454	1,375,246	1,178,553	36,000,000	0	225,000
8	187,193,208	1,483,954	1,169,958	36,000,000	0	225,000
9	185,709,254	1,591,789	1,160,683	36,000,000	0	225,000
10	184,117,464	1,698,659	1,150,734	36,000,000	0	225,000
11	182,418,805	1,804,473	1,140,118	36,000,000	0	225,000
12	180,614,332	1,909,139	1,128,840	36,000,000	0	225,000
75	12,893,479	2,143,974	80,584	36,000,000	0	225,000
76	10,749,504	2,124,935	67,184	36,000,000	0	225,000
77	8,624,569	2,106,062	53,904	36,000,000	0	225,000
78	6,518,507	2,087,353	40,741	36,000,000	0	225,000
79	4,431,154	2,068,807	27,695	36,000,000	0	225,000
80	2,362,347	2,050,422	14,765	36,000,000	0	225,000
81	311,926	311,926	1,950	36,000,000	1,720,271	225,000
82	0	0	0	34,279,729	2,014,130	214,248
83	0	0	0	32,265,599	1,996,221	201,660
84	0	0	0	30,269,378	1,978,468	189,184
85	0	0	0	28,290,911	1,960,869	176,818
95	0	0	0	9,449,331	1,793,089	59,058
96	0	0	0	7,656,242	1,777,104	47,852
97	0	0	0	5,879,138	1,761,258	36,745
98	0	0	0	4,117,880	1,745,550	25,737
99	0	0	0	2,372,329	1,729,979	14,827
100	0	0	0	642,350	642,350	4,015
101	0	0	0	0	0	0
102	0	0	0	0	0	0
103	0	0	0	0	0	0
104	0	0	0	0	0	0
105	0	0	0	0	0	0

	Tranche C			Tranche D		
1	96,500,000	0	603,125	73,000,000	0	456,250
2	96,500,000	0	603,125	73,000,000	0	456,250
3	96,500,000	0	603,125	73,000,000	0	456,250
4	96,500,000	0	603,125	73,000,000	0	456,250

(*Continued*)

263

Exhibit 12-2   Monthly Cash Flow for Selected Months for FJF-01 Assuming 165 PSA (Continued)

	Tranche C			Tranche D		
Month	Balance	Principal	Interest	Balance	Principal	Interest
5	96,500,000	0	603,125	73,000,000	0	456,250
6	96,500,000	0	603,125	73,000,000	0	456,250
7	96,500,000	0	603,125	73,000,000	0	456,250
8	96,500,000	0	603,125	73,000,000	0	456,250
9	96,500,000	0	603,125	73,000,000	0	456,250
10	96,500,000	0	603,125	73,000,000	0	456,250
11	96,500,000	0	603,125	73,000,000	0	456,250
12	96,500,000	0	603,125	73,000,000	0	456,250
95	96,500,000	0	603,125	73,000,000	0	456,250
96	96,500,000	0	603,125	73,000,000	0	456,250
97	96,500,000	0	603,125	73,000,000	0	456,250
98	96,500,000	0	603,125	73,000,000	0	456,250
99	96,500,000	0	603,125	73,000,000	0	456,250
100	96,500,000	1,072,194	603,125	73,000,000	0	456,250
101	95,427,806	1,699,243	596,424	73,000,000	0	456,250
102	93,728,563	1,684,075	585,804	73,000,000	0	456,250
103	92,044,489	1,669,039	575,278	73,000,000	0	456,250
104	90,375,450	1,654,134	564,847	73,000,000	0	456,250
105	88,721,315	1,639,359	554,508	73,000,000	0	456,250
175	3,260,287	869,602	20,377	73,000,000	0	456,250
176	2,390,685	861,673	14,942	73,000,000	0	456,250
177	1,529,013	853,813	9,556	73,000,000	0	456,250
178	675,199	675,199	4,220	73,000,000	170,824	456,250
179	0	0	0	72,829,176	838,300	455,182
180	0	0	0	71,990,876	830,646	449,943
181	0	0	0	71,160,230	823,058	444,751
182	0	0	0	70,337,173	815,536	439,607
183	0	0	0	69,521,637	808,081	434,510
184	0	0	0	68,713,556	800,690	429,460
185	0	0	0	67,912,866	793,365	424,455
350	0	0	0	1,235,674	160,220	7,723
351	0	0	0	1,075,454	158,544	6,722
352	0	0	0	916,910	156,883	5,731
353	0	0	0	760,027	155,238	4,750
354	0	0	0	604,789	153,607	3,780
355	0	0	0	451,182	151,991	2,820
356	0	0	0	299,191	150,389	1,870
357	0	0	0	148,802	148,802	930

would be 81 months for tranche A, 100 months for tranche B, 178 months for tranche C, and 357 months for tranche D.

The **principal pay-down window** for a tranche is the time period between the beginning and the ending of the principal payments to that tranche. So, for example, for tranche A, the principal pay-down window would be month 1 to month 81 assuming 165 PSA. For tranche B it is from month 82 to month 100. The window is also specified in terms of the length of the time from the beginning of the principal pay-down window to the end of the principal pay-down window. For tranche A, the window would be stated as 80 months, for tranche B, 19 months.

Let's look at what has been accomplished by creating the CMO. First, in Chapter 11 we indicated that the average life of the pass-through is 8.76 years, assuming a prepayment speed of 165 PSA. Exhibit 12-3 reports the average life of the collateral and the four tranches assuming different prepayment speeds. Notice that the four tranches have average lives that are both shorter and longer than the collateral, thereby attracting investors who have a preference for an average life different from that of the collateral.

There is still a major problem: There is considerable variability of the average life for the tranches. We will see later how this can be tackled. However, there is some protection provided for each tranche against prepayment risk. This is because prioritizing the distribution of principal (i.e., establishing the payment rules for principal) effectively protects the shorter-term tranche A in this structure against extension risk. This protection must come from somewhere, so it comes from the three other tranches. Similarly, tranches C and D provide protection against extension risk for tranches A and B. At the same time, tranches C and D benefit because they are provided protection against contraction risk, the protection coming from tranches A and B.

Exhibit 12-3   Average Life for the Collateral and the Four Tranches of FJF-01

Prepayment Speed (PSA)	Average Life for				
	Collateral	Tranche A	Tranche B	Tranche C	Tranche D
50	15.11	7.48	15.98	21.02	27.24
100	11.66	4.90	10.86	15.78	24.58
165	8.76	3.48	7.49	11.19	20.27
200	7.68	3.05	6.42	9.60	18.11
300	5.63	2.32	4.64	6.81	13.36
400	4.44	1.94	3.70	5.31	10.34
500	3.68	1.69	3.12	4.38	8.35
600	3.16	1.51	2.74	3.75	6.96
700	2.78	1.38	2.47	3.30	5.95

Accrual Bonds

In FJF-01, the payment rules for interest provide for all tranches to be paid interest each month. In many sequential-pay CMO structures, at least one tranche does not receive current interest. Instead, the interest for that tranche would accrue and be added to the principal balance. Such a bond class is commonly referred to as an **accrual tranche**, or a **Z bond** (because the bond is similar to a zero-coupon bond). The interest that would have been paid to the accrual bond class is then used to speed up the pay down of the principal balance of earlier bond classes.

To see this, consider FJF-02, a hypothetical CMO structure with the same collateral as FJF-01 and with four tranches, each with a coupon rate of 7.5%. The difference is in the last tranche, Z, which is an accrual. The structure for FJF-02 is shown in Exhibit 12-4.

Exhibit 12-5 shows cash flows for selected months for tranches A and B. Let's look at month 1 and compare it with month 1 in Exhibit 12-2. Both cash flows are based on 165 PSA. The principal payment from the collateral is $709,923. In FJF-01, this is the principal pay down for tranche A. In FJF-02, the interest for tranche Z, $456,250, is not paid to that tranche but instead is used to pay down the principal of tranche A. So the principal payment to tranche A in Exhibit 12-5 is $1,166,173, the collateral's principal payment of $709,923 plus the interest of $456,250 that was diverted from tranche Z.

The expected final maturity for tranches A, B, and C has shortened as a result of the inclusion of tranche Z. The final payout for tranche A is 64 months rather than 81 months; for tranche B it is 77 months rather than 100 months; and for tranche C it is 112 rather than 178 months.

Exhibit 12-4 **FJF-02: Hypothetical Four-Tranche Sequential-Pay Structure with an Accrual Bond Class**[a]

Tranche	Par Amount	Coupon Rate (%)
A	$194,500,000	7.5
B	36,000,000	7.5
C	96,500,000	7.5
Z (accrual)	73,000,000	7.5
	$400,000,000	

[a]*Payment rules:*

1. For payment of periodic coupon interest: Disburse periodic coupon interest to tranches A, B, and C on the basis of the amount of principal outstanding at the beginning of the period. For tranche Z, accrue the interest based on the principal plus accrued interest in the preceding period. The interest for tranche Z is to be paid to the earlier tranches as a principal pay down.

2. For disbursement of principal payments: Disburse principal payments to tranche A until it is completely paid off. After tranche A is paid off completely, disburse principal payments to tranche B until it is paid off completely. After tranche B is paid off completely, disburse principal payments to tranche C until it is paid off completely. After tranche C is paid off completely, disburse principal payments to tranche Z, until the original principal balance plus accrued interest is paid off completely.

Month	Tranche A			Tranche B		
	Balance	Principal	Interest	Balance	Principal	Interest
1	194,500,000	1,166,173	1,215,625	36,000,000	0	225,000
2	193,333,827	1,280,997	1,208,336	36,000,000	0	225,000
3	192,052,829	1,395,531	1,200,330	36,000,000	0	225,000
4	190,657,298	1,509,680	1,191,608	36,000,000	0	225,000
5	189,147,619	1,623,350	1,182,173	36,000,000	0	225,000
6	187,524,269	1,736,446	1,172,027	36,000,000	0	225,000
7	185,787,823	1,848,875	1,161,174	36,000,000	0	225,000
8	183,938,947	1,960,543	1,149,618	36,000,000	0	225,000
9	181,978,404	2,071,357	1,137,365	36,000,000	0	225,000
10	179,907,047	2,181,225	1,124,419	36,000,000	0	225,000
11	177,725,822	2,290,054	1,110,786	36,000,000	0	225,000
12	175,435,768	2,397,755	1,096,474	36,000,000	0	225,000
60	15,023,406	3,109,398	93,896	36,000,000	0	225,000
61	11,914,007	3,091,812	74,463	36,000,000	0	225,000
62	8,822,195	3,074,441	55,139	36,000,000	0	225,000
63	5,747,754	3,057,282	35,923	36,000,000	0	225,000
64	2,690,472	2,690,472	16,815	36,000,000	349,863	225,000
65	0	0	0	35,650,137	3,023,598	222,813
66	0	0	0	32,626,540	3,007,069	203,916
67	0	0	0	29,619,470	2,990,748	185,122
68	0	0	0	26,628,722	2,974,633	166,430
69	0	0	0	23,654,089	2,958,722	147,838
70	0	0	0	20,695,367	2,943,014	129,346
71	0	0	0	17,752,353	2,927,508	110,952
72	0	0	0	14,824,845	2,912,203	92,655
73	0	0	0	11,912,642	2,897,096	74,454
74	0	0	0	9,015,546	2,882,187	56,347
75	0	0	0	6,133,358	2,867,475	38,333
76	0	0	0	3,265,883	2,852,958	20,412
77	0	0	0	412,925	412,925	2,581
78	0	0	0	0	0	0

The average lives for tranches A, B, and C are shorter in FJF-02 than in FJF-01 because of the inclusion of the accrual bond. For example, at 165 PSA, the average lives are as follows:

Structure	Tranche A	Tranche B	Tranche C
FJF-02	2.90	5.86	7.87
FJF-01	3.48	7.49	11.19

The reason for the shortening of the nonaccrual tranches is that the interest that would be paid to the accrual bond is being allocated to the other tranches. Tranche Z in FJF-02 will have a longer average life than that of tranche D in FJF-01.

Thus, shorter-term tranches and a longer-term tranche are created by including an accrual bond. The accrual bond has appeal to investors who are concerned with reinvestment risk. Because there are no coupon payments to reinvest, reinvestment risk is eliminated until all the other tranches are paid off.

Floating-Rate Tranches

The CMO structures discussed previously offer a fixed coupon rate on all tranches. If CMO classes could only be created with fixed-rate coupons, the market for CMOs would be limited. Many financial institutions prefer floating-rate assets, which provide a better match for their liabilities.

Floating-rate tranches can be created from fixed-rate tranches by creating a floater and an inverse floater. We illustrate the creation of a floating-rate and an inverse-floating-rate bond class using the hypothetical CMO structure FJF-02, which is a four-tranche sequential-pay structure with an accrual bond. We can select any of the tranches from which to create a floating-rate and an inverse-floating-rate tranche. In fact, we can create these two securities for more than one of the four tranches or for only a portion of one tranche.

In this case, we create a floater and an inverse floater from tranche C. The par value for this tranche is $96.5 million, and we create two tranches that have a combined par value of $96.5 million. We refer to this CMO structure with a floater and an inverse floater as FJF-03. It has five tranches, designated A, B, FL, IFL, and Z, where FL is the floating-rate tranche and IFL is the inverse-floating-rate tranche. Exhibit 12-6 describes FJF-03. Any reference rate can be used to create a floater and the corresponding inverse floater. The reference rate for setting the coupon-rate for FL and IFL in FJF-03 is taken as one-month LIBOR.

The amount of the par value of the floating-rate tranche will be some portion of the $96.5 million. There is an infinite number of ways to cut up the $96.5 million between the floater and inverse floater, and final partitioning will be driven by the demands of investors. In the FJF-03 structure, we made the floater from $72,375,000 or 75% of the $96.5 million. The coupon rate on the floater is set at one-month LIBOR plus 50 basis points. So, for example, if LIBOR is 3.75% at the reset date, the coupon rate on the floater is 3.75% + 0.5%, or 4.25%. There is a cap on the coupon rate for the floater (discussed later).

Unlike a floating-rate note in the corporate bond market, whose principal is unchanged over the life of the instrument, the floater's principal balance declines over time as principal

---

Exhibit 12-6   FJF-03: Hypothetical Five-Tranche Sequential-Pay Structure with Floater, Inverse Floater, and Accrual Bond Classes[a]

Tranche	Par Amount	Coupon Rate (%)
A	$194,500,000	7.50
B	36,000,000	7.50
FL	72,375,000	1-month LIBOR +0.50
IFL	24,125,000	$28.50 - 3 \times$ (1-month LIBOR)
Z (accrual)	73,000,000	7.50
	$400,000,000	

[a]*Payment rules:*

1. *For payment of periodic coupon interest: Disburse periodic coupon interest to tranches A, B, FL, and IFL on the basis of the amount of principal outstanding at the beginning of the period. For tranche Z, accrue the interest based on the principal plus accrued interest in the preceding period. The interest for tranche Z is to be paid to the earlier tranches as a principal pay down. The maximum coupon rate for FL is 10%; the minimum coupon rate for IFL is 0%.*
2. *For disbursement of principal payments: Disburse principal payments to tranche A until it is paid off completely. After tranche A is paid off completely, disburse principal payments to tranche B until it is paid off completely. After tranche B is paid off completely, disburse principal payments to tranches FL and IFL until they are paid off completely. The principal payments between tranches FL and IFL should be made in the following way: 75% to tranche FL and 25% to tranche IFL. After tranches FL and IFL are paid off completely, disburse principal payments to tranche Z until the original principal balance plus accrued interest is paid off completely.*

---

payments are made. The principal payments to the floater are determined by the principal payments from the tranche from which the floater is created. In our CMO structure, this is tranche C.

Because the floater's par value is $72,375,000 of the $96.5 million, the balance is the inverse floater. Assuming that one-month LIBOR is the reference rate, the coupon rate on the inverse floater takes the following form:

$$K - L \times (\text{one-month LIBOR})$$

In FJF-03, K is set at 28.50% and L at 3. Thus, if one-month LIBOR is 3.75%, the coupon rate for the month is

$$28.50\% - 3(3.75\%) = 17.25\%$$

K is the cap or maximum coupon rate for the inverse floater. In FJF-03, the cap for the inverse floater is 28.50%.

The L or multiple in the formula to determine the coupon rate for the inverse floater is called the **coupon leverage**. The higher the coupon leverage, the more the inverse floater's coupon rate changes for a given change in one-month LIBOR. For example, a coupon leverage of 3.0 means that a 100-basis-point change in one-month LIBOR will change the coupon rate on the inverse floater by 300 basis points; a coupon leverage of 0.7 means that the coupon rate will change by 70 basis points for a 100-basis-point change in one-month LIBOR. Inverse floaters with a wide variety of coupon leverages are available in the market.

Participants refer to low-leverage inverse floaters as those with a coupon leverage between 0.5 and 2.1; medium-leverage as those with a coupon leverage higher than 2.1 but not exceeding 4.5; and high-leverage as those with a coupon leverage higher than 4.5. At the time of issuance, the issuer determines the coupon leverage according to investor desire. In FJF-03, the coupon leverage is set at 3.

Let's see how the total interest paid on the floater and inverse floater can be supported by the bond class with a coupon rate of 7.5% from which they are created. The coupon rate for the floating-rate class is

$$\text{one-month LIBOR} + 0.50$$

For the inverse floater the coupon rate is

$$28.50 - 3 \times (\text{one-month LIBOR})$$

Because the floater is 75% of the $96.5 million and the inverse floater is 25%, the weighted-average coupon rate is

$$0.75(\text{floater coupon rate}) + 0.25 \,(\text{inverse floater coupon rate})$$

The weighted average coupon rate is 7.5%, regardless of the level of LIBOR. For example, if one-month LIBOR is 9%, then

$$\text{floater coupon rate} = 9.0\% + 0.5\% = 9.5\%$$
$$\text{inverse floater coupon rate} = 28.5 - 3(9.0\%) = 1.5\%$$

The weighted-average coupon rate is

$$0.75(9.5\%) + 0.25(1.5\%) = 7.5\%$$

Consequently, the 7.5% coupon rate on the bond class from which these two classes were created can support the aggregate interest payments that must be made to them. As in the case of the floater, the principal pay down of an inverse floater will be a proportionate amount of the principal pay down of bond class C.

Because one-month LIBOR is always positive, the coupon rate paid to the floating-rate bond class cannot be negative. If there are no restrictions placed on the coupon rate for the inverse floater, however, it is possible for the coupon rate for that bond class to be negative. To prevent this, a floor, or minimum, can be placed on the coupon rate. In many structures, the floor is set at zero. Once a floor is set for the inverse floater, a cap or ceiling is imposed on the floater. In FJF-03, a floor of zero is set for the inverse floater. The floor results in a cap or maximum coupon rate for the floater of 10%. This is found by substituting zero for the coupon rate of the inverse floater in the formula for the weighted-average coupon rate, and then setting the formula equal to 7.5%.

The cap for the floater and the inverse floater, the floor for the inverse floater, the coupon leverage, and the margin spread are not determined independently. Given four of these variables, the fifth will be determined.

Planned Amortization Class Tranches

The CMO innovations discussed previously attracted many institutional investors who had previously either avoided investing in mortgage-backed securities or allocated only a nominal portion of their portfolio to this sector of the fixed-income market. Although some traditional corporate bond buyers shifted their allocation to CMOs, a majority of institutional investors remained on the sidelines, concerned about investing in an instrument that they continued to perceive as posing significant prepayment risk because of the substantial average life variability, despite the innovations designed to reduce prepayment risk.

Potential demand for a CMO product with less uncertainty about the cash flow increased in the mid 1980s because of two trends in the corporate bond market. First was the increased event risk faced by investors, highlighted by the RJR Nabisco leveraged buy-out in 1988. The second trend was a decline in the number of AAA-rated corporate issues. Traditional corporate bond buyers sought a structure with both the characteristics of a corporate bond (either a bullet maturity or a sinking fund type of schedule of principal repayment) and high credit quality. Although CMOs satisfied the second condition, they did not satisfy the first.

In March 1987, the M.D.C. Mortgage Funding Corporation CMO Series O included a class of bonds referred to as **stabilized mortgage reduction term** (SMRT) **bonds**; another class in its CMO Series P was referred to as **planned amortization class** (PAC) **bonds**. The Oxford Acceptance Corporation III Series C CMOs included a class of bonds referred to as **planned redemption obligation** (PRO) **bonds**. The characteristic common to these three bonds is that if the prepayments are within a specified range, the cash flow pattern is known.

The greater predictability of the cash flow for these classes of bonds, now referred to exclusively as PAC bonds, occurs because there is a principal repayment schedule that must be satisfied. PAC bondholders have priority over all other classes in the CMO issue in receiving principal payments from the underlying collateral. The greater certainty of the cash flow for the PAC bonds comes at the expense of the non-PAC classes, called **support** or **companion bonds**. It is these bonds that absorb the prepayment risk. Because PAC bonds have protection against both extension risk and contraction risk, they are said to provide **two-sided prepayment protection**.

To illustrate how to create a PAC bond, we will use as collateral the $400 million pass-through with a coupon rate of 7.5%, an 8.125% WAC, and a WAM of 357 months. The second column of Exhibit 12-7 shows the principal payment (regularly scheduled principal repayment plus prepayments) for selected months assuming a prepayment speed of 90 PSA, and the next column shows the principal payments for selected months assuming that the pass-through prepays at 300 PSA.

The last column of Exhibit 12-7 gives the *minimum* principal payment if the collateral speed is 90 PSA or 300 PSA for months 1 to 349. (After month 346, the outstanding principal balance will be paid off if the prepayment speed is between 90 PSA and 300 PSA.) For example, in the first month, the principal payment would be $508,169.52 if the collateral prepays at 90 PSA and $1,075,931.20 if the collateral prepays at 300 PSA. Thus, the minimum principal payment is $508,169.52, as reported in the last column of Exhibit 12-7. In month 103, the minimum principal payment is also the amount if the prepayment speed is 90 PSA, $1,446,761, compared with $1,458,618.04 for 300 PSA. In month 104, however, a prepayment speed of 300 PSA would produce a principal payment of $1,433,539.23, which is less than the principal payment of $1,440,825.55 assuming 90 PSA. So $1,433,539.23 is reported in the last column of Exhibit 12-7. In fact, from month 104 on, the minimum principal payment is the one that would result assuming a prepayment speed of 300 PSA.

Exhibit 12-7 **Monthly Principal Payment for $400 Million 7.5% Coupon Pass-Through with an 8.125% WAC and a 357 WAM Assuming Prepayment Rates of 90 PSA and 300 PSA**

Month	At 90% PSA	At 300% PSA	Minimum Principal Payment—the PAC Schedule
1	508,169.52	1,075,931.20	508,169.52
2	569,843.43	1,279,412.11	569,843.43
3	631,377.11	1,482,194.45	631,377.11
4	692,741.89	1,683,966.17	692,741.89
5	753,909.12	1,884,414.62	753,909.12
6	814,850.22	2,083,227.31	814,850.22
7	875,536.68	2,280,092.68	875,536.68
8	935,940.10	2,474,700.92	935,940.10
9	996,032.19	2,666,744.77	996,032.19
10	1,055,784.82	2,855,920.32	1,055,784.82
11	1,115,170.01	3,041,927.81	1,115,170.01
12	1,174,160.00	3,224,472.44	1,174,160.00
13	1,232,727.22	3,403,265.17	1,232,727.22
14	1,290,844.32	3,578,023.49	1,290,844.32
15	1,348,484.24	3,748,472.23	1,348,484.24
16	1,405,620.17	3,914,344.26	1,405,620.17
17	1,462,225.60	4,075,381.29	1,462,225.60
18	1,518,274.36	4,231,334.57	1,518,274.36
101	1,458,719.34	1,510,072.17	1,458,719.34
102	1,452,725.55	1,484,126.59	1,452,725.55
103	1,446,761.00	1,458,618.04	1,446,761.00
104	1,440,825.55	1,433,539.23	1,433,539.23
105	1,434,919.07	1,408,883.01	1,408,883.01
211	949,482.58	213,309.00	213,309.00
212	946,033.34	209,409.09	209,409.09
213	942,601.99	205,577.05	205,577.05
346	618,684.59	13,269.17	13,269.17
347	617,071.58	12,944.51	12,944.51
348	615,468.65	12,626.21	12,626.21
349	613,875.77	12,314.16	3,432.32
350	612,292.88	12,008.25	0
351	610,719.96	11,708.38	0
352	609,156.96	11,414.42	0
353	607,603.84	11,126.28	0
354	606,060.57	10,843.85	0
355	604,527.09	10,567.02	0
356	603,003.38	10,295.70	0
357	601,489.39	10,029.78	0

In fact, if the collateral prepays at *any* speed between 90 PSA and 300 PSA, the minimum principal payment would be the amount reported in the last column of Exhibit 12-7. For example, if we had included principal payment figures assuming a prepayment speed of 200 PSA, the minimum principal payment would not change; from month 11 through month 103, the minimum principal payment is that generated from 90 PSA, but from month 104 on, the minimum principal payment is that generated from 300 PSA.

This characteristic of the collateral allows for the creation of a PAC bond, assuming that the collateral prepays over its life at a speed between 90 PSA to 300 PSA. A schedule of principal repayments that the PAC bondholders are entitled to receive before any other bond class in the CMO is specified. The monthly schedule of principal repayments is as specified in the last column of Exhibit 12-7, which shows the minimum principal payment. Although there is no assurance that the collateral will prepay between these two speeds, a PAC bond can be structured to assume that it will.

Exhibit 12-8 shows a CMO structure, FJF-04, created from the $400 million, 7.5% coupon pass-through with a WAC of 8.125% and a WAM of 357 months. There are just two bond classes in this structure: a 7.5% coupon PAC bond created assuming 90 to 300 PSA with a par value of $243.8 million, and a support bond with a par value of $156.2 million. The two speeds used to create a PAC bond are called the **initial PAC collars (or initial PAC bands)**; in our case, 90 PSA is the lower collar and 300 PSA is the upper collar.

Exhibit 12-9 reports the average life for the PAC bond and the support bond in FJF-04 assuming various *actual* prepayment speeds. Notice that between 90 PSA and 300 PSA, the average life for the PAC bond is stable at 7.26 years. However, at slower or faster PSA speeds, the schedule is broken, and the average life changes, lengthening when the prepayment speed is less than 90 PSA and shortening when it is greater than 300 PSA. Even so, there is much greater variability for the average life of the support bond.

Exhibit 12-8   FJF-04: CMO Structure with One PAC Bond and One Support Bond[a]

Tranche	Par Amount	Coupon Rate (%)
P (PAC)	$243,800,000	7.5
S (Support)	156,200,000	7.5
	$400,000,000	

[a]*Payment rules:*

1. For payment of periodic coupon interest: Disburse periodic coupon interest to each tranche on the basis of the amount of principal outstanding at the beginning of the period.

2. For disbursement of principal payments: Disburse principal payments to tranche P based on its schedule of principal repayments. Tranche P has priority with respect to current and future principal payments to satisfy the schedule. Any excess principal payments in a month over the amount necessary to satisfy the schedule for tranche P are paid to tranche S. When tranche S is paid off completely, all principal payments are to be made to tranche P regardless of the schedule.

Exhibit 12-9 Average Life for PAC Bond and Support Bond in FJF-04 Assuming Various Prepayment Speeds

Prepayment Rate (PSA)	PAC Bond (P)	Support Bond (S)
0	15.97	27.26
50	9.44	24.00
90	7.26	18.56
100	7.26	18.56
150	7.26	12.57
165	7.26	11.16
200	7.26	8.38
250	7.26	5.37
300	7.26	3.13
350	6.56	2.51
400	5.92	2.17
450	5.38	1.94
500	4.93	1.77
700	3.70	1.37

Creating a Series of PAC Bonds

Most CMO PAC structures have more than one class of PAC bonds. We created six PAC bonds from FJF-04, which we call FJF-05. Information about this CMO structure is reported in Exhibit 12-10. The total par value of the six PAC bonds is equal to $243.8 million, which is the amount of the single PAC bond in FJF-04.

Exhibit 12-11 shows the average life for the six PAC bonds and the support bond in FJF-05 at various prepayment speeds. From a PAC bond in FJF-04 with an average life of 7.26, we have created six bonds with an average life as short as 2.58 years (P-A) and as long as 16.92 years (P-F) if prepayments stay within 90 PSA and 300 PSA.

As expected, the average lives are stable if the prepayment speed is between 90 PSA and 300 PSA. Notice that even outside this range the average life is stable for several of the PAC bonds. For example, the PAC P-A bond is stable even if prepayment speeds are as high as 400 PSA. For the PAC P-B, the average life does not vary when prepayments are in the initial collar until prepayments are greater than 350 PSA. Why is it that the shorter the PAC, the more protection it has against faster prepayments?

To understand why this is so, remember that there are $156.2 million in support bonds that are protecting the $85 million of PAC P-A. Thus, even if prepayments are faster than the initial upper collar, there may be sufficient support bonds to assure the satisfaction of

Exhibit 12-10 FJF-05: CMO Structure with Six PAC Bonds and One Support Bond[a]

Tranche	Par Amount	Coupon Rate (%)
P-A	$ 85,000,000	7.5
P-B	8,000,000	7.5
P-C	35,000,000	7.5
P-D	45,000,000	7.5
P-E	40,000,000	7.5
P-F	30,800,000	7.5
S	156,200,000	7.5
	$400,000,000	

[a]*Payment rules:*

1. *For payment of periodic coupon interest: Disburse periodic coupon interest to each tranche on the basis of the amount of principal outstanding at the beginning of the period.*
2. *For disbursement of principal payments: Disburse principal payments to tranches P-A to P-F based on their respective schedules of principal repayments. Tranche P-A has priority with respect to current and future principal payments to satisfy the schedule. Any excess principal payments in a month over the amount necessary to satisfy the schedule for tranche P-A are paid to tranche S. When tranche P-A is paid off completely, tranche P-B has priority, then tranche P-C, and so on. When tranche S is paid off completely, all principal payments are to be made to the remaining PAC tranches in order of priority regardless of the schedule.*

Exhibit 12-11 Average Life for the Six PAC Bonds in FJF-05 Assuming Various Prepayment Speeds

Prepayment Rate (PSA)	PAC Bonds					
	P-A	P-B	P-C	P-D	P-E	P-F
0	8.46	14.61	16.49	19.41	21.91	23.76
50	3.58	6.82	8.36	11.30	14.50	18.20
90	2.58	4.72	5.78	7.89	10.83	16.92
100	2.58	4.72	5.78	7.89	10.83	16.92
150	2.58	4.72	5.78	7.89	10.83	16.92
165	2.58	4.72	5.78	7.89	10.83	16.92
200	2.58	4.72	5.78	7.89	10.83	16.92
250	2.58	4.72	5.78	7.89	10.83	16.92
300	2.58	4.72	5.78	7.89	10.83	16.92
350	2.58	4.72	5.49	6.95	9.24	14.91
400	2.57	4.37	4.91	6.17	8.33	13.21
450	2.50	3.97	4.44	5.56	7.45	11.81
500	2.40	3.65	4.07	5.06	6.74	10.65
700	2.06	2.82	3.10	3.75	4.88	7.51

Exhibit 12-12 Effective Collars for Each PAC Tranche in FJF-05

Amount of Support Bonds: $156.2 Million

Tranche	Effective Collar
P-A	90–450 PSA
P-B	90–350 PSA
P-C	90–300 PSA
P-D	90–300 PSA
P-E	90–300 PSA
P-F	90–300 PSA

the schedule. In fact, as can be seen from Exhibit 12-11, even if prepayments are at 400 PSA over the life of the collateral, the average life is unchanged.

Now, consider PAC P-B. The support bonds are providing protection for both the $85 million of PAC P-A and $93 million of PAC P-B. As can be seen from Exhibit 12-11, prepayments could be 350 PSA and the average life is still unchanged. From Exhibit 12-11 it can be seen that the degree of protection against extension risk increases the shorter the PAC. Thus, whereas the initial collar may be 90 to 300 PSA, the **effective collar** is wider for the shorter PAC tranches. Exhibit 12-12 shows the effective collar for the six PAC tranches in FJF-05.

Planned Amortization Class Window

As we explained earlier, the length of time over which scheduled principal repayments are made is referred to as the window. A PAC window can be wide or narrow. The narrower a PAC window, the more it resembles a corporate bond with a bullet payment. PAC buyers appear to prefer tight windows, although institutional investors facing a liability schedule are generally better off with a window that more closely matches the liabilities. Investor demand dictates the PAC windows that issuers will create. Investor demand in turn is governed by the nature of investor liabilities.

Effective Collars and Actual Prepayments

As we have emphasized several times, the creation of a mortgage-backed security cannot make prepayment risk disappear. This is true for both a pass-through and a CMO. Thus, the reduction in prepayment risk (both extension risk and contraction risk) that a PAC offers must come from somewhere.

Where does the prepayment protection come from? It comes from the support bonds. It is the support bonds that forego principal payments if the collateral prepayments are slow; support bonds do not receive any principal until the PAC bonds receive the scheduled principal repayment. This reduces the risk that the PAC bonds will extend. Similarly, it is the support bonds that absorb any principal payments in excess of the scheduled principal payments that are made. This reduces the contraction risk of the PAC bonds. *Thus, the key to the prepayment protection offered by a PAC bond is the amount of support bonds outstanding. If the support bonds are paid off quickly because of*

Exhibit 12-13 Average Life for PAC Tranches of FJF-05 One Year from Now Assuming Various Prepayment Speeds for the First 12 Months

Speed for First 12 Months	Thereafter	PAC P-A	P-B	P-C	P-D	P-E	P-F
90 PSA	90 PSA	1.81	3.72	4.77	6.89	9.82	15.91
100 PSA	100 PSA	1.81	3.72	4.77	6.89	9.82	15.91
165 PSA	165 PSA	1.81	3.72	4.77	6.89	9.82	15.91
200 PSA	200 PSA	1.81	3.72	4.77	6.89	9.82	15.91
300 PSA	300 PSA	1.81	3.72	4.77	6.89	9.82	15.91
400 PSA	400 PSA	1.80	3.37	3.90	5.17	7.32	12.21
600 PSA	600 PSA	1.41	2.16	2.50	3.29	4.65	7.83
800 PSA	800 PSA	1.09	1.56	1.79	2.34	3.28	5.48

Speed for First 12 Months	Thereafter	PAC P-A	P-B	P-C	P-D	P-E	P-F
42 CPR	90 PSA	2.73	6.17	8.26	12.78	18.86	25.42
42 CPR	100 PSA	2.52	5.69	7.63	11.92	17.93	24.92
42 CPR	165 PSA	1.70	3.77	5.06	8.08	12.91	21.07
42 CPR	200 PSA	1.46	3.19	4.28	6.83	11.03	18.94
42 CPR	300 PSA	1.05	2.24	2.96	4.69	7.61	13.97
42 CPR	400 PSA	0.84	1.74	2.28	3.55	5.72	10.67
42 CPR	600 PSA	0.60	1.23	1.57	2.37	3.73	6.92
42 CPR	800 PSA	0.47	0.97	1.22	1.77	2.71	4.92

faster-than-expected prepayments, there is no longer any protection for the PAC bonds. In fact, in FJF-05, if the support bond is paid off, the structure is effectively reduced to a sequential-pay CMO.

The support bonds can be thought of as bodyguards for the PAC bondholders. When the bullets fly (i.e., prepayments occur) it is the bodyguards that get killed off first. The bodyguards are there to absorb the bullets. When all the bodyguards are killed off (i.e., the support bonds paid off with faster-than-expected prepayments), the PAC bonds must fend for themselves; they are exposed to all the bullets.

The top panel of Exhibit 12-13 shows what happens to the average life for all PAC tranches of FJF-05 one year from now if prepayments for the first 12 months are the speed shown and the future speed is the same as the first 12 months. For example, if the collateral prepays at 165 PSA for the first 12 months and then prepays at the same speed thereafter, the average life one year from now will be 1.81 years for tranche P-A. Notice that for all the PAC tranches the average life is still stable for the initial collar. In contrast, the second panel shows what will happen to the average life one year from now if the collateral pays at 42 CPR for the first 12 months and prepays at the indicated speed thereafter. We selected 42 CPR so that the support bonds will be paid off by the end of the first year. The structure is now effectively a sequential-pay structure and, as indicated by the average lives reported in the exhibit, there is substantial average life variability for the original PAC tranches. A comparison of the lower and upper panel clearly demonstrates the role of the support bonds.

With the bodyguard metaphor for the support bonds in mind, let's consider two questions asked by CMO buyers:

1. Will the schedule of principal repayments be satisfied if prepayments are faster than the initial upper collar?
2. Will the schedule of principal repayments be satisfied as long as prepayments stay within the initial collar?

Let's address the first question. The initial upper collar for FJF-05 is 300 PSA. Suppose that actual prepayments are 500 PSA for seven consecutive months; will this disrupt the schedule of principal repayments? The answer is: It depends!

To answer this question, we need two pieces of information. First, when does the 500 PSA occur? Second, what has been the actual prepayment experience up to the time that prepayments are 500 PSA? For example, suppose that six years from now is when the prepayments reach 500 PSA and also suppose that for the past six years the actual prepayment speed has been 90 PSA every month. This means that there are more bodyguards (i.e., support bonds) around than was expected when the PAC was structured at the initial collar. In establishing the schedule of principal repayments, it was assumed that the bodyguards would be killed off at 300 PSA, but the actual prepayment experience results in them being killed off at only 90 PSA. Thus, six years from now when the 500 PSA is assumed to occur, there are more bodyguards than expected. Thus, a 500 PSA for seven consecutive months may have no effect on the ability of the schedule of principal repayments to be met.

In contrast, suppose that the actual prepayment experience for the first six years is 300 PSA (the upper collar of the initial PAC collar). In this case, there are no extra bodyguards around. As a result, any prepayment speeds faster than 300 PSA, such as 500 PSA in our example, jeopardize satisfaction of the principal repayment schedule and increase extension risk. This does not mean that the schedule will be **busted**—the term used in the CMO market when a PAC schedule is broken. It does mean that the prepayment protection is reduced.

It should be clear from these observations that the initial collars are not particularly useful in assessing the prepayment protection for a seasoned PAC bond. This is most important to understand, as it is common for CMO buyers to compare prepayment protection of PACs in different CMO structures, and conclude that the greater protection is offered by the one with the wider collar. This approach is inadequate because it is actual prepayment experience that determines the degree of prepayment protection as well as the expected future prepayment behavior of the collateral.

The way to determine this protection is to calculate the effective collar for a seasoned PAC bond. An effective collar for a seasoned PAC is the lower and the upper PSA that can occur in the future and still allow maintenance of the schedule of principal repayments.

The effective collar changes every month. An extended period over which actual prepayments are below the upper range of the initial PAC collar will result in an increase in the upper range of the effective collar. This is because there will be more bodyguards around than anticipated. An extended period of prepayments slower than the lower range of the initial PAC collar will raise the lower range of the effective collar. This is because it will take faster prepayments to make up the shortfall of the scheduled principal payments not made plus the scheduled future principal payments.

The PAC schedule may not be satisfied even if the actual prepayments never fall outside the initial collar. This may seem surprising because our previous analysis indicated that the average life would not change if prepayments are at either extreme of the initial collar. However, recall that all of our previous analysis has been based on a single PSA speed for the life of the structure.

Let's use vector analysis to see what happens to the effective collar if the prepayments are at the initial upper collar for a certain number of months. Exhibit 12-14 shows the average life two years from now for the PAC bond in FJF-04 assuming that prepayments are 300 PSA for the first 24 months. Notice that the average life is stable at six years if the prepayments for the following months are between 115 PSA and 300 PSA. That is, the effective PAC collar is no longer the initial collar. Instead, the lower collar has shifted upward. This means that the protection from year 2 on is for 115 to 300 PSA, a narrower band than initially even though the earlier prepayments did not exceed the initial upper collar.

Providing Greater Prepayment Protection for PACs

There are two ways to provide greater protection for PAC bonds: lockouts and reverse PAC structures. One obvious way to provide greater protection for PAC bonds is to issue fewer PAC bonds relative to support bonds. In FJF-05, for example, rather than creating the six PAC bonds with a total par value of $243.8 million, we could use only $158.8 million of the

---

Exhibit 12-14 Average Life Two Years from Now for PAC Bond of FJF-04 Assuming Prepayments of 300 PSA for First 24 Months

PSA from Year 2 on	Average Life (years)
95	6.43
105	6.11
115	6.01
120	6.00
125	6.00
300	6.00
305	5.62

$400 million of collateral to create these bonds, by reducing the amount of each of the six PAC bonds. An alternative is not to issue one of the PAC bonds, typically the shorter-term one. For example, suppose that we create only the last five of the six PAC bonds in FJF-05. The $85 million for PAC P-A is then used to create more support bonds. Such a CMO structure with no principal payments to a PAC bond class in the earlier years is referred to as a **lockout structure**.

A lockout structure provides greater prepayment protection to all PAC bonds in the CMO structure. One way to provide greater prepayment protection to only some PAC bonds is to alter the principal payment rules for distributing principal when all the support bonds have been paid off. In FJF-05, for example, when the support bond in this structure is paid off, the structure effectively becomes a sequential-pay structure. For PAC P-A, this means that although there is protection against extension risk, as this tranche receives principal payments before the other five PAC bonds, there is no protection against contraction.

To provide greater protection to PAC P-A, the payment rules after all support bonds have been paid off can be specified so that any principal payments in excess of the scheduled amount will be paid to the last PAC bond, P-F. Thus, PAC P-F is exposed to greater contraction risk, which provides the other five PAC bonds with more protection against contraction risk. The principal payment rules would also specify that when the support bond and PAC P-F bond are paid off, all principal payments in excess of the scheduled amounts to earlier tranches are to be paid to the next-to-last PAC bond, PAC P-E in our example.

A CMO structure requiring any excess principal payments to be made to the longer PAC bonds after all support bonds are paid off is called a **reverse PAC structure**.

Other Planned Amortization Class Tranches

Earlier, we described how the collateral can be used to create a CMO with accrual bonds, floaters, and inverse floaters bonds. In addition, interest-only and principal-only tranches (described later) can be created. These same types of bond classes can be created from a PAC bond. The difference between the bond classes described and those created from a PAC bond is simply the prepayment protection offered by the PAC structure.

Targeted Amortization Class Bonds

A **targeted amortization class (TAC) bond** resembles a PAC bond in that both have a schedule of principal repayment. The difference between a PAC bond and a TAC bond is that the former has a wide PSA range over which the schedule of principal repayment is protected against contraction risk and extension risk. A TAC bond, in contrast, has a single PSA rate from which the schedule of principal repayment is protected. As a result, the prepayment protection afforded the TAC bond is less than that for a PAC bond.

The creation of a bond with a schedule of principal repayments based on a single prepayment rate results in protection against contraction risk but not extension risk. Thus, whereas PAC bonds are said to have two-sided prepayment protection, TAC bonds have one-sided prepayment protection. Such a bond is acceptable to institutional investors who are not overly concerned with some extension risk but greatly concerned with contraction risk.

Some institutional investors are interested in protection against extension risk but are willing to accept contraction risk. This is the opposite protection from that sought by the buyers of TAC bonds. The structures created to provide such protection are referred to as **reverse TAC bonds**.

Very Accurately Determined Maturity Bonds

Accrual or Z bonds have been used in CMO structures as support for bonds called **very accurately determined maturity** (VADM) or **guaranteed final maturity bonds**. In this case, the interest accruing (i.e., not being paid out) on a Z bond is used to pay the interest and principal on a VADM bond. This effectively provides protection against extension risk even if prepayments slow down, because the interest accruing on the Z bond will be sufficient to pay off the scheduled principal and interest on the VADM bond. Thus, the maximum final maturity can be determined with a high degree of certainty. If prepayments are high, resulting in the supporting Z bond being paid off faster, however, a VADM bond can shorten.

A VADM is similar in character to a reverse TAC. For structures with similar collateral, however, a VADM bond offers greater protection against extension risk. Moreover, most VADMs will not shorten significantly if prepayments speed up. Thus, they offer greater protection against contraction risk compared with a reverse TAC with the same underlying collateral. Compared with PACs, VADM bonds have greater absolute protection against extension risk, and though VADM bonds do not have as much protection against contraction risk, as noted previously, the structures that have included these bonds are such that contraction risk is generally not significant.

Interest-Only and Principal-Only Tranches

As we explain later in this chapter, stripped mortgage-backed securities are created by paying all the principal to one bond class and all the interest to another bond class. These two classes are referred to as the **principal-only** (PO) **bond class** and the **interest-only** (IO) **bond class**. We discuss the investment characteristics of these securities later.

CMO structures can be created so that a tranche can receive only the principal or only the interest. For example, consider FJF-01. Tranche B in this structure can be divided into two tranches, a principal-only tranche and an interest-only tranche.

Notional Interest-Only

In our previous illustrations, we used a CMO structure in which all the tranches have the same coupon rate (7.5%) and that coupon rate is the same as the collateral. In practice, the same coupon rate would not be given to each tranche. Instead, the coupon rate would depend on the term structure of interest rates and the average life of the tranche, among other things.

In the earlier CMO deals, all of the excess interest between the coupon rate on the tranches and the coupon interest on the collateral was paid to an equity class referred to as the **CMO residual**. This is no longer the practice today. Instead, a tranche is created that receives the excess coupon interest. This tranche is called a **notional IO class** and also referred to as a **structured IO**.

To see how a notional IO is created, consider the CMO structure shown in Exhibit 12-15, FJF-06. This is the same structure as FJF-02 except that the coupon rate varies by tranche and there is a class denoted IO, which is the class of interest to us.

Exhibit 12-15 **FJF-06: Hypothetical Five Tranche Sequential Pay with an Accrual Tranche and an Interest-Only Tranche**[a]

Tranche	Par Amount	Notional Amount	Coupon Rate (%)
A	$194,500,000		6.00
B	36,000,000		6.50
C	96,500,000		7.00
Z	73,000,000		7.25
IO		52,566,666	7.50
	$400,000,000		

[a]*Payment rules:*

1. *For payment of periodic coupon interest: Disburse periodic coupon interest to tranches A, B, and C on the basis of the amount of principal outstanding at the beginning of the period. For tranche Z, accrue the interest based on the principal plus accrued interest in the preceding period. The interest for tranche Z is to be paid to the earlier tranches as a principal pay down. Disburse periodic interest to the IO tranche based on the notional amount at the beginning of the period.*
2. *For disbursement of principal payments: Disburse principal payments to tranche A until it is paid off completely. After tranche A is paid off completely, disburse principal payments to tranche B until it is paid off completely. After tranche B is paid off completely, disburse principal payments to tranche C until it is paid off completely. After tranche C is paid off completely, disburse principal payments to tranche Z until the original principal balance plus accrued interest is paid off completely.*

Notice that for this structure, the par amount for the IO class is shown as $52,566,666 and the coupon rate is 7.5%. This is an IO class, so there is no par amount. The amount shown is the amount on which the interest payments will be determined, not the amount that will be paid to the holder of this bond. Therefore, it is called a **notional amount**.

Let's look at how the notional amount is determined. Consider first tranche A. The par value is $194.5 million and the coupon rate is 6%. Because the collateral's coupon rate is 7.5%, the excess interest is 150 basis points (1.5%). Therefore, an IO with a 1.5% coupon rate and a notional amount of $194.5 million can be created from tranche A. However, this is equivalent to an IO with a notional amount of $38.9 million and a coupon rate of 7.5%. Mathematically, this notional amount is found as follows:

$$\text{notional amount for 7.5\% IO} = \frac{\text{tranche's par value} \times \text{excess interest}}{0.075}$$

where

$$\text{excess interest} = \text{collateral coupon rate} - \text{tranche coupon rate}$$

For example, for tranche A,

$$\text{excess interest} = 0.075 - 0.060 = 0.015$$

$$\text{tranche's par value} = \$194,500,000$$

$$\text{notional amount for 7.5\% IO} = \frac{\$194,500,000 \times 0.015}{0.075}$$
$$= \$38,900,000$$

Similarly, from tranche B with a par value of $36 million, the excess interest is 100 basis points (1%), and therefore an IO with a coupon rate of 1% and a notional amount of $36 million can be created. But this is equivalent to creating an IO with a notional amount of $4.8 million and a coupon rate of 7.5%. This procedure is shown in the following table for all four tranches.

Tranche	Par Amount	Excess Interest	Notional Amount for a 7.5% Coupon Rate IO
A	$194,500,000	1.50	$38,900,000
B	36,000,000	1.00	4,800,000
C	96,500,000	0.50	6,433,333
Z	73,000,000	0.25	2,433,333
		Notional amount for 7.5% IO	$52,566,666

Support Bonds

The support bonds—or bodyguards—are the bonds that provide prepayment protection for the PAC tranches. Consequently, they are exposed to the greatest level of prepayment risk. Because of this, investors must be particularly careful in assessing the cash flow characteristics of support bonds to reduce the likelihood of adverse portfolio consequences due to prepayments.

The support bond typically is divided into different bond classes. All the bond classes we have discussed earlier in this section are available, including sequential-pay support bond classes, floater and inverse floater support bond classes, and accrual support bond classes.

The support bond can even be partitioned so as to create support bond classes with a schedule of principal repayments. That is, support bond classes that are PAC bonds can be created. In a structure with a PAC bond and a support bond with a PAC schedule of principal repayments, the former is called a PAC I bond or level I PAC bond or PAC1 and the latter a PAC II bond or level II PAC bond. Although PAC II bonds have greater prepayment protection than the support bond classes without a schedule of principal repayments, the prepayment protection is less than that provided PAC I bonds.

Actual Transaction

Now that we have an understanding of CMOs, let's look at an actual one. We will use a Ginnie Mae deal. The deal that we will describe is Ginnie Mae REMIC Trust 2008-004. The first five pages of the offering circular supplement are shown as Exhibit 12-16. Because Ginnie Mae is a federal government agency, it is not required to file a prospectus with the Securities and Exchange Commission.

The first page of the offering circular supplement indicates the tranches (class of REMIC securities) being offered. The total original principal balance is $375 million. Notice that the offering is a supplement to the "Base Offering Circular dated October 1, 2004." The base offering circular provides a more detailed description of the securities. Exhibit 12-17 provides four pages from the base offering circular: (1) the cover page, (2) the table of contents (two pages), and (3) Appendix I, which provides the standard abbreviations used by Ginnie Mae for the different class types. Notice that the offering circular supplement refers the reader to Appendix I of the base offering circular for the definitions of the class types—principal type and interest type.

Offering Circular Supplement
(To Base Offering Circular dated October 1, 2004)

$375,000,000

Government National Mortgage Association
GINNIE MAE®

Guaranteed REMIC Pass-Through Securities
and MX Securities
Ginnie Mae REMIC Trust 2008-004

The Securities

The Trust will issue the Classes of Securities listed on the front cover of this offering circular supplement.

The Ginnie Mae Guaranty

Ginnie Mae will guarantee the timely payment of principal and interest on the securities. The Ginnie Mae Guaranty is backed by the full faith and credit of the United States of America.

The Trust and its Assets

The Trust will own Ginnie Mae Certificates.

Class of REMIC Securities	Original Principal Balance(2)	Interest Rate	Principal Type(3)	Interest Type(3)	CUSIP Number	Final Distribution Date(4)
FA	$100,000,000	(5)	PT	FLT	38375PEQ0	January 2038
FB	50,000,000	(5)	PT	FLT	38375PER8	January 2038
FC	100,000,000	(5)	PT	FLT	38375PES6	January 2038
FI	3,019,154	6.50 %	NTL (SEQ)	FIX/IO	38375PET4	February 2008
FJ	250,000	(5)	NTL (PT)	FLT/INV/IO/SP (6)	38375PEU1	January 2038
HA	12,500,000	5.25	SUP	FIX	38375PEV9	October 2037
HB	5,000,000	5.50	SUP	FIX	38375PEW7	May 2037
HC	3,643,000	5.25	SUP	FIX	38375PEX5	May 2037
HD	1,357,000	5.50	SUP	FIX	38375PEY3	December 2037
HG	1,201,000	5.50	SUP	FIX	38375PEZ0	December 2037
HI	165,591	5.50	NTL (SUP)	FIX/IO	38375PFA4	May 2037
HT	12,500,000	5.75	SUP	FIX	38375PFB2	October 2037
PF	59,686,786	(5)	PAC I	FLT	38375PFC0	January 2038
PO(1)...	16,278,214	0.00	PAC I	PO	38375PFD8	January 2038
PY(1)...	59,686,786	(5)	NTL (PAC I)	INV/IO	38375PFE6	January 2038
QA	3,933,000	5.50	PAC II	FIX	38375PFF3	January 2038
SA	250,000,000	(5)	NTL (PT)	INV/IO	38375PFG1	January 2038
UA	7,500,000	5.50	SUP	FIX	38375PFH9	December 2037
UB	1,401,000	5.50	SUP	FIX	38375PFJ5	January 2038
Residual						
RR	0	0.00	NPR	NPR	38375PFK2	January 2038

(1) These Securities may be exchanged for MX Securities described in Schedule I.

(2) Subject to increase as described under "Increase in Size" in this Supplement. The amount shown for each Notional Class (indicated by "NTL" under Principal Type) is its original Class Notional Balance and does not represent principal that will be paid.

(3) As defined under "Class Types" in Appendix I to the Base Offering Circular. The type of Class with which the Class Notional Balance of each Notional Class will be reduced is indicated in parentheses.

(4) See "Yield, Maturity and Prepayment Considerations — Final Distribution Date" in this Supplement.

(5) See "Terms Sheet — Interest Rates" in this Supplement.

(6) Class FJ has the SP ("Special") designation in its Interest Type because its Interest Rate will change significantly at specified levels of LIBOR. See "Terms Sheet — Interest Rates" in this Supplement.

The securities may not be suitable investments for you. You should consider carefully the risks of investing in them.

See "Risk Factors" beginning on page S-6 which highlights some of these risks.

The Sponsor and the Co-Sponsor will offer the securities from time to time in negotiated transactions at varying prices. We expect the closing date to be January 30, 2008.

You should read the Base Offering Circular as well as this Supplement.

The securities are exempt from registration under the Securities Act of 1933 and are "exempted securities" under the Securities Exchange Act of 1934.

Citi

Guzman & Company

The date of this Offering Circular Supplement is January 23, 2008.

(Continued)

Exhibit 12-16   Selected Pages from the Offering Circular Supplement for Ginnie Mae REMIC Trust 2008-004 (Continued)

AVAILABLE INFORMATION

You should purchase the securities only if you have read and understood the following documents:

- this Offering Circular Supplement (this "Supplement") and

- the Base Offering Circular.

The Base Offering Circular is available on Ginnie Mae's website located at http://www.ginniemae.gov.

If you do not have access to the internet, call The Bank of New York, which will act as information agent for the Trust, at (800) 234-GNMA, to order copies of the Base Offering Circular.

Please consult the standard abbreviations of Class Types included in the Base Offering Circular as Appendix I and the Glossary included in the Base Offering Circular as Appendix II for definitions of capitalized terms.

TABLE OF CONTENTS

S-2

(Continued)

Exhibit 12-16 **Selected Pages from the Offering Circular Supplement for Ginnie Mae REMIC Trust 2008-004 (Continued)**

TERMS SHEET

This terms sheet contains selected information for quick reference only. You should read this Supplement, particularly "Risk Factors," and each of the other documents listed under "Available Information."

Sponsor: Citigroup Global Markets Inc.

Trustee: Wells Fargo Bank, N.A.

Tax Administrator: The Trustee

Closing Date: January 30, 2008

Distribution Date: The 20th day of each month or, if the 20th day is not a Business Day, the first Business Day thereafter, commencing in February 2008.

Trust Assets:

Trust Asset Type	Certificate Rate	Original Term To Maturity (in years)
Ginnie Mae II	6.5%	30

Assumed Characteristics of the Mortgage Loans Underlying the Trust Assets[1]:

Principal Balance[2]	Weighted Average Remaining Term to Maturity (in months)	Weighted Average Loan Age (in months)	Weighted Average Mortgage Rate[3]
$375,000,000	358	2	6.922%

[1] As of January 1, 2008.

[2] Does not include the Trust Assets that will be added to pay the Trustee Fee.

[3] The Mortgage Loans underlying the Trust Assets may bear interest at rates ranging from 0.25% to 1.50% per annum above the Certificate Rate.

The actual remaining terms to maturity, loan ages and Mortgage Rates of many of the Mortgage Loans will differ from the weighted averages shown above, perhaps significantly. *See "The Trust Assets — The Mortgage Loans" in this Supplement.*

Issuance of Securities: The Securities, other than the Residual Securities, will initially be issued in book-entry form through the book-entry system of the U.S. Federal Reserve Banks (the "Fedwire Book-Entry System"). The Residual Securities will be issued in fully registered, certificated form. *See "Description of the Securities — Form of Securities" in this Supplement.*

Modification and Exchange: If you own exchangeable Securities you will be able, upon notice and payment of an exchange fee, to exchange them for a proportionate interest in the related Securities shown on Schedule I to this Supplement. *See "Description of the Securities — Modification and Exchange" in this Supplement.*

Increased Minimum Denomination Classes: Each Class that constitutes a Principal Only, Interest Only, Inverse Floating Rate or Special Class. *See "Description of the Securities — Form of Securities" in this Supplement.*

Interest Rates: The Interest Rates for the Fixed Rate Classes are shown on the front cover of this Supplement.

S-3

(Continued)

Exhibit 12-16   Selected Pages from the Offering Circular Supplement for Ginnie Mae REMIC Trust 2008-004 (Continued)

The Floating Rate and Inverse Floating Rate Classes will bear interest at per annum rates based on one-month LIBOR (hereinafter referred to as ''LIBOR'') as follows:

Class	Interest Rate Formula(1)	Initial Interest Rate(2)	Minimum Rate	Maximum Rate	Delay (in days)	LIBOR for Minimum Interest Rate
FA	LIBOR + 0.48%	4.99500000%	0.48%	7.00000000%	0	0.000%
FB	LIBOR + 0.48%	4.89125000%	0.48%	7.00000000%	0	0.000%
FC	LIBOR + 0.49%	4.86063000%	0.49%	7.00000000%	0	0.000%
FJ	(3)	0.00000000%	0.00%	2.40000000%	0	(4)
PA	13.36% − (LIBOR x 2.00)	4.72124000%	0.00%	13.36000000%	0	6.680%
PB	15.03% − (LIBOR x 2.25)	5.31139500%	0.00%	15.03000000%	0	6.680%
PC	16.70% − (LIBOR x 2.50)	5.90155000%	0.00%	16.70000000%	0	6.680%
PD	18.37% − (LIBOR x 2.75)	6.49170500%	0.00%	18.37000000%	0	6.680%
PE	20.04% − (LIBOR x 3.00)	7.08186000%	0.00%	20.04000000%	0	6.680%
PF	LIBOR + 0.32%	4.63938000%	0.32%	7.00000000%	0	0.000%
PG	21.71% − (LIBOR x 3.25)	7.67201500%	0.00%	21.71000000%	0	6.680%
PH	23.38% − (LIBOR x 3.50)	8.26217000%	0.00%	23.38000000%	0	6.680%
PS	24.49333333% − (LIBOR x 3.66666667)	8.65560665%	0.00%	24.49333333%	0	6.680%
PY	6.68% − LIBOR	2.36062000%	0.00%	6.68000000%	0	6.680%
SA	6.516% − LIBOR	2.00100000%	0.00%	6.51600000%	0	6.516%

(1) LIBOR will be established on the basis of the BBA LIBOR method, as described under ''Description of the Securities — Interest Distributions — Floating Rate and Inverse Floating Rate Classes'' in this Supplement.

(2) The initial Interest Rate will be in effect during the first Accrual Period; the Interest Rate will adjust monthly thereafter.

(3) If LIBOR is less than or equal to 6.516%, (LIBOR x 400) − 2604.0%; if LIBOR is greater than 6.516%, 3912.0% − (LIBOR x 600).

(4) Less than or equal to 6.51% or greater than or equal to 6.52%.

Allocation of Principal: On each Distribution Date, a percentage of the Principal Distribution Amount will be applied to the Trustee Fee, and the remainder of the Principal Distribution Amount (the ''Adjusted Principal Distribution Amount'') will be allocated, concurrently, as follows:

1. 66.6666666667%, concurrently, to FA, FB and FC, pro rata, until retired

2. 33.3333333333% in the following order of priority:

   a. Concurrently, to PF and PO, pro rata, until reduced to their Aggregate Scheduled Principal Balance for that Distribution Date

   b. To QA, until reduced to its Scheduled Principal Balance for that Distribution Date

   c. Concurrently, as follows:

      i. 17.1620786710% to UA, until retired

      ii. 22.8827715613% in the following order of priority:

         1. Concurrently, to HB and HC, pro rata, until retired

         2. To HD, until retired

(Continued)

Exhibit 12-16 **Selected Pages from the Offering Circular Supplement for Ginnie Mae REMIC Trust 2008-004 (Continued)**

      iii. 59.9551497677% in the following order of priority:

        1. Concurrently, to HA and HT, pro rata, until retired

        2. To HG, until retired

    d. To UB, until retired

    e. To QA, without regard to its Scheduled Principal Balance, until retired

    f. Concurrently, to PF and PO, pro rata, without regard to their Aggregate Scheduled Principal Balance, until retired

Scheduled Principal Balances: The Scheduled Principal Balances or Aggregate Scheduled Principal Balances for the Classes listed below are included in Schedule II to this Supplement. They were calculated using, among other things, the following Structuring Ranges:

Class	Structuring Ranges
PF and PO (in the aggregate)	125% PSA through 400% PSA
QA	140% PSA through 400% PSA

Notional Classes: The Notional Classes will not receive distributions of principal but have Class Notional Balances for convenience in describing their entitlements to interest. The Class Notional Balance of each Notional Class represents the percentage indicated below of, and reduces to that extent with, the Class Principal Balances indicated:

Class	Original Class Notional Balance	Represents Approximately
FI(1)	$ 798,077	1.5961538462% of FB (PT Class)
	2,221,077	2.2210769231% of FC (PT Class)
	$ 3,019,154	
FJ	$ 250,000	0.1% of FA, FB and FC (PT Class)
HI	$ 165,591	4.5454545455% of HC (SUP Class)
PY	$ 59,686,786	100% of PF (PAC I Class)
SA	$250,000,000	100% of FA, FB and FC (PT Class)

(1) For the February 2008 Distribution Date; thereafter, the Notional Balance of Class FI will be zero.

Tax Status: Double REMIC Series. *See "Certain Federal Income Tax Consequences" in this Supplement and in the Base Offering Circular.*

Regular and Residual Classes: Class RR is a Residual Class and includes the Residual Interest of the Issuing REMIC and the Pooling REMIC; all other Classes of REMIC Securities are Regular Classes.

S-5

Source: *Reprinted from Offering Circular Supplement for Ginnie Mae REMIC Trust 2008-004, pages S-1 through S-5. Ginnie Mae and the Ginnie Mae logo are registered service marks of the Government National Mortgage Association and are used with permission.*

Base Offering Circular
October 1, 2004

Government National Mortgage Association
GINNIE MAE®
Guaranteed REMIC Pass-Through Securities
(Issuable in Series)

The Government National Mortgage Association Guaranteed REMIC Pass-Through Securities, which will be sold from time to time in one or more series, represent interests in separate Ginnie Mae REMIC Trusts established from time to time. The Government National Mortgage Association ("Ginnie Mae"), a wholly-owned corporate instrumentality of the United States of America within the U.S. Department of Housing and Urban Development, guarantees the timely payment of principal and interest on each Class of Securities. The Ginnie Mae Guaranty is backed by the full faith and credit of the United States of America.

The terms of each Series will be described in an Offering Circular Supplement. Each Trust will be comprised primarily of (i) "fully modified pass-through" mortgage-backed certificates as to which Ginnie Mae has guaranteed the timely payment of principal and interest pursuant to the Ginnie Mae I Program or the Ginnie Mae II Program, (ii) certificates backed by Ginnie Mae MBS Certificates as to which Ginnie Mae has guaranteed the timely payment of principal and interest pursuant to the Ginnie Mae Platinum Program, (iii) previously issued REMIC or comparable mortgage certificates or Underlying Callable Securities or (iv) previously issued Ginnie Mae Guaranteed Stripped Mortgage-Backed Securities, in each case, evidencing interests in trusts consisting primarily of direct or indirect interests in Ginnie Mae Certificates, as further described in the related Offering Circular Supplement. The mortgage loans underlying the Ginnie Mae Certificates consist of one- to four-family residential mortgage loans that are insured or guaranteed by the Federal Housing Administration ("FHA"), the U.S. Department of Veterans Affairs ("VA"), the U.S. Department of Housing and Urban Development ("HUD") or the Rural Housing Service ("RHS"), formerly the Farmers Home Administration. See "The Ginnie Mae Certificates."

Each Series will be issued in two or more Classes. Each Class of Securities of a Series will evidence an interest in future principal payments and/or an interest in future interest payments on the Trust Assets included in the related Trust or a group of Trust Assets in the related Trust. The Holders of one or more Classes of Securities of a Series may be entitled to receive distributions of principal, interest, other revenues or any combination thereof prior to the Holders of one or more other Classes of Securities of that Series or after the occurrence of specified events, in each case, as specified in the related Offering Circular Supplement.

The Weighted Average Life of each Class of Securities of a Series may be affected by the rate of payment of principal (including prepayments and payments of certain other amounts resulting from defaults) on the Mortgage Loans underlying the related Trust Assets and the timing of receipt of those payments, as described in this Base Offering Circular and in the related Offering Circular Supplement. The Ginnie Mae Guaranty of timely payment of principal and interest is not a guarantee of the Weighted Average Life of a Class of Securities or of any particular rate of principal prepayments with respect to the Mortgage Loans underlying the Trust Assets or any Trust Asset Group. A Trust may be subject to early termination under the circumstances described in the related Offering Circular Supplement.

An election will be made to treat each Trust or certain assets of each Trust as one or more real estate mortgage investment conduits for federal income tax purposes. See "Certain Federal Income Tax Consequences" in this Base Offering Circular.

THE GOVERNMENT NATIONAL MORTGAGE ASSOCIATION GUARANTEES THE TIMELY PAYMENT OF PRINCIPAL AND INTEREST ON THE SECURITIES. THE GINNIE MAE GUARANTY IS BACKED BY THE FULL FAITH AND CREDIT OF THE UNITED STATES OF AMERICA. THE SECURITIES ARE EXEMPT FROM THE REGISTRATION REQUIREMENTS OF THE SECURITIES ACT OF 1933 AND CONSTITUTE EXEMPTED SECURITIES UNDER THE SECURITIES EXCHANGE ACT OF 1934.

Offers of the Securities may be made through one or more different methods, including offerings through the Sponsor, as more fully described in the related Offering Circular Supplement. This Base Offering Circular may not be used to consummate sales of Securities unless you have received the related Offering Circular Supplement. The date of this Base Offering Circular is October 1, 2004.

Base Offering Circular - Single Family

(Continued)

| Exhibit 12-17 | Selected Pages from the Ginnie Mae Guaranteed Pass-Through Securities Base Offering Circular, October 1, 2004 (Continued) |

TABLE OF CONTENTS

(Continued)

APPENDIX I

CLASS TYPES

The following list contains standard abbreviations used to describe certain class types. Definitions of the class types may be found in Appendix II. The definitions are not intended as descriptions of the material risks associated with any Class. For a discussion of the risks associated with particular class types, investors should see "Risk Factors — Class Investment Considerations" in the related Offering Circular Supplement.

Standard Abbreviation	Category of Class Definition
PRINCIPAL TYPES	
AD	Accretion Directed
CC	Callable Class
CPT	Component
JMP	Jump
NPR	No Payment Residual
NSJ	Non-Sticky Jump
NTL	Notional
PAC	PAC (or Planned Amortization Class)
PT	Pass-Through
SC	Structured Collateral
SCH	Scheduled
SEQ	Sequential Pay
SJ	Sticky Jump
STP	Strip
SUP	Support (or Companion)
TAC	TAC (or Targeted Amortization Class)
XAC	Index Allocation
INTEREST TYPES	
ARB	Ascending Rate
DLY	Delay
DIF	Differential
DRB	Descending Rate
EXE	Excess
FIX	Fixed Rate
FLT	Floating Rate
INV	Inverse Floating Rate
IO	Interest Only
NPR	No Payment Residual
PO	Principal Only
PZ	Partial Accrual
WAC	WAC (or Weighted Average Coupon)
Z	Accrual
OTHER TYPES	
SP	Special

Source: *Reprinted from pages 1, 3, and 44 of Ginnie Mae Guaranteed Pass-Through Securities Base Offering Circular, October 1, 2004. Ginnie Mae. Ginnie Mae and the Ginnie Mae logo are registered service marks of the Government National Mortgage Association and are used with permission.*

Pages S-3, S-4, and S-5 of the offering circular supplement show the term sheet. Pages S-3 and S-4 identify the floaters and the inverse floaters in the deal. Pages S-4 and S-5 explain the allocation of principal to the classes. On page S-5, the structuring bands for the PAC bonds are explained. For classes PF and PO, the initial PAC band (i.e., the structuring range) is 125%–400% PSA; for class QA, it is 140%–400% PSA. Also shown on page S-5 is a summary of the notional classes.

Exhibit 12-18 from another Ginnie Mae publication shows the abbreviation conventions that are used for the different types of classes.

Exhibit 12-18   Ginnie Mae Class Naming Conventions for Multiclass Securities

Ginnie Mae has established the following conventions that should be followed to determine Class designations.

Type	Name[1]
Accrual	Z, ZA, ZB, ZC, etc.
Interest Only, stripped from the entire deal[2]	IO
Principal Only, stripped from the entire deal[3]	PO
Floater	F, FA, FB, etc.
Inverse Floater	S, SA, SB, etc.; match with floaters[4]
PAC1[5]	PA, PB, PC, etc.[6]
PAC1 Floater	PF
PAC1 Inverse Floater	PS
PAC1 Accrual	PZ, PU, PV, PW, PX, PY
Everything Else[7]	A through X (excluding F, I, Q, R and S)
Component[8]	Numerical suffix - A1 and A2
Certificated Regular Class (initial issuance)	Q suffix - AQ, ZQ, SQ, etc.
Residual	R, RI, RP, RR[9]

---

[1]   Triple lettering is not accepted.

[2]   An IO stripped from a Class(es) will be named with the next alphabetical lettering immediately following the Class(es) to which it is related. For example, a PAC1 IO whose Class Notional Balance is a percentage of PA, PB and PC will be named PD.

[3]   A PO stripped from a Class(es) will be named with the next alphabetical lettering immediately following the Class(es) to which it is related. For example, a PAC1 PO whose principal amount is a percentage of PA, PB and PC will be named PD.

[4]   For example: if F pays with S and SA, skip FA. The next Floating Rate Class should be FB, which will pay with SB.

[5]   The PAC range must be at least 30% PSA above and below the pricing PSA. The PAC2 range, while narrower than the PAC1 range, must still be 30% PSA above and below the pricing PSA. "PAC"s that do not meet these criteria will be called Scheduled Classes.

[6]   Refrain from using PO and PQ to avoid confusion with Principal Only Classes and Certificated Regular Classes; refrain from using PP because double lettering, with the exception of RR, is not permitted.

[7]   "I" is not used to denote any Class, with the exception of IO. "R" may not be used in any class designation, with the exception of a Residual Security.

[8]   Only Components are allowed to be alpha-numeric; no hyphens are permitted.

[9]   R — Single REMIC Residual, RI — Issuing REMIC Residual, RP — Pooling REMIC Residual, RR — Stapled Residual.

Source: *Reprinted from Government National Mortgage Association, Multiclass Structure Guide: Part I: Ginnie Mae REMIC and MX Transactions: Guidelines and Selected Transaction Documents, January 1, 2002, p. I-5-1. Ginnie Mae. Ginnie Mae and the Ginnie Mae logo are registered service marks of the Government National Mortgage Association and are used with permission.*

AGENCY STRIPPED MORTGAGE–BACKED SECURITIES

Agency **stripped mortgage-backed securities** (SMBS) are another example of derivative mortgage products. A pass-through divides the cash flow from the underlying pool of mortgages on a pro rata basis across the security holders. An SMBS is created by altering the distribution of principal and interest from a pro rata distribution to an unequal distribution. Some of the securities thus created will have a price/yield relationship that is different from the price/yield relationship of the underlying mortgage pool.

There are three types of SMBS:

- synthetic-coupon pass-throughs
- interest-only/principal-only securities
- CMO strips

Synthetic-Coupon Pass-Throughs

The first generation of SMBS were **synthetic-coupon pass-throughs**, where two securities were paid some interest and principal from a pass-through security but the distribution of interest or principal were not equal. The result was two securities with a synthetic coupon rate that was different from that of the underlying pass-through security from which they were created.

To illustrate what was done (and then we will explain why), suppose that $1 billion of pass-throughs with a 6% coupon rate are used to create two securities. Assume further that 6% is the prevailing mortgage rate and that the following two securities, A-1 and A-2, are created as follows:

A-1 receives 75% of the interest and 50% of the principal
A-2 receives 25% of the interest and 50% of the principal

This means that the principal for the two issues and the interest at issuance is

A-1 and A-2: principal = $ 1 billion × 0.5 = $500 million
A-1 interest: 0.06 × 0.75 × $1 billion = $45 million
A-2 interest: 0.06 × 0.25 × $1 billion = $15 million

The synthetic coupon rate for the two securities is then

Synthetic coupon for A-1: $45 million/$500 million = 9%
Synthetic coupon for A-2: $15 million/$500 million = 3%

How will these securities trade in the market? Assume that the prevailing market rate is 6% (which is the coupon rate on the pass-through used to create the two securities). Security A-1 will sell in the market at a premium (i.e., above par value) because its synthetic coupon rate exceeds the prevailing market rate (6%). Security A-2 will sell in the market at a discount to par value because its synthetic coupon rate is below the prevailing market rate (6%).

This is some interesting financial engineering, but why? First remember that the coupon on the collateral (i.e., the 6% coupon, $1 billion pass-throughs) is 6%. Suppose that an investor believes that this collateral will exhibit slower prepayments than expected by the market. If this investor purchases security A-1, then the investor is receiving an above-market coupon rate (9%) in a 6% interest rate environment and will do so for a longer period of time if prepayments are in fact slower than expected by the market in pricing this security. Suppose another investor anticipates just the opposite: prepayments will be much faster than expected by the market. Then security A-2 offers this investor the opportunity to receive par value when prepayment occurs for a security purchased below par value. Thus, the two securities allow investors to express different views on prepayment speeds on the same collateral (i.e., the 6% pass-throughs).

Interest-Only/Principal-Only Securities

Notice that in the synthetic coupon pass-throughs, at least some interest and principal is paid to the two securities created. In an interest-only (IO) security and principal-only (PO) security, all of the interest is allocated to the IO and all of the principal to the PO. These two SMBS are referred to as **mortgage strips**.

The PO security is purchased at a substantial discount from par value. The yield an investor will realize depends on the speed at which prepayments are made. The faster the prepayments, the higher the yield the investor will realize. In the extreme case, if all the homeowners in the underlying mortgage pool decide to prepay their mortgage loans immediately, PO investors will receive the entire principal of the pass-through immediately.

Let's look at how the price of the PO can be expected to change as mortgage rates in the market change. When mortgage rates decline below the coupon rate, prepayments are expected to speed up, accelerating payments to the PO holder. Thus, the cash flow of a PO improves (in the sense that principal repayments are received earlier). The cash flow will be discounted at a lower interest rate because the mortgage rate in the market has declined. The result is that the price of a PO will increase when mortgage rates decline. When mortgage rates rise above the coupon rate, prepayments are expected to slow down. The cash flow deteriorates (in the sense of it taking longer to recover principal repayments). Coupled with a higher discount rate, the price of a PO will fall when mortgage rates rise.

As for the IO, there is no par value. In contrast to the PO investor, the IO investor wants prepayments to be slow. The reason is that the IO investor receives interest only on the amount of the principal outstanding. As prepayments are made, the outstanding principal declines, and less dollar interest is received. In fact, if prepayments are too fast, the IO investor may not recover the amount paid for the IO.

Let's look at the expected price response of an IO to changes in mortgage rates. If mortgage rates decline below the coupon rate, prepayments are expected to accelerate. This results in a deterioration of the expected cash flow for an IO. Although the cash flow will be discounted at a lower rate, the net effect is typically a decline in the price of an IO. If mortgage rates rise above the coupon rate, the expected cash flow improves but the cash flow is discounted at a higher interest rate. The net effect may be either a rise or a fall for the IO. Thus, we see an interesting characteristic of an IO: its price tends to move in the same direction as the change in mortgage rates. This effect occurs (1) when mortgage rates fall below the coupon rate, and (2) for some range of mortgage rates above the coupon rate.

An example of this effect can be seen in Exhibit 12-19, which shows for various mortgage rates the price of (1) a pass-through, (2) a PO created from this pass-through, and (3) an IO created from this pass-through. Notice that as mortgage rates decline below some level (which would be the coupon rate on the pass-through), the price of the pass-through does not respond much. This is the negative convexity (or price compression) property of pass-throughs. For the PO security, the price falls monotonically as mortgage rates rise. For the IO security, at mortgage rates above approximately a certain rate, the

Exhibit 12-19   Relationship Between Price and Mortgage Rates for a Pass-Through, PO, and IO

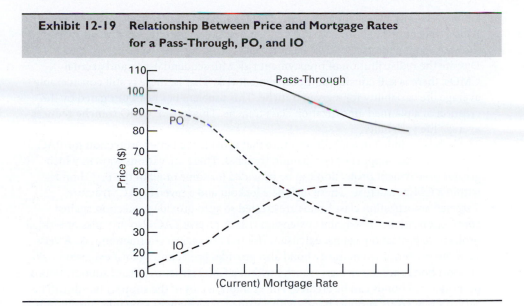

price declines as mortgage rates rise; as mortgage rates fall below that rate, the price of an IO falls as mortgage rates decline. Both POs and IOs exhibit substantial price volatility when mortgage rates change. The greater price volatility of the IO and PO compared with the pass-through from which they were created can be seen by the steepness of a tangent line to the curves at any given mortgage rate.

Collateralized Mortgage Obligation Strips

One of the classes in a CMO structure can be a principal-only or an interest-only class. These are called CMO strips or structured IOs. Earlier, we discussed how CMO strip tranches can be created.

KEY POINTS

- Agency CMOs, referred to by the agencies that issue them as REMICs, are bond classes created by redirecting the cash flows of mortgage-related products (mortgage pass-through securities).
- The creation of a CMO cannot eliminate prepayment risk; it can only redistribute the various forms of this risk among different classes of bonds called tranches.
- The credit risk of an agency CMO carries the same credit risk as that of an agency pass-through security.
- In a CMO, there are rules for the distribution of interest and principal from the collateral.
- The first CMOs were structured so that each class of bond would be retired sequentially, and hence such structures are referred to as sequential-pay CMOs. The average life of the tranches differs from that of the collateral.
- An accrual tranche allows the creation of even shorter-term and longer-term average life tranches than in a sequential-pay CMO without the inclusion of an accrual tranche.
- From any of the fixed-rate tranches, a floater and an inverse can be created.

- An interest-only and a principal-only tranche can be created from a tranche. A notional IO is a tranche created from the difference between the collateral's coupon interest and the total coupon interest paid to the tranches.
- Despite the redistribution of prepayment risk with sequential-pay and accrual CMOs, there is still considerable prepayment risk. That is, there is still considerable average life variability for a given tranche. This problem has been mitigated by the creation of a planned amortization class tranche. This type of CMO tranche reduces average life variability.
- The bonds included in a CMO structure that provide the better protection for PAC tranches are the support or companion tranches. There are various ways in which greater prepayment protection can be provided for some or all of the PAC bonds within a CMO structure. These include a lockout and a reverse PAC structure.
- Targeted amortization class bonds are created so as to provide protection against contraction risk but not against extension risk. A reverse TAC also provides one-sided protection: protection against extension risk but not against contraction risk. A very accurately determined maturity bond also provides protection against extension risk.
- Support bonds are the riskiest tranche within a CMO structure. From support bonds other types of bonds can be created. For example, a part of the support bonds can be carved up to create support bonds with a principal repayment schedule. Such bonds are referred to as PAC II or level II PAC bonds.
- An SMBS is created by assigning distribution of principal and interest of the underlying pass-through security in unequal portions to two classes of bonds. The result is that the two bonds will have a different price/yield relationship from that of the underlying pass-through.
- There are three types of SMBS: (1) synthetic-coupon pass-throughs, (2) interest-only/principal-only securities, and (3) CMO strips.

QUESTIONS

1. How does a CMO alter the cash flow from mortgages so as to shift the prepayment risk across various classes of bondholders?

2. What is the difference between a REMIC and a CMO?

3. **a.** "By creating a CMO, an issuer eliminates the prepayment risk associated with the underlying mortgages." Do you agree with this statement?
   b. Wall Street often refers to CMOs as "customized securities." Explain why.

4. In a discussion of the CMO market, the popular press sometimes refers to this sector of the mortgage-backed securities market as the riskiest sector and the pass-through sector as the safest sector. Comment.

5. Explain the effect on the average lives of sequential-pay structures of including an accrual tranche in a CMO structure.

6. What types of investors would be attracted to an accrual bond?

7. Suppose that a tranche from which an inverse floater is created has an average life of five years. What will the average life of the inverse floater be?

8. This quotation is taken from a 1991 issue of *BondWeek*:

   > First Interstate Bank of Texas will look into buying several different types of collateralized mortgage obligation tranches when it starts up its buy program sometime after the second quarter of 1991, according to Jules Pollard, v.p. Pollard said he will consider replacing maturing adjustable-rate mortgage pass-throughs with short companion tranches and planned amortization classes because the ARMS have become rich. . . . Pollard did

not provide a dollar figure on the planned investments, which will be made to match fund the bank's liabilities. When he does invest he said he prefers government-guaranteed securities or those with implied guarantees.

a. Explain the types of securities that Pollard is buying and selling.

b. Given the preference stated in the last sentence of the quotation, what issuers is he likely to prefer? What issuers would he reject?

9. Describe how the schedule for a PAC tranche is created.

10. Explain the role of a support bond in a CMO structure.

11. What was the motivation for the creation of PAC bonds?

12. Suppose that a savings and loan association has decided to invest in mortgage-backed securities and is considering the following two securities: (i) a Freddie Mac pass-through security with a WAM of 340 months or (ii) a PAC tranche of a Freddie Mac CMO issue with an average life of two years. Which mortgage-backed security would probably be better from an asset/liability perspective?

13. Suppose that a PAC bond is created assuming prepayment speeds of 80 PSA and 350 PSA. If the collateral pays at 100 PSA over its life, what will this PAC tranche's average life be?

14. Suppose that $1 billion of pass-throughs is used to create a CMO structure with a PAC bond with a par value of $700 million and a support bond with a par value of $300 million.

a. Which of the following will have the greatest average life variability: (i) the collateral, (ii) the PAC bond, or (iii) the support bond? Why?

b. Which of the following will have the least average life variability: (i) the collateral, (ii) the PAC bond, or (iii) the support bond? Why?

15. Suppose that the $1 billion of collateral in Question 14 was divided into a PAC bond with a par value of $800 million and a support bond with a par value of $200 million. Will the PAC bond in this CMO structure have more or less protection than the PAC bond in Question 14?

16. Suppose that $1 billion of pass-throughs is used to create a CMO structure with a PAC bond with a par value of $700 million (PAC I), a support bond with a schedule (PAC II) with a par value of $100 million, and a support bond without a schedule with a par value of $200 million.

a. Will the PAC I or PAC II have the smaller average life variability? Why?

b. Will the support bond without a schedule or the PAC II have the greater average life variability? Why?

17. In a CMO structure with several PAC bonds, explain why, when the support bonds are paid off, the structure will be just like a sequential-pay CMO.

18. Suppose that for the first four years of a CMO, prepayments are well within the initial PAC collar. What will happen to the effective upper collar?

19. Consider the following CMO structure backed by 8% collateral:

Tranche	Par Amount (in millions)	Coupon Rate (%)
A	$300	6.50
B	250	6.75
C	200	7.25
D	250	7.75

Suppose that a client wants a notional IO with a coupon rate of 8%. Calculate the notional amount for this notional IO.

20. An issuer is considering the following two CMO structures:

Structure I

Tranche	Par Amount (in millions)	Coupon Rate (%)
A	$150	6.50
B	100	6.75
C	200	7.25
D	150	7.75
E	100	8.00
F	500	8.50

Tranches A to E are a sequence of PAC I's and F is the support bond.

Structure II

Tranche	Par Amount (in millions)	Coupon Rate (%)
A	$150	6.50
B	100	6.75
C	200	7.25
D	150	7.75
E	100	8.00
F	200	8.25
G	300	?

Tranches A to E are a sequence of PAC I's, F is a PAC II, and G is a support bond without a PAC schedule.

a. In structure II, tranche G is created from tranche F in structure I. What is the coupon rate for tranche G assuming that the combined coupon rate for tranches F and G in structure II should be 8.5%?

b. What is the effect on the value and average life of tranches A to E by including the PAC II in structure II?

c. What is the difference in the average life variability of tranche G in structure II and tranche F in structure II?

21. **a.** What is the role of a lockout in a CMO structure?

b. Explain why in a reverse PAC bond structure the longest average life bond can turn out to be effectively a support bond if all the support bonds in the structure are paid off.

22. What type of prepayment protection is afforded each of the following: (a) a TAC bond, (b) a reverse TAC bond, (c) a VADM?

23. **a.** What is a PO security? What is an IO security?

b. How is the price of an interest-only security expected to change when interest rates change?

24. Suppose that 8% coupon pass-throughs are stripped into two classes. Class X-1 receives 75% of the principal and 10% of the interest. Class X-2 receives 25% of the principal and 90% of the interest.

a. What type of SMBS would this be?

b. What is the synthetic coupon rate on Class X-1?

c. What is the synthetic coupon rate on Class X-2?

13

Nonagency Residential Mortgage–Backed Securities

LEARNING OBJECTIVES

After reading this chapter, you will understand

- what a nonagency residential mortgage–backed security is

- how the market for nonagency residential mortgage–backed securities has changed since 2007 following the subprime mortgage crisis

- the types of loans used as collateral in nonagency residential mortgage–backed securities

- the need for credit enhancement

- the three types of credit enhancement (structural, originator provided, third-party provided)

- the cash flow for a nonagency residential mortgage–backed security and the importance of defaults, recoveries, and the timing of recoveries

- delinquency and default measures for a pool of loans

As explained in Chapter 11, the residential mortgage–backed securities (RMBS) market is divided into two sectors: agency RMBS and nonagency RMBS. The securities issued in the agency RMBS market were discussed in Chapters 11 and 12. RMBS issued in the nonagency RMBS market require that credit enhancement be provided to protect against losses from the loan pool.

The nonagency RMBS market is divided into the private label RMBS market and subprime RMBS market. Private label RMBS, also referred to as prime or residential deals, are backed by prime mortgage loans; subprime RMBS are backed by subprime loans and, prior to 2007, were commonly classified as part of the asset-backed securities sector and referred to as mortgage-related asset-backed securities. Prior to the crisis that occurred in the subprime mortgage market that began in the summer of 2007 and the subsequent housing market meltdown, private label RMBS and subprime RMBS were viewed as two distinct products and traded in separate markets. However, due to the poor performance of the underlying residential mortgage loans backing both types of nonagency RMBS, the market no longer makes a distinction between these two products. For this reason, no distinction is made in this chapter.

Nonagency RMBS, sometimes referred to as nonagency collateralized mortgage obligations (nonagency CMOs), are issued by commercial banks, thrifts, and private conduits. Private conduits purchase nonconforming mortgages, pool them, and then sell CMOs in which the collateral is the underlying pool of nonconforming mortgages. The private conduits that issue RMBS are doing what the government created the agency conduits to do for conforming loans, but without any guarantees (implicit or explicit) from the U.S. government. Nonagency RMBS must be registered with the Securities and Exchange Commission. They are rated by the same rating agencies that rate corporate and municipal debt obligations. The collateral is sold to a special purpose entity (SPE) whose critical role in a securitization transaction is described in more detail in Chapter 15. It is the SPE, also referred to as the trust, that issues the nonagency RMBS.

There was more than $1 trillion in nonagency RMBS issuance by 2006. Since then, poor collateral performance and the dramatic decline in housing prices resulted in a significant drop in issuance in 2007 and very little issuance in the three years that followed. Although market observers believe that parts of the nonagency RMBS market backed by prime loans will be revived, few believe that in the foreseeable future there will be a revival of deals backed by subprime loans. The regulatory rules regarding RMBS issuance is set forth in the Dodd-Frank Wall Street Reform and Consumer Protection Act. This act as it pertains to the securitization of RMBS requires entities that securitize loans to retain an economic interest in the underlying loans that they securitize and sets forth extensive requirements applicable to mortgage lending. More specifically, with respect to mortgage lending, there are detailed requirements concerning the compensation that can be received by mortgage originators and underwriters, servicer requirements, and underwriting standards. These requirements are intended to avoid another crisis in the nonagency RMBS market.

Despite the expected decline in issuance, there is still enough publicly traded nonagency RMBS to warrant an understanding of this sector of the bond market. As of year-end 2010, there was about $1.46 trillion of nonagency RMBS outstanding.[1] In terms of vintage—that is, the year that the deals were issued—the largest vintage years are 2005 and 2006. The third largest vintage year was 2007, but issuance in that year was far less than in the two prior years.

In this chapter, we discuss the nonagency RMBS market, focusing on the structure of the securities created, particularly on credit enhancement. We will describe the different forms of credit enhancement in this chapter and discuss them further in Chapter 15, where we discuss asset-backed securities backed by nonmortgage loans. The difference between private label RMBS and subprime RMBS is due to the complexity of the structure for dealing with credit enhancement required because of the greater credit risk associated with subprime mortgage loans. Other details about the process of securitizing loans are left for Chapter 15.

---

[1] Dapeng Hu and Robert Goldstein, "Non-Agency Residential Mortgage-Backed Securities," Chapter 31 in Frank J. Fabozzi (ed.), *The Handbook of Fixed Income Securities: 8th edition* (New York: McGraw-Hill, 2011).

COLLATERAL TYPES

As explained in Chapter 10, there are conforming and nonconforming mortgages. The former are typically collateral for agency RMBS and the latter for nonagency RMBS. We also mentioned some of the various types of mortgages that fall into the nonconforming category. The collateral backing a nonagency RMBS is set forth in the prospectus. Typically a deal will be backed by a combination of collateral types.

Below is the amount of nonagency RMBS outstanding as of year-end 2010 based on the collateral type:

- Prime loans: $318 billion
- Subprime loans: $395 billion
- Alt-A loans: $432 billion
- Second lien loans: $156 billion
- Option ARM loans: $158 billion

Prime loans are loans to borrowers viewed as having (1) a high credit quality as gauged by strong employment and credit histories, and income sufficient to pay the loan obligation without jeopardizing the borrower's creditworthiness, and (2) substantial equity in the underlying property. Subprime loans are (1) loans to borrowers viewed as having lower credit quality or (2) loans that are not a first lien on the property. Note that in our listing of the outstanding nonagency RMBS above, there is separate category for subprime and second lien loans. Alt-A loans (short for alternative-A loans) is a somewhat nebulous category of loans between prime and subprime loans.

In Chapter 10, we described adjustable-rate mortgage (ARM) loans. One type of ARM that was popular between 2001 and 2007, when ARM issuance reached its peak, was hybrid ARM loans, also referred to as **option ARM loans**. This product allowed borrowers to be able to qualify for a loan where they otherwise would not be able to do so using traditional mortgage loans. In this loan arrangement, the loan rate is fixed for a contractually specified number of years (three, five to seven, or 10 years). At the end of the initial fixed-rate period, the loan resets in a fashion very similar to that of more traditional ARM loans. The reason why these loans are referred to as "option" ARM loans is that the borrower has the option to select among payment options.

CREDIT ENHANCEMENT

Because there is no government guarantee or guarantee by a government-sponsored enterprise, to receive an investment-grade rating, nonagency RMBS must be structured with additional credit support. The credit support is needed to absorb expected losses from the underlying loan pool due to defaults. This additional credit support is referred to as **credit enhancement**. There are different forms of credit enhancement. We will describe them briefly here.

When rating agencies assign a rating to the bond classes in a nonagency RMBS deal, they must analyze the credit risk associated with a bond class. Basically, that analysis begins by looking at the credit quality of the underlying pool of loans. For example, a pool of loans can consist of prime borrowers or subprime borrowers. Obviously, one would expect that a pool consisting of prime borrowers would have less expected losses as a percentage of the dollar amount of the loan pool compared to a pool consisting of subprime borrowers.

Given the credit quality of the borrowers in the pool and other factors such as the structure of the transaction, a rating agency will determine the dollar amount of the credit enhancement needed for a particular bond class to receive a specific credit rating. The process by which the rating agencies determine the amount of credit enhancement needed to obtain a specific rating is referred to as **sizing the transaction**.

There are standard mechanisms for providing credit enhancement in nonagency RMBS. We will describe these mechanisms shortly. When prime loans were securitized, the credit enhancement mechanisms used were straightforward and, as a result, the structures were not complicated. In contrast, when subprime loans were securitized, the structures became more complex because of the need for greater credit enhancement. These more complex structures are found in certain types of asset-backed securities (ABS). For this reason, market participants classified securitizations involving subprime loans as part of the ABS market (recall that they were referred to as mortgage-related ABS) prior to 2007.

Interest rate derivatives such as interest rate swaps and interest rate caps are often employed in nonagency RMBS structures that are not allowed in agency RMBS structures. We do not cover interest rate derivatives until later chapters. Here we merely point out that they are used when there is a mismatch between the character of the cash flows for the loan pool and the character of the cash payments that must be made to the bond classes. For example, some or all of the bonds classes may have a floating interest rate, whereas all the loans have a fixed interest rate.

There are three forms of credit enhancement:

- Structural
- Originator/seller provided
- Third-party provided

Each is described in the following text.[2]

Structural Credit Enhancement

Structural credit enhancement refers to the redistribution of credit risks among the bond classes comprising the structure in such a way as to provide credit enhancements by one bond class to the other bond classes in the structure. This is achieved by creating bond classes with different priorities on the cash flow and is referred to as a **senior-subordinated structure**.

In a senior-subordinated structure, two general categories of bond classes are created: a senior bond class and subordinated bond classes. For example, consider the following hypothetical nonagency RMBS structure consisting of $400 million of collateral:

Bond Class	Principal Amount	Credit Rating
X1	$350 million	AAA
X2	$ 20 million	AA
X3	$ 10 million	A
X4	$ 5 million	BBB
X5	$ 5 million	BB
X6	$ 5 million	B
X7	$ 5 million	not rated

---

[2] For a more detailed discussion, see Chapter 7 in Frank J. Fabozzi and Vinod Kothari, *Introduction to Securitization* (Hoboken, NJ: John Wiley & Sons, 2008).

Collectively, the bond classes comprising the structure are referred to as the deal's **capital structure**. The capital structure here has the same meaning with respect to the prioritization of claims as in the standard corporation's bond structure that we described in Chapter 7. That is, senior secured debt has a prior claim over unsecured debt, while the latter has a prior claim over subordinated debt, preferred stock and equity. However, as noted in Chapter 7, in a corporate bankruptcy under Chapter 11, the priority of creditors is typically violated. This is not the case in a nonagency RMBS (nor in an ABS, which we will discuss in Chapter 15), where the priority rules are strictly enforced for the capital structure.

The bond class in the capital structure with the highest rating is referred to as the **senior bond class**. The **subordinated bond classes** in the capital structure are those below the senior bond class. The rules for the distribution of the cash flow (interest and principal) among the bond classes as well as how losses are to be distributed are explained in the prospectus. These rules are referred to as the deal's **cash flow waterfall**, or simply waterfall. Basically, the losses are distributed based on the position of the bond class in the capital structure. Losses start from the bottom (the lowest or unrated bond class) and progress to the senior bond class. For example, if over the life of this nonagency RMBS the losses are less than $5 million, then only bond class X7 will realize a loss. If the loss is $15 million, bond classes X7, X6, and X5 will realize total losses and the other bond classes will realize no losses.

Note a few points about this structure. First, the credit enhancement for bond classes is being provided by other bond classes within the structure. For example, the senior bond class, X1, is being protected against losses up to $50 million. This is because it is only until $50 million of losses are realized that bond class X1 will realize a loss. Bond class X3 has a credit enhancement of $20 million because the collateral can realize $20 million in losses before bond class X3 realizes a loss.

Second, compare what is being done to distribute credit risk in this nonagency RMBS with what is done in an agency collaterized mortgage obligation (CMO). In an agency CMO, there is no credit risk for Ginnie Mae-issued structures and the credit risk of the loan pool for Fannie Mae and Freddie Mac-issued structures has been viewed until recent years as small. What is being done in creating the different bond classes in an agency CMO is the redistribution of prepayment risk. In contrast, in a nonagency RMBS, there is both credit risk and prepayment risk. By creating the senior-subordinated bond classes, credit risk is being redistributed among the bond classes in the structure. Hence, what is being done is called **credit tranching**. Can prepayment risk also be redistributed? This is typically done in nonagency RMBS but only at the senior bond class level. That is, the $350 million of senior bond classes in our hypothetical nonagency CMO structure can be carved up to create senior bond classes with different exposure to prepayment risk.

Finally, when the bond classes are sold in the market, they are sold at different yields. Obviously, the lower the credit rating of a bond class, the higher is the yield at which it must be offered.

Most AAA bond classes have been downgraded since 2007. By collateral type, the AAA bond classes that have been downgraded by year-end 2010 were as follows: prime, 85%; subprime, 94%; Alt-A, 97%; and option ARM, 99%.[3] Many were downgraded from AAA

---

[3] Hu and Goldstein, "Non-Agency Residential Mortgage-Backed Securities."

to below investment grade. Consequently, as of year-end 2010, only a small number of outstanding nonagency RMBS have an investment-grade rating.[4]

Shifting Interest Mechanism in a Senior-Subordinated Structure

Because of the major credit concerns in subprime RMBS deals and the need to protect the senior bond class, almost all senior-subordinated structures backed by subprime loans incorporate a shifting interest mechanism. This mechanism redirects prepayments disproportionately from the subordinated bond class to the senior bond class according to a specified schedule. The rationale for the shifting interest structure is to have enough subordinated bond classes outstanding to cover future credit losses.

The basic credit concern that investors in the senior bond class have is that although the subordinated bond classes provide a certain level of credit protection for the senior bond class at the closing of the deal, the level of protection may deteriorate over time due to prepayments and certain liquidation proceeds. The objective is to distribute these payments of principal such that the credit protection for the senior bond class does not deteriorate over time.

The percentage of the mortgage balance of the subordinated bond class to that of the mortgage balance for the entire deal is called the **level of subordination** or the **subordinate interest**. The higher the percentage, the greater is the level of protection for the senior bond class. The subordinate interest changes after the deal is closed due to prepayments. That is, the subordinate interest shifts (hence the term *shifting interest*). The purpose of a shifting interest mechanism is to allocate prepayments so that the subordinate interest is maintained at an acceptable level to protect the senior bond class.

The prospectus will specify how different scheduled principal payments and prepayments will be allocated between the senior bond class and the subordinated bond classes. The scheduled principal payments are allocated based on the senior percentage. The **senior percentage**, also called the **senior interest**, is defined as the ratio of the balance of the senior bond class to the balance of the entire deal and is equal to 100% minus the subordinate interest. So, if in some month the senior percentage is 82% and the scheduled principal payment is $1 million, the senior bond class will get $820,000 (0.82 × $1,000,000) and the subordinated bond class will get $180,000 ($1,000,000 − $820,000).

Allocation of the prepayments is based on the **senior prepayment percentage** (in some deals called the **accelerated distribution percentage**). This is defined as follows:

Senior prepayment percentage + (Shifting interest percentage × Subordinate interest)

The "shifting interest percentage" in the formula above is specified in the prospectus. To illustrate the formula, suppose that in some month the senior interest is 82%, the subordinate interest is 18%, and the shifting interest percentage is 70%. The senior prepayment percentage for that month is

$$82\% + (0.70 \times 18\%) = 94.6\%$$

---

[4] In early 2010, these downgraded bond classes from various deals have been used to create a new securitized product. Since the new product involves the securitization of products that have already been part of a securitization, they are referred to as "re-securitizations." What has been done in these transactions is to create a simple bond structure in which there is a senior bond class and a junior bond class. Principal is paid to the senior bond class until it is completely paid off. Thus, the credit enhancement is structural.

Thus, if prepayments for the month are $1,000,000, then $946,000 is allocated to the senior bond class and $54,000 to the subordinated bond class.

The prospectus will provide the shifting interest percentage schedule for calculating the senior prepayment percentage. A commonly used shifting interest percentage schedule is as follows:

Year after Issuance	Shifting Interest Percentage
1–5	100
6	70
7	60
8	40
9	20
after year 9	0

The shifting interest percentage schedule given in the prospectus is the "base" schedule. The schedule can change over time depending on the performance of the collateral. If the performance is such that the credit protection is deteriorating or may deteriorate, the base shifting interest percentages are overridden such that a higher allocation of prepayments is made to the senior bond class. Performance analysis of the collateral is undertaken by the trustee for determining whether to override the base schedule. The performance analysis is in terms of tests, and if the collateral or structure fails any of the tests, this will trigger an override of the base schedule. The tests are described next.

While the shifting interest structure is beneficial to the senior bond class holder from a credit standpoint, it does alter the cash flow characteristics of the senior bond class even in the absence of defaults. The size of the subordination also matters. A larger subordinated class redirects a higher proportion of prepayments to the senior bond class, thereby short-ening the average life even further.

Deal Step-Down Provisions

An important feature in analyzing senior-subordinated bond classes or deals backed by residential mortgages is the deal's **step-down provisions**. These provisions allow for the reduction in credit support over time. As noted previously, a concern that inves-tors in the senior bond class have is that if the collateral performance is deteriorating, step-down provisions should be altered. The provisions that prevent the credit support from stepping down are called "triggers." Principal payments from the subordinated bond classes are diverted to the senior bond class if a trigger is reached. The diver-sion of principal varies from issuer to issuer. The most conservative approach is to stop all principal payments from being distributed to the subordinated bond classes. Alternatively, some issuers allow the subordinated bond classes to receive regularly scheduled principal (amortization) on a pro rata basis but divert all prepayments to the senior bond class.

There are two triggers based on the level of credit performance required to be passed before the credit support can be reduced: a delinquency trigger and a loss trigger. The triggers are expressed in the form of a test that is applied in each period. The **delinquency test**, in its most common form, prevents any step-down from taking place as long as the current over-60-day delinquency rate exceeds a specified percentage of the then-current pool balance. The **principal loss test** prevents a step-down from occurring if cumulative losses exceed a certain limit (which changes over time) of the original balance.

In addition to triggers based on the performance of the collateral, there is a **balance test**. This test involves comparing the change in the senior interest from the closing of the deal to the current month. If the senior interest has increased, the balance test is failed, triggering a revision of the base schedule for the allocation of principal payments from the subordinated bond classes to the senior bond class. Unlike a trigger that will increase the allocation to the senior bond class, there are balance tests that will increase the allocation to the subordinated bond class. This can occur when the subordinate interest improves by a significant amount. That amount is set forth in the prospectus. For example, the prospectus may set forth that if the subordinate interest doubles, the base schedule is overridden such that more is allocated to the subordinated bond class.

Originator/Seller-Provided Credit Enhancement

The originator/seller of the collateral to the SPV can provide credit support for the transaction in one or a combination of three ways:

- Excess spread
- Cash collateral
- Overcollateralization

Excess Spread

The most natural form of credit enhancement is the interest from the collateral that is not used to satisfy the liabilities (i.e., the interest payments to the bond classes in the structure) and the fees (such as mortgage servicing and administrative fees). The amount by which the interest payment from the collateral exceeds what has to be paid to the bond classes as interest and the fees that must be paid is called **excess spread** or **excess interest**. For example, assume a pool of loans has a weighted average interest rate of 8% and the originator receives a servicing fee of 1%. If the weighted-average cost of the liabilities issued is 5%, then the excess spread is 2% (8% − 1% − 5%).

The monthly excess spread can be either (1) distributed to the seller of the collateral to the SPV, (2) used to pay any losses realized by the collateral for the month, (3) retained by the SPV and accumulated in a reserve account and used to offset not only current losses experienced by the collateral but also future losses, or (4) some combination of the others. When the excess spread is retained and accumulated in a cash reserve account, the excess spread is said to be "trapped" in the deal. Any excess spread remaining after the last liability of the deal is paid off is returned to the seller of the collateral. Or, if certain conditions are satisfied, and if the cash reserve reaches a certain level, the deal prospectus may permit further excess spread to be paid to the seller of the collateral.

In prime RMBS deals, the excess spread is typically small. In contrast, in subprime RMBS deals, the loan rate on subprime loans is much higher than for prime loans because the expected losses are greater for subprime loans. Consequently, excess spread is an important source of credit enhancement for subprime RMBS.

Cash Collateral

Excess spread that we have just described is one of three ways that an originator/seller of the collateral can provide cash to absorb collateral losses. There are two other ways. First is by depositing at the time of the sale of the collateral to the SPV cash that can be utilized if the other forms of credit enhancement are insufficient to meet collateral losses. Second is by providing a subordinated loan to the SPV.

Overcollateralization

In our hypothetical nonagency CMO earlier, the liabilities are $400 million and are assumed to match the amount of the collateral. Suppose instead that the collateral has a par value of $410 million. This means that the assets exceed the liabilities by $10 million. This excess collateral is referred to as **overcollateralization** and can be used to absorb any collateral losses. Hence, it is a form of credit enhancement.

Overcollateralization was more commonly used as a form of credit enhancement in subprime deals than in prime deals. This is one of the aspects that makes subprime deals more complicated because there are a series of tests built into the structure as to when collateral can be released.

Third-Party Credit Enhancements

Prior to 2007, one form of credit enhancement, typically used in combination with the other two forms mentioned above, was some type of third-party credit enhancement. These guarantees typically included one of the following: insurance, a letter of credit, and related-party guarantees. Of course, the guarantee is only as good as the third-party guarantor. That is, third-party credit enhancements are subject to third-party credit risk—the risk that the third-party guarantor may be either downgraded or not able to satisfy its commitment.

Today, few, if any, deals are done with insurance by monoline insurers, bank letters of credit, and related-party guarantees. Monoline insurers, as mentioned in Chapter 8 where we covered municipal bonds, have been downgraded so that they are not able to guarantee triple A bond classes. Risk-based capital requirements have made letters of credit for banks unattractive. Finally, third-party-related guarantors are rare because the parent of the originator/seller is typically not triple A-rated.

CASH FLOW FOR NONAGENCY MORTGAGE–BACKED SECURITIES

In agency RMBS, the cash flow is not affected by defaults in the sense that they result in a reduction in the principal to some bond class. Rather, defaulted principal is made up by the agency as part of its guarantee. For a nonagency RMBS, one or more bond classes may be affected by defaults, and therefore, defaults must be taken into account in estimating the cash flow of a bond class. More specifically, the default rate, the loss severity (i.e., how much of the outstanding principal is lost when there is a default), and the time lag between default and recovery must be projected.

In Chapter 11, we discussed the factors that impact prepayments for RMBS focusing on agency RMBS. The three components are housing turnover, cash-out refinancing, and rate/term refinancing. We did not focus on prepayments attributable to defaults. Prior to the subprime mortgage crisis, investors assumed that the triple A senior bonds of nonagency RMBS were exposed to minimal credit risk. The performance of loans backing nonagency RMBS deals demonstrated the critical importance of assessing the factors that impact defaults.

What the subprime mortgage crisis clearly showed is that defaults are not just tied to the level of economic activity but also housing prices. Economic difficulties faced by borrowers that followed a period of rising prices provided lenders with a strong position in the collateral as long as the loan-to-value ratio (LTV) was not high. Lax lending practices and high LTVs at issuance (due to inflated appraisal values) created a situation where house price appreciation was critical for lenders to recover the outstanding mortgage balance if the borrower defaulted. Rising housing prices, in fact, avoided a default scenario and instead gave the borrower the option to sell the property and pay off the loan. In the statistics that gauge prepayment activity, such situations where default is avoided is merely reported as part of the housing turnover components of prepayment.

In contrast, the opportunity to sell the property to repay the loan is not available if the property declines below the outstanding mortgage balance (i.e., the current LTV exceeds 1 or, equivalently, the borrower has negative equity in the property). In such situations, the borrower can exercise the option to put the property to the lender. The lender has no recourse to the borrower's assets to cover any shortfall between the net proceeds received from the sale of the foreclosed property and the outstanding mortgage balance. As mentioned in Chapter 11, when this behavior is followed by a borrower who has the ability to make mortgage payments but finds no economic benefit to do so because it would take too long for the property's value to rise in order to eliminate the negative equity, it is referred to as a strategic default. This practice has increased, particularly in regions of the country where there has been a steep decline in housing prices. In Nevada, for example, where housing prices declined by as much as 60%, one study reported that almost one fourth of homeowners whose homes were foreclosed upon could afford the monthly mortgage payments.[5]

Understanding how defaults are reported is important in analyzing the performance of the collateral. The reporting of defaults differs for agency RMBS and nonagency RMBS. For the latter, seriously delinquent loans are classified as nonperforming loans. These loans are then purchased from the pool's guarantor at the full amount of the outstanding principal. The principal repaid to investors is then classified as both amortization (i.e., scheduled repayment for the portion that was due) and unscheduled principal payment for the balance that was paid. Thus, the unscheduled principal payment would be treated in agency RMBS as part of normal housing turnover.

In contrast, the reporting of nonagency RMBS is different. Once a loan moves from the delinquent category to the default category, the borrower loses possession of the property and the mortgage servicer takes possession with the purpose of selling the property. The proceeds received by the servicer reduced by the costs associated with selling the property are referred to as the **recovered principal**. The servicer must report separately traditional prepayments—which are called **voluntary prepayments**—and credit-related prepayments—which are called **involuntary prepayments**. The reason for doing this is for determining the principal payments that must be distributed to the senior bond classes and for determining the losses (i.e., shortfall between the mortgage balance and the recovered principal) that must be allocated to the subordinated bond classes.

Delinquency Measures

A delinquency is required before a loan can be classified as in default. Loans are classified as **current loans** or **delinquent loans**. A current loan is one in which the borrower has made all mortgage payments due. A **delinquent loan** is a loan where the borrower fails to

---

[5] Nevada Association of Realtors, "The Face of Foreclosure: An Analysis of the Nevada Foreclosure Crisis," 2010.

make one or more timely payments. At a certain point, a delinquent loan is classified as a **defaulted loan**.

The severity of the delinquencies in a loan pool can be grouped based on a method selected by the servicer. There are two classification methods from which a servicer can choose: the Office of Thrift Supervision (OTS) method and the Mortgage Bankers Association (MBA) method. The MBA method is more stringent than the OTS method and therefore can result in significantly different delinquencies reported for a loan pool. This is because under the OTS method, a borrower that misses one payment is classified as a current loan but under the MBA method the same loan is classified as a delinquent loan. The standard practice for prime RMBS deals is to use the MBA method (the more stringent method); the OTS method is the standard practice for subprime RMBS. The subtle definitional issues associated with classifying delinquencies in order to model defaults are important.[6]

Measuring Defaults

There are two measures used for quantifying default rates for a loan pool:

- Conditional default rate
- Cumulative default rate

The **conditional default rate** (CDR) is the annualized value of the unpaid principal balance of newly defaulted loans over the course of a month as a percentage of the unpaid balance of the pool (before scheduled principal payment) at the beginning of the month. The calculation begins with computing the **monthly default rate** (MDD) for the month as shown below:

Monthly default rate for month t

$$\text{MMD}_t = \frac{\text{defaulted loan balance in month } t}{\text{beginning balance for month } t - \text{scheduled principal payment in month } t}$$

Then, this is annualized as follows to get the CDR:

$$\text{CDR}_t = 1 - (1 - \text{default rate for month } t)^{12}$$

The monthly default rate is viewed as representing involuntary prepayments, and the CDR represents the involuntary prepayment speed calculated for nonagency RMBS. The **cumulative default rate**, abbreviated as CDX in order to avoid confusion with CDR, is the proportion of the total face value of loans in the pool that have gone into default as a percentage of the total face value of the pool.

Standard Default Rate Assumption

A standardized benchmark for default rates was formulated by the Public Securities Association (PSA). The PSA standard default assumption (SDA) benchmark gives the annual default rate for a mortgage pool as a function of the seasoning of the mortgages. The PSA SDA benchmark, or 100 SDA, specifies the following:

1. The default rate in month 1 is 0.02% and increases by 0.02% up to month 30, so that in month 30, the default rate is 0.60%.
2. From month 30 to month 60, the default rate remains at 0.60%.

---

[6] Kyle G. Lundstedt and Andrew Davidson, "Modeling Mortgage Risk: Definitional Issues," Andrew Davidson & Co., Inc., April 2005.

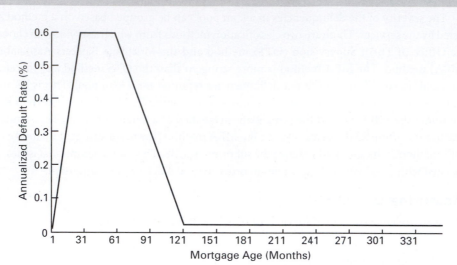

Exhibit 13-1   The PSA SDA Benchmark (100 SDA)

3. From month 61 to month 120, the default rate declines from 0.60% to 0.03%.
4. From month 120 on, the default rate remains constant at 0.03%.

This pattern is illustrated in Exhibit 13-1.

As with the PSA prepayment benchmark, multiples of the benchmark are found by multiplying the default rate by the assumed multiple. For example, 200 SDA means the following pattern:

1. The default rate in month 1 is 0.04% and increases by 0.04% up to month 30, so that in month 30, the default rate is 1.20%.
2. From month 30 to month 60, the default rate remains at 1.20%.
3. From month 61 to month 120, the default rate declines from 1.20% to 0.06%.
4. From month 120 on, the default rate remains constant at 0.06%.

A 0 SDA means that no defaults are assumed.

Prepayment Measures

Prepayments are measured in terms of the conditional prepayment rate (CPR). Borrower characteristics and the seasoning process must be kept in mind when trying to assess prepayments for a particular deal. In the prospectus of an offering, a base-case prepayment assumption is made—the initial speed and the amount of time until the collateral is expected to be seasoned. Thus, the prepayment benchmark is issuer specific. The benchmark speed in the prospectus is called the **prospectus prepayment curve** (PPC). Slower or faster prepayment speeds are a multiple of the PPC.

For example, the prospectus for a subprime mortgage deal might specify that the base-case prepayment assumption for the fixed-rate mortgages in the pool is as follows:

. . . a 100% Prepayment Assumption assumes conditional prepayment rates of 5% per annum of the then outstanding principal balance of the mortgage loans in the first month of the life of the mortgage loans and an additional 1.0% per annum in each month thereafter until the twelfth month. Beginning in the twelfth month and in each month thereafter during the life of the mortgage loans, 100% Prepayment Assumption assumes a conditional prepayment rate of 16% per annum each month.

Therefore, if an investor analyzed the deal based on 200% PPC, this means doubling the CPRs cited in the excerpt and using 12 months for seasoning.

In nonagency RMBS, two prepayment rates are projected: **voluntary prepayment rate** and **involuntary prepayment rate**. The voluntary prepayment rate (VPR) is calculated similarly to a CPR. First a voluntary monthly mortgage rate, VMM, similar to the single monthly mortality rate (SMM) described in Chapter 11, is calculated. That monthly rate is then annualized to get the VPR. Involuntary prepayment rates are quoted as CDRs as described above. The SMM for a month for a deal is the sum of the VMM and MDR for that month.

Deal-Specific Factors Impacting Cash Flow

There are deal-specific factors that impact the cash flow of a nonagency RMBS. Two important ones are servicer advances and treatment of modified loans.

Servicer Advances

In a nonagency RMBS deal the servicer has an important function, not only with respect to collecting payments due from borrowers in the loan pool and repossessing and then selling the property when there are defaults, but also in advancing principal and interest on delinquent loans. A report on mortgage servicing by Fitch found that at the market peak of 2006, mortgage servicers advanced payments on 90% of delinquent loans. As of November 2010, Fitch reports mortgage services advanced 63% for subprime delinquent loans, 88% for Alt-A delinquent loans, and 96% for prime delinquent loans.

However, there are specific conditions as to when a servicer need not make such advance payments. In most deals, the servicer is not required to advance any amount that it deems "nonrecoverable" through the foreclosure process. The policy of a servicer regarding how long it will advance against seriously delinquent loans along with the property's current LTV dictates how it will interpret the term "recoverability." Because a property's projected recovered principal depends on its current LTV, servicers typically cease advancing on loans where the current LTV is greater than a specified threshold.

Loan Modifications

A **modified loan** is one in which the terms have been altered in order to help the borrower satisfy the monthly mortgage obligation. Prior to the problems in the market, deal transactions gave the servicer the right to modify a loan but typically did not address how the modification of a loan should be handled.

Loan modification programs were established by several government agencies, along with monetary incentives to modify loans such as the Home Affordable Modification Program (HAMP) introduced in 2009. HAMP's primary goal is to reduce the monthly mortgage payments of borrowers with proven hardship to no more than 31% of income. This is to be accomplished by a combination of interest rate reduction, term extension, and payment deferral. Although it is recognized that these programs were not very successful in terms of aiding borrowers,[7] there have been a considerable number of loans in transactions that were modified. In fact, 1.2 million loans were modified under the HAMP by year-end 2010.

The key issue is how servicers treat the modified loans because that impacts the senior and subordinated transactions. As an example, consider a loan in a pool where the principal has been modified such that the principal has been deferred. The question is whether such a loan should be written off immediately as a loss and, as a result, benefit the senior bond classes. On the other hand, if the deferred principal is not recognized until the point where principal losses are realized by the trust, this would result in more interest payments made to the subordinate bond classes that would have had their principal written down.

KEY POINTS

- Nonagency RMBS are issued by entities such as commercial banks, thrifts, and private conduits. The collateral is sold to a special purpose entity that then issues the securities.
- Historically, while nonagency RMBS are classified as private label RMBS and subprime RMBS and traded in separate markets, following the subprime mortgage crisis in 2007 and the meltdown of the housing market, these two sectors are no longer viewed differently.
- Although there has been very little issuance since 2008, there is a considerable amount of nonagency RMBS outstanding backed by prime loans, subprime loans, Alt-A loans, second lien loans, and option ARM loans.
- Unlike agency RMBS, nonagency RMBS are rated by the nationally recognized rating agencies and require some form of credit enhancement to obtain a credit rating.
- The amount of credit enhancement necessary to obtain a particular credit rating is determined by the rating agencies and is referred to as sizing the transaction.
- The three forms of credit enhancement are (1) structural (senior-subordinated structure), (2) originator provided (excess spread, cash reserve, overcollateralization), and (3) third-party provided.

---

[7] The recidivism rate (i.e., the rate at which modified loans have re-defaulted) has been high. For example, a study by the Office of the Comptroller of the Currency found that more than half of borrowers whose loans had been modified had missed at least one payment six months after a lender modified their loan. There have been other studies that report similar findings.

- The cash flow of a nonagency RMBS depends on defaults and prepayments.
- Default rates are measured in terms of the conditional default rate and the cumulative default rate. A standardized benchmark for default rates was formulated by the PSA. The PSA SDA benchmark gives the annual default rate for a mortgage pool as a function of the seasoning of the mortgages.
- Prepayments are measured in terms of the conditional prepayment rate. A unique prepayment benchmark can be developed for an issuer and is referred to as the prospectus prepayment curve.
- Voluntary prepayments and involuntary prepayments must be projected in projecting the collateral's cash flow.
- The treatment of advances and modified loans by mortgage servicers has an impact on the bond classes in a nonagency RMBS deal.

QUESTIONS

1. **a.** Why is it necessary for a nonagency mortgage-backed security to have credit enhancement?
   b. Who determines the amount of credit enhancement needed?

2. What is the difference between a private label and subprime mortgage-backed security? Be sure to mention how they differ in terms of credit enhancement.

3. **a.** What is an option ARM loan?
   b. Why is it unlikely that this loan type will be originated in the future?

4. **a.** At one time, prime and subprime RMBS were traded in separate markets. Why?
   b. Why after 2007 are prime and subprime RMBS treated as one asset type?

5. **a.** What is meant by a senior-subordinated structure?
   b. Why is the senior-subordinated structure a form of credit enhancement?

6. How can excess spread be a form of credit enhancement?

7. **a.** What is the difference between credit tranching and prepayment tranching?
   b. Why would there be both types of tranching in a nonagency deal but only one type of tranching in an agency deal?

8. **a.** What is the conditional default rate?
   b. What is the cumulative default rate?

9. Why was the PSA standard default benchmark introduced?

10. Why might an interest rate derivative such as an interest rate swap or interest rate cap be used in a securitization transaction for residential mortgage loans?

11. Why is a shifting interest mechanism included in a securitization where the collateral is residential mortgage loans?

12. Suppose that for a securitization with a shifting interest mechanism you are given the following information for some month:

$$\text{subordinate interest} = 25\%$$
$$\text{shifting interest percentage} = 85\%$$
$$\text{regularly scheduled principal payment} = \$3,000,000$$
$$\text{prepayments} = \$1,200,000$$

a. What is the senior prepayment percentage for the month?

b. How much of the $3,000,000 regularly scheduled principal payment is distributed to the senior class?

c. How much of the $1,200,000 is distributed to the senior class?

13. What is the purpose of the step-down provisions in a securitization?

14. What is meant by the prospectus prepayment curve?

15. **a.** What is meant by an involuntary prepayment?
    b. Why is the distinction between a voluntary and involuntary prepayment important in a nonagency RMBS?

16. When will a mortgage servicer not advance payments for principal and interest?

17. Why does the treatment of modified loans in a nonagency RMBS deal impact the bond classes?

18. There are some mortgage loans that are balloon loans. This means that when the loan matures, there is a mortgage balance that will require financing. It is the responsibility of the borrower to obtain the refinancing. What is the added risk associated with a pool of loans backed by balloon loans?

19. Suppose that the loans in the collateral pool for a nonagency RMBS deal have a floating rate. What is the risk associated with issuing fixed-rate bond classes?

20. What is the concern with the inclusion of fixed-rate mortgage loans in the collateral pool when the liabilities are floating rate?

21. An interest rate cap allows the buyer of the cap to be compensated if interest rates rise above a reference rate. The buyer has to pay a periodic premium to obtain this protection. When an RMBS transaction has a pool of floating-rate loans, what type of protection does an interest rate cap provide?

14

Commercial Mortgage Loans and Commercial Mortgage–Backed Securities

LEARNING OBJECTIVES

After reading this chapter, you will understand

- how commercial mortgage loans differ from residential mortgage loans

- the different property types for which commercial mortgage loans are obtained

- the two indicators of performance used for evaluating commercial mortgage loans—debt-to-service coverage ratio and loan-to-value ratio

- the different types of call protection provided for in commercial mortgage loans and in a commercial mortgage–backed security

- what balloon risk is for a commercial mortgage loan and a commercial mortgage–backed security

- differences in structuring a commercial mortgage–backed and residential mortgage–backed securities transaction

- the structural features of a commercial mortgage–backed security deal

- how prepayment premiums may be distributed among bondholders in a commercial mortgage–backed security

- the difference between a single borrower/multiproperty deal and a conduit deal

- the different types of servicers in a commercial mortgage–backed securities deal

- factors to consider in the analysis of the collateral of a commercial mortgage–backed security

- why it is important to stress test a deal's structure

The mortgage market consists of residential mortgages and commercial mortgages. Residential mortgage loans are for properties with one to four single-family units. Residential mortgage–backed securities are the securities we discussed in the previous two chapters that are backed by residential mortgage loans. In this chapter, we look at commercial mortgages and securities backed by commercial mortgages—**commercial mortgage–backed securities** (CMBS).

COMMERCIAL MORTGAGE LOANS

Commercial mortgage loans are for income-producing properties. These properties include:

- multifamily properties
- apartment buildings
- office buildings
- industrial properties (including warehouses)
- shopping centers
- hotels
- health care facilities (e.g., senior housing care facilities)

A commercial mortgage loan is originated either to finance a commercial purchase or to refinance a prior mortgage obligation. Commercial mortgage loans are **non-recourse loans**. This means that the lender can only look to the income-producing property backing the loan for interest and principal repayment.

Indicators of Potential Performance

Because commercial mortgage loans are non-recourse loans, the lender looks only to the property to generate sufficient cash flow to repay principal and to pay interest. If there is a default, the lender looks to the proceeds from the sale of the property for repayment and has no recourse to the borrower for any unpaid balance. There are different risks associated with investing in each property type. Later in this chapter an excerpt from an actual CMBS transaction that describes these risks by property type will be presented.

Regardless of the property type, the two measures that have been found to be key indicators of the potential credit performance are the debt-to-service coverage ratio and the loan-to-value ratio.

The **debt-to-service coverage** (DSC) **ratio** is the ratio of a property's **net operating income** (NOI) divided by the debt service. The NOI is defined as the rental income reduced by cash operating expenses (adjusted for a replacement reserve). A ratio greater than 1 means that the cash flow from the property is sufficient to cover debt servicing. The higher the ratio, the more likely it is that the borrower will be able to meet debt servicing from the property's cash flow.

As with residential mortgage loans, studies have found that the key predictor of default is the **loan-to-value ratio**. For residential mortgage loans, "value" is either market value or appraised value. For income-producing properties, the value of the property is based on the fundamental principles of valuation: the value of an asset is the present value of the expected cash flow. Valuation requires projecting an asset's cash flow and discounting at an appropriate interest rate(s). In valuing commercial property, the cash flow is the future NOI. A discount rate (a single rate), referred to as the "capitalization rate," reflecting the risks associated with the cash flow is then used to compute the present value of the future NOI. Consequently, there can be considerable variation in the estimates of NOI and the appropriate capitalization rate in estimating a property's market value. Thus, analysts are skeptical about estimates of market value and the resulting LTVs reported for properties.

Call Protection

For residential mortgage loans, only prepayment penalty mortgages provide protection against prepayments. For commercial mortgage loans, call protection can take the following forms:

- prepayment lockout
- defeasance
- prepayment penalty points
- yield maintenance charges

Prepayment Lockout

A **prepayment lockout** is a contractual agreement that prohibits any prepayments during a specified period of time, called the **lockout period**. The lockout period can be from two to 10 years. After the lockout period, call protection usually comes in the form of either prepayment penalty points or yield maintenance charges. Prepayment lockout and defeasance (discussed next) are the strongest forms of prepayment protection.

Defeasance

With **defeasance**, the borrower provides sufficient funds for the servicer to invest in a portfolio of Treasury securities that replicates the cash flows that would exist in the absence of prepayments.[1] For example, in May 2005, the Fountainbleau Hilton in Miami was defeased. For the reason explained later when we describe CMBS, this form of prepayment protection has become the most popular.

Prepayment Penalty Points

Prepayment penalty points are predetermined penalties that must be paid by the borrower if the borrower wishes to refinance. For example, 5-4-3-2-1 is a common prepayment penalty point structure. That is, if the borrower wishes to prepay during the first year, he must pay a 5% penalty for a total of $105 rather than $100; in the second year, a 4% penalty would apply, and so on.

It has been argued that the prepayment penalty points are not an effective means for discouraging refinancing. However, prepayment penalty points may be superior to yield maintenance charges in a rising rate environment. This is because prepayments do occur when rates rise. With yield maintenance, the penalty will be zero (unless there is a "yield maintenance floor" that imposes a minimum penalty). In contrast, with prepayment penalty points, there will be a penalty even in a rising rate environment.

Yield Maintenance Charge

Yield maintenance charge, in its simplest terms, is designed to make the lender indifferent as to the timing of prepayments. The yield maintenance charge, also called the make

---

[1] Defeasance is a method used by municipal bond issuers for prerefunding a bond issue.

whole charge, makes it uneconomical to refinance solely to get a lower mortgage rate. The simplest and most restrictive form of yield maintenance charge ("Treasury flat yield maintenance") penalizes the borrower based on the difference between the mortgage coupon and the prevailing Treasury rate.

There are several methods that have been used in practice to compute the yield maintenance charge. These methods include the simple model, the bullet model, the single discount factor model, the multiple discount factor model, the interest difference model, and the truncated interest difference model.[2] To provide further protection to lenders, there are often yield maintenance floors that impose a minimum charge.

Balloon Maturity Provisions

Commercial mortgage loans are typically balloon loans requiring substantial principal payment at the end of the balloon term. If the borrower fails to make the balloon payment, the borrower is in default. The lender may extend the loan and in so doing will typically modify the original loan terms. During the work-out period for the loan, a higher interest rate will be charged, the **default interest rate**.

The risk that a borrower will not be able to make the balloon payment because either the borrower cannot arrange for refinancing at the balloon payment date or cannot sell the property to generate sufficient funds to pay off the balloon balance is called **balloon risk**. Since the term of the loan will be extended by the lender during the work-out period, balloon risk is also referred to as **extension risk**.

COMMERCIAL MORTGAGE–BACKED SECURITIES

Many types of commercial loans can be sold by the originator as a commercial whole loan or structured into a CMBS transaction. A CMBS is a security backed by one or more commercial mortgage loans. The whole loan market, which is largely dominated by insurance companies and banks, is focused on loans between $10 and $50 million issued on traditional property types (multifamily, retail, office, and industrial). CMBS transactions, on the other hand, can involve loans of virtually any size (from as small as $1 million to single property transactions as large as $200 million) and/or property type.

Issuers of Commercial Mortgage–Backed Securities

As with residential mortgage–backed securities (RMBS), CMBS can be issued by Ginnie Mae, Fannie Mae, Freddie Mac, and private entities. All of the securities issued by Ginnie Mae, Fannie Mae, and Freddie Mac are consistent with their mission of providing funding for residential housing. This includes securities backed by nursing home projects and health care facilities.

Ginnie Mae–issued securities are backed by Federal Housing Administration (FHA)–insured multifamily housing loans. These loans are called **project loans.** From these loans, Ginnie Mae creates project loan pass-through securities. The securities can be backed by a single project loan on a completed project or one or more project loans. Freddie Mac and Fannie Mae purchase multifamily loans from approved lenders and either retain them in

---

[2] For a description of these methods, see Da Cheng, Adrian Cooper, and Jason Huang, "Understanding Prepayments in CMBS Deals," Chapter 8 in Frank J. Fabozzi and David Jacob, *The Handbook of Commercial Mortgage–Backed Securities* (Hoboken, NJ: John Wiley & Sons, 1999).

their portfolio or use them for collateral for a security. This is no different from what these two government-sponsored enterprises do with the single-family mortgage loans that they acquire.

While securities backed by Ginnie Mae and issued by the two government-sponsored enterprises constitute the largest sector of the RMBS market, it is the securities issued by private entities that are by far the largest sector of the CMBS market. Typically, it is less than 3% of the market. Our focus in this chapter is on CMBS issued by private entities.

How CMBS Trade in the Market

One might think that because CMBS and RMBS are backed by mortgage loans, they would trade in a similar manner in the marketplace. That is not the case, and the primary reason has to do with the greater prepayment protection afforded to investors in CMBS compared to RMBS. We described that protection at the loan level. As will be explained, at the structure level (i.e., when the commercial mortgage loans are pooled to create a CMBS), certain tranches can be created that give even greater prepayment protection. As a result, CMBS trade much like corporate bonds.[3]

Differences Between CMBS and Nonagency RMBS Structuring

The structure of a transaction is the same as in a nonagency RMBS in that most structures have multiple bond classes (tranches) with different ratings, and there are rules for the distribution of interest and principal to the bond classes. However, there are three major differences due to the features of the underlying loans.[4]

First, as explained earlier, prepayment terms for commercial mortgages differ significantly from residential mortgages. The former impose prepayment penalties or restrictions on prepayments. While there are residential mortgages with prepayment penalties, they are a small fraction of the market.[5] In structuring a CMBS, there are rules for the allocation of any prepayment penalties among the bondholders. In addition, if there is a defeasance, the credit risk of a CMBS virtually disappears because it is then backed by U.S. Treasury securities. In fact, it is because investors like the defeasance feature for commercial mortgages used as collateral for a CMBS that defeasance has become the most popular type of prepayment protection.

The second difference in structuring is due to the significant difference between commercial and residential mortgages with respect to the role of the servicer when there is a default. In commercial mortgages, the loan can be transferred by the servicer to the *special* servicer when the borrower is in default, imminent default, or in violation of covenants. The key here is that it is transferred when there is an imminent default. The special servicer has the responsibility of modifying the loan terms in the case of an imminent default to reduce the likelihood of default. There is no equivalent feature for a residential

---

[3] See Brian P. Lancaster, "Introduction to Commercial Mortgage–Backed Securities," Chapter 23 in Frank J. Fabozzi (ed.), *The Handbook of Nonagency Mortgage–Backed Securities* (Hoboken, NJ: John Wiley & Sons, 1999).
[4] David P. Jacob, James M. Manzi, and Frank J. Fabozzi, "The Impact of Structuring on CMBS Bond Class Performance," Chapter 51 in Frank J. Fabozzi (ed.), *The Handbook of Mortgage–Backed Securities*, 6th ed. (New York: McGraw-Hill, 2006).
[5] In RMBS with prepayment penalty mortgages, traditionally, the penalties paid have been held by the servicer independent of the securitization. A more recent trend is to create a tranche that passes the penalty through to the investor (which may be either a private investor or the servicer). Investors in interest-only securities like them as a hedge.

mortgage in the case of an imminent default. The particular choice of action that may be taken by the special servicer in a commercial mortgage will generally have different effects on the various bond classes on a CMBS structure. Moreover, there can be a default due to failure to make the balloon payment at the end of the loan term. There can be differences in loans as to how to deal with defaults due to a failure to meet the balloon payment. Thus, balloon risk must be taken into account in structuring a CMBS transaction, which because of the significant size of the payment, can have a considerable impact on the cash flow of the structure. Balloon risk is not something that has to be dealt with in structuring an RMBS.

The third difference in structuring between CMBS and RMBS has to do with the role of the buyers when the structure is being created. More specifically, typically potential buyers of the junior bond classes are first sought by the issuer before the deal is structured. The potential buyers first review the proposed pool of mortgage loans and in the review process may, depending on market demand for CMBS product, request the removal of some loans from the pool. This phase in the structuring process, which one does not find in RMBS transactions, provides an additional layer of security for the senior buyers, particularly because some of the buyers of the junior classes have tended to be knowledgeable real estate investors.

Structural Features of a CMBS Transaction

To understand the features of a CMBS transaction, let's look at a hypothetical deal. Exhibit 14-1 shows the hypothetical structure. There are 18 tranches in this deal. For each tranche, the following are reported in Exhibit 14-1: ratings, the balance of the tranche ("balance"), the coupon rate, and a description of each tranche.

The tranches are classified as senior, mezzanine, and junior. The senior certificates include Class A-1, Class A-2, Class A-2F, and Class X. All but one senior tranche and the interest-only tranche have a fixed coupon rate. Assuming all of the commercial mortgage loans backing this deal have a fixed rate, this means that there is a mismatch between the interest obligation for Class A-2F and the interest obligation from the collateral. This is dealt with in this deal by using an interest-rate swap, a derivative instrument that we will discuss in Chapter 28.[6]

The principal and interest payments are distributed in descending order as follows. First the senior classes—Class A-1, Class A-2 , Class A-2F Regular Interest, and Class X— are paid. Then payments are distributed to Class B, then Class C and so on.

When there are mortgage loan losses, they are allocated in ascending order to the bond classes. For our hypothetical deal, because Class X is an interest-only security, no principal payments or loan losses are allocated to that class. However, the notional amount for Class X is reduced by principal payments or loan losses.

The credit enhancements that were described for nonagency RMBS in the previous chapter can be used in CMBS structures. Typically, the primary form of credit support is the senior-subordinated structure such as the hypothetical deal shown in Exhibit 14-1. The credit support provided for each bond class is shown in the exhibit.

---

[6] Interest-rate swaps are commonly used in structured products.

Exhibit 14-1 National Bank Commercial Mortgage

Morgage

Bond	Credit rating	Balance	Credit Support (%)	Coupon rate (%)	Description
A-1	AAA	$161,603,149	22.01	6.09	Senior fixed rate
A-2	NA	$527,811,659	22.01	6.50	Senior fixed rate
A-2F	NA	$50,000,000	22.01	2.16	Senior floating rate
B	AA	$35,576,642	18.26	6.67	Mezzanine fixed rate
C	A+	$21,345,985	16.01	6.77	Mezzanine fixed rate
D	A	$18,974,209	14.01	6.85	Mezzanine fixed rate
E	A−	$9,487,105	13.01	6.97	Mezzanine fixed rate
F	BBB+	$9,487,105	12.01	7.22	Mezzanine fixed rate
G	BBB	$18,974,209	10.01	7.32	Mezzanine fixed rate
H	BBB−	$14,230,657	8.51	7.51	Mezzanine fixed rate
J	NA	$13,281,946	7.10	6.13	Junior fixed rate
K	NA	$23,480,584	4.63	6.13	Junior fixed rate
L	NA	$2,134,598	4.40	6.13	Junior fixed rate
M	NA	$5,538,842	3.82	6.13	Junior fixed rate
N	NA	$6,788,329	3.10	6.13	Junior fixed rate
O	NA	$5,883,218	2.48	6.13	Junior fixed rate
P	NA	$23,532,872	0	6.13	Junior fixed rate
X	AAA	$948,131,109	0.99	1.09	Senior floating-rate interest only

Prepayment Protection and Distributions of Prepayment Premiums

In a CMBS structure, there are two levels of prepayment protection. The first is at the loan level. As described earlier, there are various forms of prepayment protection provided (lockouts, prepayment penalty points, yield maintenance, and defeasance). The second is at the structure level. For example, the senior tranches can be structured to pay off sequentially as described in Chapter 12 in a CMO structure.

When a defeasance takes place, there is no distribution made to the bondholders. Since there are no penalties or charges, there is no issue as to how any penalties paid by the borrower are to be distributed among the bondholders in a CMBS structure. When there are prepayment penalty points, there are rules for distributing the penalty among the CMBS bondholders. In the case of loans with a yield maintenance provision, several methods are used in practice for distributing the yield maintenance charge and, depending on the method specified in a deal, not all bondholders in a CMBS may be made whole. These methods include the principal allocation method, base interest method, bond yield maintenance method, and present value yield loss method.[7] Prepayment penalties and yield maintenance charges are referred to as **prepayment premiums**.

Balloon Risk in CMBS Deals

As explained earlier, commercial mortgage loans have a balloon maturity provision. Balloon risk, or extension risk, is the risk that the borrower will fail to refinance to meet the balloon payment. Therefore, CMBS with senior-subordinated structures face the risk that all loans must be refinanced to pay off the most senior bondholders. Therefore, the balloon risk of the most senior tranche may be equivalent to that of the most junior bond class in the deal.

There are two types of structural provisions that can be present in CMBS transactions to mitigate balloon risk: internal tail and external tail. The **internal tail** requires the borrower to document efforts to refinance the loan within one year of the balloon maturity date. Within six months prior to the balloon maturity date, the borrower must obtain a refinancing commitment. With an **external tail**, the maturity date for the CMBS issue is set to be longer than the balloon payment for the pool of commercial mortgage loans. Since this gives the borrower the time to arrange refinancing while avoiding default on the bond obligations, it is the method preferred by rating agencies.

Clean-Up Call Provisions

Every CMBS transaction has a clean-up call provision that permits the bond classes that are outstanding to purchase the remaining mortgage loans in a trust. The purpose of the clean-up call provision in all securitizations is to wind-down the transaction when the balance remaining in the transaction is too small to justify the ongoing administrative fees. Typically the clean-up call provision is limited to when the balance of mortgage loans in the mortgage pool represents 1% to 3% of the deal's original balance. Usually the price at which the remaining loans can be repurchased is the outstanding balance of the mortgage loans plus accrued interest.

---

[7] For a description of these methods, see Cheng, Cooper, and Huang, "Understanding Prepayments in CMBS Deals."

TYPES OF DEALS

The two major classifications for CMBS deals are single borrower/multiproperty deals and multiproperty conduit deals.

Single Borrower/Multiproperty Deals

As the name suggests, in a single borrower/multiproperty deal there is one borrower and multiple properties. Three key structural features in such deals are the cross-collateralization feature, cross-default feature, and property release provisions.

The **cross-collateralization feature** is a mechanism whereby the properties that collateralize the individual loans in the mortgage pool are pledged against each loan. The **cross-default feature** permits the lender to call each loan within the mortgage pool when any one property defaults. By including these two features, the principal and interest payments of all the properties are available to meet the obligations of all the loans. As a result, a shortfall on an individual loan would not make it delinquent if the principal and interest payments from other loans in the mortgage pool are not less than the amount of the shortfall.[8]

Because there is a single borrower, there is concern that the borrower can benefit by removing the best properties from the mortgage pool by prepaying the balance and selling those properties. This action would result in a deterioration of the structural protection afforded the bondholders. The objective of **property release provisions** is to protect the investor against such an action by the borrower. Two examples of a property release provision are (1) a requirement that if any property is sold, the borrower must retire more than the initial mortgage balance in the pool (say, 125%), and (2) a sale may not take place if the DSC ratios after a proposed sale are less than prior to the sale.

Multi-Borrower Deals

The second type of deal is one that involves loans by conduits. Conduits are commercial-lending entities that are established for the sole purpose of generating collateral to securitize, and the CMBS transactions that result are called **conduit deals**. The rating agencies refer to conduit transactions as **multi-borrower deals**. When a conduit deal contains one large property for more than $50 million and then smaller loans, it is referred to as a **fusion conduit deal**. In a conduit, there can be more than one originator.

Servicers

As with a nonagency RMBS, a servicer is required and plays an important role. The responsibilities of the servicer include collecting monthly loan payments, keeping records relating to payments, maintaining property escrow for taxes and insurance, monitoring the condition of underlying properties, preparing reports for the trustee, and transferring collected funds to the trustee for payment to bondholders.

Depending on the transaction, there are several types of servicers. The three most common in CMBS transactions are the sub-servicer, the master servicer, and the special servicer. The **sub-servicer** collects all payments and gathers property information, which is then sent to the master servicer. The **master servicer** is responsible for (1) overseeing the

---

[8] For an illustration of the importance of these two features, see Frank J. Fabozzi and John N. Dunlevy, *Real Estate-Backed Securities* (Hoboken, NJ: John Wiley & Sons, 2001), pp. 139–140.

deal, (2) verifying that all servicing agreements are being maintained, and (3) facilitating the timely payment of interest and principal. This last function is critical for a CMBS transaction. If a loan is in default, it is the master servicer that must provide for servicing advances. To fulfill this role, the master servicer must have the financial capacity to provide advances.

The duties of a **special servicer** arise only when a loan becomes more than 60 days past due. Typically, the special servicer has the authority to (1) extend the loan, (2) make loan modifications, (3) restructure the loan, or (4) foreclose on the loan and sell the property.

Analysis of the Collateral

Because of the nonrecourse nature of commercial mortgage loans, CMBS investors must view each property as a stand-alone business and evaluate each property using the measures discussed earlier (DSC and LTV ratios). While there are fundamental principles of assessing credit risk that apply to all property types, traditional approaches to assessing the credit risk of the collateral differ for CMBS than for nonagency RMBS. For nonagency RMBS, the loans typically are lumped into buckets based on certain loan characteristics, and assumptions regarding default rates and prepayment rates are then made regarding each bucket. In contrast, for commercial mortgage loans, the unique economic characteristics of each income-producing property in a pool backing a CMBS deal require that credit analysis be performed on a loan-by-loan basis not only at the time of issuance, but also be monitored on an ongoing basis. The starting point in the analysis is an investigation of the underwriting standards of the originators of the loans in the mortgage pool.

For all properties backing a CMBS deal, a weighted-average DSC ratio and a weighted-average LTV is computed. An analysis of the credit quality of a CMBS structure will also look at the dispersion of the DSC and LTV ratios for the underlying loans. For example, one might look at the percentage of a deal with a DSC ratio below a certain value.

In analyzing the collateral, the types of income-producing properties are examined. In general, investors prefer deals that are not concentrated in one property type. Investors are also interested in the geographical dispersion of the properties. The concern is that if the properties are concentrated in one geographical region, investors would be exposed to economic downturns that may be unique to that geographical region.

Stress Testing Structures

As noted earlier in this chapter, an analysis of the credit quality of the tranches in a CMBS involves looking at the commercial loans on a loan-by-loan basis. Rating agencies and analysts will then stress test the structure with respect to a combination of default and prepayment assumptions.

In stress testing default risk, the following three key assumptions are made. The first is the annual rate of defaults as measured by the conditional default rate (CDR). The benchmark CDRs typically used by rating agencies and analysts are those based on the default experience of commercial loans in the 1970s and 1980s. For example, it is not uncommon for analysts to assume a CDR of 2% to stress test strong deals and 3% to test weaker deals.[9]

---

[9] See Patrick Corcoran and Joshua Phillips, "Stress and Defaults in CMBS Deals: Theory and Evidence," *JP Morgan Credit Research* (June 18, 1999), p. 1.

However, Patrick Corcoran and Joshua Phillips have argued that, for a variety of reasons, the default experience of the 1970s and 1980s is inappropriate for stress testing default risk in today's CMBS market. They believe that "the modern CMBS market has benefited primarily from the tougher oversight and discipline provided by the public markets, and highlighted by rating agency leadership."[10] Specifically, there is much stronger cash coverage in deals today and reduced property cash flows.

A second important assumption is the timing of the defaults. A default can occur sometime early in the term of the loan or at the balloon date (when refinancing is required). The earlier defaults occur, the more adverse the impact will be on the performance of the deal. A third important assumption is the percentage of the loan balance that will be lost when a default occurs. This measure is called the loss severity.

To illustrate the importance of the assumptions on stress testing, Corcoran and Phillips used three stress test scenarios for a representative conduit deal to assess the impact on each bond class. Exhibit 14-2 shows the bond classes in the structure. The loans are 10-year balloon loans with a 30-year amortization. For each scenario, the loss severity assumed was 33% and no voluntary prepayments were assumed (i.e, a CPR of zero is assumed).

Exhibit 14-2   Scenario Bond Spreads

| Bond Classes | Base Case: Default Scenarios | | | |
	0 CDR 0 CPR	2 CDR 0 CPR	Model Defaults 0 CPR	Balloon Default Scenario 0 CPR
AAA-5 yr	98	93	97	98
AAA-10 yr	123	123	123	123
AA	137	137	137	137
A	160	160	160	160
BBB	195	195	195	195
BBB−	275	275	275	271
BB	575	575	575	556
B/B−	725	22	443	420
B−	950	−1585	−406	−220
UR	1706	−2921	−16	689
X	450	127	369	475

Source: *Table 2 in Patrick Corcoran and Joshua Phillips, "Stress and Defaults in CMBS Deals: Theory and Evidence," JP Morgan Credit Research (June 18, 1999), p. 5.*

---

[10] Corcoran and Phillips, "Stress and Defaults in CMBS Deals: Theory and Evidence," p. 1.

The three stress test scenarios that they analyzed are:

Scenario 1 (2% CDR Scenario): A 2% CDR per year. (For the 10-year loan pool with a 30-year amortization schedule, this means cumulative defaults over the 10-year loan of 16.7%.)

Scenario 2 (Model Default Scenario): Annual default rates over 10 years based on a model developed by Corcoran and Kao.[11] The default model produces a cumulative default rate for 10 years of 14%. However, the pattern of defaults is such that there is a delay or backloading of defaults. This scenario does not allow for the stronger DSC ratios that exist in today's CMBS market compared to those of the 1970s and 1980s.

Scenario 3 (Balloon Default Scenario): Default rates from the Corcoran–Kao model are used as in Scenario 1, producing a cumulative default rate for 10 years of 14%. However, the defaults are assumed to occur at the 10-year balloon date. Effectively, this scenario does allow for the stronger DSC ratios in today's CMBS market compared to the 1970s and 1980s.

Exhibit 14-2 shows the results of the analysis on the spread. The spread reported is a "credit-adjusted spread." This is a spread measure based on cash flows adjusted for the assumed defaults for the scenario. The second column shows the base case results—a CDR of zero. The next three columns show the results of the 2% CDR scenario, model default scenario, and balloon default scenario. As can be seen, for the B-rated tranche, the credit-adjusted spread is small in the 2% CDR scenario but roughly the same in the other two scenarios. However, even though positive in those scenarios, the spread is less than for the BB tranche. For the BBB and higher-rated tranches, the credit-adjusted spreads are equal; for the BB tranche the balloon default scenario shows a slightly lower credit-adjusted spread compared to the other two scenarios.

While the scenarios used in the Corcoran–Phillips illustration test solely for defaults, a more complete analysis recognizes that prepayments must be considered and that there is an interaction between default rates and prepayment rates linked by changes in interest rates. In stress testing, it is important to take both defaults and prepayments not due to default into account. For example, Michael Ervolini, Harold Haig, and Michael Megliola have demonstrated how credit-driven prepayment and default analysis can be used for stress testing.[12]

The model that they present specifies conditions for prepayments and for defaults. Prepayments occur when permitted and when it will result in net proceeds to the borrower (after adjusting for any prepayment penalties). So, assessing prepayments requires modeling how the yield curve will change over the investment horizon. The conditions for default occur when NOI is insufficient to meet debt service. This is modeled to assess the default possibility for each loan rather than an assumed constant CDR. Assumptions regarding when the defaults will occur and the severity of loss must be made. In addition, the refinanceability of each property is modeled.

---

[11] Patrick Corcoran and Duen-Li Kao, "Assessing Credit Risk of CMBS," Chapter 13 in Fabozzi and Jacob, *The Handbook of Commercial Mortgage–Backed Securities.*

[12] See Michael A. Ervolini, Harold J. A. Haig, and Michael Megliola, "Credit-Driven Prepayment and Default Analysis," Chapter 14 in Fabozzi and Jacob, *The Handbook of Commercial Mortgage–Backed Securities.*

▌KEY POINTS

- Commercial mortgage loans are for income-producing properties. Consequently, the lender looks only to the property to generate sufficient cash flow to repay principal and to pay interest and, if there is a default, the lender looks to the proceeds from the sale of the property for repayment.

- Two measures that have been found to be important measures of potential credit performance for a commercial mortgage loan are the debt-to-service coverage ratio and the loan-to-value ratio.

- For commercial mortgage loans, call protection can take the following forms: pre-payment lockout, defeasance, prepayment penalty points, or yield maintenance charges.

- Commercial mortgage loans are typically balloon loans requiring substantial principal payment at the end of the balloon term. If the borrower fails to make the balloon payment, the borrower is in default. Balloon risk, also called extension risk, is the risk that a borrower will not be able to make the balloon payment because either the borrower cannot arrange for refinancing at the balloon payment date or cannot sell the property to generate sufficient funds to pay off the balloon balance.

- CMBS are issued by Ginnie Mae, Fannie Mae, and Freddie Mac, and nonagencies.

- The structure of a transaction is the same as in a nonagency residential mortgage–backed security, with the typical structure having multiple bond classes with different ratings.

- There are rules for the distribution of interest and principal to the bond classes and the distribution of losses. However, there are differences in structuring transactions due to prepayment features, the role of the special servicer in the case of imminent default, and the role of potential investors when the deal is being structured.

- In a CMBS structure, there is call protection at the loan level and the structure level. When there are prepayment premiums (i.e., prepayment penalty points or yield maintenance charges), there are rules for distributing the prepayment premiums among the CMBS bondholders.

- In a CMBS deal, there are two types of structural provisions that can be present to mitigate balloon risk: internal tail and external tail.

- A CMBS trades in the market like a corporate bond rather than a nonagency RMBS because of its substantial prepayment protection at the loan and structure level.

- There are two major classifications for CMBS deals. One type is the single borrower/multiproperty deal. Three key structural features in these deals are the cross-collateralization feature, cross-default feature, and property release provisions.

- The second type of CMBS deal is the multi-borrower deal, also called a conduit deal. A conduit is a commercial-lending entity that is established for the sole purpose of generating collateral to securitize. Depending on the transactions, there are several types of servicers. The three most common in CMBS transactions are the sub-servicer, the master servicer, and the special servicer.

- Because of the nonrecourse nature of commercial mortgage loans, investors must view each property as a stand-alone business. The unique economic characteristics of each income-producing property in a pool backing a CMBS deal require that credit analysis be performed on a loan-by-loan basis not only at the time of issuance, but also monitored on an ongoing basis. The starting point is investigating the underwriting standards of the originators of the loans in the mortgage pool.

- An analysis of the credit quality of a CMBS structure will also look at the dispersion of the DSC ratios and LTV ratios for the underlying loans, the types of income-producing properties, and the geographical dispersion of the properties.

- Rating agencies and analysts will stress test the structure with respect to a combination of default and prepayment assumptions.
- In stress testing default risk, alternative assumptions are made regarding the conditional default rate, the timing of the defaults, and the percentage of the loss severity.

QUESTIONS

1. How is the net operating income (NOI) of a commercial property determined?

2. Why might an investor be skeptical about the loan-to-value ratio for a commercial mortgage loan?

3. Explain the underlying principle for a yield maintenance charge.

4. What types of prepayment protection provisions result in a prepayment premium being paid if a borrower prepays?

5. The following statement was made in a special report, "Commercial Mortgage Special Report" (September 19, 2005, p. 2), by FitchRatings: "Defeasance of a loan in a CMBS transaction is a positive credit event." Explain why.

6. In an article by Matt Hudgines, "More CMBS Borrowers Pay Off Balloon Mortgages On Time," posted on August 18, 2010, the following appeared (http://nreionline.com/finance/news/cmbs_borrowers_pay_balloon_mortgages_0818/#):

   Some 49.9% of the securitized loans that matured in July successfully met their balloon payments, according to New York-based Trepp LLC, which closely tracks the commercial mortgage–backed securities (CMBS) market. That's up more than 11 percentage points from 38.7% the previous month and is the highest level since the end of 2008.

   Later in the article, the following appeared:

   Until the fourth quarter of 2008, when financial markets experienced a meltdown following the bankruptcy of Lehman Brothers, the monthly average for the number of on-time, paid balloon payments was more than 70%, according to Trepp.

   Since the beginning of 2009, there hasn't been a month when even half of

the borrowers with CMBS loans reaching maturity were able to make their balloon payments. The average percentage for the past 12 months has been 32.2%.

Explain the relevance of this information to investors in CMBS.

7. Explain whether you agree or disagree with each of the following statements:
   a. "The largest sector of the CMBS market is securities issued by agency and government-sponsored enterprises."
   b. "Most CMBS deals are backed by newly originated commercial mortgage loans."
   c. "A fusion CMBS deal has only one single large borrower."

8. Why do CMBS trade in the market more like corporate bonds than RMBS?

9. What are the major differences in structuring CMBS and RMBS transactions?

10. In a commercial mortgage–backed security, what is the concern that the bondholders have when there is a prepayment premium paid by a borrower?

11. The following appears on the website of Chatham Financial, an advisory service:

    Kennett Square, Pa., June 21, 2010 — Chatham Financial announced today that it advised Primus Capital in the defeasance of $76.9 million in debt secured by twelve properties held in two CMBS securitizations. The defeasance of the loans, which are scheduled to mature in 2018, facilitated the sale of the 12 movie theater properties.

    Explain what is meant by a defeasance of loans.

12. Explain why commercial mortgage–backed securities do not trade like residential mortgage–backed securities in the market.

13. With respect to the mitigation of balloon risk, what is meant by
    a. an internal tail?
    b. an external tail?
14. Explain each of the following features and their significance in a single borrower/multiproperty CMBS transaction:
    a. cross-collateralization feature
    b. cross-default feature
    c. property release provision
15. a. How does a single borrower/multiproperty deal differ from a conduit deal?
    b. What is meant by a fusion conduit deal?

16. What are the typical duties of a special servicer?
17. How does the analysis of a commercial mortgage–backed security differ from that of a residential mortgage–backed security?
18. Why is it not adequate to look at the weighted-average debt-to-service coverage ratio and weighted-average loan-to-value ratio for the pool of commercial mortgage loans in assessing the potential performance of a CMBS transaction?
19. Why is it important to look at the dispersion of property types and geographical location of properties in analyzing a CMBS transaction?

15

Asset-Backed Securities

LEARNING OBJECTIVES

After reading this chapter, you will understand

- how asset-backed securities are created
- the basic structure of a securitization
- the parties to a securitization
- the primary motivation for raising funds via a securitization
- the role of the special purpose vehicle
- what a two-step securitization is
- the different types of structures: self liquidating and revolving
- the various forms of credit enhancement
- the different types of optional call provisions
- the structure of several major types of asset-backed securities not backed by residential mortgage loans
- the credit risks associated with asset-backed securities and how they are analyzed
- the implications of the Dodd-Frank Wall Street Reform and Consumer Protection Act for securitizations
- what is meant by a collateralized debt obligation, collateralized bond obligation, and collateralized loan obligation
- the structure of a collateralized debt obligation and the role of the collateral manager

In Chapters 11 through Chapter 13, we discussed securities backed by a pool of residential mortgage loans and, in the previous chapter, we discussed securities backed by commercial mortgage loans. A security created by pooling loans other than residential *prime* mortgage loans and commercial mortgage loans is referred to as an **asset-backed security** (ABS). Recall from Chapter 11 that the market classifies securities backed by subprime mortgage loans as mortgage-related ABS.

The two types of assets that can be used as collateral for an asset-backed securitization are existing assets/existing receivables or assets/receivables to arise in the future. Securitizations with existing collateral are referred to as **existing asset securitizations**. Securitizations of assets/receivables to arise in the future are referred to as **future flow securitizations**.

The types of assets that have been securitized fall into the following two general categories: (1) consumer asset–backed securities and subprime residential mortgage–backed securities (MBS), and (2) commercial asset–backed securities. Consumer ABS and subprime residential MBS securitizations include:

- home equity loans
- auto loans and leases
- credit card receivables
- competitive transaction tariff receivables charged by utility companies
- manufactured housing loans
- student loans
- other consumer loans such as home improvement loans

Commercial ABS securitizations include:

- trade receivables (e.g., health care receivables)
- equipment leasing
- operating assets (e.g., aircraft, marine cargo containers)
- entertainment assets (e.g., film rights, music publishing royalties)
- franchise loans
- small business loans

The broad-based bond market indexes include an ABS sector. The five largest subsectors within this sector are: (1) credit card receivable ABS, (2) auto ABS, (3) home equity ABS, (4) rate reduction bonds (also called stranded cost ABS), and (5) manufactured housing ABS. The commercial mortgage–backed securities (CMBS) sector, the subject of Chapter 14, is treated as a separate sector in the broad-based bond market indexes.

In this chapter, we will discuss the basic features of asset-backed securities and provide an overview of three major nonmortgage-related asset-backed security types that are not residential or commercial mortgage loans. A product that uses the securitization technology is the collateralized debt obligation (CDO). We briefly describe CDOs at the end of this chapter, although—with the exception of one form, the collateralized loan obligations (CLOs) that we described in Chapter 8—issuance of this product has ceased since 2007.

CREATION OF AN ASSET-BACKED SECURITY

To explain how an ABS is created and the parties to a securitization, we will use an illustration. Suppose that Exceptional Dental Equipment, Inc., manufactures high-quality dental equipment. While the company has cash sales, a bulk of its sales are from installment sales contracts. An installment sale contract is a loan to the buyer of the dental equipment (i.e., a dental practice) wherein the buyer agrees to repay Exceptional Dental Equipment, Inc., over a specified period of time for the amount borrowed plus interest.

The dental equipment purchased is the collateral for the loan. We will assume that the loans are all for five years.

The credit department of Exceptional Dental Equipment, Inc., makes the decision as to whether or not to extend credit to a customer. That is, the credit department will receive a credit application from a potential customer and, based on criteria established by the company, will decide on whether to make a loan. The criteria for granting a loan are referred to as **underwriting standards**. Because Exceptional Dental Equipment, Inc., is granting the loan, the company is referred to as the **originator** of the loan.

Moreover, Exceptional Dental Equipment, Inc., may have a department that is responsible for servicing the loan. As explained in previous chapters, servicing involves collecting payments from borrowers, notifying borrowers who may be delinquent, and, when necessary, recovering and disposing of the collateral (i.e., the dental equipment in our illustration) if the borrower fails to make the contractual loan payments. While the servicer of the loans need not be the originator of the loans, we are assuming in our illustration that Exceptional Dental Equipment, Inc., is the servicer.

Now let's get to how these loans are used in a securitization transaction. We will assume that Exceptional Dental Equipment, Inc., has more than $300 million of installment sales contracts. We will further assume that Exceptional Dental Equipment, Inc., wants to raise $300 million. Rather than issuing corporate bonds for $300 million, the treasurer of the corporation decides to raise the funds via a securitization. To do so, Exceptional Dental Equipment, Inc., will set up a legal entity referred to as a **special purpose vehicle** (SPV). At this point, we will not explain the purpose of this legal entity, but it will be made clearer later that the SPV is critical in a securitization transaction. In our illustration, the SPV that is set up is called DE Asset Trust (DEAT). Exceptional Dental Equipment, Inc., will then sell to DEAT $300 million of the loans. Exceptional Dental Equipment, Inc., will receive from DEAT $300 million in cash, the amount of funds it wanted to raise. DEAT obtains the $300 million by selling securities that are backed by the $300 million of loans. The securities are the asset-backed securities we referred to earlier.

The Parties to a Securitization

Let's make sure we understand the parties to a securitization. In our hypothetical securitization, Exceptional Dental Equipment, Inc., is not the issuer of the ABS (although it is sometimes referred to as the issuer because it is the entity that ultimately raises the funds). Rather, it originated the loans. Hence, in this transaction, Exceptional Dental Equipment, Inc., is called the "seller." The reason it is referred to as the "seller" is because it sold the receivables to DEAT. Exceptional Dental Equipment, Inc., is also called the "originator" because it originated the loans. The SPV in a securitization is referred to as the "issuing entity," "issuer," or "trust" in the prospectus.

While in our simple transaction Exceptional Dental Equipment, Inc., manufactured the dental equipment and originated the loans, there is another type of securitization transaction involving another company, called a **conduit**, that buys the loans and securitizes them. For example, consider the hypothetical company Dental Equipment Financing Corporation, whose business is to provide financing to dental equipment manufacturers who want to sell their equipment on an installment basis. Dental Equipment Financing Corporation would then develop a relationship with manufacturers of dental equipment (such as Exceptional Dental Equipment, Inc.) to purchase their installment contracts.

Dental Equipment Financing Corporation would then warehouse the purchased installment contracts until it had a sufficient amount to sell to an SPV, which would then issue the ABS.

There will be a trustee for the securities issued. The responsibilities of the trustee are to represent the interests of the bond classes by monitoring compliance with covenants and, in the event of default, to enforce remedies as specified in the governing documents.[1]

Two-Step Securitizations

Our above description of the parties to a securitization is for what is referred to as a "one-step securitization." For certain reasons that are not important to investors, a securitization might involve two SPVs in order to ensure that the transaction is considered a true sale for tax purposes. One SPV is called an **intermediate SPV**, which is a wholly owned subsidiary of the originator and has restrictions on its activities.[2] It is the intermediate SPV that purchases the assets from the originator. The intermediate SPV then sells the assets to the SPV that issues the asset-backed securities (i.e., the issuing entity). In the prospectus for a securitization transaction, the intermediate SPV is referred to as the **depositor**.

This type of securitization transaction, referred to as a "two-step securitization," is now commonplace. The reason for its use since 1997 is for financial reporting reasons as imposed by FASB 125. Thus, in older securitization transactions, the seller of the collateral is referred to as the "Seller" in the prospectus and prospectus supplement, but today with a two-step securitization, the same entity is identified as the "Depositor."

Let's use an example from an actual securitization transaction. Harley-Davidson Credit Corp. originates loans and uses those loans for a securitization. One such transaction is Harley-Davidson Motorcycle Trust 2007-3. In a one-step securitization, Harley-Davidson Credit Corp. would sell the loans to the SPV (Harley-Davidson Motorcycle Trust 2007-3), who would then issue the securities. However, that was not done. Instead, Harley-Davidson Credit Corp. sold the loans to Harley-Davidson Customer Funding Corp., the intermediate SPV. Then, the loans were sold to Harley-Davidson Motorcycle Trust 2007-3. Thus, in the transaction, the parties were identified as follows:

> *Seller:* Harley-Davidson Credit Corp.
> *Depositor:* Harley-Davidson Customer Funding Corp.
> *Issuing entity:* Harley-Davidson Motorcycle Trust 2007-3

In this transaction, the seller serviced the loans.

Transaction Structure

In creating the various bond classes (or tranches) in a securitization, there will be rules for distribution of principal and interest. As explained in Chapters 12 and 13, the creation of the different bond classes results in securities with different risk-return characteristics. The structure is designed to create bond classes with investment characteristics that are more

---

[1] For a further discussion of the role of the trustee in a securitization, see Karen Cook and F. Jim Della Sala, "The Role of the Trustee in Asset-Backed Securities," Chapter 7 in Frank J. Fabozzi (ed.), *Handbook of Structured Financial Products* (Hoboken, NJ: John Wiley & Sons, 1998).

[2] More specifically, it is (1) only allowed to engage in the business of purchasing, owning, and selling the receivables, and (2) restricted in various ways from entering into a voluntary bankruptcy.

attractive to institutional investors. By doing so, the entity seeking to raise funds can obtain the best price for the securities it sells (referred to as "best execution").

As explained in Chapter 13, nonagency MBS are credit enhanced. The two general forms of credit enhancement are internal and external credit enhancement. All asset-backed securities are credit enhanced. Credit enhancement levels are determined relative to a specific rating desired by the seller/servicer for a security by each rating agency. Typically in a securitization, there are at least two classes of bonds: senior bond classes and subordinate bond classes. This structure is called a senior-subordinate structure, and we described it in Chapter 13.

Role of the Special Purpose Vehicle

To understand the role of the SPV, we need to understand why a corporation would want to raise funds via securitization rather than simply issue corporate bonds. There are four principal reasons why a corporation may elect to raise funds via a securitization rather than a corporate bond. They are

1. the potential for reducing funding costs
2. to diversify funding sources
3. to accelerate earnings for financial reporting purposes
4. for regulated entities, potential relief from capital requirements

We will only focus on the first of these reasons in order to see the critical role of the SPV in a securitization.[3]

Let's suppose that Exceptional Dental Equipment, Inc., has a double B credit rating (i.e., a below investment-grade credit rating). If it wants to raise funds equal to $300 million by issuing a corporate bond, its funding cost would be whatever the benchmark Treasury yield is plus a credit spread for double B issuers. Suppose, instead, that Exceptional Dental Equipment, Inc., uses $300 million of its installment sales contracts (i.e., the loans it has made to customers) as collateral for a bond issue. What will be its funding cost? It probably will be the same as if it issued a corporate bond. The reason is that if Exceptional Dental Equipment, Inc., defaults on any of its outstanding debt, the creditors will go after all of its assets, including the loans to its customers.

Suppose that Exceptional Dental Equipment, Inc., can create a legal entity and sell the loans to that entity. That entity is the special purpose vehicle. In our illustration, the SPV is DEAT. If the sale of the loans by Exceptional Dental Equipment, Inc., to DEAT is done properly,[4] DEAT then legally owns the receivables, not Exceptional Dental Equipment, Inc. As a result, if Exceptional Dental Equipment, Inc., is ever forced into bankruptcy while the loans sold to DEAT are still outstanding, the creditors of Exceptional Dental Equipment, Inc., cannot recover the loans because they are legally owned by DEAT.

The legal implication is that when DEAT issues the ABS that are backed by the loans, investors contemplating the purchase of any bond class will evaluate the credit risk associated with collecting the payments due on the loans independent of the credit rating of Exceptional Dental Equipment, Inc. The credit ratings will be assigned to the different bond

[3] For a discussion of the other reasons, see W. Alexander Roever and Frank J. Fabozzi, "Primer on Securitization," *Journal of Structured and Project Finance,* Summer 2003, pp. 5–19.
[4] More specifically, it has to be a sale of the loans at a fair market value.

classes created in the securitization and will depend on how the rating agencies will evaluate the credit risk based on the collateral (i.e., the loans). In turn, this will depend on the credit enhancement for each bond class. So, due to the SPV, quality of the collateral, and credit enhancement, a corporation can raise funds via a securitization in which some of the bond classes have a better credit rating than the corporation itself that seeks to raise funds, and—in the aggregate—the funding cost is less than for issuing corporate bonds.

Credit Enhancements

In Chapter 13, we briefly reviewed the different forms of credit enhancement for nonagency MBS. They include structural, originator-provided, and third-party provided credit enhancement. The first two forms of credit enhancement are referred to as internal credit enhancement and the last is referred to as external credit enhancement. Also as explained in Chapter 13, third-party credit enhancement has been rare after 2007. The credit enhancement forms are used both individually and in combination, depending on the loan types that are backing the securities.

External credit enhancement involves a guarantee from a third party. The risk faced by an investor is the potential for the third party to be downgraded, and, as a result, the bond classes guaranteed by the third party may be downgraded. The most common form of external credit enhancement is **bond insurance** and it is referred to as a **surety bond** or a **wrap**. Bond insurance is a financial guarantee from a monoline insurance company requiring that the insurer guarantee the timely payments of principal and interest if these payments cannot be satisfied from the cash flow from the underlying loan pool. The principal payments will be made without acceleration, except if the insurer elects to do so.

Internal credit enhancements come in more complicated forms than external credit enhancements and may alter the cash flow characteristics of the loans even in the absence of default. Credit enhancement levels (i.e., the amount of subordination for each form of enhancement utilized within a deal) are determined by the rating agencies from which the issuer seeks a rating for the bond classes. This is referred to as "sizing" the transaction and is based on the rating agencies' expectations for the performance of the loans collateralizing the deal in question.

Most securitization transactions that employ internal credit enhancements follow a predetermined schedule that prioritizes the manner in which principal and interest generated by the underlying collateral must be used. This schedule, which is explained in the deal's prospectus, is known as the **cash flow waterfall**, or simply the **waterfall**. At the top of the waterfall would be cash flows due to senior bondholders (interest and principal, depending upon the principal repayment schedule) as well as some standard fees and expenses (e.g., administration and servicing fee). After the cash flow obligations at the top of the waterfall are met, cash flows down to lower priority classes (those, bond classes rated AA, A, BBB, and so on). The cash flows that remain after all of the scheduled periodic payment obligations are met are the **excess spread**. The excess spread is the first line of defense against collateral losses, since deals that are structured to have a large amount of excess spread can absorb relatively large levels of collateral losses. If the excess spread is fully eaten away by losses, the next lowest-rated class will begin to be negatively affected by credit losses.

The most common forms of internal credit enhancement are senior/subordinate structures, overcollateralization, and reserve funds. In Chapter 13, we described each of these forms of internal credit enhancement.

Optional Clean-Up Call Provisions

For ABS, there is an optional clean-up call provision granted to the trustee. There are several types of clean-up call provisions: percent of collateral call, percent of tranche clean-up call, call on or after specified date, latter of percent or date call, auction call, and insurer call.

In a **percent of collateral call**, the outstanding bonds can be called at par value if the outstanding collateral's balance falls below a predetermined percent of the original collateral's balance. This is the most common type of clean-up call provision for amortizing assets, and the predetermined level is typically 10%.

A **percent of bonds clean-up call** provision is similar to a percent of collateral call except that the percent that triggers the call is the percent of the amount of the bonds outstanding relative to the original amount of bonds issued. A **percent of tranche clean-up call** bases the right to call on the percent of the tranche's par value outstanding relative to the tranche's original par value.

A **call on or after specified date** operates just like a standard bond call provision. In a **latter of percent or date call**, the outstanding bond classes can be called if either (1) the collateral outstanding reaches a predetermined level before the specified call date, or (2) the call date has been reached even if the collateral outstanding is above the predetermined level. In an **auction call**, at a certain date a call will be exercised if an auction results in the outstanding collateral being sold at a price greater than its par value. The premium over par value received from the auctioned collateral is retained by the trustee and eventually paid to the seller through the residual.

In addition to the above clean-up call provisions, which permit the trustee to call the bonds, there may be an **insurer call**. Such a call permits the insurer to call the bonds if the collateral's cumulative loss history reaches a predetermined level.

COLLATERAL TYPE AND SECURITIZATION STRUCTURE

Structuring a securitization will depend on the characteristics of the underlying assets. Here we will discuss how two characteristics affect the structure: amortization and interest rate. Specifically, the structure depends on whether (1) the assets are amortizing or nonamortizing, and (2) the interest rate on the collateral is fixed or floating.

Amortizing versus Nonamortizing Assets

The collateral in a securitization can be classified as either amortizing or nonamortizing assets. **Amortizing assets** are loans in which the borrower's periodic payments consist of scheduled principal and interest payments over the life of the loan. The schedule for the repayment of the principal is called an **amortization schedule**. The standard residential mortgage loan falls into this category. Auto loans and certain types of home equity loans (specifically, closed-end home equity loans discussed later in this chapter) are amortizing assets.

The amortization schedule for the collateral can be created on a pool level or a loan level. In pool-level analysis, it is assumed that all loans comprising the collateral are identical. For an amortizing asset, the amortization schedule is based on the gross weighted average coupon (GWAC) and weighted average maturity (WAM) for that single loan. Pool-level analysis is appropriate where the underlying loans are homogeneous. Loan-level analysis involves amortizing each loan (or group of homogeneous loans).

As explained in Chapter 11, a prepayment is any excess payment over the scheduled principal payment. For an amortizing asset, projection of the cash flows requires projecting prepayments. In contrast to amortizing assets, **nonamortizing assets** do not have a schedule for the periodic payments that the individual borrower must make. Instead, a nonamortizing asset is one in which the borrower must make a minimum periodic payment. If that payment is less than the interest on the outstanding loan balance, the shortfall is added to the outstanding loan balance. If the periodic payment is greater than the interest on the outstanding loan balance, then the difference is applied to the reduction of the outstanding loan balance. Because there is no schedule of principal payments (i.e., no amortization schedule) for a nonamortizing asset, the concept of a prepayment does not apply. Credit card receivables are examples of nonamortizing assets.

Typically when amortizing assets are securitized, the collateral is fixed over the life of the structure. That is, no new assets are acquired. The collateral composition stays the same except for prepayments and defaults. Consequently, all principal received by the trust is paid out to the bond classes. The structure in this case is referred to as a **self-liquidating structure**. In the case of nonamortizing assets, for a period of time, referred to as the **lockout period** or **revolving period**, all principal received is used to purchase new collateral. Hence, new assets are being added to the collateral, and this structure is referred to as a **revolving structure**. After the lockout period, called the **amortization period**, principal received is distributed to the bond classes.

Fixed-Rate versus Floating-Rate Assets

The assets that are securitized can have a fixed rate or a floating rate. This impacts the structure in terms of the coupon rate for the bonds issued. For example, a structure with all floating-rate bond classes backed by collateral consisting of only fixed-rate contracts exposes bondholders to interest rate risk. If the reference rate for the floating-rate bond classes increases sufficiently, there could be a shortfall between the interest received from the collateral and the aggregate interest payment that must be made to the bond classes. If the collateral consists of only floating-rate contracts and the bond classes all have a fixed coupon rate, the exposure in this case is that the reference rate for the contracts will decline sufficiently so that the interest paid by the borrowers will be less than the total interest due to the bondholders.

To deal with situations where there may be a mismatch between the cash flow characteristics of the asset and the liabilities, interest rate derivative instruments are used in a securitization. The two common interest rate derivatives used are interest rate swaps and interest rate caps, both described in Chapter 28.[5]

CREDIT RISKS ASSOCIATED WITH INVESTING IN ASSET-BACKED SECURITIES

Investors in ABS are exposed to credit risk and rely on rating agencies to evaluate that risk for the bond classes in a securitization. While the three agencies have different approaches in assigning credit ratings, they do focus on the same areas of analysis. Moody's, for example, investigates: (1) asset risks, (2) structural risks, and (3) third parties to the

---

[5] For an explanation of how interest rate derivatives are used in securitizations, see Frank J. Fabozzi, Raymond Morel, and Brian D. Grow, "Use of Interest Rate Derivatives in Securitization Transactions," *Journal of Structured Finance,* Summer 2005, pp. 22–27.

structure.[6] We discuss each next. In addition, rating agencies analyze the legal structure (i.e., the SPV). We also discuss the legal issues regarding securitizations in general.

Asset Risks

Evaluating asset risks involves the analysis of the credit quality of the collateral. The rating agencies will look at the underlying borrower's ability to pay and the borrower's equity in the asset. The reason for looking at the latter is because it is a key determinant as to whether the underlying borrower will default or sell the asset and pay off a loan. The rating agencies will look at the experience of the originators of the underlying loans and will assess whether the loans underlying a specific transaction have the same characteristics as the experience reported by the seller.

The concentration of loans is examined. The underlying principle of asset securitization is that a large number of borrowers in a pool will reduce the credit risk via diversification. If there are a few borrowers in the pool that are significant in size relative to the entire pool balance, this diversification benefit can be lost, resulting in a higher level of credit risk referred to as **concentration risk**. To reduce concentration risk, concentration limits on the amount or percentage of receivables from any one borrower, region of the country, or industry (in the case of commercial assets) will be established by rating agencies. If at issuance the concentration limit is exceeded, some or all of the bond classes will receive a lower credit rating than if the concentration limit was within the established range. Subsequent to issuance, bond classes may be downgraded if the concentration limit is exceeded.

Employing statistical analysis, the rating agencies assess the most likely loss to a bond class that would result from the performance of the collateral. This is done by analyzing various scenarios that the rating agencies specify. Based on the result of the analysis, the rating agencies compute both a weighted average loss and variability of loss for each bond class. To appreciate why the variability of loss is important, suppose that a bond class has protection against a 7% loss in the value of the collateral due to defaults. To simplify the illustration, suppose that a rating agency evaluates two equally likely scenarios and that in the first scenario the loss is 6% and in the second scenario 4%. The weighted average loss is 5%. This is less than the 7% loss that a bond class has protection against and therefore the rating agency would expect that it is unlikely that the bond class will realize a loss. Let's change the two outcomes now. Suppose that the outcome of the two scenarios is that the loss is 8% in the first scenario and 2% in the second scenario. While the expected value for the loss is still 5%, the variability of the loss is much greater than before. In fact, if in the second scenario an 8% loss occurs, the bond class would realize a loss of 1% (8% loss in the scenario minus the 7% protection).

Structural Risks

The decision on the structure is up to the seller. Once selected, the rating agencies examine the extent to which the cash flow from the collateral can satisfy all of the obligations of the bond classes in the securitization. The cash flow of the underlying collateral is interest and principal repayment. The cash flow payments that must be made are interest and principal to investors,

---

[6] Andrew A. Silver, "Rating Structured Securities," Chapter 5 in Frank J. Fabozzi (ed.), *Issuer Perspectives on Securities* (Hoboken, NJ: John Wiley & Sons, 1998).

servicing fees, and any other expenses for which the issuer is liable. This is described by the structure's cash flow waterfall. The rating agencies analyze the structure to test whether the collateral's cash flows match the payments that must be made to satisfy the issuer's obligations. This requires that the rating agency make assumptions about losses and delinquencies and consider various interest rate scenarios after taking into consideration credit enhancements.

In considering the structure, the rating agencies will consider (1) the loss allocation (how losses will be allocated among the bond classes in the structure), (2) the cash flow allocation (i.e., the cash flow waterfall), (3) the interest rate spread between the interest earned on the collateral and the interest paid to the bond classes plus the servicing fee, (4) the potential for a trigger event to occur that will cause the early amortization of a deal (discussed later), and (5) how credit enhancement may change over time.

Third-Party Providers

In a securitization, several third parties are involved. These include third-party credit guarantors (most commonly bond insurers), the servicer, a trustee, issuer's counsel, a guaranteed investment contract provider (this entity insures the reinvestment rate on investable funds), and accountants. The rating agency will investigate all third-party providers. For the third-party guarantors, the rating agencies will perform a credit analysis of their ability to pay.

All loans must be serviced. Servicing involves collecting payments from borrowers, notifying borrowers who may be delinquent, and, when necessary, recovering and disposing of the collateral if the borrower does not make loan repayments by a specified time. The servicer is responsible for these activities. Moreover, while still viewed as a "third party" in many securitizations, the servicer is likely to be the originator of the loans used as the collateral.

In addition to the administration of the loan portfolio as just described, the servicer is responsible for distributing the proceeds collected from the borrowers to the different bond classes in the structure according to the cash flow waterfall. Where there are floating-rate securities in the transaction, the servicer will determine the interest rate for the period. The servicer may also be responsible for advancing payments when there are delinquencies in payments (that are likely to be collected in the future), resulting in a temporary shortfall in the payments that must be made to the bondholders.

The role of the servicer is critical in a securitization. Therefore, rating agencies look at the ability of a servicer to perform all the activities that a servicer will be responsible for before they assign a rating to the bonds in a transaction. For example, the following factors are reviewed when evaluating servicers: servicing history, experience, underwriting standard for loan originations, servicing capabilities, human resources, financial condition, and growth/competition/business environment. Transactions where there is a concern about the ability of a servicer to perform are either not rated or the rating agency may require a backup servicer.

Recent cases have made rating agencies pay even closer attention to the importance of the underlying business of the seller/originator, the strength of the servicer, and the economics that will produce the cash flows for the collateral. Primarily, this was as a result of the alleged fraud of both National Century Financial Enterprises (NCFE), a purchaser of health care receivables that were then securitized and serviced, and DVI, a securitizer of medical equipment leases. In addition, the NCFE and DVI case highlighted the need for a trustee to be more proactive if the performance of the servicer deteriorates. That is, the trustee's role should be expanded beyond the traditional function of merely performing the ongoing tests on the collateral that are set forth in the deal documents. This is, in fact, happening in recent deals where the trustee under certain circumstances can take on an expanded role. This is referred to as a **trustee event trigger**.

Potential Legal Challenges

The long-standing view is that investors in ABS are protected from the creditors of the seller of the collateral. That is, when the seller of the collateral transfers it to the trust (the SPV), the transfer represents a "true sale" and, therefore, in the case of the seller's bankruptcy, the bankruptcy court cannot penetrate the trust to recover the collateral or cash flow from the collateral. However, this issue has never been fully tested. The closest challenge was the bankruptcy of LTV Steel Company. In the bankruptcy, LTV argued that its securitizations were not true sales and therefore it should be entitled to the cash flows that it transferred to the trust. Although the case was settled and the settlement included a summary finding that the LTV's securitizations were a true sale, the court's decision to permit LTV to use the cash flows prior to the settlement is a major concern to investors.

There are also concerns regarding the outcome of a bankruptcy involving Conseco Finance. The firm filed for bankruptcy in December 2002. Conseco Finance had been the largest originator of manufactured housing loans, as well as originator of other types of asset-backed securities. At the time of filing, Conseco was the servicer for its prior securitizations, charging a servicing fee of 50 basis points. The bankruptcy court took the position that a 50 basis points servicing fee was not adequate compensation, ordering it to be increased (to 115 basis points). That increase in the servicing fee was obtained by reducing the excess spread in the securitization transactions that Conseco was servicing. As a result of a reduction in the excess spread, the credit enhancement levels for the transactions being serviced were reduced and several of the subordinate tranches in those transactions were downgraded.[7]

REVIEW OF SEVERAL MAJOR TYPES OF ASSET-BACKED SECURITIES

The three largest sectors within the ABS market that are not backed by residential mortgage loans are: (1) credit card receivable–backed securities, (2) auto loan–backed securities, and (3) rate reduction bonds. We conclude this chapter with a summary of these ABS types.

Credit Card Receivable–Backed Securities

Credit cards are issued by banks (e.g., Visa and MasterCard), retailers (e.g., JC Penney and Sears), and leading global payments and travel companies (e.g., American Express). The cash flow for a pool of credit card receivables consists of

- finance charge collections
- principal collections
- fees collected

Finance charges collected represent the periodic interest the credit card borrower is charged based on the unpaid balance after the grace period.

---

[7] For a further discussion of the implications of the Conseco Finance bankruptcy, see Frank J. Fabozzi, "The Structured Finance Market: An Investor's Perspective," *Financial Analysts Journal,* May–June 2005, pp. 27–40.

Structure of the Transaction

Credit card issuers have a large number of credit card accounts that can be pledged to a trust. The process of structuring a transaction begins with the credit card issuer setting up a trust and pledging those credit card accounts to the trust. In credit card transactions, the type of trust used is called a **master trust** and is referred to in the prospectus as the **trust portfolio**. To be included as an account pledged to the master trust, the account must meet certain eligibility requirements. New credit card accounts can be pledged to the master trust if they meet the eligibility requirements. If a credit card account in the master trust generates a receivable, that receivable belongs to the master trust.

Each series is a separate credit card deal and the trust can issue various securities or bond classes to the public. For example, a series can have a senior bond class and two subordinate bond classes. However, each series will have a different level of credit enhancement. It is the cash flow from the trust portfolio that is used to make the payments due to the bond classes for all the series.

Because a card receivable is a nonamortizing asset, it therefore has a revolving structure. During the revolving period or lockout period, the principal payments made by credit card borrowers comprising the pool are retained by the trustee and reinvested in additional receivables to maintain the size of the pool. The revolving period can vary from 18 months to 10 years. So, during the revolving period, the cash flow that is paid out to the bond classes is based on finance charges collected and fees. The revolving period is followed by the principal amortization period where the principal received from the accounts is no longer reinvested but paid to bondholders. There are various ways principal can be repaid over the principal amortization period.

There are provisions in credit card receivable-backed securities that require early amortization of the principal if certain events occur. The events are referred to as **payout events**. Such a provision, referred to as an **early amortization provision** or a **rapid amortization provision**, is included to safeguard the credit quality of the structure. The only way that the principal cash flows can be altered is by occurrence of a payout event. When early amortization occurs, the bond classes are retired sequentially (i.e., highest–rated bond class first, then the second–highest rated bond class, and so on). This is accomplished by distributing the principal payments to the specified bond class instead of using those payments to acquire more receivables. The length of time until the return of principal is largely a function of the monthly payment rate that we describe next.

Performance of the Portfolio of Receivables

The following concepts must be understood in order to assess the performance of the portfolio of receivables and the ability of the collateral to satisfy the interest obligation and repay principal as scheduled: gross portfolio yield, charge-offs, net portfolio yield, delinquencies, and monthly payment rate.

The **gross portfolio yield** includes finance charges collected and fees. **Charge-offs** represent the accounts charged off as uncollectible. **Net portfolio yield** is equal to gross portfolio yield minus charge-offs. The net portfolio yield is important because it is from this yield that the bondholders will receive interest payments. So, for example, if the weighted average coupon that must be paid to the various bond classes in the structure is 6% and the net portfolio yield for the month is 5%, there is the risk that the bondholder obligations will not be satisfied.

Delinquencies are the percentages of receivables that are past due for a specified number of months, usually 30, 60, and 90 days. They are considered an indicator of potential future charge-offs.

The **monthly payment rate** (MPR) expresses the monthly payment (which includes finance charges, fees, and any principal repayment) of a credit card receivable portfolio as a percentage of credit card debt outstanding in the previous month. For example, suppose a $600 million credit card receivable portfolio in February realized $60 million of payments in March. The MPR for March would then be 10% ($60 million divided by $600 million). The MPR is important for two reasons. First, if the MPR reaches an extremely low level, there is a chance that there will be extension risk with respect to the principal payments to the bond classes. Second, if the MPR is very low, then there is a chance that there will not be sufficient cash flows to pay off principal. This is one of the events that could trigger the early amortization provision.

Auto Loan–Backed Securities

Auto loan–backed securities are issued by the financial subsidiaries of auto manufacturers (domestic and foreign), commercial banks, and independent finance companies and small financial institutions specializing in auto loans. The cash flow for auto loan-backed securities consists of regularly scheduled monthly loan payments (interest and scheduled principal repayments) and any prepayments. For securities backed by auto loans, prepayments result from (1) sales and trade-ins requiring full payoff of the loan, (2) repossession and subsequent resale of the automobile, (3) loss or destruction of the vehicle, (4) payoff of the loan with cash to save on the interest cost, and (5) refinancing of the loan at a lower interest cost. While refinancings may be a major reason for prepayments of residential mortgage loans, they are of minor importance for automobile loans.

Prepayments for auto loan-backed securities are measured in terms of the **absolute prepayment speed** (ABS).[8] The ABS measure is the monthly prepayment expressed as a percentage of the original collateral amount. As explained in Chapter 11, the single-monthly mortality rate (SMM) is the monthly conditional prepayment rate (CPR) based on the prior month's balance. There is a mathematical relationship between the ABS and SMM. Given the SMM (expressed as a decimal), the ABS (expressed as a decimal) is obtained as follows:

$$ABS = \frac{SMM}{1 + SMM \times (M - 1)}$$

where M is the number of months after origination (i.e., loan age).

For example, suppose that the SMM is 2.1%, or 0.021, in month 32. Then the ABS is

$$ABS = \frac{0.021}{1 + 0.021 \times (32 - 1)} = 0.0127 = 1.27\%$$

Given the ABS, the SMM is obtained as follows:

$$SMM = \frac{ABS}{1 + ABS \times (M - 1)}$$

The SMM can then be converted to a CPR using the formula given in Chapter 11.

---

[8] The abbreviation *ABS* was probably used because it was the first prepayment measure used for asset-backed securities.

To illustrate the formula, suppose that the ABS is 1.5%, or 0.015, in month 26. Then the SMM is

$$\text{SMM} = \frac{0.015}{1 - 0.015 \times (26 - 1)} = 0.024 = 2.4\%$$

Illustration: DaimlerChrysler Auto Trust 2007-A

As an illustration of an auto loan–backed deal, we will look at DaimlerChrysler Auto Trust 2007-A. Information about the transaction is provided below and shown graphically in Exhibit 15-1:

> *Issuing Entity:* DaimlerChrysler Auto Trust 2007-A
> *Sponsor, Originator, Depositor, and Servicer:* DaimlerChrysler Financial Services Americas LLC
> *Monthly Servicing Fee Rate:* 1/12th of 1% per year of the aggregate principal balance of the receivable as of the first day of the prior calendar month

The loan pool consists of automobile and light-duty truck receivables purchased directly from DaimlerChrysler Financial Services Americas LLC.

The principal amount of the transaction was $1,689,500,000. The bond classes in the transaction were A-1, A-2a, A-2b, A-3a, A-3b, A-4a, A-4b, B, C, and D. All of the bond classes labeled "A" are the senior bonds. The only bond classes offered to the public were A-2a, A-2b, A-3a, A-3b, A-4a, and A-4b. The A-1 bond class was a short-term bond maturing in about a year after issuance. The principal amount for the senior bond classes offered is summarized below:

Class	Principal Amount
A-2a and A-2b	$836,000,000
A-3a and A-3b	$405,000,000
A-4a and A-4b	$448,500,000

Bond classes A-2a, A-3a, and A-4a have a fixed interest rate. Bond classes A-2b, A-3b, and A-4b are floating-rate bond classes where the reference rate is one-month LIBOR.

Because the loans in the pool of receivables were all fixed rate, this resulted in a mismatch between the cash flow (based on a fixed rate) and the payments to bond classes A-2b, A-3b, and A-4b, which require a floating-rate payment. To deal with this mismatch risk, the trust entered into an interest rate swap for each of the floating-rate bond classes. We will describe interest rate swaps in Chapter 28 and we only mention them here as an application. In the interest rate swap, the trust would pay a fixed rate (which it receives from the pool of receivables) to the counterparty and would receive from the counterparty a floating rate. In this transaction, the swap counterparty was Goldman Sachs Mitsui Marine Derivative Products, L.P.

Every month, the cash flow from the collateral is first used to pay the servicing fee and then to make payments (if any) to the swap counterparties. The principal payment distribution for the bond classes is then to the senior bond classes first. The senior bond classes are sequential pays. The principal payments made to the fixed and floating-rate bond classes are made on a pro rata basis.

Credit enhancement for the senior notes was provided by the B, C, and D bond classes as well as initial credit enhancement in the form of overcollateralization and a reserve fund. In addition, there is the excess spread, which is referred to as "excess interest collections" in the prospectus supplement.

Exhibit 15-1   Page from Prospectus Supplement for DaimlerChrysler Auto Trust 2007-A Summarizing the Transaction

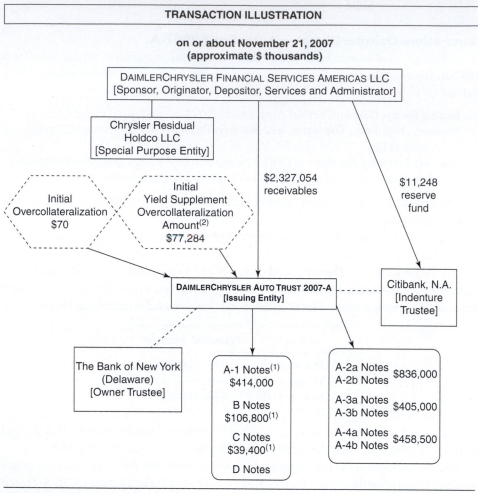

TRANSACTION ILLUSTRATION

on or about November 21, 2007
(approximate $ thousands)

DAIMLERCHRYSLER FINANCIAL SERVICES AMERICAS LLC
[Sponsor, Originator, Depositor, Services and Administrator]

Chrysler Residual Holdco LLC
[Special Purpose Entity]

Initial Overcollateralization $70

Initial Yield Supplement Overcollateralization Amount[2] $77,284

$2,327,054 receivables

$11,248 reserve fund

DAIMLERCHRYSLER AUTO TRUST 2007-A
[Issuing Entity]

Citibank, N.A.
[Indenture Trustee]

The Bank of New York (Delaware)
[Owner Trustee]

A-1 Notes[1] $414,000

B Notes $106,800[1]

C Notes $39,400[1]

D Notes

A-2a Notes
A-2b Notes $836,000

A-3a Notes
A-3b Notes $405,000

A-4a Notes
A-4b Notes $458,500

(1) Not being offered publicly or in this document
(2) The yield supplement overcollateralization amount starts at this amount and declines as set forth on page S–45 in this document.

Source: *Prospectus Supplement Dated November 21, 2007, DaimlerChrysler Auto Trust 2007-A, p. S-5.*

The prospectus supplement also provides information about the weighted average lives of the senior bond classes based on different ABS (absolute prepayment speed as defined earlier in this chapter but absolute prepayment model as defined in the prospectus supplement). Exhibit 15-2 shows the percent of the initial note principal at each payment date for the senior bond classes based on different ABS assumptions as presented in the prospectus supplement.

Rate Reduction Bonds

Rate reduction bonds are backed by a special charge (tariff) included in the utility bills of utility customers. The charge, called the **competitive transition charge** (CTC), is effectively a legislated asset. It is the result of the movement to make the electric utility industry more competitive by deregulating the industry. Prior to deregulation, electric utilities were entitled to set utility rates so as to earn a competitive return on the assets on their balance sheet. After deregulation, the setting of utility rates to recover a competitive return was no longer permissible. As a result, many electric utilities had a substantial amount of assets that they acquired prior to deregulation that would likely become uneconomic and utilities would no longer be assured that they could charge a high enough rate to recover the costs of these assets. These assets are referred to as "stranded assets" and the associated costs referred to as "stranded costs." For this reason, rate reduction bonds are also known as **stranded cost bonds** or **stranded asset bonds**. Some market participants refer to this sector of the ABS market as the "utilities" sector.

Exhibit 15-2	**Page from Prospectus Supplement for DaimlerChrysler Auto Trust 2007-A Showing for Different ABS Percentages the Percent of Note Principal Amount for the Senior Bond Classes by Payment Date**

Percent of Initial Note Principal Amount at Various ABS Percentages

Payment Date	A-1 Notes						A-2 Notes					
	0.00%	0.50%	1.20%	1.40%	1.60%	1.80%	0.00%	0.50%	1.20%	1.40%	1.60%	1.80%
Closing Date	100.00%	100.00%	100.00%	100.00%	100.00%	100.00%	100.00%	100.00%	100.00%	100.00%	100.00%	100.00%
December 2007	90.13%	87.27%	82.94%	81.60%	80.17%	78.11%	100.00%	100.00%	100.00%	100.00%	100.00%	100.00%
January 2008	81.23%	75.60%	67.07%	64.44%	61.65%	58.07%	100.00%	100.00%	100.00%	100.00%	100.00%	100.00%
February 2008	72.28%	63.97%	51.38%	47.52%	43.43%	38.78%	100.00%	100.00%	100.00%	100.00%	100.00%	100.00%
March 2008	63.27%	52.37%	35.87%	30.82%	25.50%	19.80%	100.00%	100.00%	100.00%	100.00%	100.00%	100.00%
April 2008	54.23%	40.83%	20.56%	14.37%	7.90%	1.14%	100.00%	100.00%	100.00%	100.00%	100.00%	100.00%
May 2008	45.15%	29.33%	5.44%	0.00%	0.00%	0.00%	100.00%	100.00%	100.00%	99.09%	95.34%	91.48%
June 2008	36.02%	17.88%	0.00%	0.00%	0.00%	0.00%	100.00%	100.00%	95.30%	91.19%	86.93%	82.56%
July 2008	26.84%	6.48%	0.00%	0.00%	0.00%	0.00%	100.00%	100.00%	88.01%	83.41%	78.67%	73.80%
August 2008	17.84%	0.00%	0.00%	0.00%	0.00%	0.00%	100.00%	97.69%	80.89%	75.81%	70.58%	65.20%
September 2008	8.80%	0.00%	0.00%	0.00%	0.00%	0.00%	100.00%	92.19%	73.86%	68.47%	62.93%	57.23%
October 2008	0.00%	0.00%	0.00%	0.00%	0.00%	0.00%	99.86%	87.00%	67.78%	61.97%	55.99%	49.84%
November 2008	0.00%	0.00%	0.00%	0.00%	0.00%	0.00%	96.07%	82.39%	61.79%	55.56%	49.16%	42.58%
December 2008	0.00%	0.00%	0.00%	0.00%	0.00%	0.00%	92.34%	77.78%	55.88%	49.26%	42.46%	35.46%
January 2009	0.00%	0.00%	0.00%	0.00%	0.00%	0.00%	88.58%	73.19%	50.05%	43.05%	35.87%	28.49%
February 2009	0.00%	0.00%	0.00%	0.00%	0.00%	0.00%	84.79%	68.61%	44.29%	36.95%	29.41%	21.66%
March 2009	0.00%	0.00%	0.00%	0.00%	0.00%	0.00%	80.97%	64.05%	38.62%	30.94%	23.06%	14.97%
April 2009	0.00%	0.00%	0.00%	0.00%	0.00%	0.00%	77.12%	59.50%	33.03%	25.04%	16.85%	8.44%
May 2009	0.00%	0.00%	0.00%	0.00%	0.00%	0.00%	73.25%	54.97%	27.52%	19.24%	10.75%	2.05%
June 2009	0.00%	0.00%	0.00%	0.00%	0.00%	0.00%	69.34%	50.44%	22.09%	13.54%	4.79%	0.00%
July 2009	0.00%	0.00%	0.00%	0.00%	0.00%	0.00%	65.50%	46.03%	16.81%	8.00%	0.00%	0.00%
August 2009	0.00%	0.00%	0.00%	0.00%	0.00%	0.00%	61.63%	41.63%	11.61%	2.57%	0.00%	0.00%
September 2009	0.00%	0.00%	0.00%	0.00%	0.00%	0.00%	57.74%	37.24%	6.49%	0.00%	0.00%	0.00%
October 2009	0.00%	0.00%	0.00%	0.00%	0.00%	0.00%	53.81%	32.87%	1.46%	0.00%	0.00%	0.00%
November 2009	0.00%	0.00%	0.00%	0.00%	0.00%	0.00%	49.85%	28.51%	0.00%	0.00%	0.00%	0.00%
December 2009	0.00%	0.00%	0.00%	0.00%	0.00%	0.00%	45.86%	24.17%	0.00%	0.00%	0.00%	0.00%
January 2010	0.00%	0.00%	0.00%	0.00%	0.00%	0.00%	41.84%	19.84%	0.00%	0.00%	0.00%	0.00%
February 2010	0.00%	0.00%	0.00%	0.00%	0.00%	0.00%	37.79%	15.53%	0.00%	0.00%	0.00%	0.00%
March 2010	0.00%	0.00%	0.00%	0.00%	0.00%	0.00%	33.70%	11.24%	0.00%	0.00%	0.00%	0.00%
April 2010	0.00%	0.00%	0.00%	0.00%	0.00%	0.00%	29.59%	6.96%	0.00%	0.00%	0.00%	0.00%
May 2010	0.00%	0.00%	0.00%	0.00%	0.00%	0.00%	25.44%	2.69%	0.00%	0.00%	0.00%	0.00%
June 2010	0.00%	0.00%	0.00%	0.00%	0.00%	0.00%	21.26%	0.00%	0.00%	0.00%	0.00%	0.00%
July 2010	0.00%	0.00%	0.00%	0.00%	0.00%	0.00%	17.04%	0.00%	0.00%	0.00%	0.00%	0.00%
August 2010	0.00%	0.00%	0.00%	0.00%	0.00%	0.00%	12.95%	0.00%	0.00%	0.00%	0.00%	0.00%
September 2010	0.00%	0.00%	0.00%	0.00%	0.00%	0.00%	8.90%	0.00%	0.00%	0.00%	0.00%	0.00%
October 2010	0.00%	0.00%	0.00%	0.00%	0.00%	0.00%	4.82%	0.00%	0.00%	0.00%	0.00%	0.00%
November 2010	0.00%	0.00%	0.00%	0.00%	0.00%	0.00%	0.71%	0.00%	0.00%	0.00%	0.00%	0.00%
December 2010	0.00%	0.00%	0.00%	0.00%	0.00%	0.00%	0.00%	0.00%	0.00%	0.00%	0.00%	0.00%
Weighted Average Life (years)[1]	0.46	0.36	0.27	0.25	0.23	0.21	1.99	1.61	1.19	1.10	1.02	0.94

(1) The weighted average life of a note is determined by (a) multiplying the amount of each principal payment on a note by the number of years from the date of the issuance of the note to the related payment date, (b) adding the results and (c) dividing the sum by the related initial principal amount of the note.

This ABS Table has been prepared based on the assumptions described above (including the assumptions regarding the characteristics and performance of the receivables which will differ from the actual characteristics and performance thereof) and should be read in conjunction therewith.

(Continued)

Percent of Initial Note Principal Amount at Various ABS Percentages

Payment Date	A-3 Notes						A-4 Notes					
	0.00%	0.50%	1.20%	1.40%	1.60%	1.80%	0.00%	0.50%	1.20%	1.40%	1.60%	1.80%
Closing Date	100.00%	100.00%	100.00%	100.00%	100.00%	100.00%	100.00%	100.00%	100.00%	100.00%	100.00%	100.00%
December 2007	100.00%	100.00%	100.00%	100.00%	100.00%	100.00%	100.00%	100.00%	100.00%	100.00%	100.00%	100.00%
January 2008	100.00%	100.00%	100.00%	100.00%	100.00%	100.00%	100.00%	100.00%	100.00%	100.00%	100.00%	100.00%
February 2008	100.00%	100.00%	100.00%	100.00%	100.00%	100.00%	100.00%	100.00%	100.00%	100.00%	100.00%	100.00%
March 2008	100.00%	100.00%	100.00%	100.00%	100.00%	100.00%	100.00%	100.00%	100.00%	100.00%	100.00%	100.00%
April 2008	100.00%	100.00%	100.00%	100.00%	100.00%	100.00%	100.00%	100.00%	100.00%	100.00%	100.00%	100.00%
May 2008	100.00%	100.00%	100.00%	100.00%	100.00%	100.00%	100.00%	100.00%	100.00%	100.00%	100.00%	100.00%
June 2008	100.00%	100.00%	100.00%	100.00%	100.00%	100.00%	100.00%	100.00%	100.00%	100.00%	100.00%	100.00%
July 2008	100.00%	100.00%	100.00%	100.00%	100.00%	100.00%	100.00%	100.00%	100.00%	100.00%	100.00%	100.00%
August 2008	100.00%	100.00%	100.00%	100.00%	100.00%	100.00%	100.00%	100.00%	100.00%	100.00%	100.00%	100.00%
September 2008	100.00%	100.00%	100.00%	100.00%	100.00%	100.00%	100.00%	100.00%	100.00%	100.00%	100.00%	100.00%
October 2008	100.00%	100.00%	100.00%	100.00%	100.00%	100.00%	100.00%	100.00%	100.00%	100.00%	100.00%	100.00%
November 2008	100.00%	100.00%	100.00%	100.00%	100.00%	100.00%	100.00%	100.00%	100.00%	100.00%	100.00%	100.00%
December 2008	100.00%	100.00%	100.00%	100.00%	100.00%	100.00%	100.00%	100.00%	100.00%	100.00%	100.00%	100.00%
January 2009	100.00%	100.00%	100.00%	100.00%	100.00%	100.00%	100.00%	100.00%	100.00%	100.00%	100.00%	100.00%
February 2009	100.00%	100.00%	100.00%	100.00%	100.00%	100.00%	100.00%	100.00%	100.00%	100.00%	100.00%	100.00%
March 2009	100.00%	100.00%	100.00%	100.00%	100.00%	100.00%	100.00%	100.00%	100.00%	100.00%	100.00%	100.00%
April 2009	100.00%	100.00%	100.00%	100.00%	100.00%	100.00%	100.00%	100.00%	100.00%	100.00%	100.00%	100.00%
May 2009	100.00%	100.00%	100.00%	100.00%	100.00%	100.00%	100.00%	100.00%	100.00%	100.00%	100.00%	100.00%
June 2009	100.00%	100.00%	100.00%	100.00%	100.00%	91.35%	100.00%	100.00%	100.00%	100.00%	100.00%	100.00%
July 2009	100.00%	100.00%	100.00%	100.00%	97.90%	78.80%	100.00%	100.00%	100.00%	100.00%	100.00%	100.00%
August 2009	100.00%	100.00%	100.00%	100.00%	86.16%	66.55%	100.00%	100.00%	100.00%	100.00%	100.00%	100.00%
September 2009	100.00%	100.00%	100.00%	94.28%	74.68%	54.60%	100.00%	100.00%	100.00%	100.00%	100.00%	100.00%
October 2009	100.00%	100.00%	100.00%	83.48%	63.46%	42.95%	100.00%	100.00%	100.00%	100.00%	100.00%	100.00%
November 2009	100.00%	100.00%	92.79%	72.89%	52.50%	31.60%	100.00%	100.00%	100.00%	100.00%	100.00%	100.00%
December 2009	100.00%	100.00%	82.75%	62.52%	41.80%	20.57%	100.00%	100.00%	100.00%	100.00%	100.00%	100.00%
January 2010	100.00%	100.00%	72.88%	52.37%	31.37%	9.84%	100.00%	100.00%	100.00%	100.00%	100.00%	100.00%
February 2010	100.00%	100.00%	63.19%	42.45%	21.20%	0.00%	100.00%	100.00%	100.00%	100.00%	100.00%	99.48%
March 2010	100.00%	100.00%	53.67%	32.74%	11.30%	0.00%	100.00%	100.00%	100.00%	100.00%	100.00%	90.14%
April 2010	100.00%	100.00%	44.34%	23.27%	1.68%	0.00%	100.00%	100.00%	100.00%	100.00%	100.00%	80.97%
May 2010	100.00%	100.00%	35.20%	14.02%	0.00%	0.00%	100.00%	100.00%	100.00%	100.00%	92.95%	72.11%
June 2010	100.00%	96.79%	26.23%	5.00%	0.00%	0.00%	100.00%	100.00%	100.00%	100.00%	84.44%	63.55%
July 2010	100.00%	88.05%	17.46%	0.00%	0.00%	0.00%	100.00%	100.00%	100.00%	96.58%	76.20%	55.30%
August 2010	100.00%	79.61%	9.04%	0.00%	0.00%	0.00%	100.00%	100.00%	100.00%	88.71%	68.32%	47.43%
September 2010	100.00%	71.34%	0.90%	0.00%	0.00%	0.00%	100.00%	100.00%	100.00%	81.11%	60.75%	39.91%
October 2010	100.00%	63.10%	0.00%	0.00%	0.00%	0.00%	100.00%	100.00%	93.52%	73.72%	53.45%	32.69%
November 2010	100.00%	54.89%	0.00%	0.00%	0.00%	0.00%	100.00%	100.00%	86.22%	66.54%	46.40%	25.77%
December 2010	92.91%	46.71%	0.00%	0.00%	0.00%	0.00%	100.00%	100.00%	79.10%	59.58%	39.61%	19.15%
January 2011	84.29%	38.57%	0.00%	0.00%	0.00%	0.00%	100.00%	100.00%	72.15%	52.84%	33.08%	12.85%
February 2011	75.60%	30.47%	0.00%	0.00%	0.00%	0.00%	100.00%	100.00%	65.38%	46.32%	26.83%	6.86%
March 2011	66.84%	22.40%	0.00%	0.00%	0.00%	0.00%	100.00%	100.00%	58.78%	40.03%	20.84%	1.19%
April 2011	58.01%	14.36%	0.00%	0.00%	0.00%	0.00%	100.00%	100.00%	52.37%	33.96%	15.12%	0.00%
May 2011	49.11%	6.37%	0.00%	0.00%	0.00%	0.00%	100.00%	100.00%	46.15%	28.12%	9.68%	0.00%
June 2011	40.14%	0.00%	0.00%	0.00%	0.00%	0.00%	100.00%	98.56%	40.11%	22.51%	4.51%	0.00%
July 2011	31.10%	0.00%	0.00%	0.00%	0.00%	0.00%	100.00%	91.22%	34.25%	17.14%	0.00%	0.00%
August 2011	22.48%	0.00%	0.00%	0.00%	0.00%	0.00%	100.00%	84.18%	28.77%	12.13%	0.00%	0.00%
September 2011	13.96%	0.00%	0.00%	0.00%	0.00%	0.00%	100.00%	77.28%	23.53%	7.39%	0.00%	0.00%
October 2011	5.37%	0.00%	0.00%	0.00%	0.00%	0.00%	100.00%	70.42%	18.47%	2.87%	0.00%	0.00%
November 2011	0.00%	0.00%	0.00%	0.00%	0.00%	0.00%	97.03%	63.60%	13.59%	0.00%	0.00%	0.00%
December 2011	0.00%	0.00%	0.00%	0.00%	0.00%	0.00%	88.88%	56.80%	8.89%	0.00%	0.00%	0.00%
January 2012	0.00%	0.00%	0.00%	0.00%	0.00%	0.00%	80.62%	50.05%	4.38%	0.00%	0.00%	0.00%
February 2012	0.00%	0.00%	0.00%	0.00%	0.00%	0.00%	72.30%	43.32%	0.05%	0.00%	0.00%	0.00%
March 2012	0.00%	0.00%	0.00%	0.00%	0.00%	0.00%	63.92%	36.64%	0.00%	0.00%	0.00%	0.00%
April 2012	0.00%	0.00%	0.00%	0.00%	0.00%	0.00%	55.46%	29.99%	0.00%	0.00%	0.00%	0.00%
May 2012	0.00%	0.00%	0.00%	0.00%	0.00%	0.00%	46.94%	23.38%	0.00%	0.00%	0.00%	0.00%
June 2012	0.00%	0.00%	0.00%	0.00%	0.00%	0.00%	38.36%	16.80%	0.00%	0.00%	0.00%	0.00%
July 2012	0.00%	0.00%	0.00%	0.00%	0.00%	0.00%	29.70%	10.27%	0.00%	0.00%	0.00%	0.00%
August 2012	0.00%	0.00%	0.00%	0.00%	0.00%	0.00%	20.98%	3.77%	0.00%	0.00%	0.00%	0.00%
September 2012	0.00%	0.00%	0.00%	0.00%	0.00%	0.00%	15.34%	0.00%	0.00%	0.00%	0.00%	0.00%
October 2012	0.00%	0.00%	0.00%	0.00%	0.00%	0.00%	9.64%	0.00%	0.00%	0.00%	0.00%	0.00%
November 2012	0.00%	0.00%	0.00%	0.00%	0.00%	0.00%	3.90%	0.00%	0.00%	0.00%	0.00%	0.00%
December 2012	0.00%	0.00%	0.00%	0.00%	0.00%	0.00%	0.00%	0.00%	0.00%	0.00%	0.00%	0.00%
Weighted Average Life (years)[1]	3.50	3.06	2.38	2.20	2.03	1.88	4.48	4.18	3.49	3.24	2.99	2.75
Weighted Average Life to Call (years)[1][2]	N/A	N/A	N/A	N/A	N/A	N/A	4.47	4.17	3.47	3.22	2.98	2.75
Earliest Possible Call Date	N/A	N/A	N/A	N/A	N/A	N/A	Oct. 2012	Jul. 2012	Dec. 2011	Aug. 2011	May 2011	Feb. 2011

(1) The weighted average life of a note is determined by (a) multiplying the amount of each principal payment on a note by the number of years from the date of the issuance of the note to the related payment date, (b) adding the results and (c) dividing the sum by the related initial principal amount of the note.

Source: *Prospectus Supplement Dated November 21, 2007, DaimlerChrysler Auto Trust 2007-A, pp. S-27–28.*

The CTC is collected by the utility over a specific period of time. Because the state legislature designates the CTC to be a statutory property right, it can be sold by a utility to an SPV and securitized. It is the legislative designation of the CTC as an asset that makes rate reduction bonds different from the typical asset securitized.

The CTC is initially calculated based on projections of utility usage and the ability to collect revenues. However, actual collection experience may differ from initial projections. Because of this, there is a "true-up" mechanism in these securitizations. This mechanism permits the utility to recompute the CTC on a periodic basis over the term of the securitization based on actual collection experience. The advantage of the true-up mechanism to the bond classes is that it provides cash flow stability as well as a form of credit enhancement.

DODD-FRANK WALL STREET REFORM AND CONSUMER PROTECTION ACT

Because of the turmoil that occurred in the securitization market and related sectors of the financial market, in July 2010, Congress passed the **Dodd-Frank Wall Street Reform and Consumer Protection Act**. Although the act deals with more than securitizations, we limit our discussion here to just that topic.

The key features of the act that impact securitizations are

1. The requirement that "securitizers"[9] retain a portion of the transaction's credit risk.
2. Requirements regarding reporting standards and disclosure for a securitization transaction.
3. The representations and warranties required to be provided in securitization transactions and the mechanisms for enforcing them.
4. Due diligence requirements with respect to loans underlying securitization transactions.

The specifics regarding how the above requirements should be handled were not set forth in the act. Instead, Congress delegated that responsibility and its implementation to three federal banking agencies (Federal Reserve Board, Office of the Comptroller of the Currency, and the Federal Deposit Insurance Corporation) and the Securities and Exchange Commission (SEC). With respect to nonagency RMBS, joint rules are to be specified by the three federal banking agencies, the Federal Housing Finance Agency (FHFA), and the Department of Housing and Urban Development (HUD).

The rules dealing with the amount and form of credit risk that securitizers must retain differ for securitizations that do not have "qualified residential mortgages" and those that have entirely such mortgages. For securitizations consisting entirely of "qualified residential mortgages," there are no risk retention requirements. The definition of what constitutes a "qualified residential mortgage" was delegated to the three federal banking agencies, SEC, FHFA, and HUD and takes into account the underwriting and product features of the loans and their historical performance.

Securitizers that are required to retain credit risk are not permitted to hedge (directly or indirectly) or transfer the credit risk.

---

[9] The act defines a securitizer as either an issuer of an ABS transaction or a person who organizes and initiates an ABS transaction by selling or transferring assets, either directly or indirectly, including through an affiliate, to the issuer.

COLLATERALIZED DEBT OBLIGATIONS

When the ABS market began, there was a debt product that employed the securitization technology to create a diversified pool of some asset type and issue securities backed by the cash flow of the asset pool. These debt products are called **collateralized debt obligations** (CDOs). CDOs differ from ABS as discussed earlier in this chapter in that the pool of assets is actively managed by an entity referred to as the collateral manager.

Although many types of asset classes have been used as collateral in a CDO, the following are the major ones

- investment-grade corporate bonds
- high-yield corporate bonds
- emerging market bonds
- nonagency residential mortgage–backed securities (nonagency RMBS)
- commercial mortgage–backed securities (CMBS)
- leveraged bank loans
- collateralized debt obligations

CDOs backed by the first three asset types are referred to as **collateralized bond obligations**; those backed by nonagency RMBS and CMBS are referred to as **structured finance CDOs**. CDOs backed by leveraged bank loans are called **collateralized loan obligations** (CLOs) and we discussed them in Chapter 8. Finally, CDOs backed by bond classes of other CDOs are referred to as **CDO-squared** or CDO^2.

While issuance of CDOs grew dramatically from the mid-1990s through early 2007, issuance for all but CLOs has stopped because of the dismal performance of this product. Market observers do not believe that the market for CDOs other than CLOs will be revived. It is for this reason that we limit our discussion to the basic feature of this product.[10] This review will also make the distinction between an ABS and CDO clear.

Structure of a CDO

In a CDO structure, there is a collateral manager responsible for managing the portfolio of debt obligations. The portfolio of debt obligations in which the collateral manager invests is referred to as the **collateral**. The individual issues that comprise the collateral are referred to as the **collateral assets**.

The funds to purchase the collateral assets are obtained from the issuance of debt obligations. As with ABS, the debt obligations are referred to as **tranches** or **bond classes**. The tranches include:

- senior tranches
- mezzanine tranches
- subordinate/equity tranches

A CDO may or may not have a mezzanine tranche.

---

[10] In the previous edition of this book, an entire chapter was devoted to CDOs. The chapter covered the motivation for the creation of CDOs from the perspective of the issuer.

There will be a rating sought for all but the subordinate/equity tranche. For the senior tranches, at least an A rating is typically sought. For the mezzanine tranches, a rating of BBB but no less than B is sought. The subordinate/equity tranche receives the residual cash flow; hence, no rating is sought for this tranche. There are restrictions imposed as to what the collateral manager may do and certain tests that must be satisfied for the CDO to maintain the credit rating assigned at the time of issuance.

The ability of the collateral manager to make the interest payments to the tranches and pay off the tranches as they mature depends on the performance of the collateral. The proceeds to meet the obligations to the CDO tranches (interest and principal repayment) can come from

- coupon interest payments from the collateral assets
- maturing of collateral assets
- sale of collateral assets

In a typical structure, one or more of the tranches has a floating rate. With the exception of deals backed by bank loans that pay a floating rate, the collateral manager invests in fixed-rate bonds. Now that presents a problem—paying tranche investors a floating rate and investing in assets with a fixed rate. To deal with this problem, the collateral manager uses derivative instruments in order to convert a portion of the fixed-rate payments from the assets into floating-rate cash flow to pay floating-rate tranches. In particular, interest-rate swaps are used. This instrument, which we describe in Chapter 28, allows a market participant to swap fixed-rate payments for floating-rate payments or vice versa. Because of the mismatch between the nature of the cash flows of the debt obligations in which the collateral manager invests and the floating-rate liability of any of the tranches, the collateral manager must use an interest-rate swap. A rating agency will require the use of swaps to eliminate this mismatch.

The collateral manager must monitor the collateral to ensure that certain tests are being met. There are two types of tests imposed by rating agencies: quality tests and coverage tests. In rating a transaction, the rating agencies are concerned with the diversity of the assets. Consequently, there are tests that relate to the diversity of the assets. These tests are called **quality tests**. A collateral manager may not undertake a trade that will result in the violation of any of the quality tests. There are tests to ensure that the performance of the collateral is sufficient to make payments to the various tranches. These tests are called **coverage tests** and, as explained next, if the coverage tests are violated, then income from the collateral is diverted to pay down the senior tranches.

Distribution Rules

There are three relevant periods. The first is the **ramp-up period**. This is the period that follows the closing date of the transaction where the collateral manager begins investing the proceeds from the sale of the debt obligations issued. This period usually lasts from one to two years. The **reinvestment period** or **revolving period** is where principal proceeds are reinvested and is usually for five or more years. In the final period, the collateral is sold and the debt holders are paid off.

Distribution of Income

Income is derived from interest income from the collateral assets and capital appreciation. The income is then used as follows. Payments are first made to the trustee and administrators and then to the senior collateral manager. Once these fees are paid, then the senior tranches are paid their interest. At this point, before any other payments are made, certain tests must be passed. These tests are called coverage tests, as mentioned previously. If the coverage tests are passed, then interest is paid to the mezzanine tranches. Once the mezzanine tranches are paid, interest is paid to the subordinate/equity tranche.

In contrast, if the coverage tests are not passed, then payments are made to protect the senior tranches. The remaining income after paying the fees and senior tranche interest is used to redeem the senior tranches (i.e., pay off principal) until the coverage tests are brought into compliance. If the senior tranches are paid off fully because the coverage tests are not brought into compliance, then any remaining income is used to redeem the mezzanine tranches. Any remaining income is then used to redeem the subordinate/equity tranche.

Distribution of Principal Cash Flow

The principal cash flow is distributed as follows after the payment of the fees to the trustees, administrators, and senior managers. If there is a shortfall in interest paid to the senior tranches, principal proceeds are used to make up the shortfall. Assuming that the coverage tests are satisfied, during the reinvestment period the principal is reinvested. After the reinvestment period or if the coverage tests are failed, the principal cash flow is used to pay down the senior tranches until the coverage tests are satisfied. If all the senior tranches are paid down, then the mezzanine tranches are paid off, followed by the subordinate/equity tranche.

After all the debt obligations are satisfied in full, if permissible, the equity investors are paid. Typically, there are also incentive fees paid to management based on performance. Usually, a target return for the equity investors is established at the inception of the transaction. Management is then permitted to share on some prorated basis once the target return is achieved.

KEY POINTS

- Asset-backed securities are created by pooling loans and receivables through a process known as securitization.
- The main parties to a securitization are the seller/originator (party seeking to raise funds), special purpose vehicle, and servicer.
- The motivation for issuing asset-backed securities rather than issuing a corporate bond is the potential reduction in funding cost. The key to this savings is the role of the special purpose vehicle.
- ABSs are credit enhanced to provide greater protection to bond classes against defaults. There are two general types of credit enhancement structures: internal and external.
- Internal credit enhancements include structural credit enhancement (senior/subordinate structures) and originator-provided credit enhancement (cash reserves, excess spread, and overcollateralization).

- External credit enhancements come in the form of third-party guarantees, the most common historically being bond insurance, which has not been used in deals since 2007.
- In analyzing credit risk, the rating agencies will examine asset risks, structural risks, and third parties to the structure. Based on this analysis, a rating agency will determine the amount of credit enhancement needed for a bond class to receive a specific credit rating.

QUESTIONS

1. Why is the entity seeking to raise funds through a securitization referred to as the "seller" or the "originator"?

2. In achieving the benefits associated with a securitization, why is the special purpose vehicle important to the transaction?

3. In a securitization, what is the difference between a servicer and a special purpose vehicle?

4. **a.** What is the difference between a one-step securitization and a two-step securitization?
   b. What is meant by the "depositor" in a securitization?

5. What is meant by a cash flow waterfall?

6. Explain the difference in the treatment of principal received for a self-liquidating trust and a revolving trust.

7. In a securitization, what is (a) a revolving period and (b) an early amortization provision?

8. **a.** Why is credit enhancement required in a securitization?
   b. What entity determines the amount of securities needed in a securitization?

9. Why is the MPR for credit card receivable–backed securities important?

10. What is the limitation of a third-party guarantee as a form of credit enhancement?

11. An asset-backed security has been credit enhanced with a letter of credit from a bank with a single A credit rating. If this is the only form of credit enhancement, explain whether this issue can be assigned a triple A credit rating at the time of issuance.

12. A corporation is considering a securitization and is considering two possible credit enhancement structures backed by a pool of automobile loans. Total principal value underlying the asset-backed security is $300 million.

Principal Value for:	Structure I	Structure II
Pool of automobile loans	$304 million	$301 million
Senior class	250	270
Subordinate class	50	30

a. Which structure would receive a higher credit rating and why?
b. What form of credit enhancement is being used in both structures?

13. **a.** What is meant by concentration risk?
b. How do rating agencies seek to limit the exposure of a pool of loans to concentration risk?

14. What is the difference between pool-level and loan-level analysis?

15. How do optional call provisions in a securitization differ from that of a call provision in a standard corporate bond?

16. What factors do the rating agencies consider in analyzing the structural risk in a securitization?

17. Why would an interest rate derivative be used in a securitization structure?

18. The following questions relate to auto loan–backed securities:
a. What is the cash flow for an auto loan–backed security?
b. Why are prepayments of minor importance for automobile loan–backed securities?
c. How are prepayments on pools of auto loans measured?

19. The following questions relate to credit card receivable–backed securities:

    a. What happens to the principal repaid by borrowers in a credit card receivable–backed security during the lockout period?

    b. What is the role of the early amortization provision in a credit card receivable–backed security structure?

    c. How can the cash flow of a credit card receivable–backed security be altered prior to the principal-amortization period?

    d. Why is the monthly payment rate an important measure to examine when considering investing in a credit card receivable–backed security?

20. The following questions relate to rate reduction bonds:

    a. What asset is the collateral?

    b. What is a true-up provision in a securitization creating rate reduction bonds?

21. What does the Dodd-Frank Wall Street Reform and Consumer Protection Act specify regarding a securitizer retaining credit risk in a securitization transaction?

22. How does a CDO differ from an ABS transaction?

23. **a.** If there is a shortfall in interest paid to the senior tranches of a CDO, how is the shortfall made up?

    b. If coverage tests are failed for a CDO, how is the principal received from the collateral used?

16

Interest-Rate Models

LEARNING OBJECTIVES

After reading this chapter, you will understand

- what an interest-rate model is

- how an interest-rate model is represented mathematically

- the characteristics of an interest-rate model: drift, volatility, and mean reversion

- what a one-factor interest-rate model is

- the difference between an arbitrage-free model and an equilibrium model

- the different types of arbitrage-free models and why they are used in practice

- the difference between a normal model and a lognormal model

- the empirical evidence on interest rate changes

- considerations in selecting an interest rate model

- how to calculate historical volatility

In implementing bond portfolio strategies, there are two important activities that a manager will undertake. One will be the determination of whether the bonds that are purchase and sale candidates are fairly priced. The same applies to any interest-rate derivatives that the manager may want to employ to control interest-rate risk or potentially enhance returns. Second, a manager will want to assess the performance of a portfolio over realistic future interest-rate scenarios. For both of these activities, the manager will have to rely on an interest-rate model.

Future interest rates are, of course, unknown. The description of the uncertainty about future interest rates is mathematically described by an interest-rate model. More specifically, an **interest-rate model** is a probabilistic description of how interest rates can change over time. In this chapter, we provide an overview of interest-rate models. Our focus will be on *nominal* interest rates rather than *real* interest rates (i.e., the nominal interest rate reduced by the inflation rate). At the end of this chapter, we will see how interest-rate volatility is computed using historical data.

MATHEMATICAL DESCRIPTION OF ONE-FACTOR INTEREST-RATE MODELS

Interest-rate models must incorporate statistical properties of interest-rate movements. These properties are (1) drift, (2) volatility, and (3) mean reversion. We will describe each property next. The commonly used mathematical tool for describing the movement of interest rates that can incorporate these properties is **stochastic differential equations** (SDEs). A rigorous treatment of interest-rate modeling requires an understanding of this specialized topic in mathematics. Because SDEs are typically not covered in finance courses (except in financial engineering programs), we provide only the basic elements of the subject here. It is also worth noting that SDEs are used in the pricing of options, the most well-known model being the Black-Scholes model that we will describe in Chapter 27.

The most common interest-rate model used to describe the behavior of interest rates assumes that short-term interest rates follow some statistical process and that other interest rates in the term structure are related to short-term rates. The short-term interest rate (i.e., short rate) is the only one that is assumed to drive the rates of all other maturities. Hence, these models are referred to as **one-factor models**. The other rates are not randomly determined once the short rate is specified. Using arbitrage arguments, the rates for all other maturities are determined.

There are also multi-factor models that have been proposed in the literature. The most common multi-factor model is a two-factor model where a long-term rate is the second factor. In practice, however, one-factor models are used because of the difficulty of applying even a two-factor model. The high correlation between rate changes for different maturities provides some support for the use of a one-factor model. There is also empirical evidence that supports the position that a level shift in interest rates accounts for the major portion of the change in the yield curve.[1] Consequently, our focus is on one-factor models.

While the value of the short rate at some future time is uncertain, the pattern by which it changes over time can be assumed. In statistical terminology, this pattern or behavior is called a **stochastic process**. Thus, describing the dynamics of the short rate means specifying the stochastic process that describes the movement of the short rate. It is assumed that the short rate is a continuous random variable and therefore the stochastic process used is a **continuous-time stochastic process**.

There are different types of continuous-time stochastic processes, and we describe those used in interest-rate modeling next. In all of these models, because time is a continuous variable, the letter d is used to denote the "change in" some variable. Specifically, in the models below, we will let

r = the short rate and, therefore, dr denotes the change in the short rate
t = time, and therefore, dt denotes the change in time or equivalently the length of the time interval (dt is a very small interval of time)
z = a random term and dz denotes a random process

---

[1] Note that a one-factor model should not be used in valuing financial instruments where the payoff depends on the shape of the spot rate curve rather than simply the level of interest rates. Examples would be dual index floaters and yield curve options.

A Basic Continuous-Time Stochastic Process

Let's start with a basic continuous-time stochastic process for describing the dynamics of the short rate given by

$$dr = b\,dt + \sigma\,dz \tag{16.1}$$

where dr, dt, and dz were defined above and

σ = standard deviation of the changes in the short rate
b = expected direction of rate change

The expected direction of the change in the short rate (b) is called the **drift term** and σ is called the **volatility term**.[2]

In words, equation (16.1) says that the change in the short rate (dr) over the time interval (dt) depends on

1. the expected direction of the change in the short rate (b) and
2. a random process (dz) that is affected by volatility

The random nature of the change in the short rate comes from the random process dz.

The assumptions are that

1. the random term z follows a normal distribution with a mean of zero and a standard deviation of one (i.e., is a standardized normal distribution)
2. the change in the short rate is proportional to the value of the random term, which depends on the standard deviation of the change in the short rate
3. the change in the short rate for any two different short intervals of time are independent

Based on the assumptions above, important properties can be shown for equation (16.1). The expected value of the change in the short rate is equal to b, the drift term. Notice that in the special case where the drift term is equal to zero, equation (16.1) tells us that expected value of the change in the short rate is zero. This means that the expected value for the short rate is its current value. Note that in the special case where the drift term is zero and the variance is one, it can be shown that the variance of the change in the short rate over some interval of length T is equal to T and, therefore, the standard deviation is the square root of T.

Itô Process

Notice that in equation (16.1) neither the drift term nor the standard deviation of the change in the short rate depend on either the level of the short rate and time. So, for example, suppose the current short rate is 3%, then the SDE given by equation (16.1) assumes that b is the same if the current short rate is 12%. There are economic reasons that might suggest that the expected direction of the rate change will depend on the level of the current short rate. The same is true for σ.

We can change the dynamics of the drift term and the dynamics of the volatility term by allowing these two parameters to depend on the level of the short rate and/or time. We

---

[2] A special case of the SDE described by equation (16.1) when b is equal to zero and σ is equal to one is called a standard Wiener process and is the building block for constructing models in continuous time.

can denote that the drift term depends on both the level of the short rate and time by $b(r,t)$. Similarly, we can denote the volatility term by $\sigma(r,t)$. We can then write

$$dr = b(r,t)dt + \sigma(r,t)dz \qquad (16.2)$$

The continuous-time stochastic model given by equation (16.2) is called an **Itô process**.

Specifying the Dynamics of the Drift Term

In specifying the dynamics of the drift term, one can specify that the drift term depends on the level of the short rate by assuming it follows a **mean-reversion process**. By mean reversion, it is meant that some long-run stable mean value for the short rate is assumed. We will denote this value by $\bar{r}$. So, if r is greater than $\bar{r}$, the direction of change in the short rate will move down in the direction of the long-run stable value and vice versa. However, in specifying the mean-reversion process, it is necessary to indicate the speed at which the short rate will move or converge to the long-run stable mean value. This parameter is called the **speed of adjustment** and we will denote it by α. Thus, the mean-reversion process that specifies the dynamics of the drift term is

$$b(r,t) = -\alpha(r - \bar{r}) \qquad (16.3)$$

Specifying the Dynamics of the Volatility Term

There have been several formulations of the dynamics of the volatility term. If volatility is not assumed to depend on time, then $\sigma(r,t) = \sigma(r)$. In general, the dynamics of the volatility term can be specified as follows:

$$\sigma r^\gamma dz \qquad (16.4)$$

where γ is equal to the **constant elasticity of variance**. Equation (16.4) is called the **constant elasticity of variance model** (CEV model). The CEV model allows us to distinguish between the different specifications of the dynamics of the volatility term for the various interest-rate models suggested by researchers.

Let's look at three cases for γ: 0, 1, and 1/2. Substituting these values for γ into equation (16.4) we get the following models identified by the researchers who first proposed them:

$\gamma = 0$:	$\sigma(r,t) = \sigma$	Vasicek specification[3]
$\gamma = 1$:	$\sigma(r,t) = \sigma r$	Dothan specification[4]
$\gamma = \frac{1}{2}$:	$\sigma(r,t) = \sigma \sqrt{r}$	Cox-Ingersoll-Ross specification[5]

In the Vasicek specification, volatility is independent of the level of the short rate as in equation (16.1) and is referred to as the **normal model**. In the normal model, it is possible for negative interest rates to be generated. In the Dothan specification, volatility is proportional to the short rate. This model is referred to as the **proportional volatility model**. The Cox-Ingersoll-Ross (CIR) specification, referred to for obvious reasons as the **square-root model**,

---

[3] Oldrich A. Vasicek, "An Equilibrium Characterization of the Term Structure," *Journal of Financial Economics*, 1977, pp. 177–188.

[4] L. Uri Dothan, "On the Term Structure of Interest Rates," *Journal of Financial Economics*, 1978, pp. 59–69.

[5] John C. Cox, Jonathan E. Ingersoll, Jr, and Stephen A. Ross, "A Theory of the Term Structure of Interest Rates," *Econometrica*, 1985, pp. 385–407.

makes the volatility proportional to the square root of the short rate. Negative interest rates are not possible in the square-root model.

One can combine the dynamics of the drift term and volatility term to create the following commonly used interest rate model:

$$dr = -\alpha(r - \bar{r})dt + \alpha\sqrt{r}\,dz \tag{16.5}$$

Notice that this model specifies a mean-reversion process for the drift term and the square-root model for volatility. The model given by equation (16.5) is referred to as the **mean-reverting square-root model**.

ARBITRAGE-FREE VERSUS EQUILIBRIUM MODELS

Interest-rate models fall into two general categories: arbitrage-free models and equilibrium models. We describe both in this section.

Arbitrage-Free Models

In **arbitrage-free models**, also referred to as **no-arbitrage models**, the analysis begins with the observed market price of a set of financial instruments. The financial instruments can include cash market instruments and interest-rate derivatives, and they are referred to as the **benchmark instruments** or **reference set**. The underlying assumption is that the benchmark instruments are fairly priced. A random process for the generation of the term structure is assumed. The random process assumes a drift term for interest rates and volatility of interest rates. Based on the random process and the assumed value for the parameter that represents the drift term, a computational procedure is used to calculate the term structure of interest rates (i.e., the spot rate curve) such that the valuation process generates the observed market prices for the benchmark instruments. The model is referred to as arbitrage-free because it matches the observed prices of the benchmark instruments. In other words, one cannot realize an arbitrage profit by pursuing a strategy based on the value of the securities generated by the model and the observed market price. Non-benchmark instruments are then valued using the term structure of interest rates estimated and the volatility assumed.

We will describe how this is done in the next chapter, where we will start with the price of benchmark bonds, generate a spot rate curve that matches the market prices of the benchmark bonds, and then use the model to generate the theoretical price of non-benchmark bonds. The arbitrage-free model is also used to value certain derivatives (options, caps, floors, and swaptions) using a consistent framework for valuing cash market instruments. In Chapters 27 and 28, we will see how the arbitrage-free model is used to value option-type derivatives.

The most popular arbitrage-free interest-rate models used for valuation are[6]

- the Ho-Lee model
- the Hull-White model
- the Kalotay-Williams-Fabozzi model
- the Black-Karasinski model
- the Black-Derman-Toy model
- the Heath-Jarrow-Morton model

---

[6] For a more detailed discussion including a discussion of the solution to these models, see Gerald W. Buetow, Frank J. Fabozzi, and James Sochacki, "A Review of No Arbitrage Interest Rate Models," Chapter 3 in Frank J. Fabozzi (ed.), *Interest Rate, Term Structure, and Valuation Modeling* (Hoboken, NJ: John Wiley & Sons, 2002).

The first arbitrage-free interest-rate model was introduced by Ho and Lee in 1986.[7] In the Ho-Lee model, there is no mean reversion and volatility is independent of the level of the short rate. That is, it is a normal model [i.e, $\gamma = 0$ in equation (16.4)]. The Hull-White model is also a normal model.[8] Unlike the Ho-Lee model, however, it allows for mean reversion. Thus, the Hull-White model is the first arbitrage-free, mean-reverting normal model.

The last three models listed above are lognormal models. In the Kalotay-Williams-Fabozzi (KWF) model,[9] changes in the short rate are modeled by modeling the natural logarithm of r; no allowance for mean reversion is considered in the model. It is this model that will be used in the next chapter to value bonds with embedded options. The Black-Karasinski model[10] is a generalization of the KWF model by allowing for mean reversion. That is, the Black-Karasinski model is the logarithmic extension of the KWF model in the same way that the Hull-White model is the normal model extension of the Ho-Lee model. The Black-Derman-Toy (BDT) model[11] allows for mean reversion. However, unlike the Black-Karasinski model, mean reversion is endogenous to the model. The mean reversion in the BDT model is determined by market conditions.

The Heath-Jarrow-Morton (HJM) model is a general continuous time, multi-factor model.[12] The HJM model has received considerable attention in the industry as well as in the finance literature. Many other no-arbitrage models are shown to be special cases of the HJM model. The HJM model does not require assumptions about investor preferences but instead only requires a description of the volatility structure of forward interest rates. A special case of the one-factor HJM model is derived by Jeffrey.[13]

Equilibrium Models

A fair characterization of arbitrage-free models is that they allow one to interpolate the term structure of interest rates from a set of observed market prices at one point in time assuming that one can rely on the market prices used. **Equilibrium models**, however, are models that seek to describe the dynamics of the term structure using fundamental economic variables that are assumed to affect the interest-rate process. In the modeling process, restrictions are imposed allowing for the derivation of closed-form solutions for equilibrium prices of bonds and interest rate derivatives. In these models, (1) a functional form of the interest-rate volatility is assumed, and (2) how the drift moves up and down over time is assumed.

---

[7] Thomas Ho and Sang Lee, "Term Structure Movements and Pricing Interest Rate Contingent Claims," *Journal of Finance*, 1986, pp. 1011–1029.

[8] John Hull and Alan White, "Pricing Interest Rate Derivative Securities," *Review of Financial Studies*, 1990, pp. 573–592.

[9] Andrew Kalotay, George Williams, and Frank J. Fabozzi, "A Model for the Valuation of Bonds and Embedded Options," *Financial Analyst Journal*, May–June 1993, pp. 35–46.

[10] Fisher Black and Piotr Karasinski, "Bond and Option Pricing When Short Rates are Lognormal," *Financial Analyst Journal*, July–August 1991, pp. 52–59.

[11] Fischer Black, Emanuel Derman, and William Toy, "A One Factor Model of Interest Rates and Its Application to the Treasury Bond Options," *Financial Analyst Journal*, January–February 1990, pp. 33–39.

[12] David Heath, Robert A. Jarrow, and Andrew J. Morton, "Bond Pricing and the Term Structure of Interest Rates: A New Methodology for Contingent Claims Valuation," *Econometrica*, 60, 1992, pp. 77–105. The Brace-Gatarek-Musiela model is a particular implementation of the HJM model, which corresponds to a specific choice of the volatility term: Alan Brace, Dariusz Gatarek, and Marcek Musiela, "The Market Model of Interest Rate Dynamics," *Mathematical Finance*, 7, 1997, pp. 127–155.

[13] Andrew Jeffrey, "Single Factor Heath-Jarrow-Morton Term Structure Models Based on Spot Interest Rate Dynamics," *Journal of Financial and Quantitative Analysis*, 30, 1995, pp. 619–642.

In characterizing the difference between arbitrage-free and equilibrium models, one can think of the distinction being whether the model is designed to be consistent with any initial term structure, or whether the parameterization implies a particular family of term structure of interest rates. Arbitrage-free models have the deficiency that the initial term structure is an input rather than being explained by the model. Basically, equilibrium models and arbitrage models are seeking to do different things.

While there have been many developments in equilibrium models, the best known models are the Vasicek and CIR models discussed previously and the Brennan and Schwartz,[14] and Longstaff and Schwartz models.[15] To implement these models, estimates of the parameters of the assumed interest-rate process are needed, including the parameters of the volatility function for interest rates. These estimated parameters are typically obtained using econometric techniques using historical yield curves without regard to how the final model matches any market prices.

In practice, there are two concerns with implementing and using equilibrium models. First, many economic theories start with an assumption about the class of utility functions to describe how investors make choices. Equilibrium models are no exception: the model builder must specify the assumed class of utility functions. Second, as noted previously, these models are not calibrated to the market so that the prices obtained from the model can lead to arbitrage opportunities in the current term structure.[16] These models are such that volatility is an input into the model rather than output that can be extracted from observed prices for financial instruments.

EMPIRICAL EVIDENCE ON INTEREST-RATE CHANGES

Now that we are familiar with the different types of interest-rate models, let's look at empirical evidence regarding the historical movement of interest rates. Our motivation for doing so is to help in assessing the various arbitrage-free interest-rate models. Specifically, in our review of interest-rate models, we encountered the following issues:

1. The choice between normal models (i.e., volatility is independent of the level of interest rates) and logarithm models.
2. If interest rates are highly unlikely to be negative, then interest-rate models that allow for negative rates may be less suitable as a description of the interest-rate process.

Accordingly, we present evidence regarding

- the relationship between interest-rate volatility and the level of interest rates
- negative interest rates

---

[14] Michael Brennan and Eduardo Schwartz, "A Continuous Time Approach to the Pricing of Bonds," *Journal of Banking and Finance*, 1979, pp. 133–155; "An Equilibrium Model of Bond Pricing and a Test of Market Efficiency," *Journal of Financial and Quantitative Analysis*, 1982, pp. 301–329.

[15] Francis Longstaff and Eduardo Schwartz, "Interest Rate Volatility and the Term Structure: A Two-Factor General Equilibrium Model," *Journal of Finance*, 1992, pp. 1259–1282.

[16] To deal with this, Dybvig has suggested an approach that has been used by some commercial vendors of analytical systems. See Philip Dybvig, "Bond and Bond Option Pricing Based on the Current Term Structure," in Michael A.H. Dempster and Stanley Pliska (eds.), *Mathematics of Derivatives Securities* (Cambridge, U.K.: Cambridge University Press, 1997).

Recall from Chapter 3 that the change in interest rates can be measured by either the absolute rate change (absolute value of the change in spread in basis points between two time periods) or percentage rate change (computed as the natural logarithm of the ratio of the yield for two time periods).

Volatility of Rates and the Level of Interest Rates

We will first look at the historical movement to examine the issue as to whether interest-rate volatility is affected by the level of interest rates or independent of the level of interest rates. In the former case, the higher the level of interest rates, the greater the interest-rate volatility. That is, there is a positive correlation between the level of interest rates and interest-rate volatility. If the two are independent, a low correlation would exist.

The dependence of volatility on the level of interest rates has been examined by several researchers. The earlier research focused on short-term rates and employed a statistical time series model called generalized autoregressive conditional heteroscedasticity (GARCH).[17] With respect to short-term rates, the findings were inconclusive.

Rather than focusing on the short-term rate, Oren Cheyette of MSCI Barra examined all the spot rates for the Treasury yield curve for the period from 1977 to early 1996, a period covering a wide range of interest rates and different Federal Reserve policies.[18] He finds that for different periods, there are different degrees of dependence of volatility on the level of interest rates. (Interest-rate changes are measured as absolute rate changes in Cheyette's study.) Specifically, in the high interest-rate environment of the late 1970s and early 1980s where interest rates exceeded 10%, there was a positive correlation between interest-rate volatility and the level of interest rates. However, when interest rates were below 10%, the relationship was weak. Hence, the findings suggest that since the 1980s, interest-rate volatility has been independent of the level of interest rates. These conclusions were supported in a study by Levin of the Treasury 10-year rate from 1980 to 2003 and the 10-year swap rate from 1989 to 2003.[19]

The implication is that in modeling interest rates, one can assume that interest-rate volatility is independent of the level of interest rates in an environment where rates are less than double digit. That is, in modeling the dynamics of the volatility term the normal model can be used.

Negative Interest Rates

Our focus is on nominal interest rates. While we know that real interest rates (rates adjusted for inflation) in an economy have been negative, it is generally thought that it is impossible for the nominal interest rate to be negative. The reason is that if the nominal rate is negative, investors will simply hold cash. However, there have been time periods in countries where interest rates have been negative for a brief time period, refuting the notion that investors would not be willing to lend at negative interest rates.

---

[17] See, for example, K.C. Chan, G.A. Karolyi, Francis A. Longstaff, and Anthony B. Sanders, "An Empirical Comparison of Alternative Models of the Short Rate," *Journal of Finance* 47:3, 1992, pp. 1209–1227; Robin J. Brenner, Richard H. Harjes, and Kenneth F. Kroner, "Another Look at Alternative Models of the Short-Term Interest Rate," *Journal of Financial and Quantitative Analysis*, 31, 1996, pp. 85–107; and Yacine Aït-Sahalia, "Testing Continuous Time Models of the Spot Interest Rate," *Review of Financial Studies*, 9:2, 1996, pp. 385–426.

[18] Oren Cheyette, "Interest Rate Models," Chapter 1 in *Interest Rate, Term Structure, and Valuation Modeling.*

[19] Alexander Levin, "Interest Rate Model Selection," *Journal of Portfolio Management*, Winter 2004, pp. 74–86.

For example, during the Great Depression in the United States, financial historians have identified periods where Treasury securities traded at a negative yield. Japan provides another example. In early November 1998, Western banks charged Japanese banks interest of 3 to 6 basis points to hold 2- or 3-month yen deposits that Japanese banks were unwilling to deposit with local institutions because of the perceived instability of Japan's financial system. The yield on 3-month Japanese Treasury bills during one trading day in November 1998 fell to −5 basis points, although the closing yield was positive.

It is fair to say that while negative interest rates are not impossible, they are unlikely. The significance of this is that one might argue that an interest-rate model should not permit negative interest rates (or negative rates greater than a few basis points). Yet, this may occur in a model where volatility is measured in terms of basis points—as in the normal model. In contrast, if interest-rate volatility is measured in terms of the percentage yield change (i.e., logarithm of the yield ratio), interest rates cannot be negative. Hence, a stated advantage of using an interest-rate model whose volatility is dependent on the level of interest rates is that negative returns are not possible. How critical is this assumption in deciding whether to use a lognormal model rather than a normal model? We address this in the next section.

SELECTING AN INTEREST-RATE MODEL

Cheyette provides guidance in the selection of an interest rate model. He writes:

> It may seem that one's major concern in choosing an interest-rate model should be the accuracy with which it represents the empirical volatility of the term structure of rates, and its ability to fit market prices of vanilla derivatives such as at-the-money caps and swaptions. These are clearly important criteria, but they are not decisive. The first criterion is hard to pin down, depending strongly on what historical period one chooses to examine. The second criterion is easy to satisfy for most commonly used models, by the simple (though unappealing) expedient of permitting predicted future volatility to be time dependent. So, while important, this concern doesn't really do much to narrow the choices.[20]

Moreover, as Cheyette notes, the ease of application is a critical issue in selecting an interest-rate model. While our focus in this chapter has been on describing interest-rate models, there is the implementation issue. For consistency in valuation, a portfolio manager would want a model that can be used to value all financial instruments that are included in a portfolio. In practice, writing efficient algorithms to value all financial instruments that may be included in a portfolio for some interest-rate models that have been proposed in the literature is "difficult or impossible."[21]

Based on the empirical evidence, Cheyette and Levin have concluded that the normal model is a suitable model. Cheyette argues that for typical initial spot rate curves and volatility parameters, the probability that negative rates would be generated by the model is quite small.[22] What is important from a practical perspective is not just whether the normal model admits the possibility of negative interest rates but whether negative interest rates may have a significant impact on the pricing of financial instruments. Cheyette tests

[20] Cheyette, "Interest Rate Models," p. 4.
[21] Cheyette, "Interest Rate Models," p. 4.
[22] Cheyette, "Interest Rate Models," p. 10.

this by pricing a call option on a zero-coupon bond and concluded that: "The oft raised bogeyman of negative interest rates proves to have little consequence for option pricing, since negative rates occur with very low probability for reasonable values of the model parameters and initial term structure."[23]

Levin, who empirically investigated the issue for valuing mortgage-backed securities, also concluded that the normal model, in particular the Hull-White model, is appropriate. He states: "It will not lead to sizable mispricing even in the worst mortgage-irrelevant case."[24] But, as he notes, "This conclusion, however, certainly merits periodic review."[25]

ESTIMATING INTEREST-RATE VOLATILITY USING HISTORICAL DATA

As we have seen, one of the inputs into an interest-rate model is interest-rate volatility. Where does a practitioner obtain this value in order to implement an interest-rate model? Market participants estimate yield volatility in one of two ways. The first way is by estimating historical interest volatility. This method uses historical interest rates to calculate the standard deviation of interest-rate changes and for obvious reasons is referred to as **historical volatility**. The second method is more complicated to explain at this juncture of the book. It involves using models for valuing option-type derivative instruments to obtain an estimate of what the market expects interest-rate volatility to be. Basically, in any option pricing model, the only input that is not observed in the model is interest-rate volatility. What is done in practice is to assume that the observed price for an option-type derivative is priced according to some option pricing model. The calculation then involves determining what interest-rate volatility will make the market price of the option-type derivative equal to the value generated by the option pricing model. Since the expected interest-rate volatility obtained is being "backed out" of the model, it is referred to as **implied volatility**.

We use the data in Exhibit 16-1 to explain how to calculate the historical volatility as measured by the standard deviation based on the absolute rate change and the percentage change in rates. The historical interest rates shown in Exhibit 16-1 are the weekly returns for one-month LIBOR from 7/30/2004 to 7/29/2005. The observations are based on bid rates for Eurodollar deposits collected around 9:30 A.M. Eastern time.[26] The calculation can be performed on an electronic spreadsheet. The *weekly* standard deviation is reported in the exhibit. For the absolute rate change, it is 2.32 basis points; for the percentage rate change, it is 1.33%.

The weekly measures must be annualized. The formula for annualizing a weekly standard deviation is[27]

$$\text{Weekly standard deviation} \times \sqrt{52}$$

---

[23] Cheyette, "Interest Rate Models," p. 25.

[24] Levin, "Interest Rate Model Selection," p. 85.

[25] Levin, "Interest Rate Model Selection," p. 85.

[26] The data were obtained from the Federal Reserve Statistical Release H.15.

[27] In the annualizing formula, there is an assumption made when the square root of the number of time periods in a year is used. The assumption is that the correlation between the interest rate changes over time is not significant. The term *serial correlation* is used to describe this correlation.

Exhibit 16-1 **Data for Calculating Historical Volatility: One-Month from 7/30/2004 to 7/29/2005**

Date	1-Month LIBOR (%)	Absolute Rate Change (bps)	Percentage Rate Change (%)
7/30/2004	1.43		
8/6/2004	1.49	6	4.110
8/13/2004	1.51	2	1.333
8/20/2004	1.52	1	0.660
8/27/2004	1.54	2	1.307
9/3/2004	1.59	5	3.195
9/10/2004	1.67	8	4.909
9/17/2004	1.73	6	3.530
9/24/2004	1.77	4	2.286
10/1/2004	1.77	0	0.000
10/8/2004	1.78	1	0.563
10/15/2004	1.81	3	1.671
10/22/2004	1.86	5	2.725
10/29/2004	1.90	4	2.128
11/5/2004	1.98	8	4.124
11/12/2004	2.03	5	2.494
11/19/2004	2.06	3	1.467
11/26/2004	2.11	5	2.398
12/3/2004	2.24	13	5.979
12/10/2004	2.30	6	2.643
12/17/2004	2.35	5	2.151
12/24/2004	2.34	1	−0.426
12/31/2004	2.34	0	0.000
1/7/2005	2.34	0	0.000
1/14/2005	2.39	5	2.114
1/21/2005	2.44	5	2.070
1/28/2005	2.50	6	2.429
2/4/2005	2.53	3	1.193
2/11/2005	2.53	0	0.000
2/18/2005	2.53	0	0.000
2/25/2005	2.59	6	2.344
3/4/2005	2.66	7	2.667
3/11/2005	2.71	5	1.862
3/18/2005	2.77	6	2.190
3/25/2005	2.79	2	0.719
4/1/2005	2.81	2	0.714
4/8/2005	2.85	4	1.413
4/15/2005	2.89	4	1.394
4/22/2005	2.95	6	2.055
4/29/2005	3.01	6	2.013
5/6/2005	3.04	3	0.992

(Continued)

Exhibit 16-1 Data for Calculating Historical Volatility: One-Month from 7/30/2004 to 7/29/2005 (Continued)

Date	1-Month LIBOR (%)	Absolute Rate Change (bps)	Percentage Rate Change (%)
5/13/2005	3.03	1	−0.329
5/20/2005	3.02	1	−0.331
5/27/2005	3.03	1	0.331
6/3/2005	3.08	5	1.637
6/10/2005	3.12	4	1.290
6/17/2005	3.19	7	2.219
6/24/2005	3.25	6	1.863
7/1/2005	3.28	3	0.919
7/8/2005	3.29	1	0.304
7/15/2005	3.32	3	0.908
7/22/2005	3.38	6	1.791
7/29/2005	3.44	6	1.760
Average		3.98	1.690
Weekly Variance		6.84	1.780
Weekly Std. Dev.		2.62	1.330
Annualized Std. Dev.		18.86	9.620

Source: *Federal Reserve Statistical Release H.15.*

Annualizing the two weekly volatility measures:

$$Absolute\ rate\ change: 2.32 \times \sqrt{52} = 18.86 \text{ basis points}$$
$$Logarithm\ percentage\ change: 1.33 \times \sqrt{52} = 9.62\%$$

If we use daily or monthly data to compute the standard deviation, the following formulas would be used to annualize:

$$\text{Monthly standard deviation} \times \sqrt{12}$$
$$\text{Daily standard deviation} \times \sqrt{\text{Number of trading days in a year}}$$

Note that annualizing of the daily volatility requires that the number of trading days in a year be determined. Market practice varies with respect to the number of trading days in the year that should be used in the annualizing formula above. Typically, either 250 days or 260 days are used. For many traders who use daily rates, the difference in the calculated historical annual volatility could be significant depending on the number of trading days assumed in a year. Specifically, the difference in the factor that the daily standard deviation will be multiplied by depending on the number of days assumed in the year is

Days Assumed	Square Root of Days Assumed
250	15.81
260	16.12

KEY POINTS

- An interest-rate model is a probabilistic description of how interest rates can change over time. A stochastic differential equation is the most commonly used mathematical tool for describing interest-rate movements that incorporate statistical properties of interest-rate movements (drift, volatility, and mean reversion).

- In practice, one-factor models are used to describe the behavior of interest rates; they assume that short-term interest rates follow some statistical process and that other interest rates in the term structure are related to short-term rates.

- In a one-factor model, the SDE expresses the interest rate movement in terms of the change in the short rate over the time interval based on two components: (1) the expected direction of the change in the short rate (the drift term), and (2) a random process (the volatility term).

- Interest-rate models fall into two general categories: arbitrage-free models and equilibrium models.

- For arbitrage-free models, the analysis begins with the observed market price of benchmark instruments that are assumed to be fairly priced, and using those prices one derives a term structure that is consistent with observed market prices for the benchmark instruments. The model is referred to as arbitrage-free because it matches the observed prices of the benchmark instruments.

- Equilibrium models attempt to describe the dynamics of the term structure using fundamental economic variables that are assumed to affect the interest-rate process.

- In practice, because of the difficulties of implementing equilibrium models, arbitrage-free models are used.

- The classification of a model as normal or lognormal is based on the assumed dynamics of the random component of the SDE. Normal models assume that interest-rate volatility is independent of the level of rates and therefore admits the possibility of negative interest rates. The lognormal models assume that interest-rate volatility is proportional to the level of rates, and therefore negative interest rates are not possible.

- Empirical evidence reviewed in this chapter regarding the relationship between interest rate volatility and the level of rates suggests that the relationship is weak at interest rate levels below 10%. However, for rates exceeding 10%, there tends to be a positive relationship. This evidence suggests that in rate environments below 10%, a normal model would be more descriptive of the behavior of interest rates than the lognormal model.

- Empirical tests also suggest that the impact of negative interest rates on pricing is minimal, and therefore one should not be overly concerned that a normal model admits the possibility of negative interest rates.

- Interest-rate volatility can be estimated using historical volatility or implied volatility.

- Historical volatility is calculated from observed rates over some period of time. When calculating historical volatility using daily observations, differences in annualized volatility occur for a given set of observations because of the different assumptions that can be made about the number of trading days in a year. Implied volatility is obtained using an option pricing model and observed prices for option-type derivative instruments.

QUESTIONS

1. What is meant by an interest-rate model?

2. Explain the following three properties of an interest-rate model:
   a. drift
   b. volatility
   c. mean reversion

3. What is the commonly used mathematical tool for describing the movement of interest rates that can incorporate the properties of an interest-rate model?

4. a. Why is the most common interest-rate model used to describe the behavior of interest rates a one-factor model?
   b. What is the one-factor in a one-factor interest-rate model?

5. What is meant by
   a. a normal model of interest rates?
   b. a lognormal model of interest rates?

6. Explain the treatment of the dynamics of the volatility term for the following interest-rate models:
   a. Vasicek model
   b. Dothan model
   c. Cox-Ingersoll-Ross model

7. What is an arbitrage-free interest-rate model?

8. a. What are the general characteristics of the Ho-Lee arbitrage-free interest-rate model?
   b. How does the Ho-Lee arbitrage-free interest-rate model differ from the Hull-White arbitrage-free interest-rate model?

9. What is an equilibrium interest-rate model?

10. Explain why in practice arbitrage-free models are typically used rather than equilibrium models.

11. a. What is the empirical evidence on the relationship between volatility and the level of interest rates?
    b. Explain whether the historical evidence supports the use of a normal model or a lognormal model.

12. Comment on the following statement: "If an interest-rate model allows the possibility of negative interest rates, then it is not useful in practice."

13. a. What is meant by historical volatility?
    b. What is meant by implied volatility?

14. Suppose that the following weekly interest-rate volatility estimates are computed:

    absolute rate change = 3.85 basis points
    percentage rate change = 2.14%

    a. What is the annualized volatility for the absolute rate change?
    b. What is the annualized volatility for the percentage rate change?

17

Analysis of Bonds with Embedded Options

LEARNING OBJECTIVES

After reading this chapter, you will understand

- the drawbacks of the traditional yield spread analysis

- what static spread is and under what conditions it would differ from the traditional yield spread

- the disadvantages of a callable bond from the investor's perspective

- the yield to worst and the pitfalls of the traditional approach to valuing callable bonds

- the price–yield relationship for a callable bond

- negative convexity and when a callable bond may exhibit it

- how the value of a bond with an embedded option can be decomposed

- the lattice method and how it is used to value a bond with an embedded option

- how a binomial interest-rate tree is constructed to be consistent with the prices for the on-the-run issues of an issuer and a given volatility assumption

- what an option-adjusted spread is and how it is calculated using the binomial method

- the limitations of using modified duration and standard convexity as a measure of the price sensitivity of a bond with an embedded option

- the difference between effective duration and modified duration

- how effective duration and effective convexity are calculated using the binomial method

In earlier chapters, we discussed pricing, yield measures, and price volatility for bonds without options. In Chapter 2, we saw that the price of a bond was based on the present value of its cash flow. A bond with an embedded option is one in which either the issuer or the bondholder has the option to alter a bond's cash flows. In this chapter, we look at how to analyze bonds with embedded options. Because the most common type of option embedded in a bond is a call option, our primary focus is on callable bonds. We begin by looking at the limitations of traditional yield spread analysis. Although corporate bonds are used in our examples, the analysis presented in this chapter is equally applicable to agency securities and municipal securities. In the next chapter, we will focus on the analysis of mortgage-backed securities.

DRAWBACKS OF TRADITIONAL YIELD SPREAD ANALYSIS

Traditional analysis of the yield premium for a non-Treasury bond involves calculating the difference between the yield to maturity (or yield to call) of the bond in question and the yield to maturity of a comparable-maturity Treasury. The latter is obtained from the Treasury yield curve. For example, consider two 8.8% coupon 25-year bonds:

Issue	Price	Yield to Maturity (%)
Treasury	$96.6133	9.15
Corporate	87.0798	10.24

The yield spread for these two bonds as traditionally computed is 109 basis points (10.24% minus 9.15%). The drawbacks of this convention, however, are (1) the yield for both bonds fails to take into consideration the term structure of interest rates, and (2) in the case of callable and/or putable bonds, expected interest rate volatility may alter the cash flow of a bond. For now, let's focus only on the first problem: failure to incorporate the term structure of interest rates.

STATIC SPREAD: AN ALTERNATIVE TO YIELD SPREAD

In traditional yield spread analysis, an investor compares the yield to maturity of a bond with the yield to maturity of a similar maturity on-the-run Treasury security. This means that the yield to maturity of a 25-year zero-coupon corporate bond and an 8.8% coupon 25-year corporate coupon bond would both be compared to a benchmark 25-year Treasury security. Such a comparison makes little sense, because the cash flow characteristics of the two corporate bonds will not be the same as that of the benchmark Treasury.

The proper way to compare non-Treasury bonds of the same maturity but with different coupon rates is to compare them with a portfolio of Treasury securities that have the same cash flow. For example, consider the 8.8% 25-year corporate bond selling for $87.0798. The cash flow per $100 par value for this corporate bond, assuming that interest rates do not change (i.e., assuming static interest rates), is 49 six-month payments of $4.40 and a payment in 25 years (50 six-month periods) of $104.40. A portfolio that will replicate this cash flow would include 50 zero-coupon Treasury securities with maturities coinciding with the amount and timing of the cash flows of the corporate bond. The corporate bond's value is equal to the present value of all the cash flows.

The corporate bond's value, assuming that the cash flows are riskless, will equal the present value of the replicating portfolio of Treasury securities. In turn, these cash flows are valued at the Treasury spot rates. Exhibit 17-1 shows how to calculate the price of a risk-free 8.8%

Exhibit 17-1   Calculation of Price of a 25-Year 8.8% Coupon Bond Using Treasury Spot Rates

Period	Cash Flow	Treasury Spot Rate (%)	Present Value
1	4.4	7.00000	4.2512
2	4.4	7.04999	4.1055
3	4.4	7.09998	3.9628
4	4.4	7.12498	3.8251
5	4.4	7.13998	3.6922
6	4.4	7.16665	3.5622
7	4.4	7.19997	3.4351
8	4.4	7.26240	3.3077
9	4.4	7.33315	3.1820
10	4.4	7.38977	3.0611
11	4.4	7.44517	2.9434
12	4.4	7.49135	2.8302
13	4.4	7.53810	2.7200
14	4.4	7.57819	2.6141
15	4.4	7.61959	2.5112
16	4.4	7.66205	2.4111
17	4.4	7.70538	2.3139
18	4.4	7.74391	2.2207
19	4.4	7.78888	2.1291
20	4.4	7.83434	2.0404
21	4.4	8.22300	1.8879
22	4.4	8.33333	1.7923
23	4.4	8.40000	1.7080
24	4.4	8.50000	1.6204
25	4.4	8.54230	1.5465
26	4.4	8.72345	1.4500
27	4.4	8.90000	1.3581
28	4.4	9.00000	1.2829
29	4.4	9.01450	1.2252
30	4.4	9.23000	1.1367
31	4.4	9.39000	1.0611
32	4.4	9.44840	1.0045
33	4.4	9.50000	0.9514
34	4.4	9.50000	0.9083
35	4.4	9.50000	0.8671
36	4.4	9.50000	0.8278
37	4.4	9.55000	0.7833

(Continued)

Exhibit 17-1 Calculation of Price of a 25-Year 8.8% Coupon Bond Using Treasury Spot Rates (Continued)

Period	Cash Flow	Treasury Spot Rate (%)	Present Value
38	4.4	9.56000	0.7462
39	4.4	9.58000	0.7095
40	4.4	9.58000	0.6771
41	4.4	9.60000	0.6436
42	4.4	9.70000	0.6020
43	4.4	9.80000	0.5625
44	4.4	9.90000	0.5251
45	4.4	10.00000	0.4897
46	4.4	10.10000	0.4563
47	4.4	10.30000	0.4154
48	4.4	10.50000	0.3774
49	4.4	10.60000	0.3503
50	104.4	10.80000	7.5278
Theoretical price			96.6134

25-year bond assuming the Treasury spot rate curve shown in the exhibit. The price would be $96.6134. The corporate bond's price is $87.0798, less than the package of zero-coupon Treasury securities, because investors in fact require a yield premium for the risk associated with holding a corporate bond rather than a riskless package of Treasury securities.

The **static spread**, also referred to as the **zero-volatility spread**, is a measure of the spread that the investor would realize over the entire Treasury spot rate curve if the bond is held to maturity. It is not a spread off one point on the Treasury yield curve, as is the traditional yield spread. The static spread is calculated as the spread that will make the present value of the cash flows from the corporate bond, when discounted at the Treasury spot rate plus the spread, equal to the corporate bond's price. A trial-and-error procedure is required to determine the static spread.

To illustrate how this is done, let's use the corporate bond in the first illustration. Select a spread, say, 100 basis points. To each Treasury spot rate shown in the third column in Exhibit 17-2, 100 basis points is added. So, for example, the 14-year (period 28) spot rate is 10% (9% plus 1%). The spot rate plus 100 basis points is then used to calculate the present value of $88.5474. Because the present value is not equal to the corporate bond's price ($87.0796), the static spread is not 100 basis points. If a spread of 110 basis points is tried, it can be seen from the next-to-last column of Exhibit 17-2 that the present value is $87.8029; again, because this is not equal to the corporate bond's price, 110 basis points is not the static spread. The last column of Exhibit 17-2 shows the present value when a 120-basis-point spread is tried. The present value is equal to the corporate bond price. Therefore, 120 basis points is the static spread, compared to the traditional yield spread of 109 basis points.

Exhibit 17-3 shows the static spread and the traditional yield spread for bonds with various maturities and prices, assuming the Treasury spot rates shown in Exhibit 17-1.

Exhibit 17-2 **Calculation of the Static Spread for a 25-Year 8.8% Coupon Corporate Bond**

Period	Cash Flow	Treasury Spot Rate (%)	Present Value If Spread Used Is: 100 BP	110 BP	120 BP
1	4.4	7.00000	4.2308	4.2287	4.2267
2	4.4	7.04999	4.0661	4.0622	4.0583
3	4.4	7.09998	3.9059	3.9003	3.8947
4	4.4	7.12498	3.7521	3.7449	3.7377
5	4.4	7.13998	3.6043	3.5957	3.5871
6	4.4	7.16665	3.4607	3.4508	3.4408
7	4.4	7.19997	3.3212	3.3101	3.2990
8	4.4	7.26240	3.1828	3.1706	3.1584
9	4.4	7.33315	3.0472	3.0340	3.0210
10	4.4	7.38977	2.9174	2.9034	2.8895
11	4.4	7.44517	2.7917	2.7770	2.7624
12	4.4	7.49135	2.6715	2.6562	2.6409
13	4.4	7.53810	2.5552	2.5394	2.5236
14	4.4	7.57819	2.4440	2.4277	2.4115
15	4.4	7.61959	2.3366	2.3198	2.3032
16	4.4	7.66205	2.2327	2.2157	2.1988
17	4.4	7.70538	2.1325	2.1152	2.0981
18	4.4	7.74391	2.0368	2.0193	2.0020
19	4.4	7.78888	1.9435	1.9259	1.9085
20	4.4	7.83434	1.8536	1.8359	1.8184
21	4.4	8.22300	1.7072	1.6902	1.6733
22	4.4	8.33333	1.6131	1.5963	1.5796
23	4.4	8.40000	1.5300	1.5132	1.4967
24	4.4	8.50000	1.4446	1.4282	1.4119
25	4.4	8.54230	1.3722	1.3559	1.3398
26	4.4	8.72345	1.2806	1.2648	1.2492
27	4.4	8.90000	1.1938	1.1785	1.1635
28	4.4	9.00000	1.1224	1.1075	1.0929
29	4.4	9.01450	1.0668	1.0522	1.0378
30	4.4	9.23000	0.9852	0.9712	0.9575
31	4.4	9.39000	0.9154	0.9020	0.8888
32	4.4	9.44840	0.8625	0.8495	0.8367
33	4.4	9.50000	0.8131	0.8004	0.7880
34	4.4	9.50000	0.7725	0.7601	0.7480
35	4.4	9.50000	0.7340	0.7219	0.7100
36	4.4	9.50000	0.6974	0.6855	0.6739
37	4.4	9.55000	0.6568	0.6453	0.6341
38	4.4	9.56000	0.6227	0.6116	0.6007
39	4.4	9.58000	0.5893	0.5785	0.5679
40	4.4	9.58000	0.5597	0.5492	0.5389

(*Continued*)

Exhibit 17-2 Calculation of the Static Spread for a 25-Year 8.8% Coupon Corporate Bond (Continued)

Period	Cash Flow	Treasury Spot Rate (%)	Present Value If Spread Used Is:		
			100 BP	110 BP	120 BP
41	4.4	9.60000	0.5295	0.5193	0.5093
42	4.4	9.70000	0.4929	0.4832	0.4737
43	4.4	9.80000	0.4585	0.4492	0.4401
44	4.4	9.90000	0.4260	0.4172	0.4086
45	4.4	10.00000	0.3955	0.3871	0.3789
46	4.4	10.10000	0.3668	0.3588	0.3511
47	4.4	10.30000	0.3323	0.3250	0.3179
48	4.4	10.50000	0.3006	0.2939	0.2873
49	4.4	10.60000	0.2778	0.2714	0.2652
50	104.4	10.80000	5.9416	5.8030	5.6677
Total present value			88.5474	87.8029	87.0796

Exhibit 17-3 Comparison of Traditional Yield Spread and Static Spread for Various Bonds[a]

Bond	Price	Yield to Maturity (%)	Spread (basis points)		
			Traditional	Static	Difference
25-year 8.8% Coupon Bond					
Treasury	96.6133	9.15	—	—	—
A	88.5473	10.06	91	100	9
B	87.8031	10.15	100	110	10
C	87.0798	10.24	109	120	11
15-year 8.8% Coupon Bond					
Treasury	101.9603	8.57	—	—	—
D	94.1928	9.54	97	100	3
E	93.4639	9.63	106	110	4
F	92.7433	9.73	116	120	4
10-year 8.8% Coupon Bond					
Treasury	107.4906	7.71	—	—	—
G	100.6137	8.71	100	100	0
H	99.9585	8.81	110	110	0
I	99.3088	8.91	120	120	0
5-year 8.8% Coupon Bond					
Treasury	105.9555	7.36	—	—	—
J	101.7919	8.35	99	100	1
K	101.3867	8.45	109	110	1
L	100.9836	8.55	119	120	1

[a]Assumes Treasury spot rate curve given in Exhibit 17-1.

Notice that the shorter the maturity of the bond, the less the static spread will differ from the traditional yield spread. The magnitude of the difference between the traditional yield spread and the static spread also depends on the shape of the yield curve. The steeper the yield curve, the more the difference for a given coupon and maturity.

Another reason for the small differences in Exhibit 17-3 is that the corporate bond makes a bullet payment at maturity. The difference between the traditional yield spread and the static spread will be considerably greater for sinking fund bonds and mortgage-backed securities in a steep yield curve environment.

CALLABLE BONDS AND THEIR INVESTMENT CHARACTERISTICS

Now that we know the problems with the traditional yield spread analysis, let's introduce another complexity: the callability of an issue. We begin by examining the characteristics of a callable bond. The holder of a callable bond has given the issuer the right to call the issue prior to the expiration date. The presence of a call option results in two disadvantages to the bondholder.

First, callable bonds expose bondholders to reinvestment risk, because an issuer will call a bond when the yield on bonds in the market is lower than the issue's coupon rate. For example, if the coupon rate on a callable corporate bond is 13% and prevailing market yields are 7%, the issuer will find it economical to call the 13% issue and refund it with a 7% issue. From the investor's perspective, the proceeds received will have to be reinvested at a lower interest rate.

Second, as we explain later in this chapter, the price appreciation potential for a callable bond in a declining interest-rate environment is limited. This is because the market will increasingly expect the bond to be redeemed at the call price as interest rates fall. This phenomenon for a callable bond is referred to as **price compression**.

Because of the disadvantages associated with callable bonds, these instruments often feature a period of call protection, an initial period when bonds may not be called. Still, given both price compression and reinvestment risk, why would any investor want to own a callable bond? If the investor receives sufficient potential compensation in the form of a higher potential yield, an investor would be willing to accept call risk.

Traditional Valuation Methodology for Callable Bonds

When a bond is callable, the practice has been to calculate a **yield to worst**. As explained in Chapter 3, the yield to worst is the smallest of the yield to maturity and the yield to call for all possible call dates. The yield to worst is the yield that the traditional approach has investors believing should be used in relative value analysis of callable bonds.

We explained in Chapter 3 the limitations of the **yield to call** as a measure of the potential return of a security. The yield to call does consider all three sources of potential return from owning a bond. However, as in the case of the yield to maturity, it assumes that all cash flows can be reinvested at the computed yield—in this case, the yield to call—until the assumed call date. Moreover, the yield to call assumes that (1) the investor will hold the bond to the assumed call date, and (2) the issuer will call the bond on that date.

Often, these underlying assumptions about the yield to call are unrealistic because they do not take into account how an investor will reinvest the proceeds if the issue is called. For example, consider two bonds, M and N. Suppose that the yield to maturity for bond M, a five-year noncallable bond, is 10%, and the yield to call for bond N is 10.5% assuming that the bond will be called in three years. Which bond is better for an investor with a five-year investment horizon? It is not possible to tell for the yields cited. If the investor intends to hold the bond for five years and the issuer calls the bond after three years, the total dollars that will be available at the end of five years will depend on the interest rate that can be earned from investing funds from the call date to the end of the investment horizon.

Price–Yield Relationship for a Callable Bond

As explained in Chapter 4, the price–yield relationship for an option-free bond is convex. Exhibit 17-4 shows the price–yield relationship for both a noncallable bond and the same bond if it is callable. The convex curve $a-a'$ is the price–yield relationship for the noncallable (option-free) bond. The unusual shaped curve denoted by $a-b$ is the price–yield relationship for the callable bond.

The reason for the shape of the price–yield relationship for the callable bond is as follows. When the prevailing market yield for comparable bonds is higher than the coupon interest on the bond, it is unlikely that the issuer will call the bond. For example, if the coupon rate on a bond is 8% and the prevailing yield on comparable bonds is 16%, it is highly improbable that the issuer will call an 8% coupon bond so that it can issue a 16% coupon bond. The bond is unlikely to be called, so the callable bond will have the same convex price–yield relationship as a noncallable bond when yields are greater than y^*. However, even when the coupon rate is just below the market yield, investors may not pay the same price for the callable bond than they would had it been noncallable because there is still the chance the market yield may drop further, making it beneficial for the issuer to call the bond.

As yields in the market decline, the likelihood that yields will decline further so that the issuer will benefit from calling the bond increases. The exact yield level at which investors begin to view the issue likely to be called may not be known, but we do know that there is some level. In Exhibit 17-4, at yield levels below y^*, the price–yield relationship for the callable bond departs from the price–yield relationship for the noncallable bond. Consider

Exhibit 17-4 **Price–Yield Relationship for a Noncallable and a Callable Bond**

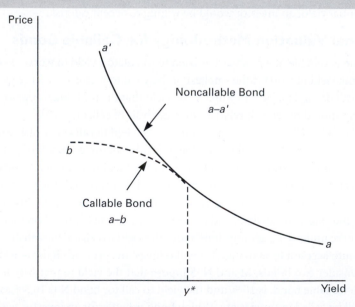

Exhibit 17-5   Price Volatility Implications of Positive and Negative Convexity

	Absolute Value of Percentage Price Change	
Change in Interest Rates	Positive Convexity	Negative Convexity
−100 basis points	X%	Less than Y%
+100 basis points	Less than X%	Y%

a bond that is callable at 104. If market yield would price a comparable noncallable bond at 109, rational investors would not pay 109 for the callable bond. If they did and the bond was called, investors would receive 104 (the call price) for a bond they purchased for 109.

Notice that for a range of yields below y^*, there is price compression—that is, there is limited price appreciation as yields decline. The portion of the callable bond price–yield relationship below y^* is said to be negatively convex.

Negative convexity means that the price appreciation will be less than the price depreciation for a large change in yield of a given number of basis points. For a bond that is option-free and exhibits positive convexity, the price appreciation will be greater than the price depreciation for a large change in yield. The price changes resulting from bonds exhibiting positive convexity and negative convexity are shown in Exhibit 17-5.

It is important to understand that a bond can still trade above its call price even if it is highly likely to be called. For example, consider a callable bond with a 10-year 13% coupon rate that is callable in one year at a call price of 104. Suppose that the yield on 10-year bonds is 6% and that the yield on one-year bonds is 5%. In a 6% interest rate environment for 10-year bonds, investors will expect that the issue will be called in one year. Thus, investors will treat this issue as if it is a one-year bond and price it accordingly. The price must reflect the fact that the investor will receive a 13% coupon rate for one year. The price of this bond would be the present value of the two cash flows, which are (1) $6.50 (per $100 of par value) of coupon interest six months from now, and (2) $6.50 coupon interest plus the call price of $104 one year from now. Discounting the two cash flows at the 5% prevailing market yield (2.5% every six months) for one-year bonds, the price is

$$\frac{\$6.5}{1.025} + \frac{\$110.5}{(1.025)^2} = \$111.52$$

The price is greater than the call price. Consequently, an investor will be willing to pay a higher price than the call price to purchase this bond.

COMPONENTS OF A BOND WITH AN EMBEDDED OPTION

To develop a framework for analyzing a bond with an embedded option, it is necessary to decompose a bond into its component parts. A **callable bond** is a bond in which the bondholder has sold the issuer an option (more specifically, a call option) that allows the issuer to repurchase the contractual cash flows of the bond from the time the bond is first callable until the maturity date.

Consider the following two bonds: (1) a callable bond with an 8% coupon, 20 years to maturity, and callable in five years at 104, and (2) a 10-year 9% coupon bond callable immediately at par. For the first bond, the bondholder owns a five-year noncallable bond and has sold a call option granting the issuer the right to call away from the bondholder 15 years of cash flows five years from now for a price of 104. The investor who owns the second bond has a 10-year noncallable bond and has sold a call option granting the issuer the right to call immediately the entire 10-year contractual cash flows, or any cash flows remaining at the time the issue is called, for 100.

Effectively, the owner of a callable bond is entering into two separate transactions. First, she buys a noncallable bond from the issuer for which she pays some price. Then, she sells the issuer a call option for which she receives the option price.

In terms of price, a callable bond is, therefore, equal to the price of the two components parts; that is,

$$\text{callable bond price} = \text{noncallable bond price} - \text{call option price}$$

The reason the call option price is subtracted from the price of the noncallable bond is that when the bondholder sells a call option, she receives the option price. Graphically, this can be seen in Exhibit 17-6. The difference between the price of the noncallable bond and the callable bond at any given yield is the price of the embedded call option.[1]

Exhibit 17-6 Decomposition of Price of a Callable Bond

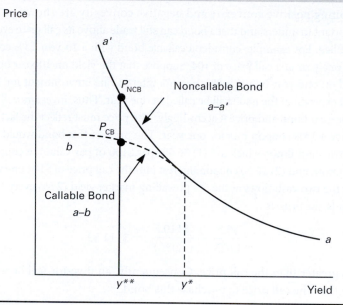

Note: At y^{**} yield level: P_{NCB} = noncallable bond price
P_{CB} = callable bond price
$P_{NCB} - P_{CB}$ = call option price

---

[1] Actually, the position is more complicated than we have described. The issuer may be entitled to call the bond at the first call date and anytime thereafter, or at the first call date and any subsequent coupon anniversary. Thus, the investor has effectively sold an American-type call option to the issuer, but the call price may vary with the date the call option is exercised. This is because the call schedule for a bond may have a different call price depending on the call date. Moreover, the underlying bond for the call option is the remaining coupon payments that would have been made by the issuer had the bond not been called. For exposition purposes, it is easier to understand the principles associated with the investment characteristics of callable corporate bonds by describing the investor's position as a noncallable bond and a call option.

The same logic applies to **putable bonds**. In the case of a putable bond, the bond-holder has the right to sell the bond to the issuer at a designated price and time. A putable bond can be broken into two separate transactions. First, the investor buys a noncallable bond. Second, the investor buys an option from the issuer that allows the investor to sell the bond to the issuer. The price of a putable bond is then

$$\text{putable bond price} = \text{nonputable bond price} + \text{put option price}$$

VALUATION MODEL[2]

Thus far, we described a way to think conceptually about bonds with embedded options. More specifically, the value of a callable bond is equal to the value of a comparable noncallable bond minus the value of the call option. In this section, a model for valuing bonds with embedded options is presented.

The valuation principles that we have discussed so far in this book are used here. Specifically, we saw two important things in Chapter 5. First, it is inappropriate to use a single rate to discount all the cash flows of a bond. Second, the correct rate to use to discount each cash flow is the theoretical spot rate. This is equivalent to discounting at a series of forward rates.

What we have to add to the valuation process is how interest-rate volatility affects the value of a bond through its effects on the embedded options. There are three models depending on the structure of the security to be analyzed. The first is a model for a bond that is not a mortgage-backed security or asset-backed security that can be exercised at more than one time over its life. An example is a 10-year corporate bond that is callable beginning three years from now on every coupon anniversary date. It is the valuation model for such a bond that is discussed in this section. The second case is a bond with an embedded option where the option can be exercised only once. An example is a callable bond that can be exercised only on a specific date. Bonds with this characteristic are issued by the government-sponsored enterprises Fannie Mae and Freddie Mac. We will discuss the approach to valuing such bonds later in this chapter. The third model is for a mortgage-backed security or certain types of asset-backed securities. The model used, the Monte Carlo simulation, is explained and illustrated in the next chapter.

We begin with a review of the valuation of bonds without embedded options.

Valuation of Option-Free Bonds

In Chapter 5, we said that the price of an option-free bond is the present value of the cash flows discounted at the spot rates. To illustrate this, let's use the following hypothetical yield curve:

Maturity (years)	Yield to Maturity (%)	Market Value
1	3.50	100
2	4.00	100
3	4.50	100

---

[2] The valuation model described in this section was first introduced in Andrew J. Kalotay, George O. Williams, and Frank J. Fabozzi, "A Model for the Valuation of Bonds and Embedded Options," *Financial Analysts Journal*, May–June 1993, pp. 35–46.

We will be simplifying the illustration by assuming annual-pay bonds. Using the bootstrapping methodology described in Chapter 5, the spot rates and the one-year forward rates can be obtained.

Year	Spot Rate (%)	One-Year Forward Rate (%)
1	3.500	3.500
2	4.010	4.523
3	4.541	5.580

Now, consider an option-free bond with three years remaining to maturity and a coupon rate of 5.25%. The price of this bond can be calculated in one of two ways, both producing the same result. First, the coupon payments can be discounted at the zero-coupon rates:

$$\frac{\$5.25}{(1.035)} + \frac{\$5.25}{(1.0401)^2} + \frac{\$100 + \$5.25}{(1.04541)^3} = \$102.075$$

The second way is to discount by the one-year forward rates:

$$\frac{\$5.25}{(1.035)} + \frac{\$5.25}{(1.035)(1.04523)} + \frac{\$100 + \$5.25}{(1.035)(1.04523)(1.05580)} = \$102.075$$

Introducing Interest-Rate Volatility

When we allow for embedded options, consideration must be given to interest-rate volatility. This can be done by introducing an **interest-rate tree**, also referred to as an **interest-rate lattice**. This tree is nothing more than a graphical depiction of the one-period forward rates over time based on some assumed interest-rate model and interest-rate volatility.

Interest-Rate Model

As explained in the previous chapter, an **interest-rate model** is a probabilistic description of how interest rates can change over the life of a financial instrument being evaluated. An interest-rate model does this by making an assumption about the relationship between (1) the level of short-term interest rates, and (2) interest-rate volatility. Standard deviation of interest rates is used as the measure of interest-rate volatility.

The interest-rate models commonly used are arbitrage-free models based on how short-term interest rates can evolve (i.e., change) over time. As explained in Chapter 16, models based solely on movements in the short-term interest rate are referred to as one-factor models

Interest-Rate Lattice

Exhibit 17-7 shows an example of the most basic type of interest-rate lattice or tree, a **binomial interest-rate tree**. The corresponding model is referred to as the **binomial model**. In this model, it is assumed that interest rates can realize one of two possible rates in the next period. In the valuation model we present in this chapter, we will use the binomial model. Valuation models that assume that interest rates can take on three possible rates in the next period are called **trinomial models**. More complex models exist that assume that more than three possible rates in the next period can be realized.

Exhibit 17-7   Three-Year Binomial Interest-Rate Tree

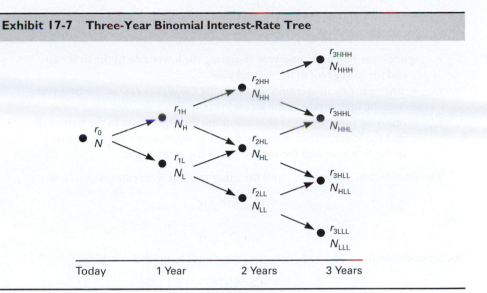

| Today | 1 Year | 2 Years | 3 Years |

Returning to the binomial interest-rate tree in Exhibit 17-7, each node (bold circle) represents a time period that is equal to one year from the node to its left. Each node is labeled with an N, representing **node**, and a subscript that indicates the path that one-year forward rates took to get to that node. H represents the *higher* of the two forward rates and L the *lower* of the two forward rates from the preceding year. For example, node N_{HH} means that to get to that node the following path for one-year rates occurred: The one-year rate realized is the higher of the two rates in the first year and then the higher of the one-year rates in the second year.[3]

Look first at the point denoted N in Exhibit 17-7. This is the root of the tree and is nothing more than the current one-year rate, or equivalently, the one-year forward rate, which we denote by r_0. In the model, a one-factor interest-rate model is assumed. More specifically, it is assumed that the one-year forward rate can evolve over time based on a random process called a **lognormal random walk** with a certain volatility.

We will use the following notation to describe the tree in the first year. Let

σ = assumed volatility of the one-year forward rate
$r_{1,L}$ = the lower one-year rate one year from now
$r_{1,H}$ = the higher one-year rate one year from now

The relationship between $r_{1,L}$ and $r_{1,H}$ is as follows:

$$r_{1,H} = r_{1,L}(e^{2\sigma})$$

where e is the base of the natural logarithm 2.71828. For example, suppose that $r_{1,L}$ is 4.074% and σ is 10% per year; then

$$r_{1,H} = 4.074\%(e^{2\times0.10}) = 4.976\%$$

---

[3] Note that N_{HL} is equivalent to N_{LH} in the second year, and that in the third year, N_{HHL} is equivalent to N_{HLH} and N_{LHH} and that N_{HLL} is equivalent to N_{LLH}. We have simply selected one label for a node rather than clutter up the figure with unnecessary information.

In the second year, there are three possible values for the one-year rate, which we will denote as follows:

$r_{2,LL}$ = one-year rate in second year assuming the lower rate in the first year and the lower rate in the second year

$r_{2,HH}$ = one-year rate in second year assuming the higher rate in the first year and the higher rate in the second year

$r_{2,HL}$ = one-year rate in second year assuming the higher rate in the first year and the lower rate in the second year or equivalently the lower rate in the first year and the higher rate in the second year

The relationship between $r_{2,LL}$ and the other two one-year rates is as follows:

$$r_{2,HH} = r_{2,LL}(e^{4\sigma})$$

and

$$r_{2,HL} = r_{2,LL}(e^{2\sigma})$$

So, for example, if $r_{2,LL}$ is 4.53%, then assuming once again that σ is 10%,

$$r_{2,HH} = 4.53\%(e^{4\times0.10}) = 6.757\%$$

and

$$r_{2,HL} = 4.53\%(e^{2\times0.10}) = 5.532\%$$

Exhibit 17-7 shows the notation for the binomial interest-rate tree in the third year. We can simplify the notation by letting r_t be the lower one-year forward rate t years from now because all the other forward rates t years from now depend on that rate. Exhibit 17-8 shows the interest-rate tree using this simplified notation.

Before we go on to show how to use this binomial interest-rate tree to value bonds, let's focus on two issues here. First, what does the volatility parameter σ in the expression $e^{2\sigma}$ represent? Second, how do we find the value of the bond at each node?

Exhibit 17-8   Three-Year Binomial Interest-Rate Tree with One-Year Forward Rates

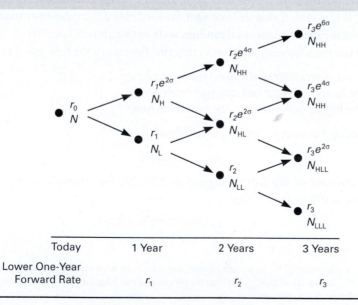

Volatility and the Standard Deviation

It can be shown that the standard deviation of the one-year forward rate is equal to $r_0\sigma$.[4] The standard deviation is a statistical measure of volatility. For now, it is important to see that the process that we assumed generates the binomial interest-rate tree (or equivalently, the forward rates) implies that volatility is measured relative to the current level of rates. For example, if σ is 10% and the one-year rate (r_0) is 4%, the standard deviation of the one-year forward rate is 4% × 10% = 0.4% or 40 basis points. However, if the current one-year rate is 12%, the standard deviation of the one-year forward rate would be 12% × 10% or 120 basis points.

Determining the Value at a Node

The answer to the second question about how we find the value of the bond at a node is as follows. First, calculate the bond's value at the two nodes to the right of the node where we want to obtain the bond's value. For example, in Exhibit 17-8, suppose that we want to determine the bond's value at node N_H. The bond's value at node N_{HH} and N_{HL} must be determined. Hold aside for now how we get these two values because, as we will see, the process involves starting from the last year in the tree and working backward to get the final solution we want, so these two values will be known.

Effectively what we are saying is that if we are at some node, the value at that node will depend on the future cash flows. In turn, the future cash flows depend on (1) the bond's value one year from now, and (2) the coupon payment one year from now. The latter is known. The former depends on whether the one-year rate is the higher or lower rate. The bond's value depending on whether the rate is the higher or lower rate is reported at the two nodes to the right of the node that is the focus of our attention. So the cash flow at a node will be either (1) the bond's value if the short rate is the higher rate plus the coupon payment, or (2) the bond's value if the short rate is the lower rate plus the coupon payment. For example, suppose that we are interested in the bond's value at N_H. The cash flow will be either the bond's value at N_{HH} plus the coupon payment or the bond's value at N_{HL} plus the coupon payment.

To get the bond's value at a node we follow the fundamental rule for valuation: The bond's value is the present value of the expected cash flows. The appropriate discount rate to use is the one-year forward rate at the node. Now there are two present values in this case: the present value if the one-year rate is the higher rate and the value if it is the lower rate. Because it is assumed that the probability of both outcomes is equal, an average of the two present values is computed. This is illustrated in Exhibit 17-9 for any node assuming that the one-year forward rate is r_* at the node where the valuation is sought and letting

V_H = the bond's value for the higher one-year rate
V_L = the bond's value for the lower one-year rate
C = coupon payment

---

[4] This can be seen by noting that $e^{2\sigma} \approx 1 + 2\sigma$. Then the standard deviation of one-period forward rates is

$$\frac{re^{2\sigma} - r}{2} \approx \frac{r + 2\sigma - r}{2} = \sigma r$$

Exhibit 17-9 Calculating a Value at a Node

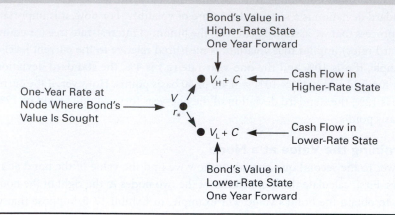

Using our notation, the cash flow at a node is either

$$V_H + C \text{ for the higher one-year rate}$$

or

$$V_L + C \text{ for the lower one-year rate}$$

The present value of these two cash flows using the one-year rate at the node, r_*, is

$$\frac{V_H + C}{1 + r_*} \text{ present value for the higher one-year rate}$$

$$\frac{V_L + C}{1 + r_*} \text{ present value for the lower one-year rate}$$

Then the value of the bond at the node is found as follows:

$$\text{value at a node} = \frac{1}{2}\left[\frac{V_H + C}{1 + r_*} + \frac{V_L + C}{1 + r_*}\right]$$

Constructing the Binomial Interest-Rate Tree

To see how to construct the binomial interest-rate tree, let's use the assumed current on-the-run yields that we used earlier. We will assume that volatility, σ, is 10% and construct a two-year model using the two-year bond with a coupon rate of 4%.

Exhibit 17-10 shows a more detailed binomial interest-rate tree because at each node the cash flow is shown. We'll see how all the values reported in the exhibit are obtained. The root rate for the tree, r_0, is simply the current one-year rate, 3.5%.

In the first year, there are two possible one-year rates, the higher rate and the lower rate. What we want to find are the two forward rates that will be consistent with the volatility assumption, the process that is assumed to generate the forward rates, and the observed market value of the bond. There is no simple formula for this. It must be found by an iterative process (i.e., trial and error). The steps are described and illustrated next.

Step 1: Select a value for r_1. Recall that r_1 is the lower one-year forward rate one year from now. In this first trial, we *arbitrarily* selected a value of 4.5%.

Exhibit 17-10   Finding the One-Year Forward Rates for Year 1 Using the Two-Year 4% On-the-Run: First Trial

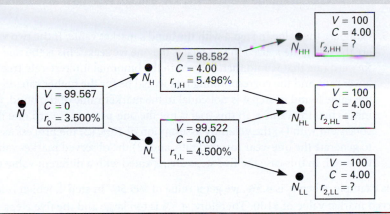

Step 2: Determine the corresponding value for the higher one-year forward rate. As explained earlier, this rate is related to the lower one-year forward rate as follows: $r_1e^{2\sigma}$. Because r_1 is 4.5%, the higher one-year forward rate is 5.496%($= 4.5\% \ e^{2\times0.10}$). This value is reported in Exhibit 17-10 at node N_H.

Step 3: Compute the bond's value one year from now. This value is determined as follows:

   3a. The bond's value two years from now must be determined. In our example this is simple. We are using a two-year bond, so the bond's value is its maturity value ($100) plus its final coupon payment ($4). Thus, it is $104.

   3b. Calculate the present value of the bond's value found in 3a using the higher rate. In our example the appropriate discount rate is the one-year higher forward rate, 5.496%. The present value is $98.582 (= $104/1.05496). This is the value of V_H that we referred to earlier.

   3c. Calculate the present value of the bond's value found in 3a using the lower rate. The discount rate used is then the lower one-year forward rate, 4.5%. The value is $99.522(= $104/1.045) and is the value of V_L.

   3d. Add the coupon to V_H and V_L to get the cash flow at N_H and N_L, respectively. In our example we have $102.582 for the higher rate and $103.522 for the lower rate.

   3e. Calculate the present value of the two values using the one-year forward rate using r_*. At this point in the valuation, r_* is the root rate, 3.50%. Therefore,

$$\frac{V_H + C}{1 + r_*} = \frac{\$102.582}{1.035} = \$99.113$$

and

$$\frac{V_L + C}{1 + r_*} = \frac{\$103.522}{1.035} = \$100.021$$

Step 4: Calculate the average present value of the two cash flows in step 3. This is the value we referred to earlier as

$$\text{value at a node} = \frac{1}{2}\left[\frac{V_H + C}{1 + r_*} + \frac{V_L + C}{1 + r_*}\right]$$

In our example, we have

$$\text{value at a node} = \frac{1}{2}(\$99.113 + \$100.021) = \$99.567$$

Step 5: Compare the value in step 4 with the bond's market value. If the two values are the same, the r_1 used in this trial is the one we seek. This is the one-year forward rate that would then be used in the binomial interest-rate tree for the lower rate, and the corresponding rate would be for the higher rate. If, instead, the value found in step 4 is not equal to the market value of the bond, this means that the value r_1 in this trial is not the one-period forward rate that is consistent with (1) the volatility assumption of 10%, (2) the process assumed to generate the one-year forward rate, and (3) the observed market value of the bond. In this case the five steps are repeated with a different value for r_1.

In this example, when r_1 is 4.5%, we get a value of \$99.567 in step 4, which is less than the observed market value of \$100. Therefore, 4.5% is too large and the five steps must be repeated, trying a lower value for r_1.

Let's jump right to the correct value for r_1 in this example and rework steps 1 through 5. This occurs when r_1 is 4.074%. The corresponding binomial interest-rate tree is shown in Exhibit 17-11.

Step 1: In this trial, we select a value of 4.074% for r_1.
Step 2: The corresponding value for the higher one-year forward rate is
4.976% ($4.074\% \ e^{2\times0.10}$).
Step 3: The bond's value one year from now is determined as follows:
    3a. The bond's value two years from now is \$104, just as in the first trial.
    3b. The present value of the bond's value found in 3a for the higher rate, V_H, is \$99.070 (= \$104/1.04976).
    3c. The present value of the bond's value found in 3a for the lower rate, V_L, is \$99.929 (= \$104/1.04074).
    3d. Adding the coupon to V_H and V_L, we get \$103.071 as the cash flow for the higher rate and \$103.929 as the cash flow for the lower rate.

Exhibit 17-11   One-Year Forward Rates for Year 1 Using the Two-Year 4% On-the-Run Issue

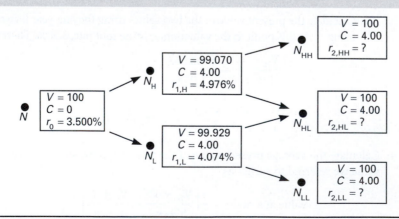

3e. The present value of the two cash flows using the one-year forward rate at the node to the left, 3.5%, gives

$$\frac{V_H + C}{1 + r_*} = \frac{\$103.071}{1.035} = \$99.586$$

and

$$\frac{V_L + C}{1 + r_*} = \frac{\$103.929}{1.035} = \$100.414$$

Step 4: The average present value is $100, which is the value at the node.
Step 5: Because the average present value is equal to the observed market value of $100, r_1 is 4.074%.

We are not done. Suppose that we want to "grow" this tree for one more year—that is, we want to determine r_2. Now we will use the three-year on-the-run issue, the 4.5% coupon bond, to get r_2. The same five steps are used in an iterative process to find the one-year forward rate two years from now. But now our objective is as follows: Find the value for r_2 that (1) will produce an average present value at node N_H equal to the bond value at that node ($98.074) and (2) will also produce an average present value at node N_L equal to the bond value at that node ($99.926). When this value is found, we know that given the forward rate we found for r_1, the bond's value at the root—the value of ultimate interest to us—will be $100, the observed market price.

It can be demonstrated that the value of r_2 that will produce that desired outcome is 4.530%. Exhibit 17-12 shows the completed binomial interest-rate tree. It is this tree that we can use to value any option-free bond or bond with embedded options.

The binomial interest-rate tree constructed is said to be an **arbitrage-free tree**. It is so named because it fairly prices the on-the-run issues.

Application to Valuing an Option-Free Bond

To illustrate how to use the binomial interest-rate tree, consider a 5.25% corporate bond that has two years remaining to maturity and is option-free. Also assume that the issuer's on-the-run yield curve is the one given earlier, and hence the appropriate binomial interest-rate

Exhibit 17-12   One-Year Forward Rates for Year 2 Using the Three-Year 4.5% On-the-Run Issue

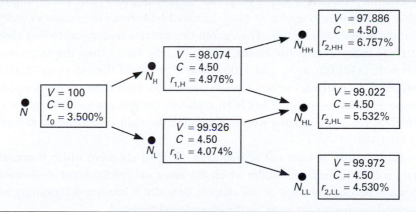

Exhibit 17-13 Valuing an Option-Free Corporate Bond with Three Years to Maturity and a Coupon Rate of 5.25%

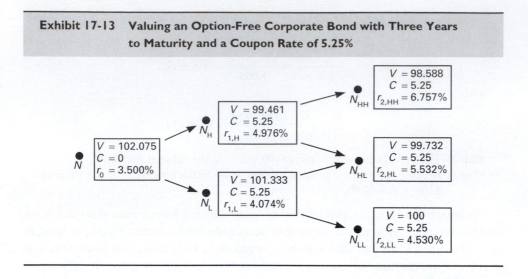

tree is the one in Exhibit 17-12. Exhibit 17-13 shows the various values in the discounting process and produces a bond value of $102.075.

It is important to note that this value is identical to the bond value found earlier when we discounted at either the zero-coupon rates or the one-year forward rates. We should expect to find this result because our bond is option free. This clearly demonstrates that the valuation model is consistent with the standard valuation model for an option-free bond.

Valuing a Callable Corporate Bond

Now, we demonstrate how the binomial interest-rate tree can be applied to value a callable corporate bond. The valuation process proceeds in the same fashion as in the case of an option-free bond but with one exception: When the call option may be exercised by the issuer, the bond value at a node must be changed to reflect the lesser of its value if it is not called (i.e., the value obtained by applying the recursive valuation formula described previously) and the call price.

For example, consider a 5.25% corporate bond with three years remaining to maturity that is callable in one year at $100. Exhibit 17-14 shows the values at each node of the binomial interest-rate tree. The discounting process is identical to that shown in Exhibit 17-13 except that at two nodes, N_L and N_{LL}, the values from the recursive valuation formula ($101.001 at N_L and $100.689 at N_{LL}) exceed the call price ($100) and, therefore, have been struck out and replaced with $100. Each time a value derived from the recursive valuation formula has been replaced, the process for finding the values at that node is reworked starting with the period to the right. The value for this callable bond is $101.432.

The question that we have not addressed in our illustration but which is nonetheless important is the circumstances under which the issuer will call the bond. A discussion of the call rule is beyond the scope of this chapter. Basically, it involves determining when it is economical on an after-tax basis for the issuer to call the bond.

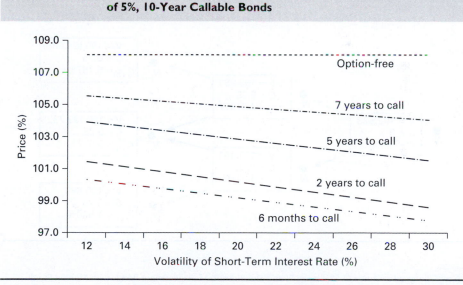

Impact of Expected Interest Rate Volatility on Price

As we have explained, expected interest rate volatility is a key input into the valuation of bonds with embedded options. To see the impact on the price of a callable bond, Exhibit 17-15 shows the price of four 5%, 10-year callable bonds with different deferred call structures (six months, two years, five years, and seven years) based on different assumptions about the expected volatility of short-term interest rates. Also shown in the

Exhibit 17-15   Effect of Interest Rate Volatility and Years to Call on Prices of 5%, 10-Year Callable Bonds

Note: *The prices are calculated using Andrew Kalotay Associates BondOAS™ using 3,000 interest rate lattices.*

exhibit is the price of a 5%, 10-year option-free bond. We observe the following from the exhibit:

- The price of the option-free bond is the same regardless of the interest rate volatility assumed. This is expected since there is no embedded option that is affected by interest rate volatility.
- For any given level of interest rate volatility, the longer the deferred call, the higher the price. Again, as expected, the value of the option-free bond has the highest price.
- The price of a callable bond moves inversely to the interest rate volatility assumed.

Determining the Call Option Value (or Option Cost)

The value of a callable bond is expressed as the difference between the value of a noncallable bond and the value of the call option. This relationship can also be expressed as follows:

value of a call option = value of a noncallable bond − value of a callable bond

But we have just seen how the value of a noncallable bond and the value of a callable bond can be determined. The difference between the two values is, therefore, the value of the call option. In our illustration, the value of the noncallable bond is $102.075 and the value of the callable bond is $101.432, so the value of the call option is $0.643.

Extension to Other Embedded Options

The bond valuation framework presented here can be used to analyze other embedded options, such as put options, caps and floors on floating-rate notes, and the optional accelerated redemption granted to an issuer in fulfilling its sinking fund requirement.[5] For example, let's consider a putable bond. Suppose that a 5.25% corporate bond with three years remaining to maturity is putable in one year at par ($100). Also assume that the appropriate binomial interest-rate tree for this issuer is the one in Exhibit 17-12. Exhibit 17-16 shows the binomial interest-rate tree with the bond values altered at two

---

Exhibit 17-16   Valuing a Putable Corporate Bond with Three Years to Maturity, a Coupon Rate of 5.25%, and Putable in One Year at 100

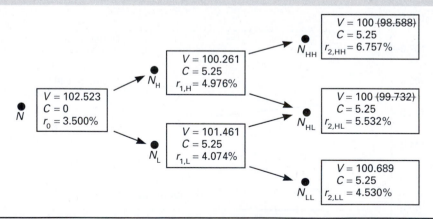

---

[5] Andrew Kalotay and George O. Williams, "The Valuation and Management of Bonds with Sinking Fund Provisions," *Financial Analysis Journal*, March–April 1992, pp. 59–67.

nodes (N_{HH} and N_{HL}) because the bond values at these two nodes are below $100, the value at which the bond can be put. The value of this putable bond is $102.523.

Because the value of a nonputable bond can be expressed as the value of a putable bond minus the value of a put option on that bond, this means that

value of a put option = value of a nonputable bond − value of a putable bond

In our example, because the value of the putable bond is $102.523 and the value of the corresponding nonputable bond is $102.075, the value of the put option is −$0.448. The negative sign indicates that the issuer has sold the option, or equivalently, the investor has purchased the option.

The framework can also be used to value a bond with multiple or interrelated embedded options. The bond values at each node are altered based on whether one of the options is exercised.

Incorporating Default Risk

John Finnerty has extended the basic binomial model just explained to incorporate default risk.[6] The extension involves adjusting the expected cash flows for the probability of a payment default and the expected amount of cash that will be recovered when a default occurs. This extension then requires the manager to estimate (1) the historical default experience of bonds with a similar rating, and (2) the expected amount that will be recovered. Empirical data collected by the commercial rating agencies and several well-known studies by Edward Altman allow a manager to do a good job of estimating this required data.

An explanation of specifically how the adjustments are made to the model is beyond the scope of this chapter. The article by Finnerty provides not only a detailed discussion of the valuation process but also illustrates how the model was applied to value a pay-in-kind debenture bond of the Bucyrus-Erie Company, an issue that was rated non-investment grade at the time of the analysis and had multiple embedded options.

Modeling Risk

The user of any valuation model is exposed to **modeling risk**. This is the risk that the output of the model is incorrect because the assumptions upon which it is based are incorrect. Consequently, it is imperative that the results of a valuation model be stress-tested for modeling risk by altering the assumptions.

A critical assumption in the valuation model is the volatility assumption. For a callable bond, a higher (lower) volatility assumption lowers (raises) its value. For a putable bond, a higher (lower) volatility assumption raises (lowers) its value.

Implementation Challenge

To transform the basic interest rate tree into a practical tool requires several refinements. First, the spacing of the node lines in the tree must be much finer. However, the fine spacing required to value short-dated securities becomes computationally inefficient if one seeks to value, say, 30-year bonds. While one can introduce time-dependent node spacing, caution is required; it is easy to distort the term structure of volatility. Other practical difficulties include the management of cash flows that fall between two node lines.

---

[6] John D. Finnerty, "Adjusting the Binomial Model for Default Risk," *Journal of Portfolio Management*, Winter 1999, pp. 93–104.

OPTION-ADJUSTED SPREAD

What an investor seeks to do is to buy securities whose value is greater than their market price. A valuation model such as the one just described allows an investor to estimate the value of a security, which at this point would be sufficient to determine the fairness of the price of the security. That is, the investor can say that this bond is one point cheap or two points cheap and so on.

A valuation model need not stop here, however. Instead, it can convert the divergence between the price observed in the market for the security and the value derived from the model into a yield spread measure. This step is necessary because most market participants find it more convenient to think about yield spread than about price differences.

The **option-adjusted spread** (OAS) was developed as a measure of the yield spread (in basis points) that can be used to convert dollar differences between value and price. Thus, basically, the OAS is used to reconcile value with market price. But what is it a "spread" over? The OAS is a spread over the spot rate curve or benchmark used in the valuation. The reason that the resulting spread is referred to as *option-adjusted* is because the cash flows of the security whose value we seek are adjusted to reflect the embedded option.

In the case of the binomial method, the OAS is a spread over the binomial interest rate tree. Some market participants construct the binomial interest-rate tree using the Treasury spot rates. In this case, the OAS reflects the richness or cheapness of the security, if any, plus a credit spread. Other market participants construct the binomial interest-rate tree from the issuer's spot rate curve. In this case, the credit risk is already incorporated into the analysis, and the OAS therefore reflects the richness or cheapness of a security. Therefore, it is critical to know the on-the-run issues that the modeler used to construct the binomial interest-rate tree.

Translating the Option-Adjusted Spread to Theoretical Value

Although the product of a valuation model is the OAS, the process can be worked in reverse. For a specified OAS, the valuation model can determine the theoretical value of the security that is consistent with that OAS. As with the theoretical value, the OAS is affected by the assumed interest rate volatility. The higher (lower) the expected interest rate volatility, the lower (higher) the OAS.

Determining the Option Value in Spread Terms

Earlier, we described how the dollar value of the option is calculated. The option value in spread terms is determined as follows:

$$\text{option value (in basis points)} = \text{static spread} - \text{OAS}$$

EFFECTIVE DURATION AND CONVEXITY

As explained in Chapter 4, money managers also want to know the price sensitivity of a bond when interest rates change. Modified duration is a measure of the sensitivity of a bond's price to interest-rate changes, *assuming that the expected cash flow does not change with interest rates*. Consequently, modified duration may not be an appropriate measure for bonds with embedded options because the expected cash flows change as interest rates change. For example, when interest rates fall, the expected cash flow for a callable bond may change. In the case of a putable bond, a rise in interest rates may change the expected cash flow.

Although modified duration may be inappropriate as a measure of a bond's price sensitivity to interest rate changes, there is a duration measure that is more appropriate for bonds with embedded options. Because duration measures price responsiveness to changes in interest rates, the duration for a bond with an embedded option can be estimated by letting interest rates change by a small number of basis points above and below the prevailing yield, and seeing how the prices change. As explained in Chapter 4, in general, the duration for *any* bond can be *approximated* as follows:

$$\text{duration} = \frac{P_- - P_+}{2(P_0)(\Delta y)}$$

where

P_- = price if yield is decreased by x basis points
P_+ = price if yield is increased by x basis points
P_0 = initial price (per \$100 of par value)
Δy = change in rate used to calculate price (x basis points in decimal form)

In Chapter 4, we showed how the application of this formula to an option-free bond gives the modified duration because the cash flows do not change when yields change.

When the approximate duration formula is applied to a bond with an embedded option, the new prices at the higher and lower yield levels should reflect the value from the valuation model. Duration calculated in this way is called **effective duration** or **option-adjusted duration**.

In general, the relationships among duration, modified duration, and effective duration are as follows. Duration is a generic concept that indicates the responsiveness of a bond to a change in interest rates. Modified duration is a duration measure in which the cash flow is not assumed to change when interest rates change. In contrast, effective duration measures the responsiveness of a bond's price taking into account that the expected cash flow will change as interest rates change due to the embedded option. The difference between modified duration and effective duration for a bond with an embedded option can be quite dramatic. For example, a callable bond could have a modified duration of 5 and an effective duration of 3. For certain highly leveraged mortgage-backed securities, the bond could have a modified duration of 7 and an effective duration of 50! The differences between modified duration and effective duration are summarized in Exhibit 17-17.

Exhibit 17-17   Modified Duration versus Effective Duration

Duration
Interpretation: Generic description of the sensitivity of a bond's price
(as a percent of initial price) to a parallel shift in the yield curve

Modified Duration
Duration measure in which it is assumed
that yield changes do not change
the expected cash flow

Effective Duration
Duration measure in which recognition
is given to the fact that yield changes may
change the expected cash flow

Similarly, the standard convexity measure may be inappropriate for a bond with embedded options because it does not consider the effect of a change in interest rates on the bond's cash flow. As explained in Chapter 4, the convexity of any bond can be approximated using the following formula:

$$\frac{P_+ + P_- - 2(P_0)}{(P_0)(\Delta y)^2}$$

When the prices used in this formula assume that the cash flows do not change when yields change, the resulting convexity is a good approximation of the standard convexity for an option-free bond. When the prices used in the formula are derived by changing the cash flows when yields change, the resulting convexity is called **effective convexity**.

Using the binomial method, the procedure for calculating the value of P_+ that should be used to calculate effective duration and effective convexity is as follows:

Step 1: Calculate the OAS for the issue.
Step 2: Shift the on-the-run yield curve up by a small number of basis points.
Step 3: Construct a binomial interest-rate tree based on the new yield curve in step 2.
Step 4: To each of the short rates in the binomial interest-rate tree, add the OAS to obtain an adjusted tree.
Step 5: Use the adjusted tree found in step 4 to determine the value of the security, which is P_+.

To determine the value of P_-, the same five steps are followed except that in step 2 the on-the-run yield curve is shifted down by a small number of basis points.

KEY POINTS

- The traditional yield spread approach fails to take three factors into account: (1) the term structure of interest rates, (2) the options embedded in the bond, and (3) the expected volatility of interest rates. The static spread measures the spread over the Treasury spot rate curve assuming that interest rates will not change in the future.
- The potential investor in a callable bond must be compensated for the risk that the issuer will call the bond prior to the stated maturity date. The two risks faced by a potential investor are reinvestment risk and truncated price appreciation when yields decline (i.e., negative convexity).
- The traditional methodology for valuing bonds with embedded options relies on the yield to worst. The limitations of yield numbers are now well recognized. Moreover, the traditional methodology does not consider how future interest-rate volatility will affect the value of the embedded option.
- To value a bond with an embedded option, it is necessary to understand that the bond can be decomposed into an option-free component and an option component.
- The binomial method can be used to value a bond with an embedded option. It involves generating a binomial interest-rate tree based on (1) an issuer's yield curve, (2) an interest-rate model, and (3) an assumed interest-rate volatility. The binomial interest-rate tree provides the appropriate volatility-dependent one-period forward rates that should be used to discount the expected cash flows of a bond. Critical to the valuation process is an assumption about expected interest-rate volatility.
- The OAS converts the cheapness or richness of a bond into a spread over the future possible spot rate curves. The spread is option adjusted because it allows for future interest-rate volatility to affect the cash flows.

- Modified duration and standard convexity, used to measure the interest-rate sensitivity of an option-free bond, may be inappropriate for a bond with an embedded option because these measures assume that cash flows do not change as interest rates change.
- The duration and convexity can be approximated for any bond, whether it is option-free or a bond with an embedded option. The approximation involves determining how the price of the bond changes if interest rates go up or down by a small number of basis points. If interest rates are changed and it is assumed that the cash flows do not change, the resulting measures are modified duration and standard convexity. However, when the cash flows are allowed to change when interest rates change, the resulting measures are called effective duration and effective convexity.

QUESTIONS

1. What are the two drawbacks of the traditional approach to the valuation of bonds with embedded options?
2. Is the static spread for a three-year 9% coupon corporate bond selling at 105.58, given the following theoretical Treasury spot rate values, equal to 50, 100, or 120 basis points?

Month	Spot Rate (%)
1	4.0
2	4.2
3	4.9
4	5.4
5	5.7
6	6.0

3. Under what conditions would the traditional yield spread be close to the static spread?
4. Why is the investor of a callable bond exposed to reinvestment risk?
5. What is negative convexity?
6. Does a callable bond exhibit negative or positive convexity?
7. Suppose that you are given the following information about two callable bonds that can be called immediately:

Estimated Percentage Change in Price If Interest Rates Change by

	−100 basis points	+100 basis points
Bond ABC	+5%	−8%
Bond XYZ	+22%	−16%

You are told that both of these bonds have the same maturity and that the coupon rate of one bond is 7% and of the other is 13%. Suppose that the yield curve for both issuers is flat at 8%. Based on this information, which bond is the lower coupon bond and which is the higher coupon bond? Explain why.

8. The theoretical value of a noncallable bond is $103; the theoretical value of a callable bond is $101. Determine the theoretical value of the call option.
9. Explain why you agree or disagree with the following statement: "The value of a putable bond is never greater than the value of an otherwise comparable option-free bond."
10. Explain why you agree or disagree with the following statement: "An investor should be unwilling to pay more than the call price for a bond that is likely to be called."
11. In Robert Litterman, Jose Scheinkman, and Laurence Weiss, "Volatility and the Yield Curve," *Journal of Fixed Income*, Premier Issue, 1991, p. 49, the following statement was made: "Many fixed income securities (e.g., callable bonds) contain embedded options whose prices are sensitive to the level of volatility. Modeling the additional impact of volatility on the value of the coupons allows for a better understanding of the price behavior of these securities." Explain why.
12. If an on-the-run issue for an issuer is evaluated properly using a binomial model, how would the theoretical value compare to the actual market price?

13. The current on-the-run yields for the Ramsey Corporation are as follows:

Maturity (years)	Yield to Maturity (%)	Market Price
1	7.5	100
2	7.6	100
3	7.7	100

Assume that each bond is an annual-pay bond. Each bond is trading at par, so its coupon rate is equal to its yield to maturity.

a. Using the bootstrapping methodology, complete the following table:

Year	Spot Rate (%)	One-Year Forward Rate (%)
1		
2		
3		

b. Using the spot rates, what would be the value of an 8.5% option-free bond of this issuer?

c. Using the one-year forward rates, what would be the value of an 8.5% coupon option-free bond of this issuer?

d. Using the binomial model (which assumes that one-year rates undergo a lognormal random walk with volatility σ), show that if σ is assumed to be 10%, the lower one-year forward rate one year from now *cannot* be 7%.

e. Demonstrate that if σ is assumed to be 10%, the lower one-year forward rate one year from now is 6.944%.

f. Demonstrate that if σ is assumed to be 10%, the lower one-year forward rate two years from now is approximately 6.437%.

g. Show the binomial interest-rate tree that should be used to value any bond of this issuer.

h. Determine the value of an 8.5% coupon option-free bond for this issuer using the binomial interest-rate tree given in part g.

i. Determine the value of an 8.5% coupon bond that is callable at par (100) assuming that the issue will be called if the price exceeds par.

14. Explain how an increase in expected interest-rate volatility can decrease the value of a callable bond.

15. **a.** What is meant by the option-adjusted spread?
b. What is the spread relative to?

16. "The option-adjusted spread measures the yield spread over the Treasury on-the-run yield curve." Explain why you agree or disagree with this statement.

17. What is the effect of greater expected interest-rate volatility on the option-adjusted spread of a security?

18. The following excerpt is taken from an article titled "Call Provisions Drop Off" that appeared in the January 27, 1992, issue of *BondWeek*, p. 2:

> Issuance of callable long-term bonds dropped off further last year as interest rates fell, removing the incentive for many issuers to pay extra for the provision, said Street capital market officials....
>
> The shift toward noncallable issues, which began in the late 1980s, reflects the secular trend of investors unwilling to bear prepayment risk and possibly the cyclical trend that corporations believe that interest rates have hit all time lows....

a. What "incentive" is this article referring to in the first sentence of the excerpt?
b. Why would issuers not be willing to pay for this incentive if they feel that interest rates will continue to decline?

19. The following excerpt is taken from an article titled "Eagle Eyes High-Coupon Callable Corporates" that appeared in the January 20, 1992, issue of *BondWeek*, p. 7:

> If the bond market rallies further, Eagle Asset Management may take profits, trading $8 million of seven- to 10-year Treasuries for high-coupon single-A industrials that are callable in two to four years according to Joseph Blanton, senior V.P. He thinks a further rally is unlikely, however....
>
> The corporates have a 95% chance of being called in two to four years and are treated as two- to four-year paper in calculating the duration of the portfolio, Blanton said....

a. Why is modified duration an inappropriate measure for a high-coupon callable bond?
b. What would be a better measure than modified duration?
c. Why would the replacement of 10-year Treasuries with high-coupon callable bonds reduce the portfolio's duration?

18

Analysis of Residential Mortgage–Backed Securities[*]

LEARNING OBJECTIVES

After reading this chapter, you will understand

- the cash flow yield methodology for analyzing residential mortgage-backed securities

- the limitations of the cash flow yield methodology

- how the effective duration and convexity are calculated for the cash flow yield methodology

- one measure for estimating prepayment sensitivity

- why the Monte Carlo simulation methodology is used to value residential mortgage-backed securities

- how interest-rate paths are simulated in a Monte Carlo simulation methodology

- how the Monte Carlo simulation methodology can be used to determine the theoretical value of a residential mortgage-backed security

- how the option-adjusted spread, effective duration, and effective convexity are computed using the Monte Carlo simulation methodology

- the complexities of modeling collateralized mortgage obligations

- the limitations of option-adjusted spread

- modeling risk and how it can be stress tested

- how the total return is calculated for a residential mortgage-backed security

- the difficulties of applying the total return framework to residential mortgage-backed securities

---

[*] Parts of this chapter are adapted from Chapters 9 and 10 of Frank J. Fabozzi, Chuck Ramsey, and Frank Ramirez, *Collateralized Mortgage Obligations: Structures and Analysis* (Buckingham, PA: Frank J. Fabozzi Associates, 1994).

There are two approaches to the analysis of residential mortgage-backed securities (including pass-throughs, collateralized mortgage obligations [CMOs], and stripped mortgage-backed securities): (1) the static cash flow yield methodology, and (2) the Monte Carlo simulation methodology. The Monte Carlo simulation methodology provides the theoretical value of a residential mortgage-backed security. That is, it is a valuation model. A product of this valuation model, as with all valuation models, is the option-adjusted spread (OAS). In this chapter, we review the static cash flow yield methodology and its limitations and then focus on the Monte Carlo simulation methodology. The framework provided in this chapter applies to agency and nonagency residential mortgage-backed securities.

STATIC CASH FLOW YIELD METHODOLOGY

The static cash flow yield methodology is the simplest to use, although we shall see that it offers little insight into the relative value of a residential mortgage-backed security (RMBS). It begins with the computation of the cash flow yield measure that we described for pass-throughs in Chapter 11. The cash flow yield is based on some prepayment assumption.

To illustrate the cash flow yield, we will use one of the CMO structures we developed in Chapter 12, FJF-06. This structure is summarized in Exhibit 12-15. Exhibit 18-1 summarizes cash flow yields according to various Public Securities Association (PSA) prepayment assumptions for the four tranches assuming different purchase prices. Notice that the greater the discount assumed to be paid for the tranche, the more a tranche will benefit from faster prepayments. The converse is true for a tranche for which a premium is paid. The faster the prepayments, the lower the cash flow yield.

Vector Analysis

One practice that market participants use to overcome the drawback of the PSA benchmark is to assume that the PSA speed can change over time. This technique is referred to as **vector analysis**. A **vector** is simply a set of numbers. In the case of prepayments, it is a vector of prepayment speeds. Vector analysis is particularly useful for CMO tranches that are dramatically affected by the initial slowing down of prepayments, and then speeding up of prepayments, or vice versa.

Exhibit 18-2 reports the cash flow yield using vector analysis for the four tranches and collateral of FJF-06. The top panel shows the cash flow yield assuming 165 PSA. Nine vectors are then shown assuming that the PSA is constant from months 1 to 36, and then changes for months 37 through 138, and again changes for months 139 through 357.

Limitations of the Cash Flow Yield

As we have noted several times already, the yield to maturity has two shortcomings as a measure of a bond's potential return: (1) It is assumed that the coupon payments can be reinvested at a rate equal to the yield to maturity, and (2) it is assumed that the bond is held to maturity. These shortcomings are equally present in application of the cash flow yield measure: (1) the projected cash flows are assumed to be reinvested at the cash flow yield, and (2) the RMBS is assumed to be held until the final payout based on some prepayment assumption. The importance of reinvestment risk—the risk that the cash flow will be reinvested at a rate less than the cash flow yield—is particularly important for many RMBS because payments come as frequently as every month. The cash flow yield, moreover, is

Exhibit 18-1 Price Cash Flow Yield Table for the Four Tranches in FJF-06

Tranche A: Orig. par: $194,500,000; type: sequential; coupon: 6.00% (fixed)

If Price Paid Is:	50.00 PSA	100.00 PSA	165.00 PSA	250.00 PSA	400.00 PSA	500.00 PSA	700.00 PSA	1000.00 PSA
90–24	8.37	9.01	9.76	10.61	11.87	12.59	13.88	15.63
91–24	8.09	8.66	9.32	10.07	11.17	11.81	12.94	14.47
92–24	7.82	8.31	8.88	9.53	10.49	11.03	12.01	13.33
93–24	7.56	7.97	8.45	9.00	9.81	10.27	11.10	12.22
94–24	7.29	7.63	8.03	8.48	9.14	9.52	10.20	11.12
95–24	7.03	7.30	7.61	7.97	8.49	8.79	9.32	10.04
96–24	6.78	6.97	7.20	7.46	7.85	8.06	8.45	8.98
97–24	6.53	6.65	6.80	6.97	7.21	7.35	7.60	7.94
98–24	6.28	6.34	6.40	6.48	6.59	6.65	6.76	6.91
99–24	6.04	6.02	6.01	6.00	5.97	5.96	5.94	5.91
100–24	5.79	5.72	5.62	5.52	5.37	5.28	5.13	4.92
101–24	5.56	5.41	5.24	5.05	4.77	4.61	4.33	3.95
102–24	5.33	5.12	4.87	4.59	4.18	3.95	3.54	2.99
103–24	5.10	4.82	4.50	4.14	3.61	3.30	2.77	2.05
104–24	4.87	4.53	4.14	3.69	3.04	2.66	2.01	1.12
105–24	4.65	4.25	3.78	3.25	2.47	2.03	1.26	0.21
106–24	4.42	3.96	3.42	2.81	1.92	1.41	0.52	−0.68
107–24	4.21	3.69	3.07	2.38	1.37	0.80	−0.21	−1.57
108–24	3.99	3.41	2.73	1.96	0.83	0.20	−0.93	−2.44
109–24	3.78	3.14	2.39	1.54	0.30	−0.40	−1.64	−3.29
Average life:	5.09	3.80	2.93	2.33	1.79	1.58	1.31	1.07
Mod. duration:	4.12	3.22	2.57	2.09	1.64	1.46	1.22	1.00
Exp. maturity:	9.40	7.15	5.40	4.15	3.07	2.65	2.24	1.82

(Continued)

dependent on realization of the projected cash flow according to some prepayment rate. If actual prepayments vary from the prepayment rate assumed, the cash flow yield will not be realized.

Yield Spread to Treasuries

It should be clear that at the time of purchase it is not possible to determine an exact yield for an RMBS; the yield will depend on the actual prepayment experience of the mortgages in the pool. Nevertheless, the convention in all fixed-income markets is to measure the yield on a non-Treasury security to that of a "comparable" Treasury security.

The repayment of principal over time makes it inappropriate to compare the yield of an RMBS to a Treasury of a stated maturity. Instead, market participants have used two measures: Macaulay duration (as explained in Chapter 4) and average life (as explained in Chapter 11).

Exhibit 18-1 Price Cash Flow Yield Table for the Four Tranches in FJF-06 (Continued)

Tranche B: Orig. par: $36,000,000; type: sequential; coupon: 6.50% (fixed)

If Price Paid Is:	50.00 PSA	100.00 PSA	165.00 PSA	250.00 PSA	400.00 PSA	500.00 PSA	700.00 PSA	1000.00 PSA
90–31	7.85	8.12	8.49	8.95	9.69	10.13	10.89	11.83
91–31	7.69	7.93	8.25	8.66	9.31	9.70	10.36	11.18
92–31	7.54	7.75	8.02	8.37	8.94	9.27	9.84	10.55
93–31	7.39	7.57	7.80	8.09	8.57	8.85	9.33	9.92
94–31	7.24	7.39	7.58	7.82	8.20	8.43	8.82	9.31
95–31	7.10	7.21	7.35	7.54	7.84	8.02	8.32	8.70
96–31	6.95	7.03	7.14	7.27	7.49	7.61	7.83	8.10
97–31	6.81	6.86	6.92	7.00	7.13	7.21	7.34	7.51
98–31	6.67	6.69	6.71	6.74	6.79	6.82	6.86	6.92
99–31	6.53	6.52	6.50	6.48	6.45	6.42	6.39	6.35
100–31	6.39	6.35	6.29	6.22	6.11	6.04	5.92	5.78
101–31	6.26	6.19	6.09	5.97	5.77	5.66	5.46	5.22
102–31	6.13	6.02	5.89	5.72	5.44	5.28	5.00	4.66
103–31	5.99	5.86	5.69	5.47	5.12	4.91	4.55	4.12
104–31	5.86	5.70	5.49	5.22	4.79	4.54	4.11	3.58
105–31	5.74	5.55	5.30	4.98	4.48	4.18	3.67	3.04
106–31	5.61	5.39	5.10	4.74	4.16	3.82	3.23	2.51
107–31	5.48	5.24	4.91	4.50	3.85	3.46	2.80	1.99
108–31	5.36	5.08	4.72	4.27	3.54	3.11	2.38	1.48
109–31	5.24	4.93	4.54	4.04	3.24	2.76	1.96	0.97
Average life:	10.17	7.76	5.93	4.58	3.35	2.89	2.35	1.90
Mod. duration:	7.23	5.92	4.78	3.84	2.92	2.56	2.11	1.74
Exp. maturity:	10.90	8.40	6.49	4.99	3.65	3.15	2.49	1.99

(*Continued*)

Static Spread

As explained in Chapter 17, the practice of spreading the yield to the average life on the interpolated Treasury yield curve is improper for an amortizing bond even in the absence of interest-rate volatility. What should be done instead is to calculate what is called the **static spread**. This is the yield spread in a static scenario (i.e., no volatility of interest rates) of the bond over the entire theoretical Treasury spot rate curve, not a single point on the Treasury yield curve.

As explained in Chapter 17, the magnitude of the difference between the traditional yield spread and the static yield spread depends on the steepness of the yield curve: The steeper the curve, the greater the difference between the two values. In a relatively flat interest-rate environment, the difference between the traditional yield spread and the static spread will be small.

Exhibit 18-1   Price Cash Flow Yield Table for the Four Tranches in FJF-06 (Continued)

Tranche C: Orig. par: $96,500,000; type: sequential; coupon: 7.00% (fixed)

If Price Paid Is:	50.00 PSA	100.00 PSA	165.00 PSA	250.00 PSA	400.00 PSA	500.00 PSA	700.00 PSA	1000.00 PSA
90–03	8.34	8.53	8.80	9.15	9.77	10.16	10.89	11.85
91–03	8.20	8.37	8.61	8.92	9.47	9.81	10.46	11.31
92–03	8.06	8.21	8.42	8.70	9.17	9.48	10.05	10.79
93–03	7.92	8.06	8.24	8.47	8.88	9.14	9.63	10.27
94–03	7.79	7.90	8.05	8.25	8.60	8.81	9.22	9.76
95–03	7.66	7.75	7.87	8.03	8.31	8.49	8.82	9.25
96–03	7.53	7.60	7.69	7.82	8.03	8.17	8.42	8.76
97–03	7.40	7.45	7.52	7.61	7.76	7.85	8.03	8.26
98–03	7.28	7.31	7.35	7.40	7.48	7.54	7.64	7.78
99–03	7.15	7.16	7.17	7.19	7.21	7.23	7.26	7.30
100–03	7.03	7.02	7.01	6.98	6.95	6.93	6.88	6.83
101–03	6.91	6.88	6.84	6.78	6.69	6.63	6.51	6.36
102–03	6.79	6.74	6.67	6.58	6.43	6.33	6.14	5.90
103–03	6.67	6.61	6.51	6.39	6.17	6.03	5.78	5.45
104–03	6.56	6.47	6.35	6.19	5.92	5.74	5.42	5.00
105–03	6.44	6.34	6.19	6.00	5.67	5.46	5.07	4.56
106–03	6.33	6.21	6.03	5.81	5.42	5.17	4.72	4.12
107–03	6.22	6.08	5.88	5.62	5.18	4.89	4.37	3.69
108–03	6.11	5.95	5.73	5.43	4.94	4.62	4.03	3.26
109–03	6.00	5.82	5.57	5.25	4.70	4.34	3.69	2.84
Average life:	12.77	10.16	7.98	6.24	4.54	3.87	3.04	2.37
Mod. duration:	8.18	7.04	5.92	4.89	3.76	3.28	2.65	2.12
Exp. maturity:	14.57	11.90	9.57	7.65	5.57	4.74	3.65	2.82

(Continued)

There are two ways to compute the static spread for RMBS. One way is to use today's yield curve to discount future cash flows and keep the mortgage refinancing rate fixed at today's mortgage rate. Because the mortgage refinancing rate is fixed, the investor can usually specify a reasonable prepayment rate for the life of the security. Using this prepayment rate, the bond's future cash flow can be estimated. Use of this approach to calculate the static spread recognizes different prices today of dollars to be delivered at future dates. This results in the proper discounting of cash flows while keeping the mortgage rate fixed. Effectively, today's prices indicate what the future discount rates will be, but the best estimates of future rates are today's rates.

The second way to calculate the static spread allows the mortgage rate to go up the curve as implied by the forward interest rates. This procedure is sometimes called the **zero-volatility OAS**. In this case, a prepayment model is needed to determine the vector of future prepayment rates implied by the vector of future refinancing rates.

Exhibit 18-1 Price Cash Flow Yield Table for the Four Tranches in FJF-06 (Continued)

Tranche Z: Orig. par: $73,000,000; type: sequential; coupon: 7.35% (fixed)

If Price Paid Is:	50.00 PSA	100.00 PSA	165.00 PSA	250.00 PSA	400.00 PSA	500.00 PSA	700.00 PSA	1000.00 PSA
90–01	7.87	7.96	8.09	8.27	8.61	8.84	9.33	10.10
91–01	7.82	7.89	8.00	8.16	8.47	8.68	9.11	9.79
92–01	7.76	7.83	7.93	8.07	8.33	8.51	8.89	9.49
93–01	7.71	7.76	7.85	7.97	8.20	8.35	8.68	9.20
94–01	7.65	7.70	7.77	7.87	8.06	8.19	8.47	8.90
95–01	7.60	7.63	7.69	7.77	7.93	8.04	8.26	8.61
96–01	7.54	7.57	7.62	7.68	7.80	7.88	8.05	8.33
97–01	7.49	7.51	7.54	7.59	7.67	7.73	7.85	8.04
98–01	7.44	7.45	7.47	7.49	7.54	7.58	7.65	7.76
99–01	7.38	7.39	7.39	7.40	7.42	7.43	7.45	7.49
100–01	7.33	7.33	7.32	7.31	7.29	7.28	7.26	7.21
101–01	7.28	7.27	7.25	7.22	7.17	7.14	7.06	6.95
102–01	7.23	7.21	7.18	7.13	7.05	6.99	6.87	6.68
103–01	7.18	7.15	7.11	7.05	6.93	6.85	6.68	6.42
104–01	7.13	7.09	7.04	6.96	6.81	6.71	6.49	6.16
105–01	7.08	7.04	6.97	6.88	6.69	6.57	6.31	5.90
106–01	7.04	6.98	6.90	6.79	6.58	6.43	6.13	5.65
107–01	6.99	6.93	6.84	6.71	6.46	6.29	5.94	5.39
108–01	6.94	6.87	6.77	6.62	6.35	6.16	5.77	5.15
109–01	6.89	6.82	6.70	6.54	6.24	6.03	5.59	4.90
Average life:	22.39	19.57	16.21	12.78	9.01	7.46	5.49	3.88
Mod. duration:	19.42	16.68	13.81	11.08	8.06	6.78	5.11	3.67
Exp. maturity:	29.74	29.74	29.74	29.74	29.74	29.74	29.74	24.24

Note: *Calculated using SFW Software, copyright © 1989 by Wall Street Analytics, Inc.*

A money manager using static spread should determine which approach is used in the calculation.

Effective Duration

Modified duration is a measure of the sensitivity of a bond's price to interest-rate changes, assuming that the expected cash flow does not change with interest rates. Modified duration is consequently not an appropriate measure for mortgage-backed securities, because prepayments do cause the projected cash flow to change as interest rates change. When interest rates fall (rise), prepayments are expected to rise (fall). As a result, when interest rates fall (rise), duration may decrease (increase) rather than increase (decrease). As we explained in Chapter 17, this property is referred to as **negative convexity**.

Exhibit 18-2   Vector Analysis of Cash Flow Yield for Four Tranches of FJF-06 and Collateral Assumptions

	Coupon (%)	Price	Cash Flow Yield at 165 PSA (%)
Tranche A	6.00	99–24	6.00
Tranche B	6.50	99–31	6.50
Tranche C	7.00	100–03	7.00
Tranche Z	7.25	100–01	7.25
Collateral	7.50	100–00	?

	Months	(1)	(2)	(3)	(4)	(5)	(6)	(7)	(8)	(9)
					PSA Vector Scenario					
	1–36	165	165	165	165	165	165	165	165	165
Tranche	37–138	50	50	300	400	400	400	400	500	600
Parameter	139–357	250	400	400	200	700	500	165	200	1000
Tranche A										
Cash flow yield		6.02	6.02	6.01	6.00	6.00	6.00	6.00	6.00	6.00
Average life		3.51	3.51	2.71	2.63	2.63	2.63	2.63	2.58	2.54
Modified duration		2.97	2.97	2.40	2.34	2.34	2.34	2.34	2.30	2.27
Tranche B										
Cash flow yield		6.52	6.52	6.48	6.48	6.48	6.48	6.48	6.47	6.46
Average life		8.51	8.51	4.82	4.39	4.39	4.39	4.39	4.11	3.91
Modified duration		6.35	6.35	4.02	3.71	3.71	3.71	3.71	3.50	3.36
Tranche C										
Cash flow yield		7.03	7.03	6.98	6.97	6.97	6.97	6.97	6.96	6.95
Average life		11.15	11.07	6.24	5.52	5.52	5.52	5.52	5.04	4.68
Modified duration		7.50	7.47	4.89	4.43	4.43	4.43	4.43	4.11	3.87
Tranche D										
Cash flow yield		7.26	7.25	7.21	7.19	7.19	7.20	7.20	7.17	7.14
Average life		17.08	15.29	11.47	10.49	9.55	11.42	10.65	8.92	7.49
Modified duration		15.44	14.19	10.28	9.19	8.76	9.56	9.26	8.01	6.98
Collateral										
Cash flow yield		7.54	7.53	7.50	7.49	7.49	7.49	7.49	7.48	7.47
Average life		10.90	10.05	6.31	5.68	5.40	5.95	5.72	5.02	4.48
Modified duration		6.47	6.25	4.50	4.14	4.07	4.21	4.16	3.82	3.55

Note: *Calculated using SFW Software, copyright © 1989 by Wall Street Analytics, Inc.*

Negative convexity has the same impact on the price performance of an RMBS as it does on the performance of a callable bond (discussed in Chapter 17). When interest rates decline, a bond with an embedded call option, which is what an RMBS is, will not perform as well as an option-free bond. Although modified duration is an inappropriate measure of interest-rate sensitivity, there is a way to allow for changing prepayment rates on cash flow as interest rates change. This is achieved by calculating the **effective duration**, which allows for changing cash flow when interest rates change.

To illustrate calculation of effective duration for CMO classes, consider FJF-06 once again. The structure is summarized in the top panel of Exhibit 18-3. The second panel provides all the data necessary to calculate modified duration and effective duration of the four tranches and the collateral. This panel shows the assumed cash flow yield and the corresponding initial price for the tranches assuming a prepayment speed of 165 PSA. The two columns following the initial prices give the new prices if the cash flow yield is changed by 25 basis points and assuming no change in the prepayment speed. The last two columns show new prices if the cash flow yield changes by 25 basis points and the prepayment speed is assumed to change; it decreases to 150 PSA if the cash flow yield

Exhibit 18-3 **Calculation of Effective Duration and Convexity for FJF-06**

Structure of FJF-06

Class	Par Amount	Coupon Rate (%)
A	$194,500,000	6.00
B	36,000,000	6.50
C	96,500,000	7.00
Z (accrual)	73,000,000	7.25
R	0	0
Collateral	$400,000,000	7.50

			NEW PRICE 165% PSA		NEW PRICE CFY	
	Cash Flow		CFY Change (bp)		Change (bp)/New PSA	
Class	Yield (%)	Initial Price	+25 bp	−25 bp	+25/150	−25/200
A	6.00	99.7813	99.0625	100.5313	99.0313	100.4375
B	6.50	100.0313	98.6250	101.5000	98.5625	101.2813
C	7.00	100.2813	98.4063	102.1875	98.3438	101.9063
Z	7.25	100.6250	98.0625	103.2500	98.0313	103.0313
Collateral	7.50	100.1250	98.7500	101.5000	98.7188	101.3438

Modified Duration/Standard Convexity and Effective Duration/Convexity

Class	Modified Duration	Effective Duration	Standard Convexity	Effective Convexity
A	2.94	2.82	25.055	−75.164
B	5.75	5.44	49.984	−174.945
C	7.54	7.11	24.930	−249.299
Z	10.31	9.94	49.689	−149.068
Collateral	5.49	5.24	0	−149.813

increases by 25 basis points, and it increases to 200 PSA if the cash flow yield decreases by 25 basis points.

Exhibit 18-3 reports the modified duration and effective duration. To illustrate the calculation, consider tranche C. The data for calculating modified duration using the approximation formula is

$$P_- = 102.1875 \ P_+ = 98.4063 \ P_0 = 100.2813 \ \Delta y = 0.0025$$

Substituting into the duration formula yields

$$\text{modified duration} = \frac{102.1875 - 98.4063}{2(100.2813)(0.0025)} = 7.54$$

The effective duration for the same bond class is calculated as follows:

$$P_- = 101.9063 \ (\text{at 200 PSA}) \ P_+ = 98.3438 \ (\text{at 150 PSA}) \ P_0 = 100.2813 \ \Delta y = 0.0025$$

Substituting into the formula gives

$$\text{effective duration} = \frac{101.9063 - 98.3438}{2(100.2813)(0.0025)} = 7.11$$

Notice that for all four tranches and the collateral, the effective duration is less than the modified duration.

The divergence between modified duration and effective duration is much more dramatic for bond classes trading at a substantial discount from par or at a substantial premium over par. To demonstrate this, we can create another hypothetical CMO structure, which differs from FJF-06 by including a PO class and an IO class made up from tranche C. Let's look at the duration for the PO class. Assuming that the cash flow yield for the PO class is 7%, based on 165 PSA, the following prices are obtained:

Initial Price	New Price		New Price	
	165 PSA 7.25% CFY	165 PSA 6.75% CFY	150 PSA 7.25% CFY	200 PSA 6.75% CFY
60.3125	59.2500	61.3750	57.6563	64.5938

The modified duration for this PO is 7.05. The effective duration of 23.01 is dramatically different.

Effective Convexity

Exhibit 18-3 reports the standard convexity and the effective convexity for the four tranches in FJF-06 and the collateral. To illustrate the convexity formula, consider once again tranche C in FJF-06. The standard convexity is approximated as follows:

$$\frac{98.4063 - 102.1875 - 2(100.2813)}{(100.2813)(0.0025)^2} = 24.930$$

The effective convexity is

$$\frac{98.3438 + 101.9063 - 2(100.2813)}{(100.2813)(0.0025)^2} = -249.299$$

Note the significant difference in the two convexity measures here and in Exhibit 18-3. The standard convexity indicates that the four tranches have positive convexity, whereas the effective convexity indicates they have negative convexity. The difference is even more dramatic for bonds not trading near par. For a PO created from tranche C, the standard convexity is close to zero whereas the effective convexity is 2,155! This means that if yields change by 100 basis points, the percentage change in price due to convexity would be

$$2{,}155(0.01)^2(100) = 21.6\%$$

Prepayment Sensitivity Measure

The value of an RMBS will depend on prepayments. To assess prepayment sensitivity, market participants have used the following measure: the basis point change in the price of an RMBS for a 1% increase in prepayments. Specifically, prepayment sensitivity is defined as

P_0 = initial price (per \$100 par value) at assumed prepayment speed
P_s = price (per \$ 100 par value) assuming a 1% increase in prepayment speed

$$\text{prepayment sensitivity} = (P_s - P_0) \times 100$$

For example, suppose that for some RMBS at 300 PSA the price is 106.10. A 1% increase in the PSA prepayment rate means that PSA increases from 300 PSA to 303 PSA. Suppose that at 303 PSA the price is recomputed using a valuation model to be 106.01. Therefore,

P_0 = 106.10
P_s = 106.01
prepayment sensitivity = $(106.01 - 106.10) \times 100 = -9$

Notice that a security that is adversely affected by an increase in prepayment speeds will have a negative prepayment sensitivity while a security that benefits from an increase in prepayment speed will have a positive prepayment sensitivity.

▌MONTE CARLO SIMULATION METHODOLOGY[1]

For some fixed-income securities and derivative instruments, the periodic cash flows are **path dependent**. This means that the cash flows received in one period are determined not only by the current and future interest-rate levels but also by the path that interest rates took to get to the current level.

In the case of mortgage pass-through securities, prepayments are path dependent because this month's prepayment rate depends on whether there have been prior opportunities to refinance since the underlying mortgages were originated. Unlike mortgage loans, the decision as to whether a corporate issuer will elect to refund an issue when the current rate is below the issue's coupon rate is not dependent on how rates evolved over time to the current level.

---

[1] Portions of the material in this section and the one to follow are adapted from Frank J. Fabozzi and Scott F. Richard, "Valuation of CMOs," in Frank J. Fabozzi (ed.), *CMO Portfolio Management* (Summit, NJ: Frank J. Fabozzi Associates, 1994). In the finance literature, several recursive valuation models (i.e., models described in the previous chapter for valuing bonds with embedded options) have been proposed. However, in practice these models have not been used.

Moreover, in the case of adjustable-rate pass-throughs (ARMs), prepayments are not only path dependent but the periodic coupon rate depends on the history of the reference rate upon which the coupon rate is determined. This is because ARMs have periodic caps and floors as well as a lifetime cap and floor. For example, an ARM whose coupon rate resets annually could have the following restriction on the coupon rate: (1) The rate cannot change by more than 200 basis points each year, and (2) the rate cannot be more than 500 basis points from the initial coupon rate.

Pools of pass-throughs are used as collateral for the creation of collateralized mortgage obligations (CMOs). Consequently, for CMOs there are typically two sources of path dependency in a CMO tranche's cash flows. First, the collateral prepayments are path dependent, as discussed previously. Second, the cash flow to be received in the current month by a CMO tranche depends on the outstanding balances of the other tranches in the deal. Thus, we need the history of prepayments to calculate these balances.

Because of the path dependency of an RMBS's cash flow, the Monte Carlo simulation method is used for these securities rather than the static method described in Chapter 17.

Conceptually, the valuation of pass-throughs using the Monte Carlo method is simple. In practice, however, it is very complex. The simulation involves generating a set of cash flows based on simulated future mortgage refinancing rates, which in turn imply simulated prepayment rates.

Valuation modeling for CMOs is similar to valuation modeling for pass-throughs, although the difficulties are amplified because, as we explained in Chapter 12, the issuer has sliced and diced both the prepayment risk and the interest-rate risk into smaller pieces called tranches. The sensitivity of the pass-throughs composing the collateral to these two risks is not transmitted equally to every tranche. Some of the tranches wind up more sensitive to prepayment risk and interest-rate risk than the collateral, whereas some of them are much less sensitive.

The objective of the money manager is to figure out how the value of the collateral gets transmitted to the CMO tranches. More specifically, the objective is to find out where the value goes and where the risk goes so that the money manager can identify the tranches with low risk and high value: the ones we want to buy. The good news is that this combination usually exists in every deal. The bad news is that in every deal there are usually tranches with low value and high risk.

Using Simulation to Generate Interest-Rate Paths and Cash Flows

The typical model that Wall Street firms and commercial vendors use to generate random interest-rate paths takes as input today's term structure of interest rates and a volatility assumption. The term structure of interest rates is the theoretical spot rate (or zero-coupon) curve implied by today's Treasury securities. The volatility assumption determines the dispersion of future interest rates in the simulation. The simulations should be normalized so that the average simulated price of a zero-coupon Treasury bond equals today's actual price.

Each model has its own model of the evolution of future interest rates and its own volatility assumptions. Typically, there are no significant differences in the interest-rate models of dealer firms and vendors, although their volatility assumptions can be significantly different.

The random paths of interest rates should be generated from an arbitrage-free model of the future term structure of interest rates. By *arbitrage-free*, it is meant that the model replicates today's term structure of interest rates, an input of the model, and that for all future dates there is no possible arbitrage within the model.

The simulation works by generating many scenarios of future interest-rate paths. In each month of the scenario, a monthly interest rate and a mortgage refinancing rate are generated. The monthly interest rates are used to discount the projected cash flows in the scenario. The mortgage refinancing rate is needed to determine the cash flow because it represents the opportunity cost the mortgagor is facing at that time.

If the refinancing rates are high relative to the mortgagor's contract rate, the mortgagor will have less incentive to refinance, or even a positive disincentive (i.e., the homeowner will avoid moving, to avoid refinancing). If the refinancing rate is low relative to the mortgagor's contract rate, the mortgagor has an incentive to refinance.

Prepayments are projected by feeding the refinancing rate and loan characteristics, such as age, into a prepayment model. In the case of a nonagency deal, the prepayments can be involuntary. By involuntary, it is meant that prepayments can arise because of a default by homeowners. Thus, in the modeling of prepayments, defaults must be projected. Modeling prepayments due to defaults involve projecting the severity of defaults (i.e., determining what the recovery rates are) and the timing of defaults. Given the projected prepayments (voluntary and involuntary), the cash flow along an interest-rate path can be determined.

To make this more concrete, consider a newly issued mortgage pass-through security with a maturity of 360 months. Exhibit 18-4 shows N simulated interest-rate path scenarios. Each scenario consists of a path of 360 simulated one-month future interest rates. Just how many paths should be generated is explained later. Exhibit 18-5 shows the paths of simulated mortgage refinancing rates corresponding to the scenarios shown in

Exhibit 18-4   Simulated Paths of One-Month Future Interest Rates

Month	Interest-Rate Path Number[a]				
	1	2	3 $\cdots$	n $\cdots$	N
1	$f_1(1)$	$f_1(2)$	$f_1(3)$	$f_1(n)$	$f_1(N)$
2	$f_2(1)$	$f_2(2)$	$f_2(3)$	$f_2(n)$	$f_2(N)$
3	$f_3(1)$	$f_3(2)$	$f_3(3)$	$f_3(n)$	$f_3(N)$
4	$f_4(1)$	$f_4(2)$	$f_4(3)$	$f_4(n)$	$f_4(N)$
$\vdots$					
t	$f_t(1)$	$f_t(2)$	$f_t(3)$	$f_t(n)$	$f_t(N)$
$\vdots$					
358	$f_{358}(1)$	$f_{358}(2)$	$f_{358}(3)$	$f_{358}(n)$	$f_{358}(N)$
359	$f_{359}(1)$	$f_{359}(2)$	$f_{359}(3)$	$f_{359}(n)$	$f_{359}(N)$
360	$f_{360}(1)$	$f_{360}(2)$	$f_{360}(3)$	$f_{360}(n)$	$f_{360}(N)$

[a]Notation: $f_t(n)$, one-month future interest rate for month t on path n; N, total number of interest-rate paths.

Exhibit 18-5   Simulated Paths of Mortgage Refinancing Rates

	Interest-Rate Path Number[a]				
Month	1	2	3 $\cdots$	n $\cdots$	N
1	$r_1(1)$	$r_1(2)$	$r_1(3)$	$r_1(n)$	$r_1(N)$
2	$r_2(1)$	$r_2(2)$	$r_2(3)$	$r_2(n)$	$r_2(N)$
3	$r_3(1)$	$r_3(2)$	$r_3(3)$	$r_3(n)$	$r_3(N)$
4	$r_4(1)$	$r_4(2)$	$r_4(3)$	$r_4(n)$	$r_4(N)$
$\vdots$					
t	$r_t(1)$	$r_t(2)$	$r_t(3)$	$r_t(n)$	$r_t(N)$
$\vdots$					
358	$r_{358}(1)$	$r_{358}(2)$	$r_{358}(3)$	$r_{358}(n)$	$r_{358}(N)$
359	$r_{359}(1)$	$r_{359}(2)$	$r_{359}(3)$	$r_{359}(n)$	$r_{359}(N)$
360	$r_{360}(1)$	$r_{360}(2)$	$r_{360}(3)$	$r_{360}(n)$	$r_{360}(N)$

[a]Notation: $r_t(n)$, mortgage refinancing rate for month t on path n; N, total number of interest-rate paths.

Exhibit 18-6   Simulated Cash Flow on Each of the Interest-Rate Paths

	Interest-Rate Path Number[a]				
Month	1	2	3	n	N
1	$C_1(1)$	$C_1(2)$	$C_1(3)$	$C_1(n)$	$C_1(N)$
2	$C_2(1)$	$C_2(2)$	$C_2(3)$	$C_2(n)$	$C_2(N)$
3	$C_3(1)$	$C_3(2)$	$C_3(3)$	$C_3(n)$	$C_3(N)$
4	$C_4(1)$	$C_4(2)$	$C_4(3)$	$C_4(n)$	$C_4(N)$
t	$C_t(1)$	$C_t(2)$	$C_t(3)$	$C_t(n)$	$C_t(N)$
358	$C_{358}(1)$	$C_{358}(2)$	$C_{358}(3)$	$C_{358}(n)$	$C_{358}(N)$
359	$C_{359}(1)$	$C_{359}(2)$	$C_{359}(3)$	$C_{359}(n)$	$C_{359}(N)$
360	$C_{360}(1)$	$C_{360}(2)$	$C_{360}(3)$	$C_{360}(n)$	$C_{360}(N)$

[a]Notation: $C_t(n)$, cash flow for month t on path n; N, total number of interest-rate paths.

Exhibit 18-4. Assuming these mortgage refinancing rates, the cash flow for each scenario path is shown in Exhibit 18-6.

Calculating the Present Value for a Scenario Interest-Rate Path

Given the cash flow on an interest-rate path, its present value can be calculated. The discount rate for determining the present value is the simulated spot rate for each month on the interest-rate path plus an appropriate spread. The spot rate on a path can be determined from the simulated future monthly rates. The relationship that holds between the simulated spot rate for month T on path n and the simulated future one-month rates is

$$z_T(n) = \{[1 + f_1(n)][1 + f_2(n)]\dots[1 + f_T(n)]\}^{1/T} - 1$$

where

$z_T(n)$ = simulated spot rate for month T on path n
$f_j(n)$ = simulated future one-month rate for month j on path n

Consequently, the interest-rate path for the simulated future one-month rates can be converted to the interest-rate path for the simulated monthly spot rates as shown in Exhibit 18-7.

Therefore, the present value of the cash flow for month T on interest-rate path n discounted at the simulated spot rate for month T plus some spread is

$$PV[C_T(n)] = \frac{C_T(n)}{[1 + z_T(n) + K]^{1/T}}$$

where

$PV[C_T(n)]$ = present value of cash flow for month T on path n
$C_T(n)$ = cash flow for month T on path n
$z_T(n)$ = spot rate for month T on path n
K = appropriate risk-adjusted spread

The present value for path n is the sum of the present value of the cash flow for each month on path n. That is,

$$PV[\text{path}(n)] = (1/360)\{PV[C_1(n)] + PV[C_2(n)] + \dots + PV[C_{360}(n)]\}$$

where $PV[\text{path}(n)]$ is the present value of interest-rate path n.

Exhibit 18-7   Simulated Paths of Monthly Spot Rates

	Interest-Rate Path Number[a]				
Month	1	2	3 $\cdots$	n $\cdots$	N
1	$z_1(1)$	$z_1(2)$	$z_1(3)$	$z_1(n)$	$z_1(N)$
2	$z_2(1)$	$z_2(2)$	$z_2(3)$	$z_2(n)$	$z_2(N)$
3	$z_3(1)$	$z_3(2)$	$z_3(3)$	$z_3(n)$	$z_3(N)$
4	$z_4(1)$	$z_4(2)$	$z_4(3)$	$z_4(n)$	$z_4(N)$
$\vdots$					
t	$z_t(1)$	$z_t(2)$	$z_t(3)$	$z_t(n)$	$z_t(N)$
$\vdots$					
358	$z_{358}(1)$	$z_{358}(2)$	$z_{358}(3)$	$z_{358}(n)$	$z_{358}(N)$
359	$z_{359}(1)$	$z_{359}(2)$	$z_{359}(3)$	$z_{359}(n)$	$z_{359}(N)$
360	$z_{360}(1)$	$z_{360}(2)$	$z_{360}(3)$	$z_{360}(n)$	$z_{360}(N)$

[a]Notation: $z_t(n)$, spot rate for month t on path n; N, total number of interest-rate paths.

Determining the Theoretical Value

The present value of a given interest-rate path can be thought of as the theoretical value of a pass-through if that path was actually realized. The theoretical value of the pass-through can be determined by calculating the average of the theoretical value of all the interest-rate paths. That is, the theoretical value is equal to

$$\text{theoretical value} = (1/N)\{PV[\text{path}(1)] + PV[\text{path}(2)] + \cdots + PV[\text{path}(N)]\}$$

This procedure for valuing a pass-through is also followed for a CMO tranche. The cash flow for each month on each interest-rate path is found according to the principal repayment and interest distribution rules of the deal. To do this, a CMO structuring model is needed. In any analysis of CMOs, one of the major stumbling blocks is getting a good CMO structuring model.

Looking at the Distribution of the Path Values

The theoretical value generated by the Monte Carlo simulation method is the average of the path values. There is valuable information in the distribution of the path values. For example, consider a well-protected PAC bond. If the theoretical value generated from the Monte Carlo simulation method is 88 and the standard deviation of the path values is 1 point, there is not a great deal of dispersion in the path values. In contrast, suppose that the model indicates that the theoretical value for a support bond is 77 and the standard deviation of the path values is 10 points. Clearly, there is substantial dispersion of the path values and, as a result, the investor is warned about the potential variability of the model's value.[2]

Simulated Average Life

In Chapter 11, the average-life measure for a mortgage-backed security was introduced. The average life reported in a Monte Carlo analysis is the average of the average lives along the interest-rate paths. That is, for each interest-rate path, there is an average life. The average of these average lives is the average life reported. As with the theoretical value, additional information is conveyed by the distribution of the average life. The greater the range and standard deviation of the average life, the more uncertainty there is about the security's average life.

Option-Adjusted Spread

As explained in Chapter 17, the option-adjusted spread is a measure of the yield spread that can be used to convert dollar differences between value and price. It represents a spread over the issuer's spot rate curve or benchmark.

In the Monte Carlo model, the OAS is the spread K that—when added to all the spot rates on all interest-rate paths—will make the average present value of the paths equal to the observed market price (plus accrued interest). Mathematically, OAS is the spread that will satisfy the following condition:

$$\text{market price} = (1/N)\{PV[\text{path}(1)] + PV[\text{path}(2)] + \cdots + PV[\text{path}(N)]\}$$

where N is the number of interest-rate paths.

---

[2] For illustrations, see Robert W. Kopprasch, "A Further Look at Option-Adjusted Spread Analysis," Chapter 30 in Frank J. Fabozzi (ed.), *The Handbook of Mortgage-Backed Securities* (Burr Ridge, IL: Irwin Professional Publishing, 1995).

Option Cost

The implied cost of the option embedded in any RMBS can be obtained by calculating the difference between the OAS at the assumed volatility of interest rates and the static spread. That is,

$$\text{option cost} = \text{static spread} - \text{option-adjusted spread}$$

The reason that the option cost is measured in this way is as follows. In an environment of no interest-rate changes, the investor would earn the static spread. When future interest rates are uncertain, the spread is less; however, because of the homeowner's option to prepay, the OAS reflects the spread after adjusting for this option. Therefore, the option cost is the difference between the spread that would be earned in a static interest-rate environment (the static spread) and the spread after adjusting for the homeowner's option.

In general, a tranche's option cost is more stable than its OAS in the face of market movements. This interesting feature is useful in reducing the computational costs of calculating the OAS as the market moves. For small market moves, the OAS of a tranche may be approximated by recalculating the static spread (which is relatively cheap and easy to calculate) and subtracting its option cost.

Effective Duration and Convexity

In Chapter 17, we explained how to determine the effective duration and effective convexity for any security. These measures can be calculated using the Monte Carlo method as follows. First, the bond's OAS is found using the current term structure of interest rates. Next, the bond is repriced holding OAS constant but shifting the term structure. Two shifts are used to get the prices needed to apply the effective duration and effective convexity formulas: In one, yields are increased, in the second, they are decreased.

Selecting the Number of Interest-Rate Paths

Let's now address the question of the number of scenario paths or repetitions, N, needed to value an RMBS. A typical OAS run will be done for 512 to 1,024 interest-rate paths. The scenarios generated using the simulation method look very realistic and, furthermore, reproduce today's Treasury curve. By employing this technique, the money manager is effectively saying that Treasuries are fairly priced today and that the objective is to determine whether a specific RMBS is rich or cheap relative to Treasuries.

The number of interest-rate paths determines how "good" the estimate is, not relative to the truth but relative to the model. The more paths, the more average spread tends to settle down. It is a statistical sampling problem.

Most Monte Carlo simulation models employ some from of **variance reduction** to cut down on the number of sample paths necessary to get a good statistical sample. Variance reduction techniques allow us to obtain price estimates within a tick. By this we mean that if the model is used to generate more scenarios, price estimates from the model will not change by more than a tick. For some very sensitive CMO tranches, more than 1,024 paths may be needed to estimate prices within one tick.

Limitations of the Option-Adjusted Spread Measure

Although the OAS measure is much more useful than the static cash flow yield measure, it still suffers from major pitfalls.[3] These limitations apply not only to the OAS for RMBS but also the OAS produced from a binomial model. First, as noted earlier, the OAS is a product of the valuation model. The valuation model may be poorly constructed because it fails to capture the true factors that affect the value of particular securities. Second, in a Monte Carlo simulation the interest-rate paths must be adjusted so that on-the-run Treasuries are valued properly. That is, the value of an on-the-run Treasury is equal to its market price or, equivalently, its OAS is zero. The process of adjusting the interest-rate paths to achieve that result is ad hoc.

A third problem with the OAS is that it assumes a constant OAS for each interest-rate path and over time for a given interest-rate path. If there is a term structure to the OAS, this is not captured by having a single OAS number. Finally, the OAS is dependent on the volatility assumption, the prepayment assumption in the case of RMBS, and the rules for refunding in the case of corporate bonds.

In addition, there is a problem with calculating an OAS for a portfolio by taking a weighted average of the OAS of the individual portfolio holdings.[4] Instead, if an OAS for a portfolio is sought, it is necessary to obtain the portfolio's cash flow along each interest-rate path. The OAS is then the spread that will make the average portfolio value equal to the portfolio's market value.

Illustration[5]

In this section, we use a plain vanilla deal to show how CMOs can be analyzed using the Monte Carlo simulation method. The plain vanilla sequential-pay CMO bond structure in our illustration is FNMA 89-97. A diagram of the principal allocation structure is given in Exhibit 18-8. The structure includes five tranches, A, B, C, D, and Z, and a residual class.

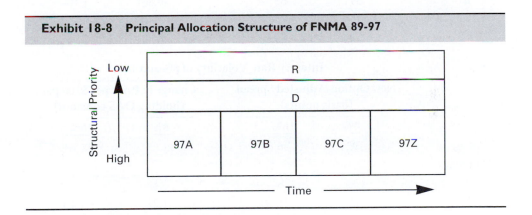

Exhibit 18-8   Principal Allocation Structure of FNMA 89-97

[3] These pitfalls have been described and documented in David F. Babbel and Stavros A. Zenios, "Pitfalls in the Analysis of Option-Adjusted Spreads," *Financial Analysts Journal,* July–August 1992, pp. 65–69.

[4] Kopprasch, "A Further Look at Option-Adjusted Spread Analysis."

[5] For additional illustrations, see Frank J. Fabozzi, Scott F. Richard, and David S. Horovitz, "Valuation of Mortgage-Backed Securities," Chapter 25 in Frank J. Fabozzi (ed.), *The Handbook of Mortgage-Backed Securities,* 5th ed. (New York: McGraw-Hill, 2001).

Tranche Z is an accrual bond, and tranche D class is an "IOette."[6] The focus of our analysis is on tranches A, B, C, and Z.

The top panel of Exhibit 18-9 shows the OAS and the option cost for the collateral and the four tranches in the CMO structure. The OAS for the collateral is 70 basis points.

Exhibit 18-9 Analysis of FNMA 89-97 Classes A, B, C, and Z (as of 4/27/90)

	Base Case (Assumes 12% Interest-Rate Volatility)	
	Option-Adjusted Spread (basis points)	Option Cost (basis points)
Collateral	70	45
Tranches		
A	23	29
B	46	41
C	59	36
Z	74	50

Prepayments at 80% and 120% of Prepayment Model
(Assumes 12% Interest-Rate Volatility)

	New Option-Adjusted Spread (basis points)		Change in Price per $100 par (holding OAS constant)	
	80%	120%	80%	120%
Collateral	70	71	$0.00	$0.04
Tranches				
A	8	40	−0.43	0.48
B	31	65	−0.86	1.10
C	53	73	−0.41	0.95
Z	72	93	−0.28	2.70

Interest-Rate Volatility of 8% and 16%

	New Option-Adjusted Spread (basis points)		Change in Price per $100 par (holding OAS constant)	
	8%	16%	8%	16%
Collateral	92	46	$1.03	−$1.01
Tranches				
A	38	5	0.42	−0.51
B	67	21	1.22	−1.45
C	77	39	1.22	−1.36
Z	99	50	3.55	−3.41

[6] This is a form of an interest-only tranche that has a nominal par value. Until 1992, all tranches in a CMO structure had to have some par value. As explained in Chapter 12, today, notional IOs are created.

Because the option cost is 45 basis points, the static spread is 115 basis points (70 basis points plus 45 basis points). The weighted-average OAS of all the tranches (including the residual) is equal to the OAS of the collateral.

At the time this analysis was performed, April 27, 1990, the Treasury yield curve was not steep. As we noted earlier, in such a yield curve environment the static spread will not differ significantly from the traditionally computed yield spread. Thus, for the four tranches shown in Exhibit 18-9, the static spread is 52 for A, 87 for B, 95 for C, and 124 for D.

Notice that the tranches did not share the OAS equally. The same is true for the option cost. The value tended to go toward the longer tranches, something that occurs in the typical deal. Both the static spread and the option cost increase as the maturity increases. The only tranches where there appears to be a bit of a bargain are B and C. A money manager contemplating the purchase of one of these middle tranches can see that C offers a higher OAS than B and appears to bear less of the risk, as measured by the option cost. The problem a money manager may encounter is that he might not be permitted to extend out as long as the C tranche because of duration, maturity, or average-life constraints.

Now let's look at modeling risk. Examination of the sensitivity of the tranches to changes in prepayments and interest-rate volatility will help us to understand the interaction of the tranches in the structure and who is bearing the risk.

We begin with prepayments. Specifically, we keep the same interest-rate paths as those used to get the OAS in the base case (the top panel of Exhibit 18-9) but reduce the prepayment rate on each interest-rate path to 80% of the projected rate.

As can be seen in the second panel of Exhibit 18-9, slowing down prepayments does not change the OAS for the collateral and its price at all. This is because the collateral is trading close to par. Tranches created by this collateral do not behave the same way, however. The exhibit reports two results of the sensitivity analysis. First, it indicates the change in the OAS. Second, it indicates the change in the price, holding the OAS constant at the base case.

To see how a money manager can use the information in the second panel, consider tranche A. At 80% of the prepayment speed, the OAS for this class declines from 23 basis points to 8 basis points. If the OAS is held constant, the panel indicates that the buyer of tranche A would lose $0.43 per $100 par value.

Notice that for all the tranches reported in Exhibit 18-9 there is a loss. How could all four tranches lose if prepayments are slowed down and the collateral does not lose value? This is because tranche D and the residual (R), which are not reported in the exhibit, got all the benefit of that slowdown. Notice that tranche Z is actually fairly well protected, so it does not lose much value as a result of the slowdown of prepayments. Tranche B by contrast is severely affected.

Also shown in the second panel of the exhibit is the second part of our experiment that tests the sensitivity of prepayments: The prepayment rate is assumed to be 120% of the base case. Once again, as the collateral is trading at close to par, its price does not move very much, about four cents per $100 of par value. In fact, because the collateral is trading slightly below par, the speeding up of prepayments will make the collateral look better while the OAS increases by only one basis point.

Now look at the four tranches. They all benefited. The results reported in the exhibit indicate that a money manager who is willing to go out to the long end of the curve, such as tranche Z, would realize most of the benefits of that speedup of prepayments. Because the four tranches benefited and the benefit to the collateral was minor, tranche D, the IOette, and the residual were affected adversely. In general, IO types of tranches will be affected adversely by a speedup.

Now let's look at the sensitivity to the interest-rate volatility assumption, 12% in the base case. Two experiments are performed: reducing the volatility assumption to 8% and increasing it to 16%. These results are reported in the third panel of Exhibit 18-9.

Reducing the volatility to 8% increases the dollar price of the collateral by $1 and increases the OAS from 70 in the base case to 92. This $1 increase in the price of the collateral is not equally distributed, however, among the four tranches. Most of the increase in value is realized by the longer tranches. The OAS gain for each of the tranches follows more or less the OAS durations of those tranches. This makes sense, because the longer the duration, the greater the risk, and when volatility declines, the reward is greater for the risk accepted.

At the higher level of assumed interest-rate volatility of 16%, the collateral is affected severely. The collateral's loss is distributed among the tranches in the expected manner: The longer the duration, the greater the loss. In this case tranche D and the residual are the least affected.

Using the OAS from the Monte Carlo simulation methodology, a fair conclusion can be made about this simple plain vanilla structure: What you see is what you get. The only surprise in this structure seems to be tranches B and C. In general, however, a money manager willing to extend duration gets paid for that risk.

TOTAL RETURN ANALYSIS

Neither the static cash flow methodology nor the Monte Carlo simulation methodology will tell a money manager whether investment objectives can be satisfied. The performance evaluation of an individual RMBS requires specification of an investment horizon, whose length for most financial institutions is dictated by the nature of its liabilities.

The measure that should be used to assess the performance of a security or a portfolio over some investment horizon is the total return that we discussed in Chapter 3. The total dollars received from investing in an RMBS consist of

1. the projected cash flow from the projected interest payments and the projected principal repayment (scheduled plus prepayments)
2. the interest earned on reinvestment of the projected interest payments and the projected principal prepayments
3. the projected price of the RMBS at the end of the investment horizon

To obtain the cash flow, a prepayment rate over the investment horizon must be assumed. The second step requires assumption of a reinvestment rate. Finally, either of the methodologies described in this chapter—cash flow yield or Monte Carlo simulation—can be used to calculate the price at the end of the investment horizon under a particular set of assumptions. Either approach requires assumption of the prepayment rate and the Treasury rates (i.e., the yield curve) at the end of the investment horizon. The cash flow yield methodology uses an assumed spread to a comparable Treasury to determine the required cash flow yield, which is then used to compute the projected price. The Monte Carlo simulation methodology requires an assumed OAS at the investment horizon. From this assumption, the OAS methodology can produce the horizon price.

To test the sensitivity of total return to various alternative assumptions scenario analysis is helpful. Its limitation is that only a small number of potential scenarios can be considered, and it fails to take into consideration the dynamics of changes in the yield curve and the dynamics of the deal structure.

Horizon Price for Collateralized Mortgage Obligation Tranches

The most difficult part of estimating total return is projecting the price at the horizon date. In the case of a CMO tranche, the price depends on the characteristics of the tranche and the spread to Treasuries *at the termination date.* The key determinants are the "quality" of the tranche, its average life (or duration), and its convexity.

Quality refers to the type of CMO tranche. Consider, for example, that an investor can purchase a CMO tranche that is a PAC bond but as a result of projected prepayments could become a sequential-pay tranche. As another example, suppose that a PAC bond is the longest-average-life tranche in a reverse PAC structure. Projected prepayments in this case might occur in an amount to change the class from a long-average-life PAC tranche to a support tranche. The converse is that the quality of a tranche may improve as well as deteriorate. For example, the effective collar for a PAC tranche could widen at the horizon date when prepayment circumstances increase the par amount of support tranches outstanding as a proportion of the deal.

Option-Adjusted Spread Total Return

The total return and OAS frameworks can be combined to determine the projected price at the horizon date. At the end of the investment horizon, it is necessary to specify how the OAS is expected to change. The horizon price can be "backed out" of the Monte Carlo simulation model.

Assumptions about the OAS value at the investment horizon reflect the expectations of the money manager. It is common to assume that the OAS at the horizon date will be the same as the OAS at the time of purchase. A total return calculated using this assumption is sometimes referred to as a **constant-OAS total return.** Alternatively, active total return managers will make bets on how the OAS will change—either widening or tightening. The total return framework can be used to assess how sensitive the performance of an RMBS is to change in the OAS.

▌KEY POINTS

- There are two methodologies commonly used to analyze all RMBS (agency and nonagency): cash flow yield methodology and Monte Carlo simulation methodology.
- The cash flow yield is the interest rate that will make the present value of the projected cash flow from an RMBS equal to its market price. The cash flow yield assumes that (1) all the cash flows can be reinvested at a rate equal to the cash flow yield, (2) the RMBS is held to the maturity date, and (3) the prepayment speed used to project the cash flow will be realized. In addition, the cash flow yield methodology fails to recognize that future interest-rate changes will affect the cash flow.
- Modified duration is not a good measure of price volatility for RMBS because it assumes that the cash flow does not change as yield changes. Effective duration does take into consideration how yield changes will affect prepayments and therefore cash flow.
- An RMBS is a security whose cash flow is path dependent. This means that cash flow received in one period is determined not only by the current and future interest-rate levels, but also by the path that interest rates took to get to the current level.
- A methodology used to analyze path-dependent cash flow securities is the Monte Carlo simulation. This methodology involves randomly generating many scenarios of future interest-rate paths, where the interest-rate paths are generated based on some

volatility assumption for interest rates. The random paths of interest rates should be generated from an arbitrage-free model of the future term structure of interest rates. The Monte Carlo simulation methodology applied to RMBS involves randomly generating a set of cash flows based on simulated future mortgage refinancing rates.

- The theoretical value of a security on any interest-rate path is the present value of the cash flow on that path, where the spot rates are those on the corresponding interest-rate path. The theoretical value of a security is the average of the theoretical values over all the interest-rate paths. Information about the distribution of the path values is useful in understanding the variability around the theoretical value.
- The average life reported is the average of the average lives from all the interest-rate paths, and information about the distribution of the average life is useful.
- In the Monte Carlo simulation methodology, the option-adjusted spread is the spread that when added to all the spot rates on all interest-rate paths will make the average present value of the paths equal to the observed market price (plus accrued interest).
- The effective duration and effective convexity are calculated using the Monte Carlo simulation methodology by holding the OAS constant and shifting the term structure up and down.
- Total return is the correct measure for assessing the potential performance of CMO tranches over a specified investment horizon.
- The static cash flow yield or Monte Carlo simulation methodology can be incorporated into a total return framework to calculate the mortgage-backed security's price at the horizon date.
- Scenario analysis is one way to evaluate the risk associated with investing in an RMBS.

QUESTIONS

1. Suppose you are told that the cash flow yield of a pass-through security is 9% and that you are seeking to invest in a security with a yield greater than 8.8%.

   a. What additional information would you need to know before you might invest in this pass-through security?

   b. What are the limitations of the cash flow yield for assessing the potential return from investing in an RMBS?

2. Using the cash flow yield methodology, a spread is calculated over a comparable Treasury security. How is a comparable Treasury determined?

3. What is vector analysis?

4. In the calculation of effective duration and effective convexity, why is a prepayment model needed?

5. The following excerpt is taken from an article titled "Fidelity Eyes $250 Million Move into Premium PACs and I-Os" that appeared in the January 27, 1992, issue of *BondWeek*, pp. 1 and 21:

   Three Fidelity investment mortgage funds are considering investing this quarter a total of $250 million in premium planned amortization classes of collateralized mortgage obligations and some interest-only strips, said Jim Wolfson, portfolio manager. . . . Wolfson . . . will look mainly at PACs backed by 9–10% Federal Home Loan Mortgage Corp. and Federal National Mortgage Association pass-throughs. These have higher option-adjusted spreads than regular agency pass-throughs, or similar premium Government National Mortgage Association-backed, PACs, he said. He expects I-Os will start to perform better as prepayments start to slow later in this quarter.

   The higher yields on I-Os and premium PACs compensate for their higher prepayment risk, said Wolfson. "You get paid in yield to take on negative convexity," he said. He does not feel prepayments will accelerate. . . .

   a. Why would premium PACs and interest-only strips offer higher yields if the market expects that prepayments will accelerate or are highly uncertain?

b. What does Wolfson mean when he says: "You get paid in yield to take on negative convexity"?

c. What measure is Wolfson using to assess the risks associated with prepayments?

6. In an article titled "CUNA Mutual Looks for Noncallable Corporates" that appeared in the November 4, 1991, issue of *BondWeek*, p. 6, Joe Goglia, a portfolio manager for CUNA Mutual Insurance Group, stated that he invests in "planned amortization class tranches, which have less exposure to prepayment risk and are more positively convex than other mortgage-backeds." Is this true?

7. What is a path-dependent cash flow security?

8. Why is a pass-through security a path-dependent cash flow security?

9. Give two reasons why a CMO tranche is a path-dependent cash flow security.

10. Explain how, given the cash flow on the simulated interest-rate paths, the theoretical value of an RMBS is determined.

11. Explain how, given the cash flow on the simulated interest-rate paths, the average life of an RMBS is determined.

12. Suppose that a support bond is being analyzed using the Monte Carlo simulation methodology. The theoretical value using 1,500 interest-rate paths is 88. The range for the path present values is a low of 50 and a high of 115. The standard deviation is 15 points. How much confidence would you place on the theoretical value of 88?

13. In a well-protected PAC structure, what would you expect the distribution of the path present values and average lives to be compared to a support bond from the same CMO structure?

14. Suppose that the following values for an RMBS are correct for each prepayment assumption:

PSA Assumption	Value of Security
192	112.10
194	111.80
200	111.20
202	111.05
210	110.70

Assume that the value of the security in the market is 111.20 based on 200 PSA. What is the prepayment sensitivity of this security?

15. An analysis of a CMO structure using the Monte Carlo method indicated the following, assuming 12% volatility:

	OAS (basic points)	Static Spread (basic points)
Collateral	80	120
Tranche		
PAC I A	40	60
PAC I B	55	80
PAC I C	65	95
PAC II	95	125
Support	75	250

a. Calculate the option cost for each tranche.

b. Which tranche is clearly too rich?

c. What would happen to the static spread for each tranche if a 15% volatility is assumed?

d. What would happen to the OAS for each tranche if a 15% volatility is assumed?

16. Why would the option-adjusted spread vary across dealer firms?

17. Explain how the number of interest-rate paths used in the Monte Carlo simulation methodology is determined.

18. Explain why you agree or disagree with the following statement: "When the Monte Carlo simulation methodology is used to value an RMBS, a PSA assumption is employed for all interest-rate paths."

19. What assumption is made about the OAS in calculating the effective duration and effective convexity of an RMBS?

20. What are the limitations of the option-adjusted spread measure?

21. What assumptions are required to assess the potential total return of an RMBS?

22. What are the complications of assessing the potential total return of a CMO tranched using the total return framework?

19

Analysis of Convertible Bonds

LEARNING OBJECTIVES

After reading this chapter, you will understand

- what a convertible bond is

- what an exchangeable bond is

- the basic features of a convertible security

- the types of convertible securities

- conversion value, market conversion price, conversion premium per share, conversion premium ratio, and premium over straight value of a convertible bond

- the investment features of a convertible security

- what the minimum value of a convertible bond is

- the premium payback period

- the downside risk associated with a convertible bond

- measures from options theory that are used for convertible bonds: delta, gamma, and vega

- the pros and cons of investing in a convertible bond

- profile of a convertible bond

- the options approach to valuing a convertible bond

- why an option pricing approach is needed to value convertible securities properly

In Chapter 7, we described convertible bonds. In this chapter, we explain methodologies for analyzing them, beginning with a review of the basic provisions of convertible bonds.

CONVERTIBLE BOND PROVISIONS

The conversion provision in a corporate bond issue grants the bondholder the right to convert the bond into a predetermined number of shares of common stock of the issuer. A **convertible bond**, colloquially referred to as a "convert," is, therefore, a corporate bond with a call option to buy the common stock of the issuer. **Exchangeable bonds** grant the bondholder the right to exchange the bonds for the common stock of a firm *other* than the issuer of the bond.

The number of shares of common stock that the bondholder will receive from exercising the call option of a convertible bond or an exchangeable bond is called the **conversion ratio**. The conversion privilege may extend for all or only some portion of the bond's life, and the stated conversion ratio may fall over time. It is always adjusted proportionately for stock splits and stock dividends. There are some convertible bonds that may have an initial nonconversion period. That period can be from six to 12 months.

Upon conversion, the bondholder typically receives from the issuer the underlying shares. This is referred to as a **physical settle**. There are issues where the issuer may have the choice of paying the bondholder the cash value of the underlying shares. This is referred to as a **cash settle**.

At the time of issuance of a convertible bond, the issuer has effectively granted the bondholder the right to purchase the common stock at a price equal to

$$\frac{\text{par value of convertible bond}}{\text{conversion ratio}}$$

Along with the conversion privilege granted to the bondholder, most convertible bonds are callable at the option of the issuer as of a certain date. This standard type of call option in a convertible bond is called an **unprotected call**. There is another type of call feature that is included in some convertible bond issues: The bond may only be called if the price of the underlying stock (or the average stock price over some number of days) exceeds a specified trigger price. This type of call is known as a **protected call**. Some convertible bonds are putable. Put options can be classified as hard puts and soft puts. A **hard put** is one in which the convertible security must be redeemed by the issuer only for cash. In the case of a **soft put**, the issuer has the option to redeem the convertible security for cash, common stock, subordinated notes, or a combination of the three. Most converts include another type of put should there be a change in control of the corporation. Typically, an investor can put the bond at par or slightly above par if a specified percent of the shares (typically 51%) is acquired by another entity. The put price is payable in cash (i.e., a hard put).

Another convertible that was at one time issued for its favorable tax treatment had a **contingent payment provision**. These were nicknamed "CoPa" bonds. Unlike a traditional convertible bond whose coupon rate is fixed over the bond's life, a CoPa bond pays a higher coupon rate if the price of the underlying stock price reaches a specified threshold (say, 125% of the conversion price).

Special Conversion Provisions

An investor must look carefully at the conversion privilege because not all bonds allow the straightforward conversion privilege described above. Two types of convertible bonds issued prior to 2008 that departed from the traditional conversion privilege are the net share settlement convertible and the contingent conversion convertible.

When the holder of a convertible bond exercises the option to convert, the traditional outcome was that the issuer exchanged the bond for the number of shares as indicated by the conversion ratio. For a convertible bond that includes a **net share settlement provision**, upon exercise of the conversion option to convert, the issuer pays the par value in cash to retire the bonds but the bond will be trading above its par value. As will be explained later in this chapter, the bond will have a conversion value. The difference between the conversion value and the par value is additional compensation owed to the holder. That difference is made up by the issuer providing shares of stock to the holder. In some convertible issues, the issuer will have the option to settle by providing a combination of cash and stock. Issuer motivation for the issuance of convertible bonds with this provision (also called a **cash-par settlement provision**) was that, from a financial accounting perspective, convertible bonds with net share settlement provisions were treated favorably in the calculation of the issuer's earnings per share. However, the changes in the financial accounting rules that were put into place in 2008 no longer made this type of financing attractive to corporations. As evidence of the popularity of these bonds before then, since 2005 when they first became popular, $120 billion of the $171 billion of U.S. convertible bonds contained this provision.[1]

In a traditional convertible bond, the holder has the right to convert at any time. With a **contingent convertible provision**, the holder only has the right to convert when the price of the underlying stock exceeds a specified threshold price for a specified number of trading days.[2] Typically, the threshold was 130% of the conversion price. (We will explain the conversion price later.) Until that time, the bondholder is not entitled to convert. Bonds with this provision, nicknamed "CoCo" bonds, were introduced in late 1999, and by 2003 accounted for more than 70% of new convertible bond issuance.[3] The reason for the popularity of a convertible bond with this provision was the tax and financial accounting advantages from the perspective of the issuer. These benefits disappeared with changes in the tax law and financial reporting requirements.

CATEGORIZATION OF CONVERTIBLE SECURITIES

The U.S. convertible bond market is by far the largest convertible bond market in the world. Most U.S. convertible bonds are issued as private placements under Securities and Exchange Commission (SEC) Rule 144A. Lehman Brothers publishes the Barclays Capital U.S. Convertible Indices. The main index is the Barclays Capital Convertible Composite

[1] "No More Net-Share Settle," *International Financing Review*, March 23, 2011. http://www.ifre.com/no-more-net-share-settle/552214.article.
[2] For those familiar with options, this type of option is referred to as a "knock-in option."
[3] Mihir Bhattacharya, "Convertible Securities and Their Valuation," Chapter 60 in Frank J. Fabozzi (ed.), *Handbook of Fixed Income Securities*, 7th ed. (New York: McGraw-Hill, 2005).

Index. The different subindexes of that index shown below indicate the different subsectors or ways to categorize the convertible bond market:

TYPE

- cash-pay bonds
- zero-coupon/original issue discount
- preferreds
- mandatories

UNDERLYING MARKET CAPITALIZATION

- small cap
- mid cap
- large cap

CREDIT QUALITY

- investment grade
- intermediate grade
- junk
- nonrated

PROFILE

- typical
- equity sensitive
- busted
- distressed

There are further breakdowns by industry sector.

With respect to "Type" of convertible security, **cash-pay bonds**, also referred to as traditional convertible bonds, are convertible bonds that pay coupon interest. **Zero-coupon convertible bonds** are like any other bonds that pay no coupon interest. A popular type of zero-coupon bond is a Merrill Lynch product called LYON, which stands for Liquid Yield Option Notes. An original issue discount (OID) convertible bond is issued at a discount from par but has some coupon interest; the coupon interest rate is a below-market rate. A **convertible preferred** is a preferred stock that can be converted into common stock. Finally, a **mandatory convertible** is a convertible security that converts automatically at maturity into shares of the issuer's common stock. This automatic conversion differs from convertible bonds where conversion is optional.

"Underlying Market Capitalization" indicates the market capitalization (or "cap") of the equity of the issuer of the convertible bond. The market capitalization of a corporation is the product of its common stock outstanding and the price per share of common stock. Credit quality is simply based on the rating of the convertible issue. According to Barclays Capital, as of mid 2009, 31% of all convertibles issued by U.S. corporations had an investment-grade rating, 32% an intermediate-grade rating, 7% a junk bond rating, and 29% were nonrated. The three largest sectors that issued convertible bonds were consumer noncyclicals (23%), financial institutions (21%), and technology (19%).

We will explain what is meant by "Profile" later in this chapter.

BASIC ANALYTICS AND CONCEPTS FOR CONVERTIBLE BOND ANALYSIS

In this section, we will describe some basic measures and concepts used in convertible bond analysis. We shall use the following hypothetical convertible bond in our illustrations:

$$\text{convertible bond} = \text{XYZ bond}$$
$$\text{maturity} = 10 \text{ years}$$
$$\text{coupon rate} = 10\%$$
$$\text{conversion ratio} = 50$$
$$\text{par value} = \$1,000$$
$$\text{current market price of XYZ bond} = \$950$$
$$\text{current market price of XYZ common stock} = \$17$$
$$\text{dividends per share} = \$1$$

We will assume that this convertible bond is neither callable nor putable.

The conversion price for the XYZ bond is

$$\text{conversion price} = \frac{\$1,000}{50} = \$20$$

Minimum Value of a Convertible Bond

The **conversion value** of a convertible bond is the value of the bond if it is converted immediately.[4] That is,

$$\text{conversion value} = \text{market price of common stock} \times \text{conversion ratio}$$

The minimum price of a convertible bond is the greater of[5]

1. its conversion value, or
2. its value as a corporate bond without the conversion option—that is, based on the convertible bond's cash flows if not converted (i.e., a plain vanilla bond). This value is called its **straight value**.

To estimate the straight value, we must determine the required yield on a nonconvertible bond with the same quality rating and similar investment characteristics. Given this estimated required yield, the straight value is then the present value of the bond's cash flows using this yield to discount the cash flows.

If the convertible bond does not sell for the greater of these two values, arbitrage profits could be realized. For example, suppose that the conversion value is greater than the straight value, and the bond trades at its straight value. An investor can buy the convertible bond at the straight value and convert it. By doing so, the investor realizes a gain equal to the difference between the conversion value and the straight value. Suppose, instead, that the straight value is greater than the conversion value, and the bond trades at its conversion

---

[4] Technically, the standard textbook definition of conversion value given here is theoretically incorrect because as bondholders convert, the price of the stock will decline. The theoretically correct definition for the conversion value is that it is the product of the conversion ratio and the stock price *after* conversion.

[5] If the conversion value is the greater of the two values, it is possible for the convertible bond to trade below the conversion value. This can occur for the following reasons: (1) there are restrictions that prevent the investor from converting, (2) the underlying stock is illiquid, and (3) an anticipated forced conversion will result in loss of accrued interest of a high coupon issue. See Mihir Bhattacharya, "Convertible Securities and Their Valuation," p. 1395.

value. By buying the convertible at the conversion value, the investor will realize a higher yield than a comparable straight bond.

Illustration

For the XYZ convertible bond,

$$\text{conversion value} = \$17 \times 50 = \$850$$

To determine the straight value, it is necessary to determine what comparable bonds are trading for in the market. Suppose that comparable bonds are trading to yield 14%. The straight value is then the price of a 10% 10-year bond selling to yield 14%. The price for such a bond would be $788.[6]

Given a conversion value of $850 and a straight value of $788, the minimum price for the XYZ bond is $850. To see this, note that if the bond is selling at its straight value rather than its conversion value, an investor could buy the bond for $788 and simultaneously sell 50 shares of XYZ stock at $17 per share. When the short sale of the stock is covered when the bond is converted, the transaction would produce an arbitrage profit of $62 per XYZ bond purchased. The only way to eliminate this arbitrage profit is for the XYZ bond to sell for $850, its conversion value.

Suppose, instead, that comparable nonconvertible bonds are trading to yield 11.8%. Then the straight value of XYZ bond would be $896. The minimum price for the XYZ bond must be its straight value in this case because that is a value higher than the conversion value of $850. To see this, suppose that the market price of the XYZ bond is $850. At this price, the yield would be about 12.7%, 90 basis points greater than comparable nonconvertible bonds. Investors would find the bond attractive. As investors buy the bond, they will bid up its price to where the new yield is 11.8%.

Market Conversion Price

The price that an investor effectively pays for the common stock if the convertible bond is purchased and then converted into the common stock is called the **market conversion price**.[7] It is found as follows:

$$\text{market conversion price} = \frac{\text{market price of convertible bond}}{\text{conversion ratio}}$$

The market conversion price is a useful benchmark because when the actual market price of the stock rises above the market conversion price, any further stock price increase is certain to increase the value of the convertible bond by at least the same percentage. Therefore, the market conversion price can be viewed as a break-even point.

An investor who purchases a convertible bond rather than the underlying stock typically pays a premium over the current market price of the stock. This premium per share is equal to the difference between the market conversion price and the current market price of the common stock. That is,

market conversion premium per share = market conversion price − current market price

---

[6] Actually, it is $788.10, but $788 will be used in our illustrations.
[7] The market conversion price is also called the **conversion parity price**.

The market conversion premium per share is usually expressed as a percentage of the current market price as follows:

$$\text{market conversion premium per ratio} = \frac{\text{conversion premium per share}}{\text{market price of common stock}}$$

Why would someone be willing to pay a premium to buy this bond? Recall that the minimum price of a convertible bond is the greater of its conversion value or its straight value. Thus, as the stock price declines, the price of the convertible bond will not fall below its straight value. The straight value therefore acts as a floor for the convertible bond price.

Viewed in this context, the market conversion premium per share can be seen as the price of a call option. As will be explained in Chapter 27, the buyer of a call option limits the downside risk to the option price. In the case of a convertible bond, for a premium, the bondholder limits the downside risk to the straight value of the bond. The difference between the buyer of a call option and the buyer of a convertible bond is that the former knows precisely the dollar amount of the downside risk, whereas the latter knows only that the most that can be lost is the difference between the convertible bond price and the straight value. The straight value at some future date, however, is not known; the value will change as the interest rate changes.

Illustration

At a market price of $950, a stock price of $17, and a conversion ratio of 50, the market conversion price, market conversion premium per share, and market conversion premium ratio of the XYZ convertible bond are calculated as follows:

$$\text{market conversion price} = \frac{\$950}{50} = \$19$$

$$\text{market conversion premium per share} = \$19 - \$17 = \$2$$

$$\text{market conversion premium ratio} = \frac{\$2}{\$17} = 0.118 \text{ or } 11.8\%$$

Current Income of the Convertible Bond versus Stock

As an offset to the market conversion premium per share, investing in the convertible bond rather than buying the stock directly generally means that the investor realizes higher current income from the coupon interest paid on the convertible bond than would be received as dividends paid on the number of shares equal to the conversion ratio. Analysts evaluating a convertible bond typically compute the time it takes to recover the premium per share by computing the **premium payback period** (which is also known as the **break-even time**). This is computed as follows:

$$\frac{\text{market conversion premium per share}}{\text{favorable income differential per share}}$$

where the favorable income differential per share is equal to[8]

$$\frac{\text{coupon interest from bond} - (\text{conversion ratio} \times \text{dividend per share})}{\text{conversion ratio}}$$

---

[8] A more precise methodology for calculating the favorable income from holding the convertible is recommended in Luke Knecht and Mike McCowin, "Valuing Convertible Securities," in Frank J. Fabozzi (ed.), *Advances and Innovations in Bond and Mortgage Markets* (Chicago: Probus Publishing, 1989). In most cases, the conventional formula presented in the text is sufficient.

Notice that the premium payback period does *not* take into account the time value of money.

Illustration

For the XYZ convertible bond, the market conversion premium per share is $2. The favorable income differential per share is found as follows:

$$\text{coupon interest from bond} = 0.10 \times \$1{,}000 = \$100$$
$$\text{conversion ratio} \times \text{dividend per share} = 50 \times \$1 = \$50$$

Therefore,

$$\text{favorable income differential per share} = \frac{\$100 - \$50}{50} = \$1$$

and

$$\text{premium payback period} = \frac{\$2}{\$1} = 2 \text{ years}$$

Without considering the time value of money, the investor would recover the market conversion premium per share in two years.

Downside Risk with a Convertible Bond

Investors usually use the straight value of the bond as a measure of the downside risk of a convertible bond because the price of the convertible bond cannot fall below this value. Thus, the straight value acts as the *current* floor for the price of the convertible bond. The downside risk is measured as a percentage of the straight value and computed as follows:

$$\text{premium over straight value} = \frac{\text{market price of the convertible bond}}{\text{straight value}} - 1$$

The higher the premium over straight value, all other factors constant, the less attractive the convertible bond.

Despite its use in practice, this measure of downside risk is flawed because the straight value (the floor) changes as interest rates change. If interest rates rise (fall), the straight value falls (rises) making the floor fall (rise). Therefore, the downside risk changes as interest rates change.

Illustration

Earlier, we said that if comparable nonconvertible bonds are trading to yield 14%, the straight value of the XYZ bond would be $788. The premium over straight value is then

$$\text{premium over straight value} = \frac{\$950}{\$788} - 1 = 0.21 \text{ or } 21\%$$

If the yield on a comparable nonconvertible bond is 11.8% instead of 14%, the straight value would be $896 and the premium over straight value would be

$$\text{premium over straight value} = \frac{\$950}{\$896} - 1 = 0.06 \text{ or } 6\%$$

OPTION MEASURES

Because a convertible bond embeds a call option on the underlying common stock, we can estimate the sensitivity of a convertible bond's price from measures used in option theory. While we will describe these measures for options on bonds in Chapter 27, here we describe some of the relevant measures that are used by practitioners in managing risk of options on common stock and how they relate to convertible bonds. We will then see how these measures are used in strategies known as convertible bond arbitrage strategies later in this chapter.

The measures we describe are

- delta
- gamma
- vega
- implied volatility

Basically, these measures relate to the factors that we will describe in Chapter 27 that affect the value of an option. The first three measures show the sensitivity of the option's price to changes in a particular factor that is known to affect the price. Several of these factors, in the case of an option on a stock, include:

- the price of the underlying stock
- the expected volatility of the underlying stock's price
- the amount of time remaining to the expiration of the option

The measures are calculated by using a theoretical model to value the price of an option (the most common for options on common stock is the well-known Black–Scholes option pricing model explained in Chapter 27) and determining how the theoretical value changes when a factor (holding all other factors constant) changes.

Delta

An option's delta measures the sensitivity of an option's price to a change in the price of the underlying. For an option on common stock, the underlying is common stock. In the case of a convertible bond, the underlying is the common stock of the issuer. Hence, a convertible bond's delta is the sensitivity of its value to a change in the underlying stock's price. (Another name used for delta is **hedge ratio** or **neutral hedge ratio**.) More specifically, delta is the ratio of the change in the convertible's value to the change in the price of the underlying shares.

The delta is used to estimate the impact of a change in the price per share of the underlying stock on the convertible bond's value as follows:

approximate change in a convertible bond's value =

$$\text{change in stock price per share} \times \text{conversion ratio} \times \text{delta}$$

For example, consider our hypothetical convertible bond, bond XYZ. The conversion ratio is 50. Suppose that the delta is 0.60. For a price change of $0.125 for the stock price per share, the approximate change in the convertible bond's value is

$$\$0.125 \times 50 \times 0.60 = \$3.75$$

Delta ranges from 0 to 1. The delta can help describe the character of the convertible bond. If the delta is 0, basically the bond is a straight bond since a change in the price of the underlying stock has no impact on the convertible bond's price. At the other end of the spectrum, a delta of 1 means that the convertible bond will mirror the movement in the underlying stock.

In option theory, delta is also known as the hedge ratio because it indicates for an option the amount of the underlying that must be shorted so that a combined long position in the option and short position in the underlying will be neutralized if there is a small change in the price of the underlying. In the case of a convertible bond, the hedge ratio is the number of stocks to short so that by owning the convertible bond and shorting the number of stocks indicated by the hedge ratio, there will be no change in value of the position if the price of the stock changes by a small amount. The combined position of the convertible bond and the short position in the stock is said to be **delta hedged**, **delta neutral**, or **market neutral**.

For example, for our hypothetical convertible bond, the delta is 0.60. Multiplying the delta by the conversion ratio of 50 gives 30. This means that 30 shares must be shorted in order to obtain a market neutral position. For example, suppose the price of the underlying shares increases by $0.125. This means the short position consisting of 30 shares of stock will lose $3.75. This is the same amount, as shown above, that the long position in the convertible bond would gain. Hence, for the combined position, there is neither a gain nor loss.

There are two important points to know about delta. First, just like duration, which we describe in Chapter 4, delta is only an approximation. That is, duration is an approximation of the price change of a bond for a small change in interest rates; delta is only an approximation of the change in the value of a convertible bond for a small change in the price of the stock.

Second, an option's delta changes over time. It changes due to a change in the price of the underlying stock and changes in the other factors that are known to affect the value of an option such as the amount of time remaining until the option expires. So, if an investor wanted to maintain a hedged position (i.e., market neutral position) in the convertible bond and short stock position, the short position would have to be changed as delta changes.

Gamma

Recall again our discussion of duration and convexity in Chapter 4. Duration is the first approximation of how the bond's price will change when interest rates change. The convexity measure shows for a larger change in interest rates what the additional change in the bond's price will be. Basically, convexity relates to the benefit associated with larger interest rate movements or interest rate volatility. In option theory, **gamma** plays the same role as convexity. In the case of a convertible bond, gamma is the additional change in the convertible bond's value for a larger change in the price of the underlying stock.

Vega

An option's **vega** is the sensitivity of the option's price to a change in expected volatility for the underlying stock. For a convertible bond, it is an estimate of the sensitivity of the convertible bond's price to a change in the expected volatility of the stock's price.

Implied Volatility

In general, the higher the expected volatility, the more valuable an option. In an option pricing model, the only unknown input that must be estimated is expected volatility. Practitioners base expected volatility on historical volatility, also referred to as realized volatility and actual volatility. A common practice in the option market is to "back out" what the expected volatility is given the observed market price for the option and the option pricing model. The volatility so obtained is referred to as **implied volatility**.

The difference between implied volatility and historical volatility often is the basis for trading strategies in the options market and is also used for that purpose in the convertible bond market. If the implied volatility is less than historical volatility, the option is viewed as cheap. In the case of convertible bonds, the bond issue is cheap if implied volatility is less than historical volatility.

It should be noted that modeling volatility is not simple and trading strategies based on volatility obviously assumes that volatility has been measured properly.

PROFILE OF A CONVERTIBLE BOND

In describing how to categorize convertible securities at the outset of this chapter, one way to categorize is by the convertible's profile. Basically, by profile, we mean the factors that dominate the performance of the convertible such as the stock price of the issuer or the level of interest rates and spreads. The categories according to the now-defunct investment bank Lehman Brothers are (1) typical, (2) equity sensitive, (3) busted, and (4) distressed.

Bhattacharya refers to a convertible as a **balanced convertible** and defines it as follows:

> Convertibles with conversion premium of 25% to 40%, and investment premium of 15% to 25% respond materially to changes in the underlying stock price as well as interest rates and credit spreads. Hence converts with these attributes, either on issuance or subsequently as a result of stock price evolution, are called *balanced* convertibles. Their hedge ratios, or equivalently, their correlation with stock price changes, range from roughly 55% to 80%.[9]

An **equity sensitive convertible**, also referred to as an **equity substitute convertible** by practitioners, is one in which the underlying stock price exceeds the conversion price of the stock. Hence, movements in the price of the stock will move the price of the convertible, and changes in yield and yield spreads will have a lesser impact. The conversion premium for such issues is low, and in the parlance of the option market, the convertible is said to be "in the money."

When the price of the underlying stock is very far below the conversion price, the convertible is said to be a **busted convertible**. The factors that primarily move a busted convertible's value are changes in yield and yield spreads. Busted convertibles typically have a high conversion premium and are said to be "deep out of the money" in option parlance.

A **distressed convertible** can be viewed as a special type of busted convertible where the price of the underlying stock has fallen so far below the conversion price that it is likely that the issuer will be forced into bankruptcy. The credit rating for such issues has been or is expected to be lowered.

PROS AND CONS OF INVESTING IN A CONVERTIBLE BOND

So far, we have presented several measures that can be used to analyze convertible bonds. Let's use the XYZ convertible bond to drive home the pros and cons of investing in a convertible bond.

Suppose that an investor is considering purchase of a stock or a convertible bond. The stock can be purchased in the market for $17. By buying the convertible bond, the investor is effectively purchasing the stock for $19 (the market conversion price per share).

---

[9] Bhattacharya, "Convertible Securities and Their Valuation," p. 1409.

Look at the outcome one month from now, assuming that XYZ stock rises to $34. An investor buying the stock would realize a gain of $17 (i.e., $34 − $17) on a $17 investment, or a 100% return. In contrast, the conversion value for the bond would be $1,700 (i.e., $34 × 50). Because the price of XYZ bond is $950, the investor would realize a return of about 79%. The return would in fact probably be slightly higher because the convertible bond would trade at a slight premium to its conversion value. The reason for the lower return by buying the convertible bond rather than the stock directly is that the investor has effectively paid $2 per share more for the stock. Thus, the investor realizes a gain based on a stock price of $19 rather than $17.

So far, we have illustrated the advantage of owning the stock rather than the bond when the price of the stock rises. Let's look at the situation where the stock declines in value to $7. The investor who buys the stock now realizes a loss of $10 per share for a return of −59%. The conversion value of the XYZ bond likewise drops, to $350 (i.e., $7 × 50). Its price, however, will not fall to that level. Recall from our earlier discussion that the minimum price of a convertible bond will be the greater of its conversion value or its straight value. Assuming that the straight value is $788, and it does not change over the one-month period, the value of XYZ bond will fall to only $788. This means that the investor realizes a loss of only 17%. The loss would be even less in fact because the convertible bond would trade at a premium to its straight value.

The critical assumption in this analysis is that the straight value does not change, although it can change for any of the reasons cited in Chapter 2. More specifically, if interest rates rise in the economy, the straight value will decline. Even if interest rates do not rise, the perceived creditworthiness of the issuer may deteriorate, causing investors to demand a higher yield. In fact, the stock price and the yield required by investors are not independent. When the price of the stock drops precipitously, as in our $17 to $7 illustration, the perceived creditworthiness of the issuer may decline, causing a decline in the straight value. In any event, although the straight value may decline, it still is a floor (albeit a moving floor) for the convertible bond price. In our illustration, the straight value would have to fall about $390 (59% loss on $950) to equal the loss on the stock purchase.

The illustration clearly demonstrates that there are benefits and drawbacks of investing in convertible bonds. The disadvantage is the upside potential given up because a premium per share must be paid. An advantage is the reduction in downside risk (as determined by the straight value), with the opportunity to recoup the premium per share through the higher current income from owning the convertible bond.

A portfolio manager is interested in the total return from holding a convertible bond. The benchmark to compare the total return is the performance of the underlying common stock. The manager must therefore examine the total return using scenario analysis.

Call Risk

Convertible issues are callable by the issuer. This is a valuable feature for issuers who deem the current market price of their stock undervalued enough that selling stock directly would dilute the equity of current stockholders. The firm would prefer to raise equity funds over incurring debt, so it issues a convertible, setting the conversion ratio on the basis of a stock price it regards as acceptable. When the market price reaches the conversion point, the firm will want to see the conversion happen in view of the risk that the price may drop in the future. This gives the firm an interest in forcing conversion, even though this is not in the interest of the owners of the security whose price is likely to be adversely affected by the call.

Takeover Risk

Corporate takeovers represent another risk to investing in convertible bonds. If an issuer is acquired by another company or by its own management (as in the case of a management-led leveraged buyout), the stock price may not appreciate sufficiently for the holders of the convertible bond to benefit from the conversion feature. As the stock of the acquired company may no longer trade after a takeover, the investor can be left with a bond that pays a lower coupon rate than comparable-risk corporate bonds.

CONVERTIBLE BOND ARBITRAGE

Because of the investment characteristics of convertible bonds that we have described in this chapter, their payoff characteristics allow the creation of different positions that can benefit from the mispricing of a convertible bond. Seeking to capitalize on the perceived mispricing of a convertible bond issue is referred to as **convertible bond arbitrage**. Here, as in many other instances in the investment management profession, the term "arbitrage" is used loosely and not in the sense of a risk-free arbitrage used in finance theory.

The large number of ways to capitalize on mispricing of convertible bonds is one of the reasons for their popularity by hedge fund managers. As a result, there are a large number of convertible bond arbitrage strategies that seek to capitalize on the insights about the various factors that impact the pricing of a particular convertible bond's price.

The first step in all convertible bond arbitrage strategies is to identify convertible bonds that are trading at a price that substantially deviates from the theoretical value indicated by the manager's convertible bond model. Hence, the process is heavily dependent on this valuation model. For those convertible bonds that are identified as substantially misvalued in the market, a position is taken in the convertible bond, the underlying common stock, and a derivative instrument needed to hedge market risks that could otherwise adversely impact the objective of the convertible bond arbitrage strategies. This is described by delta hedging, discussed earlier, to hedge against adverse movements in the price of the underlying stock. Hedging against other adverse market risks would involve taking positions in an interest-rate derivative (typically an interest-rate swap is used) and credit derivatives (typically a credit default swap is used).[10]

Attributes of Issues for Use in a Convertible Bond Arbitrage Strategy

In screening the candidate list of convertible bond issues for a convertible bond arbitrage strategy, the manager will prefer those with certain attributes for the underlying common stock and for the convertible bond issue itself. For the convertible bond itself, the following attributes are desirable in a convertible bond arbitrage: (1) good liquidity, (2) low conversion premium, (3) high convexity, and (4) low implied volatility.[11]

With respect to the underlying common stock, the following attributes are desirable: (1) high expected price volatility, (2) can be easily borrowed, and (3) pay little or no dividends. Basically, the reason for the first attribute sought for the underlying common stock is that convertible bond arbitrage strategies seek to benefit from substantial price movements for

---

[10] Interest-rate swaps and credit default swaps are described in Chapters 28 and 29, respectively.

[11] Filippo Stetanini, "Convertibile Bond Arbitrage," Chapter 48 in Frank J. Fabozzi (ed.), *The Handbook of Finance: Volume II* (Hoboken, NJ: John Wiley & Sons, 2008).

the convertible bond. This is because if the value of the embedded call option on the stock price increases, this objective can be realized and a higher expected price volatility for the stock price increases the value of the embedded option. The second attribute is desired because a short position is often created in the underlying common stock. In the equity market, it is not always simple to short individual stocks. There is a market for borrowing stocks, called the securities lending market. Some stocks are easily borrowed in the securities lending market, while others can only be borrowed at a very high cost.[12] The last attribute is desired because when borrowing the underlying stock in a securities lending transaction, no payment (in the case of a non-dividend-paying stock) or a small payment (in the case of a low-dividend-paying stock) must be made to the lender of the stock.

Types of Strategies

Stefanini identifies the following eight convertible bond arbitrage strategies that are employed by hedge fund managers: cash flow arbitrage, volatility trading, gamma trading, credit arbitrage, skewed arbitrage, carry trade, refinancing play, and late-stage restructuring play.[13] Some of these strategies are similar to strategies employed in the trading of options. We will briefly describe the first three strategies.

As noted earlier in this chapter, the cash flow from a convertible bond differs from the cash flow from a stock. The idea behind a **cash flow arbitrage strategy** is to create equivalent positions in the convertible bond and underlying stock so that any additional cash flow available from the convertible bond can be captured while eliminating or mitigating any risks. More specifically, the convertible bond is purchased with funds obtained from shorting the underlying stock.

In convertible bond arbitrage trades, typically a long position is established in the convertible bond, and simultaneously, a short position is established in the underlying stock. The number of shares shorted is such that any change in the value of the convertible bond will be equal to the change in the position of the stocks shorted. As explained earlier, this is determined by the delta of the convertible bond, and the resulting position is said to be market neutral.

The objective in a **volatility trading strategy** is that regardless of how the price of the underlying stock price changes, the mispriced convertible bond's value will outperform the value of the short position in the underlying stock's value. Hence, this convertible bond strategy is a nondirectional strategy. That is, the performance of the strategy is based purely on the volatility of the underlying stock price not the direction in which the stock price moves. Effectively, this strategy is a bet on the volatility of the underlying stock and hence the name given to this type of convertible bond arbitrage strategy, volatility trading.

As with most option trading strategies, the position of a strategy must be changed as the price of the underlying changes. Hence, in implementing this strategy, the transaction cost associated with the shorting of the stocks must be taken into account. There are risks associated with this strategy, and they can be quantified using other measures taken from option theory that will be described in Chapter 27.

---

[12] For a discussion of the securities lending market, see Frank J. Fabozzi and Steven V. Mann (eds.), *Securities Finance* (Hoboken, NJ: John Wiley & Sons, 2005).

[13] Stefanini, "Convertible Bond Arbitrage," and Filippo Stefanini, *Investment Strategies of Hedge Funds* (Chichester, UK: John Wiley & Sons, 2006).

There are option strategies that involve capitalizing on the expected change in the delta of an option. As explained earlier, gamma is a measure of the change in the delta of an option or, in the case of a convertible bond, the change in its delta when the price of the underlying stock changes. As just explained, in a volatility trading strategy, the short position in the underlying stock must be changed periodically just to keep the position market neutral. In a convertible bond arbitrage **gamma trading strategy**, instead of adjusting the short position in the underlying stock as specified by the delta, the manager takes a position based on the expected change in the delta. The expectation is to generate additional income when the stock price changes.

OPTIONS APPROACH TO VALUATION

In our discussion of convertible bonds, we did not address the following questions:

1. What is a fair value for the conversion premium per share?
2. How do we handle convertible bonds with call and/or put options?
3. How does a change in interest rates affect the stock price?

The option pricing approach to valuation described in Chapter 17 can help us answer these questions. Consider first a noncallable/nonputable convertible bond. The investor who purchases this bond would be entering into two separate transactions: (1) buying a noncallable/nonputable straight bond, and (2) buying a call option (or warrant) on the stock, where the number of shares that can be purchased with the call option is equal to the conversion ratio.

The question is: What is the fair value for the call option? The fair value depends on the factors (discussed in Chapter 27) that affect the price of a call option. One key factor is the expected price volatility of the stock: the more the expected price volatility, the greater the value of the call option. The theoretical value of a call option can be valued using the Black–Scholes option pricing model[14] or the binomial option pricing model.[15] As a first approximation to the value of a convertible bond, the formula would be

convertible bond value = straight value + price of the call option on the stock

The price of the call option is added to the straight value because the investor has purchased a call option on the stock.

Now let's add in a common feature of a convertible bond: the issuer's right to call the bond. The issuer can force conversion by calling the bond. For example, suppose that the call price is $1,030 per $1,000 par and the conversion value is $1,700. If the issuer calls the bonds, the optimal strategy for the investor is to convert the bond and receive shares worth $1,700.[16] The investor, however, loses any premium over the conversion value that is reflected in the market price. Therefore, the analysis of convertible bonds must take into account the value of the issuer's right to call the bond. This depends, in turn, on (1) future

---

[14] Fischer Black and Myron Scholes, "The Pricing of Corporate Liabilities," *Journal of Political Economy*, May–June 1973, pp. 637–659.

[15] John C. Cox, Stephen A. Ross, and Mark Rubinstein, "Option Pricing: A Simplified Approach," *Journal of Financial Economics*, September 1979, pp. 229–263; Richard J. Rendleman and Brit J. Bartter, "Two-State Option Pricing," *Journal of Finance*, December 1979, pp. 1093–1110; and William F. Sharpe, *Investments* (Upper Saddle River, NJ: Prentice Hall, 1981), Chapter 16.

[16] Actually, the conversion value would be less than $1,700 because the per-share value after conversion would decline.

interest rate volatility, and (2) economic factors that determine whether it is optimal for the issuer to call the bond.

The Black–Scholes option pricing model cannot handle this situation. Instead, the binomial option pricing model can be used simultaneously to value the bondholder's call option on the stock and the issuer's right to call the bonds. The bondholder's put option can also be accommodated. To link interest rates and stock prices together (the third question we raised previously), statistical analysis of historical movements of these two variables must be estimated and incorporated into the model.

The option pricing approach offers a great deal of promise and models have been proposed as far back as 1977.[17] In the experience of the author, the most complicated model employed by practitioners uses the Black–Scholes model and tests the sensitivity of the factors that affect any other embedded options.[18]

KEY POINTS

- A convertible bond grants the bondholder the right to convert the bond into a predetermined number of shares of common stock of the issuer. The number of shares is called the conversion ratio.
- Convertible bonds issued prior to 2008 have provisions that an investor should be aware of that are unique with respect to the conversion privilege: net share settlement provision and contingent conversion provision.
- Analysis of a convertible bond requires calculation of the conversion value, straight value, market conversion price, market conversion premium ratio, and premium payback period.
- The downside risk of a convertible bond usually is estimated by calculating the premium over straight value. The limitation of this measure is that the straight value (the floor) changes as interest rates change.
- Because a convertible bond is basically a bond with an embedded call option on the underlying stock, option theory and measures used by participants in the options market are used in describing the investment characteristics of convertibles. These measures include delta, gamma, vega, and implied volatility.
- Convertibles are classified according to their investment profile: typical convertibles (also referred to as balanced convertibles), equity sensitive convertibles (also referred to as equity substitute convertibles), busted convertibles, and distressed convertibles.
- There are several strategies that can be used to capitalize on any perceived mispricing of convertible bonds. These strategies are referred to as convertible bond arbitrage strategies.
- The option pricing approach can be used to determine the fair value of the embedded call option. The value of the call option following this approach is estimated using an equity option pricing model such as the Black–Scholes model.

---

[17] See, for example, Michael Brennan and Eduardo Schwartz, "Convertible Bonds: Valuation and Optimal Strategies for Call and Conversion," *Journal of Finance,* December 1977, pp. 1699–1715; Jonathan Ingersoll, "A Contingent-Claims Valuation of Convertible Securities," *Journal of Financial Economics,* May 1977, pp. 289–322; Michael Brennan and Eduardo Schwartz, "Analyzing Convertible Bonds," *Journal of Financial and Quantitative Analysis,* November 1980, pp. 907–929; and George Constantinides, "Warrant Exercise and Bond Conversion in Competitive Markets," *Journal of Financial Economics,* September 1984, pp. 371–398.

[18] See, for example, Mihir Bhattacharya and Yu Zhu, "Valuation and Analysis of Convertible Securities," Chapter 36 in Frank J. Fabozzi and T. Dessa Fabozzi (eds.), *The Handbook of Fixed Income Securities* (Burr Ridge, IL: Irwin Professional Publishing, 1995); and Frank J. Fabozzi, *Valuation of Fixed Income Securities and Derivatives* (New Hope, PA: Frank J. Fabozzi Associates, 1995), Chapter 9.

QUESTIONS

1. In the October 26, 1992, prospectus summary of the Staples 5% convertible subordinated debentures due 1999, the offering stated: "Convertible into Common Stock at a conversion price of $45 per share . . . . " If the par value is $1,000, what is the conversion ratio?

2. What is the difference between a soft put and a hard put?

3. Upon exercise of the conversion option for a convertible bond, all issuers must exchange shares of stock for the bond. Explain whether you agree or disagree.

4. What is a mandatory convertible?

5. This excerpt is taken from an article titled "Caywood Looks for Convertibles," which appeared in the January 13, 1992, issue of *BondWeek*, p. 7:

   > Caywood Christian Capital Management will invest new money in its $400 million high-yield portfolio in "busted convertibles," double- and triple-B rated convertible bonds of companies . . . , said James Caywood, CEO. Caywood likes these convertibles as they trade at discounts and are unlikely to be called, he said.

   a. What is a busted convertible?
   b. What is the premium over straight value at which these bonds would trade?
   c. Why does Mr. Caywood seek convertibles with higher investment-grade ratings?
   d. Why is Mr. Caywood interested in call protection?

6. Explain the limitation of using premium over straight value as a measure of the downside risk of a convertible bond.

7. This excerpt comes from an article titled "Bartlett Likes Convertibles" in the October 7, 1991, issue of *BondWeek*, p. 7:

   > Bartlett & Co. is selectively looking for opportunities in convertible bonds that are trading cheaply because the equity of the issuer has dropped in value, according to Dale Rabiner, director of fixed income at the $800 million Cincinnati-based fund. Rabiner said he looks for five-year convertibles trading at yields comparable to straight bonds of companies he believes will rebound.

   Discuss this strategy for investing in convertible bonds.

8. Consider a convertible bond as follows:

$$\text{par value} = \$1,000$$
$$\text{coupon rate} = 9.5\%$$
$$\text{market price of convertible bond} = \$1,000$$
$$\text{conversion ratio} = 37.383$$
$$\text{estimated straight value of bond} = \$510$$
$$\text{yield to maturity of straight bond} = 18.7\%$$

   Assume that the price of the common stock is $23 and that the dividend per share is $0.75 per year.

   a. Calculate each of the following:
   1. Conversion value
   2. Market conversion price
   3. Conversion premium per share
   4. Conversion premium ratio
   5. Premium over straight value
   6. Favorable income differential per share
   7. Premium payback period

   b. Suppose that the price of the common stock increases from $23 to $46.
   1. What will be the approximate return realized from investing in the convertible bond?
   2. What would be the return realized if $23 had been invested in the common stock?
   3. Why would the return on investing in the common stock directly be higher than investing in the convertible bond?

   c. Suppose that the price of the common stock declines from $23 to $8.
   1. What will be the approximate return realized from investing in the convertible bond?
   2. What would be the return realized if $23 had been invested in the common stock?
   3. Why would the return on investing in the convertible bond be higher than investing in the common stock directly?

9. A Merrill Lynch note structure called a *liquid yield option note* (LYON) is a zero-coupon instrument that is convertible into the common stock of the issuer. The conversion ratio is fixed for the entire life of the note. If investors wish to convert to the shares of the issuer, they must exchange the LYON for the stock. As a result, the conversion price increases over time. Why?

10. **a.** Suppose that a convertible bond has a conversion ratio of 20 and a delta of 0.70. For a price change of $0.125 for the stock price per share, what is the approximate change in the convertible bond's value?

    b. How many shares of the stock must be shorted in order to create a market-neutral position by holding the convertible bond and shorting the stock?

11. Why would you expect that a distressed convertible would have a delta of zero?

12. Suppose that the price of the underlying stock for a convertible bond is considerably higher than the conversion price. What would you expect that convertible bond's delta to be?

13. The following quotes are from Mihir Bhattacharya, "Convertible Securities and Their Valuation," Chapter 51 in Frank J. Fabozzi (ed.), *The Handbook of Fixed Income Securities*, 6th ed. (New York: McGraw-Hill, 2001).

    a. "Increased debt market volatility has driven home the point of *duration risk* inherent in any security with a fixed income component, including converts. The increased volatility of the spreads (over Treasury or other interest rate benchmarks) has heightened investor sensitivity to the reliability of the *fixed income floor* or *bond value* of the convert." What message is the author trying to convey to investors?

    b. "Convertibles have equity and interest rate options, and occasionally, currency options, embedded in them. Issuers and investors are becoming even more aware that option valuation is driven by, among other factors: (a) equity volatility; (b) interest rate volatility; and (c) spread volatility. In some situations the embedded options may easily be separated and valued. However, in the vast majority of cases, they interact with each other and so prove difficult, if not impossible, to separate. Investors should be aware of the inherent danger of attempting to value the embedded options as if they were separable options." Explain why the factors mentioned in the quote affect the value of a convertible bond and why the factors interact.

14. Why is a volatility trading strategy considered to be a nondirectional strategy?

15. What is the difference between a busted convertible and a distressed convertible?

16. What is a cash flow arbitrage strategy involving convertible bonds?

20

Corporate Bond Credit Analysis

LEARNING OBJECTIVES

After reading this chapter, you will understand

- the major areas of bond credit analysis: covenants, collateral, and ability to pay

- the reason why covenants must be analyzed

- what factors are considered in evaluating the ability of an issuer to satisfy its obligations

- what factors are considered in assessing a company's business risk

- why an analysis of a company must be looked at relative to the industry in which it operates

- the reasons corporate governance risk is important and how it can be mitigated

- key financial ratios

- the relationship between corporate bond credit analysis and common stock analysis

As explained in Chapter 1, credit risk encompasses three types of risk: default risk, credit spread risk, and credit downgrade risk. Since the credit rating agencies (Moody's Investors Service, Standard & Poor's, and Fitch Ratings) have well-developed methodologies for analyzing the default risk of a corporate bond, we will describe factors that they consider in this chapter. The framework for analysis that we describe in this chapter is referred to as "traditional credit analysis." In the next chapter, we will explain credit risk models for assessing credit risk and look at the potential advantage of the output of such models relative to credit ratings.

Available online at www.pearsonhighered.com/fabozzi is the appendix to this chapter, which is a report on Lear Corporation. The report was prepared by Eric Selle and Stephanie Renegar while working at Wachovia Securities. (The authors are now at JPMorgan Chase.) This comprehensive report illustrates all of the key elements discussed in this chapter (and more), and we make continual reference to the relevant portions. It should be noted that on

July 7, 2009, Lear Corporation filed petitions for relief under Chapter 11 with the bankruptcy court. On November 9, 2009, Lear emerged from Chapter 11 bankruptcy proceedings.

OVERVIEW OF CORPORATE BOND CREDIT ANALYSIS

In the analysis of the default risk of a corporate bond issuer and specific bond issues, there are three areas that are analyzed by bond credit analysts:

1. the protections afforded to bondholders that are provided by covenants limiting management's discretion
2. the collateral available for the bondholder should the issuer fail to make the required payments
3. the ability of an issuer to make the contractual payments to bondholders

In this section, we briefly describe these three areas of analysis.

Analysis of Covenants

An analysis of the indenture is part of a credit review of a corporation's bond issue. The indenture provisions establish rules for several important areas of operation for corporate management. These provisions are safeguards for the bondholder. Indenture provisions should be analyzed carefully. A general description of the indenture is found in a company's prospectus for its bond offering. However, it is often stated that the indenture provisions are only summarized. Often, the covenants are ambiguous. The analyst must pay careful attention to the definitions in indentures because they vary from indenture to indenture. For examples of a summary of a bank and bond covenant, see pages 28 to 30 in the Lear Corp. report in the Appendix found online.

The importance of understanding covenants was summarized by one high-yield portfolio manager, Robert Levine, as follows:

> Covenants provide insight into a company's strategy. As part of the credit process, one must read covenants within the context of the corporate strategy. It is not sufficient to hire a lawyer to review the covenants because a lawyer might miss the critical factors necessary to make the appropriate decision. Also, loopholes in covenants often provide clues about the intentions of management teams.[1]

There are two general types of covenants. **Affirmative covenants** call upon the corporation to make promises to do certain things. **Negative covenants**, also called **restrictive covenants**, require that the borrower not take certain actions. There are an infinite variety of restrictions that can be placed on borrowers in the form of negative covenants.

Some of the more common restrictive covenants include various limitations on the company's ability to incur debt since unrestricted borrowing can be highly detrimental to the bondholders. Consequently, bondholders may want to include limits on the absolute dollar amount of debt that may be outstanding or may require some type of fixed charge coverage ratio test. We will discuss these types of ratios later in the chapter. The two most common tests are the maintenance test and the debt incurrence test. The **maintenance test** requires the borrower's ratio of earnings available for interest or fixed charges to be at least a

---

[1] Robert Levine, "Unique Factors in Managing High-Yield Bond Portfolios," in Frank K. Reilly (ed.), *High-Yield Bonds: Analysis and Risk Assessment* (Charlottesville, VA: Association for Investment Management and Research, 1990), p. 35.

certain minimum figure on each required reporting date (such as quarterly or annually) for a certain preceding period. The **debt incurrence test** only comes into play when the company wishes to do additional borrowing. In order to take on additional debt, the required interest or fixed charge coverage figure adjusted for the new debt must be at a certain minimum level for the required period prior to the financing. Debt incurrence tests are generally considered less stringent than maintenance provisions. There could also be **cash flow tests** (or **cash flow requirements**) and **working capital maintenance provisions**.

Some indentures may prohibit subsidiaries from borrowing from all other companies except the parent. Indentures often classify subsidiaries as restricted or unrestricted. Restricted subsidiaries are those considered to be consolidated for financial test purposes; unrestricted subsidiaries (often foreign and certain special-purpose companies) are those excluded from the covenants governing the parent. Often, subsidiaries are classified as unrestricted in order to allow them to finance themselves through outside sources of funds.

Analysis of Collateral

A corporate debt obligation can be secured or unsecured. In the case of the liquidation of a corporation, proceeds from a bankruptcy are distributed to creditors based on the absolute priority rule. In contrast, as explained in Chapter 7, seldom does the absolute priority rule hold in a reorganization. What is typically observed in such cases is that the corporation's unsecured creditors may receive distributions for the entire amount of their claim and common stockholders may receive some distribution, while secured creditors may receive only a portion of their claim. Secured creditors are willing to allow distribution to unsecured creditors and common stockholders in order to obtain approval for the plan of reorganization, a plan that requires approval of all parties.

The question is then, what does a "secured position" mean in the case of a reorganization if the absolute priority rule is not followed in a reorganization? The claim position of a secured creditor is important in terms of the negotiation process. However, because absolute priority is not followed and the final distribution in a reorganization depends on the bargaining ability of the parties, some analysts place less emphasis on collateral compared to covenants and business risk. To see an example of the importance of security holders' priority of claims in a bankruptcy valuation, see page 6 of the Lear Corp. report in the Appendix.

Assessing an Issuer's Ability to Pay

In assessing the ability of an issuer to service its debt (i.e., make timely payment of interest and principal), one immediately thinks about the crunching of numbers based on the financial statements of the issuing corporation. While that is extremely important, the ability of an issuer to generate cash flow goes considerably beyond the calculation and analysis of a myriad of financial ratios and cash flow measures that can be used as a basic assessment of a company's financial risk. Analysts also look at qualitative factors such as the issuer's business risk and corporate governance risk to assess the issuer's ability to pay.

Thus, an evaluation of an issuer's ability to pay involves analysis of

1. business risk
2. corporate governance risk
3. financial risk

We describe the analysis of each of these in the following sections.

ANALYSIS OF BUSINESS RISK

Business risk is defined as the risk associated with operating cash flows. Operating cash flows are not certain because the revenues and the expenditures comprising the cash flows are uncertain. Revenues depend on conditions in the economy as a whole and the industry in which the company operates, as well as the actions of management and its competitors. Expenditures for operations are comprised of variable costs and fixed costs, and these costs depend on a myriad of factors. In the Lear Corp. report in the Appendix, the analysts who authored the report derive their model assumptions off of their estimates of the breakdown of variable and fixed costs (see page 22).

In assessing business risk, the three rating agencies look at the same general areas. Standard & Poor's (S&P) states that in analyzing business risk it considers country risk, industry characteristics, company position, product portfolio/marketing, technology, cost efficiency, strategic and operational management competence, and profitability/peer group comparisons.[2] Moody's investigates industry trends, national political and regulatory environment, management quality and attitude towards risk-taking, and basic operating and competitive position.[3] Fitch reviews industry trends, operating environment, market position, and management.[4]

An analysis of industry trends is important because it is only within the context of an industry that company analysis is valid. For example, suppose that the growth rate for a company over the past three years was 20% per year. In isolation, that may appear to be an attractive growth rate. However, suppose that over the same time period, the industry in which the company operates has been growing at 45% over the same period. While there could be many factors to explain the discrepancy in the relative performance, one might conclude that the company is competitively weak. Industry consideration should be considered in a global context. For example, consider the automobile industry. It is not sufficient to consider the competitive position of companies in this industry without taking into account their global competitive position. The need for many companies to become globally competitive increases as the barriers to international trade are broken down. For an example of the use of industry analysis to help analyze a specific credit, see pages 22 to 23 in the Lear Corp. report in the Appendix.

It has been suggested that the following areas will provide a credit analyst with a sufficient framework to properly interpret a company's economic prospects: economic cyclicality, growth prospects, research and development expenses, competition, sources of supply, degree of regulation, and labor.[5] These general areas encompass most of the areas that the rating agencies have identified for assessing business risk. We will briefly describe each of these areas.

One of the first areas of analysis is investigating how closely the industry follows gross domestic product (GDP) growth. This is done in order to understand the industry's economic cyclicality. Note, however, that economic growth as measured by the growth in GDP may not always be the most suitable benchmark for the potential growth of an industry. There are some industries that are sensitive to many economic variables, and

---

[2] Standard & Poor's Corporation, *Corporate Rating Criteria*, 2005, p. 20.

[3] Moody's Investors Service, *Industrial Company Rating Methodology*, July 1998, p. 3.

[4] Fitch Ratings, *Corporate Rating Methodology*, undated, pp. 1–2.

[5] Frank J. Fabozzi, "Credit Analysis for Corporate Bonds," Chapter 32 in Frank J. Fabozzi (ed.), *The Handbook of Fixed Income Securities* (New York, McGraw-Hill, 2005), p. 735.

often various industry sub-sectors move countercyclically or at least with different lags in relation to the general economy. For some industries, growth may be somewhat dependent on general economic growth but be more sensitive to demographic changes. Related to the analysis of economic cyclicality is the growth prospects of the industry. This requires an analysis as to whether the industry's growth is projected to increase and thereafter be maintained at a high level or is it expected to decline. The analyst develops growth scenarios to assess the implications of industry growth for the company.

To assess the growth prospects, a credit analyst will have to investigate the dependence on research and development (R&D) expenditures for maintaining or expanding the company's market position. While the company under analysis may be currently well positioned with the industry in which it operates, the lack of financial capacity to continue a technological lead or at least expend a sufficient amount of money to keep technologically current will likely result in a deterioration of its relative position in the long run (see page 8 of the Lear Corp. report in the Appendix).

A credit analyst will look at the market structure of an industry (e.g., unregulated monopoly, oligopoly, etc.) because of its implications on pricing flexibility. Moreover, market structure is important if it bears on one of the other industry factors identified previously: sources of supply. A company that is not self-sufficient in its factors of production but is sufficiently powerful in its industry to pass along increased costs is in a stronger position than a company that is in an industry where none or only a modest portion of increased costs can be passed on to customers. In the Lear Corp. report, the authors of the report describe how Lear's inability to pass on higher raw material costs has negatively affected the credit (see pages 11 and 13).

With respect to regulation, the concern should not be with its existence or absence in an industry per se. Rather, the focus with respect to regulation should be on the direction of regulation and its potential impact on the current and prospective profitability of the company. Regulation also encompasses government intervention in non–U.S. operations of a company.

A key component in the cost structure of an industry is labor. (For analysis of a company's labor situation, see "Labor-Intensive Production" and the "Restructuring Plans" sections (page 12) in the Lear Corp. report in the Appendix.) In analyzing the labor situation, the credit analyst will examine if the industry is heavily unionized and, if so, will study: (1) whether management has the flexibility to reduce the labor force, (2) when does the prevailing labor contract come up for renewal, and (3) the historical occurrence of strikes. In nonunionized companies, the credit analyst will look at the prospect of potential unionization. Also in analyzing an industry, the requirements for particular specialists are examined.

CORPORATE GOVERNANCE RISK

Corporate governance issues involve (1) the ownership structure of the corporation, (2) the practices followed by management, and (3) policies for financial disclosure. The eagerness of corporate management to present favorable results to shareholders and the market has been a major factor in several of the corporate scandals in recent years. Chief executive officers (CEOs), chief financial officers, and the board of directors are being held directly accountable for disclosures in financial statements and other corporate decisions.

The underlying economic theory regarding many of the corporate governance issues is the principal-agency relationship between the senior managers and the shareholders of corporations.[6] The agent, a corporation's senior management, is charged with the responsibility of acting on behalf of the principal, the shareholders of the corporation. In a principal-agency relationship, there is the potential for the agent not to pursue the best interest of the principal, but instead pursue a policy in its own self-interest.

There are mechanisms that can mitigate the likelihood that management will act in its own self-interest. The mechanisms fall into two general categories. The first is to more strongly align the interests of management with those of shareholders. This can be accomplished by granting management an economically meaningful equity interest in the company. Also, manager compensation can be linked to the performance of the company's common stock.

The second category of mechanism is by means of the company's internal corporate control systems, which can provide a way for effectively monitoring the performance and decision-making behavior of management. For example, it would allow the timely removal of the CEO by the board of directors who believe that a CEO's performance is not in the best interest of the shareholders. In general, there are several critical features of an internal corporate control system that are necessary for the effective monitoring of management. What has been clear in corporate scandals is that there was a breakdown of the internal corporate control systems that lead to corporate difficulties and the destruction of shareholder wealth.

Because of the important role played by the board of directors, the structure and composition of the board are critical for effective corporate governance. The key is to remove the influence of the CEO and senior management on board members. This can be done in several ways. First, while there is no optimal board size, the more members there are, the less likely the influence of the CEO. With more board members, a larger number of committees can be formed to deal with important corporate matters.[7] Second, the composition of the board should have a majority of independent directors, and the committees should include only independent directors.[8] Finally, there are corporate governance specialists who believe that the CEO should not be the chairman of the board of directors because such a practice allows the CEO to exert too much influence over board members and other important corporate actions.[9]

There are standards and codes of best practice for effective corporate governance.[10] The standards and codes of best practice go beyond applicable securities law. The expectation is

---

[6] The seminal paper on the principal-agency relationship in corporate finance is Michael Jensen and William Meckling, "Theory of the Firm: Managerial Behavior, Agency Costs and Ownership Structure," *Journal of Financial Economics* (October 1976), pp. 305–360.

[7] At a minimum, there should be an auditing committee, a nominating committee (for board members), and a compensation committee.

[8] There are two classes of members of the board of directors. Directors who are employees or management or have some economic interest as set forth by the Securities and Exchange Commission (for example, a former employee with a pension fund, the relative of senior management, or an employee of an investment banking firm that has underwritten the company's securities) are referred to as "inside directors." Board members who do not fall into the category of inside directors are referred to as "outside directors" or "independent directors."

[9] This is a position that has been taken by the Securities and Exchange Commission.

[10] The standards of best practice that have become widely accepted as a benchmark are those set forth by the Organisation of Economic Cooperation and Development (OECD) in 1999. Other entities that have established standards and codes for corporate governance are the Commonwealth Association for Corporate Governance, the International Corporate Governance Network, and the Business Roundtable. Countries have established their own code and standards using the OECD principles.

that the adoption of best practice for corporate governance is a signal to investors about the character of management. There is empirical evidence supporting the relationship between corporate governance and bond ratings (and hence bond yields).[11]

Several organizations have developed services that assess corporate governance and express their view in the form of a rating. Generally, these ratings are made public at the option of the company requesting an evaluation. One such service is offered by S&P, which produces a Corporate Governance Score based on a review of both publicly available information, interviews with senior management and directors, and confidential information that S&P may have available from its credit rating of the corporation's debt. The score ranges from 10 (the highest score) to 1 (the lowest score).[12]

In addition to corporate governance, credit analysts look at the quality of management in assessing a corporation's ability to pay. In assessing management quality, Moody's for example, tries to understand the business strategies and policies formulated by management. The factors Moody's considers are: (1) strategic direction, (2) financial philosophy, (3) conservatism, (4) track record, (5) succession planning, and (6) control systems.

FINANCIAL RISK

Having achieved an understanding of a corporation's business risk and corporate governance risk, the analyst is ready to move on to assessing financial risk. This involves traditional ratio analysis and other factors affecting the firm's financing. Next we provide a brief summary of some of the more important financial ratios: interest coverage, leverage, cash flow, net assets, and working capital. Once these ratios are calculated, it is necessary to analyze their absolute levels relative to those of the industry.

Before performing an analysis of the financial statement, the analyst must determine if the industry in which the company operates has any special accounting practices, such as those in the insurance industry. If so, an analyst should become familiar with industry practices. Moreover, the analyst must review the accounting policies to determine whether management is employing liberal or conservative policies in applying generally accepted accounting principles (GAAP). An analyst should be aware of changes in GAAP policies by the company and the reason for any changes. Since historical data are analyzed, the analyst should recognize that companies adjust prior years' results to accommodate discontinued operations and changes in accounting that can hide unfavorable trends. This can be done by assessing the trends for the company's unadjusted and adjusted results.

Interest Coverage

An **interest coverage ratio** measures the number of times interest charges are covered on a pretax basis. Typically, interest coverage ratios that are used and published are pretax as opposed to after-tax because interest payments are a pretax expense. **Pretax interest coverage ratio** is calculated by dividing pretax income plus interest charges by total interest

---

[11] See Sanjeev Bhojraj and Partha Sengupta, "Effect of Corporate Governance on Bond Ratings and Yields: The Role of Institutional Investors and Outside Directors," *Journal of Business*, 76, 2003, pp. 455–476.

[12] Standard & Poor's, *Corporate Governance Evaluations & Scores*, 2004, p. 3.

charges. The higher this ratio, the lower the credit risk, all other factors the same. If a company has a pretax interest ratio that is less than 1×, it must borrow or use cash flow or proceeds from the sale of assets to meet its interest payments. For the Lear Corp., the authors of the report define interest coverage as the ratio of EBITDA, or operating earnings (excluding noncash restructuring charges and depreciation and amortization) over consolidated interest expense.

A calculation of simple pretax interest coverage would be misleading if there are fixed obligations other than interest that are significant. In this case, a more appropriate coverage ratio would include these other fixed obligations, and the resulting ratio is called a **fixed charge coverage ratio**. An example of other significant fixed obligations is lease payments. An analyst must also be aware of any contingent liabilities, such as a company's guaranteeing another company's debt.

Rather than use pretax income, cash flow can be used, and the computed ratio is called a **cash flow ratio**. We will discuss the various cash flow ratios later.

Leverage

A second important ratio is a **leverage ratio**. While there is no one definition for leverage, the most common one is the ratio of long-term debt to total capitalization. The higher the level of debt, the higher the percentage of operating income that must be used to satisfy fixed obligations. In calculating leverage, it is common to use the company's capitalization structure as stated in the most recent balance sheet. To supplement this measure, the analyst should calculate capitalization using a market approximation for the value of the common stock. For Lear Corp., the authors of the report define the leverage ratio as the ratio of total debt to EBITDA for a trailing 12-month period.

In analyzing a highly leveraged company (i.e., a company with a high leverage ratio), the margin of safety must be analyzed. The **margin of safety** is defined as the percentage by which operating income could decline and still be sufficient to allow the company to meet its fixed obligations. (Page 6 of the Lear Corp. report in the Appendix shows the margin of safety analysis.) The degree of leverage and margin of safety varies dramatically among industries.

Recognition must be given to the company's operating leases. Such leases represent an alternative to financing assets with borrowed funds. The existence of material operating leases can therefore understate a company's leverage. Operating leases should be capitalized to give a true measure of leverage.

Two other factors should be considered: the maturity structure of the debt and bank lines of credit. With respect to the first, the analyst would want to know the percentage of debt that is coming due within the next five years and how that debt will be refinanced. For the latter, a company's bank lines of credit often constitute a significant portion of its total debt. These lines of credit should be closely analyzed in order to determine the flexibility afforded to the company. The lines of credit should be evaluated in terms of undrawn capacity as well as security interests granted. (See Exhibit 21 on page 21 of the Lear Corp. report in the Appendix for an analysis of the amount of the credit's borrowing capacity that is driven by bank covenants.) The analysis also involves a determination as to whether the line contains a "material adverse change" clause under which the bank may withdraw a line of credit.

Cash Flow

Credit analysts agree that the analysis of a corporation's cash flow is critical in assessing credit risk. This is particularly true for bonds of speculative-grade issuers because, unlike investment-grade issuers, there is greater reliance on internally generated funds during times when the issuer faces a temporty shortfall in cash.

Unfortunately, there is no uniform definition of cash flow. S&P, for example, discusses four cash flow concepts: operating cash flow, free operating cash flow, discretionary cash flow, and prefinancing cash flow. Given a cash flow measure, cash flow ratios are calculated.[13] These ratios are simply variants of the coverage ratio described earlier.

The statement of cash flows is required to be published in financial statements along with the income statement and balance sheet. The statement of cash flows is a summary over a period of time of a company's cash flows broken out by operating, investing, and financing activities. Analysts then reformat this information, combining it with information from the income statement to obtain what they view as a better description of the company's activities. S&P, for example, first calculates what it refers to as **funds from operations** (defined as net income adjusted for depreciation and other noncash debits and credits). **Operating cash flow** is funds from operations reduced by changes in the investment in working capital (current assets less current liabilities). Subtracting capital expenditures gives what S&P defines as **free operating cash flow**. It is from this cash flow that dividends and acquisitions can be made. Deducting cash dividends from free operating cash flow gives **discretionary cash flow**. Adjusting discretionary cash flow for managerial discretionary decisions for acquisition of other companies, the disposal of assets (e.g., lines of business or subsidiaries), and other sources or uses of cash gives prefinancing cash flow. As stated by S&P, **prefinancing cash flow** "represents the extent to which company cash flow from all internal sources have been sufficient to cover all internal needs."[14] In the Lear Corp. report in the Appendix, the analysts who authored the report define free cash flow as EBITDA less total interest expense, income tax expense, cash used or gained from management of working capital, capital expenditures, dividends, cash restructuring, and asset sales or purchases (see the exhibits in the report where free cash flow is computed).

Cash flow measures can then be used to calculate various cash flow ratios. The ratio used often depends on the type of company being analyzed.

Net Assets

A fourth important ratio is net assets to total debt. In the analysis of this ratio, consideration should be given to the liquidation value of the assets. Liquidation value will often differ dramatically from the value stated on the balance sheet. In addition to the assets' market value, some consideration should be given to the liquidity of the assets. A company with a high percentage of its assets in cash and marketable securities is in a much stronger asset position than a company whose primary assets are illiquid real estate. Finally, consideration should be given to several other financial variables including intangible assets, pension liabilities, and the age and condition of the plant.

---

[13] Standard & Poor's Corporation, *Corporate Rating Criteria*, 2003, p. 27.
[14] Standard & Poor's Corporation, *Corporate Rating Criteria*, 2003, p. 27.

Working Capital

Working capital is defined as current assets less current liabilities. Working capital is considered a primary measure of a company's financial flexibility. Other such measures include the *current ratio* (current assets divided by current liabilities) and the *acid test* (cash, marketable securities, and receivables divided by current liabilities). The stronger the company's liquidity measures, the better it can weather a downturn in business and reduction in cash flow.

In assessing this variable, the normal working capital requirements of a company and industry should be considered. The components of working capital should also be analyzed. Although accounts receivable are considered to be liquid, an increase in the average days receivables outstanding may be an indication that a higher level of working capital is needed for the efficient running of the operation. In addition, companies frequently have account receivable financing, some with recourse provisions. In this scenario, comparisons among companies in the same industry may be distorted. For an example of the analysis of working capital, see page 8 of the Lear Corp. report in the Appendix.

CORPORATE BOND CREDIT ANALYSIS AND EQUITY ANALYSIS

The analysis of business risk, corporate governance risk, and financial risk described previously involves the same type of analysis that a common stock analyst would undertake. Many fixed income portfolio managers strongly believe that corporate bond analysis, particularly high-yield bond analysis, should be viewed from an equity analyst's perspective. As Stephen Esser notes:

> Using an equity approach, or at least considering the hybrid nature of high-yield debt, can either validate or contradict the results of traditional credit analysis, causing the analyst to dig further.[15]

He further states:

> For those who work with investing in high-yield bonds, whether issued by public or private companies, dynamic, equity-oriented analysis is invaluable. If analysts think about whether they would want to buy a particular high-yield company's stock and what will happen to the future equity value of that company, they have a useful approach because, as equity values go up, so does the equity cushion beneath the company's debt. All else being equal, the bonds then become better credits and should go up in value relative to competing bond investments.[16]

---

[15] Stephen F. Esser, "High-Yield Bond Analysis: The Equity Perspective," in Ashwinpaul C. Sondhi (ed.), *Credit Analysis of Nontraditional Debt Securities* (Charlottesville, VA: Association for Investment Management and Research, 1995), p. 47.

[16] Esser, "High-Yield Bond Analysis: The Equity Perspective," p. 54.

KEY POINTS

- Corporate bond credit analysis involves an assessment of bondholder protections set forth in the bond indenture, the collateral available for the bondholder should the issuer fail to make the required payments, and the capacity of an issuer to fulfill its payment obligations.
- Covenants contained in the bond indenture set forth limitations on management and, as a result, provide safeguard provisions for bondholders.
- While collateral analysis is important, there is a question of what a secured position means in the case of a reorganization if the absolute priority rule is not followed in a reorganization.
- In assessing the ability of an issuer to service its debt, analysts look at a myriad of financial ratios as well as qualitative factors such as the issuer's business risk and corporate government risk.
- In assessing the ability of an issuer to service its debt, analysts assess the issuer's business risk, corporate governance risk, and financial risk. Business risk is the risk associated with operating cash flows. In assessing business risk, some of the main factors considered are industry characteristics and trends, the company's market and competitive positions, management characteristics, and national political and regulatory environment.
- Corporate governance risk involves assessing (1) the ownership structure of the corporation, (2) the practices followed by management, and (3) policies for financial disclosure.
- Assessing financial risk involves traditional ratio analysis and other factors affecting the firm's financing. The more important financial ratios analyzed are interest coverage, leverage, cash flow, net assets, and working capital.
- Some fixed income portfolio managers strongly believe that corporate bond analysis should be viewed from an equity analyst's perspective. This is particularly the case in analyzing high-yield bonds.

QUESTIONS

1. **a.** What is the difference between a positive and negative covenant?
    b. What is the purpose of the analysis of covenants in assessing the credit risk of an issuer?

2. **a.** What is a maintenance test?
    b. What is a debt incurrence test and when does it come into play?

3. Some credit analysts place less emphasis on collateral compared to covenants and business risk. Explain why.

4. Why do credit analysts begin with an analysis of the industry in assessing the business risk of a corporate issuer?

5. What is the purpose of a credit analyst investigating the market structure of an industry (e.g., unregulated monopoly, oligopoly, etc.)?

6. What should be the focus of an analyst with respect to the regulation of an industry?

7. In analyzing the labor situation in an industry in which a corporate issue operates, what should the credit analyst examine?

8. The underlying economic theory regarding many corporate governance issues is the principal-agency relationship between the senior managers and the shareholders of corporations. Explain this relationship.

9. With respect to corporate governance, what are the mechanisms that can mitigate the likelihood that management will act in its own self-interest?

10. **a.** What are corporate governance ratings?
    b. Are corporate governance ratings reported to the investing public?
    c. What factors are considered by services that assign corporate governance ratings?

11. Explain what a credit analyst should do in preparation for an analysis of the financial statements.

12. **a.** What is the purpose of an interest coverage ratio?
    b. What does an interest coverage ratio of 1.8× mean?
    c. Why are interest coverage ratios typically computed on a pretax basis?
    d. Why would a fixed-charge coverage ratio be materially different from an interest coverage ratio?

13. **a.** What is the purpose of a leverage ratio?
    b. What measures are used in a leverage ratio for total capitalization?
    c. What is the margin of safety measure?

14. Why do analysts investigate the bank lines of credit that a corporation has?

15. Explain each of the following:
    a. funds from operations
    b. operating cash flow
    c. free operating cash flow
    d. discretionary cash flow
    e. prefinancing cash flow

16. In the analysis of net assets, what factors should be considered?

17. **a.** What is meant by working capital?
    b. Why is an analysis of working capital important?

18. Why do analysts of high-yield corporate bonds feel that the analysis should be viewed from an equity analyst's perspective?

21

Credit Risk Modeling

LEARNING OBJECTIVES

After reading this chapter, you will understand

- the difficulties of measuring credit risk exposure compared to interest rate risk exposure

- there are two basic types of credit risk models: structural models and reduced form models

- what a structural model is and the link to option theory

- the basic structural model (Black-Scholes-Merton model) and its extensions (Geske model and first-passage time model)

- what is meant by default correlations and the reason for using copulas in measuring portfolio credit risk

- the basic feature of reduced-form models

- the role of the Poisson process in reduced-form models

- the differences in the two major reduced-form models: Jarrow-Turnbull model and Duffie-Singleton model

- what an incomplete information model is

Credit risk models are used in finance to measure, monitor, and control a portfolio's credit risk. In fixed-income analysis, they are also used in the pricing of credit risky debt instruments. Credit risk models are classified as either structural models or reduced-form models. There is considerable debate as to which type of model is the best to employ. This is not just a debate amongst academic theorists. Oftentimes, the parties to the debate are vendors that sell these models to asset management firms and financial institutions needing a credit risk management system.

We will provide the main elements of structural and reduced-form models in this chapter. In addition, there are structural/reduced-form hybrid models, and we will discuss one such model called the incomplete information model. A discussion of how the parameters of credit risk models are estimated is beyond the scope of this chapter.

DIFFICULTIES IN CREDIT RISK MODELING

In Chapter 4, we described how to quantify the interest rate risk of a bond and a bond portfolio. While there are complex securities where modeling the interest rate risk exposes the portfolio manager to modeling risk, quantifying interest risk exposure is less complicated than modeling credit risk exposure. Following are three reasons that this is so:

1. Credit default risk is a rare event and, as a result, the historical data needed to compute the inputs into a credit risk model (e.g., default rates and recovery rates) are considerably less in comparison to the data available for the modeling of interest rate risk where, for example, historical U.S. Treasury prices are available on a daily basis for many decades.
2. Even with the default data that are available, it is much more difficult to draw any meaningful and possibly predictive conclusions about the probability of default because of the diversity of the corporations involved (in terms of industry sector, size, and leverage) and the lack of complete information regarding corporate practices.
3. There are various causes of default by a corporate borrower—ranging from microeconomic factors (such as poor management) to macroeconomic factors (such as high interest rates and recession)—that make default hard to predict.

Moreover, while our focus in this chapter will be on credit risk modeling for U.S. corporations, applying these models to non–U.S. entities is complicated by the fact that default is not a universal concept. Every country has its own bankruptcy code to deal with defaults. Furthermore, there is no assurance that the administrators of the bankruptcy law (e.g., bankruptcy judges in the United States) will apply the law in a manner that is consistent with the bankruptcy code. For example, as explained in Chapter 7, the U.S. bankruptcy code sets forth that when a corporation is liquidated, creditors receive distributions based on the "absolute priority rule" to the extent assets are available. The absolute priority rule is the principle that senior creditors are paid in full before junior creditors are paid anything. For secured creditors and unsecured creditors, the absolute priority rule guarantees their seniority to stockholders. In liquidations, the absolute priority rule generally holds. In contrast, there is a preponderance of evidence that shows that strict absolute priority has not been upheld by the courts in corporate reorganizations.

From what we have said so far, it seems unlikely that credit risk modeling will yield fruitful and meaningful information. Yet, credit risk models have long been employed in the finance and insurance industries. The focus of the early models was on generating forecasts of default rates, credit ratings, and credit spreads (measured relative to U.S. Treasury securities).[1] From a portfolio perspective, the assumption was that credit default risk for corporate bonds is idiosyncratic and, therefore, can be diversified away

---

[1] One of the approaches was a credit scoring model using multiple discriminant analysis developed by Edward I. Altman in 1968: Edward I. Altman, "Financial Bankruptcies, Discriminant Analysis and the Prediction of Corporate Bankruptcy," *Journal of Finance* (September 1968), pp. 589–609. There were subsequent updates of the model. See Edward I. Altman, Robert G. Haldeman, and Paul Narayann, "Zeta Analysis: A New Model to Identify Bankruptcy Risk of Corporations," *Journal of Banking and Finance* (June 1977), pp. 29–54 and Chapters 8 and 9 in Edward I. Altman, *Corporate Financial Distress and Bankruptcy: A Complete Guide to Predicting and Avoiding Distress and Profiting from Bankruptcy* (New York: John Wiley & Sons, 1993).

in large portfolios containing corporate bonds. In credit risk modeling for individual corporate bonds, some risk-return measure (such as the Sharpe ratio) was used to evaluate the observed credit spreads.[2]

Since the mid 1990s, more sophisticated approaches to credit risk modeling have been proposed and made commercially available to portfolio managers. For one of these approaches that is commercially available, the theoretical foundation underlying the model dates back to the early 1970s.

OVERVIEW OF CREDIT RISK MODELING[3]

Credit risk modeling is used for

- estimating the default probability
- pricing individual corporate bonds
- measuring a portfolio's credit risk

The **default probability** (or **probability of default**) is the likelihood that a borrower will default sometime over the life of the debt obligation. By default, it is meant that the borrower fails to honor the terms of the agreement, such as the failure to make a principal or coupon payment required under the agreement, or the violation of a covenant. It is common in practice to look at the default over the next one year. The default probability is sometimes referred to as an **expected default frequency**. To estimate the default probability for one year, a credit risk model requires the following: (1) a definition of what constitutes a default event, (2) a model of investor uncertainty (i.e., what information are we uncertain about?), and (3) how that information will evolve over time.[4]

Given a credit risk model and observed market prices for corporate bonds and/or credit derivatives, a fair value for the credit spread for an illiquid or unpriced corporate bond with a given credit rating or other credit-based characteristic can be estimated. This credit spread is referred to as the **fair market credit spread**. The fair market credit spread is then used to price other credit risky assets with similar characteristics. To estimate the fair market credit spread, a credit risk model requires (1) a model that estimates recovery if a default occurs, (2) a model that shows the credit spread that investors want in order to accept systematic credit risk and idiosyncratic risk—as the spread is largely driven by uncertainty of the timing of default for this one company, and (3) a model of the risk-free rate.[5]

Measuring a portfolio's credit risk requires a model for linking the defaults of corporate bonds. One might think that this link can be estimated by looking at the correlations of defaults for corporate bond issuers in different sectors of the bond market. However, as will be explained later in this chapter, a different statistical tool is used.

---

[2] See H. Gifford Fong and Frank J. Fabozzi, *Fixed Income Portfolio Management* (Homewood, IL: Dow Jones-Irwin, 1985). One of the problems with using the Sharpe measure for corporate bond returns is the assumed symmetric return distribution. However, corporate bond returns offer an asymmetric risk-reward property. As a result, traditional risk-reward measures such as the Sharpe ratio based on variance do not cope well with credit especially for bonds that may be crossover candidates—bonds that are candidates for shifting from high-yield to investment grade.

[3] A detailed discussion of the objectives of the credit risk modeling process is provided in Donald R. van Deventer and Kenji Imai, *Credit Risk Models and the Basel Accords* (Hoboken, NJ: John Wiley & Sons, 2003).

[4] Tim Backshall, Kay Giesecke, and Lisa Goldberg, "Credit Risk Modeling," Chapter 33 in Frank J. Fabozzi (ed.), *The Handbook of Fixed Income Securities* (New York: McGraw-Hill, 2004), p. 779.

[5] Backshall, Giesecke, and Goldberg, "Credit Risk Modeling," pp. 779–780.

CREDIT RATINGS VERSUS CREDIT RISK MODELS

Recall that a long-term credit rating is a prediction of the likelihood that an issuer or issue will default and the severity of the loss. Why not simply rely on credit ratings as a forecaster of default? Van Deventer of Kamakura Corporation, a vendor of credit risk models, provides the following reasons.[6] First, ratings are discrete with a limited number of rating grades, which were described in Chapter 7. In contrast, default probabilities are continuous and range from 0% to 100%. Second, while ratings are updated very infrequently, default probabilities can be estimated on a real-time basis. Van Deventer provides an example of the downgrade of Merck (from AAA to AA–) in 2004. The downgrade came three weeks after the withdrawal of a major drug that significantly impacted Merck's stock price. Finally, there is no clear maturity for a credit rating. While there is a separate short- and long-term credit rating, credit risk models provide a default probability by maturity (i.e., a term structure of default probabilities). This provides insight into the default probabilities for different phases of the business cycle.

STRUCTURAL MODELS

In 1973, Fischer Black and Myron Scholes developed a model for the pricing of options on common stock.[7] At the end of the article, the authors discussed an application of their option pricing model to corporate bond pricing by explaining how the stockholders can be viewed as having a call option on the value of the assets with the right being granted by the bondholders. A year after the publication of this seminal article, Robert Merton extended the framework provided by Black and Scholes to analyze how it can be used to value credit risky securities such as corporate bonds.[8] We will provide the basics of what is now referred to as the Black-Scholes-Merton (BSM) model. As we review the model, we will see that there are many simplifying assumptions. There have been extensions of the BSM model to make the model more realistic and we will briefly describe them also.

The BSM model and its extensions are referred to as **structural models**. The fundamental feature that is common to all structural models is that default can be viewed as some type of option by the equity owners on the assets of the firm, and that the option is triggered (i.e., the corporation defaults) when the value of the corporation's assets declines below a certain default point.[9] The application of option pricing theory avoids the use of a risk premium and tries to use other marketable securities to price the option. The use of option pricing theory provides a significant improvement over traditional methods for valuing corporate bonds. The outputs of structural models show how the credit risk of a corporate bond is a function of the issuer's leverage and the volatility of the issuer's assets. The output of these models also provides information about how to hedge the default risk, which was not obtainable from traditional methods.

---

[6] Donald R. van Deventer, "An Introduction to Credit Risk Models," Chapter 14 in Frank J. Fabozzi, Lionel Martellini, and Philippe Priaulet (eds.), *Advanced Bond Portfolio Management: Best Practices in Modeling and Strategies* (Hoboken, NJ: John Wiley & Sons, 2006).

[7] Fischer Black and Myron Scholes, "The Pricing of Options and Corporate Liabilities," *Journal of Political Economy*, 81 (1973), pp. 637–654.

[8] Robert Merton, "On the Pricing of Corporate Debt: The Risk Structure of Interest Rates," *Journal of Finance*, 29 (1974), pp. 449–470.

[9] Because of this feature, structural models are also known as "firm-value models."

Structural models have been used by banks in making credit decisions and by bond portfolio managers. According to Wesley Phoa of Capital Group Companies, structural models have been used by bond portfolio managers in one or more of the following ways:[10]

1. to estimate a corporate bond's default risk
2. to predict rating changes (upgrades and downgrades with particular interest in downgrades)
3. for a given corporate issuer with several issues in its capital structure, to identify relative value opportunities
4. to forecast changes in corporate bond credit spreads
5. from within the corporate bond market, to identify relative value opportunities
6. to evaluate the sensitivity of corporate bond credit spreads to equity prices

In assessing the merits of structural models, these potential uses must be kept in mind. Structural models may perform well in one area of application in bond portfolio management but turn out to be useless for other applications. When considering the potential use of structural models, it is important to be aware of the underlying assumptions of the model because it is these assumptions that may limit the usefulness of a model to one or more of the six areas mentioned previously.

Fundamentals of the Black-Scholes-Merton Model[11]

In the BSM model, the following assumptions are made:

Assumption 1: A corporation has only one type of bond outstanding in its debt structure.
Assumption 2: The bond outstanding is a zero-coupon bond that matures in T years.
Assumption 3: There is a constant risk-free interest rate over the life of the bond.
Assumption 4: The payment to bondholders in the case of default of the corporation is made in accordance with the principle of absolute priority.
Assumption 5: Volatility is assumed to be constant.

Assumption 1 is obviously unrealistic, and extensions of the BSM model discussed later allow for multiple types of bond issues. Assumption 2 is important because it precludes a corporation from defaulting prior to the maturity date of the zero-coupon bond. The reason is that there are no payments that must be made and, therefore, no default based on missed payments if the outstanding debt is a zero-coupon bond. So, regardless of what happens to the value of the zero-coupon bond issued by the corporation between the time of issuance and its maturity date, there is nothing having to do with this bond that would result in a default event. Again, this assumption is unrealistic and there are models that allow for default prior to the maturity date.

To describe the model, we will let

$E(t)$ = the value of the corporation's equity at time t
$A(t)$ = the value of the corporation's assets at time t
K = the maturity value of the zero-coupon bond issued by the corporation

---

[10] Wesley Phoa, "Implications of Merton Models for Corporate Bond Investors," Chapter 16 in Frank J. Fabozzi, Lionel Martellini, and Philippe Priaulet (eds.), *Advanced Bond Portfolio Management: Best Practices in Modeling and Strategies* (Hoboken, NJ: John Wiley & Sons, 2006).
[11] For numerical illustrations of the BSM model, see Chapter 8 in Mark J. P. Anson, Frank J. Fabozzi, Moorad Choudhry, and Ren-Raw Chen, *Credit Derivatives: Instruments, Pricing, and Applications* (John Wiley & Sons, 2004).

At the maturity date of the zero-coupon bond, T, the value of the corporation's equity is $E(T)$ and the value of the corporation's assets is $A(T)$.

Now, let's look at what can happen at the maturity date of the zero-coupon bond. There are only three possible scenarios at T:

>   **Scenario 1:** Total assets exceed the maturity value of the zero-coupon bond. That is, $A(T) > K$.
>   **Scenario 2:** Total assets are less than the maturity value of the zero-coupon bond. That is, $A(T) < K$.
>   **Scenario 3:** Total assets are equal to the maturity value of the zero-coupon bond. That is, $A(T) = K$.

The value of the equity at time T, $E(T)$, is the difference between the value of the assets, $A(T)$, and the maturity value of the zero-coupon bond, K. That is,

$$E(T) = A(T) - K$$

In Scenario 1 (total assets exceed the maturity value of the zero-coupon bond), then

$$E(T) = A(T) - K > 0$$

That is, there is positive equity value, and the stockholders would be sure to pay off the bondholders in full in order to retain the corporation.

In Scenario 2 (total assets are less than the maturity value of the zero-coupon bond), then

$$E(T) = A(T) - K < 0$$

In this scenario, the stockholders would default and the bondholders would receive less than the maturity value of the bond. Effectively, the bondholders would own the corporation.

In Scenario 3 (total assets are equal to the maturity value of the zero-coupon bond), the value of the equity is zero. In this case, the stockholders would pay off the bondholders in full and own a corporation with zero value.

If we let $B(T)$ denote the value of the corporation's zero-coupon bond, then its value at the maturity date can be expressed as

$$B(T) = A(T) - \max[A(T) - K, 0] \qquad \textbf{(21.1)}$$

The notation $\max[A(T) - K, 0]$ means the maximum of $A(T) - K$ and zero. In Scenario 1, $A(T) - K$ is positive so the maximum value is $A(T) - K$ and the value of the bond is K,

$$B(T) = A(T) - [A(T) - K] = K$$

In Scenario 2, $A(T) - K$ is negative and therefore $\max[A(T) - K, 0]$ is zero. Hence, the value of the bond is

$$B(T) = A(T) - 0 = A(T)$$

In Scenario 3, the value of the bond is simply K.

If we look closely at equation (21.1) we can see why Black and Scholes viewed the value of a corporate bond in terms of the value of an option. The term $\max[A(T) - K, 0]$ in equation (21.1) is the payoff of a call option with a strike price of K that expires at T, and the underlying is the corporation's assets. Since the term enters into the equation with a negative sign, this means a short position in a call option (i.e., the sale of a call option). So the position given by equation (21.1) is that the bondholder has a long position in the corporation's assets and has sold a call option to the common stockholders on the corporation's assets. The value of a corporate bond is valued accordingly: It is the value of the total assets reduced by the value of the call option. The call option can be valued by using an option pricing model such as the Black-Scholes model.

If we rewrite equation (21.1), we have another interpretation that is useful. The equation can be rewritten as

$$B(T) = K - \max[K - A(T), 0] \qquad (21.2)$$

The results for each of the three scenarios will, of course, be the same as with equation (21.1). Again, the notation $\max[K - A(T), 0]$ means the maximum of $K - A(T)$ and zero. In Scenario 1, $K - A(T)$ is negative so the maximum value is zero, and the value of the bond is K. In Scenario 2, $K - A(T)$ is positive and, therefore, $\max[K - A(T), 0]$ is $K - A(T)$. Hence, the value of the bond is

$$B(T) = K - [K - A(T)] = A(T)$$

In Scenario 3, the value of the bond is simply K.

The term $[K - A(T)]$ is the payoff of a put option at time T written on the corporation's assets with a strike price K. Since this term enters into equation (21.2) with a negative sign, it is the payoff of a short put position. One can interpret the position given by equation (21.2) as a position in a risk-free bond reduced by the value of the put position that the stockholders sold to the bondholders on the corporation's assets.

To value the option using this approach to corporate bond valuation using an option pricing model, the following inputs are required:

1. the corporation's capital structure
2. the corporation's market value (typically derived from its stock price)
3. the volatility of the market value of the corporation (typically derived from the volatility of the stock's price)

Extensions of the Black-Scholes-Merton Model

Researchers have developed extensions of the BSM model by relaxing the assumptions. The mathematics in deriving the model becomes more complicated. Moreover, the type of option that is granted by the bondholders to the common stockholders is no longer a basic call option but rather a complex or exotic option. We do not cover such options in this book. Therefore, here we will only describe the extensions and their motivation, providing references for those who desire to study the topic further.

First, consider Assumption 1 (the corporation has only one type of bond outstanding). If the company has a series of zero-coupon bonds outstanding with different maturities, then it is quite easy for the BSM model to characterize default at different times. Geske demonstrated how this is done by using a "compound option" model.[12] A compound option is an option on another option. The main point of the Geske model is that defaults can be described as a series of contingent events and that later defaults are contingent upon

---

[12] See Robert Geske, "The Valuation of Corporate Liabilities as Compound Options," *Journal of Financial and Quantitative Analysis*, 12 (1977), pp. 541–552. Also see Robert Geske and Herbert Johnson, "The Valuation of Corporate Liabilities as Compound Options: A Correction," *Journal of Financial and Quantitative Analysis*, 19 (1984), pp. 231–232. For a numerical illustration of the Geske model, see Chapter 8 in Anson, Fabozzi, Choudhry, and Chen, *Credit Derivatives: Instruments, Pricing, and Applications*.

whether there was no prior default. Based on this notion, layers of contingent defaults build up a series of sequential compound options, one linking to the other.

Another series of models have been proposed to extend the BSM model to the case where default can occur not only at maturity but at any time prior to maturity. The underlying legal principle here is that there are typically covenants in a typical bond indenture granting the bondholders the right to restructure the corporation should the value of the corporate assets fall below a given amount, referred to as a **default barrier**. These models are referred to as **first-passage time models** with the first such model being proposed by Black and Cox.[13] In all of these models, a threshold is defined (default barrier) and default occurs when a corporation's asset value crosses that threshold. Default is viewed as a form of barrier option.[14] A barrier option is a path dependent option. For such options, both the payoff of the option and the survival of the option to the stated expiration date depends on whether the price of the underlying asset reaches a specified level over the life of the option.[15]

With respect to Assumption 3, a constant risk-free rate, Shimko, Tejima, and van Deventer extend the BSM model to allow for stochastic interest rates.[16]

Moody's KMV Model

A number of software/consulting companies have developed credit risk models based on structural models. The two most popular appear to be Moody's KMV Corporation and RiskMetric Group's CreditGrades. Both systems use the BSM model to model defaults using large databases of historical data. Here, we will describe the Moody's KMV model. This is not an endorsement of this company's products but merely to see the output of a commercial product based on the BMS model.

In the Moody's KMV methodology, information contained in equity prices and the balance sheet of corporate bond issuers is used to extract the probability of default, which it refers to as the **expected default frequency** (EDF) and is the probability of defaulting within a specified time period. So, a corporation with an EDF for a one-year time period of 3% has a 3% probability of defaulting within the next 12 months. The EDF is specific to a corporation, as any default of any security is legally applicable to all securities of the issuer (i.e., the corporation cannot "cherry-pick" which liabilities to default upon).

Moreover, each EDF can be associated with a credit spread curve and a credit rating. The credit rating assigned by the model based on market prices is called a **market implied**

---

[13] Fischer Black and John Cox, "Valuing Corporate Securities: Some Effects of Bond Indenture Provisions," *Journal of Finance*, 31 (1976), pp. 351–367.

[14] Other extensions viewing default as a barrier option include: Francis Longstaff and Eduardo Schwartz, "A Simple Approach to Valuing Risky Fixed and Floating Rate Debt," *Journal of Finance*, 50 (1995), pp. 789–819; Eric Briys and Francois de Varenne, "Valuing Risky Fixed Rate Debt: An Extension," *Journal of Financial and Quantitative Analysis*, 32 (1997), pp. 239–248; Chunsheng Zhou, "An Analysis of Default Correlations and Multiple Defaults," *Review of Financial Studies* (2001), pp. 555–576; and Ming Huang and Jay Huang, "How Much of the Corporate-Treasury Yield Spread Is Due to Credit Risk?" working paper, Stanford University, 2002.

[15] This form of barrier option is also called a "down-and-out barrier" option. There are two types of barrier options: knock-out options and knock-in options. The former is an option that is terminated once a specified value is realized by the underlying asset. A knock-in option is an option that is activated once a specified value is realized by the underlying asset. For a further explanation of barrier options, see John Hull, *Options, Futures, and Other Derivatives* (New York: Prentice Hall, 2002).

[16] David C. Shimko, Naohiko Tejima, and Donald R. van Deventer, "The Pricing of Risky Debt When Interest Rates Are Stochastic," *Journal of Fixed Income* (September 1993), pp. 58–66.

rating. Instead of being aggregated into rating classes, corporations are categorized in the Moody's KMV methodology using a "distance-to-default index" measure.

There are three steps involved in computing a firm's EDF in the Moody's KMV methodology. First, the market value and volatility of a firm's assets need to be estimated. Second, using option pricing theory applied to the valuation of corporate bonds, the distance-to-default index measure is computed. Finally, the distance-to-default index measure is combined with a large dataset of actual default rates to compute the probability of default. This last step is the major advantage of the model and what also sets it most apart from the BSM approach.

Advantages and Disadvantages of Structural Models

From a theoretical perspective, structural models analyze default based on a reasonable assumption that it is a result of the value of the corporate issuer's assets falling below the value of its debt. In addition to providing default probabilities, these models allow a bond portfolio manager to see how the credit risk of corporate debt is a function of the leverage and the asset volatility of the issuer. Accordingly, the impact of a new stock or bond offering that will change the capital structure of a corporation can be assessed.

While superior to what was previously available, there are two concerns that have been expressed about structural models: they are difficult to calibrate and computationally burdensome. We first discussed the calibration of models to market data when we discussed interest rate models in Chapter 16. Calibration is a necessary first step in fixed-income trading because it allows traders to clearly see *relative prices* and hence be able to construct arbitrage trading strategies. To calibrate a structural model to price a corporate bond requires calibration to asset volatility, asset value, face value of the corporate issuer's debt, the default barrier (in the case of first-passage time models), and the risk-free rate.[17] While some of these values required for calibration can be estimated from market data (e.g., using Treasuries to estimate the risk-free rate), many are not observable or easy to obtain. The value of a corporation is estimated from stock prices for publicly traded corporations. Determining the face value of the corporation's debt may seem simple; however, in complex capital structures involving multiple bond issues, bank debt, guarantees on debt issues by others, pension liabilities, leasing obligations, and any interest rate derivatives that the issuer may be exposed to, it is not simple. For first-passage time models, a suitable default barrier must be estimated. Because of this difficulty, it is argued that structural models are not suitable for the frequent marking to market of credit contingent securities.

What we have just described is the problem with calibration for a single corporate bond issue. When assessing the credit risk of a portfolio of corporate bonds there is a further complication when implementing structural models. One must estimate the correlation between the issuers in the portfolio. The statistical tool for doing this is described next.

From a computational perspective, the pricing of a corporate zero-coupon bond, for example, is just like pricing an option on a bond, a topic we cover in Chapter 27. However, for coupon-bearing corporate bonds the problem becomes one of pricing a compound option, a more difficult problem. To price a subordinated bond, it is necessary to simultaneously value all of the more senior debt (bonds and loans). Consequently, there is reluctance

---

[17] To truly price the bond (in the real world), we actually need the risk premium also—as the standard BSM model will produce risk-neutral spreads.

by some market participants to use structural models where there is a need for rapid and accurate pricing of corporate bonds.

The main application of structural models in practice appears to be in the area of credit risk analysis. Market participants have argued that structural models are more likely to be able to predict the credit quality of a corporate security than the reduced-form models that will be discussed later and are certainly more timely than rating agency actions or fundamental analysis described in the previous chapter. As a result, banks have found it a useful model for establishing credit lines with corporations and a useful tool in the risk analysis of portfolios of corporate bonds.

ESTIMATING PORTFOLIO CREDIT RISK: DEFAULT CORRELATION AND COPULAS

Thus far, we have discussed how structural models can be used in assessing the credit risk of an individual corporation. For a portfolio of corporate bonds, there is the risk that some event that triggers the default of one of the corporate bonds in the portfolio will adversely impact another corporate bond in the portfolio, thereby increasing the probability of the default of that second corporation. A commonly used statistical concept to gauge the dependence between two variables is correlation. In credit risk management, this type of risk is referred to as default correlation. One would expect that for corporate issuers in the same industry sector, **default correlation** is high.

Developers of credit risk models need an estimate of the default correlations in order to assess the credit risk of a portfolio and credit derivatives. The technique used to estimate the default correlation varies. For example, Moody's uses a Monte Carlo simulation of historical data on rating transitions and defaults in its analysis. Another rating agency, Fitch Ratings, uses correlations based on equity price changes.

While we just noted that correlation quantifies the dependence between two variables, it should be noted that correlation is often incorrectly used to mean any notion of dependence between two variables. However, correlation is only one of several measures in statistics used to quantify a dependence structure, and there are reasons this measure is not a suitable one in the case of credit risk modeling. One reason is that the independence of two random variables implies a correlation that is equal to zero. However, conversely, a correlation of zero does not imply independence.

To see the relevance for credit risk management, suppose that there are numerous potential suppliers of a particular part to the automotive industry. Assume that the ABC Company is one such supplier firm. From the perspective of the ABC Company, defaults of firms in the automotive industry are likely to have severe adverse economic consequence, potentially leading to its bankruptcy. Hence, from the perspective of an investor in the ABC Company's bond, there is high default risk between the ABC Company and the automotive industry. However, from the perspective of the holder of the corporate bonds of companies in the automotive industry, the default of the ABC Company is highly unlikely to have any impact on these companies. Thus, from the perspective of the automotive industry, the impact on default risk is likely to be zero.

Because of this asymmetrical dependence and other drawbacks of correlation as a measure of risk, many developers of credit risk models use different measures of dependence to understand the multivariate relationship between all of the bonds in a portfolio.

The combination of individual default probabilities (or default distributions) and their dependence is known mathematically as a "copula." The background needed to understand copulas cannot be discussed here. What is important to understand is that by using copulas rather than simple correlations to gauge the nature of the dependency between two variables, a modeler can better handle the modeling of extreme events.

REDUCED-FORM MODELS

Reduced-form models were introduced in the mid 1990s. The two most notable reduced-form models are the Jarrow-Turnbull model [18] and the Duffie-Singleton model.[19]

The major difference between reduced-form models and structural models is how default is treated. As with all economic models, structural and reduced-form models are merely an abstract simplified mathematical representation of relationships between economic variables. The variables in an economic model contain endogenous variables and exogenous variables. An endogenous variable is a variable whose value is determined within the economic model; it is referred to as a "dependent" variable because its value is dependent on the other variables in the economic model. An exogenous variable is a variable whose value is determined outside the economic model and is referred to as an "independent" variable because its value is determined independent of the other variables in the economic model. In structural models, default is endogenous; in reduced-form models it is exogenous. As it turns out, specifying defaults exogenously, as is done in reduced-form models, greatly simplifies credit risk modeling because it ignores the constraint of defining what causes default and simply looks at the default event itself. Pricing of corporate bonds with different maturities can be seen as independent, unlike structural models where defaults of longer-maturity corporate bonds of an issuer are contingent on defaults of shorter-maturity corporate bonds of that same issuer.

The key elements in reduced-form models are: (1) the default time, (2) recovery rate process, and (3) risk-free interest rate. The modeling of when a default occurs and the recovery process, if the issuer defaults, is how the reduced-form models that have been proposed differ. Accurately modeling the bankruptcy recovery process is not simple.[20] Recognition must be given to the trade-off between analytic tractability and practical applicability. Based on restrictive assumptions about the dynamics of the default and recovery processes, a closed-form solution to reduced-form models has been derived by their proposers.

The theoretical framework for reduced-form models is the Poisson process. We will provide a brief explanation of this simple stochastic process.

Poisson Process

In Chapter 16, in our description of interest rate modeling, we explained what a stochastic process is. A Poisson process is one of the most important classes of stochastic processes.

---

[18] Robert Jarrow and Stuart Turnbull, "Pricing Derivatives on Financial Securities Subject to Default Risk," *Journal of Finance*, 50 (1995), pp. 53–86.

[19] Darrell Duffie and Kenneth Singleton, "Modeling the Term Structure of Defaultable Bonds," *Review of Financial Studies*, 12 (1999), pp. 687–720. The name "reduced form" was given by Darrell Duffie to distinguish it from structural models.

[20] Three models have been proposed to model the recovery process: (1) recovery of market value, (2) recovery of face value and accrued interest, and (3) recovery of Treasury value.

To understand the Poisson process, we begin with a sequence or counter, which counts (i.e., 1, 2, . . .) the number of some defined event occurring from an initial point in time. We denote the value of this counter at time t as N_t. That is,

$$N_t = \text{number of occurences in the interval 0 to } t$$

Thus, N_t will increase by 1 for every occurrence of an event, and these increases are referred to as "increments."

The probability of an event occurring from one integer to the next over a small time interval dt is given by[21]

$$\text{Probability } [N_{t+dt} + N_{t-1} = 1] = \lambda dt$$

where the parameter λ is called the *intensity parameter* of the Poisson process. Similarly, the probability of no event occurring in the same time interval is simply given by

$$\text{Probability } [N_{t+dt} + N_{t-1} = 0] = 1 - \lambda dt$$

In reduced-form models, the event in a Poisson process is defined as a default. The intensity parameter in reduced-form models is called the **default intensity** and is a key parameter in the model. In fact, reduced-form models are also referred to as **intensity-based models** and **stochastic default rate models**. In the context of a reduced-form model, the default intensity at time t can be thought of in terms of a probability. More specifically, it is the *conditional* probability of default per unit time given that the corporation has not previously defaulted.[22] Consequently, the Poisson process basically describes the near-term default risk of a corporation.

The intensity parameter in the Poisson process can be specified in one of three ways. The first is simply as a deterministic or constant value that is independent of time t. In the previous formula that is how it is specified. The second way is to specify the intensity parameter as a deterministic function of time t. Finally, the intensity function can be specified as a random variable that depends on some exogenously specified state variables. For example, the default process can be correlated with the risk-free interest rate processes.[23] Most reduced-form models used in practice employ a stochastic intensity parameter to model the default process.

If we assume that the intensity parameter is a constant, then it can be demonstrated that the time it takes until the first default event occurs, called the **default time**, obeys an exponential distribution given by

$$\text{Probability } (T > t) = e^{-\lambda (T-t)}$$

The Jarrow-Turnbull Model

The Jarrow-Turnbull model is a simple model of default and recovery. It assumes that no matter when default occurs, the recovery payment is paid at the maturity date. By making the assumption that the recovery payment is made at maturity, Jarrow and

---

[21] Recall in Chapter 16, where we mentioned stochastic differential equations, what dt represents: dt denotes the change in time or equivalently the length of the time interval and is a very small interval of time.

[22] Because it depends on the corporation not having previously defaulted, that is why it is a conditional probability.

[23] In such cases, a special type of Poisson process known as a Cox process (or doubly stochastic Poisson process) is used. For a discussion of the Cox process, see Chapter 10 in Svetlozar T. Rachev, Christian Menn, and Frank J. Fabozzi, *Fat-Tailed and Skewed Asset Return Distributions: Implications for Risk Management, Portfolio Selection, and Option Pricing* (Hoboken, NJ: John Wiley & Sons, 2005).

Turnbull assume away any dependency between the bond price and the conditional default probability.

The basic Jarrow-Turnbull model has been extended by Jarrow, Lando, and Turnbull[24] to incorporate different credit ratings rather than just two states (default and survival). That is, instead of a single state for default (and survival), there can be a number of probabilities, each for the probability of moving from one credit rating to another credit rating. This is done by providing the probabilities for these rating movements. As explained in Chapter 7, these probabilities can be obtained from the rating transition tables published periodically by the rating agencies. Thus, these extended reduced-form models deal with migration risk of credit ratings rather than default risk.

The Duffie-Singleton Model

The assumption in the Jarrow-Turnbull model that the recovery payment can occur only at maturity rather than when default actually occurs (or soon after) so that a closed-form solution can be derived is not realistic. This is one of two major drawbacks of that model. The second drawback is that the recovery amount can fluctuate randomly over time. The recovery amount fluctuates because it depends on the corporation's liquidation value at the time of default. As a result, it is possible to have scenarios for the Jarrow-Turnbull model wherein the recovery payment may exceed the price of the bond at the time of default because the recovery rate is an exogenously specified percentage of the risk-free bonds.

In contrast, the model proposed by Duffie and Singleton (1) allows the recovery payment to occur at any time, and (2) restricts the amount of recovery to be a fixed fraction of the non-default bond price at the time of default. Because of this second assumption, the Duffie-Singleton model is referred to as a **fractional recovery model** or a **fractional recovery of predefault market value model**. The rationale for this assumption is that as a corporate bond's credit quality deteriorates, its price falls. At the time of default, the recovery price will be some fraction of the final price that prevailed prior to default, and, as a result, one does not encounter the shortcoming of the Jarrow-Turnbull model that recovery price can be greater than the price prior to default.

Advantages and Disadvantages of Reduced-Form Models

Because the default probabilities and recovery rates are exogenously specified in the model, one can use a series of risky zero-coupon bonds to calibrate out a default probability curve and hence a credit spread curve. The ability to quickly calibrate to the market so that traders can assess relative prices and construct arbitrage trading strategies is the major reason why reduced-form models are strongly favored by practitioners involved in the credit derivatives market.[25]

A criticism of reduced-form models is precisely the advantage cited by its proponents: It does not explain the economic reasoning behind default because it treats default as an exogenous event. Future refinements of reduced-form models will likely incorporate factors driving defaults into the modeling of the intensity rate and loss rate. One example

---

[24] Robert Jarrow, David Lando, and Stuart Turnbull, "A Markov Model for the Term Structure of Credit Spreads," *Review of Financial Studies*, 10 (1997), pp. 481–532.

[25] We will discuss credit derivatives in Chapter 29. For an illustration of the calibration process for the Jarrow-Turnbull model, see Chapter 9 in Anson, Fabozzi, Choudhry, and R. Chen, *Credit Derivatives: Instruments, Applications, and Pricing.*

is the linking of the intensity parameter to the value of the firm.[26] Moreover, reduced-form models suffer from the constraint that default is always treated as a surprise. This is rarely the case. Studies by the rating agencies indicate that there are very few corporate bonds that move from investment-grade quality right into default without a series of downgrades in between. Hence, default for such corporate bonds can be anticipated.

INCOMPLETE INFORMATION MODELS

In both structural and reduced-form models, no consideration is given to the fact that the information that investors use may be imperfect. In structural models, for example, firm value is based on the market evaluating correctly the value of the corporation. This could be due to off-balance sheet derivatives, lease financing, pension obligations, etc., all being based on generally accepted accounting principles but not reflecting a true economic state. Moreover, corporate scandals such as Enron, Tyco, WorldCom, and Parmalat are constant reminders that the financial information provided by corporations may be far from reflecting their true economic condition. For example, in first-passage time models, as explained earlier, a default barrier is required. Using the information supplied by Enron, Tyco, and WorldCom would have resulted in misleading default barriers.

Incomplete-information models take into account imperfect information reported in financial statements. While incomplete-information models were proffered by several researchers,[27] Giesecke and Goldberg propose a structural/reduced-form hybrid model based on incomplete information.[28] Their model, which is used by MSCI Barra, is a first-passage time model wherein it is assumed that investors do not know the default barrier. The approach allows a portfolio manager or credit analyst to include their view on the financial well-being of a company in calibrating the model to market data.

KEY POINTS

- Credit risk models are used to measure, monitor, and control a portfolio's credit risk as well as to price credit risky debt instruments.
- Credit risk models are classified as either structural models or reduced-form models.
- Options theory provides the framework for all structural models.
- The basic idea underlying structural models is that a company defaults on its debt if the value of its assets falls below a certain default point and that the value of a corporate bond can be modeled as an option on these assets. With this insight, researchers were able to apply the same principles used for option pricing to the valuation of corporate bonds using the issuer's stock price and balance sheet data.
- The Black-Scholes-Merton structural model is based on some simplifying assumptions. There have been several modifications and extensions to this model.

---

[26] Sanjiv Das and Peter Tufano, "Pricing Credit–Sensitive Debt When Interest Rates, Credit Ratings, and Credit Spreads Are Stochastic," *Journal of Financial Engineering*, 5 (1996), pp. 161–198.

[27] Darrell Duffie and David Lando, "Term Structures of Credit Spreads with Incomplete Accounting Information," *Econometrica*, 69 (2001), pp. 633–664; Umut Cetin, Robert A. Jarrow, Philip Protter, and Yildiray Yildirim, "Modeling Credit Risk with Partial Information," *Annals of Applied Probability*, 14 (2004), pp. 1167–1178; and Kay Giesecke, "Correlated Default with Incomplete Information," *Journal of Banking and Finance*, 28 (2004), pp. 1521–1545.

[28] Kay Giesecke and Lisa Goldberg, "Forecasting Default in the Face of Uncertainty," *Journal of Derivatives*, 12 (2004), pp. 14–25. For a further description of this model, see Backshall, Giesecke, and Goldberg, "Credit Risk Modeling," pp. 794–797.

- Reduced-form models do not look into the microeconomic factors of a company. Rather, they model directly the default probability or transition risk.
- The theoretical framework for reduced-form models is the Poisson process.
- The two most notable reduced-form models are the Jarrow-Turnbull and Duffie-Singleton models.
- Both structural models and reduced-form models assume that the information reported by the issuing corporations is accurate. However, corporate bankruptcies that have been attributable to fraud and opaque/inaccurate financial accounting data have made practitioners aware that when modeling credit risk, there must be consideration of the possibility that information is imperfect. This has led to the development of incomplete-information models.
- The Giesecke and Goldberg model combines the structural and reduced-form models but incorporates incomplete information.

QUESTIONS

1. Why is credit risk modeling more difficult than interest rate modeling?

2. A corporate bond portfolio manager was overhead asking: "Why do I need a credit risk model? I can get information about the probability of default from credit ratings." How would you respond to this portfolio manager?

3. What is a common feature of all structural models?

4. Give two interpretations of the value of a bond from an option's perspective.

5. Explain how the Black-Scholes-Merton model has been extended to allow for multiple bond issues in a corporation's debt structure.

6. Explain how the Black-Scholes-Merton model has been extended to overcome the assumption that default can only occur at maturity.

7. How can structural models be used by bond portfolio managers?

8. Explain each of the following:
   a. expected default frequency
   b. market implied rating
   c. distance-to-default index measure

9. How does the treatment of default in structural models and reduced-form models differ?

10. How do the Jarrow-Turnbull and Duffie-Singleton reduced-form models differ?

11. How does the Jarrow-Turnbull-Lando model differ from the basic Jarrow-Turnbull model?

12. a. How is an event defined in the Poisson process?
    b. What is meant by the intensity parameter in the Poisson process?

13. a. What is the meaning of the default intensity parameter in a reduced-form model?
    b. What are the various ways that the default intensity parameter can be modeled in a reduced-form model?

14. What is meant by default correlation?

15. What is the drawback of the default correlation measure and what alternative measure is used in measuring portfolio credit risk?

16. What is the motivation for the development of incomplete-information credit risk models?

17. Why is the calibration of a credit risk model to the market important in fixed income trading?

22

Bond Portfolio Management Strategies

LEARNING OBJECTIVES

After reading this chapter, you will understand

- what is meant by asset allocation

- the composition of a portfolio management team

- top-down and bottom-up approaches to bond portfolio management

- the spectrum of portfolio management strategies

- what is meant by a core/satellite strategy

- bond indices

- the different types of active bond portfolio strategies: interest-rate expectations strategies, yield curve strategies, yield spread strategies, option-adjusted spread-based strategies, and individual security selection strategies

- bullet, barbell, and ladder yield curve strategies

- the limitations of using duration and convexity to assess the potential performance of bond portfolio strategies

- why it is necessary to use the dollar duration when implementing a yield spread strategy

- how to assess the allocation of funds within the corporate bond sector

- why leveraging is used by managers and traders and the risks and rewards associated with leveraging

- how to leverage using the repo market

In this and the following two chapters we discuss bond portfolio management strategies. We first look in this chapter at bond portfolio strategies where the benchmark by which a manager is evaluated is a bond index. In the next chapter, we look at how to build portfolios using factor models, and in Chapter 24 we discuss liability-driven strategies.

Before we discuss bond portfolio management strategies in this chapter, we begin with a discussion of the asset allocation decision in two contexts: allocation of funds among asset classes in the capital markets and allocating funds within the bond market. We also preface our coverage of bond portfolio management strategies with a description of a bond portfolio management team.

THE ASSET ALLOCATION DECISION

Our focus in this book is on bond portfolio management. That is, given a portfolio manager's mandate to manage a specified amount of funds in fixed income products, we will look at how this should be accomplished. For example, the Oklahoma Teachers Retirement System (OTRS), a public pension fund, had assets of roughly $8.3 billion as of June 10, 2010. The long-term allocation of funds, according to the Executive Director of the OTRS, is to invest 70% in the equity market and 30% in the bond market.[1] A study by Wilshire found that other public pension funds have a similar allocation—66.8% to equities (which includes real estate and private equity) and 33.2% to fixed income.[2]

Regardless of the institutional investor, there are two important decisions to be made by an investor/client:

1. How much should be allocated to bonds?
2. Who should manage the funds to be allocated to bonds?

How Much Should Be Allocated to Bonds?

The decision as to how much to invest in the major asset classes is referred to as the **asset allocation decision**. This decision is the first decision that an investor must make. The asset allocation decision must be made in light of the investor's investment objective. The investment objective will vary by type of investor.

For institutions such as pension funds, the investment objective is to generate sufficient cash flow from investments to satisfy pension obligations. For life insurance companies, the basic objective is to satisfy obligations stipulated in insurance policies and generate a profit. Most insurance products guarantee a dollar payment or a stream of dollar payments at some time in the future. The premium that the life insurance company charges a policyholder for one of its products will depend on the interest rate that the company can earn on its investments. To realize a profit, the life insurance company must earn a higher return on the premium it invests than the implicit (or explicit) interest rate it has guaranteed policyholders.

For institutions such as banks and thrifts, funds are obtained from the issuance of certificates of deposit, short-term money market instruments, or floating-rate notes. These funds are then invested in loans and marketable securities. The objective in this case is to earn a return on invested funds that exceeds the cost of acquiring those funds. For these sorts of institutions, investment objectives are dictated essentially by the nature of their liabilities—obligations to pension recipients, policyholders, and depositors. For investment companies (mutual funds

---

[1] Brian Brus, "Oklahoma Teachers Retirement System Exec Reflects on Change," *The Oklahoma City Journal Record,* July 13, 2010.
[2] Julia K. Bonafede, Steven J. Foresti, and Russell J. Walker, "2010 Wilshire Report on State Retirement Systems: Funding Levels and Asset Allocation," Wilshire Consulting, March 3, 2010.

and closed-end funds), the investment objectives will be as set forth in a prospectus. Typically, the fund establishes a target dividend payout. Because of the importance of the nature of the liabilities in determining investment objectives, in Chapter 24 we examine this topic more closely.

Who Should Manage the Bond Portfolio?

Let's assume that an investor has made the decision to allocate a specified amount to the fixed income sector. For example, suppose that for the $8.3 billion OTRS, the committee responsible for the asset allocation decision has decided to allocate 30% to fixed income. Since the total assets are $8.3 billion, this means that $2.49 billion will be allocated to fixed income. The next decision that must be made is whether that amount will be managed by internal managers or external managers.

There are three choices: (1) use only internal managers, (2) use only external managers, or (3) use a combination of internal and external managers. Some pension funds, for example, do not have internal managers and therefore obviously must engage external managers. If external managers are hired, a decision must be made as to which managers (i.e., asset management firm) to engage.

For example, consider the largest public pension fund in the United States: the California Public Employees Retirement System (CalPERS), with approximately $228 billion in assets as of January 2011. As of early 2011, CalPERS allocated roughly 21% of its portfolio to what it refers to as "global fixed income." Of that amount, the CalPERS investment office manages all of its U.S. fixed income investments internally with two exceptions. The funds allocated to the high-yield sector (1.38% of its assets) are managed externally by the following asset management firms (as of early December 2010): TCW Asset Management Company, Colombia Investment Management, Putnam Investments, Logan Circle Partners, JP Morgan Investment Management, Artio Global Management, ING Investment Management, Nomura Corporate Research & Asset Management, and Pacific Investment Management Company. The second exception to internal management is its international fixed income investments, which are managed externally using the following asset management firms (as of early December 2010): Alliance Bernstein, Baring Asset Management, Pacific Investment Management Company, and Rogge Global Partners.

In practice, the term *asset allocation* is used in two contexts. The first is the way it is used above: allocation of funds among the major asset classes.[3] Although we have mentioned bonds and equities as the major asset classes, there is now accepted a group of assets referred to as **alternative assets**. For example, for CalPERS, the actual (as of January 31, 2011) and target allocation (as of June 2009) asset allocation amongst the asset classes defined by CalPERS is shown in Exhibit 22-1.

Our brief discussion of the asset allocation decision as described here should not suggest that this decision is not critical. In fact, studies have shown that the asset allocation decision is the most important decision impacting performance. It is just that this decision is beyond the scope of this book.

---

[3] One can define an asset class in terms of investment attributes that the members of an asset class have in common. These attributes include (1) the key economic factors influencing the value of the members of the asset class, (2) the similarity of the risk/return relationship for members of the asset class, and (3) the sharing of a common legal structure. Given these attributes, the correlation of returns of members in the asset class is high and the correlation between the returns of different asset classes would be low.

Exhibit 22-1 Asset Allocation of CalPERS: Actual as of January 31, 2011, and Target Allocation as of June 2009

Asset Class	Market Value ($ billion)	Actual Allocation (%)	Target Allocation (%)
Cash Equivalents	4.50	2.0%	2.0%
Global Fixed Income	47.50	20.8%	20.0%
AIM	32.20	14.1%	14.0%
Equity	120.30	52.8%	49.0%
Total Global Equities	152.50	66.9%	63.0%
Real Estate	16.60	7.3%	10.0%
Inflation Linked	6.80	3.0%	5.0%
Total Fund	227.90	100.0%	100.0%

Source: *http://www.calpers.ca.gov/index.jsp?bc=/investments/assets/assetallocation.xml*

The second way in which the term asset allocation is used is how the funds should be allocated, after a decision has been made to invest in a specified asset class, amongst the different sectors within that asset class. For example, in the case of equities, clients do not think in terms of equities being one large asset class. Instead, equities are classified by market capitalization (i.e., large, mid, and small capitalization stocks) and by other attributes such as growth and value stocks. In the bond market, we described the different sectors in earlier chapters in this book. Later in this chapter and in the chapters to follow, when we refer to asset allocation, it is meant in this second way.

The asset allocation among the different sectors of the bond market is made at two levels. The first is where a client must make a decision as to allocation among each sector and then, if an external money manager is to be hired, deciding on the asset management and amount to be allocated to each.

PORTFOLIO MANAGEMENT TEAM

Throughout this book we refer to the person making the investment decisions as the "manager" or "portfolio manager." In practice, while there is someone who will make the ultimate decision about the composition and therefore risk exposure of a portfolio, that decision is the result of recommendations and research provided by the portfolio management team.

An asset management firm or "shop" may manage more than just bond portfolios. A firm may manage multiple asset classes—bonds, equities, and alternative investments. The clients could include corporate, state, local, and Taft-Hartley pension funds, wealthy individuals, and insurance companies. The firm may also manage regulated investment companies (mutual funds and closed-end funds), hedge funds, and exchange-traded funds.

At the top of the investment organizational chart of the investment group is the chief investment officer (CIO), who is responsible for all of the portfolios. The CIO may or may not be a manager of a specific portfolio. Along with the CIO responsible for all portfolios is a chief compliance officer (CCO). That individual monitors portfolios to make sure that the holdings comply with the fund's investment guidelines and that there are no activities conducted by the managers of the fund that are in violation of federal and state securities laws or investment policies. This is an extremely important function and its failure to be carried out properly is one of the reasons for major problems that have occurred at some firms. In the marketing literature of an asset management firm, a key selling point is often the firm's strong internal controls.

The firm will also employ analysts and traders. The analysts are responsible for the different sectors and industries. The traders are responsible for executing trades authorized by a portfolio manager. The analysts and traders can support all of the portfolios managed by the firm or just designated portfolios. For example, a firm managing bonds and equities will hire analysts and traders who specialize in these two asset classes. The bond analysts could be assigned to all of the bond portfolios or just specific ones. If the firm, for example, manages both investment-grade portfolios and high-yield portfolios, an analyst who specializes in high-yield credit analysis might be assigned only to the latter portfolios. Of course, the insight provided by a high-yield credit analyst would be shared with other groups within the firm such as equity analysts and corporate investment-grade analysts.

A large firm may also employ an economist or an economic staff that would support all portfolios managed by the firm.

At the individual portfolio level there is either a lead portfolio manager (sometimes referred to as the senior portfolio manager) or co-managers. The lead manager or co-managers will typically be responsible for more than one portfolio. It is the lead manager or co-managers who will make the decision regarding the portfolio's interest rate exposure and the allocation of the fund's assets among the countries (if non-U.S. investments are permitted), sectors, and industries. These decisions are supported by the macroeconomic perspective adopted by the staff of analysts assigned to the portfolio.

SPECTRUM OF BOND PORTFOLIO STRATEGIES

The bond portfolio strategy selected by an investor or client depends on the investment objectives and policy guidelines. In general, bond portfolio strategies can be categorized into the following three groups:

1. Bond benchmark-based strategies
2. Absolute return strategies
3. Liability-driven strategies

Bond Benchmark-Based Strategies

There is a wide range of bond portfolio management strategies for an investor or client who has selected a bond index as a benchmark. Kenneth Volpert, head of the Taxable Bond Group at the Vanguard Group, classifies traditional bond benchmark-based strategies as[4]

- pure bond index matching
- enhanced indexing: matching primary risk factors

---

[4] Kenneth E. Volpert, "Introduction to Bond Portfolio Management," Chapter 49 in Frank J. Fabozzi (ed.), *The Handbook of Fixed Income Securities,* 8th ed. (New York: McGraw-Hill, 2012).

- enhanced indexing: minor risk-factor mismatches
- active management: larger risk-factor mismatches
- active management: full-blown active

These strategies range from low risk strategies at the top of the preceding list to high risk-tolerance strategies at the bottom. Notice that these strategies are categorized based on how much the portfolio manager departs from the primary risk factors. (We will discuss what we mean by "primary risk factors" shortly.) Basically, one can view a benchmark (bond index) as a package of risk factors. The classification of a strategy into one of the categories above depends on the degree to which a portfolio manager is allowed to depart from the quantity of risk in the benchmark. So not only is it important to understand what the risk factors are, but also how to quantify those risks.

Although we will discuss shortly the primary risk factors, we can focus on one of those risk factors now. As explained in Chapter 4, a major risk factor is the exposure of a benchmark or portfolio to changes in the level of interest rates. Duration is the quantification of this risk and that is the reason we devoted an entire chapter to discussing this measure of risk. With the first three strategies above, a portfolio manager is not permitted to deviate from the benchmark's duration. That is, even when minor mismatches in the primary risk factors are permitted in an enhanced indexing strategy, the mismatch may not occur with respect to duration. Thus, suppose that the benchmark is the Barclays Capital U.S. Aggregate Index and the duration for that index is 5. Then a portfolio manager pursuing any of the first three indexing strategies above is not permitted to construct a portfolio whose duration differs from 5.

The last two strategies above are active bond portfolio management strategies. They differ to the extent with which they allow mismatches relative to the benchmark. For example, the first of the two active strategies described above allows for some small duration mismatch. So if the benchmark's duration is 5, the portfolio might be permitted to deviate by, say, plus or minus 10%. That is, the portfolio manager may be permitted to construct a portfolio with a duration between 4.5 and 5.5 if the benchmark's duration is 5. For the full-blown active management strategy, a portfolio manager has no duration constraint. It is important to note that even if a manager pursues an active strategy, the manager may still elect to have a duration equal to that of the benchmark (i.e., pursue a **duration-matching strategy**). In such cases, it is the other primary risk factors where the manager has elected to take on risk.

In practice, it is extremely difficult to follow the first strategy above: a pure bond indexing strategy is unlike the same strategy when the benchmark is a stock market index. We'll see why in the next chapter.

Today, more often portfolio managers pursue what is referred to as a **core/satellite strategy**.[5] Basically, this strategy involves building a blended portfolio using an indexed and active strategy. The core component is a low-risk portfolio constructed using one of the indexing strategies. The benchmark for the core portfolio is a broad liquid bond market index and the core component provides broad market exposure that has basically the same

---

[5] For a further discussion of this strategy, see Noël Almenc, Philippe Malaise, and Lionel Martelinni, "Revisiting Core-Satellite Investing—A Dynamic Model of Relative Risk Management," EDHEC Risk and Asset Management Research Centre, 2004.

primary risk factor exposure as the benchmark. The satellite component is constructed using an active strategy with a benchmark that is a specialized rather than a broad liquid bond market index. It is this component of the portfolio where the manager makes bets (i.e., takes views) on the primary risk factors.

The core component provides broad market exposure and therefore captures systematic market risk or what is commonly referred to as "beta." In contrast, an active return—commonly referred to as "alpha"—is sought in the actively managed satellite portfolio. The advantage cited for the core/satellite strategy is that it provides a cost-efficient means for controlling portfolio risk relative to a benchmark. (As will be explained in the next chapter, this relative risk is referred to as tracking error.)

Absolute Return Strategies

In an **absolute return strategy**, the portfolio manager seeks to earn a positive return over some time frame irrespective of market conditions. Few restrictions are placed on the exposure to the primary risk factors. Absolute return strategies are typically pursued by hedge fund managers who employ leverage. Other absolute return managers set as their target earning a return from 150 to 400 basis points per annum over the return on cash and hence such strategies are referred to as **cash-based absolute return strategies**. "Cash" means some money market reference rate such as 3-month LIBOR. Typically, these strategies involve the use of fixed income derivatives (i.e., interest rate derivatives and credit derivatives).

Absolute return bond strategies have also been used as a complement to liability-driven strategies that we discuss next.

Liability-Driven Strategies

A bond portfolio strategy that calls for structuring a portfolio to satisfy future liabilities is called a **liability-driven strategy**. Such strategies are followed when funding future liabilities. When the portfolio is constructed so as to generate sufficient funds to satisfy a single future liability regardless of the course of future interest rates, a strategy known as **immunization** is often used. When the portfolio is designed to fund multiple future liabilities regardless of how interest rates change, strategies such as immunization, **cash flow matching** (or **dedication**), or **horizon matching** can be employed.

As part of the immunization and cash flow matching strategies, low-risk active management strategies can be employed. For example, **contingent immunization strategy** allows the portfolio manager to manage a portfolio actively until certain parameters are violated. If and when those parameters are violated, the portfolio is then immunized.

All of these strategies are the subject of Chapter 24.

BOND INDEXES

Typically, bond portfolio managers are given a mandate that involves their performance evaluation relative to a bond index. For that reason, let's discuss bond indexes here.

The wide range of bond market indexes available can be classified as broad-based market indexes and specialized market indexes. Why have broker/dealer firms developed and aggressively marketed their bond indexes? Enhancing the firm's image is only a minor reason. The key motivation lies in the potential income that the firm will generate by executing trades to set up an indexed portfolio and rebalance it. Typically, a broker/dealer charges a portfolio manager who wants to set up or rebalance an indexed portfolio a nominal amount for providing the necessary data but expects that the bulk of the trades will be executed through its trading desks. Also, by keeping the makeup of the index proprietary, those firms attempt to lock in customers to use their index.

The broad-based U.S. bond market index most commonly used by institutional investors is the Barclays Capital U.S. Aggregate Bond Index.[6] There are more than 6,000 issues in this index, which includes only investment-grade securities. The index is a market-value weighted index. That is, for each issue, the ratio of the market value of an issue relative to the market value of all issues in the index is used as the weight of the issue in all calculations. The index is computed daily. The pricing of the securities in each index is either trader priced or model priced.

Each broad-based bond index is broken into sectors. The sector breakdown for the Barclays Capital U.S. Aggregate Bond Index is

- Treasury
- Agency
- Corporate
- Mortgage pass-through
- Commercial mortgage–backed
- Asset-backed

The agency sector includes agency debentures, not mortgage-backed or asset-backed securities issued by federal agencies. The mortgage pass-through sector includes agency pass-through securities. What is not included in the index is agency collateralized mortgage obligations and agency stripped mortgage-backed securities. These mortgage derivatives products are not included because it would be double counting since they are created from agency pass-throughs. In constructing the index for the mortgage sector, Barclays Capital groups more than 800,000 individual mortgage pools with a fixed-rate coupon into generic aggregates. These generic aggregates are defined in terms of agency (i.e., Ginnie Mae, Fannie Mae, and Freddie Mac), program type (e.g., 30-year, 15-year, balloon mortgages), coupon rate for the pass-through, and the year the pass-through was originated (i.e., vintage).

The minimum amount outstanding for an issue to be included is generally $250 million. For ABS and CMBS the minimum deal size is $500 million ($25 million for tranche size); for CMBS there must be at least $300 million outstanding remaining.

The eligibility requirement based on maturity is that there must be at least one year to maturity (regardless if the issue is callable before the year). Only fixed-rate securities are included.

Understanding the eligibility requirements for inclusion in a bond index is important. Active bond portfolio strategies often attempt to outperform an index by buying noneligible or nonindex securities. For example, CMOs are not included in the

[6] Prior to November 2008, Lehman Brothers and Barclays Capital produced a variety of bond indices. In November 2008, Barclays Capital acquired the Lehman Brothers bond indices and rebranded them as Barclays Capital indices.

Barclays Capital U.S. Aggregate Bond Index for the reason described earlier. Thus, there are opportunities for buying CMO tranches if they are expected to outperform on a relative value basis.

Although we have focused on the Barclays Capital broad-based U.S. bond index, there are other indices created by that firm. For example, this includes

- Barclays Capital U.S. Intermediate Aggregate Bond Index
- Barclays Capital U.S. Treasury Bond Index
- Barclays Capital U.S. Government-Related Bond Index
- Barclays Capital U.S. Agencies Bond Index
- Barclays Capital U.S. Corporate Bond Index
- Barclays Capital U.S. Securitized Bond Index
- Barclays Capital U.S. MBS Index
- Barclays Capital U.S. ABS Index
- Barclays Capital U.S. CMBS (ERISA Only) Index

Even finer sub-indices are available. Examples are

- Barclays Capital U.S. 1–3 Year Treasury Bond Index
- Barclays Capital U.S. 3–7 Year Treasury Bond Index
- Barclays Capital U.S. 7–10 Year Treasury Bond Index
- Barclays Capital U.S. 10–20 Year Treasury Bond Index
- Barclays Capital U.S. 20+ Year Treasury Bond Index
- Barclays Capital U.S. Industrial Bond Index
- Barclays Capital U.S. Utility Bond Index
- Barclays Capital U.S. Financial Institutions Bond Index

For managers whose mandate is both Treasury and credit products (with no structured products) there are indices such as the

- Barclays Capital U.S. Government/Credit Bond Index
- Barclays Capital U.S. Intermediate Government/Credit Bond Index
- Barclays Capital U.S. Long Government/Credit Bond Index
- Barclays Capital Short-term Government/Corp Bond Index

The Barclays Capital U.S. Aggregate Bond Index is rolled up to create global bond indices.

Of course, Barclays Capital is not the only creator of broad-based and specialized bond indices. Managers in consultation with their client or their client's consultants can choose from several families of indices that are deemed appropriate for measuring the market exposure that is being sought.

THE PRIMARY RISK FACTORS

What are primary risk factors in bond indices? That is, what risk factors drive the returns on bond indexes? It is those risk factors that a portfolio manager can match or mismatch when constructing a portfolio. The mismatching is not done indiscriminately. A portfolio manager will only intentionally mismatch if the manager has information (based on research) that strongly suggests there is a benefit (in the form of outperforming a benchmark) that is expected to result from mismatching. We will also see that because of the difficulty of constructing a bond portfolio to match a bond index, a manager may be forced to mismatch.

The primary risk factors can be divided into two general types: systematic risk factors and nonsystematic risk factors. **Systematic risk factors** are forces that affect all securities in a certain category in the benchmark. **Nonsystematic risk factors** are the risks that are not attributable to the systematic risk factors.

Systematic risk factors, in turn, are divided into two categories: term structure risk factors and non-term structure risk factors. **Term structure risk factors** are risks associated with changes in the shape of the term structure (level and shape changes). **Non-term structure risk factors** include

- sector risk
- credit risk
- optionality risk

There is a further breakdown of non-term structure risk that we will describe in the next chapter, but here we describe only the three above.

Sector risk is the risk associated with exposure to the sectors of the benchmark. For example, consider the Barclays Capital U.S. Aggregate Bond Index. At the macro level, these sectors include Treasury, agencies, corporates, residential agency mortgage-backed securities, commercial mortgage-backed securities, and asset-backed securities. Each of these sectors is divided further. For example, the corporate sector (called the credit sector) is divided into financial institutions, industrials, transportations, and utilities. In turn, each of these subsectors is further divided. The financial institutions subsector, for example, is broken down into the following: banking, brokerage, financial companies, insurance, and other. For the residential mortgage market (which includes agency pass-through securities), the breakdown is as follows: Ginnie Mae 30-year MBS, 15-year MBS, conventional MBS (Fannie Mae and Freddie Mac MBS), and balloon MBS. There is an even further breakdown by the coupon range of the MBS.

Credit risk, also referred to as **quality risk**, is the risk associated with exposure to the credit rating of the securities in the benchmark. The breakdown for the Barclays Capital U.S. Aggregate Bond Index, which includes only investment-grade credits, is Aaa+, Aaa, Aa, A, Baa, and MBS. MBS includes credit exposure to the agency pass-through sector.

Optionality risk is the risk associated with an adverse impact on the embedded options of the securities in the benchmark. This includes embedded options in callable and putable corporate bonds, MBS, and ABS.

Non-systematic factor risks are classified as the non-systematic risks associated with a particular issuer, **issuer-specific risk**, and those associated with a particular issue, **issue-specific risk**.

TOP-DOWN VERSUS BOTTOM-UP PORTFOLIO CONSTRUCTION AND MANAGEMENT

There are two general approaches to construction and management of a bond portfolio: top-down and bottom-up. Typically, portfolio managers do not use a pure top-down or bottom-up approach but instead blend the elements of both in conjunction with certain considerations and constraints in constructing a portfolio.

In the **top-down approach**, a bond portfolio manager looks at the major macro drivers of bond returns (hence this approach is also referred to as a **macro approach**) and obtains a view (forecast) about these drivers in the form of a macroeconomic forecast.[7] Among the major variables considered in obtaining a macroeconomic forecast are

- monetary policy
- fiscal policy
- tax policy
- political developments
- regulatory matters
- exchange-rate movements
- trade policy
- demographic trends
- credit market conditions

For a portfolio manager who is managing a global bond portfolio, a macro forecast is required for all country markets.

Based on this assessment and forecast, the manager decides on how much of the portfolio's funds to allocate among the different sectors of the bond market and how much to cash equivalents (i.e., money market instruments). Given the amount of the portfolio's funds to be allocated to each sector of the bond market, the manager must then decide how much to allocate to each industry within a sector. In the case of bond portfolio manager who is entitled to invest in both U.S. and non-U.S. bonds, the first decision is the allocation among countries, then sectors within a country, and then industries.

A manager who follows a top-down approach often relies on an analysis of the bond market to identify those countries (if permitted), sectors, and industries that will benefit the most on a relative basis from the anticipated economic forecast. Once the amount to be allocated to each country, sector, and industry is decided, the manager then looks for the individual bonds to include in the portfolio. The top-down approach looks at changes in several macroeconomic factors to assess the expected excess return (anticipated performance over risk-free return) on securities and portfolios. The portfolio allocation amongst countries, sectors, and industries is altered as macroeconomic conditions change.

The **bottom-up approach** to active bond portfolio management focuses on the micro analysis of individual bond issues, sectors, and industries. The primary research tools used in this form of investing is credit analysis (the subject of Chapter 20), industry analysis, and relative value analysis (discussed later in this chapter). To control the portfolio's risk, risk modeling is used. The use of factor risk models is the subject of the next chapter.

ACTIVE PORTFOLIO STRATEGIES

Armed with an understanding of the primary risk factors for a benchmark we now discuss various active portfolio strategies that are typically employed by managers.

---

[7] For a more detailed description of how macroeconomic forecasts are formulated by bond portfolio managers, see Chris P. Dialynas and Ellen J. Rachlin, "The Art of Fixed Income Investing," Chapter 20 in Frank J. Fabozzi and Harry M. Markowitz (eds.), *The Theory and Practice of Investment Management: 2nd Edition* (Hoboken, NJ: John Wiley & Sons, 2011).

Manager Expectations versus the Market Consensus

A money manager who pursues an active strategy will position a portfolio to capitalize on expectations about future interest rates, but the potential outcome (as measured by total return) must be assessed before an active strategy is implemented. The primary reason for this is that the market (collectively) has certain expectations for future interest rates and these expectations are embodied into the market price of bonds. One lesson we learned in Chapter 5 when we discussed forward rates is that the outcome of a strategy will depend on how a manager's expectation differs from that of the market. Moreover, it does not make a difference if the market's expectation is correct. What is relevant is that the price of a bond embodies those expectations. The same is true for the strategies we discuss in this chapter.

Consequently, though some managers might refer to an "optimal strategy" that should be pursued given certain expectations, that is insufficient information in making an investment decision. If the market's expectations are the same as the manager's, bond prices reflect these expectations. For this reason, we emphasize the use of the total return framework for evaluating active strategies rather than the blind pursuit of a strategy based merely on general statements such as "if you expect . . . , you should pursue . . . strategy."

Interest-Rate Expectations Strategies

A money manager who believes that he or she can accurately forecast the future level of interest rates will alter the portfolio's sensitivity to interest-rate changes. As duration is a measure of interest-rate sensitivity, this involves increasing a portfolio's duration if interest rates are expected to fall and reducing duration if interest rates are expected to rise. For those managers whose benchmark is a bond index, this means increasing the portfolio duration relative to the benchmark index if interest rates are expected to fall and reducing it if interest rates are expected to rise. The degree to which the duration of the managed portfolio is permitted to diverge from that of the benchmark index may be limited by the client.

A portfolio's duration may be altered by swapping (or exchanging) bonds in the portfolio for new bonds that will achieve the target portfolio duration. Such swaps are commonly referred to as **rate anticipation swaps**. Alternatively, a more efficient means for altering the duration of a bond portfolio is to use interest-rate futures contracts. As we explain in Chapter 26, buying futures increases a portfolio's duration, whereas selling futures decreases it.

The key to this active strategy is, of course, an ability to forecast the direction of future interest rates. The academic literature, however, does not support the view that interest rates can be forecasted so that risk-adjusted excess returns can be realized consistently. It is doubtful whether betting on future interest rates will provide a consistently superior return.

Although a manager may not pursue an active strategy based strictly on future interest-rate movements, there can be a tendency to make an interest-rate bet to cover inferior performance relative to a benchmark index. For example, suppose that a manager holds himself or herself out to a client as pursuing one of the active strategies discussed later in this chapter. Suppose further that the manager is evaluated over a one-year investment horizon and that three months before the end of the investment horizon the manager is performing below the client-specified benchmark index. If the manager believes the account will be lost because of underperformance, there is an incentive to bet on interest-rate movements. If the manager is correct, the account will be saved, although an incorrect bet will result in underperforming the benchmark index by a greater amount. A client can prevent this type of gaming by a manager by imposing constraints on the degree that the portfolio's duration can vary from that of the benchmark index. Also, in the performance-evaluation stage of the investment management process described in Chapter 25, decomposing the portfolio's return into the factors that generated the return will highlight the extent to which a portfolio's return is attributable to changes in the level of interest rates.

There are other active strategies that rely on forecasts of future interest-rate levels. Future interest rates, for instance, affect the value of options embedded in callable bonds and the value of prepayment options embedded in mortgage-backed securities. Callable corporate and municipal bonds with coupon rates above the expected future interest rate will underperform relative to noncallable bonds or low-coupon bonds. This is because of the negative convexity feature of callable bonds. For the wide range of mortgage-backed securities described in Chapters 11 through 13, the effect of interest rates on prepayments cause some bondholders to benefit from higher future interest rates and others to benefit from lower future interest rates.

Yield Curve Strategies

As we explained in Chapter 5, the yield curve for U.S. Treasury securities shows the relationship between their maturities and yields. The shape of this yield curve changes over time. **Yield curve strategies** involve positioning a portfolio to capitalize on expected changes in the shape of the Treasury yield curve. In this section, we describe various ways in which the Treasury yield curve has shifted, the different types of yield curve strategies, the usefulness of duration as a measure of the price sensitivity of a bond or portfolio when the yield curve shifts, and how to assess the potential outcome of yield curve strategies.

Types of Shifts in the Yield Curve and Impact on Historical Returns

A shift in the yield curve refers to the relative change in the yield for each Treasury maturity. A **parallel shift in the yield curve** is a shift in which the change in the yield on all maturities is the same. A **nonparallel shift in the yield curve** indicates that the yields for different maturities do not change by the same number of basis points.

Historically, two types of nonparallel yield curve shifts have been observed: a twist in the slope of the yield curve and a change in the humpedness of the yield curve. All of these shifts are portrayed graphically in Exhibit 22-2. A twist in the slope of the yield curve refers to a flattening or steepening of the yield curve. In practice, the slope of the yield curve is measured by the spread between some long-term Treasury yield and some short-term Treasury yield. For example, some practitioners refer to the slope as the difference between the 30-year Treasury yield and the one-year Treasury yield. Others refer to it as the spread between the 20-year Treasury yield and the two-year Treasury yield. Regardless of how it is defined, a **flattening of the yield curve** indicates that the yield spread between the yield on a long-term and a short-term Treasury has decreased; a **steepening of the yield curve** indicates that the yield spread between a long-term and a short-term Treasury has increased. The other type of nonparallel shift, a change in the humpedness of the yield curve, is referred to as a **butterfly shift**.

Frank Jones analyzed the types of yield curve shifts that occurred between 1979 and 1990.[8] He found that the three types of yield curve shifts are not independent, with the two most common types of yield curve shifts being (1) a downward shift in the yield curve combined

---

[8] Frank J. Jones, "Yield Curve Strategies," *Journal of Fixed Income*, September 1991, pp. 43–48.

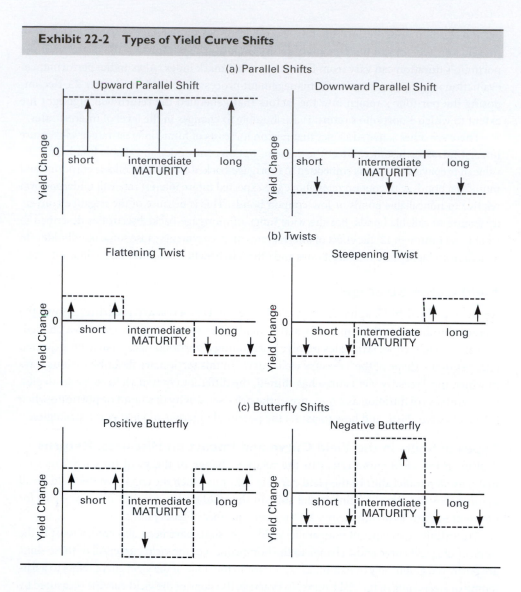

Exhibit 22-2   Types of Yield Curve Shifts

with a steepening of the yield curve, and (2) an upward shift in the yield curve combined with a flattening of the yield curve. These two types of shifts in the yield curve are depicted in Exhibit 22-3. For example, his statistical analysis indicated that an upward parallel shift in the Treasury yield curve and a flattening of the yield curve have a correlation of 0.41. This suggests that an upward shift of the yield curve by 10 basis points is consistent with a 2.5-basis-point flattening of the yield curve. Moreover, he finds that an upward shift and flattening of the yield curve is correlated with a positive butterfly (less humpedness), whereas a downward shift and steepening of the yield curve is correlated with a negative butterfly (more humpedness).

Jones also provides empirical evidence of the importance of changes in the yield curve in determining returns of Treasury securities for various maturity sectors from 1979 to 1990. He finds that parallel shifts and twists in the yield curve are responsible for 91.6% of Treasury returns, 3.4% of the return is attributable to butterfly shifts and the balance,

Exhibit 22-3   Combinations of Yield Curve Shifts

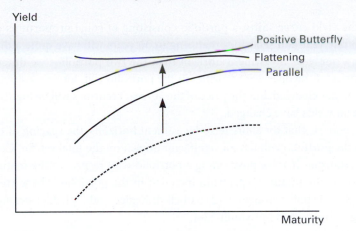

Upward Shift/Flattening/Positive Butterfly

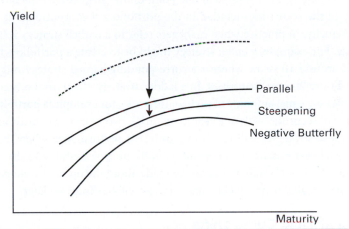

Downward Shift/Steepening/Negative Butterfly

5%, to unexplained factor shifts.[9] This discussion indicates that yield curve strategies require a forecast of the direction of the shift and a forecast of the type of twist.

Yield Curve Strategies

In portfolio strategies that seek to capitalize on expectations based on short-term movements in yields, the dominant source of return is the impact on the price of the securities in the portfolio. This means that the maturity of the securities in the portfolio will have an important impact on the portfolio's return. For example, a total return over a one-year investment horizon for a portfolio consisting of securities all maturing in one year will not be sensitive to changes in how the yield curve shifts one year from now. In contrast, the total return over a one-year investment horizon for a portfolio consisting of securities all

---

[9] These findings are consistent with those reported in Robert Litterman and Jose Scheinkman, "Common Factors Affecting Bond Returns," *Journal of Fixed Income*, June 1991, pp. 54–61.

maturing in 30 years will be sensitive to how the yield curve shifts because one year from now the value of the portfolio will depend on the yield offered on 29-year securities. As we know from Chapter 3, long maturity bonds have substantial price volatility when yields change.

When the yield curve shifts, a portfolio consisting of equal proportions of securities maturing in one year and securities maturing in 30 years will have quite a different total return over a one-year investment horizon than the two portfolios we described previously. The price of the one-year securities in the portfolio will not be sensitive to how the one-year yield has changed, but the price of the 30-year securities will be highly sensitive to how long-term yields have changed.

The key point is that for short-term investment horizons, the spacing of the maturity of bonds in the portfolio will have a significant impact on the total return. Consequently, yield curve strategies involve positioning a portfolio with respect to the maturities of the securities across the maturity spectrum included in the portfolio. There are three yield curve strategies: (1) bullet strategies, (2) barbell strategies, and (3) ladder strategies. Each of these strategies is depicted in Exhibit 22-4.

In a **bullet strategy**, the portfolio is constructed so that the maturity of the securities in the portfolio are highly concentrated at one point on the yield curve. In a **barbell strategy**, the maturity of the securities included in the portfolio are concentrated at two extreme maturities. Actually, in practice when managers refer to a barbell strategy it is relative to a bullet strategy. For example, a bullet strategy might be to create a portfolio with maturities concentrated around 10 years, whereas a corresponding barbell strategy might be a portfolio with five- and 20-year maturities. In a **ladder strategy**, the portfolio is constructed to have approximately equal amounts of each maturity. So, for example, a portfolio might have equal amounts of securities with one year to maturity, two years to maturity, and so on.

Each of these strategies will result in a different performance when the yield curve shifts. The actual performance will depend on both the type of shift and the magnitude of the shift. Thus, no general statements can be made about the optimal yield curve strategy. The framework for analyzing a yield curve strategy will be discussed later.

Duration and Yield Curve Shifts

Before discussing how to analyze yield curve strategies, let's reconsider the concept of duration and its role in approximating the price volatility of a bond portfolio when the yield curve shifts. In Chapter 4, we explained how duration is a measure of the sensitivity of the price of a bond or the value of a bond portfolio to changes in market yields. Thus, a portfolio with a duration of 4 means that if market yields change by 100 basis points, the portfolio will change by approximately 4%.

In explaining the limitations of duration, we indicated that there is an assumption made about how market yields change. Specifically, if a portfolio of bonds consists of 5-, 10-, and 20-year bonds, and the portfolio's duration is 4, what market yield is assumed to change when we say that this portfolio will change in value by 4% if yields change by 100 basis points? Is it the 5-year yield, the 10-year yield, or the 20-year yield? In fact, the assumption made when using duration as a measure of how the value of a portfolio will change if market yields change is that the yield on *all* maturities will change by the same number of basis points. Thus, if our three-bond portfolio has a duration of 4, the statement that the portfolio's value will change by 4% for a 100-basis-point change in yields actually should be stated as follows: The portfolio's

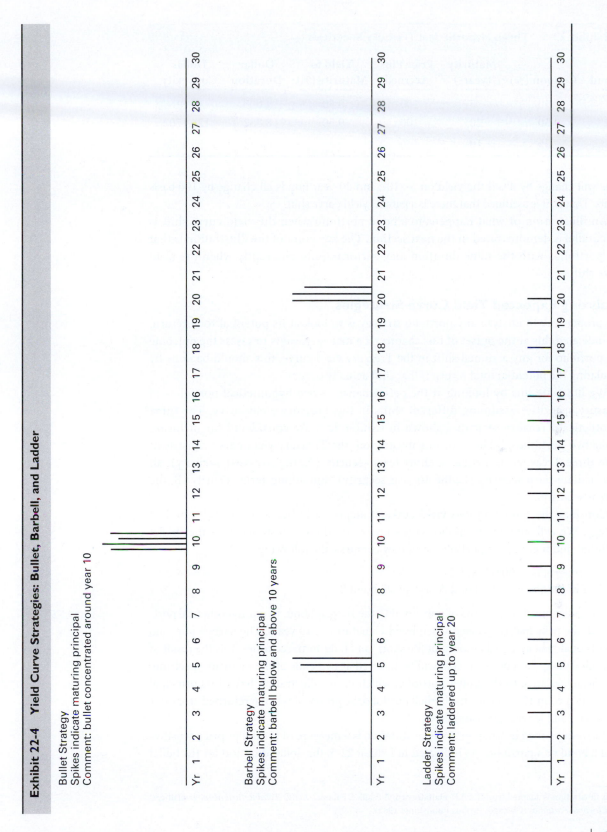

Exhibit 22-4   Yield Curve Strategies: Bullet, Barbell, and Ladder

Bullet Strategy
Spikes indicate maturing principal
Comment: bullet concentrated around year 10

Barbell Strategy
Spikes indicate maturing principal
Comment: barbell below and above 10 years

Ladder Strategy
Spikes indicate maturing principal
Comment: laddered up to year 20

Exhibit 22-5	Three Hypothetical Treasury Securities					
Bond	Coupon (%)	Maturity (years)	Price Plus Accrued	Yield to Maturity (%)	Dollar Duration	Dollar Convexity
A	8.50	5	100	8.50	4.005	19.8164
B	9.50	20	100	9.50	8.882	124.1702
C	9.25	10	100	9.25	6.434	55.4506

value will change by 4% if the yield on 5-, 10-, and 20-year bonds all change by 100 basis points. That is, it is assumed that there is a parallel yield curve shift.

An illustration of what happens to a bond portfolio when the yield curve shift is not parallel is demonstrated in the next section. The key point of the illustration is that two portfolios with the same duration may perform quite differently when the yield curve shifts.

Analyzing Expected Yield Curve Strategies

The proper way to analyze any portfolio strategy is to look at its potential total return. We indicated this at the outset of this chapter. If a manager wants to assess the outcome of a portfolio for any assumed shift in the Treasury yield curve, this should be done by calculating the potential total return if that shift actually occurs.

We illustrate this by looking at the performance of two hypothetical portfolios of Treasury securities assuming different shifts in the Treasury yield curve. The three hypothetical Treasury securities shown in Exhibit 22-5 are considered for inclusion in our two portfolios.[10] Thus, for our illustration, the Treasury yield curve consists of these three Treasury securities: a short-term security (A, the five-year security), an intermediate-term security (C, the 10-year security), and a long-term security (B, the 20-year security).

Consider the following two yield curve strategies: a bullet strategy and a barbell strategy. We will label the portfolios created based on these two strategies as the "bullet portfolio" and the "barbell portfolio" and they comprise the following:

- *Bullet portfolio:* 100% bond C
- *Barbell portfolio:* 50.2% bond A and 49.8% bond B

The bullet portfolio consists of only bond C, the 10-year bond. In our hypothetical portfolio, all the principal is received when bond C matures in 10 years. The barbell portfolio consists of almost an equal amount of the short- and long-term securities. It is the result of a barbell strategy because principal will be received at two ends of the maturity spectrum. Specifically, relative to the bullet portfolio, which in our illustration has all its principal being returned in 10 years, for the barbell portfolio the principal is being returned at shorter (five years) and longer (20 years) dates.

As we explained in Chapter 4, dollar duration is a measure of the dollar price sensitivity of a bond or a portfolio. As indicated in Exhibit 22-5, the dollar duration for the bullet

---

[10] This illustration is adapted from Ravi E. Dattatreya and Frank J. Fabozzi, *Active Total Return Management of Fixed Income Portfolios* (Chicago: Probus Publishing, 1989).

portfolio per 100-basis-point change in yield is 6.434. For the barbell portfolio, the dollar duration is just the weighted average of the dollar duration of the two bonds. Therefore,

$$\text{dollar duration of barbell portfolio} = 0.502(4.005) + 0.498(8.882) = 6.434$$

The dollar duration of the barbell portfolio is the same as that of the bullet portfolio. (In fact, the barbell portfolio was designed to produce this result.)

As we explained in Chapter 4, duration is just a first approximation of the change in price resulting from a change in interest rates. Convexity provides a second approximation. Although we did not discuss **dollar convexity**, it has a meaning similar to *convexity*, in that it provides a second approximation to the dollar price change. For two portfolios with the same dollar duration, the greater the convexity, the better the performance of a bond or a portfolio when yields change. What is necessary to understand for this illustration is that the larger the dollar convexity, the greater the dollar price change due to a portfolio's convexity. As shown in Exhibit 22-5, the dollar convexity of the bullet portfolio is 55.4506. The dollar convexity for the barbell portfolio is a weighted average of the dollar convexity of the two bonds. That is,

$$\text{dollar convexity of barbell portfolio} = 0.502(19.8164) + 0.498(124.1702) = 71.7846$$

Therefore, the dollar convexity of the barbell portfolio is greater than that of the bullet portfolio.

Similarly, the yield for the two portfolios is not the same. The yield for the bullet portfolio is simply the yield to maturity of bond C, 9.25%. The traditional yield calculation for the barbell portfolio, which is found by taking a weighted average of the yield to maturity of the two bonds included in the portfolio, is 8.998%:

$$\text{portfolio yield for barbell portfolio} = 0.502(8.50\%) + 0.498(9.50\%) = 8.998\%$$

This approach suggests that the yield of the bullet portfolio is 25.2 basis points greater than that of the barbell portfolio (9.25% − 8.998%). Although both portfolios have the same dollar duration, the yield of the bullet portfolio is greater than the yield of the barbell portfolio. However, the dollar convexity of the barbell portfolio is greater than that of the bullet portfolio. The difference in the two yields is sometimes referred to as the **cost of convexity** (i.e., giving up yield to get better convexity).

Now suppose that a portfolio manager with a six-month investment horizon has a choice of investing in the bullet portfolio or the barbell portfolio. Which one should he choose? The manager knows that (1) the two portfolios have the same dollar duration, (2) the yield for the bullet portfolio is greater than that of the barbell portfolio, and (3) the dollar convexity of the barbell portfolio is greater than that of the bullet portfolio. Actually, this information is not adequate in making the decision. What is necessary is to assess the potential total return when the yield curve shifts.

Exhibit 22-6 provides an analysis of the six-month total return of the two portfolios when the yield curve shifts.[11] The numbers reported in the exhibit are the difference in the total return for the two portfolios. Specifically, the following is shown:

$$\text{difference in dollar return} = \text{bullet portfolio's total return} - \text{barbell portfolio's total return}$$

[11] Note that no assumption is needed for the reinvestment rate because the three bonds shown in Exhibit 22-5 are assumed to be trading right after a coupon payment has been made, and, therefore, there is no accrued interest.

Exhibit 22-6   **Relative Performance of Bullet Portfolio and Barbell Portfolio over a Six-Month Investment Horizon***

Yield Change	Parallel Shift	Nonparallel Shift[a]	Nonparallel Shift[b] (%)
−5.000	−7.19	−10.69	−3.89
−4.750	−6.28	−9.61	−3.12
−4.500	−5.44	−8.62	−2.44
−4.250	−4.68	−7.71	−1.82
−4.000	−4.00	−6.88	−1.27
−3.750	−3.38	−6.13	−0.78
−3.500	−2.82	−5.44	−0.35
−3.250	−2.32	−4.82	0.03
−3.000	−1.88	−4.26	0.36
−2.750	−1.49	−3.75	0.65
−2.500	−1.15	−3.30	0.89
−2.250	−0.85	−2.90	1.09
−2.000	−0.59	−2.55	1.25
−1.750	−0.38	−2.24	1.37
−1.500	−0.20	−1.97	1.47
−1.250	−0.05	−1.74	1.53
−1.000	0.06	−1.54	1.57
−0.750	0.15	−1.38	1.58
−0.500	0.21	−1.24	1.57
−0.250	0.24	−1.14	1.53
0.000	0.25	−1.06	1.48
0.250	0.24	−1.01	1.41
0.500	0.21	−0.98	1.32
0.750	0.16	−0.97	1.21
1.000	0.09	−0.98	1.09
1.250	0.01	−1.00	0.96
1.500	−0.08	−1.05	0.81
1.750	−0.19	−1.10	0.66
2.000	−0.31	−1.18	0.49
2.250	−0.44	−1.26	0.32
2.500	−0.58	−1.36	0.14
2.750	−0.73	−1.46	−0.05
3.000	−0.88	−1.58	−0.24
3.250	−1.05	−1.70	−0.44
3.500	−1.21	−1.84	−0.64
3.750	−1.39	−1.98	−0.85
4.000	−1.57	−2.12	−1.06
4.250	−1.75	−2.27	−1.27

(Continued)

Exhibit 22-6   Relative Performance of Bullet Portfolio and Barbell Portfolio over a Six-Month Investment Horizon* (Continued)

Yield Change	Parallel Shift	Nonparallel Shift[a]	Nonparallel Shift[b] (%)
4.500	−1.93	−2.43	−1.48
4.750	−2.12	−2.58	−1.70
5.000	−2.31	−2.75	−1.92

[a] Change in yield for bond C. Nonparallel shift as follows (flattening of yield curve):

> yield change bond A = yield change bond C + 25 basis points
> yield change bond B = yield change bond C − 25 basis points

[b] Change in yield for bond C. Nonparallel shift as follows (steepening of yield curve):

> yield change bond A = yield change bond C − 25 basis points
> yield change bond B = yield change bond C + 25 basis points

*Performance is based on the difference in total return over a six-month investment horizon. Specifically,

> *bullet portfolio's total return − barbell portfolio's total return*

Therefore, a negative value means that the barbell portfolio outperformed the bullet portfolio.

Thus, a positive value means that the bullet portfolio outperformed the barbell portfolio, and a negative sign means that the barbell portfolio outperformed the bullet portfolio.

Let's focus on the second column of Exhibit 22-6, which is labeled "Parallel Shift." This is the relative total return of the two portfolios over the six-month investment horizon assuming that the yield curve shifts in a parallel fashion. In this case parallel movement of the yield curve means that the yields for the short-term bond (A), the intermediate-term bond (C), and the long-term bond (B) change by the same number of basis points, shown in the "yield change" column of the table.

Which portfolio is the better investment alternative if the yield curve shifts in a parallel fashion and the investment horizon is six months? The answer depends on the amount by which yields change. Notice that when yields change by less than 100 basis points, the bullet portfolio outperforms the barbell portfolio. The reverse is true if yields change by more than 100 basis points.

This illustration makes two key points. First, even if the yield curve shifts in a parallel fashion, two portfolios with the same dollar duration will not give the same performance. The reason is that the two portfolios do not have the same dollar convexity. The second point is that although with all other things equal it is better to have more convexity than less, the market charges for convexity in the form of a higher price or a lower yield. But the benefit of the greater convexity depends on how much yields change. As can be seen from the second column of Exhibit 22-6, if market yields change by less than 100 basis points (up or down), the bullet portfolio, which has less convexity, will provide a better total return.

Now let's look at what happens if the yield curve does not shift in a parallel fashion. The last two columns of Exhibit 22-6 show the relative performance of the two portfolios for a nonparallel shift of the yield curve. Specifically, the first nonparallel shift column assumes that if the yield on bond C (the intermediate-term bond) changes by the amount shown in the first column, bond A (the short-term bond) will change by the same amount plus 25 basis points, whereas bond B (the long-term bond) will change by the same amount shown in the first column less 25 basis points. Measuring the steepness of the yield curve as the spread between the long-term yield (yield on bond B) and the short-term yield (yield on Bond A), the spread has decreased by 50 basis points. As we noted earlier, such a non-parallel shift means a flattening of the yield curve. As can be seen in Exhibit 22-6, for this assumed yield curve shift, the barbell outperforms the bullet.

In the last column, the nonparallel shift assumes that for a change in bond C's yield, the yield on bond A will change by the same amount less 25 basis points, whereas that on bond B will change by the same amount plus 25 points: Thus, the spread between the long-term yield and the short-term yield has increased by 50 basis points, and the yield curve has steepened. In this case, the bullet portfolio outperforms the barbell portfolio as long as the yield on bond C does not rise by more than 250 basis points or fall by more than 325 basis points.

The key point here is that looking at measures such as yield (yield to maturity or some type of portfolio yield measure), duration, or convexity tells us little about performance over some investment horizon, because performance depends on the magnitude of the change in yields and how the yield curve shifts. Therefore, when a manager wants to position a portfolio based on expectations as to how he might expect the yield curve to shift, it is imperative to perform total return analysis. For example, in a steepening yield curve environment, it is often stated that a bullet portfolio would be better than a barbell portfolio. As can be seen from Exhibit 22-6, it is not the case that a bullet portfolio would outperform a barbell portfolio. Whether the bullet portfolio outperforms the barbell depends on how much the yield curve steepens. An analysis similar to that in Exhibit 22-6 based on total return for different degrees of steepening of the yield curve clearly demonstrates to a manager whether a particular yield curve strategy will be superior to another. The same analysis can be performed to assess the potential outcome of a ladder strategy.

Approximating the Exposure of a Portfolio's Yield Curve Risk

In Chapter 4, we explained the meaning and usefulness of key rate duration. A portfolio and a benchmark have key rate durations. The extent to which the profile of the key rate durations of a portfolio differs from that of its benchmark helps identify the difference in yield curve risk exposure. For example, suppose that the key rate durations for a portfolio and a benchmark are as shown below:

Year	Portfolio Key Rate Duration	Benchmark Key Rate Duration	Difference
0.50	0.173	0.149	0.024
2.00	0.361	0.600	−0.239
5.00	1.725	1.229	0.497
10.00	1.466	1.377	0.089
20.00	0.366	0.730	−0.364
30.00	0.033	0.407	−0.374
Duration	4.124	4.491	−0.367

As can be seen, the portfolio's duration is less than that of the benchmark. The portfolio has less exposure to changes in the long maturity sector (as indicated by its lower 10-year and 30-year key rate durations) and more exposure to the 5-year to 10-year maturity sector.

In addition to summary measures such as key rate duration, practitioners look at the difference in the present value of the distribution of the cash flows of the portfolio and the benchmark to get a feel for yield curve exposure.

Complex Strategies

Thus far, we have described the basics of yield curve strategies. A study by Fabozzi, Martinelli, and Priaulet finds evidence of the predictability in the time-varying shape of the U.S. term structure of interest rates using a more advanced econometric model.[12] Variables such as default spread, equity volatility, and short-term and forward rates are used to predict changes in the slope of the yield curve and (to a lesser extent) changes in its curvature. Systematic trading strategies based on butterfly swaps reveal that the evidence of predictability in the shape of the yield curve is both statistically and economically significant.

Yield Spread Strategies

As discussed in Chapter 5, the bond market is classified into sectors in several ways: by type of issuer (Treasury, agencies, corporates, and mortgage-backed), quality or credit (risk-free Treasuries, AAA, AA, and so on), coupon (high-coupon/premium bonds, current-coupon/par bonds, and low-coupon/discount bonds), and maturity (short, intermediate, or long term). Yield spreads between maturity sectors involve changes in the yield curve as discussed in the preceding section.

Yield spread strategies involve positioning a portfolio to capitalize on expected changes in yield spreads between sectors of the bond market. Swapping (or exchanging) one bond for another when the manager believes that the prevailing yield spread between the two bonds in the market is out of line with their historical yield spread, and that the yield spread will realign by the end of the investment horizon, are called **intermarket spread swaps**.

Credit Spreads

Credit or quality spreads change because of expected changes in economic prospects. Credit spreads between Treasury and non-Treasury issues widen in a declining or contracting economy and narrow during economic expansion. The economic rationale is that in a declining or contracting economy, corporations experience a decline in revenue and reduced cash flow, making it difficult for corporate issuers to service their contractual debt obligations. To induce investors to hold non-Treasury securities of lower-quality issuers, the yield spread relative to Treasury securities must widen. The converse is that during economic expansion and brisk economic activity, revenue and cash flow pick up, increasing the likelihood that corporate issuers will have the capacity to service their contractual debt obligations. Yield spreads between Treasury and federal agency securities will vary depending on investor expectations about the prospects that an implicit government guarantee will be honored.

Spreads between Callable and Noncallable Securities

Spreads that are attributable to differences in callable and noncallable bonds and differences in coupons of callable bonds will change as a result of expected changes in (1) the direction of the change in interest rates, and (2) interest-rate volatility. An expected

[12] Frank J. Fabozzi, Lionel Martellini, and Philippe Priaulet, "Exploiting Predictability in the Time-Varying Shape of the Term Structure of Interest Rates," *Journal of Fixed Income*, June 2005, pp. 40–53. Specifically, they use a robust recursive modeling approach based on a Bayesian mixture of multifactor models.

drop in the level of interest rates will widen the yield spread between callable bonds and noncallable bonds as the prospects that the issuer will exercise the call option increase. The reverse is true: The yield spread narrows if interest rates are expected to rise. As we explained in Chapter 17, an increase in interest-rate volatility increases the value of the embedded call option and thereby increases the yield spread between callable bonds and noncallable bonds. Expectations about the direction of the change in interest rates and interest-rate volatility will affect the yield spread between Treasury and mortgage pass-through securities and the yield spread between low-coupon and high-coupon pass-throughs in the same way as it affects the yield spreads for corporates.

Importance of Dollar Duration Weighting of Yield Spread Strategies

What is critical in assessing yield spread strategies is to compare positions that have the same dollar duration. To understand why, consider two bonds, X and Y. Suppose that the price of bond X is 80 with a modified duration of 5, and bond Y has a price of 90 with a modified duration of 4. Because modified duration is the approximate percentage change per 100-basis-point change in yield, a 100-basis-point change in yield for bond X would change its price by about 5%. Based on a price of 80, its price will change by about $4 per $80 of market value. Thus, its dollar duration for a 100-basis-point change in yield is $4 per $80 of market value. Similarly, for bond Y, its dollar duration for a 100-basis-point change in yield per $90 of market value can be determined. In this case it is $3.60. So if bonds X and Y are being considered as alternative investments in a strategy other than one based on anticipating interest-rate movements, the amount of each bond in the strategy should be such that they will both have the same dollar duration.

To illustrate this, suppose that a portfolio manager owns $10 million of par value of bond X, which has a market value of $8 million. The dollar duration of bond X per 100-basis-point change in yield for the $8 million market value is $400,000. Suppose further that this portfolio manager is considering exchanging bond X that it owns in its portfolio for bond Y. If the portfolio manager wants to have the same interest-rate exposure (i.e., dollar duration) for bond Y that she currently has for bond X, she will buy a market value amount of bond Y with the same dollar duration. If the portfolio manager purchased $10 million of *par value* of bond Y and, therefore, $9 million of *market value* of bond Y, the dollar price change per 100-basis-point change in yield would be only $360,000. If, instead, the portfolio manager purchased $10 million of *market value* of bond Y, the dollar duration per 100-basis-point change in yield would be $400,000. Because bond Y is trading at 90, $11.11 million of par value of bond Y must be purchased to keep the dollar duration of the position from bond Y the same as for bond X.

Mathematically, this problem can be expressed as follows:
Let

D_X = dollar duration per 100-basis-point change in yield for bond X for the market value of bond X held

MD_Y = modified duration for bond Y

MV_Y = market value of bond Y needed to obtain the same dollar duration as bond X

Then, the following equation sets the dollar duration for bond X equal to the dollar duration for bond Y:

$$\$D_X = \frac{MD_Y}{100} MV_Y$$

Solving for MV_Y yields

$$MV_Y = \frac{\$D_X}{\dfrac{MD_Y}{100}}$$

Dividing by the price per \$1 of par value of bond Y gives the par value of Y that has an approximately equivalent dollar duration as bond X.

In our illustration, $\$D_X$ is \$400,000 and MD_Y is 4; then

$$MV_Y = \frac{\$400,000}{\dfrac{4}{100}} = \$10,000,000$$

The market value of bond Y is 90 per \$100 of par value, so the price per \$1 of par value is 0.9. Dividing \$10 million by 0.9 indicates that the par value of bond Y that should be purchased is \$11.11 million.

Failure to adjust a portfolio repositioning based on some expected change in yield spread so as to hold the dollar duration the same means that the outcome of the portfolio will be affected not only by the expected change in the yield spread but also by a change in the yield level. Thus, a manager would be making a conscious yield spread bet and possibly an undesired bet on the level of interest rates.

Individual Security Selection Strategies

There are several active strategies that money managers pursue to identify mispriced securities. The most common strategy identifies an issue as undervalued because either (1) its yield is higher than that of comparably rated issues, or (2) its yield is expected to decline (and price, therefore, rise) because credit analysis indicates that its rating will improve.

A swap in which a money manager exchanges one bond for another bond that is similar in terms of coupon, maturity, and credit quality, but offers a higher yield, is called a **substitution swap**. This swap depends on a capital market imperfection. Such situations sometimes exist in the bond market owing to temporary market imbalances and the fragmented nature of the non-Treasury bond market. The risk the money manager faces in making a substitution swap is that the bond purchased may not be truly identical to the bond for which it is exchanged. Moreover, typically, bonds will have similar but not identical maturities and coupons. This could lead to differences in the convexity of the two bonds, and any yield spread may reflect the cost of convexity.

An active strategy used in the mortgage-backed securities market is to identify individual issues of pass-throughs, CMO classes, or stripped MBS that are mispriced, given the assumed prepayment speed to price the security. Another active strategy commonly used in the mortgage-backed securities market is to create a package of securities that will have a better return profile for a wide range of interest-rate and yield curve scenarios than similar duration securities available in the market. Because of the fragmented nature of the mortgage-backed securities market and the complexity of the structures, such opportunities are not unusual.

Strategies for Asset Allocation within Bond Sectors

The ability to outperform a benchmark index will depend on how the manager allocates funds within a bond sector relative to the composition of the benchmark index. As explained in the next chapter, the three major sectors of the broad-based bond market indexes are government/agencies, corporates, and mortgage-backed securities. Within the corporate sector, for example, the manager must decide how to allocate funds among the different credit ratings. (Only investment grade ratings are included in the broad-based bond market indexes.) In the case of mortgage-backed securities where only pass-through securities are included with different coupon rates, there is the decision of how to allocate funds among the different coupon issues. This is important because prepayment rates and the performance of pass-throughs will depend on the coupon issues selected by the manager.

We already discussed strategies that will affect the allocation decision among the bond sectors. Expected changes in the level of interest rates will affect the allocation of funds within the corporate and mortgage-backed securities sectors because the more attractive the call feature of a security, the worse it may perform in a declining interest rate environment due to negative convexity. Yield curve strategies would affect the maturity selection within sectors. While our previous focus was on strategies involving anticipated changes in credit spreads or OAS between sectors in the bond market, the same strategies are used in making intersector asset allocation decisions. Next we look at a framework for guiding and assessing the allocation of funds among the credit sectors within the corporate bond sector. This strategy was first suggested by Leland Crabbe.[13]

The framework relies on the historical experience of credit quality changes. This information is captured in a table referred to as a *rating transition matrix* and shows on a percentage basis how ratings on issues change over time. Exhibit 22-7 shows a hypothetical one-year rating transition matrix (table). Here is how to interpret the table. The rows indicate the rating at the beginning of a year. The columns show the rating at the end of the year. For example, look at the second row. This row shows the transition for Aa rated bonds at the beginning of a year. The number 92.00 in the second row means that on average 92.00% of Aa rated bonds at the beginning of the year remained Aa rated at year end. The value of 1.00 means that on average 1.00% of Aa rated bonds at the beginning of the year were upgraded to Aaa. The value of 0.80 means that on average 0.80% of Aa rated bonds at the beginning of the year were downgraded to a Baa rating.

From Exhibit 22-7, it should be clear that the probability of a downgrade is much higher than for an upgrade for investment grade bonds. This is the typical pattern found

Exhibit 22-7   One-Year Rating Transition Probabilities (%)

	Aaa	Aa	A	Baa	Ba	Bb	C or D	Total
Aaa	90.00	9.00	1.00	0.00	0.00	0.00	0.00	100.00
Aa	1.00	92.00	6.00	0.80	0.20	0.00	0.00	100.00
A	0.20	3.00	91.00	5.00	0.70	0.10	0.00	100.00
Baa	0.00	0.30	5.00	88.00	6.00	0.50	0.20	100.00

[13] Leland E. Crabbe, "A Framework for Corporate Bond Strategy," *Journal of Fixed Income*, June 1995, pp. 15–25 and Chapter 13 in Leland E. Crabbe and Frank J. Fabozzi, *Managing a Corporate Bond Portfolio*, Hoboken, NJ: John Wiley & Sons, 2002.

in a real-world rating transition matrix. While the historical rating transition matrix is a useful starting point since it represents an average over some study period, a manager must modify the matrix based on expectations of upgrades and downgrades given current and anticipated economic conditions.

Given the rating transition matrix that the manager expects, an *expected incremental return* can be calculated for each credit quality sector. This involves four steps. First, estimate what the spread over Treasuries will be for all ratings at the end of the investment horizon. Second, estimate the price change for upgraded and downgraded bonds based on the new spreads. Third, compute the return for upgraded and downgraded bonds based on the price change calculated in the first step and the coupon interest. Finally, calculate the expected incremental return for the credit quality sector by weighting the returns by the probabilities as given in the manager's rating transition matrix.

To illustrate this, suppose that the manager's rating transition matrix is the one shown in Exhibit 22-7. Second, suppose that the manager expects that the spreads will not change over the one-year investment horizon. Consider the Aa rated sector. Exhibit 22-8 shows the expected incremental return estimates for a portfolio consisting of only three-year Aa rated bonds. The first column shows the initial spread. The second column is the rating at the end of the investment horizon. The horizon spread is the spread over Treasuries at the end of the investment horizon for each of the credit quality sectors for the three-year maturity sector shown in the second column. For example, if there is no change in the rating, the horizon spread is the same as the initial spread of 30 basis points. An upgrade reduces the spread, a downgrade increases it. The assumption in our illustration is that the horizon spread is the same as currently observed. The fourth column shows the horizon return over Treasuries based on price change and coupon interest. The next to the last column gives the probabilities from the rating transition matrix (i.e., the second row of Exhibit 22-7). The sum of the product of the fourth and fifth columns gives the expected incremental return over Treasuries of 28.75 basis points.

There are two reasons why the expected incremental return over Treasuries of 28.75 basis points is less than the initial spread of 30 basis points. First, the probability of an upgrade is significantly less than for a downgrade. Second, the steepness of the credit spread curve at the end of the investment horizon penalizes downgrades.

Exhibit 22-8   Expected Incremental Return Estimates for Three-Year Aa Rated Bonds over a One-Year Horizon

Initial Spread	Horizon Rating	Horizon Spread	Return over Treasuries (bp) ×	Transition Probability (%) =	Contribution to Incremental Return (bp)
30	Aaa	25	38	1.00	0.38
30	Aa	30	30	92.00	27.60
30	A	35	21	6.00	1.26
30	Baa	60	−24	0.80	−0.192
30	Ba	130	−147	0.20	−0.294

Portfolio Incremental Return over Treasuries = 28.75

From this illustration, it can be seen that the incremental return over Treasuries depends on the initial spread, the change in the spread, and the probability of a rating change. While the illustrations assumed the rating transmission matrix in Exhibit 22-7 and that the spread over Treasuries at the end of the investment horizon would be unchanged from the initial spread, this will not be the case in practice. The manager will modify both assumptions based on prevailing and expected market conditions.

The framework can be extended to any maturity sector. As a result, the analysis would provide a guide for assessing relative value within each maturity sector and can also be used to assess relative value among maturity sectors for a given rating sector, a guide for assessing relative value within each maturity sector can also be used to assess relative value among maturity sectors for a given rating sector.

THE USE OF LEVERAGE

If permitted by investment guidelines, a manager may use leverage in an attempt to enhance portfolio returns. A portfolio manager can create leverage by borrowing funds in order to acquire a position in the market that is greater than if only cash were invested. For example, a manager may have cash to invest in the bond market of $50 million but wants an exposure of $200 million.

The funds available to invest without borrowing are referred to as the "equity." In our example, the equity is $50. A portfolio that does not contain any leverage is called an **unlevered portfolio**. A **levered portfolio** is a portfolio in which a manager has created leverage. The levered portfolio in this example is $200 million.

In this section, we will take a look at leverage. First, we will look at why a manager uses leverage and the measurement of the duration of a portfolio that uses leverage. Then we will look at how a manager can create leverage using the repo market.

Motivation for Leverage

The basic principle in using leverage is that a manager wants to earn a return on the borrowed funds that is greater than the cost of the borrowed funds. The return from borrowing funds is produced from a higher income and/or greater price appreciation relative to a scenario in which no funds are borrowed.

Let's first look at the higher income that may be generated from a levered portfolio relative to an unlevered portfolio. If a manager can invest $50 million earning 5% for a year but can borrow funds at a cost of 4.5% for a year, then the manager can generate for the year 50 basis points in income over its funding cost. By borrowing greater amounts, the manager can magnify the 50 basis points. This is a benefit of leveraging. The risk of leveraging is that the return generated from the borrowed funds will be less than the funding cost. In our example, the risk is that if the return from investing the amount borrowed is less than 4.5%, then there will be negative return on the funds borrowed.

The return from investing the funds comes from two sources. The first is the interest income and the second is the change in the value of the security (or securities) at the end of the borrowing period. For example, suppose our manager invests all the funds borrowed in a security that matures in one year, is selling at par, and has a coupon rate of 5%. At the end of one year (the time period we assumed in our example that the manager borrowed the funds), the return is 5% if the issuer of the security pays off the bond at par. Suppose instead that the bond is a 10-year bond that can be purchased at par and has a coupon rate of 5%. Then the return over the one-year period for which the funds are borrowed will be 5% in interest income adjusted for how the price of the bond changes at the end of one year. At the end of one year, the 10-year bond is a 9-year bond and its price will be greater than or less than par depending on market rates at the end of one year. The risk, of course, is that the change in the value of the security will decline such that the return will be negative.

There are some managers who use leverage in the hopes of benefiting primarily from price changes. Small price changes will be magnified by using leveraging. For example, if a manager expects interest rates to fall, the manager can borrow funds to increase price exposure to the market. Effectively, the manager is increasing the duration of the portfolio, a point that we will return to later.

Thus, the risk associated with borrowing funds is that the security (or securities) in which the borrowed funds are invested may earn less than the cost of the borrowed funds due to failure to generate interest income plus capital appreciation as expected when the funds were borrowed.

Leveraging is a necessity for depository institutions (such as banks and savings and loan associations) because the spread over the cost of borrowed funds is typically small. The magnitude of the borrowing (i.e., the degree of leverage) is what produces an acceptable return for the institution. For traders, individual trades typically produce small spreads over funding costs. It is the leveraging of those trades that will generate a return needed to make them attractive to traders.

Duration of a Leveraged Portfolio

Now let's look at how to calculate the duration of a fund that has borrowed money. This can be done by using an example to understand the general principle.

Suppose that a portfolio has a market value of $100 million and the manager invests the proceeds in a bond with a duration of 3. This means that the manager would expect that for a 100-basis-point change in interest rates, the portfolio's value would change by approximately $3 million. For this unlevered fund, the duration of the portfolio is 3.

Suppose now that the manager of this portfolio can borrow an additional $300 million. This means that the levered fund will have $400 million to invest, consisting of $100 million that the manager has available before borrowing (i.e., the equity) and $300 million borrowed. All of the funds are invested in a bond with a duration of 3. Now let's look at what happens if interest rates change by 100 basis points. The levered portfolio's value will change by $12 million (3% times $400 million). This means that on an investment of $100 million, the portfolio's value changes by $12 million. The proper way to measure the portfolio's duration is relative to the unlevered amount or equity because the manager is concerned with the risk exposure relative to equity. Thus, the duration for the portfolio is 12 because a duration of 12 will change the portfolio's equity value of $100 million by 12% or $12 million for a 100-basis-point change in rates.

In general, the procedure for calculating the duration of a portfolio that uses leverage is as follows:

Step 1: Calculate the duration of the levered portfolio.
Step 2: Determine the dollar duration of the portfolio of the levered portfolio for a change in interest rates.
Step 3: Compute the ratio of the dollar duration of the levered portfolio to the value of the initial unlevered portfolio (i.e., initial equity).
Step 4: The duration of the unlevered portfolio is then found as follows:

$$\text{ratio computed in Step 3} \times \frac{100}{\text{rate change used in Step 2 in bps}} \times 100$$

To illustrate the procedure, suppose that the initial value of the unlevered portfolio is $100 million and the levered portfolio is $400 million ($100 million equity plus $300 million borrowed).

Step 1: Assume that calculation of the duration of the levered portfolio finds that the duration is 3.
Step 2: Let's use a 50-basis point change in interest rates to compute the dollar duration. If the duration of the levered portfolio is 3, then the dollar duration for a 50-basis-point change in interest rates is $6 million (1.5% change for a 50-basis-point move times $400 million).
Step 3: The ratio of the dollar duration for a 50-basis-point change in interest rates to the $100 million initial market value of the unlevered portfolio is 0.06 ($6 million divided by $100 million).
Step 4: The duration of the unlevered portfolio is

$$0.06 \times \frac{100}{50} \times 100 = 12$$

How to Create Leverage via the Repo Market

A manager can create leverage in one of two ways. One way is through the use of derivative instruments. As is explained in Chapters 26, 27, and 28, interest-rate derivatives instruments can produce the same effect as leverage. The second way is to borrow funds via a collateralized loan arrangement. The two most common ways a money manager can borrow via a collateralized loan arrangement are through a reverse repurchase agreement or margin buying. The former is the most common transaction used by institutional money managers, so we discuss it next.

Repurchase Agreement

A **repurchase agreement** is the sale of a security with a commitment by the seller to buy the same security back from the purchaser at a specified price at a designated future date. The price at which the seller must subsequently repurchase the security is called the **repurchase price**, and the date that the security must be repurchased is called the **repurchase date**. Basically, a repurchase agreement is a collateralized loan, where the collateral is the security sold and subsequently repurchased. The agreement is best explained with an illustration.

Suppose a government securities dealer has purchased $10 million of a particular Treasury security. The dealer uses the repurchase agreement or "repo" market to obtain financing. In the repo market, the dealer can use the $10 million of the Treasury security as collateral for a loan. The term of the loan and the interest rate that the dealer agrees to pay are specified. The interest rate is called the **repo rate**. When the term of the loan is one day, it is called an **overnight repo**; a loan for more than one day is called a **term repo**. The transaction is referred to as a repurchase agreement because it calls for the sale of the security and its repurchase at a future date. Both the sale price and the purchase price are specified in the agreement. The difference between the purchase (repurchase) price and the sale price is the dollar interest cost of the loan.

Back to the dealer who needs to finance $10 million of a Treasury security that it purchased and plans to hold overnight. Suppose that a customer of the dealer has excess funds of $10 million. (The customer might be a municipality with tax receipts that it has just collected and no immediate need to disburse the funds.) The dealer would agree to deliver ("sell") $10 million of the Treasury security to the customer for an amount determined by the repo rate and buy ("repurchase") the same Treasury security from the customer for $10 million the next day. Suppose that the overnight repo rate is 6.5%. Then, as is explained subsequently, the dealer would agree to deliver the Treasury securities for $9,998,195 and repurchase the same securities for $10 million the next day. The $1,805 difference between the "sale" price of $9,998,195 and the repurchase price of $10 million is the dollar interest on the financing.

The following formula is used to calculate the dollar interest on a repo transaction:

$$\text{dollar interest} = (\text{dollar amount borrowed}) \times (\text{repo rate}) \times \text{repo term}/360$$

Notice that the interest is computed on a 360-day basis.

In our example, at a repo rate of 6.5% and a repo term of one day (overnight), the dollar interest is $1,805 as shown here:

$$\$9,998,195 \times 0.065 \times 1/360 = \$1,805$$

The advantage to the dealer of using the repo market for borrowing on a short-term basis is that the rate is lower than the cost of bank financing. (The reason for this is explained later.) From the customer's perspective, the repo market offers an attractive yield on a short-term secured transaction that is highly liquid.

Although the example illustrates financing a dealer's long position in the repo market, dealers can also use the market to cover a short position. For example, suppose a government dealer sold $10 million of Treasury securities two weeks ago and must now cover the position—that is, deliver the securities. The dealer can do a **reverse repo** (agree to buy the securities and sell them back). Of course, the dealer eventually would have to buy the Treasury security in the market in order to cover its short position. In this case, the dealer is actually making a collateralized loan to its customer; that is, in a reverse repo a party is lending funds. The customer may be using the funds obtained from the collateralized loan to create leverage.

There is a good deal of Wall Street jargon describing repo transactions. To understand it, remember that one party is lending money and accepting a security as collateral for the loan; the other party is borrowing money and providing collateral to borrow the money. When someone lends securities in order to receive cash (i.e., borrow money), that party is said to be "reversing out" securities. A party that lends money with the security as collateral is said to be "reversing in" securities. The expressions "to repo securities" and "to do repo" are also used. The former means that someone is going to finance securities using the security as collateral; the latter means that the party is going to invest in a repo. Finally, the expressions "selling collateral" and "buying collateral" are used to describe a party financing a security with a repo on the one hand and lending on the basis of collateral on the other.

Rather than using industry jargon, investment guidelines should be clear as to what a manager is permitted to do. For example, a client may have no objections to its money manager using a repo as a short-term investment; that is, the money manager may lend funds on a short-term basis. The investment guidelines will set forth how the loan arrangement should be structured to protect against credit risk. We will discuss this next. However, if a client does not want a money manager to use the repo agreement as a vehicle for borrowing funds in order to create leverage, it should state so.

Although in our illustration we used Treasury securities as the collateral, the collateral in a repo is not limited to government securities. Money market instruments, federal agency securities, and mortgage-backed securities[14] are also used. In some specialized markets, whole loans (i.e., individual loans that have not been securitized) are used as collateral.

Credit Risks

Despite the fact that there may be high-quality collateral underlying a repo transaction, both parties to the transaction are exposed to credit risk. Why does credit risk occur in a repo transaction? Consider our initial example in which the dealer uses $10 million of government securities as collateral to borrow. If the dealer cannot repurchase the government securities, the customer may keep the collateral; if interest rates on government securities increase subsequent to the repo transaction, however, the market value of the government securities will decline, and the customer will own securities with a market value less than the amount it lent to the dealer. If the market value of the security rises instead, the dealer will be concerned with the return of the collateral, which then has a market value higher than the loan.

Repos should be carefully structured to reduce credit risk exposure. The amount lent should be less than the market value of the security used as collateral, thereby providing the lender with some cushion should the market value of the security decline. The amount by which the market value of the security used as collateral exceeds the value of the loan is called **repo margin** or simply **margin**. Margin is also referred to as the "haircut." Repo margin is generally between 1% and 3%. For borrowers of lower credit worthiness and/or when less liquid securities are used as collateral, the repo margin can be 10% or more.

Another practice to limit credit risk is to mark the collateral to market on a regular basis. (Marking a position to market means recording the value of a position at its market value.) When market value changes by a certain percentage, the repo position is adjusted accordingly.

---

[14] A special repo called a "dollar roll" is available when the security used as collateral is a mortgage pass-through security.

One concern in structuring a repo is delivery of the collateral to the lender. The most obvious procedure is for the borrower to deliver the collateral to the lender or to the lender's clearing agent. In such instances, the collateral is said to be "delivered out." At the end of the repo term, the lender returns the collateral to the borrower in exchange for the principal and interest payment. This procedure may be too expensive, though, particularly for short-term repos, because of costs associated with delivering the collateral. The cost of delivery would be factored into the transaction by a lower repo rate than the borrower would be willing to pay. The risk of the lender not taking possession of the collateral is that the borrower may sell the security or use the same security as collateral for a repo with another party.

As an alternative to delivering out the collateral, the lender may agree to allow the borrower to hold the security in a segregated customer account. Of course, the lender still faces the risk that the borrower may use the collateral fraudulently by offering it as collateral for another repo transaction. If the borrower of the cash does not deliver out the collateral, but instead holds it, then the transaction is called a **hold-in-custody (HIC) repo**. Despite the credit risk associated with a HIC repo, it is used in some transactions when the collateral is difficult to deliver (such as in whole loans) or the transaction amount is small and the lender of funds is comfortable with the reputation of the borrower of the cash.

Another method is for the borrower to deliver the collateral to the lender's custodial account at the borrower's clearing bank. The custodian then has possession of the collateral that it holds on behalf of the lender. This practice reduces the cost of delivery because it is merely a transfer within the borrower's clearing bank. If, for example, a dealer enters into an overnight repo with Customer A, the next day the collateral is transferred back to the dealer. The dealer can then enter into a repo with Customer B for, say, five days without having to redeliver the collateral. The clearing bank simply establishes a custodian account for Customer B and holds the collateral in that account. This specialized type of repo arrangement is called a **tri-party repo**.

Determinants of the Repo Rate

There is not one repo rate. The rate varies from transaction to transaction depending on a variety of factors: quality of collateral, term of the repo, delivery requirement, availability of collateral, and the prevailing federal funds rate.

The higher the credit quality and liquidity of the collateral, the lower the repo rate. The effect of the term of the repo on the rate depends on the shape of the yield curve. As noted earlier, if delivery of the collateral to the lender is required, the repo rate will be lower. If the collateral can be deposited with the bank of the borrower, a higher repo rate is paid.

The more difficult it is to obtain the collateral, the lower the repo rate. To understand why this is so, remember that the borrower (or equivalently the seller of the collateral) has a security that lenders of cash want, for whatever reason. Such collateral is referred to as **hot** or **special collateral**. (Collateral that does not have this characteristic is referred to as **general collateral**.) The party that needs the hot collateral will be willing to lend funds at a lower repo rate in order to obtain the collateral.

Whereas these factors determine the repo rate on a particular transaction, the federal funds rate determines the general level of repo rates. The repo rate generally will be a rate lower than the federal funds rate, because a repo involves collateralized borrowing, whereas a federal funds transaction is unsecured borrowing.

KEY POINTS

- The asset allocation decision is the decision made to determine how much should be allocated amongst the major asset classes and is made in light of the investment objective.
- Once the asset allocation decision is made, the client must decide whether to use only internal managers, use only external managers, or use a combination of internal and external managers.
- The term *asset allocation* is also used after a decision has been made to invest in a specified asset class to indicate how funds should be allocated amongst the different sectors within that asset class.
- In general, there are three categories of bond portfolio strategies: bond benchmark-based strategies, absolute return strategies, and liability-driven strategies.
- Bond benchmark-based strategies include indexing–type strategies (pure bond index matching, enhanced indexing with matching of primary risk factors, and enhanced indexing with minor risk-factor mismatches) and active management–type strategies (with larger risk-factor mismatches and full-blown active).
- With a core/satellite strategy there is a blending of an indexed strategy (to create a low-risk core portfolio) and an active strategy (to create a specialized higher risk–tolerant satellite portfolio).
- An absolute return strategy seeks to earn a positive return over some time frame irrespective of any changes in market conditions that impact the bond market.
- The wide range of bond market indexes available can be classified as broad-based market indexes and specialized market indexes.
- The primary risk factors affecting a portfolio are divided into systematic risk factors and nonsystematic risk factors. In turn, each of these risk factors is further decomposed. Systematic risk factors are divided into term structure risk factors and non–term structure risk factors. Examples of non–term structure risk factors are sector risk, credit risk, and optionality risk. Nonsystematic risk factors are classified as issuer-specific risk and issue-specific risk.
- Active bond portfolio strategies seek to capitalize on expectations about changes in factors that will affect the price and therefore the performance of an issue over some investment horizon.
- The total return framework should be used to assess how changes in risk factors will affect the performance of a strategy over some investment horizon.
- Leveraging involves creating an exposure to a market in excess of the exposure that can be obtained without borrowing funds. The objective is to earn a return in excess of the cost of the borrowed funds. The risk is that the manager will earn a return less than the cost of the borrowed funds. The return on the borrowed funds is realized from the interest earned plus the change in the value of the securities acquired. The duration of a portfolio is magnified by leveraging a portfolio.
- The most common way in which a manager can borrow funds is via a repurchase agreement. This is a collateralized loan arrangement in which a party borrows funds. It is called a reverse repo agreement when a party lends funds. There is credit risk in a repo agreement, and there are mechanisms for mitigating this risk.

QUESTIONS

1. Why might the investment objective of a portfolio manager of a life insurance company be different from that of a mutual fund manager?

2. Explain how it can be possible for a portfolio manager to outperform a benchmark but still fail to meet the investment objective of a client.

3. The following two quotes are from the website for the FTIF Franklin High Yield Fund (dated December 31, 2009 (at http://www.franklintempleton .com.es/pdf/funds/fdata/0825_ksp_es.pdf):
   a. "Portfolio risk is controlled primarily through our extensive bottom-up, fundamental analysis process, as well as through security and industry diversification." What does this mean?
   b. "The overall volatility of the product (i.e., standard deviation) and tracking error versus its benchmark and peer group is monitored and projected from a top-down quantitative approach." What is meant by a top-down approach? (In the next chapter, the quantitative approach and tracking error will be discussed.)

4. **a.** What is the essential ingredient in all active portfolio strategies?
   b. Those portfolio managers who follow an indexing strategy are said to be "index huggers." Why?

5. Explain whether you agree or disagree with the following statement: "All duration-matching strategies are indexing strategies."

6. The investment objective of the Threadneedle Bond Fund is "To outperform the benchmark by 3% per annum (gross of fees) over an 18–24 month period" What type of fund is this?

7. **a.** What is meant by systematic risk factors?
   b. What is the difference between term structure and non-term structure risk factors?

8. The following is reproduced from the Prospectus of the T. Rowe Price Institutional Core Plus Fund dated October 1, 2010:

   > **Principal Investment Strategies** The fund intends to invest at least 65% of its net assets in a "core" portfolio of investment-grade, U.S. dollar-denominated fixed income securities which may include, but are not limited to, debt securities of the

U.S. government and its agencies, corporate bonds, mortgages, and asset-backed securities. Normally, the fund will also maintain a "plus" portion of its portfolio in other sectors of the bond market, including high yield, non-U.S. dollar-denominated, and emerging market securities, to seek additional value.

Under normal conditions, the fund expects to maintain an effective duration within +/–20% of the Barclays Capital U.S. Aggregate Bond Index. As of July 31, 2010, the effective duration of this index was 4.05; however, it will change over time. The fund, in the aggregate, will seek to maintain a weighted average credit rating of A− or better, based on the weighted average credit quality of the fund's portfolio securities.

Individual bond investments in the core portfolio will be investment grade, with a minimum credit quality of BBB−. Ratings will be as determined, at the time of purchase, by at least one nationally recognized statistical rating organization (NRSRO) or, if not so rated, a comparable rating by T. Rowe Price. If a security is split-rated (i.e., one rating below investment grade and one at or above investment grade), the higher rating will be used.

The plus portion of the fund's portfolio may consist of below investment-grade (junk) bonds of U.S. and other developed country companies (not to exceed 20% of net assets), below investment-grade emerging market fixed income securities (not to exceed 10% of net assets), non-U.S. dollar-denominated securities (not to exceed 20% of net assets), and convertible and preferred securities (not to exceed 10% of net assets), as well as other investments. The fund may hold non-U.S. currencies without holding any bonds or other securities denominated in those currencies.

The fund may continue to hold an investment in its core portfolio that is downgraded to below investment grade after purchase. If such rating downgrades cause high yield exposure to exceed 20% of net assets or below investment-grade emerging market securities to exceed 10%

of net assets, the fund will reduce exposure within a reasonable period of time.

In keeping with the fund's objective, it may also use futures, options, and swaps. The fund may sell holdings for a variety of reasons, such as to adjust the portfolio's average maturity, duration, or credit quality or to shift assets into and out of higher yielding or lower yielding securities or different sectors.

Discuss in detail the strategy of this fund.

9. What are the limitations of using duration and convexity measures in active portfolio strategies?

10. Next are two portfolios with a market value of $500 million. The bonds in both portfolios are trading at par value. The dollar duration of the two portfolios is the same.

Issue	Years to Maturity	Par Value (in millions)
Bonds Included in Portfolio I		
A	2.0	$120
B	2.5	130
C	20.0	150
D	20.5	100
Bonds Included in Portfolio II		
E	9.7	$200
F	10.0	230
G	10.2	70

a. Which portfolio can be characterized as a bullet portfolio?

b. Which portfolio can be characterized as a barbell portfolio?

c. The two portfolios have the same dollar duration; explain whether their performance will be the same if interest rates change.

d. If they will not perform the same, how would you go about determining which would perform best assuming that you have a six-month investment horizon?

11. Explain why you agree or disagree with the following statements:

a. "It is always better to have a portfolio with more convexity than one with less convexity."

b. "A bullet portfolio will always outperform a barbell portfolio with the same dollar duration if the yield curve steepens."

12. What is a laddered portfolio?

13. A portfolio manager owns $5 million par value of bond ABC. The bond is trading at 70 and has a modified duration of 6. The portfolio manager is considering swapping out of bond ABC and into bond XYZ. The price of this bond is 85 and it has a modified duration of 3.5.

a. What is the dollar duration of bond ABC per 100-basis-point change in yield?

b. What is the dollar duration for the $5 million position of bond ABC?

c. How much in market value of bond XYZ should be purchased so that the dollar duration of bond XYZ will be approximately the same as that for bond ABC?

d. How much in par value of bond XYZ should be purchased so that the dollar duration of bond XYZ will be approximately the same as that for bond ABC?

14. Explain why in implementing a yield spread strategy it is necessary to keep the dollar duration constant.

15. The excerpt that follows is taken from an article titled "Smith Plans to Shorten," which appeared in the January 27, 1992, issue of *BondWeek*, p. 6:

> When the economy begins to rebound and interest rates start to move up, Smith Affiliated Capital will swap 30-year Treasuries for 10-year Treasuries and those with average remaining lives of nine years, according to Bob Smith, executive V.P. The New York firm doesn't expect this to occur until the end of this year or early next, however, and sees the yield on the 30-year Treasury first falling below 7%. Any new cash that comes in now will be put into 30-year Treasuries, Smith added.

What type of portfolio strategy is Smith Affiliated Capital pursuing?

16. The following excerpt is taken from an article titled "MERUS to Boost Corporates," which appeared in the January 27, 1992, issue of *BondWeek*, p. 6:

> MERUS Capital Management will increase the allocation to corporates in its $790 million long investment-grade

fixed-income portfolio by $39.5 million over the next six months to a year, according to George Wood, managing director. MERUS will add corporates rated single A or higher in the expectation that spreads will tighten as the economy recovers and that some credits may be upgraded.

What types of active portfolio strategies is MERUS Capital Management pursuing?

17. This excerpt comes from an article titled "Eagle Eyes High-Coupon Callable Corporates" in the January 20, 1992, issue of *BondWeek*, p. 7:

> If the bond market rallies further, Eagle Asset Management may take profits, trading $8 million of seven- to 10-year Treasuries for high-coupon single-A industrials that are callable in two to four years according to Joseph Blanton, senior V.P. He thinks a further rally is unlikely, however.
>
> Eagle has already sold seven- to 10-year Treasuries to buy $25 million of high-coupon, single-A nonbank financial credits. It made the move to cut the duration of its $160 million fixed income portfolio from 3.7 to 2.5 years, substantially lower than the 3.3-year duration of its bogey. . . because it thinks the bond rally has run its course. . . .
>
> Blanton said he likes single-A industrials and financials with 9–10% coupons because these are selling at wide spreads of about 100–150 basis points off Treasuries.

What types of active portfolio strategies are being pursued by Eagle Asset Management?

18. The following excerpt is taken from an article titled "W.R. Lazard Buys Triple Bs," which appeared in the November 18, 1991, issue of *BondWeek*, p. 7:

> W.R. Lazard & Co. is buying some corporate bonds rated triple B that it believes will be upgraded and some single As that the market perceives as risky but Lazard does not, according to William Schultz, V.P. The firm, which generally buys corporates rated single A or higher, is making the move to pick up yield, Schultz said.

What types of active portfolio strategies are being followed by W.R. Lazard & Co.?

19. In an article titled "Signet to Add Pass-Throughs," which appeared in the October 14, 1991, issue of *BondWeek*, p. 5, it was reported that Christian Goetz, assistant vice president of Signet Asset Management, "expects current coupons to outperform premium pass-throughs as the Fed lowers rates because mortgage holders will refinance premium mortgages." If Goetz pursues a strategy based on this, what type of active strategy is it?

20. The following excerpt comes from an article titled "Securities Counselors Eyes Cutting Duration" in the February 17, 1992, issue of *BondWeek*, p. 5:

> Securities Counselors of Iowa will shorten the 5.3 year duration on its $250 million fixed-income portfolio once it is convinced interest rates are moving up and the economy is improving. . . . It will shorten by holding in cash equivalents the proceeds from the sale of an undetermined amount of 10-year Treasuries and adding a small amount of high-grade electric utility bonds that have short-maturities if their spreads widen out at least 100 basis points. . . .
>
> The portfolio is currently allocated 85% to Treasuries and 15% to agencies. It has not held corporate bonds since 1985, when it perceived as risky the barrage of hostile corporate takeovers.

a. Why would Securities Counselors want to shorten duration if it believes that interest rates will rise?

b. How does the purchase of cash equivalents and short-maturity high-grade utilities accomplish the goal of shortening the duration?

c. What risk is Securities Counselors indicating in the last sentence of the excerpt that it is seeking to avoid by not buying corporate bonds?

21. The next excerpt is taken from an article titled "Wood Struthers to Add High-Grade Corporates," which appeared in the February 17, 1992, issue of *BondWeek*, p. 5:

> Wood Struthers & Winthrop is poised to add a wide range of high-grade corporates to its $600 million fixed-income portfolio

. . . . It will increase its 25% corporate allocation to about 30% after the economy shows signs of improving. . . . It will sell Treasuries and agencies of undetermined maturities to make the purchase. . . .

Its duration is 4 1/2–5 years and is not expected to change significantly. . . .

Comment on this portfolio strategy.

22. Explain how a rating transition matrix can be used as a starting point in assessing how a manager may want to allocate funds to the different credit sectors of the corporate bond market.

23. What is the risk associated with the use of leverage?

24. Suppose that the initial value of an unlevered portfolio of Treasury securities is $200 million and the duration is 7. Suppose further that the manager can borrow $800 million and invest it in the identical Treasury securities so that the levered portfolio has a value of $1 billion. What is the duration of this levered portfolio?

25. Suppose a manager wants to borrow $50 million of a Treasury security that it plans to purchase and hold for 20 days. The manager can enter into a repo agreement with a dealer firm that would provide financing at a 4.2% repo rate and a 2% margin requirement. What is the dollar interest cost that the manager will have to pay for the borrowed funds?

26. Two trustees of a pension fund are discussing repurchase agreements. Trustee A told Trustee B that she feels it is a safe short-term investment for the fund. Trustee B told Trustee A that repurchase agreements are highly speculative vehicles because they are leveraged instruments. You've been called in by the trustees to clarify the investment characteristics of repurchase agreements. What would you say to the trustees?

27. Suppose that a manager buys an adjustable-rate pass-through security backed by Freddie Mac or Fannie Mae, two government-sponsored enterprises. Suppose that the coupon rate is reset monthly based on the following coupon formula:

one-month LIBOR + 80 basis points

with a cap of 9% (i.e., maximum coupon rate of 9%).

Suppose that the manager can use these securities in a repo transaction in which (1) a repo margin of 5% is required, (2) the term of the repo is one month, and (3) the repo rate is one-month LIBOR plus 10 basis points. Also assume that the manager wishes to invest $1 million of his client's funds in these securities. The manager can purchase $20 million in par value of these securities because only $1 million is required. The amount borrowed would be $19 million. Thus, the manager realizes a spread of 70 basis points on the $19 million borrowed because LIBOR plus 80 basis points is earned in interest each month (coupon rate) and LIBOR plus 10 basis points is paid each month (repo rate).

What are the risks associated with this strategy?

28. Why is there credit risk in a repo transaction?

23

Bond Portfolio Construction

LEARNING OBJECTIVES

After reading this chapter you will understand

- what the Markowitz mean-variance framework for constructing portfolios is and the limitations of applying it to bond portfolio construction

- the difference between systematic risk and idiosyncratic risk

- what tracking error is and how it is computed

- the difference between forward-looking and backward-looking tracking error

- what the cell-based approach to bond portfolio construction is and its limitations

- the difficulties associated with constructing a bond portfolio when following a bond indexing strategy

- the purpose of a multi-factor model

- how a multi-factor model can be used to identify the sources of risk of a portfolio

- how to construct and rebalance a portfolio using a multi-factor model

In the previous chapter, we provided an overview of bond portfolio management and bond portfolio strategies. In this chapter, we will see how to construct (build) portfolios. We begin with a brief review of the basic principles of the theory of portfolio selection and portfolio risk. Then we explain a key metric used in constructing, monitoring, and controlling portfolio risk: tracking error (TE). In the last two sections of the chapter we explain two approaches to portfolio construction: the cell-based approach and the multi-factor model approach.

BRIEF REVIEW OF PORTFOLIO THEORY
AND RISK DECOMPOSITION

Portfolio theory as formulated by Harry Markowitz in the early 1950s provides guidance for the construction of portfolios.[1] The Markowitz framework, also referred to as **mean-variance analysis**, states there are three parameters that are important in making portfolio selection decisions. The first is the mean or expected value of an asset's return. The second is the variance of an asset's return, and it is this parameter that quantifies the risk of an individual asset. The variance of a random variable is a measure of the dispersion or variability of the possible outcomes around the expected value (mean). In the case of an asset's return, the variance is a measure of the dispersion of the possible rate of return outcomes around the expected return. The standard deviation is the positive square root of the variance, and oftentimes in referring to this type of risk the terms *variance* and *standard deviation* are used interchangeably.

The insight of the Markowitz framework is that when assets are combined to create a portfolio, the portfolio's risk is not merely some weighted average of the risks of the individual assets comprising the portfolio. Instead, the portfolio's risk, as measured by the portfolio variance, depends on the covariance or correlation of the returns between each pair of assets comprising the portfolio. The covariance, the third input needed for the mean-variance model, is the degree to which the returns on two assets co-vary or change together. The correlation is analogous to the covariance between the expected returns for two assets. Specifically, the correlation between the returns for two assets is equal to the covariance of the two assets divided by the product of their standard deviations.

More specifically, for the simple two-asset case—assets 1 and 2—the portfolio mean (or expected return) and the portfolio variance are respectively

$$E(R_p) = w_1\, E(R_1) + w_2\, E(R_2) \tag{23.1}$$

$$\text{var}(R_p) = w_1^2\, \text{var}(R_1) + w_2^2\, \text{var}(R_2) + 2\, w_1\, w_2\, \text{cov}(R_1, R_2) \tag{23.2}$$

where

$E(R_1)$, $E(R_2)$, and $E(R_p)$ are the expected return (mean) of asset 1, asset 2, and the portfolio, respectively.

w_1 and w_2 are the weight (allocation) of assets 1 and 2, respectively, in the portfolio (i.e., market value of the respective asset as a proportion of the market value of the total portfolio) at the beginning of the period.

$\text{var}(R_1)$, $\text{var}(R_2)$, and $\text{var}(R_p)$ are the variance of asset 1, asset 2, and the portfolio, respectively.

$\text{cov}(R_1, R_2)$ is the covariance between the returns for assets 1 and 2.

Let's highlight the key points here. As can be seen from equation (23.1), the portfolio expected return is a weighted average of the expected return for the two assets. The weight is the allocation of the asset in the portfolio. Equation (23.2) shows that in contrast to the portfolio expected return, the portfolio variance is not merely a weighted average of the variance of the two assets. Instead, it also depends on the covariance.

---

[1] Harry Markowitz, "Portfolio Selection," *Journal of Finance* (March 1952), pp. 77–91.

It is easier to see the importance of the relationship for the portfolio variance given by equation (23.2) by reformulating it in terms of the correlation. The relationship between the covariance and the correlation is as follows:

$$\text{cor}(R_1, R_2) = \text{cov}(R_1, R_2)/[\text{SD}(R_1)\,\text{SD}(R_2)] \tag{23.3}$$

where $\text{cor}(R_1, R_2)$ is the correlation between the returns of asset 1 and asset 2, and $\text{SD}(R_1)$ and $\text{SD}(R_2)$ are the standard deviations of the returns of asset 1 and asset 2, respectively. From equation (23.3) we have

$$\text{cov}(R_1, R_2) = \text{cor}(R_1, R_2)\,\text{SD}(R_1)\,\text{SD}(R_2) \tag{23.4}$$

Substituting the right-hand side of equation (23.4) for the $\text{cov}(R_1, R_2)$ in equation (23.2) we get

$$\text{var}(R_p) = w_1^2\,\text{var}(R_1) + w_2^2\,\text{var}(R_2) + 2\,w_1\,w_2\,\text{cor}(R_1, R_2)\,\text{SD}(R_1)\,\text{SD}(R_2) \tag{23.5}$$

Using equation (23.5), it is easier to appreciate how the relationship between asset returns as measured by the correlation impacts the portfolio variance. The correlation measure can have values ranging from $+1.0$, denoting perfect co-movement in the same direction, to -1.0, denoting perfect co-movement in the opposite direction. Also note that because the standard deviations are always positive, the correlation can be negative only if the covariance is a negative number. A correlation of zero implies that the returns are uncorrelated. Let's look at the following three cases:

$$\text{Correlation of } +1\text{: var}(R_p) = w_1^2\,\text{var}(R_1) + w_2^2\,\text{var}(R_2) + 2\,w_1 w_2\,\text{SD}(R_1)\,\text{SD}(R_2)$$
$$\text{Correlation of } 0\text{: var}(R_p) = w_1^2\,\text{var}(R_1) + w_2^2\,\text{var}(R_2)$$
$$\text{Correlation of } -1\text{: var}(R_p) = w_1^2\,\text{var}(R_1) + w_2^2\,\text{var}(R_2) - 2\,w_1 w_2\,\text{SD}(R_1)\,\text{SD}(R_2)$$

The maximum portfolio variance occurs when there is perfect correlation (i.e., correlation of $+1$) between the return of the two assets. For correlations less than $+1$, the portfolio variance is lower. This is the well-known property of asset diversification. The minimum portfolio variance occurs when asset returns have a correlation of -1.

This mathematical property that the variance of the returns of two assets—and it holds for any number of assets—is not just the weighted average of the individual asset variances applies to another risk measure that we will discuss later in this chapter, the portfolio tracking error.

Let's take a closer look at the portfolio variance. Financial theory as well as empirical evidence tells us that the portfolio variance can be decomposed into two general categories: systematic risk and idiosyncratic risk. The **systematic risk** is the risk that impacts the return on all assets in the portfolio. **Idiosyncratic risk** is the risk that is unique to the return of the individual assets in the portfolio.[2] In a well-diversified portfolio, idiosyncratic risk can be eliminated so that the only risk remaining in the portfolio is the systematic risk.

APPLICATION OF PORTFOLIO THEORY TO BOND PORTFOLIO CONSTRUCTION

The Markowitz mean-variance framework has been applied to portfolio construction in two ways.[3] The first is at the asset class level. As mentioned in the previous chapter, investors make an asset allocation decision. This is the decision as to how to allocate funds

---

[2] This risk is also referred to as nonsystematic risk, unique risk, and residual risk.
[3] For a further discussion of the application of portfolio theory, see Frank J. Fabozzi, Francis Gupta, and Harry M. Markowitz, "The Legacy of Modern Portfolio Theory," *Journal of Investing* (Fall 2002), pp. 7–22.

amongst the major asset classes (stocks, bonds, cash, real estate, and alternative assets). This has probably been the major use of the Markowitz framework.

The second application is the use of the mean-variance framework to select securities to construct a portfolio. This is the application of interest to us here. Although the mean-variance framework has been used in equity portfolio management for a good number of years, it has seen very limited use in constructing bond portfolios. The issues associated with the application to bond portfolio management (which, except where noted, also apply to equity portfolio management) are discussed in this section. However, despite the limitations, the insights provided by the Markowitz framework were of major importance and, in recognition of his the major contribution to financial economics, Harry Markowitz was awarded the 1990 Nobel Memorial Prize in Economic Sciences.

Although investors talked about diversification in very general and casual ways, prior to the introduction of portfolio theory and the benefits of diversification, they did not possess the analytical tools to quantify risk. Markowitz explained how risk can be quantified and that the key contributor to portfolio risk was the covariance/correlation.

Moving from theory to the implementation for constructing portfolios within an asset class requires the estimation of the inputs—mean, variance, and covariance—for all of the securities that are candidates for inclusion in the portfolio. These inputs are not easily estimated and there is an entire literature dealing with the issues associated with estimation risk.[4] Moreover, the number of inputs that must be calculated for even a modest number of securities that are candidates for inclusion into the portfolio is enormous. For example, if there are N securities that can be included in a portfolio, there are N variances and $(N^2 - N)/2$ covariances to estimate. Hence, for a portfolio of just 50 securities that could be included in the portfolio, there are 1,225 covariances that must be calculated. For 100 securities, there are 4,950 covariances.

Holding aside estimation risk, the enormity of the number of estimations that must be made was clear to Markowitz. He recognized that some kind of model of covariance structure was needed for the practical implementation of the theory to large portfolios. He did little more than point out the problem and suggest some possible models of covariance. One model Markowitz proposed to explain the correlation structure among security returns assumed that the return on a security depends on an "underlying factor, the general prosperity of the market as expressed by some index."[5] In 1963, William Sharpe tested the suggestion made by Markowitz by examining how stock returns tend to go up and down together with a general stock market index.[6] Specifically, Sharpe—the co-recipient of the Nobel Prize in Economics with Markowitz—estimated using regression analysis the relationship between the return on the market index (the explanatory variable) and the return on the stock (the dependent variable). The regression model Sharpe estimated is referred to as the **single index market model** or simply the **market model**. The regression coefficient of the market model that is estimated is referred to as **beta** and is a measure of the sensitivity of a stock to general movements in the market index.

It is worth noting that when Markowitz discussed the possibility of estimating the covariance structure, the index he suggested was not required to be a market index. The market

---

[4] See Vijay Chopra and William T. Ziemba, "The Effect of Errors in Means, Variances, and Covariances on Optimal Portfolio Choice," *Journal of Portfolio Management* 19 (1993), pp. 6–12.

[5] See pages 96–101 and in particular footnote 1 on page 100 of Harry M. Markowitz, *Portfolio Selection*, Cowles Foundation Monograph 16 (New York: John Wiley & Sons, 1959).

[6] William F. Sharpe, "A Simplified Model for Portfolio Analysis," *Management Science* (January 1963), pp. 277–293.

model is a very simple factor model (i.e., a one-factor model). Today, quantitative portfolio managers use a multi-factor model to estimate the covariance structure of returns. We will discuss this model for constructing bond portfolios later in this chapter.

The use of portfolio variance as a risk measure is an issue for two reasons. The first is that it is assumed that the return distribution for securities is normally distributed. If this holds, the variance is the appropriate measure of risk. However, empirical and theoretical evidence suggests that stock returns and bond returns are not normally distributed. As a result, extensions of the Markowitz optimization framework have been suggested that include other risk measures such as skewness and kurtosis.[7] The second criticism on portfolio variance is one that follows from our discussion in the previous chapter about the objective of portfolio managers: outperforming a benchmark. The measure used with this objective is a portfolio's tracking error. This measure is the standard deviation or variance of the difference between the portfolio return and the benchmark return. We'll discuss this in more detail next. The key point is that in constructing a portfolio where there is a benchmark, the relevant risk measure is not the portfolio variance but the portfolio tracking error.

Finally, let's revisit the notion of the decomposition of portfolio total risk (i.e., portfolio variance) into systematic risk and idiosyncratic risk. Studies of the stock market indicate that it does not take more than 25 or so randomly selected stocks to remove most of the idiosyncratic risk of a portfolio.[8] That is, a randomly selected portfolio of stocks is mostly exposed to systematic risk. However, when risk is measured in terms of tracking error, it takes a considerably larger (but reasonable) number of stocks to remove idiosyncratic risk. Typically, this is not the case when dealing with bonds where the benchmark is one of the standard bond market indexes. Such indexes may include 6,500 bonds. As we will see when we discuss the approaches to constructing bond portfolios later in this chapter, typically a bond portfolio will have a large component of idiosyncratic risk.

TRACKING ERROR

When a portfolio manager's benchmark is a bond market index, risk is not measured in terms of the variance or standard deviation of the portfolio's return. Instead, as explained earlier, risk is measured by the standard deviation of the return of the portfolio relative to the return of the benchmark index. This risk measure is called **tracking error**. Tracking error is also called **active risk**.

Calculation of Tracking Error

Tracking error is computed as follows:

Step 1: Compute the total return for a portfolio for each period.
Step 2: Obtain the total return for the benchmark index for each period.
Step 3: Obtain the difference between the values found in Step 1 and Step 2. The difference is referred to as the **active return**.
Step 4: Compute the standard deviation of the active returns. The resulting value is the tracking error.

[7] See Chapter 4 in Frank J. Fabozzi, *Institutional Investment Management* (Hoboken, NJ: John Wiley & Sons, 2010).
[8] See Raman Vardharaj, Frank J. Fabozzi, and Frank J. Jones, "Tracking Error and Common Stock Portfolio Management," Chapter 10 in Frank J. Fabozzi and Harry M. Markowitz, *Equity Analysis and Portfolio Management* (Hoboken, NJ: John Wiley & Sons, 2011).

Exhibit 23-1   Calculation of Tracking Error for Portfolio A for Year X

Month	Portfolio Return (%)	Benchmark Index Return (%)	Active Return (%)
Jan	−0.02	−0.04	0.02
Feb	1.58	1.54	0.04
March	−0.04	0.00	−0.04
April	0.61	0.54	0.07
May	−0.71	−0.76	0.05
June	−0.27	−0.30	0.03
July	0.91	0.83	0.08
Aug	1.26	1.23	0.03
Sept	0.69	0.76	−0.07
Oct	0.95	0.90	0.05
Nov	1.08	1.04	0.04
Dec	0.02	0.28	−0.26
Sum			0.041
Mean			0.0034
Variance			0.0086
Standard Deviation = Tracking error			0.0930
Tracking error (in basis points)			9.30

Notes: *active return = portfolio return − benchmark index return; variance = sum of the squares of the deviations from the mean/11; (division by 11, which is number of observations minus 1); standard deviation = tracking error = square root of variance*

Exhibits 23-1 and 23-2 show the calculation of the tracking error for two hypothetical portfolios, A and B, assuming some benchmark index. The observations are monthly for Year X. Portfolio A's monthly tracking error is 9.30 basis points. Notice that the monthly returns of the portfolio closely track the return of the benchmark index—that is, the active returns are small. In contrast, for Portfolio B, the active returns are large, and therefore, the monthly tracking error is large—79.13 basis points.

The tracking error measurement is in terms of the observation period. If monthly returns are used, the tracking error is a monthly tracking error. If weekly returns are used, the tracking error is a weekly tracking error. Tracking error is annualized as follows:

When observations are monthly:
annual tracking error = monthly tracking error × $\sqrt{12}$

When observations are weekly:
annual tracking error = monthly tracking error × $\sqrt{52}$

For example, the annual tracking errors for Portfolio A and Portfolio B are:

Annual tracking error for Portfolio A = 9.30 basis points × $\sqrt{12}$ = 32.16 basis points

Annual tracking error for Portfolio B = 79.13 basis points × $\sqrt{12}$ = 274.11 basis points

Two Faces of Tracking Error

We have just described how to calculate tracking error based on the actual active returns observed for a portfolio. Calculations computed for a portfolio based on a portfolio's

	Portfolio	Benchmark Index	Active
Month	**Return (%)**	**Return (%)**	**Return (%)**
Jan	−1.05	−0.04	−1.01
Feb	2.13	1.54	0.59
March	0.37	0.00	0.37
April	1.01	0.54	0.47
May	−1.44	−0.76	−0.68
June	−0.57	−0.30	−0.27
July	1.95	0.83	1.12
Aug	1.26	1.23	0.03
Sept	2.17	0.76	1.41
Oct	1.80	0.90	0.90
Nov	2.13	1.04	1.09
Dec	−0.32	0.28	−0.60
Sum			3.42
Mean			0.2850
Variance			0.6262
Standard Deviation = Tracking error			0.7913
Tracking error (in basis points)			79.13

Exhibit 23-2   Calculation of Tracking Error for Portfolio B for Year X

Notes: *active return = portfolio return − benchmark index return; variance = sum of the squares of the deviations from the mean/11; (division by 11, which is number of observations minus 1); standard deviation = tracking error = square root of variance*

actual active returns reflect the portfolio manager's decisions during the observation period with respect to the factors that we describe later in this chapter that affect tracking error. We call tracking error calculated from observed active returns for a portfolio **backward-looking tracking error**. It is also called **ex-post tracking error, historical tracking error**, and **actual tracking error**.

A problem with using backward-looking tracking error in bond portfolio management is that it does not reflect the effect of current decisions by the portfolio manager on the future active returns and hence the future tracking error that may be realized. If, for example, the manager significantly changes the portfolio's duration or allocation to the mortgage market sector today, then the backward-looking tracking error which is calculated using data from prior periods would not accurately reflect the current portfolio risks going forward. That is, the backward-looking tracking error will have little predictive value and can be misleading regarding portfolio risks going forward.

The portfolio manager needs a forward-looking estimate of tracking error to reflect the portfolio risk going forward. The way this is done in practice is by using the services of a commercial vendor or dealer firm that has modeled the factors that affect the tracking error associated with the bond market index that is the portfolio manager's benchmark. These models are called **multi-factor risk models**. Given a manager's current portfolio holdings, the portfolio's current exposure to the various risk factors can be calculated and compared to the benchmark's exposures to the factors. Using the differential factor exposures and the risks of the factors, a **forward-looking tracking error** for the portfolio can be computed. This tracking error is also referred to as **predicted tracking error** and **ex ante tracking error**.

Given a forward-looking tracking error, a range for the future possible portfolio active returns can be calculated assuming that the active returns are normally distributed. For example, assume the following:

expected return for benchmark = 10%

forward-looking tracking error relative to benchmark = 100 basis points

From the properties of a normal distribution, we know the following:

Number of Standard Deviations	Range for Portfolio Return	Probability
1	9%–11%	67%
2	8%–12%	95%
3	7%–13%	99%

It should be noted that there is no guarantee that the forward-looking tracking error at the start of, say, a year would exactly match the backward-looking tracking error calculated at the end of the year. There are two reasons for this. The first is that as the year progresses and changes are made to the portfolio, the forward-looking tracking error estimate would change to reflect the new exposures. The second is that the accuracy of the forward-looking tracking error at the beginning of the year depends on the extent of the stability of the variances and correlations that commercial vendors use in their statistical models to estimate forward-looking tracking error. These problems notwithstanding, the average of forward-looking tracking error estimates obtained at different times during the year will be reasonably close to the backward-looking tracking error estimate obtained at the end of the year.

The forward-looking tracking error is useful in risk control and portfolio construction. The manager can immediately see the likely effect on tracking error of any intended change in the portfolio. Thus, scenario analysis can be performed by a portfolio manager to assess proposed portfolio strategies and eliminate those that would result in tracking error beyond a specified tolerance for risk.

Tracking Error and Active versus Passive Strategies

Now that we know what tracking error is, we can think of active versus passive bond portfolio strategies in terms of forward-looking tracking error. In constructing a portfolio, a manager can estimate its forward-looking tracking error. When a portfolio is constructed to have a forward-looking tracking error of zero, the manager has effectively designed the portfolio to replicate the performance of the benchmark. If the forward-looking tracking error is maintained for the entire investment period, the active return should be close to zero. Such a strategy—one with a forward-looking tracking error of zero or very small—indicates that the manager is pursing a passive strategy relative to the benchmark index. When the forward-looking tracking error is large, the manager is pursuing an active strategy.

CELL-BASED APPROACH TO BOND PORTFOLIO CONSTRUCTION

In this section and the one to follow, we explain two approaches to constructing a bond portfolio: cell-based and multi-factor modeling.

Under the **cell-based approach**, the benchmark is divided into cells, each cell representing a different characteristic of the benchmark. The most common cells used to break down a benchmark are (1) duration, (2) coupon, (3) maturity, (4) market sectors, (5) credit quality, (6) call factors, and (7) sinking fund features. The last two factors are particularly important because the call and sinking fund features of an issue will affect its performance.

For example, suppose that a manager selects the following cells to partition an investment-grade bond index that is the benchmark:

Cell 1: Effective duration range: (1) less than or equal to five years, and (2) greater than five years

Cell 2: Maturity range: (1) less than five years, (2) between five and 15 years, and (3) greater than or equal to 15 years

Cell 3: Market sectors: (1) Treasury, (2) agencies, (3) corporate, and (4) agency MBS

Cell 4: Credit quality: (1) AAA, (2) AA, (3) A, and (4) BBB

The total number of cells would be equal to 96 (= $2 \times 3 \times 4 \times 4$).

For a portfolio manager pursuing a passive strategy, the objective is to match the performance of the benchmark. Following the cell-based approach, the manager selects from all the issues in the bond index one or more issues in each cell that can be used to represent the entire cell. The total dollar amount purchased of the issues from each cell will be based on the percentage of the bond index's total market value that the cell represents. For example, if 30% of the market value of all the issues in the bond index is made up of corporate bonds, 30% of the market value of the indexed portfolio should be composed of corporate bond issues.

For a portfolio manager pursuing an active strategy, the manager will intentionally mismatch the amount allocated to specific cells where a view is taken. For example, suppose that a manager has a view that the corporate sector will outperform the Treasury sector. Then the manager will overweight the corporate sector and underweight the Treasury sector. Overweight means that if a cell's weight in the bond index is x%, then more than x% will be allocated to that cell; underweighting means that less than x% will be allocated to that cell. When allocation to a cell is the same percentage as that in the cell, the allocation is said to be neutral.

The number of cells that the indexer uses will depend on the dollar amount of the portfolio. In a portfolio of less than $100 million, for example, using a large number of cells would require purchasing odd lots of issues. This increases the cost of buying the issues to represent a cell and thus would increase the portfolio's tracking error. However, reducing the number of cells to overcome this problem would increase the portfolio's tracking error in an undesirable way.

In practice, when the cell-based approach for bond portfolio construction is used, once a model portfolio is constructed, the portfolio's tracking error can be estimated. If the tracking error is unsatisfactory, the manager must alter the portfolio so that the tracking error is within the acceptable range specified by the manager or the client. This is often not a simple process, since modifying the portfolio can result in unintended bets (or views) by changing the allocation to cells.

Moreover, the cell-based approach ignores how mismatches impact portfolio risk as a result of cross-correlation associated with the risks of each cell. For example, it is possible that there may be large mismatches between two of the cells (characteristics) but the correlation of the risks associated with the cells may result in a very small increase in the portfolio's tracking error.

Fortunately, these drawbacks of the cell-based approach can be dealt with using the more quantitative approach, the multi-factor model approach, discussed in the next section. However, before doing so, we will discuss the difficulties associated with following an indexing strategy.

Complications in Bond Indexing

As explained in Chapter 22, there are three forms of bond indexing: pure bond index matching, enhanced indexing matching primary risk factors, and enhanced indexing allowing for minor risk-factor mismatches. As we mentioned in the previous chapter, it is almost impossible to implement a pure bond indexing strategy and it is not simple to do so for the other two bond indexing strategies. We will explain why. These difficulties apply to both the cell-based and multi-factor model approaches to portfolio construction.

In a pure bond indexing strategy, the portfolio manager must purchase all of the issues in the bond index according to their weight in the benchmark index. However, substantial tracking error will result from the transaction costs (and other fees) associated with purchasing all the issues and reinvesting cash flow (maturing principal and coupon interest). A broad-based market index could include more than 6,500 issues, so large transaction costs make this strategy impractical. In addition, some issues in the bond index may not be available at the prices used in constructing the index.

Instead of purchasing all issues in the bond index, the manager may purchase just a sample of issues using the cell-based approach. This moves the strategy from being a pure bond indexing strategy to an enhanced bond indexing strategy with minor mismatches in the primary risk factors. In terms of the cell-based approach, the primary risk factors are the characteristics or cells we described earlier. Although this approach reduces tracking error resulting from high transaction costs, it increases tracking error resulting from the mismatch of the indexed portfolio and the bond index. In practice, managers who state that they pursue a bond indexing strategy typically are forced to follow an enhanced bond indexing strategy with minor mismatches in the primary risk factors.

A portfolio manager faces several other logistical problems in seeking to construct an indexed portfolio. First, the prices for each issue used by the organization that publishes the index may not be execution prices available to the indexer. In fact, they may be materially different from the prices offered by some dealers. In addition, the prices used by organizations reporting the value of indexes are based on bid prices. Dealer-ask prices, however, are the ones that the manager would have to transact at when constructing or rebalancing the indexed portfolio. Thus, there will be a bias between the performance of the bond index and the indexed portfolio that is equal to the bid–ask spread.

Furthermore, there are logistical problems unique to certain sectors in the bond market. Consider first the corporate bond market. There are typically about 3,500 issues in the corporate bond sector of a broad-based bond index. Because of the illiquidity of this sector of the bond market, not only may the prices used by the organization that publishes the index be unreliable, but many of the issues may not even be available. Next, consider the agency mortgage-backed securities market. There are more than 800,000 agency pass-through issues. The organizations that publish indexes lump all these issues into a few hundred generic issues. The portfolio manager is then faced with the difficult task of finding pass-through securities with the same risk–return profiles of these hypothetical (generic) issues.

Finally, recall that the total return depends on the reinvestment rate available on coupon interest. If the organization publishing the index regularly overestimates the reinvestment rate, the indexed portfolio could underperform the bond index by a significant number of basis points a year.

PORTFOLIO CONSTRUCTION WITH MULTI-FACTOR MODELS

Multi-factor models are statistical models that are used to estimate a security's expected return based on the primary drivers affecting the return on securities. The primary drivers of returns are referred to as **risk factors** or simply **factors**. These models are also called **multi-factor risk models** or just **factor models**.

Multi-factor models provide managers with information about the sources of risk in their portfolio. Hence, they are indispensible tools for constructing portfolios so as to realize the desired exposure to the risk factors where a manager has a view. Moreover, these models can be used to monitor and control the risk exposure of the portfolio.

Our focus is not on how to build multi-factor models for bonds.[9] Rather it is how they are used to identify the sources of a bond portfolio's risk and how to employ them to construct bond portfolios.

Risk Decomposition

Before we explain how to use a multi-factor model to construct a portfolio, let's look at how a multi-factor model can be used to identify the risk exposure of a portfolio relative to a benchmark. We will illustrate this by using the 50-security portfolio shown in Exhibit 23-3 with a market value as of February 28, 2011 of $100 million. For now, it is not important to know how this portfolio was constructed. Later we see that this portfolio was constructed using a multi-factor model combined with an optimization model.[10]

The risk exposure for this portfolio will be measured in terms of tracking error. It is therefore necessary to know what this portfolio's benchmark is. In this illustration, let's suppose that the client establishes a composite index made up of the Barclays Capital U.S. Treasury Index, Barclays Capital U.S. Credit Index, and Barclays Capital U.S. MBS Index on an equally weighted basis (i.e., each index has a one-third weight).

---

[9] For a detailed description of multi-factor models and how they are developed, see the following two chapters by Anthony Lazanas, António Baldaque da Silva, Radu Găbudean, and Arne D. Staal, appearing in Frank J. Fabozzi (ed.), *The Handbook of Fixed Income Securities, 8th Edition* (New York: McGraw-Hill, 2012): "Introduction to Multi-Factor Risk Models in Fixed-Income and Their Applications" (Chapter 46) and "Analyzing Risk from Multi-Factor Fixed-Income Models" (Chapter 47).

[10] The portfolio for this illustration, which is also discussed further later in this chapter, as well as the portfolio for Question 20 at the end of this chapter, was provided by Cenk Ural of Barclays Capital using the Barclays Capital Global Risk Model.

Exhibit 23-3 Portfolio for Enhanced Indexing Illustration

Identifier	Description	Position Amount ($)	Market Value ($)
20029PAG	Comcast Cable Communication	1,559,836	1,994,785
652478AQ	News AM Holdings	1,058,588	1,326,367
694032AV	Pacific Bell	1,704,496	1,822,829
912810FG	US Treasury Bonds	1,672,649	1,897,604
71713UAW	Pharmacia Corp	1,476,540	1,776,413
16132NAV	Charter One Bank FSB	2,902,572	3,072,449
636180BE	National Fuel Gas Co	1,477,240	1,541,351
FGB05003	FHLM Gold Guar Single F. 30yr	1,474,515	1,559,577
FNA05003	FNMA Conventional Long T. 30yr	1,885,831	1,995,455
FNA05403	FNMA Conventional Long T. 30yr	1,434,788	1,549,951
GNA04403	GNMA I Single Family 30yr	2,361,203	2,465,800
05946NAD	Banco Bradesco SA	2,572,158	3,005,201
FGB05005	FHLM Gold Guar Single F. 30yr	1,549,025	1,634,273
FNA05005	FNMA Conventional Long T. 30yr	1,715,720	1,810,938
25459HAD	Directv Holdings/Finance	1,382,619	1,442,705
FNA06006	FNMA Conventional Long T. 30yr	1,627,692	1,782,118
37247XAD	Genworth Global Funding	1,862,609	1,986,026
13062TZV	California ST	1,692,373	1,748,831
FNA05407	FNMA Conventional Long T. 30yr	1,419,504	1,522,468
742718DF	Procter + Gamble Co-Global	2,074,088	2,295,058
FGB05407	FHLM Gold Guar Single F. 30yr	1,349,686	1,447,383
827065AA	Silicon Valley Bank	2,691,482	2,815,241
126650BK	CVS Corp-Global	3,034,915	3,029,619
060505DP	Bank Of America Corp	1,694,514	1,844,418
29379VAC	Enterprise Products Oper	1,239,177	1,390,729
581557AX	Mckesson Corp	1,150,435	1,407,417
FNA04409	FNMA Conventional Long T. 30yr	2,500,251	2,560,817
FGB04409	FHLM Gold Guar Single F. 30yr	2,088,579	2,138,445
36962G4D	General Electric Capital	1,707,300	1,902,870
912810QC	US Treasury Bonds	2,487,285	2,498,155
912828LZ	US Treasury Notes	785,094	805,949
912828ME	US Treasury Notes	830,946	866,901
4521518T	Illinois ST	1,849,220	1,858,124
61747YCL	Morgan Stanley Dean Witter	2,033,984	2,090,861
912828MH	US Treasury Notes	1,844,994	1,892,304
912810QE	US Treasury Notes	2,381,534	2,439,355
912828MR	US Treasury Notes	2,663,599	2,737,153
FNA04410	FNMA Conventional Long T. 30yr	1,819,251	1,862,947

(*Continued*)

Exhibit 23-3   Portfolio for Enhanced Indexing Illustration (Continued)

Identifier	Description	Position Amount ($)	Market Value ($)
FGB04410	FHLM Gold Guar Single F. 30yr	1,671,888	1,710,444
GNB04410	GNMA II Single Family 30yr	1,650,889	1,714,891
GNB04010	GNMA II Single Family 30yr	3,189,834	3,207,290
912828MZ	US Treasury Notes	1,655,406	1,719,878
912828NK	US Treasury Notes	2,001,683	1,995,645
912828NL	US Treasury Notes	2,838,516	2,853,752
912828NR	US Treasury Notes	2,307,072	2,273,303
172967FF	Citigroup Inc	1,377,851	1,431,826
912828NV	US Treasury Notes	3,899,465	3,788,034
912828NW	US Treasury Notes	2,347,035	2,233,159
912828PA	US Treasury Notes	1,558,736	1,491,788
665859AL	Northern Trust Corp	1,825,580	1,761,105

Exhibit 23-4   Summary of Portfolio and Benchmark Sector Allocation as of February 28, 2011

Sector	Portfolio (%)	Benchmark (%)	Difference (%)
Treasury	29.5	33.3	−3.8
Government Related	3.6	6.8	−3.2
Corporate Industrials	15.1	13.9	1.2
Corporate Utilities	2.9	3.0	−0.1
Corporate Financials	19.9	9.7	10.2
Agency MBS	29.0	33.3	−4.3
Total	100.0	100.0	0.0

This is shown in the third column of Exhibit 23-4. The U.S. Credit Index includes corporate bonds and government-related securities. In Exhibit 23-4 the distribution of the U.S. Credit Index is shown in terms of corporate sectors (industrials, utilities, and financials) and government-related sectors. The U.S. MBS index includes agency pass-through securities.

The analysis of the portfolio begins with a comparison of the portfolio to that of the benchmark. Identification of the mismatches indicates where the manager has taken a view (unintentional or not). Exhibit 23-4 compares the portfolio and the benchmark in terms of the allocation to the major sectors of the benchmark. It is clear from Exhibit 23-4 that the portfolio manager is taking a positive view on the corporate sector (more specifically industrials and financials) by overweighting it, and this is achieved by underweighting the other sectors.

Although the information contained in Exhibit 23-4 about the allocation based on percentage market value of sector relative to the benchmark provides a good starting point for our analysis, the information has limited value because it is not known how the exposures to the sectors are related to the exposures to the risk factors that drive the portfolio's return. Here are three examples. First, consider the Treasury sector. In Chapter 4, we discussed the concept of contribution to portfolio duration. It is possible that the specific Treasury securities contained in the portfolio have a greater contribution to portfolio duration than the contribution to index duration of the Treasuries in the benchmark despite the underweighting of Treasuries in the portfolio. As a second example of why the manager must look beyond the percentage allocation to a sector, consider the corporate bonds in the financial sector. Corporate financials will have a contribution to spread duration in both the portfolio and the benchmark. It is possible to have an overweight of this sector in the portfolio and yet have a contribution to spread duration that is less than that of the benchmark. Finally, a portfolio's convexity relative to the benchmark will impact relative performance. It is possible to underweight the portfolio's exposure to agency MBS so as to create a portfolio with large negative convexity while the benchmark has much lower negative convexity.

It is for this reason that the portfolio manager must look beyond a naïve assessment of portfolio risk relative to the benchmark based on percentage allocation to sectors. Exhibit 23-5 provides information about the relative exposure to interest rate risk as measured by duration, spread risk as measured by spread duration, and call/prepayment risk as measured by vega, as well as the convexity. From the exhibit we observe the following:

- The duration of the portfolio slightly exceeds that of the benchmark so that the portfolio has slightly more exposure to changes in the level of interest rates.
- Due to the underweighting in Treasuries, spread duration is higher.
- The slightly higher portfolio convexity compared to the benchmark means less exposure to call and prepayment risk, which is attributable to the reduced exposure to agency MBS.
- Exposure to call/prepayment risk as measured is small and about the same for the portfolio and the benchmark.

In addition, the spread of the portfolio is 107 basis points while that of the benchmark is 57 basis points.

More information about the portfolio's relative risk exposure to interest rate risk can be obtained by looking at the contribution to duration for the portfolio and the benchmark. This is shown in Exhibit 23-6. As can be seen, the major reason for the slightly

Exhibit 23-5 Analytics for the 50-Bond Portfolio and the Composite Index (Benchmark)

Exposure	Portfolio	Benchmark	Difference
Duration	5.56	5.41	0.15
Spread duration	5.37	5.27	0.10
Convexity	0.11	0.06	0.05
Vega	−0.04	−0.03	−0.01

Exhibit 23-6   Contribution to Duration by Asset Class for the 50-Bond Portfolio

Duration	Portfolio	Benchmark	Difference
Treasury	2.14	1.77	0.37
Government Related	0.07	0.40	−0.33
Corporate	1.84	1.73	0.12
Agency MBS	1.50	1.51	−0.01
Total	5.56	5.41	0.15

longer duration of the portfolio relative to the benchmark is mainly attributable to the duration of the Treasury securities selected for the portfolio.

The analysis thus far, while helpful, is missing one important element. To understand why, suppose that a portfolio has more exposure to a risk factor than the benchmark. This would mean if that risk factor moves, the portfolio will have a greater movement than the benchmark. But the question is: to what extent does that risk factor move? Another way of asking this is: how volatile is the risk factor? For example, from Exhibit 23-5 we know that the portfolio has greater exposure than the benchmark to changes in the level of interest rates (i.e., a higher duration) but less exposure to changes in spreads (i.e., a higher spread duration). But which exposure (i.e., risk factor) has greater volatility?

To address this, the volatility of the risk factors must be taken into consideration. Exhibit 23-7 shows the monthly volatility of all the risk factor categories. Let's look at each one of these volatilities and what it means. Isolated risk in this exhibit displays the tracking error/volatility of different exposures of the portfolio in isolation. Consider first the yield curve risk of 3.9 reported in Exhibit 23-7. Yield curve risk is the risk exposure to changes in interest rates. We know from Exhibit 23-5 that the portfolio duration is greater than the benchmark (5.56 versus 5.41), but how does that translate into what it will cost the manager in terms of additional risk? That is where the 3.9 is useful. Suppose that the portfolio differs from the benchmark only with respect to its exposure to changes in the yield curve. Then the 3.9 means that this mismatch relative to the benchmark creates a risk equal to 3.9 basis points per month of volatility. That is, if interest rates were the

Exhibit 23-7   Monthly Tracking Error for Risk Factors

Risk Factor Categories	Isolated Risk/Tracking Error
Yield curve risk	3.9
Swap spread risk	2.6
Volatility risk	1.3
Government-related spread risk	0.8
Corporate spread risk	2.8
Securitized spread risk	2.5

portfolio's only net exposure, this number would be the tracking error volatility (TEV) of that portfolio versus the benchmark.

Similarly, consider the risk factor "securitized spread" in Exhibit 23-7. This risk factor is the exposure to changes in the spreads in the agency MBS market. The value of 2.5 means that if the portfolio differs from the benchmark only with respect to its exposure to changes in the spread in the agency MBS sector, then this mismatch relative to the benchmark would result in a monthly isolated tracking error of 2.5 basis points.

Notice in Exhibit 23-7 that there is a risk exposure category labeled "volatility." This risk factor is the risk associated with changes in interest rate volatility and is critical for quantifying the exposure of a portfolio or benchmark to securities with embedded options such as callable bonds and agency MBS because they are impacted by changes in interest rate volatility. Hence, the value of 1.3 is the exposure of the portfolio to the risk factor volatility. The value of 1.3 means that if the portfolio differs from the benchmark only with respect to its exposure to changes in interest rate volatility, then this mismatch relative to the benchmark would result in a monthly isolated tracking error of 1.3 basis points.

How can we determine the monthly tracking error for the portfolio given the monthly tracking error for each risk factor exposure in Exhibit 23-7? One might think that the solution is to just add up the monthly tracking errors, which would give 13.9 basis points ($= 3.9 + 2.6 + 1.3 + 0.8 + 2.8 + 2.5$). However, that is not correct because standard deviations are not additive. (We noted this earlier in the chapter when we discussed portfolio risk not being the sum of the variances of the returns for the securities in portfolio.) Assuming a zero correlation between any pair of risk factors, the portfolio isolated tracking error attributable to systematic risk is found by squaring each isolated tracking error for each risk factor, summing them, and then taking the square root. That is, for the general case where there are K risk factors

$$\text{Portfolio isolated systematic TE} = [(\text{TE}_1)^2 + (\text{TE}_2)^2 + \ldots + (\text{TE}_K)^2]^{1/2}$$

where TE denotes tracking error and the subscript denotes the risk factor.

So for the 50-security portfolio in Exhibit 23-3 whose monthly isolated tracking error for each risk factor is shown in Exhibit 23-7, the portfolio isolated systematic TE is 6.20 basis points per month as shown below:

$$\text{Portfolio isolated systematic TE} = [(3.9)^2 + (2.6)^2 + (1.3)^2 + (0.8)^2 + (2.8)^2 + (2.5)^2]^{1/2} = 6.20$$

The actual value is 6.24 and the difference is due to rounding of the intermediate values.

The assumption that there is zero correlation between every pair of risk factors is unrealistic. Obviously, to address this, correlations or covariances must be brought into the analysis. The calculation of the portfolio risk then involves the use of the variance-covariance matrix for the risk factors. Recall that in mean-variance analysis, the portfolio variance (risk) captures the diversification effect by taking into consideration the covariances. In the case of tracking error, let's consider the case where there are only two risk factors, F_1 and F_2. Then the portfolio tracking error is equal to

$$\text{Portfolio TE} = [(\text{TE}_{F1})^2 + (\text{TE}_{F2})^2 + 2\,\text{Cov}(F_1, F_2)]^{1/2}$$

where $\text{Cov}(F_1, F_2)$ is the covariance between risk factor exposures 1 and 2.

In our illustration, there are six risk factors that we denote as follows:

F_1 = Yield curve risk
F_2 = Swap spread risk
F_3 = Volatility risk
F_4 = Government related spread risk
F_5 = Corporate spread risk
F_6 = Securitized spread risk

The variance-covariance matrix is then

$$
\begin{vmatrix}
\text{Var}(F_1) & \text{Cov}(F_1,F_2) & \text{Cov}(F_1,F_3) & \text{Cov}(F_1,F_4) & \text{Cov}(F_1,F_5) & \text{Cov}(F_1,F_6) \\
\text{Cov}(F_2,F_1) & \text{Var}(F_2) & \text{Cov}(F_2,F_3) & \text{Cov}(F_2,F_4) & \text{Cov}(F_2,F_5) & \text{Cov}(F_2,F_6) \\
\text{Cov}(F_3,F_1) & \text{Cov}(F_3,F_2) & \text{Var}(F_3) & \text{Cov}(F_3,F_4) & \text{Cov}(F_3,F_5) & \text{Cov}(F_3,F_6) \\
\text{Cov}(F_4,F_1) & \text{Cov}(F_4,F_2) & \text{Cov}(F_4,F_3) & \text{Var}(F_4) & \text{Cov}(F_4,F_5) & \text{Cov}(F_4,F_6) \\
\text{Cov}(F_5,F_1) & \text{Cov}(F_5,F_2) & \text{Cov}(F_5,F_3) & \text{Cov}(F_5,F_4) & \text{Var}(F_5) & \text{Cov}(F_5,F_6) \\
\text{Cov}(F_6,F_1) & \text{Cov}(F_6,F_2) & \text{Cov}(F_6,F_3) & \text{Cov}(F_6,F_4) & \text{Cov}(F_6,F_5) & \text{Var}(F_6)
\end{vmatrix}
$$

The diagonal terms in the variance-covariance matrix are the variance or equivalently the square of the tracking error.

Further information is available to describe the risk attributes of a portfolio. The Barclays Capital's cross-asset portfolio analysis and construction system, POINT[R], is used here to provide a more detailed summary of the portfolio exposure to each of the risk factors as well as a detailed breakdown of issue/issuer exposures. Here we will simply provide an example of the type of information that can be provided.[11] Specifically, we will look at more detailed information about the general exposure of the portfolio and then focus on exposure to yield curve risk in more detail.

A summary report for the portfolio whose holdings are listed in Exhibit 23-3 is shown in Exhibit 23-8. The portfolio has only 50 positions and 25 issuers in contrast to 5,693 positions in the benchmark and 780 issuers. What this means is that the portfolio is not very well diversified and, as a result, the manager should expect a significant level of idiosyncratic risk. All of the holdings are dollar-denominated and the same is true for the benchmark. For this reason there is only one currency shown in the summary report. From our previous discussion, we know about the last five metrics reported in the analytics section of the exhibit. Average life and yield to worst are measures discussed in earlier chapters.

Exhibit 23-8 gives a breakdown of the standard deviation of the returns for the portfolio and the benchmark in terms of systematic risk and idiosyncratic risk. The portfolio has greater systematic and idiosyncratic risk than the benchmark. For the total risk of the portfolio and the benchmark, since the systematic and idiosyncratic risks are constructed so as to be independent, the standard deviation of the portfolio and benchmark can be calculated as follows:

Total risk (volatility of returns) = [(Systematic risk)^2 + (Idiosyncratic risk)^2]$^{1/2}$

The total risk for the portfolio and the benchmark using the values in Exhibit 23-8 is 125.7 and 123.6, respectively.

---

[11] A more detailed description can be found in Anthony Lazanas, António Baldaque da Silva, Radu Găbudean, and Arne D. Staal, "Multifactor Fixed Income Risk Models and Their Applications," Chapter 21 in Frank J. Fabozzi and Harry M. Markowitz, *The Theory and Practice of Investment Management* (Hoboken, NJ: John Wiley & Sons, 2011).

Exhibit 23-8 Summary Report for Illustrative 50-Bond Portfolio

A. Parameters	Portfolio	Benchmark	
Positions	50	5,693	
Issuers	25	780	
Currencies	1	1	
Market value ($MM)	100	13,615	
Notional ($MM)	95	12,851	

B. Analytics	Portfolio	Benchmark	Difference
Coupon (%)	4.65	4.39	0.26
Average life (Yr)	8.09	7.77	0.31
Yield to worst (%)	3.69	3.18	0.51
Spread (bps)	107	57	50
Duration	5.56	5.41	0.15
Vega	−0.04	−0.03	−0.01
Spread duration	5.37	5.27	0.09
Convexity	0.11	0.06	0.05

C. Volatility	Portfolio	Benchmark	Tracking Error
Systematic (bps/month)	125.4	123.5	4.6
Idiosyncratic (bps/month)	9.6	4.8	7.8
Total (bps/month)	125.7	123.6	9.0

D. Portfolio Beta	1.01		

Notice that for the benchmark, the percentage of the total risk (123.6) that is explained by the systematic risk factors (123.5) is 99.99%. For the portfolio it is 99.76% (125.4/125.7). It would therefore seem that the idiosyncratic risk is not important. This, however, is not true when dealing with the tracking error of the portfolio (volatility of the net position, portfolio vs. the benchmark). The systematic and idiosyncratic tracking error (per month) is 4.6 basis points and 7.8 basis points per month, respectively. The portfolio tracking error is

$$\text{Portfolio tracking error} = [(\text{Systematic TE})^2 + (\text{Idiosyncratic TE})^2]^{0.5}$$

Therefore, the portfolio tracking error is 9 basis points per month. Consequently, although idiosyncratic risk is minimal for the portfolio on a stand-alone basis, when risk is assessed relative to a benchmark, there is tracking error risk of 9 basis points per month. (The systematic risk is responsible for 7.8/9.0 or 87% of the total risk. As explained later, this tracking error is well within the risk budget that we assume the manager was permitted of 15 basis points per month.)

This is an extremely important point: It is the tracking error—not the idiosyncratic risk (as measured by the standard deviation of the idiosyncratic returns)—that the manager must consider in portfolio construction and monitoring. In our illustration, the portfolio tracking error is small, only 9 basis points. But the illustration could have just as easily been constructed where the systematic risk relative to the total risk (as measured by the standard deviation of returns) for the portfolio is 99.76% with a tracking error per month of 200 basis points.

As with equities where a portfolio beta is computed that shows the movement of an equity portfolio in response to a movement in some equity market index (such as the S&P 500), a beta can be computed for a bond portfolio. As shown in Exhibit 23-8, the portfolio beta is 1.01. Since the benchmark is the Composite Index, a beta of 1.01 means that if that index increases by 10%, the portfolio will increase, on average, by 10.1%.

A beta-type measure can be estimated for each risk factor. For example, consider the risk factor measuring changes in the level of the yield curve that is the portfolio's duration. A **duration beta** can be calculated as follows:

$$\text{Duration beta} = \frac{\text{Portfolio duration}}{\text{Benchmark duration}}$$

For our portfolio and benchmark, since the duration is 5.56 and 5.41, respectively (see Exhibit 23-6), the duration beta is 1.03.

While the information contained in Exhibit 23-8 gives us a starting point for understanding the portfolio's risk relative to the benchmark, further insight can be gained by looking at how the portfolio risk (as measured by tracking error) is allocated across the different (1) categories of risk factors and (2) asset classes (i.e., sectors of the benchmark).

Exhibit 23-9 provides information about the portfolio risk across the different categories of risk factors. Shown are the systematic risk and the idiosyncratic risk and the seven components of systematic risk. The second column shows the isolated tracking error. The contribution to tracking error for each group of risk factors is shown in the third column. As can be seen, the major risk exposures of the 50-bond portfolio are yield curve risk, spread risk, corporate spread risk as measured by the swap spread, and idiosyncratic risk. The fourth column gives a new metric, liquidation effect on tracking error. Barclays Capital defines this metric to be the impact to the portfolio's tracking error by hedging (i.e., eliminating) the exposure to the respective risk group. For example, consider the systematic risk. The liquidation effect on tracking error shown in the exhibit is −1.2 and is interpreted as follows: if the portfolio manager hedges

Exhibit 23-9 Detailed Monthly Tracking Error for the 50-Bond Portfolio by Risk Factor Group

Risk Factor Group	Isolated Tracking Error	Contribution to Tracking Error	Liquidation Effect on Tracking Error	Tracking Error Elasticity (%)
Total	9.0	9.0	−9.0	1.0
Systematic risk	4.6	2.3	−1.2	0.2
Yield curve risk	3.9	0.9	−0.1	0.1
Swap spread risk	2.6	0.6	−0.2	0.1
Volatility risk	1.3	0.1	0.0	0.0
Government-related spread risk	0.8	0.0	0.0	0.0
Corporate spread risk	2.8	0.7	−0.3	0.1
Securitized spread risk	2.5	0.0	0.4	0.0
Idiosyncratic risk	7.8	6.8	−4.2	0.7

the systematic risk, then the portfolio's tracking error will decline by 1.2 basis points per month. Since the portfolio's tracking error is 9 basis points per month, this means that hedging the systematic risk reduces the monthly tracking error for the portfolio to 7.8 basis points per month.

A detailed analysis of the systematic and idiosyncratic risk applied at the asset class level rather than at the individual risk factor level is provided in Exhibit 23-10. The five asset classes are shown in the first column and in the second column the underweighting or over-weighting of each asset class (referred to as the "net market weight") are shown. The last three columns report the contribution to tracking error for systematic risk, idiosyncratic risk, and total risk. The row labeled "Total" shows what we already know about the portfolio risk from earlier analysis: systematic risk of 2.3 basis points per month, idiosyncratic risk of 6.8 basis points per month, and the total risk of 9 basis points per month. The exhibit then shows how each asset class contributes to systematic, idiosyncratic, and total risk. Looking at the exhibit at a high level, idiosyncratic risk seems to be dominant compared to the systematic risk due to the small number of securities in the portfolio. It is interesting to note that the major contribution to systematic risk is coming from the Treasuries although this sector has a smaller net market weight (in magnitude) than the corporates. This is mainly due to the duration mismatch between the Treasury component of the portfolio versus the benchmark. On the other hand, Treasuries have negligible idiosyncratic risk contribution as a large proportion of variation in the return of these securities can be explained by systematic yield curve factors.

Another important observation to take away from the analysis reported in Exhibit 23-10 is that Corporates are the major contributor to idiosyncratic risk due to the overweighting of this sector, carrying relatively higher idiosyncratic risk at the individual security level. If any of these Corporate bonds selected for the portfolio performs poorly (i.e., the idiosyncratic risk is realized), then this could have a substantial adverse impact on the portfolio's performance relative to the benchmark. This highlights the significant "name" risk (i.e., risk to individual issuers) that the portfolio is exposed to.

An analysis similar to the decomposition of risk shown in Exhibit 23-9 by asset class instead of risk factor group is shown in Exhibit 23-11. Notice that the isolated tracking error for both the Treasury and corporate asset classes exceeds that of the portfolio tracking error (10.6 and 9.3 basis points per month versus 9 basis points per month). How is that possible? This occurs because exposures to certain asset classes in the portfolio are

Exhibit 23-10   Systematic and Idiosyncratic Monthly Tracking Error for the 50-Bond Portfolio by Asset Class

Asset Class	Net Market Weight (%)	Contribution to Tracking Error		
		Systematic	Idiosyncratic	Total
Total	0.0	2.3	6.8	9.0
Treasuries	−3.8	2.5	0.2	2.7
Government agencies	−1.8	−0.3	0.0	−0.3
Government non-agencies	−1.4	−0.9	0.2	−0.7
Corporates	11.4	1.0	6.0	6.9
MBS	−4.4	0.0	0.4	0.4

Exhibit 23-11   Isolated Monthly Tracking Error and Liquidation Effect for the 50-Bond Portfolio by Asset Class

Asset Class	Net Market Weight (%)	Isolated Tracking Error	Liquidation Effect on Tracking Error	Tracking Error Elasticity (%)
Total	0.0	9.0	−9.0	1.0
Treasuries	−3.8	10.6	2.9	0.3
Government agencies	−1.8	2.0	0.5	0.0
Government non-agencies	−1.4	7.2	2.9	−0.1
Corporates	11.4	9.3	−2.9	0.8
MBS	−4.4	3.4	0.3	0.0

acting as hedges to certain other asset classes (since Treasuries and Corporates could also be hedging each other). The hedging effect can be seen in the fourth column where the liquidation effect on tracking error is shown for each asset class in Exhibit 23-11.

Now let's look at the exposure of the portfolio to yield curve risk in more detail. In Chapter 5, we discussed the term structure of interest rates. Although our focus was on the Treasury yield curve, we explained that there are other interest rate benchmarks that can be used such as the swap curve. During non-crisis periods, the Treasury and swap curves tend to behave the same way. This is the not the case during periods where there is a crisis in the financial markets. This was apparent in the credit crisis of 2008. Consequently, in the Barclays Capital model, there is a different yield curve used for government products. With the exception of Treasuries, the other four asset classes have exposure to the swap spread factors on top of the Treasury curve. By decomposing the swap curve into the Treasury curve and swap spreads, the Barclays Capital model gives portfolio managers the flexibility to analyze their spread risk over the Treasury or the swap curve depending on their preferences.

There are different measures to look at the exposure to changes in the shape of the yield curve. The most common is key rate duration. In the Barclays Capital model, the six key rates are the 6-month, 2-year, 5-year, 10-year, 20-year, and 30-year. For the 50-bond portfolio and for the benchmark, these six key rate durations with respect to the U.S. Treasury curve, as well as the option-adjusted or effective convexity, are shown in Exhibit 23-12. Summing up the key rate durations for the portfolio and the benchmark gives the portfolio duration of 5.56 and benchmark duration of 5.41, which agrees with the values in Exhibit 23-8.

The fourth column shows the mismatch for the key rate duration and convexity between the portfolio and benchmark. From Chapter 4 we know how to interpret the key rate duration. It is the approximate percentage change in the portfolio value or benchmark value for a 100 basis point change in the rate for a particular maturity holding all other rates constant. In terms of mismatch, it is the approximate differential percentage change in the portfolio relative to the benchmark for a 100 basis point change in the rate for a particular maturity holding all other rates constant. For example, consider the net five-year key rate duration of 0.09. The impact on return relative to the benchmark for a 100 basis point change in five-year interest rates will be 0.09. The question then is how volatile is the five-year rate. The fifth column, labeled factor volatility, is the factor's forecasted volatility with a monthly horizon. The five-year rate, for example, has a factor volatility of 29.48 basis

Exhibit 23-12 Treasury Curve Risk for 50-Bond Portfolio

Factor Name	Portfolio	Benchmark	Net*	Factor Volatility	Return Impact of a Typical Movement		Marginal Contribution to Tracking Error
					Isolated TE	Correlated TE	
USD 6M key rate	0.11	0.11	0.01	22.20	−0.2	−0.9	2.2
USD 2Y key rate	0.59	0.64	−0.05	21.59	1.1	−1.4	3.3
USD 5Y key rate	1.53	1.43	0.09	29.48	−2.8	−1.7	5.3
USD 10Y key rate	1.39	1.51	−0.12	30.42	3.6	−2.0	6.6
USD 20Y key rate	0.98	0.91	0.07	27.84	−2.0	−2.1	6.3
USD 30Y key rate	0.96	0.82	0.14	27.18	−3.8	−2.2	6.4
USD Convexity	0.11	0.06	0.05	4.72	0.2	0.5	0.3

* Differences due to rounding.

points per month. Assuming that the factor volatility represents a typical movement for the factor (i.e., key interest rate), then the isolated impact of that movement on the return of the 50-bond portfolio (versus the benchmark) can be found as follows:

Return impact of a typical movement = − (Net key rate duration) × Typical rate movement

For example, for the five-year key rate duration, we have

Return impact of a typical movement = − (0.09) × 29.48 = −2.7 basis points per month

Looking at the 10-year key rate, we have

Return impact of a typical movement = − (−0.12) × 30.42 = 3.6 basis points per month

Recall the difference between isolated and correlated return impact. Notice that for the 10-year key rate, the isolated return impact of a typical movement in the 10-year rate is positive but when correlation between factors is considered, it is −2 basis points per month.

The last column in Exhibit 23-12, which shows the marginal contribution to tracking error, is useful for a portfolio manager who seeks to effectively reduce portfolio exposure to Treasury yield curve risk. Basically, it shows that a change of one unit exposure to the 10-year key rate changes the tracking error by 6.6 basis points per month.

Exhibit 23-13 shows the exposure of the portfolio to the change in the swap spread. The swap spread is the difference between the swap rate and the Treasury rate. All securities in the portfolio except Treasuries expose the portfolio to this risk. A comparison of the return impact based on correlated factors in the next-to-the-last columns of Exhibits 23-12 and 23-13 indicates that potential movements in swap spread factors have less impact on the portfolio than that of the Treasury curve factors.

Portfolio Construction Using a Multi-Factor Model and an Optimizer

Now that we know what information can be obtained from a multi-factor model, let's see how it can be applied to construct a bond portfolio.

Exhibit 23-13   Swap Spread Risk for 50-Bond Portfolio

Factor Name	Exposure (SS-KRD)			Factor Volatility	Return Impact Correlated	Marginal Contribution to TE
	Portfolio	Benchmark	Net			
USD 6M swap spread	0.11	0.08	0.04	19.5	−0.9	2.0
USD 2Y swap spread	0.43	0.38	0.05	11.0	−0.6	0.7
USD 5Y swap spread	0.74	0.89	−0.15	6.7	−0.5	0.4
USD 10Y swap spread	1.16	1.08	0.09	8.5	1.2	−1.1
USD 20Y swap spread	0.66	0.72	−0.06	9.9	1.7	−1.8
USD 30Y swap spread	0.21	0.40	−0.19	12.5	1.9	−2.6

As with the cell-based approach to portfolio construction, a manager has views on the various primary factors driving the return on the benchmark and wants to position the portfolio to capitalize on those expectations. The manager does this in the face of constraints in terms of the risk budget as well as any restrictions on maximum exposure to any sector, industry, or issuer. Of course, the manager almost must consider transaction costs not only when constructing a portfolio from cash but also when rebalancing a current portfolio to revise the portfolio's exposure to risk factors.

A multi-factor model is used in conjunction with an optimization model, or simply optimizer, to construct a portfolio.[12] We will assume the benchmark is the composite index shown in Exhibit 23-4. Although we have discussed the 50-bond portfolio in Exhibit 23-3 in terms of its exposure to risk factors, this portfolio was actually generated from the Barclays Capital POINT[R] Optimizer.[13]

In using an optimizer, the optimal value for all of the variables that the decision maker seeks is the output for the model. The decision maker specifies the variables (i.e., decision variables), an objective function, and constraints. Given all of that information, the optimizer finds the optimal value for all of the decision variables.

In the case of portfolio construction using a multi-factor model, the decision variables are the amounts of each security to be held in the optimized portfolio. This requires that the portfolio manager specify the universe of securities that are acceptable for inclusion in the portfolio. But more is needed than just information about the securities that may be included. The price at which each candidate security can be purchased is needed. The tradable universe that will be used are the securities included in the composite index with a minimum amount outstanding specified (it is $300 million in our illustration). There is no need for the tradable universe to be the same as the benchmark. If the portfolio manager is permitted to invest in nonindex securities, a larger tradable universe could be used such as the Barclays Capital U.S. Aggregate index. The imposition of a minimum issue size is employed to avoid inclusion of small issues into the portfolio that could potentially lead to a liquidity problem.

The portfolio manager must also specify the objective function. This is the measure or quantity that is to be minimized or maximized. In portfolio construction using multi-factor

---

[12] For an explanation of optimization models, see Dessislava A. Pachamanova and Frank J. Fabozzi, *Simulation and Optimization Modeling in Finance* (Hoboken, NJ: John Wiley & Sons, 2010).
[13] See Anuj Kumar, "The POINT Optimizer," Barclays Capital Publication, June 2010.

models, the measure to be optimized is the portfolio's tracking error. The manager wants that measure to be minimized.

The optimization of the objective function is typically done subject to constraints. These constraints may be client-imposed based on the investment guidelines, self-imposed by the manager, or imposed by regulations. The most obvious constraint is the risk budget, which imposes a maximum portfolio tracking error. Other common constraints in the initial construction of a portfolio are (1) restrictions on short selling, (2) a maximum deviation from the benchmark's duration, (3) a maximum mismatch to any one sector in the benchmark, (4) a maximum exposure to any one issuer or industry, and (5) a minimum size purchase of an issue to avoid the purchase of odd lots. If the tradable universe includes securities not included in the benchmark, a typical constraint imposed on the manager is the percentage of the portfolio that may be allocated to nonindex securities. Of course, there must be a requirement on the market value of the portfolio and an upper limit on the number of securities.

In constructing the portfolio listed in Exhibit 23-3, the following restrictions were imposed:

1. Market value of $100 million
2. No more than 50 securities in the portfolio
3. No short sales
4. The portfolio's duration must exceed the benchmark's duration by at least 0.15 but no more than 0.30.
5. Spreads between 50 and 80 basis points higher than the benchmark
6. Monthly tracking error not to exceed 15 basis points
7. Maximum under/overweight of 3% per issuer

Notice constraint 4 dealing with the portfolio duration. It is that requirement that tilts the portfolio in the direction of the portfolio manager's view to have a mismatch to the benchmark with respect to the risk factor representing curve risk. Constraint 5 is the risk budget, which permits not only a duration mismatch but a mismatch on sector allocations. Constraint 7 is imposed for diversification purposes.

It is clear from Exhibit 23-4 that the portfolio manager is also taking a positive view on the corporate sector by overweighting it and this is achieved by underweighting the three other sectors.

Portfolio Rebalancing

While it is common to illustrate portfolio construction starting with a position of cash and building a portfolio of securities, in practice the more common task is to rebalance an existing portfolio. A multi-factor model along with an optimizer can be used to efficiently rebalance the portfolio so as to realign the portfolio that has been drifting away from the characteristics of the benchmark over time (such as a change in the duration of the benchmark requiring a change in the duration of the portfolio, or an upgrade or downgrade of some issues in the portfolio) and/or tilt the portfolio to reflect a manager's new views. Rebalancing is also required when a portfolio manager receives additional funds from a client or portfolio cash inflows or when a client withdraws funds.

Rebalancing must be done so as to minimize transaction costs by reducing the need to turn over current holdings unnecessarily. The optimizer is able to evaluate the trade-off of replacing one issue held (i.e., a sale) with another issue (i.e., a purchase). The optimizer can identify a package of transactions (i.e., sells and buys) and identify the reduction (or increase) in risk that would result from the execution of those transactions so that the portfolio manager can assess the risk adjustment benefit relative to the cost of executing the transaction.

To illustrate, a detailed analysis of the portfolio's holdings shown in Exhibit 23-3 would indicate an overweighting of issuers in the banking sector. Suppose that the manager wants to limit the overweight to banks to 5% but wants to do so with no more than 15 trades. The optimizer can then be used where the inputs are the set of tradable securities and their current prices. A constraint must be added to restrict the overweight to banks to less than or equal to 5% and to restrict the number of trades to no more than 15.

Exhibit 23-14 shows the trades that would have been recommended by the optimizer at the time. The total market value of the trades was roughly $13 million. Almost half of the sales from the portfolio were for banks and they were replaced with various Treasury notes, a corporate bond, a sovereign bond, and an agency MBS.

Before the manager executes the package of trades proposed in Exhibit 23-14, there must be an evaluation of the change in risk exposure. The new systematic TE after rebalancing was 4.2 basis points (the original was 4.6 basis points); idiosyncratic TE is 7.8 basis points (same as before rebalancing); and total TE is 8.8 basis points (9.0 basis points before rebalancing). The decline in the total TE is because there are more than 50 securities in the portfolio after the rebalancing.

Exhibit 23-14   Trades for Portfolio Rebalancing

	Buys		
Identifier	Description	Position Amount ($)	Market Value ($)
912828LK	US TREASURY NOTES	3,133,909	3,235,179
912828LS	US TREASURY NOTES	2,814,967	2,924,353
489170AB	KENNAMETAL INC	1,959,720	2,087,886
94986EAA	WELLS FARGO CAPITAL XIII	1,286,097	1,360,888
912810QD	US TREASURY BONDS	1,118,189	1,111,380
465138ZR	ISRAEL STATE OF	920,297	1,097,735
912810QB	US TREASURY BONDS	1,017,169	991,185
GNG03410	GNMA II Single Family 15yr	117,277	119,672
Total			12,928,278

	Sells		
Identifier	Description	Position Amount ($)	Market Value ($)
912828NV	US TREASURY NOTES	−2,662,260	−2,586,183
16132NAV	CHARTER ONE BANK FSB	−2,203,358	−2,332,312
05946NAD	BANCO BRADESCO SA	−1,564,870	−1,828,328
827065AA	SILICON VALLEY BANK	−1,692,776	−1,770,613
912828NL	US TREASURY NOTES	−1,603,631	−1,612,239
912810QC	US TREASURY BONDS	−1,462,336	−1,468,727
912810QE	US TREASURY BONDS	−1,298,352	−1,329,875
Total			−12,928,278

KEY POINTS

- The Markowitz mean-variance model is used for asset allocation and portfolio construction. The inputs required are the mean (expected return) and variance for each security that is a candidate for inclusion in the portfolio and the covariance or correlation between each pair of securities.
- While the insights provided by Markowitz mean-variance model are important, there are several issues that limit its application to the construction of bond portfolios.
- Tracking error, or active risk, is the standard deviation of a portfolio's return relative to the benchmark index.
- There are two types of tracking error—backward-looking tracking error and forward-looking tracking error.
- Backward-looking tracking error, also called historical tracking error and ex post tracking error, is calculated based on the actual performance of a portfolio relative to a benchmark index.
- Forward-looking tracking error is an estimate of how a portfolio will perform relative to a benchmark index in the future. Forward-looking tracking error, also called predicted tracking error and ex ante tracking error, is used in risk control and portfolio construction. The higher the forward-looking tracking error, the more the manager is pursuing a strategy in which the portfolio has a different risk profile than the benchmark and there is, therefore, greater active management.
- In the cell-approach to bond portfolio construction, the benchmark is divided into cells, which are the characteristics of the benchmark. The portfolio manager then picks one or more securities to either match or mismatch a cell depending on whether the strategy is a passive or active strategy. In the latter, the mismatch is based on the manager's views.
- There are complications in constructing a portfolio for a bond indexing strategy that are not faced by equity portfolio managers who pursue an equity indexing strategy.
- Multi-factor models (also called multi-factor risk models or factor models) are statistical models that are used to estimate a security's expected return based on the primary drivers (factors) affecting the return on securities.
- The systematic risk factors in a multi-factor model include yield curve risk, swap spread risk, volatility risk, government-related spread risk, corporate spread risk, and securitized spread risk.
- The risk exposure in a factor model is measured in terms of tracking error.
- Multi-factor models combined with an optimization model are used to construct a portfolio that minimizes tracking error subject to the constraints imposed by the manager (client-imposed or self-imposed) and embodying the views of the manager.

QUESTIONS

1. What is the major insight provided by the Markowitz framework in portfolio theory?

2. Explain whether you agree or disagree with the following two statements:
   a. "It is the covariance, not the correlation, that is important in the mean-variance model for portfolio selection."
   b. "In the mean-variance framework, the variance is lower the higher the correlation between the assets in the portfolio."

3. What are the two ways in which the Markowitz mean-variance framework has been used by investors?

4. What are the difficulties of implementing the Markowitz mean-variance framework in constructing portfolios?

5. What was the purpose for William Sharpe's development of the single index market model?

6. Why is the tracking error more important than portfolio variance of returns when a portfolio

manager's performance is measured versus a benchmark?

7. What is tracking error?

8. Explain why backward-looking tracking error has limitations for estimating a portfolio's future tracking error.

9. Why might one expect for a manager pursuing an active management strategy that the backward-looking tracking error at the end of the year will deviate from the forward-looking tracking error at the beginning of the year?

10. **a.** Compute the tracking error from the following information:

Month	Portfolio A's Return (%)	Benchmark Index Return (%)
Jan	2.15	1.65
Feb	0.89	−0.10
March	1.15	0.52
April	−0.47	−0.60
May	1.71	0.65
June	0.10	0.33
July	1.04	2.31
Aug	2.70	1.10
Sept	0.66	1.23
Oct	2.15	2.02
Nov	−1.38	−0.61
Dec	−0.59	−1.20

b. Would the tracking error computed in part **a** be a backward-looking or forward-looking tracking error?

c. Compare the tracking error found in part **a** to the tracking error found for Portfolios X and Y in Exhibits 23-1 and 23-2. What can you say about the investment management strategy pursued by this portfolio manager?

11. Assume the following:

> expected return for benchmark index = 7%
> forward-looking tracking error relative to
>   index = 200 basis points

Assuming that returns are normally distributed, complete the following table:

Number of Standard Deviations	Range for Portfolio Return	Probability
1		
2		
3		

12. At a meeting between a portfolio manager and a prospective client, the portfolio manager stated that his firm's bond investment strategy is a conservative one. The portfolio manager told the prospective client that he constructs a portfolio with a forward-looking tracking error that is typically between 250 and 300 basis points of a client-specified bond index. Explain why you agree or disagree with the portfolio manager's statement that the portfolio strategy is a conservative one.

13. What is meant by tracking error due to systematic risk factors?

14. You are reviewing a report by a portfolio manager that indicates that a fund's predicted (forward-looking) tracking error is 94.87 basis points. Furthermore, it is reported that the predicted tracking error due to systematic risk is 90 basis points and the predicted tracking error due to non-systematic risk is 30 basis points. Why doesn't the sum of these two tracking error components total up to 94.87 basis points?

15. What are the drawbacks of the cell-based approach for bond portfolio construction?

16. Why is it difficult to build a portfolio in pursuing a pure bond indexing strategy?

17. How can a multi-factor risk model be used to monitor and control portfolio risk?

18. How can a multi-factor risk model be used to rebalance a portfolio?

19. In a factor model, what is meant by isolated tracking error?

20. Following is a portfolio consisting of 50 bonds
    with a market value of $100 million as of
    April 29, 2011:

Identifier	Description	Position Amount ($)	Market Value ($)
003723AA	ABN AMRO BANK NV	1,449,636	1,422,596
00104BAC	AES EASTERN ENERGY	1,682,044	1,206,446
02051PAC	ALON REFINING KROTZ	592,304	630,655
02360XAL	AMERENENERGY GENERATING	707,484	737,343
101137AD	BOSTON SCIENTIFC	1,551,232	1,656,030
12527GAA	CF INDUSTRIES INC	1,328,707	1,499,778
165167BS	CHESAPEAKE ENERGY CORP	797,314	880,013
125896BG	CMS ENERGY	1,286,476	1,337,697
251591AY	DEVELOPERS DIVERS REALTY	646,714	644,344
FGB08000	FHLM Gold Guar Single F. 30yr	2,683,702	3,040,911
FGB07001	FHLM Gold Guar Single F. 30yr	690,235	780,262
FGB06402	FHLM Gold Guar Single F. 30yr	885,600	1,004,579
FGB07002	FHLM Gold Guar Single F. 30yr	3,751,831	4,235,068
FGB05403	FHLM Gold Guar Single F. 30yr	1,411,009	1,531,707
FGB06003	FHLM Gold Guar Single F. 30yr	1,387,727	1,537,027
FGB06004	FHLM Gold Guar Single F. 30yr	633,691	700,545
FGB05011	FHLM Gold Guar Single F. 30yr	651,568	690,585
FNA07098	FNMA Conventional Long T. 30yr	884,357	1,014,899
FNA08000	FNMA Conventional Long T. 30yr	1,643,844	1,883,297
FNA05402	FNMA Conventional Long T. 30yr	1,707,042	1,854,853
FNA06402	FNMA Conventional Long T. 30yr	1,155,221	1,311,433
FNA07002	FNMA Conventional Long T. 30yr	2,241,336	2,563,939
FNA05003	FNMA Conventional Long T. 30yr	641,485	684,085
FNA05403	FNMA Conventional Long T. 30yr	3,194,556	3,469,103
FNA06003	FNMA Conventional Long T. 30yr	1,548,573	1,715,870
FNA05010	FNMA Conventional Long T. 30yr	794,384	843,855
FNA05011	FNMA Conventional Long T. 30yr	1,105,717	1,173,465
GNB04411	GNMA II Single Family 30yr	2,391,899	2,509,580
381427AA	GOLDMAN SACHS CAPITAL II	3,123,435	2,761,546
45905CAA	INTERNATL BANK RECON DEV-GLOBA	1,151,247	1,200,080
45950KBJ	INTL FINANCE CORPORATION	1,227,607	1,198,808
46513E5Y	ISRAEL STATE OF-GLOBAL	1,797,220	1,911,761
500769BR	KREDIT FUER WIEDERAUFBAU-GLOBA	3,461,061	1,012,672
500769CH	KREDIT FUER WIEDERAUFBAU-GLOBA	3,430,115	941,429
582834AM	MEAD CORP	727,352	787,191
58551TAA	MELLON CAPITAL IV	3,326,734	3,102,915
651715AF	NEWPAGE CORP	6,414,006	1,603,501
665772CE	NORTHERN STATES PWR MINN	889,932	907,113
723787AG	PIONEER NATURAL RESOURCES	945,542	1,045,275
749685AQ	RPM INTERNATIONAL INC	591,159	642,823
797440BM	SAN DIEGO GAS & ELECTRIC	957,058	856,840
784635AM	SPX CORPORATION	708,877	766,621
91311QAD	UNITED UTILITES PLC	844,170	848,272
915436AF	UPM-KYMMENE CORP	655,540	648,265

Identifier	Description	Position Amount ($)	Market Value ($)
912810PW	US TREASURY BONDS	797,859	804,588
912810QA	US TREASURY BONDS	8,725,929	7,505,533
912810QK	US TREASURY BONDS	4,408,259	4,048,097
912828PA	US TREASURY NOTES	3,507,446	3,378,751
912828PF	US TREASURY NOTES	21,453,185	20,596,365
962166AV	WEYERHAEUSER CO	750,667	871,588

The benchmark for the manager who has constructed this portfolio is a composite index consisting one-third each of the Barclays Capital U.S. Treasury index, Barclays Capital U.S. Credit index, and Barclays Capital U.S. MBS index.

Asset Class	Portfolio (%)	Benchmark (%)
Total	100.0	100.0
Treasury	36.3	33.3
Government Related	6.3	6.8
Corporate Industrials	11.0	13.9
Corporate Utilities	5.9	2.9
Corporate Financials	7.9	9.7
MBS Agency	32.6	33.3

Analytics	Portfolio	Benchmark	Difference
Duration	6.87	5.37	1.50
Spread Duration	6.77	5.27	1.50
Convexity	0.47	0.00	0.47
Vega	−0.01	−0.03	0.02
Spread (bps)	355	55	300

Duration Contribution	Portfolio	Benchmark	Difference
Total	6.87	5.37	1.50
Treasury	3.62	1.78	1.84
Gov't Related	0.92	0.41	0.51
Corporate	1.10	1.74	−0.63
Securitized	1.23	1.45	−0.22

Risk Factor Categories	Isolated Risk/ Tracking Error
Yield curve risk	40.8
Swap spread risk	2.5
Volatility risk	2.8
Gov't-related spread risk	5.3
Corporate spread risk	30.6
Securitized spread risk	5.8

Risk Factor Categories	Isolated Risk/ Tracking Error
Total	33.2
Yield curve risk	23.4
Swap spread risk	0.2
Volatility risk	0.5
Gov't-related spread risk	0.0
Corporate spread risk	10.0
Securitized spread risk	−0.8

Volatility	Portfolio	Benchmark	Tracking Error
Systematic	141.9	117.4	37.9
Idiosyncratic	19.3	4.8	18.7
Total	143.2	117.5	42.3
Portfolio Beta	1.18		

Risk Factor Group	Isolated TEV	Contribution to TEV	Liquidation Effect on TEV	TEV Elasticity (%)
Total	42.3	42.3	−42.3	1.0
Systematic Risk	37.9	33.2	−22.4	0.8
Curve	40.8	23.4	−4.3	0.5
Swap Spreads	2.5	0.2	−0.1	0.0
Volatility	2.8	0.5	−0.4	0.0
Spread Gov't Related	5.3	0.0	0.3	0.0
Spread Corporate	30.6	10.0	0.8	0.2
Spread Securitized	5.8	−0.8	1.1	0.0
Idiosyncratic Risk	18.7	9.1	−4.2	0.2

Describe in detail the risk characteristics of this portfolio. Be sure to discuss where it seems like the manager is taking views on the market.

24

Liability-Driven Strategies

LEARNING OBJECTIVES

After reading this chapter, you will understand

- the types of liabilities that an institution may face

- the two important dimensions of a liability: the amount and timing of the payment

- why the same factors that affect the risk of financial assets also affect liabilities

- the goals of asset/liability management

- the difference between an institution's accounting surplus, regulatory surplus, and economic surplus

- how assets are handled for accounting purposes

- how to use the duration of assets and liabilities to calculate the sensitivity of the economic surplus of an institution when interest rates change

- what a liability-driven strategy is

- the risks associated with mismatching portfolio assets and liabilities

- what immunizing a portfolio is

- the basic principles of an immunization strategy and the role of duration in an immunization strategy

- the risks associated with immunizing a portfolio

- what a contingent immunization strategy is and the key factors in implementing such a strategy

- the two liability-driven strategies when there are multiple liabilities: multiperiod liability immunization and cash flow matching

- the advantages and disadvantages of a multiple liability immunization strategy versus a cash flow matching strategy

- how liability funding strategies can be extended to cases in which the liabilities are not known with certainty

- what an active/immunization combination strategy is

- liability-driven strategies for defined benefit pension plans

For many institutional investors, investment objectives are influenced by the nature of the institution's liabilities. Although investors are exposed to the same types of risks when they invest in financial assets, the nature of liabilities varies from institution to institution and is therefore the key factor in a portfolio manager's selection of the asset classes to include in a portfolio.

In this chapter, we begin with the basic principles underlying the management of assets relative to liabilities, popularly referred to as **asset/liability management**. We then describe several structured portfolio strategies, strategies that seek to match the performance of a predetermined benchmark. Bond portfolio indexing, discussed in Chapter 22, is an example of such a strategy. There the benchmark is based on a bond index but matching or outperformance of that benchmark provides no assurance that the liabilities of the sponsoring institution will be satisfied. In this chapter, we discuss **liability-driven strategies** that select assets so that cash flows will equal or exceed a client's liabilities. The client's liabilities, then, serve as the benchmark for portfolio performance. Specifically, when the liability is a single liability, an immunization strategy is employed. When there are multiple liabilities, there are two strategies to choose from: multiperiod immunization and cash flow matching. In the last section of this chapter, we discuss liability-driven strategies for defined benefit pension plans.

Basically these strategies focus on being able to satisfy liabilities in the future regardless of interest rate changes and issuer defaults. Default risk is minimized by investing in only high-quality bond issues. In the case of interest rate risk, the goal is to lock in prevailing rates. Because the objective is to lock in prevailing rates, the strategies discussed in this chapter were popular when the level of interest rates was higher than they are at the time of this writing. For example, in the 1980s major pension plans such as American Airlines and Chrysler Corporation followed this type of strategy when interest rates were 15%. Locking in very low interest rates is obviously unappealing and therefore the strategies discussed in this chapter are not popular as of this writing. However, as rates rise to more normal levels, the lessons learned from failing to lock in rates will make these strategies more popular in the future.

GENERAL PRINCIPLES OF ASSET/ LIABILITY MANAGEMENT

The nature of an institutional investor's liabilities will dictate the investment strategy it will request its portfolio manager to pursue. Depository institutions, for example, seek to generate income by the spread between the return that they earn on their assets and the cost of their funds. Consequently, banking is referred to as **spread banking**. Life insurance companies are in the spread business. Pension funds are not in the spread business, in that they themselves do not raise funds in the market. Sponsors of defined benefit pension plans seek to cover the cost of pension obligations at a minimum cost that is borne by the sponsor of the pension plan. Most investment companies face no explicit costs for the funds they acquire and must satisfy no specific liability obligations.

Classification of Liabilities

A **liability** is a cash outlay that must be made at a specific time to satisfy the contractual terms of an issued obligation. An institutional investor is concerned with both the amount and timing of liabilities because its assets must produce the cash to meet any payments it has promised to make in a timely way. In fact, liabilities are classified according to the degree of certainty of their amount and timing, as shown in Exhibit 24-1. The classification assumes that the holder of the obligation will not cancel it prior to an actual or projected payout date.

The descriptions of cash outlays as either known or uncertain are undoubtedly broad. When we refer to a cash outlay as being uncertain, we do not mean that it cannot be predicted. There are some liabilities for which the "law of large numbers" makes it easier to predict the timing and/or amount of cash outlays. This work is typically done by actuaries, but even actuaries have difficulty predicting natural catastrophes, such as floods and earthquakes.

Next, we illustrate each type of risk category. The important thing to note is that just like assets, there are risks associated with liabilities. Some of these risks are affected by the same factors that affect asset risks.

Type I Liabilities

A type I liability is one for which both the amount and timing of the liabilities are known with certainty. An example is a liability in which an institution knows that it must pay $50,000 six months from now. Banks and thrifts know the amount that they are committed to pay (principal plus interest) on the maturity date of a fixed-rate deposit, assuming that the depositor does not withdraw funds prior to the maturity date.

Type I liabilities, however, are not limited to depository institutions. A major product sold by life insurance companies is a **guaranteed investment contract**, popularly referred to as a **GIC**. The obligation of the life insurance company under this contract is that for a sum of money (called a **premium**), it will guarantee an interest rate up to some specified maturity date. For example, suppose that a life insurance company, for a premium of $10 million, issues a five-year GIC agreeing to pay 10% compounded annually. The

Exhibit 24-1	Classification of Liabilities of Institutional Investors	
Liability Type	**Amount of Cash Outlay**	**Timing of Cash Outlay**
I	Known	Known
II	Known	Uncertain
III	Uncertain	Known
IV	Uncertain	Uncertain

life insurance company knows that it must pay $16.11 million to the GIC policyholder in five years.[1]

Type II Liabilities

A type II liability is one for which the amount of cash outlay is known but the timing of the cash outlay is uncertain. The most obvious example of a type II liability is a life insurance policy. There are many types of life insurance policies, but the most basic type provides that for an annual premium, a life insurance company agrees to make a specified dollar payment to policy beneficiaries upon the death of the insured. Naturally, the timing of the insured's death is uncertain.

Type III Liabilities

A type III liability is one for which the timing of the cash outlay is known but the amount is uncertain. A two-year floating-rate CD in which the interest rate resets quarterly based on a market interest rate is an example. Not surprisingly, there are also floating-rate GICs; these also fall into the type III liabilities category.

Type IV Liabilities

A type IV liability is one in which there is uncertainty as to both the amount and timing of the cash outlay. There are numerous insurance products and pension obligations in this category. Probably the most obvious examples are automobile and home insurance policies issued by property and casualty insurance companies. When, and if, a payment will have to be made to the policyholder is uncertain. Whenever damage is done to an insured asset, the amount of the payment that must be made is uncertain.

The liabilities of pension plans can also be type IV liabilities. In defined benefit plans, retirement benefits depend on the participant's income for a specified number of years before retirement and the total number of years the participant worked. This will affect the amount of the cash outlay. The timing of the cash outlay depends on when the employee elects to retire and whether the employee remains with the sponsoring plan until retirement. Moreover, both the amount and the timing will depend on how the employee elects to have payments made—over only the employee's life or those of the employee and spouse.

Liquidity Concerns

Because of uncertainty about the timing and/or the amount of the cash outlays, an institution must be prepared to have sufficient cash to satisfy its obligations. Also keep in mind that the entity that holds the obligation against the institution may have the right to change the nature of the obligation, perhaps incurring a penalty. For example, in the case of a CD, the depositor may request the withdrawal of funds prior to the maturity date. Typically, the deposit-accepting institution will grant this request but assess an early-withdrawal penalty. In the case of certain types of investment companies, shareholders have the right to redeem their shares at any time. These rights add to the uncertainty of the liability from the point of view of the financial institution.

Similarly, some life insurance products have a cash surrender value. This means that at specified dates, the policyholder can exchange the policy for a lump-sum payment.

---

[1] This amount is determined as follows: $\$10,000,000 \times (1.10)^5$.

Typically, the lump-sum payment will penalize the policyholder for turning in the policy. Some life insurance products have a loan value, which means that the policyholder has the right to borrow against the cash value of the policy. Both factors increase the uncertainty of the insurance company's liabilities.

In addition to uncertainty about the timing and amount of the cash outlays and the potential for the depositor or policyholder to withdraw cash early or borrow against a policy, an institution has to be concerned with a possible reduction in cash inflows. In the case of a depository institution, this means the inability to obtain deposits. For insurance companies, it means reduced premiums because of the cancellation of policies. For certain types of investment companies, it means not being able to find new buyers for shares.

Surplus Management

The two goals of a financial institution are (1) to earn an adequate return on funds invested, and (2) to maintain a comfortable surplus of assets beyond liabilities. The task of managing funds of a financial institution to accomplish these goals is referred to as **asset/ liability management** or **surplus management**. This task involves a trade-off between controlling the risk of a decline in the surplus and taking on acceptable risks in order to earn an adequate return on the funds invested. With respect to the risks, the manager must consider the risks of both the assets and the liabilities.

Institutions may calculate three types of surpluses: economic, accounting, and regulatory. The method of valuing assets and liabilities greatly affects the apparent health of a financial institution. Unrealistic valuation, although allowable under accounting procedures and regulations, is not sound investment practice.

Economic Surplus

The **economic surplus** of any entity is the difference between the market value of all its assets and the market value of its liabilities; that is,

economic surplus = market value of assets − market value of liabilities

Although the concept of a market value of assets may not seem unusual, one might ask: What is the market value of liabilities? This value is simply the present value of the liabilities, in which the liabilities are discounted at an appropriate interest rate. A rise in interest rates will therefore decrease the present value or market value of the liabilities; a decrease in interest rates will increase the present value or market value of liabilities. Thus, the economic surplus can be expressed as

economic surplus = market value of assets − present value of liabilities

For example, consider an institution that has a portfolio consisting only of bonds and liabilities. Let's look at what happens to the economic surplus if interest rates rise. This will cause the bonds to decline in value, but it will also cause the liabilities to decline in value. Both the assets and liabilities decline so the economic surplus can either increase, decrease, or not change. The net effect depends on the relative interest-rate sensitivity of the assets compared to the liabilities. Because duration is a measure of the responsiveness of cash flows to changes in interest rates, a duration can be calculated for liabilities in the same way in which it is calculated for assets. Thus, the duration of liabilities measures their responsiveness to a change in interest rates.

If the duration of the assets is greater than the duration of the liabilities, the economic surplus will increase if interest rates fall. For example, suppose that the current market value of a portfolio of assets is equal to $100 million, and the present value of liabilities is $90 million. Then the economic surplus is $10 million. Suppose that the duration of the assets is 5 and the duration of the liabilities is 3. Consider the following two scenarios:

Scenario 1: Interest rates decline by 100 basis points. Because the duration of the assets is 5, the market value of the assets will increase by approximately 5% or $5 million (5% × $100 million) to $105 million. The liabilities will also increase. If the duration of the liabilities is assumed to be 3, the present value of the liabilities will increase by $2.7 million (3% × $90 million) to $92.7 million. Thus, the surplus increased from $10 million to $12.3 million.

Scenario 2: Interest rates rise by 100 basis points. Because the duration of the assets is 5, the market value of the assets will decrease by approximately 5%, to $95 million. The liabilities will also decrease. If the duration of the liabilities is 3, the present value of the liabilities will decrease by $2.7 million to $87.3 million. The surplus is then reduced to $7.7 million from $10 million.

The net effect on the surplus depends on the duration or interest-rate sensitivity of both the assets and liabilities, so it is imperative that portfolio managers be able to measure this sensitivity for all assets and liabilities accurately.

Accounting Surplus

Institutional investors must prepare periodic financial statements. These financial statements must be prepared in accordance with **generally accepted accounting principles** (GAAP). Thus, the assets and liabilities reported are based on GAAP accounting. The accounting treatment for assets is governed by a relatively new accounting requirement, Statement of Financial Accounting Standards No. 115, more popularly referred to as FASB 115.[2] However, it does not deal with the accounting treatment for liabilities.

With respect to the financial reporting of assets, there are three possible methods for reporting: (1) amortized cost or historical cost, (2) market value, or (3) the lower of cost or market value. Despite the fact that the real cash flow is the same regardless of the accounting treatment, there can be substantial differences in the financial statements using these three methods.

In the **amortized cost method**, the value reported in the balance sheet reflects an adjustment to the acquisition cost for debt securities purchased at a discount or premium from their maturity value. This method is sometimes referred to as **book value accounting**. In the **market value accounting method**, the balance sheet reported value of an asset is its market value. When an asset is reported in the financial statements of an institution at its market value, it is said to be "marked to market." Finally, the **lower of cost** or **market method** requires comparison of market value to the amortized cost, with

---

[2] FASB 115 was issued in May 1993 and became effective with fiscal years beginning after December 15, 1993. On April 9, 2009, the FASB released FAS 115-2 that amends GAAP for available-for-sale and held-to-maturity debt securities. The amended FAS deals with the impairment of debt securities. Impairment is the amount by which the fair value of the security is less than its amortized cost basis.

the lower of these two values reported in the balance sheet. The value reported cannot exceed the amortized cost.

FASB 115 specifies which of these three methods must be followed for assets. Specifically, the accounting treatment required for a security depends on how the security is classified. There are three classifications of investment accounts: (1) held to maturity, (2) available for sale, and (3) trading. The definition of each account is set forth in FASB 115, and we summarize each next.

The **held-to-maturity account** includes assets that the institution plans to hold until they mature. Obviously, the assets classified in this account cannot be common stock because they have no maturity. For all assets in the held-to-maturity account, the amortized cost method must be used.

An asset is classified as in the **available-for-sale account** if the institution does not have the ability to hold the asset to maturity or intends to sell it. An asset that is acquired for the purpose of earning a short-term trading profit from market movements is classified in the **trading account.** For all assets in the available-for-sale and trading accounts, market value accounting is used. Thus, these two accounts more accurately reflect the economic condition of the assets held by the institution. Exhibit 24-2 summarizes the accounting treatment of assets as set forth by FASB 115.

When financial statements are prepared, the change in the value of assets must be accounted for. An unrealized gain or loss occurs when the asset's value has changed but the gain or loss is not realized because the asset is not sold. For example, if an asset has a market value of $100 at the beginning of an accounting period and is held in the portfolio at the end of the accounting period with a market value of $110, the unrealized gain is $10.

Any unrealized gain or loss affects the accounting surplus. Specifically, an unrealized gain increases the surplus, and an unrealized loss reduces the accounting surplus. The unrealized gain or loss may or may not affect the reported earnings.

Under FASB 115, the accounting treatment for any unrealized gain or loss depends on the account in which the asset is classified. Specifically, any unrealized gain or loss is ignored for assets in the held-to-maturity account. Thus, for assets in this account there is no effect on reported earnings or the accounting surplus. For the other two accounts, any unrealized gain or loss affects the accounting surplus as described previously. However, there is a difference as to how reported earnings are affected. For assets classified in the available-for-sale account, unrealized gains or losses are not included in reported earnings; in contrast, for assets classified in the trading account, any gains or losses are included in reported earnings. These provisions are summarized in Exhibit 24-2.

Exhibit 24-2 Summary of Key Provisions of FASB 115

Account Classification	Accounting Method for Assets	Will Affect Surplus	Will Affect Reported Earnings
Held to maturity	Amortized cost	No	No
Available for sale	Market value	Yes	No
Trading	Market value	Yes	Yes

Regulatory Surplus

Institutional investors that are regulated at the state or federal levels must provide financial reports to regulators based on regulatory accounting principles (RAP). RAP accounting for a regulated institution need not use the same rules as set forth by FASB 115 (i.e., GAAP accounting). Liabilities may or may not be reported at their present value, depending on the type of institution and the type of liability. The surplus as measured using RAP accounting, called **regulatory surplus**, may, as in the case of accounting surplus, differ materially from economic surplus.

IMMUNIZATION OF A PORTFOLIO TO SATISFY A SINGLE LIABILITY

In the balance of this chapter, we focus on liability-driven strategies. Tens of billions of dollars in pension monies went into these liability-driven strategies in the early and mid-1980s when interest rates were high because of the strong incentive to reduce pension costs by locking in these rates. The insurance industry has also made widespread use of these strategies for their fixed-liability insurance products.

We begin with a strategy referred to as an **immunization strategy.** The person generally credited with pioneering this strategy, F.M. Reddington, defined immunization in 1952 as "the investment of the assets in such a way that the existing business is immune to a general change in the rate of interest."[3]

To comprehend the basic principles underlying the immunization of a portfolio against interest-rate changes so as to satisfy a single liability, consider the situation faced by a life insurance company that sells a guaranteed investment contract (GIC). Under this policy, for a lump-sum payment, a life insurance company guarantees that specified dollars will be paid to the policyholder at a specified future date. Or, equivalently, the life insurance company guarantees a specified rate of return on the payment. For example, suppose that a life insurance company sells a GIC that guarantees an interest rate of 6.25% every six months (12.5% on a bond-equivalent yield basis) for 5.5 years (11 six-month periods). Also suppose that the payment made by the policyholder is $8,820,262. Then, the value that the life insurance company has guaranteed the policyholder 5.5 years from now is

$$\$8,820,262(1.0625)^{11} = \$17,183,033$$

When investing the $8,820,262, the target accumulated value for the portfolio manager of the life insurance company is $17,183,033 after 5.5 years, which is the same as a target yield of 12.5% on a bond-equivalent basis.[4]

Suppose that the portfolio manager buys $8,820,262 par value of a bond selling at par with a 12.5% yield to maturity that matures in 5.5 years. Will the portfolio manager be assured of realizing the target yield of 12.5% or, equivalently, a target accumulated value of $17,183,033? As we explained in Chapter 3, the portfolio manager will realize a 12.5% yield only if the coupon interest payments can be reinvested at 6.25% every six months. That is, the accumulated value will depend on the reinvestment rate.

---

[3] The theory of immunization was first set forth in F. M. Reddington, "Review of the Principle of Life Office Valuation," *Journal of the Institute of Actuaries*, 1952, pp. 286–340.

[4] Actually, the life insurance company will not guarantee the interest rate that it expects to earn, but a lower rate. The spread between the interest rate earned and the interest rate it guarantees is the return for the risk of not achieving the target return.

Exhibit 24-3   Accumulated Value and Total Return after 5.5 Years: 5.5-Year 12.5% Bond Selling to Yield 12.5%

Investment horizon (years): 5.5
Coupon rate: 0.125
Maturity (years): 5.5
Yield to maturity: 0.125
Price: 100
Par value purchased: $8,820,262
Purchase price: $8,820,262
Target accumulated value: $17,183,033

| | | | After 5.5 Years | | |
New Yield[a]	Coupon Interest	Interest on Interest	Price of Bond[b]	Accumulated Value	Total Return
0.160	$6,063,930	$3,112,167	$8,820,262	$17,996,360	0.1340
0.155	6,063,930	2,990,716	8,820,262	17,874,908	0.1326
0.145	6,063,930	2,753,177	8,820,262	17,637,369	0.1300
0.140	6,063,930	2,647,037	8,820,262	17,521,230	0.1288
0.135	6,063,930	2,522,618	8,820,262	17,406,810	0.1275
0.130	6,063,930	2,409,984	8,820,262	17,294,086	0.1262
0.125	6,063,930	2,298,840	8,820,262	17,183,033	0.1250
0.120	6,063,930	2,189,433	8,820,262	17,073,625	0.1238
0.115	6,063,930	2,081,648	8,820,262	16,965,840	0.1225
0.110	6,063,930	1,975,462	8,820,262	16,859,654	0.1213
0.105	6,063,930	1,870,852	8,820,262	16,755,044	0.1201
0.100	6,063,930	1,767,794	8,820,262	16,651,986	0.1189
0.095	6,063,930	1,666,266	8,820,262	16,550,458	0.1178
0.090	6,063,930	1,566,246	8,820,262	16,450,438	0.1166
0.085	6,063,930	1,467,712	8,820,262	16,351,904	0.1154
0.080	6,063,930	1,370,642	8,820,262	16,254,834	0.1143
0.075	6,063,930	1,275,014	8,820,262	16,159,206	0.1132
0.070	6,063,930	1,180,808	8,820,262	16,065,000	0.1120
0.065	6,063,930	1,088,003	8,820,262	15,972,195	0.1109
0.060	6,063,930	996,577	8,820,262	15,880,769	0.1098
0.055	6,063,930	906,511	8,820,262	15,790,703	0.1087
0.050	6,063,930	817,785	8,820,262	15,701,977	0.1077

[a]Immediate change in yield.
[b]Maturity value.

To demonstrate this, we will suppose that immediately after investing the $8,820,262 in the 12.5% coupon 5.5-year maturity bond, yields in the market change and stay at the new level for the remainder of the 5.5 years. Exhibit 24-3 illustrates what happens at the end of 5.5 years. The first column shows the new yield level. The second column shows the total coupon interest payments (which remains constant). The third column gives the interest on interest over the entire 5.5 years if the coupon interest payments are reinvested at the new yield level shown in the first column. The price of the bond at the end of 5.5 years shown in the fourth column is the par value. The fifth column is the accumulated value from all three sources: coupon interest, interest on interest, and bond price. The total return on a bond-equivalent yield basis is shown in the last column, according to the formula[5]

$$2\left[\left(\frac{\text{accumulated value}}{\$8,820,262}\right)^{1/11} - 1\right]$$

If yields do not change, so that the coupon payments can be reinvested at 12.5% (6.25% every six months), the portfolio manager will achieve the target accumulated value. If market yields rise, an accumulated value (total return) higher than the target accumulated value (target yield) will be achieved. This is because the coupon interest payments can be reinvested at a higher rate than the initial yield to maturity. Contrast this with what happens when the yield declines. The accumulated value (total return) will be less than the target accumulated value (target yield). *Therefore, investing in a coupon bond with a yield to maturity equal to the target yield and a maturity equal to the investment horizon does not assure that the target accumulated value will be achieved.*

Suppose that instead of investing in a bond maturing in 5.5 years the portfolio manager invests in a 15-year bond with a coupon rate of 12.5% that is selling at par to yield 12.5%. Exhibit 24-4 presents the accumulated value and total return if the market yield changes immediately after the bond is purchased and remains at the new yield level. The fourth column of the table is the market price of a 12.5% coupon 9.5-year bond (because 5.5 years have passed), assuming the market yields shown in the first column. If the market yield increases, the portfolio will fail to achieve the target accumulated value; the opposite will be true if the market yield decreases: The accumulated value (total return) will exceed the target accumulated value (target yield).

The reason for this result can be seen Exhibit 24-5, which summarizes the change in interest on interest and the change in price resulting from a change in the market yield. For example, if the market yield rises instantaneously by 200 basis points, from 12.5% to 14.5%, interest on interest will be $454,336 greater; however, the market price of the bond will decrease by $894,781. The net effect is that the accumulated value will be $440,445 less than the target accumulated value. The reverse will be true if the market yield decreases. The change in the price of the bond will more than offset the decline in the interest on interest, resulting in an accumulated value that exceeds the target accumulated value.

Now we can see what is happening to the accumulated value. There is a trade-off between interest rate (or price) risk and reinvestment risk. For this 15-year bond, the target accumulated value will be realized only if the market yield does not increase.

Because neither a coupon bond with the same maturity nor a bond with a longer maturity ensures realization of the target accumulated value, perhaps a bond with a

---

[5] The procedure for calculating the total return is given in Chapter 3.

Exhibit 24-4   Accumulated Value and Total Return After 5.5 Years: 15-Year 12.5% Bond Selling to Yield 12.5%

Investment horizon (years): 5.5
Coupon rate: 0.1250
Maturity (years): 15
Yield to maturity: 0.1250
Price: 100
Par value purchased: $8,820,262
Purchase price: $8,820,262
Target accumulated value: $17,183,033

			After 5.5 Years		
New Yield[a]	Coupon Interest	Interest on Interest	Price of Bond	Accumulated Value	Total Return
0.160	$6,063,930	$3,112,167	$7,337,902	$16,513,999	0.1173
0.155	6,063,930	2,990,716	7,526,488	16,581,134	0.1181
0.145	6,063,930	2,753,177	7,925,481	16,742,588	0.1200
0.140	6,063,930	2,637,037	8,136,542	16,837,509	0.1211
0.135	6,063,930	2,522,618	8,355,777	16,942,325	0.1223
0.130	6,063,930	2,409,984	8,583,555	17,057,379	0.1236
0.125	6,063,930	2,298,840	8,820,262	17,183,032	0.1250
0.120	6,063,930	2,189,433	9,066,306	17,319,699	0.1265
0.115	6,063,930	2,081,648	9,322,113	17,467,691	0.1282
0.110	6,063,930	1,975,462	9,588,131	17,627,523	0.1299
0.105	6,063,930	1,870,852	9,864,831	17,799,613	0.1318
0.100	6,063,930	1,767,794	10,152,708	17,984,432	0.1338
0.095	6,063,930	1,666,266	10,452,281	18,182,477	0.1359
0.090	6,063,930	1,566,246	10,764,095	18,394,271	0.1382
0.085	6,063,930	1,467,712	11,088,723	18,620,365	0.1406
0.080	6,063,930	1,370,642	11,462,770	18,897,342	0.1431
0.075	6,063,930	1,275,014	11,778,867	19,117,811	0.1457
0.070	6,063,930	1,180,808	12,145,682	19,390,420	0.1485
0.065	6,063,930	1,088,003	12,527,914	19,679,847	0.1514
0.060	6,063,930	996,577	12,926,301	19,986,808	0.1544
0.055	6,063,930	906,511	13,341,617	20,312,058	0.1576
0.050	6,063,930	817,785	13,774,677	20,656,392	0.1609

[a]Immediate change in yield.

maturity shorter than 5.5 years will. Consider a 12.5% bond with six months remaining to maturity selling at par. Exhibit 24-6 shows the accumulated value and total return over the 5.5-year investment horizon. The second column shows the accumulated value after six months. The third column shows the value that is accumulated after 5.5 years

Exhibit 24-5	Change in Interest on Interest and Price Due to Interest Rate Change after 5.5 Years: 15-Year 12.5% Bond Selling to Yield 12.5%		
New Yield	Change in Interest on Interest	Change in Price	Total Change in Accumulated Value
0.160	$813,327	−$1,482,360	−$669,033
0.155	692,875	−1,293,774	−600,899
0.145	454,336	−894,781	−440,445
0.140	338,197	−683,720	−345,523
0.135	223,778	−464,485	−240,707
0.130	111,054	−236,707	−125,653
0.125	0	0	0
0.120	−109,407	246,044	136,637
0.115	−217,192	501,851	284,659
0.110	−323,378	767,869	444,491
0.105	−427,989	1,044,569	616,580
0.100	−531,046	1,332,446	801,400
0.095	−632,574	1,632,019	999,445
0.090	−732,594	1,943,833	1,211,239
0.085	−831,128	2,268,461	1,437,333
0.080	−928,198	2,606,508	1,678,310
0.075	−1,023,086	2,958,605	1,934,779
0.070	−1,118,032	3,325,420	2,207,388
0.065	−1,210,838	3,707,652	2,496,814
0.060	−1,302,263	4,106,039	2,803,776
0.055	−1,392,329	4,521,355	3,129,026
0.050	−1,481,055	4,954,415	3,473,360

by reinvesting the value accumulated after six months at the yield shown in the first column; that is,

$$\$9{,}371{,}528\left(1 + \frac{\text{new yield}}{2}\right)^2$$

By investing in this six-month bond, the portfolio manager incurs no interest-rate risk, although there is reinvestment risk. The target accumulated value will be achieved only if the market yield remains at 12.5% or rises. Once again, the portfolio manager is not assured of achieving the target accumulated value.

If we assume there is a one-time instantaneous change in the market yield, is there a coupon bond that the portfolio manager can purchase to assure the target accumulated value whether the market yield rises or falls? The portfolio manager should look for a coupon bond so that however the market yield changes, the change in the interest on interest will be offset by the change in the price.

Exhibit 24-6	Accumulated Value and Total Return: Six-Month, 12.5% Bond Selling to Yield 12.5%

Investment horizon (years): 5.5
Coupon rate: 0.125
Maturity (years): 0.5
Yield to maturity: 0.125
Price: 100
Par value purchased: $8,820,262
Purchase price: $8,820,262
Target accumulated value: $17,183,033

		After 5.5 Years	
New Yield[a]	After 6 Months	Accumulated Value	Total Return
0.160	$9,371,528	$20,232,427	0.1568
0.155	9,371,528	19,768,932	0.1523
0.145	9,371,528	18,870,501	0.1432
0.140	9,371,528	18,435,215	0.1386
0.135	9,371,528	18,008,986	0.1341
0.130	9,371,528	17,591,647	0.1295
0.125	9,371,528	17,183,033	0.1250
0.120	9,371,528	16,782,980	0.1205
0.115	9,371,528	16,391,330	0.1159
0.110	9,371,528	16,007,924	0.1114
0.105	9,371,528	15,632,609	0.1068
0.100	9,371,528	15,265,232	0.1023
0.095	9,371,528	14,905,644	0.0977
0.090	9,371,528	14,553,697	0.0932
0.085	9,371,528	14,209,247	0.0886
0.080	9,371,528	13,872,151	0.0841
0.075	9,371,528	13,542,270	0.0795
0.070	9,371,528	13,219,466	0.0749
0.065	9,371,528	12,903,604	0.0704
0.060	9,371,528	12,594,550	0.0658
0.055	9,371,528	12,292,175	0.0613
0.050	9,371,528	11,996,349	0.0567

[a]Immediate change in yield.

Consider, for example, an eight-year 10.125% coupon bond selling at 88.20262 to yield 12.5%. Suppose that $10,000,000 of par value of this bond is purchased for $8,820,262. Exhibit 24-7 provides the same information for this bond as Exhibits 24-3 and 24-4 did for the previous bonds. Looking at the last two columns, we see that the accumulated value and the total return are never less than the target accumulated value and the target yield.

Exhibit 24-7	Accumulated Value and Total Return: Eight-Year 10.125% Bond Selling to Yield 12.5%

Investment horizon (years): 5.5
Coupon rate: 0.10125
Maturity (years): 8
Yield to maturity: 0.125
Price: 88.20262
Par value purchased: $10,000,000
Purchase price: $8,820,262
Target accumulated value: $17,183,033

		After 5.5 Years			
New Yield[a]	Coupon Interest	Interest on Interest	Price of Bond	Accumulated Value	Total Return
0.160	$5,568,750	$2,858,028	$8,827,141	$17,253,919	0.1258
0.155	5,568,750	2,746,494	8,919,852	17,235,096	0.1256
0.145	5,568,750	2,528,352	9,109,054	17,206,156	0.1253
0.140	5,568,750	2,421,697	9,205,587	17,196,034	0.1251
0.135	5,568,750	2,316,621	9,303,435	17,188,806	0.1251
0.130	5,568,750	2,213,102	9,402,621	17,184,473	0.1250
0.125	5,568,750	2,111,117	9,503,166	17,183,033	0.1250
0.120	5,568,750	2,010,644	9,605,091	17,184,485	0.1250
0.115	5,568,750	1,911,661	9,708,420	17,188,831	0.1251
0.110	5,568,750	1,814,146	9,813,175	17,196,071	0.1251
0.105	5,568,750	1,718,078	9,919,380	17,206,208	0.1253
0.100	5,568,750	1,623,436	10,027,059	17,219,245	0.1254
0.095	5,568,750	1,530,199	10,136,236	17,235,185	0.1256
0.090	5,568,750	1,438,347	10,246,936	17,254,033	0.1258
0.085	5,568,750	1,347,859	10,359,184	17,275,793	0.1260
0.080	5,568,750	1,258,715	10,473,006	17,300,471	0.1263
0.075	5,568,750	1,170,897	10,588,428	17,328,075	0.1266
0.070	5,568,750	1,084,383	10,705,477	17,358,610	0.1270
0.065	5,568,750	999,156	10,824,180	17,392,086	0.1273
0.060	5,568,750	915,197	10,944,565	17,428,512	0.1277
0.055	5,568,750	832,486	11,066,660	17,467,896	0.1282
0.050	5,568,750	751,005	11,190,494	17,510,249	0.1268

[a]Immediate change in yield.

Thus, the target accumulated value is assured regardless of what happens to the market yield. Exhibit 24-8 shows why. When the market yield rises, the change in the interest on interest more than offsets the decline in price. When the market yield declines, the increase in price exceeds the decline in interest on interest.

Exhibit 24-8　Change in Interest on Interest and Price Due to Interest Rate Change after 5.5 Years: Eight-Year 10.125% Bond Selling to Yield 12.5%

New Yield	Change in Interest on Interest	Change in Price	Total Change in Accumulated Value
0.160	$746,911	−$676,024	$70,887
0.155	635,377	−583,314	52,063
0.145	417,235	−394,112	23,123
0.140	310,580	−297,579	13,001
0.135	205,504	−199,730	5,774
0.130	101,985	−100,544	1,441
0.125	0	0	0
0.120	−100,473	101,925	1,452
0.115	−199,456	205,254	5,798
0.110	−296,971	310,010	13,039
0.105	−393,039	416,215	23,176
0.100	−487,681	523,894	36,213
0.095	−580,918	633,071	52,153
0.090	−672,770	743,771	71,001
0.085	−763,258	856,019	92,761
0.080	−852,402	969,841	117,439
0.075	−940,221	1,085,263	145,042
0.070	−1,026,734	1,202,311	175,577
0.065	−1,111,961	1,321,014	209,053
0.060	−1,195,921	1,441,399	245,478
0.055	−1,278,632	1,563,494	284,862
0.050	−1,360,112	1,687,328	327,216

Exhibit 24-9　Modified Durations of Selected Bonds

Bond	Modified Duration
5.5-year 12.5% coupon, selling at par	3.90
15-year 12.5% coupon, selling at par	6.70
6-month 12.5% coupon, selling at par	0.48
8-year 10.125% coupon, selling for 88.20262	5.18

Let's look at the characteristic of this bond that seems to assure that the target accumulated value will be realized regardless of how the market yield changes. The duration for each of the four bonds we have considered is shown in Exhibit 24-9. Recall from our earlier discussion of duration in this book that there is modified duration and effective duration. Because the bonds in our illustration are all assumed to be option-free bonds, modified duration is used. However, when portfolios include securities with embedded options, the effective duration is used. Throughout the remainder of the discussion in this chapter, when we refer to *duration* we mean the appropriate measure of duration given the types of securities in the portfolio. For most institutional portfolios, this will typically be effective duration.

Given the duration for each bond as shown in Exhibit 24-9, let's compare them to the duration of the liability. This is a simple liability because there is only one cash payment at the maturity date, and it is assumed that there is no embedded option in the liability. For an asset or a liability with only one cash flow, the duration is equal to the number of years to maturity divided by one plus one-half the yield. If the number of years to maturity is 5.5 years and the yield for a 5.5-year liability is 12.5%, then the duration is 5.5 divided by 1 plus 0.0625, or 5.18. We can see from Exhibit 24-9 that the duration of the eight-year 10.125% coupon issue has the same duration as the liability. This is the bond that assured immunization in our illustration.

This equality of the duration of the asset and the duration of the liability is the key to immunization. Generalizing this observation to bond portfolios from individual bonds, the key is: *To immunize a portfolio's target accumulated value (target yield), a portfolio manager must construct a bond portfolio such that (1) the duration of the portfolio is equal to the duration of the liability, and (2) the present value of the cash flow from the portfolio equals to the present value of the future liability.*

Often in discussions of immunization, the condition for immunization is cast in terms of Macaulay duration, a concept discussed in Chapter 4. The reason for the focus on Macaulay duration is that the bonds and liabilities are assumed to be option-free so that modified duration is appropriate and, therefore, from the relationship between modified duration and Macaulay duration, the analysis can be cast in terms of the latter.

Rebalancing an Immunized Portfolio

Our illustrations of the principles underlying immunization assume a one-time instantaneous change in the market yield. In practice, the market yield will fluctuate over the investment horizon. As a result, the duration of the portfolio will change as the market yield changes. In addition, the duration will change simply because of the passage of time.

Even in the face of changing market yields, a portfolio can be immunized if it is rebalanced so that its duration is equal to the duration of the liability's remaining time. For example, if the liability is initially 5.5 years, the initial portfolio should have a duration of 5.5 years. After six months, the liability will be five years, but the duration of the portfolio will probably be different from five years. This is because duration depends on the remaining time to maturity and the new level of yields, and there is no reason why the change in these two values should reduce the duration by exactly six months. Thus, the portfolio must be rebalanced so that its duration is five years. Six months later, the portfolio must be rebalanced again so that its duration will equal 4.5 years. And so on.

How often should the portfolio be rebalanced to adjust its duration? On the one hand, more frequent rebalancing increases transactions costs, thereby reducing the likelihood of achieving the target yield. On the other hand, less frequent rebalancing will result in the duration wandering from the target duration, which will also reduce the likelihood of achieving the target yield. Thus, the portfolio manager faces a trade-off: Some transaction costs must be accepted to prevent the duration from wandering too far from its target, but some maladjustment in the duration must be accepted or transaction costs will become prohibitively high.

Immunization Risk

The sufficient condition for the immunization of a single liability is that the duration of the portfolio be equal to the duration of the liability. However, a portfolio will be immunized against interest-rate changes only if the yield curve is flat and any changes in the yield curve are parallel changes (i.e., interest rates move either up or down by the same number of basis points for all maturities). Recall from Chapter 4 that duration is a measure of price volatility for parallel shifts in the yield curve. If there is a change in interest rates that does not correspond to this shape-preserving shift, matching the portfolio's duration to the liability's duration will not assure immunization. That is, the target yield will no longer be the minimum total return for the portfolio.

As there are many duration-matched portfolios that can be constructed to immunize a liability, is it possible to construct one that has the lowest risk of not realizing the target yield? That is, in light of the uncertain way in which the yield curve may shift, is it possible to develop a criterion for minimizing the risk that a duration-matched portfolio will not be immunized? Fong and Vasicek[6] and Bierwag, Kaufman, and Toevs[7] explore this question. Exhibit 24-10 illustrates how to minimize immunization risk.

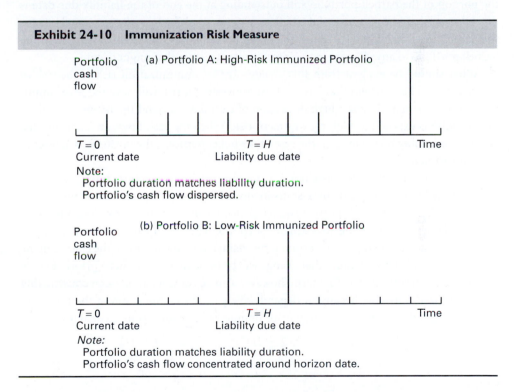

Exhibit 24-10   Immunization Risk Measure

(a) Portfolio A: High-Risk Immunized Portfolio

Portfolio cash flow

$T = 0$
Current date

$T = H$
Liability due date

Time

Note:
Portfolio duration matches liability duration.
Portfolio's cash flow dispersed.

(b) Portfolio B: Low-Risk Immunized Portfolio

Portfolio cash flow

$T = 0$
Current date

$T = H$
Liability due date

Time

Note:
Portfolio duration matches liability duration.
Portfolio's cash flow concentrated around horizon date.

[6] H. Gifford Fong and Oldrich Vasicek, "A Risk Minimizing Strategy for Multiple Liability Immunization," *Journal of Finance*, December 1984, pp. 1541–1546.
[7] G.O. Bierwag, George K. Kaufman, and Alden Toevs, "Bond Immunization and Stochastic Process Risk," working paper, Center for Capital Market Research, University of Oregon, July 1981.

The spikes in the two panels of Exhibit 24-10 represent actual portfolio cash flows. The taller spikes depict the actual cash flows generated by securities that have matured, and the smaller spikes represent coupon payments. Portfolios A and B are both composed of two bonds with a portfolio's duration equal to the liability's duration. Portfolio A is, in effect, a barbell portfolio, one composed of short and long maturities and interim coupon payments. For Portfolio B, the two bonds mature very close to the date the liability is due, and the coupon payments are nominal over the investment horizon. Portfolio B is, in effect, a bullet portfolio.

We can now see why the barbell portfolio should be riskier than the bullet portfolio. Assume that both portfolios have durations equal to the liability's duration, so that each is immune to parallel changes in the yield curve. Suppose that the yield curve changes in a nonparallel way so that short-term interest rates decline while long-term interest rates increase. Both portfolios would then produce an accumulated value at the liability due date that is below the target accumulated value because they would experience a capital loss owing to the higher long-term interest rate and less interest on interest resulting from the lower reinvestment rate when the short-term interest rate declines.

The accumulated value for the barbell portfolio at the liability due date, however, would miss the target accumulated value by more than the bullet portfolio. There are two reasons for this. First, the lower reinvestment rates are experienced on the barbell portfolio for larger interim cash flows over a longer time period than on the bullet portfolio. Second, the portion of the barbell portfolio still outstanding at the end of the liability due date is much longer than the maturity of the bullet portfolio, resulting in a greater capital loss for the barbell than for the bullet. Thus, the bullet portfolio has less risk exposure than the barbell portfolio to any changes in the interest-rate structure that might occur.

What should be evident from this analysis is that immunization risk is the risk of reinvestment. The portfolio that has the least reinvestment risk will have the least immunization risk. When there is a high dispersion of cash flows around the liability due date, the portfolio is exposed to high reinvestment risk. When the cash flows are concentrated around the liability due date, as in the case of the bullet portfolio, the portfolio is subject to low reinvestment risk.

Fong and Vasicek have developed a measure of immunization risk. They have demonstrated that if the yield curve shifts in any arbitrary way, the relative change in the portfolio value will depend on the product of two terms. The first term depends solely on the characteristics of the investment portfolio. The second term is a function of interest-rate movement only. The second term characterizes the nature of the change in the shape of the yield curve. Because that change will be impossible to predict a priori, it is not possible to control for it. The first term, however, can be controlled for when constructing the immunized portfolio, because it depends solely on the composition of the portfolio. This first term, then, is a measure of risk for immunized portfolios and is equal to

$$\frac{CF_1(1-H)^2}{1+y} + \frac{CF_2(2-H)^2}{(1+y)^2} + \cdots + \frac{CF_n(n-H)^2}{(1+y)^n}$$

where

CF_t = cash flow of the portfolio at time period t
H = length (in years) of the investment horizon or liability due date
y = yield for the portfolio
n = time to receipt of the last cash flow

The immunization risk measure agrees with our earlier graphic analysis of the relative risk associated with a barbell and a bullet portfolio. For the barbell portfolio (Portfolio A in Exhibit 24-10), the portfolio's cash flow payments are widely dispersed in time and the immunization risk measure would be high. The portfolio cash flow payments for the bullet portfolio (Portfolio B in Exhibit 24-10) are close to the liability due date so the immunization risk measure is low.

Notice that if all the cash flows are received at the liability due date, the immunization risk measure is zero. In such a case, the portfolio is equivalent to a pure discount security (zero-coupon security) that matures on the liability due date. If a portfolio can be constructed that replicates a pure discount security maturing on the liability due date, that portfolio will be the one with the lowest immunization risk. Typically, however, it is not possible to construct such an ideal portfolio.

The objective in constructing an immunized portfolio, then, is to match the portfolio's duration to the liability's duration and select the portfolio that minimizes the immunization risk. The immunization risk measure can be used to construct approximate confidence intervals for the target yield and the target accumulated value.

Zero-Coupon Bonds and Immunization

So far we have dealt with coupon bonds. An alternative approach to immunizing a portfolio against changes in the market yield is to invest in zero-coupon bonds with a maturity equal to the investment horizon. This is consistent with the basic principle of immunization because the duration of a zero-coupon bond is equal to the liability's duration. However, in practice, the yield on zero-coupon bonds is typically lower than the yield on coupon bonds. Thus, using zero-coupon bonds to fund a bullet liability requires more funds because a lower target yield (equal to the yield on the zero-coupon bond) is being locked in.

Suppose, for example, that a portfolio manager must invest funds to satisfy a known liability of $20 million five years from now. If a target yield of 10% on a bond-equivalent basis (5% every six months) can be locked in using zero-coupon Treasury bonds, the funds necessary to satisfy the $20 million liability will be $12,278,260, the present value of $20 million using a discount rate of 10% (5% semiannually).

Suppose, instead, that by using coupon Treasury securities, a target yield of 10.3% on a bond-equivalent basis (5.15% every six months) is possible. Then, the funds needed to satisfy the $20 million liability will be $12,104,240, the present value of $20 million discounted at 10.3% (5.15% semiannually). Thus, a target yield higher by 30 basis points would reduce the cost of funding the $20 million by $174,020 ($12,278,260 − $12,104,240). But the reduced cost comes at a price—the risk that the target yield will not be achieved.

Credit Risk and the Target Yield

The target yield may not be achieved if any of the bonds in the portfolio default or decrease in value because of credit quality deterioration. Restricting the universe of bonds that may be used in constructing an immunized portfolio to Treasury securities eliminates credit risk. The target yield that can be achieved, however, will be lower than that for bonds with credit risk so that the cost of funding a liability would be increased.

In most immunization applications, the client specifies an acceptable level of credit risk. Issues selected for the immunized portfolio are then restricted to those with that quality rating or higher. The more credit risk the client is willing to accept, the higher the achievable target yield, but the greater the risk that the immunized portfolio will fail to meet that target yield because of defaulted or downgraded issues. After the minimum credit risk is specified and the immunized portfolio is constructed, the portfolio manager must then monitor the individual issues for possible decreases in credit quality. Should an issue be downgraded below the minimum quality rating, that issue must be sold or the acceptable level of credit risk changed.

Call Risk

When the universe of acceptable issues includes corporate bonds, the target yield may be jeopardized if a callable issue is included that is subsequently called. Call risk can be avoided by restricting the universe of acceptable bonds to noncallable bonds and deep-discount callable bonds. This strategy does not come without a cost. Because noncallable and deep-discount bonds offer lower yields in a low-interest-rate environment, restricting the universe to these securities reduces the achievable target yield and therefore increases the cost of funding a liability. Also, it may be difficult to find acceptable noncallable bonds.

An immunized portfolio that includes callable bond issues must be carefully monitored so that issues likely to be called are sold and replaced with bond issues that have a lower probability of being called.

Constructing the Immunized Portfolio

When the universe of acceptable issues is established and any constraints are imposed, the portfolio manager has a large number of possible securities from which to construct an initial immunized portfolio and from which to select to rebalance an immunized portfolio. An objective function can be specified, and a portfolio that optimizes the objective function using mathematical programming tools can be determined. A common objective function, given the risk of immunization discussed earlier, is to minimize the immunization risk measure.[8]

Contingent Immunization

Contingent immunization is a strategy that consists of identifying both the available immunization target rate and a lower safety net level return with which the investor would be minimally satisfied.[9] The portfolio manager pursues an active portfolio strategy until an adverse investment experience drives the then-available potential return—the combined active return from actual past experience and immunized return from expected future experience—down to the safety net level. When that point is reached, the portfolio manager is obligated to immunize the portfolio completely and lock in the safety net level return. As long as the safety net is not violated, the portfolio manager can continue to manage the portfolio actively. When the immunization mode is activated because the safety net

---

[8] For a discussion of alternative objective functions, see H. Gifford Fong and Frank J. Fabozzi, *Fixed Income Portfolio Management* (Homewood, IL: Dow Jones-Irwin, 1985), Chapter 6; Peter C. Christensen and Frank J. Fabozzi, "Bond Immunization: An Asset Liability Optimization Strategy," Chapter 31 in Frank J. Fabozzi and Irving M. Pollack (eds.), *The Handbook of Fixed Income Securities* (Homewood, IL: Dow Jones-Irwin, 1987); and Peter C. Christensen and Frank J. Fabozzi, "Dedicated Bond Portfolios," Chapter 32 in Frank J. Fabozzi (ed.), *The Handbook of Fixed Income Securities*, 3rd ed. (Homewood, IL: Business One-Irwin, 1991).

[9] Martin L. Leibowitz, "The Uses of Contingent Immunization," *Journal of Portfolio Management*, Fall 1981, pp. 51–55.

is violated, the manager can no longer return to the active mode, unless, of course, the contingent immunization plan is abandoned.

To illustrate this strategy, suppose that a client investing $50 million is willing to accept a 10% rate of return over a four-year investment horizon at a time when a possible immunized rate of return is 12%. The 10% return is called the **safety net return.** The difference between the immunized return and the safety net return is called the **safety cushion.** In our example, the safety cushion is 200 basis points (12% minus 10%).

Because the initial portfolio value is $50 million, the minimum target value at the end of four years, based on semiannual compounding, is $73,872,772 [= $50,000,000 (1.05)^8]. The rate of return at the time is 12% so the assets required at this time to achieve the minimum target value of $73,872,772 represent the present value of $73,872,772 discounted at 12% on a semiannual basis, which is $43,348,691 [= $73,872,772/(1.06)^8]. Therefore, the safety cushion of 200 basis points translates into an initial *dollar safety margin* of $6,651,309 ($50,000,000 − $43,348,691). Had the safety net of return been 11% instead of 10%, the safety cushion would have been 100 basis points and the initial dollar safety margin, $1,855,935. In other words, the smaller the safety cushion, the smaller the dollar safety margin. Exhibit 24-11 illustrates the contingency immunization strategy by showing the portfolio's initial value and for two scenarios six months later.

Initially, the portfolio manager pursues an active portfolio strategy within the contingent immunization strategy. Suppose that the portfolio manager puts all the funds into a 20-year 12% coupon bond selling at par to yield 12%. Let's look at what happens if the market yield falls to 9% at the end of six months. The value of the portfolio at the end of six months would consist of (1) the value of the 19.5-year 12% coupon bond at a 9% market yield, and (2) six months of coupon interest. The price of the bond would increase from 100 to 127.34 so that the price of $50 million of these bonds would rise to $63.67 million. Coupon interest is $3 million (0.50 × 0.12 × $50 million). Thus, the portfolio value at the end of six months is $66.67 million.

Exhibit 24-11   Contingency Immunization: Two Scenarios

Initial conditions: $50 million investment
Achievable immunization rate: 12%
Safety net return: 10%
Planning horizon: 4 years
Initial investment: 20-year 12% coupon bond, selling at par to yield 12%

| | | Interest Rates | |
Scenario	Initial Rate 12%	Drops to 9% in 6 Months	Rises to 14.26% in 6 Months
Minimum target value to horizon	$73,872,772	$73,872,772	$73,872,772
Current portfolio value	50,000,000	66,670,000	45,615,776
Present value of minimum target	43,348,691	54,283,888	45,614,893
Dollar safety margin (current value – present value of minimum target)	6,651,309	12,386,112	883
Management strategy	Active	Active	Immunize

How much would be necessary to achieve the minimum target return of $73,872,772 if a portfolio can be immunized at the current interest rate of 9%? The required dollar value is found by computing the present value of the minimum target return at 9% for 3.5 years. The required dollar amount is $54,283,888 [$= $73,872,772/(1.045)^7$].

The portfolio value of $66.67 million is greater than the required portfolio value of $54,283,888. The portfolio manager can therefore continue to manage the portfolio actively. The dollar safety margin is now $12,386,112 ($66,670,000 − $54,283,888). As long as the dollar safety margin is positive (i.e., the portfolio value is greater than the required portfolio value to achieve the minimum target value at the prevailing interest rate), the portfolio is actively managed.

Suppose that instead of declining to 9% in six months, interest rates rose to 14.26%. The market value of the bond would decline to $42,615,776. The portfolio value would then equal $45,615,776 (the market value of the bonds plus $3 million of coupon interest). The required dollar amount to achieve the minimum target value of $73,872,772 at the current interest rate (14.26%) would be $45,614,893 [$= $73,872,772/(1.0713)^7$]. The required dollar amount is approximately equal to the portfolio value (i.e., the dollar safety margin is almost zero). Thus, the portfolio manager would be required to immunize the portfolio to achieve the minimum target value (safety net return) over the investment horizon.

The three key factors in implementing a contingent immunization strategy are (1) establishing accurate immunized initial and ongoing available target returns, (2) identifying a suitable and immunizable safety net return, and (3) designing an effective monitoring procedure to ensure that the safety net return is not violated.

STRUCTURING A PORTFOLIO TO SATISFY MULTIPLE LIABILITIES

Thus far, we have discussed immunizing a single liability. For pension funds, there are multiple liabilities that must be satisfied—payments to the beneficiaries of the pension fund. A stream of liabilities must also be satisfied for a life insurance company that sells an insurance policy requiring multiple payments to policyholders, such as an annuity policy. There are two strategies that can be used to satisfy a liability stream: (1) multiperiod immunization, and (2) cash flow matching.

Multiperiod Immunization

Multiperiod immunization is a portfolio strategy in which a portfolio is created that will be capable of satisfying more than one predetermined future liability regardless if interest rates change. Even if there is a parallel shift in the yield curve, Bierwag, Kaufman, and Toevs demonstrate that matching the duration of the portfolio to the duration of the liabilities is not a sufficient condition to immunize a portfolio seeking to satisfy a liability stream.[10] Instead, it is necessary to decompose the portfolio payment stream in such a way that each liability is immunized by one of the component streams. The key to understanding this approach is recognizing that the payment stream on the portfolio, not the portfolio itself, must be decomposed in this manner. There may be no actual bonds that would give the component payment stream.

---

[10] G.O. Bierwag, George K. Kaufman, and Alden Toevs, "Immunization Strategies for Funding Multiple Liabilities," *Journal of Financial and Quantitative Analysis*, March 1983, pp. 113–124.

In the special case of a parallel shift of the yield curve, Fong and Vasicek demonstrate the necessary and sufficient conditions that must be satisfied to assure the immunization of multiple liabilities:[11]

1. The portfolio's duration must equal the duration of the liabilities.
2. The distribution of durations of individual portfolio assets must have a wider range than the distribution of the liabilities.[12]
3. The present value of the cash flows from the bond portfolio must equal the present value of the liability stream.

However, these conditions will immunize only in the case of a parallel shift in the yield curve. To cope with the problem of failure to immunize because of nonparallel shifts in the yield curve, Fong and Vasicek generalize the immunization risk measure for a single liability discussed earlier in this chapter to the multiple liability case. An optimal immunization strategy is to minimize this immunization risk measure subject to the three constraints mentioned previously (duration, dispersion of assets and liabilities, and equality of present value of asset cash flow and liability stream), as well as any other constraints that a client may impose.

In a series of articles, Reitano has explored the limitations of the parallel shift assumption.[13] He has also developed models that generalize the immunization of multiple liabilities to arbitrary yield curve shifts. His research makes it clear that classical multiple-period immunization can disguise the risks associated with nonparallel yield curve shifts and that a model that protects against one type of yield curve shift may allow a great deal of exposure and vulnerability to other types of shifts.

Cash Flow Matching

An alternative to multiperiod immunization is **cash flow matching.** This approach, also referred to as **dedicating a portfolio**, can be summarized as follows. A bond is selected with a maturity that matches the last liability stream. An amount of principal plus final coupon equal to the amount of the last liability stream is then invested in this bond. The remaining elements of the liability stream are then reduced by the coupon payments on this bond, and another bond is chosen for the new, reduced amount of the next-to-last liability. Going backward in time, this cash flow matching process is continued until all liabilities have been matched by the payment of the securities in the portfolio.

---

[11] Fong and Vasicek, "A Risk Minimizing Strategy for Multiple Liability Immunization."

[12] The reason for the second condition can be illustrated using an example. Suppose that a liability stream with 10 payments of $5 million each year is funded with a zero-coupon bond with a maturity (duration) equal to the duration of the liability stream. Suppose also that when the first $5 million payment is due, interest rates rise so that the value of the zero-coupon bond falls. Even though interest rates have increased, there is no offset to reinvestment income because the bond is a zero-coupon bond. Thus, there is no assurance that the portfolio will generate sufficient cash flow to satisfy the remaining liabilities. In the case of a single liability, the second condition is satisfied automatically.

[13] Robert R. Reitano, "A Multivariate Approach to Immunization Theory," *Actuarial Research Clearing House*, Vol. 2, 1990; and "Multivariate Immunization Theory," *Transactions of the Society of Actuaries*, Vol. XLIII, 1991. For a detailed illustration of the relationship between the underlying yield curve shift and immunizations, see Robert R. Reitano, "Non-Parallel Yield Curve Shifts and Immunization," *Journal of Portfolio Management*, Spring 1992, pp. 36–43.

Exhibit 24-12 provides a simple illustration of this process for a five-year liability stream. Mathematical programming techniques can be employed to construct a least-cost cash flow matching portfolio from an acceptable universe of bonds.

Exhibit 24-12   Cash Flow Matching Process

Assume: Five-year liability stream.
        Cash flow from bonds are annual.

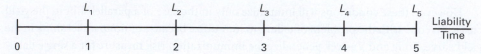

Step 1:
Cash flow from bond A selected to satisfy L_5
    Coupons = A_s; Principal = A_p and $A_s + A_p = L_5$
Unfunded liabilities remaining:

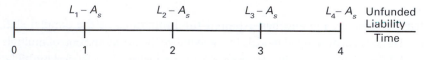

Step 2:
Cash flow from bond B selected to satisfy L_4
    Unfunded liability = $L_4 - A_s$
    Coupons = B_s; Principal = B_p and $B_s + B_p = L_4 - A_s$
Unfunded liabilities remaining:

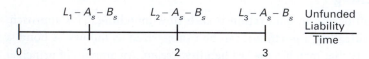

Step 3:
Cash flow from bond C selected to satisfy L_3
    Unfunded liability = $L_3 - A_s - B_s$
    Coupons = C_s; Principal = C_p and $C_s + C_p = L_3 - A_s - B_s - C_s$
Unfunded liabilities remaining:

Step 4:
Cash flow from bond D selected to satisfy L_2
    Unfunded liability = $L_2 - A_s - B_s - C_s$
    Coupons = D_s; Principal = D_p and $D_s + D_p = L_2 - A_s - B_s - C_s$
Unfunded liabilities remaining:

Step 5:
Select bond E with a cash flow of $L_1 - A_s - B_s - C_s - D_s$

The differences between the cash flow matching and multiperiod immunization strategies should be understood. First, unlike the immunization approach, the cash flow matching approach has no duration requirements. Second, with immunization, rebalancing is required even if interest rates do not change. In contrast, no rebalancing is necessary for cash flow matching except to delete and replace any issue whose quality rating has declined below an acceptable level. Third, there is no risk that the liabilities will not be satisfied (barring any defaults) with a cash flow–matched portfolio. For a portfolio constructed using multiperiod immunization, there is immunization risk due to reinvestment risk.

The differences just cited may seem to favor the use of cash flow matching. However, what we have ignored is the relative cost of the two strategies. Using the cost of the initial portfolio as an evaluation measure, Gifford Fong Associates has found that cash flow–matched portfolios, using a universe of corporate bonds rated at least AA, cost from 3% to 7% more in dollar terms than do multiperiod immunized portfolios. The reason cash flow matching is more expensive is that, typically, the matching of cash flows to liabilities is not perfect. This means that more funds than necessary must be set aside to match the liabilities. Optimization techniques used to design cash flow–matched portfolios assume that excess funds are reinvested at a conservative reinvestment rate. With multiperiod immunization, all reinvestment returns are assumed to be locked in at a higher target rate of return. Therefore, portfolio managers face a trade-off in deciding between the two strategies: avoidance of the risk of not satisfying the liability stream under cash flow matching versus the lower cost attainable with multiperiod immunization.

In the basic cash flow–matching technique, only asset cash flows occurring prior to a liability date can be used to satisfy the liability. The technique has been extended to handle situations in which cash flows occurring both before and after the liability date can be used to meet a liability. This technique, called **symmetric cash matching**, allows for the short-term borrowing of funds to satisfy a liability prior to the liability due date. The opportunity to borrow short term so that symmetric cash matching can be employed results in a reduction in the cost of funding a liability.

A popular variation of multiperiod immunization and cash flow matching to fund liabilities is one that combines the two strategies. This strategy, referred to as **combination matching** or **horizon matching**, creates a portfolio that is duration matched with the added constraint that it be cash matched in the first few years, usually five years. The advantage of combination matching over multiperiod immunization is that liquidity needs are provided for in the initial cash flow–matched period. Cash flow matching the initial portion of the liability stream reduces the risk associated with nonparallel shifts of the yield curve. The disadvantage of combination matching over multiperiod immunization is that the cost is slightly greater.

Within the immunization and dedicated cash flow strategies, some portfolio managers are permitted to manage the portfolio actively by entering into bond swaps to enhance portfolio performance. Obviously, only small bets can be made, to minimize the likelihood that the liability payments will not be satisfied.

EXTENSIONS OF LIABILITY-DRIVEN STRATEGIES

As we explained at the outset of this chapter, liabilities may be uncertain with respect to both timing and amount of the payment. In the techniques we have discussed in this chapter, we have assumed that the timing and the amount of the cash payment of liabilities are known with certainty. That is, we assume that the liabilities are deterministic.

We assume, moreover, that the cash flows from the assets are known with certainty, although you have learned that most non-Treasury securities have embedded options that permit the borrower or the investor to alter the cash flows. Thus, the models presented in this chapter are referred to as **deterministic models** because they assume that the liability payments and the asset cash flows are known with certainty.

Since the mid-1980s, a good number of models have been developed to handle real-world situations in which liability payments and/or asset cash flows are uncertain. Such models are called **stochastic models**.[14] Such models require that the portfolio manager incorporate an interest-rate model; that is, a model that describes the probability distribution for interest rates. Optimal portfolios then are solved for using a mathematical programming technique known as **stochastic programming.**

The complexity of stochastic models, however, has limited their application in practice. Nevertheless, they are gaining in popularity as more portfolio managers become comfortable with their sophistication. There is increasing awareness that stochastic models reduce the likelihood that the liability objective will not be satisfied and that transactions costs can be reduced through less frequent rebalancing of a portfolio derived from these models.

COMBINING ACTIVE AND IMMUNIZATION STRATEGIES

In our discussion of contingent immunization, the portfolio manager is permitted to manage the portfolio actively until the safety net is violated. However, contingent immunization is not a combination or mixture strategy. The portfolio manager is either in the immunization mode by choice or because the safety net is violated or in the active management mode. In contrast to an immunization strategy, an active/immunization combination strategy is a mixture of two strategies that are pursued by the portfolio manager at the same point in time.

The immunization component of this strategy could be either a single-liability immunization or a multiple-liability immunization using the techniques discussed earlier in this chapter. In the single-liability immunization case, an assured return would be established so as to serve to stabilize the portfolio's total return. In the multiple-liability immunization case, the component to be immunized would be immunized now, with new requirements, as they become known, taken care of through reimmunization. This would be an adaptive strategy in that the immunization component would be based on an initial set of liabilities and modified over time to changes in future liabilities (e.g., for actuarial changes for the liabilities in the case of a pension fund). The active portion would continue to be free to maximize expected return, given some acceptable risk level.

The following formula suggested by Gifford Fong Associates can be used to determine the portion of the initial portfolio to be managed actively, with the balance immunized:[15]

$$\text{active component} = \frac{\text{immunization target rate } - \text{ minimum return established by client}}{\text{immunization target rate } - \text{ expected worst case active return}}$$

---

[14] For a review of such models, see Randall S. Hiller and Christian Schaack, "A Classification of Structured Bond Portfolio Modeling Techniques," *Journal of Portfolio Management*, Fall 1990, pp. 37–48.

[15] Gifford Fong, *The Costs of Cash Flow Matching* (Santa Monica, CA: Gifford Fong Associates, 1981).

In the formula, it is assumed that the immunization target return is greater than either the minimum return established by the client or the expected worst-case return from the actively managed portion of the portfolio.

As an illustration, assume that the available immunization target return is 7% per year, the minimum return acceptable to the client is 5%, and the expected worst-case return for the actively managed portion of the portfolio is 2%. Then, the percentage in the active portion of the portfolio would be

$$\text{active component} = \frac{0.07 - 0.05}{0.07 - 0.02} = 0.40 \text{ or } 40\%$$

Notice from the formula for determining the active component that for any given immunization target return, the smaller the minimum acceptable return to the client and the larger the expected worst-case active return, the larger will be the percentage allocated to active management. Since the return values in the formula change over time, the portfolio manager must monitor these values constantly, adjusting and rebalancing the allocation between the immunized and active components as appropriate. As long as the worst-case scenario is not violated—that is, as long as the actual return experienced does not drop below the expected worst-case active return—the minimum return for the portfolio established by the client will be achieved.

LIABILITY-DRIVEN STRATEGIES FOR DEFINED BENEFIT PENSION FUNDS

Thus far in this chapter, we have explained liability-driven strategies where the allocation of the fund's assets is to bonds only. Certain institutional investors such as an insurance company seeking to satisfy its obligations where the liabilities are known with certainty would find that a bond-only portfolio is the most suitable to meet its investment objectives. While a defined benefit plan can use an immunization or cash flow matching strategy that has bonds only, the problem is that the liabilities are uncertain due to factors such as changes in the contractual benefits provided by the plan sponsor, the decision by plan beneficiaries to retire early, and the impact of inflation on benefits.

In recent years, several liability-driven strategies for pension funds that allow for investing outside of the bond universe have been proposed. These proposals have come about as a result of the poor performance of defined pension plans since the turn of the century due to unfavorable conditions in the capital markets and poor asset allocation decisions. More specifically, a measure of the performance of a pension fund is the funding ratio, which is the ratio of the market value of the assets to the value of the liabilities. The value of the liabilities is a suitably discounted cash flow of the liabilities (i.e., present value of the liabilities). Since the turn of the century, the funding ratios of public corporations have deteriorated.

Historically, plan sponsors have focused on the management of plan assets, using market benchmarks as a measure of performance without consideration of the relationship between the liability profile of the pension plan and the market benchmarks used. Basically, the asset allocation decision (i.e., the allocation among the major asset classes) used the mean-variance optimization model formulated by Harry Markowitz.[16] Historically, a commonly used allocation was a 60/40 stock/bond mix.

---

[16] Harry M. Markowitz, "Portfolio Selection," *Journal of Finance*, 7 (March 1952), pp. 77–91.

There are basically two camps as to what the suitable strategy is to employ in the allocation of assets for defined pension plans. One camp is a bond-only camp that favors the dedicated strategy discussed earlier in this chapter. The other camp believes that the liability characteristics of pension funds require the use of equities. Both camps, however, agree that the benchmark should be the liabilities, not general market benchmarks for major asset classes.

Basically, the camp that believes that the plan sponsor should be given the opportunity to allocate to equity argues that the mean-variance optimization framework can be used but that the liability benchmark must be incorporated into the analysis. Recall that in mean-variance optimization, a portfolio manager determines the efficient frontier. The efficient frontier is the set of efficient portfolios where an efficient portfolio is the portfolio with the highest expected return for a given level of risk. To determine which efficient portfolio to select, the Sharpe ratio is used. The Sharpe ratio is the excess return of the portfolio divided by the standard deviation of the excess return. The excess return is the difference between the expected return of the portfolio minus the risk-free rate, with the risk-free rate being a Treasury rate. Those who advocate the inclusion of equity argue that rather than measuring the excess return in terms of a benchmark such as the risk-free rate, the benchmark should be an index that reflects the liability structure of the pension plan.

Ross, Bernstein, Ferguson, and Dalio of Bridgewater Associates propose the following liability-driven strategy for a pension plan, which involves two steps.[17] First, create an immunizing portfolio. We described earlier how this is done. The purpose of this portfolio is to hedge the adverse consequences associated with the exposure to the liabilities. Second, create what they refer to as an "excess return portfolio." The purpose of that portfolio is to generate a return that exceeds the return on the immunizing portfolio. The total return for the pension plan is then

$$\text{total plan return} = \text{return on liability-immunizing portfolio}$$
$$+ \text{ return on excess return portfolio} - \text{return on liabilities}$$

The return on liabilities is the change in the present value of the liabilities. If the immunizing portfolio is properly created, its return should be close to the return on the liabilities. (Recall it is not a simple task to completely immunize.) Hence, the volatility of the liabilities is neutralized to a great extent. What remains is then the return on the excess return portfolio.

The issue associated with liability-driven strategies applied to defined pension plans must deal with risks that may not be handled adequately by investing in the major asset classes. The more obvious of the two risks is the impact of inflation on future pension liabilities. An increase in the inflation rate increases future liabilities as salaries are adjusted upwards. At one time the view was that equities were the suitable asset class for dealing with inflation. However, because of the volatility in equity prices, adverse movements in equity values may not mitigate inflation risk. The second of the two risks is **longevity risk.** This is the risk that beneficiaries may live longer and as a result future liabilities will exceed current actuarial determined liabilities.

Even prior to the decline of interest rates to low current low rates, pension plan sponsors were reluctant to embrace liability-driven strategies as reported in a 2006 survey study by Northern Trust Bank and Greenwich Associates.[18] The survey included

---

[17] Paul Ross, Dan Bernstein, Niall Ferguson, and Ray Dalio, "Creating an Optimal Portfolio to Fund Pension Liabilities," Chapter 47 in Frank J. Fabozzi (ed.), *Handbook of Finance: Volume 2* (Hoboken, NJ: John Wiley & Sons, 2008).

[18] "Implementing LDI in Pension Plans," *Point of View*, Northern Trust, January 2007. Available at http://www .northerntrust.com/pointofview/07_Jan/jan07_implementingLDI.html#.

managers of funds in the United States (1,050), United Kingdom (224), Canada (197), and Europe (217). Based on the survey study, less than 10% of plan trustees were comfortable using liability-driven strategies. There was greater adoption of these strategies outside of the United States where regulations dealing with pension accounting were much tougher. More recently, however, this has changed for U.S.-defined benefit plans in the United States according to the consulting firm of Towers Watson.[19]

KEY POINTS

- The nature of their liabilities, as well as regulatory considerations, determine the investment strategy pursued by all institutional investors. By nature, liabilities vary with respect to the amount and timing of their payment.

- The economic surplus of any entity is the difference between the market value of all its assets and the present value of its liabilities. Institutional investors will pursue a strategy either to maximize economic surplus or to hedge economic surplus against any adverse change in market conditions.

- In addition to economic surplus, there are accounting surplus and regulatory surplus. The former is based on GAAP accounting, specifically, FASB 115, and the latter on RAP accounting. To the extent that these two surplus measures may not reflect the true financial condition of an institution, future financial problems may arise.

- Liability-driven strategies involve designing a portfolio to produce sufficient funds to satisfy liabilities whether or not interest rates change.

- When there is only one future liability to be funded, an immunization strategy can be used. An immunization strategy is designed so that as interest rates change, interest-rate risk and reinvestment risk will offset each other in such a way that the minimum accumulated value (or minimum rate of return) becomes the target accumulated value (or target yield).

- An immunization strategy requires that a portfolio manager create a bond portfolio with a duration equal to the duration of the liability.

- Because immunization theory is based on parallel shifts in the yield curve, the risk is that a portfolio will not be immunized even if the duration-matching condition is satisfied. Immunization risk can be quantified so that a portfolio that minimizes this risk can be constructed.

- When there are multiple liabilities to be satisfied, either multiperiod immunization or cash flow matching can be used. Multiperiod immunization is a duration-matching strategy that exposes the portfolio to immunization risk. The cash flow–matching strategy does not impose any duration requirement. Although the only risk that the liabilities will not be satisfied is that issues will be called or will default, the dollar cost of a cash flow–matched portfolio may be higher than that of a portfolio constructed using a multiperiod immunization strategy.

- Liability-driven strategies in which the liability payments and the asset cash flows are known with certainty are deterministic models. In a stochastic model, either the liability payments or the asset cash flows, or both, are uncertain. Stochastic models require specification of a probability distribution for the process that generates interest rates.

- A combination of active and immunization strategies can be pursued. Allocation of the portion of the portfolio to be actively managed is based on the immunization

---

[19] "Towers Watson: LDI Strategies Gaining in Popularity Among U.S. Investors," June 15, 2010. Available at http://www.towerswatson.com/united-states/press/2184.

target rate, the minimum return acceptable to the client, and the expected worst-case return from the actively managed portfolio. In a contingent immunization strategy, a portfolio manager is either actively managing the portfolio or immunizing it. Because both strategies are not pursued at the same time, contingent immunization is not a combination or mixture strategy.

- The liability structure of a defined benefit pension plan is uncertain. There are two liability-driven strategies advocated for defined benefit pension plans. One approach argues that only bonds should be acquired and a dedicated portfolio strategy should be used. The other approach is a liability-driven strategy that uses bonds and equities but uses the liabilities as a benchmark in determining the best asset allocation.

QUESTIONS

1. What are the two dimensions of a liability?
2. Why is it not always simple to estimate the liability of an institution?
3. Why is asset/liability management best described as surplus management?
4. **a.** What is the economic surplus of an institution?
   b. What is the accounting surplus of an institution?
   c. What is the regulatory surplus of an institution?
   d. Which surplus best reflects the economic well-being of an institution?
   e. Under what circumstances are all three surplus measures the same?
5. Suppose that the present value of the liabilities of some financial institution is $600 million and the surplus $800 million. The duration of the liabilities is equal to 5. Suppose further that the portfolio of this financial institution includes only bonds and the duration for the portfolio is 6.
   a. What is the market value of the portfolio of bonds?
   b. What does a duration of 6 mean for the portfolio of assets?
   c. What does a duration of 5 mean for the liabilities?
   d. Suppose that interest rates increase by 50 basis points; what will be the approximate new value for the surplus?
   e. Suppose that interest rates decrease by 50 basis points; what will be the approximate new value for the surplus?

6. **a.** Why is the interest-rate sensitivity of an institution's assets and liabilities important?
   b. In 1986, Martin Leibowitz of Salomon Brothers, Inc., wrote a paper titled "Total Portfolio Duration: A New Perspective on Asset Allocation." What do you think total portfolio duration means?
7. If an institution has liabilities that are interest-rate sensitive and invests in a portfolio of common stocks, can you determine what will happen to the institution's economic surplus if interest rates change?
8. The following quote is taken from Phillip D. Parker (Associate General Counsel of the SEC), "Market Value Accounting—An Idea Whose Time Has Come?" in Elliot P. Williams (ed.), *Managing Asset/ Liability Portfolios* (Charlottesville, VA: Association for Investment Management and Research, 1991), published prior to the passage of FASB 115:

   > The use of market value accounting would eliminate any incentive to sell or retain investment securities for reasons of accounting treatment rather than business utility.

   Explain why this statement is correct. (Note that in historical accounting a loss is recognized only when a security is sold.)
9. Indicate why you agree or disagree with the following statements.
   a. "Under FASB 115 all assets must be marked to market."
   b. "The greater the price volatility of assets classified in the held-to-maturity account, the greater the volatility of the accounting surplus and reported earnings."

10. What is meant by immunizing a bond portfolio?
11. **a.** What is the basic underlying principle in an immunization strategy?
    b. Why might the matching of the maturity of a coupon bond to the remaining time to maturity of a liability fail to immunize a portfolio?
12. Why must an immunized portfolio be rebalanced periodically?
13. What are the risks associated with a bond immunization strategy?
14. "I can immunize a portfolio simply by investing in zero-coupon Treasury bonds." Comment on this statement.
15. Three portfolio managers are discussing a strategy for immunizing a portfolio so as to achieve a target yield. Manager A, whose portfolio consists of Treasury securities and option-free corporates, stated that the duration of the portfolio should be constructed so that the Macaulay duration of the portfolio is equal to the number of years until the liability must be paid. Manager B, with the same types of securities in his portfolio as Manager A, feels that Manager A is wrong because the portfolio should be constructed so that the modified duration of the portfolio is equal to the modified duration of the liabilities. Manager C believes Manager B is correct. However, unlike the portfolios of Managers A and B, Manager C invests in mortgage-backed securities and callable corporate bonds. Discuss the position taken by each manager and explain why they are correct.
16. Why is there greater risk in a multiperiod immunization strategy than a cash flow–matching strategy?
17. **a.** What is a contingent immunization strategy?
    b. What is the safety net cushion in a contingent immunization strategy?
    c. Is it proper to classify a contingent immunization as a combination active/immunization strategy?
18. What is a combination matching strategy?
19. In a stochastic liability-driven strategy, why is an interest-rate model needed?
20. Suppose that a client has granted an asset management firm permission to pursue an active/immunized combination strategy. Suppose further that the minimum return expected by the client is 9% and that the asset management firm believes that an achievable immunized target return is 4% and the worst possible return from the actively managed portion of the portfolio is 1%. Approximately how much should be allocated to the active component of the portfolio?
21. A liability-driven strategy for defined benefit pension funds is to create an immunizing portfolio and an excess return portfolio. Explain this strategy.
22. The following excerpt is from a January 18, 2008, article ("LDI strategy that is liable to work?") by Penny Green, chief executive of the SAUL Trustee Company (a U.K. firm that advises on pension management), dealing with liability-driven strategies:

    . . . there is no one asset class that precisely matches a plan's liabilities. It is the case that bonds provide a cash flow that can be used to meet the cash flows out of a pension plan. But so do equities—it is just that the cash flows from equities (dividends) cannot be guaranteed. However, bonds do not cover longevity risk or salary inflation, so bonds are not a perfect match—but neither do equities. In fact, there is no asset class at present that matches longevity risk or salary inflation. This is the trustee's dilemma that LDI strategies are supposed to resolve.

    Explain why you agree or disagree with this viewpoint.
23. In explaining how a pension fund should transition to a liability-driven investment strategy, Duane Rocheleau, managing director of Northern Trust's global investment solutions team, writes in "Implementing LDI in Pension Plans," January 2007 http://www.ntrs.com/pointofview/07_Jan/implementing-ldi-pension-plans.html:
    "**1.** Analyze and characterize the liabilities;
    2. Quantify the relationship between the assets and liabilities;
    3. Develop and implement appropriate investment strategies;
    4. Monitor the account, rebalance the assets and liabilities mix and tweak the investment strategy as necessary."

    Describe each of the above elements.

24. One of your clients, a newcomer to the life insurance business, questioned you about the following excerpt from Peter E. Christensen, Frank J. Fabozzi, and Anthony LoFaso, "Dedicated Bond Portfolios," Chapter 43 in Frank J. Fabozzi (ed.), *The Handbook of Fixed Income Securities* (Homewood, IL: Richard D. Irwin, 1991):

> For financial intermediaries such as banks and insurance companies, there is a well-recognized need for a complete funding perspective. This need is best illustrated by the significant interest-rate risk assumed by many insurance carriers in the early years of their Guaranteed Investment Contract (GIC) products. A large volume of compound interest (zero coupon) and simple interest (annual pay) GICs were issued in three- through seven-year maturities in the positively sloped yield-curve environment of the mid-1970s. Proceeds from hundreds of the GIC issues were reinvested at higher rates in the longer 10- to 30-year private placement, commercial mortgage, and public bond instruments. At the time, industry expectations were that the GIC product would be very profitable because of the large positive spread between the higher "earned" rate on the longer assets and the lower "credited" rate on the GIC contracts.
>
> By pricing GICs on a spread basis and investing the proceeds on a mismatched basis, companies gave little consideration to the rollover risk they were assuming in volatile markets. As rates rose dramatically in the late 1970s and early 1980s, carriers were exposed to disintermediation as GIC liabilities matured and the corresponding assets had 20 years remaining to maturity and were valued at only a fraction of their original cost.

Answer the following questions posed to you by your client.

a. "It is not clear to me what risk an issuer of a GIC is facing. A carrier can invest the proceeds in assets offering a higher yield than they are guaranteeing to GIC policyholders, so what's the problem? Isn't it just default risk that can be controlled by setting tight credit standards?"

b. "I understand that disintermediation means that when a policy matures, the funds are withdrawn from the insurance company by the policyholder. But why would a rise in interest rates cause GIC policyholders to withdraw their funds? The insurance company can simply guarantee a higher interest rate."

c. "What do the authors mean by 'pricing GICs on a spread basis and investing the proceeds on a mismatched basis,' and what is this 'rollover risk' they are referring to?"

25. Suppose that a life insurance company sells a five-year guaranteed investment contract that guarantees an interest rate of 7.5% per year on a bond-equivalent yield basis (or equivalently, 3.75% every six months for the next 10 six-month periods). Also suppose that the payment made by the policyholder is $9,642,899. Consider the following three investments that can be made by the portfolio manager:

Bond X: Buy $9,642,899 par value of an option-free bond selling at par with a 7.5% yield to maturity that matures in five years.

Bond Y: Buy $9,642,899 par value of an option-free bond selling at par with a 7.5% yield to maturity that matures in 12 years.

Bond Z: Buy $10,000,000 par value of a six-year 6.75% coupon option-free bond selling at 96.42899 to yield 7.5%.

a. Holding aside the spread that the insurance company seeks to make on the invested funds, demonstrate that the target accumulated value to meet the GIC obligation five years from now is $13,934,413.

b. Complete Table A assuming that the manager invests in bond X and immediately following the purchase, yields change and stay the same for the five-year investment horizon.

c. Based on Table A, under what circumstances will the investment in bond X fail to satisfy the target accumulated value?

d. Complete Table B, assuming that the manager invests in bond Y and immediately following the purchase, yields change and stay the same for the five-year investment horizon.

e. Based on Table B, under what circumstances will the investment in bond Y fail to satisfy the target accumulated value?

f. Complete Table C, assuming that the manager invests in bond Z and immediately following the purchase, yields change and stay the same for the five-year investment horizon.

g. Based on Table C, under what circumstances will the investment in bond Z fail to satisfy the target accumulated value?

h. What is the modified duration of the liability?

i. Complete the following table for the three bonds assuming that each bond is trading to yield 7.5%:

Bond	Modified Duration
5-year, 7.5% coupon, selling at par	
12-year, 7.5% coupon, selling at par	
6-year, 6.75% coupon, selling for 96.42899	

j. For which bond is the modified duration equal to the duration of the liability?

k. Why in this example can one focus on modified duration rather than effective duration?

Table A
Accumulated Value and Total Return after Five Years:
Five-Year 7.5% Bond Selling to Yield 7.5%

Investment horizon (years): 5
Coupon rate: 7.50%
Maturity (years): 5
Yield to maturity: 7.50%
Price: 100.00000
Par value purchased: $9,642,899
Purchase price: $9,642,899
Target accumulated value: $13,934,413

		After Five Years			
New Yield (%)	Coupon	Interest on Interest	Price of Bond	Accumulated Value	Total Return (%)
11.00	$3,616,087	$1,039,753	$9,642,899	$14,298,739	8.04
10.00	3,616,087				
9.00	3,616,087				
8.00	3,616,087				
7.50	3,616,087				
7.00	3,616,087				
6.00	3,616,087				
5.00	3,616,087				
4.00	3,616,087	343,427	9,642,899	13,602,414	7.00

Table B
Accumulated Value and Total Return after Five Years:
Twelve-Year 7.5% Bond Selling to Yield 7.5%

Investment horizon (years): 5
Coupon rate: 7.5%
Maturity (years): 12
Yield to maturity: 7.5%
Price: 100.00000
Par value purchased: $9,642,899
Purchase price: $9,642,899
Target accumulated value: $13,934,413

New Yield (%)	Coupon	After Five Years			
		Interest on Interest	Price of Bond	Accumulated Value	Total Return (%)
11.00	$3,616,087	$1,039,753	$8,024,639	$12,680,479	5.55
10.00	3,616,087				
9.00	3,616,087				
8.00	3,616,087				
7.50	3,616,087				
7.00	3,616,087				
6.00	3,616,087				
5.00	3,616,087				
4.00	3,616,087	343,427	11,685,837	15,645,352	9.92

Table C
Accumulated Value and Total Return after Five Years: Six-Year 6.75%
Bond Selling to Yield 7.5%

Investment horizon (years): 5
Coupon rate: 6.75%
Maturity (years): 6
Yield to maturity: 7.5%
Price: 96.42899
Par value purchased: $10,000,000
Purchase price: $9,642,899
Target accumulated value: $13,934,413

New Yield (%)	Coupon	After Five Years			
		Interest on Interest	Price of Bond	Accumulated Value	Total Return (%)
11.00	$3,375,000	$970,432	$9,607,657	$13,953,089	7.53
10.00	3,375,000				
9.00	3,375,000				
8.00	3,375,000				
7.50	3,375,000				
7.00	3,375,000				
6.00	3,375,000				
5.00	3,375,000				
4.00	3,375,000	320,531	10,266,965	13,962,495	7.54

25

Bond Performance Measurement and Evaluation

LEARNING OBJECTIVES

After reading this chapter, you will understand

- the difference between performance measurement and performance evaluation

- the various methods for calculating the rate of return over some evaluation period: the arithmetic average rate of return, the time-weighted rate of return, and the dollar-weighted rate of return

- the impact of client contributions and withdrawals on the calculated return

- the method of calculating return that minimizes the effect of client contributions and withdrawals

- why it is necessary to establish a benchmark

- how normal portfolios are created and the difficulties of creating them

- what a fixed-income performance attribution model is and why it is useful in assessing the performance of a portfolio manager

In this chapter, we will see how to measure and evaluate the investment performance of a fixed-income portfolio manager. *Performance measurement* involves the calculation of the return realized by a portfolio manager over some time interval, which we call the *evaluation period*. *Performance evaluation* is concerned with two issues. The first is to determine whether the manager added value by outperforming the established benchmark. The second is to determine how the manager achieved the calculated return. For example, as explained in Chapter 22, there are several active strategies that a fixed-income manager can employ. The decomposition of the performance results to explain the reasons why those results were achieved is called performance or return attribution analysis.

REQUIREMENTS FOR A BOND PERFORMANCE AND ATTRIBUTION ANALYSIS PROCESS

There are three desired requirements of a bond performance and attribution analysis process. The first is that the process be accurate. For example, as we will explain, there are several ways of measuring portfolio return. The return should recognize the time when each cash flow actually occurs, resulting in a much more accurate measure of the actual portfolio performance. The second requirement is that the process be informative. It should be capable of evaluating the managerial skills that go into fixed-income portfolio management. To be informative, the process must effectively address the key management skills and explain how these can be expressed in terms of realized performance. The final requirement is that the process be simple. Whatever the output of the process, it should be understood by the manager and client, or others who may be concerned with the performance of the portfolio. As we explain the process for analyzing bond performance in this chapter, these requirements should be kept in mind.

PERFORMANCE MEASUREMENT

The starting point for evaluating the performance of a manager is measuring return. As we will see, there are several important issues that must be addressed in developing a methodology for calculating a portfolio's return. Because different methodologies are available and these methodologies can lead to quite disparate results, it is difficult to compare the performances of managers. Consequently, there is a great deal of confusion concerning the meaning of the data provided by managers to their clients and their prospective clients. This has led to abuses by some managers in reporting performance results that are better than actual performance. To deal with this problem, the CFA Institute has promulgated a set of industrywide principles, referred to as Global Investment Performance Standards (GIPS), for calculating performance results and how to present those results.

Alternative Return Measures

Let's begin with the basic concept. The dollar return realized on a portfolio for any evaluation period (i.e., a year, month, or week) is equal to the sum of (1) the difference between the market value of the portfolio at the end of the evaluation period and the market value at the beginning of the evaluation period, and (2) any distributions made from the portfolio. It is important that any capital or income distributions from the portfolio to a client or beneficiary of the portfolio be included.

The rate of return, or simply return, expresses the dollar return in terms of the amount of the market value at the beginning of the evaluation period. Thus, the return can be viewed as the amount (expressed as a fraction of the initial portfolio value) that can be withdrawn at the end of the evaluation period while maintaining the initial market value of the portfolio intact.

In equation form, the portfolio's return can be expressed as follows:

$$R_P = \frac{MV_1 - MV_0 + D}{MV_0} \tag{25.1}$$

where

R_P = return on the portfolio
MV_1 = portfolio market value at the end of the evaluation period
MV_0 = portfolio market value at the beginning of the evaluation period
D = cash distributions from the portfolio to the client during the evaluation period

To illustrate the calculation of a return, assume the following information for an external manager for a pension plan sponsor: The portfolio's market value at the beginning and end of the evaluation period is $25 million and $28 million, respectively, and during the evaluation period $1 million is distributed to the plan sponsor from investment income. Thus,

$$MV_1 = \$28,000,000$$
$$MV_0 = \$25,000,000$$
$$D = \$1,000,000$$

Then

$$R_P = \frac{\$28,000,000 - \$25,000,000 + \$1,000,000}{\$25,000,000}$$

$$= 0.16 = 16\%$$

There are three assumptions in measuring return as given by equation (25.1). First, it assumes that cash inflows into the portfolio from interest income that occur during the evaluation period, but are not distributed, are reinvested in the portfolio. For example, suppose that during the evaluation period $2 million is received from interest income. This amount is reflected in the market value of the portfolio at the end of the period.

The second assumption is that if there are distributions from the portfolio, they occur at the end of the evaluation period or are held in the form of cash until the end of the evaluation period. In our example, $1 million is distributed to the plan sponsor. But when did that distribution actually occur? To understand why the timing of the distribution is important, consider two extreme cases: (1) the distribution is made at the end of the evaluation period, as assumed by equation (25.1), and (2) the distribution is made at the beginning of the evaluation period. In the first case, the manager had the use of the $1 million to invest for the entire evaluation period. By contrast, in the second case, the manager loses the opportunity to invest the funds until the end of the evaluation period. Consequently, the timing of the distribution will affect the return, but this is not considered in equation (25.1).

The third assumption is that there is no cash paid into the portfolio by the client. For example, suppose that sometime during the evaluation period, the plan sponsor gives an additional $1.5 million to the external manager to invest. Consequently, the market value of the portfolio at the end of the evaluation period, $28 million in our example, would reflect the contribution of $1.5 million. Equation (25.1) does not reflect that the ending market value of the portfolio is affected by the cash paid in by the sponsor. Moreover, the timing of this cash inflow will affect the calculated return.

Thus, while the return calculation for a portfolio using equation (25.1) can be determined for an evaluation period of any length of time, such as one day, one month, or five years, from a practical point of view the assumptions discussed previously limit its application. The longer the evaluation period, the more likely the assumptions will be violated. For example, it is highly likely that there may be more than one distribution to the client and more than one contribution from the client if the evaluation period is five years. Thus, a return calculation made over a long period of time, if longer than a few months, would not be very reliable because of the assumption underlying the calculations that all cash payments and inflows are made and received at the end of the period.

Not only does the violation of the assumptions make it difficult to compare the returns of two managers over some evaluation period, but it is also not useful for evaluating performance over different periods. For example, equation (25.1) will not give reliable information to compare the performance of a one-month evaluation period and a three-year evaluation period. To make such a comparison, the return must be expressed per unit of time, for example, per year.

The way to handle these practical issues is to calculate the return for a short unit of time such as a month or a quarter. We call the return so calculated the **subperiod return**. To get the return for the evaluation period, the subperiod returns are then averaged. So, for example, if the evaluation period is one year and 12 monthly returns are calculated, the monthly returns are the subperiod returns and they are averaged to get the one-year return. If a three-year return is sought and 12 quarterly returns can be calculated, quarterly returns are the subperiod returns and they are averaged to get the three-year return. The three-year return can then be converted into an annual return by the straightforward procedure described later.

There are three methodologies that have been used in practice to calculate the average of the subperiod returns: (1) the arithmetic average rate of return, (2) the time-weighted rate of return (also called the geometric rate of return), and (3) the dollar-weighted rate of return.

Arithmetic Average Rate of Return

The **arithmetic average rate of return** is an unweighted average of the subperiod returns. The general formula is

$$R_A = \frac{R_{P1} + R_{P2} + \cdots + R_{PN}}{N}$$

where

R_A = arithmetic average rate of return
R_{Pk} = portfolio return for subperiod k as measured by equation (25.1), $k = 1, \ldots, N$
N = number of subperiods in the evaluation period

For example, if the portfolio returns [as measured by equation (25.1)] were -10%, 20%, and 5% in July, August, and September, respectively, the arithmetic average monthly return is 5%:

$$N = 3; \; R_{P1} = -0.10; \; R_{P2} = 0.20; \; R_{P3} = 0.05$$

$$R_A = \frac{-0.10 + 0.20 + 0.05}{3} = 0.05 = 5\%$$

There is a major problem with using the arithmetic average rate of return. To see this problem, suppose that the initial market value of a portfolio is $28 million and the market values at the end of the next two months are $58 million and $28 million, and assume that there are no distributions or cash inflows from the client for either month. Then using equation (25.1) the subperiod return for the first month (R_{P1}) is 100% and the subperiod return for the second month (R_{P2}) is -50%. The arithmetic average rate of return is then 25%. Not a bad return! But think about this number. The portfolio's initial market value was $28 million. Its market value at the end of two months is $28 million. The return over this two-month evaluation period is zero. Yet the arithmetic average rate of return says that it is a whopping 25%.

Thus, it is improper to interpret the arithmetic average rate of return as a measure of the average return over an evaluation period. The proper interpretation is as follows: It is the average value of the withdrawals (expressed as a fraction of the initial portfolio market value) that can be made at the end of each subperiod while keeping the initial portfolio market value intact. In our first example, in which the average monthly return is 5%, the investor must add 10% of the initial portfolio market value at the end of the first month, can withdraw 20% of the initial portfolio market value at the end of the second month, and can withdraw 5% of the initial portfolio market value at the end of the third month. In our second example, the average monthly return of 25% means that 100% of the initial portfolio market value ($28 million) can be withdrawn at the end of the first month and 50% must be added at the end of the second month.

Time-Weighted Rate of Return

The **time-weighted rate of return** measures the compounded rate of growth of the initial portfolio market value during the evaluation period, assuming that all cash distributions are reinvested in the portfolio. It is also commonly referred to as the **geometric rate of return** because it is computed by taking the geometric average of the portfolio subperiod returns computed from equation (25.1). The general formula is

$$R_T = [(1 + R_{P1})(1 + R_{P2}) \cdots (1 + R_{PN})]^{1/N} - 1$$

where R_T is the time-weighted rate of return and R_{Pk} and N are as defined earlier. For example, let us assume that the portfolio returns were -10%, 20%, and 5% in July, August, and September, as in the first example. The time-weighted rate of return is

$$R_T = \{[1 + (-0.10)](1 + 0.20)(1 + 0.05)\}^{1/3} - 1$$
$$= [(0.90)(1.20)(1.05)]^{1/3} - 1 = 0.043$$

If the time-weighted rate of return is 4.3% per month, one dollar invested in the portfolio at the beginning of July would have grown at a rate of 4.3% per month during the three-month evaluation period.

The time-weighted rate of return in the second example is 0%, as expected:

$$R_T = \{(1 + 1.00)[(1 + (-0.50)]\}^{1/2} - 1$$
$$= [(2.00)(0.50)]^{1/2} - 1 = 0\%$$

In general, the arithmetic and time-weighted average returns will give different values for the portfolio return over some evaluation period. This is because in computing the arithmetic average rate of return, the amount invested is assumed to be maintained (through additions or withdrawals) at its initial portfolio market value. The time-weighted return, on the other hand, is the return on a portfolio that varies in size because of the assumption that all proceeds are reinvested.

In general, the arithmetic average rate of return will exceed the time-weighted average rate of return. The exception is in the special situation where all the subperiod returns are the same, in which case the averages are identical. The magnitude of the difference between the two averages is smaller the less the variation in the subperiod returns over the evaluation period. For example, suppose that the evaluation period is four months and that the four monthly returns are as follows:

$$R_{P1} = 0.04 \qquad R_{P2} = 0.06 \qquad R_{P3} = 0.02 \qquad R_{P4} = -0.02$$

The average arithmetic rate of return is 2.5% and the time-weighted average rate of return is 2.46%. Not much of a difference. In our earlier example, in which we calculated an average rate of return of 25% but a time-weighted average rate of return of 0%, the large discrepancy is due to the substantial variation in the two monthly returns.

Dollar-Weighted Rate of Return

The **dollar-weighted rate of return** is computed by finding the interest rate that will make the present value of the cash flows from all the subperiods in the evaluation period plus the terminal market value of the portfolio equal to the initial market value of the portfolio.

Cash flows are defined as follows:[1]

- A cash withdrawal is treated as a cash inflow. So, in the absence of any cash contribution made by a client for a given time period, a cash withdrawal (e.g., a distribution to a client) is a positive cash flow for that time period.
- A cash contribution is treated as a cash outflow. Consequently, in the absence of any cash withdrawal for a given time period, a cash contribution is treated as a negative cash flow for that period.
- If there are both cash contributions and cash withdrawals for a given time period, then the cash flow is as follows for that time period: If cash withdrawals exceed cash contributions, then there is a positive cash flow. If cash withdrawals are less than cash contributions, then there is a negative cash flow.

The dollar-weighted rate of return is simply an internal rate-of-return calculation and hence it is also called the **internal rate of return**. The general formula for the dollar-weighted return is

$$V_0 = \frac{C_1}{1 + R_D} + \frac{C_2}{(1 + R_D)^2} + \cdots + \frac{C_N + V_N}{(1 + R_D)^n}$$

where

R_D = dollar-weighted rate of return
V_0 = initial market value of the portfolio
V_N = terminal market value of the portfolio
C_k = cash flow for the portfolio (cash inflows minus cash outflows) for subperiod $k, k = 1, 2, \ldots, N$

Notice that it is not necessary to know the market value of the portfolio for each subperiod to determine the dollar-weighted rate of return. For example, consider a portfolio with a market value of $100,000 at the beginning of July, capital withdrawals of $5,000 at the end of months July, August, and September, no cash inflows from the client in any month, and a market value at the end of September of $110,000. Then $V_0 = \$100,000$, $N = 3$, $C_1 = C_2 = C_3 = \$5,000$, $V_3 = \$110,000$, and R_D is the interest rate that satisfies the following equation:

$$\$100,000 = \frac{\$5,000}{1 + R_D} + \frac{\$5,000}{(1 + R_D)^2} + \frac{\$5,000 + \$110,000}{(1 + R_D)^3}$$

It can be verified that the interest rate that satisfies the expression above is 8.1%. This, then, is the dollar-weighted return.

---

[1] Here is a simple way of remembering how to handle cash withdrawals: Treat withdrawals the same way as you would ordinary bonds. To compute the yield for a bond, the cash flow for the coupon payments (i.e., a cash withdrawal from the investment) is positive. Since a cash withdrawal is a positive cash flow, a cash contribution is a negative cash flow.

The dollar-weighted rate of return and the time-weighted rate of return will produce the same result if no withdrawals or contributions occur over the evaluation period and all investment income is reinvested. The problem with the dollar-weighted rate of return is that it is affected by factors that are beyond the control of the manager. Specifically, any contributions made by the client or withdrawals that the client requires will affect the calculated return. This makes it difficult to compare the performance of two managers.

To see this, suppose that a pension plan sponsor engaged two managers, A and B, with $10 million given to A to manage and $200 million given to B. Suppose that

- both managers invest in identical portfolios (i.e., the two portfolios have the same securities that are held in the same proportion)
- for the following two months, the rate of return on the two portfolios is 20% for month 1 and 50% for month 2
- the amount received in investment income is in cash
- the plan sponsor does not make an additional contribution to the portfolio of either manager

Under these assumptions, it is clear that the performance of both managers would be identical.

Suppose, instead, that the plan sponsor withdraws $4 million from A at the beginning of month 2. This means that A could not invest the entire amount at the end of month 1 and capture the 50% increase in the portfolio value. A's net cash flow would be as follows:

- For month 1: The cash flow is $6 million because $2 million (20% × $10 million) is realized in investment income and $4 million is withdrawn by the plan sponsor.
- For month 2: There is $8 million invested for the month—the $2 million of realized investment income in month 1 plus $6 million from the $10 million in month 1 minus the $4 million withdrawn. The realized income for month 2 is $4 million (50% × $8 million). The cash flow for month 2 is then $8 million plus $4 million or $12 million.

The dollar-weighted rate of return is then calculated as follows:

$$\$10 = \frac{\$6}{1 + R_D} + \frac{\$12}{(1 + R_D)^2} \rightarrow R_D = 28.4\%$$

For B, the cash inflow for month 1 is $40 million (20% × $200 million) and the portfolio value at the end of month 2 is $360 million (1.5 × $240 million). The dollar-weighted rate of return is

$$\$200 = \frac{\$40}{1 + R_D} + \frac{\$360}{(1 + R_D)^2} \rightarrow R_D = 44.5\%$$

These are different results for two managers who we agreed had identical performance. The withdrawal by the plan sponsor and the size of the withdrawal relative to the portfolio value had a significant impact on the calculated return. Notice also that even if the plan sponsor had withdrawn $4 million from B at the beginning of month 2, this would not have had as significant an impact. The problem would also have occurred if we assumed that the return in month 2 is –50% and that instead of A realizing a withdrawal of $4 million, the plan sponsor contributed $4 million.

Despite this limitation, the dollar-weighted rate of return does provide information. It indicates information about the growth of the fund that a client will find useful.

This growth, however, is not attributable to the performance of the manager because of contributions and withdrawals.

Annualizing Returns

The evaluation period may be less than or greater than one year. Typically, return measures are reported as an average annual return. This requires the annualization of the subperiod returns. The subperiod returns are typically calculated for a period of less than one year for the reasons described earlier. The subperiod returns are then annualized using the following formula:

$$\text{annual return} = (1 + \text{average period return})^{\text{number of periods in year}} - 1$$

For example, suppose that the evaluation period is three years and a monthly period return is calculated. Suppose further that the average monthly return is 2%. Then the annual return would be

$$\text{annual return} = (1.02)^{12} - 1 = 26.8\%$$

Suppose instead that the period used to calculate returns is quarterly and the average quarterly return is 3%. Then the annual return is

$$\text{annual return} = (1.03)^{4} - 1 = 12.6\%$$

PERFORMANCE ATTRIBUTION ANALYSIS

In the preceding section, we concentrated on performance measurement. Bond attribution models seek to identify the active management decisions that contributed to the portfolio's performance and give a quantitative assessment of the contribution of these decisions. Since these models look at performance relative to a benchmark, we begin with a discussion of benchmarks and then briefly describe two single index measures of performance.

Benchmark Portfolios

To evaluate the performance of a manager, a client must specify a benchmark against which the manager will be measured. There are two types of benchmarks that have been used in evaluating fixed-income portfolio managers: (1) market indexes published by dealer firms and vendors, and (2) normal portfolios.

A **normal portfolio** is a customized benchmark that includes "a set of securities that contains all of the securities from which a manager normally chooses, weighted as the manager would weight them in a portfolio."[2] Thus, a normal portfolio is a specialized index. It is argued that normal portfolios are more appropriate benchmarks than market indexes because they control for investment management style, thereby representing a passive portfolio against which a manager can be evaluated.

The construction of a normal portfolio for a particular manager is no simple task.[3] The principle is to construct a portfolio that, given the historical portfolios held by the

---

[2] Jon Christopherson, "Normal Portfolios: Construction of Customized Benchmarks," Chapter 6 in Frank J. Fabozzi (ed.), *Active Equity Portfolio Management* (New Hope, PA: Frank J. Fabozzi Associates, 1998), p. 92.
[3] See Mark Kritzman, "How to Build a Normal Portfolio in Three Easy Steps," *Journal of Portfolio Management*, Spring 1987, pp. 21–23.

manager, will reflect that manager's style in terms of assets and the weighting of those assets. The construction of a normal portfolio for a manager requires (1) defining the universe of fixed-income securities to be included in the normal portfolio, and (2) determining how these securities should be weighted (i.e., equally weighted or capitalization weighted).

Defining the set of securities to be included in the normal portfolio begins with discussions between the client and the manager to determine the manager's investment style. Based on these discussions, the universe of all publicly traded securities is reduced to a subset that includes those securities that the manager considers eligible given his or her investment style.

Given these securities, the next question is how they should be weighted in the normal portfolio. The two choices are equal weighting or capitalization weighting of each security. Various methodologies can be used to determine the weights. These methodologies typically involve a statistical analysis of the historical holdings of a manager and the risk exposure contained in those holdings.

Plan sponsors work with pension consultants to develop normal portfolios for a manager. The consultants use vendor systems that have been developed for performing the needed statistical analysis and the necessary optimization program to create a portfolio exhibiting similar factor positions to replicate the "normal" position of a manager. A plan sponsor must recognize that there is a cost to developing and updating the normal portfolio.

There are some who advocate the responsibility of developing normal portfolios should be left to the manager. However, many clients are reluctant to let their managers control the construction of normal portfolios because they believe that the managers will produce easily beaten, or "slow rabbit," benchmarks. Bailey and Tierney demonstrate that under reasonable conditions there is no long-term benefit for the manager to construct a "slow rabbit" benchmark and explain the disadvantage of a manager pursuing such a strategy.[4] In addition, they recommend that clients let managers control the benchmarks. Clients should, instead, focus their efforts on monitoring the quality of the benchmarks and the effectiveness of the managers' active management strategies.

Single-Index Performance Evaluation Measures

It is common for portfolio managers to report the following two single-index performance evaluation measures as an indicator of relative performance: Sharpe ratio and information ratio. Both measures are basically reward-risk ratios; the higher the ratio, the better is the relative performance.

The **Sharpe ratio** is a measure of the following reward-risk ratio:[5]

$$\text{Sharpe ratio} = \frac{\text{Portfolio return} - \text{Risk-free rate}}{\text{Standard deviation of the portfolio's return}}$$

That is, the Sharpe ratio is a measure of the excess return (i.e., reward) relative to the total variability of the portfolio return (i.e., risk).

[4] Jeffery V. Bailey and David E. Tierney, "Gaming Manager Benchmarks," *Journal of Portfolio Management* 19, 4 (1993), pp. 37–40.

[5] William F. Sharpe, "Mutual Fund Performance," *Journal of Business* 34 (1966, Special Supplement), pp. 119–138.

Using data from the calculation of the backward tracking error explained in Chapter 23, the **information ratio** is:

$$\text{Information ratio} = \frac{\text{Average active return}}{\text{Backward-looking tracking error}}$$

The reward in the information ratio is the average active return. As explained in Chapter 23, the active return is the difference between the portfolio return and the benchmark return. The average active return is also referred to in the information ratio as "alpha".

Performance Attribution Analysis Models

Clients of asset management firms need to have more information than merely whether or not a portfolio manager outperformed a benchmark and by how much. They need to know the reasons why a portfolio manager realized the performance relative to the benchmark. For example, suppose a pension fund engaged an external manager based on the manager's claim that return enhancement can be achieved via security selection. Suppose further that the manager did in fact outperform the benchmark by more than enough to cover management fees. Did this manager achieve the stated objective? It is not possible to know based solely on the outperformance because it is not known what specific risks relative to the benchmark that the manager took to generate the return. It is entirely possible that the outperformance was attributable to being mismatched against the benchmark's duration. In fact, it is possible that the manager could have outperformed the benchmark due to a mismatch in duration and invested in specific securities that did poorly. There is no way that the client can determine that by simply looking at the portfolio's return relative to the benchmark's return.

Not only do clients need information about why the portfolio's return differed from that of the benchmark, but so do the individuals at the asset management firm engaged by the client. At the firm level, bonuses to members of the portfolio management team[6] will be determined based on performance. Breaking down the performance to the team-member level is important for this purpose, because it impacts decisions about the advancement and retention of such personnel.

Although useful, single-index performance measures do not provide sufficient information about performance to address the questions posed earlier. The model that can be used is performance attribution analysis, a quantitative technique for identifying the sources of portfolio risk and performance so that the contributions of members of the portfolio management team can be measured and the impact on return of major portfolio decisions can be quantified.

There are several performance attribution models that are available from third-party entities. (Some of the larger asset management firms have developed their own models.) In selecting a third-party model, there are requirements that a good attribution model should possess in order to evaluate the decision-making ability of the members of the portfolio management team: additivity, completeness, and fairness.[7] **Additivity** means that the contribution to performance of two or more decision makers of the portfolio management team should be equal to the sum of the contributions of those decision

---

[6] We discussed the portfolio management team in Chapter 22.
[7] Anthony Lazanas, António Baldaque da Silva, Chris Sturhahn, Eric P. Wilson, and Pam Zhong, "Principles of Performance Attribution," Chapter 69 in Frank J. Fabozzi (ed.), *Handbook of Fixed Income Securities* (New York: McGraw-Hill, 2012).

makers. **Completeness** means that when the contribution to portfolio performance of all decision makers is added up, the result should be equal to the contribution to portfolio performance relative to the benchmark. Finally, the decision-making process is one that involves the interaction of many members of the portfolio management team. **Fairness** means that the portfolio management team members should view the performance attribution model selected as being fair with respect to representing their contribution.

Types of Performance Attribution Models

In the early 1970s, Fama suggested a framework for the partitioning of risk-adjusted portfolio performance for *equity* managers.[8] Extensions of the Fama framework were then proposed by Kon and Jen[9] and Kon[10] for mutual funds. In 1980, Dietz, Fogler, and Hardy appear to have been the first to apply performance attribution to bonds.[11] A few years later, Fong, Pearson, and Vasicek provided a more elaborate bond performance attribution model.[12]

Today, performance attribution models can be classified into three types:

1. Sector-based attribution models
2. Factor-based attribution models
3. Hybrid sector-based/factor-based attribution models.

We discuss each type below.

Sector-Based Attribution Models

The simplest model is the **sector-based attribution**, also referred to as the **Brinson model**.[13] In this model, the portfolio return relative to the benchmark is represented by two decisions: (1) the allocation of funds among the different sectors and (2) the selection of the specific securities within each sector. The first decision is referred to as the **asset allocation decision** and the second the **security selection decision**.[14]

For example, consider the following three portfolios with the return relative to the same benchmark (i.e., the active return) shown in basis points:

Decision	Portfolio A	Portfolio B	Portfolio C
Asset allocation	130	235	−45
Security selection	70	−35	245

All three managers outperformed the benchmark by 200 basis points. However, they did it in different ways. The manager of Portfolio A made the right calls both in the

---

[8] Eugene F. Fama, "Components of Investment Performance," *Journal of Finance* 27, 3 (1972), pp. 551–567.

[9] Stanley J. Kon and Frank C. Jen, "The Investment Performance of Mutual Funds: An Empirical Investigation of Timing, Selectivity, and Market Efficiency," *Journal of Business* 52, 2 (1979), pp. 263–289.

[10] Stanle J. Kon, "The Market-Timing Performance of Mutual Fund Managers," *Journal of Business* 56 (1983), pp. 323–347.

[11] Peter O. Dietz, H. Russell Fogler, and Donald J. Hardy, "The Challenge of Analyzing Bond Portfolio Returns," *Journal of Portfolio Management* 6, 3 (1980), pp. 53–58.

[12] H. Gifford Fong, Charles Pearson, and Oldrich A. Vasicek, "Bond Performance: Analyzing Sources of Return," *Journal of Portfolio Management* 9, 2 (1983), pp. 46–50.

[13] Gary Brinson and Nimrod Fachler, "Measuring Non-U.S. Equity Portfolio Performance," *Journal of Portfolio Management* 11, 3 (1985), pp. 73–76.

[14] There is also an interaction decision that results when two factors contribute to the performance of the return but vendors will fold that term into one of the other two.

allocation of funds among the different sectors and the selection of securities within each sector. Portfolio B's outperformance is attributable to the portfolio manager making a good asset allocation decision while at the same time doing a poor job of security selection. That is, the manager picked the right sectors of the benchmark to allocate funds but selected the poor performing securities within those sectors. Finally, Portfolio C's manager outperformed due to the selection of the better performing securities within a sector despite not selecting the better performing sectors.

A more detailed analysis would break down the active return from each sector and the securities within each sector. Performance attributable to security selection would probably differ by sector. For example, consider Portfolio C and assume that the 245 basis points due to security selection was such that there was a zero active return in terms of security selection for all sectors in the benchmark except for the CMBS and agency MBS sectors. Assume further that the respective active returns were 100 and 145 basis points respectively. This would indicate that the analysts responsible for the selection of the securities in these two sectors did a superb job in making security selection decisions.

Factor-Based Attribution Models

In Chapter 23, we discussed portfolio construction using factor-based models. Recall that these models determine the key common drivers of returns and their risks for the benchmark and can then be used to construct a portfolio relative to a benchmark so as to control the tracking error. These common factors are referred to as the systematic risk factors. Also as explained in Chapter 23, the primary systematic risk factors for a U.S. benchmark can be decomposed into yield curve risk (changes in the level and shape of the yield curve risk) and non-yield curve risks. The latter include swap spread risk, volatility risk, government-related spread risk, corporate spread risk, and securitized spread risk.

For example, consider the following three hypothetical portfolios all with a 110 basis point active return:

Risk Factor	Portfolio D	Portfolio E	Portfolio F
Yield curve risk	140	1	−60
Swap spread risk	0	10	20
Volatility risk	−1	9	15
Government-related spread risk	−19	2	10
Corporate spread risk	−8	48	60
Securitized spread risk	−2	40	55

The manager of Portfolio D simply made one right bet: an interest rate bet. All other bets made in the portfolio had an adverse impact on performance. In contrast, it seems that Portfolio E's manager took no view on interest rates. All the non-interest rate bets paid off, with the major one being due to bets on the risks associated with corporate credit and securitized products. The manager of Portfolio F also made the right bets on non-interest rate risk and, as did the manager of Portfolio E, the majority of the outperformance was due to the risks associated with corporate credit and securitized products. However, Portfolio F's manager made the wrong call on the interest rate bet, causing the portfolio's performance to just match that of Portfolio E's manager.

Factor-based attribution models actually allow a decomposition of the yield curve risk into level risk and changes in the shape of the yield curve. For example, for the three hypothetical portfolios just discussed, suppose that the attribution due to yield curve risk is determined to be as follows:

	Portfolio D	Portfolio E	Portfolio F
Yield curve risk	140	1	−60
Level risk	135	60	3
Shape risk	5	−59	−63

Notice that once yield curve risk is decomposed as shown above, it turns out that the manager of Portfolio E did indeed make interest rate bets. It turns out that the two bets almost offset each other so that net there was only a one-basis-point return attributable to the interest rate bet. Portfolio D's manager basically made a major duration bet but virtually no bet on changes in the shape of the yield curve. The interest rate bet by the manager of Portfolio F was on changes in the shape of the yield curve but otherwise was basically duration neutral.

Hybrid Sector-Based/Factor-Based Attribution Models

As the name suggests, a **hybrid sector-based/factor-based attribution model** combines the previous two attribution models. This model allows for much more detail regarding not only the bets on the primary systematic risk factors driving returns but also the impact of decisions with respect to sector and security selection. The level of detail in such models depends on what might be sought by the client or the portfolio manager.

▌KEY POINTS

- Performance measurement involves calculation of the return realized by a portfolio manager over some evaluation period.
- Performance evaluation is concerned with determining whether the portfolio manager added value by outperforming the established benchmark and how the portfolio manager achieved the calculated return.
- The rate of return expresses the dollar return in terms of the amount of the initial investment (i.e., the initial market value of the portfolio).
- Three methodologies have been used in practice to calculate the average of the sub-period returns: (1) the arithmetic average rate of return, (2) the time-weighted (or geometric) rate of return, and (3) the dollar-weighted return.
- The arithmetic average rate of return is the average value of the withdrawals (expressed as a fraction of the initial portfolio market value) that can be made at the end of each period while keeping the initial portfolio market value intact.
- The time-weighted rate of return measures the compounded rate of growth of the initial portfolio over the evaluation period, assuming that all cash distributions are reinvested in the portfolio. The time-weighted return is the return on a portfolio that varies in size because of the assumption that all proceeds are reinvested. In general, the arithmetic average rate of return will exceed the time-weighted average rate of return. The magnitude of the difference between the two averages is smaller the less the variation in the sub-period returns over the evaluation period.

- The dollar-weighted rate of return is computed by finding the interest rate that will make the present value of the cash flows from all the sub-periods in the evaluation period plus the terminal market value of the portfolio equal to the initial market value of the portfolio. The dollar-weighted rate of return is an internal rate-of-return calculation and will produce the same result as the time-weighted rate of return if (1) no withdrawals or contributions occur over the evaluation period, and (2) all coupon interest payments are reinvested.

- The problem with using the dollar-weighted rate of return to evaluate the performance of portfolio managers is that it is affected by factors that are beyond the control of the portfolio manager. Specifically, any contributions made by the client or withdrawals that the client requires will affect the calculated return, making it difficult to compare the performance of two portfolio managers.

- The role of performance evaluation is to determine if a portfolio manager added value beyond what could have been achieved by a passive strategy in a benchmark portfolio. The analysis requires the establishment of a benchmark.

- A normal portfolio is a customized benchmark that includes a set of securities that contains the universe of securities that a manager normally selects from and is weighted as the manager would weight them in a portfolio. Advocates claim that normal portfolios are more appropriate benchmarks than market indexes because they control for investment management style, thereby representing a passive portfolio against which a manager can be evaluated.

- Bond indexes are commonly used as benchmarks.

- Single-index performance evaluation measures include the Sharpe ratio and the information ratio. These ratios are reward-risk ratios. They have limited use because they fail to explain the reasons for relative performance.

- Performance attribution models can be used to explain why the active return of a portfolio was realized. The three types of performance attribution models available are sector-based attribution models, factor-based attribution models, and hybrid sector-based/factor-based attribution models.

❙ QUESTIONS

1. What is the difference between performance measurement and performance evaluation?

2. Suppose that the monthly return for two bond managers is as follows:

Month	Manager I	Manager II
1	9%	25%
2	13%	13%
3	22%	22%
4	−18%	−24%

   What is the arithmetic average monthly rate of return for the two managers?

3. What is the time-weighted average monthly rate of return for the two managers in Question 2?

4. Why does the arithmetic average monthly rate of return diverge more from the time-weighted monthly rate of return for manager II than for manager I in Question 2?

5. Smith & Jones is a money management firm specializing in fixed-income securities. One of its clients gave the firm $100 million to manage. The market value for the portfolio for the four months after receiving the funds was as follows:

End of Month	Market Value (in millions)
1	$ 50
2	150
3	75
4	100

a. Calculate the rate of return for each month.

b. Smith & Jones reported to the client that over the four-month period the average monthly rate of return was 33.33%. How was that value obtained?

c. Is the average monthly rate of return of 33.33% indicative of the performance of Smith & Jones? If not, what would be a more appropriate measure?

6. The Mercury Company is a fixed-income management firm that manages the funds of pension plan sponsors. For one of its clients it manages $200 million. The cash flow for this particular client's portfolio for the past three months was $20 million, −$8 million, and $4 million. The market value of the portfolio at the end of three months was $208 million.

a. What is the dollar-weighted rate of return for this client's portfolio over the three-month period?

b. Suppose that the $8 million cash outflow in the second month was a result of withdrawals by the plan sponsor and that the cash flow after adjusting for this withdrawal is therefore zero. What would the dollar-weighted rate of return then be for this client's portfolio?

7. If the average monthly return for a portfolio is 1.23%, what is the annualized return?

8. If the average quarterly return for a portfolio is 1.78%, what is the annualized return?

9. What are the difficulties of constructing a normal portfolio?

10. Suppose that the active return for a portfolio over the past year was 130 basis points after management fees. What questions would you have to ask before concluding that the manager's performance was exceptional?

11. Not only do clients find performance attribution analysis helpful but so does the chief investment officer of an asset management firm in evaluating the firm's bond portfolio team. Explain why.

12. A financial institution has hired three external portfolio managers: X, Y, and Z. All three managers have the same benchmark. A performance attribution analysis of the portfolios managed by the three managers for the past year was (in basis points):

Risk Factor	Portfolio X	Portfolio Y	Portfolio Z
Yield curve risk	−1	92	−3
Swap spread risk	20	4	20
Volatility risk	40	3	25
Government-related spread risk	35	−5	10
Corporate spread risk	−2	6	30
Securitized spread risk	−2	−4	5

The financial institution's investment committee is using the previous information to assess the performance of the three external managers. Below is a statement from three members of the performance evaluation committee. Respond to each statement.

a. Committee member 1: "Based on overall performance, it is clear that manager Y was the best performing manager given the 96 basis points outperformance."

b. Committee member 2: "All three of the managers were hired because they claimed that they had the ability to capitalize on corporate credit opportunities. Although they have all outperformed the benchmark, I am concerned about the claims that they made when we engaged them."

c. Committee member 3: "It seems that managers X and Z were able to outperform the benchmark without taking on any interest rate risk at all."

13. In discussing the performance of the external managers hired by a financial institution, the following statement was made: "The most important factor we consider in retention decisions is performance as measured by the information ratio." Comment on this statement.

26

Interest-Rate Futures Contracts

LEARNING OBJECTIVES

After reading this chapter, you will understand

- what a futures contract is
- the differences between a futures contract and a forward contract
- the basic features of various interest-rate futures contracts
- the cheapest-to-deliver issue for a Treasury bond futures contract and how it is determined
- how the theoretical price of a futures contract is determined
- how the theoretical price of a Treasury bond futures contract is affected by the delivery options
- how futures contracts can be used in bond portfolio management: portfolio duration adjustment, yield enhancement, and hedging
- how to calculate the hedge ratio and the number of contracts to short when hedging with Treasury bond futures contracts

A futures contract is an agreement that requires a party to the agreement either to buy or sell something at a designated future date at a predetermined price. In this chapter, we describe interest-rate futures contracts. Interest-rate options and options on futures are covered in Chapter 27. Interest-rate swaps and agreements are the subject of Chapter 28.

With the advent of interest-rate futures, options, swaps, caps, and floors, proactive portfolio risk management, in its broadest sense, assumes a new dimension. Portfolio managers can achieve new degrees of freedom. It is now possible to alter the interest-rate sensitivity of a bond portfolio or an asset/liability position economically and quickly. These derivative contracts, so called because they derive their value from an underlying asset, offer portfolio managers risk and return patterns that previously were either unavailable or too costly to create.

MECHANICS OF FUTURES TRADING

A **futures contract** is an agreement between a buyer (seller) and an established exchange or its clearinghouse in which the buyer (seller) agrees to take (make) delivery of something at a specified price at the end of a designated period of time. The price at which the parties agree to transact in the future is called the futures price. The designated date at which the parties must transact is called the **settlement** or **delivery date**.

To illustrate, suppose that there is a futures contract traded on an exchange where the something to be bought or sold is bond XYZ, and the settlement is three months from now. Assume further that Bob buys this futures contract, and Sally sells this futures contract, and the price at which they agree to transact in the future is $100. Then $100 is the **futures price**. At the settlement date, Sally will deliver bond XYZ to Bob. Bob will give Sally $100, the futures price.

Most financial futures contracts have settlement dates in the months of March, June, September, or December. This means that at a predetermined time in the contract settlement month the contract stops trading, and a price is determined by the exchange for settlement of the contract. The contract with the nearest settlement date is called the **nearby futures contract**. The next futures contract is the one that settles just after the nearby contract. The contract furthest away in time from settlement is called the **most distant futures contract**.

Opening Position

When an investor takes a position in the market by buying a futures contract, the investor is said to be in a **long position** or to be **long futures**. If, instead, the investor's opening position is the sale of a futures contract, the investor is said to be in a **short position** or **short futures**.

Liquidating a Position

A party to a futures contract has two choices on liquidation of the position. First, the position can be liquidated prior to the settlement date. For this purpose, the party must take an offsetting position in the same contract. For the buyer of a futures contract, this means selling the same number of identical futures contracts; for the seller of a futures contract, this means buying the same number of identical futures contracts.

The alternative is to wait until the settlement date. At that time, the party purchasing a futures contract accepts delivery of the underlying asset at the agreed-upon price; the party that sells a futures contract liquidates the position by delivering the underlying asset at the agreed-upon price. For some futures contracts that we describe in this chapter, settlement is made in cash only. Such contracts are referred to as **cash-settlement contracts**.

Role of the Clearinghouse

Associated with every futures exchange is a clearinghouse, which performs several functions. One of these functions is guaranteeing that the two parties to the transaction will perform. To see the importance of this function, consider potential problems in the futures transaction described earlier from the perspective of the two parties: Bob the buyer and Sally the seller. Each must be concerned with the other's ability to fulfill the obligation at the settlement date. Suppose that at the settlement date the price of bond XYZ in the cash market is $70. Sally can buy bond XYZ for $70 and deliver it to Bob, who, in turn, must pay her $100. If Bob does not have the capacity to pay $100 or refuses to pay, however,

Sally has lost the opportunity to realize a profit of $30. Suppose, instead, that the price of bond XYZ in the cash market is $150 at the settlement date. In this case, Bob is ready and willing to accept delivery of bond XYZ and pay the agreed-upon price of $100. If Sally does not have the ability or refuses to deliver bond XYZ, Bob has lost the opportunity to realize a profit of $50.

The clearinghouse exists to meet this problem. When an investor takes a position in the futures market, the clearinghouse takes the opposite position and agrees to satisfy the terms set forth in the contract. Because the clearinghouse exists, the investor need not worry about the financial strength and integrity of the party taking the opposite side of the contract. After initial execution of an order, the relationship between the two parties ends. The clearinghouse interposes itself as the buyer for every sale and the seller for every purchase. Thus, investors are free to liquidate their positions without involving the other party in the original contract and without worry that the other party may default. This is the reason why we define a futures contract as an agreement between a party and a clearinghouse associated with an exchange.

Besides its guarantee function, the clearinghouse makes it simple for parties to a futures contract to unwind their positions prior to the settlement date. Suppose that Bob wants to get out of his futures position. He will not have to seek out Sally and work out an agreement with her to terminate the original agreement. Instead, Bob can unwind his position by selling an identical futures contract. As far as the clearinghouse is concerned, its records will show that Bob has bought and sold an identical futures contract. At the settlement date, Sally will not deliver bond XYZ to Bob but will be instructed by the clearinghouse to deliver to someone who bought and still has an open futures position. In the same way, if Sally wants to unwind her position prior to the settlement date, she can buy an identical futures contract.

Margin Requirements

When a position is first taken in a futures contract, the investor must deposit a minimum dollar amount per contract as specified by the exchange. This amount, called the **initial margin**, is required as deposit for the contract.[1] The initial margin may be in the form of an interest-bearing security such as a Treasury bill. As the price of the futures contract fluctuates, the value of the investor's equity in the position changes. At the end of each trading day, the exchange determines the settlement price for the futures contract. This price is used to mark to market the investor's position so that any gain or loss from the position is reflected in the investor's equity account.

The **maintenance margin** is the minimum level (specified by the exchange) by which an investor's equity position may fall as a result of an unfavorable price movement before the investor is required to deposit additional margin. The additional margin deposited, called the **variation margin**, is the amount necessary to bring the equity in the account back to its initial margin level. Unlike initial margin, variation margin must be in cash, not in interest-bearing instruments. Any excess margin in the account may be withdrawn by the investor. If a party to a futures contract who is required to deposit variation margin fails to do so within 24 hours, the futures position is closed out.

[1] Individual brokerage firms are free to set margin requirements above the minimum established by the exchange.

Although there are initial and maintenance margin requirements for buying securities on margin, the concept of margin differs for securities and futures. When securities are acquired on margin, the difference between the price of the security and the initial margin is borrowed from the broker. The security purchased serves as collateral for the loan, and the investor pays interest. For futures contracts, the initial margin, in effect, serves as "good faith" money, an indication that the investor will satisfy the obligation of the contract. Normally, no money is borrowed by the investor.

FUTURES VERSUS FORWARD CONTRACTS

Just like a futures contract, a **forward contract** is an agreement for the future delivery of the underlying at a specified price at the end of a designated period of time. Futures contracts are standardized agreements as to the delivery date (or month) and quality of the deliverable and are traded on organized exchanges. A forward contract differs in that it is usually nonstandardized (i.e., the terms of each contract are negotiated individually between buyer and seller), there is no clearinghouse, and secondary markets are often non-existent or extremely thin. Unlike a futures contract, which is an exchange-traded product, a forward contract is an over-the-counter instrument.

Because there is no clearinghouse that guarantees the performance of a counterparty in a forward contract, the parties to a forward contract are exposed to **counterparty risk**. Counterparty risk is the risk that the other party to the transaction will fail to perform. That is, a party to a forward contract is exposed to credit or default risk.

Although both futures and forward contracts set forth terms of delivery, futures contracts are not intended to be settled by delivery. In fact, generally less than 2% of outstanding contracts are settled by delivery. Forward contracts, in contrast, are intended for delivery.

A futures contract is marked to market at the end of each trading day, whereas a forward contract may or may not be marked to market. Just how much variation margin may be required by one or both parties of a forward contract depends on the terms negotiated. Therefore, although a futures contract is subject to interim cash flows as additional margin may be required in the case of adverse price movements, or as cash is withdrawn in the case of favorable price movements, variation margin may or may not result from a forward contract.

Finally, the parties in a forward contract are exposed to credit risk because either party may default on the obligation. Credit risk is minimal in the case of futures contracts because the clearinghouse associated with the exchange guarantees the other side of the transaction. Other than these differences, most of what we say about futures contracts applies to forward contracts.

RISK AND RETURN CHARACTERISTICS OF FUTURES CONTRACTS

The buyer of a futures contract will realize a profit if the futures price increases; the seller of a futures contract will realize a profit if the futures price decreases. For example, suppose that one month after Bob and Sally take their positions in the futures contract, the futures price of bond XYZ increases to $120. Bob, the buyer of the futures contract, could then sell the futures contract and realize a profit of $20. Effectively, at the settlement date he has agreed to buy bond XYZ for $100 and agreed to sell bond XYZ for $120. Sally, the seller of the futures contract, will realize a loss of $20.

If the futures price falls to $40 and Sally buys the contract, she realizes a profit of $60 because she agreed to sell bond XYZ for $100 and now can buy it for $40. Bob would realize a loss of $60. Thus, if the futures price decreases, the buyer of a futures contract realizes a loss while the seller of a futures contract realizes a profit.

Leveraging Aspect of Futures

When a position is taken in a futures contract, the party need not put up the entire amount of the investment. Instead, only initial margin must be put up. If Bob has $100 and wants to invest in bond XYZ because he believes its price will appreciate as a result of a decline in interest rates, he can buy one bond if bond XYZ is selling for $100. If the exchange where the futures contract for bond XYZ is traded requires an initial margin of $5, however, Bob can purchase 20 contracts with his $100 investment. (This example ignores the fact that Bob may need funds for variation margin.) His payoff will then depend on the price action of 20 XYZ bonds, not the one he could buy with $100. Thus, he can leverage the use of his funds. Although the degree of leverage available in the futures market varies from contract to contract, the leverage attainable is considerably greater than in the cash market.

At first, the leverage available in the futures market may suggest that the market benefits only those who want to speculate on price movements. This is not true. Futures markets can be used to reduce price risk. Without the leverage possible in futures transactions, the cost of reducing price risk using futures would be too high for many market participants.

INTEREST-RATE FUTURES CONTRACTS

The two major exchanges where interest rate futures are traded are those operated by the Chicago Mercantile Exchange Group (CME Group) and Euronext Liffe.[2] The exchanges offer bond futures and short-term interest rate futures. Below is a listing of some of the interest-rate futures contracts by the CME Group and Euronext Liffe:

CME GROUP	EURONEXT LIFFE
U.S. Treasury Futures	EONIA (Euro Overnight Index Average) Futures
Eurodollar Futures	Eurodollar Futures
On-the-Run U.S. Treasury Futures	Euribor Futures
30-Day Fed Funds Futures	Euroswiss Futures
3-Month Overnight Index Swap Futures	Euribor Futures
Interest Rate Swap Futures	Euroyen Futures
	Short Sterling Futures
	Short Gilt Futures
	Medium Gilt Futures
	Long Gilt Futures
	Japanese Government Bond Futures
	Euro Swapnote Futures
	Dollar Swapnote Futures

---

[2] The CME Group was formed in 2007 with the merger of two major futures and options exchanges: the Chicago Mercantile Exchange and the Chicago Board of Trade. Liffe stands for London International Financial Futures Exchange. This exchange was acquired by the NYSE Euronext.

It is not possible to review all of these contracts, nor is it necessary since information for each is provided on the Internet by the exchange. Here we describe only two of the major contracts used for risk control by institutional investors: Eurodollar futures and U.S. Treasury futures.

Eurodollar Futures

Eurodollar futures contracts are traded on both the International Monetary Market of the Chicago Mercantile Exchange and the London International Financial Futures Exchange. The Eurodollar time deposit with a principal value of U.S. $1 million and three months to maturity is the underlying for this contract. The Eurodollar futures contract is one of the most heavily traded futures contracts in the world. It is frequently used to trade the short end of the yield curve, and many hedgers have found this contract to be the best hedging vehicle for a wide range of hedging situations.

A Eurodollar time deposit is a dollar-denominated time deposit issued outside of the United States. The interest rate paid on Eurodollar time deposits is the London Interbank Offered Rate (LIBOR) and is an add-on-interest rate. For the Eurodollar futures contract the parties are effectively agreeing to buy and sell "three-month LIBOR."

The contract is quoted on an index price basis. For example, the index price might be 94.52. From the futures index price, the annualized futures three-month LIBOR is determined as follows: 100 minus the index price. For example, a Eurodollar futures index price of 94.52 means the parties to this contract agree to buy or sell three-month LIBOR for 5.48%. Since the underlying is an interest rate that obviously cannot be delivered, this contract is a cash settlement contract.

The principal value for this contract is $1 million. A one-tick change in the index price for this contract is 0.01. That is, an index price change of, for example, 94.52 to 94.53 is 0.01 or one tick. Let's see how an index change of one tick translates into a change in three-month LIBOR. An index price change from 94.52 to 94.53 changes three-month LIBOR from 5.48% to 5.47%. In terms of basis points, a one-tick change in the index price means a 1-basis-point (0.0001) change in three-month LIBOR.

We know that simple interest on $1 million for 90 days is equal to

$$\$1,000,000 \times (\text{LIBOR} \times 90/360)$$

If LIBOR changes by 1 basis point (0.0001), then

$$\$1,000,000 \times (0.0001 \times 90/360) = \$25$$

Hence, a one-tick change in the index price or, equivalently, a 1-basis-point change in the three-month LIBOR means a $25 change in the value of the contract. So, if there is a 10-tick change in the index price or, equivalently, a 10-basis-point change in three-month LIBOR, the contract value will change by $250 (= $25 × 10).

The minimum price fluctuation for the index price is a half a tick, or $12.50. In the nearest trading month for this contract, the minimum index price fluctuation is a quarter tick, or $6.25.

The contracts are listed for March, June, September, and December (referred to as the "March cycle"), 40 months in the March quarterly cycle, and the four nearest serial contract months. A portfolio manager can take a position in this contract out to 10 years.

As explained, the Eurodollar futures contract is a cash settlement contract. That is, the parties settle in cash based on three-month LIBOR at the settlement date. Suppose that a trade occurs at 94.52 and on the settlement date the settlement index price is 95.00. From the perspective of the buyer, the index price increased. Hence, the seller must pay the buyer 0.48. Since one tick is $25 and 0.48 is 48 ticks, the buyer receives from the seller $1,200 (48 × $25). An alternative way of thinking about this is that the buyer contracted to receive a three-month interest rate of 5.42% (i.e., 100.00 − 94.52). At the settlement date, the index price is 95.00. This means a three-month LIBOR of 5.00% interest rate is available in the market. The compensation of $1,200 of the seller to the buyer is for the lower prevailing three-month LIBOR of 5.00% rather than the contracted amount of 5.48%.

To see how this contract is used for hedging, suppose that a market participant is concerned that its borrowing costs six months from now are going to be higher. To protect itself, it can take a position in the Eurodollar futures contract such that a rise in short-term interest rates will be beneficial. With this position in the futures contract, if short-term interest rates do in fact increase, future borrowing costs will rise but they will be offset (in whole or in part) from the position in the Eurodollar futures contract. A position in the futures contract that will benefit from a rise in interest rates is a short position (i.e., sell the futures contract). To see this, consider our previous illustration in the Eurodollar futures at 94.52 (5.48% rate). Suppose at the settlement date three-month LIBOR increases to 6.00% and, therefore, the settlement index price is 94.00. This means that the seller sold the contract for 94.52 and purchased it for 94.00, realizing a gain of 0.52 or 52 ticks. The buyer must pay the seller $1,300 (52 × $25). The gain from the short futures position is then used to offset the higher borrowing cost resulting from a rise in short-term interest rates.

There are similar futures contracts based on reference rates for floating rate loans in other currencies that have specifications similar to that of Eurodollar futures. For example, for euro-denominated loans, the reference rate used is typically the Euro Interbank Offered Rate (Euribor). Euribor is the rate on deposits denominated in euros and it is the underlying for the Euribor futures contact. The Euribor futures and the Eurodollar futures contracts are the most actively traded futures contracts in the world.

Treasury Futures

The most active bond derivatives contracts are the Treasury futures contracts. These contracts are classified by maturity. The underlying for the **Treasury bond futures contract** are certain Treasury coupon securities that were originally issued as Treasury bonds. **Treasury note futures** contracts include the two-year, five-year, and 10-year Treasury futures.

Treasury Bond Futures

The underlying instrument for a Treasury bond futures contract is $100,000 par value of a hypothetical 20-year 6% coupon bond. The futures price is quoted in terms of par being 100. Quotes are in *32nds* of 1%. Thus, a quote for a Treasury bond futures contract of 97-16 means 97 and 16/32nds, or 97.50.[3] So if a buyer and seller agree on a futures price of 97-16, this means that the buyer agrees to accept delivery of the hypothetical underlying Treasury bond and pay 97.50% of par value, and the seller agrees to accept 97.50% of par value. Because the par value is $100,000, the futures price that the buyer and seller agree to transact for this hypothetical Treasury bond is $97,500.

---

[3] Sometimes an apostrophe is used instead of a hyphen in the quote. For example, instead of 97-16, the quote would be 97'16.

The minimum price fluctuation for the Treasury bond futures contract is a *32nd* of 1%. The dollar value of a *32nd* for a $100,000 par value (the par value for the underlying Treasury bond) is $31.25. Thus, the minimum price fluctuation is $31.25 for this contract.

We have been referring to the underlying as a hypothetical Treasury bond. Does this mean that the contract is a cash settlement contract, as is the case with the Eurodollar futures contract? The answer is no. The seller of a Treasury bond futures contract who decides to make delivery rather than liquidate his position by buying back the contract prior to the settlement date must deliver some Treasury bond. But what Treasury bond? The CME Group allows the seller to deliver one of several Treasury bonds that the CME Group declares is acceptable for delivery. The specific bonds that the seller may deliver are published by the CME Group prior to the initial trading of a futures contract with a specific settlement date. Exhibit 26-1 shows the Treasury issues that the seller can select from to deliver to the buyer of four Treasury bond futures contracts by settlement month. The CME Group makes its determination of the Treasury issues that are acceptable for delivery from all outstanding Treasury issues that meet the following criteria: An issue must have at least 15 years to maturity from the date of delivery if not callable; in the case of callable Treasury bonds, the issue must not be callable for at least 15 years from the first day of the delivery month. In addition to the eligible issues shown in the exhibit, newly issued Treasury bonds would qualify for delivery.

The delivery process for the Treasury bond futures contract makes the contract interesting. At the settlement date, the seller of a futures contract (the short) is required to deliver the buyer (the long) $100,000 par value of 6% 20-year Treasury bond. Because no such bond exists, the seller must choose from one of the acceptable deliverable Treasury

Exhibit 26-1   Treasury Bonds Acceptable for Delivery and Conversion Factors

Coupon	Maturity Date	Mar. 2011	Jun. 2011	Sep. 2011	Dec. 2011	Mar. 2012	Jun. 2012	Sep. 2012	Dec. 2012	Mar. 2013
6 3/4	08/15/26	1.0741	1.0735	-----	-----	-----	-----	-----	-----	-----
6 1/2	11/15/26	1.0500	1.0494	1.0490	-----	-----	-----	-----	-----	-----
6 5/8	02/15/27	1.0630	1.0625	1.0618	1.0613	-----	-----	-----	-----	-----
6 3/8	08/15/27	1.0385	1.0382	1.0377	1.0375	1.0370	1.0368	-----	-----	-----
6 1/8	11/15/27	1.0130	1.0127	1.0127	1.0125	1.0125	1.0123	1.0123	-----	-----
5 1/2	08/15/28	0.9466	0.9472	0.9475	0.9481	0.9485	0.9490	0.9494	0.9500	0.9504
5 1/4	11/15/28	0.9194	0.9200	0.9208	0.9213	0.9221	0.9227	0.9235	0.9242	0.9250
5 1/4	02/15/29	0.9187	0.9194	0.9200	0.9208	0.9213	0.9221	0.9227	0.9235	0.9242
6 1/8	08/15/29	1.0136	1.0136	1.0134	1.0134	1.0132	1.0132	1.0130	1.0130	1.0127
6 1/4	05/15/30	1.0281	1.0278	1.0277	1.0274	1.0273	1.0270	1.0269	1.0265	1.0264
5 3/8	02/15/31	0.9281	0.9287	0.9291	0.9297	0.9301	0.9307	0.9311	0.9318	0.9322
4 1/2	02/15/36	0.8078	0.8087	0.8095	0.8105	0.8113	0.8123	0.8132	0.8142	0.8151
4 3/4	02/15/37	-----	-----	-----	-----	0.8398	0.8406	0.8413	0.8421	0.8427
5	05/15/37	-----	-----	-----	-----	-----	0.8718	0.8725	0.8730	0.8737
4 3/8	02/15/38	-----	-----	-----	-----	-----	-----	-----	-----	0.7918

bonds that the CME Group has specified. Suppose that the seller is entitled to deliver $100,000 of a 5% 20-year Treasury bond to settle the futures contract. The value of this bond of course is less than the value of a 6% 20-year bond. If the seller delivers the 5% 20-year bond, this would be unfair to the buyer of the futures contract who contracted to receive $100,000 of a 6% 20-year Treasury bond. Alternatively, suppose that the seller delivers $100,000 of a 7% 20-year Treasury bond. The value of a 7% 20-year Treasury bond is greater than that of a 6% 20-year bond, so this would be a disadvantage to the seller.

How can this problem be resolved? To make delivery equitable to both parties, the CME Group has introduced **conversion factors** for determining the invoice price of each acceptable deliverable Treasury issue against the Treasury bond futures contract. The conversion factor is determined by the CME Group before a contract with a specific settlement date begins trading. Exhibit 26-1 shows for each of the acceptable Treasury issues for each contract the corresponding conversion factor.[4] The conversion factor is constant throughout the trading period of the futures contract for a given settlement month. The short must notify the long of the actual bond that will be delivered one day before the delivery date.

The price that the buyer must pay the seller when a Treasury bond is delivered is called the **invoice price**. The invoice price is the settlement futures price plus accrued interest on the bonds delivered. However, as just noted, the seller can deliver one of several acceptable Treasury issues. To make delivery fair to both parties, the invoice price must be adjusted based on the actual Treasury issue delivered. It is the conversion factors that are used to adjust the invoice price. The invoice price is

invoice price = contract size × futures contract settlement price × conversion factor
+ accrued interest

Suppose that the Treasury bond futures contract settles at 94-08 and that the short elects to deliver a Treasury bond issue with a conversion factor of 1.20. The futures contract settlement price of 94-08 means 94.25% of par value. As the contract size is $100,000, the invoice price the buyer pays the seller is

$100,000 × 0.9425 × 1.20 + accrued interest = $113,100 + accrued interest

In selecting the issue to be delivered, the short will select from all the deliverable issues the one that is cheapest to deliver. This issue is referred to as the **cheapest-to-deliver issue**; it plays a key role in the pricing of this futures contract. The cheapest-to-deliver issue is determined by participants in the market as follows. For each of the acceptable Treasury issues from which the seller can select, the seller calculates the return that can be earned by buying that issue and delivering it at the settlement date. Note that the seller can calculate the return because she knows the price of the Treasury issue now and the futures price that she agrees to deliver the issue. The return so calculated is called the **implied repo rate**. The cheapest-to-deliver issue is then the one issue among all acceptable Treasury issues with the highest implied repo rate because it is the issue that would give the seller of the futures contract the highest return by buying and then delivering the issue. This is depicted in Exhibit 26-2.

In addition to the choice of which acceptable Treasury issue to deliver—sometimes referred to as the **quality option** or **swap option**—the short position has two more options

---

[4] The conversion factor is based on the price that a deliverable bond would sell for at the beginning of the delivery month if it were to yield 6%.

Exhibit 26-2   Determination of Cheapest-to-Deliver Issue Based on the Implied Repo Rate

Implied repo rate: Rate of return by buying an acceptable Treasury issue, shorting the Treasury bond futures, and delivering the issue at the settlement date.

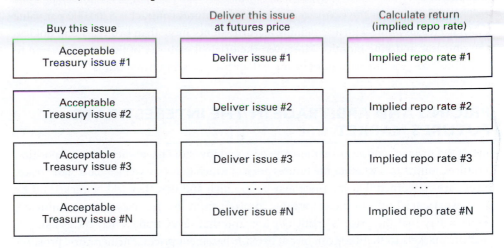

The cheapest-to-deliver issue is that which produces the maximum implied repo rate.

granted under CME Group delivery guidelines. The short position is permitted to decide when in the delivery month delivery actually will take place. This is called the **timing option**. The other option is the right of the short position to give notice of intent to deliver up to 8:00 P.M. Chicago time after the closing of the exchange (3:15 P.M. Chicago time) on the date when the futures settlement price has been fixed. This option is referred to as the **wild card option**. The quality option, the timing option, and the wild card option (in sum referred to as the **delivery options**) mean that the long position can never be sure of which Treasury bond will be delivered or when it will be delivered. The delivery options are summarized below.

Quality or swap option	Choice of which acceptable Treasury issue to deliver
Timing option	Choice of when in delivery month to deliver
Wild card option	Choice to deliver after the closing price of the futures contract is determined

Treasury Note Futures

There are three Treasury note futures contracts: 10-year, five-year, and two-year. All three contracts are modeled after the Treasury bond futures contract and are traded on the CME Group. The underlying instrument for the 10-year Treasury note futures contract is $100,000 par value of a hypothetical 10-year 6% Treasury note. There are several acceptable Treasury issues that may be delivered by the short. An issue is acceptable if the maturity is not less than 6.5 years and not greater than 10 years from the first day of the delivery month. The delivery options granted to the short position and the minimum price fluctuations are the same as for the Treasury bond futures contract.

For the five-year Treasury note futures contract, the underlying is $100,000 par value of a U.S. Treasury note that satisfies the following conditions: (1) an original maturity of not more than five years and three months, (2) a remaining maturity no greater than five years and three months, and (3) a remaining maturity not less than four years and three months.

The underlying for the two-year Treasury note futures contract is $200,000 par value of a U.S. Treasury note with a remaining maturity of not more than two years and not less than one year and nine months. Moreover, the original maturity of the note delivered to satisfy the two-year futures cannot be more than five years and two months.

PRICING AND ARBITRAGE IN THE INTEREST-RATE FUTURES MARKET

One of the primary concerns that most traders and investors have when taking a position in futures contracts is whether the futures price at which they transact will be a "fair" price. Buyers are concerned that the price may be too high and that they will be picked off by more experienced futures traders waiting to profit from the mistakes of the uninitiated. Sellers worry that the price is artificially low and that savvy traders may have manipulated the markets so that they can buy at bargain-basement prices. Furthermore, prospective participants frequently find no rational explanation for the sometimes violent ups and downs that occur in the futures markets. Theories about efficient markets give little comfort to anyone who knows of or has experienced the sudden losses that can occur in the highly leveraged futures markets.

Fortunately, the futures markets are not as irrational as they may at first seem; if they were, they would not have become so successful. The interest-rate futures markets are not perfectly efficient markets, but they probably come about as close as any other market. Furthermore, there are both very clear reasons why futures prices are what they are and methods by which traders, investors, and borrowers can and will quickly eliminate any discrepancy between futures prices and their fair levels.

There are several different ways to price futures contracts. Fortunately, all lead to the same fair price for a given contract. Each approach relies on the "law of one price." This law states that a given financial asset (or liability) must have the same price regardless of the means by which it is created. We explain here one way in which futures contracts can be combined with cash market instruments to create cash flows that are identical to other cash securities. The law of one price implies that the synthetically created cash securities must have the same price as the actual cash securities. Similarly, cash instruments can be combined to create cash flows that are identical to futures contracts. By the law of one price, the futures contract must have the same price as the synthetic futures created from cash instruments.

Pricing of Futures Contracts

To understand how futures contracts should be priced, consider the following example. Suppose that a 20-year 100-par-value bond with a coupon rate of 12% is selling at par. Also suppose that this bond is the deliverable for a futures contract that settles in three months. If the current three-month interest rate at which funds can be loaned or borrowed is 8% per year, what should be the price of this futures contract?

Suppose that the price of the futures contract is 107. Consider the following strategy:

- Sell the futures contract at 107.
- Purchase the bond for 100.
- Borrow 100 for three months at 8% per year.

The borrowed funds are used to purchase the bond, resulting in no initial cash outlay for this strategy. Three months from now, the bond must be delivered to settle the futures contract, and the loan must be repaid. These trades will produce the following cash flows:

From Settlement of the Futures Contract:	
Flat price of bond	107
Accrued interest (12% for 3 months)	3
Total proceeds	110
From the Loan:	
Repayment of principal of loan	100
Interest on loan (8% for 3 months)	2
Total outlay	102
Profit	8

This strategy will guarantee a profit of 8. Moreover, the profit is generated with no initial outlay because the funds used to purchase the bond are borrowed. The profit will be realized *regardless of the futures price at the settlement date*. Obviously, in a well-functioning market, arbitrageurs would buy the bond and sell the futures, forcing the futures price down and bidding up the bond price so as to eliminate this profit. This strategy is called a **cash-and-carry trade**.

In contrast, suppose that the futures price is 92 instead of 107. Consider the following strategy:

- Buy the futures contract at 92.
- Sell (short) the bond for 100.
- Invest (lend) 100 for three months at 8% per year.

Once again, there is no initial cash outlay. Three months from now, a bond will be purchased to settle the long position in the futures contract. That bond will then be used to cover the short position (i.e., to cover the short sale in the cash market). The outcome in three months would be as follows:

From Settlement of the Futures Contract:	
Flat price of bond	92
Accrued interest (12% for 3 months)	3
Total outlay	95
From the Loan:	
Principal received from maturing investment	100
Interest earned from the 3-month investment (8% for 3 months)	2
Total outlay	102
Profit	7

The profit of 7 is a pure arbitrage profit. It requires no initial cash outlay and will be realized *regardless of the futures price at the settlement date*. This strategy is called a **reverse cash-and-carry trade**.

There is a futures price that will eliminate the arbitrage profit, however. There will be no arbitrage if the futures price is 99. Let's look at what would happen if the two previous strategies are followed and the futures price is 99. First, consider the following cash-and-carry trade strategy:

- Sell the futures contract at 99.
- Purchase the bond for 100.
- Borrow 100 for three months at 8% per year.

In three months, the outcome would be as follows:

From Settlement of the Futures Contract:	
Flat price of bond	99
Accrued interest (12% for 3 months)	3
Total proceeds	102
From the Loan:	
Repayment of principal of loan	100
Interest on loan (8% for 3 months)	2
Total outlay	102
Profit	0

There is no arbitrage profit in this case.

Next, consider the following reverse cash-and-carry trade strategy:

- Buy the futures contract at 99.
- Sell (short) the bond for 100.
- Invest (lend) 100 for three months at 8% per year.

The outcome in three months would be as follows:

From Settlement of the Futures Contract:	
Flat price of bond	99
Accrued interest (12% for 3 months)	3
Total outlay	102
From the Loan:	
Principal received from maturing investment	100
Interest earned from the 3-month investment (8% for 3 months)	2
Total proceeds	102
Profit	0

Thus, neither strategy results in a profit. Hence, the futures price of 99 is the theoretical futures price because any higher or lower futures price will permit arbitrage profits.

Theoretical Futures Price Based on Arbitrage Model

Considering the arbitrage arguments just presented, the theoretical futures price can be determined on the basis of the following information:

1. The price of the bond in the cash market.
2. The coupon rate on the bond. In our example, the coupon rate is 12% per year.
3. The interest rate for borrowing and lending until the settlement date.
   The borrowing and lending rate is referred to as the **financing rate**. In our example, the financing rate is 8% per year.

We will let

r = financing rate
c = current yield, or coupon rate divided by the cash market price
P = cash market price
F = futures price
t = time, in years, to the futures delivery date

and then consider the following cash-and-carry trade strategy that is initiated on a coupon date:

- Sell the futures contract at F.
- Purchase the bond for P.
- Borrow P until the settlement date at r.

The outcome at the settlement date is

From Settlement of the Futures Contract:	
Flat price of bond	F
Accrued interest	ctP
Total proceeds	$F + ctP$
From the Loan:	
Repayment of principal of loan	P
Interest on loan	rtP
Total outlay	$P + rtP$

The profit will be

$$\text{profit} = \text{total proceeds} - \text{total outlay}$$
$$= F + ctP - (P + rtP)$$

In equilibrium, the theoretical futures price occurs where the profit from this trade is zero. Thus, to have equilibrium, the following must hold:

$$0 = F + ctP - (P + rtP)$$

Solving for the theoretical futures price, we have

$$F = P\big[1 + t(r - c)\big] \tag{26.1}$$

Alternatively, consider the following reverse cash-and-carry trade strategy:

- Buy the futures contract at F.
- Sell (short) the bond for P.
- Invest (lend) P at r until the settlement date.

The outcome at the settlement date would be

From Settlement of the Futures Contract:	
Flat price of bond	F
Accrued interest	ctP
Total outlay	$F + ctP$
From the Loan:	
Proceeds received from maturing of investment	P
Interest earned	rtP
Total proceeds	$P + rtP$

The profit will be

$$\text{profit} = \text{total proceeds} - \text{total outlay}$$
$$= P + rtP - (F + ctP)$$

Setting the profit equal to zero so that there will be no arbitrage profit and solving for the futures price, we obtain the same equation for the futures price as equation (26.1).

Let's apply equation (26.1) to our preceding example, in which

$r = 0.08$
$c = 0.12$
$P = 100$
$t = 0.25$

Then, the theoretical futures price is

$$F = 100[1 + 0.25(0.08 - 0.12)] = 99$$

This agrees with the theoretical futures price that we derived earlier.

The theoretical futures price may be at a premium to the cash market price (higher than the cash market price) or at a discount from the cash market price (lower than the cash market price), depending on $(r - c)$. The term $r - c$ is called the **net financing cost** because it adjusts the financing rate for the coupon interest earned. The net financing cost is more commonly called the **cost of carry**, or simply **carry**. **Positive carry** means that the current yield earned is greater than the financing cost; **negative carry** means that the financing cost exceeds the current yield. The relationships can be expressed as follows:

Carry	Futures Price
Positive ($c > r$)	Will sell at a discount to cash price ($F < P$)
Negative ($c < r$)	Will sell at a premium to cash price ($F > P$)
Zero ($c = r$)	Will be equal to cash price ($F = P$)

In the case of interest-rate futures, carry (the relationship between the short-term financing rate and the current yield on the bond) depends on the shape of the yield curve. When the yield curve is upward-sloping, the short-term financing rate will generally be less than the current yield on the bond, resulting in positive carry. The futures price will then sell at a discount to the cash price for the bond. The opposite will hold true when the yield curve is inverted.

Closer Look at the Theoretical Futures Price

To derive the theoretical futures price using the arbitrage argument, we made several assumptions, which have certain implications.

Interim Cash Flows

No interim cash flows due to variation margin or coupon interest payments were assumed in the model. However, we know that interim cash flows can occur for both of these reasons. Because we assumed no variation margin, the price derived is technically the theoretical price for a forward contract (which is not marked to market at the end of each trading day). If interest rates rise, the short position in futures will receive margin as the futures price decreases; the margin can then be re-invested at a higher interest rate. In contrast, if interest rates fall, there will be variation margin that must be financed by the short position; however, because interest rates have declined, financing will be possible at a lower cost. Thus, whichever way rates move, those who are short futures gain relative to those who are short forwards. Conversely, those who are long futures lose relative to those who are long forwards. These facts account for the difference between futures and forward prices.

Incorporating interim coupon payments into the pricing model is not difficult. However, the value of the coupon payments at the settlement date will depend on the interest rate at which they can be reinvested. The shorter the maturity of the futures contract and the lower the coupon rate, the less important the reinvestment income is in determining the futures price.

Short-Term Interest Rate (Financing Rate)

In deriving the theoretical futures price, it is assumed that the borrowing and lending rates are equal. Typically, however, the borrowing rate is higher than the lending rate. We will let

$$r_B = \text{borrowing rate}$$
$$r_L = \text{lending rate}$$

Consider the following strategy:

- Sell the futures contract at F.
- Purchase the bond for P.
- Borrow P until the settlement date at r_B.

The futures price that would produce no arbitrage profit is

$$F = P[1 + t(r_B - c)] \tag{26.2}$$

Now consider the following strategy:

- Buy the futures contract at F.
- Sell (short) the bond for P.
- Invest (lend) P at r_L until the settlement date.

The futures price that would produce no profit is

$$F = P[1 + t(r_L - c)] \tag{26.3}$$

Equations (26.2) and (26.3) together provide boundaries for the theoretical futures price. Equation (26.2) provides the upper boundary and equation (26.3) the lower boundary. For example, assume that the borrowing rate is 8% per year and the lending rate is 6% per year. Then, using equation (26.2) and the preceding example, the upper boundary is

$$F(\text{upper boundary}) = \$100[1 + 0.25(0.08 - 0.12)]$$
$$= \$99$$

The lower boundary using equation (26.3) is

$$F(\text{lower boundary}) = \$100[1 + 0.25(0.06 - 0.12)]$$
$$= \$98.50$$

In calculating these boundaries, we assume that no transaction costs are involved in taking the position. In actuality, the transaction costs of entering into and closing the cash position as well as the round-trip transaction costs for the futures contract must be considered and do affect the boundaries for the futures contract.

Deliverable Bond Is Not Known

The arbitrage arguments used to derive equation (26.1) assumed that only one instrument is deliverable. But the futures contracts on Treasury bonds and Treasury notes are designed to allow the short the choice of delivering one of a number of deliverable issues (the quality or swap option). Because there may be more than one deliverable, market participants track the price of each deliverable bond and determine which bond is the cheapest to deliver. The futures price will then trade in relation to the cheapest-to-deliver issue.

There is the risk that though an issue may be the cheapest to deliver at the time a position in the futures contract is taken, it may not be the cheapest to deliver after that time. A change in the cheapest-to-deliver issue can dramatically alter the futures price.

What are the implications of the quality (swap) option on the futures price? Because the swap option is an option granted by the long to the short, the long will want to pay less for the futures contract than indicated by equation (26.1). Therefore, as a result of the quality option, the theoretical futures price as given by equation (26.1) must be adjusted as follows:

$$F = P[1 + t(r - c)] - \text{value of quality option} \qquad (26.4)$$

Market participants have employed theoretical models in attempting to estimate the fair value of the quality option. These models are beyond the scope of this chapter.

Delivery Date Is Not Known

In the pricing model based on arbitrage arguments, a known delivery date is assumed. For Treasury bond and note futures contracts, the short has a timing and wild card option, so the long does not know when the securities will be delivered. The effect of the timing and wild card options on the theoretical futures price is the same as with the quality option. These delivery options should result in a theoretical futures price that is lower than the one suggested in equation (26.1), as shown here:

$$F = P[1 + t(r - c)] - \text{value of quality option} - \text{value of timing option}$$
$$- \text{value of wildcard option} \qquad (26.5)$$

or alternatively,

$$F = P[1 + t(r - c)] - \text{delivery options} \qquad (26.6)$$

Market participants attempt to value the delivery option in order to apply equation (26.6).

Deliverable Is Not a Basket of Securities

The municipal index futures contract is a cash settlement contract based on a basket of securities. The difficulty in arbitraging this futures contract is that it is too expensive to buy or sell every bond included in the index. Instead, a portfolio including a smaller number of bonds may be constructed to "track" the index. The arbitrage, however, is no longer risk-free because there is tracking error risk.

BOND PORTFOLIO MANAGEMENT APPLICATIONS

There are various ways in which a portfolio manager can use interest-rate futures contracts.

Controlling the Duration of a Portfolio

Interest-rate futures can be used to alter the interest-rate sensitivity of a portfolio. Portfolio managers with strong expectations about the direction of the future course of interest rates will adjust the durations of their portfolios so as to capitalize on their expectations. Specifically, if a manager expects rates to increase, the duration will be shortened; if interest rates are expected to decrease, the duration will be lengthened. Although portfolio managers can alter the durations of their portfolios with cash market instruments, a quick and inexpensive means for doing so (on either a temporary or permanent basis) is to use futures contracts.

In addition to adjusting a portfolio based on anticipated interest-rate movements, futures contracts can be used in constructing a portfolio with a longer duration than is available with cash market securities. As an example of the latter, suppose that in a certain interest-rate environment a pension fund manager must structure a portfolio to have a duration of 15 to accomplish a particular investment objective. Bonds with such a long duration may not be available. By buying the appropriate number and kind of interest-rate futures contracts, a pension fund manager can increase the portfolio's duration to the target level of 15.

To illustrate, suppose that a manager is managing a portfolio whose benchmark is the Barclays Capital Intermediate Aggregate Index, which has a duration of 3.68. Suppose further that the market value of the portfolio on March 31, 2011, was $48,109,810. The portfolio holdings are shown in Exhibit 26-3.[5] The portfolio duration is 2.97 as shown in the exhibit and is less than that of the benchmark duration of 3.68. This means that the portfolio has less interest rate exposure (for a parallel shift in the yield curve) than the benchmark.

Suppose that the manager wants to restructure the portfolio so that its duration matches that of the benchmark. That is, the portfolio manager seeks to follow a duration-matched strategy and therefore the portfolio's target duration is 3.68. For a 100 basis point change in interest rates, the portfolio's target dollar duration is then the product of 3.68% times the current market value of the portfolio. Therefore,

$$\text{portfolio target dollar duration} = 3.68\% \times \$48,109,810 = \$1,770,110$$

The current portfolio duration is 2.97, so for a 100 basis point change in interest rates,

$$\text{portfolio current dollar duration} = 2.97\% \times \$48,109,810 = \$1,428,594$$

The difference between the target and the current dollar duration for the portfolio is $341,516. This means that to get to the target portfolio duration of 3.68, the portfolio manager must increase the dollar duration of the current portfolio by $341,516.

One way to do this as we have just discussed is by taking a position in a futures contract. Buying futures contracts increases the dollar duration. The question is, What is the dollar duration of the futures contract? Let's suppose that the portfolio manager wants to use the 5-year Treasury note futures contract. The futures price on March 31, 2011, was 116.79. Based on an analysis of this contract, the portfolio manager determines that for a 100 basis point change in interest rates, the 5-year Treasury note futures contract will change by roughly $5,022.[6] If the portfolio manager buys C contracts, then the dollar duration of the futures position for a 100 basis point change in interest rates is the product of the number futures contract and $5,022; that is,

$$\text{dollar duration of futures position} = \$5,022 \times C$$

---

[5] I am grateful to Mark Paltrowitz of BlackRock Solutions for providing the hypothetical portfolio, the portfolio analytics, and the information about the portfolio resulting from using the 5-year Treasury note futures contract. The same portfolio is used in Chapter 28 to illustrate duration adjustment using interest rate swaps and swaptions.
[6] This was obtained by changing interest rates by 100 basis points and computing the average dollar price change.

Exhibit 26-3 Portfolio Used for Hedging Illustration

CUSIP	Security	Market Value	Effective Duration
00209TAA3	COMCAST CABLE COMMUNICATIONS HOLDINGS	$ 367,082	1.84
05947UES3	BACM_02-PB2	498,539	0.58
07383FX52	BSCMS_04-PWR6	481,631	3.10
07386HNQ0	BALTA_04-12	170,260	0.10
07386HPX3	BALTA_04-13	81,731	0.10
12669GHY0	CWHL_04-29	44,259	0.10
156700AJ5	CENTURYTEL INC	11,642	3.53
25179SAC4	DEVON FINANCING CORP ULC	56,686	0.50
26884AAE3	ERP OPERATING LIMITED PARTNERSHIP	58,702	5.19
3128X3F32	FHLMC	1,112,838	3.24
31359MQV8	FNMA BENCHMARK NOTES	314,068	1.82
31385JPS1	FNMA 10YR BALLOON MULTI	323,203	1.24
31385XEC7	FNMA 30YR	1,155,490	2.39
31385XQ91	FNMA 30YR	25,628	2.39
31393X4L8	FNMA_04-36	7,532	0.08
31393XRP4	FNMA_04-25	2,000	0.07
31393YRY3	FNMA_04-M1	49,167	0.84
31394DA42	FNMA_05-48	172,658	2.51
31394EBH0	FNMA_05-51	454,910	2.34
31394ERM2	FNMA_05-57	148,601	0.68
31395TXY5	FHLMC_2973	215,040	2.85
31395UM24	FHLMC_2979	597,884	2.83
31395UYX3	FHLMC_29-96	174,293	3.12
361849ZS4	GMACC_03-C3	72,523	1.24
36228CVT7	GSMS_05-GG4	470,388	3.44
36228FYY6	GSR_03-13	143,370	0.64
396789JS9	GCCFC_05-GG3	482,580	2.74
46625YDB6	JPMCC_04-CBX	152,149	0.04
46625YSG9	JPMCC_05-LDP3	416,307	3.67
471060AN3	JAPAN FINANCE ORGANIZATION FOR MUN	198,247	3.66
52108H2S2	LBUBS_05-C1	430,328	0.70
52108HUL6	LBUBS_03-C7	299,329	0.88
577778BF9	MAY DEPARTMENT STORES CO/THE	20,508	3.14
59156RAN8	METLIFE INC	122,518	3.77
652482BG4	NEWS AMERICA INC	200,980	3.36

(*Continued*)

Exhibit 26-3   Portfolio Used for Hedging Illustration (Continued)

CUSIP	Security	Market Value	Effective Duration
783764AN3	RYLAND GROUP INC	11,367	3.09
79549AJJ9	SBMVII_01-C2	199,970	0.34
831641DQ5	SBIC_03-P10B	2,385,687	1.52
872287AC1	TCI COMMUNICATIONS INC	88,550	3.69
87927VAE8	TELECOM ITALIA CAPITAL SA	77,441	2.43
87927VAL2	TELECOM ITALIA CAPITAL SA	74,839	3.24
912810ED6	TREASURY BOND	205,399	6.38
912810EG9	TREASURY BOND	457,196	6.84
912810EQ7	TREASURY BOND	1,045,939	8.81
912810EW4	TREASURY BOND	71,650	10.01
912810FB9	TREASURY BOND	362,442	10.54
912810FP8	TREASURY BOND	743,901	12.16
912828EE6	TREASURY NOTE	937,817	4.00
912828EN6	TREASURY NOTE	1,689,187	4.14
912828FF2	TREASURY NOTE	10,426,256	4.48
92344UAA3	VERIZON NEW JERSEY INC.	246,008	0.78
92553PAB8	VIACOM INC	94,764	5.30
9297667G2	WBCMT_05-C21	542,938	3.35
929766JE4	WBCMT_03-C6	324,841	1.91
94979TAA4	WFMBS_04-H	152,523	0.00
977100AA4	WI ST	141,256	1.97
BRS344PH7	FNMA 15YR TBA	1,189,283	2.17
BRS344PT1	FGOLD 15YR TBA	760,939	2.17
FG040015Q	FGOLD 15YR 2004 PRODUCTION	44,207	2.19
FG043215Q	FGOLD 15YR 2004 PRODUCTION	234,314	1.99
FG043215R	FGOLD 15YR 2005 PRODUCTION	389,860	2.00
FG050015Q	FGOLD 15YR 2004 PRODUCTION	100,219	1.59
FG050015R	FGOLD 15YR 2005 PRODUCTION	202,364	1.72
FG050030R	FGOLD 30YR 2005 PRODUCTION	342,051	3.22
FG053230R	FGOLD 30YR 2005 PRODUCTION	402,904	2.05
FG060030K	FGOLD 30YR 1999 PRODUCTION	88,299	1.56
FG060030P	FGOLD 30YR 2003 PRODUCTION	196,141	1.42
FN043215P	FNMA 15YR 2003 PRODUCTION	106,718	1.74
FN043230R	FNMA 30YR 2005 PRODUCTION	132,376	3.79
FN050015N	FNMA 15YR 2002 PRODUCTION	238,631	1.50
FN050015P	FNMA 15YR 2003 PRODUCTION	46,633	1.75
FN050030P	FNMA 30YR 2003 PRODUCTION	194,263	3.30

(Continued)

| | Exhibit 26-3 | Portfolio Used for Hedging Illustration (Continued) | | |

CUSIP	Security	Market Value	Effective Duration
FN050030R	FNMA 30YR 2005 PRODUCTION	171,727	3.15
FN053215N	FNMA 15YR 2002 PRODUCTION	586,289	1.11
FN053215P	FNMA 15YR 2003 PRODUCTION	81,430	1.90
FN053215Q	FNMA 15YR 2004 PRODUCTION	27,676	1.61
FN053215R	FNMA 15YR 2005 PRODUCTION	11,587,216	1.24
FN053230P	FNMA 30YR 2003 PRODUCTION	428,986	2.06
FN053230Q	FNMA 30YR 2004 PRODUCTION	31,671	2.06
FN060015N	FNMA 15YR 2002 PRODUCTION	14,526	1.60
FN060030P	FNMA 30YR 2003 PRODUCTION	167,591	1.36
FN063230N	FNMA 30YR 2002 PRODUCTION	111,750	0.52
FN070030K	FNMA 30YR 1999 PRODUCTION	78,974	2.18
FN070030L	FNMA 30YR 2000 PRODUCTION	30,117	2.25
GN053230P	GNMA 30YR 2003 PRODUCTION	88,083	3.52
GN060030P	GNMA 30YR 2003 PRODUCTION	131,655	3.07
GN063230L	GNMA 30YR 2000 PRODUCTION	59,712	2.78
GN063230Q	GNMA 30YR 2004 PRODUCTION	30,165	2.94
	Portfolio	$48,109,810	2.97

Note: *Obtained from BlackRock Solutions (BRS). Effective duration is term used by author. BRS uses "OAD" for option-adjusted duration.*

The portfolio manager wants the above equation to be equal to $341,516. Thus,

$$\$5,022 \times C = \$341,516$$

Solving we get

$$C = 68 \text{ contracts}$$

Thus, by buying 68 5-year Treasury note futures contracts, the portfolio manager will increase the dollar duration of the portfolio by $341,516 for a 100 basis point change in interest rates.

Since the notional amount of the futures contract is $100,000, this means that the total notional amount of the futures position is $6,800,000. The market value of the futures position given that the future price is 116.79 is equal to

$$(116.79/100) \times \$100,000 \times 68 = \$7,941,720$$

A formula to approximate the number of futures contracts necessary to adjust the portfolio duration to a target level is

approximate number of futures contracts

$$= \frac{\text{portfolio target dollar duration} - \text{portfolio current dollar duration}}{\text{dollar duration of futures contract}} \quad (26.7)$$

A negative value indicates the number of contracts that should be sold; a positive value indicates the number of contracts that should be purchased.

In our example, it is

$$\text{approximate number of futures contract} = \frac{\$1,770,110 - \$1,428,594}{\$5,022} = 68$$

Suppose instead that the portfolio manager does not want to duration match versus the benchmark but instead wants the duration to be 90% of the benchmark. Since the benchmark duration is 3.68, this means that the manager wants the portfolio's target duration to be 3.31. The portfolio target dollar duration for a 100 basis point change in interest rates is

$$\text{portfolio target dollar duration} = 3.31\% \times \$48,109,810 = \$1,592,435$$

Then the approximate number of futures contract to increase the duration is found by

$$= \frac{\$1,592,435 - \$1,428,594}{\$5,022} \approx 33$$

Hence, 33 futures contracts should be purchased.

It is important to remember that although one can match the duration of a benchmark, this does not mean that other interest rate risk attributes match the benchmark. More specifically, the duration can be matched but the convexity and key rate durations of the benchmark and portfolio can be mismatched. This is why portfolio managers will actually use other hedging instruments to neutralize differences in key rate duration and convexity.

Hedging

Although we discuss hedging as a separate application, it is nothing more than a special case of interest rate risk management where the target duration is zero. In the case of hedging a portfolio, a simple way to determine the number of futures contract to short is to use equation (26.7). The target portfolio dollar duration is zero. That is, the number of futures contract to short is found by dividing the current portfolio dollar duration by the dollar duration of the futures contract that is used as the hedging vehicle. In hedging an individual bond position, a more detailed analysis can be used. Here we describe the nuances in such hedging.

In hedging an individual bond position with futures, the hedger is taking a futures position as a temporary substitute for transactions to be made in the cash market at a later date. If cash and futures prices move together, any loss realized by the hedger from one position (whether cash or futures) will be offset by a profit on the other position. When the net profit or loss from the positions is exactly as anticipated, the hedge is referred to as a **perfect hedge.**

In practice, hedging is not that simple. The amount of net profit will not necessarily be as anticipated. The outcome of a hedge will depend on the relationship between the cash price and the futures price both when a hedge is placed and when it is lifted. The difference between the cash price and the futures price is the **basis**. The risk that the basis will change in an unpredictable way is called **basis risk**.

In bond portfolio management, typically, the bond to be hedged is not identical to the bond underlying the futures contract. This type of hedging is referred to as **cross hedging**. There may be substantial basis risk in cross hedging. An unhedged position is exposed to price risk, the risk that the cash market price will move adversely. A hedged position substitutes basis risk for price risk.

A **short** (or **sell**) **hedge** is used to protect against a decline in the cash price of a bond. To execute a short hedge, futures contracts are sold. By establishing a short hedge, the hedger has fixed the future cash price and transferred the price risk of ownership to the buyer of the futures contract. To understand why a short hedge might be executed, suppose that a pension fund manager knows that bonds must be liquidated in 40 days to make a $5 million payment to the beneficiaries of the pension fund. If interest rates rise during the 40-day period, more bonds will have to be liquidated to realize $5 million. To guard against this possibility, the manager can sell bonds in the futures market to lock in a selling price.

A **long** (or **buy**) **hedge** is undertaken to protect against an increase in the cash price of a bond. In a long hedge, the hedger buys a futures contract to lock in a purchase price. A pension fund manager might use a long hedge when substantial cash contributions are expected, and the manager is concerned that interest rates will fall. Also, a portfolio manager who knows that bonds are maturing in the near future and expects that interest rates will fall can employ a long hedge to lock in a rate for the proceeds to be reinvested.

Conceptually, cross hedging is somewhat more complicated than hedging deliverable securities, because it involves two relationships. First, there is the relationship between the cheapest-to-deliver security and the futures contract. Second, there is the relationship between the security to be hedged and the cheapest-to-deliver security.

The Hedge Ratio

The key to minimizing risk in a cross hedge is to choose the right hedge ratio. The hedge ratio depends on volatility weighting, or weighting by relative changes in value. The purpose of a hedge is to use gains or losses from a futures position to offset any difference between the target sale price and the actual sale price of the asset. Accordingly, the hedge ratio is chosen with the intention of matching the volatility (i.e., the dollar change) of the futures contract to the volatility of the asset. Consequently, the hedge ratio is given by

$$\text{hedge ratio} = \frac{\text{volatility of bond to be hedged}}{\text{volatility of hedging instrument}} \qquad (26.8)$$

As equation (26.8) shows, if the bond to be hedged is more volatile than the hedging instrument, more of the hedging instrument will be needed.

Although it might be fairly clear why volatility is the key variable in determining the hedge ratio, *volatility* has many definitions. For hedging purposes, we are concerned with volatility in absolute dollar terms. To calculate the dollar volatility of a bond, one must know the precise point in time that volatility is to be calculated (because volatility generally declines as a bond seasons) as well as the price or yield at which to calculate volatility (because higher yields generally reduce dollar volatility for a given yield change). The relevant point in the life of the bond for calculating volatility is the point at which the hedge will be lifted. Volatility at any other point is essentially irrelevant because the goal is to lock in a price or rate only on that particular day. Similarly, the relevant yield at which to calculate volatility initially is the target yield. Consequently, the "volatility of the bond to be hedged" referred to in equation (26.8) is the price value of a basis point for the bond on the date the hedge is expected to be delivered.[7]

---

[7] The yield that is to be used on this date in order to determine the price value of a basis point is the forward rate. We discussed forward rates in Chapter 5.

An example shows why volatility weighting leads to the correct hedge ratio.[8] Suppose that on December 24, 2007, an investor owned $10 million par value of the Procter & Gamble (P&G) 5.55% bonds of March 5, 2037 (CUSIP 742718DF3), and sold the March 2008 Treasury bond futures to hedge a future sale of the bonds. This is an example of a cross hedge. Suppose that

1. the Treasury 6.25% of 8/15/2023 issue was the cheapest-to-deliver (CTD) issue on the contract and was trading at 4.643% with a price of 117.719 and a conversion factor of 1.0246
2. the P&G bond was trading at 5.754% with a price of 97.127
3. the Treasury bond futures contract was at a price of 114.375. The spread between the P&G bond and the cheapest-to-deliver issue was 111.1 basis points, and it is assumed that the spread will remain the same over the period the bond is hedged.

To simplify, we assume that the anticipated sale date was the last business day for the contract, March 31, 2008.

Given the conversion factor for the CTD issue (1.0246) and the futures price for the March 2007 contract (114.375), the target forward price for the CTD issue is found by multiplying these two values; that is, the target forward price for the CTD issue is the target forward yield corresponding to a price of 117.1886. The target forward yield for the CTD corresponding to a 6.25% bond maturing 8/15/2023 with a price of 117.1886 on March 31, 2008 (the settlement date of the futures contract) is 4.670%.

Given the target forward yield for the CTD issue of 4.670%, we must determine the target forward yield for the P&G bond. To do so, we employ the assumption that the yield spread remains at 111.1 basis points. Adding this spread to 4.670% gives a target forward yield for the P&G bond of 5.781%. The target forward price for the P&G bond as of March 31, 2008, given a yield of 4.670%, a coupon of 5.55%, and a maturity date of 3/5/2037 as of the settlement date of the futures contract (March 31, 2008) is 96.768. For $10 million par value, the target forward amount is $9,678,000.

At these target levels, the price value of a basis point (PVBP) for the CTD issue is 0.1207, and for the P&G bond, it is 0.1363. As indicated earlier, all of these calculations are made using a settlement date equal to the anticipated sale date, in this case March 31, 2008. Thus, the relative price volatilities of the bonds to be hedged and the deliverable security are easily obtained from the assumed sale date and target prices.

However, to calculate the hedge ratio [equation (26.8)], we need the volatility not of the cheapest-to-deliver issue, but of the hedging instrument—that is, of the futures contract. Fortunately, knowing the volatility of the bond to be hedged relative to the cheapest-to-deliver issue and the volatility of the cheapest-to-deliver bond relative to the futures contract, we can easily obtain the relative volatilities that define the hedge ratio:

$$\text{hedge ratio} = \frac{\text{volatility of bond to be hedged}}{\text{volatility of CTD issue}} \times \frac{\text{volatility of CTD issue}}{\text{volatility of hedging instrument}} \quad (26.9)$$

where CTD issue is the cheapest-to-deliver issue. The second ratio can be shown to equal the conversion factor for the CTD issue. Assuming a fixed yield spread between the bond to be hedged and the CTD issue, equation (26.9) can be rewritten as

$$\text{hedge ratio} = \frac{\text{PVBP of bond to be hedged}}{\text{PVBP of CTD issue}} \times \text{conversion factor for CTD issue} \quad (26.10)$$

---

[8] This illustration was provided by Peter Ru of Morgan Stanley.

The hedge ratio at hand is, therefore,

$$\text{hedge ratio} = \frac{0.1363}{0.1207} \times 1.0246 = 1.157$$

Given the hedge ratio, the number of contracts that must be short is determined as follows:

$$\text{number of contracts} = \text{hedge ratio} \times \frac{\text{par value to be hedged}}{\text{par value of contract}} \qquad (26.11)$$

Because the amount to be hedged is $10 million and each Treasury bond futures contract is for $100,000, this means that the number of futures contracts that must be sold is

$$\text{number of contracts} = \text{hedge ratio} \times \frac{\$10,000,000}{\$100,000}$$
$$= 1.157 \times 100$$
$$= 116 \text{ contracts (rounded)}$$

Exhibit 26-4 shows that if the simplifying assumptions hold, a futures hedge using the recommended hedge ratio very nearly locks in the target forward amount of $9,678,000 for $10 million par value of the P&G bond.[9]

Adjusting the Hedge Ratio for Yield Spread Changes

A refinement in the hedging strategy is usually necessary for hedging nondeliverable securities. This refinement concerns the assumption about the relative yield spread between the CTD issue and the bond to be hedged. In the prior discussion, we assumed that the yield spread was constant over time. Yield spreads, however, are not constant over time. They vary with the maturity of the instruments in question and the level of rates, as well as with many unpredictable and nonsystematic factors. Because of this, the hedge ratio has to be adjusted.

The formula for the hedge ratio, equation (26.10), is revised as follows to incorporate the impact of the yield beta:

$$\text{hedge ratio} = \frac{\text{PVBP of bond to be hedged}}{\text{PVBP of CTD issue}} \times \text{conversion factor for CTD issue} \times \text{adjustment factor} \qquad (26.12)$$

Two approaches have been suggested for estimating the adjustment factor that takes into account the relationship between yield levels and yield spreads: (1) regression approach, and (2) pure volatility approach.

The regression approach involves estimating from historical data the following regression model:

$$\text{yield change on bond to be hedged} = a + b \times \text{yield change on CTD issue} + \text{error} \qquad (26.13)$$

The regression procedure provides an estimate of b, called the yield beta, which is the expected relative change in yield between the two bonds. For the two issues in question, that is, the P&G 5.55% of 3/5/2037 and the CTD Treasury issue (the 6.25% of 8/15/2003), the

---

[9] In practice, most of the remaining error could be eliminated by frequent adjustments to the hedge ratio to account for the fact that the price value of a basis point changes as rates move up or down.

Exhibit 26-4   Hedging a Nondeliverable Bond to a Delivery Date with Futures

Instrument to be hedged: P&G 5.55% 3/5/2037
Hedge ratio: 1.15
Number of contracts shorted: 116
Price of futures contract when sold at initiation of hedge: 114.375
Target forward price for hedged bond: 96.768

Actual Sale Price of P&G Bond	Yield at Sale	Yield of Treasury[a]	Price of Treasury	Futures Price[b]	Gain (Loss) on 116 Contracts	Effective Sale Price[c]
8,000,000	7.204%	6.093%	101.544	99.106	1,771,194	9,771,194
8,200,000	7.010%	5.899%	103.508	101.023	1,548,862	9,748,862
8,400,000	6.824%	5.713%	105.438	102.907	1,330,323	9,730,323
8,600,000	6.645%	5.534%	107.341	104.764	1,114,875	9,714,875
8,800,000	6.472%	5.361%	109.224	106.601	901,748	9,701,748
9,000,000	6.306%	5.195%	111.071	108.404	692,606	9,692,606
9,200,000	6.144%	5.033%	112.914	110.203	484,008	9,684,008
9,400,000	5.989%	4.878%	114.714	111.960	280,164	9,680,164
9,600,000	5.838%	4.727%	116.504	113.707	77,476	9,677,476
9,800,000	5.691%	4.580%	118.282	115.442	(123,809)	9,676,191
10,000,000	5.550%	4.439%	120.021	117.139	(320,633)	9,679,367
10,200,000	5.412%	4.301%	121.755	118.831	(516,925)	9,683,075
10,400,000	5.278%	4.167%	123.469	120.505	(711,032)	9,688,968
10,600,000	5.149%	4.038%	125.149	122.144	(901,256)	9,698,744
10,800,000	5.022%	3.911%	126.832	123.787	(1,091,785)	9,708,215
11,000,000	4.899%	3.788%	128.490	125.405	(1,279,473)	9,720,527
11,200,000	4.780%	3.669%	130.120	126.996	(1,464,047)	9,735,953
11,400,000	4.663%	3.552%	131.749	128.586	(1,648,452)	9,751,548
11,600,000	4.550%	3.439%	133.347	130.145	(1,829,358)	9,770,642

[a]By assumption, the yield on the CTD issue (6.25% of 8/15/2003) is 111.1 basis points lower than the yield on the P&G bond.
[b]By convergence, the futures price equals the price of the CTD issue divided by 1.0246 (the conversion factor).
[c]Transaction costs and the financing of margin flows are ignored.

yields for each trading day from 2/28/2007 to 12/21/2007 are shown in Exhibit 26-5 along with the daily change in yield. There is no set formula for determining the number of trading days to use. The yield beta using three different sets of trading days is summarized below:

Number of Trading Days	Yield Beta
Prior 30 trading days ending 12/21/2007	0.906
Prior 90 trading days ending 12/21/2007	0.894
Prior 218 trading days ending 12/21/2007	0.906

Exhibit 26-5 Yield and Yield Change for Each Trading Day for the P&G 5.55% 3/5/2037 and Treasury 6.25% 8/15/2023 (CTD Issue): 2/28/2007–12/21/2007

Trading Day	P&G 5.55% 3/5/2037			Treasury 6.25% 8/15/2023 (CTD issue)		
	Price	Yield	Yield Change	Price	Yield	Yield Change
2/28/2007	99.766	5.566		116.709	4.773	
3/1/2007	99.612	5.577	0.011	116.571	4.783	0.010
3/2/2007	99.975	5.552	−0.025	116.957	4.752	−0.031
3/5/2007	100.018	5.549	−0.003	116.963	4.752	0.000
3/6/2007	99.761	5.566	0.017	116.921	4.755	0.003
3/7/2007	100.039	5.547	−0.019	117.244	4.729	−0.026
3/8/2007	99.700	5.571	0.024	117.092	4.741	0.012
3/9/2007	98.841	5.630	0.059	116.151	4.816	0.075
3/12/2007	99.375	5.593	−0.037	116.557	4.783	−0.033
3/13/2007	99.878	5.558	−0.035	117.096	4.740	−0.043
3/14/2007	99.259	5.601	0.043	116.686	4.772	0.032
3/15/2007	99.417	5.590	−0.011	116.619	4.777	0.005
3/16/2007	99.361	5.594	0.004	116.548	4.783	0.006
3/19/2007	99.026	5.617	0.023	116.213	4.809	0.026
3/20/2007	99.151	5.609	−0.008	116.435	4.791	−0.018
3/21/2007	99.319	5.597	−0.012	116.702	4.770	−0.021
3/22/2007	97.990	5.690	0.093	115.708	4.849	0.079
3/23/2007	97.879	5.698	0.008	115.463	4.869	0.020
3/26/2007	97.878	5.698	0.000	115.669	4.852	−0.017
3/27/2007	97.711	5.710	0.012	115.365	4.877	0.025
3/28/2007	97.445	5.729	0.019	115.190	4.891	0.014
3/29/2007	97.487	5.726	−0.003	115.156	4.893	0.002
3/30/2007	97.165	5.749	0.023	114.830	4.920	0.027
4/2/2007	97.347	5.736	−0.013	114.948	4.910	−0.010
4/3/2007	97.207	5.746	0.010	114.788	4.923	0.013
4/4/2007	97.221	5.745	−0.001	114.870	4.916	−0.007
4/5/2007	96.885	5.769	0.024	114.568	4.940	0.024
4/6/2007	96.670	5.785	0.016	113.813	5.002	0.062
4/9/2007	96.241	5.816	0.031	113.882	4.997	−0.005
4/10/2007	96.408	5.804	−0.012	114.086	4.980	−0.017
4/11/2007	96.695	5.783	−0.021	113.925	4.993	0.013
4/12/2007	96.751	5.779	−0.004	113.955	4.990	−0.003
4/13/2007	96.512	5.796	0.017	113.718	5.009	0.019
4/16/2007	97.019	5.760	−0.036	114.100	4.978	−0.031
4/17/2007	97.653	5.714	−0.046	114.671	4.930	−0.048

(*Continued*)

Exhibit 26-5 Yield and Yield Change for Each Trading Day for the P&G 5.55% 3/5/2037 and Treasury 6.25% 8/15/2023 (CTD Issue): 2/28/2007–12/21/2007 (Continued)

Trading Day	P&G 5.55% 3/5/2037			Treasury 6.25% 8/15/2023 (CTD issue)		
	Price	Yield	Yield Change	Price	Yield	Yield Change
4/18/2007	98.047	5.686	−0.028	115.045	4.900	−0.030
4/19/2007	97.948	5.693	0.007	114.899	4.911	0.011
4/20/2007	97.849	5.700	0.007	114.820	4.918	0.007
4/23/2007	98.047	5.686	−0.014	115.016	4.901	−0.017
4/24/2007	98.386	5.662	−0.024	115.302	4.878	−0.023
4/25/2007	98.357	5.664	0.002	115.048	4.898	0.020
4/26/2007	97.776	5.705	0.041	114.574	4.937	0.039
4/27/2007	97.563	5.721	0.016	114.415	4.950	0.013
4/30/2007	98.528	5.652	−0.069	115.310	4.876	−0.074
5/1/2007	98.556	5.650	−0.002	115.278	4.879	0.003
5/2/2007	98.400	5.661	0.011	115.279	4.879	0.000
5/3/2007	98.103	5.682	0.021	114.973	4.903	0.024
5/4/2007	98.584	5.648	−0.034	115.392	4.869	−0.034
5/7/2007	98.740	5.637	−0.011	115.510	4.859	−0.010
5/8/2007	98.612	5.646	0.009	115.414	4.867	0.008
5/9/2007	98.088	5.683	0.037	114.878	4.910	0.043
5/10/2007	98.272	5.670	−0.013	115.108	4.891	−0.019
5/11/2007	97.975	5.691	0.021	114.823	4.914	0.023
5/14/2007	97.819	5.702	0.011	114.619	4.931	0.017
5/15/2007	97.493	5.726	0.024	114.373	4.951	0.020
5/16/2007	97.606	5.718	−0.008	114.435	4.946	−0.005
5/17/2007	97.067	5.756	0.038	113.910	4.989	0.043
5/18/2007	96.444	5.802	0.046	113.374	5.034	0.045
5/21/2007	96.656	5.786	−0.016	113.557	5.018	−0.016
5/22/2007	96.104	5.826	0.040	113.012	5.064	0.046
5/23/2007	95.706	5.856	0.030	112.627	5.096	0.032
5/24/2007	95.749	5.853	−0.003	112.670	5.092	−0.004
5/25/2007	95.749	5.853	0.000	112.670	5.092	0.000
5/29/2007	95.663	5.859	0.006	112.484	5.107	0.015
5/30/2007	95.870	5.844	−0.015	112.540	5.103	−0.004
5/31/2007	95.883	5.843	−0.001	112.534	5.103	0.000
6/1/2007	95.199	5.893	0.050	111.881	5.158	0.055
6/4/2007	95.739	5.853	−0.040	112.337	5.119	−0.039
6/5/2007	95.154	5.897	0.044	111.774	5.167	0.048
6/6/2007	94.659	5.934	0.037	111.664	5.176	0.009
6/7/2007	93.084	6.053	0.119	110.183	5.304	0.128

(Continued)

Exhibit 26-5 Yield and Yield Change for Each Trading Day for the P&G 5.55% 3/5/2037 and Treasury 6.25% 8/15/2023 (CTD Issue): 2/28/2007–12/21/2007 (Continued)

| Trading Day | P&G 5.55% 3/5/2037 | | | Treasury 6.25% 8/15/2023 (CTD issue) | | |
	Price	Yield	Yield Change	Price	Yield	Yield Change
6/8/2007	92.899	6.068	0.015	109.954	5.324	0.020
6/11/2007	92.640	6.088	0.020	109.854	5.332	0.008
6/12/2007	91.169	6.203	0.115	108.527	5.449	0.117
6/13/2007	92.070	6.132	−0.071	109.270	5.383	−0.066
6/14/2007	91.818	6.152	0.020	109.064	5.402	0.019
6/15/2007	92.271	6.117	−0.035	109.478	5.365	−0.037
6/18/2007	92.371	6.109	−0.008	109.679	5.347	−0.018
6/19/2007	93.037	6.057	−0.052	110.310	5.292	−0.055
6/20/2007	92.798	6.076	0.019	109.849	5.332	0.040
6/21/2007	92.213	6.121	0.045	109.336	5.377	0.045
6/22/2007	92.526	6.097	−0.024	109.581	5.355	−0.022
6/25/2007	93.353	6.033	−0.064	110.324	5.290	−0.065
6/26/2007	93.011	6.059	0.026	110.059	5.313	0.023
6/27/2007	93.060	6.056	−0.003	110.418	5.282	−0.031
6/28/2007	92.692	6.084	0.028	110.056	5.313	0.031
6/29/2007	93.880	5.993	−0.091	111.081	5.224	−0.089
7/2/2007	94.273	5.963	−0.030	111.376	5.199	−0.025
7/3/2007	93.652	6.010	0.047	110.822	5.246	0.047
7/5/2007	92.544	6.096	0.086	109.836	5.332	0.086
7/6/2007	91.908	6.146	0.050	109.304	5.379	0.047
7/9/2007	92.347	6.111	−0.035	109.718	5.342	−0.037
7/10/2007	93.848	5.996	−0.115	111.001	5.230	−0.112
7/11/2007	93.213	6.044	0.048	110.456	5.277	0.047
7/12/2007	92.791	6.077	0.033	110.095	5.309	0.032
7/13/2007	93.003	6.061	−0.016	110.221	5.298	−0.011
7/16/2007	93.895	5.992	−0.069	110.996	5.230	−0.068
7/17/2007	93.428	6.028	0.036	110.523	5.271	0.041
7/18/2007	93.971	5.986	−0.042	111.243	5.208	−0.063
7/19/2007	93.760	6.003	0.017	111.042	5.226	0.018
7/20/2007	94.450	5.950	−0.053	111.706	5.168	−0.058
7/23/2007	94.407	5.954	0.004	111.657	5.172	0.004
7/24/2007	94.464	5.949	−0.005	111.745	5.165	−0.007
7/25/2007	94.971	5.911	−0.038	112.172	5.128	−0.037
7/26/2007	96.054	5.831	−0.080	113.267	5.035	−0.093
7/27/2007	96.012	5.834	0.003	113.115	5.048	0.013
7/30/2007	92.944	6.066	0.232	112.938	5.062	0.014

(Continued)

Exhibit 26-5 Yield and Yield Change for Each Trading Day for the P&G 5.55% 3/5/2037 and Treasury 6.25% 8/15/2023 (CTD Issue): 2/28/2007–12/21/2007 (Continued)

	P&G 5.55% 3/5/2037			Treasury 6.25% 8/15/2023 (CTD issue)		
Trading Day	Price	Yield	Yield Change	Price	Yield	Yield Change
7/31/2007	94.163	5.972	−0.094	113.397	5.023	−0.039
8/1/2007	94.313	5.961	−0.011	113.388	5.024	0.001
8/2/2007	94.449	5.951	−0.010	113.570	5.009	−0.015
8/3/2007	94.855	5.920	−0.031	113.989	4.973	−0.036
8/6/2007	94.313	5.961	0.041	113.516	5.013	0.040
8/7/2007	94.380	5.956	−0.005	113.514	5.013	0.000
8/8/2007	93.587	6.016	0.060	112.173	5.127	0.114
8/9/2007	93.530	6.021	0.005	112.317	5.114	−0.013
8/10/2007	93.704	6.008	−0.013	112.541	5.095	−0.019
8/13/2007	93.708	6.007	−0.001	112.692	5.082	−0.013
8/14/2007	93.983	5.986	−0.021	113.052	5.051	−0.031
8/15/2007	93.822	5.999	0.013	112.821	5.071	0.020
8/16/2007	94.982	5.911	−0.088	113.916	4.978	−0.093
8/17/2007	93.970	5.987	0.076	113.100	5.047	0.069
8/20/2007	94.396	5.955	−0.032	113.542	5.009	−0.038
8/21/2007	94.770	5.927	−0.028	114.011	4.969	−0.040
8/22/2007	93.650	6.012	0.085	113.777	4.989	0.020
8/23/2007	94.070	5.980	−0.032	114.068	4.964	−0.025
8/24/2007	94.095	5.978	−0.002	114.220	4.951	−0.013
8/27/2007	94.526	5.945	−0.033	114.715	4.910	−0.041
8/28/2007	94.951	5.914	−0.031	114.989	4.887	−0.023
8/29/2007	95.492	5.873	−0.041	114.814	4.901	0.014
8/30/2007	95.492	5.873	0.000	114.814	4.901	0.000
8/31/2007	96.118	5.827	−0.046	115.195	4.869	−0.032
9/4/2007	96.078	5.830	0.003	115.050	4.881	0.012
9/5/2007	95.406	5.880	0.050	115.915	4.809	−0.072
9/6/2007	95.198	5.895	0.015	115.722	4.825	0.016
9/7/2007	96.560	5.795	−0.100	117.060	4.715	−0.110
9/10/2007	97.272	5.743	−0.052	117.754	4.658	−0.057
9/11/2007	97.156	5.751	0.008	117.548	4.675	0.017
9/12/2007	95.307	5.887	0.136	117.098	4.711	0.036
9/13/2007	94.495	5.948	0.061	116.326	4.774	0.063
9/14/2007	94.775	5.927	−0.021	116.500	4.760	−0.014
9/17/2007	94.902	5.917	−0.010	116.530	4.757	−0.003
9/18/2007	94.306	5.962	0.045	116.174	4.786	0.029
9/19/2007	93.665	6.011	0.049	115.308	4.857	0.071
9/20/2007	92.145	6.129	0.118	113.770	4.985	0.128

(Continued)

Exhibit 26-5 Yield and Yield Change for Each Trading Day for the P&G 5.55% 3/5/2037 and Treasury 6.25% 8/15/2023 (CTD Issue): 2/28/2007–12/21/2007 (Continued)

Trading Day	P&G 5.55% 3/5/2037			Treasury 6.25% 8/15/2023 (CTD issue)		
	Price	Yield	Yield Change	Price	Yield	Yield Change
9/21/2007	93.149	6.051	−0.078	114.270	4.943	−0.042
9/24/2007	93.026	6.060	0.009	114.396	4.932	−0.011
9/25/2007	94.718	5.931	−0.129	114.301	4.940	0.008
9/26/2007	94.613	5.939	0.008	114.199	4.948	0.008
9/27/2007	95.402	5.880	−0.059	114.877	4.891	−0.057
9/28/2007	95.281	5.889	0.009	114.877	4.891	0.000
10/1/2007	95.806	5.850	−0.039	115.284	4.857	−0.034
10/2/2007	96.055	5.832	−0.018	115.572	4.833	−0.024
10/3/2007	96.059	5.831	−0.001	115.381	4.849	0.016
10/4/2007	96.335	5.811	−0.020	115.632	4.828	−0.021
10/5/2007	94.915	5.916	0.105	114.224	4.945	0.117
10/8/2007	94.915	5.916	0.000	114.224	4.945	0.000
10/9/2007	94.915	5.916	0.000	114.224	4.945	0.000
10/10/2007	96.247	5.818	−0.098	114.224	4.944	−0.001
10/11/2007	95.952	5.839	0.021	114.039	4.960	0.016
10/12/2007	95.630	5.863	0.024	113.761	4.983	0.023
10/15/2007	95.643	5.862	−0.001	113.815	4.978	−0.005
10/16/2007	95.523	5.871	0.009	113.769	4.982	0.004
10/17/2007	97.233	5.746	−0.125	115.112	4.869	−0.113
10/18/2007	97.677	5.714	−0.032	115.608	4.827	−0.042
10/19/2007	98.915	5.625	−0.089	116.738	4.734	−0.093
10/22/2007	99.170	5.607	−0.018	116.916	4.719	−0.015
10/23/2007	98.903	5.626	0.019	116.698	4.737	0.018
10/24/2007	99.369	5.593	−0.033	117.488	4.672	−0.065
10/25/2007	99.155	5.608	0.015	117.329	4.685	0.013
10/26/2007	98.780	5.635	0.027	117.026	4.710	0.025
10/29/2007	99.034	5.617	−0.018	117.180	4.697	−0.013
10/30/2007	99.185	5.606	−0.011	117.105	4.703	0.006
10/31/2007	98.068	5.686	0.080	116.050	4.789	0.086
11/1/2007	99.589	5.578	−0.108	117.353	4.682	−0.107
11/2/2007	100.343	5.526	−0.052	118.040	4.626	−0.056
11/5/2007	99.978	5.551	0.025	117.731	4.651	0.025
11/6/2007	99.454	5.587	0.036	117.265	4.688	0.037
11/7/2007	98.263	5.672	0.085	117.235	4.691	0.003
11/8/2007	98.356	5.665	−0.007	117.585	4.662	−0.029

(Continued)

Exhibit 26-5   Yield and Yield Change for Each Trading Day for the P&G 5.55% 3/5/2037 and Treasury 6.25% 8/15/2023 (CTD Issue): 2/28/2007–12/21/2007 (Continued)

| Trading Day | P&G 5.55% 3/5/2037 | | | Treasury 6.25% 8/15/2023 (CTD issue) | | |
	Price	Yield	Yield Change	Price	Yield	Yield Change
11/9/2007	98.264	5.672	0.007	118.216	4.611	−0.051
11/12/2007	98.264	5.672	0.000	118.216	4.611	0.000
11/13/2007	99.111	5.612	−0.060	117.976	4.629	0.018
11/14/2007	98.893	5.627	0.015	117.977	4.629	0.000
11/15/2007	99.922	5.555	−0.072	119.051	4.543	−0.086
11/16/2007	100.081	5.544	−0.011	119.201	4.530	−0.013
11/19/2007	100.754	5.497	−0.047	119.890	4.475	−0.055
11/20/2007	100.504	5.514	0.017	119.916	4.473	−0.002
11/21/2007	100.727	5.499	−0.015	120.180	4.452	−0.021
11/23/2007	101.189	5.467	−0.032	120.565	4.421	−0.031
11/26/2007	103.537	5.310	−0.157	122.554	4.265	−0.156
11/27/2007	102.331	5.390	0.080	121.322	4.361	0.096
11/28/2007	101.554	5.443	0.053	120.608	4.417	0.056
11/29/2007	101.863	5.422	−0.021	121.492	4.347	−0.070
11/30/2007	101.140	5.471	0.049	120.804	4.401	0.054
12/3/2007	101.802	5.426	−0.045	121.638	4.335	−0.066
12/4/2007	101.881	5.420	−0.006	121.670	4.332	−0.003
12/5/2007	99.350	5.595	0.175	121.262	4.364	0.032
12/6/2007	98.063	5.686	0.091	120.151	4.451	0.087
12/7/2007	96.671	5.787	0.101	118.645	4.571	0.120
12/10/2007	96.317	5.813	0.026	118.244	4.603	0.032
12/11/2007	98.093	5.684	−0.129	120.015	4.461	−0.142
12/12/2007	98.142	5.680	−0.004	119.156	4.529	0.068
12/13/2007	96.989	5.764	0.084	117.981	4.624	0.095
12/14/2007	96.284	5.815	0.051	117.245	4.684	0.060
12/17/2007	96.824	5.776	−0.039	117.764	4.641	−0.043
12/18/2007	98.203	5.676	−0.100	118.801	4.557	−0.084
12/19/2007	98.796	5.634	−0.042	119.325	4.515	−0.042
12/20/2007	99.466	5.587	−0.047	119.987	4.462	−0.053
12/21/2007	97.757	5.708	0.121	118.364	4.592	0.130

Notice that the yield beta is invariant in this case to the time period used. The yield beta is approximately 0.90, and hence, the adjustment factor in equation (26.12) is 0.90.

This means that yields on the P&G bond are expected to move 10% less than yields on the CTD issue. To calculate the relative volatility of the two issues correctly, this fact must be taken into account; thus, the hedge ratio derived in our earlier example is multiplied by the factor 0.90. Consequently, instead of shorting 116 Treasury bond futures contracts to hedge $10 million par value of the P&G bond, only 105 contracts should be shorted.

The formula for the hedge ratio, equation (26.10), is revised as follows to incorporate the impact of the yield beta:

$$\text{hedge ratio} = \frac{\text{PVBP of bond to be hedged}}{\text{PVBP of CTD issue}} \times \text{conversion factor for CTD issue} \times \text{yield beta} \qquad \textbf{(26.14)}$$

The second approach for capturing the relative movement in yields and estimating the adjustment is the pure volatility adjustment. This is done by first calculating the daily change in yield for the bond to be hedged and the CTD issue. Then for the change in yield, the standard deviation is computed. The pure volatility adjustment is just the ratio of the two standard deviations. That is,

$$\text{pure volatility adjustment} = \frac{\text{std. dev. of yield change for bond to be hedged}}{\text{std. dev. of yield change for CTD issue}} \qquad \textbf{(26.15)}$$

Again, there is no set formula for selecting the number of trading days that should be used. The pure volatility adjustment using three different sets of trading days is summarized below:

Number of Trading Days	Standard Deviation for:		
	P&G Bond	CTD Issue	Pure Volatility Adjustment
Prior 30 trading days ending 12/21/2007	0.085	0.084	1.011
Prior 90 trading days ending 12/21/2007	0.064	0.060	1.064
Prior 218 trading days ending 12/21/2007	0.053	0.049	1.084

In contrast to the regression approach, one can see that the adjustment differs depending on the time period used, and in addition, the number of contracts to be shorted would be greater since the pure volatility adjustment is greater than one.

Change in the CTD Issue

The effect of a change in the cheapest-to-deliver issue and the yield spread can be assessed a priori. An exhibit similar to that of Exhibit 26-4 can be constructed under a wide range of assumptions. For example, at different yield levels at the date the hedge is to be lifted (the second column in Exhibit 26-4), a different yield spread may be appropriate and a different acceptable issue will be the CTD. The portfolio manager can determine what this will do to the outcome of the hedge.

Creating Synthetic Securities for Yield Enhancement

A cash market security can be created synthetically by taking a position in the futures contract together with the deliverable instrument. If the yield on the synthetic security is the same as the yield on the cash market security, there will be no arbitrage opportunity. Any difference between the two yields can be exploited so as to enhance the yield on the portfolio.

To see how, consider an investor who owns a 20-year Treasury bond and sells Treasury futures that call for the delivery of that particular bond three months from now. Although the maturity of the Treasury bond is 20 years, the investor has effectively shortened the maturity of the bond to three months.

Consequently, the long position in the 20-year bond and the short futures position are equivalent to a long position in a three-month riskless security. The position is riskless because the investor is locking in the price to be received three months from now—the futures price. By being long the bond and short the futures, the investor has synthetically created a three-month Treasury bill. The return the investor should expect to earn from this synthetic position should be the yield on a three-month Treasury bill. If the yield on the synthetic three-month Treasury bill is greater than the yield on the cash market Treasury bill, the investor can realize an enhanced yield by creating the synthetic short-term security. The fundamental relationship for creating synthetic securities is

$$RSP = CBP - FBP \qquad (26.16)$$

where

RSP = riskless short-term security position
CBP = cash bond position
FBP = futures bond position

A negative sign before a position means a short position. In terms of our previous example, CBP is the long cash bond position, the negative sign before FBP refers to the short futures position, and RSP is the riskless synthetic three-month security or Treasury bill.

Equation (26.16) states that an investor who is long the cash market security and short the futures contract should expect to earn the rate of return on a risk-free security with the same maturity as the futures delivery date. Solving equation (26.16) for the long bond position, we have

$$CBP = RSP + FBP \qquad (26.17)$$

Equation (26.17) states that a cash bond position equals a short-term riskless security position plus a long bond futures position. Thus, a cash market bond can be created synthetically by buying a futures contract and investing in a Treasury bill. Solving equation (26.17) for the bond futures position, we have

$$FBP = CBP - RSP \qquad (26.18)$$

Equation (26.18) tells us that a long position in the futures contract can be created synthetically by taking a long position in the cash market bond and shorting the short-term riskless security. But shorting the short-term riskless security is equivalent to borrowing money. Notice that it was equation (26.18) that we used in deriving the theoretical futures price when the futures contract was underpriced. Recall that when the actual futures price is greater than the theoretical futures price, the strategy to obtain an arbitrage profit is to sell the futures contract and create a synthetic long futures position by buying the asset with borrowed funds. This is precisely what equation (26.18) states. In this case, instead of creating a synthetic cash market instrument as we did with equations (26.16) and (26.17), we have created a synthetic futures contract. The fact that the synthetic long futures position is cheaper than the actual long futures position provides an arbitrage opportunity. If we reverse the sign of both sides of equation (26.18), we can see how a short futures position can be created synthetically.

In an efficient market, the opportunities for yield enhancement should not exist very long. But even in the absence of yield enhancement, portfolio managers can use synthetic securities to hedge a portfolio position that they find difficult to hedge in the cash market either because of lack of liquidity or because of other constraints.

Allocating Funds between Stocks and Bonds

A pension sponsor may wish to alter the composition of the pension's funds between stocks and bonds, that is, change its asset allocation. Suppose that a pension sponsor wants to shift a $1 billion fund from its current allocation of $500 million in stocks and $500 million in bonds to $300 million in stocks and $700 million in bonds. This can be done directly by selling $200 million of stocks and buying a similar amount of bonds. The costs associated with shifting funds in this manner are (1) the transactions costs with respect to commissions and bid-ask spreads, (2) the market impact costs, and (3) the disruption of the activities of the portfolio managers employed by the pension sponsor.

An alternative course of action is to use interest-rate futures and stock index futures. Assume that the pension sponsor wants to shift $200 million from stocks to bonds. Buying an appropriate number of interest-rate futures and selling an appropriate number of stock index futures can achieve the desired exposure to stocks and bonds. Futures positions can be maintained or slowly liquidated as funds invested in the cash markets are actually shifted. The advantages of using financial futures contracts are as follows: (1) Transactions costs are lower, (2) market impact costs are avoided or reduced by allowing the sponsor time to buy and sell securities in the cash market, and (3) activities of the portfolio managers employed by the pension sponsor are not disrupted.[10]

To determine the approximate number of interest-rate futures contracts needed to change the market value of the portfolio allocated to bonds we can use the following formula:

approximate number of contracts

$$= \frac{\text{dollar duration for target bond allocation} - \text{dollar duration for current bond allocation}}{\text{dollar duration of the futures contract}}$$

KEY POINTS

- A futures contract is an agreement between a buyer (seller) and an established exchange or its clearinghouse in which the buyer (seller) agrees to take (make) delivery of something at the futures price at the settlement or delivery date.
- Associated with every futures exchange is a clearinghouse, which guarantees that the two parties to the transaction will perform and allows parties to unwind their position without the need to deal with the counterparty to the initial transaction.
- A party to a futures contract must comply with margin requirements (initial, maintenance, and variation margin).
- A forward contract differs from a futures contract in that it is usually nonstandardized (i.e., the terms of each contract are negotiated individually between buyer and seller), there is no clearinghouse, and secondary markets are often nonexistent or extremely thin.

---

[10] See Roger Clarke, "Asset Allocation Using Futures," Chapter 16 in Robert Arnott and Frank J. Fabozzi (eds.), *Asset Allocation* (Chicago: Probus Publishing, 1988); and Mark Zurak and Ravi Dattatreya, "Asset Allocation Using Futures Contracts," Chapter 20 in Frank J. Fabozzi and Gregory Kipnis (eds.), *The Handbook of Stock Index Futures and Options* (Homewood, IL: Probus Publishing, 1988).

- Futures contracts are traded on short-term interest rates, the most active being the Eurodollar futures and Euribor futures. The most active bond futures are Treasury futures (Treasury bond futures and Treasury note futures).
- The theoretical price of a futures contract is equal to the cash or spot price plus the cost of carry. The cost of carry is equal to the cost of financing the position less the cash yield on the underlying security. The shape of the yield curve will affect the cost of carry.
- There are several reasons why the actual futures price will depart from the theoretical futures price. In the case of the Treasury bond futures contracts, the delivery options granted to the seller reduce the actual futures price below the theoretical futures price suggested by the standard arbitrage model.
- Buying futures adds dollar duration to a portfolio; selling futures reduces a portfolio's dollar duration.
- Interest-rate futures contracts can be used by portfolio managers to control a portfolio's duration, to hedge a portfolio or bond position, to enhance returns when futures are mispriced, and to efficiently allocate funds between stocks and bonds.

QUESTIONS

1. Explain the differences between a futures contract and a forward contract.

2. **a.** What is counterparty risk?
   b. Why do both the buyer and seller of a forward contract face counterparty risk?

3. What does it mean if the cost of carry is positive for a Treasury bond futures contract?

4. If the Eurodollar futures contract is quoted at 91.75, what is the annualized futures three-month LIBOR?

5. Suppose that an investor purchased a Eurodollar futures contract at an index price of 95.00. At the settlement date, suppose that the settlement price is 95.40. Explain whether the buyer or the seller of the futures contract receives a payment at the settlement date.

6. Explain how a market participant concerned with a decline in three-month LIBOR can hedge that risk using the Eurodollar futures contract.

7. **a.** What is Euribor?
   b. What is Euribor futures contract?

8. For a Treasury futures contract, how do you think the cost of carry will affect the decision of the short as to when in the delivery month the short will elect to deliver?

9. Explain the asymmetric effect on the variation margin and cash flow for the short and long in an interest-rate futures contract when interest rates change.

10. What are the delivery options granted to the seller of the Treasury bond futures contract?

11. How is the theoretical futures price of a Treasury bond futures contract affected by the delivery options granted to the short?

12. Explain how the shape of the yield curve influences the theoretical price of a Treasury bond futures contract.

13. Suppose that the conversion factor for a particular Treasury bond that is acceptable for delivery in a Treasury bond futures contract is 0.85 and that the futures price settles at 105. Assume also that the accrued interest for this Treasury bond is 4. What is the invoice price if the seller delivers this Treasury bond at the settlement date?

14. Suppose that bond ABC is the underlying asset for a futures contract with settlement six months from now. You know the following about bond ABC and the futures contract: (1) in the cash market, ABC is selling for $80 (par value is $100); (2) ABC pays $8 in coupon interest per year in two semiannual payments of $4, and the next semiannual payment is due exactly six months from now; and (3) the current six-month interest rate at which funds can be loaned or borrowed is 6%.
   a. What is the theoretical futures price?
   b. What action would you take if the futures price is $83?

c. What action would you take if the futures price is $76?

d. Suppose that bond ABC pays interest quarterly instead of semiannually. If you know that you can reinvest any funds you receive three months from now at 1% for three months, what would the theoretical futures price for six-month settlement be?

e. Suppose that the borrowing rate and lending rate are not equal. Instead, suppose that the current six-month borrowing rate is 8% and the six-month lending rate is 6%. What is the boundary for the theoretical futures price?

15. What is the implied repo rate?

16. Explain why the implied repo rate is important in determining the cheapest-to-deliver issue.

17. A portfolio manager wishes to hedge a bond with a par value of $20 million by selling Treasury bond futures. Suppose that (1) the conversion factor for the cheapest-to-deliver issue is 0.91, (2) the price value of a basis point of the cheapest-to-deliver issue at the settlement date is 0.06895, and (3) the price value of a basis point of the bond to be hedged is 0.05954.

a. What is the hedge ratio?

b. How many Treasury bond futures contracts should be sold to hedge the bond?

18. Suppose that without an adjustment for the relationship between the yield on a bond to be hedged and the yield on the hedging instrument the hedge ratio is 1.30.

a. Suppose that a yield beta of 0.8 is computed. What would the revised hedge ratio be?

b. Suppose that the standard deviation for the bond to be hedged and the hedging instrument are 0.9 and 0.10, respectively. What is the pure volatility adjustment, and what would be the revised hedge ratio?

19. Suppose that a manager wants to reduce the duration of a portfolio. Explain how this can be done using Treasury bond futures contracts.

20. What risks are associated with hedging?

21. How could a portfolio manager use a Treasury bond futures contract to hedge against increased interest rates over the next quarter?

22. Consider the portfolio in Exhibit 26-3. Suppose that the dollar duration of the 5-year Treasury note futures contract is $5,022.

a. What position would a portfolio manager have to take in the contract to hedge the portfolio?

b. What is the market value of the position that the portfolio manager must take?

23. Consider the portfolio in Exhibit 26-3. Suppose that the dollar duration of the 5-year Treasury note futures contract is $5,022.

a. What position would a portfolio manager have to take in the contract to obtain a portfolio duration of 4?

b. What is the market value of the position that the portfolio manager must take?

24. Suppose that an institutional investor wants to hedge a portfolio of mortgage pass-through securities using Treasury bond futures contracts. What are the risks associated with such a hedge?

25. The following excerpt appeared in the article, "Duration," in the November 16, 1992, issue of *Derivatives Week*, p. 9:

> TSA Capital Management in Los Angeles must determine duration of the futures contract it uses in order to match it with the dollar duration of the underlying, explains David Depew, principal and head of trading at the firm. Futures duration will be based on the duration of the underlying bond most likely to be delivered against the contract....

a. Explain why it is necessary to know the dollar duration of the underlying in order to hedge.

b. Why can the price value of a basis point be used instead of the dollar duration?

26. You work for a conservative investment management firm. You recently asked one of the senior partners for permission to open up a futures account so that you could trade interest-rate futures as well as cash instruments. He replied, "Are you crazy? I might as well write you a check, wish you good luck, and put you on a bus to Las Vegas. The futures markets are nothing more than a respectable game of craps. Don't you think you're taking enough risk trading bonds?" How would you try to persuade the senior partner to allow you to use futures?

27

Interest-Rate Options

LEARNING OBJECTIVES

After reading this chapter, you will understand

- the basic features of interest-rate options contracts
- why over-the-counter interest-rate options are used by institutional investors
- what futures options are, their trading mechanics, and the reasons for their popularity
- the differences between options and futures
- the basic option positions
- the factors that affect the value of an option
- what the intrinsic value and time value of an option are
- the relationship between the price of a put and a call option
- the limitations of applying the Black–Scholes option pricing model to options on fixed-income securities
- how the arbitrage-free binomial model can be used to value options on fixed-income securities
- how the Black model is used to value an option on an interest-rate futures contract
- measures to estimate the sensitivity of the option price to the factors that determine the price
- what implied volatility is
- how implied yield volatility is computed
- how to calculate the duration of an option
- how futures options can be used to hedge

In this chapter, we explain the various types of interest-rate options, their applications to portfolio management, and how they are priced.

OPTIONS DEFINED

An **option** is a contract in which the writer of the option grants the buyer of the option the right to purchase from or sell to the writer a designated instrument at a specified price within a specified period of time. The writer, also referred to as the seller, grants this right to the buyer in exchange for a certain sum of money called the **option price** or **option premium**. The price at which the instrument may be bought or sold is called the **strike** or **exercise price**. The date after which an option is void is called the **expiration date**. An **American option** may be exercised at any time up to and including the expiration date. A **European option** may be exercised only on the expiration date.

When an option grants the buyer the right to purchase the designated instrument from the writer, it is called a **call option**. When the option buyer has the right to sell the designated instrument to the writer (seller), the option is called a **put option**. The buyer of any option is said to be **long the option**; the writer (seller) is said to be **short the option**.

The maximum amount that an option buyer can lose in such a transaction is the option price. The maximum profit that the option writer (seller) can realize likewise is the option price. The option buyer has substantial upside return potential, whereas the option writer has substantial downside risk. We will investigate the risk/reward relationship for option positions later in this chapter.

DIFFERENCES BETWEEN AN OPTION AND A FUTURES CONTRACT

Notice that options differ from futures contracts, in that the buyer of an option has the right but not the obligation to perform, whereas the option seller (writer) has the obligation to perform. In the case of a futures contract, both the buyer and the seller are obligated to perform. Also notice that in a futures contract, the buyer does not pay the seller to accept the obligation; in the case of an option, the buyer pays the seller the option price.

Consequently, the risk/reward characteristics of the two contracts are also different. In a futures contract the long position realizes a dollar-for-dollar gain when the price of the futures increases and suffers a dollar-for-dollar loss when the price of the futures decreases. The opposite occurs for the short position. Options do not provide such a symmetric risk/reward relationship. The most that a long may lose is the option price, yet the long retains all the upside potential, although the gain is always reduced by the option price. The maximum profit that the short may realize is the option price, but this position has substantial downside risk.

TYPES OF INTEREST-RATE OPTIONS

Interest-rate options can be written on cash instruments or futures. At one time, there were several exchange-traded option contracts whose underlying instrument was a debt instrument. These contracts are referred to as **options on physicals**. The most liquid exchange-traded option on a fixed-income security is the CME Group's option on Treasury bonds. For reasons to be explained later, options on futures have been far more popular than options on physicals. In recent years, market participants have made increasingly greater use of over-the-counter (OTC) options on Treasury and mortgage-backed securities.

Certain institutional investors who want to purchase an option on a specific Treasury security or a Ginnie Mae pass-through can do so on an OTC basis. There are government and mortgage-backed securities dealers who make a market in options on specific securities. OTC (or dealer) options typically are purchased by institutional investors who want to hedge the risk associated with a specific security. For example, a thrift may be interested in hedging its position in a specific mortgage pass-through security. Typically, the maturity of the option coincides with the time period over which the buyer of the option wants to hedge, so the buyer is usually not concerned with the option's liquidity. Besides options on fixed-income securities, there are OTC options on the shape of the yield curve or the yield spread between two securities (such as the spread between mortgage pass-through securities and Treasuries, or between double A corporates and Treasuries).

Exchange-Traded Futures Options

An option on a futures contract, commonly referred to as a **futures option**, gives the buyer the right to buy from or sell to the writer a designated futures contract at a designated price at any time during the life of the option. If the futures option is a call option, the buyer has the right to purchase one designated futures contract at the exercise price. That is, the buyer has the right to acquire a long futures position in the designated futures contract. If the buyer exercises the call option, the writer (seller) acquires a corresponding short position in the futures contract.

A put option on a futures contract grants the buyer the right to sell one designated futures contract to the writer at the exercise price. That is, the option buyer has the right to acquire a short position in the designated futures contract. If the put option is exercised, the writer acquires a corresponding long position in the designated futures contract.

Mechanics of Trading Futures Options

Exercising a Futures Option

As the parties to the futures option will realize a position in a futures contract when the option is exercised, the question is: What will the futures price be? That is, at what price will the long be required to pay for the instrument underlying the futures contract, and at what price will the short be required to sell the instrument underlying the futures contract?

Upon exercise, the futures price for the futures contract will be set equal to the exercise price. The position of the two parties is then immediately marked to market in terms of the then-current futures price. Thus, the futures position of the two parties will be at the prevailing futures price. At the same time, the option buyer will receive from the option seller the economic benefit from exercising. In the case of a call futures option, the option writer must pay the difference between the current futures price and the exercise price to the buyer of the option. In the case of a put futures option, the option writer must pay the option buyer the difference between the exercise price and the current futures price.

For example, suppose that an investor buys a call option on some futures contract in which the exercise price is 85. Assume also that the futures price is 95 and that the buyer exercises the call option. Upon exercise, the call buyer is given a long position in the futures contract at 85 and the call writer is assigned the corresponding short position in the futures contract at 85. The futures positions of the buyer and the writer are immediately marked to market by the exchange. Because the prevailing futures price is 95 and the exercise price is 85, the long futures position (the position of the call buyer) realizes a gain of 10, while the short futures position (the position of the call writer) realizes a loss of 10. The call writer pays the exchange 10 and the call buyer receives from the exchange 10. The call buyer, who now has a long futures position at 95, can either liquidate the futures position at 95 or maintain a long futures position. If the former course of action is taken, the call buyer sells a futures contract at the prevailing futures price of 95. There is no gain or loss from liquidating the position. Overall, the call buyer realizes a gain of 10. The call buyer who elects to hold the long futures position will face the same risk and reward of holding such a position, but still has realized a gain of 10 from the exercise of the call option.

Suppose instead that the futures option is a put rather than a call, and the current futures price is 60 rather than 95. Then if the buyer of this put option exercises it, the buyer would have a short position in the futures contract at 85; the option writer would have a long position in the futures contract at 85. The exchange then marks the position to market at the then-current futures price of 60, resulting in a gain to the put buyer of 25 and a loss to the put writer of the same amount. The put buyer who now has a short futures position at 60 can either liquidate the short futures position by buying a futures contract at the prevailing futures price of 60 or maintain the short futures position. In either case the put buyer realizes a gain of 25 from exercising the put option.

Margin Requirements

There are no margin requirements for the buyer of a futures option after the option price has been paid in full. Because the option price is the maximum amount that the buyer can lose, regardless of how adverse the price movement of the underlying instrument, there is no need for margin.

Because the writer (seller) of an option has agreed to accept all of the risk (and none of the reward) of the position in the underlying instrument, the writer (seller) is required to deposit not only the margin required on the interest rate futures contract position if that is the underlying instrument, but also (with certain exceptions) the option price that is received for writing the option. In addition, as prices adversely affect the writer's position, the writer would be required to deposit variation margin as it is marked to market.

Reasons for the Popularity of Futures Options

There are three reasons why futures options on fixed-income securities have largely supplanted options on physicals as the options vehicle of choice for institutional investors. First, unlike options on fixed-income securities, options on Treasury coupon futures do not require payments for accrued interest to be made. Consequently, when a futures option is exercised, the call buyer and the put writer need not compensate the other party for accrued interest.

Second, futures options are believed to be "cleaner" instruments because of the reduced likelihood of delivery squeezes. Market participants who must deliver an instrument are concerned that at the time of delivery the instrument to be delivered will be in short supply, resulting in a higher price to acquire the instrument. As the deliverable supply of futures contracts is more than adequate for futures options currently traded, there is no concern about a delivery squeeze. Finally, in order to price any option, it is imperative to know at all times the price of the underlying instrument. In the bond market, current prices are not as easily available as price information on the futures contract.

Specifications for the Actively Traded Futures Options

There are options on all of the futures contracts described in Chapter 26. All futures options are of the American type. If the option buyer elects to exercise early, he or she must notify the clearing corporation, which then randomly selects a clearing member that must select a short from among its customers.

The Treasury bond futures contracts have delivery months of March, June, September, and December. In Chapter 26, we described the delivery process and the choices granted to the short. There are futures options that expire in the next three regular quarterly expiration months. Trading of futures options on Treasury bonds stops in the month prior to the underlying futures contract's delivery month. The day in that month in which the futures options stop trading is the first Friday preceding, by at least five days, the first notice day for the Treasury bond futures contract.

To compete with the OTC option market, **flexible Treasury futures options** were introduced. These futures options allow counterparties to customize options within certain limits. Specifically, the strike price, expiration date, and type of exercise (American or European) can be customized subject to CBOT constraints. One key constraint is that the expiration date of a flexible contract cannot exceed that of the longest standard option traded on the CBOT. Unlike an OTC option, where the option buyer is exposed to counterparty risk, a flexible Treasury futures option is guaranteed by the clearing house. The minimum size requirement for the launching of a flexible futures option is 100 contracts.

INTRINSIC VALUE AND TIME VALUE OF AN OPTION

The cost to the buyer of an option is primarily a reflection of the option's intrinsic value and any additional amount over that value. The premium over intrinsic value is often referred to as **time value**.

Intrinsic Value of an Option

The intrinsic value of an option is the economic value of the option if it is exercised immediately. Because the buyer of an option need not exercise the option, and, in fact, will not do so if no economic gain will result from exercising it, the intrinsic value cannot be less than zero.

Call Options

The intrinsic value of a call option on a bond is the difference between the bond price and the strike price. For example, if the strike price for a call option is $100 and the current bond price is $105, the intrinsic value is $5. That is, if the option buyer exercises the option and sells the bond simultaneously, the option buyer would realize $105 from the sale of the bond, which would be covered by acquiring the bond from the option writer for $100, thereby netting a $5 gain.

When a call option has intrinsic value, it is said to be **in-the-money**. Our call option with a strike price of $100 is in-the-money when the price of the underlying bond is greater than $100. When the strike price of a call option exceeds the bond price, the call option is said to be **out-of-the-money** and has no intrinsic value. An option for which the strike price is equal to the current bond price is said to be **at-the-money**. Both at-the-money and out-of-the-money options have an intrinsic value of zero because it is not profitable to exercise the option.

Put Options

For a put option, the intrinsic value is equal to the amount by which the bond price is below the strike price. For example, if the strike price of a put option is $100 and the current bond price is $92, the intrinsic value is $8. That is, the buyer of the put option who exercises the put option and buys the bond simultaneously will net $8 because the bond will be sold to the writer for $100 and purchased in the market for $92.

When the put option has intrinsic value, the option is said to be in-the-money. For our put option with a strike price of $100, the option will be in-the-money when the bond price is less than $100. A put option is out-of-the-money when the current bond price exceeds the strike price. A put option is at-the-money when the strike price is equal to the bond price.

Time Value of an Option

The time value of an option is the amount by which the option price exceeds the intrinsic value. The option buyer hopes that at some time prior to expiration, changes in the market yield will increase the value of the rights conveyed by the option. For this prospect, the option buyer is willing to pay a premium above the intrinsic value. For example, if the price of a call option with a strike price of $100 is $9 when the current bond price is $105, the time value of this option is $4 ($9 minus the intrinsic value of $5). If the current bond price is $90 instead of $105, the time value of this option is $9 because the option has no intrinsic value.

There are two ways in which an option buyer may realize the value of a position taken in the option. First, the investor may exercise the option. In the case of a futures option, by exercising the buyer will be assigned a position in the underlying futures contract at the current futures price and be paid by the writer any difference between the current futures price and the strike price. The investor can sell the futures contract at the current price. For example, for our hypothetical call option with a strike price of $100 and an option price of $9, in which the current futures price is $105, the option buyer can exercise the option. This will produce a long position in the futures contract currently at $105. The call writer will pay the buyer $5 (the difference between the current futures price of $105 and the strike price of $100). By simultaneously selling the underlying futures for $105, the option buyer will realize $5.

The second way of realizing the value of an option position is by selling the call option for $9. Obviously, this is the preferable alternative because the exercise of an option will cause the immediate loss of any time value (in this case, $4).

Whether any option will be exercised prior to the expiration date depends on whether the total proceeds at the expiration date would be greater by holding the option or by exercising and reinvesting any cash proceeds received until the expiration date.

PROFIT AND LOSS PROFILES FOR SIMPLE NAKED OPTION STRATEGIES

To appreciate the opportunities available with interest-rate options, the profit and loss profiles for various option strategies must be understood. We begin with simple strategies in only one option on a bond, which are referred to as **naked option strategies**. That is, no other position is taken in another option or bond. *The profit and loss profiles that we present assume that each option position is held to the expiration date and not exercised earlier.* Also, to simplify the illustrations, we assume that there are no transactions costs to implement the strategies.

The four naked option strategies that we illustrate are (1) long call strategy (buying call options), (2) short call strategy (selling or writing call options), (3) long put strategy (buying put options), and (4) short put strategy (selling or writing put options).

Long Call Strategy (Buying Call Options)

The most straightforward option strategy for participating in an anticipated decrease in interest rates (increase in the price of bonds) is to buy a call option on a debt instrument. This is called a **long call strategy**. To illustrate this strategy, assume that there is a call option on a particular 8% coupon bond with a par value of $100 and 20 years and one month to maturity. The call option expires in one month and the strike price is $100. The option price is $3. Although this option is an option on a cash market security, the principles apply equally to futures options.

Suppose that the current price of the bond is $100 (i.e., the bond is selling at par), which means that the yield on this bond is currently 8%. As the strike price is equal to the current price of the bond, this option is at-the-money. What would the profit or loss be for the investor who purchases this call option and holds it to the expiration date?

The profit and loss from the strategy will depend on the price of the bond at the expiration date. The price, in turn, will depend on the yield on 20-year bonds with an 8% coupon, because in one month the bond will have only 20 years to maturity. Exhibit 27-1 shows the price of a 20-year 8% coupon bond for interest rates ranging from 4% to 12%. Five outcomes are possible:

1. If the price of the bond at the expiration date is less than $100 (which means that the market yield is greater than 8%), the investor would not exercise the option. (Why bother exercising the option and paying the option writer $100 when the same bond can be purchased in the market at a lower price?) In this case, the option buyer will lose the entire option price of $3. Notice, however, that this is the maximum loss that the option buyer will realize, no matter how far the price of the bond declines.

2. If the price of the bond is equal to $100 (which means that the market yield is unchanged at 8%), no economic value will result from exercising the option. As in the outcome when the price of the bond is less than $100, the buyer of this call option will lose the entire option price, $3.

3. If the price of the bond is greater than $100 but less than $103 (which means that the market yield is less than 8% but greater than 7.70%—see Exhibit 27-1), the option buyer will exercise the option. By exercising, the option buyer purchases the bond for $100 (the strike price) and can sell it in the market for a higher price. Suppose, for example, that the market yield is 7.8%, so that the price of the bond is about $102 at the expiration date. The buyer of this call option will realize a $2 gain by exercising the option, offset by the $3 cost of purchasing the call option. Hence, $1 is the total loss on this strategy. If the investor fails to exercise the option, the $3 is lost.

4. If the price of the bond at the expiration date is equal to $103 (a market yield of about 7.70%), the investor will exercise the option. In this case, the investor breaks even, realizing a gain of $3 on the bond, which offsets the cost of the option, $3. Although there is no net gain, the price of the option is recouped.

5. If the price of the bond at the expiration date is greater than $103 (a market yield of less than 7.70%), the investor will exercise the option and realize a profit. For example, if the price of the bond is $113 because the market yield has declined from 8% to 6.8%, exercising the option will generate a profit on the bond of $13. Reducing this gain by the cost of the option ($3) means that the investor realizes a net profit of $10 on this strategy.

Exhibit 27-1 Price/Yield Relationship for a 20-Year 8% Coupon Bond

Yield	Price	Yield	Price
4.0	154.71	8.1	99.02
4.2	151.08	8.2	98.05
4.4	147.56	8.3	97.10
4.6	144.15	8.4	96.16
4.8	140.85	8.5	95.23
5.0	137.65	8.6	94.32
5.2	134.56	8.7	93.42
5.4	131.56	8.8	92.53
5.6	128.66	8.9	91.66
5.8	125.84	9.0	90.80
6.0	123.11	9.1	89.95
6.1	121.78	9.2	89.11
6.2	120.47	9.3	88.29
6.3	119.18	9.4	87.48
6.4	117.91	9.5	86.68
6.5	116.66	9.6	85.89
6.6	115.42	9.7	85.11
6.7	114.21	9.8	84.34
6.8	113.01	9.9	83.59
6.9	111.84	10.0	82.84
7.0	110.68	10.2	81.38
7.1	109.54	10.4	79.96
7.2	108.41	10.6	78.58
7.3	107.30	10.8	77.24
7.4	106.21	11.0	75.93
7.5	105.14	11.2	74.66
7.6	104.08	11.4	73.42
7.7	103.04	11.6	72.22
7.8	102.01	11.8	71.05
7.9	101.00	12.0	69.91
8.0	100.00		

Exhibit 27-2 shows the profit/loss in tabular form for the buyer of the hypothetical call option, and Exhibit 27-3 portrays it graphically. Although the break-even point and the loss will depend on the option price and the strike price, the shape shown in Exhibit 27-3 will hold for all buyers of call options. That shape indicates that the maximum loss is the option price, yet there is substantial upside potential.

It is worthwhile to compare the profit and loss profile of a call option buyer to a long bond strategy in the same bond. The payoff from the strategy depends on the price of the

Exhibit 27-2   Profit/Loss Profile for a Long Call Strategy

Assumptions:
Call option price: 3
Strike price: 100
Time to expiration: 1 month

At Expiration Date:			At Expiration Date:		
Market Yield	Price of Bond	Net Profit	Market Yield	Price of Bond	Net Profit
4.0	154.71	51.71	8.1	99.02	−3.00
4.2	151.08	48.08	8.2	98.05	−3.00
4.4	147.56	44.56	8.3	97.10	−3.00
4.6	144.15	41.15	8.4	96.16	−3.00
4.8	140.85	37.85	8.5	95.23	−3.00
5.0	137.65	34.65	8.6	94.32	−3.00
5.2	134.56	31.56	8.7	93.42	−3.00
5.4	131.56	28.56	8.8	92.53	−3.00
5.6	128.66	25.66	8.9	91.66	−3.00
5.8	125.84	22.84	9.0	90.80	−3.00
6.0	123.11	20.11	9.1	89.95	−3.00
6.1	121.78	18.78	9.2	89.11	−3.00
6.2	120.47	17.47	9.3	88.29	−3.00
6.3	119.18	16.18	9.4	87.48	−3.00
6.4	117.91	14.91	9.5	86.68	−3.00
6.5	116.66	13.66	9.6	85.89	−3.00
6.6	115.42	12.42	9.7	85.11	−3.00
6.7	114.21	11.21	9.8	84.34	−3.00
6.8	113.01	10.01	9.9	83.59	−3.00
6.9	111.84	8.84	10.0	82.84	−3.00
7.0	110.68	7.68	10.2	81.38	−3.00
7.1	109.54	6.54	10.4	79.96	−3.00
7.2	108.41	5.41	10.6	78.58	−3.00
7.3	107.30	4.30	10.8	77.24	−3.00
7.4	106.21	3.21	11.0	75.93	−3.00
7.5	105.14	2.14	11.2	74.66	−3.00
7.6	104.08	1.08	11.4	73.42	−3.00
7.7	103.04	0.04	11.6	72.22	−3.00
7.8	102.01	−0.99	11.8	71.05	−3.00
7.9	101.00	−2.00	12.0	69.91	−3.00
8.0	100.00	−3.00			

Exhibit 27-3   Profit/Loss Diagram for a Long Call Strategy

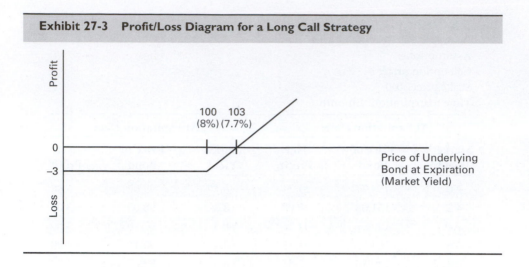

bond at the expiration date, which, in turn, depends on the market yield at the expiration date. Consider again the five price outcomes given previously:

1. If the price of the bond at the expiration date is less than $100 (market yield rises above 8%), the investor would lose the entire option price of $3. In contrast, a long bond position will have one of three possible outcomes:
   a. If the price of the bond is lower than $100 (market yield greater than 8%) but higher than $97 (market yield less than about 8.3%), the loss on the long bond position will be less than $3.
   b. If the price of the bond is $97 (market yield of about 8.3%), the loss on the long bond position will be $3.
   c. If the price of the bond is lower than $97, the loss on the long bond position will be more than $3. For example, if the price at the expiration date is $80 because the market yield has risen to 10.4%, the long bond position will result in a loss of $20.
2. If the price of the bond is equal to $100 because the market yield is unchanged, the buyer of the call option will realize a loss of $3 (the cost of the option). There will be no gain or loss on the long bond position.
3. If the price of the bond is higher than $100 because the market yield has fallen below 8% but lower than $103 (market yield above 7.70%), the option buyer will realize a loss of less than $3, while the long bond position will realize a profit.
4. If the market yield falls to about 7.70% so that the price of the bond at the expiration date is equal to $103, there will be no loss or gain from buying the call option. The long bond position will produce a gain of $3.
5. If the price of the bond at the expiration date is higher than $103 because the market yield has fallen below 7.70%, both the call option purchase and the long bond position will result in a profit. However, the profit for the buyer of the call option will be $3 less than that on the long bond position. For example, if the market yield falls to 6.8% so that the price of the bond is $113, the profit from the long call position is $10 and the profit from the long bond position is $13.

Exhibit 27-4 compares the long call strategy and the long bond strategy. This comparison clearly demonstrates the way in which an option can change the risk/return profile available to investors. An investor who takes a long position in the bond realizes a profit

Exhibit 27-4   Comparison of a Long Call Strategy and a Long Bond Strategy

Assumptions:
Current price of bond: 100
Call option price: 3
Strike price: 100
Time to expiration: 1 month

At Expiration Date:		Profit		At Expiration Date:		Profit	
Market Yield	Price of Bond	Long Call	Long Bond	Market Yield	Price of Bond	Long Call	Long Bond
4.0	154.71	51.71	54.71	8.1	99.02	−3.00	−0.98
4.2	151.08	48.08	51.08	8.2	98.05	−3.00	−1.95
4.4	147.56	44.56	47.56	8.3	97.10	−3.00	−2.90
4.6	144.15	41.15	44.15	8.4	96.16	−3.00	−3.84
4.8	140.85	37.85	40.85	8.5	95.23	−3.00	−4.77
5.0	137.65	34.65	37.65	8.6	94.32	−3.00	−5.68
5.2	134.56	31.56	34.56	8.7	93.42	−3.00	−6.58
5.4	131.56	28.56	31.56	8.8	92.53	−3.00	−7.47
5.6	128.66	25.66	28.66	8.9	91.66	−3.00	−8.34
5.8	125.84	22.84	25.84	9.0	90.80	−3.00	−9.20
6.0	123.11	20.11	23.11	9.1	89.95	−3.00	−10.05
6.1	121.78	18.78	21.78	9.2	89.11	−3.00	−10.89
6.2	120.47	17.47	20.47	9.3	88.29	−3.00	−11.71
6.3	119.18	16.18	19.18	9.4	87.48	−3.00	−12.52
6.4	117.91	14.91	17.91	9.5	86.68	−3.00	−13.32
6.5	116.66	13.66	16.66	9.6	85.89	−3.00	−14.11
6.6	115.42	12.42	15.42	9.7	85.11	−3.00	−14.89
6.7	114.21	11.21	14.21	9.8	84.34	−3.00	−15.66
6.8	113.01	10.01	13.01	9.9	83.59	−3.00	−16.41
6.9	111.84	8.84	11.84	10.0	82.84	−3.00	−17.16
7.0	110.68	7.68	10.68	10.2	81.38	−3.00	−18.62
7.1	109.54	6.54	9.54	10.4	79.96	−3.00	−20.04
7.2	108.41	5.41	8.41	10.6	78.58	−3.00	−21.42
7.3	107.30	4.30	7.30	10.8	77.24	−3.00	−22.76
7.4	106.21	3.21	6.21	11.0	75.93	−3.00	−24.07
7.5	105.14	2.14	5.14	11.2	74.66	−3.00	−25.34
7.6	104.08	1.08	4.08	11.4	73.42	−3.00	−26.58
7.7	103.04	0.04	3.04	11.6	72.22	−3.00	−27.78
7.8	102.01	−0.99	2.01	11.8	71.05	−3.00	−28.95
7.9	101.00	−2.00	1.00	12.0	69.91	−3.00	−30.09
8.0	100.00	−3.00	0.00				

of $1 for every $1 increase in the price of the bond as the market yield falls. However, as the market yield rises, this investor loses dollar for dollar. So if the price decreases by more than $3, this strategy will result in a loss of more than $3. The long call strategy, in contrast, limits the loss to only the option price of $3, but retains the upside potential, which will be $3 less than for the long bond position.

We can use this hypothetical call option to demonstrate the speculative appeal of options. Suppose that an investor has strong expectations that market yields will fall in one month. With an option price of $3, the speculator can purchase 33.33 call options for each $100 invested. Thus, if the market yield declines, the investor realizes the price appreciation associated with 33.33 bonds of $100 par each (or $3,333 par). With the same $100, the investor could buy only one $100 par value bond and realize the appreciation associated with that one bond if the market yield declines. Now, suppose that in one month the market yield declines to 6% so that the price of the bond increases to $123.11. The long call strategy will result in a profit of $670.26 ($23.11 × 33.33 − $100), a return of 670% on the $100 investment in the call options. The long bond strategy results merely in a profit of $23.11, a 23% return on $100.

It is this greater leverage that an option buyer can achieve that attracts investors to options when they wish to speculate on interest-rate movements. It does not come without drawbacks, however. Suppose that the market yield is unchanged at the expiration date so that the price of the bond is $100. The long call strategy will result in the loss of the entire investment of $100, whereas the long bond strategy will produce neither a gain nor a loss.

Short Call Strategy (Selling or Writing Call Options)

An investor who believes that interest rates will rise or change very little can—if those expectations prove correct—realize income by writing (selling) a call option. This strategy is called a **short call strategy**.

To illustrate this option strategy, we use the same call option we used to demonstrate the long call strategy. The profit and loss profile of the short call strategy (the position of the call option writer) is the mirror image of the profit and loss profile of the long call strategy (the position of the call option buyer). That is, the profit (loss) of the short call position for any given price of the bond at the expiration date is the same as the loss (profit) of the long call position. Consequently, the maximum profit that the short call strategy can produce is the option price. But the maximum loss is limited only by how high the price of the bond can increase (i.e., how low the market yield can fall) by the expiration date, less the option price. Exhibit 27-5 diagrams the profit and loss profile for a short call strategy.

Long Put Strategy (Buying Put Options)

The most straightforward option strategy for benefiting from an expected increase in interest rates is to buy a put option. This strategy is called a long put strategy.

To illustrate this strategy, we will assume a hypothetical put option for an 8% coupon bond with a par value of $100, 20 years and one month to maturity, and a strike price of $100 that is selling for $2. The current price of the bond is $100 (yield of 8%); hence the put option is at-the-money. The profit or loss for this strategy at the expiration date depends on the market yield at that time. The following outcomes are possible:

1. If the price of the bond is higher than $100 because the market yield has fallen below 8%, the buyer of the put option will not exercise it because exercising would mean selling the bond to the writer for a price that is lower than the current market

Exhibit 27-5   Profit/Loss Profile Diagram for a Short Call Strategy

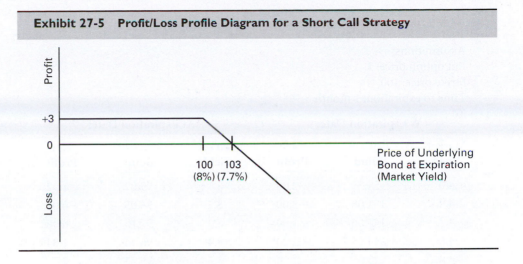

price. Consequently, a loss of $2 (the option price) will result from the long put strategy. Once again, the option price represents the maximum loss to which the buyer of the put option is exposed.

2. If the price of the bond at expiration is equal to $100 because the market yield has remained at 8%, the put will not be exercised, leaving the long put position with a loss equal to the option price of $2.

3. Any price for the bond that is lower than $100 because the market yield has risen above 8% but higher than $98 (market yield of approximately 8.2%) will result in a loss; exercising the put option, however, limits the loss to less than the option price of $2. For example, suppose that the market yield rises to 8.6%, resulting in a price of $99.03 for the bond at the expiration date. By exercising the option, the option buyer will realize a loss of $1.03. This is because the buyer of the put option can sell the bond, purchased in the market for $99.03 to the writer for $100, realizing a gain of $0.97. Deducting the $2 cost of the option results in a loss of $1.03.

4. At a $98 price for the bond (a market yield of roughly 8.2%) at the expiration date, the long put strategy will break even: The investor will realize a gain of $2 by selling the bond to the writer of the option for $100, offsetting the cost of the option ($2).

5. If the market yield rises above 8.2% so that the price of the bond is below $98 at the expiration date, the long put position will realize a profit. For example, if the market yield rises 260 basis points (from 8% to 10.6%), the price of the bond at expiration will be $78.58. The long put strategy will produce a profit of $19.42: a gain of $21.42 on the bond less the $2 option price.

The profit and loss profile for the long put strategy is shown in tabular form in Exhibit 27-6 and in graphic form in Exhibit 27-7. As with all long option positions, the loss is limited to the option price. However, the profit potential is substantial, the theoretical maximum profit being generated if the bond price falls to zero.

Once again, we can see how an option alters the risk/return profile for an investor by comparing it with a position in the bond. In the case of a long put position, it would be compared with a short bond position, because both strategies realize profits if market yields rise (the price falls). Suppose that an investor sells the bond short for $100. The

Exhibit 27-6 Profit/Loss Profile for a Long Put Strategy

Assumptions:
Put option price: 2
Strike price: 100
Time to expiration: 1 month

Market Yield	At Expiration Date: Price of Bond	Net Profit	Market Yield	At Expiration Date: Price of Bond	Net Profit
4.0	154.71	−2.00	8.1	99.02	−1.92
4.2	151.08	−2.00	8.2	98.05	−0.05
4.4	147.56	−2.00	8.3	97.10	0.90
4.6	144.15	−2.00	8.4	96.16	1.84
4.8	140.85	−2.00	8.5	95.23	2.77
5.0	137.65	−2.00	8.6	94.32	3.68
5.2	134.56	−2.00	8.7	93.42	4.58
5.4	131.56	−2.00	8.8	92.53	5.47
5.6	128.66	−2.00	8.9	91.66	6.34
5.8	125.84	−2.00	9.0	90.80	7.20
6.0	123.11	−2.00	9.1	89.95	8.05
6.1	121.78	−2.00	9.2	89.11	8.89
6.2	120.47	−2.00	9.3	88.29	9.71
6.3	119.18	−2.00	9.4	87.48	10.52
6.4	117.91	−2.00	9.5	86.68	11.32
6.5	116.66	−2.00	9.6	85.89	12.11
6.6	115.42	−2.00	9.7	85.11	12.89
6.7	114.21	−2.00	9.8	84.34	13.66
6.8	113.01	−2.00	9.9	83.59	14.41
6.9	111.84	−2.00	10.0	82.84	15.16
7.0	110.68	−2.00	10.2	81.38	16.62
7.1	109.54	−2.00	10.4	79.96	18.04
7.2	108.41	−2.00	10.6	78.58	19.42
7.3	107.30	−2.00	10.8	77.24	20.76
7.4	106.21	−2.00	11.0	75.93	22.07
7.5	105.14	−2.00	11.2	74.66	23.34
7.6	104.08	−2.00	11.4	73.42	24.58
7.7	103.04	−2.00	11.6	72.22	25.78
7.8	102.01	−2.00	11.8	71.05	26.95
7.9	101.00	−2.00	12.0	69.91	28.09
8.0	100.00	−2.00			

Exhibit 27-7   Profit/Loss Profile Diagram for a Long Put Strategy

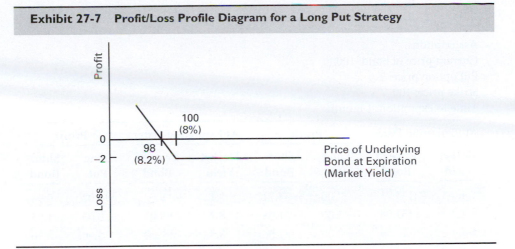

short bond position would produce the following profit or loss as compared with the long put position:

1. If the price of the bond increases above $100 because the market yield declines, the long put option will result in a loss of $2, but the short bond position will realize one of the following:
    a. If the price of the bond is lower than $102 because the market yield has fallen to below 7.80%, there will be a loss of less than $2.
    b. If the price of the bond is equal to $102, the loss will be $2, the same as for the long put strategy.
    c. If the price of the bond is higher than $102, the loss will be more than $2. For example, if the price is $125.84, because market yields declined to 5.8%, the short bond position will realize a loss of $25.84, because the short seller must now pay $125.84 for a bond sold short at $100.
2. If the price of the bond at expiration is equal to $100 because the market yield is unchanged, the long put strategy will realize a $2 loss, and there will be no profit or loss on the short bond strategy.
3. Any price for the bond that is lower than $100 but higher than $98 (market yield of about 8.2%) will result in a loss of less than $2 for the long put strategy but a profit for the short bond strategy. For example, a price of $99.02 (market yield of 8.1%) will result in a loss of less than $2 for the long put strategy but a profit for the short bond strategy. For example, a price of $99.02 (market yield of 8.1%) at the expiration date will result in a loss of $1.02 for the long put strategy but a profit of $0.98 for the short bond strategy.
4. At a $98 price for the bond at the expiration date, the long put strategy will break even, but the short bond strategy will generate a $2 profit.
5. At a price below $98 (market yield greater than 8.2%), both strategies will generate a profit. However, the profit will always be $2 less for the long put strategy.

Exhibit 27-8 is a tabular comparison of the profit and loss profile for the long put and short bond strategies. Whereas the investor who pursues a short bond strategy participates in all the upside potential and faces all the downside risk, the long put strategy allows the investor to limit the downside risk to the option price while still maintaining upside

Exhibit 27-8 **Comparison of a Long Put Strategy and a Short Bond Strategy**

Assumptions:
Current price of bond: 100
Put option price: 2
Strike price: 100
Time to expiration: 1 month

At Expiration Date:		Profit		At Expiration Date:		Profit	
Market Yield	Price of Bond	Long Put	Short Bond	Market Yield	Price of Bond	Long Put	Short Bond
4.0	154.71	−2.00	−54.71	8.1	99.02	−1.02	0.98
4.2	151.08	−2.00	−51.08	8.2	98.05	−0.05	1.95
4.4	147.56	−2.00	−47.56	8.3	97.10	0.90	2.90
4.6	144.15	−2.00	−44.15	8.4	96.16	1.84	3.84
4.8	140.85	−2.00	−40.85	8.5	95.23	2.77	4.77
5.0	137.65	−2.00	−37.65	8.6	94.32	3.68	5.68
5.2	134.56	−2.00	−34.56	8.7	93.42	4.58	6.58
5.4	131.56	−2.00	−31.56	8.8	92.53	5.47	7.47
5.6	128.66	−2.00	−28.66	8.9	91.66	6.34	8.34
5.8	125.84	−2.00	−25.84	9.0	90.80	7.20	9.20
6.0	123.11	−2.00	−23.11	9.1	89.95	8.05	10.05
6.1	121.78	−2.00	−21.78	9.2	89.11	8.89	10.89
6.2	120.47	−2.00	−20.47	9.3	88.29	9.71	11.71
6.3	119.18	−2.00	−19.18	9.4	87.48	10.52	12.52
6.4	117.91	−2.00	−17.91	9.5	86.68	11.32	13.32
6.5	116.66	−2.00	−16.66	9.6	85.89	12.11	14.11
6.6	115.42	−2.00	−15.42	9.7	85.11	12.89	14.89
6.7	114.21	−2.00	−14.21	9.8	84.34	13.66	15.66
6.8	113.01	−2.00	−13.01	9.9	83.59	14.41	16.41
6.9	111.84	−2.00	−11.84	10.0	82.84	15.16	17.16
7.0	110.68	−2.00	−10.68	10.2	81.38	16.62	18.62
7.1	109.54	−2.00	−9.54	10.4	79.96	18.04	20.04
7.2	108.41	−2.00	−8.41	10.6	78.58	19.42	21.42
7.3	107.30	−2.00	−7.30	10.8	77.24	20.76	22.76
7.4	106.21	−2.00	−6.21	11.0	75.93	22.07	24.07
7.5	105.14	−2.00	−5.14	11.2	74.66	23.34	25.34
7.6	104.08	−2.00	−4.08	11.4	73.42	24.58	26.58
7.7	103.04	−2.00	−3.04	11.6	72.22	25.78	27.78
7.8	102.01	−2.00	−2.01	11.8	71.05	26.95	28.95
7.9	101.00	−2.00	−1.00	12.0	69.91	28.09	30.09
8.0	100.00	−2.00	0.00				

potential. However, the upside potential is less than that for a short put position by an amount equal to the option price.

Short Put Strategy (Selling or Writing Put Options)

The last naked option position that we shall consider is the short put strategy. The **short put strategy** involves the selling (writing) of put options. This strategy is employed if the investor expects interest rates to fall or stay flat so that the price of the bond will increase or stay the same. The profit and loss profile for a short put option is the mirror image of that for the long put option. The maximum loss is limited only by how low the price of the bond can fall by the expiration date less the option price received for writing the option. Exhibit 27-9 graphically depicts this profit and loss profile.

To summarize, long calls and short puts allow the investor to gain if bond prices rise (interest rates fall). Short calls and long puts allow the investor to gain if bond prices fall (interest rates rise). An investor would want to use each strategy under the following circumstances:

Circumstance	Strategy
Very bullish	Buy call
Slightly bullish	Write put
Slightly bearish	Write call
Very bearish	Buy put

Considering the Time Value of Money

Our illustrations of the four naked option positions do not reflect the time value of money. Specifically, the buyer of an option must pay the seller the option price at the time the option is purchased. Thus, the buyer must either finance the purchase price of the option or, if the proceeds do not have to be borrowed, lose the interest that could be earned by investing the option price until the expiration of the option. The seller, in contrast, assuming that the option price does not have to be used as margin for the short position, has the opportunity to invest this option price.

Exhibit 27-9   Profit/Loss Profile Diagram for a Short Put Strategy

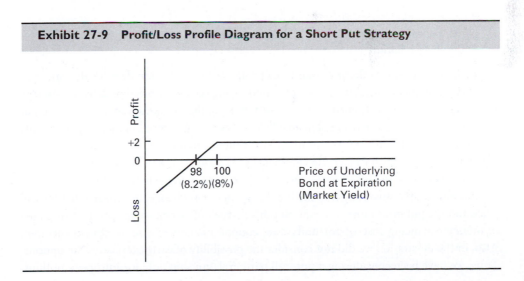

The profit profiles of the naked option positions change when the time value of money is taken into consideration. The break-even price for the buyer and the seller of an option will not be the same as in our illustrations. The break-even price for the underlying instrument at the expiration date is higher for the buyer of the option; for the seller, it is lower.

We also ignored the time value of money in comparing the option strategies with positions in the underlying instrument. In this case, we did not consider the fact that when the underlying instrument is a cash market coupon security, coupon payments may be made between the time the option is purchased and the option's expiration date. When these coupon payments are received, they can be reinvested. Thus, reinvestment income must be factored into the analysis of an option position. Also, the effects of financing costs and opportunity costs on the long or short bond positions, respectively, must be factored into the analysis. For the sake of simplicity, however, we shall ignore the time value of money throughout the remainder of this chapter.

PUT–CALL PARITY RELATIONSHIP AND EQUIVALENT POSITIONS

Is there a relationship between the price of a call option and the price of a put option on the same underlying instrument, with the same strike price and the same expiration date? There is. To see this relationship, which is commonly referred to as the **put–call parity relationship**, let's use an example.

Previous illustrations have used a put and a call option on the same underlying instrument (a bond currently with 20 years and one month to maturity), both options having a strike price of $100 and one month to expiration. The price of the underlying bond is assumed to be $100. The call price and put price are assumed to be $3 and $2, respectively. Consider the following strategy:

- Buy the bond at a price of $100.
- Sell a call option at a price of $3.
- Buy a put option at a price of $2.

This strategy, therefore, involves the following:

- Long the bond.
- Short the call option.
- Long the put option.

Exhibit 27-10 shows the profit and loss profile at the expiration date for this strategy. Notice that no matter what the price of the underlying bond at expiration date, the strategy produces a profit of $1. Ignoring the cost of financing the long position and the long put position, this situation cannot exist in an efficient market. The actions of market participants in implementing this strategy to capture the $1 profit will result in one or more of the following consequences, which will tend to eliminate the $1 profit: (1) an increase in the price of the bond, (2) a decrease in the call option price, and/or (3) an increase in the put option price.

In our example, assuming that the bond price does not change, this means that the call price and the put price must be equal. But this is true only when we ignore the time value of money (financing cost, opportunity cost, coupon income, and reinvestment income). Also, in the illustration we did not consider the possibility of early exercise of the options. Thus, we have been considering a put–call parity relationship only for European options.

> **Exhibit 27-10   Profit/Loss Profile for a Strategy Involving a Long Bond Position, Short Call Option Position, and Long Put Option Position**

Assumptions:
Current price of bond: 100
Price of call option: 3
Call strike price: 100

Price of put option: 2
Put strike price: 100
Time to expiration: 1 month

At Expiration Date:

Market Yield	Price of Bond	Profit from Long Bond	Price Received for Call	Price Paid for Put	Overall Profit
5.0	137.65	0*	3	−2	1
6.0	123.11	0*	3	−2	1
7.0	110.68	0*	3	−2	1
7.9	101.00	0*	3	−2	1
8.0	100.00	0	3	−2	1
8.1	99.02	0‡	3	−2	1
9.0	90.80	0‡	3	−2	1
10.0	82.84	0‡	3	−2	1
11.0	75.93	0‡	3	−2	1

*If the price of the bond is more than the strike price, the buyer of the call option will exercise the option.
‡If the price of the bond is lower than the strike price, the investor will exercise the put option.

Ignoring the time value of money and considering European options, the outcome from the following position must be one of no arbitrage profits:

$$\text{long the bond} + \text{short call option} + \text{long put option} = 0 \qquad (27.1)$$

In terms of price, it can be shown that there will be no arbitrage profits at any time (not just expiration) if

$$P_{po} = P_{co} + S - P_b \qquad (27.2)$$

where

P_{po} = price of put option
P_{co} = price of call option
S = strike price of option
P_b = current price of the underlying bond

and the strike price and expiration date are the same for both options. This relationship is one form of the put–call parity relationship for European options when the time value of money is ignored. It is approximately true for American options. Considering the time value of money, the put–call parity relationship for coupon bonds is

$$P_{po} = P_{co} + PV(S) + PV(\text{coupon}) - P_b \qquad (27.3)$$

where

$PV(S)$ = present value of the strike price
$PV(\text{coupon})$ = present value of the coupon payments

Equivalent Positions

Working with equation (27.1), we can identify equivalent positions; that is, positions that will provide the same profit profile. For example, subtracting the long put position from both sides of equation (27.1), we have

$$\text{long the bond} + \text{short call option} = -\text{long put option} \qquad (27.4)$$

But the position on the right-hand side of equation (27.4) is the same as a short put position. Therefore,

$$\text{long the bond} + \text{short call option} = \text{short put option} \qquad (27.5)$$

We will see later in this chapter that a covered call position, which is a long bond position plus a short call option position on the same bond, has the same profit profile as a short put option position. This is what equation (27.5) states. Owning callable securities is equivalent to a long bond position plus a short call position. Thus, these securities will have a payoff similar to a short put position. But remember, the equivalent position holds only for European options, and a more precise relationship requires that the time value of money be considered.

Manipulating equation (27.1) gives us the following equivalent positions:

$$\text{short the bond} + \text{short put} = \text{short call}$$
$$\text{long the bond} + \text{long put} = \text{long call}$$
$$\text{short the bond} + \text{long call} = \text{long put}$$
$$\text{long call} + \text{short put} = \text{long the bond}$$
$$\text{long put} + \text{short call} = \text{short the bond}$$

Thus, an investor can synthetically create any of the positions on the right-hand side of these equations by taking the two positions indicated on the left-hand side.

OPTION PRICE

Six factors will influence the option price:

1. current price of the underlying instrument
2. strike price
3. time to expiration
4. short-term risk-free interest rate over the life of the option
5. coupon rate on the bond
6. expected volatility of yields (or prices) over the life of the option

The impact of each of these factors may depend on whether (1) the option is a call or a put, (2) the option is an American option or a European option, and (3) the underlying instrument is a bond or a futures contract on a bond.

Current Price of the Underlying Instrument

For a call option, as the current price of the underlying instrument increases (decreases), the option price increases (decreases). For a put option, as the current price of the underlying instrument decreases (increases), the option price increases (decreases).

Strike Price

All other factors being constant, the higher the strike price, the lower the price of a call option. For a put option, the opposite is true: The higher the strike price, the higher the price of a put option.

Time to Expiration

For American options (both puts and calls), all other factors held constant, the longer the time to expiration, the higher the option price. No general statement can be made for European options. The impact of the time to expiration on European options will depend on whether the option is a put or a call.

Short-Term Risk-Free Interest Rate over the Life of the Option

Holding all other factors constant, the price of a call option on a bond will increase as the short-term risk-free interest rate rises. For a put option, the opposite is true: An increase in the short-term risk-free interest rate will decrease the price of a put option. In contrast, for a futures option, the price of both a call and a put option will decrease if the short-term risk-free interest rate rises.

Coupon Rate

For options on bonds, coupons tend to reduce the price of a call option because the coupons make it more attractive to hold the bond than the option. Thus, call options on coupon-bearing bonds will tend to be priced lower than similar call options on non–coupon-bearing bonds. Conversely, coupons tend to increase the price of put options.

Expected Volatility of Yields over the Life of the Option

As the expected volatility of yields over the life of the option increases, the price of the option will also increase. The reason is that the greater the expected volatility, as measured by the standard deviation or variance of yields, the greater the probability that the price of the underlying bond or futures contract will move in the direction that will benefit the option buyer.

MODELS FOR PRICING OPTIONS

Several models have been developed for determining the theoretical value of an option. These models are referred to as option pricing models. There are models for valuing options on bonds and options on bond futures. We discuss these various models in the following text.

Models for Valuing Options on Bonds

First, we will discuss models for valuing options on bonds (i.e., options on physicals). In the equity options area, the most popular model is the Black–Scholes option pricing model.[1] This model, however, is limited in pricing options on bonds, as we shall see next. A more appropriate model that takes into account the yield curve builds on the valuation procedure described in Chapter 17, where we introduced a binomial interest-rate tree.

---

[1] Fischer Black and Myron Scholes, "The Pricing of Corporate Liabilities," *Journal of Political Economy*, May–June 1973, pp. 637–659.

Black–Scholes Option Pricing Model

By imposing certain assumptions (to be discussed later) and using arbitrage arguments, the **Black–Scholes option pricing model** computes the fair (or theoretical) price of a European call option on a non–dividend-paying stock with the following formula:

$$C = SN(d_1) - Xe^{-rt}N(d_2) \tag{27.6}$$

where

$$d_1 = \frac{\ln(S/X) + (r + 0.5s^2)t}{s\sqrt{t}} \tag{27.7}$$

$$d_2 = d_1 - s\sqrt{t} \tag{27.8}$$

where

ln = natural logarithm
C = call option price
S = current stock price
X = strike price
r = short-term risk-free interest rate
e = 2.718 (natural antilog of 1)
t = time remaining to the expiration date (measured as a fraction of a year)
s = standard deviation of the stock return
$N(\cdot)$ = cumulative probability density [the value of $N(\cdot)$ is obtained from a normal distribution function that is tabulated in most statistics textbooks]

With the exception of the cash payments, notice that the factors that we said earlier influence the price of an option are included in the formula. Cash payments are not included because the model is for a non–dividend-paying stock.

The option price derived from the Black–Scholes option pricing model is "fair" in the sense that if any other price existed, it would be possible to earn riskless arbitrage profits by taking an offsetting position in the underlying stock. That is, if the price of the call option in the market is higher than that derived from the Black–Scholes option pricing model, an investor could sell the call option and buy a certain number of shares in the underlying stock. If the reverse is true, that is, the market price of the call option is less than the "fair" price derived from the model, the investor could buy the call option and sell short a certain number of shares in the underlying stock. This process of hedging by taking a position in the underlying stock allows the investor to lock in the riskless arbitrage profit. The number of shares necessary to hedge the position changes as the factors that affect the option price change, so the hedged position must be changed constantly.

Computing the Price of a Call Option on a Zero-Coupon Bond

Because the basic Black–Scholes formula as given by equation (27.6) is for a non–cash-paying security, let's apply it to a zero-coupon bond with three years to maturity. Assume the following values:

strike price = \$88.00
time remaining to expiration = 2 years
current price = \$83.96
expected return volatility = standard deviation = 10%
risk-free rate = 6%

Note that the current price is $83.96, which is the present value of the maturity value of $100 discounted at 6% (assuming a flat yield curve).

In terms of the values in the formula,

$$S = 83.96$$
$$X = 88.00$$
$$t = 2$$
$$s = 0.10$$
$$r = 0.06$$

Substituting these values into equations (27.7) and (27.8) yields

$$d_1 = \frac{\ln(83.96/88) + [0.06 + 0.5(0.10)^2]2}{0.10\sqrt{2}} = 0.5869$$

$$d_2 = 0.5869 - 0.10\sqrt{2} = 0.4455$$

From a normal distribution table,

$$N(0.5869) = 0.7124 \text{ and } N(0.4455) = 0.6720$$

Then, from equation (27.6),

$$C = 83.96(0.7214) - 88[e^{-(0.06)(2)}(0.6720)] = \$8.116$$

There is no reason to suspect that this estimated value is unreasonable. However, let's change the problem slightly. Instead of a strike price of $88, let's make the strike price $100.25. Substituting the new strike price into equations (27.7) and (27.8):

$$d_1 = \frac{\ln(83.96/100.25) + [0.06 + 0.5(0.10)^2]2}{0.10\sqrt{2}} = -0.3346$$

$$d_2 = -0.3346 - 0.10\sqrt{2} = -0.4761$$

From a normal distribution table,

$$N(-0.3346) = 0.3689 \text{ and } N(-0.4761) = 0.3170$$

Then, from equation (27.6),

$$C = 83.96(0.3689) - 100.25[e^{-(0.06)(2)}(0.3170)] = \$2.79$$

Thus, the Black–Scholes option pricing model tells us that this call option has a fair value of $2.79. Is there any reason to believe that this is unreasonable? Well, consider that this is a call option on a zero-coupon bond that will *never* have a value greater than its maturity value of $100. Consequently, a call option struck at $100.25 must have a value of zero. Yet, the Black–Scholes option pricing model tells us that the value is $2.79! In fact, with a higher volatility assumption, the model would give an even greater value for the call option.

Why is the Black–Scholes model off by so much in our previous illustration? The answer lies in its underlying assumptions. There are three assumptions underlying the Black–Scholes model that limit its use in pricing options on interest-rate instruments. First, the probability distribution for the return assumed by the Black–Scholes option pricing model permits some probability—no matter how small—that the return can take on any positive value. But in the case of a zero-coupon bond, the price cannot take on a value above $100, and, therefore, the return is capped. In the case of a coupon bond, we know that the price cannot exceed the sum of the coupon payments plus the maturity value. For example, for a five-year 10% coupon bond with a maturity value of $100, the price cannot be greater than $150 (five coupon payments of $10 plus the maturity value of $100). Thus, unlike stock returns, bond prices have a maximum return. The only way that a bond's return can exceed the maximum value is if negative interest rates are permitted. This is not likely to occur, so any probability distribution for prices assumed by an option pricing model that permits bond prices to be higher than the maximum bond value could generate nonsensical option prices. The Black–Scholes model does allow bond prices to exceed the maximum bond value (or, equivalently, allows negative interest rates). That is one of the reasons why we can get a senseless option price for the three-month European call option on the three-year zero-coupon bond.

The second assumption of the Black–Scholes option pricing model is that the short-term interest rate is constant over the life of the option. Yet the price of an interest-rate option will change as interest rates change. A change in the short-term interest rate changes the rates along the yield curve. Therefore, to assume that the short-term rate will be constant is inappropriate for interest-rate options. The third assumption is that the variance of prices is constant over the life of the option. Recall from Chapter 4 that as a bond moves closer to maturity its price volatility declines. Therefore, the assumption that price variance is constant over the life of the option is inappropriate.

We have illustrated the problem of using the Black–Scholes model to price interest-rate options; we can also show that the binomial option pricing model based on the price distribution of the underlying bond suffers from the same problems.

Arbitrage-Free Binomial Model

The proper way to value options on interest-rate instruments is to use an arbitrage-free model that takes into account the yield curve. These models can incorporate different volatility assumptions along the yield curve. The most popular model employed by dealer firms is the Black–Derman–Toy model.[2]

We have already developed the basic principles for employing this model. In Chapter 17, we explained how to construct a binomial interest-rate tree such that the tree would be arbitrage free. We used the interest-rate tree to value bonds (both option-free bonds and bonds with embedded options). But the same tree can be used to value a stand-alone European option on a bond.

To illustrate how this is done, let's consider a two-year European call option on a 5.25% three-year Treasury bond with a strike price of 99.25. We will assume that the yield for the on-the-run Treasuries is the one in Chapter 17 and that the volatility assumption is 10% per year. Exhibit 17-13 shows the binomial interest-rate tree along with the value of the Treasury bond at each node. It is a portion of that exhibit we use to value the call option. Specifically, Exhibit 27-11 shows the value of our Treasury bond (excluding coupon interest) at each node at the end of year 2. There are three values shown: 98.5884, 99.7328, and 100.6888. Given these three values, the value of a call option struck at 99.25 can be determined at each node. For example, if in two years the price of this Treasury bond is 98.5884, then because the strike price is 99.25, the value of the call option would be

[2] Fischer Black, Emanuel Derman, and William Toy, "A One-Factor Model of Interest Rates and Its Application to Treasury Bond Options," *Financial Analysis Journal*, January–February 1990, pp. 24–32.

Exhibit 27-11   Valuing a European Call Option Using the Binomial Method

Call Option:
expiration: 2 years
strike price: 99.25
current price: 102.075
volatility assumption: 10%

Underlying: 3-year, 5.25% Treasury

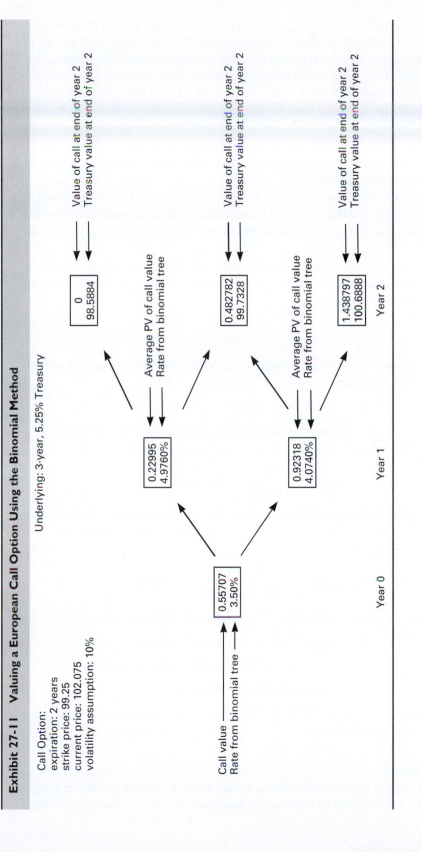

Value of call at end of year 2
Treasury value at end of year 2

| 0 |
| 98.5884 |

Average PV of call value
Rate from binomial tree

| 0.22995 |
| 4.9760% |

Value of call at end of year 2
Treasury value at end of year 2

| 0.482782 |
| 99.7328 |

Call value
Rate from binomial tree

| 0.55707 |
| 3.50% |

Average PV of call value
Rate from binomial tree

| 0.92318 |
| 4.0740% |

Value of call at end of year 2
Treasury value at end of year 2

| 1.438797 |
| 100.6888 |

Year 0   Year 1   Year 2

zero. In the other two cases, because the price two years from now is greater than the strike price, the value of the call option is the difference between the price of the bond and 99.25.

Exhibit 27-11 shows the value of the call option two years from now (the option expiration date) for each of the three nodes. Given these values, the binomial interest-rate tree is used to find the present value of the call option. The backward induction procedure is used. The discount rates are those from the binomial interest-rate tree. For years 0 and 1, the discount rate is the second number shown at each node. The first number at each node for year 1 is the average present value found by discounting the call option value of the two nodes to the right using the discount rate at the node. The value of the call option is the first number shown at the root, $0.55707.

The same procedure is used to value a European put option. This is illustrated in Exhibit 27-12 assuming that the put option has two years to expiration and that the strike price is 99.25. The value of the put option two years from now is shown at each of the three nodes in year 2.

To demonstrate that the arbitrage-free binomial model satisfies the put–call parity relationship for European options given by equation (27.3), let's use the values from our illustration. We just found that

$$P_{po} = 0.55707$$
$$P_{co} = 0.15224$$

In Chapter 17, we showed that the theoretical price for the 5.25% three-year option-free bond is 102.075. Therefore,

$$P_b = 102.075$$

Also in Chapter 17, we showed the spot rates for each year. The spot rate for year 2 is 4.01%. Therefore, the present value of the strike price of 99.25 is

$$PV(S) = \frac{99.25}{(1.0401)^2} = 91.7446$$

The present value of the coupon payments are found by discounting the two coupon payments of 5.25 by the spot rates. As just noted, the spot rate for year 2 is 4.01%; the spot rate for year 1 is 3.5%. Therefore,

$$PV(coupon) = \frac{5.25}{1.035} + \frac{5.25}{(1.0401)^2} = 9.9255$$

The put–call parity relationship as given by equation (27.3) is repeated as follows:

$$P_{po} = P_{co} + PV(S) + PV(coupon) - P_b$$

Substituting the values into the right-hand side of the relationship, we find that

$$0.55707 + 91.7446 + 9.9255 - 102.075 = 0.15217$$

The put value that we found is 0.15224. The discrepancy is due simply to rounding error. Therefore, put–call parity holds.

Implied Volatility

Option pricing models provide a theoretical option price depending on the six factors discussed earlier. The only one of these factors that is not known and must be estimated

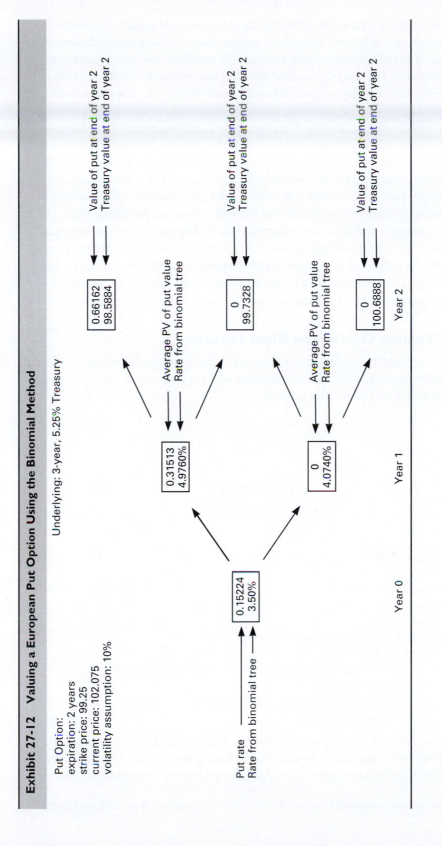

Exhibit 27-12 Valuing a European Put Option Using the Binomial Method

Put Option:
expiration: 2 years
strike price: 99.25
current price: 102.075
volatility assumption: 10%

Underlying: 3-year, 5.25% Treasury

| 0.66162 | Value of put at end of year 2 |
| 98.5884 | Treasury value at end of year 2 |

| 0 | Value of put at end of year 2 |
| 99.7328 | Treasury value at end of year 2 |

| 0 | Value of put at end of year 2 |
| 100.6888 | Treasury value at end of year 2 |

| 0.31513 | Average PV of put value |
| 4.9760% | Rate from binomial tree |

| 0 | Average PV of put value |
| 4.0740% | Rate from binomial tree |

| 0.15224 | Put rate |
| 3.50% | Rate from binomial tree |

Year 0   Year 1   Year 2

is the expected volatility of yield or price over the life of the option. A popular methodology to assess whether an option is fairly priced is to assume that the option is priced correctly and then, using an option pricing model, estimate the volatility that is implied by that model, given the observed option price and the other five factors that determine the price of an option. The estimated volatility computed in this manner is called the **implied volatility**.

For example, suppose that a portfolio manager using some option pricing model, the current price of the option, and the five other factors that determine the price of an option computes an implied yield volatility of 12%. If the portfolio manager expects that the volatility of yields over the life of the option will be greater than the implied volatility of 12%, the option is considered to be undervalued. In contrast, if the portfolio manager's expected volatility of yields over the life of the option is less than the implied volatility, the option is considered to be overvalued. Although we have focused on the option price, the key to understanding the options market is knowing that trading and investment strategies in this market involve buying and selling volatility. Estimating the implied volatility and comparing it with the trader's or portfolio manager's expectations of future volatility is just another way of evaluating options. If an investor uses expected volatility to compute the fair value of the option, the option will appear cheap or expensive in exactly the same cases.

Models for Valuing Options on Bond Futures

The most commonly used model for futures options was developed by Fischer Black.[3] The model was initially developed for valuing European options on forward contracts. The value of a call and put based on the Black model is

$$C = e^{-rt}[FN(d_1) - XN(d_2)]$$
$$P = e^{-rt}[XN(-d_2) - FN(-d_1)]$$

where

$$d_1 = \frac{\ln(F/X) + 0.5s^2t}{s\sqrt{t}}$$

$$d_2 = d_1 - s\sqrt{t}$$

ln = natural logarithm
C = call option price
P = put option price
F = futures price
X = strike price
r = short-term risk-free interest rate
e = 2.718 (natural antilog of 1)
t = time remaining to the expiration date (measured as a fraction of a year)
s = standard deviation of the return
$N(\cdot)$ = the cumulative probability density. The value for $N(\cdot)$ is obtained from a
        normal distribution function.

There are two problems with this model. First, the Black model does not overcome the problems cited earlier for the Black–Scholes model. Failing to recognize the yield curve means that there will not be a consistency between pricing Treasury futures and options on

---

[3] Fischer Black, "The Pricing of Commodity Contracts," *Journal of Financial Economics*, March 1976, pp. 161–179.

Treasury futures. Second, the Black model was developed for pricing European options on futures contracts. Treasury futures options, however, are American options.

The second problem can be overcome. The Black model was extended by Barone-Adesi and Whaley to American options on futures contracts.[4] This is the model used by the CBOT to settle the flexible Treasury futures options. However, this model was also developed for equities and is subject to the first problem noted previously. Despite its limitations, the Black model is the most popular option pricing model for options on Treasury futures.

Computing Implied Volatility

Despite the many limitations and inconsistent assumptions of the Black model for valuing futures options, it has been widely adopted by traders for computing the implied volatility from options on Treasury bond futures options. These implied volatilities are also published by some investment houses and are available through data vendors.

When computing implied volatilities of yield from Treasury bond futures options, the process is more complex than those for options on individual stocks or stock indexes. Remember that the options are written on futures prices. Therefore, the implied volatilities computed directly from the Black model are implied *price* volatilities of the underlying futures contract. Converting implied price volatilities into implied yield volatilities requires the calculation of the duration of the corresponding cheapest-to-deliver Treasury bond. We know from Chapter 4 that

$$\text{approximate percentage price change} = \text{duration} \times \text{change in yield}$$

This same relationship holds for price volatility and yield volatility. Therefore,

$$\text{price volatility} = \text{duration} \times \text{yield volatility}$$

Solving for yield volatility, we have

$$\text{yield volatility} = \text{price volatility/duration}$$

Selection and Interpretation of Implied Volatility

Is there one implied yield volatility that should be used in practice? It has been amply documented that the implied volatility for the same expiration month varies by strike price. However, since the late 1980s the pattern that has been observed is not random. Instead, the relationship is as follows: the implied volatility for both in-the-money and out-of-the money options with the same expiration date is higher than the implied volatility for at-the-money options with the same expiration date. Because the U-shaped curve that exists if the strike price is plotted on the horizontal axis and the implied volatility on the vertical axis looks like a smile, the relationship is referred to as **volatility smile**.[5] More recently, however, the pattern that has been observed between the strike

---

[4] Giovanni Barone-Adesi and Robert E. Whaley, "Efficient Analytic Approximation of American Option Values," *Journal of Finance,* June 1987, pp. 301–320.

[5] For an empirical analysis of the economic determinants of the volatility smile for interest rate options, see Prachi Deuskar, Anurag Gupta, and Marti G. Subrahmanyam, "The Economic Determinants of Interest Rate Option Smiles," *Journal of Banking and Finance* 35, 2 (2008), pp. 714–728.

price and implied volatility indicates that the implied volatility decreases with the strike price, a pattern referred to as **volatility skew**.

If implied yield volatility is not constant, which one should be used? Standard practice suggests that the implied volatility of the at-the-money or the nearest-the-money option should be used.

How do we interpret the meaning of implied volatility? For example, what is the meaning of an "implied yield volatility of X%"? To interpret this number, one needs to be aware that this number is extracted from the observed option price based on some option pricing model such as the Black model. As a result, the meaning of this number not only depends on the assumption that the market correctly prices the option, but also the fact that the market prices the option in accordance with the model used to compute the implied volatility. Neither of these assumptions needs to hold. In fact, most probably, both assumptions are unrealistic. Given these assumptions, one may interpret that the option market expects a *constant* annualized yield volatility of X% over the life of the option (i.e., to the option's maturity date).

SENSITIVITY OF OPTION PRICE TO CHANGE IN FACTORS

In employing options in an investment strategy, a portfolio manager would like to know how sensitive the price of an option is to a change in any one of the factors that affect its price. Here we look at the sensitivity of a call option's price to changes in the price of the underlying bond, the time to expiration, and expected volatility.

Call Option Price and Price of the Underlying Bond

Exhibit 27-13 shows the theoretical price of a call option based on the price of the underlying bond. The horizontal axis is the price of the underlying bond at any point in time.

Exhibit 27-13 Theoretical Call Price and the Price of the Underlying Bond

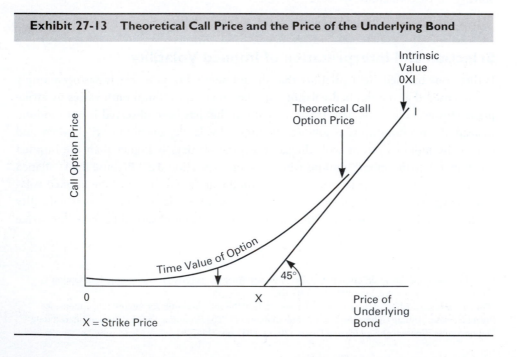

The vertical axis is the call option price. The shape of the curve representing the theoretical price of a call option, given the price of the underlying bond, would be the same regardless of the actual option pricing model used. In particular, the relationship between the price of the underlying bond and the theoretical call option price is convex. Thus, option prices also exhibit convexity.

The line from the origin to the strike price on the horizontal axis in Exhibit 27-13 is the intrinsic value of the call option when the price of the underlying bond is less than the strike price because the intrinsic value is zero. The 45-degree line extending from the horizontal axis is the intrinsic value of the call option once the price of the underlying bond exceeds the strike price. The reason is that the intrinsic value of the call option will increase by the same dollar amount as the increase in the price of the underlying bond. For example, if the strike price is $100 and the price of the underlying bond increases from $100 to $101, the intrinsic value will increase by $1. If the price of the bond increases from $101 to $110, the intrinsic value of the option will increase from $1 to $10. Thus, the slope of the line representing the intrinsic value after the strike price is reached is 1.

Because the theoretical call option price is shown by the convex line, the difference between the theoretical call option price and the intrinsic value at any given price for the underlying bond is the time value of the option.

Exhibit 27-14 shows the theoretical call option price but with a tangent line drawn at the price of p^*. The tangent line in the figure can be used to estimate what the new option price will be (and, therefore, what the change in the option price will be) if the price of the underlying bond changes. Because of the convexity of the relationship between the option price and the price of the underlying bond, the tangent line closely approximates the new option price for a small change in the price of the underlying bond. For large

Exhibit 27-14   Estimating the Theoretical Option Price with a Tangent Line

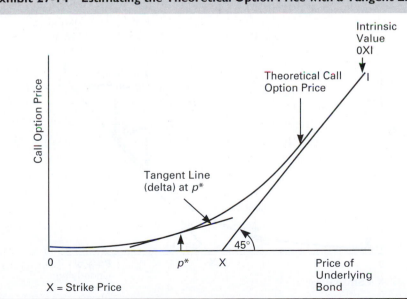

changes, however, the tangent line does not provide as good an approximation of the new option price.

The slope of the tangent line shows how the theoretical call option price will change for small changes in the price of the underlying bond. The slope is popularly referred to as the **delta** of the option. Specifically,

$$\text{delta} = \frac{\text{change in price of call option}}{\text{change in price of underlying bond}}$$

For example, a delta of 0.4 means that a $1 change in the price of the underlying bond will change the price of the call option by approximately $0.40.

Exhibit 27-15 shows the curve of the theoretical call option price with three tangent lines drawn. The steeper the slope of the tangent line, the greater the delta. When an option is deep out of the money (i.e., the price of the underlying bond is substantially below the strike price), the tangent line is nearly flat (see Line 1 in Exhibit 27-15). This means that delta is close to zero. To understand why, consider a call option with a strike price of $100 and two months to expiration. If the price of the underlying bond is $20, its price would not increase by much, if anything, should the price of the underlying bond increase by $1, from $20 to $21.

For a call option that is deep in the money, the delta will be close to 1. That is, the call option price will increase almost dollar for dollar with an increase in the price of the underlying bond. In terms of Exhibit 27-15, the slope of the tangent line approaches the slope of the intrinsic value line after the strike price. As we stated earlier, the slope of that line is 1.

Thus, the delta for a call option varies from zero (for call options deep out of the money) to 1 (for call options deep in the money). The delta for a call option at the money is approximately 0.5.

Exhibit 27-15 Theoretical Option Price with Three Tangents

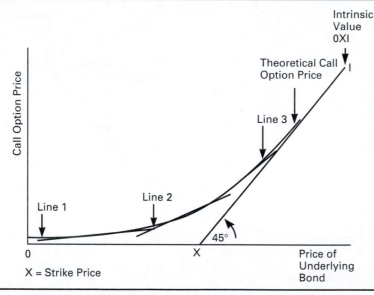

The curvature of the convex relationship can also be approximated. This is the rate of change of delta as the price of the underlying bond changes. The measure is commonly referred to as **gamma** and is defined as follows:

$$\text{gamma} = \frac{\text{change in delta}}{\text{change in price of underlying bond}}$$

Call Option Price and Time to Expiration

All other factors constant, the longer the time to expiration, the greater the option price. Because each day the option moves closer to the expiration date, the time to expiration decreases. The **theta** of an option measures the change in the option price as the time to expiration decreases, or equivalently, it is a measure of **time decay**. Theta is measured as follows:

$$\text{theta} = \frac{\text{change in price of option}}{\text{decrease in time to expiration}}$$

Assuming that the price of the underlying bond does not change (which means that the intrinsic value of the option does not change), theta measures how quickly the time value of the option changes as the option moves towards expiration. Buyers of options prefer a low theta so that the option price does not decline quickly as it moves toward the expiration date. An option writer benefits from an option that has a high theta.

Call Option Price and Expected Interest Rate Volatility

All other factors constant, a change in the expected interest rate volatility will change the option price. The **kappa** of an option measures the dollar price change in the price of the option for a 1% change in the expected price volatility. That is,

$$\text{kappa} = \frac{\text{change in option price}}{1\% \text{ change in expected price volatility}}$$

Duration of an Option

The modified duration of an option measures the price sensitivity of the option to changes in interest rates. The modified duration of an option can be shown to be equal to

$$\text{modified duration for an option} =$$

$$\text{modified duration of underlying instrument} \times \text{delta} \times \frac{\text{price of underlying instrument}}{\text{price of option}}$$

As expected, the modified duration of an option depends on the modified duration of the underlying bond. It also depends on the price responsiveness of the option to a change in the underlying instrument, as measured by the option's delta. The leverage created by a position in an option comes from the last ratio in the formula. The higher the price of the underlying instrument relative to the price of the option, the greater the leverage (i.e., the more exposure to interest rates for a given dollar investment).

It is the interaction of all three factors that affects the modified duration of an option. For example, a deep-out-of-the-money option offers higher leverage than a deep-in-the-money option, but the delta of the former is less than that of the latter.

Because the delta of a call option is positive, the modified duration of an interest rate call option will be positive. Thus, when interest rates decline, the value of an interest rate call option will rise. A put option, however, has a delta that is negative. Thus, the modified duration is negative. Consequently, when interest rates rise, the value of a put option rises.

HEDGE STRATEGIES

Hedge strategies involve taking a position in an option and a position in the underlying bond in such a way that changes in the value of one position will offset any unfavorable price (interest rate) movement in the other position. We discuss two popular hedge strategies here: (1) the protective put buying strategy, and (2) the covered call writing strategy. In this section, we demonstrate these two strategies using futures options. The exercise is worthwhile because it shows how complicated hedging with futures options is and the key parameters involved in the process. We also compare the outcome of hedging with futures and hedging with futures options.[6]

Hedging Long-Term Bonds with Puts on Futures

Investors often want to hedge their bond positions against a possible increase in interest rates. Buying puts on futures is one of the easiest ways to purchase protection against rising rates. To illustrate this strategy, we can use the Procter & Gamble (P&G) bond that we used in Chapter 26 to demonstrate how to hedge with Treasury bond futures. In that example, an investor held the P&G 5.55% 3/5/2037 and used Treasury bond futures to lock in a sale price for those bonds on a futures delivery date. The par value of the P&G bond owned and to be hedged is $10 million. Now we want to show how the investor could have used Treasury bond futures options instead of Treasury bond futures to protect against rising rates.

Recall that in the previous chapter we used a Treasury bond futures contract with settlement in March 2008. We will use a put option on that same Treasury bond futures contract. The put options for this contract expire on February 22, 2008. Recall that the cheapest-to-deliver (CTD) issue for the Treasury bond futures contract was the Treasury 6.25% 8/15/2023.

In the example (summarized at the top of Exhibit 27-16), the P&G bond was selling at a yield of 5.74% and the CTD Treasury issue for the March 2008 contract was trading at 4.643%. For simplicity, we assumed that this yield spread would remain at 111.1 basis points. To hedge, the investor must determine the minimum price that he wants to establish for the P&G bond. In our illustration, it is assumed that the minimum price is 96.219 per bond or $9,621,900 for $10 million of par value. Thus, 96.219 becomes the target forward price for the P&G bond. But the investor is not buying a put option on the P&G bond. Rather, he is buying a put option on a Treasury bond futures contract. Therefore, in order to hedge, the investor must determine the strike price for a put option on a Treasury bond futures contract that is equivalent to a strike price of 96.219 for the P&G bond.

This can be done with the help of Exhibit 27-17. We begin at the top left-hand box of the exhibit. Because the minimum price is 96.219 for the P&G bond, this means that the

---

[6] The illustrations in this section were provided by Peter Ru of Morgan Stanley.

Exhibit 27-16   Hedging a Nondeliverable Bond to a Delivery Date with Puts on Futures

Instrument to be hedged: P&G 5.55% 3/5/2037
Hedge ratio: 1.15   No. of contracts: 115
Strike price for puts on futures: 114.000
Target minimum price for hedged bonds: 96.219
Put option price per contract: $192

Actual Sale Price of P&G Bonds	Futures Price[a]	Value of 115 Put Options[b]	Cost of 115 Put Options	Effective Sale Price[c]
8,000,000	99.139	1,709,040	22,678	9,686,362
8,200,000	101.054	1,488,827	22,678	9,666,149
8,400,000	102.946	1,271,207	22,678	9,648,529
8,600,000	104.812	1,056,651	22,678	9,633,973
8,800,000	106.647	845,619	22,678	9,622,941
9,000,000	108.469	636,036	22,678	9,613,358
9,200,000	110.265	429,516	22,678	9,606,838
9,400,000	112.042	225,118	22,678	9,602,440
9,600,000	113.787	24,502	22,678	9,601,824
9,800,000	115.519	0	22,678	9,777,322
10,000,000	117.237	0	22,678	9,977,322
10,200,000	118.938	0	22,678	10,177,322
10,400,000	120.608	0	22,678	10,377,322
10,600,000	122.269	0	22,678	10,577,322
10,800,000	123.908	0	22,678	10,777,322
11,000,000	125.522	0	22,678	10,977,322
11,200,000	127.135	0	22,678	11,177,322
11,400,000	128.721	0	22,678	11,377,322
11,600,000	130.303	0	22,678	11,577,322

[a] These numbers are approximate because futures trade in even *32nds*.
[b] From 115 × $1,000 × Max[(114 − futures price), 0].
[c] Does not include transaction costs or the financing of the options position.

investor is attempting to establish a maximum yield of 5.821%. This is found from the relationship between price and yield: Given a price of 96.219 for the P&G bond, this is equivalent to a yield of 5.821%. (This gets us to the lower left-hand box in Exhibit 27-17.) From our assumption that the yield spread between the P&G bond and the CTD issue is a constant 111.1 basis points, setting a maximum yield of 5.821% for this bond is equivalent to setting a maximum yield of 4.710% for the CTD issue. (Now we are at the lower box in the middle column of Exhibit 27-17.)

Given the yield of 4.710% for the CTD issue, the minimum price can be determined (the top box in the middle column of Exhibit 27-17). Since the CTD issue is the Treasury 6.25%

Exhibit 27-17   Calculating Equivalent Prices and Yields for Hedging with Futures Options

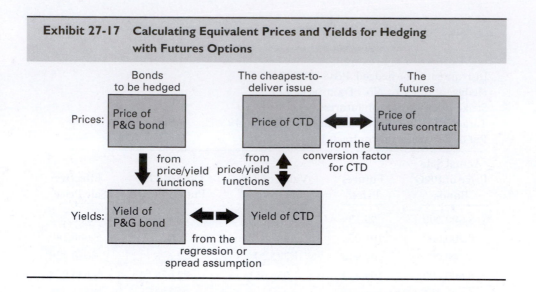

8/15/2023, a 4.710% yield means a target forward price for the CTD issue of 116.8044. The corresponding futures price is found by dividing the price of the CTD issue by the conversion factor. This gets us to the box in the right-hand column of Exhibit 27-17. Because the conversion factor for the CTD issue is 1.0246, the futures price is about 114.373 (116.8044 divided by 1.0246). Based on the availability of strike prices, a futures price of 114.000 is used. This means that a strike price of 114.000 for a put option on a Treasury bond futures contract is roughly equivalent to a put option on the P&G bond with a strike price of 96.219.

The foregoing steps are always necessary to obtain the appropriate strike price on a put futures option. The process is not complicated. It involves simply (1) the relationship between price and yield, (2) the assumed relationship between the yield spread between the hedged bonds and the CTD issue, and (3) the conversion factor for the CTD issue. As with hedging employing futures illustrated in Chapter 26, the success of the hedging strategy will depend on (1) whether the CTD issue changes, and (2) the yield spread between the hedged bonds and the CTD issue.

The hedge ratio is determined using equation (26.10) of Chapter 26 because we will assume a constant yield spread between the bond to be hedged and CTD issue. To compute the hedge ratio, we calculate the price values of a basis point at the option expiration date (assumed to be February 22, 2008) and at the yields corresponding to the futures strike price of 114.000 (4.710% yield for the CTD issue and 5.821% for the P&G bond). The price value of a basis point per $100 par value for the P&G bond and the CTD issue were 0.1353 and 0.1208, respectively. This results in a hedge ratio of 1.148 for the options hedge, or 1.15 with rounding.

This means 115 put options on the Treasury bond futures contract expiring on February 22, 2008, and with a strike price of 114 should be purchased. At the time of the hedge, December 24, 2007, the price quote for this put option was 1.972. This means the dollar cost of each option is $197.2. Since 115 contracts are purchased, the total cost of the put options (ignoring commissions) is $22,678.

To create a table for the protective put hedge, we can use some of the numbers from Exhibit 26-4 of Chapter 26. The first column in Exhibit 27-16 repeats the numbers in the first column of Exhibit 26-4; the second column in Exhibit 27-16 is the futures price and differs slightly from the fifth column of Exhibit 26-4 because of different settlement dates. The rest of the columns in Exhibit 27-16 are computed. The value of the put options shown in the third column of the exhibit is easy to calculate because the value of each option at expiration is just the strike price of the futures option (114) minus the futures price (or zero if that difference is negative), all multiplied by $1,000. Let's see why by looking at the first row that corresponds to a futures price of 99.139. Since the strike price for the put option is 114.000, this means the value of the put option is 14.861(114.000−99.139). This is per $1,000 par value. But the par value for the Treasury bond futures contract is $1 million. Hence, the 14.861 must be multiplied by $1,000. Thus, the value of the contract is 14.861 times $1,000 or $14,861. Since 115 contracts were purchased, their total value is $1,709,015. The value of the 115 put options shown in the third column of $1,709,040 differs by $25 due to rounding in earlier calculation.

The cost of the 115 put options is shown in the next-to-last column. The effective sale price for the P&G bonds is then just the actual market price for the bond, plus the value of the 115 put options at expiration, minus the cost of the 115 put options. The effective sale price is shown in the last column of the exhibit. This effective sale price is never less than $9,601,824. Recall that we established a minimum price of $9,621,900. This minimum effective sale price is something that can be calculated before the hedge is ever initiated. (As prices decline, the effective sale price actually exceeds the projected effective minimum sale price of 96.219 by a small amount. This is due to rounding and the fact that the hedge ratio is left unaltered, although the relative price values of a basis point that go into the hedge ratio calculation change as yields change.) As prices increase, however, the effective sale price of the P&G bond increases as well; unlike the futures hedge shown in Exhibit 26-4, the options hedge using puts protects the investor if rates rise but allows the investor to profit if rates fall.

Covered Call Writing with Futures Options

Unlike the protective put strategy, covered call writing is not entered into with the sole purpose of protecting a portfolio against rising rates. The covered call writer, believing that the market will not trade much higher or much lower than its present level, sells out-of-the-money calls against an existing bond portfolio. The sale of the calls brings in premium income that provides partial protection in case rates increase. The premium received does not, of course, provide the kind of protection that a long put position provides, but it does provide some additional income that can be used to offset declining prices. If, on the other hand, rates fall, portfolio appreciation is limited because the short call position constitutes a liability for the seller, and this liability increases as rates go down. Consequently, there is limited upside potential for the covered call writer. Of course, this is not so bad if prices are essentially going nowhere; the added income from the sale of options is obtained without sacrificing any gains.

To see how covered call writing with futures options works for the bond used in the protective put example, we construct a table much as we did before. With futures selling around 114.375 on the hedge initiation date, a sale of a 120 call option on futures might be appropriate. The price for the March call options with a strike of 120 expiring on 2/22/2008 was 0.512 or $51.20. As before, it is assumed that the hedged bond will remain at a 111.11 basis point spread off the CTD issue. The number of options contracts sold will be the same, 115.

Exhibit 27-18 shows the results of the covered call writing strategy given these assumptions. To calculate the effective sale price of the bonds in the covered call writing strategy, the premium received from the sale of the call options is added to the actual sale price

Exhibit 27-18 **Hedging a Nondeliverable Bond to a Delivery Date with Calls on Futures**

Instrument to be hedged: P&G 5.55% 3/5/2037
Hedge ratio: 1.15 No. of contracts: 115
Strike price for calls on futures: 120.000
Expected maximum price for hedged bonds: 103.785
Call option price per contract: $51.2

Actual Sale Price of P&G Bonds	Futures Price[a]	Liability of 115 Call Options[b]	Premium of 115 Call Options	Effective Sale Price[c]
8,000,000	99.139	0	5,888	8,005,888
8,200,000	101.054	0	5,888	8,205,888
8,400,000	102.946	0	5,888	8,405,888
8,600,000	104.812	0	5,888	8,605,888
8,800,000	106.647	0	5,888	8,805,888
9,000,000	108.469	0	5,888	9,005,888
9,200,000	110.265	0	5,888	9,205,888
9,400,000	112.042	0	5,888	9,405,888
9,600,000	113.787	0	5,888	9,605,888
9,800,000	115.519	0	5,888	9,805,888
10,000,000	117.237	0	5,888	10,005,888
10,200,000	118.938	0	5,888	10,205,888
10,400,000	120.608	69,902	5,888	10,335,986
10,600,000	122.269	260,978	5,888	10,344,910
10,800,000	123.908	449,427	5,888	10,356,461
11,000,000	125.522	635,003	5,888	10,370,885
11,200,000	127.135	820,568	5,888	10,385,320
11,400,000	128.721	1,002,866	5,888	10,403,022
11,600,000	130.303	1,184,850	5,888	10,421,038

[a] These numbers are approximate because futures trade in even *32nds*.
[b] From $115 \times \$1{,}000 \times Max[(\text{futures price} - 120), 0]$.
[c] Does not include transaction costs or the financing of the options position.

of the bonds, and the liability associated with the short call position is subtracted from the actual sale price. The liability associated with each call is the futures price minus the strike price of 120 (or zero if this difference is negative), all multiplied by $1,000. The middle column in the exhibit is just this value multiplied by 115, the number of options sold.

Just as the minimum effective sale price could be calculated beforehand for the protective put strategy, the maximum effective sale price can be calculated beforehand for the covered call writing strategy. The maximum effective sale price will be the price of the hedged security corresponding to the strike price of the call option sold, plus the premium received. In this case the strike price on the futures call option was 120. A futures price of 120 corresponds to a price of 122.9520 (from 120 times the conversion factor of 1.0246) and a corresponding yield of 4.126% for the CTD issue. The equivalent yield for the P&G bond is 111.11 basis points higher, or 5.3271%, for a corresponding price of 103.273. Adding on the premium received, 0.512, the final maximum effective sale price will be about 103.785 or $10,378,500. As Exhibit 27-18 shows, if the hedged bond does trade at 111.11 basis points over the CTD issue as assumed, the maximum effective sale price for the P&G bond is, in fact, slightly more than that amount. The discrepancies shown in the table are due to rounding and the fact that the position is not adjusted, even though the relative price values of a basis point change as yields change.

Comparing Alternative Strategies

In Chapter 26 and in this chapter, we reviewed three basic hedging strategies for hedging a bond position: (1) hedging with futures, (2) hedging with out-of-the-money protective puts, and (3) covered call writing with out-of-the-money calls. Similar but opposite strategies exist for those whose risks are that rates will decrease. As might be expected, there is no "best" strategy. Each strategy has advantages and disadvantages, and we never get something for nothing. To get anything of value, something else of value must be forfeited.

To make a choice among strategies, it helps to lay the alternatives side by side. Using the futures and futures options examples from this chapter, Exhibit 27-19 shows the final values of the portfolio for the various alternatives. It is easy to see from Exhibit 27-19 that

Exhibit 27-19   Alternative Hedging Strategies Compared

Actual Sale Price of Bonds	Effective Sale Price with Futures Hedge	Effective Sale Price with Protective Puts	Effective Sale Price with Covered Calls
8,000,000	9,767,401	9,686,362	8,005,888
8,200,000	9,745,273	9,666,149	8,205,888
8,400,000	9,725,761	9,648,529	8,405,888
8,600,000	9,709,339	9,633,973	8,605,888
8,800,000	9,696,472	9,622,941	8,805,888
9,000,000	9,685,066	9,613,358	9,005,888
9,200,000	9,676,751	9,606,838	9,205,888
9,400,000	9,670,575	9,602,440	9,405,888
9,600,000	9,668,215	9,601,824	9,605,888
9,800,000	9,667,281	9,777,322	9,805,888
10,000,000	9,668,034	9,977,322	10,005,888
10,200,000	9,670,700	10,177,322	10,205,888
10,400,000	9,676,990	10,377,322	10,335,986
10,600,000	9,684,253	10,577,322	10,344,910
10,800,000	9,694,165	10,777,322	10,356,461
11,000,000	9,706,975	10,977,322	10,370,885
11,200,000	9,719,797	11,177,322	10,385,320
11,400,000	9,735,913	11,377,322	10,403,022
11,600,000	9,752,347	11,577,322	10,421,038

if one alternative is superior to another alternative at one level of rates, it will be inferior at some other level of rates.

Consequently, we cannot conclude that one strategy is the best strategy. The manager who makes the strategy decision makes a choice among probability distributions, not usually among specific outcomes. Except for the perfect hedge, there is always some range of possible final values of the portfolio. Of course, exactly what that range is, and the probabilities associated with each possible outcome, is a matter of opinion.

KEY POINTS

- An option grants the buyer of the option the right either to buy (in the case of a call option) or to sell (in the case of a put option) the underlying asset to the seller (writer) of the option at the strike (exercise) price by the expiration date.

- The option price or option premium is the amount that the option buyer pays to the writer of the option.

- An American option allows the option buyer to exercise the option at any time up to and including the expiration date; a European option may be exercised only at the expiration date.

- Interest-rate options include options on fixed-income securities and options on interest-rate futures contracts, called futures options. The latter are the preferred vehicle for implementing investment strategies.

- Because of the difficulties of hedging particular bond issues or pass-through securities, many institutions find over-the-counter options more useful; these contracts can be customized to meet specific investment goals.

- The buyer of an option cannot realize a loss greater than the option price and has all the upside potential. By contrast, the maximum gain that the writer (seller) of an option can realize is the option price; the writer is exposed to all the downside risk.

- The option price consists of two components: the intrinsic value and the time value. The intrinsic value is the economic value of the option if it is exercised immediately (except that if there is no positive economic value that will result from exercising immediately, the intrinsic value is zero). The time value is the amount by which the option price exceeds the intrinsic value.

- Six factors influence the option price: (1) the current price of the underlying bond, (2) the strike price of the option, (3) the time remaining to the expiration of the option, (4) the expected price volatility of the underlying bond (i.e., expected interest-rate volatility), (5) the short-term risk-free interest rate over the life of the option, and (6) coupon payments.

- An option pricing model determines the theoretical or fair value of an option. There are option pricing models for options on bonds (i.e., options on physicals) and options on bond futures.

- The two models used to value options on bonds are the Black–Scholes option pricing model and the arbitrage-free binomial option pricing model. The limitations of the former when applied to options on bonds are that it fails to incorporate the yield curve in the model and does not recognize that there is a maximum price that a bond can reach.

- The most common model to value an option on a bond futures contract is the Black model.

- The two popular strategies using options are protective put buying and covered call writing.

QUESTIONS

1. An investor owns a call option on bond X with a strike price of 100. The coupon rate on bond X is 9% and has 10 years to maturity. The call option expires today at a time when bond X is selling to yield 8%. Should the investor exercise the call option?

2. When the buyer of a put option on a futures contract exercises, explain the resulting position for the buyer and the writer.

3. An investor wants to protect against a rise in the market yield on a Treasury bond. Should the investor purchase a put option or a call option to obtain protection?

4. What is the intrinsic value and time value of a call option on bond W given the following information?

$$\text{strike price of call option} = 97$$
$$\text{current price of bond W} = 102$$
$$\text{call option price} = 9$$

5. "There's no real difference between options and futures. Both are hedging tools, and both are derivative products. It's just that with options you have to pay an option premium, whereas futures require no upfront payment except for a 'good faith' margin. I can't understand why anyone would use options." Do you agree with this statement?

6. What arguments would be given by those who feel that the Black–Scholes model does not apply in pricing interest-rate options?

7. You are the senior portfolio manager of an institutional account. You are reviewing the response of a junior member of your portfolio management team to a client who inquired about the use of options and futures. Four paragraphs in the letter to the client are reproduced below.
   a. "The substantial interest-rate volatility is forcing many of our clients to grant us authorization to employ options to hedge their bond portfolios." Explain why such movements in interest rates would motivate clients to authorize their portfolio managers to use options.
   b. "We believe options are a prudent choice because should the market move against us if we purchase an option for your account, the only

negative is that the option expires worthless, and all we have only lost for your account is the option price paid." Comment on the accuracy of this statement.
   c. "As an alternative, we could use another type of derivative to hedge a bond portfolio: futures contracts. We are reluctant to use this type of derivative because futures cost more, and there is tremendous downside risk; that is there is no limit on the amount of losses that might be realized for your account before we get out of the futures position." Comment on the accuracy of this statement.
   d. "The overall strategy involved in using options is straightforward. If we are concerned about interest rates rising but do not want to do a major rebalancing of your portfolio, we simply take a position in put options." Why might put options be a preferable means of altering the a bond portfolio rather than rebalancing the portfolio?

8. What are the differences between an option on a bond and an option on a bond futures contract?

9. What is the motivation for the purchase of an OTC option?

10. Does it make sense for an investor who wants to speculate on interest-rate movements to purchase an OTC option?

11. "I don't understand how portfolio managers can calculate the duration of an interest-rate option. Don't they mean the amount of time remaining to the expiration date?" Respond to this question.

12. **a.** What factors affect the modified duration of an interest-rate option?
    b. A deep-in-the-money option always provides a higher modified duration for an option than a deep-out-of-the-money option. Comment.
    c. The modified duration of all options is positive. Is this statement correct?

13. How is the implied volatility of an option determined?

14. **a.** What are the delta and gamma of an option?
    b. If the implied price volatility of a call option on a Treasury bond futures contract is 10.0 and the duration of the CTD issue is 8, what is the implied yield volatility?

15. Explain why the writer of an option would prefer an option with a high theta (all other factors equal).

16. In implementing a protective put-buying strategy, explain the trade-off between the cost of the strategy and the strike price selected.

17. Here is an excerpt from an article titled "Dominguez Barry Looks at Covered Calls," appearing in the July 20, 1992, issue of *Derivatives Week*, p. 7:

    > SBC Dominguez Barry Funds Management in Sydney, with A$5.5 billion under management, is considering writing covered calls on its Australian bond portfolio to take advantage of very high implied volatilities, according to Carl Hanich, portfolio manager. The implied price volatility on at-the-money calls is 9.8%, as high as Hanich can ever remember. . . .

    In response to rising volatility, Hanich is thinking about selling calls with a strike of 8.5%, generating premium income. "I'd be happy to lose bonds at 8.5%, given our market's at 8.87% now," he said.

    Explain the strategy that Hanich is considering.

18. Determine the price of a European call option on a 6.5% four-year Treasury bond with a strike price of 100.25 and two years to expiration assuming: (1) the arbitrage-free binomial interest-rate tree shown in Exhibit 27-11 (based on a 10% volatility assumption), and (2) the price of the Treasury bond two years from now shown at each node.

19. Determine the price of a European put option on a 6.5% four-year Treasury bond with a strike price of 100.25 and two years to expiration assuming the same information as in Exhibit 27-12.

Interest-Rate Swaps,
Caps, and Floors

LEARNING OBJECTIVES

After reading this chapter, you will understand

- what an interest-rate swap is

- the relationship between an interest-rate swap and forward contracts

- how interest-rate swap terms are quoted in the market

- how the swap rate is calculated

- how the value of a swap is determined

- how a swap can be used by institutional investors

- how a structured note is created using an interest-rate swap

- what a swaption is and how it can be used by institutional investors

- what a rate cap and floor are, and how these agreements can be used by institutional investors

- the relationship between a cap and floor and options

- how to value caps and floors

- how an interest-rate collar can be created

In Chapters 26 and 27, we discussed how interest-rate futures and options can be used to control interest-rate risk. There are other contracts useful for controlling such risk that commercial banks and investment banks can customize for their clients. These include (1) interest-rate swaps and options on swaps, and (2) interest-rate caps and floors and options on these agreements. In this chapter, we review each of them and explain how they can be used by institutional investors.

INTEREST-RATE SWAPS

In an **interest-rate swap**, two parties (called **counterparties**) agree to exchange periodic interest payments. The dollar amount of the interest payments exchanged is based on a predetermined dollar principal, which is called the **notional principal amount**. The dollar amount that each counterparty pays to the other is the agreed-upon periodic interest rate times the notional principal amount. The only dollars that are exchanged between the parties are the interest payments, not the notional principal amount. In the most common type of swap, one party agrees to pay the other party fixed-interest payments at designated dates for the life of the contract. This party is referred to as the **fixed-rate payer** or the **floating-rate receiver**. The other party, who agrees to make interest rate payments that float with some reference rate, is referred to as the **floating-rate payer** or **fixed-rate receiver**. In practice, these parties are typically referred to in terms of whether they are paying or receiving the fixed rate. That is, the parties are typically referred to as the fixed-rate payer and fixed-rate receiver. The frequency with which the interest rate that the floating-rate payer must pay is called the **reset frequency**.

The reference rates that have been used for the floating rate in an interest-rate swap are those on various money market instruments: the London Interbank Offered Rate, Treasury bill rate, commercial paper, banker's acceptances, certificates of deposit, the federal funds rate, and the prime rate. The most common is the London Interbank Offered Rate (LIBOR). LIBOR is the rate at which prime banks offer to pay on Eurodollar deposits available to other prime banks for a given maturity. Basically, it is viewed as the global cost of bank borrowing. There is not just one rate but a rate for different maturities. For example, there is a one-month LIBOR, three-month LIBOR, and six-month LIBOR.

To illustrate an interest-rate swap, suppose that for the next five years party X agrees to pay party Y 10% per year, while party Y agrees to pay party X six-month LIBOR (the reference rate). Party X is a fixed-rate payer, while party Y is a fixed-rate receiver. Assume that the notional principal amount is $50 million and that payments are exchanged every six months for the next five years. This means that every six months, party X (the fixed-rate payer) will pay party Y $2.5 million (10% times $50 million divided by 2). The amount that party Y (the fixed-rate receiver) will pay party X will be six-month LIBOR times $50 million divided by 2. If six-month LIBOR is 7%, party Y will pay party X $1.75 million (7% times $50 million divided by 2). Note that we divide by two because one-half year's interest is being paid.

Later, we will illustrate how market participants can use an interest-rate swap to alter the cash flow character of assets or liabilities from a fixed-rate basis to a floating-rate basis, or vice versa.

Entering into a Swap and Counterparty Risk

Interest-rate swaps are over-the-counter instruments. This means that they are not traded on an exchange. An institutional investor wishing to enter into a swap transaction can do so through either a securities firm or a commercial bank that transacts in swaps.[1] These entities can do one of the following. First, they can arrange or broker a swap between two

---

[1] Do not get confused here about the role of commercial banks. A bank can use a swap in its asset/liability management or a bank can transact (buy and sell) swaps to clients to generate fee income. It is in the latter sense that we are discussing the role of a commercial bank in the swap market here.

parties that want to enter into an interest-rate swap. In this case, the securities firm or commercial bank is acting in a brokerage capacity.

The second way in which a securities firm or commercial bank can get an institutional investor into a swap position is by taking the other side of the swap. This means that the securities firm or the commercial bank is a dealer rather than a broker in the transaction. Acting as a dealer, the securities firm or the commercial bank must hedge its swap position in the same way that it hedges its position in other securities that it holds. Also it means that the dealer (which we refer to as a **swap dealer**) is the counterparty to the transaction. Goldman, Sachs, for example, is a swap dealer. If an institutional investor entered into a swap with Goldman, Sachs, the institutional investor will look to Goldman, Sachs to satisfy the obligations of the swap; similarly, Goldman, Sachs looks to the institutional investor to fulfill its obligations as set forth in the swap. Today, swaps are typically transacted using a swap dealer.

A risk that the two parties take on when they enter into a swap is that the other party will fail to fulfill its obligations as set forth in the swap agreement. That is, each party faces default risk. The default risk in a swap agreement is called **counterparty risk**. In fact, counterparty risk is more general than the default risk for only a swap agreement. In any agreement between two parties that must perform according to the terms of a contract, counterparty risk is the risk that the other party will default. With futures and exchange-traded options, the counterparty risk is the risk that the clearinghouse established to guarantee performance of the contracts will default. Market participants view this risk as small. In contrast, counterparty risk in a swap can be significant.

Because of counterparty risk, not all securities firms and commercial banks can be swap dealers. Several securities firms have actually established subsidiaries that are separately capitalized so that they have a high credit rating, which permits them to enter into swap transactions as a dealer. Thus, it is imperative to keep in mind that any party who enters into a swap is subject to counterparty risk.

Interpreting a Swap Position

There are two ways that a swap position can be interpreted: (1) as a package of forward/futures contracts, and (2) as a package of cash flows from buying and selling cash market instruments.

Package of Forward Contracts

Consider the hypothetical interest-rate swap described earlier to illustrate a swap. Let's look at party X's position. Party X has agreed to pay 10% and receive six-month LIBOR. More specifically, assuming a $50 million notional principal amount, X has agreed to buy a commodity called six-month LIBOR for $2.5 million. This is effectively a six-month forward contract in which X agrees to pay $2.5 million in exchange for delivery of six-month LIBOR. If interest rates increase to 11%, the price of that commodity (six-month LIBOR) is higher, resulting in a gain for the fixed-rate payer, who is effectively long a six-month forward contract on six-month LIBOR. The fixed-rate receiver is effectively short a six-month forward contract on six-month LIBOR. There is therefore an implicit forward contract corresponding to each exchange date.

Consequently, interest-rate swaps can be viewed as a package of more basic interest-rate control tools, such as forwards. The pricing of an interest-rate swap will then depend on the price of a package of forward contracts with the same settlement dates in which the underlying for the forward contract is the same index.

Although an interest-rate swap may be nothing more than a package of forward contracts, it is not a redundant financial instrument, for several reasons. First, maturities for forward or futures contracts do not extend out as far as those of an interest-rate swap; an interest-rate swap with a term of 15 years or longer can be obtained. Second, an interest-rate swap is a more transactionally efficient instrument. By this we mean that in one transaction an entity can effectively establish a payoff equivalent to a package of forward contracts. The forward contracts would each have to be negotiated separately. Third, the interest-rate swap market has grown in liquidity since its establishment in 1981; interest-rate swaps now provide more liquidity than forward contracts, particularly long-dated (i.e., long-term) forward contracts.

Package of Cash Market Instruments

To understand why a swap can also be interpreted as a package of cash market instruments, consider an investor who enters into the following transaction:

- Buy $50 million par of a five-year floating-rate bond that pays six-month LIBOR every six months.
- Finance the purchase by borrowing $50 million for five years on terms requiring 10% annual interest rate paid every six months.

The cash flows for this transaction are shown in Exhibit 28-1. The second column of the table shows the cash flow from purchasing the five-year floating-rate bond. There is

Exhibit 28-1 Cash Flow for the Purchase of a Five-Year Floating-Rate Bond Financed by Borrowing on a Fixed-Rate Basis

Transaction: Purchase for $50 million a five-year floating-rate bond: floating rate = LIBOR, semiannual pay; borrow $50 million for five years: fixed rate = 10%, semiannual payments

Six-Month Period	Floating-Rate Bond[a]	Borrowing Cost	Net
0	−$50	+$50.0	$0
1	+ (LIBOR$_1$/2) × 50	−2.5	+ (LIBOR$_1$/2) × 50 − 2.5
2	+ (LIBOR$_2$/2) × 50	−2.5	+ (LIBOR$_2$/2) × 50 − 2.5
3	+ (LIBOR$_3$/2) × 50	−2.5	+ (LIBOR$_3$/2) × 50 − 2.5
4	+ (LIBOR$_4$/2) × 50	−2.5	+ (LIBOR$_4$/2) × 50 − 2.5
5	+ (LIBOR$_5$/2) × 50	−2.5	− (LIBOR$_5$/2) × 50 − 2.5
6	+ (LIBOR$_6$/2) × 50	−2.5	+ (LIBOR$_6$/2) × 50 − 2.5
7	+ (LIBOR$_7$/2) × 50	−2.5	+ (LIBOR$_7$/2) × 50 − 2.5
8	+ (LIBOR$_8$/2) × 50	−2.5	+ (LIBOR$_8$/2) × 50 − 2.5
9	+ (LIBOR$_9$/2) × 50	−2.5	+ (LIBOR$_9$/2) × 50 − 2.5
10	+ (LIBOR$_{10}$/2) × 50 + 50	−52.5	+ (LIBOR$_{10}$/2) × 50 − 2.5

[a] The subscript for LIBOR indicates the six-month LIBOR as per the terms of the floating-rate bond at time *t*.

a $50 million cash outlay and then 10 cash inflows. The amount of the cash inflows is uncertain because they depend on future LIBOR. The next column shows the cash flow from borrowing $50 million on a fixed-rate basis. The last column shows the net cash flow from the entire transaction. As the last column indicates, there is no initial cash flow (no cash inflow or cash outlay). In all 10 six-month periods, the net position results in a cash inflow of LIBOR and a cash outlay of $2.5 million. This net position, however, is identical to the position of a fixed-rate payer.

It can be seen from the net cash flow in Exhibit 28-1 that a fixed-rate payer has a cash market position that is equivalent to a long position in a floating-rate bond and a short position in a fixed-rate bond—the short position being the equivalent of borrowing by issuing a fixed-rate bond.

What about the position of a fixed-rate receiver? It can be easily demonstrated that the position of a fixed-rate receiver is equivalent to purchasing a fixed-rate bond and financing that purchase at a floating rate, where the floating rate is the reference interest rate for the swap. That is, the position of a fixed-rate receiver is equivalent to a long position in a fixed-rate bond and a short position in a floating-rate bond.

Terminology, Conventions, and Market Quotes

Here we review some of the terminology used in the swaps market and explain how swaps are quoted. The date that the counterparties commit to the swap is called the **trade date**. The date that the swap begins accruing interest is called the **effective date**, and the date that the swap stops accruing interest is called the **maturity date**.

Although our illustrations assume that the timing of the cash flows for both the fixed-rate payer and fixed-rate receiver will be the same, this need not be the case in a swap. Also, the way in which interest accrues on each leg of the transaction differs because there are several day-count conventions in the fixed-income markets.

The terminology used to describe the position of a party in the swap markets combines cash market jargon and futures jargon, given that a swap position can be interpreted as a position in a package of cash market instruments or a package of futures/forward positions. As we have said, the counterparty to an interest-rate swap is either a fixed-rate payer or fixed-rate receiver. These positions can be described in the following ways:

Fixed-Rate Payer	Fixed-Rate Receiver
Pays fixed rate in the swap	Pays floating rate in the swap
Receives floating in the swap	Receives fixed in the swap
Has bought a swap	Has sold a swap
Is long a swap	Is short a swap
Is short the bond market	Is long the bond market

The first two expressions above that describe the position of a fixed-rate payer and fixed-rate receiver are self-explanatory. To understand why the fixed-rate receiver is viewed as short the bond market and the fixed-rate receiver is viewed as long the bond market, consider what happens when interest rates change. Those who borrow on a fixed-rate basis will benefit if interest rates rise because they have locked in a lower interest rate, but those who have a short bond position will also benefit if interest rates rise. Thus, a fixed-rate payer can be said to be short the bond market. A fixed-rate receiver benefits if interest rates fall. A long position in a bond also benefits if interest rates fall, so terminology describing a fixed-rate receiver as long the bond market is not surprising.

Another way to describe the position of the counterparties to a swap is in terms of our discussion of the interpretation of a swap as a package of cash market instruments. That is,

Fixed-rate payer: A position that is exposed to the price sensitivities of a longer-term liability and a floating-rate bond.

Fixed-rate receiver: A position that is exposed to the price sensitivities of a fixed-rate bond and a floating-rate liability.

The convention that has evolved for quoting swaps levels is that a swap dealer sets the floating rate equal to the index and then quotes the fixed rate that will apply. To illustrate this convention, consider a 10-year swap offered by a dealer to market participants shown in Exhibit 28-2.

The offer price that the dealer would quote the fixed-rate payer would be to pay 8.85% and receive LIBOR "flat" ("flat" meaning with no spread to LIBOR). The bid price that the dealer would quote the fixed-rate receiver would be to pay LIBOR flat and receive 8.75%. The bid-offer spread is 10 basis points.

The fixed rate is some spread above the Treasury yield curve with the same term to maturity as the swap. In our illustration, suppose that the 10-year Treasury yield is 8.35%. Then the offer price that the dealer would quote to the fixed-rate payer is the 10-year Treasury rate plus 50 basis points versus receiving LIBOR flat. For the fixed-rate receiver, the bid price quoted would be LIBOR flat versus the 10-year Treasury rate plus 40 basis points. The dealer would quote such a swap as 40–50, meaning that the dealer is willing to enter into a swap to receive LIBOR and pay a fixed rate equal to the 10-year Treasury rate plus 40 basis points, and it would be willing to enter into a swap to pay LIBOR and receive a fixed rate equal to the 10-year Treasury rate plus 50 basis points. The difference between the Treasury rate paid and received is the bid-offer spread.

Calculation of the Swap Rate

At the initiation of an interest-rate swap, the counterparties are agreeing to exchange future interest-rate payments, and no upfront payments by either party are made. This means that the swap terms must be such that the present value of the cash flows for the payments to be made by the counterparties must be equal. This is equivalent to saying that the present value of the cash flows of payments to be received by the counterparties must be equal. The equivalence of the cash flows is the principle in calculating the swap rate.

For the fixed-rate side, when a swap rate is determined, the payments of the fixed-rate payer are known. However, the floating-rate payments are not known because they depend on the value of the reference rate at the reset dates. For a LIBOR-based swap, the

Exhibit 28-2	Meaning of a "40–50" Quote for a 10-Year Swap When Treasuries Yield 8.35% (Bid-Offer Spread of 10 Basis Points)	
	Fixed-Rate Receiver	**Fixed-Rate Payer**
Pay	Floating rate of six-month LIBOR	Fixed rate of 8.85%
Receive	Fixed rate of 8.75%	Floating rate of six-month LIBOR

Eurodollar futures contract (discussed in Chapter 26) can be used to establish the forward (or future) rate for three-month LIBOR. Given the cash flow based on the forward rate for three-month LIBOR, the swap rate is the interest rate that will make the present value of the payments on the fixed-rate side equal to the payments on the floating-rate side.

The next question is: What interest rate should be used to discount the payments? As explained in Chapter 5, the appropriate rate to discount any cash flow is the theoretical spot rate. Each cash flow should be discounted at a unique discount rate. Where do we get the theoretical spot rates? Recall from Chapter 5 that spot rates can be obtained from forward rates. It is the same three-month LIBOR forward rates derived from the Eurodollar futures contract that can be used to obtain the theoretical spot rates.

We will illustrate the procedure with an example.[2] Consider the following terms for our swap:

- A swap starts today, January 1 of year 1 (swap settlement date).
- The floating-rate payments are made quarterly based on actual/360.
- The reference rate is three-month LIBOR.
- The notional amount of the swap is $100 million.
- The term of the swap is three years.

The quarterly floating-rate payments are based on an actual/360-day count convention. This convention means that 360 days are assumed in a year and that in computing the interest for the quarter the actual number of days in the quarter is used. The floating-rate payment is set at the beginning of the quarter but paid at the end of the quarter—that is, the floating-rate payments are made in arrears.

Suppose that today three-month LIBOR is 4.05%. Let's look at what the fixed-rate payer will receive on March 31 of year 1—the date when the first quarterly swap payment is made. There is no uncertainty about what the floating-rate payment will be. In general, the floating-rate payment is determined as follows:

$$\text{notional amount} \times (\text{three-month LIBOR}) \times \frac{\text{no. of days in period}}{360}$$

In our illustration, assuming a non-leap year, the number of days from January 1 of year 1 to March 31 of year 1 (the first quarter) is 90. If three-month LIBOR is 4.05%, then the fixed-rate payer will receive a floating-rate payment on March 31 of year 1 equal to

$$\$100,000,000 \times 0.0405 \times \frac{90}{360} = \$1,012,500$$

Now the difficulty is in determining the floating-rate payment after the first quarterly payment. That is, for the three-year swap there will be 12 quarterly floating-rate payments. So, while the first quarterly payment is known, the next 11 are not. However, there is a way to hedge the next 11 floating-rate payments by using a futures contract. Specifically, the futures contract used to hedge the future floating-rate payments in a swap whose reference rate is three-month LIBOR is the Eurodollar futures contract. We discussed this contract in Chapter 26, and we will show how these floating-rate payments are computed using this contract.

---

[2] This illustration is taken from Frank J. Fabozzi, *Fixed Income Analysis for the Chartered Financial Analyst Program* (New Hope, PA: Frank J. Fabozzi Associates, 2000), pp. 609–621.

We begin with the next quarterly payment—from April 1 of year 1 to June 30 of year 1. This quarter has 91 days. The floating-rate payment will be determined by three-month LIBOR on April 1 of year 1 and paid on June 30 of year 1. There is a three-month Eurodollar futures contract for settlement on June 30 of year 1. That futures contract provides the rate that can be locked in for three-month LIBOR on April 1 of year 1. For example, if the futures price for the three-month Eurodollar futures contract that settles on June 30 of year 1 is 95.85, then as just explained, the three-month Eurodollar futures rate is 4.15%. We will refer to that rate for three-month LIBOR as the forward rate. Therefore, if the fixed-rate payer bought 100 of these three-month Eurodollar futures contracts on January 1 of year 1 (the inception of the swap) that settle on June 30 of year 1, then the payment that will be locked in for the quarter (April 1 to June 30 of year 1) is

$$\$100,000,000 \times 0.0415 \times \frac{91}{360} = \$1,049,028$$

(Note that each futures contract is for $1 million and hence 100 contracts have a notional amount of $100 million.) Similarly, the Eurodollar futures contract can be used to lock in a floating-rate payment for each of the next 10 quarters. It is important to emphasize that the reference rate at the beginning of period t determines the floating rate that will be paid for the period. However, the floating-rate payment is not made until the end of period t.

Exhibit 28-3 shows this for the three-year swap. Shown in column (1) is when the quarter begins and in column (2) when the quarter ends. The payment will be received at the end of the first quarter (March 31 of year 1) and is $1,012,500. That is the known floating-rate payment as explained earlier. It is the only payment that is known. The information

Exhibit 28-3 Floating Cash Flow Based on Initial LIBOR and Eurodollar Futures

(1) Quarter Starts	(2) Quarter Ends	(3) Number of Days in Quarter	(4) Current 3-Month LIBOR	(5) Euro-dollar Futures Price	(6) Futures Rate	(7) Period = End of Quarter	(8) Floating Cash Flow at End of Quarter
Jan 1 year 1	Mar 31 year 1	90	4.05%			1	1,012,500
Apr 1 year 1	June 30 year 1	91		95.85	4.15%	2	1,049,028
July 1 year 1	Sept 30 year 1	92		95.45	4.55%	3	1,162,778
Oct 1 year 1	Dec 31 year 1	92		95.28	4.72%	4	1,206,222
Jan 1 year 2	Mar 31 year 2	90		95.10	4.90%	5	1,225,000
Apr 1 year 2	June 30 year 2	91		94.97	5.03%	6	1,271,472
July 1 year 2	Sept 30 year 2	92		94.85	5.15%	7	1,316,111
Oct 1 year 2	Dec 31 year 2	92		94.75	5.25%	8	1,341,667
Jan 1 year 3	Mar 31 year 3	90		94.60	5.40%	9	1,350,000
Apr 1 year 3	June 30 year 3	91		94.50	5.50%	10	1,390,278
July 1 year 3	Sept 30 year 3	92		94.35	5.65%	11	1,443,889
Oct 1 year 3	Dec 31 year 3	92		94.24	5.76%	12	1,472,000

used to compute the first payment is in column (4), which shows the current three-month LIBOR (4.05%). The payment is shown in the last column, column (8).

Notice that column (7) numbers the quarters from 1 through 12. Look at the heading for column (7). It identifies each quarter in terms of the end of the quarter. This is important because we will eventually be discounting the payments (cash flows). We must take care to understand when each payment is to be exchanged in order to properly discount. So, the first payment of $1,012,500 will be received at the end of quarter 1. When we refer to the time period for any payment, the reference is to the end of the quarter. So, the fifth payment of $1,225,000 would be identified as the payment for period 5, where period 5 means that it will be exchanged at the end of the fifth quarter.

Now let's turn to the fixed-rate payments. The swap will specify the frequency of settlement for these payments. The frequency need not be the same as the floating-rate payments. For example, in the three-year swap we have been using to illustrate the calculation of the floating-rate payments, the frequency is quarterly. The frequency of the fixed-rate payments could be semiannual rather than quarterly.

In our illustration, we will assume that the frequency of settlement is quarterly for the fixed-rate payments, the same as with the floating-rate payments. The day count convention is the same as for the floating-rate payment, actual/360. The equation for determining the dollar amount of the fixed-rate payment for the period is

$$\text{notional amount} \times \text{swap rate} \times \frac{\text{no. of days in period}}{360}$$

It is the same equation as for determining the floating-rate payment except that the swap rate is used instead of the reference rate (three-month LIBOR in our illustration).

For example, suppose that the swap rate is 4.98% and the quarter has 90 days. Then the fixed-rate payment for the quarter is

$$\$100,000,000 \times 0.0498 \times \frac{90}{360} = \$1,245,000$$

Exhibit 28-4 shows the fixed-rate payments based on an assumed swap rate of 4.9875%. (Later, we will see how the swap rate is determined.) The first three columns of the exhibit show the same information as in Exhibit 28-3—the beginning and end of the quarter and the number of days in the quarter. Column (4) simply uses the notation for the period. That is, period 1 means the end of the first quarter, period 2 means the end of the second quarter, and so on. Column (5) shows the fixed-rate payments for each period based on a swap rate of 4.9875%.

Given the swap payments, we can demonstrate how to compute the swap rate. At the initiation of an interest-rate swap, the counterparties are agreeing to exchange future payments and no upfront payments by either party are made. This means that the swap terms must be such that the present value of the payments to be made by the counterparties must be at least equal to the present value of the payments that will be received. In fact, to eliminate arbitrage opportunities, the present value of the payments made by a party will be equal to the present value of the payments received by that same party. The equivalence (or no arbitrage) of the present value of the payments is the key principle in calculating the swap rate.

Since we will have to calculate the present value of the payments, let's show how this is done. As explained earlier, we must be careful about how we compute the present value

Exhibit 28-4 Fixed-Rate Payments Assuming a Swap Rate of 4.9875%

Quarter Starts	Quarter Ends	Days in Quarter	Period = End of Quarter	Fixed-Rate Payment If Swap Rate Is Assumed to Be 4.9875%
Jan 1 year 1	Mar 31 year 1	90	1	1,246,875
Apr 1 year 1	June 30 year 1	91	2	1,260,729
July 1 year 1	Sept 30 year 1	92	3	1,274,583
Oct 1 year 1	Dec 31 year 1	92	4	1,274,583
Jan 1 year 2	Mar 31 year 2	90	5	1,246,875
Apr 1 year 2	June 30 year 2	91	6	1,260,729
July 1 year 2	Sept 30 year 2	92	7	1,274,583
Oct 1 year 2	Dec 31 year 2	92	8	1,274,583
Jan 1 year 3	Mar 31 year 3	90	9	1,246,875
Apr 1 year 3	June 30 year 3	91	10	1,260,729
July 1 year 3	Sept 30 year 3	92	11	1,274,583
Oct 1 year 3	Dec 31 year 3	92	12	1,274,583

of payments. In particular, we must carefully specify (1) the timing of the payment, and (2) the interest rates that should be used to discount the payments. We already addressed the first issue.

In constructing the exhibit for the payments, we indicated that the payments are at the end of the quarter. So, we denoted the timing of the payments with respect to the end of the quarter.

What interest rates should be used for discounting? Every cash flow should be discounted at its own discount rate using a spot rate. So, if we discounted a cash flow of $1 using the spot rate for period t, the present value would be

$$\text{present value of \$1 to be received in } t \text{ period} = \frac{\$1}{(1 + \text{spot rate for period } t)^t}$$

As explained in Chapter 5, forward rates are derived from spot rates so that if we discounted a cash flow using forward rates rather than a spot rate, we would come up with the same value. That is, the present value of $1 to be received in period t, can be rewritten as

$$\text{present value of \$1 to be received in period } t =$$

$$\frac{\$1}{(1 + \text{forward rate for period 1})(1 + \text{forward rate for period 2})\cdots(1 + \text{forward rate for period } t)}$$

We will refer to the present value of $1 to be received in period t as the **forward discount factor**. In our calculations involving swaps, we will compute the forward discount factor for a period using the forward rates. These are the same forward rates that are used to compute the floating-rate payments—those obtained from the Eurodollar futures contract. We must make just one more adjustment. We must adjust the forward rates used in the formula for the number of days in the period (i.e., the quarter in our illustrations) in the same way that we made this adjustment to obtain the payments. Specifically, the forward rate for a period, which we will refer to as the **period forward rate**, is computed using the following equation:

$$\text{period forward rate} = \text{annual forward rate} \times \frac{\text{days in period}}{360}$$

For example, look at Exhibit 28-3. The annual forward rate for period 4 is 4.72%. The period forward rate for period 4 is

$$\text{period forward rate} = 4.72\% \times \frac{92}{360} = 1.2062\%$$

Column (5) in Exhibit 28-5 shows the annual forward rate for all 12 periods (reproduced from Exhibit 28-3) and column (6) shows the period forward rate for all 12 periods. Note that the period forward rate for period 1 is 90/360 of 4.05%, which is 90/360 of the known rate for three-month LIBOR.

Also shown in Exhibit 28-5 is the forward discount factor for all 12 periods. These values are shown in the last column. Let's show how the forward discount factor is computed for periods 1, 2, and 3. For period 1, the forward discount factor is

$$\text{forward discount factor} = \frac{\$1}{1.010125} = 0.9899764$$

For period 2,

$$\text{forward discount factor} = \frac{\$1}{1.010125 \times 1.010490} = 0.9796991$$

Exhibit 28-5   Calculating the Forward Discount

(1) Quarter Starts	(2) Quarter Ends	(3) Number of Days in Quarter	(4) Period = End of Quarter	(5) Forward Rate	(6) Period Forward Rate	(7) Forward Discount Factor
Jan 1 year 1	Mar 31 year 1	90	1	4.05%	1.0125%	0.9899764
Apr 1 year 1	June 30 year 1	91	2	4.15%	1.0490%	0.9796991
July 1 year 1	Sept 30 year 1	92	3	4.55%	1.1628%	0.9684383
Oct 1 year 1	Dec 31 year 1	92	4	4.72%	1.2062%	0.9568960
Jan 1 year 2	Mar 31 year 2	90	5	4.90%	1.2250%	0.9453159
Apr 1 year 2	June 30 year 2	91	6	5.03%	1.2715%	0.9334474
July 1 year 2	Sept 30 year 2	92	7	5.15%	1.3161%	0.9213218
Oct 1 year 2	Dec 31 year 2	92	8	5.25%	1.3417%	0.9091244
Jan 1 year 3	Mar 31 year 3	90	9	5.40%	1.3500%	0.8970147
Apr 1 year 3	June 30 year 3	91	10	5.50%	1.3903%	0.8847147
July 1 year 3	Sept 30 year 3	92	11	5.65%	1.4439%	0.8721222
Oct 1 year 3	Dec 31 year 3	92	12	5.76%	1.4720%	0.8594708

For period 3,

$$\text{forward discount factor} = \frac{\$1}{1.010125 \times 1.010490 \times 1.011628} = 0.9684383$$

Given the floating-rate payment for a period and the forward discount factor for the period, the present value of the payment can be computed. For example, from Exhibit 28-3 we see that the floating-rate payment for period 4 is $1,206,222. From Exhibit 28-6, the forward discount factor for period 4 is 0.9568960. Therefore, the present value of the payment is

$$\text{present value of period 4 payment} = \$1,206,222 \times 0.9568960 = \$1,154,229$$

Exhibit 28-6 shows the present value for each payment. The total present value of the 12 floating-rate payments is $14,052,917. Thus, the present value of the payments that the fixed-rate payer will receive is $14,052,917, and the present value of the payments that the fixed-rate receiver will make is $14,052,917.

The fixed-rate payer will require that the present value of the fixed-rate payments that must be made based on the swap rate not exceed the $14,052,917 to be received from the floating-rate payments. The fixed-rate receiver will require that the present value of the fixed-rate payments received be at least as great as the $14,052,917 that must be paid. This means that both parties will require a present value for the fixed-rate payments to be $14,052,917. If that is the case, the present value of the fixed-rate payments is equal to the present value of the floating-rate payments and, therefore, the value of the swap is zero for both parties at the inception of the swap. The interest rates that should be used to compute

Exhibit 28-6 Present Value of the Floating-Rate Payments

(1) Quarter Starts	(2) Quarter Ends	(3) Period = End of Quarter	(4) Forward Discount Factor	(5) Floating Cash Flow at End of Quarter	(6) PV of Cash Flow
Jan 1 year 1	Mar 31 year 1	1	0.9899764	1,012,500	1,002,351
Apr 1 year 1	June 30 year 1	2	0.9796991	1,049,028	1,027,732
July 1 year 1	Sept 30 year 1	3	0.9684383	1,162,778	1,126,079
Oct 1 year 1	Dec 31 year 1	4	0.9568960	1,206,222	1,154,229
Jan 1 year 2	Mar 31 year 2	5	0.9453159	1,225,000	1,158,012
Apr 1 year 2	June 30 year 2	6	0.9334474	1,271,472	1,186,852
July 1 year 2	Sept 30 year 2	7	0.9213218	1,316,111	1,212,562
Oct 1 year 2	Dec 31 year 2	8	0.9091244	1,341,667	1,219,742
Jan 1 year 3	Mar 31 year 3	9	0.8970147	1,350,000	1,210,970
Apr 1 year 3	June 30 year 3	10	0.8847147	1,390,278	1,229,999
July 1 year 3	Sept 30 year 3	11	0.8721222	1,443,889	1,259,248
Oct 1 year 3	Dec 31 year 3	12	0.8594708	1,472,000	1,265,141
				Total	14,052,917

the present value of the fixed-rate payments are the same interest rates as those used to discount the floating-rate payments.

Beginning with the basic relationship for no arbitrage to exist,

$$\text{PV of floating-rate payments} = \text{PV of fixed rate payments}$$

The formula for the swap rate is derived as follows. The fixed-rate payment for period t is equal to

$$\text{notional amount} \times \text{swap rate} \times \frac{\text{days in period } t}{360}$$

The present value of the fixed-rate payment for period t is found by multiplying the previous expression by the forward discount factor for period t. That is, the present value of the fixed-rate payment for period t is equal to

$$\text{notional amount} \times \text{swap rate} \times \frac{\text{days in period } t}{360} \times \text{forward discount factor for period } t$$

Summing up the present value of the fixed-rate payment for each period gives the present value of the fixed-rate payments. Letting N be the number of periods in the swap, the present value of the fixed-rate payments can be expressed as

$$\text{swap rate} \times \sum_{t=1}^{N} \text{notional amount} \times \frac{\text{days in period } t}{360} \times \text{forward discount factor for period } t$$

The condition for no arbitrage is that the present value of the fixed-rate payments as given by the preceding expression is equal to the present value of the floating-rate payments. That is,

$$\text{swap rate} \times \sum_{t=1}^{N} \text{notional amount} \times \frac{\text{days in period } t}{360} \times \text{forward discount factor for period } t$$

$$= \text{present value of floating-rate payments}$$

Solving for the swap rate gives

$$\text{swap rate} = \frac{\text{present value of floating-rate payments}}{\sum_{t=1}^{N} \text{notional amount} \times \frac{\text{days in period } t}{360} \times \text{forward discount factor for period } t}$$

Note that all the values to compute the swap rate are known.

Let's apply the formula to determine the swap rate for our three-year swap. Exhibit 28-7 shows the calculation of the denominator of the formula. The forward discount factor for each period shown in column (5) is obtained from column (4) of Exhibit 28-6. The sum of the last column in Exhibit 28-7 shows that the denominator of the swap rate formula is \$281,764,281. We know from Exhibit 28-6 that the present value of the floating-rate payments is \$14,052,917. Therefore, the swap rate is

$$\text{swap rate} = \frac{\$14,052,917}{\$281,764,281} = 0.049875 = 4.9875\%$$

Given the swap rate, the swap spread can be determined. For example, since this is a three-year swap, the convention is to use the three-year on-the-run Treasury rate as

Exhibit 28-7 Calculating the Denominator for the Swap Rate Formula

(1)	(2)	(3)	(4)	(5)	(6)	(7)
Quarter Starts	Quarter Ends	Number of Days in Quarter	Period = End of Quarter	Forward Discount Factor	Days/360 × Notional	Forward Discount Factor × Days/360
Jan 1 year 1	Mar 31 year 1	90	1	0.98997649	0.25000000	24,749,412
Apr 1 year 1	June 30 year 1	91	2	0.97969917	0.25277778	24,764,618
July 1 year 1	Sept 30 year 1	92	3	0.96843839	0.25555556	24,748,981
Oct 1 year 1	Dec 31 year 1	92	4	0.95689609	0.25555556	24,454,011
Jan 1 year 2	Mar 31 year 2	90	5	0.94531597	0.25000000	23,632,899
Apr 1 year 2	June 30 year 2	91	6	0.93344745	0.25277778	23,595,477
July 1 year 2	Sept 30 year 2	92	7	0.92132183	0.25555556	23,544,891
Oct 1 year 2	Dec 31 year 2	92	8	0.90912441	0.25555556	23,233,179
Jan 1 year 3	Mar 31 year 3	90	9	0.89701471	0.25000000	22,425,368
Apr 1 year 3	June 30 year 3	91	10	0.88471472	0.25277778	22,363,622
July 1 year 3	Sept 30 year 3	92	11	0.87212224	0.25555556	22,287,568
Oct 1 year 3	Dec 31 year 3	92	12	0.85947083	0.25555556	21,964,255
					Total	281,764,281

the benchmark. If the yield on that issue is 4.5875%, the swap spread is 40 basis points (4.9875% − 4.5875%).

The calculation of the swap rate for all swaps follows the same principle: equating the present value of the fixed-rate payments to that of the floating-rate payments.

Valuing a Swap

Once the swap transaction is completed, changes in market interest rates will change the payments of the floating-rate side of the swap. The value of an interest rate swap is the difference between the present value of the payments of the two sides of the swap. Three-month LIBOR forward rates from the current Eurodollar futures contracts are used to (1) calculate the floating-rate payments, and (2) determine the discount factors at which to calculate the present value of the payments.

To illustrate this, consider the three-year swap used to demonstrate how to calculate the swap rate. Suppose that one year later, interest rates change as shown in columns (4) and (6) in Exhibit 28-8. Column (4) shows the current three-month LIBOR. In column (5) are the Eurodollar futures prices for each period. These rates are used to compute the forward rates in column (6). Note that the interest rates have increased one year later since the rates in Exhibit 28-8 are greater than those in Exhibit 28-3. As in Exhibit 28-3, the current three-month LIBOR and the forward rates are used to compute the floating-rate payments. These payments are shown in column (8) of Exhibit 28-8.

In Exhibit 28-9, the forward discount factor is computed for each period. The calculation is the same as in Exhibit 28-5 to obtain the forward discount factor for each period. The forward discount factor for each period is shown in the last column of Exhibit 28-9.

Exhibit 28-8   Rates and Floating-Rate Payments One Year Later If Rates Increase

(1)	(2)	(3)	(4)	(5)	(6)	(7)	(8)
Quarter Starts	Quarter Ends	Number of Days in Quarter	Current 3-Month LIBOR	Euro-dollar Futures Price	Futures Rate	Period = End of Quarter	Floating Cash Flow at End of Quarter
Jan 1 year 2	Mar 31 year 2	90	5.25%			1	1,312,500
Apr 1 year 2	June 30 year 2	91		94.27	5.73%	2	1,448,417
July 1 year 2	Sept 30 year 2	92		94.22	5.78%	3	1,477,111
Oct 1 year 2	Dec 31 year 2	92		94.00	6.00%	4	1,533,333
Jan 1 year 3	Mar 31 year 3	90		93.85	6.15%	5	1,537,500
Apr 1 year 3	June 30 year 3	91		93.75	6.25%	6	1,579,861
July 1 year 3	Sept 30 year 3	92		93.54	6.46%	7	1,650,889
Oct 1 year 3	Dec 31 year 3	92		93.25	6.75%	8	1,725,000

Exhibit 28-9   Period Forward Rates and Forward Discount Factors One Year Later If Rates Increase

(1)	(2)	(3)	(4)	(5)	(6)	(7)
Quarter Starts	Quarter Ends	Number of Days in Quarter	Period = End of Quarter	Futures Rate	Period Forward Rate	Forward Discount Factor
Jan 1 year 2	Mar 31 year 2	90	1	5.25%	1.3125%	0.98704503
Apr 1 year 2	June 30 year 2	91	2	5.73%	1.4484%	0.97295263
July 1 year 2	Sept 30 year 2	92	3	5.78%	1.4771%	0.95879023
Oct 1 year 2	Dec 31 year 2	92	4	6.00%	1.5333%	0.94431080
Jan 1 year 3	Mar 31 year 3	90	5	6.15%	1.5375%	0.93001186
Apr 1 year 3	June 30 year 3	91	6	6.25%	1.5799%	0.91554749
July 1 year 3	Sept 30 year 3	92	7	6.46%	1.6509%	0.90067829
Oct 1 year 3	Dec 31 year 3	92	8	6.75%	1.7250%	0.88540505

In Exhibit 28-10, the forward discount factor (from Exhibit 28-9) and the floating-rate payments (from Exhibit 28-8) are shown. The fixed-rate payments need not be recomputed. They are the payments shown in Exhibit 28-4 for the swap rate of 4.9875%, and they are reproduced in Exhibit 28-10. Now the two payment streams must be discounted using the new forward discount factors. As shown at the bottom of Exhibit 28-10, the two present values are as follows:

Present value of floating-rate payments	$11,459,496
Present value of fixed-rate payments	$ 9,473,392

Exhibit 28-10 Valuing the Swap One Year Later If Rates Increase

(1)	(2)	(3)	(4)	(5)	(6)	(7)
Quarter Starts	Quarter Ends	Forward Discount Factor	Floating Cash Flow at End of Quarter	PV of Floating Cash Flow	Fixed Cash Flow at End of Quarter	PV of Fixed Cash Flow
Jan 1 year 2	Mar 31 year 2	0.98704503	1,312,500	1,295,497	1,246,875	1,230,722
Apr 1 year 2	June 30 year 2	0.97295263	1,448,417	1,409,241	1,260,729	1,226,630
July 1 year 2	Sept 30 year 2	0.95879023	1,477,111	1,416,240	1,274,583	1,222,058
Oct 1 year 2	Dec 31 year 2	0.94431080	1,533,333	1,447,943	1,274,583	1,203,603
Jan 1 year 3	Mar 31 year 3	0.93001186	1,537,500	1,429,893	1,246,875	1,159,609
Apr 1 year 3	June 30 year 3	0.91554749	1,579,861	1,446,438	1,260,729	1,154,257
July 1 year 3	Sept 30 year 3	0.90067829	1,650,889	1,486,920	1,274,583	1,147,990
Oct 1 year 3	Dec 31 year 3	0.88540505	1,725,000	1,527,324	1,274,583	1,128,523
			Total	11,459,496		9,473,392

Summary	Fixed-Rate Payer	Fixed-Rate Receiver
PV of payments received	11,459,496	9,473,392
PV of payments made	9,473,392	11,459,496
Value of swap	1,986,104	−1,986,104

The two present values are not equal; therefore, for one party the value of the swap increased while for the other party the value of the swap decreased. Let's look at which party gained and which party lost.

The fixed-rate payer will receive the floating-rate payments. These payments have a present value of $11,459,496. The present value of the payments that must be made by the fixed-rate payer is $9,473,392. Thus, the swap has a positive value for the fixed-rate payer equal to the difference in the two present values of $1,986,104. This is the value of the swap to the fixed-rate payer. Notice that when interest rates increase (as they did in the illustration analyzed), the fixed-rate payer benefits because the value of the swap increases.

In contrast, the fixed-rate receiver must make payments with a present value of $11,459,496 but will only receive fixed-rate payments with a present value equal to $9,473,392. Thus, the value of the swap for the fixed-rate receiver is −$1,986,104. The fixed-rate receiver is adversely affected by a rise in interest rates because it results in a decline in the value of a swap.

The same valuation principle applies to more complicated swaps that we describe later in this section.

Duration of a Swap

As with any fixed-income contract, the value of a swap will change as interest rates change. Dollar duration is a measure of the interest-rate sensitivity of a fixed-income contract. From the perspective of the party who pays floating and receives fixed, the interest-rate swap position can be viewed as follows: long a fixed-rate bond + short a floating-rate bond. This means that the dollar duration of an interest-rate swap from the perspective of a fixed-rate receiver is simply the difference between the dollar duration of the two bond positions that make up the swap; that is,

$$\text{dollar duration of a swap} = \text{dollar duration of a fixed-rate bond}$$
$$- \text{dollar duration of a floating-rate bond}$$

Most of the dollar price sensitivity of a swap due to interest-rate changes will result from the dollar duration of the fixed-rate bond because the dollar duration of the floating-rate bond will be small. The closer the swap is to the date that the coupon rate is reset, the smaller the dollar duration of a floating-rate bond.

The implication here is that to increase the dollar duration of a portfolio, a manager should enter into a swap as the fixed-rate receiver. This is economically equivalent to leveraging the interest rate risk exposure of the portfolio and thereby adding dollar duration. By entering into a swap as the fixed-rate payer, instead, the manager reduces the dollar duration of the portfolio.

Application to Portfolio Risk Control

In Chapter 26, we explained how to use futures to alter the risk exposure of a portfolio to changes in interest rates (i.e., alter a portfolio's duration). Earlier in this chapter we explained how an interest-rate swap is equivalent to a portfolio of forward/futures contracts. Therefore, it should be no surprise that interest-rate swaps can be used to provide the same duration-adjustment mechanism as futures contracts as illustrated in Chapter 26. In our explanation of the duration of an interest-rate swap, we described how a position in a swap can either increase dollar duration (by being a fixed-rate receiver) or decrease dollar duration (by being a fixed-rate payer).

Let's illustrate the use of how an interest-rate swap can be used to alter the duration of a portfolio. We will use the example in Chapter 26 for the portfolio shown in Exhibit 26-3. Here is a recap of the situation. The manager of a portfolio with a market value as of March 31, 2011, of $48,109,810 has a benchmark that is the Barclays Capital Intermediate Aggregate Index. On March 31, 2011, the duration of the index and the portfolio were 3.68 and 2.97, respectively. The manager wants to restructure the portfolio so that the portfolio's duration matches that of the benchmark. That is, the portfolio manager seeks to follow a duration-neutral strategy and therefore the portfolio's target duration is 3.68. We know that for a 100 basis point change in rates:

portfolio target dollar duration = 3.68% × $48,109,810 = $1,770,441
portfolio current dollar duration = 2.97% × $48,109,810 = $1,428,861

The difference between the target and the current dollar duration for the portfolio is $341,580. This means that to get to the target portfolio duration of 3.68, the portfolio manager must increase the dollar duration of the current portfolio by $341,580 for a 100 basis change in interest rates.

On March 31, 2011, the manager decides to use a 5-year interest-rate at-the-money (i.e., par) swap. The swap rate is 2.42%. Since the objective is to increase the dollar duration, this involves the manager entering into a swap as the fixed-rate receiver. It can be shown that the dollar duration for a notional amount of $7,699,779 is $340,881. Hence a 5-year interest-rate swap with that notional amount combined with the current portfolio will result in a new dollar duration for the portfolio of $1,769,475, which is close to the target dollar duration needed to obtain a portfolio duration of 3.68.

Application of a Swap to Asset/Liability Management

So far, we have merely described an interest-rate swap and looked at its characteristics. Here, we illustrate how they can be used in asset/liability management. Other types of interest-rate swaps have been developed that go beyond the generic or "plain vanilla" swap described, and we describe these later.

An interest-rate swap can be used to alter the cash flow characteristics of an institution's assets so as to provide a better match between assets and liabilities. The two institutions we use for illustration are a commercial bank and a life insurance company.

Suppose that a bank has a portfolio consisting of five-year term commercial loans with a fixed interest rate. The principal value of the portfolio is $50 million, and the interest rate on all the loans in the portfolio is 10%. The loans are interest-only loans; interest is paid semiannually, and the principal is paid at the end of five years. That is, assuming no default on the loans, the cash flow from the loan portfolio is $2.5 million every six months for the next five years and $50 million at the end of five years. To fund its loan portfolio, assume that the bank is relying on the issuance of six-month certificates of deposit. The interest rate that the bank plans to pay on its six-month CDs is six-month LIBOR plus 40 basis points.

The risk that the bank faces is that six-month LIBOR will be 9.6% or greater. To understand why, remember that the bank is earning 10% annually on its commercial loan portfolio. If six-month LIBOR is 9.6%, it will have to pay 9.6% plus 40 basis points, or 10%, to depositors for six-month funds and there will be no spread income. Worse, if six-month LIBOR rises above 9.6%, there will be a loss; that is, the cost of funds will exceed the interest rate earned on the loan portfolio. The bank's objective is to lock in a spread over the cost of its funds.

The other party in the interest-rate-swap illustration is a life insurance company that has committed itself to pay a 9% rate for the next five years on a guaranteed investment contract (GIC) it has issued. The amount of the GIC is $50 million. Suppose that the life insurance company has the opportunity to invest $50 million in what it considers an attractive five-year floating-rate instrument in a private placement transaction. The interest rate on this instrument is six-month LIBOR plus 160 basis points. The coupon rate is set every six months. The risk that the life insurance company faces in this instance is that six-month LIBOR will fall so that the company will not earn enough to realize a spread over the 9% rate that it has guaranteed to the GIC holders. If six-month LIBOR falls to 7.4% or less, no spread income will be generated. To understand why, suppose that six-month LIBOR at the date the floating-rate instrument resets its coupon is 7.4%. Then the coupon rate for the next six months will be 9% (7.4% plus 160 basis points). Because the life insurance company has agreed to pay 9% on the GIC policy, there will be no spread income. Should six-month LIBOR fall below 7.4%, there will be a loss.

We can summarize the asset/liability problems of the bank and the life insurance company as follows:

BANK:

1. Has lent long term and borrowed short term.
2. If six-month LIBOR rises, spread income declines.

LIFE INSURANCE COMPANY:

1. Has lent short term and borrowed long term.
2. If six-month LIBOR falls, spread income declines.

Now let's suppose the market has available a five-year interest-rate swap with a notional principal amount of $50 million. The swap terms available to the bank are as follows:

1. Every six months the bank will pay 8.45% (annual rate).
2. Every six months the bank will receive LIBOR.

The swap terms available to the insurance company are as follows:

1. Every six months the life insurance company will pay LIBOR.
2. Every six months the life insurance company will receive 8.40%.

What has this interest-rate contract done for the bank and the life insurance company? Consider first the bank. For every six-month period for the life of the swap agreement, the interest-rate spread will be as follows:

Annual Interest Rate Received:	
From commercial loan portfolio	10.00%
From interest-rate swap	six-month LIBOR
Total	10.00% + six-month LIBOR
Annual Interest Rate Paid:	
To CD depositors	six-month LIBOR
On interest-rate swap	8.45%
Total	8.45% + six-month LIBOR
Outcome:	
To be received	10.00% + six-month LIBOR
To be paid	8.45% + six-month LIBOR
Spread income	1.55% or 1.55 basis points

Thus, whatever happens to six-month LIBOR, the bank locks in a spread of 155 basis points. Now let's look at the effect of the interest-rate swap on the life insurance company:

Annual Interest Rate Received:	
From floating-rate instrument	1.6% + six-month LIBOR
From interest-rate swap	8.40%
Total	10.00% + six-month LIBOR
Annual Interest Rate Paid:	
To GIC policyholders	9.00%
On interest-rate swap	six-month LIBOR
Total	9.00% + six-month LIBOR
Outcome:	
To be received	10.00% + six-month LIBOR
To be paid	9.00% + six-month LIBOR
Spread income	1.0% or 100 basis points

Regardless of what happens to six-month LIBOR, the life insurance company locks in a spread of 100 basis points.

The interest-rate swap has allowed each party to accomplish its asset/liability objective of locking in a spread.[3] It permits the two financial institutions to alter the cash flow characteristics of their assets: from fixed to floating in the case of the bank, and from floating to fixed in the case of the life insurance company. This type of transaction is referred to as an **asset swap**. Another way the bank and the life insurance company could use the swap market would be to change the cash flow nature of their liabilities. Such a swap is called a **liability swap**.

Of course, there are other ways that two such institutions can accomplish the same objectives. The bank might refuse to make fixed-rate commercial loans. However, if borrowers can find someplace else willing to lend on a fixed-rate basis, the bank has lost these customers. The life insurance company might refuse to purchase a floating-rate instrument. But suppose that the terms on a private-placement instrument offered to the life insurance company were more attractive than those available on a comparable-credit-risk floating-rate instrument, and that by using the swap market the life insurance company can earn more than it could by investing directly in a five-year fixed-rate bond. For example, suppose that the life insurance company can invest in a comparable-credit-risk five-year fixed-rate bond with a yield of 9.8%. Assuming that it commits itself to a GIC with a 9% rate, this would result in spread income of 80 basis points, less than the 100-basis-point spread income it achieves by purchasing the floating-rate instrument and entering into the swap.

Consequently, not only can an interest-rate swap be used to change the risk of a transaction by changing the cash flow characteristics of assets or liabilities, but under certain circumstances, it can also be used to enhance returns. Obviously, this depends on the existence of market imperfections.

Creation of Structured Notes Using Swaps

As explained in Chapter 7, corporations can customize medium-term notes for institutional investors who want to make a market play on interest rate, currency, and/or stock market movements. That is, the coupon rate on the issue will be based on the movements of these financial variables. A corporation can do so in such a way that it can still synthetically fix the coupon rate. This can be accomplished by issuing an MTN and entering into a swap simultaneously. MTNs created in this way are called **structured MTNs**.

The following illustration demonstrates how an interest-rate swap can be used to create a structured note in which the coupon rate floats inversely with LIBOR; that is, an inverse floater. As we explained in Chapter 8, an inverse floater can be created from a fixed-rate security by creating a corresponding floater. By using an interest-rate swap, it is not necessary to create the floater.

To see how this can be done using an interest-rate swap, let's assume the following. The Arbour Corporation wants to issue $100 million of a five-year fixed-rate MTN. The firm's banker indicates that the yield it would have to offer is 6.10%. However, it recommends that the corporation issue an inverse-floating-rate MTN and proposes the following two transactions:

Transaction 1: Issue $100 million of a five-year inverse-floating-rate MTN with a coupon payment that resets every six months based on the following formula: 13% – LIBOR.

---

[3] Whether the size of the spread is adequate is not an issue for us in this illustration.

Transaction 2: Enter into a five-year interest-rate swap with its banker with a notional principal amount of $100 million in which semiannual payments are exchanged as follows:

Arbour Corporation pays LIBOR.

Arbour Corporation receives 7%.

Notice that Arbour Corporation's MTN is an inverse-floating-rate note because as LIBOR increases, the coupon rate decreases. However, although the MTN may have an inverse floating rate, the combination of the two transactions results in a fixed-rate financing for Arbour Corporation, as follows:

Arbour Corporation Receives:	
From its banker for swap	7%
Arbour Corporation Pays:	
To MTN holders	13% − LIBOR
To its banker for swap	LIBOR
Net payments:	(13% − LIBOR) + LIBOR − 7% = 6%

The advantage of this structured MTN is that the issuer was able to obtain a funding cost of 6% rather than 6.1% if it issued a fixed-rate MTN. By using other types of swaps (equity and currency), any type of coupon rate can be created.

Variants of the Generic Interest-Rate Swap

Thus far, we have described the plain vanilla or generic interest-rate swap. Nongeneric or individualized swaps have evolved as a result of the asset/liability needs of borrowers and lenders. These include swaps where the notional principal changes in a pre-determined way over the life of the swap and swaps in which both counterparties pay a floating rate. There are complex swap structures such as options on swaps (called **swaptions**) and swaps where the swap does not begin until some future time (called **forward start swaps**). We discuss all of these swaps next.[4] What is important to appreciate is that these swap structures are not just "bells and whistles" added to the plain vanilla swap to make them more complicated, but features that managers have found that they need to control interest-rate risk.

Varying Notional Principal Amount Swaps

In a generic or plain vanilla swap, the notional principal amount does not vary over the life of the swap. Thus, it is sometimes referred to as a **bullet swap**. In contrast, for amortizing, accreting, and roller coaster swaps, the notional principal amount varies over the life of the swap.

An **amortizing swap** is one in which the notional principal amount decreases in a predetermined way over the life of the swap. Such a swap would be used where the principal of the asset that is being hedged with the swap amortizes over time. For example, in our illustration of the asset/liability problem faced by the bank, the commercial loans are assumed to pay interest every six months and repay principal only at the end of the loan

---

[4] See Geoffrey Buetow, Jr., and Frank J. Fabozzi, *Valuation of Interest Rate Swaps and Swaptions* (New Hope, PA: Frank J. Fabozzi Associates, 2001).

term. However, what if the commercial loan is a typical term loan; that is, suppose it is a loan that amortizes. Or, suppose that it is a typical mortgage loan that amortizes. In such circumstances, the outstanding principal for the loans would decline and the bank would need a swap where the notional principal amount amortizes in the same way as the loans.

Less common than the amortizing swap are the accreting swap and the roller coaster swap. An **accreting swap** is one in which the notional principal amount increases in a predetermined way over time. In a **roller coaster swap**, the notional principal amount can rise or fall from period to period.

Basis Swaps and Constant Maturity Swaps

The terms of a generic interest-rate swap call for the exchange of fixed- and floating-rate payments. In a **basis swap**, both parties exchange floating-rate payments based on a different reference rate. As an example, assume a commercial bank has a portfolio of loans in which the lending rate is based on the prime rate, but the bank's cost of funds is based on LIBOR. The risk the bank faces is that the spread between the prime rate and LIBOR will change. This is referred to as **basis risk**. The bank can use a basis swap to make floating-rate payments based on the prime rate (because that is the reference rate that determines how much the bank is receiving on the loans) and receive floating-rate payments based on LIBOR (because that is the reference rate that determines the bank's funding cost).

Another popular swap is to have the floating leg tied to a longer-term rate such as the two-year Treasury note rate rather than a money market rate. One of the parties to the swap would pay the two-year Treasury rate, for example, and the counterparty would pay LIBOR. Such a swap is called a **constant maturity swap**. The reference rate for determining the yield on the constant maturity Treasury in a constant maturity swap is typically the Constant Maturity Treasury (CMT) rate published by the Federal Reserve. Consequently, a constant maturity swap tied to the CMT is called a **Constant Maturity Treasury swap**.

Forward Start Swap

A **forward start swap** is a swap wherein the swap does not begin until some future date that is specified in the swap agreement. Thus, there is a beginning date for the swap at some time in the future and a maturity date for the swap. A forward start swap will also specify the swap rate at which the counterparties agree to exchange payments commencing at the start date.

For example, on April 21, 2011, the 10-year Treasury rate was 3.40% and the 10-year swap rate was 3.49%. On the same day, the forward swap rate was

2-year	4.42%
3-year	4.74%
5-year	5.08%
10-year	5.13%

So, for example, consider the 2-year forward start swap on a 10-year swap. For this contract, the counterparties agree to enter into a 10-year interest-rate swap two years from April 21, 2011, and the swap rate for that swap will be 4.42%.

Swaptions

There are options on interest-rate swaps. These swap structures are called **swaptions** and grant the option buyer the right to enter into an interest-rate swap at a future date. The buyer of the swaption must pay the swaption seller a fee, the swaption price or premium. The time until expiration of the swap, the term of the swap, and the swap rate are specified. The swap rate is the strike rate for the swaption. A swaption can have either an American- or European-style exercise provision.

There are two types of swaptions—a payer swaption and a receiver swaption. A **payer swaption** entitles the option buyer to enter into an interest-rate swap in which the option buyer pays a fixed rate and receives a floating rate. In a **receiver swaption** the swaption buyer has the right to enter into an interest-rate swap that requires paying a floating rate and receiving a fixed rate.

The convention used to describe a swaption is as follows: "A×B" where A is the number of years when the option expires and B is the number of years (term) of the swap if the option is exercised. This is also described as an "A into B" swaption. For example, a 3×10 European swaption (also described as a "3 into 10" swaption) is one in which the swaption buyer has the right three years from now to enter into a 10-year interest rate swap.

As we explained in describing options in Chapter 27, an option can be in-the-money (ITM), at-the-money (ATM), or out-of-the-money (OTM). The terminology applies based on how the strike price differs from the prevailing market price of the underlying. The same holds for swaptions. Typically dealers quote ATM swaptions based on an assumed volatility. ITM and OTM swaptions quotes are based on higher volatilities than ATM options.

How is a swaption used? We can see its usefulness by looking at two of the applications of a swap given earlier: controlling the duration of a portfolio and asset-liability management.

Controlling interest rate risk. In Chapter 27 we illustrated how to use futures options to control the interest rate risk of an individual bond. Let's look at how a swaption can be used to create an option-type payoff for the bond portfolio that was used in Chapter 26 to show how to use futures to change duration, and earlier in this chapter to show how to use swaps for the same purpose.

Let's look at the type of position that must be taken. Recall in the illustration that the manager wants to increase the interest rate risk exposure of the portfolio. With a futures contract this is done by buying Treasury futures and with an interest rate swap this accomplished by being the fixed-rate receiver. Using an option-type instrument such as a swaption, the manager wants a nonlinear payoff whereby if interest rates decline, the portfolio will have a payoff similar to the benchmark that has a duration of 3.68. Yet, if interest rates rise, the portfolio does not decline in value by as much as a portfolio with a duration of 3.68. Increasing upside potential but limiting downside risk is what character-izes option-type instruments such as a swaption. Of course, this is not free; it requires the payment of a fee, the swaption premium.

What position in the swaption should the manager take? Since the manager wants to add duration to the portfolio and a fixed-rate receiver swap will add duration, this means that the manager would buy a receiver swaption (i.e., receive fixed and pay floating). Suppose on March 31, 2011, the manager decides to use a 1×5 ATM receiver European swaption with a strike rate (swap rate) of 3.26%. Assuming a 115 basis point volatility, the cost of a receiver swaption that would be needed to produce the desired interest rate exposure is $307,705 (the notional amount of the receiver swaption is $14,487,071). The dollar duration that would be added to the portfolio using the receiver swaption would be $340,881 (the same as in the fixed-rate swap).

Asset-liability management. To illustrate how a swaption can be used in asset-liability management, let's return to the bank–insurance company example. The bank makes the fixed-rate payments in the interest-rate swap (10%) using the interest rate it is earning on the commercial loans (10%). Suppose that the commercial loan borrowers default on their obligations. The bank will then not receive from the commercial loans the 10% to make its swap payments. This problem can be addressed at the outset of the initial swap transaction by the bank entering into a swaption that effectively gives it the right to terminate or cancel the swap. That is, the bank will enter into a receiver swaption—receiving fixed of 10% so as to offset the fixed rate it is obligated to pay under the initial swap. In fact, the borrowers do not have to fail for the swap to have an adverse impact on the bank. Suppose the commercial loans can be prepaid. Then, the bank has a similar problem. For example, suppose rates on commercial loans decline to 7% and the borrowers prepay. Then, the bank would be obligated to make the 10% payments under the terms of the swap. With the proceeds received from the prepayment of the commercial loans, the bank may be able to invest only in similar loans at 7%, for example, a rate that is less than the bank's obligations.

❙ INTEREST-RATE CAPS AND FLOORS

An **interest-rate agreement** is an agreement between two parties whereby one party, for an upfront premium, agrees to compensate the other at specific time periods if a designated interest rate, called the **reference rate**, is different from a predetermined level. When one party agrees to pay the other when the reference rate exceeds a predetermined level, the agreement is referred to as an **interest-rate cap** or **ceiling**. The agreement is referred to as an **interest-rate floor** when one party agrees to pay the other when the reference rate falls below a predetermined level. The predetermined interest-rate level is called the **strike rate**.

The terms of an interest-rate agreement include:

1. the reference rate
2. the strike rate that sets the ceiling or floor
3. the length of the agreement
4. the frequency of settlement
5. the notional principal amount

Suppose that C buys an interest-rate cap from D with the following terms:

1. reference rate is six-month LIBOR
2. strike rate is 8%
3. agreement is for seven years
4. settlement is every six months
5. notional principal amount is $20 million

Under this agreement, every six months for the next seven years, D will pay C whenever six-month LIBOR exceeds 8%. The payment will equal the dollar value of the difference between six-month LIBOR and 8% times the notional principal amount divided by 2. For example, if six months from now six-month LIBOR is 11%, D will pay C 3% (11% minus 8%) times $20 million divided by 2, or $300,000. If six-month LIBOR is 8% or less, D does not have to pay anything to C.

In the case of an interest-rate floor, assume the same terms as those for the interest-rate cap we just illustrated. In this case, if six-month LIBOR is 11%, C receives nothing from D, but if six-month LIBOR is less than 8%, D compensates C for the difference. For example, if six-month LIBOR is 7%, D will pay C $100,000 (8% minus 7% times $20 million divided by 2).

Interest-rate caps and floors can be combined to create an interest-rate collar. This is done by buying an interest-rate cap and selling an interest-rate floor. Some commercial banks and investment banking firms write options on interest-rate agreements for customers. Options on caps are **captions**; options on floors are called **flotions**.

Risk/Return Characteristics

In an interest-rate agreement, the buyer pays an upfront fee, which represents the maximum amount that the buyer can lose and the maximum amount that the writer of the agreement can gain. The only party that is required to perform is the writer of the interest-rate agreement. The buyer of an interest-rate cap benefits if the underlying interest rate rises above the strike rate because the seller (writer) must compensate the buyer. The buyer of an interest rate floor benefits if the interest rate falls below the strike rate, because the seller (writer) must compensate the buyer.

To better understand interest-rate caps and floors, we can look at them as in essence equivalent to a package of interest-rate options. Because the buyer benefits if the interest rate rises above the strike rate, an interest-rate cap is similar to purchasing a package of call options on an interest rate or purchasing a put option on a bond. The seller of an interest-rate cap has effectively sold a package of call options on an interest rate or sold a package of put options on a bond. The buyer of an interest-rate floor benefits from a decline in the interest rate below the strike rate. Therefore, the buyer of an interest-rate floor has effectively bought a package of put options on an interest rate or a package of call options on a bond from the writer of the option.

Once again, a complex contract can be seen to be a package of basic contracts, or options in the case of interest-rate agreements. Captions and flotions can be viewed as options on a package of options.

Valuing Caps and Floors[5]

The arbitrage-free binomial model described in Chapter 17 can also be used to value a cap and a floor. This is because, as previously explained, a cap and a floor are nothing more than a package or strip of options. More specifically, they are a strip of European options on interest rates. Thus, to value a cap, the value of each period's cap, called a **caplet**, is found and all the caplets are then summed. We refer to this approach to valuing a cap as the **caplet method**. (The same approach can be used to value a floor.) Once the caplet method is demonstrated, we will show an easier way of valuing a cap.

To illustrate the caplet method, we will use the binomial interest-rate tree used in Chapter 17 to value an interest rate option to value a 5.2%, three-year cap with a notional amount of $10 million. The reference rate is the one-year rates in the binomial tree. The payoff for the cap is annual.

There is one wrinkle having to do with the timing of the payments for a cap and floor that requires a modification of the binomial approach presented to value an interest rate option. This is due to the fact that settlement for the typical cap and floor is paid

---

[5] The presentation here is based on the framework provided by Professor Donald Smith of Boston University.

Exhibit 28-11 Binomial Interest Rate Tree with Dates and Years Identified

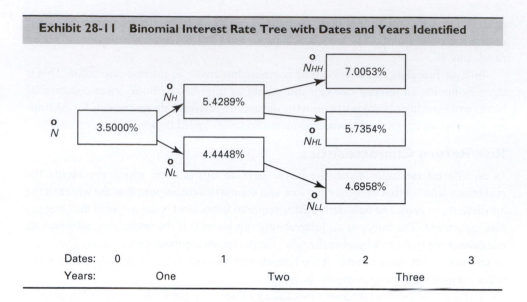

Dates:	0		1		2		3
Years:		One		Two		Three	

in arrears. As explained elsewhere, this means that the interest rate paid on a financial instrument with this feature is determined at the beginning of the period but paid at the end of the period (i.e., beginning of the next period). We will use Arabic numbers for dates (i.e., Date 0, Date 1, Date 2, and Date 3) and words for years (i.e., Year One, Year Two, and Year Three) to avoid confusion regarding when a payment is determined and when it is made. Exhibit 28-11 shows the binomial interest rate tree with dates and years.

Using Exhibit 28-11, we can understand what is meant by payment in arrears. Consider Date 1. There are two interest rates, 4.4448% and 5.4289%. Suppose today, Date 0, that an investor enters into an agreement whereby if a reference rate at Date 1 exceeds 5.2%, the investor will receive at Date 2 the difference between the reference rate and 5.2% multiplied by $10 million; if the reference rate is less than 5.2% nothing is received. This agreement specifies payment in arrears. For example, consider at Date 1 the interest rate (reference rate) of 5.4289%. Then there would be a payoff of

$$(5.4289\% - 5.2000\%) \times \$10,000,000 = \$22,890$$

The payment of $22,890 would be made at Date 2.

With this background, we will first show how to use the caplet method to value the three-year cap.

Caplet Method

Consider first the value of the caplet for Year One, which is shown in panel a in Exhibit 28-12. At Date 0, the one-year rate is 3.5%. Since it does not exceed the cap rate of 5.2%, the payoff is zero.

We now move on to the Year Two caplet as shown in panel b in Exhibit 28-12. There are two interest rates at Day 1: 4.4448% and 5.4289%. If the interest rate is 4.4448% on Date 1, there is no payoff because the rate is less than 5.2%. If the interest rate is 5.4289%, there is a payoff, as explained earlier. The payoff is $22,890 and will be made at Date 2.

The payoff at Date 2 is either $0 or $22,890. These values have to be discounted back to Date 0. The discounting requires first discounting back to Date 1 and then discounting

Exhibit 28-12   Value a Cap Using the Caplet Method

a. Value of the Year One Caplet at 5.20%

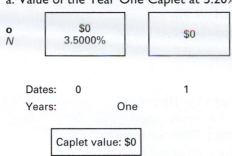

| Dates: | 0 | | 1 |
| Years: | | One | |

Caplet value: $0

b. Value of the Year Two Caplet at 5.20%

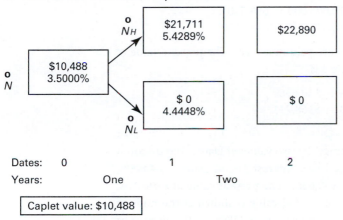

| Dates: | 0 | | 1 | | 2 |
| Years: | | One | | Two | |

Caplet value: $10,488

c. Value of the Year Three Caplet at 5.20%

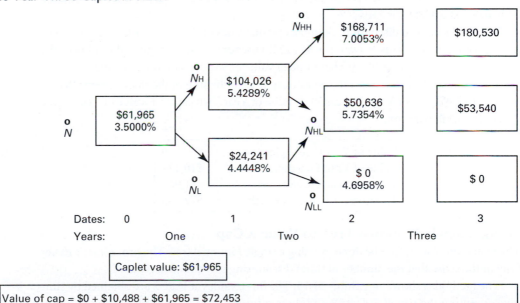

| Dates: | 0 | | 1 | | 2 | | 3 |
| Years: | | One | | Two | | Three | |

Caplet value: $61,965

Value of cap = $0 + $10,488 + $61,965 = $72,453

back to Date 0. At each date, the present values are averaged because of the assumption that both payoffs are equally likely.

What discount rate should be used? The discount rate that should be used is the one at the node at the date where the interest rate is to be discounted back to. For example, the payoff of $22,890 at Date 2 should be discounted at 5.4289% to get the present value at Date 1. The present value is $21,711 (=$22,890/1.054289) and is shown at the node in Panel b. Obviously, the present value of the $0 payoff is $0. The average of these two present values at Date 1 is $10,855.5.

The present value at Date 1 is then discounted back to Date 0 by using 3.5%. The present value is $10,488.41 (=$10,855.5/1.035). The rounded value of $10,488 is shown at Date 0.

Panel c of Exhibit 28-12 shows the valuation of the Year Three caplet. There are three interest rates shown at Date 2: 4.6958%, 5.7354%, and 7.0053%. There is no payoff if the interest rate at Date 2 is 4.6958%. For the other two interest rates, the payoff is

$$(5.7354\% - 5.2000\%) \times \$10,000,000 = \$53,540$$
$$(7.0053\% - 5.2000\%) \times \$10,000,000 = \$180,530$$

These payoffs are shown at Date 3 because they are paid in arrears. The present value of these two payoffs on Date 2 to be received at Date 3 is

$$\$53,540/1.057354 = \$50,636$$
$$\$180,530/1.070053 = \$168,711$$

These present values are shown at Date 2.

Moving backwards to Date 1, we have to average the two values at Date 2 and discount back at the corresponding interest rate. For the lower interest rate at Date 1, 4.4448%, the average value at Date 2 is $25,318 =($0 + $50,636). The present value at Date 1 is, therefore, $24,240.56 (=$25,318/1.044448). The rounded value is shown at the node at Date 1. Similarly, the average value for the higher interest rate, 5.4289%, is the average of $50,636 and $168,711, which is $109,673.5. The present value at Date 1, discounting back $109,673.5 at 5.4289%, is $104,026.

The final step is to discount back to Date 0 the values of the two payoffs at Date 1. The average of the two payoffs at Date 1 is $64,134. Discounting at 3.5% gives the value of the Year Three caplet of $61,964.73. The rounded value of $61,965 is shown in Panel c.

The value of the three-year interest rate cap is then the sum of the three caplets; that is, value of cap = value of Year One caplet + value of Year Two caplet + value of Year Three caplet. In our illustration,

Value of Year One caplet:	$ 0
Value of Year Two caplet:	$10,488
Value of Year Three caplet:	$61,965
Three-year interest rate cap:	$72,453

Using a Single Binomial Tree to Value a Cap

The valuation of a cap can be done by using a single binomial tree. The procedure is easier only in the sense that the number of times discounting is required is reduced.

The method is shown in Exhibit 28-13. The three values at Date 2 are obtained by simply computing the payoff at Date 3 and discounting back to Date 2. These are the values shown for Date 2 in panel c of Exhibit 28-12.

Exhibit 28-13 Valuing a Cap Using a Single Binomial Tree

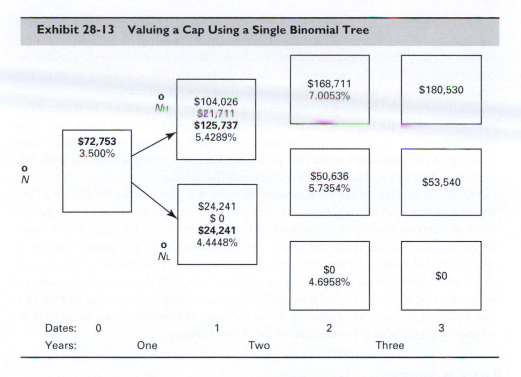

Dates:	0	1	2	3
Years:		One	Two	Three

Let's look at the higher node at Date 1 (interest rate of 5.4289%). The top number, $104,026, is the present value of the two Date 2 values that branch out from that node. It is computed in the same way as in panel c in Exhibit 28-12. The number below it, $21,711, is the payoff of the Year Two caplet on Date 1 as calculated in Exhibit 28-12. The third number down at the top node at Date 1 in Exhibit 28-13, which is in bold, is the sum of the top two values above it. It is this value that is then used in the backward induction. The same procedure is used to get the values shown in the boxes at the lower node at Date 1.

Given the values at the two nodes at Date 1, the bolded values are averaged to obtain $74,989 [=($125,737 + $24,241)/2]. Discounting this value at 3.5% gives $72,453. This is the same value obtained from using the caplet approach.

Valuing a Floor

An interest rate floor can be valued using the two approaches just illustrated for valuing a cap except that there is a payoff when the interest rate is less than the strike rate. In the case of a floor, the value for the floor for any year is called a **floorlet**. The sum of the floorlets is the value of the floor. Alternatively, a floor can be valued using a single binomial tree.

Applications

To see how interest-rate agreements can be used for asset/liability management, consider the problems faced by the commercial bank and the life insurance company we discussed in demonstrating the use of an interest-rate swap.[6] Recall that the bank's objective is to lock in an interest-rate spread over its cost of funds. Yet because it borrows short term, its cost

---

[6] For additional applications in the insurance industry, see David F. Babbel, Peter Bouyoucos, and Robert Stricker, "Capping the Interest Rate Risk in Insurance Products," Chapter 21 in Frank J. Fabozzi (ed.), *Fixed Income Portfolio Strategies* (Chicago: Probus Publishing, 1989).

of funds is uncertain. The bank may be able to purchase a cap, however, so that the cap rate plus the cost of purchasing the cap is less than the rate it is earning on its fixed-rate commercial loans. If short-term rates decline, the bank does not benefit from the cap, but its cost of funds declines. The cap, therefore, allows the bank to impose a ceiling on its cost of funds while retaining the opportunity to benefit from a decline in rates.

The bank can reduce the cost of purchasing the cap by selling a floor. In this case the bank agrees to pay the buyer of the floor if the reference rate falls below the strike rate. The bank receives a fee for selling the floor, but it has sold off its opportunity to benefit from a decline in rates below the strike rate. By buying a cap and selling a floor, the bank has created a predetermined range for its cost of funds (i.e., a collar).

Recall the problem of the life insurance company that guarantees a 9% rate on a GIC for the next five years and is considering the purchase of an attractive floating-rate instrument in a private placement transaction. The risk that the company faces is that interest rates will fall so that it will not earn enough to realize the 9% guaranteed rate plus a spread. The life insurance company may be able to purchase a floor to set a lower bound on its investment return, yet retain the opportunity to benefit should rates increase. To reduce the cost of purchasing the floor, the life insurance company can sell an interest-rate cap. By doing so, however, it gives up the opportunity of benefiting from an increase in six-month LIBOR above the strike rate of the interest-rate cap.

▌KEY POINTS

- An interest-rate swap is an agreement specifying that the parties exchange interest payments at designated times.
- In a generic interest-rate swap, one party will make fixed-rate payments (called the fixed-rate payer), and the other will make floating-rate payments (called the fixed-rate receiver), with payments based on the notional principal amount.
- Asset and risk managers use interest-rate swaps to alter the duration of a portfolio, alter the cash flow characteristics of their assets or liabilities, or to capitalize on perceived capital market inefficiencies.
- A swap position can be interpreted as either a package of forward/futures contracts or a package of cash flows from buying and selling cash market instruments.
- The swap rate is computed by finding the rate that will make the present value of the cash flow of both sides of the swap equal. The value of an existing swap is equal to the difference in the present value of the two payments.
- The interest-rate sensitivity or duration of a swap from the perspective of a floating-rate payer is just the difference between the duration of the fixed-rate bond and duration of the floating-rate bond that compose the swap. Most of the interest-rate sensitivity of a swap will result from the duration of the fixed-rate bond since the duration of the floating-rate bond will be small.
- Nongeneric swaps include swaps where the notional amount changes in a predetermined way over the life of the swap (amortizing, accreting, and roller coaster swaps) and swaps in which both counterparties pay a floating rate (basis swaps and Constant Maturity Treasury swaps).
- There are complex swap structures, such as swaps where the swap does not begin until some future time (forward start swaps) and options on swaps (swaptions).
- Swaptions can be used to create a portfolio with option-type payoffs that will have the desired duration if rates move in a favorable direction but limit adverse movements

when interest rates move in the opposite direction. The cost of creating such a favorable risk-return relationship is the cost of the swaptions.

- An interest-rate agreement allows one party for an upfront premium the right to receive compensation from the writer of the agreement if a designated interest rate is different from a predetermined level.
- An interest-rate cap calls for one party to receive a payment if a designated interest rate is above the strike rate. An interest-rate floor lets one party receive a payment if a designated interest rate is below the strike rate.
- An interest-rate cap can be used to establish a ceiling on the cost of funding; an interest-rate floor can be used to establish a floor return. Buying a cap and selling a floor creates a collar.
- A cap and a floor can be valued using the binomial model.

QUESTIONS

1. Suppose that a dealer quotes these terms on a five-year swap: fixed-rate payer to pay 4.4% for LIBOR and fixed-rate receiver to pay LIBOR for 4.2%.
   a. What is the dealer's bid-ask spread?
   b. How would the dealer quote the terms by reference to the yield on five-year Treasury notes?

2. Give two interpretations of an interest-rate swap.

3. In determining the cash flow for the floating-rate side of a LIBOR swap, explain how the cash flow is determined.

4. How is the swap rate calculated?

5. Suppose that a life insurance company has issued a three-year GIC with a fixed rate of 10%. Under what circumstances might it be feasible for the life insurance company to invest the funds in a floating-rate security and enter into a three-year interest-rate swap in which it pays a floating rate and receives a fixed rate?

6. How can an interest rate swap be used to reduce the duration of portfolio to match the duration of a benchmark?

7. A portfolio manager buys a swaption with a strike rate of 4.5% that entitles the portfolio manager to enter into an interest-rate swap to pay a fixed rate and receive a floating rate. The term of the swaption is five years.
   a. Is this swaption a payer swaption or a receiver swaption? Explain.
   b. What does the strike rate of 4.5% mean?

8. The following appeared on a quote sheet:

   "Receiver Swaption: An option to receive the fixed leg of a swap (i.e., long receiver is long duration).
   Payer Swaption: An option to pay the fixed leg of a swap (i.e., long payer is short duration)."

   a. Explain why for the receiver swaption the part is long duration.
   b. Explain why for the payer swaption the part is short duration.

9. The manager of a savings and loan association is considering the use of a swap as part of its asset/liability strategy. The swap would be used to convert the payments of its portfolio of fixed-rate residential mortgage loans into a floating payment.
   a. What is the risk with using a plain vanilla or generic interest-rate swap?
   b. Why might a manager consider using an interest-rate swap in which the notional principal amount declines over time?
   c. Why might a manager consider buying a swaption?

10. Consider the following interest-rate swap:
    - The swap starts today, January 1 of year 1.
    - The floating-rate payments are made quarterly based on actual/360.
    - The reference rate is three-month LIBOR.
    - The notional amount of the swap is $40 million.
    - The term of the swap is three years.

a. Suppose that today three-month LIBOR is 5.7%. What will the fixed-rate payer for this interest rate swap receive on March 31 of year 1 (assuming that year 1 is not a leap year)?

b. Assume the Eurodollar futures price for the next seven quarters is as follows:

Quarter Starts	Quarter Ends	No. of Days in Quarter	Euro-dollar Futures Price
April 1 year 1	June 30 year 1	91	94.10
July 1 year 1	Sept 30 year 1	92	94.00
Oct 1 year 1	Dec 31 year 1	92	93.70
Jan 1 year 2	Mar 31 year 1	90	93.60
April 1 year 2	June 30 year 2	91	93.50
July 1 year 2	Sept 30 year 2	92	93.20
Oct 1 year 2	Dec 31 year 2	92	93.00

Compute the forward rate for each quarter and the floating-rate payment at the end of each quarter.

c. What is the floating-rate payment at the end of each quarter for this interest-rate swap?

11. a. Assume that the swap rate for an interest-rate swap is 7% and that the fixed-rate swap payments are made quarterly on an actual/360 basis. If the notional amount of a two-year swap is $20 million, what is the fixed-rate payment at the end of each quarter assuming the following number of days in each quarter?

Period Quarter	Days in Quarter
1	92
2	92
3	90
4	91
5	92
6	92
7	90
8	91

b. Assume that the swap in question a requires payments semiannually rather than quarterly. What is the semiannual fixed-rate payment?

c. Suppose that the notional amount for the two-year swap is not the same in both years. Suppose instead that in year 1 the notional

amount is $20 million, but in year 2 the notional amount is $12 million. What is the fixed-rate payment every six months?

12. Given the current three-month LIBOR and the Eurodollar futures prices shown in the table below, compute the forward rate and the forward discount factor for each period.

Period	Days in Quarter	3-Month LIBOR	Current Eurodollar Futures Price
1	90	5.90%	
2	91		93.90
3	92		93.70
4	92		93.45
5	90		93.20
6	91		93.15

13. a. Suppose that at the inception of a five-year interest-rate swap in which the reference rate is three-month LIBOR, the present value of the floating-rate payments is $16,555,000. The fixed-rate payments are assumed to be semiannual. Assume also that the following is computed for the fixed-rate payments (using the notation in the chapter):

$$\sum_{t=1}^{10} \text{notional amount} \times \text{swap rate} \times \frac{\text{days in period } t}{360} \times \text{forward discount factor for period } t = \$236,500,000$$

What is the swap rate for this swap?

b. Suppose that the five-year yield from the on-the-run Treasury yield curve is 6.4%. What is the swap spread?

14. An interest-rate swap had an original maturity of five years. Today, the swap has two years to maturity. The present value of the fixed-rate payments for the remainder of the term of the swap is $910,000. The present value of the floating-rate payments for the remainder of the swap is $710,000.

a. What is the value of this swap from the perspective of the fixed-rate payer?

b. What is the value of this swap from the perspective of the fixed-rate receiver?

15. Suppose that a savings and loan association buys an interest-rate cap that has these terms: The reference rate is the six-month Treasury bill rate; the cap will last for five years; payment is semiannual; the strike rate is 5.5%; and the notional amount is $10 million. Suppose further that at the end of a six-month period, the six-month Treasury bill rate is 6.1%.

a. What is the amount of the payment that the savings and loan association will receive?

b. What would the seller of this cap pay if the six-month Treasury rate were 5.45% instead of 6.1%?

16. What is the relationship between an interest-rate agreement and an option on an interest rate?

17. How can an interest-rate collar be created?

18. Value a three-year interest rate floor with a $10 million notional amount and a floor rate of 4.8% using the binomial interest-rate tree shown in Exhibit 28-11.

29

Credit Default Swaps

LEARNING OBJECTIVES

After reading this chapter, you will understand

- how a credit derivative differs from an interest-rate derivative

- what a credit default swap is and how a credit event can be defined

- what a credit event is and the special definitions for credit events for asset-backed securities

- the mechanics of a CDS contract including the calculation of the swap premium

- the difference between a single-name credit default swap and an index credit default swap

- approximating the value of a single-name credit default swap

- what an asset swap is and its link to valuing a single-name credit default swap

- what is meant by the implied default probability for a credit default swap and what are the underlying assumptions to compute it

- the different types of index credit default swaps

- the economic interpretation of a credit default swap

- how a credit default swap can be used to control a portfolio's credit risk

The interest-rate derivatives discussed in the previous three chapters can be used to control a major primary risk inherent in bond portfolio management: interest-rate risk. Another major primary risk is credit risk. As explained in Chapter 1, credit risk encompasses default risk, credit spread risk, and downgrade risk. To control a portfolio's exposure to credit risk, credit derivatives can be employed. While there is a wide range of credit derivative products, by far the most commonly used product is the credit default swap (CDS) because it is probably the simplest form of credit risk transference among all credit derivatives.

There are two types of CDS: single-name CDS and index CDS. Regardless of the type of CDS, there are two parties to the contract: a credit protection buyer and a credit protection seller. For a fee, the credit protection seller is providing the credit protection buyer protection against some "credit event" on "something." The key terms in a CDS that must be specified in trade documentation are the definition of a "credit event" and the "something" for which credit protection is being provided. The "something" for which credit protection is being provided is the reference entity or reference obligation. The **reference entity** is the issuer of the debt instrument for which credit protection is being sought. The **reference obligation** is the particular debt issue for which the credit protection is being sought. For example, a reference entity could be Ford Motor Credit Company. The reference obligation would be a specific Ford Motor Credit Company bond issue. In a single-name CDS, there is only one reference entity or one reference obligation. In an index CDS, there is a standardized basket of reference entities. The payment made by the credit protection buyer to the credit protection seller is called the CDS spread or swap payment.[1]

With respect to the definition of a credit event, there is not just one event but several potential events that will adversely impact the value of a reference obligation or all of the debt of a reference entity. These credit events are spelled out in the documentation for a CDS trade. Prior to 1998, the development of the credit derivative products was hindered by the lack of standardization of legal documentation. Every trade (i.e., the buying and selling of a credit derivative contract) had to be customized. In 1998, the International Swaps and Derivatives Association (ISDA) developed a standard contract that could be used by parties to trades of a credit derivatives contract. While the documentation was primarily designed for CDSs, the contract form is sufficiently flexible so that it can be used for other types of credit derivatives.

In this chapter, we describe the different types of CDS, the basics of CDS valuation for a single-name CDS, and how a CDS can be used to control risk. We begin with the critical element in a CDS: the definition of a credit event.

CREDIT EVENTS

A CDS has a payout that is contingent upon a **credit event** occurring. The ISDA provides definitions of what credit events are. The IDSA's initial focus with respect to defining credit events was for corporate and sovereign debt. As the trading of CDSs on single tranches of asset-backed securities and municipal debt grew, the IDSA introduced definitions for credit events when these two asset types were the underlying of a contract.

The *1999 ISDA Credit Derivatives Definitions* (referred to as the "1999 Definitions") provides a list of eight credit events: (1) bankruptcy, (2) credit event upon merger, (3) cross acceleration, (4) cross default, (5) downgrade, (6) failure to pay, (7) repudiation/moratorium, and (8) restructuring. These eight events attempt to capture every type of situation that could

---

[1] In earlier chapters we explained how the loan of an issuer is priced off of some reference rate plus a spread, typically LIBOR plus a spread. Some issuers now have the option to have their loan rate determined by the rate in the CDS market. For example, Honeywell International in 2011 entered into a five-year $2.8 billion credit line with several banks that contained such a provision.

cause the credit quality of the reference entity to deteriorate, or cause the value of the reference obligation to decline.

Bankruptcy is defined as a variety of acts that are associated with bankruptcy or insolvency laws. **Failure to pay** results when a reference entity fails to make one or more contractual payments when due. When a reference entity breaches a covenant, it has defaulted on its obligation. When a default occurs, the obligation becomes due and payable prior to the scheduled due date had the reference entity not defaulted. This is referred to as an **obligation acceleration**. A reference entity may disaffirm or challenge the validity of its obligation. This is a credit event that is covered by **repudiation/moratorium**.

The most controversial credit event that may be included in a credit default product is the restructuring of an obligation. A **restructuring** occurs when the terms of the obligation are altered so as to make the new terms less attractive to the debt holder than the original terms. The terms that can be changed would typically include, but are not limited to, one or more of the following: (1) a reduction in the interest rate, (2) a reduction in the principal, (3) a rescheduling of the principal repayment schedule (e.g., lengthening the maturity of the obligation) or postponement of an interest payment, or (4) a change in the level of seniority of the obligation in the reference entity's debt structure.

The reason why restructuring is so controversial is that a protection buyer benefits from the inclusion of restructuring as a credit event and feels that eliminating restructuring as a credit event will erode its credit protection. The protection seller, in contrast, would prefer not to include restructuring since even routine modifications of obligations that occur in lending arrangements would trigger a payout to the protection buyer. Moreover, if the reference obligation is a loan and the protection buyer is the lender, there is a dual benefit for the protection buyer to restructure a loan. The first benefit is that the protection buyer receives a payment from the protection seller. Second, the accommodating restructuring fosters a relationship between the lender (who is the protection buyer) and its customer (the corporate entity that is the obligor of the reference obligation).

Because of this problem, the *Restructuring Supplement to the 1999 ISDA Credit Derivatives Definitions* (the "Supplement Definition") issued in April 2001 provided a modified definition for restructuring. There is a provision for the limitation on reference obligations in connection with restructuring of loans made by the protection buyer to the borrower that is the obligor of the reference obligation. This provision requires the following in order to qualify for a restructuring: (1) there must be four or more holders of the reference obligation, and (2) there must be consent to the restructuring of the reference obligation by a supermajority (66 ^{2}/$_3$%). In addition, the supplement limits the maturity of reference obligations that are physically deliverable when restructuring results in a payout triggered by the protection buyer.

As the credit derivatives market developed, market participants learned a great deal about how to better define credit events, particularly with the record level of high-yield corporate bond default rates in 2002, and with sovereign defaults, particularly the experience with the 2001–2002 Argentina debt crisis. In January 2003, the ISDA published its revised credit events definitions in the *2003 ISDA Credit Derivative Definitions* (referred to as the "2003 Definitions"). The revised definitions reflected amendments to several of the definitions for credit events set forth in the 1999 Definitions. Specifically, there were amendments for bankruptcy, repudiation, and restructuring.

The major change was to restructuring, whereby the ISDA allows parties to a given trade to select from among the following four definitions: (1) no restructuring; (2) "full" or "old" restructuring, which is based on the 1998 Definitions; (3) "modified restructuring," which is based on the Supplement Definition; and (4) "modified-modified restructuring." The last choice is new and was included to address issues that arose in the European market.

Not all of the eight definitions of credit events just described for corporate and sovereign issuers are applicable to municipal issuers. The three that are used as credit events in municipal CDSs are bankruptcy, failure to pay, and restructuring. Because credit events may not apply to all types of municipal bonds, the ISDA's standardized confirmation for municipal CDSs requires that the parties to a trade specify the type of municipal bond that is the underlying one for a trade. The ISDA confirmation provides the following three choices for the type of municipal bond: (1) those backed by the full faith and credit of the municipal government (full faith and credit obligations), (2) those paid from funds on hand (general fund obligations), and (3) those backed by specific revenue streams (revenue obligations).

Credit Events for an Asset-Backed Security

CDSs are written on asset-backed securities (ABSs) and referred to as ABS CDSs. As explained in Chapters 13, 14, and 15, ABSs include a wide range of asset types. Recall that the convention in the marketplace prior to 2007 was to classify those residential mortgage-backed securities where the collateral was a pool of subprime mortgage loans as part of the ABS market and not the MBS market. Consequently, much of the CDSs written on ABSs involved subprime mortgage pools.

There are unique aspects of an ABS that required a modification of the ISDA documentation with respect to credit event definitions when the reference entity is an ABS tranche.[2] In June 2005, the ISDA released what it refers to as its **pay-as-you-go** (PAUG) template for ABS. The focus was on cash flow adequacy of the ABS structure rather than the potential for bankruptcy. (Recall from Chapter 15 that the issuer of an ABS is not a corporation but a bankruptcy-remote trust.) Accordingly, the ISDA PAUG template provided the following three credit events that focus on cash flow adequacy for ABS transactions:

- *Failure to pay.* The underlying reference obligation fails to make a scheduled interest or principal payment.
- *Writedown.* The principal component of the underlying reference obligation is written down and deemed irrecoverable.
- *Distressed ratings downgrade.* The underlying reference obligation is downgraded to a rating of Caa2/CCC or lower.

As can be seen, unlike a CDS where the reference entity is a corporation where a credit event is intended to capture an event of default, the PAUG template seeks to capture any non-default events that impact the cash flow of the specific reference ABS tranche.

---

[2] For a more detailed discussion of the differences between a corporate CDS and an ABS CDS that calls for the modification of the definition of credit events, see Chapter 6 in Laurie S. Goodman, Shumin Li, Douglas J. Lucas, Thomas A. Zimmerman, and Frank J. Fabozzi, *Subprime Mortgage Credit Derivatives* (John Wiley & Sons, 2008).

SINGLE-NAME CDS

In a **single-name CDS**, there is only one reference entity or reference obligation. There are single-name CDSs written on a

- corporate debt issuer (bonds or leverage loans)
- sovereign issuer
- municipal bond issuer
- tranche of an asset-backed security

To explain the mechanics of a single-name CDS we will use an illustration for a CDS written on a corporate bond issuer. In the illustration, we will assume that the reference entity is XYZ Corporation and that issuer has only one bond issue outstanding. The underlying for the CDS is $10 million par value of the XYZ bond issue. As with interest-rate derivatives such as swaps, caps, and floors, a CDS involves a notional amount, which is $10 million in our illustration.

Assume that the swap premium—the payment made by the protection buyer to the protection seller—is 200 basis points. The standard contract for a single-name CDS calls for a quarterly payment of the swap premium. The quarterly payment is determined using one of the day count conventions in the bond market. The day count convention used for CDSs is actual/360, the same convention as used in the interest-rate swap market. A day count convention of actual/360 means that to determine the payment in a quarter, the actual number of days in the quarter is used and 360 days are assumed for the year. Consequently, the swap premium payment for a quarter is

quarterly swap premium payment =

$$\text{notional amount} \times \text{swap rate (in decimal)} \times \frac{\text{actual no. of days in quarter}}{360}$$

For example, assume a hypothetical CDS where the notional amount is $10 million and there are 92 actual days in a quarter. Since the swap premium is 200 basis points (0.02), the quarterly swap premium payment made by the protection buyer would be

$$\$10,000,000 \times 0.02 \times \frac{92}{360} = \$51,111.11$$

In the absence of a credit event, the protection buyer will make a quarterly swap premium payment over the life of the swap. If a credit event occurs, two things happen. First, there are no further payments of the swap premium by the protection buyer to the protection seller. Second, a **termination value** is determined for the swap should a credit event occur. The procedure for computing the termination value depends on the settlement terms specified in the swap agreement. This will be either physical settlement or cash settlement. The market practice for settlement for single-name CDSs is physical delivery.

With **physical settlement** the protection buyer delivers a specified amount of the face value of bonds of the reference entity to the protection seller. The protection seller pays the protection buyer the face value of the bonds. Unlike in our hypothetical illustration for XYZ Corporation, where only one issue of the reference entity was assumed to be outstanding, in the real world all reference entities have many issues outstanding and therefore there will be a number of alternative issues of the reference entity that the protection buyer can deliver to the protection seller. These issues are known as **deliverable obligations**.

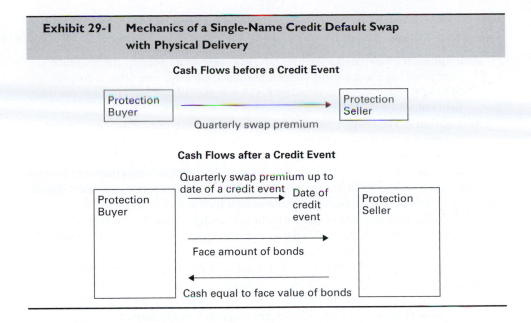

Exhibit 29-1   Mechanics of a Single-Name Credit Default Swap with Physical Delivery

The swap documentation will set forth the characteristics necessary for an issue to qualify as a deliverable obligation. Recall that for Treasury bond and note futures contracts described in Chapter 26, the short has the choice of which Treasury issue to deliver that the exchange specifies as acceptable for delivery. The short will select the cheapest-to-deliver issue, and the choice granted to the short is effectively an embedded option. The same is true for physical settlement for a single-name CDS. From the list of deliverable obligations, the protection buyer will select for delivery to the protection seller the cheapest-to-deliver issue.

Exhibit 29-1 shows the mechanics of a single-name CDS. The cash flows are shown before and after a credit event. It is assumed in the exhibit that there is physical settlement.

An alternative to the standard CDS contract that specifies physical settlement is a **fixed recovery CDS**. The type of CDS eliminates the uncertainty on the recovery rate by fixing at the time of the trade a specific recovery value. With a fixed recovery CDS, if a credit event is triggered by the reference entity, the protection seller makes a cash settlement that is equal to 100 minus the specified fixed recovery rate.

Approximating the Value of a Single-Name CDS

Let's look at the general principles for pricing or valuing single-name CDSs on a corporate bond issuer.[3] By valuing or pricing we mean the determination of the fair value of the CDS spread. The general principle is that there is a relationship between the cash and the derivatives market. We have already seen this in our discussion of the pricing of interest-rate derivative instruments in previous chapters.

We begin with a set of simplifying assumptions. Refining pricing models for CDSs then involves analyzing how, when the assumptions are relaxed, the model must be modified.

---

[3] For a more detailed discussion, see Ren-Raw Chen, Frank J. Fabozzi, and Dominic O'Kane, "The Valuation of Credit Default Swaps," in Frank J. Fabozzi (ed.), *Professional Perspectives on Fixed Income Portfolio Management: Volume 4* (Hoboken, NJ: John Wiley & Sons, 2003).

Here are eight assumptions we will need to value a single-name CDS with a maturity of *T* years for a reference entity:

Assumption 1: There exists a floating-rate debt obligation issued by the reference entity that has a maturity of *T* that is trading at par value and offers a coupon rate of LIBOR plus a spread denoted by *F*. (That is, the coupon reset formula for this debt obligation is LIBOR + *F*.)

Assumption 2: The coupon payment dates for the floating-rate debt obligation are the same as the dates that payments must be made to the protection seller of the single-name CDS.

Assumption 3: A market participant who wants to borrow funds to acquire the floating-rate debt obligation in Assumption 1 can do so at the repurchase agreement (repo) rate. Moreover, the repo rate is available for a time period equal to *T* (the maturity of the floating-rate debt obligation). The borrowing rate for the repo (i.e., the repo rate) is LIBOR + *B*, where *B* is the spread over LIBOR and this borrowing rate applies to all market participants.

Assumption 4: If a credit event occurs, it occurs one day after a coupon payment date.

Assumption 5: The CDS requires physical settlement, and the floating-rate debt obligation in Assumption 1 is the cheapest-to-deliver issue to satisfy delivery.

Assumption 6: There is no difficulty in shorting bonds in the market.

Assumption 7: There are no transaction costs.

Assumption 8: There is no counterparty risk with respect to the counterparty in the CDS and the counterparty in the repurchase agreement.

The reason why these assumptions are important will become clear as we discuss the valuation model.

We want to know how the CDS premium (denoted by S), of a single-name CDS with a maturity of *T* for some reference entity is determined. Consider the following strategy:

- Buy the floating-rate debt obligation with maturity *T* issued by the reference entity.
- Fund the purchase of the floating-rate debt obligation by borrowing for the life of that debt obligation (which is also the term of the CDS), *T*, in the repo market.
- To hedge the credit risk associated with the floating-rate debt obligation, purchase protection by buying a CDS with a maturity of *T* on the reference entity.

As we will see, this strategy is equivalent to a default-free investment. (Remember that by Assumption 8, there is no counterparty risk.)

Let's look at the payoff for the two possible scenarios:

- no credit event occurs
- a credit event occurs.

If no credit event occurs, then the floating-rate debt obligation matures. Over the life of the debt obligation, the interest earned is equal to LIBOR + *F* each period (by Assumption 1). The cost of borrowing (i.e., the repo rate) for each period is LIBOR + *B* (by Assumption 3). Hence, LIBOR + *F* is received from ownership of the asset and LIBOR + *B* is paid out to borrow funds. The net cash flow is therefore what is earned: *F* − *B*. That is, under our simplifying assumptions, the strategy will have a payoff of *F* − *B* in the no credit event scenario.

Consider next what would happen if there is a credit event. By Assumption 5, there is physical delivery of the floating-rate debt obligation. This means that the floating-rate debt obligation is delivered to the credit protection seller (i.e., the seller of the single-name CDS).

By Assumption 4, the credit event occurs right after the floating-rate debt obligation's coupon payment is made. Hence, there are no further coupon payments and no accrued CDS payment. The proceeds obtained from the CDS protection seller are used to repay the amount borrowed to purchase the floating-rate debt obligation. Hence, the repo loan has been repaid. As a result, we have the same payoff for this strategy as in the scenario where there is no credit event: $F - B$.

For no arbitrage to occur for our strategy and with our set of eight simplifying assumptions, the CDS spread, S, must be equal to the payoff under both scenarios, $F - B$. Thus, a first approximation of the CDS spread is the difference between the spread over LIBOR at which the reference entity could issue a par floating-rate debt obligation (F) and the spread over LIBOR to borrow funds in order to purchase that floating-rate debt obligation (B).

This first approximation provides a starting point for market participants as to where a CDS should trade. We say that this is an *approximation* because of the simplifying assumptions that were made. One of the assumptions that should be noted because it basically provides the economic rationale for a CDS is the assumption that the repo rate is constant over the term of the CDS (Assumption 3). (This will be explained later in this chapter when an economic interpretation of a CDS is provided.) We know from our discussion of the repo market in Chapter 22 that there is not one repo rate. For example, one can borrow overnight (i.e., overnight repo) or for a longer period (term repo). Typically, however, the repo rate is a shorter term rate. That is, one cannot borrow in the repo market at a fixed rate for several years. However, by entering into a CDS, one is effectively locking in a borrowing rate for the term of the CDS. Hence, this is the attraction of a CDS.

In practice, we know that Assumption 1 may not hold. That is, for corporate issuers that are reference entities for a single-name CDS, there is not likely to be a floating-rate debt obligation trading at par. For this reason, market participants look to the asset swap market because it allows a market participant either to swap the cash flow characteristics of an asset from a fixed to a floating rate or vice versa. It is in the asset swap market for par asset swaps where a proxy for the spread over LIBOR (F) can be obtained. Hence, the first approximation for a single-name CDS is the difference between the asset swap spread (from the par asset swap market) and the spread over LIBOR in the repo market.

Asset Swaps

Because of the importance of asset swaps in pricing single-name CDSs, we describe this type of swap here. As explained in the previous chapter, an investor can use an interest-rate swap to change the cash flow nature of a bond owned to the desired cash flow characteristics sought by an investor—fixed to floating rate or floating to fixed rate. When an investor owns an asset and converts its cash flow characteristics, the investor is said to have created an **asset swap**. A common asset swap is for an investor to buy a credit-risky bond with a fixed rate and convert it to a floating rate. If the issuer of the bond defaults on the issue, the investor must continue to make payments to the counterparty of the interest-rate swap (i.e., the swap dealer) and is therefore still exposed to the credit risk of the issuer.

Let's now illustrate a basic asset swap. Suppose that an investor purchases $10 million par value of a 7.85%, five-year bond of a BBB-rated corporation at par value. The coupon payments are semiannual. At the same time, the investor enters into a five-year interest-rate swap with a dealer where the investor is the fixed-rate payer and the payments are made semi-annually. Suppose that the swap rate is 7.00% and the investor receives six-month LIBOR.

Let's look at the cash flow for the investor every six months for the next five years:

Received from bond:	7.85%
− Payment to dealer on swap:	7.00%
+ Payment from dealer on swap:	6-month LIBOR
Net received by investor:	0.85% + 6-month LIBOR

Thus, regardless of how interest rates change, if the issuer does not default, the investor earns 85 basis points over six-month LIBOR. Effectively, the investor has converted a fixed-rate BBB five-year bond into a five-year floating-rate bond with a spread over six-month LIBOR. Thus, the investor has created a synthetic floating-rate bond. The purpose of an asset swap is to do precisely that: create a synthetic credit-risky floating-rate security.

While in our description of an asset swap the investor bought the credit-risky bond and entered into an interest-rate swap with a dealer, an asset swap typically combines the sale of a credit-risky bond owned to a counterparty at par and with no interest accrued, with an interest-rate swap. This type of asset swap structure or package is referred to as a **par asset swap**. If there is a default by the issuer on the credit-risky bond, the asset swap transaction is terminated and the defaulted bonds are returned to the investor plus or minus any mark-to-market on the asset swap transaction. Hence the investor is still exposed to the issuer's credit risk.

The coupon on the bond in the par asset swap is paid in return for LIBOR, plus a spread if necessary. This spread is the **asset swap spread** and is the price of the asset swap. In effect the asset swap allows investors that pay LIBOR-based funding to receive the asset swap spread. This spread is a function of the credit risk of the underlying credit-risky bond.

To illustrate this asset swap structure, suppose that in our previous illustration the swap rate prevailing in the market is 7.30% rather than 7.00%. The investor owns the bonds and sells them to a dealer at par with no accrued interest. The asset swap agreement between the dealer and the investor is as follows:

- The term is five years.
- The investor agrees to pay the dealer semiannually 7.30%.
- The dealer agrees to pay the investor every six months six-month LIBOR plus an asset swap spread of 30 basis points.

Let's look at the cash flow for the investor every six months for the next five years for this asset swap structure:

Received from bond:	7.85%
− Payment to dealer on swap:	7.30%
+ Payment from dealer on swap:	6-month LIBOR + 30 basis points
Net received by investor:	0.85% + 6-month LIBOR

In our first illustration of an asset swap, the investor is creating a synthetic floater without a dealer. The investor owns the bonds. The only involvement of the dealer is as a counterparty to the interest-rate swap. In the second structure, the dealer is the counterparty to the asset swap structure and the dealer owns the underlying credit-risky bonds. If there is a default, the dealer returns the bonds to the investor.

CDS Implied Default Probabilities

CDS spreads reflect the market's view on the default probability associated with the reference entity and the amount that will be recovered should a default occur. In the early days of the CDS market, the following naïve relationship was used to back out default probabilities from the observed CDS spread:

$$\text{Observed CDS spread in bps/10,000} =$$
$$(1 - \text{Assumed recovery rate}) \times (\text{Assumed default probability})$$

Note that in the above formula, we use default probability. What this means when using a CDS is not necessarily a bankruptcy but, more broadly, it is the probability of realizing a credit event.

Given an assumed recovery rate, then an **implied default probability** can be obtained by solving the above equation for the default probability:

$$\text{Implied default probability} = \frac{\text{Observed CDS spread in bps/10,000}}{(1 - \text{Assumed recovery rate})}$$

So, for example, if the observed five-year CDS spread for a corporation is 500 basis points and the assumed recovery rate is 40%, then the implied default probability is 8.33% as shown below:

$$\text{Implied default probability} = \frac{500/10,000}{(1 - 0.40)} = 0.0833 = 8.33\%$$

Notice that the higher the recovery rate assumed, the higher the implied default probability for a given CDS spread. So, for example, if a 60% recovery rate is assumed, the implied default probability is 12.5%.

Market players will employ an industry standard fixed recovery rate depending on the underlying to obtain the implied default probability. For example, the market practice is to assume a higher recovery rate for loans compared to corporate bonds and higher recovery rates for municipal bonds than for corporate debt.

As the CDS market has matured, it has become widely recognized that the formula given above for the implied default probability is only a very rough approximation of the default probability. The formula fails to take into account several factors that impact CDS spreads, such as bid-ask spread and counterparty risk.[4] Moreover, it assumes that the recovery rate is correct and constant over time.

More sophisticated models for computing the implied default probability are used today. These models employ the credit risk models described in Chapter 21. However, when using any implied default probability, it is important to understand that the value is generated from a model and that the model makes assumptions and requires estimated values for the model inputs.[5] Singh and Spackman provide good examples of the misuse

---

[4] The extraction of information is not simple due to other factors in pricing such as liquidity and counterparty risk in a CDS trade. For the importance of these factors, see Ren-Raw Chen, Frank J. Fabozzi, and Ronald Sverdlove, "Corporate Credit Default Swap Liquidity and Its Implications for Corporate Bond Spreads," *Journal of Fixed Income* 20, 2 (2010), pp. 31–57; Xiaoling Pu, Junbo Wang, and Chunchi Wu, "Are Liquidity and Counterparty Risk Priced in the Credit Default Swap Market?" *Journal of Fixed Income* 20, 4 (2011), pp. 59–79; and Navneet Arora, Priyank Gandhi, and Francis A. Longstaff, "Counterparty Credit Risk and the Credit Default Swap Market," Working paper, UCLA, 2009.

[5] This is important not for just extracting information from observed CDS prices but in other applications involving observed prices. The calculation of implied volatility from observed option prices is probably the best known example. In Chapter 27, where we discussed the Black–Scholes option pricing model applied to the pricing of options on bonds, we identified the assumptions of the model and how some of the assumptions are inappropriate with respect to pricing options on bonds.

of default probabilities extracted from CDS spreads based on industry standard fixed-recovery assumptions during distressed economic periods.[6]

INDEX CDS

An **index CDS** is a CDS written on a standardized basket of reference entities and includes CDS written on[7]

- Corporate debt issuers
- Sovereign government issuers
- Municipal debt issuers
- Tranches of asset-backed securities
- Tranches of commercial mortgage–backed securities

The mechanics of an index CDS are slightly different from that of a single-name CDS. As with a single-name CDS, a swap premium is paid. However, if a credit event occurs, once the accrued payment to the credit event date is paid, the swap premium payment ceases in the case of a single-name CDS. In contrast, for an index CDS, the swap payment continues to be made by the protection buyer. However, the amount of the quarterly swap premium payment is reduced. This is because the notional amount is reduced as a result of a credit event for a reference entity.

For an index CDS, every six months a new index series is created by the index provider. At that time, the specific composition of the reference entities in each new series is determined and a new premium level determined for each maturity. With the exception of tranches on structured transactions, swap premiums on an index CDS are exchanged once a quarter on or about the 20th day of March, June, September, and December. For the index CDS discussed below, Markit Group Ltd., a London-based organization, administers the indices.

Index CDS Written on Corporate, Sovereign, and Municipal Debt Issuers

The two most actively traded index CDS (denoted by CDX) on corporate bonds for reference entities in North America are the North America Investment Grade Index (denoted by CDX.NA.IG) and the North America High Yield Index (denoted by CDX.NA.HY). There are 125 reference entities with an investment-grade rating for the CDX.NA.IG; the CDX.NA.HY has 100 corporate reference entities that have a non-investment grade rating. For European corporate bonds, the most active index CDS is the iTraxx Europe, which has 125 corporate reference entities. All three index CDSs use equal weighting of the reference entities. So for the CDX.NA.IG and the iTraxx Europe each reference entity is 0.8% of the index while for the CDX.NA.HY each reference entity is 1% of the index.

The three index CDXs above are available in maturities from one to 10 years, with the greatest liquidity at 5-, 10-, and 7-year maturities. As for what constitutes a credit event,

---

[6] From Manmohan Singh and Carolyne Spackman, "The Use (and Abuse) of CDS Spreads During Distress," International Monetary Fund, Working Paper WP/09/62, March 2009.

[7] There are also basket default swaps that have reference entities selected by one of the counterparties. That is, unlike an index CDS, a basket default swap has a customized basket of reference entities. This type of CDS was commonly used in structured credit products to create synthetic collateralized debt obligations, issuance of which has ceased.

it differs for the North American indices and the iTraxx Europe index. For the North American indices, only bankruptcy and failure to pay are credit events, despite the fact that modified restructuring is commonly a credit event in the North American market. For iTraxx Europe, bankruptcy, failure to pay, and modified-modified restructuring are credit events.

The three index CDSs have sub-indices are that are also traded. For example, the North America Investment Grade Index has five industry sub-indices on which a CDX is written (consumer, energy, financials, industrials, and technology/media/telecom).

In addition to index CDSs on corporate bond issuers, there is an index CDS on leveraged loans (denoted LCDX). What differentiates the LCDX from the corporate bond CDX such as the CDX.HY is that the LCDX references a collection of loans (i.e., any/all outstanding senior secured bank debt of the reference issuer).

There are index CDSs written on sovereign governments in regions throughout the world. A partial listing of these index CDSs, denoted by SovX, is given below:

- iTraxx SovX Western Europe Index: 15 reference entities from the Eurozone region plus the United Kingdom, Denmark, Norway, and Sweden.
- iTraxx SovX CEEMEA Index: 15 reference entities in Central and Eastern Europe, Middle East, and African countries.
- iTraxx SovX Asia Pacific Index: 10 reference entities from the Asia and Oceania regions.

The SovX indices have 5-year and 10-year maturities and the underlying currency is the U.S. dollar.

There is an index CDS written on 50 municipal entities (denoted by MCDX) ranging from general obligation debt to revenue bonds from municipal authorities (excluding tobacco and health care bond issues). The issues must be BBB– (S&P), Baa3 (Moody's), or BBB– (Fitch) or above and not be on negative watch.

Index CDSs Written on Tranches of ABSs

As explained in Chapter 10, home equity loans are residential mortgage loans to borrowers with an impaired credit history or where the lender's claim is not a first lien on the mortgaged property. Such loans are more commonly referred to as subprime mortgage loans. The ABSs created are called subprime mortgage ABS. The index CDSs written on these ABS transactions are called ABX.HE. The index includes 20 home equity loan deals from the "top 20" issuers at the time.

Recall in our discussion of nonagency RMBS in Chapter 13 that there are tranches in a deal, each tranche having a separate rating. Typically there are tranches in subprime transactions with the following five ratings: AAA, AA, A, BBB, and BBB–. The ABX.HE has five separate sub-indices representing the five credit ratings that are appropriately referred to as ABX.HE.AAA, ABX.HE.AA, ABX.HE.A, ABX.HE.BBB, and ABX.HE.BBB–. Each sub-index consists of the corresponding tranche of the 20 ABS deals in the ABX.HE. A position in an ABX.HE sub-index is therefore equivalent to a position in each of the 20 tranches comprising the index.

The mechanics of an ABX.HE differ from those of the other index CDSs described previously beyond that of defining of a credit event. The other index CDSs we have described exchange payments quarterly. In the case of the ABX.HE, the protection buyer makes the swap payment monthly based on the notional amount. The notional amount will decline over time due to the amortization of the tranches. The protection buyer receives payments from the protection seller in the case of a credit event, which as explained earlier results from an interest shortfall, principal shortfall, or writedowns. However, unlike the other index CDSs, under the PAUG template a trigger event such as a writedown and interest shortfall may be reversed in a subsequent period. That is, the protection buyer would have to reimburse the protection seller in such instances.

Index CDSs Written on Tranches of Commercial Mortgage-Backed Securities

There are index CDSs written on deals of commercial mortgage–backed securities (CMBSs). This index CDS, denoted by CMBX, consists of deals from 25 CMBS transactions. As with the ABX.HE, there are sub-indices based on tranche ratings. The PAUG template is used as with the ABX.HE.

ECONOMIC INTERPRETATION OF A CDS AND AN INDEX CDS

To appreciate the potential application of a CDS and an index CDS to control a portfolio's credit risk that will be discussed in the next section, let's look at the economic interpretation of these derivative products from the perspective of the credit protection seller and the credit protection buyer.

Credit Protection Seller

Consider first the credit protection seller in a single-name CDS. What is the equivalent position of the credit protection seller in the cash market? For illustration purposes, we will assume that the reference obligation is bond ABC. If an investor buys bond ABC, then the investor will have the following cash flow:

Cash outlay equal to bond ABC's price, P_0.
Semiannual cash inflows equal to one half of bond ABC's annual coupon rate.

The semiannual coupon payments will be received as long as bond ABC does not default.

If the investor sells bond ABC at time T, then there will be a cash inflow equal to bond ABC's sale price, P_T. Suppose that at time T an adverse event occurred causing bond ABC's price to fall below the purchase price paid by the investor (i.e., $P_T < P_0$). The investor then realizes a loss equal to the $P_T - P_0$.

Let's look at the cash flow for the credit protection seller where the reference obligation is bond ABC. This party to the CDS receives a quarterly payment equal to the CDS spread. That is, there is a cash inflow equal to the quarterly swap payment. However, the swap payments are made only if bond ABC does not trigger a credit event. Thus, as with an investor who buys bond ABC, there are periodic cash inflows as long as there is no adverse credit event that stops the payments (default in the case of owing the cash bond and credit event in the case of a CDS). So far, it seems like this cash flow characteristic of the protection seller's position is similar to that of the buyer of a cash bond.

Let's now suppose that a credit event occurs. The protection seller must make a payment to the protection buyer. This payment represents a cash outlay or loss for the protection seller. But consider that there is a loss that occurs for the investor who buys bond ABC if an adverse event occurs. Once again, this cash flow attribute is similar for both the protection seller and an investor in a bond.

Consequently, the protection seller has an economic position that is analogous to an investor in a cash bond (i.e., an investor who owns a bond). This makes sense since both the protection seller and the investor who is long a cash bond are buyers of the bond issuer's credit risk.

There is an important difference in terms of funding the two positions and this should not be surprising at this point of our understanding of derivative instruments. Notice that the purchase of a long position in a bond requires that the investor make a payment equal to the bond's purchase price. In contrast, obtaining the same exposure to the credit risk of a bond by selling protection via a CDS does not require a cash outlay. Because it is unfunded, obtaining exposure to a bond by selling protection on that bond via a CDS is a leveraged position.

Although we have described the economic position for the protection seller in a single-name CDS, the same holds for the protection seller in an index CDS. In this case, the protection seller is taking a long leveraged position in a standardized basket of reference names.

Credit Protection Buyer

It should be no surprise that if the protection seller in a CDS has a position analogous to a long position in the cash bond, then the protection buyer in a CDS has a position analogous to a short position in a cash bond. Let's see why, once again using a single-name CDS where the reference obligation is bond ABC.

If an investor shorts bond ABC, then the investor will have the following cash flow:

Cash inflow equal to bond ABC's price, P_0
Semiannual cash outflows equal to one half of bond ABC's annual coupon rate

The semiannual coupon payments will be made by the investor because the short is responsible for reimbursing the party that it borrowed the bond from an amount equal to the coupon payment. This payment occurs as long as bond ABC does not default.

If the investor buys bond ABC at time T to cover the short position, then there will be a cash outflow equal to bond ABC's sale price, P_T. Suppose that at time T an adverse event occurred causing bond ABC's price to fall below the price the investor sold the bond short (i.e., $P_T < P_0$). The investor then realizes a gain equal to the $P_0 - P_T$.

Let's look at the cash flow for the credit protection buyer where the reference obligation is bond ABC. This party to the CDS makes a quarterly payment equal to the CDS spread. That is, there is a cash outflow equal to the quarterly swap payment. However, the swap payments are made only if bond ABC does not trigger a credit event. Thus, as with an investor who shorted bond ABC, there are periodic cash outflows as long as there is no adverse credit event that stops the payments (default in the case of shorting the cash bond and credit event in the case of a CDS). This cash flow characteristic of the protection buyer's position is similar to that of a short seller of a cash bond.

Let's now suppose that a credit event occurs. The protection buyer no longer must make any payment to the protection seller. Instead, there is a payment that the protection buyer receives if a credit event occurs that is analogous to the gain received by the short seller of bond ABC if an adverse event occurs. Once again, this cash flow attribute is similar for both the protection buyer and an investor who has shorted the bond.

Consequently, the protection buyer has an economic position that is analogous to a short position in a cash bond.

USING CDSs FOR CONTROLLING CREDIT RISK

The economic interpretation of a CDS just described, coupled with our understanding of the role of derivatives in general as described in the three prior chapters, will help us understand how portfolio managers can use both single-name CDSs and index CDSs. Recall that derivatives can be used to control risk (hedging being a special case of risk control where risk is eliminated) and provide a more transactionally efficient vehicle for doing so. Also, there is the potential to enhance return by doing relative value trades between the cash and CDS market. Here we focus exclusively on the risk control aspect of CDS.

Consider a single-name credit CDS written on a corporate reference entity. The liquidity of the CDS market compared to the corporate bond market makes it more efficient to obtain exposure to a reference entity by taking a position in the CDS market rather than in the cash market. What position should be taken in the CDS market to obtain exposure to a reference entity? As explained in the previous section, a portfolio manager would sell protection (i.e., be the protection seller in a CDS) since that is analogous to a long position.[8] Creating a long position may be easier in the CDS market given its liquidity.

For a portfolio manager seeking a leveraged position in a corporate bond, this can be done with a CDS since the economic position of a protection seller is equivalent to a leveraged position in a corporate bond. Of course, a portfolio manager can create leverage using a repo as explained in Chapter 22. However, there are disadvantages to using a repo to obtain leverage. First, the funding cost is not a fixed spread over LIBOR because the spread required by lenders can change. By using a CDS, a portfolio manager obtains a fixed financing rate (i.e., fixed in terms of a spread to LIBOR). Second, a repo is a short-term financing arrangement with financing that can be withdrawn by the lender on short notice. In contrast, a CDS provides an embedded permanent financing feature for the life of the CDS. Finally, with a repo there is a haircut or margin imposed by the lender whereas in CDSs there is 100% financing. Obviously, these advantages also apply to index CDSs.

A portfolio manager can shed the exposure to a particular corporate issuer held in a portfolio by buying protection via a single-name CDS. A reasonable question is why a portfolio manager may want to do using a CDS rather than merely selling the bond in the cash market. One reason for less liquid corporate bond names is that conditions in the cash market may be such that it is difficult for the portfolio manager to sell the current holding of a corporate bond of an issuer for which the manager has a credit concern.

Suppose a portfolio manager has a view that an issuer not included in the portfolio will have difficulties in the future and wants to take a position based on that expectation.

---

[8] The major factor that influences the use of a municipal CDS as a substitute for a cash market position is that of federal income tax treatment. As explained in Chapter 8, the interest for most municipal bonds is exempt from federal income taxation. This is not the case for the swap spread received by the protection seller as of this writing, although the Internal Revenue Service has yet to officially opine on the tax treatment of a CDS. This is clearly a disadvantage for portfolio managers who want to consider selling protection as an alternative to owning the bond. Portfolio managers of tax-exempt municipal bond funds, for example, cannot at this time sell protection as an alternative to buying the cash bond. However, there are participants in the market such as hedge fund managers who are not concerned with this difference in the tax treatment. Instead, they have other objectives when using a municipal CDS to efficiently take a credit position.

Of course, that position would be for the portfolio manager to take a short position in the bond of that issuer if shorting is permitted. However, shorting bonds in sectors in the cash market other the Treasury market is often difficult. The equivalent position can be obtained by entering into a CDS as the protection buyer. Similarly, this can be done for entire sectors using index CDSs.

What we have described previously for index CDSs is that a portfolio manager can gain credit exposure for a standard basket of reference entities by selling credit protection; a portfolio manager can reduce exposure for a standard basket of reference entities by buying credit protection. Thus, adjusting index CDS positions allows a portfolio manager to alter credit exposure to the bond market.

This use of index CDSs is particularly valuable for portfolio managers of small bond portfolios. We emphasized in earlier chapters on bond portfolio management that managing a portfolio relative to a bond index involves considerable idiosyncratic risk because all of the issues in a broad-based bond index cannot be purchased given the large number of issues in a typical index. One way of gaining exposure to a larger number of reference entities in a bond sector that comprises a broad-based bond index is via an index CDS.

What is important to note is that while CDSs do offer leveraging opportunities for a portfolio manager who is permitted to do so, no leveraging need occur if the funds that would have been used to purchase the reference entities are placed in cash rather than used to purchase other reference entities. We made the same point in discussing interest rate futures and swaps. If a portfolio manager uses a derivative for the purpose of leveraging, that can be easily identified by looking at a portfolio's key risk measures. In the case of interest-rate futures and swaps, this can be seen in the portfolio's duration. In the case of CDSs, it will show up in the portfolio's spread duration.

KEY POINTS

- Interest-rate derivatives can be used to control interest-rate risk with respect to changes in the level of interest rates. Credit derivatives can be used to control credit risk.

- By far, the most dominant type of credit derivative is the credit default swap wherein the protection buyer makes a payment of the swap premium to the protection seller; the protection buyer receives a payment from the protection seller only if a credit event occurs.

- The payments for a CDS depend on the triggering of a credit event. The International Swaps and Derivatives Association documentation for a trade defines potential credit events. The most controversial credit event is restructuring.

- There are special credit event definitions for CDSs written on tranches of asset-backed securities (the pay-as-you-go definitions).

- There is only one reference entity or reference obligation in a single-name CDS, and these contracts are written on a corporate debt issuer (bonds or leverage loans), sovereign issuer, tranche of an asset-backed security, and municipal bond issuer.

- The value of a single-name CDS can be approximated by the difference between the asset swap spread (from the par asset swap market) and the spread over LIBOR in the repo market. An asset swap structured by a dealer firm involves an investor selling a fixed-rate credit-risky bond to the dealer firm and receiving floating-rate payments.

- A CDS valuation model can be used to obtain the implied default probability for a reference entity. However, the probability calculated depends on the validity of the model and the estimated inputs.
- A CDS written on a standardized basket of reference entities is called an index CDS; this type of CDS is written on corporate debt issuers, sovereign government issuers, municipal debt issuers, tranches of asset-backed securities, and tranches of commercial mortgage–backed securities.
- Unlike a single-name CDS where the contract terminates upon the triggering of a credit event, for an index CDS, the swap payments continue if a credit event for one of the reference entities is triggered. However, the swap payments are reduced because of the lower notional amount resulting from the removal from the index of the reference entity for which a credit event was triggered.
- The economic interpretation of the credit protection seller is that it is analogous to a leveraged position in the reference entity (in the case of a single-name CDS) or the standardized basket of reference entities (in the case of an index CDS). For the credit protection buyer, the position is analogous to a short position in the reference entity or reference entities.
- Single-name CDSs can be used to alter the credit risk exposure of reference entity. Typically liquidity is greater in the CDS market than in the cash market and it is easier to short in the CDS market. An index CDS can be used to adjust the credit exposure of a portfolio: increasing credit exposure by being the credit protection seller and decreasing credit exposure by being the credit protection buyer.

QUESTIONS

1. How does the role of a credit derivative differ from that of an interest-rate swap in terms of controlling risk?
2. Why is a portfolio manager concerned with more than default risk when assessing a portfolio's credit exposure?
3. What is meant by
   a. a reference entity?
   b. a reference obligation?
4. What authoritative source is used for defining a "credit event"?
5. Why is "restructuring" the most controversial credit event?
6. Why does a credit default swap have an option-type payoff?
7. Comment on the following statement:

   "Restructuring is included in credit default swaps and therefore the reduction in a reference obligation's interest rate will result in the triggering of a payout. This exposes the protection seller to substantial risk."

8. All other factors being constant, for a given reference entity and a given scheduled term, explain whether a CDS using full or old restructuring or modified restructuring would be more expensive.
9. The focus in an asset-backed securities CDS is on the cash-paying ability of the collateral and not on bankruptcy. Why?
10. a. For a single-name credit default swap, what is the difference between physical settlement and cash settlement?
    b. In physical settlement, why is there a cheapest-to-deliver issue?
11. For a single-name CDS with the following terms, indicate the quarterly premium payment.

Swap Premium	Notional Amount	Days in Quarter	Quarterly Premium Payment
a. 600 bps	$15,000,000	90	
b. 450 bps	$ 8,000,000	91	
c. 720 bps	$15,000,000	92	

12. In the ISDA's pay-as-you-go template, why might there be payments by the credit protection buyer to the credit protection seller beyond that of the swap premium?

13. How do the cash flows for an index CDS differ from that of a single-name credit CDS?

14. How does one approximate the CDS spread for a single-name CDS on a corporate entity?

15. **a.** What is an asset swap?

    b. In pricing a single-name CDS, what information does the par asset swap market contain?

16. The following is an excerpt from "MCDX Municipal CDS index on the rise," *Credit Default Swap Market Reporting*, July 1, 2010 (http://blog.creditlime .com/2010/07/01/municipal-cds-index-rising/)

    > "The 5-year MCDX increased from 115 bps to 209 bps during the period from April 20 to June 11, 2010 and had nearly doubled 11 days later when it closed at 226.5 bps on June 22. Between September 28, 2009 and April 20, 2010, the index had only increased from 90 bps to 115 bps.
    >
    > The reason for the rise has been obvious, if not evident in CDS market prices, for quite a while now. Ballooning municipal deficits and lower revenues are creating fiscal problems for many states across America. California and Massachusetts have both announced probes (though mostly inconclusive to date) into municipal CDS trading while Illinois has seen its credit default swaps achieve the status as riskiest state in America."

    a. What is meant by a five-year MCDX?

    b. What is the link between the "ballooning municipal deficits and lower revenues" and the increase in CDS spreads?

17. You see the following statement in a popular business periodical:

    > "The credit-default swap spread on Greece is now 1,340 basis points. This means that there is a 68% probability that within five years Greece will default."

    a. How is the "68 percent probability of default" obtained?

    b. What assumptions must be made to use this probability estimate of default?

18. **a.** Explain how a single-name CDS can be used by a portfolio manager who wants to short a reference entity.

    b. Explain how a single-name CDS can be used by a portfolio manager who is having difficulty acquiring the bonds of a particular corporation in the cash market.

19. How are index CDSs used by portfolio managers?

20. How can a client determine if a portfolio manager is using a CDS for leveraging in such a way to increase the portfolio's risk relative to a bond index?

Index

Credits

Chapter 7: page 170: "Royal Bank of Canada Supplemental Prospectus," January 26, 2010. Copyright © 2010 by Royal Bank of Canada. Reprinted by permission.

Chapter 8: page 187: Published by the Idaho State Treasurer's Office. Copyright © by the Idaho State Treasurer's Office. Reprinted by permission.

Chapter 9: pages 191 and 192: OECD GLOSSARY OF TERMS by OECD. Copyright © 2008 by OECD Publishing. Reprinted with permission. http://dx.doi.org/10.1787/9789264055087-en.

Chapter 11: page 233: MORTGAGE BACKED SECURITIES PROGRAM, PROSPECTUS, January 1, 2006 by Fannie Mae. Copyright © 2006 Fannie Mae. Reprinted by permission; page 236: FANNIE MAE SINGLE-FAMILY MBS PROSPECTUS, June 1, 2007, by Fannie Mae. Copyright © 2006 Fannie Mae. Reprinted by permission; page 238: FREDDIE MAC MORTGAGE PARTICIPATION CERTIFICATES PROSPECTUS. Copyright © 2007 Freddie Mac. Reprinted courtesy of Freddie Mac; page 256: FANNIE MAE PROSPECTUS SUPPLEMENT, October 1, 2005. Copyright © 2005 by Fannie Mae Corporation. Reprinted with permission.

Chapter 12: page 260: COLLATERALIZED DEBT OBLIGATIONS: STRUCTURES AND ANALYSIS by Frank J. Fabozzi and Chuck Ramsay. Copyright © 1999 by John Wiley & Sons, Inc. Reprinted by permission of the publisher; page 284: "Offering Circular Supplement for Ginnie Mae Remic Trust," October 1, 2004. Copyright © 2004 by the Government National Mortgage Association (Ginnie Mae). Reprinted by permission; page 289: "Ginnie Mae Guaranteed Pass-Through Securities Base Offering Circular," October 1, 2007. Copyright © 2007 by the Government National Mortgage Association (Ginnie Mae). Reprinted by permission; page 292: "Ginnie Mae REMIC and MX Transactions: Guidelines and Selected Transaction Documents," January 1, 2002. Copyright © 2007 by the Government National Mortgage Association (Ginnie Mae). Reprinted by permission; page 296: BONDWEEK MAGAZINE, 1991. Copyright © 1991 by Institutional Investor. Reprinted by permission.

Chapter 15: page 344: "Prospectus Supplement for DaimlerChrysler Auto Trust 2007-A Summarizing the Transaction." Copyright © 2007 by TD Auto Finance, LLC. Reprinted by permission; page 345: "Prospectus Supplement for Daimler Chrysler Auto Trust 2007-A Summarizing the Transaction." Copyright © 2007 by TD Auto Finance, LLC. Reprinted by permission.

Chapter 17: page 394: "Call Provisions Drop Off" from BONDWEEK MAGAZINE, January 27, 1992. Copyright © 1992 by Institutional Investor. Reprinted by permission; page 394: "Eagle Eyes High-Coupon Callable Corporates" from BONDWEEK MAGAZINE, January 20, 1992. Copyright © 1992 by Institutional Investor. Reprinted by permission.

Chapter 18: page 416: "Fidelity Eyes $250 Million Move into Premium PACs and I-Os" from BONDWEEK MAGAZINE, January 27, 1992. Copyright © 1992 by Institutional Investor. Reprinted by permission.

Chapter 19: page 434: "Caywood Looks for Convertibles" from BONDWEEK MAGAZINE, January 13, 1992. Copyright © 1992 by Institutional Investor. Reprinted by permission; page 434: "Bartlett Likes Convertibles" from BONDWEEK MAGAZINE, October 7, 1991. Copyright © 1992 by Institutional Investor. Reprinted by permission.

Chapter 22: page 466: "Asset Allocation of CalPERS," January 31, 2011, by California Public Employees' Retirement System. Copyright © 2011 by CalPERS. Reprinted by permission; page 497: "Prospectus for the T. Rowe Price Institutional Core Fund," October 1, 2010. Copyright © 2010 by T. Rowe Price Associates, Inc. Reprinted by permission of T. Rowe Price Associates, Inc.; page 498: "Smith Plans to Shorten" from BONDWEEK MAGAZINE, January 27, 1992. Copyright © 1992 by Institutional Investor. Reprinted by permission; page 498: "MERUS to Boost Corporates" from BONDWEEK MAGAZINE, January 27, 1992. Copyright © 1992 by Institutional Investor. Reprinted by permission; page 499: "Eagle Eyes High-Coupon Callable Rates" from BONDWEEK MAGAZINE, January 20, 1992. Copyright © 1992 by Institutional Investor. Reprinted by permission; page 499: "W.R. Lazard Buys Triple Bs" from BONDWEEK MAGAZINE, November 18, 1991. Copyright © 1992 by Institutional Investor. Reprinted by permission; page 499: "Securities Counselors Eyes Cutting Duration" from BONDWEEK MAGAZINE, February 17, 1992. Copyright © 1992 by Institutional Investor. Reprinted by permission; page 499: "Wood Struthers to